RETRIEVAL & RENEWAL
Ressourcement
IN CATHOLIC THOUGHT

The middle years of the twentieth century marked a particularly intense time of crisis and change in European society. During this period (1930-1950), a broad intellectual and spiritual movement arose within the European Catholic community, largely in response to the secularism that lay at the core of the crisis. The movement drew inspiration from earlier theologians and philosophers such as Möhler, Newman, Gardeil, Rousselot, and Blondel, as well as from men of letters like Charles Péguy and Paul Claudel.

The group of academic theologians included in the movement extended into Belgium and Germany, in the work of men like Emile Mersch, Dom Odo Casel, Romano Guardini, and Karl Adam. But above all the theological activity during this period centered in France. Led principally by the Jesuits at Fourvière and the Dominicans at Le Saulchoir, the French revival included many of the greatest names in twentieth-century Catholic thought: Henri de Lubac, Jean Daniélou, Yves Congar, Marie-Dominique Chenu, Louis Bouyer, and, in association, Hans Urs von Balthasar.

It is not true — as subsequent folklore has it — that those theologians represented any sort of self-conscious "school": indeed, the differences among them, for example, between Fourvière and Saulchoir, were important. At the same time, most of them were united in the double conviction that theology had to speak to the present situation, and that the condition for doing so faithfully lay in a recovery of the Church's past. In other words, they saw clearly that the first step in what later came to be known as *aggiornamento* had to be *ressourcement* — a rediscovery of the riches of the whole of the Church's two-thousand-year tradition. According to de Lubac, for example, all of his own works as well as the entire *Sources chrétiennes* collection are based on the presupposition that "the renewal of Christian vitality is linked at least partially to a renewed exploration of the periods and of the works where the Christian tradition is expressed with particular intensity."

In sum, for the *ressourcement* theologians theology involved a "return to the sources" of Christian faith, for the purpose of drawing out the meaning and significance of these sources for the critical questions of our time. What these theologians sought was a spiritual and intellectual communion with Christianity in its most vital moments as transmitted to us in its classic texts, a communion that would nourish, invigorate, and rejuvenate twentieth-century Catholicism.

The *ressourcement* movement bore great fruit in the documents of the Second Vatican Council and deeply influenced the work of Pope John Paul II.

The present series is rooted in this renewal of theology. The series thus understands *ressourcement* as revitalization: a return to the sources, for the purpose of developing a theology that will truly meet the challenges of our time. Some of the features of the series, then, are a return to classical (patristic-medieval) sources and a dialogue with contemporary Western culture, particularly in terms of problems associated with the Enlightenment, modernity, and liberalism.

The series publishes out-of-print or as yet untranslated studies by earlier authors associated with the *ressourcement* movement. The series also publishes works by contemporary authors sharing in the aim and spirit of this earlier movement. This will include any works in theology, philosophy, history, literature, and the arts that give renewed expression to Catholic sensibility.

The editor of the Ressourcement series, David L. Schindler, is Gagnon Professor of Fundamental Theology and dean at the John Paul II Institute in Washington, D.C., and editor of the North American edition of *Communio: International Catholic Review,* a federation of journals in thirteen countries founded in Europe in 1972 by Hans Urs von Balthasar, Jean Daniélou, Henri de Lubac, Joseph Ratzinger, and others.

RETRIEVAL & RENEWAL

IN CATHOLIC THOUGHT

VOLUMES PUBLISHED

Mysterium Paschale
Hans Urs von Balthasar

The Heroic Face of Innocence: Three Stories
Georges Bernanos

Maurice Blondel: A Philosophical Life
Oliva Blanchette

The Letter on Apologetics and *History and Dogma*
Maurice Blondel

Prayer: The Mission of the Church
Jean Daniélou

On Pilgrimage
Dorothy Day

We, the Ordinary People of the Streets
Madeleine Delbrêl

The Discovery of God
Henri de Lubac

Medieval Exegesis, volumes 1 and 2:
The Four Senses of Scripture
Henri de Lubac

Opening Up the Scriptures:
Joseph Ratzinger and the Foundations of Biblical Interpretation
José Granados, Carlos Granados, and Luis Sánchez-Navarro, eds.

Letters from Lake Como:
Explorations in Technology and the Human Race
Romano Guardini

Divine Likeness: Toward a Trinitarian Anthropology of the Family
Marc Cardinal Ouellet

The Portal of the Mystery of Hope
Charles Péguy

*In the Beginning:
A Catholic Understanding of the Story of Creation and the Fall*
Joseph Cardinal Ratzinger

*In the Fire of the Burning Bush:
An Initiation to the Spiritual Life*
Marko Ivan Rupnik

*Love Alone Is Credible:
Hans Urs von Balthasar as Interpreter
of the Catholic Tradition*, volume 1
David L. Schindler, ed.

Hans Urs von Balthasar: A Theological Style
Angelo Scola

The Nuptial Mystery
Angelo Scola

MAURICE BLONDEL

A Philosophical Life

Oliva Blanchette

WILLIAM B. EERDMANS PUBLISHING COMPANY
GRAND RAPIDS, MICHIGAN / CAMBRIDGE, U.K.

© 2010 Oliva Blanchette
All rights reserved

Published 2010 by
Wm. B. Eerdmans Publishing Co.
2140 Oak Industrial Drive N.E., Grand Rapids, Michigan 49505 /
P.O. Box 163, Cambridge CB3 9PU U.K.

Library of Congress Cataloging-in-Publication Data

Blanchette, Oliva.
Maurice Blondel : a philosophical life / Oliva Blanchette.
p.   cm.
ISBN 978-0-8028-6365-2 (pbk.: alk. paper)
1. Blondel, Maurice, 1861-1949.   I. Title.

B2430.B584B63   2010
194 — dc22
[B]

2009040899

www.eerdmans.com

To the Memory of

Mademoiselle Nathalie Panis

*faithful disciple and collaboratrix
in Blondel's legacy to the philosophical world*

Contents

Acknowledgments   xv

PART ONE
The Journey Inward   1

I. Breaking into the Intellectual Scene   3
   The Beginning of a Confrontation   5
   The Philosophical Testing of Religion   9
   Testing the Philosophical Authenticity of a Method   13
   A Grudging Recognition   20

II. Awakening to the Divine Light in Human Action   25
   Early Family Life   25
   Early Education   29
   The Turn to Philosophy   32
   The Rite of Passage at the École Normale   36
   The Interior Life for a Dissertation on Action   43
   The Labor of Drafting a Philosophical Dissertation   49
   Final Consolidation of the Philosophical Argument   57

III. The Original Philosophy of the Supernatural   63
   A Philosophy of Human Action   65
   The Critique of Superstition   68

	The Necessity of Choosing in the Face of God	71
	The Necessary Hypothesis of a Supernatural	76
	Grounding the Phenomenon of Action in Being	88
IV.	**The Vocation to Philosophy**	**95**
	The Thesis on the *Vinculum Substantiale* of Leibniz	95
	Rethinking a Vocation	97
	Wrestling with the Source of Immanence in Modern Philosophy	105
	Resolution and Settlement into a Familial and Academic Life	117
V.	**Discourse on Method for Philosophy of Religion**	**122**
	The Philosophical Inadequacy of Given Approaches to Apologetics	124
	The Essential Point at Issue in Philosophy of Religion	133
	The Mutual Renewal of Perspectives in Philosophy and Religion	144
	The Separation of Philosophy from Religion in Descartes	162
	The Transfer from Lille to Aix-en-Provence	163
VI.	**Crisis of Modernity for Catholic Apologetics**	**167**
	Inaugurating a Tenure at Aix	167
	Impending Clouds of Controversy	172
	Getting Beyond the Dichotomy of Idealism and Realism	175
	Thoughts for a New Book on Apologetics	178
	Conversations with von Hügel	181
	Confrontation with Loisy over Historical Criticism	182
	The Crisis of Christian Consciousness in the Modernist Controversy	190
	The Need for Reconciliation of History and Dogma	192
	The Critique of Dogmatic Extrinsicism	194
	The Critique of Historical Criticism	196
	Tradition as Reconciliation of History and Dogma	202
VII.	**The Broader Social Involvement**	**210**
	The Idea of a Realistic Logic of Action	210
	A New Starting Point for the Discipline of Philosophy	216

Social Initiatives ... 223
In Defense of Social Catholicism ... 233
The Rejection of Monophorism ... 242
The Fight Against Any Political Alliance with *L'Action Française* ... 249
The Revenge of the Monophorists ... 257

VIII. The Philosopher of Aix ... 261
Uneasy Relations with a Secular University Administration ... 262
The World of a University Professor ... 265
Introducing Aquinas into Modern Philosophy ... 267
Recognizing Ancient Sources Still at Work Within Modern Cartesianism ... 272
The More Systematic Exploration of Philosophy ... 275
The Spiritual Outlook in Teaching ... 276
Summering in Burgundy ... 278
The War Years and After ... 280
The Conversion of Ali Mulla ... 282
The Disappearance of *L'Action* (1893) ... 285
Renewed Discussions of the Method of Immanence ... 288
Continuing the Work of Delbos ... 290
The Critique of Reactionary Intelligence ... 292
The Comparison to Jansenism ... 302
The Philosophical Problem of Mysticism ... 305

IX. The Philosophical Itinerary ... 322
The Demise of *Action Française* ... 322
Looking Back ... 324
The Two Kinds of Knowing ... 327
Toward a Concrete Ontology ... 330
The Question of a Supernatural Destiny ... 334
The Necessity of Joining the Human and the Divine ... 337
Heterogeneity Without Separation ... 340
Love for Both Country and Humanity ... 344
The Historical Enigma of Leibniz's *Vinculum Substantiale* ... 346
Critique of the Bergsonian *Élan Vital* ... 353

CONTENTS

X. The Question of a Catholic Philosophy	357
The Philosophical Retrieval of Saint Augustine	359
Defense Against the Backlash of Would-Be Separate Philosophy	379
The Case for a Catholic Philosophy	384
Philosophical Reassurance from the Side of Religion	392
Confronting the Refusal of Any Properly Christian Philosophy	397
Overcoming the Catholic Resistance to the Idea of Catholic Philosophy	403

PART TWO
The Systematic Summation   413

XI. The Question of Thought	420
Real Cosmic Thought	425
Organic and Psychic Thought	428
The Invention of Thinking Thought Through Language	430
The Problem of Knowledge	436
The Constitutive Act of Thinking and Its Principles of Reasoning	439
Insufficiency and Aspiration to a Higher Order in Rational Thinking	442
The Problem of God for Rational Thinking	446
The Turn Toward a Need for Practical Resolution	450
XII. The Responsibilities of Thought	453
The Noetic and Pneumatic Duality of Thought	454
The Radical Alternative in Relation to Our Final Fulfillment	458
Insufficiency and the Metaphysical Problem of the Infinite	462
Rational Responsibility at the Brink of Mystery	467
A Paradoxical Logic for Natural and Supernatural Cooperation	472
Doing Justice to the Human Spirit with the Divine Cooperation	476
Going Forward with Dispositions of Readiness to Accept a Positive Offer of Supernatural Grace from Religion	481
Purgative, Illuminative, and Unitive Stages in Thought's Progression	485
Circumincession of Thought, Being, and Action	489

Contents

XIII.	**Ontology of Consolidation in Being In, Through, and Of Itself**	493
	The Search for True Being from Matter to Organic Life	501
	The Search for True Being in Interpersonal Life	505
	The Search for Being in the Universal Becoming	508
	The Central Probe into Being In, Through, and Of Itself	510
	Aporiai Concerning What Being in Itself Is	515
	Aporiai Concerning Created Being as Such	522
	The Idea of an Ontological Normative for Created Beings	528
	Normative Ontological Exigencies in Matter, Life, and Personality	533
	Ontological Consolidation of Finite Spirits, and of the World, in the Perfection of the Infinite Spirit	538
XIV.	**Action as Cooperation with the First Cause**	547
	The Initial Conception of Essential Acting and Action	550
	In Search of an Authentic Action	553
	The Human Sphere of Action	558
	Aporiai on the Triune Mystery of Pure Acting	564
	The Immanent Life of the Totally Transcendent Pure Acting	573
	Creation and the Acting of Secondary Causes	584
XV.	**The Original Philosophy of Action Revisited**	595
	Sameness and Difference of Method	596
	Restructuring the Argument	603
	Worldly Ingredients and Internal Parturition of Action	608
	Deployment of the Internal Act into the Ethical Sphere of History	621
	The Perversion of Transcendence in Superstition	630
	Ascent to True Transcendence in Authentic Religion	638
	The Supernatural as Exotic but Supreme Sphere for Human Action	648
XVI.	**The Expanded Philosophy of the Supernatural**	657
	Incommensurability of the Supernatural in Transcendence	661
	The Interweaving of Philosophical Enigma and Christian Mystery	664

Triune Life as Inscrutable Essence of the One, True God	669
The Mystery of a Supernatural End for the Created Spirit	677
The Mystery of Supernaturalization for the Enigmatic Rational Creature	683
The Mystery of the Incarnate Divine Mediator and the Enigma of a Constant Mediating Function	689
Historical Realization of the Supernatural Ordinance in the Face of Man's Sinful Rebellion	697
The Enigma of Reparation for Sins Culminating in the Mystery of Redemption	710
The New Mystery of History as an Immediate Consequence of the Redemption	719
XVII. Symbiosis of the Human and the Divine in History	**724**
The Supernatural Life as Made Manifest in the Glorious Mysteries	727
The Supernatural Life as Continued in the Church	738
Tradition and Magisterium	744
Symbiosis of the Natural and the Supernatural in Its Sacramental Ordering	749
The Paradoxical Ethic of the Beatitudes	764
The Christian Outlook on the Last Things in Human Life	768
XVIII. Christian Spirit and Historical Civilization	**774**
Insufficiency of the Modern State	776
The Spiritual Basis of Human Sociability	779
Threefold Level of Human Sociability	781
Normative Immanence of Spiritual Transcendence	785
Church: Visible and Invisible	790
Christian Existentialism	792
The Philosophical Exigencies of Christianity	798
Index of References to Blondel's Works	**804**
Name Index	**812**
Analytical Index	**816**

Acknowledgments

This book comes out of a lifelong interest in the life and the work of Maurice Blondel that began in the early 1950s when I was an undergraduate student in philosophy under André Hayen, then a teacher at the Jesuit House of Philosophical Studies in Louvain, Belgium. Hayen not only taught us a lot of Blondel, but also got us to work on the first bibliography of Blondel's works, published under Hayen's name a few years after Blondel's death in 1949. Much of what I learned from working with Hayen during those early years of enthusiasm in Blondelian studies has gone into the writing of this book, as did also what I found coming from *Les Amis de Maurice Blondel,* who were publishing anew the early works of Blondel, which had long been out of print at the time, and running symposia on his legacy as a Master in philosophy that were published in issues of *Les Etudes Blondéliennes.*

But the book owes most to Mademoiselle Nathalie Panis, who was at the center of this flurry of activity around the recently departed Blondel, as the one who had collaborated most closely with him during the final years of his life, when he was working on what he wanted to be his final legacy, and who was then Curator of the Blondel Archives still being kept in Blondel's family residence in Aix-en-Provence.

I did not know her at the time of my studies in Louvain, but I got to know her much better later on when I started visiting those archives as a young professor in the late 1960s or early 1970s, while they were still under her care in Aix. She introduced me to those archives and showed me a lot of what still had to be uncovered in them, while urging me to begin translating *L'Action* (1893) into English, ever mindful of spreading Blondel's influence abroad from France.

It was later on that I got to know her best, however, and all that she knew about Blondel, when I began working on that translation while on sabbatical at the Camargo Foundation in Cassis on the French Riviera not far from Aix, where

Mademoiselle Panis was still living and promoting the thought of Blondel, even though the Blondel Archives had been moved to Louvain-la-Neuve.

That is when I started to go visit with her every week to talk about Blondel and what he had done during his long career as a philosopher. She became the source for most of the details that have found their way into this book about his early life, his family relations, his students, the retinue of correspondents with whom he was engaged for the better part of his life, his relations with colleagues in the university, his relations with authorities in the church, his dealings with the progressive Social Catholics and with the reactionary Action Française, and a host of other matters, including how she and Blondel worked together for years to get his Trilogies written and published.

This book is in many ways the story of Blondel's life as told by Blondel himself to Mademoiselle Panis during these many years of working together on a personal as well as an intellectual level. I am happy to acknowledge my indebtedness to her by dedicating the book to her memory as both disciple of the one she liked to call *Maître* and as collaboratrix in pulling his final works together. The story of how she did all this with Blondel is told in this book.

Another source I am happy to acknowledge my debt to is the very comprehensive Analytical and Critical Bibliography of all of Blondel's works, compiled by René Virgoulay and Claude Troisfontaines, which I used in drawing up the Index of cited works for this book. This bibliography, arranged in chronological order, tells the story of Blondel's work in capsule form. I used it extensively in deciding what to include and what to leave out in the story of Blondel's life as told in this book.

Finally, I would like to acknowledge the help I got in gathering relevant facts and texts from the first Director of the Blondel Archives after they were moved to Louvain-la-Neuve, again Prof. Claude Troisfontaines, and from Geneviève Mosseray, staff archivist, both of whom were very generous with their time and their resources in response to my inquiries on site as well as by mail. Without their help, and the help of others familiar with the contents of the archives, like Emmanuel Tourpe, I would not have gotten as good a look as I did into Blondel's early religious orientation in a devout Catholic family before the dawning of his philosophical interests as a student at the Lycée in Dijon and at the École Normale Supérieure in Paris.

I am grateful to all these people and many others for what they have contributed to this book. I hope I have done justice to these contributions and I accept responsibility for any shortcomings in taking full advantage of them all.

OLIVA BLANCHETTE
Boston College
February 14, 2010

PART ONE

The Journey Inward

Maurice Blondel can best be understood as a philosopher, but as a philosopher who sought to expand the scope of philosophy, so that it would include the most authentic religious spirit as it is lived in human thought and action. He was a religious man who had to think his religious life philosophically. But at the same time he was a philosopher for whom religion, even in its supernatural aspect, had to be seen as a necessary part, not only of human life itself, but also of philosophical reflection on that life.

In this resolve Blondel found himself at odds with both sides of the antireligious atmosphere that ruled in French intellectual life at the end of the nineteenth century, those who attacked religion or relegated it to something insignificant in rational life, and those who defended religion and asserted its right to propagate in secular society. At first he was seen as a defender of religion in philosophy in a University that was resolutely secular, and as a threat to the autonomy of reason. As the defenders of reason feared for their conception of philosophy, the defenders of religion, who were mostly Catholic in France at the time, as was Blondel, rejoiced in having a champion of religion at the University. But this joy soon turned to suspicion on the part of some, when it became clear how Blondel proposed to "defend" religion, not by cutting reason short, as even many philosophers were quite willing to do in the spirit of neo-Kantianism, but by extending its power of inquiry into the very idea of supernatural religion, thus apparently bringing the very content of such religion, supposedly the exclusive domain of a theology based on revelation, under the domain of critical philosophy. This was not what the established theologians of the time had had in mind as a proper defense of religion, and while philosophers found some reassurance in Blondel's protestations concerning the philosophical nature of his method, theologians began to fear for the autonomy of their own method in discoursing about religion.

Blondel left neither side complacent about its method in trying to bring them together into the unity of a single method which was essentially philosophical, but which was also no less essentially open to the transcendence of the supernatural in religion. This was clear from the two important publications that appeared under his name in the 1890s, the thesis on *Action* of 1893 and the so-called *Letter on Apologetics* of 1896. In the first he took issue with the attitude of the University and philosophy regarding religion. In the second he took issue with certain interpretations of his "defense" of religion and certain ways of dealing with questions of religion that were not in keeping with the exigencies of modern philosophy, as he claimed his was. In short, it could be said that in breaking into the intellectual scene of his day Blondel was breaking it up as it was established on either side of the controversy over religion, by beginning a new journey inward to the human spirit that was at once philosophical and religious.

I

Breaking into the Intellectual Scene

A new mode of religious thinking was in the offing, launched as a philosophical dissertation on *Action* at the Sorbonne. Before we go into this mode of thinking as it appears in *L'Action* of 1893, it is interesting to note how Blondel first presented himself to the University and how it first reacted to him and his claim to establish supernatural religion as a legitimate and necessary domain for philosophical inquiry.

Blondel first came to Paris in November 1881, at the age of twenty. He had gained admission to the highly touted École Normale Supérieure through a rigorous competitive exam that was carried on in France every year. He came from the provincial city of Dijon. He was from a well-established family of lawyers and notaries, professional people who gave their children a good bourgeois and Christian education, an example of work well done, a concern for doing the right thing, and even a certain taste for discreet but active proselytizing. He had done his studies at the Lycée of Dijon, the regular state-run school, and not at a Catholic school, and had spent his last year in intense preparation for the very competitive national admission examination that was the only way of access to the École Normale, then and still considered a Mecca for intellectuals in France.

At the École Normale, Blondel was to learn to think. Henri Bergson and Émile Durkheim had just finished the year before he came there. Victor Delbos and Pierre Duhem, along with many others less well known, were to be his classmates. What he was to learn, however, was not exactly congenial to his way of thinking or to his convictions. Among the faculty he found a deep-seated rationalism that was essentially anti-religious, though two, Émile Boutroux and Léon Ollé-Laprune, were themselves avowed Christians who supported him in his religious interests. Among the student body, he found a general skepticism derived from Renan, and from a waning scientism as well as a loss of confidence in the power of reason to deal with concrete questions of the meaning of life.

Philosophy seemed to be fixated on sensations and ideas as if they were "realities cut up into pieces and stabilized" where, as he was to put it later on, Blondel "could not help but see in them something pseudo-concrete, artificially solidified abstractions" (1928a, 19).

Blondel tells of an incident on the very first day of his stay at the École Normale that typifies how he was received and how he was to respond. The school was run as a closely regimented fraternity at the time and, at registration, newcomers were put through all sorts of initiation rites by the upper classmen. Among the questions one had to answer was that of religious affiliation, to which Blondel declared that he was a practicing Catholic. This was of some consequence for the discipline of the school, since practicing Catholics were allowed to leave the school at a certain time on Sunday mornings in order to attend mass at a nearby church, whence they got their nickname, *les talas*, which was short for *ils vont à la messe*. Blondel, who was just arriving from the province and from his family, was somewhat taken aback by the reaction of one of his classmates upon hearing his declaration: "Well now, how can a boy who seems intelligent still call himself *tala* (catholic)?" But he was not at a loss for an answer. "Thank you for the compliment and for the added quip," he said. "I have every intention, not just of seeming, but of being intelligent" (1928a, 20-21). It is this intention, as he adds, that he would try to actualize in his life at the school, in keeping with a need to see clearly, even as a *tala*, according to an aim that is radically philosophical. For Blondel it would become important to think, not just religiously, but also in a philosophical mode, as he was to learn at the École Normale.

In order to bring this intention to fruition Blondel realized that he had not only to push reason further forward into a consideration of the religious question, but also to pull it back to a more concrete consideration of life itself in action. It is thus that, at the beginning of his second year at the École Normale, on November 5, 1882, as he recalled quite precisely (1928a, 34), he began to focus on *action* as the subject for his dissertation. In doing so he was going back to Aristotle, for, as he also recalled, he was pulling together various texts in the *Metaphysics* and the *Ethics* in which action *(to ergon)* was spoken of as that which unifies in a way that is supra-discursive and charged with the infinite, as well as that which adds precision and perfection to a being (1936, 324-25). But in doing this he was reintroducing into the discourse of philosophy a term or a reality that had long been lost sight of at the end of the nineteenth century in France. In fact, when the classmate sitting next to him in study hall saw his notes, he could only exclaim: "A thesis on Action, great scot! What could that be? The term *action* does not even appear in the *Dictionnaire des sciences philosophiques* of Adolphe Franck," the only one available at the time (1928a, 34). Blondel's readiness to innovate in philosophy was not lost on this classmate.

But this readiness to innovate was not as readily accepted by the University.

When Blondel came to register the subject for his thesis, which appeared to him all the more justified by reason of the astonishment it was provoking, he was told by the secretary, after consultation of the competent authorities, that no one saw how there could be in *action* matter for a philosophical thesis. A more sympathetic observer, Lucien Herr, who was librarian at the École Normale and a specialist in Hegel, would later remark on how few proper names would figure in such a thesis, since it would have to be cut out of whole cloth as an original pattern, which was exactly what Blondel had in mind (1928a, 35). Thanks to the intervention of Boutroux, with whom Blondel had discussed his project and who agreed to serve as *patron* for the thesis, the subject was finally accepted and Blondel was ready to begin making his point for a philosophy of religion as something supernatural.

He finished his work at the École Normale in November 1884, armed with the Aggrégation, which entitled him to teach at the level of the Lycée. After short stints in different places, he ended up in October 1886 as professor of philosophy at the Lycée of Aix-en-Provence, where he stayed until July 1891. This was a time for working on the dissertation as well as for teaching. But in October 1891 Blondel took time off from teaching in order to devote himself exclusively to work on his dissertation. He retired to an old farmhouse owned by his family in the wine country of Burgundy and began pulling together preliminary notes and drafts in view of what was to be the final draft. This was a time of intense concentration for him in which he drew his inspiration, not just from the philosophy he had learned in school, but also from spiritual authors such as St. Bernard, St. Paul, and Pascal, with whom he was personally familiar. From these as well as from Leibniz, of whom Blondel was especially fond and on whom he was writing his secondary Latin dissertation, he learned not only how to examine his conscience, but also how to reflect on the order of intelligibility and discipline to be found in any genuinely human action and conduct of life.

The Beginning of a Confrontation

Among the notes he wrote early on in this process is one, apparently addressed to his teacher Ollé-Laprune, that is especially revelatory of how he was approaching his subject. It reads as follows:

> There is something to be defined, something that seems to be properly Christian; and it is in a way that is very concrete, through an analysis, not of the will, not of activity, but of action, that I would like to try to do this. It is true that in order to act we must think well; it is truer still, and more evangelical, to say that in order to think well we must act well. To this are connected,

through a link that I can barely grasp at the moment, different thoughts on passion, on the *letter* (of a law), and the possibility or the usefulness of a revelation. (*Notes Semailles* 1886-87)

The movement of the thought is clearly religious in its origin, but the effort is to bring it back to a clearly defined philosophical discourse by a critical reflection on characteristically human action and all that it implies rationally. In the final product of his reflection Blondel hardly mentions this evangelical dimension of his inspiration at the beginning. He chooses rather to call it an *Essay on a Critique of Life and a Science of Practice*, which is more in keeping with the philosophical nature of the work. It is only in the end that he argues for a necessity of the kind of supernatural he had in mind from the beginning. But it was this ending that was to pull his readers in the University up short and stiffen them in their fear for reason in the face of this reappearance of religion as a necessary dimension of life in philosophy.

Blondel submitted his dissertation to the Sorbonne in May 1893, not in person but by mail from Dijon. From the distance of the province he could not realize the full extent of the reaction it would provoke in Paris. It was only when he arrived in Paris shortly before the defense, scheduled for Wednesday, June 7, 1893, that he began to feel the opposition he was to encounter. Boutroux had been the only reader of the manuscript, and the one to approve it. He explained to Blondel the bitter criticisms he had drawn upon himself from his colleagues by this approval. These colleagues were so irritated upon reading such an unusual dissertation, that he advised Blondel to try by all means possible to visit the other members of the jury at their homes, before the defense, so that they could vent their anger in private rather than in public.

Blondel had encountered this kind of irritation once before in his academic career, at the time of the final aggregation exams of the École Normale, when he, along with the leader of the class, was refused passage twice, because their dissertations were thought to be too personal and too doctrinal. Blondel in particular was accused of being a *voltigeur*, one who flits from one question to another too quickly. According to one commentator, the candidates had made the mistake of not sticking close enough to an elementary pedagogy, such as is expected from a teacher at the level of the Lycée. But this time, with his doctoral dissertation, there was more at issue than just style. There was also the question of what he was advancing.

Blondel did make the rounds of the board as suggested by Boutroux. He tells of one member taking umbrage at the fact that this entire thesis had been prepared without his having been apprised of it, and spoke for others when he wondered where Blondel was coming from. "Here is what people would like to know: are you all by yourself, coming in from the wild, or are you the spokesman or even the instigator of a concerted campaign against the conception we have here of philosophy and its role?" (1928a, 48-49). Blondel was so genuinely surprised by the question or the suspicion, that his interlocutor saw immediately what he was in fact, not a loner coming in from the wild, but simply someone who was candid about what he thought. His ingenuousness earned him another ally on the board, who would later remark that he too, along with Boutroux, was becoming a martyr for Blondel.

What actually happened in private with the other members of the board we do not know. But we do know what happened in the public defense of the thesis, from a long report on the *Soutenance* published in 1907 under the name of J. Wehrlé, a classmate of Blondel at Normale who had left to enter the seminary and become a priest, but based on notes originally written by Blondel himself on the day after the defense itself. The notes themselves have recently been published alongside the published text of 1907 in the first volume of Blondel's *Oeuvres Complètes* (1995, 691-745). Blondel himself wrote the revision for publication as well as the original notes, even though he had it published under his friend's name, who added only one remark of his own at the end of the conclusion concerning their recently deceased teacher, Ollé-Laprune. Blondel seems to have decided to publish this account of the defense in the heat of the Modernist controversy we shall speak of later, in order to remind his Catholic accusers about what side he was on and where he was coming from.

In this report we learn that the defense lasted from three until seven-fifteen in the evening, somewhat longer than such exercises usually went at the time, and that it was more than usually well attended by an interested public. The discussion itself, though heated at times, was carried on well within the bounds of philosophical civility. Though the report gives no indication of it, Blondel seems to have led off with a few introductory remarks, the tenor of which we can gather from handwritten notes on a neatly folded sheet of paper still to be found at the Archives, in which Blondel explains what he was about in his thesis — remarks that lead spontaneously to the line of questioning with which Boutroux appears to begin rather abruptly in the published account. In the introductory remarks, he goes immediately to the point of the supernatural. "My aim has been to constitute a philosophy which, though quite distinct from the supernatural order, would be its natural and necessary underpinning. There has to be one, and there is none." The point is carefully worded in order to take into account the exigencies of both philosophy and theology with regard to the idea of the supernatural.

In order to constitute such a philosophy of the supernatural, Blondel sees himself as having to steer a course between two philosophies very much in vogue in his day, Thomism and Kantianism. While recognizing the force of the Thomistic synthesis, especially for believers, he did not think it met the exigencies of modern thought because it threw too many questions, religious, philosophical, and scientific, into the same pot, without confusing them to be sure, but still without recognizing the reciprocal suspicion that existed among them. At this time Blondel saw Thomism as proposing only a juxtaposition of these three elements, a descriptive anatomy that found its persuasive force in the solidity and the amplitude of its exposition. But it did not meet the preoccupations of modern thought, which had been turned around by Kant's Critique. Whatever Thomism was responding to in the thirteenth century was no longer the spirit or the approach of thoughtful people in his day and age. What was once a method of proof had become only a method of exposition and confirmation for truths now called into question.

On the other hand, however, Kantianism, with its substitution of moral life for Hellenic intellectualism, which some had thought of as the definitive arrival of the Christian spirit in thought, was even less of an answer to the philosophical question of the supernatural than Thomism. This was not the way for Christian truth to go. For Blondel what had to be found was a way between intellectualism and fideism that would determine a perspective at once absolutely natural and absolutely in conformity with the supernatural order, so that, without minimizing the validity of nature and of reason itself, one could also be brought to see the necessity of the supernatural order within the natural, in such a way that the natural order would then be viewed as subordinated. "Between these two orders there is neither a simple juxtaposition, nor an opposition, nor yet a continuity. Independent, the two are in solidarity for man; impossible to get along without them both and impossible to arrive at them. The natural order exists, and yet the supernatural order penetrates it; to refuse to rise to this higher order is not only to renounce a free gift, it is to deprive and to mutilate oneself" (1995, 691-745).

This is the relation that Blondel was trying to define with demonstrative precision, first by presenting a synthesis of the entire natural order, in order to show both its solidity and its inevitable shortcoming, and then by elaborating on the idea of the supernatural on the basis of its necessity as part of the determinism of human action. The starting point was a conception of truth, not only as something to be sought intellectually, but also as something giving rise to an alternative for the will, something to be embraced or rejected, where rejection entailed a privation rather than just intellectual neutrality. The effort was not to impose the truth dogmatically, but rather to let the truth speak for itself in whatever state of consciousness there was, even those that seemed most at odds with Blondel's. The method, then, had to be negative in the first instance, to show how those who seek to evade the truth and its exigencies actually posit it in the act of doing so. But it also had to show inevitability in the total determinism of action, so that one cannot stop at any step along the way as a palliative. The point was to open up the entire realm of the necessary toward which we are drawn as human beings, without mysticism. Finally, the method had to be charitable, because no state of soul could be omitted. Instead of trying to take the place of others, it had to let others take their own place and come to their own judgment in the light of truth. "The force of the proof is in them, in what is understood better perhaps by those I am fighting than by those I am defending" (1995, 691-745).

The focus of the method then was on the determinism of the act, prescinding from its qualities, since all of these could be included. Everything was to follow from an internal analysis of the act's content, namely, its organic relations along with its contraries. But the synthesis to which this consideration of the necessary in human action led was not merely intellectual, something merely to be viewed. It was also an alternative to be resolved, a means of action, so that this means, or this mediator, should be constituted objectively, or as the truth itself which grounds the entire determinism as real. "Only a divine Mediator can realize this conception of objective truth."

The Philosophical Testing of Religion

With this sweeping affirmation as background, then, Boutroux led off the questioning by likening Blondel to St. Augustine, St. Bernard, or Malebranche, and asking him what sort of a mystic he was: one of the Hellenic sort or one of the ascetic sort. Given what Blondel had just said about Hellenic intellectualism and mysticism, the question was loaded. It went to the heart of Blondel's method. Though he actually speaks of mysticism in passing in the dissertation, he did not want to admit that he was a mystic of any sort, if by mysticism one understands looking for the end of action beyond the necessity that is part of the determinism of human action. As a philosopher, he was looking for the end of action within action itself, as it is given spontaneously and as we posit it voluntarily. He was situating himself within human action, in other words, not to add a new dimension to it, but only to discover its exigencies and to measure up to all its necessary expansion. For him the true force of philosophy was to fall back on this internal spring of the will in action in order to watch how, slowly but surely, it reaches its effects. The task of philosophy is to bring someone to be true to this inner will in complete good faith. In this sense, philosophy had to be positive rather than mystical, even though in the end it does give rise to a religious expectation.

Satisfied that Blondel was arguing only as a philosopher, or focusing only on what is real rather than on some idea to which reality had to be brought into conformity, Boutroux then turned to the principle of Blondel's argument. What is, could be understood as either the object proposed to the will by nature, or as the will itself with its aspirations, or else as both at the same time. If there is a conflict between the two, by what principle or method can they be reconciled? Pessimism takes its principal argument from this contradiction to conclude to the nothingness of human action, whereas Blondel uses the same contradiction to arrive at the opposite conclusion, namely, that there is some being in human action. "You claim," Boutroux tells Blondel, "that the conflict ceases the moment we come to the right idea both of the end truly sought by the will and of the total reality with which this will is in relation. According to you, what we will definitively, whether we know it or not, is the substitution within us of the divine willing for our own willing; and the nature of things is fundamentally nothing more than the series of means that we must will to accomplish our destiny" (1907c, 82).

The problem with this, according to Boutroux, is that it appears more as an interpretation than as an observation of reality, an interpretation that proceeds from a presupposition surreptitiously introduced into the heart of the problem to be resolved. In other words, there seems to be some secret postulate that inspires and sustains the entire dialectic, which Boutroux sums up as follows: "to follow your argument, we have to admit that the human will is not content with any finite object and that it is oriented toward a good that it encounters nowhere in the nature of things. Willing the infinite, isn't that the point of departure and as it were the *petitio principii* of your inquiry? And, with the infinite in hand, is it any wonder that you then eliminate all the contradictions of the finite?" (1907c, 82).

Blondel admits that willing the infinite was indeed the key issue for him, but not as a postulate or as a point of departure. It was for him the point of arrival for philosophical research. The question for Blondel is indeed to see whether or how willing the infinite is a point of departure and a real principle for the spontaneous activity of human life. In defense of his argument, he says he must not suppose the infinite as either present or absent. When it arises through the interplay of mental determinism as hypothesis, or when it is proposed to conscience through education or history, we have first to oppose ourselves to it, as Blondel claims he does in the beginning of his argument. Hence the negative character of his method, which seemed to be the best way to proceed scientifically, that is, the method of admitting nothing as real, unless one were forced to do so, and admitting only as much as one has to incrementally at each step of the argument, so that in the end one is left with a system of interconnected affirmations, gradually leading up to the point of bringing before reflected thought, and to the option of the will, what was already present at the origin of a movement that was at first evasive.

Blondel likens his method to that of Descartes's methodical doubt. Just as the latter had sought new reasons for doubting, Blondel sought to bring into philosophy new moral attitudes and still barely determined stances in the face of the problem of human destiny, including aestheticism, dilettantism, and immoralism. His aim was to start from what was furthest removed and lowest in willing of any kind, in order to go further and higher with it than had been done before. Unlike Descartes's methodical doubt, however, which was the individual attitude of only one mind, Blondel had to take all the diversity of human consciences into account and set them in motion, even if they feigned not to start from the whole. Unlike the "methodical doubt," which was restricted to an intellectual difficulty that was partial and artificial, the philosophy of action had to do with the question of life, or the question of the whole. We step out of methodical doubt as from a fiction, Blondel adds, whereas we must dwell in action as we must in reality. Thus, what was only a problem of knowledge becomes at once a problem of the will, of being, and of salvation.

In short, the question raised by Blondel in defining the relation of knowing, doing, and being was no longer just the Cartesian question, nor merely the Kantian question. It was the question of destiny concerning the price of life, the truth of God, the human being's accord with the universal conditions of experience, science, and existence, and our participation in the transcendent good. Moreover, Blondel insisted, it was the philosophical question itself as a whole, since it was a question of the relation between the natural order and the supernatural as such. Thus, even at this moment of judgment on the philosophical validity of his argument, Blondel was challenging the very idea of what was called "separate philosophy," that is, a philosophy that could ignore the question of religion or the supernatural. This is a point he would make even more emphatically later on in discussing his method of immanence in the *Letter on Apologetics*.

In counterpoint to Blondel's reply here, Boutroux objects in the name of what might be termed a more rational philosophy. Even if we admit that there is in human willing an aspiration that no finite object could spontaneously satisfy, do we have to ratify this desire and second this movement, which may be unreasonable and chimerical? Do we have to try to leap beyond nature? Is there not another solution suggested by ancient philosophical wisdom, which is neither presumption nor abdication, but simply a regulation of desire according to the object accessible to our will that avoids all *hubris*, instead of vainly trying to make our willed end equal to the infinite principle of desire?

The idea of equality between willed object and the spontaneous power of willing mentioned here was central to Blondel's philosophical argument for the necessity of the supernatural. If it is impossible for any willed object in the order of nature to equal the projected infinite power of willing, the argument goes, then we have to admit a necessity of the supernatural to satisfy the principle of projected equality found at the heart of human willing. Blondel's contention was that this principle of equality was itself rational and that it made the idea of the supernatural appear as something necessary for reason itself. It is this principle that sends the will, so to speak, out of itself in search of an object that will be the equal of its power. In pursuit of this search, it finds various objects that satisfy this principle in part at least, and that the will, therefore, has to will necessarily.

But within the natural order it finds none that will satisfy the principle of equality in willing fully. At the limit of the natural order, we are left with the conclusion that it is necessary to go further, but that it is impossible for us to do so on our own. The constant recurrence of superstition in human action is a sign of this necessity, but the falsity or the pretentiousness of idolatry is an indication of the impossibility for human willing, left to its devices to go beyond the natural order, that is, without the added help of something supernatural.

Boutroux's objection thus touched on the very point of this necessity of something supernatural, while admitting the point of its impossibility for us. If one can confine one's willing to possible objects, then one does not have to admit any necessity of the supernatural. But Blondel's reply is that this is precisely what we cannot do, without pretension and without self-contradiction. In the dissertation he explains how, in spite of the strange paradox of the act, it is impossible to will infinitely without willing the infinite. But he also demonstrates the ineluctable consequences of such an abstention or, more exactly, of this systematic rejection of something necessary. Far from being more modest or "rational," such a refusal is an act of self-sufficiency in secret contradiction with itself. We do not suppress what we reject. In the logic of life the contraries remain implicated diversely in the conclusion that results from our free choice in the face of having to either will or not will the infinite.

To see how all this works itself out more cogently in Blondel's argument, we must read the dissertation itself more carefully, as Boutroux shows he had done in raising these objections. Before concluding his part of the examination, he turns to some more specific questions about Blondel's understanding of *action*. If action, as Blondel sees it, is a principle of synthesis that develops and enriches being, is it not rather, in the eyes of others, something more negative that determines being, exhausts it, narrows it in a sort of practical mechanism fixed by a literalness that kills the spirit? This was an allusion to the constraints of a literal practice on the human spirit of the sort that Blondel was defending as part of the necessity of the supernatural. In response, Blondel grants something of this negative aspect of action for the human spirit, in the sense of a certain deterioration that can set in, to limit and absorb the one acting. But this is so only because, in order to act in a human way, one must consort with other agents. We know well only what we have done, and we enter into communication with others and ourselves only at the cost of some onerous adaptations. Even in seeming to drain us and pull us out of ourselves, however, action still enriches us, fortifies us, and nourishes our dreams and aspirations by making them better and truer. In reality, what goes out of us brings back to us what is outside of ourselves, as an end to be attained, and makes immanent for us the entire series of the means by which we tend from our principle to our end.

Another difficulty had to do with the way Blondel relates determinism and freedom in his dialectic of action, where he distinguishes between a determinism antecedent to and leading up to the use of our free will and a determinism consequent to this use. The latter determinism is the one Blondel follows in its ascendance from one object of the will to another that is always higher, all the way up to the infinite. In this determinism, Blondel finds what is for him the originality of his method, which frees him from a philosophy merely of the idea and opens him up to a philosophy of action that reintegrates everything within itself, without compromising the use of free will and without misconstruing the absolute oppositions that result from the ultimate moral option before God. Blondel's phenomenology of action, starting from the central act of willing itself and reaching out to the very confines of the universe, consists precisely in the articulation of this determinism or necessity consequent upon the very act of willing.

Boutroux's final difficulty has to do with the way Blondel relates this science of the subject with the so-called objective or more positive sciences, where determinism appears to be opposed to freedom. Blondel's answer takes him to the heart of his phenomenological method, as we shall see in conjunction with his use of the method in *L'Action* (1893). The point he wishes to make in the defense is that he is trying to describe the universal concrete, including the description itself and the effort of the will each at its proper place in the whole phenomenon. He defends himself against any sort of idealism as well as against any premature realism that tends to reify different aspects of the phenomenon independently of one another.

In the end, Boutroux, who was the only examiner to have read the entire dissertation from beginning to end carefully, finds it rich and solid. Though he still has some reservations about the way Blondel tends to subordinate knowledge to action, he recognizes that on the whole the considerable effort has succeeded, the key word for saying that the thesis was accepted and approved.

Testing the Philosophical Authenticity of a Method

None of the other examiners was to raise as cogent a series of objections as Boutroux did. Paul Janet finds Blondel's thought obscure and his style even more obscure. He declares having spent one hour on one page and still not having understood it. At this rate, he calculates, he would have needed forty-five days to read the whole thesis. He finds it too personal, lacking in what he calls the value and the objective bearing of ideas. But once he has given up trying to follow the argument, he finds interesting things and sometimes charming reflections on each page, as with the *Parerga* of Schopenhauer, which far surpass the work as a whole.

Blondel feels deeply bothered by this criticism. He apologizes for the faults he is responsible for. But he answers only to the extent that the criticism reflects on the value of his method. He grants that it has always been the honor of French philosophy, from Descartes on, to be clear. But he adds that not any clarity will do for his purpose. Blondel notes that, even according to Descartes, there is a certain clarity that is often deceiving and dangerous, giving an illusion of understanding to whose who do not understand, by masking the real complexity of things. The complete understanding of Cartesian thought is no less laborious than that of Hegelian thought.

For his own part Blondel did not wish to be understood in any simplistic way. To be sure, style must be an instrument of precision. But it must also convey a complete sense, nothing more nor less, of the inevitable difficulty of things, even to the extent of putting off impatient or presumptuous minds who think they can grasp and penetrate everything without any competence. This was not said as an excuse for his obscurity. "If I have rewritten certain parts of my work six or seven times," he says, "it was not for the pleasure of remaining obscure" (1907c, 88). He had tried to reduce the difficulties of interpretation that depend on imperfections of expression as much as he could. But he had no hope or intention of eliminating every obstacle. Style is not just an opening for others to access one's thought. It is also a protection against their hasty judgments. "To be understood neither too soon nor too late, that would be the just mean" (1907c, 88). Hence Blondel regrets the pleasure some might take in running through this book, as some would do later on, looking only for random pious thoughts, after having given up trying to grasp its logic. To run through a book in this way, he says, is to look in it only for what one already knows. Moreover, he adds, confronting Janet as the adversary he knew him to be, "I was more concerned to be understood by those I criticize than by those whose beliefs and teachings I share" (1907c, 88).

Janet, however, does not take up this challenge of a systematic understanding in Blondel's work. He goes on only to pick out two or three of the details he had found interesting on one page or another and to raise some question about each, leaving the question of the argument as a whole in the dark, as it had been before Blondel's attempt to refocus on it in response to Janet's first criticism. What we find in Blondel's response, however, is the reason why his work as a philosopher is always difficult to follow, even in its early and more vigorous form. While trying to be clear in his expression, he also wanted to remain true to the complexity of things and of the human subject in action. To do this he had to be systematic or scientific in his method. This is what makes him difficult or impossible to follow, if one is not prepared to understand the development of his argument as a whole. In his way of thinking the structure of the whole is more important than any particular detail brought up along the way.

With Henri Marion we come to a more sympathetic examiner, the one willing to become a martyr among his colleagues, along with Boutroux, for the one defending his dissertation, by speaking of his book as nobly inspired. For

Marion what was surprising was that it contained so little moral instruction on how to live well, as one would expect from a "science of practice," as its subtitle indicated. Here and there, there are signs that Blondel could have done this quite well. Why did he not do more of it?

Far from making excuses for not doing more of this moralizing on details of our duties or of the learned application that the good man must make of his goodness, Blondel insists that this would have been contrary to his deliberate intention. "Your disappointment is explained, therefore, not by omission on my part, but by my aiming to demonstrate the chimerical and superstitious character of any attempt to directly ground a self-sufficient morality and to constitute an absolutely autonomous science" (1907c, 90). Blondel's intention was not to formulate anything like Kant's *Groundwork for a Metaphysics of Morals*, but rather to demonstrate the futility of any attempt to ground such morality in the will alone or in pure practical reason.

In fact, Blondel even apologizes for including any moral appeals to duty, not because he looks down on such instruction, but rather because such appeals tend to distract from his single-minded thought, which was that action cannot be defined, restricted, or organized purely within the natural order, no matter how extended or idealized we suppose it to be. In other words, or in terms of the principle Blondel invokes in his determination of what is at stake in human action, the true meaning of life and the true goodness of action is found only if, implicitly or explicitly, we tend and adhere to the one thing that finally makes our willed will equal to our willing will, which, for Blondel, could only be something supernatural.

In his Introduction to this *Science of Practice*, Blondel is careful to distinguish it from what he calls *Practical Science*. Practical Science is what we come to or learn, simply from following our conscience and putting our moral sense into practice, without stopping to raise critical questions as to the validity of our principles. It is the realm where we discover the obligation to follow our conscience and the solid value of duty accomplished for its own sake. If one could be completely sincere and faithful in following the principles of one's conscience, one would eventually learn what these principles mean ultimately for human destiny. But one is not always certain of being completely sincere or faithful in one's practice, or one is not always prepared to wait until the end before discovering the ultimate meaning of one's action. Practical Science needs to be supplemented by a more reflective and critical science of this practice in its actuality. What are the conditions for our doing what we have to do in the world? This is the question for the Science of Practice, as distinct from Practical Science. If our acts are morally valid only by reason of the final and total intention to which they are expressly or confusedly subordinate, then it is incumbent on the Science of Practice to determine how these acts will commune with this will or this life whence they derive their ultimate value and, as it were, their soul.

If Blondel's conclusions in the Science of Practice appear to be purely negative, in the sense that human action is not sufficient unto itself, or that it does not have within itself alone its ultimate rule and its ultimate end, so that there is no autonomous moral science and no legitimately separate philosophy, it is only because moral science and philosophy are meant to set aside illusions, which, for all their rational nobility, are nevertheless illusions, if they pretend to be self-sufficient. The science of life cannot be grounded as science, or practice cannot be grounded as sufficient, without surpassing the natural order of the will itself, the phenomenon of duty, or even any metaphysical conception of human being. Without reference to something supernatural, Blondel wants to claim, our way of thinking and living remains incoherent and superstitious.

Marion protests that it is unjust to bunch together, under one common reproach of superstition, the devotee of duty and the savage fetishist, as Blondel does in his chapter on superstitious action as well as in his reply to Marion's question. Blondel, however, comes to the defense of the savage, who, if his will is sincere and straightforward, also serves some good no less than the more enlightened devotee of pure duty. From the beginning, in his defense of Practical Science as distinct from and prior to the Science of Practice, Blondel has scrupulously maintained the rightness of simple folk who can only act according to the light of their conscience, without any critical discussion of their action. They learn from their action itself. What Blondel takes exception to is the sort of middling stance of those who, while profiting from the partial light we have on the end of human life, close themselves off from any new light or any new exigency that might come from something higher than ourselves. In this, he claims, there is usurpation by a thought that is incompetent by itself to define the true end of man, so that the spontaneous efforts of conscience are perverted. If we can admire all those who go forward without sinning against the light, and who devote themselves to a work of personal and social salvation, no matter where they are coming from, we must be severe in our judgment of those who have the superstition of action for the sake of action or of intention for the sake of intention, and who then stop themselves or stop others along the road where we must always go forward without presuming that we have arrived.

The fourth examiner, Victor Brochard, expresses his regrets that he had not had time to study closely and to verify the systematic unity of Blondel's construction, because the date of the defense had been moved up by three weeks. He recognizes that it is important to keep track of this systematic unity in Blondel's work. But he focuses on two links in the chain of Blondel's argument that he has had time to examine, the connection between determinism and freedom and the place of metaphysics in this dialectic, two key points in Blondel's argument.

With regard to the connection between determinism and freedom, Blondel explains how he understands the generation of the idea of freedom from determinism itself, through the mediation of another idea, the idea of the infinite in consciousness. Brochard brings up two difficulties with regard to this. First, Blondel's use of the term *infinite* seems equivocal and, second, since there is nothing in reality that corresponds to what Blondel calls the idea of the infinite, it does not follow that our freedom is real.

In answer, Blondel explains that, at the point where the connection between determinism and freedom is being made, there is no need for the kind of objective realism the objection presupposes. If the claim were that the determinism of facts, on the one hand, and moral freedom, on the other, are absolute realities in themselves, there would be no way of connecting them and the objection would be insoluble. But that is not the claim in Blondel's phenomenological method, which prescinds from any ontological preoccupation and from any assertion whatsoever, whether realist or idealist. At the point of his argument where "freedom" is seen as flowing necessarily from "determinism," the aim is simply to unfold the sequence of ideas tied to one another in the internal consciousness of action, and to disclose the implicit assertions contained in our explicit assertions. In other words, in his phenomenology Blondel is only describing the solidarity and the generation of ideas that flow from one another, even when they appear as supposedly incompatible realities. Before coming to any examination of the ontological bearing of such implicit assertions, Blondel still has to inventory a whole set of other ideas that also flow from these two intertwined ideas in human consciousness, ideas that we also inevitably affirm in our conscious action. This is how he sees the necessary connection between determinism and freedom. He sums up his case as follows:

> I show that action, if we reflect on it at all, concerns the total order of things; that, for us to have the idea of our action, we must have the idea of a transcendent initiative, the idea of an infinite (for the infinite, in scientific language, is no more than the notion of some incommensurability); the consciousness of this very transcendence is tied to the very consciousness of a freedom; and this consciousness of freedom, whatever use we make of it, whether fictitious, apparent, or authentic, marks with its imprint the entire series of conscious states that follow and the entire sequence of the determinism wherein what we call (for we are speaking here of appearances) the creations and the productions of our will take place. (1907c, 93)

Brochard then asks Blondel what degree of consistency or reality he attributes to sense objects, to the truths of the positive sciences, or to any of the successive terms of the universal chain he rolls out. Is Blondel, for example, a monadist? Blondel continues his answer in the same vein as before. Of course, sense objects are. Moreover, the invincible trust we have in the reality of all the objects of scientific knowledge, metaphysics, and morality is well founded. But it is not in isolation, or partially, that we can resolve any properly ontological problem. No single link in the chain can bear the answer to this problem by itself. All the links can be seen as real only if, while marking their irreducible heterogeneity on the one hand, we also take note, on the other hand, of their interdependence and of the necessity to bring them all back to their single and common reason for being. Hence the need to consider the entire chain of objects of consciousness before asking what degree of consistency or reality we can attribute to any one of them in particular, or what variety there is of real and distinct beings or objects. To ask whether Blondel is a monadist is like asking a chemist whether he still believes in phlogiston.

With regard to the point about metaphysics as part of the dialectic of action, Blondel answers that metaphysics too must enter into the series of objects for consciousness to consider in its action. Blondel prescinds from the variety of metaphysical systems one could bring up. He merely shows that any metaphysical system is necessarily the principle of an original dynamism in action, and that it inevitably confers upon our acts a character of transcendence. In the end, however, any metaphysical conception is bound to come back, in a second moment of the dialectic, in connection with the idea of God and proofs for his existence. But even there it does not remain static. Even the idea of God has to enter into the dynamism of action, as it gives rise to an alternative for the will: to be God *with* God or to be God *against* God. From this alternative, where the will has to pronounce itself as for or against God, there then follows a *metaphysics to the second power*, so to speak, a fundamentally realist metaphysics that then presents being, no longer as simply an object constituted by logical contours we can know from the outside and see as equal to the pure idea, but rather as a truth and goodness in which we participate more by conforming ourselves to it interiorly. In saying this, as well as in preparing his introductory remarks for the defense, Blondel was thinking of the final chapter he intended to add to the dissertation he was defending, which was to be on action as the bond between thought and being.

It was for the final examiner, Gabriel Séailles, to raise what must have appeared to him the most delicate question. Not wishing to trample on any sincere convictions of one defending a philosophical dissertation, he still wanted to question what he thought were the theological problems Blondel was raising at the end.

This was indeed a touchy question for Blondel, but not in the sense that Séailles was thinking. Far from fearing to be criticized as a believer in Catholicism, Blondel feared much more to be mistaken for a theologian. "The inspiration of my work is in no way theological," he answered immediately. "I have made every effort to go as far as reason can and must go, without transgressing into any domain external to philosophy. What is rational must, without any scruple, be subjected to unremitting criticism. Hence the conclusion at which I arrive must not become the occasion for mistaking my intentions, my method, and the very meaning of these conclusions" (1907c, 96).

What Blondel wanted above all else was a philosophical discussion of religious questions, something that was singularly lacking in France at the end of the nineteenth century, unlike in Germany or England. This was for him a mutilation of philosophy, calling for reason itself to reclaim an essential part of its domain. What was required for this philosophical reclaiming was also a philosophical method that would follow action in its real and actual development, in a critical and scientific way in order to make explicit what is implicit in human action as a whole and in order to make ourselves equal to ourselves.

Having followed such a method in his dissertation, Blondel now wanted his conclusions to be understood purely as philosophical. By showing that neither man nor nature alone can bring action to its completion, he argues that action which is fully consistent with its secret wish for autonomy "must subordinate itself to an action beyond that which it can prescribe for itself, to a higher order than any that thought can construct or justify for itself, and to a religious expectation, a supernatural truth, a literal practice" (1907c, 96).

In doing this, however, and in showing how we have the power and the duty to discern the order that would correspond to this religious predisposition within ourselves, or to discern how and at what price we come to adhere to supernatural dogmas and precepts, Blondel made no claim of entering into the supernatural itself as a philosopher, or of discovering what is its content. That would have been to betray both philosophy and theology, the latter of which has articles of faith for its principles, not purely rational truths. In other words, it would have been contradictory to conclude that action can find completion only in accepting a heteronomy, and then do as if one could philosophically deduce or promulgate, on the basis of this conclusion, the data of revelation, which are what they are and which answer our need only in that they are not drawn from ourselves or from philosophy. To define the conditions that render such data discernible, acceptable, and assimilable is in no way to produce, to discover, or to explain them.

In that case, then, Séailles asks, how can we say that the human will and the triumph of freedom come to completion in a literal submission, and how can autonomy convert itself into pure heteronomy without committing suicide? To appreciate this paradox, Blondel answers, we do not even have to consider the properly supernatural order. One simply has to recognize that we cannot sincerely will infinitely without willing the infinite. The question comes down to this: How can we will the infinite? How can we appropriate it to ourselves without first renouncing ourselves, "without letting go of ourselves to bring ourselves back to the very source of our being and without abandoning ourselves to this movement which takes us from God to God? We do not acquire the infinite as a thing," as the dissertation had already tried to make clear (1893a, 313).

"We make room for it in ourselves, through sacrifice and devotion, by liberating ourselves from the exclusive attachment to self and to the finite" (1907c, 97).

We can do this, Blondel adds, without having the real and onerous heteronomy of duty and faith contradicting the legitimate autonomy of the will, and without taking away our responsibility for lacking in submission, when we go against the very light of consciousness and conscience.

Séailles grants this up to a certain point, but then brings up the final objection of the afternoon. When Blondel speaks of the death of action and the sanction that follows from it, supposedly something like hell, how can he be so ruthless, as if the heavenly Father were to reject one of his creatures in a way that no earthly father would do for a wayward child? How can we excuse, or even understand, such a suffering inflicted from the outside, as if by an external constraint or a brutal vengeance?

Yes, Blondel agrees, the suffering would be immoral and cruel, as well as in vain, if it were imposed only from the outside. But this hypothesis is the opposite of what Blondel has claimed in his argument. In showing how the will can pervert its own movement directing it to its end, Blondel has indicated in what sense this perversion of the will itself is definitive, and how the sanction is drawn from the will itself, from the internal strength of the movement that was directing it to its true end, so that, as Bossuet had said, hell is sin itself. In this as in everything else, Blondel is only listening from within for the echo of voices from the outside. To be punished, the one who is guilty does not need to be changed or crushed. It is enough for him to see in the depths of himself, to feel his emptiness fully, to suffer the lack of that of which he has deprived himself.

A Grudging Recognition

All this took place on a Wednesday afternoon in June 1893. It was articulated in defense of a thesis that had been elaborated largely in solitude and meditation on the meaning of life itself, in order to open up the scope of philosophy to the fullness of human existence and to a dimension of supernatural transcendence. It was aimed at an audience that had largely and systematically closed itself off from any such dimension through a rationalist and immanentist presupposition illustrated by Séailles' objection. Most importantly, it was geared to arrive at its own end by strictly philosophical or rational means, so that philosophers themselves as philosophers would have to recognize the rational ground of its conclusions.

In one sense, Blondel's momentous effort was successful. He did prove, to the satisfaction of his examiners, that his method was indeed philosophical and that he was worthy of being recognized as a philosopher. In spite of their misgivings about his conclusions, the board of examiners was unanimous in officially granting Blondel its seal of approval, the title of *Docteur ès Lettres,* which he had been seeking as an entry into teaching philosophy on the level of the University.

In another sense, however, Blondel's effort was not successful, for, when he came to apply quite candidly for a teaching post at the University level, he found that the misgivings about his conclusions overshadowed whatever approval he had gained in the defense of his method. Without even letting him sit down, the Administrator told him that "given the attitude I had adopted by denying philosophy all its value and all its rational autonomy in order to arrive at a pure and exclusive supernaturalism, his responsibility as a public servant did not allow him to give me a position" (1928a, 49). Blondel could only protest that this was the exact opposite of what he had done. In fact, as he had said in his defense, far from restricting the scope and freedom of philosophy, his effort was to restore to philosophy, with a philosophical method, the highest part of its natural realm of investigation.

But the protestation was of no avail. Blondel was offered a job teaching history at a Lycée. He declined the offer, declaring himself unworthy of it. As a result he found himself involuntarily unemployed for two years, until another intervention by Boutroux, this time before the Minister of Education, who forced the Administration to offer him a University post. The fact that it eventually turned out to be in Aix-en-Provence, almost as far away from Paris as possible, was perhaps not purely incidental. The abiding misgivings of a largely antireligious University concerning his philosophy were no doubt still there to keep him as far away as possible from the City of Lights in France, the Mecca of its intellectual life.

It is interesting to note how the misgivings of philosophers themselves were expressed more cogently in a brief note on the final version of the dissertation after it was published in November 1893, penned by Léon Brunschvicg for the newly founded *Revue de Métaphysique et Morale.* According to Brunschvicg, in a phrase that Blondel would take very much to heart in the years to come, when he would have to continue defending his standing as a philosopher, modern rationalism has been led by its analysis of thought to make the *notion of immanence* the basis and the very condition for any philosophical doctrine. Contrary to this, however, according to Brunschvicg, Blondel has focused on action in order to show that in every human act there is an inevitable transcendence and that, starting from nothing and even from the negation of any moral problem, one can arrive at a necessity for a literal practice of religion, so that the universality of philosophical problems is *transposed* into the practical order and resolved by the force of this transposition.

Brunschvicg concedes a certain originality to Blondel's method, especially in the continuous tension it creates between the description of phenomena and the impossible effort to contain them in a fixed order. But he adds that, notwithstanding his sincerity, his breadth of conception, and his dialectical subtlety, Blondel will still find among the defenders of the rights of Reason courteous but resolute adversaries (1951, 99).

What Blondel saw in this note, however, was not just a courteous adversarial relationship, but a tendency to continue excluding him, without further examination, from the field of free thought and rational discourse. What he wanted more than anything else was precisely to introduce into this field of rational discourse a religious scope that was being excluded in France. In defense of his endeavor, Blondel compares philosophy in France with philosophy in England and in Germany, where religion has long been a subject of rational discussion. He speaks of a certain voluntary mutilation of philosophy in France, in its refusal to entertain religious questions. Though he represents a Catholic viewpoint in France, as a philosopher he is intent only on extracting "from Catholicism the entire rational element it contains," just as Germany has long sought to do with its Protestant forms of religion (1951, 101).

This was not to say that Blondel expected no opposition in the rational discourse he was proposing. What he wanted was to open up a scientific discussion in which religious questions could be aired on the level of ideas, even where oppositions are recognized, instead of just on a level of blind emotions. His intention was also to bring rationalism itself back into what it denied and what denies it. The question for him was to determine the relation of what we know rationally with what surpasses this order of understanding, without misusing either what is known or what is unknowable, and without any false positivism or mysticism. Hence Brunschvicg's suggestion that Blondel was overly enamored of mysteries was contrary to what Blondel himself thought he could extract philosophically from religion, its very rational core.

By placing the order of grace above the order of nature, Christianity had introduced a certain historical consciousness to the effect that human beings cannot find, within themselves or by themselves, all the truth necessary for life. In the eyes of the young Blondel, the Scholastics had understood the order of grace as superimposed on the order of nature, so that the two orders, supernatural and natural, remained exterior to one another. At the origin of modern thought, these two separated currents, stemming from different origins, became a problem rather than a solution with regard to the relation between them. In rejecting the idea of any rational preparation for faith, Protestantism came to view the relation between the two orders as a juxtaposition, with the tendency for one to become exclusive of the other. Hence comes Brunschvicg's "notion of immanence as the basis and the very condition for all philosophy," and the corollary of two parallel series between life and thought, or between belief and science, without any communication between the two. Knowledge only makes us conscious of the mystery in which we find ourselves. The practice of life, on the other hand, plunges us into it as in darkness.

What Blondel was proposing was a new way of relating the supernatural to the natural through action. In the latter, he writes, "the two orders that had been superimposed, juxtaposed, and opposed, are composed, and compenetrate one another" (1951, 102). In studying action, he was not merely reacting against a narrow rationalism centered only on ideas and thought. Nor was he merely transposing philosophical questions into practical questions, as Brunschvicg was suggesting. He was bringing out the transcendent truths implied in action without abandoning the notion of immanence so essential to modern rationalism. This immanence of action as well as of thought remained his own point of departure, his method, as he would argue later in the *Lettre* of 1896, as well as the spirit of his conclusion. In this he did not think he was shrinking from or compromising natural morality, but rather expanding it to new dimensions. To be sure, what we think and what we do by ourselves is only a part of what happens in us. But this part is coextensive with the whole. This is why, Blondel says, "I can study what seems to surpass the human being's proper role, without going outside the role of philosophy, because I do not go outside our human action. In looking at action, reason discovers more than in looking at reason, without ceasing to be rational. And if I speak of the supernatural, it is still a cry of nature, a call of moral consciousness, and an exigency of thought that I am expressing" (1951, 102).

The point of Blondel's philosophy, however, was not to show how the two orders, natural and supernatural, do in fact compose in history and human experience. That would have taken him beyond what he considered the proper role of philosophy. It was rather to show a certain necessity for the supernatural in our action, so that this necessity, not the supernatural itself, has a character of immanence that enables us to grasp it as natural. In asserting such a necessity, through an immanent affirmation of the transcendent, we do not in any way prejudge the transcendent reality of the immanent truths. What we do is open the way for a critical examination of the subjective conditions for accepting, or rejecting, the supernatural, which can be understood only as something necessary for us, and yet as strictly impossible for us to achieve by ourselves.

It is this insistence on the insufficiency of reason and natural morality by itself that made Blondel suspect among philosophers. But it was the rationality of his argument for this insufficiency that eventually won him acceptance as a philosopher, though it did not always win acceptance of his conclusions regarding the necessity of the supernatural. This same argument, in spite of the first enthusiasm with which it was received among embattled Catholics, would also eventually get him into difficulty with a number of theologians as well as philosophers, after the *Lettre* of 1896 in which he elaborated further on the *method of immanence* he was now adumbrating for Brunschvicg. But at the end of 1893, when Blondel was still waiting for an opening into the University, he was thinking of his role as one of bringing the absolute rights of reason and the privileges of a positive faith together on a common ground, where believers and unbelievers alike could be at leisure to discuss, without undue passion, the great interests that impassioned them. This was the peace hoped for, not just provisionally, but lasting enough to allow individuals, certain in their conscience, to enter into discussion, without fear of offending others in their conscience, and with respect for the truth that all were seeking, rationalists as well as anti-rationalists, religious as well as anti-religious.

Blondel would eventually win greater acceptance among philosophers with his *Lettre* of 1896, as Brunschvicg would later acknowledge. But Blondel was to do so not without antagonizing a number of religionists who had first thought of him as an ally against the rationalists. Before we come to that, however, let us flash back to Blondel's origins and to the dissertation that was the occasion for this daring and dramatic entrance into the intellectual life of France at the turn of the twentieth century. In one sense, what prepared him for such an entrance is a confidence that grew quietly within him in a staunchly Catholic family and in a city rich with its own culture, so that he was not easily intimidated by the more renowned lights of Paris.

II

Awakening to the Light of the Gospel in Human Action

Early Family Life

Maurice Blondel was born in Dijon, the capital city of Burgundy in France, on November 2, 1861. In later life he would add the precision that it was at seven in the morning, about the time when the Catholic liturgy was celebrating the office of the dead. In this, as people who knew him personally have noted, he saw a symbol: this birth at the moment when the memory of the dead was being kindled could only mean a continuity of life, the prolongation of a line. This is why, as he would say himself, he understood early in life that he had been given to his family in order to continue its traditions. The date and the hour of his deliverance from the maternal womb imposed on him a duty of fidelity, something he was conscious of all his life, even as he came to think that innovation was the best way of preserving tradition.

The family into which he was born was in fact one of long and very strong tradition in the Catholic faith of France. In a *Mémorial* of the family that he prepared for the hundredth birthday of his older sister, Thérèse, Blondel himself was able to trace its lineage, thanks especially to records of properties owned by the family over the centuries, all the way back to the thirteenth century, where he found one Jehan Blondel, a yeoman in the service of the Duke of Burgundy, who had gone to negotiate with the Great Turk for the liberation from captivity of one of the Duke's sons. The family was not part of the nobility, but they had prospered in the service of the Dukes of Burgundy and maintained themselves in prominence as lawyers and notaries. In the nineteenth century they were part of the established bourgeoisie in legal and notarial circles who felt responsible, not just for public service, but also for the propagation of their robust faith in the face of a rising secularism.

The father of the family was a notary, a highly esteemed profession that enjoyed a certain prestige in the community. Through his practice he came into contact with many people, among whom he exerted an appreciable influence. The mother was a gentle person, mistress of the household, retiring and quite refined, with a very subtle spirit. She too was a Blondel, first cousin to her husband, educated in the same strong religious tradition as he was. Her son, Maurice, remembered her as an exceptional *cuisinière*, in the best of Burgundian custom. He also remembered her as having had an important part in his religious formation at home, along with her husband, who was especially leery of the growing anti-religious sentiment in the public life that surrounded them. It was she, apparently, who pushed to have the children attend the state Lycée of Dijon for their education, rather than the private religious college, not without some misgiving from the father, who was afraid that the children might lose their faith in these militantly secular institutions. It was she too who wrote to all her children several times a week as long as she was alive, to keep them posted about the goings on in the family and to inquire about their life, and who got them all to stay in touch with one another, by writing frequently in those days before the telephone, when the postal service in France was still speedy and efficient.

Blondel was the last of four children, the Benjamin of the family. The oldest was the sister, Thérèse, who was born eleven years before Maurice and who was to outlive him by a few months, having gone three months beyond her hundredth birthday. Then came two other sons, Edouard, who was to become a notary like his father and who was to manage the affairs of his brothers and sister as well as take over the father's practice in Dijon, and George, who was to follow a more intellectual career as a Germanist and an economist in Paris, after having defended his own dissertation on German economics less than a year before Maurice defended his in philosophy.

Of the four, Edouard died in 1923, relatively young by the family standards, while George died in 1948, less than a year before Maurice, who lived to be 87. The family knew of several relatives, besides Thérèse, who had lived over one hundred years, which gives rise to the observation that, though many may have been of fragile health in the Blondel stock, as Maurice himself would feel he was most of his life, there was also in it a power for longevity and lucidity into a ripe old age, way beyond the average life expectancy of their time.

Not uncharacteristically for the family, the older sister was chosen as godmother for her youngest brother. She is the one who chose his name, Maurice, and she took her responsibility for her godchild quite seriously. Later in life Maurice would joke that he had had three mothers as a child, his birth-mother, his aunt Marie, and his sister-godmother, all of whom showered special attention on the last and seemingly most genial of the children. The aunt was a sister of his mother, who was very well educated and spoke several languages, having studied with the nuns of the Visitation all the way to the highest classes, as was not uncommon among certain women in the eighteenth and nineteenth centuries. She had thought of becoming a religious herself, but her fragile health deterred her. She took special care of the last born while the mother attended to the other business of the house and took care of the older children. As for Thérèse, she never married, so that she was always there for her godchild-brother even later in life, especially when he was suffering from unjust and unsympathetic accusers of his philosophy. She used to say that Maurice should have been an entomologist, rather than a philosopher, so that he would not have had to endure so much misunderstanding and run the risk of being condemned by the Church to which the whole family, including Maurice, were loyally devoted.

Maurice was thus born into a large, closely knit family, which included other uncles and aunts and cousins who followed and shared one another's lives. Among these the uncle Hyppolite is worth mentioning, the father's brother, who had been a magistrate under the Third Empire. Uncle Hyppolite had a son, André, who was Maurice's age and who was to rise to great heights as a prominent physicist, while Maurice would be experiencing his difficulties with the witch-hunt against Modernism. Both Hyppolite and his brother, Maurice's father, shared a contempt for the Republic, which they referred to as *la gueuse*, the reprobate. They were not monarchists, but they did not approve of the general drift of the Republic, especially as it moved away from and against religious institutions. This is why later on, as their sons showed signs of pursuing careers in the state University system, they would be reluctant in giving their approval.

In the meantime, however, they raised their children to be good responsible citizens as well as fervently religious people, as was typical in the well-established circle of Christian bourgeois families of their time who thought of themselves as defenders of the Faith. The children were taught to take pride in work well done and to care about doing things right. Concern for the poor was an integral part of this care, so that there was always some attempt to include some of the less fortunate in the activities of the family. This was part of the family's missionary spirit that Maurice imbibed from his earliest years. It was not an ostentatious spirit. It was discreet and quiet, but it was real and effective, showing itself in what were called the works of mercy. The family always had its "poor" to reach out to, as Maurice always would later on wherever he went, whether as a student in Paris or as a professor in Aix. All this was done unpretentiously, without affectation. It was part of an atmosphere that was warm and serene, filled with self-confidence, good humor, and simplicity. It was all part of what one did as a believer making one's way in the world in view of an ultimate reunion with God. What counted more than success and fame, and what was expected of all, was a certain professional conscientiousness and a commitment to religious life in the Catholic Church.

To all appearances, the young Maurice seems to have responded quite positively to all this ambient spirit and to the special attention he got as the youngest and perhaps the most genial child. He grew up in a large house near the center of Dijon that reflected the standing of the family, with its courtyard and even its cloister and, for vacation time, in another house in Saint-Seine sur Vingeanne, about thirty miles from Dijon in the wine country of the Côte d'Or, where he would later spend the better part of his time in seclusion writing his dissertation. Though the house in Dijon was big, however, it was well filled by the family, which included the maternal grandmother, until Maurice was thirteen, as well as the aunt Marie. As the youngest of the family, he did not have a room of his own to sleep or to work in until he was fourteen. While his older brothers and sister each had a room of their own, because they were more advanced in their studies, Maurice would be found doing his schoolwork in his parents' room or even in his father's receiving room, where clients would notice him and worry about disturbing him.

Maurice was given pets to care for as a child, including a guinea pig and a lamb, which he remembered in later life as following him wherever he went. But he also found many more pets on his own during his stays at the country-home of Saint-Seine. He showed an early fascination with spiders, ants, and other insects, which eventually blossomed into a hobby of collecting and raising caterpillars and butterflies brought back to Saint-Seine from all parts of France, a hobby he kept up until he was twenty-two years old, in his first year at Normale, at which time he donated his collection of seventy-two boxes of butterflies to the Museum of Dijon, thus foregoing the career of entomologist his sister thought might have been preferable for him during the time of his difficulties with certain theologians. For his own part, as he was to say later in life, it is from this early fascination with insects that Blondel thought his later concern for a philosophy of the concrete would derive.

There is a picture at the Archives of Maurice at age three showing him wearing a sort of dress-jumper down to his knees; his left hand, on a parlor chair, holds a large metal ring, and his right hand holds a stick to make it run. This kind of dress for very young boys apparently was still customary among bourgeois families of the time in France. The picture shows the young boy gazing steadily into the camera, willing to stop and pose for the picture but ready to go on with his play. There are also other pictures of him several years later, including one when he was making his first solemn communion at age thirteen, in a rather formal suit with trousers, showing him as a little gentleman who can look into the camera with aplomb and let himself be photographed without fuss or embarrassment, a boy very much at ease in his family setting. Though he had no story to tell about robbing an orchard just for the malice of it in later life, as Augustine did, he did remember raising his two fists to his aunt Marie as the first act in which he became conscious of having done something wrong.

Early Education

Bright as he was, he also resisted learning to read and write. It was not until he was seven years old, when he was already in primary school, that his mother and his aunt Marie finally cajoled him into learning to read by telling him that, if he did not learn, his ears would grow long like those of a cartoon character called Célestin, who did not learn to read, hardly an auspicious beginning for one who would later spend so much time each day reading and writing, until he could not longer see well enough to read and write for himself.

After three years in a religious primary school, shortly before his ninth birthday, Maurice moved on to the Lycée of Dijon. This is when the preference of the mother seems to have prevailed over the hesitation of the father, to place their son in a secular school. It was the beginning of an association with the state educational system that was to last the rest of Blondel's life. At the Lycée, Blondel first went through an eight-year grinding course of classical studies that was typical of these public schools at the end of the nineteenth century in France. This included eight years of Latin and German as well as French, eight years of mathematics along with geography and history, six years of Greek, and four years of science. It was hard work, but the young Blondel thrived on it. It included a lot of dissertation writing as well as translating and doing themes in different languages year in and year out. This is where he learned to write and speak well.

Each year, at the distribution of the prizes, he would come out first in most of his subjects, especially those having to do with literature, writing, and history. In mathematics and science he frequently came out only second, in competition mainly with his good friend, Maurice Léna, who was the son of the principal and with whom he would continue to correspond in later life. For each first prize, Blondel's mother had agreed to give him a special reward. Each year the whole family attended the distribution of prizes, including uncle Hyppolite and cousin André, who was attending the local Jesuit college. Comparisons were made and a friendly rivalry developed between the two cousins. The uncle would tease Maurice for being too timid, and perhaps for being too submissive to the Republic, in contrast to cousin André, who was more combative.

Anyone familiar with Blondel later on, especially at the defense of his dissertation at the Sorbonne, might have found this suggestion of timidity in him somewhat surprising. But later on in life he did remember himself as having been very timid as a child. It was not until his stay at the École Normale Supérieure in Paris that he overcame this timidity. It is perhaps in this context that we can understand his recollection that "he had had no adolescence." He had gone from childhood to manhood without much of the turmoil that adolescents usually go through. In any event, at the defense of his dissertation he was combative enough to impress his uncle, not only with the force, but also with the spiritual content of his answers, which took the uncle by surprise and led him to say that henceforth he would take his nephew as his spiritual director.

Along with his childhood timidity, Blondel also spoke of a certain sensitivity toward all sorts of living things, especially those of the sort with which he had had living contact. It is this sensitivity that led to a source of great embarrassment for him as a young boy, when he fainted at the sight of a guinea pig being dissected in a laboratory class. He was reminded of a similar guinea pig that he had had as a pet, along with the lamb, and he had to be carried out of the lab.

No doubt, the quality and the kind of education each cousin was getting was a subject of frequent discussion in the family. But each pursued his course of studies to the end, at the Lycée and at the Jesuit college respectively, and each ended up going on to one of the Grandes Écoles in Paris afterwards, one in physics and one in philosophy. One of the differences between them, Maurice later recalled, is that while he was accepted to only one of them, the Normale, his cousin André was accepted to all three of them, the Polytechnique and the Centrale as well, and chose to go to the latter.

In the meantime, however, Maurice was not just pursuing a rigorous course of academic study. He was also growing into an intense interior life, led especially by his mother and his aunt Marie. For him this meant a life centering on the Eucharist and the Catholic liturgy, which he would later think of as a philosophy in act, in the context of his dissertation (1961c, 223). This was before the days of frequent Communion, now taken for granted among Catholics, but it was a time when the young Blondel got into the habit of attending morning Mass frequently and of participating in the other hours of the daily prayer of the Church, including Vespers or evening prayer.

He was thirteen years old when he made his First Solemn Communion, an occasion for a family reunion and celebration as well as an important step in his life of devotion and union with God. It was something he had aspired to, to have within himself the very source of the Christian life on earth, and it was something for which he prepared with a special retreat. He tells of having had an almost sensible feeling of the presence of Christ when the day came, and of wanting to get away from the hubbub of the family in the evening for a quiet time by himself. He went into the park of Dijon for a solitary walk in order to find himself alone with Jesus within him, to meditate upon this new presence of the divine within him. It was shortly after mid-June, on the Feast of the Sacred Heart, and there he saw the light of fireflies playing all about him in the dark. He marveled at this transparency in the insects, but he marveled even more at the transparency of what was happening within himself. "I have much more than they within myself," he said to himself. "I carry within my heart the Son of God, the Son of the living God, for He is mine now." This was an extraordinary contact for him, and it kept him awake for the night. It made him long for Communion thereafter and ask for permission to take Communion each time he went to confession. It also endeared to him the priest entrusted with the care of the *talas* at the École Normale later on, who used to encourage them to receive Communion as often as they could get to Mass.

The time of a First Communion in the Blondel family was one, not just for receiving, but also for giving and sharing the gift received with the less fortunate. In the case of Maurice, this meant sharing with the young *ramoneur,* or chimney sweep, whom he had seen climbing into the chimneys of his family home, a boy his own age named Augustin who became his brother of Communion. Boys this age were very good as *ramoneurs* because they were small enough to climb up the chimney itself with their twig brooms, from which they emerged all black with soot. The sight of these young boys his age coming out of the chimney all black in contrast with himself, whom no one would allow even close to the chimney lest he dirty himself, made him cry the first time he saw it and it made him choose one of them as his brother of Communion. This meant that the family took on the responsibility for preparing this "brother" for First Communion along with their son, through catechism and a special retreat. It also meant that the family took on the expenses of clothing and special insignia required for a dignified participation in the solemn event of a First Communion mass.

All this Maurice entered into, not just for First Communion, but also for years afterward when he continued to write to Augustin, to share with him some of the education he was getting but which children of the poor like Augustin had no hope of getting. In keeping with this same spirit, he also joined with his brothers, while all three were together at the Lycée, to form a small school of their own, for teaching other children how to read who were kept from school because they had to go to work at a very young age, whether as shepherds in the country or as *ramoneurs* in the city, not to mention other tasks for which children could be used.

At age thirteen Blondel had his first personal experience of death and loss, something he would commemorate the rest of his life on February 5. It was the death of his maternal grandmother, which affected his entire family profoundly at a time when he was most sensitive to everyone around him. This is something he comes back to in his personal diary on the thirteenth anniversary of this death, in 1889, as his first mourning, *mon premier deuil,* where he remembers people, his entire family, experiencing an emptiness in their life and in a well-balanced system of habits. "It is themselves that they mourn," he writes. "They are diminished and torn. Then, little by little, compensations are established and the hole is covered over" (1961c, 173). It is also something that he recounts in great detail to his wife in their first year of marriage in 1895, so that she "would know all the origins of his heart" (1966b, 21). What he remembers of his grandmother is that she was the one who brought him to catechism and taught him so well what a good conscience is. She had been the stalwart woman of the house who had nursed her daughter, Blondel's *tante Marie*, back to health from typhoid fever. She had also been the one who would give him change so that he could give to the poor. Blondel watched her weaken and take to her bed. He rejoiced when she seemed to rally for a day or two. But then the entire family felt devastated when she took a turn for the worse. As the youngest of the family, he had to wait alone in his mother's room during those last moments, but when he was finally allowed into the room of death he found everyone in tears, especially aunt Marie and her brother, uncle Louis, who both felt especially abandoned by the loss of their mother. In his own sobbing, Maurice felt that he was crying as much for his aunt Marie as for his grandmother.

At age fourteen Blondel was advanced enough in both the Christian life and in the command of Latin to be writing verse on Christmas Eve, in his anticipation of the new coming of Christ. Some of this he also recalls years later in his diary at a time when he was already a teacher and beginning intensive work on his dissertation. In a meditation on Christmas Eve he prays to become again a little child in order to understand and to receive Jesus, to become again a good and docile schoolboy intent on doing his work at every moment, and to "keep whole this love that I felt during the wait for my first midnight masses, when in order to pass the time of the vigil I would compose Latin verses, quite proud of my original turns of phrase: *O sic nos Jesum quis non redamaret amantem* (Who would not love Jesus in return who loves us so)" (1961c, 292).

Blondel finds in Jesus the way to reconcile docility to the divine teaching with the authority of one who is to teach. At age twenty-seven, when he had lost the insouciance and suppleness of a child, Blondel would discover a weight to be borne in the world that he had not suspected as a submissive and sheltered child, who has not yet found the freedom of those who love purely. He asks how to live this life of hidden struggles "between a prevenient and affective docility and a laborious independence, because I have to play at one and the same time the role of child and of master, of apprentice, as you did in your familial home, and of doctor." In one sense this was to be the struggle of Blondel's life as a Christian philosopher. As a Christian he had to lead a life of docility in faith, from which he would learn what he had to teach as an independent philosopher of human life.

The Turn to Philosophy

At the end of the eight-year stage at the Lycée, in July 1878, Blondel was awarded the Bachelor of Letters in Rhetoric at age seventeen. In the final year of rhetoric, there was included a basic course in philosophy, in which Blondel was initiated into the study of psychology, ethics, and aesthetics, and for which he wrote a dissertation on the right to punish. But the more intense study of philosophy came in the following year, at the end of which he was awarded the Bachelor of Letters in Philosophy. This capstone year of the Lycée included a continuation of the study of classical literature, along with the study of philosophy. During that year he had Alexis Bertrand as a teacher, from whom he acquired an interest in Maine de Biran, a contemporary of Rousseau who had written in a critical vein on perception and on physical effort, and who was highly touted at the end of the nineteenth century in French philosophy as an earlier version of the Kantian critique. One of Blondel's special assignments at the École Normale later on would be to make a presentation on Maine de Biran, both for his classmates and for one of his first classes to college students. Maine de Biran's ideas on physical effort would also figure prominently in the part of the dissertation on *Action* having to do with implementation of one's intentions.

After the Lycée Blondel matriculated at the Faculty of Letters of Dijon ostensibly to complete his studies in Science and begin studies in Law, in keeping with the prevailing attitude of the family, but he was lured away from Law into Philosophy by the Dean of the Faculty, Henri Joly, who was a specialist in Leibniz. By July 1880 he had completed the requirements for the *License ès Lettres* in Philosophy along with those for a Bachelor of Science. In the awarding of degrees at the end of the year Blondel was given a very special mention along with his friend Léna. "The School was particularly pleased with the examinations of Mr. Léna and even more with those of Mr. Blondel. Mr. Blondel surpassed the average by twenty-seven points. It was one of the most brilliant and solid examinations that the School has seen in a long time."

It was not until three years later, in November 1883, that Blondel completed the requirements for his Bachelor of Law, but by then he was already well advanced in the path of philosophy, having worked intensively in philosophy for another year at Dijon in preparation for the competitive examinations for admission to the École Normale Supérieure, and having been admitted to that School, in philosophy, in August 1881, the first in his family to even think of seeking a career in philosophy at the University level. In the *Itinéraire*, later on, he makes it a point to say that the bishop of Dijon encouraged him to go to Normale, in spite of certain fears from his parents, in pursuit of this career (1928a, 15).

The idea of a *vinculum substantiale* which Blondel found in Leibniz at Dijon turned out to be a key original idea for his own philosophy. He was to come back to it at the École Normale with Boutroux. It became what Blondel would later refer to as *une des cellules-mères de ma pensée* — one of the mother-cells of my thought. The idea had first come to him in a lecture course at Dijon in the winter of 1879, as he recalled, when Joly devoted one of his lectures to the correspondence between Leibniz, late in life, and a certain Father Des Bosses of the Society of Jesus, having to do with ways of conceiving the real presence of Christ in the Eucharist. Unlike most other historians, Joly thought that Leibniz was quite serious in coming up with the hypothesis of a *vinculum substantiale* as a "metaphysical possibility" to account for a higher kind of reality over and above the monads and the relatively idealist conception of a pre-established harmony between them.

According to Joly, Leibniz was haunted by the need to restore the notion of substance metaphysically in opposition to the Cartesian reduction of substance to a fragment of extension. For Leibniz, extension had to be considered a mere phenomenon and could not account for the ultimate reality of things. To make his point he argued from the human soul conceived as a substance par excellence down to the simplest material things which make up the universe and which he called monads. But having come to these monads, Leibniz was then faced with the problem of bringing them together in some kind of order, whence his idea of a harmony for each of these substances closed in upon itself, a kind of parallelism between the external mechanism of perceived phenomena and the internal dynamism of the intelligible monads pre-established by God. Still, according to Joly, it was this idea of the pre-established harmony that was brought into question at the end of his life by Leibniz in response to Des Bosses as inadequate to account for the reality of phenomena. How can such an abstract harmony of substantial points in the universe account for a real composition in substances? Are composites merely a sum of simpler analytical elements (or monads), or is there in them a principle of synthetic unity that is proper to them?

This was the question raised in the correspondence with Des Bosses and, according to Joly, it was taken seriously by Leibniz, because it raised an important difficulty for his system. At first, Leibniz had had recourse to the idea of a dominant monad pulling together the subordinate monads like a herd. But a herd as such only represents a mental unity, leaving the composite substance only with the reality of its monads and their harmony, that is, as little more than an aggregate of substances and not as a substance in itself. What comes up in the correspondence with Des Bosses is an attempt to provide a more metaphysical answer to this question with the idea of a *vinculum substantiale* or a substantial bond that would account better for the original synthetic unity of a composite substance.

Just what Leibniz meant by such a *vinculum* and whether he took it seriously in his own thought, and not just as a means of placating his correspondent, became a matter of controversy in the interpretation of Leibniz and his system, a controversy in which Blondel would intervene on the side of his teacher. Joly made the point that theological questions such as that of the Eucharist had an important influence in the elaboration of Leibniz's system, at the beginning of his attempt to restore the idea of substance against the Cartesians as well as at the end with the hypothesis of a *vinculum substantiale*. In the question of the *vinculum*, this was no doubt something apt to catch the attention of the young Blondel, who was already quite devoted to the Eucharist as a Catholic. But it was not the theological aspect of the debate that fascinated him. It was rather the general bearing of the idea as it related to a higher kind of metaphysical realism, beyond the idealism of a pre-established harmony among phenomena.

To understand how this idea became a mother-cell for Blondel's own thought, we have only to see how he speaks of it later on, in 1930, in the letter of introduction to the French version of his study of this "Historical Enigma of the *Vinculum Substantiale* According to Leibniz and the Beginning of a Higher Realism."

> The explanation of the reasons for the *vinculum* in Leibniz corresponded to a need, still very vague, but already very vivid in me for a spiritual realism, opposed to any idealist symbolism or abstract individualism. What I saw, under this hypothesis provoked by the questions of a Catholic religious and by the spontaneous meditations of Leibniz, was, not a theological problem restricted to an aspect of Eucharistic dogma, but the justification of "incarnate truths," the rehabilitation of the letter and of practice, the primacy of what is ulteriorly actualized as well as one over what is cut up by analysis and reduced to prior elements or abstractions, the efficiency of the final cause and the original value of action, the bond of nature and thought, the real union of spirits forming something like a *body*, like a " new substance," like a composition more *one*, more *substantial* than the elements it dominates and which it elevates to its higher unity: *unum corpus multi sumus*. (1930a, vii-viii)

To be sure, not all of this was clearly in the thought of Leibniz, or in that of Joly, or even perhaps in the thought of the young candidate for the *License* at the time. But it was clearly fermenting in his mind, imbued with a devotion to the Eucharist as Mystical Body of Christ, as he worked on this correspondence between Leibniz and the Jesuit Des Bosses, following his own preoccupation with establishing a spiritual metaphysics and the spiritual value of a religious practice. Though the abbreviated and coded notes he took would later prove to be undecipherable even to himself, as he was to admit later on in a letter to Boutroux (1961a, 9-10), he continued to mull over the subject and to lose himself in it, bringing to it all sorts of preoccupations he was trying to sort out for himself, including those connected with what was to become his dissertation on *Action*, in which many of these same ideas would be laid out systematically and independently of Leibniz. For this reason he was happy to hear Boutroux lecture on the same enigma of Leibniz at Normale and to have it accepted as the subject for his Latin dissertation, a fitting companion to the French dissertation on *Action*, for the *Docteur ès Lettres* at the Sorbonne.

The Rite of Passage at the École Normale

Eventually, then, after his years of preparation for the admission exam to the École Normale Supérieure in Dijon and after his success in the competition, Blondel moved on to Paris in pursuit of his career in philosophy. This was an important passage in several ways. It was a move from "the province" to the City of Light which shines forth for all the provinces, in a country that is singularly divided between one city and all that surrounds it as "provincial." To move to Paris is always an important event for a French man or woman, which is why one is always reluctant to leave the City once one has gone there. Attached as he was to his family and to his Burgundian roots, Blondel was surely elated as well as apprehensive about the move.

Intellectually too it was an important move. In Paris, away from the shelter and support of his family, he found himself in a more universal flow of intellectual life, one that included many currents alien to his own religious and moral bent, not to mention those that were frankly in opposition to it. These included positivism, critical idealism, symbolism as well as dilettantism and pessimism, variations of which were found among the elite student body of the École Normale. Moreover, Blondel found himself the only member of his class coming directly from the province. All the others had already spent one or two years at the *Grands Lycées* of Paris preparing for the rigorous admission exam in which they had had to compete for admission to the highly touted School. Blondel was arriving as a surprise even to his own classmates.

Part of the passage into Normale included initiation rites that all new arrivals had to go through, which sometimes could go to dangerous or embarrassing extremes, as in most schools of this kind the world over. This was not exactly to the liking of our rather prim newcomer from the provinces. But he had been warned to go along with the farce by his friend from Dijon in second year, Jules Dussy. Otherwise he would be hounded for weeks until he was forced to undergo even worse trials. As it turned out he was given a task he could acquit himself of fairly easily. He was wrapped in a sheet, as in a Roman toga, and he was told to conduct an interview with one of the personages whose statues stand atop the École, namely, Rollin the grammarian. Blondel proceeded to berate him for giving students so much grief with language and for not leaving things well enough alone. It was enough to amuse his tormentors and to get by them into the regular flow of the school.

He moved right into the flow, where he was to learn to philosophize ever more rigorously. For a roommate he chose to go with a Jew by the name of Beer, the grandson of a rabbi who had none of his forebears' religious convictions, and with whom Blondel remained in communication for the rest of his life. This was to the chagrin of a Catholic friend, André Pératé, the future art historian, whom he had just met and with whom he was to remain a fast friend for years to come. Again Blondel's idea was to get to know better the mind of people who did not think as he did. Among his fellow students there were other Catholics, other *talas,* like himself, with whom he became very good friends, not only by reason of their devotion to Sunday mass, which it was not always easy to be excused from study hall for, depending on who was director of the school, but also by reason of other activities such as working with the poor at the St. Vincent de Paul Society as well as discussion about the place of religion in one's intellectual life.

One of the students from those early days at Normale who stood out in Blondel's mind years later was one who one day raised the question: Why should anyone interested in the universal truths of reason, and living according to the universal principles of reason, as any rational being should, show any interest in some obscure individual who lived nineteen hundred years ago in a remote part of the Roman Empire? Blondel repeats this question in a note at the beginning of *Le problème de la philosophie catholique* published in 1932, but does not identify the student. In an earlier note not meant for publication, written while he was working on the question of apologetics in the early 1900s, he identifies him as Charles Bourdel, and adds, perhaps with some consolation, that he died in 1904 having received the sacraments of the Catholic Church.

The reference in the question was to Christ, of course, and the question challenged the relevance of anything he might have said or done to anyone's rational philosophy of life. Even if there was an individual such as the one portrayed in the Gospels, what difference could that make to a philosopher intent on leading his life according to rational principles? Or, put in another way, what could philosophy possibly have to do with such an individual that it could not discover through its own resources?

What was implied in the question was a complete separation between philosophy and religion, especially a religion based on a special revelation such as Christianity. While religion might have its own questions, philosophy could have nothing to do with them. It had to remain separate and autonomous, self-sufficient in its own rational view of life. But this was not the way Blondel experienced or understood either philosophy or religion. In his life as a Christian, philosophy and religion were intimately intertwined, even when the religion entailed faith in the historical Jesus as the Lord. While other Catholics and Christians might be willing to settle for a separate philosophy for themselves as well as for non-believers, Blondel was not prepared to accept such a separation. For him the separation was based on an inadequate view of reason and of philosophy, one that rejected *a priori* any question having to do, not only with a particular religion, but also with anything concrete and singular. His was another view of philosophy, one that was not less, but more rational in its concern for the ultimate meaning of real life, one that he would have to develop from scratch in the very critical milieu in which he found himself, but one that would try to answer the question raised by his fellow student in philosophy concerning the historical Jesus as something not irrelevant to philosophy.

Hence it was a certain missionary spirit, the spirit expressed in the Gospel command: "Go, and teach all nations," that led Blondel to undertake a new way in philosophy and to cast about for an appropriate subject of inquiry for this new way. His religion gave him the motivation, but his reason would have to supply the method. He had already gotten some inkling of how this might be done with his study of the *vinculum* in Leibniz, but the idea was not yet clear enough in his mind. He had to learn more about the ways of doing philosophy, as he was to do at Normale. But while others might be learning only ways of a philosophy separate from life, he was learning ways of going beyond such a stunted philosophy back to a more concrete consideration of life itself.

In this endeavor he was not completely alone. He had the support and the example of one of his principal mentors at Normale, Léon Ollé-Laprune, who was also a fervent Catholic opposed to the idea of a separate philosophy. In his work on Moral Certitude, Ollé-Laprune had argued for a certain match between the moral exigencies of human life and the teachings of Christian life, something that Blondel would later refer to as a method of convenience or *convenance* (1896a, 20-22). But this would not satisfy the exigencies of philosophy in matters of religion as Blondel understood them. It was too purely contemplative of a fact that was established in one's life. It presupposed an act of faith in the revealed teachings along with a commitment in practice, and it merely described or gave testimony to the kind of harmony that resulted from this combination of morality and religion. It presented a living system, but it did not show enough of the rational articulation for such a system.

With Ollé-Laprune, Blondel was thus encouraged in his attempt to overcome the separation between philosophy and religion, but he did not find an adequate method for doing so philosophically. He was also encouraged to pursue his study of Maine de Biran and of Pascal, who had been the first to work at overcoming this separation between philosophy and religion in modern thought. Pascal became very dear to Blondel, both as an example and an inspiration, but he too would prove insufficient in Blondel's quest for a philosophical method to deal with questions of religion. As he was to write to his friend Valensin later on, Pascal helped him to free himself from any pretense of going back analytically to "first principles." At the same time, however, he found Pascal's "simplistic opposition of the three orders [of reason, of the heart, and of faith] insufficient, his residue of Jansenism unbearable, his criterium of 'joy, joy, tears of joy' false" (1965a, 178). For Blondel the issue had to be joined, not on the level of mystical experience, but on the level of reason, for that is where the combat had come to be situated in modern philosophy (1896a, 95).

It is through Émile Boutroux, his other mentor at the École Normale, that Blondel would develop his sense of the exigencies of a philosophical method.

Boutroux had written on the contingency of the laws of nature and on the idea of natural law, and in his courses he would insist especially on the rational articulation of the various systems he would expose. With Boutroux, Blondel became conscious of the various problems one has to face with determinism in human action and of different ways of dealing with these problems in the emergence of a spiritual life of freedom. Through him he also had an opportunity to revisit the question of the *vinculum substantiale* in Leibniz as part of the exercises in which Boutroux would have students make presentations before the whole school. Other authors whom Blondel also chose to treat were Theognis, among the ancients, le Play, among the moderns, along with Maine de Biran and Pascal, with whom he had already begun to familiarize himself in Dijon.

From the project on Leibniz, Blondel would derive the subject for his secondary dissertation. It is altogether significant, however, that while Blondel dedicated his primary dissertation on *Action* to Ollé-Laprune, he chose Boutroux as his director for it, in order to assure its greater philosophical rigor and also perhaps to aim it directly at one whom he felt he had to convince. Boutroux was the kind of man Blondel had to convince in his endeavor, for as he was to tell Valensin later, "I was trying to envision explicitly what it was that was stopping such a well-informed and straightforward intelligence as Émile Boutroux's on the path of faith or of religious practice; and I was preoccupied with saying something appropriate for such needs, something that could and would count for such souls" (1965a, 175).

Among his fellow students at the École Normale to whom Blondel felt especially obliged later on was Victor Delbos, who later became a prominent historian of philosophy and died at an untimely age in 1916. Delbos arrived at the School one year after Blondel, but they became very good friends who shared in one another's philosophical work. A Catholic, like Blondel, Delbos also shared with him a keen metaphysical sense. And while Blondel was working on his dissertation on *Action*, Delbos was working on a study on Spinoza and the evolution of Spinozism in German philosophy that he published the year Blondel defended and published his dissertation. Each one knew of the other's work through correspondence and mutual criticism and, through Delbos, Blondel gained a more intimate knowledge of Spinoza, whom he came to view as a key figure in the development of modern philosophy, including German philosophy from Kant to Hegel, especially with regard to the question of immanence and transcendence.

As a historian, Delbos shared Blondel's systematic concern with the question of immanence and transcendence and, as a systematic philosopher, Blondel was able to share in Delbos's historical explorations into the question, as it came to characterize modern philosophy, as we shall see in Blondel's review of Delbos's book when it came out. From Delbos, Blondel learned more about what he would later refer to as the philosophical exigencies of modern philosophy in matters of religion.

The normal course of studies at the École Normale Supérieure included two more years of intense classical studies in Latin and Greek as well as in modern literature and systematic philosophers. This was followed by a third year in which students went through stages of student teaching, as they prepared for the final examination in view of the *Agrégation*, which was the certification for teaching at the level of the Lycée. This was the opportunity for Blondel to learn to teach philosophy or, as he would have put it himself, to transform his learning into an action of communicating with others.

In his diary for March 26, 1884, he writes of his anxiety as he was introduced to his first class, and his near panic when he was left alone with his students. "It seemed as if I were being enclosed in a cage of wild animals. I remained mute for a long time, while a student read the list of his classmates, not daring to think that I would have to speak, fearful in advance that the sound of my voice would provoke the unleashing of a storm or the avalanche of a mountain, musing as if in a dream or through a veil that I was seeking in vain to thicken, that I would have to fill in by myself a class of two hours" (1966b, 48). He had planned to speak of Descartes's biography, but he found out that this had already been done for this class. So he spoke of the "history of his spirit." In a second session, later in the day, he commented haltingly on books VIII, V, and VI of the *Nicomachean Ethics*. Later on, upon reading the papers of his students, he was surprised at how much he had gotten across in his fumbling remarks, and at the way he had come across before his students. "I did not realize my character could be so dominating, and my manner and speech so imperial."

Blondel was no longer the timid boy he had been before coming to Normale. He discovered in himself a new courage, a new strength, a presence of mind ready to face up to the task of teaching, and he thanked God for it. At the end of his third year at Normale, however, having successfully met the test of teaching, he was to encounter another setback in his quest for a chance to pursue a career in teaching philosophy. As we have already mentioned, he failed the examination for the *Agrégation*, along with his classmate, Rauh, also a *tala*, who was at the head of the class. The examination consisted of two parts, one written and one oral, but the two friends, who were at the head of the class, never got to the oral part. They were blocked at the written part and prevented from going any further. Boutroux was surprised and furious at this failure of his two star students in philosophy and asked to see the examination papers. After reading them himself he advised his students that they had not been pedagogical enough. They had been too concerned with presenting their personal ideas and had gone off like *voltigeurs*, flying eagles eager to show off their power, but not yet ready to settle down to the more pedestrian task of teaching. Boutroux advised them to go back and prepare themselves better in private and to do more work in the library before coming back for a second try the next year. This was something Blondel had to do because, without the *Agrégation*, there would be no possibility of teaching philosophy at either the college or the University level, even if he got a doctorate.

Blondel spent the first part of the next academic year in Rome with two friends, Paul Favre and André Pérate, his former classmate at Normale, who were now enrolled as students in the French School of Rome, studying art and the history of art. With them he explored the many wonders of the Eternal City. He returned to Dijon at the beginning of 1885 and, in February, moved back to Paris to begin preparing once again for the *Agrégation* exam. There he found his friend Victor Delbos to work with, who was still in his third year at Normale. Knowing that a lot of emphasis was placed on Kant and Kantianism, he concentrated on him and on German philosophy, something that would serve him well later on, both in the writing of his dissertation and in his conception of the exigencies of modern philosophy.

In the summer he failed the exam a second time. Once again it was the written exam that did him in and he did not get to the oral. It appears that he had run himself into the ground in his final months of preparation and was sick with a fever at the time of taking the exam. His doctor had advised him against going, but it was an opportunity that came only once a year and Blondel hated to pass it up. He had to return to the summer home of his family at Saint-Seine sur Vingeanne, no doubt to nurse his wounds one more time, both physically and psychologically.

Encouraged by his teachers, he was determined to keep on trying, and he got some reassurance concerning his eventual success when he was asked to begin teaching as a substitute at the Lycée of Chaumont in the Fall. This was the beginning of his teaching in the state school system and it lasted for a full trimester, at which point the regular teacher returned to his post. He had some thirty students for whom he was the sole teacher of philosophy. Not only was he well received, but when he was observed by an inspector charged with supervising the quality of teaching he was commended for his excellent pedagogy, a commendation that was to serve him well throughout the rest of his teaching career. The experience was enough to convince Blondel that he was made for teaching and that he had to have students. He immediately began asking for another post, even though he still did not have his *Agrégation*, at which point he began to experience the kind of resistance he would find later on because of his religious convictions and his resolve to hold forth on them philosophically.

He had to return to his family, where he began once again to prepare for the *Agrégation* exam one more time under the distant direction from Paris of Ollé-Laprune. This was a very difficult period for the young philosopher and aspiring professor having to face up to a hostile University due to his religious convictions. Few people in his family could appreciate the rigors of a University career in philosophy for one such as Blondel. Most were oriented to more mundane and practical endeavors such as law or the administration of economic affairs or, as far as the University was concerned, to the more natural or social sciences. But even as he wondered about the meaning of this suffering and humiliation for himself in his preparation for some future action, he continued to work in preparation for the *Agrégation,* which was finally granted to him in August 1886. This time he took the written part of the exam in Toulouse, where he was replacing a teacher on leave, and having passed it he was then summoned to Paris to take the oral before the high command of the University system who held the reins for deciding who was to teach and who was not to teach. There he had to pick a subject out of a hat with Lachelier. What he got was life, *la vie.* Then, after three hours for preparing what he wanted to say, he made his presentation. This time he was in good form and in the proper frame of mind to satisfy his examiners. He passed, finally, and was given the much needed and much desired *Agrégation.*

To God first in his diary entry for September he writes: "Thank you for the deliverance," and then typically he adds: "Thank you also for the two years of servitude. I thank you for the success, and I thank you for all the circumstances that accompanied it. Passed the *agrégation* in the last place." This was a place to which the young Blondel was not used to, and he felt humiliated. In this he felt that God had preserved him "from complacency, from all vain joy, and almost from any sort of rejoicing." He had seen within himself a certain vanity, "always avid to be afflicted by slights, forgetfulness, murmurings, and the commentaries of the world" (1961c, 84).

Once freed of this burden that had hung over him for two years, however, Blondel could then count on getting a permanent position of his own, teaching philosophy. This began in October 1886 as a spot in Montauban, where he was appointed as the regular teacher for the year in one of the few parts of France that was still relatively Protestant. His first night in town was spent entirely fighting off fleas in the cheap hotel where he had taken up lodging on first arriving. He went to his first class the next day without having slept and then found himself a better room with a Protestant family for the rest of his stay. He was not to stay there very long, however, but upon his departure three weeks later his landlady was to commend him for not being like many other Catholics, whom she had found generally lacking in seriousness and prone to invite less than honorable persons, including women, to their rooms. Catholic though he was, Blondel was not like those others.

The reason for his sudden departure from Montauban so early in the trimester had nothing to do with his teaching, but rather with a crisis that had developed in another lycée, the *Lycée Michelet* in Aix-en-Provence, one of the places Blondel had asked for, besides Dijon, rather than Toulouse, Avignon, or Montauban. There within two weeks of the beginning of class, the young professor originally assigned to teach philosophy had come to the point of being challenged to a duel by students in his class. He had to be sent away immediately. Blondel's reputation from Chaumont for being able to control a class served him in good stead. He was called to come and take the situation in hand. Though he was twenty-five years old, he looked like he was barely twenty. The director couldn't believe his eyes when he saw this replacement arrive, someone so young to step into such an explosive situation. But Blondel let the director speak his peace, only to say that he had been sent by Lachelier, the director of higher education, and that he would not need the special assistance watching over his class which the director was promising him.

Instead he went out directly into the schoolyard and started mixing with the students, who mistook the newcomer as one of them. It was only when time came to file into class that he stepped aside and then proceeded to introduce himself as their new professor of philosophy, taking plenty of time to allow each student to introduce himself by name and to say a few things about himself, assuring all of them that he wanted to get to know them and to teach them something during this most important year of philosophy for them at the Lycée. It was a good beginning and there was never any question of any more challenges to a duel. Blondel was to spend three good years of teaching at Aix, which endeared him to his students and which endeared Aix to him, during which time he could also start thinking seriously of his dissertations for the doctorate that still lay ahead of him.

The Interior Life for a Dissertation on Action

The general subject of "action" was already approved from the years at the École Normale Supérieure, but there was more to be done about specifying what was to come under that subject. On September 16, 1886, even before going to his teaching assignment at Montauban, Blondel had written to Boutroux in order to renew contact and to confirm his intention of pursuing his interest in action and in the *vinculum substantiale* in Leibniz for his doctoral dissertations at the Sorbonne.

In this letter he admits to still being unclear as to precisely what was going on in Leibniz and in the correspondence with Des Bosses, but he thinks there is something worth studying there that has not been given sufficient attention. With regard to action, he is also still vague, but his intention is to "inquire how action is enlightened by thought, and how it also enlightens thought and guarantees its sincerity, which it takes from thought and which it adds to thought" (1961a, 10). In this regard Blondel situates himself with reference to both Aristotelianism, which, according to him, tended to depreciate practice and subordinate it to thought, and Kantianism, which separated thought and action and exalted the order of practice to the detriment of thought. Between the two, he writes to Boutroux as he had previously written to Ollé-Laprune, "there is something to be defined, and it is in a very concrete way, through the analysis of action, that I would like to determine that" (1961a, 10).

Admittedly, in his own mind this was only a beginning and quite provisional, but in another letter a few months later to the Dean at the Sorbonne, in which he was seeking approval for the subjects of his two dissertations, he showed just how concrete he intended to be in his analysis of action. After the title: *Action,* he adds the subtitle: "a study of the nature of the operation *ad extra* and of the value of literal practice." Though he was thinking of human action as flowing from thought, Blondel was thinking of it also as something quite external and as having some religious overtones in its relation to thought, as any Frenchman would understand at the end of the nineteenth century in reading the expression *pratique littérale.* This shows the religious as well as the concrete orientation of his thought from the beginning.

Like most beginners in a dissertation project, Blondel was leaping ahead immediately to the conclusion he wanted to arrive at. Though he repeated the more general indications of his orientation with reference to Aristotelianism and Kantianism that he had written of to Ollé-Laprune and Boutroux, the subtitle did not sit well with the Dean, or the School "in whose name he was responding." While the title, *Action,* was admitted, the subtitle was rejected as "truly barbaric" and "too annoying" (1961a, 13). Though the subject was not rejected outright, the candidate was advised to find something less provocative to put down as his subtitle. Blondel would accede to this demand, but he would not back down from the sort of conclusion he was driving at, for, as we shall see, the dissertation does end with a defense of the value of a literal practice as part of the necessity of the supernatural.

Having established his claim to the subjects for his two dissertations, Blondel could then settle down to his teaching at the Lycée and begin to give some thought to how he would approach the question of *action.* He felt daunted by the responsibility of teaching, to begin with, but also even more by the task he was undertaking in his study of action. His first thought in studying action is associated with the Gospel because, as he writes, "in the Gospel the power to manifest love and to acquire God is attributed to action alone," whereas in our day "we no longer are able to suffer in order to act and to produce. There is no heart. People know, understand, refine, contemplate, enjoy; but they do not live," whereas in the Gospel we read: "in Him was life and the life was the light of men" (1961c, 85). It is on this *life,* which contains a light of its own, that Blondel wished to reflect in order to arrive at a better understanding of the truth. And it is in connection with this light that he immediately struck a chord about truth which for some would be a cause of scandal later on toward the end of his dissertation. "The old logic was too narrow; it has fallen apart.

Truth is no longer *adaequatio rei et intellectus:* we no longer live on clear ideas. But truth remains, and the truth that remains is living and acting; it is *adaequatio mentis et vitae*" (1961c, 86). The task was to unpack the fullness of this truth from life itself, which for Blondel was to be the key to his philosophy as well as to the Gospel.

We see here how Blondel thought of his philosophy not only as a Christian philosophy from the very beginning, but also as more radically Christian than anything he had seen before. "People have merely appropriated pagan philosophy to Christianity," he writes; "as for a properly Christian philosophy, one issued from the Gospel itself, there is none" (1961c, 86). His would have to issue from the Gospel itself, not by way of textual exegesis but by way of reflection on life itself. Even his choice of *action* as the subject for his dissertation on the occasion of a reading of Aristotle, he thought of as having been inspired by the Christian Spirit within him. For, as he writes later on in his diary, "I must consider the philosophical subject which You have inspired me to treat as essential and, so to speak, as unique" (1961c, 349). Through this subject, or through a Science of Practice, he thought there was something to be learned by abstract thought. "Philosophy is enlightened by practice and practice has no other light, no other way that is perfect than You, oh straight and moving way" (1961c, 349). This was the way that Blondel was trying to follow interiorly in his own life and which he thought had to be presented philosophically according to the exigencies of modern philosophy, or to the ways of modern thought, which appeared so divergent from what was for him the one true way.

His aim, then, was to create an opening for this Christian philosophy of the Gospel itself in modern thought. He felt bound by the Christian truths he was to touch upon as philosopher. As for the *apologia* he was to make for them, he thought there were other ways of presenting or defending them. "There are a hundred thousand ways of justifying them better. My system, if I had one, would be according to its form only one system like others, only one of the ways to give access to the truth: but how I would like to provide a place for Christian philosophy, only to have it alongside the others, and it would show its advantage of itself" (1961c, 150). What Blondel was looking for was not a philosophy that would take the place of Christian truths, but one that would somehow transcend what philosophy can arrive at on its own. It was rather to open up a position in philosophy through which the light of the Christian revelation could pour in. For this he thought some kind of philosophical system was necessary, but he was at pains to provide such a system that would be true to philosophy without impinging on the surpassing truth of revelation.

At the same time he felt that he had to turn philosophy around from its high intellectual pretensions to something more humble, more down to earth. Instead of seeking the truth only on high, among universal laws, philosophy should also seek truth among the regular steps we must follow to elevate ourselves in practice as well as in theory to what is our true good. Such steps are usually taken apart from any pride of spirit, sheltered from the ignorance and error of a vain philosophy, as they are for the multitude of holy souls led by grace down paths that are more direct and mysterious. For Blondel what was called for was a philosophy of this humble sort of holiness, one that would follow its path of growth and learning. "As the life of the body expresses psychological states, the light of reason follows a course parallel to the supernatural illuminations. Hence there is a trace to be discovered that will allow the intelligence of the learned to slowly and humbly reach the heights of the little ones" (1961c, 203). Even if these "little ones" about whom the Gospel spoke were not as numerous as Blondel might have supposed, they were surely there to be seen in his life and it was from them, or from their practice, that he wished to develop his Science of Practice as opening the way for the highest kind of spiritual practice and truth.

In this reversal of reason, however, he did not see an abandonment of reason, but rather a perfecting of reason to a higher degree. For all their humility in practice, the little ones, as Blondel understood them, were not living in darkness. They were masters of the truth. They possessed it. They were submissive to it. They were enlightened by it, they were using it, they were enjoying it, and they were acting in it, not because they had come to it of themselves, but because Truth itself, the living Truth in person, had deigned to give himself to them. In following this Truth "the believer is not confined because he has a light, a faith, which he has not produced alone by himself, but which he has freely sought after and has found by an act of his spirit and which he preserves by the firmness of his decision" (1961c, 277). Far from feeling confined in his life of faith, Blondel felt more liberated and more expansive in his view upon the world than he could have been otherwise. "No, the believer is not confined, because the faith itself is infinitely broad; and far from inclining him to narrow his thought, it forces him to open it up; it enables him to plunge lovingly into the plenitude of the divine secret; it forces him always to look at how far short his thought falls, to admit the contrary aspects of a reality broader than our knowledge, namely, what God knows, so that he [the believer] may act in proportion to this almighty science" (1961c, 277).

This was a view of the life of faith that could barely be appreciated by modern philosophy at the end of the nineteenth century. But it was the view that the young Blondel wanted to present and to justify in the eyes of this philosophy. The problem for him was to find a way in which this could be done philosophically, or according to the demands of reason itself. This is the problem he had set himself for his dissertation on *action* and to which he was finally turning concretely as he was beginning to teach in his own right at Aix in 1886. For him it was a problem he had to resolve philosophically or according to natural reason, but the effort itself remained for him also an act in the service of the supernatural, as he had put it at the beginning of his meditation on what he wanted to do with his life as a Christian.

There he had entertained three ways of serving the supernatural: "either, in the intellectual order that invades it and seems to repress it, make a place for it in philosophy, in the theory of the human spirit, through the impulse of ideas that are healthy, reserved, really scientific; or, make a place for it in social and political action, by introducing it through example, through speech, through discussion and personal influence, into the traditions of the people, the mores of national life, into legislation and practical reason; or, call on it to reanimate the generosity of passions, the shriveled hearts, the enthusiasm of sentiment that is dampened by the abuse of the material, the positive, the scientific, in order to bring forth a Christian Rousseau" (1961c, 23). As a believer and as the son of a family oriented to action in the public domain as well as the private, Blondel could entertain all three of these ways of serving the supernatural in the modern world — a world that seemed intent on closing itself up in its own mastery of the material, the positive, and the scientific as well as in its own ideas. But what he chose for himself, not without some consternation from his very Christian family, was the first way, the way of philosophy that seemed to lead him into the lions' den of modern, anti-religious, and anti-Christian intellectualism, not without including something of the second way, in social and political action, which he would go into in his defense of the Catholic social movement and his opposition to the inroads of *Action Française* in the national life of France.

In a way, his choice of philosophy was a daring choice, but one he had to make good on in intellectual terms. Having finished his philosophical formation at the École Normale and having been finally accepted as a teacher of philosophy in the academy, he now had to deliver on the service he had chosen.

Part of his effort in this service was keeping a diary on his own interior life in his submission to the supernatural as a Christian. This is something that had occurred to him while he was still very young and that he had begun to do during his year of philosophy at the Lycée in Dijon after reading a few pages of Pascal's *Pensées*, in which he had found something of himself. This he did, he admits (1961c, 11), in a surge of emulation with the naïveté and gravity of one who thought that some day others might be reading him. In the notebook he bought especially for this purpose in March of 1880, during his year of the Licentiate at Dijon, he wrote down, first, the traces of his past life, his most distant memories, and then the most recent events. Then came a more personal and intimate part in which he wrote candidly of himself and his ideas, what he was at that time, and where his attempts at philosophical originality as well as his pious impressions were leading him (1961c, 12). But unfortunately, and most regrettably in his own mind, always avid to recall its past states, the entire notebook was lost one day on a trip up to Fourvières in Lyon.

A year later, in April 1881, in a note in which he tells of this first start and this loss, he resolves once again to start keeping a diary for himself alone in which he would keep track of where he was interiorly in a sort of prayerful consideration and of confession before God. But it was not until after he had decided on *Action* as the subject of his dissertation that he began to follow this resolve effectively, almost day by day, but with occasional interstices at times because of discouragement or because of travels, that is, in November 1883, exactly ten years before he was to publish his dissertation. The *Carnets* that resulted, and from which we have been quoting in trying to follow Blondel's thought, tell of his interior life as a Christian, on which he was beginning to reflect as a philosopher. They are the humble expression of the light and the truth he was experiencing as a man of faith, the philosophy of the Gospel living within him, from which he was to proceed in the intellectual and critical articulation of his Science of Practice.

In a way these diaries speak of the true source of Blondel's philosophy hidden in the mystery of his Christian life of devotion and self-sacrifice to the supernatural, as we have been trying to bring out. But they do not tell of the philosophy itself that was emerging from this source. This philosophy is found in another set of writings which Blondel was developing in view of the dissertation itself and which correspond more to the rigorous exigencies of reason. In these writings he was trying to bring to a modern scientific expression "the ancient Christian discipline of moral life, an entirely original and unique science, suspended not from a postulate of the spirit, but from the hypothesis of a gift from on high that all implicitly admit and from a gift of the heart that many refuse; a science that will be the one that will never pass away and that is the revelation of faith to reason, or of practice to being in its entirety; a science that has its own proper object, the free being, its own method, a complete experimentation, its own logic, the conquest of all the contrary aspects of the ample truth" (1961c, 322).

Among the sources that inspired him in this search for this new science of the ancient Christian tradition, Blondel mentions not only the Gospels but also St. Paul, whose account of the disparity between what I will and what I do would have a direct bearing on the dialectic of action, and St. Bernard, in whom Blondel found a singular way of combining grace, or the will of God, and free will in human action. Bernard is one of the few authors he cites at some length in *L'Action* (1893). Typically enough, Blondel's interest in Bernard, a fellow Burgundian, had begun when he started reading him on the occasion of centenary celebrations of the great saint in Dijon. But Bernard was only one of many ascetic and mystical writers with whom he was nourishing himself as a matter of regular practice. We find him occasionally citing Kempis's *Imitation of Christ* in his diaries or in letters to friends. And we find him taking up the *Spiritual Exercises* of St. Ignatius of Loyola while he was working on his dissertation. In his diary he makes a special note of having bought the book on March 19, 1891. He then begins the practice of reading these *Exercises* regularly, including the daily particular examination of conscience they recommend (1961c, 396). What he finds valuable in these *Exercises* is "not their content, but their method, less what they give us ready made than what they make us produce" (1961c, 402). He was to keep coming back to these *Exercises* later on in life. What he found in all this "spiritual reading" was a certain freedom of spirit that made him feel at odds with the intellectual world in which he found himself. "The more I wanted to be of my times, the more I was trying to surround myself, for my studies, with an atmosphere that has no time: a philosophy of fresh air and of full humanity that one could breathe in the twentieth century as well as in the second or the twelfth" (1928a, 20).

The Labor of Drafting a Philosophical Dissertation

The task of transposing this rich experience of a spiritual life into a science, however, was not to come easily. Often, when Blondel turned to this task of developing an argument philosophically, he found himself dry and arid, as he says repeatedly in his diaries. He felt at a loss for what to say or how to proceed, with none of the flow that came more readily in his life of faithful devotion. This was for him part of the mortification that is necessary for a true service to the supernatural. It had to yield something that was not just personal to him individually, but something more universal, something any critical intelligence could understand and follow, even if it did not issue automatically into a deliberate practical choice in life itself.

What came first were notes taken randomly on thoughts that occurred while Blondel was teaching or reading or reflecting on how to proceed. These he would later call his *notes semailles*, seminal notes that would have to germinate and coalesce together later on in a more systematic arrangement. Many of the catchphrases from these notes, such as the one on truth conceived as an *adaequatio mentis et vitae* rather than as an *adaequatio intellectus et rei*, would later find their way into the text of the dissertation. But they could not be left in a state of disarray, as Pascal's *Pensées* had been, due to his untimely death. Blondel was aiming at something systematic, something scientific.

Nor could they be left as something merely added on to a philosophy already fully constituted in its autonomy. For Blondel a true philosophy of the supernatural could not be something just tacked on to a natural philosophy, after the fact. "Christian philosophy is still almost nothing if it is content with superimposing upon natural truths other higher truths. What is this juxtaposition or this addition which leaves fragments scattered about, pieces that seem to form a whole, a philosophy that has undoubtedly no culmination but seems to have a foundation? It is necessary to enter into the internal drama of thought . . . and show that everything that one has built up falls into ruin, if the faith does not reappear at the foundation once we arrive at the summit . . ." (1961c, 356).

This is what Blondel felt he had to show: how a supernatural faith appears in the very grounding of philosophy, by showing how action, or the act, "is a naturalization of the ideal or of the supernatural in the real and the phenomenal" (1961c, 342). By reflecting on the real, or being, as it appears in what he would later call the phenomenon of action, he had to rise to the highest culmination of human action in the face of the infinite, and there show the necessity of a presence of something supernatural which could not be defined philosophically but had to be affirmed in its necessity as a principle of being for action.

To do this, the seminal notes, which brought up many different aspects of the phenomenon of action, had to be organized into some kind of an argument that would show this necessity of a principle at the end. The very necessity of coming to an end in this reflection had to be shown. On October 12, 1888, Blondel began writing what he referred to as a beginning of the French thesis, while he was still teaching in the Lycée in Aix. The complete title he gave for this first essay was: "*Action. Study on the metaphysics of science and morality and on the nature of religious practice. The science of action,*" as cited from unpublished notes in a study of the Genesis of L'Action by Raymond Saint-Jean (1965b, 67). In this we see, not only how action was to be the center of attention for Blondel's early enterprise, but also how metaphysics was part of his original outlook from the very beginning, even though in the final version of the 1893 dissertation, the metaphysical dimension would be left in the background and integrated as only a final moment in the total dialectic of action on the way to a final resolution of the conflict of action in the face of God.

Immediately, as Blondel takes note of this beginning in his diary, he also writes of a lack of taste for the task ahead and a certain discouragement. But he draws an important lesson from this lack of taste and encouragement for the task. "Is it for me that I am doing this? The less there will be of me, the better it will be. I must not think of myself in this for a moment" (1961c, 148). The more he works on the thesis, the more he feels discouraged. But then he adds: "What does it matter if it is worth nothing, will I have less merit for it? I must remain detached from everything I think and everything I say" (1961c, 150). What Blondel is aiming at is a rigorous work in philosophy, but he is not sure yet of how this will be carried off. He only knows that it cannot depend merely on his own individual feeling of accomplishment. It must be something of universal or scientific validity. Furthermore, he is doing a work in the service of the supernatural as a man of faith, which is all the more reason for not having it depend on his individual feelings. In keeping with the ascetic tradition out of which he comes, Blondel not only knows he has to overcome his discouragement, but also that he must get beyond his purely personal feelings, in order to arrive at work of both universal and supernatural validity.

By the end of 1888 he had only thirty-four pages written. He was too busy with his teaching to do more on the dissertation. At the end of the school year in 1889 he asks for and obtains a leave of absence from teaching in order to devote himself completely to the work of his dissertations. To this end he moves back into his family's country house at Saint-Seine and sets himself up in the *mansarde* where he was to do most of the work of pulling his dissertation together. "I am inaugurating my unassuming mansarde of Saint-Seine, facing my beautiful prairie, my new installation for work, and I find in this the pleasure of a child" (1961c, 237). He can hear the noises coming up from people busy below in the house, and he can look out on the play of birds and of the two swaying pines planted by his grandfather. But before his little window opening out on the wide, wide world, he feels quite alone. The first thing he does is pray and, for all the grandeur of the panorama before him and of the task ahead of him, he can think of nothing better to say than the "humble rosary." "To be both below and above at the same time; to belittle nothing in the details and to love the whole ensemble with a close love. . . . The fact is that, for reflection, we need an ample nourishment: the spirit needs a broad base in reality, so that too minute an analysis or a detail too close to oneself will not prevent it from unfolding itself freely" (1961c, 237). From this place, then, within earshot of bustling family activities in which he continued to take part, Blondel feels more ready to face his difficult task of joining the universal to the particular of his experience.

His first few months were spent in an intensive reflection, going over his accumulated notes and putting them in order, and trying to devise a plan for the whole. After a trip to Paris in October, where he met with Charles Maurras, a future adversary with whom he found very little community of spirit, due to an "infantile presumption of a pretentious spirit and a strange narrowness in these broadminded intellectuals" (1961c, 68), and with his more congenial master, Ollé-Laprune, who was on the verge of publishing his own work on *Philosophy and the Present Time,* addressed to the same kind of audience that Blondel had in mind, he took up once again work on the draft of his dissertation where he had left off after the thirty-four pages he had written the year before, this time "with greater facility and satisfaction than he would have thought possible" (1961c, 266).

Far from becoming a complete recluse upstairs in his *mansarde,* however, Blondel continued to join in various activities that occupied others in the country house. With his uncle Louis, he planted a grove of trees near the house. With others, he let himself be dragged into hunting expeditions about the countryside, even though this does not seem to have been much to his liking. What he did in these sorties was not so much hunt as continue to ruminate on his dissertation, as he tells us on one occasion when he came up with a new plan.

According to this plan, there would have to be a "preparation" in order to establish the precise truth of phenomena in the intellectual and moral order, and in order to argue for a higher domain than that of the senses and to rise above the psychophysical, without denying its legitimacy and the interest there is in it. Then would come the "thesis" itself, the value of action, the "properly psychological, moral, mystical study where the facts of the soul are considered as beings no less real and no less concrete, even as more precise and more true than sensible beings and mathematical abstractions" (1961c, 269). Then there would be a "discussion," the more critical part, to be followed by a "conclusion," "resolutions," and "practical consequences," all according to a scientific method, along with an indication of immediate applications according to a philosophical and Christian *agendum*.

This is not exactly how it would all turn out in the final draft of the dissertation, but it shows the kind of ruminating Blondel was going through during the Fall of 1889 at Saint-Seine. There is not much of it that got written down in these weeks, but the effort continued. In his diary Blondel speaks of the difficulty in sustaining a strictly dialectical and logical effort to pull together the elements of our intellectual and moral personality. "For there is labor only through resistance, action only through the effort of vanquished and victorious multiplicity, triumph only through a defeat. We need a logic at once more broad and more determinate, more conciliating and more exclusive than the logic of clear thought, to serve as a logic of action" (1961c, 273).

Finding that perhaps he was being pulled away from his *mansarde* too often, Blondel had to resolve explicitly to spend four hours each day working on his thesis, regardless of how well or poorly things were going, and not to let "family obligations" or correspondence with others, ever voluminous for him all his life — with most of the members of his large family, with former classmates, former professors, former students, and many others — serve as an excuse for setting aside his primary task in the midst of discouragement or aridity. Thanks to the concerted effort of this discipline, he was able to bring his first draft, begun in the final months of 1888, to completion in January of 1890, one year after he left off working on it at Aix.

The precise details of that draft need not detain us here. What is important, however, is to note that the draft begins by focusing on the *infinite* that is contained in thought and action, something that will be central to the argument of the final draft. The infinite is received and expressed in thought; it is given and produced in action. Through thought we attain the infinite only symbolically. Through action we situate ourselves effectively in the infinite. That is why only action can settle the problem of our destiny, and not thought or intention. For thought to have an infinite value, it would have to express the infinite really, rather than just symbolically. Action, even in the finite being, has an infinite value. Though our knowledge is imperfect, we act effectively in the absolute. Hence the necessity to study action, over and above thought.

Just how the idea of the infinite arises in human consciousness and knowledge would be the subject of careful analysis in the final draft of the dissertation, after different attempts to exclude it have been overcome. So too with the consciousness of freedom, which follows from this idea of the infinite, and with how free action flows from the subject in search of an object equal to its principle, until it comes face to face with the actual Infinite. But this line of thought is only vaguely adumbrated here in the first draft, which is divided into three parts: (1) action within the acting being, (2) action in the milieu where it is produced, where it is the bond among souls, the ground for family and nation, and where it transfigures the universe by the mediation of moral life, and (3) the response from outside the agent, where the cost and the value of practice and the nourishing role it has for thought will be considered. Many of the elements found in the final draft are already laid out in this first draft, but only loosely and in a rather static fashion that does not dialectically or logically integrate the natural and the supernatural together yet.

Once this first draft was completed, Blondel went off to Paris again in February 1890, perhaps to show the draft around and get some comments on it. He visited with his venerated Master again, Ollé-Laprune, who was still working on his own book, *Philosophy and the Present Time,* and left him a copy of the draft. When he returned, Ollé had had time to consider the scaffolding of the thesis. He told Blondel that he would need a new sort of formation at age thirty in order to carry the thesis off. But Blondel also sensed that they were not talking on the same intellectual or critical wavelength. He was reluctant to criticize his old Master, but at the same time he recognized that his own effort had to be one of much greater philosophical rigor if he was to argue for a necessity of the supernatural, and not just how the supernatural happens to correspond to the highest aspirations of the human spirit, as Ollé was doing.

On this trip Blondel also went to renew acquaintance with a former classmate from the École Normale Supérieure who had left to become a priest, the one he refers as "his dear Wehrlé," who would remain very devoted to him and who would later try to help him continue his work of publication, unfortunately without much success, after Blondel became blind. There Blondel found encouragement for his work and even a certain amount of self-satisfaction, which always made him suspicious of his motivation. "For there is nothing absolutely good except what we do not want, what God wants in us and of us" (1961c, 336).

Another advantage of this trip was a chance to get at some books not accessible to him from Saint-Seine. This was a chance for him to do some reading that would help him formulate his ideas, including "vertiginal books such as Schelling's *Transcendental Idealism,* the theological writings of Boehme, the speculative mysticism of Meister Eckhart, and others" (1961a, 20). Many of these he brought back with him to Saint-Seine in March, but he had to race through them because they were due back as soon as possible. He had to "devour them, which made digestion painful."

Upon his return to Saint-Seine, however, in addition to this reading, Blondel also tried a new approach to the writing of his dissertation, one that he would have to resort to in later life for composing his major works after he went blind. This time it took the form of dictation to a young secretary who was only fifteen years old. The strategy was to force himself to go forward anyway, even when things were not going very well. Every afternoon he had his little fifteen-year-old secretary write from twelve to fourteen pages, which he dictated: philosophy off the cuff, as he referred to it, which drained him of energy quickly. The antithesis in which he found himself was one of fullness and emptiness. He had never before experienced this feeling of indigestion and exhaustion to the same degree. Nevertheless, he was able to say that "he was not too dissatisfied with the collaboration with my gentle scribe: I imagine that he could understand [what I am saying], and I try not to scandalize him too much. This is the edition for children, the third redaction that will have to be followed by three or four more" (1961a, 20).

Blondel calls this the third redaction because he seems to be counting his personal diary, the *Carnets Intimes,* as a first redaction, prior to the one we have referred to as the first draft. This, however, was only his second attempt at formulating a plan for the dissertation. The exercise went on from March 12, 1890, to April 2, hardly enough to yield anything but a very schematic outline.

Again, we do not have to go into the details of this brief and hurried redaction, the whole of which is still to be found at the Blondel Archives, written in the hand of the young scribe. Given the manner in which it was laid out, under the pressure of direct sustained dictation lasting several hours at a time each day, as scheduled for several weeks, the results were not what one would expect of a carefully crafted philosophical text or what he knew he would have to produce for his dissertation at the Sorbonne. But Blondel was not entirely disappointed with this brief but concerted collaboration with his young scribe. What speaking directly to someone fifteen years old gave him was a much more concrete and existential way of approaching the question of how to show the necessity of a supernatural dimension in human action. Instead of starting from a discussion of the relation between the finite and infinite in action, Blondel spoke more directly of how the question of human destiny arises necessarily in human life and how it is answered, one way or another, but inevitably in each human being's life. We have to choose. We have to sacrifice. We have to act, and in doing so we have to decide what we shall make of ourselves. The problem of life is to know to what or to whom we have to give ourselves.

Before this existential problem two different attitudes are possible: either submit oneself simply to one's moral conscience without giving in to only partial truths or false evidences in life, or else hold ourselves in reserve and wait for the problem to be resolved intellectually before consenting to act freely. In the face of action, when it comes to answering the question of one's destiny, according to Blondel speaking to his young secretary, the two attitudes are somehow in an equal state of quandary. The sophisticated intellectual has no advantage over the simple soul just following her own conscience. "In the most elementary act, there is more infinite than in transcendent speculations; the poor woman who lives literally in conformity with precepts of commitment that she judges quite clear, even though she does not understand them, has more of the spirit of truth than all the philosophers in the world; she has the spirit without pretending to it. They pretend to it without having it" (1961c, 340). In the long run the simple soul who follows her conscience has as good a chance of discovering the truth about her destiny as any other. This is a way Blondel himself had been following in his own life and which he hoped to justify philosophically in his dissertation. But it was not the way he could follow for the dissertation itself, which was to be addressed to philosophers and intellectuals as well as to simple souls.

For the dissertation Blondel had to adopt more of the second attitude, that of holding back assent and trying to resolve the intellectual question before consenting to act. For this he had to look more immediately for a critical and scientific resolution of the problem, without denying the validity of the first attitude. His task then was to constitute a science of action according to a "truly scientific method" that would satisfy the exigencies of philosophy, in order to arrive at a critical solution to the problem of human destiny. He had to constitute what he would call a "Science of Practice," to complement the "Practical Science" of the simple soul in the first attitude, and for this he had to reflect critically on the practice of life as he found it within himself and around him, even among those whose principles seemed to be most at odds with his own. For a Science of Practice must have universal validity.

In doing this he was not turning away from taking direct action, but rather he was beginning to focus on it intellectually in order to bring out all that it actually contains within itself. In the end he would discover that a purely intellectual or speculative answer to the problem of action cannot be given. Existentially one still, and always, has to resort to action to find a more complete solution. The science of action still had to fall back on what can be discovered only in practical science. But the science of action will have at least served the purpose of defining the terms of the problem more clearly for a more critical consciousness.

This distinction between the Science of Practice, which Blondel was endeavoring to construct for the philosophers, and the Practical Science, which we learn from the experience of life, as well as the relation between the two, not only came to him as he was speaking to his young scribe but also found its way into the dissertation of 1893, both in the Introduction and in the final solution relating to the supernatural. It became the way for keeping his focus on action in the concrete, even in the most speculative dimension of his critical science, so much so that Blondel never departed from it even in his later version of this Science of Practice in 1936, where he left untouched the original version of the introduction, with this distinction in it and with how the philosophy of action relates to ordinary life or practical science.

After this rather exhausting interlude of work through dictation, Blondel came to realize that he needed a much more elaborate plan for his work. In May and June of 1890 he proceeded to work on such a plan. In fact, he came up with three plans: one, where he refers primarily to his first draft; second, a complementary plan, where he refers to the first part of his diaries and to his seminal notes; and finally, after having reviewed his entire life and all his diaries, a third plan which was more complete and would guide him in a new composition that would express more of the spiritual *élan* that had been gathering within him through growth in the Practical Science of his own life.

In the first plan Blondel comes back to the idea of the necessity of action and the necessity of a special science of action that has to be distinguished from every other science, according to an original method of its own. After that the plan is divided into five parts. The first deals with objections or suppositions that in action there is not a subject matter for any science, especially the objection as found in nihilism. There the intention is to show that faith in the nothingness of everything implies faith in God. The second part is to be a synthesis of being and the phenomenal, in order to overcome the limitations of positivism, empiricism, and evolutionism, by bringing reflection to focus on the subjective. The third part is to develop the synergy between the subjective and the objective within the human subject through effort and the labor of actualizing our will in our body. The fourth part, titled "exodus, exergy, co-energy," is to show how action reaches out to others as a sign and as a call to cooperation, and how it inevitably has incalculable repercussions in our social life. The fifth and final part, titled "telergy and the-ergy," is to study how all of this immanence of action in the world of experience is transcendentalized in relation to God by a certain cooperation between human and divine action, by a supernaturalization of nature, and by an incarnation of the subjective in the objective such as we find in Christ, so that we could also speak of a "christergy" or of a "cosmoanthropotheergy."

All this displays a certain formalism of ideas in the way Blondel was lining up his argument. But it is only the summation of a plan, and its shows the complexity of the way in which Blondel was approaching his speculative problem of action.

The second or complementary plan follows the same outline as the first, but with an important variation in the approach. There, in part one, the insistence is to be on showing that there is something to be studied scientifically in action, for example, to overcome nihilism. In part two, the insistence will be on showing that there is a subjective life, including reflection, reason, and will, over and above what is studied in the merely positive or mathematical sciences. Part three will continue this more phenomenological approach to the constitution of a personal subject through what Blondel calls synergy and miergy. Part four is to insist on how there has to be a collaboration of subjects in our cosmic setting, and part five will come back to the "the-ergy" of the first plan as a transition from nature to grace.

The formalism of the first plan is still apparent in the second plan, but there is added an attempt to show the necessity of moving from one level of action to the next, which will figure more prominently in the final version. Given this new insistence on showing that there is always something more to be considered in action, what was spoken of earlier as "christergy" at the end of the first plan is now expanded into a sixth part of its own. There the idea will be to show "in what sense the objective does not exist unless it is tied into the subjective, and in what sense the subjective does not exist unless it is tied into reason, and in what sense reason does not exist unless it is tied into the incarnate Word.... Apart from faith in Christ, reason, whatever effort it makes to raise itself, falls back into sleep, dreaming and emptiness" (1965b, 126). A purely symbolic logic will not suffice. What is called for in action is the reality that surmounts contradictions, like that of the Word made flesh.

This insistence on Christ by name was not to be pursued in later plans and drafts of the dissertation, except briefly in the thesis project, which no doubt picked up for a moment on this last part of the complementary second plan as Saint-Jean suggests (1965b, 161). The explicit reference to Christ had too much of a theological ring, in that it appeared to presuppose faith in Christ as the incarnate Word. As such it was not in keeping with his intent to pursue only a philosophical argument, although reference to a Mediator would always remain as a crucial part of the argument with regard to the necessity of the supernatural.

The third plan, which was much more complete and studded with references to the diaries, combined the first two into six carefully articulated parts with subsections outlining the various stages of the argument in greater detail. In it we see the structure of the final dissertation coming clearly into shape. The final part no longer refers to Christ by name, though the argument for the necessity of the supernatural to bring action to completion is maintained. It is now titled "a philosophical critique of revelation," and it includes not only a critique of the idea of a supernatural revelation, but also a philosophical exposition of the idea of mediation, redemption, and sanctification.

Final Consolidation of the Philosophical Argument

With these plans laid out before him, Blondel then began to work on what he called his *projet de thèse* on June 15, 1890, as he notes in his diary (1961c, 360). This was the beginning of work over the long haul, but it was frequently interrupted, first by a trip in the summer to Oberammergau, to attend the famous passion play that was enacted every tenth year by the entire village, followed by an extended vacation in Germany. Then there was also a stage of teaching at the *Lycée Stanislas* in Paris, where he had to replace an ailing professor from January 7, 1891, until March 31. As always in his teaching, he found there a good response from his students.

It was there also that Blondel first came into contact with a group of Catholics interested in social questions, all of whom were students in his class. They rallied around him and would later found a journal of their own called *Le Sillon*, to take issue with *Action Française* and other more conservative elements within the Church. Quite a correspondence developed between them, which was to continue after Blondel returned to Saint-Seine and would lead up to the founding of their journal in 1890-91. The journal was later condemned in 1910 under Pius X, when the conservative reaction set in within the Church. Blondel would then think that the group had been too anxious in seeking official approval from religious authorities, so that it was trapped without any other recourse for a revival when the condemnation came (1957b, 177).

After each interruption, however, thanks to his written plans, Blondel was able to pick up immediately where he had left off, so that early in April 1891, barely three weeks after getting back to his *mansarde*, he could write in his diary: "Finished with the green redaction of my thesis" (1961c, 401). What was in fact finished was a text of some two hundred handwritten pages of prose still only laying out his project.

Most of this text was an elaboration of analyses suggested in the plans, following a cumulative development of what there is in action, starting from saying that there is something in action, against nihilism, and then focusing on the phenomenon of action as something original with consciousness. From the analysis of consciousness in action, the text goes on to follow the expansion of action in collaboration with others who are also in action, and in the constitution of social wholes such as the family and the nation, reaching out to the very limits of humanity.

It is at this point that Blondel first hits upon a phrase that will become a key to his argument later on. Speaking of how we act with reference to the universal, even if we are not completely conscious of it, he writes: "The willing will is tending toward the universal, which it approaches by going through different states of unstable equilibrium." Then he adds that this expansive movement of the willing will is not to be confused "with the reflective movement of the willed will" (1965b, 153f.).

The idea of this twofold will seems to have struck Blondel like a bolt of lightning. In the margin he notes that he must insist on it more, because it lies at the heart of the entire chapter. While it appears late in the dialectic of this draft, in the final draft it will be brought in much earlier, at the point of the first reflection on the conscious origins of action, and it will then serve as the principle for moving forward from one sphere of action to the next, in search of an end that will satisfy the aspiration of the willing will and bring the willed will into conformity with the willing will. Later on, in this draft of the thesis, it enables Blondel to speak more easily of a certain inequality between what we know and what we are, what we do and what we will (1965b, 158), an inequality that forces the will always to go beyond any finite point explicitly willed in its expansion, even if it be that of the entire universe, in search of what is ultimately understood as an infinite.

In the *projet* Blondel also follows through with his idea of doing a critique of religion as well as of any idea of dogmatic revelation. In this he appears to be consciously espousing the movement of modern anti-religious philosophy, but his point is to show that the demolition of religion falls itself under the rubble of the demolition. If there is nothing more to justify fully the immense effort of human beings already described, will not the very effort of constituting science itself or any rational critique, the family, society, and everything else human, simply collapse into nothingness, starting from nothing, achieving nothing, and going toward nothing? For anyone who can see beyond nihilism, the religious dimension of action cannot be dismissed, nor can it be reduced to something merely natural or rational, even if it be the power of the conscious subject of action. The aim was to show that there has to be something more in human action than just the subject alone.

All this, however, still was not what Blondel intended to submit to his director, Émile Boutroux. While it contained most of what he wanted to say, it still did not have a sufficiently critical or philosophical form. Conscious of this, Blondel showed different parts of his manuscript to several of his friends, one of whom, Gabriel Audiat, told him that the first forty-two pages had to be redone. To another, his friend Jules Dussy, who had been a year ahead of him at Normale, then teaching physics in Dijon, he sent his chapter on empirical science. Meanwhile he started once more to pour through his notes and his diaries, in search of new angles to bolster his new idea of a dialectic of two wills and to focus on what was to become the structure of his argument. In August 1891, while on a mountain climbing expedition in Switzerland, he came to a close brush with death, which must have sobered him even more with regard to his project. By November of the same year he was ready to start on the draft he was to submit to Boutroux, and from then on, until May 8, 1892, there were six months of intense uninterrupted work according to a schedule that enabled him to count the weeks and days of his deliverance. On March 17 he writes: "One more month before the great day of my deliverance" (1961c, 455).

What he added to his dissertation during these months was to be of greatest importance for its philosophical value, especially at the end where he tackles the question of religion and of the supernatural. In view of this, he adds an important clarification in the Introduction (1893a, xx-xxi) on the scientific character of his endeavor as it is based on the sincere will. Later on, in the transition between Part II, on nihilism, and Part III, on the phenomenon of action, which begins with a discussion of empirical science, he adds another important clarification on the natural inclination of the will. Before the chapter on mathematical science, he adds a chapter on sense perception, and after it he goes to great pains to show how the mediation of a subject, the acting scientist, is necessary for the constitution of objective science itself, thus making a science of the subject itself necessary even from the standpoint of objective science.

In his articulation of the science of the subject itself, he develops the idea of moral obligation early on, in connection with his analysis of the subjective conception of action, and he shows how resistance to the will is inevitable in the psychological implementation of any decision. He adds a development of almost ten pages on the necessity of the *cité* or the *patrie* for the perfection of action and later on, still within the immanent order of action, he reworks his articulation of the different levels of morality, one natural and the other more properly moral, before going on to the metaphysical dimension of action, all as part of the universal dimension which human action must encompass.

More significantly still, he then reshapes the rest of his argument, including his critique of superstition as part of the phenomenon of action, while keeping only his positive treatment of religion and of the supernatural as the final part of the dialectic. As part of this positive treatment, Blondel gives more attention to the positive transcendence of the will in what he calls the conflict between the death and the life of action. The idea of an alternative before God, the possibility of saying *yes* or *no*, is now emphasized, with a more explicit consideration of the possibility of saying *no* as well as *yes*, including the consequences of this *no*. Finally, in the chapter on the necessity of religious practice, he adds some important clarification on how this necessity is to be viewed scientifically in philosophy even in the context of a supernatural, which by definition surpasses any scope attainable by philosophy.

None of this, which can be so easily summarized *post factum* by comparing the draft finally submitted to Boutroux with the earlier *projet*, came easily for Blondel. Each point had to be gained by a struggle against discouragement. The very abundance of the diaries, notes, drafts, dictations, and plans, made the struggle for strict philosophical rigor even more difficult, because the final form of the argument seemed so sparse in comparison to the life from which it was extracted. It seemed as though he had so little to say philosophically. At the end of a day's work he often felt like uttering "a cry of misery and lassitude." Yet at the same time he prayed for abandonment with regard to results: "I would accept to have in my labor nothing but pain and disgust, in order that you might render it fruitful even without my knowing it . . ." (1961c, 433). It is God whom he wants to work through his philosophy. He feels "harassed and anguished by the weight of the task undertaken. The only good there is is in adoring you, remembering with repentance and mockery the moments of foolish presumption" (1961c, 434).

At the same time, however, all this only reinforced the conception of action he wished to convey. Doing the dissertation itself was an action of "descending a little into the tomb of labor. If we did not take it as a mortification, it would be in vain and impossible" (1961c, 455). This theme of mortification would figure prominently in the final stage of the dialectic of action, with God as the highest point one can reach in truly human action. It was part of Blondel's own experience in producing this supreme act of his philosophy.

By the beginning of May 1892, after nearly six months of steady tortuous labor, the draft was ready to be presented to Boutroux. Blondel delivered it personally to his mentor in Paris and then, while waiting for Boutroux's judgment, went off on a trip to Belgium, Germany, and Austria. Part of his concern during this trip was to begin work on his second dissertation, on Leibniz, now that the first and more important one on *Action* was more or less completed. To this end he visited libraries in Hanover, Leipzig, Köln, and Düsseldorf, where the works of Leibniz were to be found, and consulted with archivists, who were able to furnish him with some unpublished texts of Leibniz and with information concerning the person of Des Bosses (1930a, xii). He took careful notes on his readings and continued his correspondence with the archivists after returning to Saint-Seine in mid-July 1892.

The report of Boutroux on the primary dissertation, addressed to the Dean, with a copy sent to the candidate, arrived at Saint-Seine on July 31. It was essentially one of approval, but with some suggestions for amendment in order to bring out the structure of the argument more prominently. Boutroux speaks of the work as quite personal and vivid. "It is a metaphysical meditation where reasoning is an effort of the soul itself to arrive at the clear intelligence of truth from which it expects joy. . . . The basis for the thesis is rich and solid. It is on the side of the form that it still leaves something to be desired; the development tends to be a bit long and cumbersome" (1961a, 21). The comment shows that Boutroux has seen clearly how Blondel's science of practice is rooted in his own practical science. Blondel's reaction was one of satisfaction, though not without some suspicion as to the motive of this satisfaction: "If only the indifferent satisfaction I feel could be attributed to virtue! I desire to take heart again in my interior life; grant me this . . ." (1961c, 464).

Secure in the thought that work on his primary dissertation was coming to a successful completion, Blondel then turned his hand to writing his secondary dissertation on Leibniz at the beginning of August. Earlier, while lining up his subject matter with Boutroux at Normale, he had expressed some doubt and some confusion as to whether he was not reading too much of his own philosophy and his own preoccupations into these obscure texts of Leibniz (1961c, 47-

48), but now he felt more confident about what was to be found in Leibniz, as well as what he had to say for himself. The writing, in Latin, went very fast and, quite unlike what happened for the primary dissertation, it did not go through any complicated stages of drafts, projects, and plans. It all seems to have come together in a single draft that was completed in less than four months and personally deposited at the Sorbonne on November 23 at nine in the morning (1961c, 469).

A week later Blondel returned to Saint-Seine to continue work on the final revision of the much longer thesis on *Action*. Clearly, he sensed that he had anticipated quite well what was expected of him according to the exigencies of philosophy. Boutroux was looking only for some further clarifications as to the form of his argument. But it was with the same old trepidation and fear of not being up to the task he had set for himself, and with the same idea of his work as a mortification and as a death to self, that Blondel then took up the final push for the draft that would be submitted to the whole jury and defended at the Sorbonne.

The differences between this last draft before the defense and the one initially submitted to Boutroux were not as considerable as those between the draft submitted to Boutroux and the *projet* that had preceded it. They were mainly further refinements on the different stages of the argument, with numbered summation paragraphs inserted at key points. But what was included that had not been there before was a discussion of proofs for the existence of God, or for the necessary idea of a Necessary Being, as part of the conclusion for the resolution of the conflict between death and life in human action. This reference to material more familiar to his philosophical readers would help to reassure them with regard to the philosophical intent of the dialectic, although it would not satisfy their negative expectation with regard to religion.

On April 14, 1893, Blondel notes that he had come to the last word of his provisional conclusion, exactly six months after beginning this final revision. His first act is to refer the entire work back to God: "May everything be brought back to you, including the end, especially the end, since along the way I have so often stolen your gift" (1961c, 484). Nine days later, April 23, he notes again: *fin de ma thèse,* and repeats the next day his offering of the work back to God, since it should have belonged to him from the very beginning (1961c, 486). In the meantime he must have gone over the last details of the redaction, as he asks for patience over the irritations that came from finding so many failings in one's work. On May 11, he brings an end to this fretting in private by launching his thesis "in its public life," that is, by delivering it into the hands of Boutroux and the jury before whom he was to appear one month later in Paris to defend it. We already know the kind of commotion this public launching was to evoke. Let us now have a closer look at what was contained in this dissertation as a result of all this labor.

III

The Original Philosophy of the Supernatural

We have seen how Blondel defended his philosophy of the supernatural in the philosophical forum of the Sorbonne and in the pages of the *Revue de Métaphysique et Morale*. We have seen how this philosophy grew out of a very austere systematic reflection on Blondel's own experience, which was at once human or rational and religious. But we have not yet seen in what this philosophy consists in its articulation. This is what we must now pause to consider in its original version because it represents a very important milestone in the intellectual life of Maurice Blondel, an accomplishment that, for the rest of his life, he took great pains to defend and to explain, and to shelter from any undue condemnations from either philosophy or religion. If he did not allow it to be reprinted during his lifetime, even though it was out of print within two years after its publication and the demand for it was great well into the twenties and thirties, it was not because he thought less of it. In later life he spoke fondly of it as his cathedral, which he hated to see dismantled into *morceaux choisis* or selected passages, and for which he would have been loath "to make the sacrifice of Abraham," as he put it once to his secretary. He simply did not want to risk giving more occasion for having it denounced over and over again before a court that had steadfastly refused to condemn it, even at the height of the Modernist crisis.

It is true that Blondel published a second version of *L'Action*, one that was part of his Trilogy on Thought, Being, and Action, in 1936-37. This second version was a two-volume work, the second of which was a reprise of the original dissertation, with important modifications, but the first of which was a more metaphysical consideration of the problem of secondary causes in relation to the Pure Act. But this was far from being a simple reproduction of the original argument, which had been worked out much more concretely and passionately, and was much more clearly focused on the experience of human action, in its original version, without the more metaphysical considerations that were in keeping with the context of the later Trilogy. In fact, the context of the Trilogy allowed Blondel to leave out from the second version of *L'Action* certain parts that were integral to the original version, which had to stand on its own, without the prior consideration of *Thought* and *Being*. Moreover, along with the Trilogy in the 1930s, Blondel was also planning another three-volume work on *Philosophy and the Christian Spirit*, which would take up some of the more explicit supernatural themes that the young Blondel had felt obliged to bring in at the end of his dissertation. These could therefore be left out of the second version, so that if we wish to find Blondel's philosophy of the supernatural in its pristine and in its most unified form we must go back to the dissertation of 1893.

This is not to say that the first version of Blondel's philosophy of action is the truer version or that it represents the more authentic form of his thought, as many have argued. Blondel himself would later have something to say about this, since it is the second version of *L'Action* that he chose to publish later in his own lifetime, and not the first. But it is to say that it represents a version that does not appear anywhere else in his writings precisely as it does in this one, as the culmination of his first efforts to think through the unity of his life as both natural and supernatural. It is the original philosophy of the supernatural as first conceived by him. It has its own difficulties, as evidenced by the comments of the examiners at the defense and of later readers who would frequently misconstrue what Blondel was trying to say, but it has the advantage of having been written at a time when Blondel still had his youthful vigor, with the ability to read and write for himself. The later works suffer stylistically, if not in substance, from the complicated way in which they were written because of Blondel's blindness.

In any event it is this original version of Blondel's philosophy of action that we wish to present here, however briefly. *L'Action* of 1893 is a very complex book. It covers a lot of ground, both with regard to the different philosophical attitudes it takes on and to the entire order of nature it attempts to cover. It goes into the entire order of human existence, social as well as personal and individual, the political as well as the familial, as the springboard for speaking better of the supernatural and its necessity. It offers many new insights into the way of conceiving human life, psychological as well as ethical. But we shall not attempt to go into these here. We shall only run through this order of the dialectic in the natural order as it relates to the supernatural, much as Blondel did when he began his presentation of his dissertation at the defense by saying according to an archival note cited earlier: "My aim has been to constitute a philosophy which, though entirely distinct from the supernatural order, would be the natural and necessary underpinning of this order."

First, we shall review how Blondel brings philosophy to focus on human action and what he focuses on in human action as the principle for its dialectical unfolding. Second, we shall show how this brings him to a radical critique of superstition, and even of any idea of natural religion as such, since that too can amount to a kind of superstition. Third, we shall examine how he proceeds to the affirmation of God as the necessary being of action, and how this affirmation places every human being in a position of having to choose between saying *yes* or *no* to God, at the core of one's action. Finally, we shall show how he argues from this that the thought of the supernatural necessarily arises with regard to the question of human destiny, and that this thought, if it is actualized in human action through a gratuitous initiative on the part of God, necessarily entails a revelation, a mediation, and a religious practice for the human being.

A Philosophy of Human Action

Let us begin, then, with his modest beginning in human action. How does Blondel bring philosophy to focus on human action, something that was not as easily done in France at the end of the nineteenth century as we might suppose today? The book opens with a very fundamental question: "Yes or no, does human life make sense, and does man have a destiny?" (1893a, 3 [vii]). From this question the entire movement of thought develops for anyone interested in pursuing the question with Blondel. It is the question Blondel asks himself and invites any philosopher to raise, for it is from this question that the question of religion and the question of the supernatural must eventually arise for philosophy.

But Blondel does not immediately leap forward into this question of the supernatural. Far from it, he is stepping back into a consideration of human action as a whole, as the subtitle he finally settled upon indicates: *A Critique of Life and a Science of Practice*. Critique is the mode of examination proper to philosophy and this Critique of Life is supposed to yield a Science of Practice that is critically established. Early on, in his Introduction, Blondel makes an important distinction between *practical science* and *the science of practice*. The point of the distinction is twofold. The first is to recognize the validity of the science of those who learn the meaning of life directly through practice by following the light of their *conscience* simply, without raising any critical or scientific questions about life as a whole. One does not have to be a critical philosopher in order to come to an understanding of life and of destiny. But one can raise this question critically and philosophically, and Blondel argues why one must do so at times, which is the second point he wants to make in order to get his Science of Practice underway as distinct from the more direct Practical Science, which comes to fruition only after a lifelong experience. As a Science of Practice, philosophy becomes a critical reflection on human action and on its meaning as it has already developed in practice.

In order to make this reflection as critical and as scientific as possible from its very inception, Blondel first shows, against the *dilettante,* or what Kierkegaard called the aesthetic attitude, that there has to be a question of action, that it must be taken seriously, and that an answer must be sought. Then, against the *nihilist* attitude of a Schopenhauer, he argues that the answer cannot be purely negative, but rather that it must be *something positive.* In each case, he argues from something that is hidden in the action or the attitude of the dilettante or of the nihilist. But this part of the argument need not detain us here.

It is with the *something positive* of human action that we must be more concerned, for this brings us to what Blondel calls the *phenomenon of action,* or what actually appears in action for us to reflect on. Here again, as with dilettantism and nihilism, Blondel admits nothing into the investigation unless it proves itself necessary. Having shown that we must admit *something positive* in human action, he first takes this in the minimal sense that was admitted by *positivism,* namely, the object of the positive sciences. But he goes on to show that this is not enough, because the object of the positive sciences is itself constituted by the action of a *subject* who brings observation and mathematical analysis together in that object. In other words, the science of the object presupposes a subject who is no less real than the object, and who becomes the object of its own science in the science of the subject, as the originator of action. Here again Blondel argues from something hidden in the positivist attitude, but this time it is the *subject* in action, as he will understand it in the rest of the book, that comes into view. And it is here, namely, in Stage Two of Part III, on *The Phenomenon of Action,* the longest part of the book, divided into five Stages, that we must begin to follow more carefully what he brings up, for it is out of the principle that is established here that the rest of the dialectic of action will unfold, and that the question of the supernatural will arise at the end.

After bringing out the elements of consciousness in Stage One, in connection with the positive sciences, Blondel finally turns to reflect on how action is conceived in consciousness. What is at issue now is not just the fact of consciousness, which can be observed objectively along with other facts, but the *act* of consciousness, which is at the origin of human action. In a remarkable analysis of the spontaneous dynamism of motives and mobiles in our consciousness that give rise to the possibility of deliberation and choice in human consciousness, he comes to focus on this act as following from the determinism of mobiles and motives itself, but as constituting a new synthesis, or a distinct act that prepares and launches a series of new acts (1893a, 114-15 [109]). In a second moment of reflection, he shows how this consciousness of a new act results from a certain conflict or interplay between different and contrasting motives for action, each of which is partial in contrast to the others and to the whole that contains them all, namely, reflection or reflective consciousness as such. This reflection results from the partial character of the antagonistic states, but "this plurality of the solitary and opposed states is possible only through the immanent action of a power able to embrace all the multiplicity of the contraries in a higher unity, and which we have to call *reason*" (1893a, 117 [112]).

Further reflection upon *reason,* which contains the entire system of rival reasons for action, distinguishes it from all particular reasons, and sets them all in balance, because reason sees that each of them, a portion in a whole, is only one motive among others, and like others, or just one of many. This then brings out a dimension of reason itself, which transcends all such partial motives and is somehow infinite. "The consciousness of a motive did not occur without the presence of other motives; the consciousness of the multiple reasons for acting did not occur without at least a confused view of their opposition and of the system they form; the consciousness of these contrasts in the midst of an organic unity does not occur without the thought of what is inaccessible to relation and to limitation, without the known and possessed presence of an absolute, without the regulative idea of the infinite" (1893a, 122 [117]).

The point that Blondel is making here is not that there exists an absolute or an infinite. In fact, he explicitly withholds any such affirmation of absolute reality. The only thing that is taken to exist at this point in the phenomenology of action is the act of consciousness itself, in which the idea of the infinite does appear, as reason sets action in an entirely new sphere of freedom and self-determination. "Consciousness finds its explanation and its total reason only in a principle irreducible to the facts of consciousness as well as to sensible phenomena; it is conscious of its own initiative only by attributing a character of infinitude and transcendence to itself" (1893a, 123 [119]). Freedom is itself a certain power of the infinite to transcend any finite motive for action that comes with the idea of the infinite in reason. "In short, in order to act we have to participate in an infinite power; to be conscious of acting we have to have the idea of this infinite power and the idea of the infinite; and this synthesis is what we call freedom" (1893a, 125 [121]).

If we take this freedom of the subject by itself, apart from its relation to the plurality of partial motives for action within the totality of consciousness, as some existentialists have done, it might appear to be something absolute in reality, a shot out of the blue, so to speak, separate from everything that precedes it in consciousness. But that is not how it appears in the phenomenon of action for Blondel. "Necessarily produced before consciousness, freedom is necessarily exercised" (1893a, 128 [124]). While affirming the reality of this freedom as a result of the determinism of action, Blondel sees it as still having to actualize itself within the same determinism, or rather within a new kind of determinism that is no longer antecedent to the will, but consequent to it. Freedom in human action is never purely formal or absolute. It is real only in being exercised through deliberation and choice among particular motives or mobiles. It finds itself in the interplay of a plurality of motives, and inevitably it places itself in one of them.

This is a necessity within the phenomenon of freedom itself which the will must embrace, and which "authorizes the science of free action, or that even constitutes its object" (1893a, 130 [126]). But it is a necessity that also gives rise to a certain disproportion within the initial act of freedom itself. In choosing a particular motive, the will, which entails an infinite power, finds itself confined within a particular object. "It posits itself before itself as object, as goal, as particular end, above the other motives by right, among the other motives in fact, *una e multis*" (1893a, 134 [132]). The object willed, or as Blondel says more generally, the *willed will*, is no longer equal to the power of willing, or as Blondel also says, to the *willing will*. It is in relation to this inequality within the will itself that Blondel formulates his dialectical principle for the development of the phenomenon of action from this point on and for judging what is at issue in its ultimate dimension.

To understand this principle, we must understand that freedom, as it is initially given in action, is not the fullness of freedom. It is only a first freedom, which has yet to actualize itself more fully, as the very idea of the infinite in it suggests. This ideal of freedom to be actualized can be formulated in terms of an equation between the *willed will* and the *willing will*. It would be actualized only if the willed will were equal to the willing will. As it stands initially at this point in the phenomenon of action, however, the will is far from equal to itself. In fact, through its decision, it is so caught up in a particular motive that it must begin to seek beyond this particular motive, in search of an object that will be more proportionate to its infinite power of willing. It is this desire for a more proportionate object for its willing, which is part of the spiritual dynamism of the human being, that sets each individual on his way.

It is the same desire or the same principle that guides Blondel in the dialectical unfolding of the phenomenon of action starting from this central point of individual self-conscious action. For in the choice of any particular action, there is always an unknown, something mysterious, to be discovered in the pursuit of the choice itself. It is the purpose of the Science of Practice to make this unknown known as much as possible, and to let it disclose itself. In keeping with the scientific resolve not to let anything into the investigation unless it proves itself necessary, the dialectician proceeds little by little to explore this mysterious realm, which opens up before freedom as part of what has to be integrated in the whole of what one is seeking in seeking the equation between the willed will and the willing will.

The Critique of Superstition

From this threshold of consciousness and freedom as a new and transcendent initiative in human action, Blondel goes on to examine how it expands and develops through the voluntary operation, first, from the intentional effort to the first exterior expansion of action (Stage Three), then, from individual action to social action (Stage Four), and finally, from social action to superstitious action (Stage Five). At each stage he shows what the will must integrate as part of what it wills necessarily, but at each stage he also shows that what is willed at each intermediary stage is still not equal to the power of willing. Thus he goes from individual effort to the constitution of a personal life, from personal life to the constitution of social life, first in the family, then in the nation, and finally in humanity as a whole. He even goes on to the extension of action to the universe as a whole, in what he calls the tiered forms of morality. But in all of this the will still does not find anything to equal its own infinite power of willing. Superstition appears at the end as an attempt to force this equation by placing the infinite in something finite. It is important to understand how this happens as part of the phenomenon of action, and how it fails to do what it purports to do, because the necessity of the supernatural will appear precisely out of the consciousness of this inevitable failure.

"In voluntary action, as it is given in fact, there subsists an element whose mysterious fecundity is exhausted by none of the forms of personal, social or moral life, since, after having brought into this abyss of the human will all the grandeurs of science, of consciousness, of affections, of ideas, of duties, there remains a vacuum, since, no matter how stretched the enveloping lines may be, the circle cannot be closed" (1893a, 285 [305]). This is the element that is associated with the infinite power of the will and that the Science of Practice still has to explore. But it is also the element that superstition exploits in its own way in a false attempt to close the circle of human action in upon itself. "This infinitude which he obscurely feels within and which he needs in order to be what he wants to be, what he is already in desire and intention, the subject draws from himself; he presents to himself, under the form of a symbol or an idol, his own need for completion and perfection; he adores the incommunicable and inexhaustible life whose latent source he bears within himself. It is at the very heart of voluntary action, then, that a mystery resides, and we do not escape the desire of mastering it" (1893a, 286 [306]).

Superstition appears at the limit of the phenomenon of action, where the lines of expansion would seem to open up into infinity. But at the same time it brings us back to the center of consciousness, where we first discover the presence of the infinite as a power that transcends any particular motive for action, and as an ideal to direct reason in deliberation and choice. What the critique of superstition shows, however, is a certain misdirection in the use of this power and this idea that appears most obviously in certain primitive forms of action, such as fetishism, where "the surplus of the human act that always exceeds sensible facts and social life" is assigned to an object which, "finite and insufficient like the others, would not of itself have the capacity to receive the homage man claims to give it, but which, precisely because of its smallness, satisfies man's double need both to create and master his god" (1893a, 287 [307]).

But fetishism is only one form of the superstitious attitude in action. Blondel goes on to show how it appears in the many ritual acts and ceremonials that accompany human behavior from birth to death, in political life as well as in domestic life. He shows also how it appears even in those who claim to be liberated from all superstition, in an apotheosis of Reason or in the attempt at a positive religion of Humanity. But most importantly, he shows how this attitude of superstition, "instead of juxtaposing itself by a positive cult to other distinct acts, more subtly and less visibly insinuates itself into all the forms of practice, thought, science, metaphysics, art, natural morality; so that, precisely where it seems dead, for lack of apparent object and positive cult, it comes back to life more imperceptibly and more imperiously" (1893a, 291-92 [313]). Thus he traces this presence of superstition in Kant's own sense of duty for the sake of duty, and in the metaphysician's own sense of the divine and the natural religion that he draws from this immanent sense. Of the latter he writes: "Does he not transform the metaphysical phenomenon, which he has interiorly at his disposal, into a substance, into a Being which he thinks he has at his disposal exteriorly? . . . Even when he condescends to prescribe special acts toward the first being which his reason acknowledges, he thinks that prayer and adoration proceed from his thought alone and from his will; and these actions, which he calls religious, are, like the others, rid of all parasitic form and all obscure and sacramental rite. His superstition is to make believe that he has none and to think he lives only by clear ideas and rational practices" (1893a, 293 [314-15]). All this is to be understood, as we shall see, in contrast to the more truly religious attitude that Blondel will bring out in relation to the transcendent and the supernatural.

In fact, Blondel traces this superstitious attitude into every form of human endeavor, that of the evolutionist, that of the socialist, that of the scientist, and even that of the criticist who ends up making a cult of action itself. His aim is to unearth it in all its most subtle forms, so that it may be recognized for what it is and criticized in the most radical fashion, for action cannot end in any kind of superstition, not even that of action itself. But the point of Blondel's criticism is not to remain purely negative. It is rather to open the way to a pure sense of religious expectation. "For if he stays only with negative conclusions, if he takes satisfaction in them, . . . if he is triumphant for having dug within himself an abyss deep enough to bury, once and for all, his action and all things, the impious critic is not yet impious enough. He still retains the superstition of not having any; he remains an idolater" (1893a, 297 [319]). The only way to get beyond superstition is to "penetrate further and puncture this last idol, the only one man could still cling to in order to convince himself that he is fully self-sufficient" (1893a, 297 [319]). It is this attitude of self-sufficiency that is the ultimate obstacle to the religious expectation Blondel wants to open up at the very end of the expansion of human action. To get beyond rational self-sufficiency is to come into a surplus that remains after all the possibilities of human action have been exhausted, a surplus that "does not have to be added to willed action; it is already there, and in positing it, the will whence the act proceeds requires its use" (1893a, 297 [319]). It is from this sense of a surplus within human action itself that Blondel draws a positive conclusion from his criticism of superstition in all its forms, a conclusion that is doubly imperious: "It is impossible not to recognize the insufficiency of the whole natural order and not to feel an ulterior need; it is impossible to find within oneself something to satisfy this religious need. It is *necessary;* and it is *impracticable.* Those are, in brutal form, the conclusions of the determinism of human action" (1893a, 297 [319]).

From this impossibility of satisfying our religious need in the determinism of human action, or from its impracticability, one cannot argue to the impossibility of any ulterior satisfaction or any ulterior revelation in what we now have to think of as the mystery of action. For that too would be a sectarian negation, another form of idolatry glorying in human infirmity, or of being satisfied with not being able to satisfy oneself. One simply has to recognize the need as a matter of fact and as a matter of necessity from the will itself. "All attempts to bring human action to completion fail; and it is impossible for human action not to seek to complete itself and to be self-sufficient" (1893a, 299 [321]). This is the conclusion that follows from Blondel's reflection on the entire phenomenon of action, a conclusion that excludes any possibility of being satisfied with any doctrine of immanence, but methodically opens the way to a further question, the question of finding some satisfaction for the radical need of transcendence in human action, from a source other than the human will itself. This is a question that arises necessarily at the end of reflection upon the entire phenomenon of action, given the insufficiency of superstition in any of its forms and the impossibility of self-sufficiency for any willed will of the human being. But it is a question that must be dealt with, not just in relation to what is immanent in human action, but also in relation to what remains irreducibly transcendent to this natural order of the will.

The Necessity of Choosing in the Face of God

In his first approach to the idea or the power of the infinite within the phenomenon of action, Blondel dealt with it only as something that appeared alongside other more particular ideas and powers, dominating them in a certain way but still embodying itself in them and giving rise to a need for expansion. It was viewed only as part of the phenomenon, and the question of its *being* was strictly held in reserve, that is, as contemporary phenomenology would say, it was put in parentheses. But for Blondel the parenthesis was not meant to remain indefinitely in suspense. It had to be lifted once we reach the limits of the phenomenon of action, and the question of being had to be faced as a result of the need that remains at the limit of the phenomenon, in relation to the transcendent or to what Blondel refers to as the *necessary being of action*.

In raising this question, however, Blondel comes back to his original question about human destiny and how the terms of this problem are inevitably and voluntarily posited. Given the crisis in which human action finds itself at the limit of its phenomenon, or the natural order, the necessity of going further and the impracticability of its doing so by itself, it is driven back into its very core where it finds itself powerless to produce itself as something that is totally self-sufficient and to escape the *necessity* of willing. This is the core where the power of the infinite appears and where it seems to impose itself, as something totally involuntary and tyrannical. Can this ultimate contradiction of the will be overcome?

Blondel explores this question by describing the conflict in which the will finds itself in three moments. In the first moment the will is seen as contradicted and vanquished. Human action appears to abort. This is the experience in which the will appears as not having willed itself and as caught up in a determinism, which is not willed by it, but which is prior to it and more profound in its very being. Blondel insists on the contradiction in its most abstract form: the will is forced to will itself. In this it might think of itself as simply absurd, as Sartre did. But Blondel sees in this a suffering of the will which, beyond this abstract form, takes many shapes in experience. There is the suffering, not only of deprivation, but also of satiety. There is the suffering that we experience from the inside and that seems to eat away at our very freedom. And finally, there is the suffering of not being able to undo our past acts. All this Blondel sees as signs of the ultimate suffering of the will, which is at first launched as a victorious conqueror, but in the end seems to fail by the very grandeur of its ambition, since it cannot will itself as will.

In the second moment of this conflict, however, Blondel finds a higher will implied in this fact of contradiction, not just the willed will that experiences the frustration, but also the willing will in all its purity. "And this mechanism only manifests the necessity in which the will finds itself of willing itself and positing itself. The being that we have, we undergo; but at the same time we cannot fail to adopt it as something in complete accord with our will" (1893a, 309 [333]). He argues to this higher will by his method of implication. The experience of life and death, the experience of suffering and failing, is not just a fact of experience. These are facts "only by way of contrast, by the effect of an internal opposition between the willed and the willing will" (1893a, 310 [334]). What is implied in this is a higher pretension, an antecedent initiative of the will itself, in which the will adheres to its own nature. But in this adherence to its nature, it comes up against a real content whose amplitude reflection has not yet equaled. The conclusion of the negative results of action, the impossibility of stopping and the impossibility of going on, or of finding satisfaction by ourselves, is thus, not that we must go back, but rather that we must go forward into something more than what the phenomenon of action has been able to encompass, something in comparison to which the phenomenon seems only nothing.

Thus Blondel comes to the third moment of this conflict at the heart of human action, the inevitable transcendence toward the *One Thing Necessary*. "It is this conflict that explains the forced presence of a new affirmation in consciousness; and it is the reality of this necessary presence that makes possible in us the consciousness of this very conflict" (1893a, 314 [339]). In this moment Blondel shows how we come to affirm the One we call God at the very summit of action, and how this affirmation in turn resolves the conflict out of which it comes into an alternative, for, by reason of the presence of this thought of God in it, human action inevitably acquires a transcendent character.

Our concrete effort to make the willed will equal to the willing will is nothing other than our striving to achieve the perfection of our freedom according to the essential structure of the human will. Freedom is not merely something we have by nature. It is also something we achieve by the personal exercise of our will. The dynamic principle that makes us free in our actual condition demands this effort on our part, and in willing anything, we will this dynamic principle. In this concrete effort to achieve the perfection of freedom, man inevitably comes face to face with the Infinite, the Transcendent. There is an abyss that separates the willed will from the willing will, an infinite abyss that must be bridged, and that can be bridged only by him. That is why the determinism of action necessarily leads to the option for or against God. The intention of every free act inevitably traverses the entire universe of action only to face God in the end, before whom we cannot but adopt an attitude of acceptance or rejection toward him.

"The idea of God (whether we know how to name Him or not) is the inevitable complement of human action; but human action also has its inevitable ambition to reach and to use, to define and to realize in itself, this idea of perfection" (1893a, 326 [354]). All that has gone before in the Science of Practice is thus summed in this alternative. "Man, by himself, cannot be what he already is in spite of himself, what he claims to become voluntarily. Yes or no, will he will to live, even to the point of dying, so to speak, by consenting to be supplanted by God? Or else, will he pretend to be self-sufficient without God, profit by His necessary presence without making it voluntary, borrow from Him the strength to get along without Him, and will infinitely without willing the Infinite?" (1893a, 327 [354-55]).

The choice is man's, at the summit of his action. The total determinism of action is organized in consciousness in view of this most decisive moment of freedom. It is necessary because the determinism inevitably introduces the alternative into our consciousness. But it is at the same time free, because which of the alternatives is to be actualized depends on our option. It is by my fundamental option that I become what I will to be. Whatever may be its outcome, I can only blame myself for it. In the last analysis, freedom is not absorbed in determinism; it is rather the total determinism of the phenomenon of action that is suspended from this supreme alternative: either exclude from ourselves any will but our own, or give ourselves over to the being that we are not as to the unique means of salvation. The necessity for man to opt before God, to be god without God and against God or to be god with God and through God (1893a, 328 [356]), manifests his fundamental will to be, and to be what he wills to be. Thus, this final alternative of action enables us to will fully our own will and hence to escape the apparent tyranny of a will that is not willed. But at the same time it also has its necessary consequences for man and his destiny, which Blondel goes on to determine by showing how each side of the alternative is to be understood as an outcome of human action.

On one side there is the *death of action* through the refusal of anything that surpasses the natural order in action. Through the infinite power of his will man has a vocation to something higher than anything that can be found in any finite motive for action. Blondel explains how the refusal of this vocation is possible through the mechanism of any particular choice where the power of willing is experienced. As we saw earlier, in the initial reflection on the conception of action, the universal or infinite good we aspire to always appears under the guise of limited ends that solicit the will. "To the extent that its presence moves the will, as the principle and efficient cause of a life avid to open itself out, the good truly keeps its infinitude; to the extent that, before thought, it proposes itself as an object to be conquered or as the final cause of action, it is no longer anything more than a partial and limited motive" (1893a, 334 [361]). A choice is always the choice of a particular motive that is part of a natural order. But in the choice more is invested than just this or that particular motive. The whole of one's infinite power is brought into play. And if one chooses to limit the use of this infinite power to some particular object, whether it be something outside the self, or even the self itself, one chooses death for this action, a death that is akin to superstition, in that it places the infinite in something finite. It chooses the sufficiency of self or of some other object in the natural order, when it knows this to be insufficient.

Blondel also shows how this refusal of a higher good is not just the abdication of an optional surplus for man, but an abdication of something necessary for man's own good, exercised by the indestructible power of the will itself. It is a perversion that endeavors to capture the infinite in the finite, the eternal in time, and to naturalize the absolute in the relative. From the standpoint of what is done materially or in the natural order, the act may appear moderate and perishable, or trivial. But from the standpoint of the power that goes into it, it is of infinitely greater consequence and has to be judged in the light of that power. Man has been launched to infinity through his will. "The extent of the fault is measured by the energy of the movement more than by the end to which it tends; and the offense has a bearing only because the divine offended one is struck with all the power that is supposed to go to Him" (1893a, 340 [369]). Moreover, to the extent that man uses this infinite power to limit himself only to the natural order and uses all of this power in this act of self-limitation, he not only abandons any thought of a higher destiny, but also condemns himself to this limitation forever, and God ratifies this solitary will. "His natural state is to be unchanged. And not to be changed, is the irremediable abortion of his destiny" (1893a, 343 [372]).

On the other side of the alternative, however, there is the *life of action*. Blondel describes this life in terms of a positive devotion to all that is in conformity with conscience, a generous and humble abnegation, through which we accept another will at the heart of our own will. "Whatever may be the natural value of the motive that solicits the will, it must be muffled before a truly moral price is restored to it." In terms of the mechanism of choice in self-determination, "there is only one way to reconcile contraries and to dominate opposed desires: it is to sacrifice the diverse alternatives, even the one we will choose; it is to come back to it only through a higher feeling than the natural attraction that was soliciting us" (1893a, 348 [378]). Only in this way can we realize the absolute in ourselves, not as coming from our own will, but as coming from the will of the truly Absolute.

This we can understand naturally, even though we may not understand all that God actually wills for us. Over and above mere renunciation, the life of action also has to be a life of suffering and sacrifice, something that is truly disconcerting for self-will, a scandal for our freedom. But this suffering is necessary and good for the will, because "it keeps us from becoming acclimatized to this world and leaves us here with a kind of incurable discomfort" (1893a, 351 [381]). In fact, if we are to recognize the will of Another within our own, we must somehow die to ourselves in order to rise again to life and to draw the principle of action from its truly original source. The spontaneous life of man is still too natural. His reflected life, the willed will, is already a break from this merely natural life. But if this reflected life does not recognize a higher source still for the perfection of its life, it has no way of ever making the willed will equal to its willing will. Only by going through God can it find this equality of itself with itself, which is what it wills in all sincerity. It is not that man must abandon all willing of his own. In fact, he must will all that he can and as much as he can the perfection of his own action. But he must also understand that he cannot achieve this perfection by himself or by some natural necessity of his will. He must understand that this action of his, while necessary, is still radically insufficient and he must expect everything as coming from God. "In a sense, action has to be entirely from man, but it must first be willed as entirely from God" (1893a, 354 [385]).

It is important to note that in this characterization of the life of action, Blondel is not trying to describe any positive content of this life as coming from God. This is something that remains hidden in the mystery of action. He has argued that action cannot stay enclosed in the natural order and that man must recognize the necessary presence of God at the origin of his will, something he is called to consent to, but can also reject. In consenting to this immanence of the Transcendent, he is not only acknowledging his fundamental passivity in relation to God, but also coming to the highest perfection of his activity. But this perfection is not something he can achieve by himself, nor is it something he can naturally demand from God. It is something he can only recognize as necessary for himself and as totally free from the side of God. We can only live in a prayerful expectation of what God wills for us, who in turn gives himself only to those who are open to him. The best that philosophy can do is show "how we can offer ourselves and open ourselves to the equivalents of perfect action" (1893a, 346 [375]), not lead us into it. But this is already quite a lot, if we think about it, and it opens the way for a further consideration of the properly supernatural, based on a new Revelation as part of what might enter into this necessity for something higher for the perfection of human action. Just as action itself cannot be enclosed in a strictly natural order, so also the philosophy of action must show the necessity, not only of the presence of God in action, but also of whatever God might will freely and graciously on his part for our action.

The Necessary Hypothesis of a Supernatural

Thus, finally, we come to what may properly be termed Blondel's philosophy of the supernatural. It is something that comes at the end of his philosophy of action, but it is something not purely optional for this philosophy. Since what we are looking for in action is the equation of the willed will with the willing will, and since we have not found this equation realized in any natural or human terms, we must look further, if there is any suggestion that such an equation might be found in other terms. Hence, the necessity to philosophize about the supernatural in any inquiry about human destiny that does not stop short of anything that might provide an answer to the question of complete satisfaction for a will seeking equality with itself.

Blondel is not unaware that this question of the supernatural arises historically in a context where the idea of a supernatural revelation has been advanced. He does not make much of this fact in *L'Action* of 1893, though he does make a good deal of it in the *Lettre* of 1896. Blondel is more concerned with developing the philosophical outlook that is necessary for understanding such a fact in the phenomenon of action and for seeing how it relates to the philosophical exigencies in the question of human destiny. This is the point that would be made explicitly in the *Lettre* of 1896, but it is already built into the argument implicitly here and later on, where Blondel speaks of exigencies (1893a, 362 [393], 367 [399], 383 [416], 386 [421]). Nevertheless, in approaching the question of the supernatural in 1893, in addition to the idea of a completely sincere practice of life, which he has been developing in order to show the necessity of some higher life for man, Blondel also mentions witnesses, "perhaps importunate and indiscreet, but whose state of soul has some claim on the sympathetic curiosity we have for so many others" (1893a, 359 [390]). These witnesses are the Christian believers whom the high-minded of our "historical and scientific civilization" tend to disdain, even as the latter show some interest in more remote religions, and it is the idea of the supernatural of the former which, Blondel argues, it is not scientific to exclude in a completely sincere Science of Practice.

For Blondel there is always something mysterious in human action, something that does not always appear to the clear light of consciousness, even apart from the question of the supernatural. The effort of the Science of Practice has been to open a way through to some of this mystery, and to bring out some of its content in the immanent order of nature. At the summit, however, this science is forced to recognize that part of this mystery is buried in the will of Another, to whom we can have no direct access in philosophy. It is not that philosophy has no knowledge of God, or of how man is necessarily brought to an alternative in the face of God. It is simply that philosophy has no way of knowing *what* is happening, so to speak, on the side of God. It only knows that, for man to reach the equation of his willed will with his willing will, he must go through God, and that God makes this equation real for man in whatever way he wills. It also knows that whatever God wills for this equation, it becomes a matter of necessity for man, since willful failure or rejection of what would make the equation, even if it is supernatural, is tantamount to rejecting what man wills most fundamentally in his willing will.

This is already a lot for philosophy to be able to say. But as to saying in *what* the equation would consist, especially as coming from God, philosophy has nothing to say. That is for religion to say. The highest that philosophy can rise at the summit of action is to determine the attitude of religious expectation, which should characterize man in his highest confrontation with God. And it is through this attitude of religious expectation that philosophy can raise the question of the strictly supernatural, and of how it relates to nature or to what is properly human.

In the Blondelian perspective the supernatural remains a strict mystery. Nothing can be said of its essence or of its content by the philosophical method of immanence he is following. In fact, even to say that it *is* surpasses philosophy. This is something the philosophy of the supernatural itself will bring out. Yet philosophy has a way of talking about this mystery, which appears at the end of the critique of superstition, and which is repeated at the end of the alternative in which man finds himself face to face with God. "Absolutely impossible and absolutely necessary for man, that is properly the notion of the supernatural" (1893a, 357 [388]). Philosophy cannot give birth to what would be contained in such a reality, but it can show its *necessity,* without touching on its reality or even its possibility, as Blondel insists, even in raising the question. Against the doctrine of immanence, Blondel has reintroduced the notion of transcendence and of a relation to the absolutely Transcendent in human action. At this point, the metaphysician might be tempted to introduce a notion of natural religion. But Blondel is suspicious of what would turn out to be just another immanentist notion of religion. As we saw, he views such notions as still a kind of superstition, in that they try to fit the infinite into finite ideas of metaphysicians. Though he recognizes a distinction between the strictly supernatural and the merely transcendent, so to speak, which can still be affirmed naturally or metaphysically, he moves immediately into the question of the supernatural based on faith, understood as imposing itself on our thought and our will, for it is in this necessary relationship that he finds the point of encounter for philosophy and true religion, beyond all superstition. After a general criticism of superstition in all its forms, including what are called natural religions, one cannot go back and treat the religion "that condemns all superstition by presenting itself as of superior origin" (1893a, 360 [392]), a claim that sets it apart as *religion,* as if it were not supernatural. Nor can one legitimately treat this religion as if it were just another superstition, thus restoring to superstition a value that is denied of true religion, as if all cults were equal. One simply has to recognize that the claim to rely purely on *faith* rather than any purely natural form of action is consistent, not only with a religion that is truly of divine origin, but also with the exigencies of a philosophical understanding of such a supernatural hypothesis.

The first point in this understanding is that the hypothesis of the supernatural, though it may appear historically for the philosopher, is not purely optional for him, just as the call to a higher life at the summit of action is not purely optional for a will still seeking perfect equality with itself. Blondel has gone to great pains in order to show that human action cannot be complete in the natural order alone. The entire dialectic of action "results in making us conscious of an incurable disproportion between the élan of the will and the human end of action" (1893a, 358 [390]). The equation required by the dynamic principle of action remains both necessary and impracticable for man alone. The implications of this condition, in which man finds himself at the end of his action, have led to the acknowledgment of God, the Transcendent, and now, by the complete reversal of perspective implied in this acknowledgment, or by the attitude of religious expectation now seen as required for the fullness of human freedom, the supernatural, if it is, has to be understood as *necessary* for man, since it flows *ex hypothesi* from the will of him on whom the perfection of action depends totally, and to whom man must conform his will to be completely sincere with himself. While it is thus absolutely necessary for man, it remains absolutely impossible for him, since it depends on the added liberality of God. There is no exigency for it in the natural order, where the only exigency is that man consent to the will of God in coming to his ultimate destiny. But Blondel's aim is for philosophy to understand how the supernatural order, if it is and whatever it is, so penetrates the natural order in human action that, free in its origin, it becomes necessary for man.

How does he proceed in doing this? First of all, he shows how many of the objections raised against the Christian idea of supernatural religion are incompetent and inconsistent with the very idea of the supernatural and the exigencies of philosophy itself. Then he goes on to show how it is the role of philosophy to rectify the will to the very end, by looking always and everywhere for what would be in conformity with the primitive aim of this will. In doing so he shows how philosophy comes into contact with religion or theology, but without transgressing into the domain of either religion or theology, even as it deals with the question of the supernatural. This contact implies a certain cooperation between the two disciplines, so to speak, but a cooperation in which each retains its autonomy and independence. In this sense philosophy can be understood as the handmaid of theology, but it is so only if it remains free: *non adjutrix nisi libera*. On the other hand, however, and this is the new twist that Blondel gives, not just to the old adage, but to modern philosophy as a whole: Philosophy is not free unless it is a handmaid of religion: *non libera nisi adjutrix* (1893a, 361 [393]). In other words, philosophy is not fully free, unless it raises the question of a supernatural religion, which comes as a result of its understanding of its own powerlessness and its own insufficiency at the summit of its power.

In raising this question, however, philosophy proceeds with its own critical power, as it did with the attitude of superstition at the end of the phenomenon of action. In fact, it returns to the phenomenology of action and inquires whether the means offered by supernatural religion to bring action to its perfection are in keeping with the structure of action itself as we understand it concretely. Thus, just as, in approaching the conception of action in the natural order, Blondel prescinded from every premature affirmation regarding the ontological status of the infinite, so also in approaching the supernatural he prescinds from any affirmation as to the actual existence of any supernatural means to bring action to perfection, in order to examine only how such means would relate to the phenomenon of human action as understood philosophically. In other words, Blondel's philosophy of the supernatural is primarily a phenomenology, which is like the phenomenology of action, in that it holds the question of being in reserve until the entire phenomenon has been laid out in all its determinism, but unlike that phenomenology in that it recognizes that it can never answer the question of the necessary being of this supernatural phenomenon, as philosophy can with regard to the necessary being of action, since that answer can only come from faith, or in religion itself, not in philosophy. Given this reservation, however, which is essential to its competence, philosophy can then proceed most critically in its examination of the phenomenon of supernatural religion and how it can make its appearance in human action. In this sense it can also be quite normative, not for religion itself, since *ex hypothesi* the supernatural depends on the will of God, but for human action as such, insofar as this action comes under a supernatural order.

The phenomenology of the supernatural thus begins in the same way as the phenomenology of the subject began, with how an idea is generated within us. For the hypothesis in question, the idea has to be taken as one of *revelation* from outside the subject and his world as a whole. First, Blondel studies the mechanism by which our idea of revelation is generated within us in accordance with the hypothesis that this revelation is supernatural in its source. Then he analyzes the way man has to give his assent to this revelation. And finally he shows how faith in this revelation inevitably expresses itself in an exterior practice, still in accordance with the rational exigencies of the hypothesis that this way of life is strictly supernatural. He does not make use of any content of revelation in all this, for that is the proper function only of theology or religion. What he works with is the necessary relation of the natural order in action to the supernatural that has been established.

As something intended for the illumination of human reason, revelation entails something of an idea. In order to reach us in our conscious activity, this idea has to go through the mechanism by which all our ideas become conscious. We have seen Blondel distinguish a twofold aspect in this mechanism: first, some exterior force that penetrates into the field of consciousness through the inferior determinism of our nature and, second, the lower dynamism of the spirit which assumes the content of these exterior forces into its own process of idealization, where a mobile becomes a motive for action. A similar distinction has to be made in the process by which an idea is revealed to us. First, the revelation appears in an exterior symbol that comes from the outside. Second, the sense of this exterior sign has to be interiorized so that it becomes meaningful for the subject. All this has to be seen as part of a single human activity in which revelation is taking place.

Here, one might be tempted to think of a certain psychology of faith that would examine the mechanism whereby all this might happen within the subject, but that is not the concern of Blondel's phenomenology of the supernatural. Just as the phenomenology of the subject began with the moment in which consciousness already has ideas, taking the archaeology or the birth of these ideas for granted, while reflecting on the necessary relation between the interior and the exterior, so also the phenomenology of the supernatural begins from the supposition of a revelation, and proceeds to reflect on the relation between the exterior sign of a revelation and the interior movement wherein the sign becomes an idea for the subject. The dynamism of consciousness is an act that issues from the forces of nature and transforms itself in becoming master over its conditions, in order to create a voluntary intention that inevitably expresses itself in the exterior determinism from which it has arisen. No idea, not even one of revelation, can exercise any influence on us or become truly ours unless it becomes part of this internal process. What is important for Blondel, therefore, is to show how an idea, even one of revelation, becomes ours personally and consciously, so that it can take hold of us and exercise an influence as a motive in our voluntary action.

His point is not to minimize the exterior sign of revelation, but rather to show how it relates to something interior to the subject as well, and perhaps even more. By itself, the exterior sign has a double meaning, depending on the interior disposition of the subject. It can "offer the infinite only under the guise of the finite" (1893a, 364 [395]). To those who are well disposed toward or receptive of the infinite within themselves, it is a sign that is welcome. To those who are not so disposed, but are more inclined to be self-sufficient or satisfied with something in the natural order, it is a sign of irritation to be repelled. "That is why what subdues and illumines some is also what hardens and blinds others. *Signum contradictionis*" (1893a, 364 [396]). It could not be otherwise, according to Blondel, "precisely because the sovereign originality of the interior life admits only what it has somehow digested and vivified" (1893a, 364 [396]). If man were completely determined by an exterior sign, even one of revelation, there could be no freedom, no exercise of any option in accepting or rejecting the supernatural. *Faith* could not be a free or human act. But if Faith is to be supernatural, the difficulty is to understand how the One whose essence and whose will have been recognized as inaccessible to man alone makes himself accessible through the senses, and how his presence can be recognized through this obscure relation of the interior with the exterior.

In this regard we may be inclined to think of miracles as especially helpful in revealing a special presence of the divine. Blondel thinks of them as a challenge to common reason, always ready to settle down into a routine of what one ordinarily expects in experience. But for the miraculous, the same difficulty arises as for any external symbol. It is effective only inasmuch as one grasps, not the sensibly marvelous in it, but its symbolic sense. At bottom, there is nothing more in the miracle than in the least ordinary fact, but conversely, in a supernatural order there is nothing less in the most ordinary fact than in the miracle. "And that is the meaning of those exceptional shocks that incite reflection to more general conclusions. What they reveal is that the divine is not just in what seems to surpass the accustomed powers of man and of nature, but everywhere, even where we readily think that man and nature are sufficient unto themselves" (1893a, 365 [396]).

Thus it is not from some external revelation above, on the hypothesis that there is one, or from natural phenomena alone, that the idea of revealed precepts and dogmas arises in us. "It is from an interior initiative that this notion springs forth" (1893a, 365 [397]), the religious expectation that characterizes man at the summit of his action where he finds himself in the presence of God. The question for Blondel is: "How could this quite subjective disposition recognize on the outside whether there actually is a nourishment prepared to calm this appetite for the divine?" (1893a, 365 [397]). If the need is not felt, the question cannot be asked, and the signs of an answer cannot be recognized for what they are. All this follows from the way Blondel presents the need for some intervention from the Infinite, in the fundamental option where man is seeking a final solution to the equation of his will with itself. If man cannot find this equation alone or by the power of nature alone, but only through God, will God offer an additional help, one that will surpass the one man already has in the natural power of his will? Hence the idea of something more and properly supernatural coming from God, and not from ourselves or from nature as we already have it.

In this, however, we must recognize a radical reversal of perspective that can no longer be reduced to a merely subjective disposition. If our need for God is supernatural, we cannot want him as he is already within us, through the infinite power he communicates to our will. We can only want him as he wills to give himself in a supernatural way. Thus, what is required of us in the need for the supernatural is a radical dispossession of ourselves, wherein we are raised above ourselves. This entails an abnegation of self that does not go without suffering, since this operation, to be supernatural, has to crucify the complacency of self-will or self-love, and open the way within man to a new love for man which is from God. "The great effort of the heart is to believe in God's love for man. And whoever has grasped why man can and wills to be divinely loved, as if he were the god of God Himself, is no longer surprised that the way of annihilation and mortification is the route of the fullness of love" (1893a, 366 [398]). Thus the understanding of the supernatural pushes one step further what Blondel earlier described as the alternative of life for action, all the way to the point of accepting everything as coming only from God, including the very need or the aspiration for the supernatural that philosophy has been affirming.

From this understanding of the supernatural gift, Blondel derives three essential exigencies that could be characterized as rational or natural. The first stems from the fact that any divine revelation would have to propose itself as independent of human initiative, so that reason itself would have to judge it as false, if it failed to require of us an unavoidable sacrifice of self. Such a salutary disposition, however, cannot be related back only to the effort of the human will, since the supernatural as such cannot proceed from ourselves. "Even the *élan* of the search that brings us to God, then, has to be, in its principle, a gift . . . an indispensable mediation. . . . There is a revelation, therefore, given and received, only through a *mediator*" (1893a, 367 [398]), necessary for the very conception of a supernatural. This is the first essential exigency that follows from the idea of the supernatural.

The second exigency has to do more with bringing human action to its consummation. If there is nothing in man, nothing in the natural order that reaches the perfection of action and attains God, then "to make God the end of man according to the imperious need of our will . . . we need a help, an intercessor, a pontiff to be the act of our acts. . . . It is by Him alone that our will can equal itself to itself and hold on to everything in between, from its principle to its end" (1893a, 367 [399]). This is the second exigency that follows from the idea of the supernatural.

The third exigency has to do more with the reparation of our actions, which, as we have seen, are of eternal consequence. "To annihilate evil, therefore, we need a power and an expiation of which we can never find in ourselves the smallest part. . . . The mind boggles before the enormity of such a necessary task. To give, to preserve, and to restore life, we need a savior" (1893a, 367 [399]). All these are supreme exigencies which man is incapable of satisfying, but whose necessity reason can see, without understanding their possibility, since simply to be conceived they already suppose an inspiration that does not come from man alone.

Beyond these exigencies, however, which are, so to speak, the objective conditions for the satisfaction of man's subjective need for the supernatural, there is one final difficulty to be overcome, which is to understand how revelation acts in man and gives itself the proper guaranties for believing in it. "In order to be believed as it has to be believed, the revealed doctrine must itself furnish its reasons for belief and bring its own certitude, as a supernatural gift" (1893a, 368 [400]). For Blondel, this means that the revelation can never become totally clear to us, as something that comes only from us might be, but that, even in being communicated to us, it remains mysterious in its depth. What then can we make of the revelation if we cannot understand it?

It is here that the mediating power of action makes itself manifest in its highest form for Blondel. "For on the one hand, it is through the channel of action that the revealed truth penetrates deep into thought without losing anything of its supernatural integrity; and, on the other hand, if believing thought, as obscure as it remains amid the rays of faith, fans out from its inaccessible center, has any meaning and value, it is because it ends up in action and finds in literal practice its commentary and a living reality" (1893a, 368 [400]). Action is decisive in both the reception of the gift and in the use we make of the gift. It can be so precisely because it remains mysterious in its very depths. It is the place where God and man act together, when God intervenes and man responds in obedient faith. There is no natural reason for acts that are done purely out of faith, especially when they seem to require a complete disappropriation of self. Without faith one would not produce such strange actions. But there is a natural reason for perhaps experimenting with such actions, in that man is searching for complete sufficiency in his action, and he cannot find this sufficiency in himself alone or in anything his reason can devise. Could not such supernatural actions contain the ultimate indispensable experiment for man to discover all that is involved in what he thinks of as his destiny?

To perform such religious actions truly as they ought to be performed, one has to have faith. But for the one without faith, Blondel urges the natural reason which he has developed in the dialectic of action, not with the idea that this performance would necessarily bring faith, for the performance would still be motivated only by natural reason, whereas faith is a motivation of supernatural origin, a gift from God. Nor is it merely a matter of taking a plunge blindly, keeping the eye of reason tightly closed. Rather it is a matter of entering with eyes wide open more deeply into the mystery of action, in keeping with man's deepest and sincerest wish, and discovering there how God is not only present but acting in accordance with his own will. From a natural standpoint, such an act is quite appropriate, even if nothing more is discovered. In fact, if there is the possibility that something more might be discovered, such an act would be required by the generosity of man's spiritual *élan*, since that would be the only way in which the divine light can make itself known. For if God acts in this action, then the act "is richer by an infinity than that which precedes it" (1893a, 371 [403]).

Philosophy thus shows how practice can arrive at faith, without giving faith as such. But can it show as well how faith can arrive at practice? This is the final question that Blondel tackles in this original philosophy of the supernatural, in considering the value of literal practice and the conditions of religious action in the present life. If revelation and faith introduce a new life into man, they do not separate him from himself and from his action in the world. If they transform human action from the inside out, they do not eliminate what is human in it. As we have just seen, the action of faith is a joint action of God and man. Does philosophy have anything more to say about the exigencies of the supernatural in this action? As we have also seen, there is a consequent determinism that follows upon man's willful act. Is there also a consequent determinism that follows upon the supernatural act of faith? Can there be faith without a practice and, if there has to be a practice, how can this practice remain truly supernatural, and not become merely human and thus fall back into superstition?

What is at issue for Blondel is how the hypothetical gift of the supernatural is to be acquired integrally by man and somehow naturalized in human action. It might seem unacceptable and unintelligible at first sight, that the divine intervention should be embodied in some sensible nature or that the supernatural should have a natural expression. Blondel, however, argues that such embodiment is necessary as part of the determinism of action, which philosophy has to bring out to its very end. We shall see how he does so without compromising the very supernaturalness on which he wants to insist in this very necessity.

But first let us see how he argues that this expression of the supernatural life in external acts is not only necessary, but also a progression in the life of faith itself. Here again the phenomenology of the supernatural parallels that of the subject. Just as he had argued earlier that, for the intention of act to find itself and its true fullness, it must go out of itself into an external act and so embody itself, so also here the act of faith, for all its elevation above man, must go out of itself and inspire a faith in acts. The truly religious soul is like the truly moral soul: it cannot be satisfied with a pure intention that does not find its realization in action. "To be sure, they are infinitely right, these religious souls, in finding repugnant recipes and mechanical applications that profane their ineffable feeling. But if they are raised above niggardly superstitions, they are wrong nevertheless in not recognizing that the point they are happy to have reached is still only a middle ground, and there remains for them some progress to obtain" (1893a, 375 [408]). Blondel wishes to show these would-be pure souls that the deepest faith still has to find its perfection in very precise acts and that, "if there is a letter where only death and corruption dwell, there is a necessary one that carries with it life and salvation" (1893a, 375 [408]).

The point that Blondel makes is that action not only harbors within it a profound mystery, but also that it brings a richness of life that consciousness cannot always clearly perceive. Consciousness itself rises from it, as does the coveted gift of revelation. But the mediation of action is not finished once consciousness has emerged, or once faith in revelation has come to the fore. "Its mediation is not passing, but permanent. It is the perpetual means for interior conversion and the instrument of the kingdom of faith. For, in a way that is incomprehensible, it makes the meaning of a still obscure faith flow to the very marrow of the bones, and it runs through the mysterious ways that bring to the light of reflection the shrouded truths by which it is nourished" (1893a, 376 [408]). Included in these mysterious ways for Blondel are not only the most common practices of a religious community, but also the very spirit of that community as it is inspired by God. It is in practice that the two orders, natural and supernatural, which otherwise seem incommunicable, are tied together. True faith, then, does not consist in clinging interiorly to truths perceived only in part, as to an idol, but in letting go and finding further expression in a practice inspired by precepts and prescriptions that seem to clash with this interior purity. "Just as, in the dynamism of reflection, thought, which is the fruit of the experience of life, so also faith, which could be called the divine experience within us, is the origin of an activity that concerns the whole man and makes him produce, through all his members, the belief he lives by" (1893a, 378-79 [411]). In this way it is not only a vivifying force, but also a "slow work of transubstantiation and conversion" that takes place in our desires and our appetites, and in the social body as a whole. It gives rise to a discipline and a tradition and through its action "the lowest and the most obscure parts, which express the need of the organism and the reverberations of the universe, rise to faith and cooperate in the human and divine work that comes to completion in us" (1893a, 380 [413]). Without this action the synthesis we are seeking is not brought to perfection.

What Blondel concludes from this is that some kind of practice is absolutely necessary for faith, but at the same time he understands this necessity as only natural. To see it as only natural is to see it as inadequate and vain from the standpoint of the supernatural. As such, it is still not what justifies and brings action to perfection. It only reduces the supernatural once again to the natural. We cannot abandon the idea of a necessity of a practice for religious faith, but at the same time we must recognize the absolute inanity of all human practice. Hence we must go one step further in recognizing the necessity of a practice for the supernatural, and see it as having to come from the divine will itself. "On the one hand, no act naturally born of religious belief perfects or equals its dignity. On the other hand, faith is possible only under the species of a defined letter and through the efficacy of a practical submission; and the true infinite could be immanent only in action; it is therefore a necessity for this action itself to be the object of a positive precept, and for it to start, no longer from the movement of our nature, but from the divine order" (1893a, 382 [416-17]). This follows only from a strict understanding of the supernatural still compatible with necessity as understood in the Science of Practice. Only the idea of a positive precept of the divine can save the true practice of religious faith from every semblance of superstition. In this respect Blondel takes exception, not only to Kant's idea of religion within the bounds of reason, but also to every critique of positivity in the Christian religion such as that of Hegel. Positivity is the very condition for preserving and keeping what is truly transcendent and supernatural in religion, without reducing it to some immanent necessity of nature.

At the same time, however, this positivity from the divine is the only way in which we can have the infinite in the finite, without losing it in superstition. "We must have the infinite as finite; and it is not for us to limit it; otherwise we would be lowering it to our size. It is up to this infinite alone to bring itself within our comprehension and to condescend to our littleness in order to exalt us and broaden us to its immensity" (1893a, 384 [418]). The paradox, as Kierkegaard would have noted, is that the Infinite does place himself not only in a particular individual, but also in the least of our actions, when we do them out of faith. But this is still in accord with reason, Blondel argues, if the precept or the command comes from a source other than the will of man: "infinite greatness can accommodate itself to our infinite smallness; the divine is more than universal, it is particular at each point and wholly in each" (1893a, 384 [418]).

There remains only one more point to be made before Blondel brings his philosophy of the supernatural to a close. We have seen how the ordinary relation between thought and action is preserved in religious practice, in that faith has to sink into the members and assimilate the organism of action to itself. We have also seen how it is completed in that through the positive precept, and only through it, there is, by hypothesis, a perfect equation between the spirit and the literal form wherein it expresses itself. What remains to be seen is how this ordinary relation between thought and action is reversed in religious practice, "for, unlike habitual acts, where thought precedes the sensible operations and imperfectly penetrates the organism that realizes it on the outside, here it is the sensible sign that obscurely contains the light whose invisible center thought seeks to discover little by little" (1893a, 385 [419]). Earlier, Blondel has suggested that, for one who does not have faith, performing the acts of faith could perhaps be a way of learning, through the mediation of action itself, what is contained in the life of faith. Here he argues that the acts performed out of faith, or the literal practice formally commanded, have to contain the divine life itself, whether one perceives it as such or not, so that in the sacramental act of faith we not only receive the divine life within ourselves but we are ourselves taken up into this life. "It seems that in obeying the precept we make the eminent truth which it expresses come down into us. That is true; but we also transform and raise into that truth the act it prescribes" (1893a, 385 [420]). In spite of its external and natural trappings, the act takes place entirely in the absolute. "The literal precept is, so to speak, more living and more spiritual than the spirit it takes hold of. We absorb it into ourselves, and it is the one that absorbs us into it" (1893a, 385-86 [420]).

Thus, what there is in the sacramental life of faith is a double assimilation of two infinitely different lives, of the divine by the human and, more profoundly still, of the human by the divine, a new synthesis of the human and the divine, which takes place through a kind of annihilation or an emptying of the infinite into the finite and a reformation or a refiguration of what is natural to man, so that man becomes capable of giving birth to God in some way, and of making him rise from his annihilation, through the effort of his good will complying with the divine precept. In this symbiosis of the human and the divine, which insinuates the divine even into the humblest of human functions, Blondel recognizes the final fulfillment of the equation that was originally discovered as the dynamic principle of action in the phenomenology of the subject. In other words, Blondel sees this as the necessary end to what the Science of Practice has been looking for from the beginning. "To go to the end of the determinism of the exigencies of human action and of the chain of the relations necessary for the completion of our destiny, then, God has to offer Himself to us as if annihilated, so that we may restore to this apparent nothingness its fullness" (1893a, 386 [421]). This is in accordance with what we have to conceive and hope for in seeking to make our willed will equal to our willing will and, by giving himself in the humblest of ways in a sacramental operation, God makes it possible for the faithful to will fully all that is contained in the infinite *élan* of his will. To be sure, this equation is still veiled in the mystery of action, even for the man of faith, but Blondel insists that only in action does man find complete illumination regarding the infinite. "The true infinite is less in knowledge than in life; it is neither in facts, nor in sentiments, nor in ideas; it is in action" (1893a, 387 [422]). And it is only in an action that unites the divine and the human, as in the sacramental operation, that man can come to the perfection of the infinite principle which launches him to the infinite. It is not for philosophy to say whether God actually gives himself so as to make such action possible for man, or even to say how it is possible. It is for philosophy to say only that, if such a gift is proffered even freely by God, it becomes necessary for man in the light of the equation he is seeking to actualize through his action.

With this consideration of a literal practice as necessary for a revealed supernatural religion, then, Blondel had come to the end of his philosophy of the supernatural as found in the dissertation of 1893. He had made a place in modern thought for a Christian philosophy as he understood it, including the "operation *ad extra* and the value of literal practice," which had been found too barbaric and too annoying in the subtitle he had originally submitted with his proposal to the Sorbonne in 1887.

Grounding the Phenomenon of Action in Being

In one way, Blondel had completed his task, at least to his own satisfaction if not to the satisfaction of the opponents of any religious thought in philosophy. This is why, no doubt, he felt justified in submitting his dissertation, with this chapter on literal practice as the last chapter, to the judgment of the jury, not counting a few pages of conclusion on the logic of action and on the nature of his Science of Practice in relation to the Practical Science of life itself, even though he had originally written an additional chapter on "the universal and eternal consistency of action" for the version he had submitted to Boutroux in 1892.

In another way, however, he had not completed his task as a philosopher, because for him there was more to be said about how the supernatural somehow capped the conception of reality itself. The point of the omitted chapter, originally submitted to Boutroux, had been to consider, from the standpoint of the end attained, how the philosophy of action is renewed, or has to be seen in the light of a new foundation, "for, far from having to reject or crush all the successive stages through which we ascend to divine life, it is only by taking up again the universal reality on which action has nourished itself that the human person perfects its role, which is the role of being the total bond of things, of giving them the life and the form that completes their being and is their true reason" (1961d, 41). The idea was that, from the perspective of the supernatural, philosophy could then view reality in the light of its truly divine foundation and ground it as a new creation through the supernatural Mediator.

This was to go even further than Blondel had come up to that point. It was not just to show the necessity of the supernatural in reason itself, but also to show how the natural order has to be subordinated to the supernatural order, and how reason has to be subordinated to faith, so that the whole of human experience in the world is grounded ultimately in the supernatural activity of God and human being together, or of God in human being and human being in God. This is how Blondel was thinking that philosophy had to be properly Christian or Catholic, in the proper meaning of the term as well as in its more universal meaning, *kath holou,* if it were to remain faithful to the entirety of its task, in keeping with the idea that philosophy is not free unless it is in the keeping of religion, *non libera nisi adjutrix.*

It is with this idea of philosophy that he would later develop his philosophy of the Christian spirit. But in 1892 he had made only five short points, which he put in a note as follows. First, I show that man finds himself fully and has his real consistency only in God, and not just in the universe. Second, I examine how the human personality and individuality, even when it is caught up in the divine immensity, is constituted in its own being and substance without being absorbed or losing its own foundation. Third, I study how the absolute reality of the person and the individual presupposes, and at the same time grounds, the substantial truth of a social communion and a bond of perfection that binds men effectively to one another. Fourth, I consider the total concept of the universe in a new way, so that where we have seen up to now only a phenomenon, we can henceforth discover what there is, in appearance itself, of true being and substantial reality. Fifth, I argue that, thanks to the vivifying and substantiating role of perfected action, a universal and eternal life is constituted for everyone who wills to the end the fullness of willing. This is not exactly what Spinoza and Leibniz had in mind when they spoke, respectively, of the absolute infinite substance or of a *vinculum substantiale* in the universe, but it is the way in which Blondel had appropriated these fundamental ideas of modern philosophy to his own philosophy of the supernatural.

What it all meant for Blondel was that, after a regressive analysis of all that goes into human action from its humble beginnings in the body all the way up to the "one thing necessary," or the necessary being of action, one then had to take a more synthetic view of all that had been found in the analysis. His idea was to show "action as a consummation of universal reality," as he notes in another draft of what he still had to do. "We have just seen how everything contributes to action; we must finally show how perfected action [i.e., human action that has been penetrated by divine action] perfects everything else and consummates universal reality by raising this necessary fact into an absolute truth and by constituting into beings the means whose interconnection the will has recognized" (Archives f. 654). From being consummated, human action becomes consummating. What was only a series of means taken step by step for action, now has to appear as a system of simultaneously ordered beings.

In the end, therefore, according to Blondel, the systematic philosophy of action had to become a philosophy of being. Or again, as he writes to his friend Delbos, himself a metaphysician in his own right as well as a historian of Spinozism at the time, "I have always hoped to ground facts in reason and to raise them into the absolute truth, these relations whose determinism I have long studied. In short, after having attempted to show all that is immanent to action as a necessity of fact, I would like to posit, apart from the will, as beings what up to now I had posited before thought only as means, as absolute truths what were still only relations dependent on our action" (Archives f. 655).

Clearly, this is a different kind of question than the one of human destiny, which gives rise to the philosophy of action and its consummation in the conception of a perfected or supernatural action. But it was a question Blondel saw as necessary at the end of his first philosophy of the supernatural in action. It was a question that would later give rise to his Trilogy on *Thought, Being,* and *Action,* which is why it is good for us to dwell on it here briefly, in order to see how the later philosophy would only flow from the earlier one. In terms of Kantian philosophy, it was a necessity of going from a critique of practical reason to a critique of pure reason, and Blondel was very conscious, not only of the importance of reversing the order of Kant, but also of the necessity to do so at the end of a critique of life. This was for him the way of reinstating metaphysics and ontology in a critical way.

Why he decided not to include his first attempt to make this ontological turn in the dissertation he submitted to the Sorbonne is not clear from anything that can be found in his ample notes or correspondence, let alone his published works. No doubt, he felt that his manuscript of 1892 fell too far short of what he wanted to accomplish. His thinking about the being of action had to mature further. But the reaction to the dissertation in June 1893 incited him to think again about omitting this last, more ontological dimension of his thinking. He felt too many had missed the metaphysical import of his science of action, while insisting only on its psychological and moral aspects. Boutroux, who had read the omitted final chapter, did raise a question of being in connection with mysticism at one point in his interrogation, but it was not explored in any critical way. In any event, Blondel decided to exercise the right he had reserved with the publisher to revise and to add a final chapter to the final version of the book to be published.

It was most likely his friend Delbos, whose judgment he valued more than anyone else's, who brought Blondel back to his original idea of an ontology at the end of the philosophy of action. It is not certain whether Delbos read the original manuscript of *L'Action* as submitted to Boutroux. He seems to have had in hand only a copy of the book as it was submitted for the defense, judging from his initial reaction to the end of what he had seen. "Moreover," he writes, "if you redo the conclusion (it would be useless to redo it only for this motive), couldn't you insist *a bit more* on the culminating ideas of the thesis and on the steps you have taken? Your conclusion is almost too new in relation to what comes before" (1961d, 58). This appears to have been the reaction of one who has gone directly from the chapter on religious practice to the conclusion of the book on the logic of action, without seeing the chapter on the "universal and eternal consistency of action."

The only objection to the whole Delbos says he may have, is that Blondel does not leave enough room for metaphysics. In the dissertation, Blondel speaks of metaphysics only as a moment in the development of action, where it is considered more for what it does for action than for what it is according to its intrinsic validity. Delbos agrees with Blondel in holding back from a metaphysics that tends to inflate itself into a religion, "but it seems that [metaphysics] has more to do than just raise action [to a higher level] or prepare it: it may have to consecrate action, or better still to justify it" (1961d, 60). For Delbos, metaphysics should play the role of *rationalizing* the dialectic of action, which expresses only the *needs* of action too much to have, by itself, a complete value. "Perhaps you have conceived action as the necessary *fact*, whose consequences you have to deploy in all their complexity. Shouldn't you posit this fact positively as a truth in itself and not for us? Before expressing itself in religious faith, the subordination of human action to God can and should be posited metaphysically: Religion makes efficacious what reason already affirms" (1961d, 60).

These final remarks, written in a letter dated May 14, 1893, came too late to affect Blondel's dissertation submitted to the Sorbonne, since that was already in print, but they did play into Blondel's own thinking about the need for a more synthetic conclusion about the *being* of action to complement his dialectical analysis of action. They go a long way to explain the kind of modification that was brought to the omitted final chapter after the defense, before it was reinserted in the book destined for the general public. In the 1892 version, the final chapter had been written in a tone that was much more religious than metaphysical, though a brief attempt had been made in the fourth point to pass from a purely phenomenological viewpoint to something more ontological. In the final printed version of November 1893, what emerges much more prominently is the metaphysical or ontological aspect of Blondel's synthetic view of action and its determinism. This is affirmed from the very beginning of the chapter, in connection precisely with the concatenation of necessary means that has been brought out by the dialectical analysis. It is in viewing the totality of this necessity of means that we come to understand the absolute truth of the whole universe of experience as imposing itself in being and as a sanction for action itself. This, according to Blondel, corresponds to the popular understanding of being, or of the real as the whole.

Blondel first makes this point within the dialectic of action in relation to the knowledge we have of the whole, prior to the option we are brought to by this knowledge. In this there is already an expression of absolute truth in relation to being, with regard to what he calls "the necessary being" of action. But then he goes on to show how this knowledge bifurcates into something privative or something more positive still, depending on whether one says *no* or *yes* in the option before this Necessary Being, or God. Action, as it follows from this fundamental option, brings a new and more concrete knowledge, which is no less metaphysical than the one prior to the option, but there is more to be found in the one who says *yes* to the Necessary Being than the one who says *no*. What the one who says *no* discovers is that he falls short of his destiny, deprived of the good he is aiming at, a deprivation that constitutes the sanction for his negative decision in his willed action. What the one who says *yes* discovers is an open view on the Necessary Being itself now accepted in action, a sort of metaphysical view to the second power that is receptive to whatever the transcendent Necessary Being may bring to action.

Having made this rather complicated point about different moments in one's metaphysical knowledge with reference to being in the concrete, Blondel then goes on to reintroduce the necessary conception of the supernatural as part of this metaphysical view. In this he is returning to what he had set out to do in the original version of the chapter, but now he is more intent on bringing out the metaphysical aspect of this knowledge, without excluding the religious, by insisting on objective existence as well as absolute truth and reality, and by showing "the practical necessity of raising the ontological problem which brings us to the ontological solution of the practical problem" (1893a, 389 [425]).

There is no question of our trying to follow this convoluted argument in detail here. Suffice it to say that Blondel saw it as a necessary part of his philosophy of action even at its summit, where it relates necessarily to the religious and to the supernatural. The argument shows that Blondel was intent on thinking of religion, or religious action, as a critical philosopher, and not as a believer or as a theologian or a mystic, believer and perhaps mystic though he was. Much of what he would have to say later on about Thought and Being as well as Action, and about the Christian Spirit, would evolve from the questions he grappled with in this final chapter of *L'Action* (1893). If the chapter did not turn out as clearly as he would have liked, it is because he was too rushed to meet his publication deadline of November. What he wanted to get at was far more complex than he perhaps realized at the time, and his attempts to run through the problem anyway led him to formulations that would lead to misunderstandings and that he would later regret.

What Blondel was trying to do, in effect, was meet certain exigencies of rationalist thought with regard to a metaphysical outlook that was essentially immanentist, but in answering these exigencies he was too quick in introducing questions and answers that were too specifically Christian. As he would recognize later on, the chapter was too equivocal. It did not satisfy the rationalists, who thought he was unduly throwing Christian language into a pot of classical problems, and it succeeded only in irritating many Catholic theologians, who thought he was unduly intruding into their theological domain. Blondel was trying to enter into the perspective of his rationalist critics in order to bring them around to his own view concerning the Transcendent and the necessity of the supernatural, but this backfired: it left many with the impression that Blondel himself was an immanentist. The distinction between the doctrine of immanence and the method of immanence, which Blondel would later make in the *Lettre* of 1896, was not yet clear in anyone's mind.

Delbos's response to the new chapter was more positive, though guarded. When he had suggested a more metaphysical outlook to Blondel, he had had a conception of his own in mind. What Blondel produced turned out to be quite different from what he had anticipated. After reading the final version of the chapter to be published, he wrote back to Blondel, apparently responding to specific questions Blondel had sent him. "I answer your questions briefly: first, I recognize that I was of no use to you, and it is you who have developed what you still had to say. Second, what you have added brings your book to completion and confirms its meaning. Third, with your way of understanding action you could not raise or deal with these problems before the end. Fourth, therefore I approve the addition of this chapter. Fifth, this chapter serves to tie *your* philosophical way of dealing with *your* subject back to the general way of understanding the philosophical problem" (1961d, 62).

This was the judgment of one who was not only a friend, but also an eminent historian of philosophy who had just completed his own book on Spinozism and its evolution in German philosophy, which Blondel himself was reading at the time he was completing his dissertation, an important fact to keep in mind in reading the young Blondel, since Spinoza, along with Schelling and Hegel, was for both young friends and budding philosophers the philosopher of immanence par excellence to be overcome. Just as Blondel surprised his friend in the way he did this in 1893, so also he would continue to surprise both friend and foe with his resourcefulness in dealing with the vital problems of Action, Thought, and ultimately of Being in this life as well as for eternal life.

What Blondel discovered in the effort to write this final chapter of *L'Action* in 1893 was that he had much more to say than could be said within the constraints he had imposed on himself for his dissertation. The more synthetic view he had in mind as the complement for his analysis of Action would have to be expanded to include more on Thought and Being as well as Action. As he was writing that final chapter, he came to realize that he would have to begin his own philosophy all over again, without confining himself to a rationalist method that was too narrow to contain it. It is then perhaps that he began to realize what he would later write in describing his *Itinerary:* "Without the career necessity that forced me to publish *L'Action* and to make of this fragmentary draft an academic exercise, I believe this book, or rather this chapter, would not have seen the light of day" (1928a, 63). This was written in 1928, when Blondel was already contemplating the scheme for his Trilogy and for the work on the Christian Spirit that was to follow it, where the philosophy of action would be included as only a part of a greater whole, one more congenial for a proper conception of the supernatural.

IV

The Vocation to Philosophy

The Thesis on the *Vinculum Substantiale* of Leibniz

The thesis on Action was not the only one Blondel had to defend on that fateful day in June 1893. It was the one that was more controversial and got most of the attention. But there was also a secondary thesis, in Latin, on the idea of the *vinculum substantiale* in Leibniz: *De Vinculo substantiali et de substantia composita apud Leibnitium, hanc thesim Facultati Literarum Parisiensi proponebat Mauritius Blondel*. This thesis and the discussion of it are not even mentioned in the review of the defense as a whole we have seen. It seems to have gone largely unnoticed amid the controversy about the first thesis. Blondel was to publish a French adaptation of it later on under the title *Une énigme historique: Le "Vinculum Substantiale" d'après Leibniz et l'ébauche d'un réalisme supérieur*, at the end of his teaching career in 1930, but even then it did not attract much attention.

Nevertheless, the idea of the *vinculum substantiale*, as we have seen, was to play an important part in the development of Blondel's philosophy, including his dialectic of Action. In the Latin thesis Blondel does three things. First, he examines three arguments given by interpreters against taking the hypothesis of the *vinculum* seriously as a part of Leibniz's philosophy. It was argued that Leibniz was not sincere in his correspondence with the Jesuit Des Bosses, especially because it seemed to revolve around the idea of transubstantiation in connection with the Catholic dogma of the Eucharist, something that Leibniz himself did not believe in. Blondel responds that this reading of Leibniz is not convincing and that it fails to take into account how this question of the *vinculum* occurs, not in the middle, but at the end or at the summit of Leibniz's system as something that remains to be dealt with, much as the question of ontology remained to be dealt with at the end, or at the summit, of his own phenomenology of action. In the second place, he maintains that the idea did not revolve principally around the question of transubstantiation. In fact the question of transubstantiation was only a side issue in the context of a more general Scholastic discussion about how composite substances, which could not be reduced to mere monads, were constituted. Finally, he argued that, far from being at odds with the *Monadology*, as this extrinsic criticism claimed, it was rather a final step in the evolution of the Leibnizian system, something that Leibniz had to think about if he was to take seriously the problem of composite substances that were irreducible to simple monads.

Having argued against these extrinsic considerations of interpreters, Blondel goes on to an internal criticism of the texts written by Leibniz himself that show Leibniz grappling personally with this question of a *vinculum substantiale* for composite substances — one a "secret meditation," which had just come to light in the critical edition of Leibniz at the time that Blondel was examining this discussion, in which, prior to any correspondence with Des Bosses, Blondel found Leibniz already asking himself this question at the end of his system; and the other, the final letter to Des Bosses, in which Leibniz argues that the idea of the *vinculum* is not to be confused with any idea of a monad, including the idea of the dominant monad in a unified set of monads, but rather that the idea is to be taken as referring to something real or substantial in an organic being that is not merely an aggregate of simple bodies. Blondel shows that, far from just trying to accommodate his Jesuit correspondent with regard to transubstantiation, Leibniz had to argue against him and to answer his objections to the idea of the *vinculum* as part of his system.

In the third and final part of the thesis, Blondel goes into a more general discussion of this idea of the *vinculum substantiale* as it appears at the end of the Leibnizian system, in a shift away from its earlier idealism based only on a pre-established harmony among self-enclosed monads in the mind of God, toward a realism of the composite substances themselves as actually willed into existence by God. He brings out two labyrinths in the thought of Leibniz that anticipate some of the later Kantian antinomies, one in relation to the continuous and discontinuous, and the other in relation to determinism and freedom. It is in this final chapter that we discover how Leibniz's idea of the *vinculum substantiale*, which came to the German philosopher late in life, opened a way for Blondel in his own philosophy of action, where he had to deal with both the question of the continuous and the discontinuous in passing from a purely objective or mathematical science to a subjective science, and the question of determinism and freedom in showing how there could still be a science of action even though each individual subject was free and original in its initiative (1893b, 48-96).

The reader for this Latin dissertation had been, not Boutroux, but Victor Brochard. In his report to the Dean, dated January 2, 1893, Brochard spoke of it as a serious and conscientious study shedding light on an interesting and little-known part of Leibniz's system. He said the author gave proof of knowing and understanding the system well, with his numerous and well-chosen references. The style was clear and the argumentation was sufficient and well articulated, all things one looks for in a philosophy dissertation. The only reservation expressed had to do with the last chapter, where Blondel was expanding in his own way on the significance of this final aspect of Leibniz's system. There the reader, Brochard, would like to find more clarity, if possible. But on balance he had no problem in approving the work for the required visa from the Dean (1930a, xii-xiii).

It is important to note, however, that in adopting a more realistic attitude with regard to the late Leibniz, Blondel was taking issue not only with other extrinsic critics of the significance of the *vinculum* for Leibniz's thought, but also with his own teacher, Boutroux, from whom he had gotten his general understanding of the Leibnizian system at Normale. Needless to say, this difference of opinion regarding the understanding of the *vinculum* did not go unnoticed at the defense. Boutroux led the charge against the candidate's interpretation, insisting on a purely idealist interpretation of Leibniz, with the candidate pushing for his more realist interpretation of the final push toward a recognition of something substantial in composite things themselves. Blondel did not argue that Leibniz clearly affirmed this idea of a *vinculum substantiale*, which allowed for some plausibility in Boutroux's persistent idealist reading of the system. But in raising the question or entertaining the hypothesis of a *vinculum substantiale* in things themselves, Blondel saw Leibniz as opening the way toward a more realistic philosophy that he, Blondel, was more ready to follow than his own more idealist teacher. Though he was not able to convert his teacher in this regard any more than in the matter of the necessity of the supernatural in human action, he was nevertheless able to convince him and the rest of his jury that he was indeed worthy to be deemed a solid philosopher in the accepted sense of the term. Boutroux would later commend Blondel, after his paper on an "Elementary Principle for a Logic of the Moral Life" at an International Congress held in Paris in 1900, under the presidency of Boutroux, for introducing this new and more realistic dimension of action into the philosophical debate.

Rethinking a Vocation

Blondel's defense of both his theses on June 7, 1893, proved successful. He was awarded the *Docteur ès lettres* on the force of his ability to defend his ideas philosophically. But this did not allay the anti-religious fears of those whom he had convinced of his ability to think philosophically. To his great consternation and mortification, as he called it (1961c, 487), on June 13, when he approached

Dean Liard in search of a teaching post on the University level, he was denied any possibility of getting one on the grounds that "his way of understanding the problem of philosophy and morality was destructive of the method and the conception for which the Director of Higher Education had to assure respect" (1961c, 487, note).

Blondel's challenge to the established way of doing philosophy was not sitting well with the academic authorities. His protestation was that, far from restraining the scope and the free inquiry of philosophy, he was "trying to restore to philosophy by means of a philosophical method the highest part of its natural domain of investigation, so that, wishing to make this higher and all too abandoned floor of the edifice more habitable to philosophers, [he] was not demolishing, but on the contrary wanted rather to consolidate its foundations whose necessary and unshakable structure he was far from compromising, in order that [philosophy] might go higher and have a higher bearing" (1928a, 49-50), namely, with regard to religion itself.

It was a wasted effort, at least at first, for Blondel's philosophical move to a higher ground was generally understood as anti-philosophical. And so he found himself totally frustrated in the purpose for which he had labored so long and hard, to be as philosophical as he could and push philosophy to the limits of its capacity in dealing with the religious question. He found himself wondering what he could do with his life. For, until that time in his life, he had not stopped to ponder too long on what he should do, even though way back he had surprised his family by seeking admission to the École Normale Supérieure, which ordinarily meant opening the way to a University career. Unlike his classmate and fellow *tala*, Jean Wehrlé, who left Normale to enter the seminary and become a priest, Blondel had stayed the University course, gone out to teach philosophy at the level of the Lycée, and had come back to successfully defend two dissertations. All this was preliminary to getting a University chair in philosophy, which was now being denied him.

This denial, however, was not the only reason why he was wondering what to do with his life. There was still an unanswered question in his own interior life as to what his vocation was to be, in other words, as to whether he should become a priest or not. Everything in him, his family background, his own deep religious convictions, his intellectual and reflective bent, pointed in the direction of this idea, as he indicates when he finally pauses to start pondering the question. In fact, the question had already begun to emerge in his own meditations as he was nearing the end of work on his dissertation. Even before the defense of his thesis, he feels the hour of decision approaching for him and he asks "for light, courage, and living action, in place of his languishing and dead pusillanimity. *Da vim, da viam, da lucem, da salutis exitum*" (1961c, 487). The Latin itself suggests an aura of the priesthood for a frequent communicant in a Church that was still conducting its liturgy entirely in that language. The shock and the humiliation of being refused a University chair only underlined for him the necessity of being ready and open for anything that God might call him to, while he hangs in a sort of no man's land, no longer driven by the task that had absorbed him so completely in the past few years and waiting to see what was to come, if anything, from the University.

At the same time, however, Blondel began to notice something else welling in his heart from the solitude of his retreat at Saint-Seine, a desire for companionship that he speaks of in a *mémoire* drawn up August 21, 1893, after he had finished writing the final chapter of his book to be published in November, addressed to Abbé Bieil, the Superior of the Sulpician Seminary in Paris, whom Wehrlé had recommended to Blondel to help guide him in choosing his vocation. The part of the *mémoire*, in which he speaks of new desire in his heart, was omitted in the version of it published at the end of volume one of the *Carnets Intimes*, though it has since been brought to light with the publication of the entire *mémoire* under the title of *"Mémoire" à Monsieur Bieil: Discernement d'une vocation philosophique* (1999). Blondel makes a point of including this stirring note as part of the facts to be taken into account in his decision. "I find myself in a greater quandary than ever," he writes, "inasmuch as in the past few months I have felt little by little the question of my future become complicated in an unforeseen way. I would hesitate to insist on this minor unspoken drama, which could only be a figment of my imagination, if I did not have to make everything known, and if it were not possible that it could be a surge destined to bring me toward a solution before which I would still be inclined to pull back" (1999, 83).

Blondel prefaces his narrative of his internal drama by recalling how, up to the past few months, he had always considered, in a rather abstract and impersonal way, religious celibacy and the sacerdotal state as "the only fulfillment and the perfect conclusion of manly virtue. Without focusing on this feeling of exclusion, I was inclined to regard every other state as an imperfection and almost as a falling away, in relation to the normative type that the priest appeared to be for me. But little by little I have come to understand that there is only one thing absolutely good, and that it is not this or that dignity, this or that quality no matter how excellent, but the will, the design God has for each one: to accomplish in oneself this entire will, whatever it be and wherever it places us. That is, for each individual, the good itself. Nevertheless I was not thinking of applying this rule to myself in particular. I saw only how *one* could get married, but I did not see how *I* could do so" (1999, 83).

It is in conjunction with this movement of ideas that a new feeling began to develop within himself, at first without being noticed, which redoubled the force of the ideas by determining their application. Blondel explains that he had long known, though only slightly, a certain Mademoiselle B, whose family was well known to his own. Because of her piety, her reserve, and her simplicity, he thought of her as oriented toward religious life. But as work on his theses was drawing to an end and as the moment of decision was approaching, he could not help taking note of this young woman who lived nearby, attended the services of the same parish, assisted his sister Thérèse in teaching catechism to children, and whose path he was crossing every day. At first he refused to attach any importance to this feeling that he thought of as a figment, and he resolved to act absolutely as if he felt nothing real in it. But looking back on it, he writes that the refusal to admit this feeling as real was not without great effort, troubled as he was with the probable consequences of any long delay in taking action.

What he told himself was typical of this steadfast intellectual. "Inasmuch as I have long since resolved to finish the work I had begun and to defend my theses before seeking counsel and arriving at a determination, I will remain faithful to my aim. I do not wish to be more hurried for *her* than I have been, than I am with God. I shall not consult anyone before having finished my present work. Whatever results from this delay, I accept it all, placing everything in the hands of Providence" (1999, 84). But less than two weeks before the defense of the theses, on May 23, Blondel remembers quite vividly, he learned that Mademoiselle B had just become engaged. "I felt as if a life were ending in me. The blow was painful; but as hard as it was, I did not regret the delay or the silence I had forced on myself, because I judged it reasonable and necessary" (1999, 84). Leaving himself in the hands of Providence, he was thinking that God would know where to lead him as he had been asking in spite of himself. He tried to wish that the troubling event would take place, and he prayed that *they* would be happy. But he did not relinquish the feeling. Given the seriousness of the families involved, there was little hope that the engagement, though public, would be broken, but Blondel harbored the secret thought that it might be. He repelled the thought as chimerical and needlessly troubling, but still without keeping himself from imagining what embarrassment he would find himself in if this unlikely rupture were "to present itself suddenly before me as a sign or as renewed and accrued temptation" (1999, 84). Blondel was not at a loss for imagining different possibilities for himself at this crucial moment of his life.

He went on with the business of defending his theses in Paris, where his success encouraged him to look forward to a career in advancing his ideas on philosophy and the supernatural. Then he came back to Saint-Seine to rework his final chapter and to let the sadness left in him by the troublesome engagement dissipate, thinking that two months of free and solitary work would better prepare him for the consultation he had decided to undertake before the end of September. Back in the country, he felt that, "in spite of the wound of May 23 which seemed to preclude any dream of a human future" (1999, 85), he could not hurry his inner thought of the priesthood, ever present, ever fleeting. As he was thinking of a future development of his thoughts, however, lo and behold, on July 20, again Blondel remembers the exact date, "the *unlikely* news was casually announced to me. On the eve of the date arranged for the wedding of Mademoiselle B, at the moment of departure for the civil ceremony, the secret behavior of the *fiancé* was revealed. The rupture was immediate" (1999, 86). To Blondel, of course, this was anything but casual. He felt himself penetrated by a strange impression of joy and anguish, both distinct and mixed together and, after that, a renewal of the same struggle within himself at the approaching moment of decision. Once again, however, Blondel resolved not to hurry anything. He continued working on his revision, which would take him to the end of August, while allowing either the calm to come back or the trouble to continue, without moving up the time of consultation. Thinking of the story of the young Tobit, he handed over to the disposition of God all the possible consequences of this new delay.

These are facts about himself that Blondel had to think about as he was coming to his decision. He tells his consultant: "I can indicate the turmoil of the feelings that are churning within me well enough. But I am not good at interpreting these internal sentiments. I am afraid of being exposed to all sorts of illusions about myself" (1999, 87). Blondel only wants his consultant to be aware of these troubles within himself as well as the other idea, that of the priesthood, which is still at work within him. He goes on to analyze at much greater length how this competing idea in his consciousness has led him to the point where he now finds himself, having to decide which way to go with the rest of his life.

Nothing more ever came of this internal episode for Blondel relating to Mademoiselle B. He would later marry someone else. But the secret experience did open him up to something important and real within himself that he had not been inclined to take seriously before. This is how he writes of it in his diary on August 21, two days after beginning to write his *mémoire* to Abbé Bieil: "It seems at times that I need, quite urgently, painfully so, a soul who would reassure me against myself, who would gaily bear my sadnesses, who would mercifully redress my unreasonable collapses, who would understand and refute, by the simplicity of an inviolable tenderness that nothing can discourage, my unravelings and my paralyzing complications. Will you have me meet such a soul, or must I sacrifice this deep desire?" (1961c, 493). No doubt, Mademoiselle B remains hidden in the background, but Blondel is now reflecting only on the strong desire he feels for human companionship in life.

In the *mémoire* Blondel speaks at much greater length of the idea of the priesthood that he also has to contend with, how it has been with him since as far back as he can remember, and how it has led him to where he is. It is something he picked up as a child at home, with his mother and a profoundly Christian aunt who had been a nun, and at a convent where he used to go play as a child, and also from a priest with whom he used to go on walks. Naturally serious and meditative as he was, he did not feel it was something inspired in him from the outside but rather the expression of a spontaneous aspiration or of a personal reflection (1961c, 545).

In spite of this idea, however, when the Jesuit school opened in Dijon while he was already at the Lycée, and in spite of what would have been the preference of his parents, he chose to finish his rhetoric and his philosophy at the secular *lycée*. What kept him there, he writes, was the desire "to know the state of soul of the enemies of the faith, in order to be able to have a more efficacious action on them" (1961c, 546). What was motivating him was not just the idea of the priesthood as such, but the idea of a future apostolate associated in his mind with the idea of the priesthood. The only way in which this idea influenced him at that time was to orient him away from the particular sciences, for which he had a certain attraction, and from eventually going to the École Polytechnique, where his cousin who was attending the Jesuit school would end up, toward more literary and especially philosophical studies, which he found even more attractive.

Still with the same idea of the priesthood in mind, after the Lycée Blondel went on to pursue his *License ès lettres* in Dijon, which again was not where his parents would have preferred him to go, but which was in keeping with the logic of his secret aim. As a concession to his parents, he also did a baccalaureate in sciences and a baccalaureate in law, the more traditional areas of his pragmatically oriented family, but his real and more absorbing interest was in doing philosophy and eventually plunging himself more deeply into the University milieu by applying for admission to the École Normale Supérieure in Paris. This was like going into the very bastion of the enemies of the faith, but the apostolic motivation was there to strengthen his resolve and embolden him. "Without even noticing the strangeness of the means, it seemed to me that this School (known to me only by name), which filled me and everyone around me with awe, was the way I had to take to arrive at my ends, to arm myself against those whom I wanted to hear the truth, to acquire a more direct and a more profound knowledge of these erring minds and these sincere unbelievers for whom my adolescent dream was to dissipate their prejudices by talking their own language" (1961c, 546). While the family saw a certain danger in following such a course of action within the stronghold of the enemy, the Catholic chaplain at the Lycée who would later become Rector at Catholic University of Lyon encouraged him to seize upon the opportunity of admission, which came as a surprise to everyone.

We have already seen how this resolve led Blondel to plunge more deeply into the spirit of modern philosophy and learn to speak its language even as he tried to make it admit something it would not admit, at least not in the French University of the time. But Blondel tells his consultant that he never felt any qualm of conscience or experienced any regret over this decision to attend the École Normale. Quite the contrary, the same idea of a mission that inspired the decision also inspired how he chose the subject for his dissertation, how he wrote the dissertation, and how he approached his teaching of philosophy at Chaumont, at Montauban, at Aix-en-Provence, and at Stanislas College. Always it was with an attitude of caring for the souls of his readers and his hearers.

In the end, however, when he had successfully defended his dissertation and had been awarded the title of *Docteur ès lettres*, with its implied certification as a University professor, it appeared that this idea of the priesthood, which had been motivating him all along, had been leading him further and further away from actually entering the priesthood. This is what occurs to Blondel at this juncture in his life as he feels the need to come to a decision about his future. The idea has never led him to take any concrete steps to actually enter the way that would have brought him to ordination, as his friend Wehrlé had done after their first year at the École Normale, "precisely because the apostolic aim that it filled me with has always found its direct application elsewhere than in it" (1961c, 549). He had not run away from it. It had remained ever present to him, inspiring him to make a generous use of his life. It was something he could not let go of. And yet whenever he had focused on it directly, it always seemed to recede in the background or to disappear, only to reaffirm itself whenever he seemed ready to let go of it. This is the question that he had to answer for himself as he approached his thirty-second birthday, whether he should go on to actually seek the priesthood or not, conscious that he was coming of age both as a philosopher and as a man with a mission.

Until now he had comported himself as one who was to stay in the way of philosophy, the laity, and the University, to which he was committed and where he felt that it was good to be. On the other hand, thanks to this very idea of the priesthood, he had also maintained a certain attitude of independence in thought, word, and conduct, so that, if necessary, he could immediately leave the University. He could always afford this independence financially, but it would not have been possible for him without the other idea of the priesthood in the back of his mind. The two ideas, that of a University career in philosophy and that of the priesthood, simply converged in his mind, feeding one another and keeping him in suspense as to what the final form of his vocation was to be. The problem was that the two could not be both actualized in any direct way in his life. He had to come to a decision, and that is why he was coming to consult his spiritual confidant.

The dilemma, as he understood it, was intimately connected with the philosophy of religion and of the supernatural he was coming to enunciate in the University. On the one hand, he felt comfortable with this philosophy. This is where he wanted to exercise his influence, on the level of reason itself even in the supernatural interest of souls. As he writes in his *mémoire* at the height of his emotional crisis while he was working on that ambiguous final chapter, "though I had hoped to put into the book I was finishing the principal part of my apologetical thought, I saw surging within me precise new projects to work on; I could see an entire plan of Christian philosophy opening up before me. Even as I was going forward in the final version of this first work of some xxv + 495 pages, it appeared to me to be as only the Prolegomena of other complementary treatises" (1999, 86). This was to be for him a furtherance of the original philosophy of the supernatural, and not a theology. Formed as he had been by philosophy with other critical minds, he did not feel at ease dealing with docile people who were too ready to accept ideas passively. He felt he had better access to more critical intelligences accustomed to discussing their more active and philosophical thoughts, as the reception of his dissertation had proven, where he had revealed his thought indicting the idea of a philosophy separate from religion and showing the philosophical necessity of a religious practice. In this way he thought he could do more to bring young minds closer to the Church than by a more direct priestly ministry, for which he did not feel particularly suited, either as a preacher or as a celebrant of liturgy. With regard to this side of the dilemma, the question before him was whether he should go on pursuing this movement he was already engaged in or whether he should not go back to the idea from which it had started — the idea of a priestly mission. Given his insistence on the natural and philosophical side of the relation with religion, he had to ask himself whether he had not absorbed too much of the naturalist attitude.

On the other hand, he had nothing but the highest esteem for the vocation of the priesthood and even for what the idea had meant for him in the development of his philosophy up to now. "Never without it could I have been raised to the philosophical conception that has tied me to the Christian truth and that has drawn me to go as far as reason can go, as far as it has to go in order to arrive at the pure religious expectation" (1961c, 555). Now that this level of philosophy had been attained, however, it seems that the idea of the priesthood receded in the background, even apart from the new kind of human desire for companionship he was beginning to experience within himself. Blondel was certain that the idea had not been given to him in vain. He was grateful to God for giving it to him, and to all those who fostered it in him, who would be saddened and for whom he would feel grief if it were not realized. But the moment he began to settle in his mind for only a lay form of apostolate, there was a resurgence of the idea in his conscience that he could not ignore. On this side of the dilemma it was the dignity of the priestly vocation, and the kind of intimacy with Christ that it implied, that captured his religious imagination. To be chosen for such a vocation was not something he would want to ignore even as a philosopher. The question was whether he had been chosen and whether he would have to sacrifice, not just the natural aspirations and tendernesses he had begun to dream of with a companion-soul, but more importantly all that the thought of the priesthood had inspired him to do and to project as a layman and as a philosopher, all his designs of ministry, all that it had led him to think of as the reason of his life. The thought of this double abnegation of himself was for him a cause of both panic and fascination. It was the thought he had to weigh at this moment in his life. Would he be ready for this extreme sacrifice, if it were called for?

We do not know how the priest on whom all this was placed for decision took it in. We only know what was his recommendation, given to Blondel at the *Grand Séminaire* of Saint Sulpice in Paris on September 17, only eight days after the *mémoire* had been handed to him in Dijon, and what was the reaction of Blondel to this recommendation, which he looked upon as an expression of the will of God for him. It was a moment of liberation from the uncertainty he was experiencing about the direction his life was taking and a moment of freedom to continue to run in the way of the Lord. "I received the order to run, with dilated soul, in your ways and to serve you in the world by abandoning myself completely to your paternal management, without regrets, without defiance, knowing that there are many mansions in the domain of the Heavenly Father and that all is possible for you" (1961c, 494). It was the religious confirmation he needed for the rational choice he had been making all along, a promise that he could succeed in his lay apostolate of interpreting the Christian spirit in terms of modern critical thought.

Wrestling with the Source of Immanence in Modern Philosophy

Having been liberated from the idea of actually becoming a priest, there is no sign that Blondel went back to do anything in pursuit of Mademoiselle B. Perhaps she entered religious life after her unfortunate experience. Perhaps Blondel himself did not want to appear to be taking undue advantage of a woman just left standing at the altar. Or perhaps he was simply still too timid to take action in this newly discovered realm of engagements, where family relations had as much of a role as personal emotions. We only know that Blondel found himself once again squarely before the emptiness of having been refused the chair he needed to pursue his mission, not knowing what to do or where to turn. From the depths of the abyss he cried out to God: "I am repressed everywhere. I had hoped to be called to your priesthood: no. I had passionately wished to be appointed to some teaching post from which I could exercise an apostolate: no. I had entertained the possibility of a project proposed to me, one that I was already enhancing with all my imagination: and it is no, always no. I have to hold back, not go forward, remain still in suspense. It is very painful: not to be able to settle one's life down, nor one's spirit, nor one's heart; to arrive at the age of a man without even being a child with a designated task and place" (1961c, 496). He was to remain in this state of suspense for many months, as he watched the vacant philosophy chairs being filled one after the other, the one he would have liked very much at Aix-en-Provence going on Christmas Eve, and the last one open for that year going on January 14. What was he to do with his philosophy of action?

He did not give up the intense intellectual life he had begun to lead in the solitude of his *mansarde* at Saint-Seine. For one thing, he still had to see his work through to publication. He had earlier arranged for one hundred forty-six copies of the text he submitted for the defense at the Sorbonne, but he had reserved the right to complete the text starting from page 401. Though the publisher actually printed two hundred copies of that first version, which were sold to the public, contrary to Blondel's wish, Blondel felt compelled to add the long final chapter on the relation between knowing, being, and action, in order to counteract the anti-metaphysical impression many were taking from the first version. This explains why there were two versions of *L'Action* published in 1893, one of 433 pages in June, and a second, more definitive one of 495 pages in November, of which 750 copies were printed.

After the publication he remained on the lookout for reviews, given that the defense had not gone unnoticed in the broader philosophical circles. The book was awaited and Blondel knew that it would undergo the scrutiny of reviewers, just as it had undergone the scrutiny of the examiners at the Sorbonne. One brief notice of barely one page in the *Revue de Métaphysique et Morale* especially caught his attention, because it misrepresented once again, as earlier at the defense, his truly philosophical intent. The note was unsigned, though Blondel would later learn that it had been written by Léon Brunschvicg. Blondel's letter of rejoinder was addressed to the editor, Xavier Léon, in an effort once again to correct what he thought was a tendentious and mistaken interpretation of his work. Blondel's letter was much longer than the original note, which was published as a substitute for a much longer review that had never materialized. The rejoinder is worth looking at for a moment, not just as an another example of how Blondel had to defend himself against being dismissed as a philosopher, but also as an indication of how he was beginning to reflect on his method in a way that would lead to the important *Lettre* of 1896, in which he would allay the fears of philosophers, including Brunschvicg, but incur the suspicion and the wrath of many religiously minded authors who would not approve of the way he was defending the necessity of religion, especially after seeing Blondel's critical appraisal of the standard ways of defending religion they took for granted.

In his rejoinder Blondel acknowledges the penetration with which the note described his way of transposing philosophical problems from the domain of thought to the domain of action. But he regrets the kind of opposition he immediately encounters with regard to the conclusions he is led to through this transposition. He is told that he will find adversaries who are courteous but resolute in their defense of reason. What concerns Blondel, however, is not so much the opposition, but the conception of reason on which it is based. "Modern rationalism," he is told, "has been led, through the analysis of thought, to make the notion of immanence the basis and the very condition of all philosophical doctrine" (1951, 99-100). He is also told that his conclusions concerning religion are purely dogmatic and that they infringe on the rights of reason.

Blondel appreciates this courteous opposition, but he does not wish to be set aside by it. He wishes to defend himself by showing that it is misguided and that, far from derogating from the rights of reason, he is only trying to bring into the realm of its critical examination something that has been unduly excluded from it. He points out that philosophy has undergone a certain mutilation in France in its refusal to entertain questions concerning religion, unlike in England and Germany, where philosophy of religion has thrived, though not always in a way that Blondel would agree with. He understands that such questions can be especially delicate in France because of the contentiousness with which they are usually attended among warlike factions, for or against religion, usually assumed to be the Catholic one. What he wants to do in France for philosophy is something like what was done in Germany in relation to Protestantism, which according to him has a more easily detachable form of philosophy. His intention is one of peaceful discussion, where people can not only come together and tolerate one another, but also illuminate one another in spite of their differences, and one of conquest, not against reason, but for reason, since he is trying to restore to it what fanaticism has falsely taken away from it, thereby "introducing rationalism into what it was denying and what was denying it" (1951, 101).

To do this it was important for Blondel to enter precisely into the notion of immanence that philosophy claimed for itself as a result of its modern development, apart and cut off from Christian theology and religion, which for its part had also followed its own development apart and cut off from philosophy. But a mere rapprochement between the two lines was not enough. Instead of just superimposing on one another, or just juxtaposing them, let alone opposing them, he had to show how they had to compenetrate and compose with one another, without taking anything away from the notion of immanence that had come to define modern philosophy. That, he says, "is my point of departure, my method, the spirit of my conclusion; it is not a matter of reaction or a simple transposition but a new extension of this rationalism and a synthesis formed with elements that had not yet been assimilated" (1951, 102). If he speaks of the supernatural in the end, it is only as it relates to what is natural in human action. In doing so he is not transgressing against philosophy. He is only overcoming the dualism of modern thought between philosophy and religion. Nor is he transgressing against religion or faith, since "by his immanent affirmation of the transcendent he is in no way prejudging the transcendent reality of these immanent truths" (1951, 103). He was only making it philosophically possible to discuss freely questions that concern even the most positive of religions, without calling it into question and without having to pronounce oneself on what it offers, or usurping what it reserves to itself.

Just how this is to be done concretely was already exemplified in the thesis on *Action*, but it remained to be explained in greater detail in the *Lettre* that Blondel was not yet contemplating. He ends this letter of January 1894 by expressing a certain trust in the irenic power of philosophy which, while respecting the independent critical ability of each, can also bring people of different persuasions together in the search for truth, the whole truth, and nothing but the truth, instead of seeking only exclusive or sectarian domination. The trust was not misplaced, for the response of Xavier Léon was immediate and welcoming. The letter was published in the next issue of the *Revue de Métaphysique et Morale* and very well received by its philosophical readers. Brunschvicg himself wrote a few lines of welcome and, as Blondel tells us in the *Itinéraire* (1928a, 50), from then on he began to feel that he was no longer disqualified in the mind of those who were most qualified in philosophy, even though this was not yet true in the mind of the University administrators. Who knows? Perhaps these philosophers were relieved finally to have someone before them on the side of religion who understood their exigencies and, as the young Blondel had wanted to learn to do from the beginning, spoke their language.

About a year later, Blondel's thesis was to receive a much more favorable review in the December issue of the *Revue Philosophique* written by his friend Victor Delbos. This one is worth noting in passing because Delbos and Blondel, as we have seen, not only shared the same religious spirit, as well as the same concern for rigorous philosophy, but also had frequently discussed one another's work while it was in progress. In fact, Delbos had sent Blondel a copy of the review before it appeared, and Blondel had thanked him warmly for showing how he enters into the flow of philosophy, and for representing him so clearly before the philosophical world. What you do, he writes, "is rescue me from a sort of excommunication, keeping people from seeing me as an intruder, one who is suspect, a false brother, and making a University career undoubtedly more easy for me" (1961a, 62). Though he tentatively suggests a few minor changes in the text, he congratulates Delbos for offering "a properly philosophical transcription of pages that did not succeed in showing that simple, calm, and luminous character" of this summation.

In his review Delbos picks up from Brunschvicg's idea of a transposition of terms for the ensemble of philosophical questions. But he argues that this is in keeping with one of the essential preoccupations of modern thought, one of whose principal ambitions has consisted in finding a rapprochement between what is *intelligible* and what is *given*, by expanding its original idea of an impenetrable spirit more and more, so that it could include the real. According to Delbos, this could not be accomplished by a deductive speculation, which could only yield an idea of experience rather than experience itself. Nor was the ontological necessity of the Absolute or the moral necessity of Duty sufficient to ground a philosophy of the real. What was needed was a fact, "a fact at once primordial and ultimate that would contain in itself alone or that would be able to require of itself alone all that is indispensable for it to be fully" (1951, 105). Such a fact, according to Delbos, was the will understood in its broadest meaning as the will to be. It is this *fact* that *Action* purported to study in its transposition.

Delbos's review follows the argument of the book as a series of transpositions required by the will starting from the very first manifestation of will, in the will not to will. At the point where the moral law is introduced, he makes the point that, far from being the expression of a transcendent imperative, this law is grounded in a concrete movement of the will, the very same movement that goes from a purely formal idea of freedom to its actualization in the body and the external world, from the individual to the social, and eventually embraces the entire universe of experience. According to Delbos, "M. Blondel excels in describing all the facts of moral contagion and social solidarity, those phenomena of natural or reflected sympathy that manifest in ever higher degrees of complication and richness the primordial will to be" (1951, 107).

In passing, Delbos shows how metaphysical thought enters into this expansion as the effort to explain what *is* by means of what *ought* to be, so that its ideas have to be understood as real, ideal, and practical at the same time, in other words, as relating to action. After reviewing the state of superstition, which is a spontaneous and natural, but critically untenable, attitude of the human spirit, Delbos goes on to present Blondel's authentically religious attitude as an immanent will to be that relates to the transcendent God. "That is where M. Blondel has recourse to the notion of revealed dogmas and of literal practice, not that he is attempting to do an apologetic work; he merely wishes to develop the connection of phenomena of the particular order which, in the consciousness of a Catholic Christian, establish the relation of man to God" (1951, 109). In other words, Blondel is still only developing the fact of willing to be, and how God enters into this willing, if he does, supernaturally.

As we know, Delbos showed his review to Blondel before submitting it to the *Revue Philosophique*, so that his reference to apologetics here is in keeping with Blondel's thinking at the time, two years before the so-called *Letter on Apologetics*, which is itself an editorial misnomer as we shall see. This was yet another way of insisting on the philosophical intent of the work as distinct from any properly theological intent. Delbos ends his review by returning to the idea of these continuous transpositions in action that bring about a reconciliation. "Thus in action and through action are reconciled experience and logic, practice and science, and the perception of the phenomenon along with the affirmation of Being" (1951, 111). The modern metaphysics of the understanding had tried to explain the passage from fact to idea and from idea to fact, which is the philosophical problem par excellence, but it had tried to do so as if it were itself the source of this double movement. The true role of metaphysics, which Delbos wants to maintain along with Blondel, is to show "how this double movement takes place on its own initiative, without ever absolutely subordinating one to the other the two terms between which it produces itself, how it realizes by itself the law by which it deploys itself, how it regulates and completes its own self" (1951, 111). This is no doubt an allusion to the final complicated chapter of *L'Action*, which he had had a hand in shaping, as well as another attempt to emphasize the genuinely philosophical intent of the work.

In the meantime, however, Blondel had already published his own review of Delbos's book, which had appeared about the same time as *L'Action*, on *The Moral Problem in the Philosophy of Spinoza and in the History of Spinozism* in the June 1894 issue of *Annales de Philosophie Chrétienne*. The two friends had previously corresponded about this work as well. It was a *Mémoire* written for a competition before the Academy of the Moral and Political Sciences in 1891, and shared in the appreciation of the development of modern philosophy that it represented. Delbos had failed to win any of the three prizes awarded by the Academy, but Blondel had encouraged him to publish the work just the same. In response Blondel wrote an article titled "One of the Sources of Modern Thought: The Evolution of Spinozism," which he published under the pseudonym of Bernard Aimant. It was more than just an account of what was in the book. It was an appropriation of Delbos's account of the development of Spinozism in German philosophy all the way to Hegel, and a prolongation of it in the direction of his own philosophy of action. In this review, he also gave an account of how the notion of immanence had taken hold in modern philosophy and how it called for a transcendence at the end of it. Hence it is worth our pausing to look into this review here, both as a continuation of the philosophical thrust toward transcendence in the dissertation, or of the response to the challenge from the notion of immanence which was said to be the basis and the very condition of modern philosophy, and as a preview for the more important *Lettre* of 1896 which was to elaborate much more completely on the method of immanence that Blondel was advancing.

We do not know how much of Spinoza or Hegel Blondel actually read on his own in the way that we know he read Leibniz. He surely had to become acquainted with both of them in the normal course of events during his years at the École Normale. We do know that another one of his classmates had shown a special interest in Spinoza in the same way that he had done for Leibniz, enough to chose for his own secondary, Latin thesis the question of "how the doctrine which Spinoza held about faith was coherent with the whole of his philosophy." Blondel mentions this dissertation by his friend Frédéric Rauh, defended in 1890, in a bibliographical footnote at the beginning of his article. Both of his friends, Rauh as well as Delbos, seem to have been concerned with the question of faith in relation to the Spinozistic system of metaphysics, as Blondel himself would have been. In any event it does appear that it is through Delbos's *Mémoire* that Blondel came to his best appreciation of Spinoza and Hegel, and all the rest of systematic metaphysics in between the two, as well as of how his own philosophy relates back to them and to the immanentistic tone they set for modern philosophy.

Quite significantly for Blondel, Delbos, as his title indicates, focuses on the moral problem in Spinoza and in the history of Spinozism. The centrality of this problem for Spinoza is not always evident because the method of exposition, which is deductive *more geometrico*, and from the top down, does not in fact reproduce the method of invention by which Spinoza came to his system. According to Delbos, the moving force in Spinoza's search was a concern with the problem of human happiness and a determination to resolve this problem with the resources of thought alone. In other words, underlying Spinoza's pantheism, there is a radical anthropomorphism and the supposition that a scientific or strictly rational understanding of reality is sufficient for life. The thought that is adequate to reality is what confers beatitude. With this as his principle, Spinoza can then go on to elaborate his system in ontological terms, so that the moral problem is then absorbed into the metaphysical problem and what is still called an *Ethic* takes the shape of a metaphysics of Absolute Substance.

Once we understand this hidden principle of Spinoza's thought, we can also understand the development of that thought as it centers on Substance or the infinite Object, which encompasses all thought and all reality, inasmuch as it is posited absolutely as the whole. Everything else, where we seem to find some difference or negation, or some appearance of substance even within ourselves, has to be brought back to the one absolute and eternal Substance. The only way in which individuals or the modes of extension and thought can be understood as real or as being is by seeing them as derivative from the Substance, a derivation that partakes of the necessity of Substance itself. However, since such a derivation is necessary from the standpoint of the Substance itself, what is derived becomes a finite expression of the infinite Substance. What makes this possible is that the nature of the Substance "can produce itself through the essence of the human soul considered under the form of Eternity." The quotation is from the end of the *Ethics*, but Delbos concludes from it that "there is, consubstantial with the God who *is* from all eternity, a God which *becomes* from all eternity" (1894a, 267). In this Delbos finds a reemergence of the hidden human principle underlying Spinoza's thought which had seemed to be subordinated to the metaphysical problem of the whole, so that Spinoza's anthropomorphism becomes the very essence of his monism.

What remains unexplained in Spinoza's system is the necessity of a development in the absolute Substance. Spinoza admits this without deducing it, and he posits it in Being without explaining it. Why is there such a necessity?

According to Delbos, at the moment when Spinoza gave every appearance of excluding from the Substance he was affirming any human determination, he was still conceiving it, under the influence of his ethical preoccupation, as a being that makes itself and that becomes, like a living and acting subject. Instead of relating the mode to the substance, Spinoza was in fact relating the substance to the mode. It is from a transposition such as this that German idealism would later follow, as can be seen in a very perceptive remark of Schelling: "it is in the autonomous affirmation of the I that philosophy has found its *hen kai pan*; it is from this affirmation that it has lived, even when it was not conscious of it; and Spinoza, unbeknownst to himself, was conceiving the not-I under the form of the I when he was positing it as the absolute principle" (1894a, 267-68). What Spinoza was doing in fact was projecting the human into the divine and then bringing the divine back into the human. The claim was that there was a perfect coincidence between the two and that it could be grasped adequately by the understanding without any residue of mystery.

In German idealism what had been only the hidden principle in Spinoza's system was brought to the forefront. Leibniz had a role in the transference of Spinoza's idea to the soil of German thought in that he shared the same rational spirit of reconciliation between reason and nature, freedom and necessity, Being and beings. But the ball started rolling with Lessing, who spoke of the world as resulting from the fact that Perfection is not content with being actually, but must necessarily become, under the form of progress, in particular beings that develop their powers little by little. This idea, which was taken up in different ways by Jacobi, Herder, Schiller, Goethe, and others, presented a new matter and a new content that Spinoza had not considered for the development of Absolute spirit, the historical development of humanity under whatever form it would take as science, art, philosophy, morality, or religion. In this way Spinozism was to be transformed and broadened so that it would eventually turn its effort to understanding history as well as the nature of things under one and the same law. As such, it remained intimately connected with the continuing history of modern thought.

To do this, Spinozism had to go through the crucible of the Kantian critique, but it found in it the means of prolonging itself in the *Foundations for a Metaphysics of Morals*. Though the two philosophies seemed radically opposed to one another, one starting from an affirmation of absolute Being or the infinite Object, knowledge of which was denied by the other, and the other starting from an affirmation of the free activity of the Subject and the unending realization of pure Duty, they nevertheless converged in two things, the hidden moral principle at the heart of Spinoza's system and Kant's willingness to let the thing in itself subsist. "In considering duty as an absolute, in affirming the autonomy of the will, in placing the synthetic activity of practical reason above the analytical results of the understanding, Kant was only taking as the principle of an original system the postulate that was still hidden at the heart of Spinozism; whereas Spinoza, at the origin of the *Ethics*, had already placed in evidence the absolute of the object that Kant was allowing to subsist invincibly" (1894a, 275). Thus, the hidden moral principle of Spinoza's philosophy was enabled to work its way into German philosophy by a sort of immanent operation, which first applied the monist idea to the conception of duty and of moral freedom, and then moved on to restore an integral Spinozism in the form of an absolute Knowing of absolute Being.

At this point in his account of this evolution of Spinozism, Blondel adds a critical remark about French philosophy in his day. "If in France too many minds have stopped at the doctrine of Kant, it is perhaps time to show that, since the *Critique of Practical Reason*, thought has moved on" (1894a, 275). It has done so, first through Fichte, who criticized Kant for his timid and inconsistent idealism in letting the thing in itself subsist opposite the subject. Fichte transferred the being of substance into action and the infinite of reality into the idea, thus arriving at a new monistic conception of the subject, an ethical pantheism rather than an ontological pantheism. But, according to Blondel, following Delbos, this was done in a one-sided way that insisted only on the subject and downplayed the side of the object.

Schelling would refer more explicitly back to Spinoza and give more consideration to the object, although he would argue that the absolute cannot be conceived simply as object, but rather more as something pertaining to an act apart from all relation or all limitation, in a sort of intuition as into a self. In Spinoza there is still a lack of adequation between form and matter, subject and object. Schelling posits an immediate adequation of subject and object, thereby eliminating all dualism between duty and Being. For finite being, he deduces the necessity of becoming and the impossibility of being immediately what it must be necessarily, and so he arrives at a conception of the real, not as a simple phenomenon or appearance, but as an effective production of spirit. Idealism and realism are equally grounded in a principle of identity. The finite and the infinite, being and becoming, are so intimately connected that it is the Perfect itself, or God, that needs to become in order to be. As principle, God is not yet what he is as end. The metaphysics of the absolute becomes what Schelling calls a transcendental theogony.

Thus, the idea of becoming within the absolute, which Spinoza had tried to absorb totally into the unity and the immobility of being, reappears with Schelling as taking the first place in the absolute. In the culmination of this evolution of Spinozism with Hegel, this idea "not only becomes the first of many truths, but the only one; since for him the unity of the finite and the infinite is not only an affirmation among all others, it is the thought that promotes all truth, the one whose meaning has only to be developed dialectically for it to be truth itself" (1894a, 327). Spinoza had tried to make the finite, evil, and free will disappear into a unity conceived in its abstract form. Hegel pushes this Spinozist notion of immanence to the limit. On the one hand, he argues that what is negation with regard to the immediate truth admitted by Spinoza has a necessary reality, so that the necessity of the contingent is established, and becoming is conceived as the concrete and synthetic expression of the Idea: all that is real is rational. On the other hand, since nothing happens that is not the determinate expression of Reason, not only is every event an expression of the Idea, but the Idea itself does not come to completion in any event: all that is rational is real. Starting from his Logic, Hegel is thus brought to reconstruct ideally the twofold world of nature and spirit, the very becoming that is being. According to Delbos and Blondel, this was the end to which the thought of Spinoza tended from the beginning. Or as Hegel put it in the Preface to his *Phenomenology of Spirit*, the idea of absolute Substance was only calling for this movement of subjectivity.

What this meant for Delbos and Blondel was a reassertion of the anthropomorphic principle hidden in Spinoza's objective pantheism, a reabsorption of Being into our being and, under the pretense of making us immanent to it, making it immanent to us. It was the triumph of the ethical problem over the ontological problem and of reason over the meaning of life, whose content was now supposedly totally encompassed within the understanding, the apotheosis of reason. Since he restricts himself only to the history of Spinozism, Delbos sees no need to go beyond this Hegelian system, which has dialectically developed and exhausted its meaning, though he draws his own philosophical conclusions from this analysis of the notion of immanence. Blondel goes one step further to show how such conclusions follow from the method implied in this kind of systematic historical thought.

We see in all this the wide scope that the idea of modern philosophy had for Blondel, including German as well as French thought. But what is more important for Blondel is to see how a method of philosophizing emerges from this systematic thought, even if the various forms it has taken appear obsolete. What survives from Spinoza's main idea is the notion of immanence, which had been invoked against his own philosophy. What this means ultimately is that the monism of Spinoza or of Hegel tends more and more to confine the metaphysical problem to the conditions of human knowledge. What is given forth as the real absolute and as the becoming of Being appears, not so much as the truth of Substance or as the history of the divine, but rather as the closely followed interplay of our representations, or as the interconnection of phenomena. "In the phenomenon, if we think of it carefully, there is truly the subject to which the Hegelian dialectic in the ultimate analysis is applied, there is the true notion of science which this philosophy of the absolute has elaborated" (1894a, 331). If the doctrine of Spinoza survives, it is as a sort of phenomenism that focuses no longer on an intelligible essence of things, conceived under a form of abstract universality and eternity, but on facts and the necessary connection between them methodically defined by thought. Being and knowing coincide in the phenomenon and in the scientific law that defines it.

This is the method that has been called "the immanent critique," which owes much more to Spinoza than to Kant, and the idea of which is that every act, every product of man or of nature has its value as well as its reality determined by the ensemble of which it is a part. The attempt to reduce things to a single higher exemplar is, according to Spinoza, to subordinate them to our empirical individuality. There is only one way to judge anything: it is to understand; and to understand everything, to explain everything, is to make the contingent and the irrational enter into line with necessity and reason. For his part, Hegel has taught us how to respect and understand facts, how to find the absolute of scientific law, not in an abstract generality, but in a total *fieri* and in each concrete detail. The basis for the idea lies in the supposition that in every state of nature and spirit, the infinite is present, so that without going outside the fact we must determine within it the internal relations that constitute its truth and make up its law.

Blondel distinguished three phases in the development of this idea of an immanent critique. At its origin, with Spinoza, it appears to exclude all limitation, everything diverse, multiple, or finite, as an illusion in comparison to the absolute Unity. In this phase the critique is entirely negative. With Hegel, the idea of necessity becomes transformed: instead of being pure identity, it is an identity of contradictories; it encompasses what denies it and absorbs what limits it. The contingent and the accidental are brought into the order and the power of the critique. Henceforth, instead of eliminating, the immanent critique integrates into the flow of universal necessity the most heterogeneous forms of life and thought. To understand, for Hegel, is to include in Being everything that seems to come from it as something that develops it. In its third phase, the critique pulls these two contrasting views of Spinoza and Hegel together into a new way of thinking: "Instead of thinking that to understand everything is to include everything either in the relative or in the absolute, we come to see that to understand the whole of a fact is to mark in the relative itself absolute differences. Thus, without denying the principles of the critical method, without betraying the notion of immanence, without ceasing to place ourselves inside facts and acts to explain them, it appears to be possible to judge them absolutely and to find within them the ground for a radical discernment; . . . the notion of a transcendent rule, criterion, or truth imposes itself in the very name of a fully developed immanence" (1894a, 335).

This is the rule or the truth that Blondel attempted to lay out in his own Philosophy of Action through his method of immanence. It is also the rule or the truth that Delbos attempts to explicate in his historical critique of Spinozism. But in this critique of the immanent critique, the two friends are not just trying to return to an older, more static conception of the absolute. Rather, they are moving the critique forward so that it may become more fully philosophical in accordance with the wish of Hegel, who thought that the ultimate philosophy in the order of time is the result of all the preceding philosophies, containing all their principles and bringing them all to fulfillment.

What this implies, however, is a certain transformation or, as was said earlier, a transposition of the philosophical problem itself into something that the immanent critique had not yet entertained. It is not enough just to understand. Even if it can penetrate everything, the understanding is not everything. It cannot take the place of action, even when it makes it intelligible, whereas action is what justifies the radical differences in human destinies and the absolute qualifications of good and evil in human works. Through action, a principle of transcendent truth and reality becomes immanent in us, even though the thought that discovers this immanence does not take the place of the necessity, or does not change anything in the character of this transcendent. Far from divorcing himself from the sweep of modern thought, then, Blondel espouses it in order to show that it must go beyond itself and find its ultimate truth in something more than just itself.

The modern claim is that thought can be sufficient unto itself and that it can take the place of action. At the heart of the enterprise is the desire or the need to see the problem of life absolutely resolved by the effort of man alone. Now, what belongs to us more than anything else is, not reality itself or things, but our representation of things, phenomena. Hence, if the problem is to be resolved by the effort of man alone, it must also be done by the effort of thought. Hence the immanent critique of modern thought comes to a doctrine of immanence that implies an exclusively speculative solution to the problem, as if the notion of immanence were restricted to pure thought alone. The supposition is that through thought alone human being can become equal to the fullness of its being and its duty.

We have seen how Blondel argued systematically against this supposition in his dialectic of action. Here he makes three brief points in relation to three of the modern philosophers he has been considering. Against Kant he makes the point that one cannot derive positive obligations or the matter of any precise duty from a purely formal conception of autonomy. We cannot will ourselves fully without willing, through the mediation of the infinite Being, the universal order. Against Spinoza he makes the point that we can never attain the happy state of union or adequation with the absolute without the painful intrusion of an infinite that dilates us and seems to make us split open. There is heterogeneity between what we are and what we will most fundamentally. Against Hegel he makes the point that there is never a complete coincidence between our thought and our action. There is in each one of them a principle of transcendence that forces them to surpass themselves, and keeps them from ever constituting themselves in a state of a closed and impenetrable world. Even the most adequate thought does not take the place of action, something that Blondel thinks Christianity had made clear by giving precedence to action over thought. But here he makes the point in terms of speculative thought itself. "Every speculative system is surpassed by a progress of speculation, and the only one that can contain a definitive truth is the one that does not look for its completion within itself, because it concludes to action, and because it determines its practical exigencies. If we do not grasp a system except by surpassing it, we do not grasp truth, we do not possess it, we do not live by it, except by acting" (1894a, 340).

In this way Blondel brings out how his own science of practice is in continuity with the immanent critique of modern philosophical thought, not by settling into it as in a closed system, but by calling it to a renovation through its relation to action in the concrete. Through action "the mystery of the real is immediately present to us, it is ourselves; and in discovering, according to the exigencies of the rationalist critique, what is immanent in us, we are inevitably brought to recognize the necessity of the transcendent truths that are in it" (1894a, 340-41). After this tour of modern philosophy with Delbos, Blondel finds himself just where he thinks he has to be with his philosophy of action, as we saw Delbos suggest earlier in his review of *L'Action*.

Resolution and Settlement into a Familial and Academic Life

In the meantime another year was advancing and there was still no word from the Ministry of Education. Blondel remained at a loss as to what to do with his career. He continued to correspond with his many friends and with others who wrote to him about *L'Action*, including Lasson, the editor of Hegel in Germany, who had written a very favorable review of *L'Action*, in marked contrast to the general reaction of philosophers in France. Throughout all this, he continued to feel distressed and mortified at being forced back into himself. He was nearing his thirty-second birthday and he had fulfilled all the requirements, but he was still unsure as to whether his career could take off. He was being kept at bay. He felt useless and impotent. But he refused to despair. He took his frustration as an occasion to take the long view of things and to purify himself of any vain intention. "I have this crazy ardor to be heard, to have disciples, but it is more for myself than for you, since you waited thirty-three years before satisfying the first desire of your heart consumed with the divine fire of apostolic love. Hence I wish to sacrifice all this desire for a natural influence, all this ardor for a spiritual fecundity, all ambition of mastering, and to write, to speak only as if I were before you, because that is the most efficacious way of thinking, acting, or teaching for all and in all" (1961c, 527).

One thing of a more positive nature that did happen during this time is that Blondel met the woman who would soon come to share in the ups and downs of his interior life, at Quincy-le-Vicomte, where he was visiting his friend Adéodat Broissard. Rose Royer was the sister-in-law of Broissard, whose wedding Blondel was attending. She was the youngest daughter not only of another solid well-to-do Catholic family, but also of a mother with a certain religious or mystical temperament of her own. The mother was not slow in recognizing in Blondel a very suitable young man for her youngest daughter and in encouraging the two to become better acquainted. On August 23, 1894, Blondel writes of a double visit to Quincy, which leads him into thinking of no longer belonging to himself alone and of having to come to a decision, one that was still in suspense ever since his first encounter with the desire for human companionship. He prays once again to know the will of God and to have the courage to follow it. He wishes to be guided only by God.

A proposal is made, and the day after his thirty-second birthday, on November 3, he begins to thank God for granting him such a loving soul. He is confounded that he should deserve such a gift: "It is the first, the only time that someone loves me. Will I be able to pay back such a joy?" (1961c, 358). The next day he writes again: "I have never thought that anyone could love me. What a sweet discovery!" In quick and somewhat surprising fashion for someone as cautious, one who had hardly begun thinking of marriage only a few months earlier, the formal engagement is announced less than ten days later, on November 14, and the wedding takes place one month after that, on December 12, in Quincy-le-Vicomte.

This is an indication that Blondel could be very decisive in matters of practical importance, notwithstanding his propensity to meditate at great length on the mystery of such action. The marriage did not of course bring him any closer to overcoming the obstacle to his academic career, but it did take him out of the solitude of his *mansarde*, where he had spent so much of his time in the past five or six years ruminating about his dissertation and what to do about his philosophical mission, whenever he was not away in Paris or on a trip elsewhere. This time he was leaving to join with someone with whom he was beginning to share his interior life as well as an external family life.

At this time, even the *Carnets Intimes* began immediately to take a new form, for henceforth they were to be written, no longer solo, but *à deux*, with husband and wife each contributing. We do not know what Rose wrote in these *carnets*, since only what Maurice wrote, or selections thereof, has been included in the second volume, which begins with the date of the marriage with the Latin heading, *Sequentia itineris ad Deum*, continuation of the journey to God, with the added notation: "a tenderness that will grow always up to the eternity of the divine love" (1966b, 15).

In the first few pages of this second volume, Blondel gives the itinerary of a trip that was to bring the newlyweds to Rome. First, a few days in Paris, then return to Dijon, with a side trip or a pilgrimage to Fontaines-les-Dijon, birthplace of St. Bernard. Then down to Aix-en-Provence for a few days, where they celebrated Christmas at the church that was to be their parish church later on, Saint Jean-de-Malte. Then down to Marseilles and the coast of the Riviera into Italy. In Rome they found Blondel's friends once again, Favre and Pératé, who were ready to help their friend show his wife all there was to be seen. While in Rome the couple had a private audience with the Pope, Leo XIII, about whom Blondel writes in the glowing terms of a true believer, as of one who is so close to God, another Christ on earth. Blondel would later look back on this visit as a first indication of the Church's approval of his writing.

While in Rome, however, Rose became ill and Maurice ended up doing some of the visiting by himself, which he would then narrate to Rose. Through it all he feels quite changed by the love of another, as one who is being led into new depths, though he is afflicted by this sickness of his wife. He feels tempted to devote himself softly, *mollement*, to only loving her, but he tells her that he must also pursue his work. "You know it, you want it: I must work. . . . You will strengthen me, you will support me against myself. You will make me understand the words of St. Paul, apparently so hard, but quite profound, that woman is made for man and not man for woman, since he is made for the service of God. That is how man manifests his love by associating the one he loves, through sacrifice and dedication, to the work that she could not understand without him just as he could not achieve it without her" (1966b, 25). The sentiment is hardly that of a feminist, but it is addressed directly to his wife, who seems to have acquiesced completely in it, as someone with her upbringing would. It would be repeated later in Lille, after they were settled into his first teaching assignment. "You have been given to me to aid me, according to the great primitive law of marriage. *Adjutorium meum*. My beloved aid!" (1966b, 43). What was paramount in the sentiment for Blondel was, not so much a domination, as the love that brought them together in the service of God, which for him always had an apostolic intent beyond the family.

While in Rome they learn that Rose has become pregnant. This is barely a few months after they have come to know one another. Blondel would have wished for a longer period of engagement. He would also have liked a longer time alone with his Rose, in order to form her in a more leisurely fashion, as he writes (1966b, 26), but God has willed otherwise. Blondel has to start thinking of paternity immediately, with some fear and trembling as he begins to think of the child to be born. They begin to think of their future home and of buying some things for that home, objects of art that Favre helps them to find.

On March 20 they leave Rome on their journey back to France. They stop in Florence along the way and arrive back in the Blondel family home in Dijon on March 29. After Easter, two weeks later, he takes Rose for the first time back to Saint-Seine. "In this place where I have dreamed so much, thought so much, meditated so much, o my God, here she is then, the one whom you have given me to love! How she changes me, and how she changes everything around her and around me. Thank you, my Rose, for being so good for all and for everything" (1966b, 39). They were back in the place from which Blondel had launched his mission, but there was still no word as to whether this mission would be received.

The word did come finally several days later, on May 2, when Blondel received an appointment to teach at the University of Lille for the end of the school year. The impasse was over. What brought this about was once again an intervention of Boutroux, who happened to be related to the newly appointed Minister of Education, Raymond Poincaré. Through the Minister's brother, Lucien, Boutroux let it be known that Blondel was being unjustly deprived of an appointment he deserved, and asked that the interdict against him be lifted by the University administration. At first, Lille was only a temporary appointment, but it was renewed in July for the next academic year. Blondel was finally admitted where he could begin pursuing his mission as a recognized philosopher. One week later they are in Lille, where Blondel finds a cathedral dedicated to Saint Maurice, in which to renew his own dedication "to the philosophical and apostolic mission that [God] has invested him with" (1966b, 41).

In Lille, for the first time, they find an abode of their own where they can settle in and do some entertaining of their own. Among the first ones to come for dinner were old friends from Normale, Paul Favre and Pierre Duhem. Blondel gets his first sense of being the master of a household when he signs his first lease, conscious as always that they must live in the world according to the Christian family tradition. He takes great care, perhaps too much even in his own mind, in looking for furniture that will be suitable for bringing children up in such a tradition. He is even elated when he finds a Louis XIII bed that, though perhaps a bit of a luxury, he thinks will serve this noble purpose. In keeping with everything he had learned at home, Blondel was becoming a careful administrator of property for his own family, where a child of their own was soon to be born.

As the trimester was coming to an end, late in July, Blondel's appointment at Lille was renewed without further ado from the administration. His place in the University was now officially recognized. When the courses came to a close at the end of July, the Blondels returned to Burgundy for the rest of the summer and into the fall, where they found themselves taken up once again in the activities of their extended families, and where they found support in the final weeks of Rose's pregnancy. While Rose was enduring her final days of labor, Maurice was fretting nearby, not only thinking of the child they were awaiting, but agonizing over the mystery of new life and already addressing the child yet to be born. As the labor is prolonged, he writes in the diary: "I feel even to the point of panic the solemnity of this hour when you will be born. I find myself as though annihilated before the mystery of life and death that surrounds every birth, I fall under the weight of my powerlessness and the powerlessness of every human being, and facing this moment, inevitable as my last hour will be, I enter into an agony before God who alone is powerful" (1966b, 54). Their son Charles was born in Quincy the day after he wrote this on October 17. Rose was relieved. Maurice was elated. And typically, right after the birth, she asked that he go kneel before the Blessed Sacrament to sing in his heart a *Te Deum* of thanksgiving and of blessing to God.

V

Discourse on Method for Philosophy of Religion

At the same time as Blondel was thus launching his family life and getting started in his University teaching career, he was also following the reactions to his dissertation on *Action* on the side of religion as well as on the side of philosophy. This brought him deeper into the question of apologetics than he had perhaps anticipated as a philosopher. In March and April 1894, not long after his dissertation had appeared, he had reviewed, rather favorably, a work titled *Lettres d'un curé de campagne* published under the name of Yves Le Querdec, a pseudonym for the religious apologist Fonsegrive, defending the work of moral and social renewal in society by the Church in the face of an ever suspicious and hostile laicism. This was the kind of work Blondel himself would later champion, against a certain reactionary conservatism in the Church, in favor of friends and relatives, as well as former students of his, in Catholic social movements. In September 1895, just as he was beginning to think of his courses for the coming year at Lille, he came across an article on the new trends in philosophical apologetics, in which he figured prominently, but which he could not accept as representing his views correctly.

The article had appeared in a prominent journal at the time called the *Annales de Philosophie Chrétienne*, which appeared to correspond to what Blondel was about, written by its new and supposedly progressive Director, Abbé Denis. Not liking what he saw attributed to him, he immediately asked for the opportunity to exercise his right of reply, indicating that, while he might be willing to speak of his philosophy as "apologetical," he did not think of it as an apologetics, as this was usually understood at the time, where philosophy was taken as only an instrument or a means subservient to theology, not as a discipline in its own right. Moreover, he wanted to insist that, while his method was exclusively rational, it did not remain simply in the "psychological sphere," as Denis was suggesting, nor was it restricted to "taking the soul by its intimate needs or with morally and socially fitting reasons." Such a strategy, according to Blondel, could "not reach minds like those of our contemporaries nourished in the school of criticism except through arguments of another order" (1896a, 4). Blondel had taken more strictly rational means to bring philosophy and religion together in his dissertation on *Action*, and this is what he thought had to be explained to the readers of the *Annales*.

From this initiative came one of Blondel's important early works, his discourse on method, in which he would define himself very carefully as a philosopher, and not as a theologian doing apologetics. Its title was chosen with great precision: *Letter on the Exigencies of Contemporary Thought in Matters of Apologetics and on the Method of Philosophy in the Study of the Religious Problem*, where emphasis was placed on the second part of the title rather than the first. The idea was to bring the question of apologetics back to the exigencies of modern critical thinking and to proceed from there in devising a method for raising the problem of religion within philosophy. This was a task one had to face up to in any religious apologetics, but which unfortunately was not being faced by would-be religious apologetes, not even the Director of the *Annales de Philosophie Chrétienne*. Blondel wanted to explain how he had tried to face up to it in his philosophy of action. As he writes at the beginning of the Letter itself, "There is always an advantage in not confusing competences: allow me to say to those who think they are doing philosophy that they are not doing any, and to shock certain minds who are certain of their faith, because my aim is not to put off those who perhaps have no other certitude than that of their incredulity" (1896a, 6). What is called for in the presence of such incredulous minds is not just some pious persuasion; it is a conviction that is "not merely reasonable but strictly and, if I may say so, technically rational. How is the problem to be raised so that it truly pertains to philosophy? By what method, without distorting the objects either of reason or of faith, can the investigation be brought to the critical point where the debate is settled?" (1896a, 7). These are the questions Blondel wanted to clarify, without confusion or any admixture of ideas taken from here, there, and everywhere.

It is important to note that what was at issue from the outset for Blondel was a matter of supernatural faith in the concrete Christian or Catholic sense, and not just some abstract form of natural religion, which he had spoken of in *L'Action* as just another form of superstition. It was this supernatural aspect of religion that was the problem to be solved for philosophy. The Letter was published in six long installments from January to July 1896 in the *Annales de Philosophie Chrétienne*, reaching the proportions of a short book. It is divided into three main parts, one in which he passes in review six approaches to apologetics that he finds wanting from the standpoint of philosophy, and two other parts in which he tries to show how the point that is wanting has to be made philosophically and how this can bring about a certain reconciliation between philosophy and supernatural religion as well as within each one of these two heterogeneous disciplines of one and the same spirit.

The Philosophical Inadequacy of Given Approaches to Apologetics

The first approach Blondel looks at is one he calls false philosophy in the service of apologetics, which is not to be confused with a philosophy that is false. Here Blondel names no one. Nor does he describe any specific method at any length. He is only denouncing those who presume to be doing philosophy in apologetics but in fact do not even have a philosophy to bring to the task. They are only puffed-up spirits going up against other puffed-up spirits; they do not deserve the respect of anyone in search of the truth and have no sense of the mysterious depths of human destiny. Such apologists are the first ones to need conversion to the Christian spirit of radical rational inquiry. For his part, in *L'Action*, Blondel had endeavored to be as critically philosophical as possible in accordance with the strictest exigencies of modern philosophy.

The second method brought up is one that proceeds by an abusive extension of the sciences into the realm of philosophy and apologetics. Here the problem is not a lack of seriousness of thought, but rather an inclination to reconcile science, metaphysics, and religion, starting only from the data of the positive sciences as if they were the expression of absolute reality. According to Blondel, the time when mathematics, or physics, or biology appeared to have a direct philosophical bearing has passed. These sciences have to do only with systems of more and more complex relations based on conventions or hypotheses that are subject to verification or application in facts, not in any critical reflection on the human spirit. For Blondel, they belong to an order of discourse that is quite distinct from that of metaphysics. There is not even any question of agreement or disagreement between the two, regardless of what differences there might be in philosophical discourse itself. It is futile to try to make any direct connection between the two.

This is not to say that the sciences have nothing to say about the vital questions that affect our human destiny, but to do so they require a philosophy of science that would take us out of the strict domain of these sciences into a discourse more directly related to questions relating to human destiny. That is not what we find in attempts to find in the "sciences" material elements for a metaphysical construction of the kind we find in such naïvely positivistic apologetics, but rather a misunderstanding of both science and metaphysics. In *L'Action*, Blondel had gone to great pains to show how one has to pass from a merely positive science of the object to a more critical science of the subject in order to arrive at a proper science of human action.

As Blondel comes to the third method of apologetics, he notes that the first two simply have to be rejected because they are ineffective and not without some peril. Not so with the other four that he is about to criticize. These, he says, have a certain value and certain advantages in that they are accessible to many minds. He is prepared to approve of them, but on the condition that their value not be exaggerated and their character not be denatured into something they are not.

The third method, then, is that of apologists who see their task as two-pronged: on the one hand, answering the objections of rationalism against the supernatural, and on the other hand, considering Christianity as a historical fact to be examined according to the canons of a critical evaluation of witnesses. According to Blondel, there are three difficulties this method runs into. First, the connection between these two sets of arguments is not essentially philosophical. Second, even if the arguments concerning the fact of Christianity have the greatest historical validity, it does not follow, according to both reason and faith, that they are apodictic with regard to the order revealed. Strictly speaking, philosophy is not in any position, nor does it have any competence for indicating an actual presence of the supernatural. Blondel was careful to avoid any such claim for philosophy in *L'Action,* even while arguing for a necessity of the supernatural. Third, if philosophy has less to say in the domain of empirical facts, it has and can have more to say in the domain of ideas and rational criticism.

It is all well and good to overcome the negations of rationalism. But after that, it is not enough to scrutinize the history of the Christian fact to bring the reason of the philosopher around to conversion. One still has to show why it is necessary for the philosopher to consider such a fact and to examine whether such a fact does not affect one's conscience, whereas it may be legitimate for one to show no interest in many other real facts. This objection to the third method of apologetics harkens back to the question that had been raised by one of Blondel's fellow students at the École Normale Supérieure, who asked why he "should feel obliged to inquire into and take into account a particular fact that took place 1900 years ago in an obscure corner of the Roman Empire, while [he] glories in ignoring so many great contingent events, curiosity about which would impoverish [his] interior life" (1932, 11). Blondel's difficulty with this third method is that it shows nothing of the *necessity* of inquiring into such supernatural facts for a rational being in search of his true destiny, or of recognizing the supernatural character of such facts if they happen to be given. "It is not enough to establish the *possibility* and the *reality* of the supernatural separately; one must still show the *necessity for us* to adhere to this reality of the supernatural" (1896a, 13). As long as this necessary connection has not been made, apologetics will have no bearing on minds that raise the exigencies of the philosopher to their legitimate extreme.

This does not mean that philosophy has to be in a position to bring faith into the soul of the philosopher. In this regard, his philosophy was in complete agreement with Christian theology. Faith itself can only be a supernatural gift beyond anything philosophy could produce by itself. Reduced to human means and natural ways, philosophy can only show two things with regard to such a gift: one cannot pass up such a gift with impunity, if it is offered, and at the same time one cannot come into possession of such a gift by oneself. The gift has to be both necessary and impracticable for the purely rational being, which is the point Blondel had tried to make most emphatically in his dialectic of action. To the extent that faith transcends the certitude of philosophy, philosophy does not and cannot pronounce itself on the matter of fact. But it does have to determine the spiritual dispositions that make way for a proper appreciation of the facts and a practical discernment of truths advanced from outside itself as articles of faith. What philosophy has to do before the fact can be received interiorly, or be seen as necessary by reason, is demonstrate an internal need and a sort of demanding appetite within us that prepares us for such a paradoxical gift, if it is offered.

Blondel's teacher, Léon Ollé-Laprune, had come close to producing such a response to the philosophical question about the fact of the supernatural. But, according to his student, he had not gone far enough in arguing for a certain openness of the soul to a higher life in its moral ideal. He had shown certain affinities between Christianity and our moral nature, so that Christianity could appear desirable to the human soul by reason of its beauty and goodness. Such a method of convergence, so rich in the resources it taps into, especially in the one who advances it from a position of faith as well as of philosophy, had a real attraction for Blondel, who was after all a man of faith as well as a philosopher. But it still did not satisfy his exigencies as a philosopher. It said too much on the side of faith and too little on the side of philosophy. It did not determine the relations between the natural order and the supernatural order precisely enough.

Blondel focuses on this method of the intellectual and moral convergence of Christianity with human nature developed by his teacher as the fourth method of apologetics, whose persuasive efficacy he admires but whose philosophical rigor he finds insufficient, as he had begun to think already when he was preparing to write his dissertation. The idea of this method starts from an analysis of our human needs and our powers of knowing and loving, in order to show how the dogmas of faith can be recognized as providing a harmonious answer to these aspirations. Such a method has been used by many in many different ways, using different aspects of what we aspire to and different responses one can find in the Gospels or in the Church. It provides many arguments that are useful in creating a presumption in favor of the Christian religion serving as a complement or as a full satisfaction for the nature essential to human being. But that is all they do. According to Blondel, they do not provide a properly philosophical apology for Christianity. In fact, such arguments can be very deceiving and even dangerous, if we do not know how to keep their claims in check. The method may work for some who are already favorably disposed, but not for those who are not so favorably disposed and who claim to be guided only by the power of reason. What is proposed is not essentially philosophical, nor can it be, nor must it claim to be.

For Blondel, what is essentially philosophical about this fourth kind of argument is that it has to do with something that has to be thought of as supernatural. But the method tends to consider the supernatural only from a natural standpoint. The notion of the supernatural is left in the dark or too ambiguous. If it is brought out as strictly supernatural, then it has to be thought of as outside the pale of rational investigation, so that the method ceases to be either truly apologetic or properly philosophical. Again, the relation between the supernatural and the natural is left without definition. If one tries to explain how Christianity can be binding on us in the same way as moral obligations are binding, one is still only within the scope of the human. If one tries to insist that it is binding strictly because it is supernatural, then the question becomes one of knowing precisely how something that is supposedly supernatural should come to be thought of as binding on nature.

According to Blondel, this is the question a truly apologetic philosophy has to answer. It is the question he had tried to come to in his dialectic of action. It is the question that Catholic orthodoxy itself forces him to, when it says that, though the gift of the supernatural is offered quite gratuitously on the part of God, it cannot be rejected with impunity on the part of the human being. It is also the question at which modern philosophy will put up its greatest resistance to the supernatural, for how can anything be rationally demanded of nature that is not part of nature itself? Finally, it is the question for which the method of convergence has no proper answer, for even if it supposes some resolution of the problem it cannot justify its solution philosophically. The answer it offers to the question of apologetics remains alien to the method used.

This is not to say that the method has no demonstrative force whatsoever. For the believer it can have demonstrative force. That was the force of the argument in the writings and in the life of Ollé-Laprune, as Blondel could see quite well in this person of faith. But for the unbeliever it has no more force than that of a witness to a certain harmony of life, an invitation to come and see and taste. It can work, if we start from the noble fact of Christian life. With the hypothesis of something that completely surpasses the domain of philosophy, one supposes the supernatural as present in life and then finds the reflected expression of it in thought. But in modern philosophy this is not what we find. There one finds disbelief or unbelief in both theory and practice. There one has to "suppose the supernatural as absent from life, in order to show that it is postulated by thought and action" (1896a, 21).

This is the point where any philosophy with an apologetic intent must insist. And to do so it must borrow its strength from the very attitude of resistance to the supernatural in modern philosophy. It must show the *necessity* of the supernatural as something immanent to human life itself. If there is a supernatural destiny for human being, it cannot be a matter of legitimate indifference or of innocent neutrality. To refuse it, if it is offered, would not be for human being a mere privation, but a positive failure, a fault, because what one rejects is something already present even in the life closed off from faith. Unless one can show this rationally, one cannot touch the truly philosophical spirit.

The fifth method to be criticized is that of Le Querdec, whose book Blondel had previously reviewed favorably. Supposedly this method differs from the method of convergence just examined and resembles more the method Blondel used in *L'Action,* as this will be defined more exactly in part two of the *Lettre,* but Blondel puts it through the same philosophical test as the other methods. Whereas the previous method argued from a certain conformity between Christianity and the most profound aspirations of human nature, this method starts more from a soul in search of itself, bereft of any rule of thought or any direction for life, in order to show how it is "invincibly" led to recognize that life cannot be led without the doctrine of life that only Christianity, and more precisely Catholicism, can provide.

This method goes further than the preceding one by maintaining that Christianity *alone* can satisfy all the artistic, intellectual, moral, and social needs of the human being. It proceeds by way of elimination, by flushing out every adversary from his position, and it systematically determines all the essential conditions of life, so that through this complete inventory it forms an organized synthesis. It applies the scientific methods of both absence and presence. But in the end it runs into the same philosophical difficulty as the method of convergence. It fails to define exactly the relation of the natural order with the supernatural order. Worse still, it presents certain additional difficulties that go against certain rights of reason and certain necessary susceptibilities of theology.

The method simply identifies or reduces Catholicism to life, as if revelation only confirmed or fulfilled nature without bringing anything new or unforeseen, anything heterogeneous or unhoped for. Le Querdec merely adapts Catholicism to the needs of life, as if the prescriptions of religion did nothing more than cover the dictates of conscience and the lessons of moral experience. It only juxtaposes Christian dogma as something parallel to the necessities of sensible, intellectual, moral, and social life, which is both to go too far, since Christianity creates new needs that it satisfies through its gratuitous gift, beyond anything we could expect from nature alone, and not far enough, because there is more than a parallelism to be defined in the relation between the two orders. In arguing that Catholicism satisfies all the aspirations of nature, it can only conclude to its natural and human truth, and in offering it as something truly supernatural, it is stepping beyond the premises of the argument.

At the root of all these difficulties is one that is more fundamental still from a strictly philosophical point of view. Like all the others, Le Querdec still does not take the life that is closed off from the supernatural for what it is, nor does he consider the different attitudes possible for the soul facing the decisive question from which the secret of its destiny springs. Instead of accepting the fact of a thought and an existence without faith and without grace, in order to seek in it what is present there in the very absence of the supernatural, and looking into each one for the criterion by which to judge for oneself according to a law of autonomy, it resorts to merely persuasive and prescriptive exhortation. It analyzes life only to impose something heteronomous on it, without taking into account that this external addition is not philosophically justified either in its form or in its content. What Blondel was looking for was a science applicable to any conscience universally, a science that would be complete and decisive for the inevitable solutions of the problem of human destiny, but what he found in this method was only a new tactic of accommodation without any apologetic or metaphysical doctrine of its own concerning human moral being.

This brings Blondel to a sixth and final method of apologetics to be criticized under the norms of Blondel's conception of philosophy. This is the method Le Querdec still referred to as the one most objective and most apt to convince the universality of human beings, even though it was no longer fitting "in the distorted view of our contemporaries." It was the more classical or dogmatic method, dubbed traditional, that was still most widely used in Catholic circles, namely Thomism. It was also the method whose advocates would be most vehement in their reaction to Blondel's critique and in their attack on his own more demanding philosophical method. In criticizing this method Blondel was conscious that he was treading on some very sensitive ground, but he was doing so in good faith as a loyal and faithful member of the Church, conscious of its theological as well as its rational exigencies. His tone was perhaps too sharp, coming from one trained in the University rather than the seminary, but he had no way of anticipating the bitterness of the reaction his intervention would provoke among the self-appointed defenders of the faith against reason in Thomism.

The method or the doctrine in question was the one usually proposed at the beginning of theology in seminaries in the treatise on religion. It can be summed up as follows: reason demonstrates the existence of God; this God could have revealed himself; history proves the fact of revelation, as it also proves the authenticity of Sacred Scripture and the authority of the Church. Hence, it is concluded, Catholicism is established on a truly scientific rational ground.

Apart from the appeal to historical sources, which pertain to another order of consideration than philosophy, what we have in this method is a complete and harmonious exposition of truth that is very rich and appealing. What it offers, according to Blondel, is a description of an *object*, both natural and supernatural, of knowledge and of faith, in a powerful synthesis capable of producing an irresistible conviction in spirits that are ready for it. In a time when metaphysical and theological ideas could be taken more for granted, it could be used to show the intimate cohesion of the truth in its many aspects. This is a purpose that Thomism served very well in its day. But in the modern day and age it is no longer seen as serving such a purpose. It is thought of as too "*static*, as a sort of super-imposition of elements without any movement for passing from one to the other, as an inventory but not as an invention capable of justifying, through the dynamism that arouses them, the ascensions of thought. Once one has entered into it and if one accepts its principles, one can be assured within oneself; and from the center of this fortress, one finds oneself armed to repel attacks and to overcome objections concerning details. But one has to enter in" (1896a, 27-28). Therein lies its difficulty for the modern philosophical mind, which contests many of the principles from which this synthesis starts. A merely triumphant exposition of the system will not do. When it comes to modern philosophy, we are still in a militant and suffering life, and, for Blondel, it would be a progress in Christian thought to understand this.

We might ask at this point what precisely Blondel has in mind when he speaks of "Thomism." Was it the Thomism of St. Thomas or was it more a modern Thomism in reaction, not against, but in response to modern rationalism? At the time when he was writing this *Lettre* it does not seem that he had studied much of St. Thomas, as he had St. Bernard or St. Paul, though he did invoke him in his diaries as the patron saint of Christian intellectual life. This was in keeping with the renewal in Thomistic studies strongly advocated by Leo XIII, whom Blondel revered as standing in the place of Christ for him, and whose reign had begun in 1893, the year he had defended his thesis. The only direct contact Blondel seems to have had with Thomism up to this time was with the kind of scholastic manual prevalent in Catholic seminaries at the end of the nineteenth century, supposedly written *ad mentem sancti Thomae*, but using a logic of layers in reality, one natural and one supernatural, which was far from anything to be found in St. Thomas's own writings. Blondel had reviewed such manuals in logic while he was still a licentiate student in Dijon, and it was to such manuals that he was referring now in criticizing the fortress mentality of Thomism, which was having the effect of keeping people out of the Church rather than getting them in.

The reason for this, as Blondel saw it, was that it was aiming in the wrong direction. "Let us not waste our time rehearsing arguments that are known, offering an *object*, when it is the *subject* who is not disposed" (1896a, 28). Arguments must be brought to bear, not on the side of divine truth, but on the side of human preparation for the gift. Moreover, this is not just a matter of temporary expediency. This role of subjective preparation is of primary importance, one that is essential and permanent, if it is true that the action of the human being cooperates with that of God. Far from just bemoaning the supposed errancies of modern thought and the alleged sickness of its reason, Blondel sees in this movement of human thought something that God might be using for the growth of the human spirit into a new horizon, something in which we can discern a labor of new life and thought, something that Christians can latch onto in its immense effort, in order to shed light in it, to help it grow and not to let it stop short in its opposition to divine truth, and even in order for Christians themselves to grow with it in their own understanding of this divine or supernatural truth. In his own efforts to defend revealed religion in terms of modern philosophy Blondel had in fact come to a better understanding of that religion, something that many of his religious adversaries were not always able to appreciate.

All this was in keeping with the conception of modern philosophy that he shared with Delbos, his fellow Catholic philosopher, and that we have seen expressed in the earlier article on the evolution of Spinozism. In the *Lettre*, Blondel points to this evolution in broader historical terms, going back to medieval Scholasticism, and at the same time in terms of the relation between the supernatural and the natural, which he says is crucial to a proper understanding of the problem. At the origin, in scholasticism, there were three layered zones, so to speak: at the bottom, the one where reason was quite at home; at the top, the one where faith alone reveals the mystery of divine life and of human life called to the divine banquet; and in the middle, an area of mutual understanding and encounter, with reason discovering imperfectly what faith illumines and confirms of the more important natural truths. It was in this middle area that, thanks to the community of *objects* recognized on both sides, two currents of thought coming from different sources intermingled with one another without becoming confused one with the other. But, according to Blondel, there was not yet any question about the subjective possibility or the formal compatibility of the two orders.

Eventually this medieval dualism of reason and faith would begin to appear more as a problem than as a solution for the question of the relation between philosophy and religion. In a violent reaction against the intellectualism of Aristotle and Scholasticism, Protestantism would reject the very idea of a rational preparation for faith, first by razing the edifice of reason and freedom, and then by letting the entire structure reemerge on its own, but without seeing in it anything like an infrastructure for a higher life. In other words, it eliminated the middle area of earlier Scholasticism, now thought of as an area of conflict rather than concord. The orders of the natural and the supernatural, which had been previously *superimposed,* were thus left in mere *juxtaposition* without any communication or intelligible connection between the two. It was then only a matter of time before reason, left by itself on the side of knowledge, would begin to think it could find immanent within itself, as in the case of Spinoza, all the truths necessary for reason, and thereby end up radically excluding the world of faith. From juxtaposition, philosophy thus moved to *opposition* and incompatibility with anything supernatural.

This is how Blondel thinks modern rationalism came to its *notion of immanence* as the condition of all philosophy, going back to the expression used by Brunschvicg in first commenting on *L'Action*. He will come back to this understanding of the progression of thought from the Middle Ages to modern times in presenting his own *method of immanence* as it picks up from this progression. But now he is concerned only with showing how a mere repetition of old affirmations, supposedly from the thirteenth century, not only excludes us from understanding the spirit of our times, but even prevents us from finding the old equilibrium that is now shaken by new distinctions and new problems not previously entertained. "To think literally today as if we were five hundred years ago is inevitably to think in another spirit than that of those times" (1896a, 31). Little did Blondel know at the time how much the modern-day Thomists he was thinking of were no longer thinking as St. Thomas had in fact thought.

Blondel recognizes that there may have been a spontaneous equilibrium at one time, but now we have only a *hybrid* compromise and a precarious accord. When one looks at the dogmatic arguments combining reason, history, and revealed theology, one has to keep in mind the heterogeneity of data whose very reality, let alone their accord, is in question. "If the synthesis no longer appears in the consciousness of our contemporaries with the same ease as formerly, it is not just because of our contemporaries; it is because there is truly a doctrinal lacuna to be filled, a lacuna that has been made evident by the adversaries of the Christian idea. Nor must these contemporaries be blamed for calling attention to it, because after all we should not expect them to think something sufficient and satisfying from the standpoint of method when it is not" (1896a, 31). That lacuna remains in the modern version of the ancient apologetic and leaves intact the problem of what is now the core of religious philosophy.

Whether Blondel's grasp of the medieval synthesis between the natural and the supernatural was entirely adequate is something that could be questioned. His view was not based on an extensive knowledge of any of the earlier Scholastic theologians. It was based more on a neo-Scholastic rendition of that synthesis which, according to Blondel's own general remark about the difference between the spirit of our times and the spirit of earlier times, was not exactly in the spirit of the former times. Blondel would later regret the inadequacy of his view on Thomism as expressed in the *Lettre*, after having read more of St. Thomas himself and after seeing how Aquinas could be read in a way that was more in keeping with the modern problematic of religion. But the critical point of the lacuna that remains at the heart of the traditional apologetic, as it was being presented at the end of the nineteenth century, was a valid and an important one, as irritating as it was for many theologians at the time, because it called attention to something that was being ignored in philosophy, and that could no longer be ignored, if anything like a valid case were to be made for any revealed religion, such as the Catholic religion, in philosophy.

The Essential Point at Issue in Philosophy of Religion

Having completed his critique of the six methods up for criticism, Blondel then turns, in the second part of this discourse on method, to a more positive treatment of what was for him the precisely philosophical point in the religious problem, namely, that of the relation between the natural and the supernatural, and the method for dealing with it. The problem to be solved from the standpoint of apologetics is that the supposedly philosophical arguments advanced no longer seem to work in the general movement of contemporary minds. It is not enough to complain of a lack of proper orientation in this movement or an absence of readiness to receive a truth that is ready-made for them. It is more important to face up to the critical exigencies of these minds and to address them in the full force of their resistance to any idea of the supernatural. From this, Blondel thinks, will come not only a better confrontation of the problem of religion as it presents itself in modern philosophy, but also a better appreciation of what is at stake in the idea of the supernatural, even by those who feel called to defend it. There is something to be learned about the supernatural, even from the critical exigencies of philosophy itself that appear to be opposed to it as something imposed from outside.

The aim of Blondel is not so much to restore ancient or medieval positions, now seen as untenable, but rather to find new and more solid ones in the thought that has shown the weakness of the old positions. To do this Blondel proposes three steps: (1) determine the precise point to which the development of philosophical thought has brought the debate; (2) determine the method that will enable him to deal with this decisive point; and (3) determine the character or the sense of the conclusions that can be drawn from this method so that the exigencies of both philosophy and theology can be met. From this he hopes to show how the growing demands of contemporary thought are not only legitimate, but also useful and in conformity with the Catholic as well as the philosophical spirit.

(1) The first question then is how to raise the philosophical question with regard to religion, so that religion is not seen as only an alternative philosophy, and so that philosophy is not absorbed into religion. On the one hand we have the claim of complete autonomy on the part of philosophy as expressed in the notion of *immanence,* or the idea that nothing can enter into human being that

does not somehow come from it or does not somehow correspond to a need of expansion within it. On the other hand there is the understanding that there is nothing Christian or Catholic that is not properly *supernatural*, not just in a metaphysical sense of something transcendent whose affirmation would still be immanent, but in the sense of something to be imposed on human thought and will that is impossible for human being to draw from itself.

It is important to keep in mind that Blondel is thinking of a strictly Catholic idea of the supernatural here, rather than any looser idea that would not see any necessity in the idea, for this is where the greatest point of conflict is situated and where the debate must be brought to bear if a proper solution to the problem of religion is to be found in philosophy. The first point for him is to show how philosophy and religion come into contact with one another through this radical conflict, before trying to show how there may be some agreement within the supposed conflict. Without highlighting this first point of conflictual contact, there is no way of proceeding that is philosophically valid. It is not enough to show how the gift of the supernatural might satisfy the aspirations of certain noble souls. Anything we can draw from ourselves as human falls short of what we have to and can only receive supernaturally. If we look only for what we can draw from ourselves, we will not meet the real difficulty. We will only turn our back on it, "since it is not the object or the gift that is the obstacle but the form and the fact of it. . . . Not to have it as received and given, but as found and coming from us, is not to have it at all: and that is precisely the scandal of reason" (1896a, 35). It is this very *notion of immanence* that one must address in the philosophical question of religion.

Blondel goes on to bring out different ways in which the scandal can be seen as even greater than it first appears. This is not just a matter of fact or of a truth to be believed along with others. It is a matter of what is right or what ought to be. If we do not enter through this door of accepting something that is not from ourselves in any way, we cannot be Christian. And yet to enter this door "we must admit that, incapable of saving ourselves, we are capable of damning ourselves forever; and that the gratuitous gift, free and elective in its source, becomes for the one to whom it is offered inevitable, imposed and obligatory, so that there is apparently no symmetry between the alternatives, since in the end what we cannot do by ourselves becomes imputable to us personally if we have not done it and since a gratuitous gift is changed into a strict debt" (1896a, 36). How can a philosophy that insists on its own immanent autonomy accept such a claim on the part of religion? Will not religion have to back off from this claim if it is to find any acceptance in philosophy?

Not for Blondel. Quite the contrary, for him it is only through such a claim on the part of religion that a point of intelligible communication can be established with a philosophy that claims to be autonomous in its immanence. In this claim he finds a certain definition of the relation between the natural and the supernatural that he thought was lacking in the earlier methods of apologetics. If the gift of the supernatural were something indifferent to our nature and our reason, if it were left only as something superimposed from the outside, without penetrating into the order of nature itself, then the problem of a strictly supernatural religion, which is the problem to be solved for Blondel, would remain radically inconceivable for philosophy. It is only through a Revelation — one that reaches down into the conscience of a human being and considers a neutral or a negative attitude in the face of its gratuitous offer as a positive failure and a kind of hostile culpability — that contact is made, that the difficulty explodes, and that the problem arises. "For if it is true that the exigencies of the Revelation are grounded, we cannot say that we are still entirely at home within ourselves: and of this insufficiency, this incapacity, this exigency there has to be some trace in human being purely as human being as well as some echo in the most autonomous philosophy" (1896a, 37). It is this trace or this echo of the supernatural within the human being that must be sought if any meeting of philosophy and religion is to be found. It is this trace and this echo that Blondel had sought to articulate in his dialectic of action.

But it is important to understand that according to Blondel we can come to this meeting only if we insist on the radical claim of the Catholic teaching that the gift, gratuitous though it be on the part of the giver, becomes obligatory on the part of the one to whom it is offered. The question is not one of a few fragmentary ideas or of one particular dogma or another. Nor is it one of exposing the whole of a historically defined teaching, let alone of facts or of particular persons. The problem is not one of objects to be believed in, but of believing itself under its formal and integral aspect. "If we do not go to the extremity of the most precise and most challenging exigencies of full Catholicism, we do not have the means even of rationally conceiving the meeting or the coexistence of a religion that is not simply a human construction with a philosophy that is unwilling to abdicate or to be absorbed into the ineffable" (1896a, 38).

If we compare this position with that of Hegel in *The Phenomenology of Spirit* concerning the relation between faith and pure insight and the ensuing struggle between them in the Enlightenment, we can see how Blondel has no less comprehensive demands for philosophy than his German predecessor in the philosophy of religion. Philosophy has to have its word with regard even to the supernatural. But we see also how Blondel's position differs radically from Hegel's, the modern immanentist philosopher par excellence in the view of Delbos and Blondel, by insisting on the irreducible heterogeneity of religion and faith in its source with regard to anything in human thought and will. The spirit of religion, properly understood as supernatural at the same time as necessary, cannot be understood as something purely immanent, or even as transcendent in some vague metaphysical sense. It must be understood as from beyond anything human reason can comprehend, something from *jenseits,* to use the term Hegel wished to avoid at all costs for anything in his philosophy, but as something that reason itself must acknowledge as something from beyond. Short of this, one cannot properly understand the problem of religion in philosophy without absorbing religion into philosophy, as Hegel did, or philosophy into religion, as many Catholic apologists were trying to do. Blondel was trying to negotiate a true meeting between the two without watering down the fundamental claims of either side.

(2) This brings him to the second part of his task, which is to establish a method for dealing with the precisely philosophical point of the religious problem in a way that is appropriate and useful for the modern spirit. Given the *notion of immanence* that has come to characterize modern philosophy, Blondel calls for a *"method of immanence"* to be applied integrally and rigorously in the examination of the problem of human destiny. For him such a method is capable not only of defining the difficulty but also of resolving it. And through such a method the solution as well as the problem itself can be understood only by forcing us to be equally faithful to both philosophy and Catholic orthodoxy, "or better still by forcing philosophy as well as orthodoxy to remain faithful to itself" (1896a, 38).

In what does this method consist? Not in insisting from the beginning that human being finds within itself and by itself all the truth necessary for life or that its complete happiness can come only from itself, for that would be to prejudge the question and start from a conclusion. Nor does it consist in adopting the spirit of criticism by excluding any transcendent reality, or by setting human subjectivism up as an absolute, for that only plays on a certain ambiguity in the words *immanent* and *transcendent*. To be sure, the idea we have of transcendent truths and exigencies is immanent, but before we can pronounce on the bearing of these immanent ideas we must first determine what it is precisely that we do think. In other words, according to Blondel, "We must open up the integral series of our inevitable ideas and our solidary conceptions, independently of the apparent mutilations or the partial restrictions that are introduced into it by the superficial intervention of our reflected decisions, as this series is produced under the preoccupation with ontological and moral problems" (1896a, 39). The aim of the method then is to focus on the totality of our thoughts in their mutual implication, including the thought of the transcendent, as it all relates to action and life. The method will consist "in bringing about in consciousness itself the equation of what we appear to think and will and do with what we do, will, and think in reality, so that in the factitious negations or the ends artificially willed can still be found the profound affirmations and the irrepressible needs they imply" (1896a, 39).

This is the method Blondel had used to develop the ascending dialectic in *L'Action*, the method he is now reflecting on as a whole in the *Lettre*. It is the method he thinks is becoming more and more the method of philosophy in his day. Even if it appears to degenerate into a science for the initiate or into technical subtleties, as religious apologists might be inclined to think, we must recognize that it tends to generate more and more clearly a knowledge that is specifically distinct from others, and hence technical in some sense. It is a method that Blondel thinks one has to follow if one is to arrive at any philosophically valid results in any domain, including that of religion.

His program for it is reminiscent of the way Delbos had characterized the Spinozistic system:

> Its proper work is to criticize one by the other the phenomena that make up our interior life, to adjust them, to study the connection between them, to develop their integral determinism, to see what principles are required by thought and action, to define what are the conditions on which we are forced to hang the reality of the objects and means of salvation we inevitably conceive, to study for example our idea of God, not insofar as it is God, but insofar as it is our necessary and efficacious thought of God, or further still to analyze the conception we are led to within ourselves of revealed beliefs and practices, not insofar as it is a religious and redemptive Revelation, but insofar as we can discover a type for them in conformity to our needs, in short, without claiming to add anything that [this philosophical work] is not and cannot give. (1896a, 39-40)

This final reservation is to suggest that religion is more and does give more in action than philosophy can discern, but the entire list of what philosophy is about and how far it can penetrate into the system of our thoughts, including those about God, is an indication of how far Blondel wishes to take philosophy in "the immanent affirmation of the transcendent, even of the supernatural, without prejudging in any way the transcendental reality of the immanent affirmations" (1896a, 40). Philosophy has to do with a critique of all our ideas, including those about God and religion, without transgressing into the light that comes only with faith in a Revelation and with a religious practice.

From this *method of immanence* comes what Blondel thinks is the only religious philosophy possible, one that is truly religious and one that is truly philosophical, to the surprise no doubt both of philosophers and of theologians. It remains for him to show how this is so on both sides of the divide between the two. On the side of philosophy he writes that the interconnected system of our ideas brings out how the very notion of immanence is not realized in our consciousness without the effective presence of the notion of the transcendent. Insofar as the method of immanence is limited to determining the dynamism of our representations, without having to pronounce itself at first on whether they are subjective or objective, it has only to analyze this inevitable idea of a dependence of human reason and will on a possible heteronomy with all the consequences that it implies. If the problem of the supernatural results from the labor of our thought itself, it cannot be said that it is inconceivable or inadmissible in philosophy. "It is on the contrary the very condition of philosophy precisely as it now presents itself in its intransigent independence" (1896a, 41). This is the extremity to which free thought and exclusive rationalism have come: what was proposed as a religious thesis now appears as a necessary philosophical hypothesis on which they depend logically for existence. Pushing philosophy to the totality of what it has to think means to show its lack of completeness if it remains enclosed within itself alone. In this respect, Blondel aims to go all the way to the end of philosophy and to remain strictly philosophical.

In doing this, however, he insists at the same time that we are not going beyond the exigencies of our own rational consciousness in speaking of a supernatural, so that the supernatural remains in conformity with the idea we have of it only insofar as it remains beyond our human grasp. "In determining the genesis of the idea of revelation or in indicating the necessity of revealed dogmas or precepts we can never do anything more than draw frames without content, for which nothing from ourselves can fix the reality or fill the abstract sketch" (1896a, 41). Content in the frames that philosophy draws is what faith teaches. But such content is also something that reason itself requires. By definition, the supernatural is not only a necessary hypothesis for philosophy. It is also something we cannot put into practice by ourselves. Where religious faith expresses a certain fullness, philosophy can only offer an empty concept. But in this radical difference the two coincide in what both have ultimately to talk about.

Theology, for its part, cannot admit that philosophy reaches the *reality* of the supernatural order, or that it denies its truth, or even that it admits its *intrinsic possibility*, for even this would be too much and too little. Philosophy cannot know anything of the intrinsic possibility of the supernatural, since that would be to know its essence, which by definition is beyond philosophy's capacity to know. But it must still affirm the necessity of the supernatural, if it is freely offered. Nor can theology admit that philosophy declares itself indifferent or alien to the supernatural, or simply juxtaposes itself to the supernatural, by judging itself self-sufficient and satisfied with its self-enclosed inviolability. There is only one relation that it requires and that is the one which "the method of immanence determines by considering the supernatural, not as real in its historical form, nor as simply possible as if it were only an arbitrary hypothesis, nor as gratuitous or up to one's willingness to accept as a gift, something proposed without being imposed, nor as something fitting or appropriate for human nature, for which it would be only a supreme flourishing, nor again as ineffable to the point of not having any root in our thought and our life, but, in keeping with the very precision of the scientific spirit which, concerned neither with the merely possible nor with the real, owes us neither more nor less than the necessary, but as indispensable as well as inaccessible to human being" (1896a, 42-43). Such is the essential relation of necessity between the supernatural and the natural that Blondel had found lacking in the earlier methods of apologetic, a lack that made them inadequate as philosophy, and a lack that Blondel could now define with his method of immanence.

(3) To speak of a necessity of the supernatural in relation to the natural, however, would appear to bridge the difference between the two orders temerariously, and to illegitimately force the freedom of the divine gift into the determinism of human action, which would be contrary to the very idea of the supernatural in both philosophy and theology. Blondel devotes the third and final section of this presentation of his philosophical method to explaining why, even with this notion of necessity, there is no transgression into the domain of theology in his method or any absorption of the supernatural into the natural, by reflecting more deeply on the method and on the character of the only philosophical conclusions that are rationally and theologically legitimate in relation to Christianity.

First, with regard to necessity, he refers back to the kind of science of practice he had tried to elaborate in *L'Action*. To say that such a science owes us nothing more or less than the "necessary" is not to take the word in an ontological sense, as if it had to do with an absolute existence or a truth whose contrary would imply a contradiction. It is only to take note of how our thoughts are inevitably organized according to an interconnected system. This is the determinism that enables philosophy to constitute itself as a science. In this context, to say that the supernatural appears as necessary at the same time as inaccessible for the philosopher is not to deny the freedom of either the one offering or the one to whom the gift is offered, nor is it to absorb the reality of the supernatural into the determinism of nature. What is necessary is that, without trying to specify how this takes place concretely for any single individual, the thoughts and acts of each human being come together in the form of a drama whose dénouement sooner or later but inevitably raises the decisive question of one's destiny. In every decision that we take, in every choice that we make according to the full determinism of our will, we "implicitly pass through the point where a fundamental option becomes possible and where, lacking any other light, that option becomes necessary and decisive between the solicitations of the hidden God and those of the ever present egoism" (1896a, 44).

What Blondel means by this, as he had tried to show in *L'Action*, is that, for the human being aspiring to some completion of his being through action, or in search of a willed object that will be equal to the infinite power of its willing will, the idea of the supernatural appears as a necessary hypothesis when we come face to face with God, whose idea also appears as necessary in deliberate action, just as it has its own effect on the will, making it necessary to say either *yes* or *no* to God in a fundamental option that can open us to God and whatever his will may be for our being, or else close us off from God in opposition to our will's most profound and sincere aspiration. What is necessary is neither the choice of a *yes* or a *no* that we might say to God, nor what God might in fact be willing on his part, but the *option* we are left with in the face of God and the hypothesis that God might offer more for the completion of our being than what human nature could achieve by itself.

What is also necessary is the thought that, if God were to offer a supernatural gift in addition to the gift of nature, such a gift, no matter how gratuitous on the part of God, would entail some obligation to accept on the part of the human being, since it would be in keeping with its own natural aspiration for a completion that is necessary for human nature and yet beyond the capacity of human nature to attain by itself. To say *yes* to God in the ultimate option brings infinitely more than one would suppose if one were to think of it as only the contrary of *no*. Nevertheless "it is no less true that the *no* injures the point of insertion prepared [for the supernatural] and the natural exigencies of the soul" (1896a, 45). One can reject one's destiny, but one cannot escape from it. Such is the meaning of the necessity that ties the two heterogeneous orders together without misrepresenting the independence of one from the other.

The necessity discerned in this science of practice does not posit any real continuity between the order of reason and the order of faith. Far from absorbing the supernatural into the natural, philosophical science can only affirm the supernatural as something beyond the capacity, the merits, or the exigencies of our nature. It affirms it as hypothetically necessary only by recognizing the ultimate insufficiency of human nature left to itself, which leads it to the felt need for something more and makes it possible for us, not so much to produce or to define this more, but rather to recognize it and to receive it as necessary for the perfection of our being in action, if it is offered. Blondel speaks of this felt need and insufficiency in theological terms as a baptism of desire "which, in the absence of any explicit revelation, remains accessible and necessary for the human being and, with revelation itself, is like the human sacrament immanent to the divine operation" (1896a, 44-45). The method of immanence serves to show not only how the supernatural is necessary for the completion of human being, but also how human being enters into the gift, if it is offered, only by the human being's own decisive initiative in accordance with its own autonomy.

Having shown the necessary relation of the supernatural order with the natural order, Blondel then turns his attention to showing how they remain irreducibly heterogeneous to one another, so that philosophy cannot transgress into the domain of theology, and conversely theology cannot transgress into the domain of philosophy, a point that was to irritate a number of theologians who fancied their method more philosophical than it actually was. This is an important point for us to understand here because it explains in what sense Blondel always thought of himself as a philosopher, and not as a theologian, even in dealing with religion and the supernatural or, later on, the Christian Spirit.

The idea is to understand how far one can go with the philosophical method of immanence. Its conclusions are valid only as far as the method can reach. While this includes any matter of scientific necessity, as has already been shown, "the reality or the realization of what is proposed as necessary is subordinated to another element which remains foreign to the science" (1896a, 46). Science, including the science of practice, is not a substitute for practice itself, nor does it cover everything that is hidden in practice where the secret of the relation between the soul and God is decided. In other words, according to the very meaning of the hypothetical necessity that has been defined, it follows that the legitimate bearing of our philosophical conclusions stops at the door of the real operation wherein alone the human and the divine act, or nature and grace, can come together. Consequently, according to Blondel, philosophy remains and can only remain on this side of the mysterious union, and it is this reservation that he proceeds to explain in all that it implies.

To begin with, philosophy is not addressed to members of a Church as such, but to human beings precisely as human beings. What is philosophical antecedes, encompasses, and surpasses any distinction of Church membership. Philosophy is not in the business of imposing obligations on anyone, as a Church might do for its adherents. Philosophy is in the business of studying as comprehensively as possible the possible attitudes of people and of extracting from these attitudes their immanent spring and their necessary consequences. The only thing it has to teach is what can be seen through critical reflection in what they do and what they are in themselves.

This limitation does not allow philosophy ever to pass judgment on any individual conscience. For Blondel the evangelical precept, "thou shalt not judge," is an absolute for philosophy. Even as an integral science of practice, it cannot trespass on the incommunicable teaching of practice alone. This is why in studying the supernatural, though philosophy cannot pronounce itself on its *de facto* presence, its historical form, or its actual operation, philosophy can freely discuss questions that concern even the most positive of religions without calling any particular religion into question, without pronouncing itself on what it offers, and without usurping what religion reserves only for itself. Even in the context of a Christian society, philosophy has to abide by these limitations in the free reign of its critique, recognizing the limits beyond which its conclusions cannot reach. No matter how far it can go in determining the insufficiencies of our nature and in going to the end of reason's demands or life's prayers, it is in no position to cross over into the domain of religion itself in practice. Already in 1896, long before the question was to be discussed in the 1920s and 30s, Blondel is saying that there is no more of a "Christian philosophy" than there is a Christian physics, at least not in the sense it was understood at the time by some, who claimed that philosophy could be applied to Christianity in the same measure as Christianity could pass judgment on the very people who ignored or excluded it. Usurpation on either domain from the other side could not be justified philosophically.

But the question whether there is a philosophical apologetic for Christianity remained. Having criticized earlier forms of apologetics, which all made philosophical claims, Blondel had to answer this question very carefully in order to avoid the kind of transgression he was criticizing in the relation between philosophy and theology. His first answer to the question is *no*, there is no philosophical apologetic, if the question implies that philosophy is engaged in the service of religion and its conclusions are homogeneous, or continuous with, or subordinated to those of theology. This would be to require that philosophy make its own assertions that exceed its competence or the limits of its conclusions, as we have just seen, and thereby sacrifice its method and its scientific autonomy.

On the other hand, however, given everything that Blondel had said concerning the question of religion and its necessity in philosophy, his answer also had to be *yes*, but not in the sense that was taken for granted by the other forms of apologetics previously criticized from a philosophical standpoint. The nature of the questions raised and the conclusions reached in classical theological apologetics is not the same as those of philosophy. Nevertheless philosophy has an essential role to play in apologetics that only it can play by setting aside the prejudicial objections that block the route for apologetics, by determining the notion of the supernatural, and by bringing to light the exigencies and the insufficiencies of nature. In this way it can open the way to apologetics, which is a theological discipline, but it cannot enter into it without going beyond the limits imposed upon it by its scientific character as a discipline. If it can be called more apologetic than all the other disciplines, it is only because it goes to the extremities of reason and will not have anything to do with heteronomy of any kind except one in which it would find "the guarantee, the dependence or the extension of its own autonomy" (1896a, 48). This is a tack that had not been taken previously in apologetics before Blondel and that in his mind was a strictly philosophical method of immanence.

To make this clear Blondel distinguishes two ways of doing philosophy, one that he calls "philosophoidal" and the other more strictly philosophical. The first is the one usually used in apologetics. It does not go back to the ultimate questions and proceeds dialectically from principles that are not dialectically established. The second constitutes an integral system of notions all of which are equally criticized, without any importation from outside, and with its own proper foundations and its relative sufficiency. The second is of course the method of immanence that Blondel has been at pains to describe. Now he insists that it cannot properly penetrate into the domain of the other forms of apologetics any more than it can allow them to penetrate into its own. To allow for this sort of interpenetration would be to introduce into rational critique something heterogeneous and irreducible to it as well as to betray the heteronomous aspect of the supernatural given only in practice and faith, if it is given. This is the distinction that would enable Blondel to maintain later on that, in treating the Christian Spirit as a philosopher, he was not doing theology.

It might appear then that Blondel is insisting on a kind of "separate philosophy," the very thing that he had set out to fight against, following his teacher Ollé-Laprune, albeit more systematically than he. But such is not the case. The philosophy Blondel is arguing about is one that, far from eliminating the religious problem, puts all its effort into showing "that religion cannot be eliminated from human life and that philosophy is not free, is not complete, is not itself if it does not face up to it at its most acute point" (1896a, 49). What Blondel is arguing for is a clear distinction of scientific domains between philosophy on the one hand and theology on the other, where apologetics properly belongs. If theology is right in refusing any intrusion of philosophy into its domain, then philosophy is right in refusing any intrusion of theology into its domain, especially when the intrusion is anything less than a strictly rigorous philosophy. The distinction, which is one of formal aspects in science, and not one of separation in reality, is for the good of both philosophy and theology. Those who are not philosophical or theological enough to see the difference must be made to understand that a confusion of the two domains does not properly serve either philosophy or religion. Nor does a separation of the two, or a mere juxtaposition.

In response to theologians, who are rightly jealous of their domain, Blondel explains that philosophy can play its very apologetic role for religion only if it remains impartial and free. "It represents all and nothing but the part of human being, but a part that is essential" (1896a, 50) if the human act is to coexist with the divine act, and if reason and nature are to remain immanent in the order of grace. Philosophy will serve the cause of religion all the better only "if it is not changed into an apologetic." This is a distinction that the more theologically inclined interpreters of Blondel (Bouillard, de Lubac, Saint Jean) have not always had clearly in mind, thereby reintroducing a theological confusion into his philosophy that he had tried to avoid, even in what could be called his apologetic intent. It is a distinction that was probably better understood by earlier theologians like Aquinas, but tends to get lost in the reaction of modern theology against modern philosophy or rationalism. Here Blondel reasserts this distinction in no uncertain terms, repeating a phrase he had already used near the end of *L'Action*, which combines both the religious intent of his philosophy and its autonomy as a philosophical discipline: *Non libera nisi adjutrix, non adjutrix nisi libera philosophia* (1896a, 50-51). Philosophy is not free unless it helps and does not help unless it is free.

While he is insisting primarily on the autonomy of philosophy here, we should also keep in mind how important the other side of the relation with religion was for him. Unlike many others who were given to complaining about the deleterious effects of modern philosophy with regard to the religious spirit, Blondel found that this philosophy could lead to a better understanding and appreciation even of the supernatural. If we look back on the apostolic intent that led him to pursue a career in philosophy at the Lycée in Dijon and then later on at the École Normale Supérieure, namely, to become familiar with the thought of those whom he originally thought of only as opposed or indifferent to his religion, we can see how far this pursuit of philosophy has brought him. Having gone outside the protective walls of religious institutions for his philosophy, he learned how a seemingly secular and anti-religious philosophy could itself be brought into the service of religion, as Aquinas in his day had done with regard to the philosophy of Aristotle.

Blondel did this by going into the strictest exigencies of philosophy as a discipline and by coming out at the other end in his conclusions as more favorable to supernatural religion than had been thought before. In doing this he had shocked many philosophers. But he had also learned from them, and not from theologians, not only how to overcome the "prejudicial objections" to religion, but also how to philosophize in a way that was authentic and autonomous in accordance with the critical exigencies not just of modern philosophy, but of any true philosophy. Having made his case for religion in *L'Action*, in the *Lettre* he was now making a case for the philosophy he had learned, much to the irritation of certain theologians, whose philosophy was half-hearted at best and ineffective, if not downright injurious to the faith, for minds imbued with the modern critical spirit, even as he was in his own religious mind.

The Mutual Renewal of Perspectives in Philosophy and Religion

The remarkable thing is not so much that Blondel did not lose his faith by his exposure to modern philosophy, but rather that he gained in this faith, not in spite of philosophy, but through it, in a way that many theologians could not appreciate. What he found by pushing modern thought to the fullness of all that was implied in its action was a renewal of perspective in his own religious faith. He brings this out in the third part of the *Lettre*, where he speaks at some length of the mutual renewal of perspectives in philosophy and religion through the fully consequent action of modern thought as he had experienced it. For Blondel to have come out of modern philosophy in the way that he did, however, he had to develop a view of philosophy that was new to both philosophers and theologians in his time. It is this view that he explains in the third part of the *Lettre* along with the renewal of perspective in the Christian faith that he calls for.

Up to this point he was discussing the question of method only as a particular problem in the study of religion. What he saw coming out of this discussion, however, was the idea that the problem of religion as such had become an essential part of philosophy in general as it has developed in the past five hundred years. What he wants to do in the third part of the *Lettre*, then, is sum up the teaching of this development in order to show how there is no going back to ancient forms of philosophy in doing apologetics any more than in philosophy itself. Until now he has also been considering the problem of religious philosophy as if it were only a special difficulty in philosophy. What he wants to do now is show that, far from being subordinate, partial, or determined by conditions independent from it, this problem is both dominant and determinant for philosophy, if philosophy goes to the end of the consequences of its modern form. In passing he repeats, rather sharply this time, his criticism of those who are keeping this movement of thought at arm's length with their old Scholastic pseudo-philosophical ideas, or who only want to restore ancient Reason or ancient Philosophy. All such efforts, he thinks, are doomed to failure and regression. He wants to show now the mutual renewal and the reciprocal advancement of philosophical thought and of the Christian Spirit in modern times, even though they start off as being opposed to one another, just as Aristotelianism had once appeared opposed to the Christian Faith in the thirteenth century, as he understood the uneasy amalgamation between the two to have been at that time.

For Blondel, things have come to the point where "in order to do philosophy without ceasing to be Christian or to be a Christian without ceasing to be a philosopher, one no longer has the right to start secretly from one's faith in order to make believe one arrives at it and one no longer has the power to put one's beliefs discretely to the side of one's own thinking" (1896a, 53). The two, doing philosophy and thinking as a Christian, have to come together in the unity of one thought, as they had done for Blondel in his journey through modern thought, with the understanding that philosophy itself has to be totally reconstituted, away from its anti-religious stance, in a way that can lead to both a "religious progress of philosophical thought in its entirety and a human progress of religious consciousness or of the understanding itself of Christianity" (1896a, 53).

This was a tall and complicated task to end his *Lettre* with. Blondel begins executing it by showing first how philosophy has been transformed little by little and has been determined precisely in itself under what he refers to as the "unrecognized and repressed idea of Christianity." What he means by this "Christian idea" at the heart of modern philosophy is puzzling at first sight, but it is an important part of what he wants to bring out with regard to the religious dimension of philosophy. Also puzzling are the two theses that he enunciates at the outset: first, philosophy has not yet been fully constituted as a science, and second, there has not yet been a properly Christian philosophy. What has been called such is neither entirely philosophical nor entirely Christian. But all this may be clarified and justified by the schematic overview of the development of philosophy as a whole in modern times, in conjunction with a corresponding human growth of the Christian spirit that should go with this philosophical development.

Blondel begins this overview by going back to the conception of reason and philosophy that was prevalent among the Scholastics in the Middle Ages as derived from the Greeks, which, according to him, contained the germ of all the struggles of reason against the Christian idea that were to follow. What Scholastic philosophy represented for him was largely an accommodation of an earlier free Hellenic speculation, corrected in part and completed, but not essentially renewed, in the light of a new teaching of a higher order, namely, a *sacra doctrina* based on revelation. What Blondel saw in this philosophy imported from Hellenism was a tacit postulate that philosophy could encompass the whole of truth and reality, and that it contained within itself the first and last word of all things in a sort of divine sufficiency. He quotes from the tenth Book of the *Nicomachean Ethics* to show how Aristotle, the Philosopher for the Middle Ages, thought of speculative reason as somehow divine. The combination between philosophy and theology then could be made rather easily in terms of a *logos*, which was not only an expression of reason but also a name for the God in Christianity, the God who reveals himself as *Logos*, but not without some confusion as to how the union should take place.

Blondel did not see how Scholasticism had ever challenged the tacit postulate of divinization in Greek philosophy. Hence, looking back on that union he could not see it except as an unstable hybrid bound to fall apart in due time. It appeared to work for a time, as philosophy was discovering new horizons for itself in which to exercise its reign beyond the purely human. At first, reason did not take note of the restriction imposed on it by faith. It accepted it in exchange for the broader scope now opened before it. But when philosophy eventually came back to its own postulate, namely, that it is the act of rational contemplation that constitutes the divine life in human being, an act that has its beginning and its end in ourselves, or that metaphysics alone, seen as the complete science of being, not only contains being but also procures it and salvation as well, the union was bound to fall apart. The medieval equilibrium between philosophy and theology could only be provisional. "The philosophical spirit that engendered Scholasticism is the very spirit that took arms against it" (1896a, 57). It was a resurgence of Greek rationalism turned against the theology that had tried to absorb it. But, for Blondel, it was a resurgence with a new twist, one that, "in working on itself, will contribute to the progress of Christian philosophy" (1896a, 57). In his view, neo-Scholastic attempts to revive the ancient philosophy in defense of Scholasticism could only be misguided and philosophically ineffective, not to say deleterious to the Christian Spirit as such. What was needed was a resurrection in philosophy rather than a mere revival of its ancient form.

Put in the simplest of terms, Scholasticism had taken in a matter that was not acceptable by ancient reason and a form that was unable to contain its object. The two were bound to fall apart and rise in opposition to one another. Attempts to keep them together were perilous to either side, in the way that each one was conceived. The break came with Luther, who repudiated the intellectualism of Aristotle and of Scholasticism for the sake of faith, thus setting reason free to run its own course in Protestantism. In his own way, Luther was authenticating "the very form under which rationalist reason could pretend to its absolute empire, as if it were all or nothing" (1896a, 58). Blondel does not mention Hegel here, but if we call to mind his understanding of the evolution of Spinozism as presented by Delbos, we can see how Hegel, who himself viewed Luther as a precursor for his own spirit, appears as the culmination of the general sweep of ideas Blondel presents here. The difference between Hegel and Blondel in the interpretation of this sweep is that, while Hegel was inclined to absorb Christianity in his philosophy, Blondel was to argue for a total transcendence of the supernatural in historical and positive Christianity as the necessary culmination of philosophy itself.

Here in the *Lettre,* he insists on how philosophy was to fare as a result of its breakup with faith and revelation in the Christian context. This is where we begin to see how the presence of the Christian idea, unrecognized at first and repressed, continued to exert its influence in this philosophy, once Scholasticism had opened reason up to the immensity of the horizons of faith. The situation in philosophy could never again be what it had been before: "By the mere fact that emancipated philosophy tends, as it had previously, to maintain that thought is what is most divine and that it has within itself its own sufficiency, it is already no longer as it had been. It proposes for itself, unbeknownst to itself, an ideal that is not from it alone" (1896a, 58). From this follows a series of errant trials and attempts to reach its promised land wherein, while vindicating its full independence and transforming itself according to a law of autonomy, "it is in reality wrought by the Christian idea against which it is struggling: in triumphing, it comes back to [this idea], but quite otherwise than it had left it, vanquished in its apparent victory, victorious in its apparent defeat" (1896a, 59). What was happening in effect, according to Blondel, was a reworking and a transforming, according to its own internal law of development, of a rationalism that had been unduly submissive under Scholasticism and had now become illegitimately hostile to religion. How does he see this as having happened in modern philosophy?

First he contrasts the point of departure in the sixteenth century with the point of arrival in his own time, or in his own philosophy, as he had come to understand this process with Delbos. On the one hand philosophy sets out to take over everything without any thought of restricting itself or criticizing itself. It claims to attain objects in themselves and to apprehend truth to the point of complete identity with being and life. On the other hand we later find philosophy tending more and more to specify, to criticize, and to limit itself. "This is to say, it no longer takes knowledge as a complete substitute for effective existence; of its own accord, thought, even if as thought it were adequate to reality or identical with being, is no longer sufficient to make us equal either to ourselves or to things" (1896a, 59). In other words, if every speculative system can be surpassed by a progress in speculation, the only doctrine that can have any definitive truth at its core is one that does not look for its sufficiency within itself. Theoretical solutions can be satisfying only insofar as they call for something other than themselves in manifesting the necessity and in defining the conditions of a life and of a thought that are fully consistent with their internal law. This kind of insufficiency could be found even in Hegelian philosophy, as it wonders which way the World Spirit will move after the embodiment it has taken in modern rationalist society.

In going from the first to the last of these two forms of philosophy many intermediate steps had to be taken. In reviewing them Blondel finds both an immense human effort of elaboration of ideas and a certain divine wisdom and providence leading the way, something to be taken advantage of. Once philosophy had broken away from theology at the beginning of the modern era, without yet having the idea of supplanting faith, it did not yet understand that, without theology alongside it, it would have to replace the supernatural with some other kind of transcendent. It naïvely applies itself to the study of the natural order, to the scientific knowledge of things by a critique of immediate sensation, as in Bacon, and to the discovery of the power that comes with knowing the hidden laws of nature. Inspired by its own internal movement, it reestablishes itself in the world of metaphysics and flatters itself with inventing "the true method to arrive at the knowledge of all things the spirit is capable of," as in Descartes, still claiming to remain on the level of human being as human, and not yet attacking faith, but already claiming as its empire not only nature but also the whole of thought, will, and action. Finally, with Spinozism it reveals its pretension to a total and absolute hegemony by secularizing religion itself and offering from within itself the complete equivalent of faith so as to lead human being to beatitude on its own resources, without noticing that such a method of immanence gives rise not only to a monism such as that of Spinoza, but also to one that is at the same time a cryptic anthropomorphism, as Schelling had remarked with regard to Spinoza.

At this point in the *Lettre*, Blondel continues with a brief summary of the evolution of Spinozism, now viewed as the embodiment of philosophy, through Kant and Schelling, much as we have seen him do in his discussion of

Delbos's book, down to the phenomenism of Taine, which supposedly tries to remain totally non-committal in matters of ontology and transcendence, but which still claims to have the last word in its scientific and phenomenist conception of things, intent only on eliminating everything it does not find within itself, and on grounding this exclusion, or this principle of contradiction, on the absolute of a truth and a being fully possessed, contrary to its own implicit supposition. What Blondel sees as the upshot of this movement in modern thought is the same general conclusion he had previously come to with Delbos concerning this kind of thought; it is a movement that "does not cease considering these states of consciousness or these internal phenomena as realities, immanent realities to be sure, yet realities that are complete and sufficient in their kind, so that it never takes note of something else that is essential, namely, how in our most immanent thought and action there is something heterogeneous or transcendent to the knowledge we have of it, something that is the very logical condition for the scientific viewpoint in which it claims to take its stand" (1896a, 63). It is on this heterogeneous or transcendent *something* that Blondel had tried to focus in his Science of Action, a something that he thought science could not supplant with its notion of pure immanence. Here in the *Lettre* he only says that science or philosophy is not called to penetrate this something, whether to affirm it or to deny it; it has only to study the idea of it, with everything that it implies.

What follows from all this, according to Blondel, is that to oppose either the transcendent to the supernatural or the immanent to the transcendent is always to suppose that speculative conclusions are beings or realities equal to life as lived or to thought as act, "realities" that are substituted for actual life and thought, as if knowledge of the given reality were itself the only true reality. Contrary to this view, Blondel maintains that the fundamental principle on which philosophy depends as a speculative science is that the integral knowledge of thought and of life does not supplant and does not equal the action of thinking and of living. "What is the case is that, on the one hand what is immanent to us as living action and thought still remains transcendent to the reflective or philosophical view we have of it, and on the other hand, this philosophical knowledge itself constitutes a phenomenon that is ulterior and transcendent with respect to what it represents" (1896a, 64). In other words, the *action* of life and of thought transcends what we can conceive of it philosophically, but what we do conceive as merely given in it thereby leads us to ever-expanding horizons. Instead of opposing these contrasting terms, or wanting to have either one or the other play the role of reality to the other's role of appearance, we must see them as solidary in the surge of action and "determine under what conditions we come to conceive that they are equally realized such as they are, both as constituting our knowledge and also as constituted by our knowledge" (1896a, 64).

This is the determination of the interplay between thought and action that

Blondel had tried work out at the end of *L'Action,* with his philosophy of the supernatural, by showing how philosophy itself has to limit its own competence and to insert its own dynamism into the total determinism it studies. To do this is not to undermine philosophy as a science or take away from its universal competence from the standpoint of its *method of immanence.* It is rather to point out how it can find within itself what surpasses it or, as Blondel calls it, "a transcendent immanent." In showing that our immanent action remains transcendent to any equilibrium provisionally attained by it, and to any knowledge extracted from it, he was furnishing philosophy with both a matter and a form that it was lacking before, the only matter and the only form that in their mutual adaptation could constitute it in accordance with its essence as universal philosophy.

On the one hand, "its precise object and its ever present ideal is to determine the content, the internal relations, and the exigencies of action, without ever claiming to satisfy its demands even when it defines them rigorously according to a law of necessity. On the other hand, inasmuch as it is not satisfied with itself, it contributes to stimulate the movement from which it has issued, thus opening before it an infinite field for accomplishment, without losing the benefit of its reserve with regard to the mystery of action and of its precise conclusions in the face of the exigencies of life" (1896a, 66).

In saying all this, Blondel clearly had his own philosophy of the supernatural in mind, in which he thought he was resolving the fixed oppositions he found in earlier forms of thought, so as to make them compatible at once with both scientific philosophy and Christian philosophy. Only at the end of this evolution of modern thought was the ancient conception of the hegemony or the *autarkeia* of philosophical reason finally overcome by the progress of reason itself to heights that it could not anticipate by itself.

In the *Lettre,* Blondel was thus making the case for what he had said earlier in defense of his effort as essentially philosophical, but as an effort to expand the scope of philosophy so as to include the idea of the supernatural, as well as of the natural, within the limits of its competence, something that no one had done before precisely as he did, not by reducing faith or the actual content of religion to a philosophical concept, but by bringing philosophy to recognize its own limitations and its own need to face up to what it could conceive only as a necessity beyond itself in the concreteness of action, and beyond its competence to discern as a reflective knowledge.

Here, however, in the *Lettre,* he was making the case for religious thinkers, mainly Catholic, who had their own misgivings with regard to any excessive use of reason, as Blondel knew they would have with regard to his own rational efforts regarding the mysteries of religion, even though these efforts were no longer directed against religion or faith, as the self-enclosed modern rationalism had been earlier. He was not sure these Catholic theologians would welcome his defense, and so in conclusion of his assessment of the evolution of modern reason he proceeds to offer what he thinks will be reassuring remarks for the Catholic conscience as well as for rational speculation at the intersection of exigencies between the two.

The first concluding remark has to do with the function of philosophy, which is to determine the content of thought and the postulates of action, but without proffering the being whose notion it studies, without containing the life whose exigencies it analyzes, and without realizing that which it necessarily conceives as real. Philosophy must indicate that from which it ultimately suspends everything it affirms and, though it is itself a living force and an integrating element of things, it must stop short even before what it requires of itself, keeping in mind that it cannot satisfy its own demands. This critical capacity to limit itself is what is new to philosophy. It presupposes a prodigious integration of thoughts and the accumulated effort of both philosophical reflection and Christian consciousness.

On the other hand, however, given this abstention from any claim to provide an effective solution to its demands, philosophy must not abstain from examining any solution that may be demanded or postulated. It must enter into the study of the most precise phenomena of religious life, no less than it must those of sense perception, for example. As long as it keeps the formal meaning of its conclusions within the limits of its method of immanence, as indicated, it is free to entertain Christian data in the same way as other data without claiming to supplant any of them. In order to be integral according to its own exigencies, it must examine them as part of the integral determinism of action, recognizing that it cannot be sufficient unto itself in any respect with regard to action, least of all with respect to the supernatural. "For were it ideally parallel or identical with the real or the effected act and the being thought of, it must always keep in mind that in us concrete thought and lived life are transcendent in relation to our immanent knowledge itself of the transcendent and even of the supernatural" (1896a, 67). The example for doing just this is to be found in Part V of *L'Action*, in which Blondel had explored the idea of the supernatural, not just as a hypothetical necessity for bringing human action to completion, but also as implying a necessity for revelation, for a mediator, and for a religious practice.

Finally, in this function of relating to one another all the aspects of the integral determinism of human action, philosophy is not reduced to a merely explanatory role. It is also in a position to pass some judgment, without recourse to any criterion outside of itself. "In the transcendent of immanent thought and action, it finds an internal principle of absolute judgment; and in the interconnection that makes of the phenomena it studies a solidary whole, it discovers a source capable of communicating to all its conclusions a character of necessity" (1896a, 67). This is in keeping with its scientific character based on a logic deeply ingrained in our will, whose actual exigencies it has only to discern as implied in what we think and as posited in what we do effectively. Without going into the diversity of details and appearances of individual lives, it can show how each human destiny forms a unique problem, and it can make manifest the necessity from which hangs the solution as a whole. "Without this character of internal necessity, which, in expressing the ultimatum to which we subordinate ourselves in acting, defines at the same time our true responsibility, the severity of the sanction could not be justified" (1896a, 68). What Blondel is referring to here is the idea of the sanction of eternal punishment that is attached to the gratuitous gift of the supernatural, if refused, as understood in Catholic teaching. This, he thinks, has to be justified philosophically in a way that so far only his philosophy can do, by affirming that there is something necessary in moral and religious life, without compromising the meaning of freedom and grace, and by admitting the punishments of this life and the next without violating the notion of equity and goodness.

In saying all this, Blondel knows that he will be accused of exaggerating the achievements of modern philosophy. He defends himself by saying that we cannot go on ignoring these achievements. Nor can we go only halfway with them. The advantages that can be derived from them are for the benefit, not only of philosophy itself, in specifying its scientific character and its sovereign autonomy in its own proper domain, but also of the Christian spirit, "if we understand that these advantages are due to the hidden power and as it were the constraint of the Christian idea" (1896a, 69). After having indicated the progression of free thought under this influence of the Christian idea, it remains for him to show what the Christian conception itself now humanly owes to this free philosophy, through a mutual perfecting of religious consciousness or conscience by the progress of free philosophy.

Far then from accusing modern philosophy of being tendentious, it has been necessary to reproach it with not going far enough in the direction that it has been tending. If it becomes fully consequent with its principles, its conclusions can be seen as quite fitting for the Christian spirit or, better still, as opening us up to that spirit, of which Blondel must say that, "if it has been a cause of progress, it is itself in progress in humanity" (1896a, 69). This aspect of human progression in the Christian Spirit is usually overlooked by theologians. But Blondel wants to insist on it as a philosopher. No matter how divergent philosophy and theology may otherwise appear, if we give each of these two disciplines of the human spirit more reason than they imagine for themselves in separation from one another, we come to a harmonious and solid understanding of both, not by compromise or by suppression of one discipline or the other, but by a more profound coming together of contrasting aspects, several of which Blondel proceeds to explicate.

(1) The first has to do with the very use of reason in either philosophy or

theology. Insofar as, faithful to its method of immanence, philosophy limits its bearing to the internal determinism of thought and action without encroaching on the real order or supplanting it, it enables us to understand that analytical or explanatory formulas do not exhaust their object or that there is more to life than what is contained in science or in abstract reason. As such this method leaves open a place where dogma or a higher teaching can govern thought and life, and speak in the absolute. In this sense, even when they speak of the natural order, theological teachings have a bearing and a meaning that is quite different from what can be said in philosophy, without being merely superimposed. It is not that there is no reasoning in theology. It is rather that reasoning there starts from very different principles than those from which it starts in philosophy, much as reason starts from different principles in the positive sciences.

Blondel speaks of a certain supernatural empiricism, a kind of human reasoning that starts from dogmas and revealed data that are like an experience of the divine, in order to constitute a sacred science. There, in theology, reason is properly an *ancilla theologiae*, a handmaid of theology, as it is also in positive science a handmaid of nature and science. But as such, theology is applying reason to elements that are foreign to philosophy, leading to truths that are distinct from those that are only rationally obtained even when they seem to cover the same matter. In contrast to this, philosophy, bereft of any such alliance with a foreign teaching, consists not in the heteronomous application of reason to a matter or an object, given either by sense or by revelation, but in the autonomous application of reason to itself. As such it is not an intellectual realism in juxtaposition to the legitimate objectivism of faith or in competition with it. It is simply a rational activity in its own right, different from the rational activity of theology, which, as autonomous, is concerned with the totality of ideas as determined in relation to human action. What Blondel says about the "theological rational" here as distinct from the "philosophical rational" is similar to what Aquinas had said about theology in distinguishing *sacra doctrina* as a science from philosophy at the beginning of the *Summa Theologiae* and the various Books of the *Summa contra Gentiles*, without confusion between the two orders but also without separation. But what Blondel finds among the theologians of his day is a certain confusion concerning the legitimate exigencies of philosophy, similar to the confusion that existed in the seventeenth century between the rational in the physics of a Galileo and the rational in theology in keeping with orthodox teaching.

What follows from this formal distinction between philosophy and theology as rational disciplines is a broadening of the scope or the competence of philosophy with regard to the transcendent and the supernatural. As long as it was thought that philosophy absorbed the reality of what it knew, it could not be thought of as touching Christian dogma, nor even as studying the simple notion of the supernatural or of revealed practices, without taking them over or denaturing them, as happened, for example, in Protestant countries. In saying this Blondel surely had Hegel in mind, who attempts to absorb Christian dogmas as representations in his conceptualizing of absolute knowing. However, Blondel was also thinking of how philosophy had been kept at bay from religion in Catholic countries like France, thus keeping away from the living thought of philosophy the question of "the whole of man," or of what he earlier referred to as the religious problem. Was this to say that Catholicism was incompatible with the philosophical spirit? Quite the contrary, Blondel thinks: as long as we do not reduce philosophy to a theological rationalism and as long as we do not stop at certain provisional forms of philosophy now dead and left behind by an ulterior development of thought. Catholicism has been the invisible advocate of a further development of thought "and a more profound labor of reason, by opposing any attempt to find a proper equilibrium anywhere short of where it should be found ultimately, that is, in God or the supernatural, and by constraining philosophy to continue searching for itself long enough to find itself as scientifically constituted" (1896a, 72).

This is an intricate way of saying that the method of immanence, previously described for philosophy as having to do only with the necessary, and not with the merely possible or the real itself in human action, had emerged only in relation to Catholicism with its doctrine concerning the strictly supernatural, as both gratuitous on the part of God and necessary on the part of human being. This is what made philosophy truly consequent with itself in raising the question of the supernatural. Beyond the point where certain vague religious doctrines were taken to be philosophical, there came the doctrine of Catholicism concerning the supernatural from which it appeared that philosophy had nothing to learn, but from which, at least as now conceived by Blondel, it not only could take up very precise questions of properly Christian conscience without denaturing them, but it also had "to examine them in the same spirit as all the questions whose close interconnection make up one and the same determinism" (1896a, 72-73). This is why, at the end of his dissertation, Blondel had gone into the philosophy of the supernatural, and why he was now thinking of philosophy as a whole as having to do so. What he arrived at was not a dogma of Catholic faith, but something rational, consonant with that faith and necessary from the standpoint of philosophy, the ultimate aspiration in reason from which human thought and action should not shrink. Thus philosophy and theology became more intimately linked than ever, but without confusion and without any false separation between the two.

(2) The second of the contrasting aspects between philosophy and theology discussed by Blondel has to do with the way theologians have a tendency to overstep their legitimate authority when they pronounce themselves in philosophy. Blondel admits a certain certitude and fixity in what is to be held by faith and in what can be derived rationally from the revealed truths in a theological

synthesis. But he does not admit that this authorizes the theologian to say whatever he wants in a rational pseudo-theology and to condemn as heretical whoever does not go along with him in the more mutable science of philosophy. What pertains only to human science, even in theology, must not be confused with what is of divine inspiration. Nor must the theologian think that, when he begins to speak philosophically, he is the only one to know the truth even about God or the supernatural, or that he automatically knows it better than philosophers. In matters of human science, including his own, the theologian must allow for legitimate differences of opinion and deal with them in a properly philosophical manner. In a time of confusion and ignorance concerning religion, the theologian's primary task is more one of exposing the logical synthesis of Catholic dogma in its determinate unity and its rich simplicity, leaving philosophy to those who are more familiar with its exigencies as a human science, or at least making sure that, when he speaks of the aspirations of human thought he speaks only as a philosopher, subject to critical evaluation like any other, without any admixture of his role as a theologian.

(3) In a third point of contrast, Blondel speaks of how reason can be used in theology as well as in philosophy, but in a way that is different from philosophy and that leaves ample room for philosophy's more autonomous development. Theology as a discipline is constituted by uniting reason and faith in order to explain what is said in Revelation and organize a certain system of demonstrations. As such it gives rise to a certain theological rationalism surpassing philosophy, as exemplified in St. Thomas Aquinas, although not in the pseudo-philosophical rationalism of more recent Scholasticism. In being joined to the objects of Revelation, reason is elevated to a higher perfection. In its theological use it gives rise to what Blondel calls the philosophy of faith and the rationalism of the supernatural. Nevertheless, granted the legitimacy of this theological use, reason does not cease to have its own proper use in philosophy, which is of a different order, requiring a different method, with its own freedom to intervene in the discussion of the serious problems of life, its own initiative, and its own duty to renew its theories through an effective progress of its definitions.

(4) This leads to a fourth point of contrast, where even a philosophy of the supernatural is seen as more variable and subject to discussion in its definition of the conditions it judges necessary for solving the problem of human destiny, and as reaching to a wider diversity of human spirits in their conduct of life, including many who have no inkling of a Revelation. In contrast to this variability, however, for those who have faith in a Revelation, it is appropriate to have more precise ideas of defined teachings and obligatory practices. The status of believers in a Revelation is bound to be different from that of non-believers. Hence there has to be a certain openness with regard to the way the spirit may blow in the concrete operation of different souls, at the same time as a certain

rigor and necessity with regard to the letter of the law and religious practices as an authentic condition for salvation, or as a necessity of effective Mediation and Redemption.

(5) The fifth point of contrast leads directly into what would become a key issue in the modernist crisis that was soon to erupt into the open. On the one hand, inasmuch as philosophy does not penetrate the real mystery of action or the secret relations of the human soul even with itself, it is never in any position to judge anyone absolutely on the basis of merely external forms of thought and life. It cannot know what obstacles are encountered interiorly, or what light may be given. It only knows that faith and salvation are accessible to all, but it does not know under what conditions *in concreto*. Philosophy is not in the business of fixating any of these conditions: "It is the merit and the beauty of the philosophical method of immanence to place in each one what each one is to be judged by" (1896a, 80). Each one is the law to himself. However rigorous this internal judgment may have to be in itself, the method of immanence allows for a complete liberality of spirit and heart in the order of truths that determine our destiny in accordance with the Gospel injunction: Thou shalt not judge.

On the other hand, however, the same method enables us to understand the formal necessity of raising the religious problem in human action and of coming to a solution for it. "What conscience invincibly requires to remain sincere and consequent with itself is not optional" (1896a, 81). Moreover, not only do these religious exigencies of thought impose themselves indispensably in accordance with an internal determinism, but also, once they have been positively determined and practically recognized from the exterior, these formal exigencies become necessary in a way that is material and literal. "It would not be legitimate to look for a new meaning in dogmas or a broader significance in precepts, or to gloss over established laws of discipline, or to interpret, according to the caprices of an individual devotion, as if they were simple inspirations of a particular consciousness projected symbolically into facts, the authentic signs and the positive exigencies of the supernatural order" (1896a, 81). Blondel quotes the First Vatican Council in support of his position, but while insisting on a complete liberality of spirit in refusing to judge others in their internal forum, he is also prepared to condemn "all the accommodations of liberalism" (1896a, 82) that would water the exigencies of the supernatural order down to merely human proportions. It is the elaboration of this contrast that will lead him to take issue with both modernists and extrinsicist defenders of Christian tradition in his article on History and Dogma eight years later, in 1904.

(6) The sixth point of contrast focuses on another aspect of how judgment may or may not intervene with regard to the outcome of human action. Philosophy shows how the core of anyone's moral being somehow escapes human judgment and its insufficient clarity of thought, so that we can never be absolutely certain of the moral worth of any action in the concrete. Rules and con-

demnations, even those that might be divinely inspired, always remain abstract and general, so that we can never be completely lucid as to the merit or the culpability of any particular action of another or of ourselves, leaving us always open to the duty of loving and respecting the other as well as ourselves, even when a particular case has been denounced as a scandal.

By the same token, however, philosophy also obliges the religious apologist to consider himself no less at issue than the non-believer in the argument for the necessity of raising the question of religion and of giving an answer to it. "What is at issue is not just a theoretical adherence of the mind to a dogma external to us, but the practical introduction of a vivifying truth into our heart and our conduct, a truth that, better practiced, is better known, and better known, is more demanding as it becomes more liberal and more helpful" (1896a, 83). For Blondel the task of apologetics was as much a work of personal purification in the acceptance of the supernatural in one's life as it was an attempt to explain one's religious stance to others in a way that was scientifically acceptable. This was already clear from his own reflection in the *Carnets Intimes* on what he was doing in writing his dissertation on *Action*. In the *Lettre*, it is now understood as an integral part of his method of immanence. "A truly philosophical apologetic is the work made visible, the permanent and personal work of an internal conversion. In short, as it was necessary to condemn the false separatism that isolates the religious problem from philosophical problems, it is necessary to condemn the false separatism that isolates the speculative work of thought from the ascetical efforts and the laborious teaching of life" (1896a, 84). In this appropriation of the religious problem as part of philosophy, Blondel finds a manifest progress for his own Christian consciousness as well as that of any other.

(7) In the seventh point of contrast, Blondel comes back to the scientific character of the method of immanence. As such it is only an indirect way of dealing with the supernatural. It does not try to include any revealed data, or to set itself up in juxtaposition to such data, by restricting itself to a simplistic or merely descriptive inventory of heterogeneous elements. Using a complex and binding argument, it runs through the flow of one and the same determinism that seeks to reintegrate in our willed action all that is posited and postulated by the spontaneous thrust of our action. Instead of offering the reality of a solution to the religious problem, it has only to show that we cannot avoid the problem legitimately and with impunity. In doing so, however, the philosophical conclusions it arrives at with regard to the religious problem, by reason of the reservation just mentioned, express a certain necessity and constitute an apodictic demonstration. This is more than what earlier methods of apologetics had done, starting as they did from more realist or ontological claims. In order not to encroach on the supernatural, such methods had to avoid any directly philosophical study of the notion of the supernatural, and re-

strict themselves to showing the usefulness of revelation by indicating how, without revelation, essential truths concerning human life would be too rarely known, known too late in life, and too intermixed with errors, stock arguments that go back to Aquinas and, through him, to Maimonides. Through the method of immanence, Blondel could now understand his philosophical conclusions as expressing internal exigencies of conscience, and therefore as apodictic, including the total religious postulate of action. Without encroaching in any way on the reality of the supernatural, these consequences follow from proofs that are precise and scientifically necessitating for any rational being.

(8) From the notion of a certain necessity of the supernatural in human action, there follows an eighth contrast concerning the relation between the natural and the supernatural. In considering the supernatural only insofar as the notion of it is immanent in us, and in viewing natural reality as transcendent to the knowledge we have of it, philosophy helps us understand better how we cannot do without nature as well as how we cannot hold ourselves to it. The human order has its part in all there is, and has its sufficiency in nothing. Our natural being is indestructible and, in its radical insufficiency, human action remains coextensive to the action of God in the order of the supernatural. Blondel quotes St. Bernard to this effect on the relation between grace and free will. At the same time, however, it follows that human being can have a certain power over God, can say *no* to him as well as *yes* to letting him in. "The supernatural vocation of man implies that sin is murderous of God" (1896a, 88), at least in the sense that the Savior would have to suffer and die and that this death would have to be willingly and lovingly acknowledged. Moreover, "for this necessary and freely redemptive oblation to be efficacious in each person, each one has to consent to it and cooperate in the salutary expiation which, sufficient and superabundant in itself, is incomplete in us without us" (1896a, 88). Human being is not only radically incapable of achieving its supernatural ends by itself; it also has the truly tremendous power of taking advantage of God by choosing either to die, without being annihilated, or to follow him in life. Such are the consistency and dignity of human being in its extreme infirmity with respect to the supernatural.

(9) Finally we come to the ninth contrast, which follows from this momentous power to choose in the face of the supernatural. Left to itself, human being remains closed to the higher life, whose source it does not have within itself. Yet if it is not changed by it, at least according to the Catholic teaching Blondel is reflecting on, it is condemned. This is what appears most shocking to the modern consciousness in the Catholic notion of the supernatural. But in this Blondel finds the proper mark, from the standpoint of the concepts whose interconnections alone philosophy has to study, and from the standpoint of the absolute distinction between the natural and the supernatural. In the ultimate alternative one is faced with, before God or the supernatural, the opposed solu-

tions of *yes* or *no* are not symmetrical. The *yes* lets in a surplus that is infinitely superior to what the *no* brings, which results in a positive failing to achieve one's destiny. This is what philosophy can understand of the distinction between the supernatural and the natural.

This same understanding, however, can also give us a more profound view of the connection and the harmony between the two orders. Insofar as human being has its part in all there is and its sufficiency in none of it, its acts cannot find their adequation by themselves. The counterpart of this in the totality of experience is that perhaps we cannot attain being in anything without going at least implicitly through the one who, as the origin and the bond of all there is, is the universal *Réalisant,* the one who makes everything real. It could be thought that this universal "realizer" is nothing more than God as creator. But Blondel has something more in mind, in this context of a philosophy of the supernatural.

In *L'Action* he had spoken generally of the necessity of a Mediator, having decided halfway through the redaction to stop using the name of Christ formally. Here, in the *Lettre*, where he is addressing theologians as well as philosophers, he reintroduces the name of the Word Incarnate in order to show how philosophy might incline to go to one side rather than the other in the theological dispute over the "motive" for the Incarnation, whether it was intended only in view of a reparation for original sin or whether it was intended as part of the original plan of creation to include the mystery of the Man-God.

Theologians had different arguments for coming down on either side of this dilemma. But Blondel saw a philosophical reason for coming down on the second side of this dilemma, as a condition for understanding the integral order of things. If a simple decree of creation from the First Cause is not enough to account for how we conceive of sensible phenomena or elementary physical existence as real, and if we are unable to complete our action or to remedy our faults, or even to have a vivid and real idea of God, without requiring a Mediator, then it would seem that philosophy would require something distinct both from nature and from God as its creator, in order to conceive the effective realization of the integral order of things, which for Blondel would have to be the humanity of Christ.

Thus, after having set aside all questions of fact or of persons, in order to define the notion of the supernatural, Blondel is brought back by his method to the necessity of considering under its most precise form the need for the concrete reality of the Word, the necessity of "preparing in this one point, that only the philosopher can reach, the insertion of the historical apologetic, and of justifying the necessity for human being to study, to accept, to make live within oneself one fact among all others, the divine fact of Christianity. And thus this sublime postulate of philosophical reason would be in accord with the most human of sciences, with history, as well as with the highest teaching of theology" (1896a, 90-91). Thus, by showing how philosophy has to relate to the concrete of historical actuality, Blondel fulfils his own apologetic intention as he originally conceived it in the face of the philosophical indifference to religion in general, or to the historical Christ in particular, an indifference he had encountered at the École Normale Supérieure, but he does so in a way that was strictly philosophical, and without confusion with either history or theology, as he would try to make clearer later on in arbitrating between the objective extrinsicism of certain theologians and the subjective historicism of modern exegetics in reading the Gospel stories of the life and teaching of Jesus, by means of the traditional way of joining History and Dogma.

What remains for him to do in the *Lettre* is to show how the conflict between rationalism and Catholicism can be resolved to the common advantage of both philosophy and Christian consciousness, in the sense that both fundamentally call for one another in their integral development, instead of being opposed to one another. What Blondel sees is a certain reconciliation between the idea of philosophy and the Christian idea, marking an end to the conflict between the two in the last four or five hundred years, but a reconciliation in which the Christian idea is not absorbed in philosophy and philosophy is not absorbed in the Christian idea even as it treats of the Christian idea. What lies dead on the battlefield at the end of this struggle is neither the idea philosophy should have of itself nor the Christian idea, but only a certain idea of philosophy that one might identify with Spinozism or Hegelianism in modern times, but that Blondel identifies with the idea that he thought the Scholastics had borrowed from the ancient Greeks, as explained earlier, the idea of human reason divinized and the idea of a certain naïve realism, at once ontological and intellectual, followed by a certain self-sufficiency in metaphysics that tended to reduce being or what there is in action to our thought of it. This was the idea of philosophy that he thought the neo-Scholastics were trying to revive, not realizing that it was the enemy of the Christian idea, and that he thought of, not only as having come to an end in modern philosophy, but also as simply false philosophy. By the same token, what was also dead was the middle term through which that ancient idea of philosophy had been coupled with the Christian idea, the middle term, or the lack thereof that Blondel had criticized earlier in the *Lettre*.

What survived or, better still, what triumphed in this reconciliation was a new idea of philosophy, the one that Blondel had opposed to the indifferent or the anti-religious attitude he had found in the University, and the one that he had just shown had emerged under the secret influence of the Christian idea present in modern philosophy ever since the breakup of the unstable synthesis of the Middle Ages. What Blondel saw was that exclusive rationalism, or what he also calls bastard philosophism, eventually comes to realize its own limitation in a way that is quite in conformity with the profound exigencies of Christianity. To oppose these latter-day transformations of philosophy, as some

Christian apologists were doing, is to labor against those who are laboring on the side of the Christian spirit and opening up new avenues for it. "It has taken the whole of a slow and laborious evolution of thought to open up the truthful perspective, to engender the only method that allows for the constitution of integral philosophy in integral Christianity" (1896a, 92). It would be a mistake to want to restore what is now dead from the old School and to fall once again under the twofold criticism "that killed Christian pseudo-philosophy with a metaphysics of transcendence and that killed rationalist pseudo-philosophy with the doctrine of immanence, itself surpassed" (1896a, 92).

In writing this, Blondel has in mind the kind of total transposition of philosophical questions that had originally shocked Brunschvicg as a philosopher upon reading *L'Action* in 1893. Catholics could find some comfort in the kinds of philosophical conclusions he had arrived at in the dissertation. But in the *Lettre* Blondel wants to insist that these conclusions have to be understood in the light of the method or the way they are arrived at, which is not as easy or as simple as some sympathizers were supposing. In other words, they had to be understood as a matter of philosophy taken as rational science, and not just as a matter of psychology or of accommodation to Christian ideas. Failure to appreciate the rigorousness of this method should not give rise to any vague fears and suspicions. For the method also meets with the most serious exigencies of the Catholic idea of the supernatural as necessary for human salvation. In fact, Blondel insists, it is truly philosophical only by meeting these Catholic exigencies, so that, far from being considered only an outlaw in the world of philosophy, Catholicism should be seen as the only truly rational form of religion.

Blondel was very demanding of philosophers as well as of Christians. His was not a vague general philosophy of religion. It was a Catholic philosophy, indeed a French Catholic philosophy. The kind of philosophy of religion he found in German Protestantism was not rigorous enough for him. It was carried along too quickly by the swiftness of its logic. The agreement it had reached with a certain precarious philosophism was still too hasty and easy. If a truer philosophy of religion was slower to appear in France, it was because it had to contend with the "properly Catholic idea" (1896a, 94), which includes a necessity of the supernatural and its binding obligation on the human will, if it is offered. For Blondel, however, this proved to be an advantage for philosophy itself by forcing it to be more rigorous in its exploration of the notion of religion as something other than philosophy in human action, and as something properly supernatural, that is, as something the source of which is not in human nature alone. To do this he had to expand the scope of philosophy as it had come to be understood in France at the end of the nineteenth century, but he was also able to give philosophy a greater autonomy of its own in exploring, not just the idea of human existence as such, but also the Christian idea as immanent in the human, without betraying its radical transcendence. From this new way of philosophizing would come his later work both in the Trilogy on *Thought, Being,* and *Action,* and in the two volumes on *Philosophy and the Christian Spirit.* But many more things were to happen to him in this new conception of philosophy for both philosophers and Christians before any of this could come to fruition.

The Separation of Philosophy from Religion in Descartes

Blondel finished working on the *Lettre* on June 8, 1896, much relieved after this intense intellectual effort. "I have to breathe a little," he writes in his diary, "and refresh myself in the life of the heart and of piety" (1966b, 58-59). This is the life he always had to reflect on as a philosopher. The courses for the year were drawing to their end. But Blondel was not yet ready to return to Quincy for the summer. Though he does not mention it in his diary, he must also have been working on another article at this time, on "The Christianity of Descartes," which the editor of *La Revue de Métaphysique et Morale* had requested of him for a special issue on Descartes in July 1896. Knowing Blondel's own orientation as a philosopher toward Christianity, the editor thought his view of Descartes's orientation might be of some interest to readers, especially since Pascal's negative reaction to Descartes on the question of religion was well known.

Blondel was pleased to be asked to participate in this forum of philosophers. It was a sign that he was coming to be accepted as one. He did not disappoint the editor or the readers of the *Revue.* He argues that Descartes was sincerely a man of faith as well as a man of reason, but that we cannot be certain of this merely from the external circumstances of his life or from any explicit protestations on his part under circumstances where anything less would have troubled the kind of tranquility he so ardently wished to preserve for himself in his contentious age. Blondel argues that the case must be made from an internal critique of the Cartesian system itself.

In making this case, however, he brings out how Descartes kept his faith in the Infinite separate from what he thought he could do with reason alone. For Descartes the Infinite was reserved for God alone, something pertaining to the divine understanding that the human understanding could not fathom. His was an agnostic conception of the Infinite, but one accompanied by a rationalist conception of the scientific method, without any connection between the two, except for the fact that the idea of God was used quite positively as a necessary ground for the kind of positive science he was looking for in the world. It is this transcendent immanence of the Infinite in Descartes's system that assures us of the sincerity of his faith in God, but it is the same immanence that also allows him to think as if there were no God in his system and as if a human being were sufficient unto itself, without ever having to think of God in himself or as necessary for the perfection of human thought or human will.

Though Descartes thought of his philosophy as more compatible with his Christian faith than the earlier Scholastic admixture of Aristotelian physics and metaphysics, he was also instrumental in establishing a certain separation between faith and reason, as well as between intellect and will, and between divine understanding and human understanding, a separation that could not be bridged except by divine revelation. For Descartes, according to Blondel, there could be no thought of entering into the mystery of the supernatural rationally because reason was concerned only with finding its way about in this world.

Blondel was thus reading Descartes with his own method for a philosophy of religion clearly in mind. What he found in Descartes was a genuine believer, but one who showed no concern for thinking through the unity of faith and reason in his life. "The profound deficiency of his Christianity is to have set on one side the absolute mystery that only the will can attain through grace, and on the other the absolute clarity of thought that takes satisfaction in its own complete sovereignty; it is to suppress all rational preparation for faith, all the labor of reason within faith, and all intelligence of faith . . . it is to establish a radical heterogeneity between divine understanding and human understanding, and between our understanding and our will; it is to admit the sufficiency of man purely as man, along with the imperturbability of the Christian in his faith, as if there were no cross-over problems or questions of the soul; it is to juxtapose a double equilibrium with equal fixity, without concern from the heart or thrust from thought where only a constantly moving equilibrium is possible" (1896b, 56).

In one sense, then, by reason of this profound dualism in his thought, Descartes could remain orthodox in his belief. In another sense, however, whenever he felt the necessity to accommodate his reason and his faith to one another or to bring some reasoning to his faith, he found himself at odds with orthodoxy, by reason of the alleged self-sufficiency of his philosophy and science, and the total independence of his ethics. For Blondel himself the intent was instead, not to disconnect the questions of religion from the questions of philosophy and to remain with the constantly moving equilibrium between the two in his life. In this, he thought he was remaining true both to philosophy, which he argued could not be self-sufficient, even in its own terms as it relates to the Infinite, and to his Christian faith.

The Transfer from Lille to Aix-en-Provence

Blondel left Lille that July confident that he was finally being accepted as a philosopher, but little aware of the storm that was brewing on the side of religion from his critique of standard or established methods in apologetics. He returned to Lille in the fall, but only for a month or two. Perhaps by some kind of premonition, on Christmas Eve he reminisces about his visit to Aix-en-Provence with Rose two years earlier, when they were on their way to Rome, not to mention the years he had spent there earlier as a teacher of philosophy at the Lycée. He begins to think that, as the years bring a more vivid consciousness of Christian life and its charms, he will have to "establish a more durable homestead and be more careful in doing God's work," and he prays, with Rose, for the blessing of the newborn Child of "this new era of our life" (1966b, 59). Four days later, he is appointed *Chargé de Cours* at the Faculty of Letters in Aix.

This time he has the feeling that this is the beginning of a more permanent appointment soon to become a full professorship. On January 31, 1897, he gives his inaugural lecture at Aix-en-Provence, "the first offering of his public teaching. Happy to inaugurate this teaching here in this city that I know and that I love as an adoptive homeland and where I find old friends, whose loyalty is already ten years old" (1966b, 59-60). So sure is he of the permanence of this appointment, that they immediately proceed to buy a house, at 15 rue Roux-Alphéran, into which they move on February 19, and which they have blessed on March 19. This is the house where he was to bring up his family and work until his death, a house that remains in the family to this day, marked by the city of Aix as the residence of Maurice Blondel. The speed with which they could do this is an indication of the financial means the Blondels had at their disposal. Once established in their own house, they could then finish the work of creating an appropriate setting for a good Christian family life already begun in Lille. This is the house also where their two other children were to be born, Elisabeth, on November 12, 1898, and André, on December 26, 1902.

There is not much to be said about the way Blondel brought up his family, except that it was in the very strong Catholic tradition that both he and Rose had received from their families. He fretted over the birth of each one of his children as much as Rose labored. Giving birth was never easy for her and it was in her own maternal home in Quincy that she preferred to do it, leaving Maurice to fret by himself in Aix.

The house in Aix was one befitting a well-to-do bourgeois family, with large well-appointed receiving rooms on the ground floor, a combination library and *bureau de travail*, along with some living space, on the second floor, and other rooms on the upper floors. The family lived mostly on the upper floors, while the ground floor was reserved more for entertaining. There was also a small garden in the back. Later on they would also buy a small house on a hillside in the country about a half-hour's walk away in the direction of Mont Sainte-Victoire. There they would have occasion to see a little-known painter at the time, Paul Cézanne, on some of his many sorties that would make Mont Sainte-Victoire famous. Later on, when working on his *Itinéraire Philosophique* with Frédéric Lefebvre, Blondel would take great delight in showing this *Bastidon* with its magnificent view of Mont Sainte-Victoire and its cypress trees, which he had planted himself, as he had done earlier at Saint-Seine with his uncle Louis, while working on his dissertation.

The management of the household was left largely in the hands of Rose, who would take care of things as well as see to the education of the children. In due time, they would send their children, not to the Lycée or public school, where Blondel himself had gone, but rather to private Catholic schools, officially referred to as *écoles libres*. Blondel had found an apostolic reason for going to secular, largely anti-religious schools for himself. It was to learn how the adversary thinks in order to reach him all the better. But apparently he could find no such reason for sending any of his children to non-Catholic schools. We do not know who had the preponderant say in this decision about schools, Rose or Maurice. But we do know that later on, in an evaluation, one of Blondel's deans would complain that he was not sending his children to the public school system, but to the rival Catholic school system. The ideological split between the two systems remained throughout most of Blondel's teaching career, notwithstanding his efforts to bridge the gap through irenic rational discourse.

It does not appear that Blondel's wish to continue the intimate diaries of his interior life with Rose, *à deux*, got very far. Nothing of what Rose wrote, if she did write anything, has been published by the family, and the diary form of the journals comes to an end shortly after Elisabeth was born in 1898, after one or two years of relatively sparse entries. On January 17, 1898, he writes: "Let us continue to open ourselves to one another, to profit from one another, to develop one by the other" (1966b, 62). But the couple seem to experience some frustration in doing so, as if Rose felt somehow left out by her husband's efforts to move forward. "Question me more," he adds, "and tell me freely your thoughts, your desires: I cannot always tell what interests you or by what means I could interest you in my preoccupations. I am frequently obliged to meditate at length on problems that are not easy to acquaint you with. And it was one of Abbé Huvelin's anticipations that there would be some stress for us to love one another as if through a cloud that I would never be able to clear from my thought and my brow..." (1966b, 62). Later on that same year he feels the need to force himself to write regularly, when the moment has come after long periods of slow incubation. He feels obsessed by a constant philosophical preoccupation, which is the form of duty and mortification that is imposed on him. At times he feels he should give Rose more time, but then he feels that "he has the obligation to attend to his work of thought and philosophical apostolate" (1966b, 63).

The idea of an intellectual apostolate that led him into philosophy remains with him, and he finds some justification for his concentration on his work in the thought of St. Paul that "the woman should accept that her husband should devote himself directly to the obligations and duties of his state of life, as she herself devotes herself to her husband and her children, without having the reciprocity of affection, which should be perfect, express itself in the same way on one side or the other" (1966b, 63). Thus, Blondel suffers from the tension he feels between himself and his wife, when it seems he is not paying sufficient attention to her or to her task in life, but he accepts it as part of the suffering he must endure as a family man totally devoted to a public spiritual task he cannot entirely share with his wife. He also saw it as a suffering for Rose along with other ailments, from which he too suffered. This was one of the permanent difficulties of his life which he listed later on, in 1909, in some retreat notes, along with the difficulties of his poor health and constantly recurring lassitude, and the difficulties of his life as an educator, a writer, an apologist, where he had to give so much attention to his children and to his students (1966b, 133).

VI

Crisis of Modernity for Catholic Apologetics

Inaugurating a Tenure at Aix

Upon his arrival at the University of Aix, Blondel had a very keen sense of his new duties as a professor of philosophy. With the idea that this was to be a more permanent assignment for him came also a new sense of urgency in meeting the demands of his students and his public audience in Aix. From the damp, swampy climate of Lille in Flanders he had longed for "the sunny brightness of Provence, the light of Attica," as he writes in a letter to his friend and former classmate from Dijon, Maurice Léna, but once installed in his new post, he had to face up to four courses or sets of conferences, not only at Aix, but also at Marseilles, not to mention the countless papers he would eventually have to read, and oral exams he would have to hear. At first he was hardly able to plan a day or two ahead of time what he was to say or do in each lecture.

At Lille, while he was working on his own Discourse on Method, he had given a course on the method of philosophy, as it distinguishes itself from the empirical sciences below, and from religion above it. He had also brought out this concern for method among the philosophers he taught in his course on the history of philosophy, while doing another course on analogy in psychology, logic, and metaphysics. In Aix he decided to start from a more fundamental conception of philosophy as it relates to life in the concrete, for him the true content of philosophy.

In his inaugural lecture he speaks of the joy there is in communicating to other spirits what one thinks is a truth and of the high honor there is in such a mission for a professor of philosophy. His first concern will be, not so much to promote the noble pleasures of thought or to satisfy the simple curiosity of erudition, but rather to expose his own rational convictions for the understanding and critical appreciation of his hearers. Moreover, this role or this action was not to be confined to the purely speculative or intellectual, confined to the study of the conditions of intellectual probity and of properly philosophical method, without reference to life and the way we conduct our life. For him there was no purely speculative or exclusively intellectual action. Born from life, thought returns to life, in order to shed light on it and enrich it with new characteristics, just as it receives in turn lessons from life. The two, thought and life, could not be separated, like two organisms apart from one another, or like two self-enclosed systems. They had to come together, which is why he was proposing to study the actual movement of moral ideas in the present time.

His aim was not to pursue a statistical study of ideas or of the variation of crimes, or to do a history of "virtue" in France, or to figure out whether France was in decadence or not, since it is always difficult and perhaps futile to try to measure the external morality of acts, let alone to judge the degree of internal good will and effort among human beings. All this would not be a good way to enter into the spirit of an age, nor did it correspond to the true historical method Blondel intended to follow. His point was not to look on from the outside, or to judge from on high, or to exclude anything that might contradict a previously adopted system, for that would be to step out of life, which alone is fertile. The true historical method, which he had begun to practice in writing his dissertation and which he had tried to describe in the *Lettre,* on the proper method for proceeding in the philosophy of religion, consisted in discerning the labor of gestation that is forever stirring humanity and to profit from this immense effort, to shed light on it and to foster it toward its true end, even in the doctrines that seem opposed to his own. By entering into the views of different people, as Blondel had done by immersing himself in modern secular philosophy, one could pass through many individual errors, incomplete views, and the particular deficiencies of one spirit or another, only to come out into a broader truth and a richer harmony of thought, for in all of our thoughts and in all of our actions there is always a part that surpasses our intentions and our reflections, and this part, which does not excuse us from personal responsibility, makes it possible for us to progress, to go beyond the decadence of doctrines that may be true, through the apparent and passing triumph of doctrines that may be false. The city of truth is often built of stones that were initially stacked up against it.

We see how Blondel was intending to pursue his own mission of communicating truth in much the same way as he had followed in getting to his new position as professor. In his inaugural lecture he insisted on the rational character of this way, in keeping with the exigencies of the University, which had finally accepted him as a legitimate spokesman, but he made the point of keeping the way systematically open to life and to action, in which more was contained than had yet been brought to light in ideas and thought, or even perhaps could be brought to the light of still-too-human ideas. This way of doing philosophy as a University professor seemed appropriate, not only for his own purposes, but also for the examination of contemporary problems in the thought and the intellectual movements of his day. After a period of disintegration and decomposition through analysis and official dogmatisms of different stripes, he saw an effort emerging toward a new concentration of thought and new tendencies to be brought to completion and to be brought into focus. His ambition as a professor was to summon his hearers to take part in this work of reconstitution, not to reimpose any sort of dogmatism, but rather to take part in the movement of living ideas so as to find the means of thinking and acting in common with others, in freedom and in a union, with independence. All this had to be understood as part of the role the University had to play in the general education of the nation.

In the pursuit of this goal Blondel did not think one could start only from the abstract systems of philosophers. He thought he had to start from the thought of anyone who had experienced the exhilaration of thinking and from the immediate and most accessible knowledge of people, even in approaching the more technical problems of philosophy, in order to stay close to what is simple, living, and practical. In philosophy itself, Blondel found three general attitudes that tended to keep it separate from practical reality. One was the claim that the idea is simply equal to the real, like a static or photographic reproduction of the real, which left nothing more to be thought. This attitude could take the form of realism or idealism, but in either case it could be thought of as a philosophy of the object, of which neo-Thomism was a primary example at the end of the nineteenth century, the neo-Thomism he found too domineering and intolerant of other forms of rational thought. The second attitude was the counterpart of the first, where the idea was thought of as not equal to the real, but rather as the construction of a new reality, a sort of epiphenomenon. This was a philosophy of the subject, but one that drifted into fideism, like a kite cut loose from its string. Third was the agnostic claim that the idea was mystery, a philosophy of universal relativity and positivity.

Each one of these attitudes, according to Blondel, had its own ramifications in the way of thinking of the moral life. If knowledge is equal to the object itself, one is forced into intolerance or materialism. If it is nothing other than itself, one is forced into pure formalism. If it is only relative, one is forced into practical positivism or mysticism. Blondel's idea of philosophy was not that he had to choose one of these attitudes, but rather that he had to reject all of them as artificial solutions to an artificial problem. For him, instead of opposing thought and reality to one another in a sort of fixed relation, one had to consider thought as having issued from life, as in contact with the real, as something real itself, and as preparing new forms of reality. "Wrested from action, which unites us to things and incorporates them to ourselves," as he put it in this unpublished inaugural lecture of 1897, "thought tends to enrich action, to enrich it, and to communicate to it a character that is ever more free, to elevate it above the mechanical impulses and the spontaneous tendencies which it employs and brings into the service of its ideal ends."

On the one hand, knowledge is something more than what is known. What is known within ourselves, in turn, is something more than our knowledge. And there is reciprocal progress and promotion of both thought and life. What we have to understand is that, in the unique series that makes up the drama of our existence and the problem of our destiny, our ideas make up one of the links that is intimately tied to all the links of the chain. Far from keeping us in a closed conception of life, action always has a new element to bring to thought, just as thought has new lights and new obligations to bring to action. The moving circle of the two never stops and is never closed. The task of philosophy, as Blondel understood it, was to enter into this movement in order both to add to it and to receive from it more of the truth it was concerned with.

To be sure, the execution of this task would include criticizing certain forms of thought that fell short of this high goal of truth in life, such as aestheticism, pessimism, positivism, rationalism, socialism, moralism, and so on. But he would do so by showing in each case how a new elaboration of life emerges before us, along with a profound transformation of philosophical consciousness itself, only to lead finally to the problem that has come to dominate more and more and to inspire secretly all others: Where and how can we find the truth necessary for life and the life in conformity with truth? Thus we see how the conception of philosophy that had inspired Blondel in the articulation of his dissertation continued to inspire him in the conception of his task as a professor of philosophy. The only difference between this new moment in his life and the earlier moment was that he no longer felt that he was doing battle against an established idea of philosophy, but rather that he was contributing to the life of the University and thereby of the nation. His role was now more one of initiating people to what was living and vivifying in the thought of those who were working for the common good, a role of mediation and education for the public consciousness, having to give and also to receive a great deal from the collaboration, from the resistances, and from the objections from whatever quarter, in an atmosphere of good faith and sincerity ready to face up to the seriousness of the highest questions one can raise in life.

Blondel's initial appointment in Aix, in December 1896, was as *chargé de cours*, but the understanding was that this was to be followed by further promotions. The next year, in December 1897, he was named adjunct professor, and again one year later, in January 1899, he was named titular professor of philosophy for the University of Aix-Marseilles. This was the only University chair in philosophy in that part of France, which Blondel was to occupy for the next thirty years, and from which he was to oversee the teaching of philosophy for a vast region that included the cities of Nice, Toulon, and Avignon, including even the island of Corsica. Besides the public lectures he inaugurated as early as

January 1897, Blondel was also responsible for giving graduate courses in Marseilles as well as in Aix, and for hearing state exams in philosophy in diverse places, in different parts of southeastern France and in Corsica. It was not until later on, near the end of his career, that he was assigned a *maître de conférences* to assist him in discharging some of these duties as University professor for the region. Needless to say, as he wrote to his friend and former classmate from Dijon, Maurice Léna, Blondel had a lot to do to get his four courses or sets of conferences going in both Aix and Marseilles at the beginning of his first semester, having to wonder for the first time what he would have to say from one day to the next and how he would get the refined society of Aix interested in the kind of "Intellectual Probity" he wanted to pursue with them. Writing from his newly acquired home in February 1897, he could now express a certain relief at having left behind the damp climate of Lille and at finding once again the azure sky of Provence, its verdant foliage, and the cross of Mont Sainte-Victoire.

In his graduate courses, his concern was not just to speak well of philosophy and of philosophers, but also to engage his students in actively philosophizing. He began each class by eliciting their response to what had been spoken of in the preceding class. He would be remembered later on as one with a strong faith in ideas and with a great care for elevating intelligences and forming consciences. His first concern in each course, and even in each class, was to engage his students in the discussion of ideas and not to settle for just storing up phrases in their memory. It was to get them involved in the movement of ideas, and then to nourish and guide the movement forward. He required them, not only to answer specific questions, but also to make presentations in class for their fellow students to respond to. And in addition to all this, he also assigned a regular regime of writing for all his students, which he would read assiduously and comment on quite personally, taking each student at his word.

In his first full year of teaching at Aix, he had a young Jesuit priest, Henri Brémond, sitting in on all his courses. Brémond was doing his final year of spiritual formation, called Tertianship, in Aix, and would become a loyal disciple as well as a regular correspondent with Blondel for years to come, discussing not only the movement of ideas in France and in the Church, but also how Blondel should defend himself against his attackers while promoting his more progressive ideas. Brémond had been quite taken up with the reading of *L'Action* and aspired to developing the spirit that he found in it. A year or two later, Blondel would have another student, Auguste Valensin, who had been enthralled by *L'Action* and who would himself join the Jesuits, following Blondel's recommendation. He too was to become a regular correspondent with Blondel during his long course of studies as a Jesuit, and through him Blondel would come into contact with many other Jesuits, like Pierre Teilhard de Chardin, Gaston Fessard, and Henri de Lubac, all of whom were greatly influenced by Blondel. Through his teaching, Blondel not only touched the minds of his students, but also affected their entire life, opening them up to new dimensions of spirit, much as he had thought he wanted to do when he was thinking of launching himself in his intellectual ministry for both believers and unbelievers. His teaching was his ministry to the spirit of the people who came to hear him as well as read him.

A few years after he was exercising this ministry in Aix-en-Provence, the chair of philosophy in Dijon became vacant once again, as it had during the time when he was still looking for his first appointment. When Blondel heard of this in January 1899, he applied for it with great tribulation, knowing that the University authorities would be reluctant to allow him back so close to home, in a city where his all-too-Catholic family was still very influential. Within the month he found out that Dijon was indeed denied to him. He felt deeply hurt by the decision, not only because he thought of it as unjust, but also because of the pain it would cause his parents. He was even tempted to submit his resignation to the University for a moment, as he wrote to Brémond (1970, 160), but then he thought better of it, realizing that it was only a temptation against the vocation where he thought God still wanted him. One has the suspicion that Blondel was denied the post at Dijon, not only because it was close to his place of origin, but also because it was dangerously close to Paris. From the standpoint of the University administration, it appears to have been thought better to keep him in Aix, where his influence, which was still feared by anti-religious authorities, could be kept at a distance from the intellectual Mecca of France. In any case, Aix is where Blondel was to spend the rest of his career as a teacher, where he would come to be known as the philosopher of Aix.

Impending Clouds of Controversy

During these early years at Aix, however, he had to contend with much more than his new duties as a professor. He had to contend with the intellectual storm that had been stirred by the *Lettre* on apologetics, in addition to the storm stirred by his dissertation. In fact, as Blondel seemed to be finding a certain peace and recognition among his colleagues in philosophy, he was experiencing much greater turmoil and rejection from the side of religion. His somewhat scathing *Lettre* had bruised quite a few egos in the field of apologetics, and they had begun to exact some retribution. Among the latter was, first of all, Blondel's own beloved and much revered teacher, Léon Ollé-Laprune, whose apologetical method had been characterized as lacking in rational rigor. From all indications, Ollé-Laprune, who was getting along in years, was anything but happy over the way his own student had treated him. We know a little of what went on between the two friends through another friend who had been a student of Ollé with Blondel and who had become a priest, Jean Wehrlé, another one of Blondel's many regular correspondents over the years.

In a letter to Blondel dated October 20, 1896, Wehrlé expresses surprise at the degree of hostility he encountered from Ollé when he tried to broach the subject of Blondel's idea of a rigorous apologetics. Ollé was visibly pained and scandalized. Even when Wehrlé tried to express his sympathy by saying such things as, "if Blondel's theory is true," or "Blondel may be wrong," Ollé still appeared to be harsh, almost *méchant*, he who was generally so gentle. The understanding was that, if Blondel was wrong, then one would have to declare an irreducible incompatibility between the teaching of the Church and the necessary exigencies of contemporary thought. Ollé did not want to have Blondel condemned any more than did Wehrlé, but he did think that he should be made to feel he had exceeded appropriate courtesy and said things he should not have said (1969a, 44-45).

It is doubtful that Blondel ever had to confront Ollé as directly with his ideas as Wehrlé did, but there appears to have been some reconciliation between the two in due course. Not only did Ollé not want to have his former student condemned, but he came to his defense against certain attacks, as Madame Ollé-Laprune would later attest, in an interview with *L'univers*, in May 1907, setting the record straight about what her husband had done to protect Blondel against the attacks of a certain preacher named Coubé in 1897. With regard to the authorities in Rome, Ollé is also said to have asked the French Cardinal Perraud to intervene with the Pope on behalf of his friend who, he thought, as many others did, was running the risk of being condemned. For his part, Blondel was later to accept writing the death notice for Ollé, at the request of Ollé's wife and son, where he spoke more positively of his method in a way that, as Delbos would explain later on, transubstantiated the thought of Ollé to make it enter into the more rigorous sort of philosophy that Blondel was advocating (1969b, 509). In the death notice, and in the book that he later wrote on the thought of his former teacher, Blondel more than made up for the offense he had committed against him.

But Ollé's reaction was not to be the most serious problem Blondel brought on himself with his *Lettre* of 1896. While allaying the fears of the University concerning his philosophy of religion, by insisting on the strictly rational aspect of his method, he also antagonized many in the neo-Scholastic or Thomistic camp in philosophy, which he had criticized as inadequate in resolving the philosophical question in the matter of apologetics. This was a reaction that would not be so easily allayed, and which carried a lot more weight in the Church than Ollé-Laprune did, a reaction that not only objected to Blondel's method, but also did not shrink from accusing him of heresy, an accusation that Blondel could not take lightly as a Catholic and as a loyal member of the Church. Blondel now had to face a political problem within the Church in the same way that he had had to face one within the University.

The first and the most serious attack from the neo-Scholastics came from a Dominican, M.-B. Schwalm, O.P., in the September 1896 issue of the *Revue Thomiste*, barely three months after the last installment of the *Lettre* had appeared in the *Annales de Philosophie Chrétienne*, in an article titled "Les illusions de l'idéalisme et leurs dangers pour la foi." In this article Schwalm characterizes Blondel's method as a "Kantian method pushed to its last phenomenist consequences: speculative reason knows that we have ideas, it does not know whether these ideas correspond to anything whatsoever outside of ourselves. It is practice, action, that teaches it the objective truth of what it thinks" (*Revue Thomiste* IV [1896], 413). Schwalm had picked up the Kantian flavor of Blondel's argument, which was pervasive in the philosophy of the University at the time Blondel was a student at the École Normale, but he had not picked up how Blondel was trying to overcome the idealism or the subjectivism of this method through a more realist philosophy of action in the concrete.

Schwalm saw Blondel as just another young upstart coming out of Normale and going out across France to propagate the Kantian philosophy of their teachers in the lycées. What was worse in the case of Blondel, according to Schwalm, was that he was now trying to infiltrate the Church and replace Scholastic philosophy with idealism. He argued that Blondel's method of immanence was not a method, that it did not respond to the exigencies of modern thought, and that it led to religious solipsism. With regard to apologetics, it undermined the certitude of supernatural facts in the face of reason and it led to an incompatibility between Faith and Reason. One of the things that rankled Schwalm, and many others, was not only Blondel's manner in the *Lettre*, but also the fact that he had never gone to a clerical school of philosophy or theology, and that he now appeared to be trying to tell the clerics, most of them his seniors in religion, how to do their philosophy and theology. Many would criticize him on that basis alone, without reading much of what he had written, just for daring to propose something different than what they had been thinking. If it was different, Blondel was told at one point, it had to be wrong and unorthodox. But Schwalm did better than that. He examined Blondel's method and its application in *L'Action* and found both wanting from a standpoint he thought of as realist, or as getting us beyond just ideas into reality itself.

Blondel felt not only that he had to defend himself but also that he had to answer Schwalm philosophically. This he tried to do orally with Father Schwalm, when he met him at an international congress of Catholic intellectuals in Fribourg, Switzerland, in August 1897. They spoke twice for over five hours, in a conversation where Blondel tried to make Schwalm realize what he was doing philosophically, at which time Schwalm is said to have admitted he had not entirely understood exactly what Blondel was up to as a philosopher. Later on Blondel would recall an expression Schwalm repeated several times in response to his explanations: *Vous me faites revenir de Pontoise*, an old

Burgundian expression, meaning that you are taking me down paths where I feel lost. Blondel did not succeed in conciliating Schwalm entirely, but he did get him to tone down his criticism somewhat, as others in the Dominican Order more favorable to Blondel were suggesting.

It is a fact that Blondel had shown his manuscript of *L'Action* to another Dominican, Reginald Beaudoin, O.P., in Aix, even before he submitted it to Boutroux, to see if there was anything objectionable in it from the standpoint of religion. Blondel knew that he was going out on a limb in religion as well as in philosophy, and he wanted some reassurance that he was not offending against anything in religion. Beaudoin had reassured him that there was nothing against Catholic teaching in what he was saying. He reassured him again when Blondel was faced with the accusations of his Dominican confrère, as he would continue to reassure him later on at the height of the Modernist Crisis in 1904 and 1905. By that time Père Beaudoin would have become the Assistant to the Superior General of the Dominicans in Rome, and he would also be able to assure Blondel that he was not considered suspect in Rome and that neither *L'Action* nor any of his other writings were on any official list for review. One suspects that Beaudoin probably had a lot to do with keeping Blondel's works off such lists, because in the denunciatory politics of the time there were probably many who were trying to have Blondel's work added to those lists. Blondel and his wife lived in the fear that he would be condemned in those years of free-flowing theological accusations and denunciation. Such a condemnation would have wounded them both very profoundly as fervent Catholics, so much so that she pleaded with him often to renounce all this work on apologetics and to go on to something less controversial.

Getting Beyond the Dichotomy of Idealism and Realism

But Blondel would not renounce, just to play it safe. He saw this work as part of his mission, which he was anxious to pursue within the Church, and not outside of it. In November 1898, he published a more systematic response to Schwalm without referring to Schwalm explicitly, in an article titled "L'Illusion idéaliste," in the journal that had been the first to recognize his philosophical standing, *Revue de Métaphysique et Morale*. In his correspondence with Brémond, Blondel complains of the tremendous weight he had to bear in writing this article. He had to twist and turn and agonize spiritually over it. It was like trying to lift Mont Sainte-Victoire with a crowbar. It was directed not only at Schwalm, but also at others who did not know that they were themselves victims of the idealist illusion in accusing others of idealist illusion. It did not mention any names, nor did it discuss any doctrine in particular. It only discussed the problem of getting beyond the idealist illusion for people who were supposedly realists as well as for idealists. Even after he was finished with it Blondel was profoundly unhappy with it, but he let it go, hoping that it would help others come back from the Pontoise of exclusive realism as well as exclusive idealism.

In the article Blondel argues that both idealism and realism are natural attitudes of thought that, far from being exclusive of one another, must be seen as integrated in a broader conception of thought that transcends them both. Both are deceiving, if reflection reduces them to static formulas that separate them from one another and from the dialectical movement that holds them together. But both are also well founded, in the sense that they constitute a moment in the internal determinism and a spring in the dynamism in the spiritual life. What Blondel proposes to do therefore is, first, to show the impossibility of thinking either of these two attitudes in isolation from one another, since both suffer from a certain form of intellectualism, and then, bring them back to a new sort of equilibrium in thought as it relates to action or to the act of thinking itself. In this he hopes not only to transpose such traditional problems, or merely to juxtapose his solution to that of others, but rather to extend the philosophical tradition itself into a new realm, the realm of trying to equate thought to action, or to its own act.

Blondel shows the impossibility of maintaining a pure realist position without falling back into thinking of ideas as real things. But then he also shows the impossibility of maintaining a pure idealist position without reference to some real thing in itself, as Kant had to do. Either way one is left floating somewhere between Aristotle and Plato or between Kant and Spinoza, caught in the intellectualist illusion of an impasse between the inescapable poles of subject and object or of thought and thing. As a way out of the impasse Blondel proposes a two-stage strategy, one that he had followed in *L'Action* itself.

First, before examining the validity of any one of our thoughts taken in isolation from one another, we must examine systematically the entire complexus of our thoughts as they relate to one another, in their differences as well as in their similarities, in order to clarify and to understand what it is that we think most profoundly and scientifically. What this will bring out into the clear light of consciousness is everything that we have to think necessarily as it relates to reality. What it will also bring out, which leads into the second stage of the strategy, is that this idea or this complexus of ideas is not necessarily equal to reality, especially if we think of reality as human action. There is always a certain distance that separates our knowledge from the state of the world it expresses, and our idea from the action toward which it tends. Blondel's crucial point is never to forget that all thought is at once *act* and *knowledge*. If we separate knowledge from its act and try to reify it in this abstraction, we lose sight of its limitation even as it relates to reality. If we think that our idea is adequate to reality, or reduce action to our idea of action, we close off thought from what more there is to learn from action, whence the illusion of idealism as well as of realism. Thought is what opens up action to the new dimension of spirit in the world. There is learning that takes place in this new dimension, but the learning is never meant to be fixed or absolutized at any given moment in some idea that we can store once and for all. It is always an incitement to learn more by entering more deeply into action.

The problem with both realism and idealism, both forms of what at this time Blondel calls *intellectualism*, meaning an exclusive insistence on ideas apart from how they relate to action, is that they both "take the *fact* of thought in itself, separated from the very *act* of thinking, considered not as a residue or as an echo of life that is at once physiological and moral, generic and individual, but as a reality up in the air, uprooted from its vital origins, mutilated in its natural ramifications, studied like an immobile mummy like unto itself" (1898, 120). The solution to the problem of both realism and idealism for Blondel is to bring thought back into its proper critical role as part of action and life. This, he thinks, is in keeping with the most authentic tradition of philosophy, alluding no doubt to the *philosophia perennis* that Schwalm wanted to call him back to.

"L'Illusion idéaliste" does not seem to have done much to change Blondel's situation with regard to his theological critics, most of whom remained fixed in their objectivist or "realist" ideas. Blondel was far from happy with it because it was too condensed. It made for difficult reading even for the most disciplined philosophical spirit. It may have mollified Schwalm somewhat, but it had little or no effect on scores of other objectivist critics who would continue to level accusations of neo-Kantianism and subjectivism well into the twentieth century, never showing any appreciation for the fact that Blondel was trying to move philosophy beyond subjectivism as well as objectivism or beyond the sterile opposition between the two. Blondel saw this as necessary not only for philosophy itself, but also for laying a rational groundwork for religious apologetics or, beyond apologetics, as he was already beginning to think of it, for a proper philosophy of the Christian spirit.

In the waning years of the nineteenth century, however, he was totally absorbed with the question of religion as a question of apologetics, because of his *Lettre* on the subject and the strong reactions it had provoked both for and against his proposal. He felt he had to answer his critics on the side of religion, as he had done on the side of philosophy, but more importantly he felt he had to complete the task he had only begun by laying out the philosophical requirements for a truly rational apologetics in keeping with the exigencies of modern thought. The latter task he owed to the many rejuvenated spirits who had read *L'Action* and saw it as a step, not only in convincing the irreligious of the necessity for religion, but also in revising the understanding of the role of religion in their own spirit.

Thoughts for a New Book on Apologetics

Inexperienced as he was in the politics of religious controversy within the Catholic Church, the violence of the reaction to his *Lettre* came as a surprise to Blondel. Attacks on his method came from many sides, though mostly from an objectivist perspective that was quite uncritical of itself. He took notes to keep track of all the objections, with the intention of answering all of them. At the same time he began to think of what would be required, besides a philosophy like that of *L'Action*, for a more complete apologetics of the Catholic religion, thus crossing over into the domain of theology, which in the *Lettre* he had recognized had to be kept distinct from the domain of philosophy. Thus, even before writing "L'Illusion idéaliste," he had begun to think of writing a new book on the entire subject of apologetics, in which he would answer his critics and then apply his method to the development of a complete apologetics that would meet the exigencies of modern thought. This is something he would come back to repeatedly in the next four or five years, in the heat of controversy, even though the book never came to fruition. From this project, and the notes he wrote himself in preparation for it, much as he had done in writing *L'Action*, would come many of the ideas he would develop late in his life in *Philosophie et Esprit Chrétien*.

The first title he jotted down for the book he was projecting says a lot about the orientation of his thinking: *La Religion, Essai d'une critique de la religion — Le Problème de l'apologétique et le procès philosophique du Catholicisme*. This says that he was still intent on thinking only as a philosopher and not as a theologian or a believer, though he was surely a philosopher who wanted to think through his faith. More than a Critique of Life, as *L'Action* had been, this was to be a Critique of Religion and, more specifically, of Catholicism, in answer to the problem of apologetics, which for Blondel was a problem of bringing the critical thinker to a more positive appreciation of religion. As he would write later on, in his notes to himself, theology presents the object of faith and shows its internal coherence, whereas apologetics looks to how the subject can assent to that object, or why he must assent to it. The apologist needs to understand the full scope of this task in order to be efficacious. Blondel's purpose was to raise the critical problem for apologetics itself as Locke, Hume, and Kant had raised the critical problem of rational speculation. For Blondel, this implied a critique of self as well as a critique of others. Put in more personal terms, in the same note, the question was one of asking simply how a believer, convinced of the truth of the Gospels, and wishing to communicate the divine gift of his faith, can and must proceed in order to reach and win over other spirits, rather than just defend institutions. Put in these terms, he would have preferred to call his book, not so much an apologetics, but rather a normative and fundamental theory of adherence to religious truth.

The context for the book at the time was that of the debate over apologetics, into which he had dropped something like a bomb with his *Lettre* of 1896. The debate was continuing to rage about him, with his method very much in question. He continued taking notes on objections to his method and writing outlines for the work. In his papers going from 1897 to 1901, we find no fewer than six or seven outlines for this book, along with copious notes on what was to be its content, depending on where the debate on apologetics was going at the time and where he was in his thinking about it. With all his other duties as a professor of philosophy, which included, besides teaching and reading and hearing exams, participating in the World Congress of Philosophy in 1900 as well as in the discussions of the National Society of French Philosophers under Lalande, and writing notices for the latter's *Vocabulaire Technique de Philosophie,* he could not let go of it because of his concern for finding a proper apologetic for the Church that would meet the exigencies of modern critical thought. It was part of his sense of mission as both a philosopher and a believer.

In these papers we find references to articles by opponents to his method such as Schwalm and Gayraud, a former Dominican then priest-member of the National Assembly, who fancied himself still a theologian and proper defender of the faith. We find references also to more sympathetic people like Brémond, Laberthonnière, Beaudoin, von Hügel, and even Loisy, most of whom Blondel was in correspondence with. We see Blondel asking himself what to do about Thomism in a special way and we see him turn to reading St. Thomas himself, perhaps for the first time. There is a notebook dating from around April 1899, filled with reflections on texts from Book I of the *Summa Contra Gentiles,* from the Commentary on the *Peri Hermenias,* and from some of the *Opuscula* of St. Thomas. Blondel was beginning to discover St. Thomas for himself, long before he read Interpretations by Rousselot and other commentators able to adapt to the modern critical view of philosophy, and he was not finding himself at odds with what he was reading. At one point, with reference to the *Summa Theologiae,* II-II, qq. 171-74, he notes, no doubt with some glee, that for Aquinas there is no revelation that is merely received and repeated passively. Adherence implies moving with a revelation.

In the plan set down during February and March 1901, he has a long list of attitudes that must be overcome, besides that of empiricism with its insistence on facts that smacks of fetishism: the historicism of Loisy, the scientism of Frémont, the ethicism of Bourget, or the aestheticism of Chateaubriand and Huysmans, the vitalism of Fonsegrive, the intellectualism of Ollé, the socialism of Brunetière and Lacordaire, and the ideologism of Gayraud. Just to deal with all of these would have been a volume in itself, but Blondel also had a more constructive part in mind that he does not say anything about. In another plan, dated August 2, 1901, now titled *L'Apologétique et l'esprit chrétien,* he gives a more systematic outline in five parts, each with its own discussion of objections and responses: I. The Transnatural State; II. Insufficient Intellectualism; III. The Intellectual Examination Which Is Non-Realist *a parte Dei*; IV. How to Prove; V. The Vital Point of the Problem of Faith.

The language of the headings is tentative, but it reveals something of the new ways in which Blondel was beginning to think of his subject, ways that would lead him to think in other terms than strictly apologetics, and more in terms of spirit as a principle of thought and life. Thus he was coming to ask himself in his notes: "Is there a specifically Christian spirit? And if this Christian spirit is, as it claims, a supernatural gift, how can it unite with the human spirit? If it is not from man, how does it come about that man cannot reject it without impunity?" This was the vital point to be made, having to do with the Catholic teaching "that the human being, conscious of his acts, and master of his will, does not escape from the necessity of being either saved or damned; that the Roman Church is the sole depository of divinely revealed teachings and practices; and that outside it there is no salvation." One can think of this teaching as forcing man to become religious, as one forces a child to be hardworking or a citizen to be respectful, but he adds in another note, "This conception of man's relation to Revelation is radically insufficient. It misconstrues what is essential about the supernatural. It does not even touch on the problem." The problem is not one of applying external force, but of internal discovery or disclosure, and of showing how the human spirit must remain systematically open to such disclosure. If one cannot show that there is a certain inquietude for the supernatural in the human spirit, there is no way of proving anything in apologetics. But if one can prove such an inquietude, one can then go on to speak more positively as a philosopher of the Christian spirit. All this thought of the supernatural can be inserted into the hiatus that is left open by philosophy between thought and life, where philosophy does not close in upon itself and is not exhausted in the act by which we come to live and know as human beings.

Blondel, however, was slow to shape his notes and his reflections into the book he kept intending to write during these years of mounting crisis. He was keeping abreast of everything that was being written in the debate about apologetics. After the *Lettre* of 1896, he did not publish anything more about the question, except for "L'Illusion idéaliste," which was only indirectly related to the question of apologetics, but he kept close watch on everything that was being published and on the rumored threats of condemnation in Rome and elsewhere. The mentality of denunciation among Catholic theologians that prevailed at the time weighed heavily on his spirit. But it did not keep him from engaging in prolonged discussion with others who were also at odds with the established ways of presenting religion to the modern critical mind, several of whom were in sympathy with Blondel's method, even though they were not always in agreement with his more orthodox views on how to proceed and how to think about the supernatural, and none of whom were strictly philosophers as he was.

Conversations with von Hügel

Among Blondel's correspondents was Baron Friedrich von Hügel, a family man much like Blondel with a profound spiritual life, a sense of mission in the world, and devotion to the Church, though he was more of a mystic and less a philosopher than Blondel. Nine years Blondel's senior, he traveled widely around Europe and maintained contacts everywhere he went, in England and in Italy as well as in Germany and France, among the clergy and the hierarchy as well as among more detached innovators like Loisy and Tyrrell. Blondel was introduced to von Hügel by his friend Paul Fabre when he was visiting Rome with his new bride in 1895, and the two soon discovered a kinship of spirit between them.

Von Hügel read *L'Action* and became an enthusiastic supporter of what the book was about. He brought it with him to England where he had his friends read it and he wrote back to Blondel not only to express his admiration, but also to ask questions about it. It became for him the book everyone should read to understand the place of religion in the modern world. Later on, when the *Lettre* on Apologetics came out he became even more enthusiastic and kept asking for reprints to distribute among his friends. He introduced it to philosophers like Father Giovanni Semeria in Italy and professor Rudolph Eucken in Jena. Eucken not only liked the book, but also got his student Max Scheler interested in it; Scheler in turn wrote to Blondel in 1902 to ask him to become a contributor to *Kant Studien*. Blondel declined, for fear of being further branded as a neo-Kantian, explaining that he was working on a larger work of his own on Apologetics and the Christian Spirit.

When the attack of Schwalm appeared shortly after the publication of Blondel's *Lettre* on Apologetics, von Hügel wrote to sympathize with Blondel and advised him not to launch a counterattack, but rather to let his ideas find their way more peacefully. But he did offer to have some of his friends in Rome intervene on Blondel's behalf, if that proved necessary. It is through von Hügel that Tyrrell came to read both *L'Action* and the *Lettre* shortly after he had been removed from teaching in the Jesuit scholasticate of Stonyhurst for being too much of an ardent Thomist in a nest of Suarezians (1960a, 22). In February 1899, von Hügel was to spend a week with Blondel in Aix conversing about many subjects of mutual interest and making the acquaintance of Blondel's friends. In their conversations and in their letters, von Hügel would try out new ideas about how to read Scripture, or about the personality or the consciousness of Jesus in relation to his divinity, but Blondel would tend to be more reserved in his reactions, more cautious in his ways of speaking to the modern mind about these religious matters. It was through von Hügel that *L'Action* was introduced to American Bishop Spalding, and to a certain Miss Margaret Froude, who was not only brought back to God by it, but also wanted to translate it into English in 1900 (1960a, 31). It was also von Hügel who kept urging Blondel to re-edit *L'Action,* complaining already in 1901 that he could no longer find copies of it anywhere to give to his friends (1960a, 42).

Confrontation with Loisy over Historical Criticism

Besides von Hügel, Blondel also entered into correspondence with the Abbé Alfred Loisy during this period of mounting crisis. Loisy was seen by many as a leading light among Catholic Scripture scholars in France during this time, the first to appear as equal to Protestant scholars and historians like Harnack in Germany, although some of his publications had already incurred the wrath of some theologians who had him removed from teaching at the Institut Catholique de Paris in 1893, leaving him to survive and to continue his work on his own, with the help of the pastor of a small town called Bellevue, where he took up residence in the rectory. Feeling a certain sympathy with Loisy, because the same people who had attacked Loisy were now attacking him, Blondel had sent him an offprint of the *Letter on Apologetics* not long after it came out in 1896. Loisy had reciprocated by sending him one of his own writings. In February 1897, after having read the *Lettre,* Loisy wrote to Blondel speaking of the *Lettre* as a manifesto similar to his own that he had sent him. "We are innovators," he wrote. "Your philosophy can be understood with my exegesis. It is even said that they have been disavowed as heterodox, and have escaped (let us hope) the censures that some wanted to have imposed on them" (1960a, 35). Loisy was especially struck by the claim of autonomy for philosophy that came at the end of the *Lettre* and repeated the same claim for historical criticism, without including the complementary claim about how these autonomous disciplines still had to be at the service of supernatural religion, if not abstract theology as such. "We are preaching in the desert, I am afraid," Loisy added, "caught between the fanatics of science and the rationalists of faith. This does not prove that we are in the wrong, on the contrary. Only it is quite natural that we are considered unbearable, temerarious, and slightly at odds with the common sense, that is, the sense in charge of routine." Loisy wanted Blondel to know that he was not alone in his predicament. He told him of his own *Revue d'Histoire et de Littérature réligieuse,* which he had launched and to which he was inviting Blondel to contribute. But Blondel did not take him up on that, fearing he would only get himself deeper in trouble with his critics in the Church if he did.

No more came of this first exchange between these two innovators. A brief but more intensive correspondence was to develop several years later when Loisy published his book *L'Évangile et l'Église* in November 1902. At the time the initiative came through the Abbé Jean Wehrlé, Blondel's former classmate at the École Normale Supérieure who had left the school to enter the seminary and become a priest. Needless to say, Wehrlé had not lost his intellectual interests, especially as they concerned religion, and he remained close to Blondel in thought as well as affection. After reading Loisy's little book, he became quite enthusiastic about it and urged Blondel to read it before anything else. "It is, in the strictly religious order, a work of incalculable bearing in my humble opinion. I admire it, I praise it, I recommend it without reservation. It sketches with you the program for the future. The plan of exegetical and theological renovation will take place on the program of both of you" (1960a, 48).

Blondel did not need this invitation to read the book. He had already read the book and written to Loisy about it, raising certain questions and reservations about its method and its content concerning the consciousness of Jesus with regard to his divinity. In reply to his friend Wehrlé, Blondel began to elaborate on these reservations and to point out how Loisy could be understood as perhaps undermining the true faith in the supernatural aspect of religion and in the divinity of Christ. With Wehrlé, and with others as well, he kept coming back to two points that were a matter of concern to him.

The first was the question of historical method that, as we have seen, had to be autonomous, according to Loisy. What bothered Blondel about this was not so much that the method had to be autonomous, but rather that for Loisy it also had to be kept separate from any question of transcendence in human action, which according to Loisy could not be a matter of fact for historical observation. This idea of separation between disciplines sounded to Blondel like the same kind of separation he had tried to overcome in philosophy with regard to the question of religion. It implied a certain self-sufficiency in a particular discipline closed in upon itself. In the historical method, it implied that science could give an adequate account of facts without going beyond the determinations of externally observable fact, without reference to anything internal in human historical accomplishment, let alone to any presence of divine intervention in history. For Blondel this meant another kind of naturalism or immanentism which, far from being neutral, was exclusive of the supernatural in history. For him, just as human action could not close in upon itself, to the exclusion of the supernatural, so also the history of Revelation and more particularly the history of Christ cannot be closed in *(ne boucle pas)* "within the order of purely historical explanation.... Exegesis leaves everywhere an open hiatus and the theory of a separate Critique sufficient unto itself is here absolutely deceptive" (1960a, 58), no less than a separate, self-sufficient philosophy as such would be. Blondel saw in Loisy's attempt to maintain a totally separate historical method an implied metaphysics of determinism confined to observable circumstances that was reductively Spinozistic (1960a, 74), something materialistic as well as idealistic, even though the idea of the Necessary Substance was left out of the picture. Needless to say, Loisy had never pushed the thought of his method this far, but Blondel thought that at some point he would have to philosophically.

The second concern Blondel had with the understanding of Loisy had to do with something that seemed to follow from the application of this separate historical method to what it tells us about the consciousness of Christ. Loisy focused his study of Christ on the Synoptic Gospels, explicitly leaving out John's Gospel as too theological rather than historical and factual. From the study he seemed to conclude that the consciousness of Christ was more or less like any other human consciousness, or like the consciousness of his early disciples, who were of course the ones through whom we came to know him, and that he had to grow into the consciousness of his divinity, or of his special relation to divinity. What Loisy was saying was not entirely clear in abstract theological terms, but Blondel saw in it a certain dissonance with what he thought was the Catholic belief in the divinity of Christ, recognizing that this question of the consciousness of Christ was very difficult to sort out for one who believed that Christ was both God and Man at the same time. Blondel was not satisfied with the way standard theology had sorted it out, but he was not happy with the way Loisy was going about it either. He had his own way of showing how the Word took on a truly human consciousness through what he called his Panchristism, but he did not think this way was accessible to a historical method kept separate from philosophy. Speaking as an apologist, one had to learn to speak of Christ as in the world, but not as of the world, as coming from the Father and as returning to the Father, and as taking on the condition of all human beings, including that of learning, suffering, and dying, in order to raise them all to a new, supernatural life. With his purely external or objective historical method, Loisy was incapable of speaking in this way of Christ.

These reservations of Blondel were at first addressed to Wehrlé and other friends who were sympathetic to Loisy, not to Loisy himself. Wehrlé was somewhat surprised by them, since he knew that Blondel was also quite sympathetic to Loisy and his work, and he was not immediately convinced that they were well grounded. He went to visit Loisy at Bellevue and came away with great admiration for the man, not only because of his work but also because of the way he was enduring being ostracized and even persecuted. Gayraud, the would-be theologian-deputy who had earlier attacked Blondel, was now launching another of his obtuse and violent attacks against Loisy, which would eventually force Cardinal Richard of Paris to condemn *L'Évangile et l'Église* publicly, even though the Cardinal would have preferred not to do so. Blondel and Wehrlé began to feel even sorrier for Loisy, knowing what he was going through, even though Loisy agreed to withdraw an order for a second printing of the book.

Wehrlé still was not convinced that Loisy could not be interpreted in a more acceptable way, but neither of them thought Blondel should remain silent in the situation in order not to abandon Loisy in his plight. Early in February, 1903, Wehrlé discovered, through another abbé who was also sympathetic to Loisy and other disciples of his, that Loisy, basically, did not believe in the divinity of Christ in the Catholic sense: his opinion was that Christ was indeed the most divine man who divinized himself little by little. Nor did he believe in the Resurrection in the sense in which it was understood in the Church (1960a, 71). This discovery saddened Wehrlé. He praised Blondel for having called attention to this departure of Loisy from the teaching of Christian tradition early on, and for having warned him from the beginning about his enthusiasm for Loisy. But it did not turn the two of them against Loisy. They still continued to sympathize with him and to admire his work. But they now began to think of how they might reach out to him in order to bring him around to a more acceptable way of pursuing this delicate task of a modern apologetic, or of presenting the true face of Catholicism to the modern critical mind.

Blondel had not been in direct contact with Loisy for some time. It did not appear right to them that he should now all of a sudden write to begin instructing him. Instead they agreed that Blondel should write a long letter analyzing Loisy's work, and summarizing the misgivings he had about it to Wehrlé, which Wehrlé would then send on to Loisy, while Blondel would write a brief note of sympathy to Loisy, telling him also of the letter to Wehrlé that would be sent to him. It was a subterfuge typical of Blondel to get a critical dialogue going without offending Loisy any more than he had already been offended by his censors. It worked. Loisy responded to the letter to Wehrlé directly to Blondel and there followed an exchange of three or four letters in February and March 1903, on the difficulties of Loisy's method and its results.

In the initial letter sent through Wehrlé, Blondel begins by recognizing the aptness and the fecundity of Loisy's central thesis to the effect that the Catholic Church is the legitimate offspring of the Gospel through the continuity of a living logic and through the powerful plasticity of an organism capable of maintaining the profound analogies, while suppressing the seeming resemblances, so that at each moment of its history it is what it has to be in order to subsist without cease. He notes also how Loisy does well to oppose a realistic and a dynamic method, one that is objective and truly historical or properly scientific, and one that remains open to indefinite renewals for the future, with all the suppleness and variety of life, to Harnack's more idealistic and static procedures, still caught in a Scholastic and doctrinaire apologetic. Not to recognize this approach and not to praise its author would be to be blind and unjust.

Without doubt, Blondel was in full sympathy with Loisy and his work of a "historical apology for religion" (1960a, 82, 87) in opposition to that of Harnack. He was also in sympathy with the implication Loisy himself saw in his work, which was not to deny any dogma, but rather a "necessity of revising all theological teaching from the standpoint of history in order to make it positively more true and, from the standpoint of philosophy, to make it theoretically more intelligible," as Loisy himself would put it in his reply (1960a, 85). The problem Blondel found in Loisy's work was that it did not show enough critical reflection on its method for it to be incontestable and valid and to avoid all dangerous ambiguities, especially with regard to its historical object. For Blondel it is not clear where precisely Loisy is starting from, the consciousness Christ had of himself or the consciousness those who wrote about him had of him. In fact, Loisy seems to confuse the two and to bring the first down to the second, as if Christ had the same limited view of his mission or of an imminent Parousia as his first disciples did at the beginning. In this regard Blondel maintained that the historical subject matter of Loisy's work was not defined specifically enough and that it was too mixed up with other connected problems that were subordinate or antecedent to the central one.

Moreover, Loisy cannot plead that he is only "a poor decipherer of texts," as if he could systematically avoid any incursion into different levels, whether metaphysical or theological. Metaphysics and theology are not simply higher levels hovering above or separate from history, which one can set aside while doing a purely positive history, especially not when one is doing a history of Christian religion. Blondel detects two distinct attitudes with regard to metaphysics and theology in Loisy: on the one hand, there is supposedly no metaphysics or theology at the origin of exegetical work, and yet in the end of the investigation both do show up; on the other hand, since the transcendent and the theological are not in any way a matter of history, or of critical observation, the exegete legitimately and definitively confines himself to texts and facts. "In this way, 'methodical doubt' seems to become a 'systematic and doctrinal neutrality'" (1960a, 76). In other words, the doubt itself becomes a metaphysical and even an anti-philosophical position. For Blondel the doubt is methodical only if it remains provisional and fictional; the scientist cannot avoid being a human being. The second attitude "is false, pernicious, ruinous, because [the first attitude] must necessarily lead us, through the mediation of philosophical problems, to the problems of Christology and theology" (1960a, 77).

Finally, Blondel makes the point that Loisy cannot properly disclaim any Christology in his work, as Loisy had done with Wehrlé. One cannot write about the Gospel and the Church without encountering some Christology in the facts. Given this kind of fact in history, one cannot avoid the question of a transcendent Christology and confine oneself within the determinism of a purely historical explanation. To be sure, the question of the Christ-God's knowledge and consciousness presents a formidable problem for any interpretation of the Gospels, especially if one wants to avoid mere docetism with regard to Christ's humanity. But it is a question that cannot be avoided. Loisy himself does not get around it and the solutions toward which he appears to incline appear to Blondel theologically, philosophically, and even historically unjustifiable. Even if we prescind from Christ's divinity at first, the fact of his human consciousness presents an inescapable transcendent dimension for historical science to take into account, a dimension that itself opens into the question of how he was conscious of his divinity. To ignore this question in an apologetic of the Christian religion is to take a stand against the very divinity of the historical Christ. Blondel himself does not claim to understand how the unity of the two natures in Christ was realized in history. He only thinks that the supernatural aspect of this unity cannot be ignored in a properly historical account of the origins of Christian religion.

In this challenge to Loisy's apologetic Blondel recognizes that he may not be understanding Loisy's thought correctly. He says he is only asking for clarification of assertions and claims that seem ambiguous to him. He is not himself advancing any philosophical or theological thesis as much as trying to "insinuate at least some doubt in [Loisy's] mind as to the legitimacy, the indisputability of his attitude, of his procedures, his still very scholastic anti-philosophism," as he writes to Wehrlé (1960a, 80). The strategy was to open up new avenues of thought for Loisy to defend himself and to resolve his ambiguities in a sense more in keeping with the exigencies of faith in a supernatural, or in the divinity of Christ, without reneging on his work up to then. Would Loisy accept to pursue these new avenues? Would he see them as quite in keeping with his historical apologetic in the context of the abuse that was being heaped upon him by a theology resolutely fixed in quite unhistorical categories, while insisting, as Gayraud did, that "our faith is a question of historical fact" (1960a, 57), not understanding anything of what was implied in such an assertion with regard to the immanence of the transcendent in history?

In his reply, addressed directly to Blondel, on February 11, 1903, Loisy shows that he is not ready yet to move in any direction such as that suggested by Blondel. Instead he disavows any kind of necessity in his historical account of the origins of Christianity. Whatever can be said of Christ comes to us from historical witnesses who were not determined to go one way or another in their account, and who were not the equal of Christ in his consciousness as historical agent. That is all Loisy has to go on as an exegete, though he totally discounts the witness John as too theological rather than historical. He explains that he has been forced into a stance of total separation for his preliminary work of true history by an overbearing theology that claims to know everything, without having examined or discussed any of the texts and the facts in question. As for the idea that Jesus could have had a consciousness of his divinity from his conception on, he claims that that can only be a fiction from the standpoint of the historian. For his part, Loisy does not recognize any signs of such a consciousness in the Synoptic Gospels, the only ones he considered properly historical. He expects condemnation from Rome, not from the Biblical Commission, which apparently was not alarmed at his case, but from some other Commission, perhaps the Index, where someone who had it in for him had more influence.

In his reply, now addressed directly to Loisy on February 15, Blondel takes a more conciliating tone, recognizing Loisy's justified hostility toward the aprioristic "theologism" they both deplored and expressing his agreement with the general intent of his work to overcome the "intellectual fixism" that had overtaken theological thought in the Church. He excuses himself for not wanting to go as fast as Loisy in this task of renewal. He lists a number of moot positions concerning historical exegesis, the kind of metaphysics and theology that should follow from it, evangelical eschatology, the human experience of Jesus as described in the Synoptics, the ineffable character of his divine personality, and even the necessity of revising the traditional teaching of the Church philosophically, in order to render it more intelligible, and using history to make it more positively exact and more understanding of the past, "more faithful to the duty of spiritual resurrection and of sympathetic intimacy, without which we know humanity only as a coach driver knows the houses of a city" (1960a, 88-89). But then Blondel comes back to what continues to trouble him in Loisy's attitude toward Christology and toward method.

It is not enough, according to Blondel, just to reject the despicable *a priori* dogmatism and theologism in order to confine oneself to the methodical skepticism of the historian. We must also critically reflect on the conditions for a *science of Revelation* and of any sacred literature. Blondel distinguishes three parts to the problem. First, there is history which, according to the precise effort of its comprehension and autonomy, is not in any position to discern the supernatural as such, even if, by hypothesis, the supernatural is immanent to the series of facts. The supernatural as such remains transcendent to the series. Second, however, the historian does not escape the necessity of being human and doing some metaphysics, nor perhaps does he escape the duty of being Christian. As such, he too, like any other human being, inevitably has to come to ultimate questions concerning humanity, including Christianity as well, as Blondel had try to show in *L'Action*.

Philosophy alone cannot discern the reality or the irreality of objects of religious faith such as those of Christianity, but it can show the necessity of raising the question of religion in human terms. In the third place, one can then make the hypothesis that there truly has been a Revelation, or that there has not been any, and one has to examine the conclusions that one can draw from either hypothesis.

In the hypothesis of a positive Revelation, "if a truly divine Word has resounded in a human word, it is necessary, for these words to make sense, that a continuous and permanent development should imitate little by little through its indefinite richness the infinite plenitude of the gift. This gift, which is *totum simul*, like eternity, cannot render itself except in the small change of time through accretions that, while seeming to bring something new, only *rediscover*, or recover successively, the initial unity, the infrangible ingot" (1960a, 91). From this, Blondel concludes that the thesis on "development," where many see only some heterodox novelty, is the very condition for the intelligibility and the reality of a Revelation, although this idea of development had to be determined very precisely with respect to the understanding of the Revelation, as Blondel himself would do later on in *History and Dogma* with the idea of *tradition.*

Assuming that the divine truth is given in the past, one cannot get back to it directly by the merely historical method. One can only get to it by the totality of the ongoing life of a human community, which has given it expression in different ways and at different times in history. Even the first expression of such a truth, as close as we suppose it to be to the original fact, is only a rudimentary sketch, humanly faithful and divinely synthetic, but still encapsulated and more enigmatic than later developments. Human beings can enter into the divinely revealed truth only progressively, as the first disciples of Jesus had to do, and each expression of that truth at any given time in history can only be a partial expression of a truth that cannot be fixed in any one of them. What is needed is a divine assistance to keep each successive expression in tune with the identical Eternity present in the fluctuations of time. "Hence the criterium that will enable us to recognize the divinity of the Gospel and the Church will be this continuity which you [Loisy] have so well brought to light, this living unity in diversity, this global view that keeps you from extracting a partial idea, a local aspect from it, not any more than we can judge of a plant from its first bud, often quite different from the leaves that are to follow" (1960a, 42).

Blondel sees this insistence on historical continuity as following from the hypothesis of a divine Revelation. If, however, we go with the hypothesis of no Revelation, then religious life is left to feed on a more or less diffuse faith with more or less concentrated virtual foci sustained by more or less learned constructions. In this case, religion and faith are reduced to historical determinism and facts that, as full as one wants to imagine them, are never anything more than facts. One may decipher, from one stage to the next, like an archaeologist, some handwriting of God in the various layers of human consciousness that have accumulated, but not the Word of the God who is literally the Emmanuel, God with us. In this second hypothesis the autonomy of historical studies is no longer merely a method. It is a doctrine, and one that supplants the others.

In thinking through the logical consequences of these two hypotheses concerning the fact of Revelation, Blondel is not only laying out how he thinks development in the understanding of a divine Revelation has to be understood, and how history itself is essential to this learning process in faith. He is also pointing out the importance of starting from a proper understanding of the divine or the eternal consciousness as the source or the origin of this Revelation in Christ, for a properly Christian apologetic based on some historical understanding. If one ignores or prescinds from this divine aspect of the problem from the start, by insisting on using only a purely external historical method based on observation and nothing more, then one is no longer doing a Christian apologetic or an apologetic in keeping with the divine origin of the Church. The general thesis of Loisy in *L'Évangile et l'Église* had been to show that the Church is a continuation of the Gospel, so that if Harnack admitted the divinity of the Gospel, as he did, he would also have to admit the divinity of the Church. In the process, however, by resorting exclusively to an autonomous or separate historical method, Loisy was ignoring or even denying, according to the logic of the second hypothesis just presented, the divinity of Christ, thus defeating his very apologetic purpose. This is what Blondel was trying to point out to Loisy, without denying the legitimacy of the historical method for the study of Christian religion and the idea of a development of dogma it entailed.

What Blondel was pointing to in Loisy was a certain philosophical lacuna in his apologetic, similar to the one he had found in the more objectivist and intellectually fixed methods of apologetics criticized in the *Lettre*. Loisy, too, was too much of an objectivist in separating the historical method from theology or from philosophy altogether in studying the origins of Christianity. This is what kept him from raising the human question of religion or of the human being's concern for his ultimate destiny, let alone the question of the supernatural as present in history. What he needed was a philosophy of subjectivity to show how such questions arise necessarily for the human being. Loisy shows that he gets Blondel's point, when he mischievously remarks that "you are reproaching me for not having put your philosophy into my history, and I could plead many reasons for not having done so, the best of which being that your philosophy is still in large part unpublished whereas my history, alas, is all too published" (1960a, 96). The major work on apologetics Blondel had been talking about, even to Loisy as well as to others, had yet to be published, though much of what he was bringing up in this discussion with Loisy would have been part of it.

Loisy was not disposed to pick up on that philosophical part of the argument. The discussion went on for several more long letters, but it concentrated mostly on the different ways of reading the Gospels and interpreting the historical consciousness of Jesus as expressed in those documents. Loisy sent Blondel some unpublished essays concerning his work, which Blondel found much clearer and encouraging than a lot of what had been published. In the end, after three or four letters from each one to the other, the discussion ended amicably, without much rapprochement, but with the understanding that much more had to be done on either side.

The Crisis of Christian Consciousness in the Modernist Controversy

While this exchange was going on between Blondel and Loisy, there was also another one going on between Blondel and von Hügel on the same subject, the autonomy of history and the consciousness of Christ, and on a new Christology that von Hügel was developing. This exchange, too, resulted in a standoff, although the correspondence between von Hügel and Blondel did not stop there. The correspondence showed how Blondel could be interested in new ideas as part of the development of the Christian understanding of Revelation. There were many others like him, priests and seminarians as well as laymen, who were similarly interested in these modern new ideas and who felt more shaken in their loyalty to the Church than Blondel or Wehrlé were. The official Church, for its part, seemed preoccupied only with presenting a solid front of ideas, fixed in the past and intransigent in their supposedly objective fixity. There was ferment in many quarters and fear among some, that the Church was losing the battle for souls to what was coming to be called modernism. Condemnations like those of Loisy and Tyrrell were not helping because many critical minds were persuaded that some development in Christian ideas was not only inevitable, but also necessary even from the standpoint of religion itself.

Blondel and his friends, like Wehrlé and Fernand Mourret, Director at the Saint Sulpice Seminary in Paris, were worried not only that many critical, inquiring minds were being kept away from the Church by the obtuse attacks of a Gayraud on anything having to do with modern critical thought, but also that many who were already in the Church were being driven out needlessly because of this unfortunate attitude among established influential theologians. Blondel had resolved not to publish anything more on the controversial subject after the initial reaction to his *Lettre*, and his encounter with Schwalm, until he could come out with the extensive work he was projecting on Apologetics and the Christian Spirit, in which he would try to expose everything he thought had to be done for religion in the face of modern critical thought. He had not been entirely silent in the public debate, for, besides his voluminous correspondence with many who were involved in it, he also adopted the subterfuge of an interview by a friend of his, Monsignor F. Mallet of Aix, published in 1901 under Mallet's name, to clear up accusations of naturalism and subjectivism being leveled against him, both of which were the exact opposite of what he was trying to get to philosophically.

In November 1903, however, Wehrlé and Mourret began to suggest that now was perhaps the time for Blondel to break his silence and intervene publicly in the debate, if only to stop the hemorrhaging within the Church because of this confrontation between two intransigent sides, that of fixated theologians and that of criticist historians. The two friends were concerned with the care of souls in this crisis and they thought Blondel could reconcile the anxiety of many, by showing how orthodoxy and modern critical thinking could be brought together without offending against either one of them, a role he was still more than willing to play, as he had done in the past. The only fear they had was that, by intervening again publicly, Blondel might once again open the floodgate of attacks against him personally, as well as give the appearance of abandoning their friend Loisy, whose work they still thought highly of.

Blondel put himself at the disposal of his two priest friends. He would let them decide if and when he should intervene. There were rumors of an impending condemnation of Loisy from Rome and they thought it would be good if Blondel published something before that, to at least palliate the blow to Loisy and to avoid the impression that Blondel would be only adding to the forthcoming blow. The condemnation came sooner than expected, but they reasoned that it was still opportune for Blondel to intervene, to soften the blow at least for those who were looking on, troubled by this condemnation of something that seemed like a step forward in the understanding of the Faith. So it is that Blondel began to work on an article on the "philosophical lacunae of modern exegesis" that would arbitrate between the two sides and suggest a way out of the impasse, to be published in *La Quinzaine,* a widely read journal under the direction of Fonsegrive, one of the apologists whom Blondel had criticized eight years earlier in the *Lettre.*

The Need for Reconciliation of History and Dogma

Blondel had plenty of material to work with, his correspondence with Loisy, along with the accumulated notes for his projected work on Apologetics and the Christian Spirit. The article took shape quickly. Things fell into place easily, but it began in a way that would once again bring down the wrath of those watchdog theologians operating from their fortress of a fixed objectivism. Blondel felt he had to begin with a critique of this objectivism, to be fair not only to the modern critical side but also to the supernatural aspect of the question itself. Knowing that this was a dangerous thing to do in the context of Church politics at the time, from his experience after the *Lettre* on Apologetics of 1896, he submitted part of his article to Mourret, to see if he would still think it opportune to risk the wrath of the embattled theologians, for he had no intention of publishing the article without including that first part. Mourret, as we see in an almost daily exchange of letters among all three — Blondel, Mourret, and Wehrlé — hesitated, but Blondel went on writing and completed the article to his satisfaction in a few weeks. When Mourret and Wehrlé saw the whole thing they felt reassured, especially by the third part, which emphasized the crucial role of *Tradition* in the development of dogma, thus compensating somewhat for any strategic misgivings about the first part criticizing fixated objectivism in theology.

The article that resulted from this effort is the only substantive publication that was to come from this tormented period of Blondel's reflection on the question of Apologetics in the Catholic Church and the Christian Spirit. The book that he still says he is preparing on the *Christian* Spirit, in the introduction, would not appear until decades later, long after this trouble about apologetics had subsided and after he had published a more complete philosophical prolegomenon for it in his trilogy on Thought, Being, and Action. The article of 1904 would deal with only a part of the more complex problem he had been reflecting on, the part concerning the Biblical problem in the context of modern historical studies, but still a part that was closely related to all the rest and remained focused on the essential question to be resolved, namely, how the supernatural relates to the natural and the historical in the understanding of faith in a divine Revelation.

With reference to the Biblical problem, this question comes down to understanding how a supernatural Faith is somehow based on historical facts, and how historical facts somehow open the way to a Supernatural Faith, notwithstanding the distance or the disproportion that seems to lie between our scientific knowledge of facts, on the one hand, and Faith in a supernatural Revelation, on the other. Everyone who is concerned with the Biblical problem, among Catholics at least, agrees that there has to be a connection between the essential teachings of the Church and historical facts, such as those narrated in the Bible, and that a precise historical knowledge of facts and texts is in the interests of a true understanding of the Faith. But there is a sharp difference of opinion on how we come to know what is revealed about the supernatural, where each side reproaches the other of endangering religion and hurting it in both spirit and letter. The question for Blondel is to see why such an opposition has arisen among people who supposedly share the same faith and how it can be resolved in a manner that is in keeping with both reason and theological Faith.

To do this, it is not enough to appeal directly to facts and texts, because each side does that, only to worsen the confrontation, without finding any way out of the impasse. Nor is it enough to determine the legitimate claims of the historical method, and of the rules for interpreting official documents, because these claims and rules would be understood differently by each side, so that they are part of the problem to be resolved, which has to do with how Christian facts and Christian beliefs are to be related to one another. If the two coincided perfectly in the light of direct experience or complete evidence, there would be no problem. But everyone agrees that "between facts and beliefs there is a double step, and a going back and forth to go through above two obscure intervals: for, if it is true that the historical facts are at the basis of the Catholic faith, they do not engender it by themselves, nor are they sufficient to justify it totally; and reciprocally, the Catholic faith and Church authority go back to guarantee the facts and to extract from them a doctrinal interpretation that is imposed on the believer as itself a historical reality, though on other grounds than those the historian judges by" (1904, 152).

To justify this kind of circularity, without turning it into a vicious circle, one must go beyond the brute facts or the dogmatic ideas, not by appealing immediately or exclusively to the intervention of grace, but by going to a principle of explanation and movement that accounts for this double passage from historical data to faith and "from Faith to truly objective affirmations and realities that constitute a Sacred History inserted at the heart of banal history and incarnating the ideas in the facts" (1904, 152). The question for Blondel is where to find the light and the force that allows for taking this double step that effectuates a synthesis of history and dogma, while respecting both their mutual independence and solidarity. It is a question that had yet to be raised by either of the two opposing factions in the problem of Biblical interpretation among Catholics. Before coming to what he thinks is the ground for an adequate solution to the question respecting both sides of the problem, in the final part of the article, he pauses to examine the two solutions that were in contention with one another in the minds of Catholics at the time, both of which he characterizes as inadequate in themselves and incompatible with one another.

Typically, Blondel names no one as associated with either one of these solutions. He is interested only in examining the method that is implied in either one of these solutions, and that on each side is only presupposed, without being critically examined. What he wants to do is bring out the internal logic of these solutions, even though they are not always entirely consistent and logical in their procedures, in order to show where and how they fall short in dealing with the problem of a historically grounded faith in something truly supernatural. From the content of the argument, from its own historical context, and from the correspondence we have alluded to, it is easy to see that Blondel had in mind people like Gayraud on one side and Loisy on the other, but he invites the reader to think more in terms of pure positions, for which he uses "barbaric neologisms" to call attention to them, and to highlight the exclusive character of each position. One he calls *extrinsicism* and the other, *historicism*, two solutions to "the essential problem arising today for Christian consciousness, two solutions diversely incomplete, but equally perilous for the faith; they are two extreme opposites, but belonging to the same genus, founded on similar habits of mind, suffering from analogous philosophical lacunae, making one another worse by their very conflict" (1904, 154). For Blondel it is important to sort out the logic of these two positions in the ongoing crisis of Christian consciousness, in order to arrive at a better understanding of where the solution to the problem lies.

The Critique of Dogmatic Extrinsicism

With regard to *extrinsicism*, Blondel begins by asking how it approaches the question of relating facts and dogmas, the study of Scripture, the justification of their value, how they are to be interpreted, and, in a word, how it comes to "the determination of the Christian Supernatural" (1904, 155). Ultimately, for him, the question has to come down to how the supernatural relates to the natural in history, for a religion that claims to be supernaturally inspired.

For *extrinsicism* the approach is very simple. All it looks for from facts are signs for the senses and proofs for common sense. Once the signs are proffered it takes only a rudimentary reasoning to draw from them a demonstration for the divine character of the ensemble to which these significant facts belong. Fortified by this reasoning, one can then settle into the universal conclusion one was looking for and close in on one's stance, in the place where supposedly history has led one. History's role in the process is strictly provisional and, once the abstract conclusion of divinity is reached, history is simply set aside and ignored without regard for whatever else it might have to tell us about the supernatural.

As a matter of fact, Blondel argues, *extrinsicism* never really goes into history. It only extracts some abstract ideology from it that it then presents as the object of faith, as if that were all there is to the true Christian faith. For it, "historical facts are nothing more than a vehicle whose interest is limited to the apologetic use one can make of them; for, whether it is a question of this miracle or that miracle, as long as it is *a* miracle the argument remains the same. And this argumentation itself considers the supernatural only as a sign *(signe)* and a command *(consigne)*, without any right, power, will, or interest in looking either for the bond there might be between this miraculous character and the particular historical event in which it is dressed, or for the essential connection that might exist between the facts and the ideas, or for the liaison that can and must tie our own thought and life to these objective data" (1904, 156). Such a rudimentary way of reasoning, which is supposed to make us take the first step from facts to dogmas, convinces no one, least of all those who place their faith in reason, in the letter's learned and complex methods, in the richness of reality, and in the depth of spiritual life. It cannot help to implant in us and justify the total exigencies of a religion that lays claim to the whole human being. It leaves all the key relations extrinsic to one another: the relation of the sign to the thing signified, the relation of facts to the dogmatics superimposed on them, the liaison of our thought and our life to truths that are proposed from the outside. It separates facts and dogmas in such a way that they can only remain at odds with one another, whence the defensive and ultimately defeatist attitude it takes in the face of modern historical studies, which, on their side, reveal so much more of the facts narrated in Scripture and of the way the narration itself came to be historically.

Concerned only with the "bare fact" that God has acted and spoken, and not with what God has done and said through human instruments, even excluding from the argumentation on which the authority of the Bible is supposedly founded any consideration of the historical and natural aspect of the facts, *extrinsicism* can only be shocked at the internal criticism of texts and the curiosity of historians wherever these are not strictly subordinated as part of *extrinsicism*'s apologetic argument and claim some independence for themselves, even if it be provisional. All that counts in the Bible for *extrinsicism* is some external seal of the divine. It cannot be bothered by the details or with the human condition and the relative sense of what it merely presumes is an absolute science. It can only take texts according to the letter and reduce them to the exigencies of its own dogmatic ideology, in a sort of fundamentalism that takes only its own limited understanding in the present for granted, instead of what might have been the original intent of the text as divine teaching.

Borrowing a phrase from Loisy, Blondel points out that this attitude gives the impression of people who think they know everything before having examined anything. Blondel sees them more as mystical ideologues whose ambition is imposing their particular systems on the concrete truth of history, before taking refuge in a know-nothing policy, as they continue to teach the less educated folk who still take their word as "gospel truth." This method might have seemed acceptable as long as we knew little or nothing about the historical circumstances in which the facts narrated in the Bible took place, or the narratives themselves came to be written, but the development of modern historical and philological science makes it highly suspect even as an interpretation of what has been revealed in these historical facts. For Blondel, this obscurantism becomes a challenge, not just to *extrinsicism*, or to any kind of apologetic, but also to any human being trying to lead a life according to Christian faith in a historical revelation, as many were who were troubled by the discoveries of modern historical science. These were the people whom Mourret and Wehrlé had principally in mind in urging Blondel to intervene in the debate over modern historical science and faith in ancient dogmas.

The Critique of Historical Criticism

This consideration of *extrinsicism*, however, was for Blondel only a preamble to the more important consideration of *historicism*, which was to take up a much greater part of the article "History and Dogma." It was an adaptation of some of the criticisms he had made earlier in the *Lettre* of the objectivist forms of apologetics now in the context of historical studies of the Bible. It was a necessary preamble, however, inasmuch as *historicism* itself can only be understood in relation to the method to which it is opposed in apologetics, and whose difficulties in the face of modern research it wants to overcome. Unfortunately, according to Blondel, the remedy it offers only aggravates the difficulties and brings with it a large dose of false as well as bad philosophy. This is what he wants to explain in his long consideration of what he calls *historicism*, the insistence on studying Christian facts only according to the canons of strict historical observation.

What could be more natural and more in keeping with the habits of the positive spirit, as well as more compatible with the confidence of Christian faith itself, than to consider face to face the historical and philological data of the Biblical problem in order to produce, through such an independent study, an irresistible force of conviction in favor of the supernatural that is incarnate in the long course of Revelation? If there is a supernatural anywhere, it is in the realities of history. Let us look for it where it is, and not just in the abstract reasoning of ideologists who try to wrap it up in neat little packages, and thereby turn the reality of history into nothing more than an allegory. Instead of looking for dogma and its abstract formulation in history, let us look into history itself for the dogma that will come to life, movement, and fullness again in it. The role of the apologist in this case will not be to post some small sign of reassurance before the gate of some theological palace; but rather to give testimony in the historical experience of humankind to the truth of God ever present, ever acting in the world and in the Church.

All this appears well and good, but Blondel points out that it is still only a way of raising the question. It is not a solution to the question of how a supernatural Revelation appears in history. There is still the problem of how we go from facts to dogma, where everyone agrees that the Christian facts are not sufficient for Christian beliefs. If the apologist claims to be a pure historian of facts, what is the ground for adding anything to his account of the facts? Will the flow of his critical history be powerful enough to carry the infinite burden of an ancient Faith and all the richness of Catholic dogma? This is not just a problem of apologetics or of method in relating faith to science. It is also a problem of being reasonable in the conduct of one's life and thought, and it is from this standpoint of a reasonable approach to life, that is, as a philosopher, that Blondel will begin his criticism of *historicism*, before going on to show the dangers it runs into as an apologetic for the Christian Faith.

He begins with a critique of historical science itself, not to deny its competence or its autonomy, but to show how it is relative to other sciences and to other standpoints that ultimately have to encompass the whole of human life. It cannot set itself up as a metaphysics of the whole on the basis of its method alone. Nor can it merely juxtapose itself to other sciences and their results in a formal and extrinsic way. The historian is never merely a historian. He or she is also a human being who must integrate the ontological fragment of his domain into an ontology or a view of human life as a whole. What he or she sees *as a human being in history* is more than what can be seen according to the positive methods of observation. What the historian is looking at "is the entire aspect through which humanity enables us to grasp in observable manifestations the interior labor that is taking place *within*, manifestations which, by modifying one another mutually, by inserting themselves into the world, and by ceaselessly undergoing the repercussions of even those most foreign facts on human being, no doubt form a coherent whole but still do not furnish a total or sufficient explanation of the least detail. . . . What [the historian] does not see and what he must know that escapes him is therefore the Spiritual reality whose historical phenomena, no matter how determinable as a complete sketch subsisting without its model, do not represent or exhaust the whole of action" (1904, 167-68).

As Blondel had tried to bring philosophy back to the question of human life as a whole in *L'Action,* so he now says the historical critic must also do. Action is what constitutes human history in its spiritual dimension, a dimension that cannot be grasped by merely external historical observation. "Real history is made up of human lives; and human life is metaphysics in act. To claim that one can constitute historical science apart from all preoccupation with the ideal, even to claim that the lower part, or the kitchen of history, can be, in the strict sense of the term, a positive observation, is, under the guise of an impossible neutrality, to let oneself be dominated by partisanship" (1904, 168). No doubt, the historian has to learn to remain within the limits of his or her discipline, but he or she must also recognize that in doing so, he or she is also following a philosophy that may or may not call for critical examination of the ultimate meaning of facts and what they reveal in relation to human life as a whole and its destiny. If the historian does not heed this call *as a human being,* then he or she is taking a stand against any such critical examination beyond that of ascertaining the facts and nothing but the facts.

In that case it becomes impossible to see how anyone can do history with any sort of apologetic intent. It is also clear that such a refusal to raise any ultimate questions, beyond the limited domain of merely historical observation, is itself a philosophical position that excludes any rational inquiry into the spiritual meaning of facts. This is what Blondel wants to point out with regard to *historicism,* when it insists exclusively on its historical method of observation, even if it does not formulate such an exclusive philosophy explicitly, or appears to want to do the contrary in its apologetic intent. Once it adopts its exclusive stance within the method of external historical observation, it cannot take into account the spiritual meaning of facts, let alone any supernatural meaning relating to faith and dogma. It can only arrive at a certain natural determinism of facts in history. From a certain scientific determinism, it then "concludes to a sort of dialectical evolutionism that thinks it has penetrated the spiritual secret of the living chain of souls on the grounds that it has verified the external welding of links that are only its corpse" (1904, 171-72).

Blondel sums up this philosophical criticism of *historicism* under four theses, before turning to apply these theses to the fundamental problems of Christianity itself as a historical religion. First, it reduces real history, that is, the action and the life of human beings in themselves as spirit, to historical phenomena, that is, to what can be observed and recorded historically. Second, it replaces the actor or the agent in history with the external and phenomenal act. Third, it sees only the action of phenomena that have been expressed, not the side of action that remains hidden. Finally, it reduces history to some sort of evolution with only a mechanical explanation and little or no human, let alone a divine, initiative.

Each one of these theses will have its repercussions in the debate about how *historicism* handles the crucial questions that come up in the historical evaluation of Biblical facts and teachings. The first will elucidate how historical criticism tends to reduce the real Christ, that is, the one who actually lived and dwelt among men and women, to the "historical Christ," that is, to the record we have of his life and action in the documents left by his first disciples. The second thesis will elucidate the connection between the "historical Christ" and his first witnesses. The third thesis will elucidate the connection between the Gospel and the Church (which Loisy quite rightly insisted on). The fourth thesis will elucidate "the connection between Revelation and Tradition, the relations of the diverse moments of the Church among themselves, and the very notion of the Christian Supernatural itself" (1904, 173). The necessary idea of the supernatural, which Blondel always associates with Catholicism, remains for him the touchstone for evaluating whether an apologetic is philosophically valid, as well as in keeping with the spiritual content of Faith itself, namely, its teaching or dogma. He will argue that *historicism*, as a structure of history and apologetics, is at odds with Catholic supernaturalism by reason of its philosophical insufficiencies. It is no more capable of preparing anyone to take the step from fact to faith, let alone taking the step itself, than the *extrinsicist* apologetic, because it remains locked in a naturalist or an immanentist attitude, by reason of its exclusive focus on facts as matters of external observation.

The main difference between the *historicist* apologetic and the *extrinsicist* apologetic was that, instead of focusing on one or two miraculous episodes taken in isolation, and reasoning abstractly from that to the truth of Christianity, as *extrinsicism* did, it looked more to the whole phenomenon of Christianity in history, its concrete realities, from the person of Christ to the Church which prolongs him in the world today. "Instead of asking ourselves in ideological language: How, at any particular point in the series, can we pass from the empirical data to the knowledge of a supernatural order? We are told to rediscover the real Christ and to consider the Gospel, the Church, its dogmas and its sacraments as living and continuous articulations" (1904, 174). All this sounds well and good to Blondel, but the difficulties begin when we try to implement the method. The whole cannot be known except in the details, and it is difficult to see how one can go from the details as observed to a comprehension of the whole as supernatural. How does the critical historian try to effect this passage? What particular facts does he start from? What questions does he raise about these facts? Does he raise all the relevant questions? These are the questions that the critical philosopher must ask of the critical historian intent on doing an "apology through history alone."

Blondel has no intention of going into the concrete, historical details of the historicist's argumentation, or the way he exercises his particular craft as a historian. The question for Blondel is to see whether the application of this historical method allows for a proper raising of the question of the supernatural, as required for an apologetic of the Catholic Faith. At issue is a twofold displacement, one from the abstract to the concrete, and the other from the details to the whole of the phenomenon. Before going on to a critique of the enterprise of the historical apologetic as a whole, he pauses to verify what he thinks of as three or four principal anchors for the synthesis in the historical documents.

The first question is how do we come to know "the real Christ" as distinct from "the historical Christ," that is, Christ as he is disclosed through historical documents that are more or less contemporaneous to when he lived or shortly thereafter? Is the historical method used by the exegete sufficient to bring out all that he was, or is there another means besides just deciphering the portrait of him drawn by his first witnesses, such as might emerge from the total effort of the generations that have believed in him from the very beginning up to now? For Blondel this distinction is a decisive one, which "secretly affects all the rest of the inquiry" (1904, 177). Where does the inquiry begin, from Christ as he was in himself, in which case the thought that Christ was God takes precedence over everything else, or from Christ as he was perceived by his first disciples, in which case one can stay with the thought that Christ was only a man, albeit superior to all others? To which Christ must the Church be tied: the one who founded a tradition of devotion and adoration as the Lord, or the one who is portrayed in the historical documents?

These are distinctions which may not occur to the critical historian, but which Blondel deems necessary for an apologist of the Catholic faith in a supernatural presence of God in history. If "from the beginning and for all the rest we were to prescind from the Christological problem to limit ourselves to studying the repercussions occasioned by Christ in the human consciousness and the worldly events of time, thus pinning Him down in His past and sealing His tomb under the sediments of history, we would be considering only the natural aspect of His work as real and effective; we would be removing from Him all the influence that a teacher communicates to his immediate disciples, without their being able to transmit this influence by their narratives; and by ignoring this action of a presence that perpetuates itself under forms that escape historical observation in part, we would all the more be excluding the question of the properly supernatural mode of this mysterious person; we would be suppressing from His acts all their moral and ontological character by depriving them of the explicit aim and forethought that can give His life, His death, and His work an absolute meaning" (1904, 180).

Another question is the one about how to interpret the crisis of growth occasioned by the disappointment of the first Christian community, when their dream of imminent Parousia failed to be realized, whence came a new kind of continuation of the Church on earth, instead of the Parousia. Was that just a matter of historical determinism, as the historical criticist is inclined to think, or was it rather a transposition into the spiritual meaning of the Revelation and the love of Christ as the Lord? Is historical determinism as understood by the critical historian sufficient to account for the continued presence of Christ in his Church, or did the Church then discover a new dimension of the divine present in its history that it had not yet been conscious of?

On a more intellectual note, there was also the crisis of growth and development when the Christian community encountered the speculations of ancient cultures in its dogmatic elaboration of Revelation. Were the dogmatic formulations that came in those early centuries of the Church mere adaptations to the philosophy of the time, or were they new incarnations in history of ideal exigencies going back to a fullness of truth in the original deposit of Faith? Again, these are distinctions that the critical historian is ill equipped to make, but they are crucial for coming to a proper apologetic of the Christian way of life. In making them, Blondel is beginning to suggest something of what will be the solution to the apologetic problem that historicism cannot access or take seriously, namely, the idea of a Christian *tradition* going back to Christ himself, of which historical documents such as the Gospels, or later dogmatic formulations, are still only a partial expression.

In his critique of the purely historical apologetic as a whole Blondel begins by distinguishing three meanings of the word *fact*: first, it refers to a chronological succession of events; second, it refers to an intelligible continuity that the historian adds to this chronology; third, and most importantly for an apologetic of the Church, it refers to a spiritual continuity among individuals and generations who make history. Hence the universal problem of interpretation when faced with historical facts. The apologist is one called to present an interpretation that will favor the truth of a supernatural Christian religion. Is the critical historian in any position to make such an interpretation? Is he not more inclined to deny any idea of "an absolute incarnate in time; of the presence in the series of things of an action capable of realizing the infinite; of a consciousness that would remain human without ceasing to be divine; of a supernatural mystery entirely contained, at one point in time and space, in the most humble forms of nature; of one risen from the dead who would show the appearances and the sensible reality of a natural life" (1904, 187)? It is of such paradoxes that the Christian apologist has to be able to speak.

He may try to do so by insisting that the entire phenomenon of Christ and his Church in history is something miraculous, or by tracing everything in the phenomenon back to a divine origin. But he finds himself in an impossible situation as an apologist for the supernatural, if he adheres strictly to his method of historical science. If he claims to grasp the supernatural directly through external observation, he falls into a double contradiction with regard to the passage from fact to faith; he is constrained to a purely natural order of facts taken as a matter of observation and he is forced to exclude the supernatural. This, for Blondel, is in the logic of the relation between the supernatural and the natural. As long as the *historicist* adheres exclusively to his method, he can only abdicate any concern for the supernatural, or betray it totally by reducing it to something purely immanent to history. In short, the *historicist* denies any distinction of the supernatural as such and reduces Christianity to a merely natural religion, which for Blondel is not true religion, but rather a form of idolatry, as he argues in *L'Action*.

Tradition as Reconciliation of History and Dogma

Thus, after confronting a historical lacuna in the *extrinsicist* method of apologetics, Blondel confronts a philosophical lacuna in the *historicist* approach, a lacuna that must be filled, if any sort of historical apologetic for a supernatural Christianity is going to work. This is a lacuna, not in Catholic life itself or in the practice of the Church, as Blondel sees it, but in the theoretical justification generally offered for it by shortsighted apologists. In what does this lacuna consist, and how can it be remedied, in the modern crisis of Christian consciousness that so many were undergoing at the turn of the twentieth century in the face of modern critical thought? This is the question he proposes to answer in the third and final part of the article, as a solution to the crisis, by introducing the idea of *Tradition* as playing a vital role in the life of the Church, and by grounding it philosophically as a necessary component of human action in the historical transmission of a spiritual life, even though it is not entirely open to the scrutiny of an external or merely positive historical observation. Blondel's aim is to show how the Christian tradition, or Sacred History, can be seen as constituting a form of science in its own right for the mysterious life that sustains and illuminates it. This is the positive part of the article that convinced Mourret and Wehrlé that the article should be published, in spite of any risk to Blondel of further abuse from theologians who were too established in their old ways and who might find some reassurance in seeing him defend such a venerable principle of the Church.

The idea of *Tradition* that Blondel wishes to advance, however, is not just any idea of tradition, especially not one that would only add one more piece of evidence for the critical historian to consider exteriorly or objectively. It is an idea that must solve the problem of joining together history and dogma in a meaningful way, without compromising the relative independence of each side, the problem that neither *extrinsicism* nor *historicism* has been able to solve in their opposition to one another. The fact is, this crucial idea for the continued presence of the Christian life in history was being ignored by both sides. The thing that Blondel wants to do first with this idea is lay it out in its fullness according to the vital role it plays in the Church, the sort of original progressiveness it represents. Then he wants to bring out whence it draws its force and on what it is grounded, when it knows history otherwise and better in certain respects than the critical historian, and when it knows dogma otherwise and better than the speculative theologian. Once this philosophical foundation for *Tradition* in the life and practice of the Church has been brought to light, he can show how this *Tradition* can solve the problems that the debate over a historical apologetic for the Christian has brought up.

With regard to the idea of *Tradition,* Blondel is careful to point out that it is not merely an external transmission, principally oral, or a recording of historical facts, received truths, communicated teachings, sacred practices, and ancient customs. Such an idea could hardly resist the withering analysis of critical history, which could bring out gaps in this transmission as well as differences in what has been said or done at different times in the checkered history of Christianity. Tradition is not just another "text" that parallels Scripture. It does not merely record things that were said explicitly, or prescribed expressly, or done deliberately in the past by people whose clearly formulated ideas we try to reconstitute precisely as they were originally formulated. All this is part of *Tradition,* but *Tradition* itself is more. *Tradition* also bears within it a great deal that has not and cannot be translated into a written language or that cannot be immediately and integrally converted into an intellectual expression. Thus, no matter how much of it we may come to know through historical research, we can never set *Tradition* aside as something merely of the past. It is an ongoing transmission of a spiritual life with a power of conservation. "This power of conservation is at the same time one that is acquiring; it discovers and formulates truths which the past has lived, without having been able to enunciate or define them explicitly; it enriches the intellectual patrimony by doling out little by little the total deposit [of faith] and by making it fructify" (1904, 204).

What it preserves from the past is not just its intellectual aspect, but also its vital reality. It may ground itself in texts at times, but at the same time, and primarily, it grounds itself on something other than texts, on an experience that is always in *act* and that enables it to produce and to judge its own texts rather than just be subservient to them. At work in this historical effort of *Tradition* is "any one who lives and thinks as a Christian, whether it be the saint who perpetuates Jesus among us, or the historian who strives to go back to the pure sources of Revelation, or the philosopher who strives to open up the ways of the future and to prepare the perpetual rebirth of the Spirit of newness" (1904, 205), even as the progress of this diffuse labor is concerted and stimulated by an authority and a consciousness that is divinely assisted.

Blondel has no problem relating this social dynamic of tradition in history to a teaching authority in the Church, but he does not see the authority as the only part that is divinely assisted, nor does he see its role as restricted to preserving past or fixed expressions of Christian teaching and life. The challenge of Christian *Tradition* in human history is ever to speak anew the divine truth it harbors from its origins, in order to advance this truth to the spirit of human beings, always with an eye to its origin in the real Christ, who was God in history, so that the absolute truth, or the supernatural, of the Christian way will not be sold short or restricted to any particular expression in history, which is always human and relative, or natural. It enacts its own living synthesis of history and dogma, to which neither *extrinsicism* nor *historicism* can do justice.

What this means from the standpoint of our knowledge of revealed truth and of the One who reveals, is not only that *Tradition* goes further than Scripture, but also that it has a competence of its own for penetrating more deeply into this truth. The next question for Blondel, then, is to show in human or rational terms how this specifically religious knowledge is grounded. "What rational guaranty, what philosophical justification can be invoked in it against the fantasies of individual representation and the illuminism of excessive intuitions or deductions? There has to be here, no matter how supernatural its object and its mode of action, a natural point of leverage and application for *Tradition*" (1904, 208). To find this point Blondel looks to the way the Church proceeds in its elaboration of *Tradition*.

The Church does not proceed purely by a learned historical research into its past, though the validity of such research is not excluded. Nor does it proceed in a purely dialectical fashion in the manner of a philosophy that constructs itself through an analysis and a synthesis of well-balanced concepts, though it does adapt itself to the diverse forms of intellectual culture, and sometimes borrows from philosophical systems the language it needs to give its teaching all the precision it wants in a given civilization, without ever subordinating itself to any particular system. Nor does it proceed by a sort of empirical mysticism, without being able to justify its decisions, even when the reasons it gives are not the only ones, nor perhaps the most essential ones.

The Church speaks with an independent authority, but it addresses itself to intelligence as much as to docility, "vindicating the rights of reason because it wants to teach a truth that can be communicated. Everywhere therefore its supernatural wisdom is illuminated by natural lights, surrounds itself with natural precautions, and determines natural operations" (1904, 209).

Inasmuch as Tradition itself in the Church makes a normal use, up to a point, of natural activity, and consequently requires some rational justification, it is important for Blondel to look for the secret source of this labor and the principle of its explanation in a philosophy of action that studies the many, regular, and methodically determinable ways in which a clearly formulated knowledge manages to express more and more fully the profound realities that nourish it. In *L'Action*, Blondel had tried to work out such a clearly formulated knowledge in terms of strictly rational human life as such, referring only to the mysterious depth of human action as it yields its secrets to critical reflection. Here he is concerned with showing how *Tradition* in the Church follows a similar procedure in reflecting, not only on what the ancients or early fathers in the Faith actually thought and expressly formulated, but also on the deeper deposit of Faith upon which the ancient fathers themselves were reflecting and upon which every succeeding generation of believers still has to reflect. What grounds *Tradition* as a rational knowledge of a supernatural religious life that is revealed and communicated across the generations in history is this ability to go back to its profoundly divine origin, both in the present and in the past, in order to draw out a teaching that is ever new and supernatural as well as grounded in a real history, and that has its beginning in One who was both God and man at the same time.

One of the important consequences of thinking of *Tradition* as grounded in this way, however, is that it can no longer be thought of as merely static or fixed in some particular expression of the past, no matter how ancient. For Blondel, this is as it should be, especially in the hypothesis of a supernatural religion based on a positive Revelation. "A truly supernatural teaching is conceivable and viable only if the initial gift is a sowing capable of progressive and continuous growth" (1904, 213). Blondel notes that Christ revealed himself without any sort of fixity. He wrote nothing, and what was written about him by his first disciples was only a human translation, which, even if taken literally, remains incomplete and immobile, or rather comes to us through the spirit of men of a certain race and a certain time. The only way we can come to understand the Real Christ better and assimilate him little by little is by a labor that is fed by two things, the moral life of human beings and, as it is said in John 15:26, the suggestions of the invisible Spirit, who is present simultaneously in all moments of duration and in all forms of civilization. "Thus, far from the idea of 'development' being heterodox, as many believers fear, it is fixism (both that of the historian who claims to have seized upon the truth of Revelation in its first redaction and that of the speculative type ready to lay hold of infinite reality in a closed synthesis, as if at a particular moment of history the spirit of man had drained the spirit of God), yes, it is 'fixism' that is a virtual heresy" (1904, 213).

To attain Christ, if he is truly the incarnate Word, to justify dogmas, if they express the absolute, we cannot simply go back up the chain of historical determinism to some primitive text or meaning, "for to look immediately for the last word in a first echo is to settle *a priori*, and without discussion, the question of the supernatural character of the initial witness, and to settle it in a way that is inevitably negative" (1904, 214). The idea of the supernatural remains a touchstone even for understanding the development of dogma in *Tradition*. "Only a progressive and synthetic march... can imitate by its indefinite progress the infinite richness of the God who both reveals Himself and remains hidden" (1904, 214).

With this idea of a progressive Christian Tradition, as modern as it is ancient, Blondel finds himself far removed from both the *extrinsicist* and the *historicist*. As "traditionalist" as the extrinsicist might appear, he neglects the role of *Tradition* as it must be understood in a historically grounded supernatural religion. And as "scientific" as the historicist may be, he cannot get back to the true sense of the Christian *Tradition* in its plastic force and its transformative activity. What is at issue is not just some sacred stone cast down from heaven to be passed on from generation to generation, nor is it an accumulation of sediments from centuries of human thought. It is more a spiritual community in the process of constituting itself historically on the basis of a Revelation and a life that surpasses its own human, historical, and natural capacity.

In conclusion to this presentation of Tradition, Blondel goes on to show how *Tradition* in its living form resolves the problem of method that was raised in the opposition between *extrinsicism* and *historicism* and how it can answer the questions that arise in the conflict between the two. With regard to the problem of method, he writes: "Dogmas cannot be justified by historical science alone, nor by any dialectic ingeniously applied to texts, nor by the effort of individual life; but all these forces contribute and are concentrated in *Tradition*, whose divinely assisted Authority is the organ of an infallible expression" (1904, 218). The Christian community of believers has yet to learn the fullness of the Truth that has been revealed to it. It has yet to make itself equal to the Deposit from which it has its origin. If it is going to meet the most intellectual demands of modern critical thought, it must go back to this immense effort of Faith in Jesus to express itself in dogmas, or in a teaching that has adopted human and natural means discernible to reason, in order to go beyond them. This is necessary not only for the apologetic to be successful in the face of modern critical thought, but also for the concrete exercise of thought and the real history of a spiritual Faith to be true to its own self.

In answer to particular questions raised in the debate between *extrinsicists* and *historicists*, Blondel points out how we must get beyond the separation between the conclusions of historical science and ecclesiastical definitions or pious practices, in order to discover how they come together, in their relative independence, in a certain solidarity of life within the community of believers. Similarly, the action of Christ must be taken not just as having given rise to a movement of religious consciousness, as if the Christian life were only a truth that can be summed up in some ideal formulation. It must be taken also as a reality in itself, an end as much as a means, corresponding to a metaphysical role, through the Incarnation, in elevating human life for those who believe to a new dimension of being, something truly divine and supernatural. Nor must this new dimension of supernatural life be thought of as something merely juxtaposed or superimposed extrinsically on nature, without any historical interest in nature itself for this new life, or as a mere concentration of the divine within nature that does not transcend nature itself, or what is accessible in it to an intellectual elite. Rather, it must be viewed as a relation of love and devotion that adheres to the person of Christ as he is in himself, beyond anything that can be expressed of him in human terms, and which makes it impossible for any human being to find his or her equilibrium in the human order alone.

In this way, Blondel brings the crisis that had been provoked by the emergence of positive Biblical studies in the Church back to the question that he had been working on from the beginning: how to make the case for a supernatural religion in the court of a highly critical intelligence, without merely juxtaposing the supernatural to the natural in an exterior fashion, and without compromising the absolute transcendence of the supernatural even in history. In *L'Action*, he had gone as far as he could in making this case without getting into any explicit reference to matters of Faith in the Christian supernatural. L'Action was never meant by him to be a complete apologetic, but only a philosophical preamble. In the *Lettre* on Apologetics he had tried to explain why such a philosophical preamble, proving the necessity of the supernatural from a rational standpoint, if it were offered as a gift, had to be a part of any apologetic effort.

His intention during the years that followed the crisis provoked by the *Lettre* of 1896 had been to produce a book that would encompass all that would be required for a complete apologetic, in theology as well as philosophy. But that remained mostly in a state of outlines and notes when the crisis over the historical study of the Bible and the use of such study for apologetic purposes broke out within the Catholic Church, and he decided to write his article "History and Dogma." At this point the crisis could no longer be viewed in merely philosophical terms, as it had been viewed in *L'Action* and in the *Lettre*, since it now entailed references to matters of explicit belief or dogmas, such as the divinity of Christ and the actual teaching and practice of the Church. In this article Blondel had to deal with explicit beliefs and the way they are justified, but his role was still to sort out philosophically how we go about thinking of such beliefs and how they can be justified.

It is in this way that he brings out the crucial importance of *Tradition*, or the lived experience of the believing community with its own *Practical Science*, for any sort of critical thinking within the Faith. As a matter of fact, he had already spoken briefly of tradition as a part of communal action in his *Science of Practice*, but only in general philosophical terms. Here, in "History and Dogma," he had to speak of it more specifically as an aspect of action for a community of believers grounded in the history of Jesus. In refocusing the debate on a proper understanding of the Christian Tradition, Blondel was showing how resourceful his philosophy of action could be in bringing rational human beings to a more complete appreciation of the truth in supernatural religion as well as in human history. At the end of the article he also begins to suggest how this philosophy of action can be developed into a sort of Panchristism for one who believes in Christ as incarnate Word and as Redeemer of humankind, something he had begun to think of in his earlier reflections on apologetics and in his discussions with Loisy, but that did not come to fruition at this time.

Blondel never actually published the work on apologetics he kept making plans for between 1896 and 1904. The article on History and Dogma was the only important work he published on the subject at this time. No doubt, his prolonged reflection on the problem of apologetics in the Church during a time when his own thinking was in question, as well as that of others, helped to produce the clarity and the force with which he was able to deal with the question of the relation between historical fact and faith in a teaching about the supernatural, but the problem of apologetics as such had to remain unresolved in his own mind.

His intention was always to speak only as a philosopher, and not as a theologian, even when he spoke of what theology was trying to do in apologetics. There is no question that there was an apologetic intent in his philosophy of action, but not in the sense of providing a complete apologetic argument as envisioned in what was called fundamental theology. That was something that only a theologian could formulate, since for Blondel, as for the theologian, such an argument had to include data of revelation or what were already matters of Faith. In his reflection on any apologetic task for a supernatural Religion claiming to have historical roots in human action, and seeking to insert itself into the history of souls, he was intent only on bringing out the exigencies of modern critical thought in any attempt to raise this question of Religion. He was trying to show critically why the question has to arise and why, from the standpoint of human action alone, it has to be answered in the affirmative. It was for others, namely theologians, to speak more positively of the historical facts and of the dogmas that could be derived from those facts.

The little that he did write about History and Dogma, as they relate to the critical evaluation of what is contained in *Tradition* as the action of the Christian community in its historical course, proved helpful to many who were experiencing a crisis of faith as well as of intelligence, and even to theologians who would begin to think differently of the development of dogma in later years. But the threats and the fears, which were quite real and not just imagined, from self-appointed watchdogs who could accept no other way of expressing or arguing for the truth of Catholicism than their own fixed way, kept Blondel from ever bringing his own thoughts on apologetics for Christian religion to completion. His treatment of *extrinsicism* in the article on History and Dogma only exacerbated the threats and fears, even though there was never, either at the time or subsequently, any official pronouncement on the part of Church authorities condemning Blondel, or casting the least doubt about his teaching, let alone his good intentions, much as his detractors tried to provoke such pronouncements.

Daring as he was against any sort of closed-mindedness, whether secular or religious, he still felt intimidated by intellectual bullies who had a semblance of authority in a bully press. Blondel wanted to be a defender of the true Church, the one with a soul, and not just the one that could impose itself with a heavy hand, so that all those with a rational soul could come to believe in it, and he was grateful that many in the Church recognized this. But the opposition of others, with some semblance of authority in the eyes of many in the Church, made him suffer and even doubt the rightness of what he was arguing for at times. Many would say that, in his later philosophy, he would give in too much to these critics of his attempts to bring religion into the modern mode of thought. Whether or how much this is true remains to be seen, but one thing is clear: the severity of the opposition took a lot out of his initial brashness in the *Lettre* and in *L'Action*. The later version of *L'Action*, in 1936, would be considerably toned down in comparison with the earlier version of 1893. A lot of what he had begun to think of the Christian spirit as a critical philosopher in the context of this struggle over Apologetics would later come out in a new and less polemic form in his volumes on *Philosophy and the Christian Spirit*.

VII

The Broader Social Involvement

In addition to his perhaps exaggerated preoccupation with apologetics on the religious front at the turn of the century, and with reactionary theologians who would not accept the philosophical point he was trying to make with regard to the personal problem of religion in modern thought, Blondel was also pursuing his more normal mission as a philosopher on a broader social sphere in the University and in the public affairs of France. Besides his regular courses and seminars at Aix and Marseilles, and hearing exams in various places in southern France as the titular professor for the region, he also participated actively in the International Congress of Philosophy organized by Xavier Léon, publisher of the *Revue de Métaphysique et Morale*, with whom Blondel was already familiar, in Paris from August 1 to 5, 1900, in conjunction with the Paris World Fair.

The Idea of a Realistic Logic of Action

For this Congress he chose to try to break new ground for a Logic of Action on the basis of the dialectic he had presented in his dissertation. He had begun to think of such a Logic shortly after he had finished writing the last chapter of the published version of *L'Action*, on "the bond of knowledge and action in being," in the summer and fall of 1893. During the winter, while he was still waiting for an appointment to the University, still isolated in the *mansarde* at Saint-Seine where he had written his blockbusting work, he began to think of broadening earlier conceptions of logic, such as those of Aristotle and Hegel, in terms of a critical study of action. The idea was to work towards a more fundamental canon of logic that would justify and amend these earlier systematizations of logic in a more general form of logic, embracing both formal logic and applied logic, rooted in the very exercise of thought and action. This was to be a more concrete kind of logic that would "encompass all the forms of thought or action and dominate all the abstract distinctions of science and life" (1960b, 9), a logic of Practical Science, so to speak, that grounds not just the Science of Practice, but also all other intellectual activity in human life.

In a draft that he had begun to develop at Saint-Seine, as early as 1894, he tried to show how formal or analytical logic cannot be understood as a purely analytical process. At the heart of every formal process of logic "there is always an act, always an initiative of a spirit that is inventive and constructive, always a synthesis; and it is in this somehow creative construction that one must find the regulative law that governs, through its antecedent, its immanent and subsequent action, the creations of thought and life" (1960b, 11). Until now, logical analysis has been viewed as purely *a priori*. It should also be viewed as *a posteriori* in the sense that it exploits the initial data of spontaneity and nourishes itself on the substance of activity. What needs to be brought out is the fundamental core of life thinking and acting in us that vivifies this analytical process from the inside out.

Applied logic, in contrast to formal logic, is often presented as only a question of methodology in science. One is seen as inductive, while the other is seen as deductive, without a sense of unity between the two. For Blondel the two have to be seen as integral and solidary parts of a single mental organism, but not in the way that Hegel saw this organism, that is, as an abstract construction of the concrete. The logic of experimentation needs to be grounded in a more fundamental logic that ties heterogeneous phenomena together in a synthesis, not just according to a principle of non-contradiction, but according to a principle of complementarity and solidarity in reality — whence the synthetic character of the causal link that binds them all in a single determinism — all of which presupposes a fundamental assertion of being. So that, where there appears to be only an inventive synthesis, there is in fact an analysis that is regressive from the standpoint of reality and progressive from the standpoint of knowledge. It is on this last point that, according to Blondel, Hegel's logic falls short by confusing logic with metaphysics. In its most fundamental sense, logic does not have to be either idealist or realist. It has only to depict empirically, and interpret scientifically, the way thought relates to reality. It can do this through mediation, so that the fundamental logic of the concrete will appear, not as a dialectic of ideas only, but as a dialectic of actions.

Blondel does not seem to have gone beyond this initial sketch of a few pages for his idea of a new logic to ground the older formal and applied logic in 1894, but he returned to the scheme six years later when he started thinking of what to present as his contribution to the International Congress of Philosophy in 1900, organized by Xavier Léon, publisher of the *Revue de Métaphysique et Morale,* and presided over by Émile Boutroux, the patron of Blondel's dissertation. For the Congress he came at the idea of a fundamental concrete logic by way of an "elementary principle for a logic of moral life" which was to be at the same time the "key to a general logic" (1903, 123-24). There he recognized that modern philosophy had broadened the scope of its abstract dialectic to include more of the richness of spirit and things. However, the tendency has been still to subordinate the real to the rational, as well as life and history to an idealist dialectic, if not to oppose the moral order, with its own type of certitude, to the speculative order and to the norms of thought, leaving us with the problem of understanding how the introduction of ideas into facts, or of facts into ideas, modifies the logic of abstract thought and the determinism of concrete reality. This is the problem of overcoming the hiatus between formal logic and applied logic, as he had seen it earlier, but now it is approached from the standpoint of the moral life, which for Blondel appears as a unity of idea and body, or of spirit and nature, but which, because of the formalism in the Kantian idea of morality, are kept apart as a free intention on the side of the will and as mere insertion in the determinism of physical and psychological forces. According to this perspective, if there is to be a Logic, there has to be an inflexible necessity that forges nature to its demands and that science can fasten onto. If there is to be a Morality, there has to be an original insertion of autonomous acts on the part of man, a freedom and an exemption from any logical determinism. How can these two seemingly irreconcilable points of view be brought together in the unity of our concrete moral life, and how can they be reconciled within one and the same general logic?

In order to show how they are in fact reconciled concretely in one and the same human activity, Blondel starts off by showing how the very ideas of formal logic, such as the notions of *contradictory, contrary, relative,* and *other,* all emerge systematically, in the way we come to exercise our own free activity, from the conflict of different desires and possibilities in our consciousness, in which we have to choose what we are going to be, as we decide what we are not going to be. From this comes the idea of *otherness,* and of *opposition* between different possibilities, as well as the possibility of contrary solutions. "The *contrary* solutions are contrary among themselves, not primarily because of an intellectual abstraction, but as the result of a concrete and qualitative opposition, which not only differentiates the series from the *others,* but also brings them into a clash with one another on the basis of how they are in accordance or not, with the orientation of our tendencies (1903, 130). The psychological dynamism in which this takes place had been described in a key stage of the Phenomenon of Action, in the dissertation of 1893. In this context, the very notion of *contradiction* is brought in concretely, in the way we come to think of actions done in the past as no longer able *not to be.*

If we isolate these logical notions from their vital origins, we run the risk of reducing logic merely to a matter of words or, as said today, word games, which

Blondel dubbed logology. This is not what Aristotle had in mind in developing his own formal logic, as if reality had to be squeezed into the empty forms of the understanding, without any possibility of a real dialectic and a moral logic. Instead, one has to see formal logic as a useful obstacle, a salutary test, and a necessary springboard for the development of a moral life. If it is brought back to its vital origins and subordinated to its moral ends, the logic of contradiction will find its relative truth, its natural role, and its subalternate legitimacy. "There is no purely formal logic because there is no idea that is not an act, no thought that is not thinking, no analysis that is not founded on a mental synthesis: the formal accord of thought thought with itself implies a labor of material adequation on the part of thinking thought in search of all its content." This is the real dialectic that echoes the dialectic of action. The distinction we see here for the first time in Blondel between thought thought and thinking thought is one that will figure prominently in his later systematic work on Thought.

Blondel goes on to show how this real dialectic relates back to the notion of *sterēsis* as found in Aristotle, in the sense that it implies the privation of something due or natural, or a certain exigency that may be accepted or rejected by a *yes* or a *no* but that may not be done away with. If formal logic excludes the contradictory, real logic does not exclude the possibility of contrary states that may be in contradiction with the laws of thought. Even errors are still living thoughts. There is a logic even of disorder, which is a logic of life itself. Blondel even enunciates some of the laws of this logic, such as the law of initial alogism and of spontaneous polylogism, the law of solidarity among discordant forces, the law of compensations, the determination of logico-ethical criteria, in which thought itself comes into possession of itself by becoming equal to itself, and the law of final reintegration or of total loss, where positive *sterēsis*, instead of contradiction, is seen as the extreme opposite of being. What is required to manifest the elementary principle of this logical life of the spirit is to bring abstract thinking back into contact with thinking and acting thought, that is, thought in action.

As it happened, however, Blondel did not get a chance to read his paper at the Congress. His turn to speak came late in the day on August 2 and there was time only for him to give a summary of it. Nor was there any time for any discussion from the audience. The full text of the paper was published only three years later in the Acts of the Congress. Nevertheless, his philosophy of action and even his logic was far from being left out of the discussion at the Congress. Leon Brunschvicg's paper, on the day after Blondel's was scheduled, in a session presided over by Henri Bergson, was aimed at Blondel's earlier paper "The Idealist Illusion," written to placate Schwalm and others who were accusing Blondel of idealism. Brunschvicg's paper was a defense of idealism as a living philosophy of spirit, against Blondel's claim that idealism was inadequate to meet the exigencies of action, just as the idea of action is inadequate to action itself. Blondel's objection, however, was not to the idea of a living philosophy of spirit as such, but to any attempt to limit that life to the sphere of pure ideas. "In a word, to understand spirit in a complete and concrete way, one must admit that thought is not everything, that life is heterogeneous to thought and that it enables us to raise in a certain way the problem of origins and even the problem of being" (1926d, 314). It is well and good to recognize the clarity of ideas in reflection, but it is important also to recognize that surrounding this light there is a penumbra, and that in this penumbra there is perhaps a living activity that is not reducible to pure understanding.

In the debate, people took different sides. Brunschvicg and Weber defended the purer form of idealism, but others, including Bergson, Le Roy, Milhaud, and others, took the side of Blondel. Many began to speak of the philosophy of action, of living and acting thought, as the philosophy of the future, including Boutroux in his closing speech for the Congress as a whole, as Blondel notes in a letter to Brémond (1970, 312). Blondel was able to find a certain amount of satisfaction and vindication at this Congress, unlike in other circles, in this willingness to accept his attempt to broaden the scope of the critical philosophy of spirit, to include action as an opening to the question of origin and the question of being.

Another way Blondel made his presence felt in philosophical circles at this time was his participation in the elaboration of André Lalande's *Vocabulaire Technique et Critique de la Philosophie*, which was launched at the International Congress of Philosophy in 1900 and was to be completed only in 1922, in other words over a period that would cover the better part of Blondel's teaching career. Blondel had actually met Lalande in 1891, while he was still working on his dissertation and while Lalande was still a second-year student at the École Normale Supérieure. Both found themselves together at Aix-les-Bains for a cure, Blondel for a bout with rheumatism and Lalande for a broken arm that he had sustained while coming to the defense of the Director of the École Normale, Rollin the grammarian, at the time, against a rampaging student who wanted to kill him. Blondel enjoyed hearing Lalande tell the story. During the weeks they spent at the baths together they became good friends, and it was a matter of course that Lalande would welcome his friend's participation in the work of compiling the *Vocabulaire*, especially after the impact that Blondel had had at the International Congress.

The work of compilation for the *Vocabulaire* was carried on by the *Société française de philosophie*, which met regularly in Paris under the direction of Lalande and went through all the words that were to be included, from A to Z. Blondel never attended any of the meetings in Paris, where Brunschvicg seemed to have an important say in what went into the *Vocabulaire*, but he was a regular correspondent along with many others, who would respond to the drafts that were circulated far and wide in the provinces and even abroad. The definitions that went into the vocabulary were a matter of consensus, but Lalande also included footnotes reproducing pertinent remarks from the correspondents as well as an echo of the discussions in Paris.

This is how Blondel came to figure prominently in an instrument of philosophical work that was to be used not only in France but also in many other countries for decades to come. It should come as no surprise that his name appears for the first time under the letter A at the word he had finally restored to the philosophical lexicon, Action, but which as he had been reminded, did not even appear in the standard dictionary of philosophy in France during the nineteenth century, when he came to register it as the subject for his dissertation. Given the kind of attention that the word had commanded at the International Congress, the committee had gone to great trouble to spell out the nuances that could be attached to it, including one sense that might be construed as the one Blondel wished to give it, namely, "everything that is not intelligence insofar as it is considered as constituting a kind of reality that is distinguished from intelligence." One can see the hand of Brunschvicg in this crafting of the definition from an intellectualist point of view.

Blondel could not be satisfied with this. In the letter quoted by Lalande he writes: "By *action* I understand what encompasses intelligence, preceding and preparing it, following it and going beyond it; hence what in thought is an internal synthesis rather than an objective representation" (1926d, 341). In Appendix A, of the *Vocabulaire*, Blondel is further quoted as saying: "I do not admit that the word *action* designates something EXTERIOR, something definitively refractory, something essentially impenetrable to intelligence; I admit that intelligence is INTERIOR to action, that it tries little by little to equal it, to explicate it, and that it must in the end orient and govern it" (1926d, 342). Contrary to the intellectualist position, Blondel maintains that the problem of logic is only an aspect of the problem of action, as he had argued in his paper at the International Congress. At the same time, however, he suggests that his position is a sort of *panlogism*, "a total reintegration of life in thought, which then sanctions it" (1926d, 343). Hence the idea of *alogical*, which is suggested with regard to action, appears to be inexact, since Blondel's intention is to establish a general logic of which Aristotelian, Baconian, and Hegelian logic would each be only a particular case. If he appears to be anti-intellectualist, Blondel claims, it is only because he wants to reclaim for rationality domains that the philosophy of pure ideas excludes.

Interestingly enough, in Appendix B, Blondel is quoted as suggesting the neologism *pragmatism*, to designate his approach to philosophy, presumably in opposition to *intellectualism*, as this term was understood at the time. To admit that word of Blondel, however, Brunschvicg responds, would be to follow him on his own terrain and to consecrate a doctrine that in reality we do not admit.

It is perhaps this suggestion of Blondel that led the ever-alert William James to seek out Blondel and to ask him for his copy of *L'Action*, long since out of print and unavailable anywhere in bookstores. Blondel lent him his copy for close to a year, but it soon became apparent to both men that what each one understood by "pragmatism" were two rather different things. James returned the book admitting that he could not understand its method of implication, or its logic, while admitting that there was something there worth looking into further. Blondel would later ask that the Appendix with the remark about "pragmatism" be withdrawn from the later edition of the *Vocabulaire*, because of the twist that had been given to it in the American version of "pragmatism."

Blondel's contribution to the word *action* in Lalande's *Vocabulaire* in 1902 was only the first of many that were to follow. In 1903 he contributed remarks to words under B and C, like *béatitude, bien, certitude, concepte, concrétion, conscience, criticisme, croyance,* and many others. And he would continue to do so through the years, especially where there was any question having to do with the philosophy of religion, such as, for example, the words *faith, grace, immanence, miracle, mystery,* and *mysticism*. To take up all of these contributions of Blondel to the *Vocabulaire* would be to find a fairly comprehensive exposition of Blondel's philosophy according to a chronological as well as an alphabetical order since they were stretched out over a period of some twenty years.

A New Starting Point for the Discipline of Philosophy

Blondel's idea of developing a fundamental general logic of action to encompass more the particular logics such as those of Aristotle or Hegel was never brought to fruition. The article published in the acts of the International Congress of 1900, and the remarks on such a logic at the word *action* in Lalande's *Vocabulaire* were all that ever came of that project. Like Hegel, Blondel had felt the need to develop a whole new logic to go with his philosophy of thought in act as well as of action, but he appears to have been diverted from elaborating such a logic as he saw fit by his preoccupation with apologetics, and with placating the theologians who could not understand what he saw as the philosophical exigencies for a critically valid apologetics. Later on, in his more systematic Trilogy, beginning with two volumes on *La Pensée*, when he would finally come around to pursuing his own thought in the matter of these philosophical exigencies, he would focus more on "thought" than on "logic," picking up on the distinction and the relation between *thinking thought* and *thought thought* which he had begun to speak of in the article "The Elementary Principle for a Logic of the Moral Life," realizing that the logic he was thinking of was one associated more with the activity of thinking thought than with the more formal or notional aspect of thought thought. In his work on *L'Être et les êtres*, he would transpose this idea of a fundamental logic of the concrete into a Normative for the consolidation of beings in progress through human beings in history, and even recall, in an *Excursus,* parts of that earlier General Logic as opening the way to an Ontological Normative (1935, 468-85).

Before Blondel was to move on to this later phase of his thinking, however, or to any other important philosophical business, there was still one more adjustment, or one more *mise au point,* with regard to the new approach to philosophy through human action, or with regard to "the starting point for philosophical research," which he thought had to be made and which he published in a double article in the *Annales de Philosophie Chrétienne* in 1906. This was to be the last of the important articles he published, in this early stage of his thinking, on method in philosophy. In many respects, this article was a follow-up on the two earlier articles, "The Idealist Illusion" and "The Elementary Principle for a Logic of the Moral Life," but it also broke new ground in trying to redefine, in an existential way, the approach or the point of departure for philosophy as a systematic or a technical discipline.

The problem, as Blondel conceived it, consisted in bringing together a general view of philosophy as having to do with the whole of human experience and a more specific view of philosophy as requiring a technical discipline that sets it off, not only from the common sense view that people have of human life, but also from other scientific disciplines, so that philosophy, far from cutting itself off from the spontaneous and natural movement of life, can find a way of inserting itself in the ongoing common effort of humanity and thus become a work of life as well as a work of science.

To make his point, Blondel begins by making a distinction between two fundamental kinds of knowing, one of which he will call *prospective* and the other *reflective.* The first he describes as a kind of direct knowing that takes place or is presupposed in any kind of deliberate action. This is a knowing that is oriented toward the future, toward the ends that I am pursuing in my actions, and is quite synthetic in that it encompasses the different aspects of finality that are actually governing my choices of action. It is immediate and an integral part of my labor, so closely subordinated to the ends that I am anticipating, that I do not even think of detaching this knowledge from the ends themselves. It is tied to our life as a whole and to the future that we anticipate for ourselves. It is synthetic and practical in character, but it can also grow in clarity and precision as we advance in life. This is the kind of knowing Blondel had characterized as "Practical Science" in the introduction to *L'Action* in 1893, in order to distinguish from it the "Science of Practice" he was about to embark upon. Here he is characterizing it as a direct kind of knowing that grounds our reasonable activity in the way that prudence governs it. It is essentially attentive to the concrete work toward which we are tending in an action that is evidential and providential.

In contrast to this direct kind of knowing is the more reflective kind of knowing, which we tend to associate with formal analysis of conditions from which we begin as agents. This is a more retrospective kind of knowing, turned toward results previously obtained or procedures previously used. It proceeds by an analysis that fragments the whole of past experience and of nature into different facts now seen as separate from one another. While many view this reflective or analytical kind of knowing as the primary form, Blondel insists that it is derivative and secondary to the more direct kind of knowing. But it is an original kind of knowing with its own orientation, differing from that of direct knowing in deliberate action. It is abstract in the sense that, in its consideration of different facts, it prescinds from the concrete sense in which action is directed and from the real causes that motivate that action. It is in contrast to this abstract analytical form of knowing that the first, more direct kind of knowing can be spoken of as intuitive, albeit in a practical and synthetic way. Reverting to his earlier way of speaking, adopted from Spinoza, Blondel speaks of this reflective knowing as knowledge that is known *(connaissance connue)* in contradistinction from the knowing and acting knowledge *(connaissance connaissante et agissante)* directly associated with deliberate action. Clearly, reflective knowledge has to do with things already constituted in their being, while prospective knowledge has more to do with the progression of things in becoming. But more importantly for Blondel, reflective knowledge fragments and generalizes the different objects it focuses on, in abstraction from the place or the role they play concretely in action, while the direct, prospective knowledge, which becomes all the more clear as it becomes more synthetic, envisions the entire nature of things as the series of means that it unifies and subordinates in the light of its ends.

Given these two fundamental kinds of knowing, neither of which Blondel wants to belittle, one can then ask what kind of knowing philosophical knowing is. Can it be constituted in the mode of reflective, analytical thought as a special discipline like any other science? Or given the universal, prudential scope that is usually associated with the idea of philosophy, must it busy itself only with the "final end of man" and nourish itself only on the *angst* of souls worrying about the depths of their nature and the mysteries of their future?

Before trying to give a more positive answer to these questions, Blondel pauses to examine three false points of departure for philosophy that tend to confuse action itself with the idea of action, as Descartes did, or practical knowing with the consciousness we have of it, or, in terms of the introduction to *L'Action*, the science of practice with practical science itself. Blondel is setting up to represent his method of laying out the logic or the dialectic of Practical Science in his Science of Practice, which can then only feed back into action or Practical Science, elevating it to a higher order of spiritual achievement. But before he does that, he looks at three false systematic ways of starting philosophy, with which he wants to take issue.

The first is one that proceeds from reflection, as he has just described it, and develops, on the basis of perceptions and notions that come from reflection, diverse kinds of metaphysics but only of the idea. This is an instinctive way of starting that will have to be part of any true beginning in doing philosophy as a systematic discipline. But taken by itself, it only fragments reality artificially into an object of thought that it tends to reify simply as thought, as if reality and the idea of reality were the same. This first approach abstracts from the concrete reality that gives rise to inquiry. It reduces the *act* to a fact taken as the sum of an indefinite multiplicity of facts. It only produces a scheme of factitious abstractions, each of which it then tries to reify as ontological. Even if it were to complete the circle of its reflection, it could never exhaust the antecedent knowledge of the human being in act. In fact, it can never complete such a circle, but is forever condemned to run off indefinitely in its different orders of research, without any assignable limit. As a philosophy exclusively of reflection, even when it claims to be realist, it remains a philosophy of the idea, resting on an initial and latent fideism, which it cannot justify and whose origin it cannot determine rationally.

The second kind of false start in philosophy Blondel looks into is that of an exclusively critical attitude, usually aimed at the foregoing way of exclusive reflection on ideas. This is the way that had become prevalent in France after Kant. But Blondel sees in it only another form of exclusive reflection, focused no longer on any object of understanding, but rather on the moral subject. Far from abandoning the old form of rationalism, it merely changes the matter of its reflection. It abstracts and isolates the *fact* of morality, in order to submit it to a method of inquiry that is exclusive. It too remains a fideism of ideas that starts from derivative forms of reflection and action. It is still lacking in a starting point that is distinctive and original for a positive philosophy.

The third kind of false start in philosophy Blondel brings up is one that was emerging in France at the turn of the century and that had appeared as an ally of Blondel at the International Congress of Philosophy in 1900, in the argument against idealism, but from which Blondel still wanted to distinguish his own way of starting in philosophy. This a way that was associated with Bergson. Blondel characterizes it as starting from an immediate psychological intuition rather than any analytical reflection. The idea was to come back to intuition, rather than any datum of reason, even that of practical reason, or to turn analysis against analysis, in order to grasp the life of spirit in its nascent state without losing contact with it. Blondel is quite in sympathy with this new way of starting philosophy, but he still sees in it a subtle danger of missing the true starting point for philosophy, if one simply excludes reflection in the same way as reflection previously excluded the concrete act of thinking in action. In being exclusive of reflection, psychological intuitionism is only transforming what might have been the true *prospection* of action into a simple reflection. It remains a form of intellectualism with its own ontological pretensions of immediate insight into reality. There is no way for thought to develop in this view, because thought is still seen abstractly as only an instrument of action, once again as if the idea of practice took the place of practice itself, which is where thought has to develop reflectively as well as prospectively. "At the point of departure of all the sciences, all the arts, all the industries there is a need to be satisfied, a need without which reflection would never have produced itself nor produced anything else. But at the same time, action does not produce itself, it does not produce its useful effects, except by way of a reflection that gives it its means and that, as it enables it to attain its successive ends, helps it to discern and to pursue its higher end" (1906b, 356-57).

It makes no sense then, to isolate practical knowledge from speculative knowledge. The two have to move forward together so that each has its starting point in the other at different stages of human action, with action promoting thought at one point and thought promoting action at another. Blondel devotes the second installment of his article on the point of departure for philosophical research to show us how this can be done without detriment to either prospection or reflection, as two irreducible fundamental forms of human knowing.

The problem for Blondel is to understand how philosophy is to be constituted as a technical discipline, while continuing to insert itself in the common promotion of humanity. Stated more precisely in terms of human knowing, the question is to see how knowing in *act* always proceeds by way of fragmentary reflection and of total prospection simultaneously, where both the abstractions of speculative analysis and the intuitions of practical synthesis remain inseparable, as irreducible aspects of one and the same process. When considered from the side of reflection, philosophy appears "as a technical discipline and as a speculative search for real truth," but it begins "only when, instead of focusing successively on partial data, as if they could be isolated, or instead of raising independent problems in the face of distinct objects, as if they could be solved separately, it subordinates its investigation expressly to the single and inevitable problem that the relation between consciousness and action raises within us" (1906b, 226). In other words, reflection becomes strictly philosophical only when it takes its task to be initially one of elucidation of the integral synthesis of prospection, without any of its usual premature ontological pretensions.

On the other side, from the standpoint of prospection as a work of invention and practical direction, philosophy begins only when, "instead of limiting itself to the global intuition that is initially sufficient for spontaneous action, or to the particular aims that mask without suppressing it, the general inclination of the will, it understands and puts into practice its duty of spelling out letter by letter the book of life written within us, of bringing out its directive ideas, of foreseeing and preparing its *dénouement*" (1906b, 226). In other words, once again, prospection becomes strictly philosophical only when it takes its task to be initially that of reintegrating within itself all the fragmentary achievements of reflection, without any premature moral or religious conclusions apart from a methodical and progressive consideration of every aspect of the synthesis in all of its ramifications. In this way, philosophy, which is at once reflective and prospective, can be understood as human life itself becoming conscious and directive, conferring on thought all the role it has to play and only the role it can play, legitimately, working toward the equation of knowing and existing, and simultaneously developing the reality of our being amid other beings as well as the truth of beings within us.

It is not easy to adopt this strictly philosophical stance from the side of both reflection and prospection at the same time in a way that is not reducible to common sense or uncritical knowledge, or even to Practical Science as such, even though Philosophy is a critical and technical attempt to elucidate the content of practical knowledge as a whole. Blondel goes on to elucidate how philosophy has to proceed from each one of the two sides of knowing he has distinguished. What he describes is more or less the method he had followed in *L'Action* of 1893, with its attempt to spell out, from one stage to the next, what we think systematically in acting as human, thoughtful beings, without claiming to exhaust everything we actually know prospectively and even reflectively. In this way the reflective moment of philosophy can never close in upon itself at some fixed point. It has to remain systematically open to all that action can bring to it for further reflection.

This does not mean that philosophy is anarchical, or without principle, but rather that its principle must be to become equal to action. Action, with all that is implicit in it, is philosophy's proper object, and the aim of reflective philosophy is to render the implicit in prospective knowledge explicit in consciousness as such, and so to strive toward a progressive coincidence between the two. Its point of departure is the systematic affirmation of the actual inadequation within ourselves, and of the solidarity of all the problems that concern our being, and beings in general. To the extent that in the end thought falls short of the fullness of action, philosophy then has to subordinate itself to effective action and become a part of practice itself. It must join its speculative effort with the ascetical method of deliberate action, which brings us to viewing philosophy from the side of prospective knowing as well as reflective knowing.

Philosophy cannot remain a purely reflective and analytical science. It has always been popularly thought of as having something to do with practice, or with life as a whole, and Blondel could not agree more. This is why he had turned to action for his philosophical dissertation and why he had begun with the question: "yes or no, does human life make sense, and does man have a destiny?" His idea was to arrive at a totally unified synthetic view, or science of action, having to do with the whole of life, not just for the sake of doing a systematic science as such, but also for the sake of going beyond this speculative moment of science, systematically back to the prospective moment of knowing in human action as such. In one sense the science of philosophy is not distinct from the philosophy of life, but in another sense that is not less true, knowledge itself constitutes a real progress in life. Philosophy aims not only at explaining human life, but also at making it more human. It has recourse to the analyses of reflection in search of a richer, more comprehensive, and more synthetic intuition into life. "It is not by reflecting on reflection and its objects, it is by acting according to our reflected ideas and our objective knowledge that we arrive at thinking better and at making our consciousness more equal to our being and to beings. The method of intellectual invention is not ideological, but positive and practical" (1906b, 245).

Thus, far from being anti-intellectual in any radical sense, Blondel was for a different kind of intellectualism than one that stopped short at ideas. He was for taking ideas back into action methodically and systematically, including the idea of God, in order to advance toward new intuitions into the problem of human destiny and the question of being, by composing scientific analyses with vital syntheses. At the end of the second installment of the article, he gathers his thought, in answer to the initial question of how philosophy arises as a technical discipline in the face of human life, in a sort of definition: "Philosophy is the integration, special and technical through its form, universal and popular through its matter, of all the hierarchized efforts of human life to realize our being in realizing beings and the being in us, that is in knowing them, in adapting ourselves to them, and in assimilating them to us" (1906b, 249). It is not just a representation or a projection of life. It brings life itself closer to its term, to a discovery and an increase in its riches, its responsibilities, and its sanctions. It is not able to make explicit all that is implicit or at stake in its research at any given moment, because what is at stake is ever in motion on the road of life. But, starting from the concrete situation of human existence in action, it can bring out what remains unknown in it by "determining the equation of the profound movement that bears us along, or the spontaneous exigencies that solicit us with the progress of our science and the term of our will" (1906b, 249). Blondel accepts the idea of philosophy as apprenticeship for death, which he finds in Plato and Spinoza, but he understands the apprenticeship as an anticipation of true life, that is, of a life that is for us indivisibly knowledge and action. For Blondel, philosophy had to be a personal work, no less than a universal work, a work of the human spirit as well as an academic technical work.

In the articles on the *Starting Point for Philosophical Research*, Blondel no longer refers to the Logic of Aristotle or the Logic of Hegel, nor does he speak of a Logic of Action as such. He speaks rather of knowing as a whole and of thought as it relates to action. Perhaps he had come to think that the idea of logic still connoted too much of the intellectualism or the idealism he was trying to overcome, but without falling into the anti-intellectualism he could see in Bergsonism. Instead of "logic of action," he chose rather to speak of *prospective knowing*, which was an integral part of self-conscious action, much as Kierkegaard had come to speak of subjective truth, which had to do with decision making in relation to one's eternal salvation, in contradistinction from having to do with merely objective truth.

In *L'Action* of 1893, Blondel had argued for the necessity of a subjective science or a science of the subject, over and above any positive or objective science, in order precisely to bring the human subject to the question of a final alternative in the face of one's eternal destiny. Unlike Kierkegaard, however, he had not tried to keep these kinds of knowing separate from one another. He had tried to enlist the power of reflective knowing, or his Science of Practice, in the service of Practical Science or prospective knowing, just as he had used the practical science or the prospective knowing in self-conscious action as the starting point for his reflective knowing or his Science of Practice. In the articles on the *Starting Point for Philosophical Research*, he was speaking of the practical science in any existential subject more explicitly, as a kind of knowing, a prospective knowing, to be correlated to reflective knowing, or to "philosophical research," just as philosophical research or reflection into human subjectivity had to be correlated to the prospective or practical knowing of human action, so that philosophy could not escape from the question of one's eternal destiny. Thus the way was open to start his systematic Trilogy, not with a Logic, but with a reflection on Thought or knowing as a whole, with its two sides of prospection and reflection, in its relation to Action.

Social Initiatives

In some respects the articles on the *Starting Point* marked a culmination of Blondel's early reflection on philosophical method, which had begun with his articles on *Apologetics* exactly ten years earlier, in 1896. By then he was well established as a Philosopher in Aix and in the *Société Française de Philosophie*. However, Blondel was not just a philosopher of action. He was also a man of action, as evidenced by his missionary approach to the University and to his doctoral dissertation, and by his concern for developing an effective Christian apologetic appropriate for the modern spirit. We know that he kept up with his corporal as well as spiritual works of mercy in Aix, as he had been taught to do as a boy by his family in Dijon. We also know that he continued his active participation in social movements to reshape society according to ideals of the Christian spirit, which had begun as early as 1889, while he was still working on his dissertation, when, with a student of his, Charles Combe, the son-in-law of Ollé-Laprune, and a classmate of his, Adéodat Boissard, he participated in the foundation of an avant-garde review named *Le XXe Siècle,* whose purpose was to explore social questions. Blondel was also proud of having helped a group of his students from the Lycée Stanislas, where in 1891 he had taught as a substitute for three months, found a journal of their own, called *Le Sillon,* which was to have significant impact on social issues in years to come.

In Aix, he became a regular contributor to *La Croix de Provence,* a Catholic opinion newspaper under the direction of Henri Boissard, a friend from the days of Blondel's earlier stay in Aix as a teacher of philosophy at the Lycée Mignet from 1886 to 1889, who was also the father of his friend and brother-in-law, Adéodat Boissard, married to his wife's sister. The elder Boissard was a man very much like Blondel's father and uncle Louis, a staunch Catholic committed to influencing public life under the régime of a not-so-Catholic Republic, not by direct political action, but more socially in relation to growing problems affecting ordinary people and workers. He had been a magistrate in Dijon, but had been dismissed for finding against the State in a case that involved a religious institute. He had then become a member of the bar in Aix-en-Provence, where he launched his *Croix de Provence* in 1890.

Blondel began writing for the newspaper under pseudonyms, so as not to appear to be invoking his authority as a professor of the University, or perhaps also so as not to incur any recriminations from the University itself. After the elder Boissard died in December 1897, Blondel became much more involved in the day-to-day running of the newspaper in order to help with the transition to a new director. He wrote the necrology for Boissard and then, for the next two or three years, contributed numerous articles and editorials on diverse subjects such as peace, the Dreyfus affair, public and private or free education, elections, the public spirit, patriotism, the Chamber of Deputies, crime, Franco-German relations, the influence of Pope Leo XIII in France, and, on December 30, 1900, the beginning of a new century. Many of the articles were not signed, but those that were went under such names as *La Rédaction, L'Alpin, Le Patriote, Le Brave, Graindeblé,* and even *A Reader.*

Blondel was very concerned about being discovered as the author of these pieces and, when he saw that he was in danger of being identified with one of the names, for example, *L'Alpin,* as he writes to his friend Brémond, the name would disappear. A list of these contributions of Blondel to *La Croix de Provence* is given in Annexe I of the Blondel Bibliography, volume one. The list is well authenticated but it may not be complete, given the hide-and-seek atmosphere in which they were written. It shows the wide diversity of public affairs Blondel was interested in as a man of action. His later interest in the Catholic social action movement would pick up from where he left off with *La Croix de Provence,* after his good friend, the canon Mallet, who was to help him in his other game of hide-and-seek with Catholic apologists, became the official director of *La Croix de Provence.* Later on Blondel would also become a regular contributor to another weekly journal, *Le Petit Éclaireur,* put out by a group of Social Catholics, as they called themselves, from 1906 to 1914.

During this time, however, after the *Letter on Apologetics* in 1896 leading up to the article "History and Dogma" in 1904, Blondel's attention was drawn much more by the controversy over apologetics within the Church itself that he had provoked. Blondel felt misunderstood and even calumniated. He was hurt by the criticisms and accusations leveled against him, but he was not discouraged or afraid that he might be off on a wrong track. After trying to set the record straight in his own name, he responded more by silence or by using the name of friends like the canon Mallet to explain what his true position was. He was convinced that the resistance of his opponents was due to a lack of information, or a scholastic prejudice, and he longed for a forum or a periodical that would do battle on his side to influence Catholic opinion, the clergy, and even public opinion in general.

There were, of course, the *Annales de Philosophie Chrétienne,* where the articles on Catholic apologetics had first appeared. They were under the direction of the Abbé Charles Denis, but Blondel and his friends, Wehrlé and Mourret, were wary of this abbé, who thought of himself as an ally and sought to include as much of Blondel as possible in his own writings, but who could not be trusted to get things straight, at least not as Blondel thought of them. It was Denis's misunderstanding of the method in *L'Action* that had initially provoked Blondel to write the *Letter on Apologetics,* but Denis had never quite gotten the point of what Blondel thought had to be done in apologetics in keeping with the most fundamental Christian tradition. Blondel did not trust Denis, nor did he want too much of his "collaboration" in trying to find a way through the modernist crisis. Even the *Annales,* with Denis as their director, could not be trusted to keep the record straight.

When, however, in 1905, Denis died and the continuation of the *Annales* came into question, Blondel seized on the opportunity to buy up the title and rights of the journal from Denis's estate in order to continue its Christian and even Catholic presence in the realm of philosophical and religious publication. In buying the journal Blondel had in mind keeping it under better control in both philosophy and religion, and he chose, to work with him, Lucien Laberthonnière, an Oratorian priest who was about his age and who had been an ardent enthusiast of the philosophy of action since 1894, when he had first read *L'Action,* shortly after it was published. The two had corresponded and had become good friends. Blondel had been especially pleased to find a priest who understood what he was about so well, and Laberthonnière had become even more enthused with the new philosophy of religion when he had read the *Lettre sur les exigences de la pensée contemporaine en matière d'apologétique.* The two shared in the same intellectual missionary spirit and in the desire to update Christian thinking according to the exigencies of modern thought, not in order to set old dogmas aside, but rather to bring out what was spiritually most fruitful in them. The two could also complement one another, since one had been trained in the modern secular tradition of philosophy while the other had been trained in the more ecclesiastical tradition of theology.

The arrangement for the *Annales* was to be that Blondel would oversee philosophical contributions to the journal, while Laberthonnière would oversee the more religiously oriented contributions. In announcing their program in the October issue of 1905, they announced their intention to think and to act both as philosophers and as Christians. "We are convinced," they went on to say, "of the necessity of approaching philosophically all the problems of which it can be said that they are matters of the soul, of examining philosophically even and especially the foundations of religion, not with the fatuity of using a power or exercising a right, but with the consciousness of fulfilling a duty" (1905a). With regard to authority in the Church, they recognized that "if it is true that . . . men cannot do without the Church and what it has to offer from on high, neither can the Church do entirely without men and what we can bring to it humbly from below . . . so that there is a work going on incessantly in the Church through the cooperation of the faithful and even, in some sense, of all of humanity . . ." (1905a). The idea was to act as Christians in the world of human spirit under the guidance of the Church, but according to a method that was critically philosophical.

Needless to say, both would be frequent contributors in this new venture. Instead of choosing a director for the review, Laberthonnière was named secretary for the redaction, while Blondel's role as owner and co-director remained more in the background. In fact, Blondel did not let it be known publicly that he had become the new owner, or that he had any part in its direction until much later. Of the two, Laberthonnière was much more fiery and much more intransigent in his criticism of reactionary theologians. Blondel would exert a moderating influence on him, to ward off any undue criticism or especially any condemnation from ecclesiastical authorities, at a time when opponents to their work were forever denouncing people to Rome and seeking condemnations against anyone who would not submit to the detractor's narrow, abstract idea of Christianity, or just dared to speak in a different voice. The journal did not back off from what had become the controversial issues of the modernist crisis in the Catholic Church, knowing that thinking Christians had to come to terms with these issues in a much more positive way than just blanket condemnations of everything modern and liberal or progressive. Blondel's friends and confidants, Wehrlé and Mourret, were completely in support of this new joint venture in presenting the Christian supernatural viewpoint in a way that was congenial to the exigencies of a modern critical spirit.

It will be remembered that Blondel had already published his blockbusting articles of 1896 on the philosophical exigencies for an effective Christian apologetics in these *Annales*. The article on "the idealist illusion," even though it was in response to objections from a Thomist to his own method in apologetics, had been more appropriately placed in the *Revue de Métaphysique et Morale,* since it was addressed more to philosophers than to theologians. On the other hand, the articles on history and dogma had been sent to *La Quinzaine,* a Catholic review under the direction of Fonsegrive, where it would reach more of the young Catholic intellectuals and seminarians who were looking for a way out of the impasse that had developed between intransigent *extrinsicism* in the Church and intransigent *historicism* among the modernists. Upon taking over the *Annales* with Laberthonnière, however, Blondel began to aim most of his writing toward the journal, as did its new secretary for the redaction. This is where he placed his two articles on *Le point de départ de la recherche philosophique* in January and June 1906, as an important methodological statement about the kind of philosophy that was to characterize the new orientation of the journal as well as his own philosophy.

Typically, however, this was to be the only major contribution that he would sign with his own name during his years of collaboration with the *Annales,* no doubt because he thought of it as pure philosophy rather than the more mixed kinds of subjects that he was to tackle as a Christian philosopher. In fact, Blondel chose to write under several pseudonyms according to different subjects. Under the name of Bernard de Sailly, in memory first of St. Bernard, a compatriot from Dijon, and second, of lands in Flanders once owned by Blondel's forbears, he began to revisit his conception of the philosophy of action, in 1905 and 1906, along with his ideas of philosophy of religion and of apologetics. Only Laberthonnière and Mourret were apprised of his identity under this name.

As part of the Bernard de Sailly articles, Blondel argued against Le Roy's notion of the miracle and its place in a philosophy of religion, thus showing a more factual view of miracles than he was credited for. This should be seen in the context of the earlier articles on the "Point de Départ," which had been aimed in part at correcting Le Roy's excessively facile way of manipulating ideas in philosophy as well as in religious thinking. Interestingly enough, under the same name he also revisited, in 1913, his old argument with the Dominican, Schwalm, in connection with an article by Schwalm on whether faith is reasonable, published posthumously, where Blondel finds a certain rapprochement or a certain appropriation of ideas that Schwalm had formerly reproached Blondel for using. It seems that Schwalm was rescinding some of his adamant extrinsicist attitude toward the end of his life, and that perhaps a certain meeting of minds was possible to constitute an integral apologetics that would include the proper development of internal attitudes as well as external historical facts. Unfortunately, Schwalm's intellectual heirs among the Dominicans would not pick up on this more accommodating tendency toward concern for internal attitudes in their continual opposition to Blondel.

Similarly, Blondel availed himself of another name he had used previously in offering clarifications and corrections as to what were his true intentions in philosophy and in apologetics, namely, that of the canon Mallet, who had taken over *La Croix de Provence,* and who had published previously as his own in various ecclesiastical journals explanations that Blondel had written himself, during the time when he had vowed to keep silence on the issue of apologetics. In the *Annales* Blondel reverts back to Mallet's name to publish some of his recent discoveries with Laberthonnière concerning Cardinal Dechamps, whose work on apologetics had been very influential in the First Vatican Council. In resurrecting this work of Dechamps, which did not allow for a separation between the rational motives for credibility and the concrete motives for faith, Blondel was looking for a well-placed ally in the hierarchy of the Church to bolster his own efforts at renewing apologetics according to the exigencies of modern thought, but not without a certain criticism of the Cardinal's method, which was lacking in a precise notion of philosophy and in a proper theory of knowledge. Coincidentally, Blondel was also using Mallet's name for his submission in an essay contest to another journal, *La Revue du Clergé français,* on a related matter, namely, on faith and science. The essay won the prize, though one can wonder if it would have, if its true author had been known.

In this essay Blondel analyzes the act of faith concretely as a passage from mere credulity, as something abstractly rational in itself, to an obligation to believe concretely based on motives proper to the will as well as those proper to the intellect. He also defends the logical autonomy of science in its own sphere, which is abstract, while arguing that in the concrete science depends on higher values and higher judgments, adumbrated in a reflection on action in its integrity or wholeness. Originally written as two articles in 1906, the essay was later reworked and published as a single piece in 1907 as part of a collection on Science et Religion, still under the name of Mallet. In the following year, 1908, as so often proved to be the case, Mallet, meaning Blondel, had to come back to the subject in the *Revue du Clergé,* to answer criticisms and to offer further precisions on the threefold role of the will, as it relates to intelligence in action. Misunderstanding in thinking about the act of supernatural faith comes from considering only one of these roles in isolation from the others.

Besides these articles on faith, Blondel also published in May 1907, let us recall, the account of his *soutenance de thèse* with which we began this book, fourteen years after the original event, as if to remind people of where he was coming from in these contentious times among Catholics, and whose side he was on in the question about religion. The piece, as we noted earlier, was published under the name of Wehrlé, but it had been written by Blondel himself on the basis of notes taken at the defense itself. It does not seem to have made much difference on those who were opposed to his ideas, except perhaps to make them more dogged in their pursuit of one who appeared so close and yet so wrongheaded in their view.

It must not be thought that the running was smooth for the new administration of the *Annales de Philosophie Chrétienne*. While Blondel, under the pseudonym of Bernard de Sailly, was arguing against Le Roy's loose conception of the miracle, for a proper understanding of the supernatural in history, he was also finding that Laberthonnière was giving in too much to Le Roy's loose way of thinking in the philosophy of religion and apologetics. Le Roy had his own Bergsonian way of arguing for Christianity and was gathering about him a kind of Society for Religious Studies, to which Laberthonnière was attracted. Blondel felt he had to warn his collaborator at the *Annales* against getting involved with that kind of study, which was lacking in intellectual rigor as well as a clear concept of the supernatural acceptable to the Church. Wehrlé, who had participated in the work of this Society, had felt that he had to quit it, as he saw Le Roy's influence growing in it and, in a letter to Blondel, bemoaned too much of the same kind of fluidity in Laberthonnière's writing, much as he admired and sympathized with it (1969a, 351). With Mourret, Wehrlé anticipated the condemnation that would fall upon Le Roy's book, *Dogme et Critique*, published in May 1907, and the kind of shadow this would cast on the Society for Religious Studies. Wehrlé even warned Blondel himself against giving in too much to Laberthonnière's way and urged Blondel to stick to his own way of thinking as much more precise conceptually and more in keeping with the teaching of the Church.

What was not anticipated by the circle of friends associated with the *Annales*, however, was the condemnation that fell on Laberthonnière himself when two of his books, *Essais de philosophie religieuse* (1903) and *Le réalisme chrétien* (1905), were placed on the *Index* of forbidden books. This was a blow that struck Blondel to the quick, on the very day in which he was to spend the night at his father's bedside, who died the next morning, April 9, 1906. In writing to his friends on that same day Blondel spoke of these two events in the same breath, as it were, asking for prayers for both his father and his friend, who would be severely afflicted by this condemnation, as one who was only trying to work for the acceptance of the Church among thinking people, as a loyal son. The condemnation was seen as a blow, not only to Laberthonnière personally, but also to the *Annales*, of which he was the Secretary for Redaction. It was something that affected not only Laberthonnière's, but also Blondel's conscience, along with their very consciousness of who they were as Catholics and what they were about as apostles for the Catholic Church.

Wehrlé, concerned though he was always for thinking with the Church, argued that the *Index* itself did not have to be taken seriously as a matter of conscience. "It is an outdated institution, which no longer has, which no longer can have any validity in the internal forum of Christian conscience" (1969a, 157). What Blondel and his priest friends saw in the condemnation was the act of an angered bishop, by the name of Thurinaz, taking it out on Laberthonnière, with whom he had had some controversy, by reaching for the button in Rome that would silence his adversary. The fact is that the books being condemned had previously received the *imprimatur* of other bishops who had no less authority than the offended bishop. Nevertheless, the fact was also that the authority of the Church, which Blondel and his friends respected with utmost care, was now seen as having been invoked in an attempt to silence, not only Laberthonnière, but also the *Annales de Philosophie Chrétienne*.

This was something that they had to deal with in conscience, lest they show disrespect for the very kind of authority in teaching that they were trying to defend. To their credit as philosophers of a supernatural religion, Blondel and Laberthonnière showed proper deference to this authority of the Church in the *Annales*, and went on with their work, without admitting that they had been silenced, as one particular bishop would have liked. Blondel, who always suffered interiorly from this kind of fulmination from on high, saw it as the kind of suffering one has to expect when the natural has to make way for the supernatural in one's own action, even that of defending the Church, or more personally, when the self has to make way for God in oneself.

A more serious challenge to their work arose from Rome, however, when a little over a year later, on September 8, 1907, the anti-modernist encyclical letter of Pius X, *Pascendi Dominici Gregis*, came out. Once again, Blondel felt severely grieved, even crushed, by this document, even more than by the earlier condemnation of Laberthonnière. This time the condemnation came directly from the supreme authority of the Church in a way that could not be ignored in conscience, but it named no one in particular, neither Blondel, nor Laberthonnière, nor even any of the modernists who had been previously identified as such and condemned, such as Loisy or Tyrrell or von Hügel. All that the encyclical did was give a general and vague indication of a system of thought branded as "modernist" among people who were generally thought of as philosophers, believers, theologians, historians, critics, apologists, or reformers. It was a blanket statement that could be used by anyone in the Church to point the finger of accusation against anyone else whose ideas they did not like, a triumph of extrinsicism of the worse kind, seemingly bringing the Pope around to its own narrow exclusive outlook. Blondel knew that the encyclical would be used precisely in this way against himself and many others by reactionary thinkers in the Church, and he wept with his friends at the damage this would do to countless souls in search of the truth of the Catholic faith.

Reportedly, the doctrinal part of the encyclical was written by a scholastic theologian by the name of Joseph Lemius, the Superior General of the Oblates of Mary Immaculate, who later wrote his own *Catechism on Modernism*, and it provided a perfect handle for obsessive theologians to come out swinging against anyone who did not think of the Church and its teaching in a purely extrinsicist way, precisely as they did. Blondel and his friends were dismayed by this new wave of trouble that was being heaped upon them. They knew that, as loyal sons of the Church, they would have to face up to this seeming condemnation of their work politically within the Church, in order to continue publishing the *Annales de Philosophie Chrétienne*. But they also knew that they had nothing to do with what was being condemned, even though they could not say this publicly, for fear of having their words twisted around so that the words would appear like insubordination. After a careful and apprehensive reading of the encyclical, for Blondel was always in fear of being pulled back and having to retract in his attempts to advance the thinking of the Church, he came to realize that it had to do only with doctrines he had himself criticized, whether in philosophy, history, or apologetics, and that it did not touch on anything that he had written or said in his philosophy of action or in his decade-long controversy over apologetics. Once again Blondel and Laberthonnière, in consultation with their priest friends and supporters, had to find a way of showing proper deference to the authority of the Church in the *Annales*, in order to continue with their work of publication.

The closest thing in the encyclical that could have been associated with Blondel, given his earlier insistence on the need for a method of immanence, was an allusion to the error of "vital immanentism." But Blondel found in the encyclical three different ways of talking about *immanence*, one that was said to be irreproachable, and two others that were condemned. Blondel had no trouble concurring in the condemnation, while insisting that he had spoken of immanence only in the irreproachable way, referring to St. Thomas's method in the *Summa contra Gentiles* and to Cardinal Dechamps in support of his own approach to transcendence through immanence. With the encyclical, he recognized that the method of immanence could be used recklessly, or in a way that defeated the purpose of arguing for transcendence, as had been done by some overly enthusiastic readers of *L'Action*, against whom Blondel had initially written his *Letter on Apologetics*, but that, if used properly, it should overcome any doctrine of immanence, or the idea that human nature and reason have to be confined within themselves, without any opening to the supernatural, as Blondel had argued against rationalists and non-believers, not to mention certain theologians, who also thought of human nature and reason as totally self-sufficient even in the knowledge of God, thus unwittingly rendering God himself totally immanent.

What became clear to Blondel was that the encyclical was stuck in rehashing an old Scholastic and abstract way of posing the problem of the relation between "human nature" and the "supernatural order," which had little or nothing to do with his own way of approaching the problem concretely in terms of the human situation in history. To be sure, he felt bombarded by this abstract and divisive Scholasticism of states, but this time he resolved not to attack it in return. "In short," he wrote to Wehrlé, "let us abandon all litigious language; let us leave behind these positions turned toward the 'moderns'; instead, caught within the place under assault with our brothers, let us labor, with gentleness and patience, to illuminate them, to arm them for the future. In conscience, I do not think I am obliged to renounce interiorly any of my hopes. And I am even confident that, through mysterious ways, the present suffering, this awful pain of being calumniated before the world by the highest authority, this infinitely more bitter grief in thinking of the anguish of so many souls and of the suffering of Our Lord Himself, will bear fruit" (1969b, 383). Blondel was not giving in to the Scholastic way of presenting problems, which was still too abstract and intellectualist, as some have suggested with regard to the "later Blondel," but rather he was learning to temper his language more carefully, realizing once again, as he had at the end of the *Letter on Apologetics,* that, if he was to convert the modern spirit to Catholicism he would have to begin by converting Catholics themselves to the true Catholic spirit, which is a spirit of peace and reconciliation, even with reason and the world, and not a spirit of contention and hostility.

In the interest of doing this he began to speak of the concrete state of affairs for souls in the world who were estranged from God, for whatever reason, and yet who were called to a life of supernatural union with God, as is the belief of Catholicism, as a *transnatural* state, a state that is neither purely natural, closed in upon itself, nor fully supernatural, explicitly accepting the gift of supernatural grace, but a state in spiritual tension from the natural to the supernatural, which Blondel thought could be brought out in human experience by psychological and social analysis as well as by philosophical argument concerning the necessity of transcendence in human action. This idea of a *transnatural* state followed directly from his earlier idea of Panchristism in the concrete. Blondel would develop it further in his defense of the Social Catholics against accusations of "sociological modernism" coming from the still bellicose camp of intransigent extrinsicist Catholics, and he would resort to it in his later philosophy in speaking of the Christian Spirit as it inserts itself in the drama of human history. It would be taken up later on in the century by Catholic existential theologians like Karl Rahner and Henri de Lubac, which shows that Blondel's confidence in his progressive Catholic ideas was not misplaced, especially not after Pope John XXIII and the Second Vatican Council.

Another idea that emerged in the immediate sequel to *Pascendi,* and that would also figure prominently in his later defense of the Social Catholics against accusations of modernism from those who would then be designated as *monophorists,* was a clearer way of distinguishing the position of the philosophers of action and of the Social Catholics from both the modernists on one side and the extrinsicists on the other. In a letter to Mourret dated September 24, 1907, two weeks after the publication of the encyclical, he writes: "The more I reflect on this, the more I see that what is struck down is the doctrine of *efference* or of emergence in all its forms. For my part, I have never professed anything but a doctrine of *afference*. Now, they speak only about the *afference* of the external gift; whereas I equally take into account the *afference* of the internal gift. It is true that they have not seen the possibility or the utility of speaking about the afference of the internal gift; but that is precisely what comes into question, and nothing will keep it from happening that there is there a problem that will present itself over and over again under a thousand concerted forms; an inevitable and salutary problem, albeit one naturally disagreeable for a certain authoritarian instinct born of an exclusive extrinsicism. In this sense, the avenues remain open before us, even though, for the moment, we are paralyzed" (1957a, 360).

We see here, in this idea of a *double afference* of the Christian supernatural, one internal as well as one external, the internal one having been totally ignored by the writers of *Pascendi* as well as by the extrinsicists, in spite of its clear presence in the tradition of the Church going back to the Fathers, a way of opening up the avenue Blondel will use to defend the action of the Social Catholics in the modern world as authentically Christian, and as even more consistently supernatural than anything proposed by their exclusively extrinsicist adversaries in the Church, who had no way of showing how the supernatural can enter into the natural in human history. We shall see more of how Blondel uses this idea in determining how the Christian supernatural relates to the natural in history, in order to show how the Social Catholics of France, following the social teaching of Leo XIII in *Rerum Novarum*, which was being largely ignored by most Catholics at the time, were distinguishing themselves, not only from the exclusively extrinsicist Catholics, who were shunning any discussion of social problems, except to solve them by a reimposition of order from on high, through the monarchy if necessary, but also from any form of modernism based on a doctrine of mere efference from human nature or subjectivity, or of atheistic, i.e., purely immanentist socialism. This would not be an easy thing to do philosophically, but Blondel would do it along the lines of this idea of a *double afference* that began to emerge in his reflection in the aftermath of the shock from *Pascendi Dominici Gregis*, thinking of the "flock of the Lord" as including, not only those who already believed, but also all those of the masses of the poor who were now estranged from the Church and effectively abandoned by society as a whole.

In Defense of Social Catholicism

It could be said that Blondel's most significant contribution to the *Annales de Philosophie Chrétienne* during the time of his ownership was the series of articles he published on the subject of social reform defending the work of the *Semaines*

Sociales de Bordeaux in 1909 and 1910, which were then brought together into a single volume under the title of *Catholicisme Social et Monophorisme: Controverses sur les Méthodes et les Doctrines,* and distributed at the expense of the author. This is a side of Blondel's early work that is less well known, but was tremendously important to him as both a philosopher and a man of action.

The *Semaines Sociales* were a sort of itinerant university that met each year in a different city, bringing together Catholic professionals, social scientists, and clerics from around France, to study and to formulate resolutions for social problems of the time. They were organized by Marius Gonin, publisher of the *Chronique sociale du Sud-Est,* and Adéodat Boissard, then a professor of law at the Institut catholique de Paris, and under the very spiritual leadership of Henri Lorin. The annual gatherings had begun in Lyons in 1904 and then continued in the summer of each year in a different city, with Bordeaux as their site in 1909. By then their work had become well known and it had come under the attack of conservative Catholics, who accused them of sociological modernism as well as of hostility to the "true interests" of the Church. Blondel's brother, Georges, a sociologist, was a regular participant in these *Semaines,* while Maurice himself only followed their work with great interest, having attended only the sessions in Dijon in 1906, before the one in Bordeaux. He would lecture himself at this itinerant university only much later on, in 1928, after the end of his teaching career in the university, and in 1947, near the end of his life.

Having had some experience with these accusations of modernism, he felt called to come to the defense of these Social Catholics and their work, once again to set the record straight concerning what they were up to, and to justify the principles of their action both as a philosopher of action and as a loyal son of the Church, in accordance with the fundamental tradition he had insisted in bringing out in "History and Dogma." The social dimension of action he was to defend had formed an integral part of the total Phenomenon of Action he had elaborated in *L'Action* of 1893, and now he was called to elaborate on that part of the Phenomenon of Action further in both philosophical and Christian terms, as they pertained to the action of social Catholics. In defending this action, he would adopt the same strategy he had followed in defending his method in apologetics and in rejecting pure intellectualism, or modernism, even in matters of Faith.

As in most of his other contributions to the *Annales,* Blondel did not use his own name in signing these articles on Catholic Socialism. This time, however, he did not use a name that might be construed as someone else's name. He wrote only as *Testis,* as a witness to what was going on in the action of the Social Catholics. Part of the reason for not using his own name in this case, as he explained to his Jesuit friend Valensin (1957b, 99-100, 125), was to avoid having people prejudge what he had to say on the basis of what they thought about him and his philosophy already, whether favorable or not. Another part of the reason was that, since he was not a sociologist, he did not want to get too personally involved in a debate that extended beyond his own professional competence. For other reasons as well, many of his Social Catholic friends were not too comfortable in having their cause too closely associated with Blondel and with other causes that had caused him so much difficulty in earlier phases of the modernist crisis, for the charge of modernism was once again being trotted out against the efforts of the Social Catholics. Moreover, because of poor health at the time, he was not sure he would be able to finish the task himself, so that someone else, like Laberthonnière, might have to carry it through to the end, as Laberthonnière did in fact with certain details of the final draft. As a matter of fact, Blondel had originally thought of having the articles signed *Testes amici*, friends giving witness, as he wrote to his friend Wehrlé (1969b, 415), given that he was counting on Laberthonnière's collaboration, at whose house in Loctudy he had gone to spend ten days after the *Semaine* in Bordeaux. But in the end Laberthonnière's collaboration had been limited to the level of conversation and touch-ups on the galley proofs of the final version. At any rate, Blondel chose a name that was not meant to fool anyone in its transparency, even though it did help to deflect from his person the kind of wrath that was later visited on Laberthonnière by the adherents of *Action Française*, who were to come in for some severe criticism in these articles as much as in any of Laberthonnière's writings. In his own mind, Blondel was only associating himself as an impersonal witness united in desire with the One who is alone "*Testis verus et unicus*," an allusion to Christ that he had used in the conclusion to his dissertation as submitted to the Sorbonne in the summer of 1893, but had omitted from the final published version.

In the introduction to the articles, Testis recalls the general conditions of the situation in which the Social Catholics are called to work, encouraged by Leo XIII's encyclical *Rerum Novarum* of 1891 and the "instauration" of Pius X, the reigning pontiff, in the face of a triumphant Statism and of a menacing Syndicalism, not to say a rising atheistic Socialism. The aim is to find a solution to the social problems of the day, especially those of impoverished and much-abused workers, by reinforcing the legitimate worldly aspirations of people without denying their higher spiritual and even religious aspirations. This is the kind of purpose Blondel was well attuned to, for having tried to do the same with regard to the problems of modern philosophy.

Testis sets out to do three things: first, to lay out the twofold method of the Social Catholics, which is at once social and Catholic or scientific and religious; second, to analyze the recent criticisms, both philosophical and theological, that have been leveled at the *Semaines Sociales* and sort them out in terms of their validity, or lack thereof; and third, indicate the different kinds of confusion from which it is incumbent upon all to liberate themselves in dealing with these complex social problems. The greater and the more biting part of the discussion was to focus on the criticisms of the Catholic opponents and their allies leveled against the action of the Social Catholics, beginning from the second of seven installments, plus several appendices and some final reflections on the "system of alliances merely for the sake of results" envisioned by the Catholic opponents, who were siding with *Action Française,* whose leader, Charles Maurras, was a professed atheist contemptuous of religion. Before entering into this more defensive part of his argument, Blondel had to present the methods and the operative principles of the Social Catholics as something positive to resonate with in his own criticism of the opponents' methods and principles as well as alliances.

Testis begins by showing how the participants in the *Semaines Sociales* use a method that presents a surprising combination and a paradoxical complexity of principles and procedures. On the one hand, they seem inspired only with specifically Christian principles, revealed truths, and supernatural premises that preside over the destiny of souls and societies. On the other hand, they study very carefully and minutely the natural conditions of human labor with a keen sense of positive realities and contingent circumstances, a precise concern with historical and juridical transformations, a docile confidence in the solutions that seem dictated by the force of things and by the very development of the most profoundly human sentiments, and an optimistic faith in the suppleness of life itself, all of which adds up to an experimental sort of research in the purely natural order and with purely scientific means. The problem with this sort of twofold method is to see how one can practice it without verging, either into a "supernaturalism" or a "fideism" that betrays the consistency proper to the natural order and its relative value, or into a naturalist humanitarianism that smacks of "immanentism" not to say a certain complicity with atheistic "revolutionary Socialism" in opposition to both Church and State. Blondel was not unaware of the claims of "scientific socialism" in its dealings with the social problem.

Testis tries to make sense of this paradoxical method by first of all pointing out that it is not a matter of deducing one set of principles from the other, nor of inducing certain fundamental dogmas and laws from certain factual data. These are only abstract intellectual procedures that do not represent real and concrete relations in life. What is at issue is how to come to grips with the integral reality of human beings in their personal and social lives as it has developed historically, without separating the spiritual from the material and without ignoring what religion tells us about the fall of man and the ongoing redemption inaugurated by Christ. This is not to lose sight of the logical discontinuity and the metaphysical heterogeneity between the natural and the supernatural orders, but rather to seek out how they compenetrate one another in the real historical order, through "concordances" and "coincidences" that are a matter of observation in human life and that can be used in dealing with the social problem.

In a society that has long since abandoned its identification with Christian religion, the purpose is not so much to work out an apologetic for the Christian teaching as such, but rather to rediscover this teaching as it relates to matters of historical fact. Testis cites four *constatations* or observations of fact in which the two orders, supernatural and natural, can be seen as coming together. The first is the rather Augustinian observation that disorder or disorientation in society ultimately stems from a lack of proper ordering to the "One Thing necessary" in spirit, even though this is often ignored by those who are adversely affected by the disorder. The second observation is that facts have a way of bringing out truths about the human situation, even if we are not always aware of the origin or the reasons that bear these truths out. The third observation is that what is restored or what is developed by this popular elaboration of truths is not only some incidental measure or some particular palliative or other, but an entire conception of human relations, and an order that is founded, no longer merely on the brutal interplay of material forces, but rather on a moral element, an idea of equity, which the Social Catholics call the principle of social justice, as a replacement for the individualist and mercantilist conception of freedom. Finally, the fourth observation is that, under this tutelage of these necessities of daily life and the ethical desire to ground the social order once again on justice, people of good faith and good will are led to respect Christianity once again, and even to ratify, in the name of the vital conditions of human beings and of society as a whole, some of the prescriptions of the Decalogue and of the Church, or better still, to find in the Gospel itself the supreme guaranty of justice and of the moral conditions for peace, along with social stability and prosperity. Testis speaks of this sequence of observations as a kind of secular experience and a method of absence wherein, by a sort of convalescence and resurgence, we witness a sweeping movement of conversion, so to speak, and find, in going from the bottom up, some of the ideas that have come to us from above, but whose meaning and savor we had lost.

The purpose of this method is to look for a certain historical convergence of truths that both come to us from on high and emerge from our secular experience as a society. Instead of trying to suppress or to ignore the latter as Christians, the Social Catholics are more interested in embracing the emerging truth and in fostering its emergence further, up to the point of showing its Catholic as well as natural validity. The reasons or the reasoning that they use in their observation of facts are both natural and supernatural. As Christians oriented by grace, they believe in the supernatural destiny of human beings in such a way that all our gifts and abilities, natural as well as supernatural, are seen as serving the attainment of our final end, while, as human beings and citizens, they feel authorized and obliged to encourage all the efforts of humanity, in a quest for a better future and a more just society, using science and all other natural as well as political means at their disposal. The method Blondel was finding operative among the Social Catholics in what could be called their sociology was very much like the method he had proposed in the third part of his *Letter on Apologetics* for the philosophy of religion. It was a method of looking for the truth already implied in the actual practice and aspirations of society, with the help of teaching based on revelation from on high. It was a method that conformed both "with the method of Christ revealing the Good News to the world and with the tradition of the Church when it maintains the consistency proper to nature and the force of reason as well as their inability to produce and discern the supernatural order, or even to require it with precision" (1909, 13). It brings together the two orders, natural and supernatural, not as an idea in the speculation of theoreticians, but as a practice in the unity of a conduct among human beings who are both citizens and Catholics as well, or as a matter of good conscience and simple common sense.

One would hardly expect other Catholics to object to the use of such a method in the development of a social practice worthy of human aspirations as well as of divine teaching, but objection there was, especially from extrinsicist theologians who admitted only a juxtaposition between the supernatural and the natural, instead of a living compenetration, or who saw the Christian supernatural only in what is proposed from the outside and abstractly recognized as such, and not in any anonymous stimulations or interior solicitation of grace that is preordained, coordinated, or even subordinated subjectively within human beings to the objective teaching of the Church. Testis illustrates the kind of coordination he has in mind with the example of how two social scientists, an economist and a jurist, one of them his friend Boissard, work toward a better logical organization of labor law and the code for strikes from a social standpoint that takes issue with the failed policy of modern liberal individualism but is in keeping with their own aspirations of brotherly love as Christians.

The difficulty with this kind of method in the practice of social science is that it presupposes a certain kind of corresponding philosophy that can put the relations between the revealed order and the natural order in proper perspective, which it is not the task of these social practitioners to develop as such, but is rather the task of a philosopher willing to examine the work and the principles of action of those in actual practice. Recognizing that this is somewhat beyond the scope of his ordinary activity as a philosopher, Testis proposes nevertheless to pursue this examination of a method in social practice, in support of the social practitioners, at least to the extent of answering some of the objections to their work.

With this understanding of the aim, the method, and the conclusions of the Catholics associated with the *Semaines Sociales,* one might be surprised that there was opposition to them on the part of other Catholics. But there was quite vociferous opposition, based on a set of ideas that was diametrically opposed to the ideas of the Social Catholics. Coming from philosophy, Testis sets out to analyze the two opposing sets of ideas implied in this confrontation, and to contrast them with one another as they appear in the actual practice of each side. What he finds in the *Semaines Sociales* is a practical instantiation of the problem raised by the "philosophers of action" in the theoretical order of apologetics. What he finds in their Catholic opponents is another set of ideas, one that juxtaposes the natural and the supernatural, and one that looks for solutions to practical problems only from extrinsically imposed principles from on high, without any attempt to see how the supernatural already penetrates the natural in the actual historical order of human development and conversion. What Testis will focus on first, then, before getting into a direct counterattack against the opponents of the Social Catholics, is the intellectual element that presides over each side in contrast with that of the other.

He begins by enunciating three fundamental theoretical propositions that he finds implied in the practice of the *Semaines Sociales*. The problem is for Catholics to find a way of dealing with a society and a civilization that has become totally cut off from Christianity. How can such a society be won back to Christianity or rechristianized? This is the question that makes the debate between the two sides interesting from the standpoint, not only of strategy, but also of our very understanding of Christianity as a historical movement. The idea of the Social Catholics was to reestablish contact, not so much with the intellectuals, who had become estranged from Christianity, as had been the aim of the Philosophy of Action, but rather with the people and the masses of workers who had completely lost touch with Christianity, and to enter into the problems they had to solve, not in order to offer them ready-made solutions, but rather to seek out with them solutions that would meet their own aspirations for a better future, solutions of progress, of fraternal justice, of solidarity, solutions that were solidly in the initiatives of people themselves, unlike those dictated by either liberal revolutionary individualism on one side or by atheistic socialism on the other. Among those personal aspirations and initiatives, because he is talking about the action of men of faith as well as of science, Testis wants to include those that go beyond the natural order, toward a transcendent order, as a culmination of social equity and of human brotherhood, so that the Christian order could once again appear as the keystone for the new order in the making.

The first proposition implied in the action of Social Catholics is one having to do with the relation between thought and action. Actions follow from logically defined ideas and geometrically contoured theories, but not everything is decided on the level of abstract ideas, as if human beings were pure intellects. There is more going on in individual and social practice than has been defined by clear ideas, and it is part of human thought to look for this more that is to be found or discovered in human practice itself and to integrate it into one's science, according to a more complex logic of action, of the sort Blondel had defined in his articles on method. The danger is for the understanding to stick only with its abstractions and to try to impose them as causes, or as utopias, on action. This danger has to be compensated for with a more positive and relative wisdom derived from action itself or, as we might also say, from experience. Thus the Social Catholics can be seen as more attentive to the more profound and sincere movements of the masses than to the lucubrations of intellectuals, politicians, or again revolutionary individualists. They know that practice is not just an application of theory. It also contains reasons and lights that speculation alone cannot replace, and from which speculation itself has to learn. In other words, beyond abstract speculation, there has to be a certain "conversion" to this deeper reason of action at work in human endeavors, which means a certain "interior preparation, a subjective disillusionment, a lesson from life that opens the soul to the lesson of thought, the authority of facts, the light of history, or the word of God" (1909, 28).

This is not to belittle the importance of speculation or ideas, of which the Social Catholics had many, but rather it is to put these ideas, and speculation itself, back in contact with integral reality, both as directing and as learning from practice in order to better direct. Hence the importance of a social science elaborated by reflection on practice that is not purely ideological, but that can also give new direction in action toward a better future, such as the science being developed by the Social Catholics, as men of both reason and faith.

Along with this dynamic philosophy of thought and action, Testis posits a second proposition as underlying the action of Social Catholics, one that, without denying the distinction of beings and the hierarchy of orders that compose the universe, insists on the solidarity and the continuity among them. The illusion of any exclusive ideology is to think that it can isolate not only ideas, as if they were intellectual atoms or logical blocs, but also things themselves, under the pretext that their concepts are seen as defined separately from one another. It is also to parcel out different levels of reality into compartments that are simply juxtaposed. The opposite truth, which the Social Catholics embrace, is that to distinguish orders of reality is not to disunite them, that lower degrees of reality serve as springboards for higher degrees, and that the higher degrees are really the final causes of the world, which is not just a pastiche of juxtaposed events, but a single order in which the unity of the divine plan circulates. Nor is there a simple juxtaposition between a rational order built up in metaphysics and a natural religion on one side, and a supernatural order merely tacked on from the outside as an afterthought. Classical economics, according to Testis, has erred on this score no less than philosophical rationalism, in maintaining a wall of separation between the two orders. Reality must be seen for all that it is humanly speaking, that is, as relating to the heart and the aspirations of man, and not just to his abstract and fixed ideas, which for the Social Catholics had to include some divine resemblance as well as justice on earth.

This brings Testis to his third and most delicate point, the one that dominates everything in the debate between the two Catholic sides. Most people readily admit that economic problems tie into moral problems and that human elements find their way into the mechanisms of brute forces, but few are prepared to admit, as Testis and the Social Catholics claim, that there are religious dimensions to these problems, and that adequate solutions to them cannot be found without some Christian input. In fact, the extrinsicist Catholics of the right find this idea scandalous, while the more secular minded find it edifying but hardly convincing. Yet, the Social Catholics do not want to be merely tolerated in their religious belief, by restricting their action to the positivism of some earthly outcome. In the face of objections from both right and left, they will not lose sight of the fact that we are all called to a supernatural destiny, which entails some kind of obligation on the part of everyone, not just believers. They think of their intervention in history as both secular and religious at the same time. For, "since what is at stake is man such as he is, *in concreto,* in his living and total reality, not in a simple hypothetical state of nature, there is nothing that closes man off in himself, not even in the simply natural order" (1909, 32).

This is the position Blondel had argued for in a philosophy that Testis now sees implied in the action of the Social Catholics. It does not take anything away from the validity and the relative solidity of human science and initiative, as Blondel had also argued in the *Letter on Apologetics,* but it does say that at their summit they ultimately open up, both by their stability and their insufficiency, to the supreme truth and the transcendent force, as well as to the real indispensability of the one thing necessary to bring them to completion. The point of this ultimate reference to God even in social action is, of course, denied by atheists, or largely ignored by most modern secular agents, especially those referred to as revolutionary individualists by Testis, but it is one the Social Catholics wanted to make, as they took part in the debates on how to solve the social problems of their time, unlike their Catholic opponents who thought only of keeping themselves aloof from such secular debate.

These three points sum up the philosophy and theology implied in the method of the *Semaines Sociales,* as Testis sees them. He characterizes the method as an *integral realism,* in the sense that it tries to integrate every aspect of reality into its initiative. It speaks of ideas as having a subjective life, as communicating concretely and singularly with physical, social, and religious reality, and not just as having an abstract logical validity. Far from being satisfied with a notional realism that fixates and separates different orders of reality into separate generic compartments, it looks for ways of communication, both ascending and descending, without any confusion of stages, in man's itinerary to God. It does not think of the supernatural order, as gratuitous and as absolutely transcendent as it is, as merely superimposed on the natural order, but rather as somehow supposed and concretely "preposed" in human experience. What sets the Social Catholics off from their strident Catholic opponents more than anything else is precisely this final point about the supernatural, for they look for the presence of the supernatural, not only as coming from on high through external Revelation, but also, as Testis puts it, as substantially constituted in human life through the Incarnation and Redemption, and as reaching souls, not merely as visible facts and mysteries to be believed, but also invisibly through a grace that "actions" men from below, so to speak, in order to draw them out of every self-imposed enclosure and to raise them above themselves. There are the *two* kinds of *afference* for the supernatural that Social Catholics want to tap into, according to Testis, while their Catholic opponents, who will be dubbed "monophorists," look to only one of the two afferences, the external one from on high, which they then mutilate by reducing it to their own fixed preconceptions, and by juxtaposing it to any human order as an ideology to be imposed by purely external authority.

All this is but an expansion of Blondel's philosophy into social action as well as into individual action, presented as a justification for the method of the Social Catholics in their approach to social problems. The only thing that is added that was not in the original dissertation is the direct reference to the supernatural order and to the teaching of the Church, as part of what is to be considered in seeking solutions that are in keeping with the Good News of love and friendship as well as with the principles of justice and liberation. In this respect the method of the Social Catholics had something "apologetic" about it, for those who were hostile or indifferent toward the Church, in the search for solutions to social problems, but Blondel had also worked out a philosophy for this aspect of the method in his Letter on Apologetics. All Testis now had to do was show how that philosophy was being applied in questions pertaining to both the natural and the supernatural order as concretely related to one another in human experience, or in history.

The Rejection of Monophorism

In contrast to this philosophy of the Social Catholics, Testis then lays out three propositions that define the attitude of their Catholic opponents as the exact opposite of the three we have just summed up. In this view, first, ideas are seen as simply capturing all of reality into intellectual atoms that are supposedly copies and substitutes for what is essential in things. All one has to do with such fixed ideas is combine them into more complex ideas, without any allowance for evolution or clarification coming from action or progressive experience. Second, given this conception of fixed ideas, reality is then chipped into hermetically sealed orders, so that there is no understanding of how the physical order relates to thinking being, or of how the economic order relates to the moral order of subjects, or of how the social order in its own natural and rational right relates to a still higher end than anything found in the natural order. Third, in this view the supernatural is taken only as a gratuitous superposition from a purely extrinsic dictate, addressed to a purely obediential potency that is entirely passive, without any thought of an interior gift, or afference, that could and should require some cooperation from the internal subjective agent. According to this view, everything is played out on a level of externally defined ideas, without any reference to the living tradition of spirits in movement, where God is also at work renovating the earth, as he is at work in human reason renovating the spirit.

This purely extrinsic view of the supernatural is very coherent and simple. It is even more powerful polemically than the more complex and even subjective view of the Social Catholics, who want to take the secular experience of mankind into account as well as the external teaching of Christianity. But Testis will turn this polemic of the monophorists against itself in his defense of the Social Catholics and their method, which is no less opposed to modernism and to modern liberal individualism than any of the Catholic opponents on the right. It is important to keep in mind here that Testis was in fact responding to an attack on the Social Catholics of the *Semaines Sociales,* accusing them of modernism, in a book entitled *Le Modernisme sociologique* by a right-wing cleric named J. Fontaine, and in an article titled "La foi catholique" by another abbé named Gaudeau, not long after the condemnation of modernism of 1907. Testis and the Social Catholics, convinced that they were deeply imbedded in the tradition of the Church, did not accept being branded in this way and sought rather to turn the tables on these self-proclaimed defenders of a purely external tradition. With the philosophical grounds for the debate now clearly laid out, Testis was ready to proceed to his counterattack on the basis of a better understanding of Christianity as a social movement in history, and not just as a set of abstract ideas fixed in some individual's mind at one particular moment.

As Blondel had criticized Thomism earlier in its general approach to apologetics, Testis begins by criticizing the simplistic ideas of philosophy and reason found in the standard manuals used in most Catholic seminaries, from which many of the arguments against the Social Catholics are taken, in the absence of any sort of critical social theory. What Testis criticizes is a certain naïve realism of ideas or, more precisely, a certain notional realism that sees nothing but a perfect correspondence between ideas or representations of things and the things themselves, or between ideas and realities. This time, however, thanks to his own reading of Aquinas, and to the writings of Rousselot on the Intellectualism of Aquinas that had recently begun to appear, Testis can now appeal to the medieval *Doctor Eximius,* then taken as the *Doctor Communis* in the Church since Leo XIII, against these manualists who stultify Christianity as well as philosophy. He can also argue that this naïve notional as well as natural realism, which is on the lips of so many zealous but self-proclaimed defenders of the faith, is not only a caricature of philosophy, but also a "denaturation" of tradition itself. It is nothing more than a realism of some individual's fixed notions, or again a "realistic notionalism," which distorts every aspect of reality it touches, whether it be that of science and life, that of the social order, or more importantly in the religious context, that which concerns the nature and the bearing of our natural knowledge of God, a notionalism that becomes the pretense for attacking the Social Catholics and accusing them of modernism at the moment when they are only following through with the teaching of Leo XIII in *Rerum Novarum*.

Testis goes into a detailed analysis of this compartmentalization of reality according to fixed ideas and of the way it distorts the reality of orders, including that of the Church, united and in continuity with one another in concrete actuality, no matter how they have to be distinguished conceptually. He appeals to Aristotle as well as to Aquinas and the authentic tradition of the Church, including Cardinal Dechamps and the First Vatican Council, with regard to our natural knowledge of God's existence.

Regarding the third level of principles distinguished earlier, namely, the one having to do with the relation between the natural and supernatural in human experience, Testis works out a systematic contrast between the two Catholic positions confronting one another, that of the Social Catholics and that of their intransigent opponents, which can be summed up in this way: Can we say that humanity is in fact moved and as it were raised up by a grace which, though anonymous or pseudonymous, can lead it in the direction of a gift from on high offered by Revelation and proposed by the Church, or do we have to say that there is nothing supernatural except what comes through express presentation by an external authority for a receptacle that is bereft of all spontaneity of its own?

Clearly, at this point the debate has shifted from philosophy to theology, or at least to the use of philosophy in theology, much as it had shifted when Blondel had had to criticize certain ways of doing apologetics in a purely extrinsicist way, without regard for the need to develop the interior dispositions of subjects to recognize the offer of a supernatural gift, if offered, as rational and ethical. Now Testis turns against the kind of manual theology, modeled on the simplistic philosophy manuals, to show how separating the two orders of reality, natural and supernatural, as if they were "logical concepts or intellectual atoms and then juxtaposing the rationalism of a thought that is supposedly sufficient to know God to the supernaturalism of a faith that is pure receptivity of an external given" (1909, 60) is contrary to good theology as well as good philosophy.

If one starts with this stilted way of understanding the supernatural as well as the natural, it becomes impossible to understand how there can be any opening to the supernatural in the order of nature itself, any kind of fermentation that raises it upward, nor to understand how the supernatural can descend into nature or make itself something to be sought without abolishing itself as supernatural. To settle for this kind of separatism between the two orders, according to Testis, is to fall into a twofold error in the eyes of Christian theology. It is to reason as if all non-believers were in a state of *pure nature*, which is not, has never been, and cannot be properly specified according to any data of experience. Or else it is to tacitly admit that not all men are called to a supernatural destiny, which is formally contrary to the teaching of the Church. What Testis proposes is to call the state of non-believers, for whatever reason, which is neither a state of pure nature nor a state of grace, a *transnatural state*, to mark the tension of a destiny affected by a fall and at the same time moved internally by a second calling. This is the kind of inquietude that Augustine and Malebranche spoke of concerning man in the absence of God and the supernatural. To deny that there is any such inquietude in nature and in man is to exclude even the possibility of a real vocation to the supernatural for a non-believer, that is, a vocation that is internally discernible through reflection on one's own aspirations as a rational being.

Testis does not maintain that one can have a direct consciousness of this sort of *transnatural state,* so to speak. "It remains secret, veiled, unspeakable; it does not make itself known or recognized from the inside by name, by definition, or in its proper being. But it does determine certain psychological facts that are knowable as such, verifiable and usable facts, facts that entail a responsibility, of which there can be a science, with a determination of their logic and a guidance for their use" (1909, 63). It is a function of Christian philosophy and Christian social science to focus on these facts as indicating a need for a higher life within man, as he exists in the concrete historical order. Without this conscious, albeit anonymous, element of the divine call within, there could be no reasonable and moral response on the part of an intelligent free will. These are internal facts that must be reckoned with along with the external facts of Revelation from on high, and that alone make any reception of the salvific Revelation rational as well as free.

When Testis situates this debate among Catholics in the context of the modernist crisis, as his opponents had already done, he comes up with a new way of characterizing these opponents, similar to the way Blondel had characterized his supposedly orthodox opponents in the debate about apologetics and in "History and Dogma." In those recent controversies many had thought that there were only two alternative positions in question, that of immanentism, which had been rightly condemned because it made everything in religious development and Christian evolution come from below and from the obscure depths of human consciousness, and the position that simply repelled the foregoing "modernist" position by insisting on the exterior gift exclusively, or on the revelation from on high, or on the authority addressing itself to a pure receptivity and a passive obedience, without reference to anything given internally to human beings.

Testis, however, is not satisfied with this purely formal and abstract dichotomy concerning the "supernatural" as something either purely internal to man or something purely external. For him, the view that everything in Christianity comes from the outside, *extrinsecus,* which recalls the term Blondel had used earlier in the controversy over apologetics, is no less erroneous than the view according to which everything comes from the inside by a sort of *efference,* a flowing out of. In opposition to both of these one-sided views, Testis prefers to speak of a twofold *flow* to humanity, a double *afference,* as we saw earlier, one internal and one external, both from God who takes these two ways to enter into human consciousness. This is the view of one who thinks that there is something to be learned internally as well as externally through action. It is also the view of Christians, like the Social Catholics, who think that there is something to be learned from the secular experience of men in their approach to social problems, whereas the view of their Catholic opponents was that of a single *afference* from the outside in opposition to the pure *efference* of immanentists, which all Catholics clearly reject, including Testis and the Social Catholics.

At this point Testis coins the word that was to provide the title for this set of articles in the offprint that gathered them together in a book subtitled *Le Monophorisme.* Using two Greek words, *monos,* meaning single or sole, and *phora,* meaning something brought forth, Testis makes up the word to characterize the view of a single, one-sided *afference* for the supernatural gift from God, one that is purely external and in no way internal. The intention was to stigmatize this view as erroneous in itself, and as leading to many other errors in social practice, because it considered God's gift as coming only, or solely (*monos*), one way, that is, exclusively by external dictation and sense coercion, in contrast to the more traditional view of *double afference* from both inside and outside human consciousness, with effects that could be discerned interiorly as well as exteriorly, so that one could think of human aspirations for a more just society and a better future as coming from God as well as from human nature and initiative, and so that the social teaching of the Church could be seen, at least by Social Catholics, as an essential part of the divine mission in the world, coming from on high to bolster and complete what could be discovered internally or historically by human reason in its striving for dignity.

For the doctrine of *double afference,* the immanent movement of the soul, even penetrated by supernatural stimulation, does not have the power of discerning its origin and its final end by itself, but neither does an objective truth alone, by the mere fact that it is imperatively imposed on the mind, have the power of making itself accepted and assimilated. There are two facts to be discerned or verified, as Dechamps put it, one within ourselves and one without, two facts in search of one another in order to meet and embrace one another. The internal fact is no more entirely natural than the external fact, which includes the signs of Revelation.

This doctrine reconciles the intimacy of a spiritual life with the necessary function of a teaching authority, without sacrificing any aspect of the Christian mysteries at work in the world, even in the striving of the poor for justice and a better future. It brings into play "both the invisible gift, of which the Incarnation and Redemption are a source flowing out even to the souls most ignorant of the supernatural, and the illuminating gift of Revelation which presents for our reason, for our intelligent and free adherence, for our moral use, for our total adoration, this order substantially constituted by Christ the mediator and divinizer" (1909, 65). This is why the participation of the Social Catholics in the struggle for social justice of the masses can be seen as a religious work at the same time as it is secular, and as working toward the conversion of humanity to its true spiritual end and at the same time a better future in this world.

Testis defends this doctrine of *double afference* against any accusation of immanentism and, in fact, turns the tables on the accusers by showing that, with their doctrine of a single afference, which they only juxtapose to the doctrine of mere efference or immanentism, as a mirror image of it, they end up arguing and acting as if everything had to be resolved in some external political power struggle, without reference to any moral, spiritual, or transcendent supernatural order. Testis shows how this happens because of the way monophorists compartmentalize their ideas and the different spheres of their activity. Whatever they propose to do externally is totally divorced from anything internal or spiritual, "indifferent or hostile to everything that is subjective interiority and personal spontaneity" (1909, 92). One could even say that, "to the extent that monophorism would triumph, the Catholic apostolate would be sterilized, the religious sense perverted, Christian piety denatured" (1909, 93). Hence, it is important to understand how monophorism comes to its political stance in a power struggle.

Testis raises three essential questions in order to shed light on this process. First, given the separation of the stages of human life and the supposed self-sufficiency of each, how do they come into relation with one another, and how does a lower order come to know a higher order? Second, according to the nature of this relation, considered only as possible and legitimate, how is the higher order supposed to act on the lower order? And third, since this theoretical thesis cannot in fact be realized or put into practice, what other principle will come into play in establishing alliances and determining who or what is the enemy to be excluded whether in social practice or in political action?

In elaborating on the first question, Testis shows that, given its compartmentalization of the natural and supernatural into separate, juxtaposed realms, without any sense of compenetration between them, monophorism is left with the idea that the supernatural order can never be anything but accidental, something extrinsically proposed and imposed on human knowledge for acceptance. This kind of notional exclusivism between orders is found even in the way monophorists relate the different orders of thought and science within the order of nature itself, without any sense of unity or solidarity among them. All that counts in this view is a certain kind of legalism or formal literalness. With regard to the supernatural, the natural is first regarded as if it had nothing to do with the supernatural. But once the supernatural is supposedly seen as having given proof of its existence, reason is not seen as liberated from its own self-sufficiency, but only as having to submit blindly. "Reason remains captive of its own formal linkage in a place where it has nothing, absolutely nothing more to see. It no longer exists to understand and control. It exists only to obey and to proclaim the agnosticism that is imposed on it as reasonable" (1909, 96). Thus, while monophorism seems to affirm the validity of natural reason and science, it is only to withdraw this validity, or to set it aside, when it comes to any question of the supernatural and its irrationally logical domination over the natural.

It is as if thought were nothing but a "system of valves" or of hermetically sealed compartments for the monophorists. The system makes it impossible to see how reason can ascend interiorly or spontaneously to the comprehension of anything strictly supernatural, even after the question of the supernatural has been raised. And at the same time it precludes the possibility of understanding how the supernatural perfects the natural, as Aquinas would have said, or how the natural "is assumed by the supernatural and rises into it," as Testis now puts it, hearkening back to an old Patristic expression, where Christ was said to have assumed human nature. When it comes to the question of how the higher order is supposed to act on the lower order, all the monophorist can say is purely "by command, by an exclusively notional way, meant only to enthrone the higher order rationally by conferring on it a rationally exercised dictatorship without any control, . . . as if in the name of reason, but without having to give any reason for anything" (1909, 98). All this is bad enough, but it gets worse when the truth of the supernatural is reduced to one's own simplistic understanding, "quite humanly, and only to arrive finally at a supernaturalism that is both irrational and rationalized, an anthropomorphic theocracy, which one always disavows while constantly trying to put it in practice" (1909, 98-99), which explains why the monophorists are prepared to back such overbearing movements as *Action Française,* no matter how atheistic they may be. Such oversimplification, or all-too-*human* simplification of the relation between the supernatural and the natural, or between the divine and the human, has always led to disasters in the history of the Church: the confiscation of civil liberties or the mobilization of all forces in a society for purely "religious" motives, the organization, not only of a politics that is exclusively "religious," but also of a "religion" that is purely political, and the pursuit of a dream of temporal "Empire" spiritually confronting the secular power as nothing more than another secular power. Testis denounces this sort of theocratic tendency as a theological enormity and political insanity, especially the monophorist tendency to identify itself as the authority in the Church, taken as a purely political entity, and to stand in the place of the truly religious Authority. What it represents is a "perversion of the religious sense, the transvaluation of everything Christian" (1909, 107). It transforms religious politics into political religion. Worse still, it tries to make of *believers* nothing more than a political party under its tutelage, a party to mobilize and to direct against non-believers, as if non-believers were nothing but enemies or objects of contempt, thinking that it thereby shows itself to be all the more "supernatural," when in fact it turns the *believer* into nothing but a citizen. This is the kind of abstractionism that makes possible different kinds of political alliance, even with avowed and militant atheists, who share the same conception of authority, one that is contemptuous of democracy and of the masses in movement toward a more just society.

The Fight Against Any Political Alliance with *Action Française*

This brings us to the third essential question that has to be raised with the monophorists, namely, that of the principle that lies at the base of their choice of political alliances. We can see now in what this principle consists. It has little to do with their exclusive preoccupation about doctrinal intransigence, but everything to do with their concern for the triumph of the most imposing authoritarianism possible. In this, Testis sees the return of the *old man* who, "under the pretext of thinking about religion, is involved only in doing politics, under the august mantle of Christ" (1909, 115). What results from it is a "murderous transvaluation" of Christian values, which must now be brought to light for the conscience of the monophorists as well as of others.

Testis illustrates how this transvaluation of Christian values takes place in two ways, first, in the way the monophorists relate to the prevalent individualistic liberalism of modern society and, second, in the way they ally themselves with a professedly atheistic neo-monarchism, for purposes of getting positive results in their desire to impose their own order. Starting from the idea of a society totally unified in spirit, religiously as well as morally, which is for them an absolute *thesis,* they recognize the necessity of positing what they call a *hypothesis,* which is really an antithesis, in the case of our troubled modern societies, namely, a thesis of what we would now call pluralism, given the division of spirits. In the context of the Christian supernatural as part of the spiritual value in question, this counter-thesis appears to concede too much, in its willingness to sacrifice certain spiritual ideas to political expediency, and too little, in not recognizing a hypothetical right for human persons in the spiritual realm. If the monophorist is consistent with his initial thesis, Testis argues, he must recognize the absolute right of individual liberty, apart from all spiritual content, a right "of liberty that is independent of any truth and any precise use, a right of liberty as an object, an idol no less tyrannical and an entity no less vain than the one you were trying to free yourself from" (1909, 119).

In other words, the individualist liberal, with his systematic tolerance for anything any individual may think or want, is no less an absolutist than his monophorist opponent. Both suffer from the same kind of abstractionism with regard to action, which is always social as well as individual. Testis is not opposed to the idea of respecting the inviolable freedom of conscience, but he is opposed to the doctrinaire liberalism that absolutizes individuals as isolated spiritual atoms open to external manipulation from all sides, or otherwise cast adrift each one for itself. "The authoritarian posits the hypothesis as the error to be accommodated with; this other and erroneous principle implied in the hypothesis is then taken as the thesis for the liberal, who, drawn along by logic, does not notice that he is treating subjective liberty as an object that is abstract, fixed, and absolute, that he thereby excludes the thesis of the authoritarian and considers it false, and that, under the pretext of setting up as material principle of government the entirely formal principle of a freedom that is only a bare power of contraries, he implies a radical indetermination, even an assimilation of truth with error, a nihilism of orientation, a neutrality in which all individual attempts to move nullify one another; under the guise of respect for all, he ends up in this cruelty of economic and religious individualism, in this fratricidal abstentionism that goes on repeating in a thousand forms: 'Am I my brother's keeper?'" (1909, 120-21).

Monophorism was opposed to secular liberalism, to be sure, but it was also compromised with it in adopting its individualist perspective and in pursuing a policy of neutrality in the struggle for economic justice, and in taking sides with liberalism in its opposition to the Social Catholics and their policy of intervening in the struggle, but without falling into the aberrations of "revolutionary syndicalism" or "atheistic socialism," another logical offshoot of the defunct secular individualism. Unable to get anywhere against liberalism, except to grant its principle of absolute individualism and non-intervention, or laissez-faire, in the internal forum of conscience, and not wishing to remain too isolated and powerless, monophorists had to look for an ally at least in the external forum of brute facts and to prescind from all questions of belief and unbelief in finding instrumental auxiliaries it could use just to get results. Thus it is that they turned to the neo-monarchist movement of *Action Française* under the leadership of Charles Maurras, a militant unbeliever who was happy to get this support from Catholics, as long as they did not try to bring God or Christ into the picture. In neo-monarchism, they found a kindred authoritarian spirit, so to speak, even though it was atheistic.

The idea was to use neo-monarchism in order to get themselves into positions of authority, but what they achieved in this way was anything but Christian or Catholic. They, who accused the Social Catholics of being dupes of those whose spirit they were trying to rechristianize, did not see that they were themselves the dupes being used by the neo-monarchists and, in the process, betraying the very Christian spirit they were supposedly trying to instill. By insisting only on external authority and an order imposed by brute force from the outside, without reference to any interior gift or any internal rule, they were in fact demoralizing and dechristianizing society, and turning Catholicism into a war machine or an instrument of terrestrial rule under the guise of so-called "law and order."

What was at issue, according to Testis, was "a question of principle, a question of life which, poorly raised and poorly resolved by doctrinal liberalism, is even more poorly raised and more poorly resolved here, where it is thought that, if we set aside ideas that divide and beliefs that remain different, we can ground an *entente* [only] on [getting] results" (1909, 125). In this Testis finds a serious problem of conscience when it comes to resolving economic, social, and political problems that are integral to human life as such. For one cannot find a Christian way of resolving these problems by simply embracing the monarchist way of establishing order, discipline, and authority. To be sure, order, discipline, and authority are a legitimate concern in the historical relations and the social contingencies of any nation, "but to the extent that such concerns about the role, the conditions, the future of political power get complicated by a thesis and are cast in the mold of an absolutist method and theology, there is denaturation of both the political meaning and the Catholic meaning by a hybridization of the Temporal and the Spiritual" (1909, 127), or what was called earlier a transvaluation of Christian values. Concerning such hybridization, Testis will argue (a) that it implies a total failure in maintaining what is properly supernatural in human experience, (b) that in fact, and as could easily be seen from the very logic of its starting point, it takes from Catholicism only what is not in the spirit of Catholicism, and worse still (c) it opens the way to a perversion of the meaning of truth, the meaning of Christianity, and the meaning of religion. In arguing his points, Testis shows how it is the monophorists who are the immanentists, not the Social Catholics or the philosophers of action. Their immanentism follows from their way of separating practice from theory and juxtaposing the supernatural and the natural. He also shows how *religious faith* gets reduced to a purely political faith, such as that of an atheist like Maurras, for whom there is no other metaphysics than one of the senses. For such a faith what counts is order in a passive discipline that materializes even the moral virtues by measuring them according to social utility. What is especially repugnant to it is any idea of the infinite, or the transcendent, characterized by Maurras as absurd, shameful, and obscene chaos. The only reason why Maurras is willing to accept Catholics on his side is that he thinks they have proposed the only idea of God that is tolerable in a well-policed State.

What is astounding to Testis is that Maurras was spoken of as a "Catholic atheist." It was even said that he was a "Catholic in the marrow of his bones," or that he was animated by "the true spirit of the Church." What could anyone be thinking of as "Catholic" or as "the Church" in saying such things of one who was so resolutely and lucidly atheist and pagan, not to say outright anti-Christian? One could only be thinking of a power structure in the world that could be used as a political force supposedly to "get results." This would explain why someone could write that this Catholic atheist "has nothing more at heart than to make the Church triumph, if not in souls, at least in society." But this can only be a "catholicism" without Christianity, without any of its transcendent claims, without God and without Christ, a residue of Catholicism that is aristocratic and tranquilizing for the privileged, as it is neutralized for the underprivileged. This is not the Catholicism to which the Social Catholics were trying to convert those who were bereft of justice and hope in the established social system. It was only the "catholicism" of individuals who wanted to resume command over the masses, rather than convert them to a higher sense of their own dignity and of their calling as children of God.

After showing this perversion of the social sense of discipline and authority that follows from monophorism, Testis then goes on to show the perversion of the sense of justice and of charity that equally flows from it, including a vitiating deformation of the Catholic conscience. Here he takes the offensive against the monophorists who are forever accusing the Social Catholics of following false ideas, whose falseness they do not suspect, and of falling in with modernism and doing the work of the "revolution that will make us regress all the way back to ancient paganism." He argues that, on the contrary, it is the monophorists who are led by all-too-human ideas, which they take to be pious but are nonetheless altogether pagan and quite anti-Christian, as they poison the Christian conscience with their abstractions and their reactionary spirit.

Testis begins his reply by referring to the sense of human fraternity, which Christianity has instilled among men in a way that is profoundly supernatural as well as natural, a sense that illuminates the thought and warms the heart of the Social Catholics. But for the monophorists this smacks too much of the revolution, and they reproach the Social Catholics for speaking of this from a supernatural point of view, that of charity, even more than from a natural point of view, that of justice. Monophorists ignore all the language of brotherhood in the Gospel, and allow only for a very distant brotherhood traced all the way back to Adam, not unlike what Nietzsche would have said. Testis calls this a "paganism of the natural man" (1909, 148), which, when it gets beyond the immediate family, becomes *lupus lupo,* an expression that discredits wolves as well as men. Monophorism has tenderness only for entities, a "sort of metaphysical identity which is at the root of the human personality," not for actual persons. Testis argues that, even if one wants to maintain this ancient thesis about a natural and moral diversity among men which Aristotle made use of to justify slavery, at least, from a supernatural point of view, we have to say that there is neither slave nor master, neither barbarian not Greek. All are called to the banquet of Christ, who died for all, so that we have to speak of a fraternal grandeur of the human person "in the sublime equivalence of the infinite" (1909, 149), an idea dear to Testis but rejected by Maurras as barbaric. Far from accepting the Maurrasian conception of human nature, Social Catholics look rather to a nature that is oriented to a plenitude of peace, justice, and social harmony, but which, troubled in this pursuit in its concrete historical state, needs the truths and the graces of Christianity to reveal, to sustain, and to perfect man in his advance toward God. In neglecting this fraternal spirit among men inspired by Christianity, monophorism is simply reverting back to the individualistic naturalism advocated by modern liberalism, without any sense of the social dimensions of the human spirit, let alone the fraternal dimension of the Christian Spirit.

From the notion of fraternity Testis then moves on to the notion of equality, another notion advocated by the revolution, and so rejected by monarchists and monophorists. To speak of men as equal in dignity goes one step further than to speak of them merely as brothers. It implies a moral dimension, an equality that must be taken into account in conscience, a dimension that brings into question the inequalities among men, natural or acquired, that monophorists prefer to take as absolute, in a regime of castes and privileges. They are "so far from suspecting that, behind all the natural and acquired inequalities which diversify merits and respects to the extreme, there is nevertheless a *spiritual equivalence,* that they can admit even less among Christians a *supernatural value* that supersedes with the height of the infinite all the earthly inequalities" (1909, 152-53). They are so obsessed against egalitarianism that they deny the universal salvific will of God, as well as all exhortations to equality in the New Testament. There are distinctions of inequality, both natural and acquired, to be recognized among human beings, but it is anti-rational and anti-Christian to absolutize them into a system of castes or, more exactly, of outcastes. It is also anti-rational and anti-Christian to posit two kinds of political regime, one for the outcastes and the have-nots under oppression at the bottom, due to a belittling of everything, persons and things, and one for the haves, who prize their possessions above all else.

Such a political attitude, according to Testis, is based on more profound social prejudices, pseudo-scientific ideas, and worldly idols that come together in the mind of monophorists as well as monarchists to undermine the Christian as well as the natural sense of justice, not to mention charity or friendship. According to the positivist anthropology of the monarchists, which the monophorists embrace, there is an irreducible *class of the poor* so that "the frontiers that separate the social classes are more definite and more impossible to cross than those that separate any two of the most dissimilar peoples" (1909, 156). It is supposedly a general and permanent fact that there is "a duality of races in every nation, a fact implicated in the very constitution of the human animal." Moreover, this fact is supposedly consecrated by the Gospel itself, when we are told that "the poor you always have with you," as if this were a supernatural as well as a natural necessity. Why then work to help the poor out of their poverty? Is that not contrary to the will of God as well as to nature? The only work that is acceptable on the part of the privileged classes, or of the capitalists in modern society, is one of directing or managing the poor in their supposedly irremediable poverty. It will also be to keep them quiet at their rank in the "sacred order," so that "the social hierarchy will be respected and the acquired situations will remain untouchable on the foundation of a wisely orthodox political economy" (1909, 159). Everything has to be organized for the progress of private property and for the salvation of capitalism.

All this is the critique, not of a socialist, but of a Social Catholic who is at once rational and critical about what is to be done in the Christian spirit about the underprivileged. Testis presents it as the spirit that animates M. Lorin, the leader of the *Semaines Sociales,* who "is waging today's battle against liberalism, in the face of a double hostility, that of the party that revolutionary individualism has brought to power, and that of the unconscious but tenacious liberalism among most of the conservatives. And it is in waging this actual battle that he is preparing the victories of tomorrow against socialism, because socialism is nothing more than an exalted and reversed individualism, without any other roots than egoism, fiercely avid of pleasures, which mystically projects its dream toward an idol of earthly paradise and future humanity" (1909, 161). We see here something of the course that the Social Catholics were trying to steer in France in the early years of the twentieth century, and that Testis was trying to defend in opposition, not only to laissez-faire liberalism on one side and atheistic socialism on the other, but also to many conservative Catholics who were all too anxious to side with monarchism and the restoration of the *ancien régime* as the only way compatible with Christianity, or to settle for a materialist conservatism and a bourgeois Gospel that was all too comfortable with capitalism.

For many Catholics at the time, revolution still meant the revolution of individualist liberalism, and not the later revolution advocated by a rising Communism against this bourgeois revolution. Blondel and the Social Catholics, whose struggle he espoused and defended, were looking for a less violent, a more pacific way of solving the grinding social problems of their day, one that they would have insisted was more Christian even than what the supposedly Catholic monophorists were advocating, one less warlike, one less ready to just strike back against their persecutors, one less contemptuous of the people they were trying to help find justice, one more accepting of democracy as a political regime, one more ready to find direction from below and from within, as well as from above and from without, according to a doctrine of *double afference* for the supernatural as it enters concretely and historically into the natural order.

In the end, Testis insists on the importance of maintaining the distinction between rendering unto God the things that are God's and rendering unto Caesar the things that are Caesar's, as prescribed by Christ in the Gospel, as a way of preventing pretentious individuals from arrogating to themselves an authority that can only be God's. "In the present condition of our earthly trial, this distinction perpetually fraught with difficulties is the secret and the safeguard of the spiritual life. Even with the best of intentions, arbitrary simplification and unification, decreed and imposed according to the most idealistic views, run the risk of falling back into interests and sentiments above which we are supposed to rise. Monophorism, which, in the abstract, appears as the height of the supernatural, falls back into pure naturalism, and at one and the same time, suppresses both the human sense of goodness and the Christian sense of detachment and love" (1909, 178). The Social Catholics, on the other hand, whatever else they may hold in particular and however debatable may be some of the applications they champion, "represent an essential truth, a salutary initiative, an attitude, the only attitude that is simply and integrally Christian: for they maintain, in their method and in their acts, the *double afference* to be reconciled speculatively and unified vitally, the double burden of science and faith, of nature and of grace, of experimental research and the inspirations of the Church; they contribute in bringing back the problem from the domain of abstractions, where it is irritating and without solution, to the concrete terrain, into the domain of facts and consciences" (1909, 178-79). They render the Church and society an immense service "by setting aside that artificial and sterile method in order to study, in one and the same person who is our self, the double role of citizen and Christian, of economist and believer, of pilgrim in this world and devotee of eternity" (1909, 179). One could hardly find a more Augustinian way of reconciling the tension between the City of Man and the City of God in our own historical circumstances and showing the wonderful things that God has wrought for man through the Incarnation and Redemption.

In his original plan for these articles on the method of the Social Catholics, Testis had intended to include a more positive and edifying part on work actually being done as well as social doctrine actually being taught, but now he reserves that for another series of articles, a series that, unfortunately, was never written by our philosophical critic. At the end of the volume that gathers these articles together he adds a number of appendices in which he deals with some of the replies of the monophorists, and others, who had been taken to task in the articles, including Pedro Descoqs, S.J., who was not a monophorist, as Testis acknowledged from the beginning, but who had written in *Études* in defense of a regime of alliances with the militantly atheistic *Action Française*.

The monophorists tried to deflect the accusatory arrow of Testis by saying that the arrow was aimed at the authority of the Church itself, but Testis defends the legitimate authority of the Church against the attempted takeover by self-appointed ecclesiastical bigots. He appeals to that legitimate authority in his argument for a double historical afference in the way the supernatural is inserted into the natural. To Descoqs he points out that he had explicitly left his person out of the question in discussing the regime of alliances "purely for the purpose of getting results," independently of all spiritual interpretation, but if Descoqs feels personally offended by the argument against the idea, then it must be that it was in fact his personal idea. Testis cannot do anything about that, but he does point out that what he was arguing about scrupulously as a philosopher of religion was "a question of principle, of right and of method, in no way a question of fact or of politics. On the one hand, I considered the intrinsic nature of 'an alliance by results,' so as to determine what this formal principle inevitably implies in its material content. On the other hand, I examined how, through the effect of the combination alone, the elements brought together in this way come out denatured, whatever these elements might be" (1909, 214). What was at issue was a certain system of ideas, a mixture of positivism and of theocracy, that seemed pernicious to true religion as well as to human nature, and nothing else. Descoqs's personal objections can only be seen as tangential to the essential point at issue, or else as simply twisting the argument back against himself personally.

Quite ironically, probably not knowing the true identity of Testis, Descoqs cites the case of Blondel working with Payot, his Dean at the State University of Aix-Marseilles, whose anti-religious views were well published, as an example of the kind of alliance on the basis of results alone he had had in mind. Testis points out, however, that, after careful consultation with M. Blondel, there was no such alliance in which philosophy and religion end up purely subordinated to the interests of an anti-Christian ideology. In fact, it was an important part of M. Blondel's role as a philosopher of religion at the University to show not only the philosophical necessity of religion, but also that the interests of both philosophy and religion transcend those of the State. There was no such effort on the part of monophorism, but only a tendency to submit its will for order to the will of an anti-Christian humanist, leaving aside all questions of spiritual transcendence, let alone the infinite value of personal life announced by Christianity. Monophorism would be satisfied with getting the external result of an order imposed "from on high," even if it were atheistic and anti-religious, which is why the philosopher of religion as well as of action had to be critical of it.

The Revenge of the Monophorists

The Testis articles were Blondel's last major contribution to the *Annales de Philosophie Chrétienne*. They were also his last major attempt to explain his conception of the relation between the natural and supernatural in the context of apologetics, and attempts to rechristianize French society in the early part of the twentieth century before the onset of World War I. They were not successful in bringing any of the monophorists around to his way of thinking about Christianity. Blondel and his friends saw these self-styled defenders of the faith as hopelessly mired in a simplistic, layered conception, which only juxtaposed the supernatural to the natural and imposed it extrinsically on subjects who were supposed to be purely passive in their reception of this gift from on high or, more exactly, in their reception of an exclusively extrinsic way of presenting the gift, as if it had nothing to do with the interior life of people. But the articles did reach many Catholics who needed to hear about this way of insertion for Christianity into the spiritual movement of history, not only among the Social Catholics, in whose defense they were written, but also among some Scholastic philosophers and theologians who began to rethink their own conception of natural reason in relation to the supernatural, or to God, as well as to the modern natural and social sciences.

It is during these years with the *Annales*, after the Testis articles, that Blondel began to encounter a new voice among opponents to his way of doing philosophy of religion, who would remain in pursuit of Blondel, both publicly and privately, for most of the rest of his life. This was the Dominican, Father Reginald Garrigou-Lagrange, who was picking up where his Dominican predecessor, Fr. Schwalm, had left off, but without much of the latter's philosophical finesse. Garrigou began going back over certain lines in *L'Action* of 1893, which he found objectionable, and attacking Blondel's orthodoxy all over again. At first it was what Blondel had said about proofs for the existence of God and then it was about his theory of the knowledge of being and his idea of an integral apologetic. Each time Blondel answered by showing how Garrigou had misunderstood or missed the point of what Blondel was saying, but each time the explanation never managed to penetrate the misunderstanding in Garrigou's mind. What bothered Blondel most about all this was not so much the misunderstanding in the mind of an influential Dominican in Rome, but the fact that the misunderstanding was being taught in the seminaries of Rome, and from there being broadcast to all seminaries around the world, as if it were the only teaching of the Church. Garrigou was influential in drawing up the *Oath against Modernism*, which was to be taken by all seminary teachers and students for decades to come, and in seeing that it was enforced. His attacks on Blondel, along with his own manual on apologetics, which became a standard in seminaries, were a part of this enforcement against a man who was deprived of any voice in seminaries by these very attacks. This was a pattern that Garrigou was to follow against many others through the decades, including seminary professors who did not conform to his abstract and extrinsicist way of thinking in philosophy or theology.

Another author who weighed in against Blondel at this time, in 1913, was another Jesuit, Joseph de Tonquédec, in a book on *Immanence*, excerpts of which were published in the *Revue pratique d'Apologétique* and in *Études*. There, it was not only Blondel himself who was brought into question, but also those who had tried to explain or defend his method, like the two Valensin brothers, Albert and Auguste, both Jesuits, the latter of whom had been the student of Blondel and remained in constant correspondence with him; he published the article on the Method of Immanence in the *Dictionnaire apologétique de la Foi catholique,* one of the rare instances in which something favorable to Blondel on apologetics had found its way into a mainstream work of theology. Once again, the level of discourse in this exchange between de Tonquédec and Blondel is not very elevated. Blondel finds that he is once again dealing with a misunderstanding that is probably incorrigible. Without trying to explain himself one more time, he settles for saying that what he said is not what he is said to have said, and that the difference is very important for a proper understanding of the question of immanence and transcendence in the Christian tradition.

In addition to this sparring with the likes of Garrigou and de Tonquédec, Blondel was also continuing his annual contributions to Lalande's *Vocabulaire Technique de la Philosophie,* where he was better understood and gratified for being taken seriously as a philosopher. By 1911 the discussion was down to words like *miracle, mystery* and *mysticism*. Blondel had many precisions to bring to these themes with some religious connotation. In fact, during this time, except for the Testis articles, Blondel appears to have been withdrawing more and more from the direct confrontations with exclusively extrinsicist theologians, which had been an important part of his activity during the ten years preceding *Pascendi,* and confining himself more and more to what he called the question of technical philosophy. He was not abandoning his earlier interest in the philosophy of religion, or even apologetics. Instead he was gearing up for the long haul in the debate over these questions with non-believers as well as believers. After all these years of relatively narrow focus on the question of apologetics, he felt the need to go back to a more systematic approach to philosophy that would underpin his philosophy of transcendence in human action, apart from all the heated controversy he had been experiencing since 1896, not to say 1893. What happened with the *Annales de Philosophie Chrétienne* left him no doubt as to the wisdom of this choice.

The new series of the *Annales de Philosophie Chrétienne* under the direction of Blondel and Laberthonnière was to last eight years, until 1913, when the Catholic allies of *Action Française* were finally able to touch the button in Rome once again, this time to have the entire series placed on the *Index* of forbidden books and to place Fr. Laberthonnière under a formal interdict to ever publish again on matters of philosophy and theology. Blondel's expression for the condemnation was that Laberthonnière had been guillotined, silenced once and for all. If it had been generally known who Testis was, whose articles were not the last of what the *Annales* had had to say about *Action Française*, perhaps he too would have been condemned. After Testis, the *Annales* had followed with a more direct criticism aimed at *Action Française* signed by Laberthonnière himself. This apparently proved to be the last straw for the neo-monarchists who had the ear of Rome, so that they called for the condemnation, which was handed down without even a hearing from the accused.

This was Church politics at its worst, crushing down one of its own. There was no chance of appeal, but it did become a serious matter of conscience not only for Laberthonnière, but also for Blondel and the circle of friends who rallied around them and the *Annales,* all firm believers in the authority of the Church, which they thought they were supporting by their action. An intense debate ensued, not on whether they would submit, but how they would do it. If Laberthonnière resigned as Secretary for the Redaction, as he would have to, if he were to accept being silenced, the *Annales* would have to be reorganized. The question became whether they should reorganize or simply go out of existence, since Laberthonnière did resign, once again as a loyal son of the Church, but also quite heroically, since everyone knew that he was being sacrificed to a cause that was not even Christian in spirit, but rather quite anti-Christian, as Testis and Laberthonnière had tried to show.

In a note that was debated at some length between Laberthonnière, Mourret, Brémond, and Blondel, the *Annales* of May-June 1913 expressed their "feelings of submission and of active docility" and their willingness to reform themselves, for "the future remains open." This they followed with an announcement of provisional suspension until October, which was not well received in Rome. The accusers wanted a total shutdown, which is what Mourret had been suggesting from the beginning. The accusers got what they wanted, thanks to the loyalty of the group itself to the supernatural teaching authority of the Church, for which Maurras had only contempt.

In the final issue of October 14, 1913, the Committee of Redaction, with the full collaboration of Laberthonnière, announced to its readers and subscribers that they would have to defer indefinitely, beyond the postponement originally announced, the resumption of publication, in order to reorganize themselves even more completely than they had foreseen. In fact, the *Annales de Philosophie Chrétienne* were never to appear again, and thus ended not only a very original periodical of Christian philosophy that Blondel had fostered and supported even with his own money, but also his own profound involvement in the sort of give-and-take over apologetics and religion he had been engaged in for almost twenty years. The end of the journal was a loss to the Church as well as to philosophy, the likes of which has never been replaced. The loss also affected the relations between Blondel and Laberthonnière, which had never been an easy friendship.

Tension between the two grew over the years, or at least between the followers of each one, until the year of Laberthonnière's death in 1932. Some would later think that Blondel abandoned Laberthonnière to the wolves, thinking that Blondel had always supported him in everything that he did and wrote before that, and some would even go so far as to say that Blondel caused his death by a letter of criticism he had written to him. Needless to say, Blondel felt very uncomfortable to be thought of in this way by friends of his friend, but he knew that this tension between him and Laberthonnière had not begun only with the condemnation. It had begun much earlier, when Blondel would disagree and take issue with some of Laberthonnière's ideas and attacks on certain authorities in the Church. It has also been said that only Laberthonnière was touched by the condemnation, because the Church could be "more indulgent" toward a young lay professor, but not toward a priest supposedly trained in precise and rigorous theology. On the other hand, it could also be said that the identity of Blondel as the owner and the one ultimately responsible for the *Annales*, not to mention his own authorship of the Testis articles, was not generally known. In any case, Blondel and his friends never thought that any of his writings had come under the condemnation, but rather that he continued to enjoy the support and approval of many in high authority in the Church, something Blondel and his family valued immensely as a consolation against the threats or rumors of threats that were constantly circulating about him.

VIII

The Philosopher of Aix

The story of Blondel's involvement in the modernist crisis within the Catholic Church is a long and complicated one, as we have been seeing. It started with his *Letter on Apologetics* in 1896, which had a lot to do with provoking the crisis by reason of the controversies it led to with those whose methods in apologetics were being challenged, and it was still going on in his defense of Catholic social action against those he called the monophorists in the Church. The end of this involvement, in which he felt much maligned as well as misunderstood, can be seen as having come with the closing of the *Annales de Philosophie Chrétienne,* after which he was able to enter into a much less turbulent period of his life and concentrate more on his own philosophical development.

The irony in all this controversy that took up so much of his time and energy is that Blondel found himself addressing mainly theologians and other religious authorities rather than the philosophers he had originally intended to address on the question of religion. This deviation in his career, so to speak, is something he brought on himself by the kind of innovation he was proposing in the philosophy of religion as well as by his criticism of the more established methods of apologetics or ways of promoting the interests of the Church intellectually as well as socially. Amid the barrage of objections and outright rejections he experienced within the Church, without much of a hearing about what he was actually saying, he discovered that he would have as much of a task converting Christians to what he thought was the true understanding of Christianity for the modern world and the modern spirit as converting non-Christians.

He also discovered that he would have to temper his language as he tried over and over again to explain what he was about in the philosophy of action of his dissertation of 1893, which had brought him into prominence for both Christians and non-Christians, and to defend his way of presenting the problem of religious conversion to the supernatural as something internal and subjective for the spirit as well as something external and objective. The work he kept projecting in outline on Christian apologetics during these controversial years was never brought to completion, partly because he was forever defending himself against attacks from those he called extrinsicists and monophorists on the side of religion as well as those who only wanted to secularize or naturalize religion as something purely human and historical, but also partly because he was not really interested in doing apologetics as such, which is more of a theologian's work, and which he viewed more as a Scholastic exercise for the converted than as an effort to reach those in need of conversion in their interior life both within and without the Church, including himself and his friends in their struggle to realize the Christian religion in the modern world.

What Blondel came to realize, with the help of Wehrlé, at the end of this highly contentious period within the Church, when they were contemplating having to stop publishing the *Annales de Philosophie Chrétienne*, is that what he was trying to do in the philosophy of religion would not come to any serious effect in the spirits of people in the sort of stand-up knock-down battles he had been engaging in alongside Laberthonnière, with adversaries to the right and to the left. It would have a lasting effect only in a more serene atmosphere of quiet reflection on the Catholic life as lived by the community of faith in history itself. It would also require a more complete development of the metaphysical perspective within which such a reflection had to take place and mature. Much of what actually came from his own reflections on the question of Christian religion during this contentious period would indeed come to fruition, not immediately in the form of the book on apologetics he was contemplating, but much later when his copious notes, outlines, and partial drafts would take the shape of a Trilogy on *Thought, Being,* and *Action,* followed by a three-volume work on *Philosophy and the Christian Spirit.* The thought for such a more systematic consideration of the philosophical problem of religion was already emerging in bits and pieces during this period of looking back on his work of 1896 and of 1893 and it would continue to develop at a more leisurely pace in the course of his teaching at Aix until it would all come together in one final surge of activity after retiring from teaching, when he would finally publish the whole of what he had been contemplating from the beginning.

Uneasy Relations with a Secular University Administration

In the meantime, after the demise of the *Annales,* Blondel, now well into his forties, had other things to think about besides these questions of apologetics, both as a professor of philosophy in the University and as a father of young children just starting out in their own life. His firstborn, Charles, had come in 1895, when he was still in Lille. His daughter Elisabeth was born shortly after the family moved to Aix, in 1899. The third and last child, André, was born in 1902. Blondel did not have to worry about supporting them financially. He had inherited wealth to live on as well as his salary. But he did have to worry about how and where they were to be educated outside the family, as his own parents had had to worry about where he should be educated, when the official school system was anything but favorable to their Christian faith. The great divide between the State school system and the Catholic private school system, recognized as *libre*, one staunchly irreligious and the other equally protective of religion for students committed to their charge, still existed and required a choice on the part of parents like the Blondels.

Like his parents, Maurice Blondel preferred to commit his children to the Catholic school system rather than the State system. In Aix, he had a choice, since there was a Catholic college as well as the State Lycée where he had taught in the 1980s, which had not been the case when he had started at the Lycée in Dijon. The Jesuit college in Dijon opened only after he had been launched in his studies, at which time we saw his cousin André switch over from the Lycée to the Jesuit college while Maurice stayed on at the Lycée, for apostolic reasons that became clear only later on. In the case of his children there does not seem to have been anything like the missionary spirit that had made their father stay at the Lycée even after the opportunity to attend a Catholic college presented itself, so off to the Catholic college they went to get their spiritual formation at the same time as their academic formation.

This did not go unnoticed by the State University authorities where Blondel was then employed, as we see from a note placed in his academic folder in 1912 by the rector of the University, Payot, to the effect that "MB is having his children brought up by our adversaries, at the Catholic college of Aix, which is in competition with the Lycée." Nothing more is said, but the fact that this is noted is an indication that Blondel's Catholic convictions still did not sit well with the administrators of a University system that had been so reluctant to grant him a chair to begin with, even after he had obtained the highest degree of recognition as a philosopher from a jury of philosophers. What was expected, on the side of the State system as well as on the side of the Catholic system, was exclusive loyalty to one side or the other, but Blondel never bought this kind of exclusive loyalty on either side. He thought both sides should be loyal to one another as well as to their own selves, as he was trying to show in his own pursuit of a State University career without hiding his Catholicism under a bushel basket but rather by insisting on it precisely as a philosopher. He knew that there was a lot to be learned from the State system, especially about how to philosophize, but he chose to send his children to the Catholic schools for what they had to teach about the Catholic faith in addition to philosophy, which added a bit to the handicap he experienced in the eyes of the bureaucrats in the University system.

There was also another handicap Blondel suffered under in his University career, that of poor health, which forced him to take prolonged leaves of absence. This too was noted in his academic folder by Payot. Rather surprisingly for a recently appointed professor, barely two years after becoming titular professor at Aix, Blondel obtained a leave of absence of five years, from 1901 to 1906, for reasons of health. This was at the height of the modernist crisis, during which time Blondel was in correspondence with Loisy, von Hügel, and others as well as his priest friends Wehrlé and Mourret concerning what to do in the crisis, while meditating on his own intervention in the debate with *Histoire et Dogme*, which came out in 1904, so that he could not be thought of as completely incapacitated. In fact, one might even speculate that part of the reason for this leave of absence in his own mind was to allow him more time and energy to deal with these questions of apologetics for the Catholic Church in which he was so heavily involved. But the fact is that Blondel did suffer from a severe neuritis, probably aggravated by the tension he and his wife felt under recurring threats or at least fears of his being condemned by the Church, and he did go to a spa at Grasse to find relief from his pain. The neuritis never left him. It was frequently referred to in his correspondence with others and stayed with him for the rest of his days, with varying degrees of ups and downs.

Blondel never let this fragility of health completely immobilize him. If he could not keep up with his professional duty of teaching, he could still keep up with his many other activities, which included a voluminous correspondence almost every day with journals and other individuals seeking his opinion on different questions concerning religion, as well as reading, meditating, taking copious notes, and writing on the burning questions of the day. What he actually produced even during this time of forced leisure from his functions as titular professor is an indication of an enormous capacity for work in a career that was advancing on several fronts at the same time.

What was not appreciated by the University authorities was the full extent and value of Blondel's contribution to the debate over Christian apologetics. In 1919 and 1920 it was thought that Blondel was not publishing enough for fear of antagonizing ecclesiastical authorities. Another note Payot placed in his academic folder speaks of him as "eloquent, exercising a real action on students, but a somewhat narrow action. Has not published anything serious since his dissertation." For Payot, most of what Blondel had published, starting from the *Letter on Apologetics* in 1896 and going on to his articles on the *Idealist Illusion* and the *Starting Point of Philosophy*, not to mention articles on Descartes and Malebranche as well as the one on History and Dogma, did not count as what was expected of a University professor of philosophy. Nor did Payot realize how much Blondel had run the risk of censure from "ecclesiastical authorities" in most of these writings for going against what many thought was the authentic teaching of the Church. The only thing Payot could show was a continuing indifference to questions of religion from the perspective of a narrowly conceived idea of philosophy.

It is true that perhaps Blondel was not publishing enough on other aspects of his philosophy during these first two decades of the twentieth century, as he would acknowledge in part later on in his *Itineraire Philosophique*, due to his more pressing preoccupation with the question of Christian apologetics and the controversies this led him into with theologians rather than with philosophers. But it is not true that he was not broadening his outlook to include questions on thought, being, and action that even Payot might have considered more germane to philosophy. This is clear from the content of his teaching both before and after the long leave of absence he took from his functions as a University professor from 1901 to 1906.

The World of a University Professor

In thinking about this leave of absence, and other, shorter ones that he also took later on, it is important to keep in mind all the functions a titular professor of philosophy had to exercise in the University. Blondel was the only titular professor of philosophy in his part of France during most of his thirty years of active duty at Aix. It was not until near the end of his career that he was assigned even a *Chargé de Cours* to assist him. As titular professor of philosophy he was responsible for overseeing the teaching of philosophy in the entire region, which included cities like Marseilles, Nice, Toulon, Avignon, and the island of Corsica. Blondel was expected to read written exams and hear oral exams in most of these places, on the undergraduate level as well as the graduate. He also had to write reports periodically on the state of philosophy teaching in the region, which he did with great care about the inadequacies he and his fellow examiners found both with regard to what was being taught and the spirit in which it was being taught. Along with this, of course, he also had to prepare his own courses each year and follow his own students at both Aix and Marseilles. If we keep all this in mind, we can understand better why Blondel would ask for a leave of absence when he felt more than ordinarily indisposed by the neuritis that afflicted him most of his life.

As titular professor of philosophy for the Faculty of Letters of Aix-Marseilles, Blondel was responsible for the entire graduate program in philosophy as well as the preparation of students for the Licentiate, for the Diploma in Higher Studies, and for supervising Doctoral Dissertations. There were times when he had as many as seventy students under his direction, including sixty-seven who were still registered with him when he retired. For most of his career he had to take care of all this business more or less by himself. It was not until the final years of his teaching at Aix that he was assigned a *Maître de Conférences* to assist with the teaching.

The titular professor of each regional Faculty like Aix had to offer three kinds of courses, two for graduate students and one for the general public. For the graduate students there were courses in the history of philosophy as well as more systematic courses referred to as *enseignement doctrinal*, where the professor was expected to present more of his own ideas in the different areas of philosophy. It was up to the titular professor to set the program according to a two-year cycle for the Licentiate students and, during his tenure, each Faculty or titular professor had a certain latitude in choosing what would be taught and what would be the matter for the exams. In addition it was also up to the titular professor to assign themes for monthly dissertations, which Blondel took great care in formulating in view of getting students to think for themselves and which he read and commented on meticulously in a sort of ongoing dialogue with each student, sometimes bringing the dialogue with a particular student into the classroom when he deemed it would be helpful to all in the class.

In choosing the matter for both the historical and the doctrinal courses, and in actually teaching them, Blondel always had in mind that he was forming philosophers who were supposed to be able to think for themselves and who would be future teachers of philosophy. In the history courses, with master historians in mind like Boutroux, his former teacher, and Delbos, his friend and classmate from Normale, then professor at the Sorbonne in Paris, he took care that the students would come into contact with each philosopher in his own language and come to grips with the internal coherence of each doctrinal synthesis. Moreover, in teaching the different approaches to philosophy according to its different historical and doctrinal aspects, he was especially concerned with showing the continuity among them as different endeavors within a tradition of genuine philosophizing that is more than just a juxtaposition of more or less disparate systems and specialties. Far from being a relativist in showing the originality of different philosophical systems, he tended rather to defend the philosophical spirit against the temptation to dissolve its unity into extremes of specialization or a formal heterogeneity of disciplines. Along with the treatment of authors from the past, he would frequently include courses on the current trends of the day in philosophy.

In the doctrinal courses he would expose more his own personal thinking on different questions, but always with the idea of opening up and revivifying the teaching of the philosophical tradition. His aim was not to indoctrinate students, but to elicit their critical thinking on the philosophical questions being debated in the new developments of science and civilization. He was far more interested in having his students start out on their own than in just repeating what they had heard from him. Knowing that he had strong views of his own in matters that could affect the conscience of his students, he was especially careful to respect the freedom of each conscience and to avoid every act of dogmatic proselytism. What he was looking for was a seriousness of purpose among the students as well as the professor in the development of ideas that would lead to intellectual maturity. He cared little for the kind of indifference or "tolerance" that seems disinterested in vital questions from a sort of contemptuous disdain for the diversity of doctrines, judged from on high, so to speak, as all equally narrow subjective curiosities. He took the discussion of philosophical problems seriously, and he expected his students to do the same, whether they came to agree with him or not. This is how he had responded to his own professors and this is how he wanted his own students to respond to him in the mode of critical philosophy.

Courses in the history of philosophy usually included authors from two periods, ancient and modern. Each year a certain number of authors were assigned in the program from each period. Typically this would include one part or another of Plato or Aristotle, Socrates, Plotinus, Stoicism, or Epicureanism in ancient philosophy, and Descartes, Pascal, Malebranche, Berkeley, Stuart Mill, Maine de Biran, Schopenhauer, or even a contemporary like William James in modern philosophy. Descartes was often taken as the pivotal author around whom to discuss other authors. In 1898-99, for example, Blondel lectured on Pascal as both Cartesian and anti-Cartesian. The next year he followed this up with a course on the evolution and deformations of Cartesianism in the seventeenth and eighteenth centuries.

Introducing Aquinas into Modern Philosophy

One of his important innovations in the historical program was the introduction of medieval authors like Thomas Aquinas and Albert the Great as early as 1910-11, long before Gilson had made this a *sine qua non* for the history of philosophy. His own interest in these authors had stemmed from his confrontation with the modern Scholastics he had encountered and whose philosophical inadequacies he had criticized, but it was also part of his more inclusive conception of philosophy than the one then prevalent in the French University. Blondel lectured extensively on Aquinas over a period of six or seven years, beginning in 1911-12. He realized that having Aquinas on the program of graduate studies for philosophy at the University was something new that required special attention. For himself it was an exploration into a part of Aquinas's philosophy that he had not found among the neo-Thomists he had been critical of earlier in the discussion of method in apologetics, but that in fact came closer to his own way of promoting an ascending movement toward God and the supernatural philosophically.

What struck him about Aquinas was the power and scope of his analysis using Aristotle's fourfold theory of movement as well as the detail he could encompass in this movement through the universe toward its single ultimate end, God. For him this was the *hapax* of Aquinas's philosophy, namely, "that it was detailed and systematically applied to an enormous complexus of theoretical and practical solutions that were generally intertwined and coherent" (course notes, 121). Blondel saw Aquinas's method as indirect, but working toward a growing precision focused on the immovable final end, God in his own essence, as that to which the creature was to be assimilated in an act of intelligence and will. He admired the description of action as a universal fact seen, not just from the outside, but more from the inside as a synthesis aiming at an end, where "intention," whether conscious or not, was not just a matter of objective observation, but also of subjective aim, whether through nature or through intelligence. He took delight in finding the same kind of aporia in Aquinas that he had argued for at the end of his reflection on the phenomenon of action between a necessity of fulfilling a religious need and an impossibility of doing so through human initiative alone. In Aquinas, the aporia or antinomy par excellence, according to Blondel, was that between an intellect with a natural desire to see God, a desire that was not in vain and therefore somehow necessary, and an intellect whose natural capacity was not such that it could see God or attain him on its own, whence the necessity of a supernatural gift for man, if he was to attain his natural end.

In his first years of lecturing on Aquinas, Blondel focused mainly on Part Three of the *Summa contra Gentiles,* which has to be understood not just as a philosophical argument but also as a theological elaboration of how God acts and governs in the world in accordance with how nature works and how intellectual beings provide for themselves under the divine providence. Part Three of the *Summa contra Gentiles* presupposes that the perfection of the divine Nature in itself has been established, in Part One, and that the power of this Nature is the creator and Lord of all that there is, as shown in Part Two. Part Three picks up from this production of things and goes on to show how God rules in this world by directing all things toward their final end, which is, of course, himself. As theology, the argument is framed from the standpoint of God, so to speak, but this makes Blondel uncomfortable as a philosopher because he finds St. Thomas perhaps too set in his theological ways, or perhaps not keen enough on how we have to remain in search of God even after he has revealed himself, as Augustine was so much more mindful of in his *Confessions.* Even though Aquinas acknowledges that God remains unknown to us, Blondel notes, his method is "always metaphysical, didactic and synthetic: not only do the first two parts [of the *Summa contra Gentiles*] place us in the absolute, but still we see the ascending movement [of the Third Part toward God] as it is seen from on high, from the higher term [of the movement], with full clarity" (course notes, 135).

In typical Scholastic fashion, St. Thomas never renounces his habit of citing texts and authorities, thus leaving Blondel with the impression of relying more on authority than on rational argument. Nor does Aquinas enter into the state of mind of the ignorant or the unbelievers, as Blondel tried to do so much in his own argument. In this respect Blondel found Augustine more congenial to his way of thinking than Aquinas and, not knowing much about how Aquinas had completed Augustine's theory of divine illumination with his own theory of an intellect endowed with its own natural light and principles, he would have preferred a theory of interior illumination to what he saw as only an abstractive and ratiocinative procedure in Aquinas that lent itself to the kind of extrinsicism and authoritarianism he found among the Thomists of his day.

Blondel was not unaware of Rousselot's early work on *The Intellectualism of Saint Thomas* which, in 1908, had opened up a whole new dimension in Aquinas's way of thinking. Blondel read the book carefully and found in it still many unresolved aporia in a theory of knowledge that could encompass the quiddity of things as abstract and universal but not individuals in their aspiration for the good. What he learned from Rousselot, and others like him, was that there was more to the philosophy of St. Thomas than what he had been led to believe by his early Dominican adversaries and the so-called Thomist manuals. At one point he began to muse that someone should write a book on just what Thomism is supposed to be. For his own part, he thought there was a lot in St. Thomas that should be preserved as truth to be promoted in modern philosophy and a lot that should be let go, even though he did not think that Thomists were doing a very good job of this in his day.

He was quite struck by Aquinas's own experience at the end of his life when he recognized that so much of what he had written was useless chaff, *paleae*, which Blondel interpreted as referring to the abstractive side of his thought. "We should be able to take up the work of St. Thomas," he wrote, "at the moment where he recognizes himself that all that he had written was only *paleae* and where he refused to go on dictating. We should have the abnegation to make discursive thought (for which there is an intense distaste in anyone who senses its deficiencies) serve speculative and practical wisdom" (course notes, 120). Instead of clinging to the objective literality of his words, we should look rather to the truth of the orientation of thought that they channel. With reference to the infinite, he writes, we must recognize that it is not something "to be run through by some discursive action, as abstract thought supposes, but action itself is *apeiron ti*, something infinite, as a synthesis grounded in first causality. From this we see the heterogeneity of action and thought, of the intelligent human cause and of the active presence of God. The work that St. Thomas has done from the standpoint of being and intelligence remains to be done from the standpoint of love and the will" (course notes, 120). In this sense, he saw his own work on action, not as opposed to, but as complementing that of Aquinas.

After two years of lecturing on Aquinas alone and Part Three of the *Summa contra Gentiles,* in 1913 Blondel began to lecture on a comparison between Thomism and Cartesianism in both his graduate courses and his public lectures, in order to bring out better the relevance of Thomas's philosophy to modern philosophy. This was in keeping with his own understanding of how the history of philosophy should be done by a philosopher and for philosophical purposes. The reason for studying the history of philosophy was not just to satisfy a certain historical curiosity about former philosophers, or even just to initiate ourselves to a living and renascent world such as that of Aquinas, but also to uncover a historical source that enables us to understand the development of modern thought as well as another teaching that, in its richness and fecundity, can help us to form our own thinking. The reason for introducing Aquinas into the historical program at Aix had been to fill a lacuna in the historical consciousness of the University. The reason for proceeding by way of a comparison between two systems like Cartesianism and Thomism was to better the understanding of each system, according to the saying that to comprehend is to compare. The reason for going from Descartes to Aquinas was to go from a thought that was better known and more accessible to the students to one that was less well known and less attractive. Though there was something artificial in this confrontation between two thinkers who were separated by more than three hundred years and two quite different worlds, so that St. Thomas and the Scholastics could be viewed as adversaries of Descartes, still the comparison of these respective positions presented a certain doctrinal interest in preparing new ways for philosophy in the future.

In his presentation of Descartes and Aquinas, Blondel drew two contrasting sketches going in opposite directions from one another. For Aquinas the aim was to grasp the hierarchy of beings and to disclose the divine plan, in order to bring out the distinction and the end of all things, including human beings. "He [Aquinas] took all the material and rational order of the world as an underpinning for the Christian order and considered all the grandeurs of this world only in the perspective of the future life and the supernatural solution" (course notes, 178). If Aquinas ran the risk of following Aristotle in philosophy at a time when Aristotle was being condemned by authorities in the Church, it was because he found in the Philosopher the way of making manifest rationally, not only the preambles of faith, but also much of what was taught in the Christian faith as a whole. What St. Thomas did, according to Blondel in these lectures, was to capture all the forces of Hellenic speculation and science and to use them in the service of Christian supernaturalization. This was no longer the oversimplified view of an uneasy combination or juxtaposition of Greek rationalism with Christian theology that Blondel had advanced in the *Letter on Apologetics* before studying St. Thomas in the flesh, so to speak. In reading Aquinas himself Blondel had learned that the medieval synthesis of philosophy and theology did not have to be understood in the disjointed or extrinsicist way he had seen it done earlier. In the medieval view, Blondel nevertheless recognized, everything converged on the end and, though there was a true interest in the world as it is, it was taken more as springboard for the beyond, with a certain detachment and without much concern for changing it for the better through science, as would be the case with Descartes.

In his sketch of Descartes, Blondel presented the father of modern philosophy as diametrically opposed to this otherworldly view of Aquinas, as totally concentrated on conquering this world and the forces of nature, as indicated by the subtitle of the *Discourse on Method*. It was not as if Descartes had lost the Christian faith in God or anything supernatural, as some have argued. Blondel had argued to the contrary in his earlier article on Descartes. Far from abandoning the idea of God, Descartes used it as a metaphysical backup for his idea of man and of the world of nature. But he had no more to do with the idea of God than that. In his philosophy and science he put his back to it to construct his mechanistic view of the world, leaving aside not only the idea of God but also any idea of a final cause for the world as a hierarchy of beings. His approach to the world, according to Blondel, was that of a positivist who, under the guise of giving each order its due, ends up "reversing the hierarchy of things, placing the things of this world and scientific mastery of them in the forefront" and, perhaps without realizing it too clearly, using God only to go to the world and to install himself in it permanently, quite unlike St. Thomas, "who used the world only to go to God, and to our immortal and supernatural destinies" (course notes, 179).

Thus, in the view of Blondel by the time of his lectures on Thomism and Cartesianism, it was Descartes who separated philosophy from its Christian moorings in medieval Scholastic thought and set modern philosophy up in opposition, not only to Scholasticism, but also to the consideration of the religious dimension in human experience, unlike what had been the case even in ancient philosophy. Even without abandoning his Christian faith and his idea of Christian salvation through grace, Blondel thought, Descartes established the idea that philosophy and science had to be kept separate from religion and faith, an idea that was to prevail even among later Scholastics as well as more secular thinkers.

The question for Blondel, after sketching these two contrasting historical views of philosophy and science, was whether the finalist conception, which had not been absent in the Greek form of rationalism, and the new scientific conception were as incompatible as they were made out to be. Does one have to reject the whole of the other in adopting one or can one adopt a scientific view without abandoning the finalist view? In adding his positivist view of science to the human patrimony, Descartes was also arguing for the extermination of the finalist view, *exterminanda*, as Spinoza would say more explicitly later on. But can one stay with only a positivist view of science, if one wants to do a critique of life and human existence as a whole? On the other side, if one adopts a finalist view or a religious view of human destiny, does one have to resist the positivist view of science put forth in Cartesianism and modern philosophy? What history teaches us, according to Blondel, is how such views came to be opposed to one another. What we have to learn or work out for ourselves is perhaps how they can be made, not only compatible, but even complementary and necessary for one another in a broader science of human action that would include the moral, religious, and the supernatural astir in human initiative along with the positive findings of research into the mechanisms of the world and of the soul. Even in doing the history of philosophy, Blondel was never too far away from questions he was interested in raising as a philosopher.

Recognizing Ancient Sources Still at Work Within Modern Cartesianism

This is clear not only from his courses but also in an article on Malebranche he published during this time when he was lecturing on Thomism and Cartesianism. In this article, titled *The Anti-Cartesianism of Malebranche*, Blondel argues that Malebranche, in spite of a great enthusiasm for Descartes and his way of thinking, was fundamentally opposed to the Cartesian mode of philosophy and science by the direction that he took in thinking about God, a direction that had previously been that of neo-Platonism and Scholastics like Aquinas.

Blondel here makes a distinction that will figure prominently in his own thinking in years to come between two vitally united elements that mutually determine one another in any truly organized system of thought, one of which informs the other as the original principle of synthesis and animation. "On one side there is an ensemble of conceptions that can be expressed analytically and appears communicable from one mind to another through discursive procedures, like matter that passes from hand to hand. On the other side there is an attitude of the entire spiritual being, a disposition that is at once congenital and acquired, which constitutes the deeper person of the philosopher, the nature of his spirit, his vision and his will for life, his principal inspiration and his final aspiration, something that does not have to be the object of any reflection to be the very spring of his method, the transubstantiating nourishment of his teaching, the highest stake in what he is looking for" (1966a, 62-63). The distinction is well worth pondering here because it suggests something about the two sides of thought that Blondel was beginning to work out during this time in view of his own systematic work on Thought. It allows us to see how Malebranche could be quite Cartesian on a certain conceptual level of his thought but also quite anti-Cartesian at the same time on a more profound level, as Blondel explains.

Historians of philosophy as well as philosophers themselves, according to Blondel, tend to look more to the first of the two elements just mentioned, the one that is more visible and manageable. It is from this side that Malebranche appears indebted to Descartes for a large part of the apparatus in his thought. The more decisive element of his teaching, however, is the one that expresses "the secret of the heart that is ignored, the intimate life of the spirit, as it were the soul of the soul"; and because philosophy is not pure intellectuality, but in effect a "thing of the soul, it is this spiritual tendency that determines the sense of the intellectual elements more than it is modified by them, as active as they might otherwise be by their own logical force" (1966a, 63). It is from this second aspect of his thought that Malebranche contradicts Descartes and turns everything he borrows from Descartes conceptually around in a direction that Descartes had deliberately turned his back on.

In his effort to free philosophy and science from bondage to Scholasticism, Descartes had separated philosophy, not only from theology, but also from positive religion and from any concern for our final ends or problems relative to eternal life. He chose to ignore, not only everything supernatural and mystical, according to Blondel, but also "any spiritual science studied for its own sake and methodically cultivated as a force of interior transformation for the soul" (1966a, 64). His philosophy became a concern only with mastering the world positively in order to solidify his knowledge of nature and thereby increase indefinitely our successful interventions and accommodations in the mechanism of this universe.

Malebranche, on the other hand, not only does not separate philosophy or science from the religious kind of concern, but goes even further than the traditional way of according philosophy or reason with faith and with Christianity. For him metaphysics and speculative, ascetical, and mystical theology are not only reunited but fused together by a "constant identification of the Word [spoken of in St. John's Gospel] and Reason, of positive Revelation and the teaching of the interior Master, of the supernatural life with the essential return of the finite spirit to the infinite principle of all truth and all activity. Descartes braced his back against God, without ever considering Him as end, in order to go to the world and science. Malebranche turns his back on the world in search of God, [to find] in Him light and nourishment for the soul. He is a contemplative for whom philosophy has no other purpose, no other principle, no other urge except to lead our fundamental inclination to its divine end; it is a means of entering into the vision that is salvific" (1966a, 65). Blondel is far from agreeing with the way Malebranche fuses philosophy back into theology, after Descartes had separated the two, nor does he think that philosophy can be reunited with the religious concern, let alone the supernatural of Christian Revelation, as readily as Malebranche would have it even within the framework of Christian philosophy. He is only pointing out that, even in using the concepts of Cartesian philosophy, he is in contradiction with the entire worldly thrust of that philosophy in its separation from any otherworldly concern.

Blondel shows how, in all the major ideas that Malebranche appears to be taking from Descartes, the idea of God, extension, or the soul, there is a constant reversal of perspective in the way he treats them. God is not just the creator who wills the world and guarantees our idea of it. He is an essence, the infinite focal point of all essences, all ideas, in whom all created beings are represented. Extension is understood, not just as something external and material, but also as intelligible and hence as eternal, immense, and necessary, the immensity of God himself. The soul is taken to be, not just clear and distinct in itself, but also as something in movement, in search of itself and unable to find itself except in the divine Essence. Even the "principle of clear and distinct ideas," which Malebranche finds so compelling in Descartes, is turned into a need for spiritual purification and contemplation. Descartes's scientific and rationalist method is turned into an ascetic and speculative method intent on God above everything else. Where Descartes thought philosophy had to be purely natural, Malebranche did not hesitate to turn it into something quite religious, or to see religion, including the Christian religion, as something perfectly philosophical. For this reason, Blondel points out, Malebranche could appeal as much to Plotinus as to Descartes, thus reinstating a finalist perspective that Descartes had taken pains to banish from science and philosophy.

What is surprising about all this, if we look to the deeper, more vital movement of Malebranche's thought that Blondel brings out in opposition to the purely secular movement of Descartes' thought, is that such a post-Cartesian form of metaphysics could have emerged so soon after the rise of Cartesianism itself even within the Cartesian conceptual framework itself. It took someone concerned with the philosophy of religion, as Blondel was, to bring out this deeper side of Malebranche's thought in its opposition to the Cartesian rationalism and immanentism. Even if there was no one to take up this call to a new philosophy of religion immediately after Malebranche, and even if there were some problems with this philosophy that should be pointed out, as Blondel later wrote in his introduction to a work on Malebranche by Delbos, published posthumously by Wehrlé (1924), "it did open the way to the more recent initiatives that bring precision to the methods of apologetics and determine the philosophical aspect under which the problem of positive and supernatural religion can and must be raised." What Blondel found in Malebranche's anti-Cartesianism was in some respects a precursor to his own attempts to develop a philosophy of the supernatural. Malebranche was for him an early sign that the Christian idea remained hidden in the heart of modern philosophy, as he had begun to suggest twenty years earlier in the *Letter on Apologetics*.

The More Systematic Exploration of Philosophy

If we turn now to the more doctrinal side of Blondel's teaching, in addition to his teaching on the history of philosophy, we find that he was at first concerned with offering more or less standard courses such as an Introduction to the Study of Philosophy, having to do with philosophy as a whole and with method, in 1906-07, his first year back from his long leave of absence. The next year he focused more on Metaphysics and its method as well as on the idea of truth as sanction. The next two years he lectured on the Normative Sciences, first in philosophy in general, and then in thought and in life. Each year he included a course on current trends in philosophy along with the courses on the more classical authors in the history of ancient and modern philosophy. One year he lectured on the Elements of Psychology, another, on the Problem of Conscience, while keeping up with the more basic themes of classical philosophy.

Little by little, however, as he was beginning to broaden the scope of the history of philosophy to include medieval authors like Aquinas, he also began to focus on themes he was more personally interested in developing for his own philosophy and that would figure more prominently in the Trilogy on Thought, Being, and Action he was already contemplating. As early as 1912 he began lecturing on Thought for a couple of years under the guise of a theory of knowledge and a critical epistemology. In 1914 he turned to the critical problem of knowledge, which he also spoke of as a normative logic, while addressing the problem of happiness and final ends in the moral and religious destiny of human being. Then, in 1915-16, he offered a course in the Philosophy of Being, an analysis of the degrees of reality as well as a search for the meaning and the content of concrete existence, which he referred to as a sketch of effective ontology, striving always to take each theme beyond a merely static consideration toward something more dynamic in being as well as in thought. This too went on for two years at the same time as he was introducing his students to Nietzsche and the Will to Power.

Thus, by the end of World War I, Blondel had moved into a cycle of systematic courses that he would repeat once or twice over the coming years, until his retirement from teaching in 1926. In these courses he was in effect sharpening his own thinking still in anticipation of the projected Trilogy. In fact, it was during another prolonged leave of absence from teaching for reasons of health, from 1922 to 1924, that he actually began writing what would later appear as the first volume of *La Pensée*.

In all these courses Blondel was concerned with what he would have called the technical formation of his students in philosophy as well as developing his own technical philosophy. Each year, however, as titular professor of philosophy for the region of Aix-Marseilles, he also had to give a less technical kind of course for the general public as well as graduate students. In these courses he would choose a more general theme relating to the spirit of people who came to hear him in fairly large numbers. In 1914, the first year of the War with Germany, he lectured on German thought and the lessons to be derived from the War. The next year he lectured on the task of philosophy at the present time and "on our intellectual duties" as citizens. In the third year of the War, it was "on our new duties and on the future of France," always with a patriotic bent in everything he had to say. But by the last year of the War, he was back to more typically philosophical themes. In fact, the title of the public course for 1917-18 was *Pensée et Action*. This was the first time that Blondel publicly went back to his dissertation of 1893, after twenty-four years, this time with as much emphasis on thought as on action. Perhaps he felt that by this time the War had put enough distance between him and the spirit of recrimination that had dogged him and his work during the first decade of the century prior to the War. In any event, it does not seem that the lectures ignited any new explosions against him of the sort he had experienced earlier during the Modernist Crisis.

The Spiritual Outlook in Teaching

In later years, after the War, he lectured on the traditions of French philosophy and its resources for the future, on the spiritual legacy of the seventeenth century and the new orientations of philosophic thought, on conscience and the psychological bases of moral education, and in the end on the philosophy of St. Augustine on the occasion of coming centennial celebrations. There was even one course for Americans right after the War, the content of which was not recorded. In all of these courses Blondel was interested in influencing the spiritual outlook of his public toward a more thoughtful assumption of personal responsibility in the conduct of their life as citizens and as fully human beings, which of course, in his view, included a religious dimension as well as a national dimension. He wanted to inspire as well as to edify.

This was true even for his graduate students whom he had to form philosophically, not just in a technical sense but also in a spiritual sense, for the two had to go together for him. One of his regrets as a professor, as he wrote near the end of his teaching career, was that he could never know enough about the secret of these young minds whom he had to teach and love, which ones were looking for a word of life or a viaticum for eternity, who would preserve an inextinguishable fervor for an expression of light and affection, and which ones, in their politeness and even their desire to please, were and would be of those who are dry, climbers, forgetters, disdainers, dead souls (course notes, 346). What bothered him was that one could never tell which ones belonged to which spiritual preference. Help me to speak the language that you need to hear, he would say secretly to them, the language that perhaps unwittingly you are already speaking within yourself.

Each class, we are told by those who were his students, instead of immediately launching off in a lecture, he would begin by exploring what questions were arising in the minds of the students from what had been said in earlier classes. Firm as he was in his own ideas, he wanted to hear what they were thinking in response to what he was proposing. He wanted to hear their questions and would always try to answer them before going on to something else. What would happen very frequently was that, in answering, Blondel would take them far beyond what they were thinking in asking the question. He was opening up new avenues of thought for them, which would leave them to wonder perhaps about all that was going on in their own minds in asking these questions. Students were appreciative of these efforts to get them going in their own thinking and to give answers that would encourage them to think for themselves. What they saw before them was a teacher who fervently wanted to help them in this way and who would regret it if he failed to do so.

Jacques Paliard, who was a student of his beginning in 1909 and who would later succeed Blondel in the chair of philosophy at Aix, tells of a kind of awe that would come over the class at times when Blondel would wax eloquent on something that had not yet occurred to them in their very questioning. They came to realize that, as a saying of André Gide went, when one asks a question of a philosopher and gets an answer, one no longer understands what one was asking. But Blondel was not interested in just astounding his students. He was concerned with answering them in a meaningful way for them, and when he did not succeed, a kind of disappointment would come over him. In one of the discussions among the students that always followed these classes, where they would go over what had been said or done in class, one of them once made the remark, over a glass of beer, that "Blondel was not happy with the answer he gave us today. I imagine him, after the class, getting down on his kneeler to make an act of humility." This student understood the spirit in which Blondel approached his teaching. He taught philosophy by example in action as well as by word of mouth.

Blondel enjoyed teaching. It was for him as much a pleasure as a duty. He deeply regretted having to take those long leaves of absence from teaching because of his neuritis, and he did so only as a last resort. Many times when the pain in his arms was too severe for him to go to the University, he would hold his classes at his house in rue Roux-Alphéran. From this his students learned that philosophy required a certain asceticism as well as intellectual discipline. He had the reputation of being, not only eloquent, but also challenging and demanding of his students, as was clear from the way he dealt with the monthly dissertations he so carefully assigned. He would read these, first, for the kind of academic erudition and rigor they were supposed to display, and second, for the kind of philosophical supposition they were making without perhaps saying so. In his interviews with the students he would begin by recognizing all that was good about the dissertation, underlining what was solid and worth retaining, but then there would also come a dreaded moment when he would try to go deeper into the student's own orientation in his thinking and spiritual being. What he wanted to see was whether a student was fixed in his way of thinking, which was frequently still rather shortsighted and static, or whether he was ready to move toward a broader, more dynamic perspective on life and thought as a whole. Not everyone was clearly aware of what was supposed to be going on in this second moment in the evaluation of a dissertation, but it was enough to keep anyone from settling too easily into the comfort of concepts that were still far from adequate to the fullness of life and action.

Blondel thought a lot about the influence he was having on his students, and he realized that it was not always what he thought it to be. He had the feeling that he was sowing ideas without knowing where or how they would fall, and that they did not always turn out the way he was expecting. Things he insisted on and developed at great length before intelligences he thought quite receptive at the time did not take root and left students ungrateful to a degree that he had not foreseen. On the other hand, he was struck by the abiding faithfulness of a few others whom he had barely attended to, and by the vitality that sometimes isolated and incidental thoughts had acquired in them. Given the way he thought of philosophical communication in such a concrete way, he was left to wonder at the complexity of any sort of intellectual causality, with its mixture of cooperation and resistance, always active and always passive at the same time in many different ways.

Summering in Burgundy

Blondel, however, had many other people to think about besides his students during these years of professorship. There was his extended family, and that of his wife, as well as his own more immediate family living and growing with him in Aix. Every summer during the long vacation, when his presence in Aix was not required, Blondel would move his family back to Burgundy to maintain closer contact with both families in his place of origin. As we have seen, this is what he did from Lille and this is what he continued to do from Aix-en-Provence, going north when most would be going south but mainly going from the city to the country. For years the family would move into the home of his in-laws at Quincy-le-Vicomte, where Blondel first met his wife, Rose, while attending the wedding of his friend, Adéodat Boissard, to Rose's older sister Jeanne. Each summer both daughters would move back into their mother's house with their families, which meant that Blondel and Boissard could continue to share in one another's interests. This went on for almost fifteen years, until 1913, when the Royer house was no longer large enough to accommodate both growing families. That is when Blondel bought a property in nearby Magny-la-Ville, which is where he was to summer for the rest of his life, preparing his courses for the coming year as he had done for his dissertation years before at Saint-Seine. It was a large house surrounded by a fairly extensive park. The property of Saint-Seine had passed on to his unmarried sister Thérèse at the death of their parents. From Magny he would carry on his business, including his voluminous correspondence, as he did from his home on rue Roux-Alphéran in Aix during school, always keeping his correspondents posted on where to reach him and at what time. His parents died a few years after he had established himself in Aix, his mother in 1901 and his father in 1906. But the family always remained close and interested in one another's work in the way that their mother had encouraged them to be by her constant correspondence with all of them, no matter where they were, far or near.

His sister Thérèse, for example, was well aware of his tribulations with theologians during the modernist crisis and worried about a possible condemnation as well. She would say that Maurice could have avoided all these troubles if he had become an entomologist, in keeping with his early interest in butterflies, instead of a philosopher. With his brother Georges, a Germanist in language and economics, he attended the Passion Play of Oberammergau, after which he wrote to describe his own experience as a pilgrim in 1890 and then the dramatic psychology of the Passion Play itself in 1900. He also collaborated in his brother's historical and critical study of *The Drama of the Passion of Oberammergau*, first published in 1900 and updated in 1910, where, in opposition to certain critics of the pageant for its lack of proper historical objectivity, he argued for it as an authentic representation of the Christian Spirit for the modern world with genuine apologetic merit. Blondel was always more impressed with the humble practice of faith within a tradition than the supposedly more critical studies of abstract theoreticians and biblical criticists.

On the side of his wife, the mother, who was a fervently religious person with some mystical aspirations, must also have worried greatly about her son-in-law and his relation with authorities in the Church, which also added to Blondel's own fear of condemnation. The general attitude on both sides of his extended family surely had a lot to do with his decision to stop publishing on the question of apologetics under his own name shortly after the *Letter on Apologetics*, not to mention the fear of his own wife who, more than anyone else, wanted him to stop writing on the entire subject altogether. At one time in 1899, shortly after an Encyclical Letter addressed to the Clergy of France warning against certain Catholics who were following a certain subjectivistic philosophy that denied reason the right of affirming anything beyond its own operations, a philosophy that was the exact opposite of what Blondel was advancing but was nevertheless being attributed to him by certain people, while Blondel himself was away in Germany, Mme. Blondel had personally written to his friend Brémond, begging him to use his influence on her husband to dissuade him from writing on these questions and telling him how sick such condemnations would make him when they fell on others all around him (1970, 236). If he had ever been named in any such condemnation, as Laberthonnière was, or if he had even felt personally attacked by any one of them, it would have been for both of them, and for the rest of their families, a profound spiritual crisis for their life as devout Catholics.

Mme. Blondel perhaps did not have the same sense of mission as her husband regarding the necessity to speak out, not only against those who denied having any interest in the Church, but also against those within the Church who were refusing to face up to the exigencies of modern thought on the subject of religion and, by their closed-mindedness, excluding the very possibility of many sincere thinkers, searchers Blondel would call them, ever approaching the truth of any supernatural claims of religion. He, along with Wehrlé and Mourret, felt that many, within the Church as well as without, needed to hear what he had to say as a philosopher of religion just to save their faith. That is why he chose to put himself through the kind of tribulation he underwent, even though it was at the expense of his health and that of his wife, who perhaps suffered most of all during these years of tension and religious anxiety within their own conscience. Blondel always felt confident that he was saying nothing that was contrary to the teaching of the Church, knowing full well that others like Loisy and von Hügel were going against that teaching, and knowing also where the difference between himself and them lay, but his wife could not see that kind of difference. She only felt the fear of that big club many theologians like to wield over pious folk when they do not agree with their every word, let alone dare to present an opposing point of view.

It is not clear whether their children suffered as much from this troubling fear that hung over the parents during those years of the Modernist Crisis. They were still very young during the height of the Crisis between 1904 and 1907. Charles was barely ten years old, Elisabeth seven or eight, and André was three or four. They were only coming into their teens when the *Annales de Philosophie Chrétienne* was forced to cease publication in 1913 and their father emerged from the ordeal intellectually intact and ready to carry on his work within the Church as well as without in a less contentious atmosphere.

The War Years and After

Then came the War of 1914, which forced everyone to start thinking of different kinds of problems than those that had preoccupied French Catholics during the time of their religious and intellectual crisis. For the parents it meant a new kind of worry about how their children would get caught up in this conflagration. For the children it meant a new challenge about what to do with their lives. Only Charles was old enough to actually go to war. He was assigned to the front in Lorraine, where he became part of a machine-gun brigade and found himself in the thick of battle for months on end. Back home the family kept track of him as best they could, mostly with what he would write about his whereabouts, and they marveled at his ability to endure this endless mucking around in rain and mud under fire apparently without any of the disastrous ill-effects this would have brought on the frail health of either one of his parents. It was with a huge sigh of relief and pride that on November 26, 1918, after the Armistice, Blondel wrote to Brémond: "Charles is safe! In the worst of dangers up to the last days; a new citation from the Corps of the Army for having captured a battery of 105. Now, he is trekking around in Belgium, disgusted with these fastidious marches in the mud, finding this life of ambulatory garrison and proper alignment, without the seasoning of peril, lethal. Those heroes!" (1971a, 357).

During the last year of the war, however, things were not going so well for the mother of this hero, perhaps from worrying over him in his deathly peril as she had worried about her husband in his intellectual wars with certain elements of the Church. Rose Royer-Blondel fell seriously ill to the point that her husband had to begin looking for a place where she could be cared for more adequately than could be done at home. He even asked his friend Brémond to inquire in the area of Pau, near the French Pyrenees, where Brémond was living at the time working on his monumental work on the history of religious sentiment in the seventeenth century, whether an appropriate house could be found for the ailing mother. Brémond did find something, but the family opted for another place closer to home in the Alps and more accessible for family visits. Mme. Blondel did go there, but she could not get used to the altitude because of a chronic heart condition. She stayed only a few weeks in June and then went to Burgundy to be cared for by her mother. It was during this time that Blondel found himself in the odd situation of having to go to Corsica to hear exams, not being able to find anyone to take his place, and having to bring Elisabeth and André with him so as not to leave them at home alone. Thus daughter and son were left to hang around the Hotel Vizzanova while their dad sat hearing state exams for students from the local Lycée (1971a, 355). After that, they all went back to Burgundy to join in the caring for the mother.

When time came for Blondel to go back to Aix in the fall for his courses, it would seem that the mother went back with them and that Elisabeth became the principal caregiver for her at home. In a letter to Brémond on December 16, Blondel speaks of Elisabeth as "our Providence. Without her I do not know what we would become" (1971a, 364). But he wonders how long she can hold up. She did, but the mother kept losing ground. She died on the morning of March 7, 1919, "after many months of cruel sufferings and terrible apprehensions, though in her very last hours she had the grace of an almost joyous peace and a very gentle confidence.... For more than a year, her life has been only a torture, and all of our existence was suspended to her. What an emptiness! Elisabeth has spent herself with a heart, a courage, a tact that touched her mother profoundly. Charles, alas, is in Alsace [still in the army]. André is shaken" (1971a, 371). Brémond knew the family very well from the early days when he attended Blondel's courses in Aix and had frequent visits with them, and Mme. Blondel had asked for his prayers in a special way.

Blondel was thus left to worry about his children alone as they were thrusting out into adulthood. Charles was demobilized from the army only in September 1919, after spending months driving all around Germany in a Mercedes trying to find out what had happened to prisoners of war, already beyond the reach of his father. Blondel wondered if and how he would settle down to a more sedate life after all this time in an automobile. "What will he do now," he asked himself, "in the humble solitude of Magny," the place of their summer home in Burgundy. "Pray for this grownup child," he asked Brémond, "whom I do not have the light and the strength to guide" (1971a, 392). Blondel never learned to drive a car himself, which made him all the more scared when he saw, first Elisabeth, and then André get their own driving permits when they were barely seventeen. What could a parent do in the face of fascination with such risky machines? Blondel longed to keep a firmer hand over his children, but he could feel them escaping his grasp. Disappointed in not being able to teach his younger son much philosophy, *"mon grand silencieux,"* he called him, the great silent one, he had some hope that perhaps Abbé Ali Mulla, a former student and now a close friend of the family as well as Blondel's godchild, would be able to teach him something about it at the Catholic college of Aix (1971a, 392).

The Conversion of Ali Mulla

Ali Mulla was in fact an important member of Blondel's extended spiritual family by this time and was to remain so for the rest of his life. He was of Turkish origin, the son of a Muslim Ayatollah on the island of Crete. He and his brother had been sent to Aix by their father to complete their education at the lycée. The father had wanted Ali to study law at Aix after the lycée, much as Blondel's own parents had wanted him to study law at the lycée in Dijon, but Ali, as had happened with his teacher, got interested in philosophy more than in law and went on to get his licentiate in philosophy rather than in law. Ali had begun to show some interest in Catholicism at the lycée by attending the Catholic chaplain's classes on religion and by attending mass on occasion. Then he became even more interested as he entered into Blondel's philosophy at the graduate faculty, which in turn opened him up further to the truth of Christianity. This was in keeping with Blondel's general intent as a philosopher, but when in 1904 Ali approached him to tell him that he wanted to become a Christian, Blondel appears to have been embarrassed by this turn of events in the conscience of his Muslim student. What would Ali's parents think of all this and where were those who were responsible for him in France? Blondel did not think that Ali should act in this regard without consulting with them.

For once the apologetic side of his philosophy appeared to be having some effect in bringing a student who was anything but a Christian to raise the question of faith in Christianity, but he did not pounce on this result uncritically. He took Ali's desire as a very serious step that should not be taken lightly, even though he probably welcomed it as a Christian. He questioned Ali about his faith in the Muslim tradition and what was to become of that and, when he was convinced that Ali was prepared to move away from that, he did not immediately move in himself to start directing Ali into the new way he was beginning to explore for himself. This was not something he felt he could do simply as a philosopher. What Ali needed was a director for his conscience, which calls for a discernment beyond that of philosophy alone, and Blondel thought that others would be better qualified to do that. He urged Ali to go speak with a priest, more specifically to the Director of the Catholic college, and other Christian friends who would help him to test the spirit that was moving him more authentically in concrete terms of the new life he was thinking of embracing.

Ali did just that. He sought further instruction and was soon ready to take the final step of becoming a Catholic in 1905. For his godfather, at baptism, he chose Blondel and so became Blondel's godchild in the supernatural life, something neither of them ever failed to appreciate. For godmother, he chose another friend, Félicie Boissard, who was the sister of the founder of the *Semaines Sociales* in France and who would bring her own personal touch to Ali's education as a Catholic. At his baptism Ali chose Paul for his Christian name, but Blondel continued to call him Ali for the rest of his life. From then on they remained devoted to one another as father and son. Conscious of Blondel's and his godmother's high esteem for the priesthood as a sort of apex for the Christian life, Ali went on to study for the priesthood, as other students of Blondel had done. Blondel helped him to find the better seminaries for his studies, first Saint Sulpice in Paris and then a seminary for delayed vocations nearer Aix, and after Ali's ordination he helped him find his teaching position in philosophy at the Catholic college in Aix by arguing with the Archbishop of Aix, Ali's local ordinary superior, that Ali was an intellectual and that he was unhappy working in a parish where his being a Turk did not sit well with a pastor who was perhaps all too French.

Ali thus became a teacher of philosophy not far from where his master in philosophy and his father in faith had his own chair. This, however, was to last only for two years. Other things were happening in Blondel's family and one of them would lead to Ali's appointment to a teaching position in Rome. Elisabeth was the first of Blondel's children to get married, in 1921. She married Charles Flory, who became President of the Catholic Association of French Youth in 1924. This in turn led to their going to Rome to meet with the newly elected Pope Pius XI, and Elisabeth's father went with them. While there Blondel began to hear of the new Pope's intention to launch a new Pontifical Oriental Institute to foster better relations with the Eastern Christian Churches and he thought immediately of his godchild, Ali Mulla. What better man could be found than he to teach at such an Institute, one who brought together both cultures, East and West, in his own personality? He knew Turkish and Arabic as well as French, Latin, and Greek, and he had an intimate knowledge of Islamic life. Blondel went to the newly appointed Director of the Institute, a Jesuit by the name of d'Herbigny, and told him he had just the man for him to teach languages and Islamology. It did not take long for d'Herbigny to be persuaded, and Ali was soon transferred to Rome to start teaching at the Oriental Institute. Shortly thereafter he was named a Monsignor, Prelate of the House of His Holiness, so that he would have the proper credentials to attend his first congress on Islamology in London at the beginning of what was to be a long career for Monsignor Paul Mulla at the Oriental Institute in Rome, which ended with his death in 1957, six years after Blondel's death.

The two friends, however, did not lose contact with one another by reason of this separation. Quite the contrary, Blondel found a new presence in Rome that he welcomed and nurtured to help him keep track of which way the intellectual winds were blowing in the Eternal City, something he had not had before, while Mulla did his best to shelter and to defend the interests of his teacher and godfather against those who were still attacking him. The flow of correspondence between the two has not been published, at the request of Ali himself, who did not like the haste with which Blondel's correspondence with others had been published so soon after Blondel's death, but it was abundant, a lot of it having to do with warnings to Blondel about attacks and possible condemnations from the likes of Garrigou-Lagrange, who lorded over most of the major seminaries in Rome during most of Blondel's teaching career and after.

Mulla even went to Garrigou to defend his master and to try to explain how Garrigou was misunderstanding him, but all he ever got out of him was an admission that he had not read or could not read *L'Action* and that all his criticisms of Blondel were based on certain phrases that had been pointed out to him and taken completely out of context. Mulla understood that Garrigou and the likes of him in Rome were not about to let go of their suspicion of Blondel, and this is what he kept communicating to his godfather in Aix, warning him against giving any of these powerful but misguided adversaries the least opportunity to pounce on him, as reissuing the 1893 dissertation would have done. This concern of Mulla had a lot to do with Blondel's refusal to allow any second edition of *L'Action* of 1893 to appear as long as he was alive, and it was still there after Blondel's death when Mulla warned the family against reissuing it immediately after Blondel's death. Perhaps Mulla's fear of condemnation was exaggerated, but it did affect Blondel all his life, perhaps not without reason. In any case, it was fortunate that by the time of the second printing of *L'Action* (1893) most of Blondel's adversaries or enemies in Rome had also died.

The Disappearance of *L'Action* (1893)

For most of his life, however, this fear of condemnation was very real for Blondel. He knew that there were many who wanted him and his work condemned and who kept circulating rumors that he had been condemned, or that he had at least been forbidden from putting out a second edition of *L'Action*. None of these rumors were true, but in defending himself against them he did not mention the fear. He had other reasons as well for not allowing a second edition of *L'Action* as it had appeared in 1893, reasons having to do with the general intellectual context in which it was cast and certain confusions of expression in the long complicated final chapter that had been added somewhat hastily after the defense for the version destined to the public. He explained these reasons in a letter of protestation to a Florentine editor who had just published an unauthorized translation of *L'Action*, which not only violated his rights as an author but also associated him with intentions that were contrary to his own, "at the risk of compromising religious interests that are infinitely more serious than anything personal to me" (1921a). In other words, Blondel did not want his work used against the Church, as this Italian group was doing. This circumstance did not sit well with his fear of condemnation from Rome, but also it perpetuated some obscurity about his work that he wanted to clear up before letting it out to be published again.

In the letter, which was published in 1921 under the title *Un rapt,* Blondel explains that his refusal to have *L'Action* re-edited should not be interpreted as a disavowal of the thesis of 1893. Against the Italian translator, he reaffirms that it has never been taken out of circulation, and against Parodi, who had written in 1919 to the effect that Church authorities were preventing Blondel from re-editing his dissertation, that a second printing has never been blocked by ecclesiastical authority or by fear of censure. His reason for delaying a re-edition was simply that the thesis of 1893 was only one chapter, and not a summation, and that it was necessary to provide some "preparation, complement and counterweight" for it by inserting it in a Trilogy that he was working on (1921a). Blondel would make the same point a year later in a letter to *l'Ami du clergé*, which was repeating this rumor of an interdiction against re-editing *L'Action*, adding that on the contrary, in 1912 his own bishop in Aix had been expressly charged by

Pius X to reassure him against all attacks about his orthodoxy, which in the mind of the Pontiff was "certain" (1922).

One of the readers who looked in vain for *L'Action* after it went out of print was William James. James had become interested in Blondel by reading the latter's article, "Le point de départ de la recherche philosophique," in the *Annales de Philosophie Chrétienne* of 1906 and one by Bernard de Séailles titled "La tâche de la philosophie d'après la philosophie de l'action" in a subsequent issue, not knowing that in fact both articles were by Blondel himself but recognizing in them one and the same inspiration. James at this time was also interested in Bergson, whose books were readily available, unlike Blondel's book, which he had begun to hear about but could not find anywhere, whether in a library or a bookstore. As a last resort, in November 1907, he wrote to Blondel himself to ask if he knew where some idle copy might be found or, failing that, "if he could be so obliging (and trouble-taking) as to send me a copy by mail which I would return after reading. You have struck a magnificent note in the *Annales de Philosophie Chrétienne*. I have copied whole pages of your words" (1958, 42). Knowing that the book could not be found anywhere, Blondel sent him his personal copy, the only one he had, which James kept for several months and tried to read, as much as a bout with influenza would let him.

In his letter to Blondel upon returning the book he admits to some difficulty in understanding. James realized that really understanding it would require much more time and effort than he had been able to give it. Nevertheless, he did see a certain similarity of results between Blondel's work and his own. Both ended up talking about religion. But James noticed also that there was a very marked difference in the approach to religion between them, as Blondel himself had realized earlier when he had thought of calling his philosophy pragmatic but backed off from that when he realized how the term was being used in American pragmatism. James, for his part, comes to this remarkable reflection on his attempt to enter into Blondel's thought: "I find it terribly hard to *emboîter le pas* [fall in step] with your [Blondel's] writing. In spite of the rare felicity of much of your expression, you remain to me esoteric. I feel that a whole human *life*, intellectual, practical, moral, and religious, expresses itself through your formulas, but to me they are so abstruse and complex as to be almost a foreign tongue. I will not attempt to *débrouiller* [sort out] the differences and difficulties which I have found in details. To do so properly, I should have to *piocher* [dig into] the book and read it several times. At present you belong for me to the race of absolutely original, probably prophetic, thinkers with whom one feels that one must some day settle one's accounts" (1958, 43). James had perceived exactly what Blondel had tried to do in his book, "express a whole human life, intellectual, practical, moral and religious," but he had been unable to follow this expression in its systematic ascension to something higher than a merely empirical life.

Blondel was not surprised by this avowal of disorientation from James, as he would note later on, recalling this brief encounter with one of the leaders of American pragmatism who was particularly interested in religion. "While professing a *Pluralism*, which is itself quite antipathetic to my *unitary* purpose, James, in opposition to all my efforts, uniformizes the observation of religion on the level of empirically known facts, without even suspecting that it could or should be otherwise, without noticing that the secret of destiny cannot be sought without impunity through an inquiry into temporal and spatial things, without having the sense that any solution found in such an extension of phenomenal experience, be it in the realm of spiritism, would be the very negation of what one would be claiming to discover in this way. For, if there is a religious life and a higher existence, it presupposes not so much a prolongation as a change of state, not so much a subliminal depth of natural forces as a spiritual ascension and a moral transfiguration whose reality no positive observation of the senses or of science can detect" (1928a, 49-50 or 24-25). Merely empirical or pragmatic studies cannot but miss the point of the kind of religious life that Blondel was trying to justify, not abstrusely, as James thought, but concretely by reflection on one's own interior life of intelligence and will.

There were many others besides James who looked in vain for a copy of *L'Action*, which had become impossible to find, and who hit upon another way of making it available to many students in philosophy as well as in seminaries, many of whom kept looking for it over the decades, namely, by typing it over and reproducing the typescript for distribution. At least two complete copies of the book were made, one by seminarians at Saint Sulpice in Paris, where Blondel's friend and confidant, Mourret, happened to be Director, and one by philosophy students who were preparing for the École Normale Supérieure at a school in Lyon called *la Khagne*, whence their name, *les Khagneux*. Neither of these two copies or their reproductions was ever officially sanctioned by anyone, but Blondel did not object or disapprove of them. They circulated widely and clandestinely in all sorts of circumstances even during the First World War.

One copy is known to have turned up in the trenches, when a priest medic gave it to a fellow soldier by the name of Jean Rimaud, a Jesuit Scholastic and friend of Valensin, who reported the incident to Blondel (1965a, 62). Rimaud had the copy bound by his father and later went on to study philosophy at Aix. Copies are also known to have circulated widely in France and Belgium during the 1920s and 30s, spreading Blondel's influence among young French intellectuals. While the *Khagneux* made an official presentation of their script to Blondel, with the signature of all who had participated in doing the typing, these reproductions made their way into seminaries as well as colleges, where they were read mostly in secret, sometimes by flashlight at night, as one American philosopher, Fr. Norris Clarke, S.J., recalls doing when he was in the seminary for French Jesuits on the Isle de Jersey. Some seminarians were known to have been dismissed for getting caught reading the book, but most who did came away from it refreshed in their thinking. Among the *Khagneux* there were many who later became philosophers and teachers in their own right, like Aimé Forest. From Saint Sulpice and the readers of its copy came the interpreter of Blondel's thought whom he would trust most at the end of his life, Jean Trouillard, a Sulpician priest who became a renowned scholar of Plotinus and who was to introduce Blondel to yet another who would also become a trusted interpreter, Henry Duméry. There is no telling how much influence these unofficial reproductions of *L'Action* had in the revival of the Christian spirit among intellectuals in France and other French-speaking countries during the 1920s and 30s, but they did keep Blondel's philosophy from completely disappearing in the face of the ban on him that prevailed in most Catholic seminaries. Through them Blondel made many more friends in philosophy and theology than he or those in Church officialdom perhaps realized.

Renewed Discussions of the Method of Immanence

Blondel, nevertheless, was not alone in the defense of his ideas about method in the philosophy of religion and the supernatural. In 1910, while Blondel was working on the Testis articles in defense of the Social Catholics against the monophorists and the would-be allies of *L'Action Française*, Jean Wehrlé was working on an article on the method of immanence. He had been asked to write the piece for the prestigious *Dictionnaire apologétique de la Foi catholique* (DAFC), under the direction of the Jesuit A. d'Alès. Wehrlé worked on this article completely on his own, without consulting Blondel in any way. When he submitted the article to d'Alès, however, it was rejected for the DAFC, for not being severe enough against Blondel's alleged immanentism, fideism, and naturalism. Wehrlé had in fact defended Blondel against any such accusations, explaining how Blondel had been opposed to immanentism and modernism from the start as well as against the extrinsicism that Blondel saw as the flip side of immanentism. Wehrlé took great pains to explain the different ways in which one could speak of a doctrine of immanence and of a method of immanence that could be used to oppose the doctrine of immanentism, but it was all to no avail for those who had only one way of thinking of immanence, that is, the extrinsicist way. For Blondel, writing to his Jesuit friend, Valensin, it felt as if they were going back to the days before the Dominican Schwalm, who had first attacked Blondel but who at least had come to some understanding of Blondel's approach as different from both immanentism and extrinsicism (1957b, 180).

Wehrlé was bitterly disappointed by this refusal of his article, perhaps even more than Blondel. Blondel himself, who had received a copy of it only after it had been turned down by d'Alès, was not entirely happy with it, because it presented his effort as conditioned by the character of "subjectivity" in modern philosophy. This interpretation he objected to because it did not go back far enough. "For," he wrote, "I do not position myself in the *subject* to begin with (which presupposes a conceptual distinction and a work of fractious understanding); I position myself prior to this dichotomy, in action which is immediation, synthesis of subject and object, an operation that is real and prospective, but not yet an analytical and reflective knowledge." Blondel was always careful to point out precisely where he stood, and he did not feel his friend had come precisely to that place in describing his method. But he still would have been happy to see Wehrlé's article appear in the DAFC, especially since Wehrlé had gone to the trouble of showing antecedents to Blondel's way of distinguishing between natural and supernatural in Cajetan and Suarez as well as in St. Thomas. He was pleased when Wehrlé decided to publish it anyway as a small book under his own name, which was favorably received by many prominent theologians as well as criticized by others who could not be placated.

D'Alès, in the meantime, did not abandon his project of including an article on immanence or on the method of immanence in his Dictionary, as Valensin told Blondel. He found someone else who would do the article, whose name Valensin did not know, but when that fell through, d'Alès addressed himself to Valensin's brother, Albert, who was a professor of theology. This proved to be quite fortunate for both the younger Valensin, who was about to be ordained a priest, and his philosophical mentor. It certainly was better than getting de Tonquédec, who was rumored to have been asked and who would have used the opportunity to continue his attack on Blondel. At least they could be assured of getting a fair hearing with the older Valensin and also perhaps have a say in the final outcome, which is in fact what happened. Two articles on Immanence were published in the DAFC in 1912, one on the Doctrine of Immanence by Albert Valensin alone, and the other on the Method of Immanence by both brothers, Albert and Auguste. Auguste discussed at great length what should go into the article on method with his brother, and it was agreed that when it came to the positive exposition of the method, Blondel's former student Auguste should do the writing. Not only was Blondel kept abreast of what was going into the work, he was also allowed to have some input, so that his own view would be represented more faithfully. This article too was favorably received by many prominent theologians and became a key piece in the ongoing controversy over apologetics, but it was also the occasion for more recriminations on the part of the intransigents.

Another piece worth mentioning from this time is one by Jacques Paliard, who was just finishing his studies with Blondel at Aix, on "Whether knowledge, at the limit of its perfection, abolishes conscience or consciousness," which appeared in two installments in the *Annales de Philosophie Chrétienne* in December 1911 and January 1912. The articles were an elaboration of a Mémoire presented at the Faculty of Aix for the Diploma of Higher Studies on a subject that Blondel had suggested. They were an echo of one of his courses that Paliard had developed in his own way, where, in very Blondelian fashion, he tries to go beyond realism and idealism into what he calls "an integral intuitionism" and where he anticipates some of Blondel's later ideas on Being and beings. Blondel's secretary, Mlle. Panis, tells us that Blondel himself later told her that he had personally looked over and completed this study by Paliard at the moment of its publication. The piece tells us something of what Blondel was doing in his philosophy courses during this time of heated controversy with theologians over how the Church should present itself in the modern way of thinking.

Moreover, after the disappearance of the *Annales de Philosophie Chrétienne* in 1913, Blondel was not left long without an outlet for publication that was sympathetic to his views. Already during the discussions about what to do about continuing with the *Annales* or with something else like them, some names had been suggested to replace Laberthonnière as Director or to start another journal. Among these, that of Paul Archambault, a former student of Blondel and contributor to the *Annales,* seems to have met with the approval of most, even though the decision was taken not to continue with the *Annales* as they had been previously constituted. It is Archambault who seems to have kept alive the idea of a new review to take up where the *Annales* had left off. A first attempt to start such a review was made immediately in 1914 by Archambault, but it had to be dropped after the first issue because of the War. In 1918 and 1919 this idea of a new review was revived, once again by Archambault as much as by anyone else, and this time, with the approval of Blondel and most of his friends, including Brémond, the review was launched under the title *La Nouvelle Journée,* with Archambault as director and with a lead article by Brémond. Blondel agreed to be on the editorial board, but not to get involved in the day-to-day running of the review, as he had done for the *Annales.*

Continuing the Work of Delbos

During the War, in July 1916, Blondel lost his very close friend, Victor Delbos, not as a war casualty, but as a result of an infectious myocarditis brought on by pleurisy. Delbos died suddenly at the height of his career at the Sorbonne. Less than two months earlier he had presented a paper for Blondel at the Academy of Moral and Political Sciences in Paris in favor of changing to daylight saving time in the summer, a subject that fascinated Blondel during these years. Blondel spoke of Delbos as "the perfect friend" to his other friends. His death was a public loss, he wrote, but "for me it is a profound affliction: for thirty-five years our friendship, absolutely heartfelt and open, had not known a moment of coolness; it was always more profound and more intimate" (1965a, 66). Both were profoundly Christian in their thinking and, though Delbos had never professed his Christianity as aggressively as Blondel in the University, he had always supported him in doing so, thinking of the philosophical problem of religion in the same way as he did. For Blondel, Delbos had always been the one he listened to most in the criticism of his ideas. Ever since they had published their first important books on the same day in 1893, Blondel on *Action*, Delbos on *Spinozism*, they had been on the same philosophical wavelength and had always reinforced one another. Blondel sensed that he had lost an important ally in his mission as a philosopher, even though Wehrlé, their other mutual friend from the days of Normale, thought that Delbos was too non-committal in his work as an academic.

Blondel was asked by Delbos's wife to write the notice for her husband in the *Annuaire des anciens élèves de l'École normale supérieure Paris,* which appeared in 1917. In it he wrote of Delbos as a believing philosopher, a man of conviction, but even then of utmost reserve. "At a time when so many men and even scientists spread themselves out beyond their competence, he gave an admirable example of prudence, discretion, impartiality, modesty" (1917, 191). Wehrlé, who had attended many of his lectures at the Sorbonne, added: "he was a saint in his order, that of reason." On the other side of the picture, however, Delbos, always a careful writer about everything he worked on, left many manuscripts of lectures and books that remained unpublished. One of the jobs that Blondel took on at this time, along with Wehrlé, was that of bringing many of these to publication. This became one of the many things Blondel would be doing for several years after the War, going through the manuscripts of his friend and writing introductions for the different volumes in which they would be published. It included introductory notes for a series of articles on Art by Delbos and one on the Kantian Factors in German Philosophy at the Beginning of the XIXth Century as well as *avertissements* for volumes on Figures and Doctrines of Philosophers in 1918, French Philosophy in 1919, and a Study of Malebranche in 1924. In addition there were also articles on Delbos's work on Spinoza that Blondel had been closely associated with and one on the Catholicism of V. Delbos that Blondel shared very intimately. In all this Blondel was not only prolonging the work of his friend after his death but also deepening his own acquaintance with the history of modern philosophy.

In addition to all this there was also, of course, the continuing participation in the work on the *Vocabulaire technique et critique de la philosophie* being carried on in the *Bulletin de la Société française de Philosophie* under the direction of Lalande. Blondel remained a regular correspondent with the group that included, among others, Bergson and Lévy-Bruhl, and still met mainly in Paris. He had begun with the word *Action* in 1902 and stayed with the work each year as it moved down the alphabet, making observations and clarifications that he thought opportune or necessary in this elaboration of a technical vocabulary for philosophy. By 1917 they had come to the word *Supernatural*, where Blondel explained the Christian sense of a divine communication where there is nothing commensurate to "nature." In 1922 they had come to the end of the alphabet with the word *Will (volonté)*, at which point Blondel explained his distinction between the willed will and the willing will, and the word *Truth (vrai)*, where he distinguished different levels that specify the truth for us: formal, abstract, mathematical, physical, psychological, moral, metaphysical. The next year they went back to the letter A and started over again with the word *Abnegation*, which Blondel tied back to its Christian origins in the Gospel as well as to the mystic Tauler and to Leibniz.

The Critique of Reactionary Intelligence

With all of this activity within the University at Aix-Marseilles and in the broader circles of philosophy, including religious philosophy, to which his original dissertation had given a new impetus in France, Blondel steadily drew attention to his work and to his idea of philosophy as having to do with life in the concrete. He attracted students to Aix and many became followers or promoters of the same kind of philosophizing in their own teaching and in their publishing. Paul Archambault was very typical of such promoters both in his teaching of philosophy at the level of the lycée and in his publication of *La Nouvelle Journée*, with many collaborators from different disciplines but of similar intellectual orientation. Though Blondel did not publish regularly in this review, as he had done for the *Annales*, he was very much a part of it in spirit and inspiration. When asked he also contributed some key articles, as for example in a controversy that Archambault had launched against a certain kind of intellectualism associated with Maurras and his review, *L'Action Française*, the old nemesis of Blondel and Laberthonnière.

What occasioned the controversy was a manifesto published in the newspaper *le Figaro* on July 19, 1919, *pour un parti de l'intelligence*, "for a party of intelligence," signed by Maurras, Massis, Maritain, and Bainville. This was a resurgence of the reactionary, anti-modernist movement in favor of law and order under the monarchy, as the title of Maritain's book in 1922 clearly indicates, *Antimoderne*. In response to this presumption of "intelligence" on the part of those who thought their concepts gave them an exhaustive grasp of reality, and therefore the right to rule, Archambault gathered a group of writers who would argue that this was only a false intellectualism and that it did not suffice in any field of intellectual endeavor, whether in art and literature, the social order, the knowledge of God, or philosophy. There is more to intelligence than what the party of intelligence thinks there is. Needless to say, Blondel was asked to do the piece on philosophy, which appeared last in the series of articles first published in *La Nouvelle Journée* in 1920 and 1921 and later published as a single *Cahier de la Nouvelle Journée* under the title, "Le procès de l'intelligence," the title of Blondel's article, an indictment of "intelligence" as understood by Maritain and other prominent anti-modernists.

In this article Blondel proceeds very systematically. The idea is not to speak of intelligence as a process, but rather to do a critical reflection on intelligence as it is understood by the party of intelligence, to bring it before the court of reason, *faire le procès de l'intelligence,* to see if it meets the criteria for what it is to know fully. Blondel begins by evoking the classical understanding of intelligence going back to Spinoza and Aristotle as a kind of organization or genius given in nature, like the intelligence of flowers, and then as a certain internal finality of spirit that is an infinitely plastic and totally assimilative power of adaptation according to different degrees of being. In the latter sense it is thought that it is immersed in reality: it starts from an immediation, it tends and aspires toward a union, not just a *representation,* nor just a *présence,* but an *intussusception,* an organic taking-in that is compenetration and assimilation. Then he indicates some of the different degrees that the exercise of this power can take.

First there is the intelligence of adaptation to the circumstances of real life, a sort of perpetual improvisation that requires a presence of mind, a kind of *savoir-faire* that is a mixture of analysis and intuition where natural instincts are no longer sufficient to solve the problems of life. Then there is the intelligence of drawing certain positive principles from this improvisation in life, a certain organizational empiricism that is quite caught up with this order of phenomena and that is nevertheless a set of notions from which deductions can be made apart from facts themselves. This is a purely instrumental intelligence that turns nature around to its own ends. Beyond this empirical intelligence, and presupposed in it, is a higher use of intelligence that is not limited to being a representation of things and is not ready-made in them but rather contains them, comprehends them, illumines them, dominates them, an intelligence that in the apparent real seeks and claims to find a real that is more real, an intelligence that is attuned to being. This is an intelligence that goes beyond the abstraction of essential or generic elements from data that are always singular, beyond the power of understanding or intellect, as it has been called by certain "intellectualists," beyond the purely notional that can be extracted from reality.

What we have to understand as fully intelligent beings is that our notions are abstracted from reality. They are not the equal of reality, nor is there any intellectual intuition into the concrete and intimate unity of unique singular beings. Nor does the analysis of things that are related to one another, which is still notional as well as relational, make up for this lack of intellectual intuition into beings themselves. There is more to intelligence than this kind of perception and conception relative to things; there is an intelligence of higher truths and principles whose role seems to be to keep it from stopping at objects that cannot satisfy it. It is this higher kind of intelligence, which Blondel characterizes as *real knowledge (connaissance réelle)*, that he sets out to elucidate in contradistinction from *notional knowledge (connaissance notionelle)*.

In notional knowledge we fabricate a world of representations, something made up for certain limited purposes. In real knowledge what we seek is not representations, images, symbols, phenomena, but a living presence, an effective action, an intussusception, an assimilating union, reality. This is what intelligence ultimately aspires to even in the absence of an intellectual intuition, which "intellectualists" are too ready to resign themselves to in our present state of knowledge. Real knowledge is not a realism of notions or concepts based on some putative correspondence between representations or formal relations and things. Nor is it a way of taking possession of things to organize them in some positivist order of control. It is a recognition of a higher order of being given in a world that contains it only in a finite way. The intelligence of higher truths and principles alerts us to a certain disorientation between ourselves and the world of phenomena; it gives rise to a metaphysical wonder and a moral consciousness that cut us loose for speculation and action in a broader sense that somehow sets phenomena aside, as Plato suggests. This is intelligence in the etymological sense of reading into the heart of beings, *intus legere*, rather than just tying them together exteriorly, *inter ligere*. The question then is to see how such intelligence can come to be for us in our present historical state.

For Blondel this becomes a question of method or methods in real knowing. He notes that, historically speaking, there has been a certain oscillation between excessive confidence in the abstract notional knowing that has been described and an excessive rejection of it, neither of which does justice to its value as clarification of truth. On the other hand, to safeguard the freshness and richness of burgeoning reality, there has also been a tendency to reject any attempt to draw sharp conceptual lines in the analysis of reality and to give oneself over completely to sentiment, to the heart, to the will, or to belief, to the point that intelligence ceases to be knowledge at all. But none of these tendencies does justice to real knowledge, which has to be arrived at dialectically. Nor is it enough to simply oppose intuition and intelligence, as if the two terms did not refer etymologically to some penetration of light into the core of reality. For Blondel what is necessary is, first, to determine that there is another light than the one put forth in the "age of enlightenment"; second, to show that this light entails a method, that it makes possible an original knowledge, that it bears on the real, and that it constitutes intelligence in the best sense of the term; and third, to maintain, within the heterogeneity of functions and lights, the unity of spirit (1921b, 249).

In carrying out the elaboration of this threefold necessity concerning the light of real knowledge, Blondel first refers to three philosophers who have insisted on this kind of enlightenment as distinct from that of notional knowledge, Augustine, Pascal, and Newman, all of whom had previously struck him as advocating for this kind of intelligence that went beyond merely analytical knowing. Instead, no doubt to the surprise of many of his readers, he chooses to follow St. Thomas in what he says about judgment by way of connaturality as distinct from judgment by way of knowledge arrived at by logical analysis, a judgment that is based on the disposition of a subject as much as on the representation of an object. What he has in mind is not just some particular judgment about one thing or another, but the entire dialectical process by which one arrives at a fully intelligent judgment about reality as a whole.

Following Aquinas step by step, he summarizes the dialectic of this judgment by way of connaturality according to five stages. First, at the point of departure there is a knowledge through affinity *(cognitio per affinitatem)*, a knowledge of presence and direct action that builds up a certain secret acquaintance with things parallel to and in support of analytical thinking. This is the knowledge that one acquires from experience and education. It makes us intelligent by a certain resonance within ourselves that opens us up to the action of other beings present to us. Next, there is a knowledge that can be elaborated further, but not in the way of abstract science through theoretical study. This second stage of judgment is by way of inclination *(per modum inclinationis)*, where inclination suggests a kind of leaning toward the other where love makes us more intelligent than just abstract analysis. Augustine, Pascal, and Newman all speak of this stage in real knowing, but Blondel insists more on St. Thomas, where he speaks of one having the habit of a certain virtue as being able to judge more properly about what is to be done according to that virtue even than another who has been instructed in moral science but does not have the virtue.

Beyond this there is a third stage, that of judgment by compassion *(per compassionem)*, which turns the subject around or decenters him. "Notional knowledge abstracts from beings what is in keeping with the logical needs and the egoistic interests of our subjective thought and our individual autocentrism; real knowledge, for its part, lends itself to beings as they are *(se laisse faire par les êtres tels qu'ils sont)*, puts itself in unison with their fundamental harmonics, resonates and sympathizes with them" (1921b, 260). What Blondel speaks of as compassion here, Hegel speaks of as mutual recognition in his *Phenomenology of Spirit*, and the decentering that takes place away from the isolated individual has the same effect for Blondel as it does for Hegel. Not only does it reverse the egocentric curve of the subject away from self toward others; it also opens it up to the infinite. "Compassion is intelligent: as we discern more original spirits and discover around ourselves more profound life, we truly have more penetration, more science of human beings, more personal richness, more breadth and interiority" (1921b, 260). In this metaphysical experience of other beings, intelligence becomes infinitely more plastic.

In its fourth dialectical stage, which Blondel calls judgment by passion *(per passionem)*, intelligence pushes its opening to the limit of its capacity. More than any particular compassion, the passion of intelligence is a disposition that makes us coextensive to the action and the being of others, according to the order and the plan of a reason and will that is higher than all the particularities of experience. According to the formula of the Schools, intelligence is apt for becoming all things, that is, for suffering them all, for letting itself be realized, informed, actualized by what it is ordered to know. This is so not only with regard to things in general, but also with regard to human beings and the divine. However, it is not so without the complement of a fifth stage of intelligence, which is one of cooperation as well as passion. One does not suffer from another unless there is some tendency that has been unfolded or repressed, without some affection, without consciousness. One suffers in reaction and in this reaction, which is an activity that comes into play under the influence and with the help of other subjects, themselves also in act, there is yet more intelligence to be acquired. This is knowledge by action and synergy *(per actionem et synergiam)*. "Action, with the kind of light, precision, discernment, circumspection, obligations that it entails, is the solid milieu that can be illumined where we can learn what we have to know absolutely about reality itself. . . . Action is therefore the condition of real knowing, the organ that can be educated and the instrument of precision that is methodologically appropriate for the work of a realist intelligence" (1921b, 265).

In this dialectic of real knowledge, or of a realist intelligence that goes all the way to the end of its exigencies, we have a description of what Blondel had spoken of briefly as "practical science" in contradistinction from the "science of practice" he was about to embark on in his dissertation on *Action*. There the point of the distinction had been to bring out the validity of his science of action in analytical terms, while affirming the validity of the practical science that can be acquired by acting according to the light of our conscience as it develops in experience. Here, in "Le procès de l'intelligence," the point was to bring out how intelligence is at work in this concrete practical science and how, by reason of its realism, it can go further than merely notional intelligence. The dissertation had been an exercise in discursive intelligence drawing out the system of ideas implied in the phenomenal or the natural order of human action that leads up to the necessity of saying yes or no to God, and the necessity of saying yes or no to a supernatural gift from God, if it were offered. As such it was drawing its light from the actual practice of human beings, but, as only a philosophical or scientific reflection on the phenomenon of action, it could go only so far on a notional level. In the end, the science of action had had to yield once again to the priority of practical science in action itself, to the realist intelligence from which the critical reflection had begun, where there could be more to be learned than critical analysis alone could uncover.

In the final chapter of the dissertation, titled "The bond of knowledge and action in being" and added to the dissertation only after the defense, he had attempted to bring out this realist aspect of intelligence in action, which he had been careful to abstract from in his argument by insisting that he was dealing only with a system of given phenomena or ideas (1893a, 101). But this attempt, coming from a deeply critical attitude with regard to any ontological affirmation, had not been entirely successful. It left many with the impression that he was still an idealist or an anti-realist, when in fact he was trying to get beyond any idealist-realist dichotomy. In "Le procès de l'intelligence," the distinction is made from the standpoint of notional and real knowledge, but notional knowledge is still understood as terminating in the mind, without any direct ontological reference, while real knowledge begins and develops completely with such a reference to being as other. Blondel has simplified his argument about the ontological bearing of real intelligence in action and shown how it is in keeping with the traditional understanding of intelligence as it is exercised concretely in human practice, with its own origin, its own discourse, its own methods, its own lights and its own results, that are quite distinct and irreducible to those of representational or merely notional knowledge.

The point of differentiating real knowledge from notional knowledge in the life of the spirit, however, is not to exclude notional knowledge from that life or to deny its validity as part of that life. It is only to keep notional knowledge from absorbing, obscuring, or contaminating real knowledge, and to avoid the danger of "rationalizing the spiritual life, or canonizing the temporal and carnal order, as if the metaphysics of the sensible were moving on the same plain and were in composition with the sense of the invisible and with the kingdom of incarnate Wisdom" (1921b, 275). Once that spiritual difference or heterogeneity between the two kinds of knowledge has been established, Blondel goes on to argue how they must come together in the unity of a single life. For him the great philosophical need of his time was perhaps to reinstate the synthesis of intelligence, to pull discursive thought and intuition back together, not to isolate, oppose, or dismember these two sides of one and the same organism. In fact, Blondel attaches a certain importance to defending the value of notional knowledge as an essential aspect of the human spirit because he sees in it a way of maintaining personal consciousness and of solving the problem of distinguishing individual spiritual beings within the intimate union that is their life by showing how a spirit comes into possession of itself as it takes in the total order or the universality of beings notionally.

Blondel was aware of the latter problem at the time of his writing this critical reflection on the life of intelligence because he was also working on the manuscript of Delbos on post-Kantian philosophy and the German idealist metaphysicians. He refers to this article, soon to be published in the *Revue de Métaphysique et Morale*, as giving examples of different idealist conceptions of intelligence as only canonizing an abstract dialectic in which individual spirits disappear and a pure anthropomorphism in which the transcendence of the divine is absorbed into something immanent. In affirming the unification of spirit in real knowing, or what Hegel might have called absolute knowing, Blondel did not want to lose sight of the identity of individual spirits, and he found the way of maintaining this identity precisely in the personal way of exercising notional intelligence starting from what is given in one's experience and to be conceived anew in the thinking of individuals in their effort to make clear and distinct choices leading to clear and perfect intelligence of all there is to know. Hence he insisted on two things in the exercise of human intelligence: first, that the lower uses of human intelligence are not possible, are not real in us except by the efficacious presence of its higher powers; and second, that the highest function of intelligence presupposes in us the exercise of subalternate powers, a going through middle phases: "even more," he writes, "at the very end of its perfection, real or possessing knowledge does not eliminate, without retaining something useful or even indispensable from it, the work of this imperfect intelligence that proceeds *per speculum et phantasmata et notiones, tanquam in aenigmate*" (1921b, 281). It is the mutual implication of these two sides in the spiritual exercise of human intelligence that assured, not only its transcendence beyond the merely given in experience, but also the perdurance of the distinct individual consciences in this transcendence.

In making these points about the genesis of the human spirit in action, Blondel was painfully aware that he was being all too schematic. He regrets that he has to be so brief and that he has had to scratch too much of what he had originally written for the purposes of this critical reflection on intelligence, where intelligence had to prove itself on two fronts, that of discursive thought and that of a more global intuitive thought based on affinity, inclination, compassion, passion, and action or synergy with other beings. He refers to a more systematic work where he hopes to prove more adequately these points he is trying to make about human thought and the human spirit, clearly, his work on *La Pensée*, which he was already projecting but which was not to appear for another twelve years. In the meantime he has to satisfy himself with showing how the universality of a horizon coextensive to the domain of being can be reconciled with the singular viewpoint of a personal consciousness, how one has to emerge from the confused indetermination of life in order to reflect, interiorize oneself, take hold of oneself, without ceasing to commune with the conditions that have made this reflection possible and that sustain the initiative of the intelligent person in possession of itself, how the fundamental dependence and the real independence of the spiritual agent can both be safeguarded, and at the limit showing how in perfect union this agent is all the more itself, without absorption. To do all this one has to discern the respective role of both notional and real knowledge and understand how irreducibly heterogeneous and complementary they are to one another in the genesis of science, metaphysics, and morality, each of which entails an act of the subject as well as a conception of questions to be answered.

The self-proclaimed "party of intelligence" were not slow to respond to this attempt to extend the intelligence of intelligence beyond the limits of the rational ordering of experience and politics envisaged in *L'Action Française.* They characterized it as an obscene chaos, a degradation of all the spiritual hierarchies resulting from the Reformation, the Revolution, and Romanticism. Blondel published a quick polemical reply in *La Nouvelle Journée,* playing on the theme of clouded spirits, but soon found himself being attacked on a more philosophical and religious front by his fellow Catholic, Jacques Maritain, who had his own fixed views on intelligence and how St. Thomas should be read. Maritain lectured in Aix and published an article in the *Revue de Philosophie,* in 1923, attacking Blondel's conception of real knowledge in "Le procès de l'intelligence," supposedly on Thomistic grounds but without departing from the empiricist conception of reason he shared with Maurras.

Needless to say, he rejected Blondel's interpretation of St. Thomas, who, according to Maritain, does not think of the concept as a representation and does not think of knowledge by connaturality as applying to God, but only to the singular in the practical realm. The only way in which knowledge by connaturality could be applied to God would be in the supernatural order, but to speak of that in philosophy is to transgress against something that pertains only to infused supernatural wisdom. Maritain was arguing for the same kind of separation or static juxtaposition between the natural order and supernatural order that Blondel had been opposed to from the beginning in the debate over apologetics.

Worse still, in a letter to Brémond, Maritain accused Blondel of heresy and blamed Brémond for following in this Blondelian heresy in his studies on mysticism. "The heresy in question was simply the confusion of the natural order and supernatural order, the transposition of mystical knowledge into the order of natural or philosophical knowledge, the hybridation of natural knowledge and infused wisdom" (1971b, 74-75). It is this accusation, coming now from a Catholic layman like himself, that irritated Blondel the most and against which he sought once more to defend himself as he had done before against clerics, especially certain Dominicans of the *Revue Thomiste,* whose game he now found Maritain to be playing.

What the problem comes down to, as Blondel sees it, is a certain fear of "naturalizing the supernatural." In his reply, addressed to Maritain through Brémond, Blondel points out that no one has insisted more on the impossibility of philosophy ever intruding into the divine secret than he has. Blondel is totally in agreement with Maritain's religious stance in this regard. But he asks himself why Maritain is so much afraid in this regard, since Blondel himself has made this point about the unknowability of the supernatural through natural means alone in so many of his writings. The reason lies in Maritain's immediate identification of what Blondel speaks of as real knowledge with some extraordinary mystical experience instead of the more common kind of experience that Blondel had referred to in his description of the methods of real knowledge.

If for Maritain there is nothing normal about "real knowledge," then either it is pie in the sky, that is, not knowing, or it is supernatural. For him there is only one kind of natural knowing, and that has to be notional, not real. The result is that natural knowing is reduced to notional knowing or kept enclosed within it, without any aspiration to knowing other beings or God beyond what we have conceived of them. Such knowing is satisfied with affirming its concepts as real without any sense that there is more to beings than what we have conceived of them. In other words, there is only notional knowing or else there is supernatural mystical knowing based on direct communication from God.

Maritain is not interested in finding out how there can be communication from God, or reception of such communication in an intelligent being, if there is not some aspiration to real knowledge in natural intelligence, whether such knowledge would be deemed natural or supernatural. The only kind of intelligence he recognizes is one that reduces everything to the natural order as conceived, or to its notional order, so that, even if there is the thought of a transcendent or a supernatural order, there is no way of relating it to human intelligence except as some other order like the natural order already conceived that remains extrinsic and closed to human intelligence. If there is only one kind of knowing for human beings, instead of the two that Blondel has tried to distinguish, then one is left without any opening in human intelligence to the transcendent and the supernatural, and one is forced to think of the supernatural order as another order, opposed to the natural order, but of the same kind. This is why Maritain is bound to think of any attempt to speak of the supernatural in philosophy or according to reason as naturalizing the supernatural. The heresy he attributes to Blondel is one that occurs in his own way of thinking and of reducing all real knowledge to notional knowledge. If one maintains the distinction of real knowledge as a way of entering into being itself by affinity or connaturality or action, one cannot only maintain an order of nature but one can also come to understand how a supernatural order could supervene as a fulfillment for the natural.

For Maritain, there is no way of coming to the supernatural intelligently, as Blondel was trying to do in his philosophy of action by following the inclination that is connatural to the rational will in all its sincerity. There is only the fear that to speak of the supernatural rationally or philosophically, that is, according to an abstract, reifying notional order, is to preempt illegitimately on something that has to be kept apart, a secret that cannot be communicated or learned irrespective of how it is revealed. In his philosophy of religion Blondel was concerned more with showing, not only that the Christian supernatural cannot be naturalized, but also that there is an opening for it in human intelligence and nature that cannot be denied by any false sufficiency of merely rational speculation. Without such an opening, rationally demonstrated, there could be no true philosophy of religion, let alone of the Christian spirit.

In the letter to Brémond that provoked this reaction from Blondel, Maritain had sung the praises of Thomism as explaining quite simply the difference between philosophical knowing, which was natural and perfectly rational, and mystical knowing, which was supernatural and based on a presence or a connaturality of grace. But Blondel could not be convinced that intelligence in St. Thomas could be reduced to such notional oversimplification, one that not only absolutized abstract notions but also maintained a wall of separation between what could be known by natural intelligence and what could be known by divine illumination, so that a connection between the two could never be established. It was for him another kind of monophorism or extrinsicism that keeps intelligence at bay from any sort of religious experience. Maritain's way of explaining things fit very well into the modern rationalist program of Maurras and his party of intelligence, but Blondel doubted that it did justice to St. Thomas's intelligence of the relation between the two orders of philosophy and religion.

Maritain's thought, or that of the Dominicans at the *Revue Thomiste*, did not represent for Blondel the whole of Thomism. With his friend Duhem, he thought of Maritain's way of thinking as neither true to the spirit of St. Thomas nor as adequate to meet the problems of modern rational thought. He was well aware of other ways of reading St. Thomas that were far more congenial to his own way of interpreting him in the matter of real knowing, like those of Rousselot on the intellectualism of St. Thomas, of Scheuer and Maréchal, Jesuit teachers of philosophy in Louvain who had been in correspondence with him, and Guy de Broglie, S.J., "On the Place of the Supernatural in the Philosophy of Saint Thomas," a study that appeared quite opportunely in 1924 in the *Recherches de Science religieuse* showing that, contrary to the thesis of other Thomists at the time, who only juxtapose a pure nature, closed in on itself, and a supernatural totally unknowable to reason, St. Thomas had developed the theme of a natural desire to see God, something that would be quite supernatural, in a context that was strictly philosophical. This was all stuff on which a theory of real knowledge as distinct from notional knowledge could be reconstructed. It left Blondel wondering whether anyone had yet come to an adequate interpretation of the *Doctor Communis* in all this neo-Thomism. What he felt was that the tendency of certain Thomists, like Maritain and his Dominican friends, whose concern was to fix only on certain notions or certain formal aspects of St. Thomas's philosophy while leaving out all references to common sense and to the flow of life in the concrete, not to mention knowledge by connaturality in action, was selling Thomism short and perhaps undermining the value of its renewal in relation to problems of contemporary thought.

Blondel began writing a reply to Maritain addressed to the *Revue de Philosophie,* but he never finished that. He also saw a certain symmetry between Maritain's position and that of Jansenism in the seventeenth century in that both presented themselves as paragons of morality and erudition in the purity of Christian life, but he did not pursue this way of associating his adversary with a doctrine that had been condemned by the Church. For the moment he satisfied himself with a private letter of reply addressed to Maritain through Brémond, urging Brémond to break this reply to Maritain as gently as possible, even though Maritain would later publish several editions of his criticism of Blondel in a book titled *Reflections on Intelligence and on Its Proper Life.* The tension between the two Catholic lay philosophers would remain, both with regard to their respective conceptions of philosophy, not to mention of Thomism itself, and with regard to political orientation, for Maritain continued his collaboration in the movement of *L'Action Française,* something that Blondel considered scandalous as well as anti-Christian. Blondel would continue to oppose the participation of Catholics in such a movement and he would later answer Maritain on his conception of philosophy, without naming him, in a long article on the philosophical problem of mystical experience.

The Comparison to Jansenism

For the moment, Blondel went on to other things, pursuing his own work on the philosophical problem of Thought itself, which remained uppermost in his mind. In 1923, during a two-year leave of absence from teaching for reasons of health, he published his volume on Ollé-Laprune, the fulfillment and the future of his work, in which he reproduced his earlier notice on the life and work of his teacher followed by an appraisal of this work and its prolongation as well as some unpublished writings. In the same year he came back to a more extended study combining both the themes of the relation between the natural and the supernatural, on the one hand, and of notional and real knowledge, on the other, in an article on the Jansenism and the Anti-Jansenism of Pascal, published in the *Revue de Métaphysique et de Morale.* This was an indirect way of getting back at Maritain along with his conception of the supernatural by enlisting Pascal as well as St. Thomas on the side of real knowledge and a proper intelligence of the relation between the natural and the supernatural.

In this article Blondel presents Jansenism as totally absorbed in abstract notional thinking in its appreciation of the spiritual life and as totally supernaturalizing the natural, or naturalizing the supernatural, in speaking of the way human nature had been totally subjugated to the supernatural before the Fall and was now totally subjugated to evil after the Fall. Even redemption was spoken of as another subjugation to the Savior, without any acknowledgment of human nature and will as having anything to do in the work of salvation. In its relation to the supernatural, the human being was understood as purely passive or as totally vitiated by evil, incapable of any initiative of its own toward its own fulfillment or deprived of any notion of spiritual fulfillment. Christianity, with all its elevation above the passions, was understood as something that could only be imposed from outside of human nature and will by absolute mortification in the face of a divine election that was purely arbitrary. One could only accept a loving offer of salvation in fear and trembling for oneself, without enjoyment of any kind, much less by responding.

This is hardly an adequate description of the Jansenist way of life and its conception of the Christian imposition, but Blondel saw it as something buried at the core of its understanding. He saw it also as something to which Pascal was converted in his first Christian fervor, in a second conversion, inasmuch as Pascal, once he had begun to take religion seriously, was taken in for a time by this extremely serious and exclusive kind of religious practice. He became a partisan of it and used his genius in his famous *Provincial Letters* to attack its enemies, the Jesuits, in a way that branded them for centuries as false Christians, casuists, liars, and advocates of mental reservation. But this partisanship with the Jansenists did not last long, according to Blondel. Pascal did not finish the *Letters* as projected. He began to think differently of Christianity and underwent a third conversion, the one in which he began to pull some Thoughts together in view of a more positive apologetic for the Christian religion, his famous *Pensées*, which he was still working on at his untimely death. In his article, Blondel shows how Pascal, step by step, broke out of the narrow notional intelligence of Christianity in Jansenism into a broader more real intelligence of the living Christian tradition that included a more positive appreciation of human nature, reason, and will.

Starting from the Jansenist thesis about how human nature is ruled by concupiscence, whether good or bad, Blondel shows how Pascal understands this more concretely in terms of inclinations that can be formed by an education of one's sensibility. Starting from the Jansenist thesis that fallen man has been struck with blindness regarding his final end and the most essential truths, Blondel shows how Pascal, always ready to deflate claims of any pretentious thought, does not annihilate reason, but rather elevates what has been depreciated excessively: "in its place, he glorifies thought, which constitutes the greatness of man, the principle of morality, the dignity of an order infinitely higher than the carnal powers and all the immensity of silent space" (1923, 117). Starting from the Jansenist thesis about how the human will is enslaved by concupiscence, he shows how Pascal teaches us a strategy for willing in action and through action, so that life can rise from moving body to spirit, so that the will becomes an agreeable organ of trust, a vehicle of light through faithful practice as a kind of second nature. Starting from the Jansenist thesis that man can do absolutely nothing by himself to reach God, by reason of the Fall, he shows how Pascal, even while rejecting any idea of a natural religion that would be self-sufficient or the idol of certain philosophers who think they have captured the secret of God with their ideas, brings out a more profound religious sentiment, that of "the infinite distance which, even independently of any fall, leaves God beyond the normal grasp of any creature whatever, as the one, consequently, who loves freely and who alone can fill the abysses, but who would no longer be goodness and truth if He suppressed them" (1923, 117). Pascal places God high above man to make us aspire to rise all the higher, with the necessary grace from on high, not to leave us in the depths.

Starting from the thesis that before the Fall nature was supernaturalized and after the Fall it was denatured, which exaggerated the immanence of what was necessary for salvation and made it the one thing necessary, Blondel shows how Pascal corrected this falsification and opened it to a completely different horizon, not by going back to ancient texts about the mysterious dawn of humanity, but by reflecting on his own experience, or by reflecting on the perpetual drama that takes place in every man when God makes himself known as a universal presence at every point, in every soul, in his singular goodness. This is not just a matter for the understanding. It is a matter of responding to a gift of love from the bottom of one's soul. Pascal also resonated with the Jansenist thesis according to which the principles and means of salvation are absolutely beyond our grasp, but not in a purely extrinsicist way. As Blondel puts it, Pascal was a spiritual realist and, as such, he insisted more than anyone "on the historical, substantial, ontological character of the conditions and of the very sources of man's supernatural destiny" (1923, 120), namely, the Incarnation and the living spiritual tradition that has come down to us from it. If we cannot rightly stay at a stage of nature and reason alone, "it is not because of a necessity inherent in our humanity, but because of the advent, both internal as well as external, of a gift that is really, historically, gratuitously divine," which has to be seen in the light of a living tradition, in a practice, as much as in propositions enshrined in texts.

In the Introduction to *L'Action* in 1893, Blondel had set aside Pascal's idea of the wager, the idea of playing heads or tails over nothingness and eternity, because that already presupposed that we had to wager. Blondel wanted to ask first whether we had to wager anything or to act seriously at all. In the article on Pascal thirty years later he shows how Pascal led up to the necessity of such a wager or an option in the face of the supernatural from the standpoint of human reason and will, contrary to anything that had ever occurred to the Jansenists. Pascal was a Jansenist in some sense, if we keep in mind the moral reasons and the historical pretexts invoked by Jansenism in analyzing the tragic dimension of the Christian drama to keep it free of any moral or religious adulteration. But Pascal was even more of an anti-Jansenist, if we consider the secret basis of his doctrine, the methods of his thought, even of his style, the dispositions and the ultimate orientations of his soul. As Blondel had argued that Malebranche was radically anti-Cartesian in the fundamental orientation of his thought, even though he was enamored of Descartes's ideas and principles, so also now he was arguing that Pascal was fundamentally anti-Jansenist in his way of thinking even though he resonated with many Jansenist themes about the human condition, with or without the Christian supernatural. In both cases the argument rode on a distinction between notional intelligence and real intelligence, or between reasons of reason and reasons of the heart that reason knows not of, as Pascal might have put it, which gave priority to real knowing over notional knowing without losing sight of the complementarity between the two.

Real knowing is the one that reaches out to other beings in action and to all that might be disclosed in that reality for the achievement of human fulfillment, whether natural or supernatural. In this article Blondel was drawing out the express tendencies of Pascal's thought in a more systematic or, as he says, a more technical way than Pascal had left his thoughts on apologetics at the end of his life, in relation to either philosophy or theology. By disengaging this work from its Jansenist trappings, Blondel thought he was restoring it to itself and its true value and bringing out its authentic and unexhausted meaning. In Pascal, Blondel thought he had found, as in an ingot, "all that has been minted after him, and even better, because he unites in one simple view, because he integrates into one single balanced organism all the discoveries and the initiatives of critical epistemology, of religious psychology, of new philosophy, of exegesis and apologetics, all the most recent studies on tradition, on ascetical and mystical life, each one in its place, in its rank, in its order, so as to constitute, without any technical appearance, an ensemble worthy of technical consideration and precision" (1923, 126-27). In other words, Blondel had found in Pascal an apologetic for the Christian life that vibrated with all the exigencies of modern critical thought, the kind he had not found in the Catholic Church in 1896 or during the modernist crisis or now in Maritain for that matter. What he found in Maritain was a kind of Jansenist extrinsicism that kept the supernatural notionally separate from anything in human nature as well as an inability to relate human intelligence or human nature positively to the reality of other spiritual beings and to the divine Being as he presents himself in human history.

The Philosophical Problem of Mysticism

Blondel resumed his teaching at Aix-Marseilles in 1924-25 with a course on *La Pensée,* the work he had begun writing during his leave of absence and to which he kept referring in his articles on the two kinds of knowing, notional and real, and on Pascal and Jansenism. His other courses had to do with ancient philosophy and modern philosophy, with Descartes, Leibniz, and Spinoza as the focus of attention. At the same time, however, his attention turned to another problem that was being debated in French circles at the time, namely, the problem of mysticism or, as he preferred to think about it, the problem of mystical life, *la mystique,* which he took to be an aspect of religious or supernatural life in its highest form. At the defense of his dissertation, when Boutroux had asked him what sort of a mystic he was, happy or sad, Blondel had responded that he was not a mystic, which would have been prejudicial to his standing as a philosopher of human life in the concrete. This did not mean, however, that he had no interest in the problem of authentically mystical life any more than it meant he had no interest in supernatural life as such.

When debates arose in the Société française de Philosophie concerning mystics like Theresa of Avila, St. John of the Cross, and others, in 1905, for example, he intervened to make the point that mystical states were not purely subjective or psychological or natural phenomena. Again, twenty years later, in 1925, when another reader of his, Jean Baruje, wrote of the noetic problem in the mystical experience before the same Société, on the occasion of the publication of another book on St. John of the Cross, he intervened to insist that mystical union with God was not just a metaphysical return to one's First Principle, but rather an ascension or a passing over into a supernatural order, much as action passes over beyond reflection, or what is infused by God passes over beyond what is acquired by human achievement. What Blondel was concerned about as a philosopher was defending the specificity of mystical life as such, not just another *ism,* as in "mysticism," which "indicates not facts or realities, but abstractions and tendentious, even exclusive, explanations" (1925, 2-3). His interest was focused on the experience of mystical life among real mystics, not just on some abstract idea of it. The problem that this presented for him was how it could be spoken of in philosophy, for he thought of this mystical life as strictly supernatural, and even as exceptional within the order of the supernatural itself according to theological reason, so that its content had to be thought of as something doubly beyond the pale accessible to rational investigation and criticism. How could philosophy legitimately tackle such a problem without transgressing against both its own natural order and that of the supernatural as such?

Blondel, however, did not shrink from tackling the problem. It was exactly the same kind of problem as the one he had tackled at the end of his dissertation on *Action* and for which he had worked out a method in his *Lettre* of 1896. It was also a problem that his recent study on the two kinds of knowledge, notional and real, could help him to resolve in a way that could do justice to both the philosophical spirit and the mystical spirit. Blondel played an active part in planning the volume on the subject that *La Nouvelle Journée* put out in 1925. It was he who selected a piece from Delbos on German mysticism from an unpublished course titled "preparation for modern philosophy." It was he also who invited contributions for the volume from Monsignor Paul Mulla, on Muslim mysticism, and from Henri Brémond, who had so much to do with mysticism in his literary and psychological history "of the religious sentiment" in seventeenth-century France, neither of whom, unfortunately, was able to meet the deadline for the volume. Other contributors who did make the deadline were other friends of Blondel, Jean Wehrlé, who wrote on the life and teaching of St. John of the Cross, Jacques Paliard, who wrote on Maine de Biran, and an anonymous author, who wrote on pagan and Christian mysticism.

Blondel's contribution heads the volume. It opens with the question: By what method and in what measure is the problem of mystical life accessible to the examination of philosophy, and what can the contribution of philosophy be in this domain? Blondel recognizes a resurgence of interest in mystical life and perhaps a resurgence of mystical life itself. He recognizes also different ways of characterizing this sort of life that are often obscure and confused, and that require some clarification and critical evaluation in order to distinguish authentic mystical life from "false mysticism," or any sort of illusion or imaginary representation that many are too prone to take as "mystical." True mystics may be able to distinguish themselves from any false representation of what mystical life consists in, but rational philosophy can also serve to sort out the true from the false in this regard, and thereby serve not only the science of mystical life, but also, even more paradoxically, the reality of that life itself in what is suprarational about it. Needless to say, this will require a certain delicacy on the part of reason, if it is not to betray either reason itself or the object of its consideration, but Blondel thinks the risk has to be taken in order to bring philosophy to the highest point of its own actualization as it considers a higher realm of spirit that it cannot penetrate or encompass, no matter how real it may be in itself. The question for him is thus once again one of method for dealing with this utmost extreme of religious philosophy. It is good, he writes, to "look into what is the higher question, from the viewpoint of reason, that serves to pull together and elucidate the other questions: By what method do we arrive at that question, and to what extent can we answer it?" (1925, 5).

Typically, Blondel begins his investigation by passing in review different methods that have been used in the study of mystical states. The point is not to inventory the content of mystical life, or to describe any of its stages or laws, or to furnish any theological rules for the discernment of spirits. That is not matter for philosophical discussion as such. Philosophy here is limited to a formal question of method, one that can be enunciated as follows: "Is there any aspect under which the critique of reason and philosophical examination have a normal purchase on properly mystical states? And if so, what is this aspect? What use can there be, whether for philosophy, or for mystical life itself and for spiritual life, in studying it?" (1925, 7). What is the part played by the human being who is fully human in this mystical life, where even cooperation seems to be out of the question, if the human being is not to remain a stranger and inert in this higher life? Blondel sees a double interest in pursuing this question: first, to define, from below and from the side of philosophy, mystical life in what is specific and unique about it, and second, to explore the extreme limits of the philosophical domain so often unduly constricted from the right and the left, even from below as well as from above.

The first method for studying mystical states that Blondel passes in review is one that would claim to place facts said to be mystical outside the pale of reason altogether, to declare them simply irrational, obscure, a matter of abnormal excitation, vague, occult, esoteric, or whatever else might be said to declare them as absolutely different from anything rational. Such a view, Blondel argues, is contrary not only to the proper object of a mystical state of consciousness, but also to the philosophical spirit itself. For him, as he intends to prove, a mystical state has to do, not with obscurity or illuminism, not with anything subliminal or supraliminal, nor with some hodgepodge of subjective perspectives, but with a positively determinate and methodologically determinable mode of spiritual life and internal light. It implies a prior and concomitant use of intellectual and intelligent dispositions along with a very conscious and personal willing, and a moral ascetic according to degrees that can be observed and measured, even though the state is attributed to a singular action on the part of God. In short, far from being obscure and sepulchral, the mystical state of consciousness is one of supreme clarity and of resurrection to a new life that prolongs the movement of reason itself, albeit beyond anything reason can attain by its own efforts.

Next, Blondel looks at two methods of purely external observation that, when applied to facts marked as mystical, reduces them to a matter of observation and deprives them of what is internally specific about them, one purely naturalist and the other purely supernaturalist, each in opposition to the other and exclusive of the other. These are two extremes of one and the same fault in methodology, though they start from opposite suppositions as to what is to be taken as real. Blondel begins by arguing against the naturalist supposition, which takes only what can be observed externally as real. Against this supposition, he argues that it does not in fact, and it cannot by right, specify properly mystical facts by a purely external observation. If the naturalist holds himself to a purely objective method of examination, he cannot even raise the problem of a mystical experience as such, let alone resolve it, because he is leaving out an essential ingredient of the experience as mystical. If he tries to hold himself to the objective aspect of the experience and to his scientific naturalism, he will have to exclude or make an exception of the internal aspect of the fact that is irreducible to merely objective data. If on the other hand he entertains the hypothesis that internal or subjective facts are also positive data, no less real, no less capable of being specified than the others, he will have to abandon his purely objective method in order to enter more deeply into the fact he is studying. In other words, he will have to abandon the walled-off enclosure of his naturalism.

Blondel's argument here is like the one he used in *L'Action* of 1893 in passing from a purely objective conception of science to one that takes the subject on its own grounds, a science of the subject as acting on his own initiative freely. Here, however, the action he wants to point to is not one that originates from the subject as such but from an other than the subject, one that the subject does perceive as real internally, one that raises the subject to a new height of consciousness as it is taken in by a kind of intussusception, rather than a purely spontaneous excitation that only drains the subject of energy. This is how mystics feel and understand their experience. For them the essential characteristic of their state is that it is what Blondel calls an *afference*, a term he had begun to use in connection with the supernatural in his argument against the monophorists, meaning something brought in from an other, or what the mystics themselves speak of as a *passivity*, with the idea that any attempt to induce such a state on one's own, without the *afference* from an other, would be illusory and counterproductive. To recognize this internal aspect of the mystical experience as part of the fact, however, is to open up an entirely new avenue of psychological and moral investigation that opens up properly philosophical, metaphysical, and religious problems in an analysis that is still quite positive and realist, though not purely psychoanalytical in an objective sense. To enter into this avenue of investigation one has to leave behind any purely naturalist supposition about the reality of mystical experience as a matter of objective fact.

But what of the purely supernaturalist supposition about the reality of mystical experience to be investigated according to a scientific and experimental method applied quite extrinsically to the facts of mystical states of consciousness? How would that differ from the purely naturalist supposition, and can it go any further into the psychological and moral investigation that is required by such facts? To be sure, this supernaturalist approach takes exception to the purely naturalist attitude, in claiming mystical experience as a privileged sort of experience, as a matter of supernatural fact or state of consciousness, and in vehemently denying, implicitly or explicitly, that there can be any real or any legitimate human preparation for such an experience, that is, any philosophical aspect in the life and science of mystics. But at the same time it resolutely places itself on the same formal terrain as naturalism by appealing to the same method of positive or external observation of phenomena, without any reference to internal criteria in consciousness itself, or any intrinsic criteria of reason to specify or study this mystical state of consciousness. In other words, contrary as it may claim to be to naturalism, it remains in the same genus of science or investigation and suffers from the same shortcomings in its examination of what it claims are real mystical states. Either it lets mystical phenomena, which it wants to sublimate, fall back into the promiscuity of banal facts or, like its naturalist counterpart, it is forced to pass on into the common principles of psychological and rational discernment that it was trying to avoid.

The worst thing about pure supernaturalism, however, in Blondel's view, is that it wants to set up barriers between what it considers natural and rational, on the one hand, and anything supernatural, on the other. In the case of mystical experience this implies a double barrier. First, there is the barrier of separation between ordinary Christian life and grace, already deemed supernatural, on the one hand, and anything natural, on the other. Then, there is the barrier between mystical life itself, which is seen as an addition to the Christian life itself, and any kind of ordinary life, Christian or natural. Blondel argues that both of these barriers must be knocked down by philosophical investigation without giving any pretext to the legitimate fear of intrusion from the side of reason into the supernatural. This must be done not only for the sake of philosophical reason which has a normal role to play in anything human, but also for the sake of theological reason itself in the interest of arriving at a higher, more precise, more supernatural, even more mystical notion of the unitive way of contemplation. What is at issue for Blondel is the very conception of mystical life when it is seen as only tacked on extrinsically to normal life, *du postiche*, as if it had nothing to do with the normal aspiration of ordinary human or Christian life, or as if there were no preparation for it in everyday human and Christian life itself, whether in natural gifts accessible to reason or in supernatural gifts of ordinary grace. Given its empirical method of observation, the pure supernaturalist approach is reduced to treating the mystical life only in terms of sensible data and natural facts such as visions, raptures, ecstasies, and all manner of extraordinary perturbations, without any principle for discerning between the bizarre, the strange, the pathological, and a life that is authentically sane and holy. Moreover, it is forced to represent the *supernatural* only as something preternatural, sensible, and affective, taking what is accessory to mystical experience as what is principal in it, with the practical consequence of preventing certain generous souls, who might otherwise be internally disposed, from entering in the way of mystical graces. Philosophy can do better than this in discerning what is essential to authentic mystical life and in leading up to it, not as to a wall but as to an opening into a new light that it cannot produce on its own.

However, not every method in philosophy can do this or even admit that it can be done. After indicating the insufficiency of any objective or observational method for the study of mystical states of consciousness, whether from the standpoint of pure naturalism or pure supernaturalism, Blondel turns to the examination of more reflective methods where the role of reason in the study of mystical experience is exclusively subordinated to certain theses of a supernatural order without admitting any direct or spontaneous concern on the part of philosophy. This was in fact the kind of method that was being advocated by Maritain, with his own brand of Thomism, in his own studies on mysticism and in his criticism of Blondel's approach through the idea of real knowing as distinct from merely notional knowing. Blondel had never responded publicly to Maritain's criticism of this realist intellectual approach presented in "Le procès de l'intelligence." Here in the article on the philosophical problem of mystical states of consciousness, Blondel addresses the problem without naming Maritain, since he does not wish to argue against anyone personally, but only against certain ideas formally. Merely citing phrases from Maritain's writings, he takes occasion not only to defend his idea, but also to show the insufficiency of what Maritain has to offer in the study of both the supernatural and the mystical.

In the method advocated by Maritain and certain other Thomists at the time of this debate, Blondel found a threefold barrier drawn up against philosophy on this subject of mystical experience. The first consisted in restricting the role of reason, in what concerns mystical experience, to certain abstract deductions starting from speculative theses in theology having nothing to do with the experience itself. This restriction was based on a certain theory of knowledge that alleged that human intelligence can function properly only with reference to material things, as if it were confined within a vault, without the possibility of communicating with regard to spiritual realities, much less anything supernatural. According to this theory, as Blondel quotes from it, "even our supernatural life, in its actual form, takes place entirely by means of representative ideas," that is, ideas that can be expressed only in function of material data, so that even "the theological virtues [of faith, hope, and charity] can come into contact with God only through ideas furnished by the external and sensible teaching of Revelation" (1925, 22). In this theory there can be no intellectual sense of spiritual reality or anything immaterial, only of material reality. This is why, according to this theory, there can be no intellectual sense of the supernatural or the mystical, both of which are above spiritual realities as such. This is also why this theory finds itself imprisoned in metaphors and literalness when it comes to speaking of the supernatural and the mystical.

Against this theory, Blondel once again argues that it cannot hold, and that even its proponents do not hold themselves to it. If there is a Revelation to a human intelligence, it cannot be just an X, something that remains unknown. It has to be something that is knowable and that becomes known to human intelligence, not just as some idea abstracted from matter, but as something real in itself in a spiritual dimension, something to which human intelligence is open in being open to all that is real. Even the proponents of this restrictive theory of knowledge admit this, when they speak of saints knowing certain things with certitude, but they cannot account for it in their theory of knowledge or of human intelligence. For them human knowing can only be abstract and representative of material things, with only some room for reflection and ratiocination on these abstractions added on. It remains purely notional, Blondel would say, and fails to account for any truly *real knowing* in any degree or in any order, whether natural, supernatural, or mystical, of the kind he had tried to present in his earlier assessment of human intelligence. Blondel is reminded here of the Thomistic manuals in epistemology he had already criticized earlier so severely for their accumulation of nonsense upon nonsense. He sees there an affirmation of the aptitude of the human spirit to grasp being, but the aptitude is allowed to play only with regard to matter, so that all real knowledge of spiritual realities is relegated to some future order. For the present moment we are left with only a material conception of either the spiritual or the mystical. There is no recognition of any real knowledge of spirit in the making that can be a normal preparation for the spiritual life and might even serve as a vehicle for mystical graces, so that, if there is any thought of anything supernatural in human life, it can only be thought of as adventitious or as purely extrinsic to that life, not as an elevation of it.

The second barrier to mystical life set up against philosophy by Maritain is from the side of connaturality, on which Blondel, following St. Thomas, had sought to base what he spoke of as *real knowing*. According to Maritain's theory, connaturality is something only in the order of affection, not of knowledge, and the connaturality appropriate for supernatural or mystical life is exclusively supernatural. Is such a theory of connaturality sufficient to explain the intrinsic concurrence of some divine intervention within the concrete experience of mystics, or to show how and how far and under what form it penetrates and appears in someone's consciousness and illuminates one's judgment? Strangely enough, this theory admits that something is necessary to penetrate intelligence at what purports to be a summit of experience, a sort of contact with the deity. "It concedes, therefore, that some *medium* which penetrates 'nature' under some 'knowable' form is 'necessary'" (1925, 28), but it has no way of accounting for this necessity or this knowability. For it, the point of contact is infrarational, merely affective, subjective, without any possibility of transcendence, "a poor 'substitute' which is not in a position to precede or complete, to open up or to fill notional knowledge, but which disappears before it, once it has grasped the intelligible natures, a sort of return to a lower realm, a vicarious and subalternate function that must be relegated, like a valet, to a lower office" (1925, 28).

This is not the kind of knowledge by connaturality that Blondel had tried to describe in his assessment of intelligence, both real and notional, if it is knowledge at all, though the theory does explain why Maritain could not but misunderstand what Blondel was saying about some intelligence of the supernatural in the context of *real knowing* as distinct from *notional knowing*. Here he brings back this notion of real knowing to the fore as a normal and constant form of spiritual nourishment, a kind of concrete knowledge that is at once vital and intelligent underlying the work of reflection, and without which we cannot account as much as we can and must for "either the genesis of faith in a rational being, or the insertion of a supernatural motive for faith amid the rational motives of credibility, or the reception of mystical graces in a human being" (1925, 29). When it comes to connaturality in the natural order, we cannot settle for something inferior, affective, or practical, without any intellectual character and without any real bearing. We must insist, according to Blondel, on a real knowledge by connaturality, one that is truly a knowledge, one that functions normally in the natural order, with a rational character, a value that is at once practical and contemplative, and has an objective bearing. Moreover, we must insist "that there is both solidarity and heterogeneity between the role of this knowledge in the natural order and its role, indispensable in fact, in the supernatural order, and even more so in the properly mystical order for which it contributes in opening the way and in specifying its character" (1925, 30).

What Blondel objects to in Maritain's theory of knowledge is that it remains stuck within the narrow walls of notional knowing, without recognizing what there is that is provisional within these notional constructions and that requires a more complete, a more realist kind of knowing. One cannot object that this sort of *real knowing* is diffused or confused, lacking in precision, or vague, or without determination, or affective and subjective, from which there is nothing to be gained for a knowledge that is worthy of the name. To entertain such an objection, Blondel argues, one has to have misunderstood three points. First, one has to imagine that knowledge by connaturality is given once and for all as an impenetrable and immovable block, without any relation to the experiences of life and the analyses of reflection. Second, one has to imagine that notional knowledge can do without synderesis and without the habits of thought furnished by nature or acquired by competence and, conversely, that real knowledge does not profit in clarity and precision thanks to the development of analytical and discursive science, all of which is doubly false. Third, one has to imagine that real knowledge by connaturality has no method of its own, no means of cultivation, no *organon*, which is triply false, as Blondel had tried to show, in presenting the diverse methods of knowledge by connaturality, again following St. Thomas. Real knowledge by connaturality is very much of a knowledge *in via*, but one whose view is simple and one, always capable of broadening itself and finding new light for itself. Blondel compares this kind of knowing to that of a Mozart, who could hear the whole of a symphony in the unique idea that was its soul, or that of a mathematician, who can intuit as one a whole series of demonstrations, thus joining together the spirit of geometry and the spirit of finesse. What differentiates real knowledge by connaturality from these particular kinds of knowledge, such as that of the music composer or the mathematician, is that it reaches out to the entire order of reality, including individuals in the concrete as well as universal ideas about them.

What must be overcome, however, is the idea that knowledge by connaturality can come into play only in the supernatural order, as Maritain's one-sided theory of knowledge claims, from which flows the idea that any claim to knowledge by connaturality in the natural order or through reason must be a usurpation by philosophy of something that belongs only to theology and mystical consciousness itself. To say anything else, supposedly, is to pierce the eye of sacred doctrine, which has no greater duty than to keep the intrusions of curiosity and human effort out of the secret domain of grace. This is another part of the second barrier that Blondel has set out to knock down before going on to show how philosophy can treat of mystical states of consciousness, no matter how extraordinary and supernatural, on the basis of real knowledge by connaturality in the natural order. In fact, Blondel argues that, without some notion of real knowledge by connaturality in the philosophical order as such, one cannot properly specify what is supernatural or mystical in the consciousness of the mystic. Far from sabotaging the supernatural idea of knowledge by connaturality, the idea of a real knowledge by connaturality in the natural order of human action preserves it and purifies it as a transcendent form of knowledge that cannot be acquired naturally. It is not Blondel who strikes at the eye of a sane sacred doctrine, but those who would keep all human knowing and willing away at a distance from reality and from the Word who reveals himself in this consciousness of reality as a whole.

The third barrier to be knocked down concerns a very fine point on the difference between acquired virtues and infused graces, such as those of a mystic. It may be granted that connaturality, of one kind or another, is the terrain on which the supernatural meets with the profound powers of the human being, and that this meeting takes place at the summit of spiritual life, beyond any discursive power of analysis and abstraction, though still with intellectual and moral components. But then an exception is made with regard to the properly mystical experience, where philosophy is not allowed to have any say in the specification of this state. Thus, it is conceded that the powers of the human spirit can contribute to the preambles of faith, of ascetical culture, and of exercises of piety in ordinary Christian life, even with some knowledge by connaturality in the development of this supernatural life. But once this concurrence has been given and the higher stage of life has been attained, philosophical inquiry or activity can go no further, whether in discerning or procuring anything whatsoever about the passage from the supernatural *in genere,* or as something habitual in Christian life, to a properly mystical state, or from *the acquired* to *the infused.*

Blondel recognizes that there is some important sorting out to be made at this highest level of spiritual life. There are legitimate fears of intrusion into what has to be thought of as a Holy of Holies, false fears to be overcome, initiatives to be justified, but this should serve only to safeguard the incomparable originality of the mystical order "which appears to be able to be clarified against all confusion and rigorously specified only by a more complete investigation and a more exact differentiation between the acquired and the infused. Mystical life indirectly presupposes, with faith, the preambles of faith, but it also has *preambles* which are directly proper to it and connected with it" (1925, 41). Just as the supernatural is not exclusive of some cooperation on the part of human initiative, so also the mystical experience is not exclusive of some spiritual participation on the part of the mystic, for, as Blondel argues, "even in the most humble acts of the interior life, be they childlike, there are seeds the earthly germination of which is mystical life; at the summit of this transforming union, the operations of nature do not necessarily or totally lose their function" (1925, 42). One can still mark the difference between this infusion of the divine into the spirit of the mystic without excluding the gaze of reason upon what remains a human response to an extraordinary grace.

Having set aside these barriers erected to keep reason and philosophy away from the mystical life of spirit, Blondel then goes on to speak more positively of this life as much as he can as a philosopher. Even if he cannot replicate this life within himself on the basis of human reason alone, he can still admire how far human intelligence can be brought with its secret powers to recognize that the divine summit of contemplation is infinitely higher, more inaccessible, and purer, than one can imagine it from below amid the confusion of murky ideas. There are two dangers to be avoided in speaking of properly mystical life, one, to exaggerate the continuity between this life and ordinary spiritual life, and the other, to isolate it from or hold it aloof from human life or even from ordinary Christian life. Blondel sees mystical life as a prolongation of what we are aiming at in our knowledge and our action and as the highest expansion of the life of faith in this life, even though it is incommensurable with any light we can acquire on our own with the powers given to us by nature or by the ordinary graces of Christian life. One must appreciate not only what is heterogeneous and incommensurable about this mystical life, but also what is still in conformity with reason and with everything normal about the human spirit, in the preparations and in the accompaniments that go with mystical life defined according to its rigorous specificity and truly understood, ratified, and loved in all that is gratuitous and demanding, free and passive, in it at one and the same time.

Blondel claims that there are three things for the philosopher to understand in relation to this sublime life: first, the final emptiness or openness of all sensible and notional knowledge, of all connatural and real knowledge, of all acquired contemplation, no matter how far developed they may be in their apparent plenitude; second, the positive and true plenitude of infused contemplation as such, even in the apparent emptiness and the total, but provisional, withdrawal from everything else there is; and third, the absence of any common measure between whatever can come from man and what comes from an infused gift and an operative grace. With the understanding of these three points, he adds, it remains possible, legitimate, and useful to inquire into a knowledge of a certain kind in this experience of the mystic which, while enabling us to see that there is nothing purely adventitious or arbitrary in authentic mystical life, still shows us at the same time "what there is about this life that is original, transcending, supra-normal (without being abnormal), and, so to speak, unnaturalizable" (1925, 46). Blondel concludes the essay by elaborating on these three points in a way that is reminiscent of the way he concludes his dissertation on Action.

First, he shows how human science and action inevitably fall short in their own aspiration and, in so doing, open up an experiential and philosophical clearing for a mystical life as well as a supernatural life. This is shown from the standpoint of real and connatural knowledge as well as notional knowledge, neither of which can come to completion without going through God. There is a certain necessity in man to go through God in coming to some perfection of knowing and acting, a necessity of referring to God, not just in some abstract metaphysics, but in a real way by connaturality, not as if God were another object one can capture and go through, but as one who is the source of all being and has it in his will to reveal the ultimate secret of being. Philosophy has it in its power to speak of this secret, not as if it could know what it is in God, but only as a hypothetical necessity that could resolve the ultimate mystery of life.

Second, Blondel shows how the infused graces of mystical life not only implicate, bind, and use the lower powers of the human being, but also implicate, penetrate, and liberate the higher, secret powers of the human spirit. There is nothing in mystical infused gifts and special operative graces, in this divine taking over, so to speak, or this divine possession, that does not add up to a liberty of perfection, after which the heroic soul was longing. There is here the passivity of a pure act that constitutes the contemplative union of light and love. The truly realized contemplation in its unitive and concrete form is never merely infused, "for it is the sovereign operative grace that, in place of the discursive mode and the prefigurative syntheses, substitutes a mode, which is not abnormal, but supra-normal or prenormal, one that anticipates future forms of the spiritual life, a configuration partially consummated with the Christ, an incarnation through a real extension: freed from the partialities of our present knowledge, the mystic is elevated (at times even in his organic, sensible, and intellectual life), into a state of divine unity and conformity" (1925, 52), anticipating in this life, if only for a moment, the ultimate unity and conformity with God in the next life.

In his third and final point, Blondel shows how reason survives and still functions in these highest forms of mystical union. Human, rational consciousness and will are not annihilated in this mystical union with the divine. That would be to misrepresent the message of love and recognition in this union that gives it its true meaning as a *grace*. The grace is not a creation, as if from nothing, but a renovation and an elevation that transforms the one being graced, including its intelligence and will. Nature and reason are not taken away, but reborn to a new life. In support of this, Blondel quotes from Saint John of the Cross, to the effect that mystical states are in accord with the perfect use of reason, require it, consecrate it, even when they surpass it and apparently contradict it. Whatever the struggles and the tumult may have been on the way up, speaking from experience as well as from science, St. John of the Cross also teaches that, at the highest degree of mystical life, everything becomes peace: no more ecstasies, no more binding or alienation of powers; in the extreme mortification, there is a holy freedom rendered to sensible life itself which uses the world as if not using it.

Such is the high esteem Blondel shows for the mystical life as a philosopher even as he recognizes that philosophy alone cannot make the first step to enter into this life without the prior offering from God which, if given, will bind him rationally as well as lovingly. It is a mistake, and a misrepresentation of the mystical life itself, to put down reason and philosophy in order to raise that life higher. Without a proper philosophy of transcendence and of real knowledge by connaturality, one cannot come to a proper appreciation of how sublime mystical life can be, as it elevates reason and will. Without some form of reason and will there can be no authentic mystical experience that is human as well as divine. It is to the credit of Blondel to have highlighted this human element in the theandric experience of mystics and to have demonstrated the hypothetical necessity of some infused gift into the soul for the possibility of such an experience, as something that is in conformity with the deepest aspirations of the human spirit.

In the end Blondel excuses himself for having made his argument so technical about such a vital subject. He recognizes that, though his argument has been formulated from the standpoint of a Christian life already conceived as supernatural, one can still conceive of the extraordinary gifts of mystical grace as being offered outside the Church as well as in the Church. In his generosity, God is not bound to stay within what Christians consider the normal channels of grace, especially since the mystical graces are extraordinary by their very nature, so to speak. Blondel is more than ready to recognize authentic mystical experience beyond the pale of Christian institutions, thanks to his positive philosophy of the spiritual life as such. As a philosopher of the supernatural and of mystical life, he welcomes the interest, among Christians, in studying mystical states of consciousness among Muslims and other non-Christians. He sees it, not as a betrayal of the Christian or Catholic identity he starts from in his inquiry into the special graces of mystical states in this world, but rather as a way of broadening the way in which one can relate to the mystery revealed by Christ in the Incarnation, who is the Word addressed to all human beings in their humanity. "There can be mystics outside the visible body of the Church, anonymously and pseudonymously, but there cannot be any without the soul of the Church, without a real participation in graces from Christ, which have nothing in common with the exaltation of blind forces" (1925, 59). The important thing, humanly speaking, is to respond to these graces wherever they are presented.

The theme of the article on mystical states of consciousness was the highest Blondel ever reached for in his critical philosophy of religion, touching not only on the supernatural, the content of which already exceeds the capacity of reason to comprehend, but also on operative graces and infused gifts that are exceptional even according to the norms of ordinary supernatural life. It was daring, and yet it was measured, using reason itself to specify a real domain of spiritual life that could not be naturalized or rationalized, but that had to be admired for the new way in which reason was actualized. The position of Blondel was very much like that of Johannes de Silentio in Kierkegaard's *Fear and Trembling*, who was in admiration of Abraham, or of the man of faith, as one in a spiritual state he could not achieve through the philosophical movement of infinite resignation, except that Blondel thought of this admiration, not as a divestiture of reason, but as a rational act par excellence capable of recognizing the perfection of reason itself in the spiritual gracefulness of the mystic.

The article on mystical life was also the last important systematic work Blondel published before the end of his teaching career at the University of Aix-Marseilles along the lines of the method he had laid out for the philosophical study of the supernatural in the *Lettre* of 1896, and in opposition to the same kind of false dichotomy between the natural and supernatural he had originally encountered in Thomism now being perpetuated by Maritain. In the same year, 1925, he was called upon to write necrologies for two more of his friends and allies in the battle for a post-modern or a post-immanentist philosophy, one for Chanoine F. Mallet of Aix, who had stood in for Blondel on several occasions during the heated debates over Christian apologetics when Blondel did not want to go into print under his own name, and the other for Henri Joly, who had lured Blondel away from law into philosophy at the Faculty of Letters in Dijon before going on to the Sorbonne and then the Collège de France in Paris.

In January 1926, Blondel wrote a response to a Report by Léon Brunschvicg, his one-time adversary, on the conditions of existence for the graduate teaching of philosophy especially in the provinces, in which the Paris-based philosopher criticized a too-thin scattering of resources and personnel and proposed a better concentration of these in fewer places. As one with thirty years of experience teaching in the provinces, Blondel agreed with his Paris colleague, recognizing that the position of the solo professor of philosophy such as his in Aix-en-Provence had become unviable. But he added a more careful assessment of the situation to be remedied. In the effort to raise the general culture and to strengthen the scientific value of candidates for the license in philosophy, people have confused "general culture" with "an encyclopedic examination that is inevitably primitive," and have subjected "scientific value" to a specialization that is "cut up in snippets, premature, anti-philosophical." Ever conscious that philosophy is itself a critical way of thinking, a kind of spiritual life, as well as a knowledge about philosophers, Blondel proposes a reorientation of the teaching of philosophy itself toward a licentiate program on "the philosophical spirit" as such, no matter where it is to be given, to which could be added a certificate of specialization that would vary according to the different universities (1926a).

What gratified him more than anything else perhaps, as he approached the end of his teaching career, was the foundation of the *Société d'Études philosophiques du Sud-Est*, many of whose members were former students of his, including the founder himself, Gaston Berger. Blondel was elected Honorary President and wrote a prelude for the first issue of their *Bulletin* in which he hailed the advent of this new Society of philosophy, highlighting the fact that it was due primarily, not to professionals in philosophy, but to industrialists, merchants, and businessmen. This was a reminder to him that, even in constituting philosophical research, with all its technical and formal precision as well as its concern for the realities to be taken into account and brought into line, it is important to keep in mind the limits of philosophy itself, "not to consider it as furnishing by itself all the light and the force necessary for life, in other words, to see that, if it has to raise problems and if it has its word to add on all of them, it cannot determine or provide by itself all the solutions" (1926b). He also delighted in commenting on Jacques Paliard's communication in this first issue of the *Bulletin* on a theme he had treated himself at some length early in his career, the conflict between idealism and psychology. He warns against taking the opposition between subject and object, or between conscious life and thoughtful activity as either primordial, definitive, or irreducible. Summing up the results of his own research in recent years, he adds that he has found that one must, on the one hand, go back upstream from consciousness, as it comes to the clarity of its own light, to its subterranean sources and the conditions of its life, and on the other hand, look past the present clear and distinct idea, to the prolongations and the complements of this notional knowledge, whose fixed contours are only a provisional stage in the life of the spirit (1926c). Thus, Blondel was handing on the baton of teaching to those who would succeed him in philosophy at Aix and in the southeast of France, but very well aware that he still had a very important part of his own work ahead of him, perhaps the most important part, which he had been planning for many years.

Blondel had resumed his duties as professor and holder of the chair in philosophy at Aix-Marseilles in 1924, after his two-year leave of absence, but he soon began to experience a new difficulty in fulfilling these duties, in addition to his neuritis and poor health in general. An important part of these duties included hearing oral exams, the number of which for his region was on the rise. In 1925 it went up to seventeen thousand (1971b, 204). But Blondel was finding it more and more difficult to hear. He was able to make up for his deafness in part by his ability to see, but that too eventually gave way in March 1926, when he suffered a severe hemorrhage in the retina of his right eye that not only caused permanent damage to the right eye but also impaired his ability to focus with his left eye. The hemorrhage left the retina scarred, so that he could no longer see anything he tried to look at with his right eye without finding distortions and lacunae, as if through a glass or a mirror that distends and caricatures objects. All that was left for the right eye was a certain confused peripheral vision that allowed him to see what he was not looking at, but not what he tried to look at, like the writing on a page or the face of a friend. The left eye was also afflicted with some macular degeneration, but it still retained the possibility of some distinct vision, although weak and very tenuous. At best, Blondel still had some capacity to read with his left eye, which required shutting the image from his right eye, under very restricted conditions of lighting, paper, color, and typographical characters. But the effort was such a strain and so painful that he could keep it up only for a few minutes at a time (1966b, 335ff.).

Blondel thus found himself unable to read and write, as well as unable to hear. Elisabeth had to come to his rescue to help him with his work and his correspondence, at least for a time. Attempts were made to clear up the scar in the retina of the right eye and to restore some balance in his vision, but to no avail. Treatments were stopped in October, and by February 1927, it was clear that there would be no amelioration. Blondel would have to continue struggling to focus with his left eye, and depending on others for most of his reading and writing. Without someone with him at Aix or at Magny-la-Ville, the summer home in Burgundy, Blondel was quite helpless to carry on any of his work. At first Elisabeth, who came from Paris with her two children, did most of the reading and writing for her father, helping him especially with his correspondence, but eventually her brothers, Charles and André, did their share as well. Brémond, ever the faithful correspondent who knew everyone in the family well, amused them by making comments about her in his letters, doing as if she were not there to read them to her father, and to transmit the response. Blondel was suffering, not only from not being able to work, but also from not being able to see his loved ones, his children and his grandchildren, except in distorted and grotesque images. There was no question that he could continue on as professor at the University. He had to resign. The more important question for him was whether, and how, he would be able to bring to fruition the life work in philosophy he had envisioned for himself at the time of his vocation to philosophy while he was still working on the last chapter of his dissertation, and that he had kept before his mind during his long teaching career. He began to worry about the philosophical testament he wanted to leave and so he began to practice dictation, as he had once done while working on his dissertation, in anticipation of the treatises in Christian philosophy he still had in mind to write.

IX

The Philosophical Itinerary

With his retirement from teaching in 1926, Blondel was far from thinking that his work was finished. In fact, he still had not published any of the works he had been planning for twenty or thirty years, to give a better and more complete idea of his philosophy. Borrowing a phrase Loisy had used about him early in the modernist crisis, when they were in correspondence with one another, he felt he was still largely unpublished, as he put it in his interview with Frédéric Lefèvre not long after resigning from his professorship (1928a, 47). If anything, he felt more liberated than ever to pursue that final labor, even though he realized that his growing problems with seeing and hearing would make that work more difficult than it would have been while he was still teaching.

The Demise of *Action Française*

One of the first things Blondel chose to attend to, however, in his first year of release from teaching, was the demise of *Action Française*, or at least its condemnation by Rome, published on December 15, 1926, in *Osservatore Romano*. It was well known that Blondel and Laberthonnière had long been adamantly opposed to the participation of Catholics in this movement, as well as to the movement itself, in the *Annales de Philosophie Chrétienne*. For them the movement was serving neither the good of France nor the good of the Church in France, even though it did enlist many Catholics, including many bishops and clergy, in its attempt to restore an essentially atheistic imperial order, by external force if necessary. The opposition of Blondel and his friends had continued in the pages of *La Nouvelle Journée*. It is not surprising, then, that when the condemnation finally came, *La Nouvelle Journée* organized a special *Cahier* on the debate that was coming to an end — *Un grand débat catholique et français:*

Témoignages sur l'Action Française — and that Blondel had a large part in organizing the collection of essays. His name does not appear in the volume, but he actually wrote the article attributed to Marcel Breton, a pseudonym, and collaborated in the one attributed to Étienne Gallois, another pseudonym for someone else who was killed by a student while he was working on the article. Blondel had not only inspired this author to write; he also completed and finished his work. He also collaborated on another piece by a young professor of philosophy from Toulon, on Maurras as an intellectual dictator.

In the "Breton" article, titled "The conclusions of a personal experience," Blondel describes the experience of a Catholic, not his own, who was at first seduced by Maurrasism, but later was liberated from this seduction in submitting to the condemnation. In a loose imitation of Pascal's *Provincial Letters,* Blondel has a pious and learned chanoine quoting certain anti-modernist passages from the Decree *Lamentabili* and the Encyclical *Pascendi* by Pius X, thus turning the old accusations that had once been used by the sympathizers of *Action Française* against him, back against them. In the end he has a philosopher-historian draw up a Syllabus of eighty propositions, in imitation of a document by Pius IX condemning modern errors in the mid-nineteenth century, taken from what he calls the "political physics" of Maurras, "philosophical and historical errors of method and doctrine, namely, on the criterion of truth and the discernment of competencies, on the relation of the political order with the other human disciplines and with metaphysical truths, on the relation of the two Powers and on the essential notions that ground public life, social peace, and the accord between philosophy and Christian teaching" (1927, 177). In a letter to Brémond, Blondel, wondering whether his friend has recognized his hand, admits that he may be overstepping himself in adopting this style (1971b, 281).

The "Gallois" article was more straightforward and aimed directly at the philosophical stance of Maurras's partisans. It focuses on "organizational empiricism," another way of characterizing Maurras's method in politics used by Blondel, and on a kind of pseudo-Thomism that had been used to bolster this imperialistic *real Politik.* No one was named, of course, but Maritain was not slow to realize that the barb was aimed at him. Maritain wrote a vehement letter of protest to Archambault, the editor, against the calumnies he was liable to endure, even though he was not named. In his own defense, Maritain published a work on the Primacy of the Spiritual, in which he proposed a theocracy that was in essential agreement with Maurras's organizational and dictatorial empiricism, except for the fact that he was willing to submit to the spiritual authority of the Pope, which Maurras had absolutely no inclination to do. Maritain remained a partisan of extrinsic imposition from on high in spiritual as well as political matters, which is perhaps why Blondel thought he could call him a pseudo-Thomist. But Maritain was not alone in this partisanship. There were many others in the clergy and among the bishops who felt that, if Maurras had submitted to the Pope, he would have retained the allegiance of most genuine Catholics. For them this was only a matter of a power struggle in which they had lost, not of a better understanding of how to exercise one's Christian responsibility in the world (1971b, 288).

Blondel took great pleasure in the fact that this Tenth Cahier of *La Nouvelle Journée* did not go unnoticed in Rome. He was especially pleased to learn that the Pope himself had read the volume and found in it the kind of support he was looking for from Catholics in France. "To have the Pope as reader," he wrote perhaps coyly to Brémond, "is something I've always ambitioned" (1971b, 281). But more than just read, the Pope also recommended the book to the bishops who came to Rome. He had inquiries made as to the true identity of the writers and made a point of having the Nuncio write Blondel a letter of "august thanks for a presentation whose reading caused the Holy Father a vivid satisfaction" (1971b, 288). This was recognition from Rome that Blondel was far from having experienced before. It is something he would have wished for his friend Laberthonnière as well, who had been an early ally in the struggle against the pernicious and anti-Christian spirit of Maurrasism, but who was still smothered under the earlier prohibition, brought on by the partisans of *Action Française* in France and in Rome, from publishing anything on this or any other issue in the life of the Church in France.

Looking Back

During all this commotion about *Action Française,* when many Catholics were forced to question their allegiance to a movement that had turned against the Pope as well as against Christ, Blondel was being approached from another side for an interview about his ideas that would be published in a widely read journal called *Les Nouvelles Littéraires,* edited by Frédéric Lefèvre. Lefèvre for some time had been running a series of articles based on interviews with prominent figures in the world of letters and the arts. This interview with Blondel was to be something more in the literary style of Brémond, who had already been interviewed a few years earlier, on the occasion of his being received in the Académie Française, but Blondel accepted in the hope that it would be a chance to speak more positively about his philosophy, a way of Brémondizing or Platonizing, as he told his friend, without getting into the more technical aspects of his thought. The idea was to have an hour of conversation with the Philosopher of Aix and then to publish what would come of this in *Les Nouvelles Littéraires.*

Blondel did his best to charm the literary editor and succeeded beyond all expectations. The hour stretched out into many hours and many days, all the way up to four hundred hours. In it Blondel got the chance to speak of his early work in philosophy, its origins and sources, its place in relation to Bergsonism and to the pragmatism of William James, the genesis of his dissertation on Action and how it was received in philosophical circles, as well as his present situation as far as his work was concerned overall. He explained how he felt that he still had much more to express, thoughts that he had been ruminating for more than forty years, but that he dreaded having to express all too briefly before an all-too-large public. The best that he could do under the circumstances was suggest something of what he had in mind about Thought, and about Being, and about the Christian Spirit, by way of metaphors that would help uninitiated readers enter into his frame of mind as a philosopher. What resulted was a short book that can serve as an excellent initiation into the philosophy of Blondel without dwelling on the more technical and systematic aspects of this work, especially those that were to come out only later on in the Trilogy on Thought, Being, and Action, and in the three volumes on Philosophy and the Christian Spirit. Blondel himself, not Lefèvre, ended up writing this book, for in the end that editor was so overwhelmed by all that he had heard that he asked Blondel to put all that they had spoken of in writing, including the questions as well as the answers.

Late in 1927, when all this was going on, Blondel could still see enough with his left eye to do this himself. Two installments of the "interview" were published on November 12 and 19, 1927, in *Les Nouvelles Littéraires*, but most of it came out the following year as a short book titled *L'Itinéraire philosophique de M. Blondel: Propos recueillis par Frédéric Lefèvre*. To fill out the publisher's minimum requirement of pages for the book, Blondel even had to write a Preface for what was being presented as an actual interview. The text of the articles that appeared in 1927 was from Blondel, but not the subtitles added by the editor, which were not to Blondel's liking at all. On the other hand, the text of the book, *Itinéraire*, was almost entirely from Blondel's hand, except for a few paragraphs on Marcel Jousse and his theory of language as mimetic, which Blondel did not find particularly interesting. Hence the special interest of the book, where Blondel was able to put some order in the questions, and formulate them more precisely, as he thought they should be put, to give himself a better opportunity to say what he wanted to say.

The book is divided into three sections, each with a setting of its own. The first is situated in Blondel's study at rue Roux-Alphéran in Aix, and deals mainly with Blondel's memories of his early years in philosophy, the encouragement he received from his bishop to go to the École Normale in Paris, his experiences there as a young Catholic from the provinces, his desire to pursue philosophy as a technical and autonomous discipline, and his eagerness to extend the scope of its domain beyond the narrow rationalist limits he found at its core, among his teachers and his classmates, so that it would include questions of religion and other more concrete aspects of life. What he wanted was a more unified and coherent conception of human life as a whole, not just a discussion of abstract ideas. He explained the difference between his approach and that of his contemporary, Bergson, as well as that of American pragmatism, which, even in its treatment of religion, hardly ever entered into the internal spirit of the movements it was satisfied to observe externally. But he says little or nothing of the years of opposition to his method in the study of religion he encountered within the Catholic Church before, during, and after the modernist crisis, especially on the part of extrinsicist theologians, not to say Thomists, who had no idea of the exigencies of modern philosophy, as he put it in the *Lettre* of 1896, in the philosophical study of religion.

Instead, in a rare use of technical terms for this essay, he tries to explain how his philosophy is a philosophy of the concrete in bringing *the universal* and *the singular* together in experience, instead of leaving them separate in the abstract as the *general* and the *individual*, where supposedly there could be no science of the individual. To illustrate his point, Blondel uses the image of a hank of yarn, un *écheveau*, which has to be disentangled by pulling on the different strands that one can get a hold of. There are many loops to begin from, but one has to watch the knots that form as one pulls on any of them, and one has to examine how all these knots, or essences, relate to one another and to the whole in order to come to a better understanding of the hank, or of life and the world, as a whole. A philosophy of the concrete tries to unravel all these different ways in which life, or reality, presents itself in their singularity in view of arriving at a better judgment about them in the light of a whole that is universal.

Blondel goes out of his way to mention by name many of the teachers, friends, and colleagues who influenced and supported him in his way of doing philosophy. But he names none of the censors. All he has to say about them is that, if he had understood himself as they often understood him, he would have been even more severe against himself than they were. In reaction to them, he "could say in all simplicity that, if I have had to be more precise in my expressions, to rectify them, and to complete them, I have always remained, spontaneously as well as deliberately, faithful to the first direction that I am continuing to follow without much looking back" (1928a, 33). What the censors took to be a certain strength among themselves, Blondel saw more as a sclerosis, and what they believed was a weakness in others, he took to be more a crisis of growth. When asked why there was not more talk about his philosophy among professional philosophers and historians of contemporary movements in ideas, he mused that perhaps it was bound to be so, because in his case there was a whole process of thought that had to be taken in, from beginning to end, where everything has to be sorted out, without stopping at any particular moment along the way. This is not something one can easily sum up in a survey, especially when it presents itself as a challenge to the standard ways of doing philosophy.

Blondel regrets, however, that he has been branded perhaps too exclusively as the "philosopher of action," even though he had used the expression himself. In the *Itinerary* he makes the point that his dissertation on *Action* in 1893 did not represent the entire scope of his philosophical project even at that time as he had said expressly in his Mémoire to M. Bieil, even as he was writing the final chapter for the version to be published. It was only a part of what he was thinking that he had to publish to meet an academic requirement. "Without this necessity for my career, which forced me to publish *Action* and make of this beginning fragment a school exercise, I doubt very well that this book, or rather this chapter, would have come to the light of day even now" (1928a, 63). In 1927 Blondel saw his original dissertation much more clearly as only a part of his whole philosophy, even though already in 1893 he had tried to correct for its apparent one-sidedness by adding a chapter on "being as the bond of knowledge and action." For the future he was thinking of it as something that would appear at the end, as a complement, of a Trilogy on Thought, Being and Action, now taken as a metaphysical problem prior to its being taken as an existential problem. Blondel refers to this broader scope of his philosophical project only at this point of the interview. Taking his lead from the interviewer, he tries to show how his thought relates to other movements of thought in modern industrial society, in literature, and in esthetics. He brings the first part of the interview to a close by insisting on art in general, as one of the key ways of access to the reality of a genuine spiritual life.

The Two Kinds of Knowing

The second part of the interview, now moved out to the countryside at Blondel's *bastidon*, the diminutive name used by the people of Provence for a little house of refuge in the countryside. Blondel's was in the outskirts of Aix less than a half-hour's walk from the house on rue Roux-Alphéran, on the way out to Mont Sainte-Victoire, where Cézanne also used to go out to paint his beloved Provençal countryside. At this point the interview turns mainly to aesthetics, Lefèvre's preferred domain, though Blondel uses it to introduce his own peculiar spiritual chemistry of thought, as Lefèvre calls it. There could be no question of exposing in a few moments his entire theory of thought, which was already spread out over six hundred pages of notes waiting to be pulled together. This is something he had never even tried to do even with his students, to avoid disorienting them or losing them amid views that were not yet sufficiently worked out. But here, now that he could no longer read his own notes, he would accept the challenge of saying something about these views as they relate to art and to language.

Using his metaphor of the hank of yarn, he explains how the two kinds of knowing, notional and real, can be distinguished in their very unity. As one pulls on a strand of the yarn one comes up with knots and entanglements. These are like notional knobs, so to speak, that must be understood, problems to be resolved, but not independently of the unity and the continuity of the whole. Nor can the whole be understood without a patient unraveling of these intermediate fixities in order to bring out little by little, in real knowledge, the subtle and tenuous thread that leads us prudently to string all the parts together, so that we can then pull things together and loosen them in order and in joy, without cutting anything out. What Blondel wants to do is make sense of this problem of method in what he thinks has yet to be achieved: "never to get lost in the abstract as one uses it, never to lose sight of or contact with the concrete" (1928a, 80). It is not enough to suppose, theoretically, that the string of yarn has no end, or that it has two ends, or that it is obviously possible to find these two ends: "one must effectively assure oneself of this, prior to and in order to begin a positive work. As long as we do not have this preoccupation and this care to undo the knots, to untie each hitch, to safeguard the integrity of the thread, whether it be one or many, and, in a word, to return from the abstract to the concrete and to stay there, we sin mortally against the philosophical spirit by a sort of fraudulent abuse of confidence and of bastard science" (1928a, 81).

Blondel alludes to many different ways in which thought has been analyzed, going back to Descartes and Maine de Biran. He refers to Freud, who was deaf to the higher sounds of the human spirit. Lefèvre intervenes with an explanation of Jousse's theory of language as mimetic, to which Blondel adds his own reflections on the experience of the way people who are deaf, dumb, and blind come to an intelligent self-consciousness without the benefit of sight and hearing, starting, Blondel thinks, from an intellectual activity rooted in the spontaneous initiative and organic activities of concrete human beings in action. What he wants to point out, however, as he had done frequently in his courses, where he had studied the emergence of thought among the deaf, dumb, and blind, is that in these organic activities there is already a spiritual life coming into play, organizing "the rhythm of the organic activity, the signs of representative knowing, the movements of a conquering initiative, as well as the tendencies and the beginning of a real and possessive knowledge" (1928a, 97). For him literature and art, which operate at the junction of the organic or the vital and the spiritual, are important for bringing out this spiritual *élan* of thought. Philosophy itself, "like life, remains pallid and mechanical, if the literary and esthetic sense, if the spirit of finesse and of poetry do not come in to ease and to broaden the rigid structures of a thought which, for lack of art, would remain artificial and without interiority, without plenitude, without *sursum*" (1928a, 105).

Philosophy, however, according to Blondel, distinguishes two forms of intellectual life, a discursive and a unitive form, or two kinds of thought, one that is *representative*, which develops and organizes itself in all of our perceptive, discursive, and constructive life through sense experience, science, art, metaphysics, and one that is a *presence*, which is nutritive, assimilative, and unitive. Both forms or kinds of thought are essential to an integral intellectual life. There is no unitive or real knowledge without discursive and representational or notional knowledge. Nor does notional or discursive knowledge find its fulfillment apart from real or unitive knowledge. Moreover, it is important to understand the distinction and the relation between the two properly, not quite as Paul Claudel, the dramatist-poet, has represented the two spirits or the two thoughts in us as a marriage between *animus*, the analytical part of the soul, and *anima*, the more intuitive part. For Blondel this metaphor was both incomplete and inexact.

It is incomplete because, for Blondel, one had to go back and study the birth and the infancy of these supposed lovers who seem so much at odds with one another that one might doubt their ability to cohabit with one another. One also has to sort out the causes of their conflict and bring a remedy to this contentiousness, because these strange cohabitants cannot get along without one another any more than Siamese twins. It is not enough to distinguish two kinds of thought. It is necessary to explain and to regulate their cohabitation, to define the tissue that binds them together, and thus to avoid frictions and irritations, in order to assure their peaceful and fruitful cooperation. This had been one of Blondel's main preoccupations, a theme on which he had thousands of notes that had yet to be scored as a musical harmony.

Claudel's metaphor is also inexact in many different ways, according to Blondel, especially in that it misrepresents the marriage that is to take place. In thought, the two terms said to be conjoined do not start off by existing apart from one another. Their appearance, their distinction, and their opposition are derivative of deeper causes that must be scrutinized in the way that knowing relates to being. The being to be known comes before the knowing to be realized, and is never quite reducible for us to the knowing, since we never come to the end of the least of our ideas nor the least of concrete beings. Hence the two thoughts that cohabit in us cannot in the actual conditions of our intelligence come together in a perfect copulation, or fuse into a sort of monocular vision. But Blondel has an even more surprising *coup de théatre* for Claudel: *animus*, the male principle, is not at all the spouse, or even the fiancé of *anima*, not because *anima* is not nubile, but because *animus*, with his frigid and dry understanding, is only a messenger, a representative of the distant, invisible, royal Spouse. *Anima* is the queen, and it is she whose affair it is to know Being. It would be a mistake for her to get so taken up with the ambassador, rather than the mysterious Suitor, who has not yet shown himself, the one whom the poet has only a premonition of, without touching him, and by whom the mystic may be touched, but without vision, the one who risks being supplanted by the arrogant character of *animus,* who is charged only with announcing and representing him.

Blondel does not wish to calumniate *animus*. For, if *animus* remains faithful to his mission, which is still great and indispensable, he watches over the fiancée, defends her against false suitors, reassures her about the faithfulness of one who is Absent, adds to her dowry all the reasonable things that she becomes ardently involved in as she waits for the promised one. For her part, *anima* yearns to consummate the union of thought and being, but her love must remain chaste and reserved. Her future happiness and fecundity can come only at a high price, for she can be filled with true being only by submitting to the rigorous conditions in force, as long as she has not departed for the country of the Spouse. This is the myth one has to tell, according to Blondel, if one is going to express the true drama of thought in this world. It is also a myth that can lead into what was for him the most original aspect of his philosophy, which was to unify two problems ordinarily kept separate from one another: "to reach Being and to fulfill our destiny, to realize being in ourselves and to constitute a concrete ontology" (1928a, 121).

Toward a Concrete Ontology

The third part of the interview is represented as taking place on the steep inclines of Mont Sainte-Victoire, further out still than his *bastidon* from the ordinary place of intellectual work, something Blondel could hardly have been able to do physically at this time, given the condition of his eyes, but would symbolize the difficulty of the ascent he now wanted to make with his interlocutor. The question was to see how a concrete ontology can be constituted. Modern ontology as Blondel saw it, has fallen into a crevasse, as it were, by settling for an ontology that is only a chapter, the most abstract one, of a general theory or a theory of being in general. The problem is to pull it out of this crevasse by a twofold rehabilitation, first, of abstract and discursive understanding, which leads to being, but does suffice to grasp it, and then, of concrete knowledge, which tends to grasp being, but still does not exhaust it, while the two together tend to aver to its irreducible originality.

There are three points to be made, Blondel says. First, being is not entirely captured even in the most defined notions we can formulate of it, since notions bear only on the *general,* and not on the concrete and subsistent *singular.* Second, being is not entirely in our concrete knowledge, as realist as it may be; "the action of presence of the beings of which we are most certain never gives us a complete representation of their indefinite singularities, nor of their inexhaustible interior richness, actual or future." This would be so especially of other human beings in our experience, though not exclusively. Third, then, between our two ways of knowing, the analytical and representative on the one hand, and on the other hand, the vital and intellectual certitudes, which the spirit of finesse and unitive contemplation can increase without limit, there is this domain of real being, illuminated by these two ways of knowing and consequently made accessible to the outlook of spirit and to its grasp. This domain is thereby more certain than any thought, for Blondel, even though it remains irreducible to what we can know of it from outside in any sort of logical and fixed delineation. In short, he concludes, the real is knowable, but the *known* is not the whole of the *real.*

The aim then is to get beyond merely notional knowledge, in order to arrive at a reasonable certitude, and "even a sort of singular science of reality, a reality that is not only represented within us by our percepts and our concepts, but a reality that is authentically *present,* so to speak, to itself, to other beings, and to our action. When I love a friend, and when I ask myself *why,* I may enumerate his qualities and analyze the reasons for my affection, but there always remains the principal thing to be added, in saying with Montaigne: because it is he and because it is I" (1928a, 128-29). Human knowledge is not to be cut short at the notional and the general. It has to include a rule of goodness in the singular as well as a rule of truth.

What Blondel is arguing for here, as the basis of his concrete ontology, is, over and above notional knowledge, the same kind of real knowledge he had argued for in "Le procès de l'intelligence." Notional knowledge does not exhaust what there is to be known, what there is, or what is essential or substantial in subsistent realities. Nor does it exhaust our power of intellectual knowing, of reasonable speculation, of certitude, or of objective determinations. There are reasons that reason ignores, as Pascal said, and we must remove the blindfold toward those reasons. These are reasons beyond the ratiocinative reason of *Animus,* but that are not unknowable to the spirit of finesse and of love, of *Anima.* Lefèvre, however, who was a follower of Maritain more than of Blondel, not to mention other more literary figures like Valéry, is quick to challenge the intellectual aspect of the knowledge Blondel is affirming, over and above notional knowledge. There are those who affirm that "intelligible natures" are one and the same in the mind and in things in a purely formal way, or that metaphysical knowledge by abstraction is incurably deficient, to the point that it is only by art and poetry that we attain the real and the divine in nature and the soul. This view of science is often traced back to Aristotle, who said that there is science only of the general. But Blondel is not satisfied with saying that even of Aristotle, as if Aristotle had had no sense of "the progressive human effort toward a knowledge that comes ever closer to the concrete" (1928a, 131). To accept such a view is to shortchange both the resources of thought and the richness of true being, which can be compensated for by real knowledge, bearing on more than what is simply formal or formally "intelligible."

This real knowledge of human intelligence is a knowledge by connaturality, as we have seen Blondel explain in "Le procès de l'intelligence," but there are those, like Maritain, who call themselves "partisans of intelligence," and yet deny that there is anything intelligent in this sort of union by connaturality. For them, even when such union is supernatural or mystical, it is purely affective, even though, when they admit the natural possibility of an "acquired contemplation," they imply precisely that, beyond abstractive thought, there is a unitive mode of true knowledge and of reasonable activity. What Blondel objects to is the artificial exclusiveness that goes with this kind of rational ontology, which is then compensated for by an appeal to our affective and poetic powers, to speak more concretely about the real. The problem is that "this real, this divine, set apart from any precise and verified knowledge, can only be for our reason a world apart, mythology, false gods" (1928a, 133). This is, for Blondel, a weird combination of abstract metaphysics and aesthetics, which, even when it tries to interpret the true art and spirit of the Middle Ages, which it claims to complete, cannot understand its teaching, "where concrete, direct and contemplative knowledge was able to express and communicate vitally what discursive science enunciates and shrivels, a teaching that comes from the integral real by actively and nutritively, so to speak, uniting knowledge, admiration and love" (1928a, 133). In a century of positivism, pragmatism, and aestheticism, the so-called partisans of intelligence tend to ostracize philosophy and thereby to misrepresent the aesthetic as well as the religious spirit.

Others, like Valéry and Gentile, have criticized the general ontology of modern philosophy as deceitful and ambivalent with regard to what it talks about, but they have sought a remedy, not in what Blondel calls real knowledge, but in a new kind of ideality that they fabricate, a new sort of transcendence that realizes itself into a substance of being which is act, a transcendent which was not and which will no longer exist the moment we turn our attention from it. This is what Blondel sees in Gentile's *attualisme*. It is an effort that proceeds from our being, but does not go to being, or at the most it goes to a being manufactured by our thought and our hands: "a poetry truer than history, which alone is true, but which remains fiction; a liberated art; a thought that cuts thinking thought from all thought thought" (1928a, 137), to use an expression that Blondel would explain at great length later on in *La Pensée*. In the place of a discredited "realist" metaphysics of concepts, we are left with an idealist metaphysics that reduces the real transcendence of Being to something purely immanent, the very thing Blondel wanted to defend against from the beginning in his philosophy of religion. Blondel compares this to a black hole in the rock on the flank of Sainte-Victoire, something to be gotten out of. After denouncing those who call *real* what is only a false intelligible, we must not fall into the hole of naming *transcendent* what is purely immanent, only another idol.

Blondel warns against the idea of thinking of the transcendent only as something exterior and prior to time and space. For him the transcendent is something we must arrive at as a perpetual and inexhaustible novelty, by going forward, through a spiritual prospection and promotion. It is something we look forward to in the future, not just in the past. If modern idealism rejects the idea of a being exterior or transcendent to our spirit, if it can no longer consider intelligible a "real knowledge" that would be only a projection of our thinking thought, a creation of the subject, without any conformity with an object posited in itself prior to it, it is because it goes too far in applying a principle that is quite true in itself but is open to abuse.

The principle is that to be is essentially to act, or to be active. To claim that one knows this real being in a way that is purely passive and representational of it as it is, is to miss the mark altogether. It is even to enunciate an unintelligible proposition. Because in identifying *passive* with *active*, not only do we denature the active, but we also imply, in the same affirmation, contradictory terms that we present as similar and adequate. "True being, then, cannot be known as real except by an active thought that assimilates itself to it, not by reflecting it inertly, but by reinstituting it in itself" (1928a, 142). Blondel has no quarrel with this thus far. Where the abuse and the error come in is when one adds that, unable to know the real except *through* a thought that is active, we know it really only *as* subjective action, as immanent creation, as ideal production.

Heidegger is mentioned along with Gentile as one who falls into this way of thinking of real being as purely immanent to our creative activity of thought (1928a, 142). The suggestion of a connection between Heidegger and Gentile had been made by a young Italian philosopher by the name of Ernesto Grassi, from the University of the Sacred Heart of Milan, who had come to spend two months in Aix in 1927, to sort out with Blondel how Blondel's method differed from that of Gentile (1969b, 610). The next year Grassi wrote to Blondel from Germany about having found "in Marbourg, another Gentile in the person of Heidegger, ex-Catholic turned to immanentism" (1965a, 142), which led Blondel to ask Valensin if he knew this philosopher whose reputation was growing. It will be recalled that Heidegger's own critique of abstract ontology and metaphysics, *Being and Time*, was published about the time of this interview, but it is very unlikely that Blondel could have had any firsthand knowledge of it at this time. All that Blondel knew about Heidegger was this suggestion of Grassi about an immanentism akin to that of Gentile, which, of course, Blondel was bound to be opposed to. To counteract it, he falls back on the traditional principle of a passivity in the intellect that is not merely inert, but rather requires to be set in motion by a reality already in act, as in the ordinary experience of a mutual recognition between two human beings, or the extraordinary experience of a mystic directly illuminated by the super-essential Godhead.

The key notion in this idea of active knowing is that of *assimilation to*, rather than representation of. This assimilation has its own originality and its own methods, which were described as the norm for real knowing in the critique of intelligence as merely notional. Far from being something irrational, or an obscure affective connaturality, a simple projection of our immanent life, or a subjective pseudo-creation *ad modum recipientis*, it is a way in which our intelligent and active life reinstates within itself, "*ad modum recepti entis*, the reality with which its function is to communicate and assimilate itself to" (1928a, 143). Real knowing is not just a passive inert reception of what there is; it is more a "realizing" within ourselves of what being is in itself: it is a receiving and an accepting in which we realize ourselves in it through an active and total conforming to its order.

The Question of a Supernatural Destiny

The question that arises then for Lefèvre is one that keeps recurring for Blondel's philosophy, especially in the light of the way it has been appropriated in Italy, where it has been widely read by immanentist idealists like Croce and Gentile: How can Blondel maintain that reality is not reducible, is not identical to the real knowledge he claims to acquire of it? How can he knowingly say that being is still something beyond his knowing, to which his knowing must conform? Blondel sees in this the ultimate knot to be unraveled in the drama of the human spirit, which is both philosophical and religious. Leaving aside the religious aspect of the drama for a moment, he considers the philosophical aspect, where we find a constant going back and forth from thought to being and from being to thought, or, more tragically, from the immanent to the transcendent and from the transcendent to the immanent, without ever finding equilibrium, rest, or progress. The history of philosophy is replete with attempts to put this ever-recurring dilemma to rest, through monism, or dualism, or pluralisms of all sorts. Blondel has what he thinks is a new method to solve this problem, one that will consider being as having three faces, a *unitary trinitarism*, alluding once again to his forthcoming Trilogy.

To answer the question more immediately here, however, he explains how he was brought to think of being in this way spontaneously, "through the analysis of thought and action, through the conflict and the solidarity of notional knowledge and concrete knowledge" (1928a, 146). At the end of his reflection on these irreducible terms and realities of human experience, "he was led to reinstate, in its indispensable function and in its original fullness, the third term that is often left unspoken or mentioned only for the form" (1928a, 146-47). This is what he had done, for example, in the final chapter of *L'Action* added to the original dissertation before its final publication, although not as successfully as he might have wished. This is what he had done also in the systematic cycle of courses he used to give at Aix, by including lectures on being, along with those on thought and action. This is what he was intending to do more successfully, he hoped, in the Trilogy, by including a volume on Being between the volumes on Thought and Action. But in the meantime he is satisfied with showing how the kind of distinction he keeps running into between thought and action, or between notional knowing and real knowing, is akin to the real distinction posited by the Scholastics between essence and existence in any created being.

"If we transpose and interpret this distinction on the plain where our analysis of thought places us [we get this]: knowledge by notion (knowledge-essence) always presupposes and carries some concrete datum, some effective activity, some real outlook; it does not begin, it does not develop, it does come to completion only by itself; nor does it complete itself in real knowledge, which is of another kind. Symmetrically, real knowledge (knowledge-existence) is never for us personal and true knowledge without evoking and using some notional knowledge; it is not to be confused with notional knowledge, even if it does not get along without it, nor does it rest on it or find its crowning moment in it. Solidary and incommensurable, the two knowledges, even as twinned, that we acquire of our being or of other beings are never the whole of our being or the whole of the being of anything" (1928a, 148). Then, as if to show how he has answered Lefèvre's question by this appeal to the classical distinction between essence and existence in real created beings, he adds: "Hence [the two knowledges] do not take away the need of an original science corresponding to the ever maintained originality of being; they even contribute to a better manifestation of the necessity and irreducibility of this grounding of thought, as the two flanks of a vault call for the capstone they hold up, but which will hold them up even more" (1928a, 148). In the fissure that is thus maintained in created being as well as in human thought, Blondel claims, all the highest pretensions of idealism and immanentism are drained. One is left with a sense of being as something other than just thought and to be confronted thoughtfully by thought in action. From this arises a whole new dimension of human experience for philosophy to explore, the dimension of religion.

The fissure we are left with at the heart of finite being and of human thought is not just another crevasse to be crossed over in our ascent to the completion of human thought, as Lefèvre tries to imagine. It is a fissure to be opened up and to explore, one that we cannot close, but rather one that is salutary and congenial to any created spirit, inasmuch as any finite being capable of knowing that it is and that things exist can never fully satisfy its desire to know what things are and what it is itself. "Science, metaphysics, religion, all arise through this felicitous wound; and through it also will enter the only satisfying answers, if there are any" (1928a, 149). Just as at the end of his philosophy of action, Blondel was left with the question of the supernatural as the only thing that could completely satisfy the aspiration of the will to become the equal of itself, so also at the end of his philosophy of being he is left with the question of a totally transcendent Being, who may or may not reveal himself otherwise than he has already revealed himself in the beings of our experience, including ourselves.

In this sense, his philosophy is neither agnostic when it comes to affirming the totally transcendent Being, nor is it properly mystical, as he had insisted from the beginning at the defense of his dissertation, and as he had explained more recently in specifying what a properly mystical consciousness is. But philosophy is interested in exploring critically the human aspect of any religious experience, even if it be deemed supernatural or of strictly divine origin, as he had done a year or two earlier, for example in examining the properly philosophical aspect of the problem of mystical consciousness. In doing so, he writes, "What I had in mind precisely was to set aside false solutions [to the problem], to bring reason to its highest reaches, to delineate its limits, but also to vindicate its right to examine and its critical and positive role in a domain where, to be sure, it does not enter alone, but from which it cannot be excluded with impunity, even though it cannot of itself demand that there be such a domain, nor even discern, when it is, all that it is" (1928a, 150). At this point in his life, when he ventures to speak of the supernatural in any way, Blondel has learned not only to be very precise, but also to be very cautious not to give any appearance of trespassing on the territory of theologians, or even of spiritual directors in the mystical life. But he has not given up his idea of speaking of the Christian Spirit as a philosopher, which is what he wants to lead up to in this last part of the interview, by insisting on the problem of being as a problem of order in the ascent of the human spirit toward its ultimate Good.

In its critical reflection on this ascent of the human spirit, or on its search for an object that will make it equal to itself in willing and in knowing, philosophy is brought to the idea, not only of God, which can still be thought of as natural, but also of something strictly supernatural, something that can originate only from the side of God and that is not in any way demanded by nature, but still is the only thing that could solve the problem of how the human spirit can become the equal of itself. This is the supernatural as understood in the Christian Spirit, which Blondel tries to distinguish formally from the natural, and is specified as inaccessible, in its content, to philosophy, even as it argues for its necessity, if the human spirit is to reach its perfection.

The philosopher does not invent this idea. It has appeared historically in the progression of the human spirit, from an initiative that transcends history itself, but as something that the philosopher must take into account in its specificity as part of the human experience. It is a spirit that, even though it is *not from our nature*, is nevertheless *in our nature*. Blondel's purpose is not only to mark off what is inaccessible about it to human philosophy, or to indicate the limits of philosophy, but also to free reason thereby to move about this spirit more fully than it has dared to up to now, without reducing it once again to a merely philosophical spirit, as Spinoza or Hegel might be thought to have done. In the Christian Spirit, there is thus a convergence of theology or of faith in the supernatural and of philosophy from the standpoint of nature that is a matter of historical fact. Blondel wants to speak of the historical fact as *transnatural* in relation to the experience and to the concrete truth of human destiny, no less than a theology rooted in the supernatural. This is how he proposes to dispel the supposition "that human being, as historical and psychological observation studies it, is in a 'state of pure nature,' wherein it would be sufficient unto itself, or else be capable (in order to become the superman it confusedly and imperiously aspires to be) of supernaturalizing itself on its own power" (1928a, 158), as Nietzsche would seem to have claimed.

If human being is *de facto* in a *transnatural* state, and if it is possible to understand this philosophically, one can understand Nietzsche's proclamation of a need for a transvaluation of values through an overman. Blondel would see this as another sign of how the Christian idea has come to inform modern philosophy. But far from seeing in this a proclamation of the "death of God," he would argue, to the contrary, that it requires an affirmation of God as totally transcendent and supernatural, along with a desire to become somehow the equal of God, either *with* God, by letting him in and restoring him within ourselves, or *against* God, by using the power of divinization he gives us to reject him. For Nietzsche there was no separate philosophy; there was only the atheist philosophy of the overman, who, not incidentally, was anti-Christian as well. For Blondel there was no separate philosophy also, but for the opposite reason, which even Christians were still inclined to ignore. Philosophy could not stop at a natural affirmation of God, as if in a sort of self-sufficient "natural theology." In affirming God as totally transcendent Being, and as source of all being, it had to confront God, on the supposition that God could act somehow "supernaturally" toward human being, with human being having to respond positively or negatively to this act, by a *yes* or a *no*, and suffer the eternal consequences of this its ultimate choice. For Blondel, this became the question of supernaturalization, at least as a hypothetical necessity for human being, that is, as something human being has to accept, if it is offered, because it is in keeping with the concrete historical human being's highest aspiration in its *transnatural* state.

The Necessity of Joining the Human and the Divine

There is a tendency among Christian thinkers to oppose two different kinds of synthesis in confronting what we come to know by Faith with what we know by Reason and by Conscience. One tends to stabilize rational philosophy as if it were something complete in itself, so that the supernatural life can appear in it only as a burden or as an intrusion. The other tends to absorb human wisdom into the irradiation of revelation and grace, to the point that the knowledge and the realities of reason and of nature seem to evanesce. Gilson, for example, has presented two such syntheses in the Christian philosophy of the thirteenth century, the first personified in St. Thomas, and the second personified in St. Bonaventure, each of them consistent within itself and yet incompatible with the other, both of them legitimate as opposed aspects of a broader truth. But Blondel is not prepared to settle for such a double attitude in the relation between Reason and Faith. What he has in mind is, "through a more unitive attention to both at once, a certain transmutation of rational elements and even of mystical elements, which, while irreducibly heterogeneous to one another, still do not entail a double responsibility in our conscience or in the concrete homogeneity of a single destiny that is obligatory" (1928a, 160). St. Bernard, whom Blondel was reading while writing his dissertation, and whom he cites at the crucial point of this union between the natural and the supernatural, between freedom and grace, offers excellent examples of a reflection directly inspired by concrete experience, where there is no conflict between the two, and where there is a sort of intellectual peace of soul and reconciliation in a close cooperation and a mutual expansion amid a rich variety. Instead of giving in to the rationalism and immanentism of modern philosophy, Blondel was more interested in seeing how philosophy could progress in its union with the Catholic faith.

From a standpoint of historical criticism and notional science, Blondel finds three different conceptions that seem in competition with one another in Christianity when pushed to their extremes. For one conception, the God required by the religious sense appears as a mysterious Transcendence, a will to Power, an absolute Subject set apart from all anthropomorphism, a Master who relates everything to himself. For the second conception, which is often closely associated to the first, this God, to be feared and served, is the Object *par excellence*, the perfect "Intelligible," the principle of all essences and existences, the Ocean of being and truth, from which everything draws its water and to which everything returns to be absorbed finally in unity or in vision. The third conception is that of the Good News, which has not ceased emerging and growing in the Christian consciousness of God as Charity, according to the word of St. John: *Deus caritas est*. For Blondel all these conceptions represent diverse ingredients that have always been present implicitly in Catholic thought. Where any of them is lacking, there is no authentic Christianity. Unlike Hegel who, in his early writings, plays the third, as the Spirit of Christianity, off against the first, as the Spirit of Judaism, in order eventually to settle only with the second conception, as the Absolute Spirit of Science, where the distinction between human being and divine being seems to disappear, Blondel insists that all three are essential for an integral understanding of the relation between God and human being in action.

None of these conceptions must be understood as exclusive of the other, not even that of Charity, or of a loving relation between the human individual and God with eternal ramifications. For it would be a mistake to put forward the idea of God as *charity* all by itself, leaving aside the God of fear who makes demands, or the God of light and of truth, thereby reducing God to something like the equal of the human spirit. God's love is an exacting love. If God humanizes himself out of love for human beings, it is in order "to divinize us, not metaphorically, not mimetically, not anthropomorphically, but inflexibly, 'foolishly,' by crossing the metaphysical abyss, by reversing moral impossibilities, by communicating paradoxically, through grace and within the forum of personal secrets and inviolable wills, what is incommunicable by nature but still in an order of things, of joys and of goods that can be handed over and given in accordance with all propriety" (1928a, 163-64). Blondel moves spontaneously into a language of paradox, much as Kierkegaard did, to express how the individual of Faith relates to the God he is responding to, but not without an attempt to express philosophically all that is involved in such a relationship in terms of what is natural and what is supernatural, what is free will and what is grace.

Like Kierkegaard also, Blondel explains that one cannot enter into such a relationship without "fear and trembling." There are some who think they are magnifying the divine goodness by excluding from our human vocation the idea of a radical mortification, and appealing to a unique primordial generosity in our nature that would only have to expand through moral effort and religious praise, whereas, in fact, Blondel points out, "this alleged amplification of a spiritual ideal and overflowing charity lowers and mutilates both the gift of God, which is not something that can be created and transmitted, since it is God himself, and the dignity, the grandeur, the efficaciousness of man, since man does not will and must not will to remain only one who is obliged, a servant, a debtor: what God has taken pains to do for man, man must somehow take pains to do for God: *se ipsum exinanivit*" (1928a, 164). Man must empty himself in order to make room for God within himself, but he must do so himself. This is the only way for divine goodness, not only to raise us up from the state of sin, but also to raise us up to friendship and adoption, or to fulfill the nuptial union of *Anima* with its intended Spouse.

At this point in the interview Lefèvre raises a question that Blondel says goes to the deepest and the most decisive secret of our being, the point where our entire being is set in motion. Why is it that, in order to receive the highest gift that communicates the divine life, we have to receive and then sacrifice a first gift, a rational nature, a properly human life? Why couldn't there have been a single complete gift from the beginning, if it is true that nothing is impossible to God? The answer for Blondel depends on how we conceive our own desire and our own dignity in being assimilated to the pure Act and to infinite Charity. We cannot merely receive and undergo even the highest largesse from God. To reach happiness we have to act and give as well. What we have to act with and give, however, is the first gift of our natural being, this original being which, for us to cooperate actively in our divine genesis, we have to offer up in holocaust to a love and for a love that is stronger than death and sin, "an apparent negation which is in reality the most radical affirmation, which alone makes it possible *denuo nasci* (to be born anew), from which comes a new being whose supernatural advent is prepared and enabled by this natural and consented passing away. The first gift is necessary therefore so that there can be a second one infinitely greater; for this second gift, which cannot be in us as nature, seems to repress only to move us forward; it appears to require a passivity of us only to make of us an activity that is pure and victorious over any lower receptivity" (1928a, 166). On the other hand, if we were to be satisfied with exercising only our first gift, if we tried to exercise only our initial gift of conceiving and willing God in our own human way, we would be fabricating no more than some anthropomorphic imitation, a cheap reproduction of the assimilation we are ultimately seeking. Supernaturalization is not a suppression, but an elevation of human action to a new level of effectiveness, in keeping with the highest aspiration of human nature itself.

If this process of deification is to be understood properly, according to Blondel, two things must be kept clearly in mind. First, God must remain God, that is, the One who is Unique, Incommunicable, Sovereign Master, and who lowers himself only toward the humble. Secondly, for the triumph of this deifying love to take place, neither can God infuse nor can man accept such an elevation without some test being imposed and gone through that goes to the quick of one's soul in a transforming union. The story of Abraham, as Kierkegaard saw it, is an excellent example of such a test for the man of Faith who does not cease to act rationally in acting graciously. What Kierkegaard spoke of in lyrical terms, Blondel was trying to speak of more in rational terms, in order to show that abstract or notional philosophy did not have the last word about the Christian Spirit.

Heterogeneity Without Separation

Once the intimate union of theandric action in the Christian life has been brought to the fore, however, with the individual human being's active cooperation along with God's, the scruples begin to arise once again about whether Blondel is not confusing the supernatural and the natural, the divine and the human, by not keeping them separate as others do, in keeping with what they think appears more traditional and orthodox. But Blondel protests that he is no less scrupulous about being traditional and orthodox and in maintaining the distinction and the radical heterogeneity of the strictly supernatural/divine and the strictly natural/human. The problem is to see who is the more traditional and orthodox, in keeping with the living tradition of the Church.

If we stay at a level of abstract ideas and notional thought, it may be that separation is the only word that will preserve Faith and Reason, the supernatural and the natural, each in its own integrity. But these are only incomplete ideas in comparison to the vital and spiritual functions of an authentic Christian life. One must get past these truncated ideas into the real tradition of the Church and the real intelligence of that tradition. "When we have an incomplete notion of the supernatural, and when we cut short the resources of intelligence, that is when we are reduced to patchwork and oppositions, which may be indispensable in abstractive analysis, but which do not preclude intimate cooperation" (1928a, 169). The fact is, according to Blondel, that there is not within us a plurality of forms and destinies. The heterogeneity of nature and of the supernatural is such that, for anyone who is forewarned, they cannot be confused. The real problem to be raised, the one that is more urgent, is the reverse of the one that is usually brought up. Instead of fearing to confuse the natural and the supernatural, we should rather fear not to unite them enough, and to make of Christianity something merely tacked on exteriorly to human life, without penetration. "It is only when we do not know how to unite that we become especially concerned with confusing" (1928a, 169). If humanity appears to be losing interest in Christianity, it is perhaps because too often it has been torn from the inner workings of the human spirit. Communication of spirits has to be reestablished, but without confusion or reduction of the one to the other.

Going back to the metaphor of the hank of yarn, then, Lefèvre points out that, with this union of the supernatural with the natural in real historical life, Blondel seems to have wrapped everything together around the Catholic solution, even though it is without denying the absolute transcendence of Christianity. How does that differ from any form of immanent evolutionism, such as one finds in Hegel, who is not mentioned by name but who lurks in the background here along with Spinoza, who is mentioned? For Blondel, this dialectical immanentism is still based only on a juggling of notions that have no real moral content, and none of the religious experience one finds in the concrete. It does not enter into the existential *mêlée* where one has to face up to one's destiny. Evolutionism only sees things as coming from the bottom up, but philosophy has a different idea of what comes last in the spiritual experience, one that is quite traditional and quite rational at the same time. "Everything seems to happen from below, but everything really proceeds from above; and nothing would be either knowable, or real, if everything were not drawn toward an assumption" (1928a, 170).

To illustrate, Blondel goes back to the other metaphor of the capstone and the vault. The capstone appears to come last, because we begin by building the walls and holding them up with supports. We might try to imagine that the capstone will be put in place from below, but it cannot be so. It has to be set down from above. This does not mean, however, that we have first to imagine, as others seem to suppose who oppose evolutionism, that the capstone was first hung up in mid-air, separate from the buttresses of the vault, without coming to rest on them. What we have to imagine is that, in the end, it is the capstone that holds up the vault more than it is held up by the vault, for without it everything would fall to pieces.

Nor does Blondel think that he has tied the two ends of the string of life together into a neat set of concepts. For him ideas, even the idea of the supernatural in union with the natural, has to flow into action, just as action has to flow back into thought. Philosophy, even pure philosophy, has to conclude in action. It does not dispense with having to act, and to act on one's own in the face of all that is known. Blondel expresses a special affection for his students who became men of action in all walks of life in a world that seems to make little of any spiritual elevation. He also makes the point that the Christian Spirit should not be locked up in the local historical contingencies of our Western logic and our notional culture. Beyond notional logic and systematized thought, there is a "language known by all," which finds expression in many diverse cultures, a language that is anonymously Christian perhaps, and ecumenical, but a language that even the Church may recognize as coming to meet its own: "two symmetrical histories that end up meeting little by little and that, like the prodigal son returned to his reconciled brother, will eventually embrace, be it at infinity" (1928a, 182).

Blondel thought of himself as trying to communicate in this "language known by all" from his dissertation on, as he wrote to his friend Valensin not long after this interview with Lefèvre, in answer to a question about the sources of his thought. In that *language,* he sought to find "the elementary truths that make up the intellectual atmosphere of intelligences and that we do not attend to any more than the air we breathe, even though we could not live without them. It seems that such truths, such truisms are poor, vague, or rare: well, it is not so. My aim has been to show that these 'implications,' underlying the most diverse uses of thought, the most opposed theories, form a continuous series, a coherent ensemble, a richness of life and science that no other can replace or equal, and, in fact, I have never found in any philosopher either the execution or the beginning of a similar complexus, ending in a unity that is intelligible and total" (1965a, 176). Blondel was well aware that he had arrived at a system of his own, but one built on the common truths implied in the language used by all who tried to live thoughtfully and responsibly, and were systematically open to all that could be spoken truthfully, including the religious and supernatural.

In this he thought of his philosophy as Catholic in two senses, Catholic in the sense of true to the Church's articulation of the supernatural, and catholic in the sense of accessible to anyone who has the use of reason, "the language known by all."

Reverting back to the allegory of the interview as an ascent of Mont Sainte-Victoire, Blondel notes that Lefèvre has kept pushing him constantly toward the slippery paths of aesthetics in this presentation of his ideas for a literary public, whereas he would have been "much more at ease on the wider roads of science and epistemology, of ethics and pedagogy, of sociology, where we are in the grips of so many urgent difficulties, especially that of the value of our scientific civilization" (1928a, 175). For Blondel this is a civilization that has been destabilized, despiritualized, and dechristianized; it needs a new and a better spirit, which, of course, is something he was trying to revivify. In the Preface, which Blondel was asked to write for the book version of the interview, he thanks Lefèvre for the opportunity to present his ideas on what he thinks this spirit should be for the modern world or the world at large.

The *Itinéraire* was the last work of any length Blondel was able to work on directly with his own eyes, or at least with his left eye. In 1927 he still had some use of this eye, difficult as that was because of the total distortion of images coming from his right eye, but even that was a strain that he could keep up only for a few minutes at a time. For his correspondence, the constant flow of which seems never to have abated, he had to rely more and more on others, to write for him as well as to read, even though he did retain the ability to write with his own hand long after he could no longer see or reread what he was writing. At first, his daughter Elisabeth came to his rescue. She moved in with him from Paris with her children for a time and helped him to carry on his work and, when she wasn't there, his sons, Charles and André, would take turns helping out. Charles was married by this time and had his own family in Paris, as well as his work at the Conseil d'État, which called for a good bit of traveling to different parts of Europe. André, the last born and whose health had been fragile, was still living at home with his father, that is, either in Aix during the school year or in Magny-la-Ville, in his beloved Burgundy, during vacations, but André was busy working for his doctorate in Law and preparing his Aggrégation. Among the three of them, they were able to keep the father going for a time, but as his sight failed more and more, and as the pressure to get more things done mounted, they eventually had to start thinking of hiring other secretaries to work with him on a regular basis, especially during the times when none of them could be with him.

Amazingly, it does not seem to have crossed Blondel's mind that he should cut back on any of his activities because of his growing visual difficulties, except for the teaching. He was more determined than ever to get his book on *Thought* out, even though he was at a loss as to how he would be able to do this. Hence his great joy when his friend Wehrlé, ever an admirer of his former classmate and devoted to helping him fulfill his mission in the intellectual apostolate, offered to help him write the book in its final form. There was already plenty of copy to work on from earlier years, but in the winter of 1927 Blondel began to add to that in view of a first redaction, mostly notes and nuggets of ideas ranging over a wide spectrum of what Blondel had in mind. This in turn was followed by a second redaction the following year, including material on Being and the Christian Spirit, all of which only added more to the papers Blondel would have to send to his friend to work on. All told, according to a count later made in the Blondel Archives, there were 1,200 pages, not counting inserted notes, plus 500 pages of clarification as to what Blondel intended (1954, 9). It was a heavy block of papers, literally as well as figuratively, for Wehrlé to sift through.

Love for Both Country and Humanity

In the meantime Blondel was invited to lecture at the *Semaines Sociales de France* in the summer of 1928, the theme of which was to be "the Law of Charity, principle of social life." These were the same *Semaines Sociales* whose work and philosophy Blondel had defended against the monophorists and partisans of *Action Française* in the *Annales de Philosophie Chrétienne* in 1910. In 1928, the *Semaines* were to take place in Lyon. Blondel accepted to speak on *Patrie et Humanité*, a subject that would continue to set the partisans of a one-sided "integrist" nationalism back on their heels. His son Charles read the lecture for him before the assembled itinerant university.

The problem, as Blondel saw it, was one of reconciling love of country and love of humanity in a historical situation of growing contacts and tension among nations. The traditional way of grounding this twofold love in terms of concentric circles of unequal radii around an individual appears to him inadequate to meet the social and international problems we have to face in the modern world. It is not enough simply to maintain that we must love family more than ourselves, country more than family, and humanity more than country, as if only extension counted, and not what is to be comprehended in the love. Such a principle would yield only a vague and abstract humanitarianism without content. There has to be another way of grounding the spontaneous love and the reasoned obligation every individual should feel toward his or her nation and toward all other human beings, one that will allow for differences to appear and for conflicts to be resolved. Traditional arguments have been given about how individuals have to fit into limited societies such as particular nations by reason of necessity and will, or about how the human being is a political animal, but these arguments have not been able to resolve the problem of how conflicts of interest arise among nations and how the constant recurrence of wars in history keeps undermining humanity by requiring that, to bolster the good and the interests of one particular society, we must shed blood and give up our obligation to the whole of humanity, or to moral persons as such, for the sake of only a part, to the exclusion of many others. How then can patriotism be reconciled with true humanitarianism without falling into an illusory pacifist internationalism?

It is not enough merely to justify the social fact or political organization in general, according to Blondel. We must also take into account what is unique about each Country *(Patrie)* in relation to other countries, even if that means that each country is inclined to behave as if it were the only true country or, as Hegel might have put it, to behave as if it had the unique right to embody the spirit of humanity in a particular moment of history. The inculcation of civic duties within a people tends to make us love and exalt only one country, our own, without making us recognize and love what Blondel thinks of as the legitimate and providential diversity of many countries and nations. It seems that we can understand how we can be devoted to our own country, but not how others may be just as devoted to another country quite different in spirit from ours. This is a form of collective egoism, focused on only one country among others, which is no less destructive of the social fabric than individual egoism within any particular country. In inculcating the obligation to devote oneself to one's own country, which remains for Blondel an essential part of everyone's human good, even unto death, we must also inculcate a more enlightened spirit, a heart willing to recognize the standpoint of other peoples, in the measure that these diverse peoples represent an original and legitimate aspect of human culture and of the social ideal to be realized.

Far from minimizing the importance of other cultures than his own in his social philosophy, as other French or European philosophers tend to do, Blondel recognizes the importance of other cultures in their own historical originality and diversity as essential to everyone's human good, without denying the particularity and originality of one's own standpoint in relation to that of others. What is normal and salutary for Blondel is a multiplicity of peoples within humanity as a whole to make up a harmonious concert of differences and to express all the interior riches of the human spirit historically in a variety of notes and forms in art, literature, and social and political structures that are irreducible to one another. Through this we can understand better how every nation has a right to defend itself against intrusions from the outside, to preserve its own ideal, which is important for humanity as a whole. But we can also understand how the good of humanity is promoted, not by war or the reduction of one nation to the other, but by a free exchange from the one to the other, in a union that respects all consciences, traditions, and spiritual aspirations. For Blondel the otherness of human beings, not just as individuals but also as peoples, becomes an essential factor in the consideration of the ideal historical good to be realized.

All this, according to him, can be said independently of the Christian Revelation. But when one adds to it this new *Catholic* spirit with its principle of universal love that has become part of the historical fact and has elevated human aspirations to new heights, one finds new and more compelling reasons for inculcating a higher spirit of love for solving the mounting problems of strife and justice among nations as well as within nations. The work of the Christian social activists, concerned with keeping the law of true Christian charity operative in the world, whom Blondel was addressing, was not something imported from without human historical consciousness. It was something already operative in history, not only nationally in France, but also internationally across all cultural borders. To the opponents of this work, both within the Church and without, Blondel's defense of it appeared as lacking in patriotism altogether and falling in with materialist internationalism. All the distinctions he tried to make about the diversity and the irreducible otherness and richness of human cultures as part of the historical and spiritual good of peoples were wasted on them. All they saw in this rich cultural and spiritual diversity other than their own was some lowest common denominator, very much like that of the materialist collectivists, not the higher form of a Catholic international spirit Blondel had in mind with respect for all peoples and their civilizations.

The Historical Enigma of Leibniz's *Vinculum Substantiale*

As if just getting out his major work on *Thought* were not enough for him at this time of such visual difficulties, even to read and write for himself, Blondel also decided to rework his original Latin dissertation on the *vinculum* of Leibniz and to put it out in French. At this, Wehrlé, who was already working on the notes for *La Pensée*, began to protest. For him the work on *La Pensée*, as an expression of Blondel's more fundamental synthesis, was much more pressing and should not be put off any more. But Blondel had been asked by Valensin for a French version of his work on the *vinculum* to be published by the Jesuit periodical *Archives de Philosophie*, and Blondel felt he could not say no to that. Actually there had been a time, not long after the defense, when there had been a question of translating Blondel's work, and the correspondence between Leibniz and the Jesuit Des Bosses on which it was based, into French, but the project had been dropped at the premature death of the editor interested in publishing it, as Blondel explains in his *lettre d'envoi* for the volume to his friend Valensin. He welcomes this second chance to see his original Latin work come out in French, since the insight of Leibniz into the idea of a necessary *vinculum substantiale* to complement his Monadology had been a key element, *une cellule-mère*, for his own original philosophy of action.

What he was to come out with at this later date, however, was more than just a translation of the original Latin dissertation. It was to be more an adaptation of that work into terms that could serve as an introduction to the more ample systematic work that he was now contemplating at the end of his career. Blondel could not just translate an earlier work verbatim. He had to adapt it to how he understood the problem of Thought at this time, and show how Leibniz had both opened up such a problem in his correspondence with Des Bosses and failed to answer it adequately. This, no doubt, pacified Wehrlé, who eventually was called to work on editing this text, with Valensin, as well as on the more copious mass of notes for *La Pensée*.

In the original title of the Latin dissertation Blondel had spoken simply of the *vinculum substantiale*, and of the *composite substance*, in Leibniz. He had taken Leibniz at his word and had argued that Leibniz had been serious in advancing this hypothesis, to account for the reality of complex organic beings as something more than just an external or a mechanical arrangement of those substantial points of force he called monads. According to the young Blondel, Leibniz had not been just playing up to his Jesuit correspondent and the Catholic idea of Transubstantiation associated with the dogma of the real presence of Christ in the Eucharist. On the contrary, according to Blondel still, Leibniz had been looking for a way out of the idealism with which he was left at the end of his criticism of the Cartesian idea of substance as extension and its concomitant mechanism. As long as he thought only of simple monads as real substances, Leibniz had no way of understanding more complexly organized beings, except as accidental arrangements lacking in any substantial identity of their own other than of the self-enclosed monads of which they were made up. His idea of a pre-established harmony among monads could not satisfy this exigency of something more real, something more substantial, in the organic being itself, nor could the idea of a dominant monad that would remain separate from the other monads, all of them in their own substantiality, within the one organic being. Leibniz had to find another way of accounting for the identity of organic beings in their originality as a different kind of being. He had to move from what Blondel saw as the idealism of a pure monadology to something more realistic regarding complex organic beings. Hence his idea of a different kind of substance, one that would be a bond, a *vinculum*, rather just a monad, without reverting back to mere extension and mechanism, something that would determine the reality of organic beings as different degrees of being.

This is an idea that Leibniz came to only at the end of his life, as he was struggling to make his idealistic system more realistic in the face of organically unified beings. It was in the logic of his metaphysical system that, according to Blondel, when Leibniz was faced with the problem of these complex organic beings, whose identity could not be reduced to that of a monad or a mere configuration of monads. It was not occasioned merely by a controversy about the real presence of Christ in the Eucharist, even though it might have some relevance in interpreting the mystery in that dogma, in which Leibniz did not believe in any case. Using personal notes of Leibniz himself and the final part of the correspondence with Des Bosses, after the question of the Eucharist had been set aside, Blondel argued that Leibniz was bound to take this idea seriously as part of his metaphysical system, if he was interested in accounting for the original identity of complex organic beings, over and above that of the simple monads he posited at the base of his system. In any case, it was also an idea that Blondel seized upon for his own systematic study of action, as a bond or a bonding in which human experience could be unified into a singular identity relating to its destiny.

What Blondel did with the idea, however, even in 1893, was not exactly what Leibniz had done with it in his discussions with Des Bosses. Unlike Leibniz, Blondel did not think of it immediately as something substantial. He thought of it as a bond that would pull the human agent together as a subject and as something to be studied in its own right, as a subject initiating action, and not just as another object in the world. The question of its substantiality, or of any ontological commitment in the distinction between objective representation and subjective act in any state of consciousness, was systematically set aside in favor of a phenomenological method that would elaborate only on the necessary connection between the different states of a consciousness and their contents in the search for an object that would equal its power to act. Only after the universal phenomenon of action had been laid out according to its dialectical necessity, would the question of its necessary being be raised and answered with regard both to the Necessary Being itself and to the being of the phenomenon of action. This enabled Blondel to explore the entire phenomenon of human action as a whole, including the fundamental option before God, without facing up to the kind of ontological commitment Leibniz appeared to be making immediately with his idea of a *vinculum substantiale*. From this also came the impression of idealism and subjectivism which many would derive from the dissertation, and which Blondel tried to correct for, at the suggestion of Delbos, by adding a final chapter arguing that being was the ultimate bond of thought and action. At that point in his original dialectic, Blondel had returned to the question of substantiality for action, as the *vinculum* that unifies our universal experience, but his answer to it had left much to be desired in terms of the metaphysical realism he was trying to get back to.

Blondel realized this by the time he returned for his second look at his original study of the *vinculum substantiale* in Leibniz, and he realized also that perhaps his difficulty was due to not having been critical enough of the way Leibniz had tried to move from an idealist position centered on monads to a more realist position centering on composite substances, and a *vinculum substantiale* unifying monads into a higher kind of being. His own reflections on the relation between reflection and prospection as the point of departure for philosophical research, on the relation between notional knowing and real knowing, and even on mystical consciousness as a problem for philosophy, along with the supernatural in general, had brought him to a new awareness of what was required for the critical kind of realism he was driving at, and that he thought Leibniz had also been driving at toward the end of his life. What he saw then was that perhaps Leibniz had not gotten as far in this push toward a higher realism as he had originally supposed, but that he had at least opened the way toward such a realism. This is why Blondel now spoke of the *vinculum substantiale* as a historical enigma in the title for this second work on Leibniz, seeing in that enigma only an *ébauche*, a preparatory sketch, for a higher realism, not a completed passage into a higher order of knowing and of being.

In this revision of his work, Blondel continued to think of Leibniz and his hypothesis of the *vinculum* as offering a way around Kant's *Critique of Pure Reason,* for the development of philosophical realism. Using Leibniz as a model for inquiring into speculative problems, he thought he could "avoid the criticist impasse, discern the error in method and the hybrid conceptions that lead to antinomies, and open the way to a realist metaphysics without illusion and without exclusion, while meeting all the requirements of positive science, rational speculation, and religious faith" (1930a, xvii). This is why he had accepted to interrupt his own more systematic work on Thought and Being and to pursue this lateral study, as he explains to Valensin, who had asked only for a simple translation of the earlier work, with perhaps a few additional remarks on Blondel's early Panchristism he was hoping to hear more about in connection with the discussion that had taken place on the Eucharist between Leibniz and Des Bosses. Just as the earlier work on Leibniz could be read as an introduction to the philosophical problem of action, as Blondel had treated it in his dissertation, so too now this second work on the *vinculum* could be read, along with the *Itinerary,* as an introduction to the forthcoming threefold metaphysics of Thought, Being, and Action.

In the revision Blondel still thinks of Leibniz as a critical philosopher, opposed to the naïve realism or to the dogmatism of the understanding as well as of sense knowledge. Leibniz had rejected Descartes's idea of substance as extension, which was based on a purely geometrical understanding of matter. He had also rejected the tendency to confer "reality" on what our senses and the physical sciences present us with in the order of phenomenal qualities and quantities. Leibniz had gone deeper than these flat surfaces to find reality, or substantiality, in monads that could not be perceived directly by the senses or the understanding, but had to be conceived as unique points of force in matter, each self-enclosed, but each also reflecting within itself the harmony of all monads in the universe. According to Blondel, Leibniz would have rejected the flat dogmatism of Wolff and of the Enlightenment, no less than Kant did (1930a, 87). In fact, he thought of Leibniz as even more radical than Kant or Fichte in his critical idealism, in that Leibniz could be critical of the relativism and immanentism to which this critical idealism could lead, and raise anew the question of substance beyond where his first critical reflection had led him, the monad. In raising the hypothesis of a *vinculum substantiale* as a way of accounting for an active composition of material elements into a higher degree of reality, Leibniz was still trying to resolve a metaphysical problem that no critical analysis could solve. In this Blondel felt that he was being awakened not only from the dogmatic slumber of modern philosophy from Descartes to Locke, but also from the later critical prejudice of Hume and Kant, where problems are still formulated in a one-sided way that remains essentially idealistic and leads only to false antinomies (1930a, 59).

This was still the lesson to be learned from Leibniz, according to Blondel: how to go from a metaphysics that was closely implicated with the method of the modern physical sciences based on observation and mathematical calculation, to a metaphysics of a broader, more spiritual order. But it was a lesson that did not go far enough in Leibniz himself, as he struggled to find a language for such a broader, more comprehensive metaphysics of wholeness in living, organic things.

In his Latin dissertation Blondel had argued that Leibniz had been serious in this struggle, but he had never claimed that Leibniz had succeeded in finding the language he needed for the higher realism he was aiming at. Leibniz remained too attached to the mathematical symbolization at which he excelled. He was an algebrist who dreamed of a universal language that would express all ideas in technical terms and arrive at an exact science of nature, thought, and feeling. Hence, Blondel writes, "He remains readily attached to the notional side, he gets caught up in his notations and representations, and he shows us God himself as a transcendent calculator: *dum Deus calculat, mundus fit . . . mathesi quidam divina*" (1930a, 72). Leibniz was unable to shake loose from the fascination with mathematical representation, for which he had criticized Descartes, unlike Pascal, another master mathematician, who had learned to go from the spirit of geometry to the spirit of finesse or, as Blondel puts it, using a term originally applied to his own philosophy by Brunschvicg, "to effect a true transposition of perspective such as the one in Pascal's teaching on the incommensurability and the subordination of the three domains constituted respectively by the values of the flesh, the domain of spirit, and the order of charity, each one of these orders having its proper content, its original beauty, its special infinitude, each one keeping its distinct place, its particular reason for being, its mysterious relation with the others" (1930a, 76).

Blondel also suggests that, despite the infinite subtlety of his mind and his readiness to inquire into new possibilities for the world, including those proposed by Christianity, for which he felt no affinity as a secular humanist, Leibniz was perhaps lacking in an interior life of his own. He was too taken up with ideas, which remained abstract and unreal for him, which made it difficult for him to enter into the real knowledge that moves us as *spirit*. This is why he had to struggle so much to find the proper language for expressing the bond he was trying to get at, and why he "got lost in metaphors that only prove both the fundamental sincerity and the ineffectiveness of his effort to go beyond the deceptive dogmatism of the senses and of consciousness, and also that of analytical reason and of purely intellectual intuition" (1930a, 75).

It is good that Leibniz struggled with this hypothesis of a *vinculum substantiale*. It showed that he was open to a higher form of realism than the one associated with his analytical science and metaphysics. It is also good that he was unable to settle on any technical language for this new idea for him, Blondel adds. If he had settled on any particular language he had at his disposal, it probably would have been too analytical, too abstract, too exclusively notional, too focused on physical reality, at the expense of the higher reality he was trying to get at. It would have closed off the opening to the higher metaphysics that was called for as well as to the possibility of reintroducing any question of religion and the supernatural, as Blondel was always interested in doing. It is the very openness of the hypothesis of some new reality such as a *vinculum substantiale* that makes the intellectual effort of Leibniz interesting to Blondel, not the technical language in which it was cast, which only ties it to a discursive metaphysics incapable of expressing the real knowledge that is coming into view in the opening.

It is in fact this opening at the summit of Leibniz's metaphysical system that was most interesting for Blondel, what he called *un trou par en haut*, a hole at the top, or what Leibniz had also spoken of as a "need" or an "exigency" (1930a, 78), an opening that somehow had to be filled by something like a *vinculum*. The question for Blondel was how to characterize this filling, this new metaphysical content, more positively. Was it enough to speak of it as a *vinculum substantiale* or could something more positive be said about it in its transcendence over its physical constituents? The *vinculum* was supposed to explain, to unify, to realize composite organic beings. That was understood. But where does it come from, Blondel asks. "What is its origin? It can emerge from below, or it can descend from above. Immanence or Transcendence, there is the tragic alternative."

One has to opt, but Leibniz remains "enigmatic" (1930a, 88). On the one hand, he could say that the *vinculum* comes to be a sort of spontaneous generation from a coalescence of "substantial atoms," which condition is in its very essence, so that it is nothing more than a "quasi-substance," an ontological adjunct nominally attached to an abstraction. On the other hand, even if one says that it has an origin, this has to be understood as of a higher kind of origin, for only thus can it be seen as something really new, a transcendent being, which in the order of time may be posterior to the conditions of its existence, but in the order of being is prior to these practically and chronologically determining conditions. In the second case the *vinculum* takes its place at the summit of a hierarchy of being, as if occupying a throne prepared for it but otherwise left empty, or like the capstone in a vault that pulls it together as a whole. What Blondel notes is that Leibniz was never able to choose clearly between these two conceptions in his correspondence with Des Bosses, whence the enigmatic character of this final hypothesizing.

For his part, Blondel had clearly chosen for the side of transcendence in this dilemma over the enigmatic *vinculum* of Leibniz. That is why he chose to study action, which was to be for him the *vinculum* for the whole of human experience and which was to start from the transcendence of the human subject over the conditions of its existence in thoughtful deliberation and free choice. At one point, Blondel expresses wonder that Leibniz did not think of doing this himself in his constant search for new solutions to new problems. But Blondel also brings up another reason why Leibniz was unable to make this choice, namely, in the way he thought about God intervening in the world order. There were two parts to this also. One had to do with the science and the idealist metaphysics of the monadology, which spoke of efficient causes as the object of the divine understanding. The other had to do with final causes, the effect of the divine will which manifests the sovereign freedom that realizes the most perfect world with the most essences, the order in which the *unio metaphysica* and the *vinculum substantiale* has its place as a new and the supreme perfection. At first sight it might appear that these two sides of the divine intervention in the world are well coordinated in Leibniz, one having to do with metaphysical necessity based on the understanding and the other having to do with moral necessity based on the will. But Blondel argues that in Leibniz's way of thinking about moral necessity and the order of finality, they end up being opposed to one another.

To be sure, Leibniz tried to uphold some moral necessity as irreducibly distinct from a metaphysical necessity of essences, but according to Blondel this moral necessity was still governed by a fundamental determinism. "Even when [Leibniz] appeals to the divine will or when he speaks of human liberty, all these grand words and these grand things were always tied for him to a predestination, to a metaphysical calculus, to a radical intellectualism. This is why the *vinculum,* in this perspective, results fundamentally from the substances it is supposed to unify" (1930a, 91).

In other words, even when Leibniz draws the line of efficient causes all the way back to God, the *vinculum* is still seen as coming only from below, from the essences affirmed in an idealistic metaphysics. "To confer on the *vinculum* a reality with a truly original and transcendent character, Leibniz would have had to see in it less an effect of power and a progress of intelligence than a generosity of love on the part of God" (1930a, 91). In other words, for Leibniz to understand how the *vinculum* truly descended from above, to see it as transcendent and transcending, he would have had to effect a total reversal of perspective in his thinking on how the world relates to God, in freedom and love on the part of both God and the human being, in some communication rather then just some abstract pre-established harmony. If Leibniz had insisted on the reality of the *vinculum* as the effect of God's will, without this reversal of perspective, he would have had to take away from the reality of the monads as the object of intelligence, to see in them only possibles, a reality of essences, resulting not only in absolute idealism but also in some kind of intellectualist pantheism. On the other hand, to attribute some substantial reality to the *vincula*, it was not enough to see them as pure effects of the divine will, and so to verge into an absolute and arbitrary voluntarism, as others have done before and after Leibniz, but Leibniz was not one to go overboard on that side of the balance. In his hypothesizing about the *vinculum* as real, he was only raising a problem that he could not resolve from his purely intellectualist point of view.

The problem Leibniz was raising called for a passage from immanence to transcendence or, as Blondel also puts it, for a passage from a consideration only of efficient causes in some sort of essentialism to a consideration of finality in creation itself as a communication from God and as an assimilation to God. Blondel gives Leibniz full credit for raising this problem in modern metaphysics, in the face of a mounting critical attitude that would dogmatically dismiss all such problems, but not for finding any solution that would be adequate to the real knowledge in which transcendence becomes a matter of prospection, as Blondel had spoken of this in his article on the "Point of Departure for Philosophical Research." Instead, Leibniz found himself with just another form of analytical reflection where concrete data and metaphysical realities are reduced totally to component parts of one kind or another, without any relation to a higher unity or a radically new identity in being.

Critique of the Bergsonian *Élan Vital*

On the occasion of the critique of the late Leibniz, Blondel turns for a moment to a similar critique of a certain "New Philosophy," derived from Bergson and advocated by Edouard Le Roy, another Christian philosopher whom Blondel had disagreed with before. There, he expresses certain reservations on Bergson's philosophy similar to those he was making on the Leibnizian hypothesis of the *vinculum*. In a milieu saturated with science and criticism, with analyses and with abstractions, Blondel welcomes Bergson's new attempt to drop these heavy leaden shoes and to seek higher perspectives on reality where the whole takes precedence over the elements and where the end takes precedence over the means. Such a reversal, which is scandalous to analytical reason, fascinates that other reason which scoffs at reason. It follows a train of thought similar to the one Leibniz was following in raising the question of the *vinculum,* except that, instead of taking satisfaction in a clockwork metaphysics based on a pre-established harmony among a multitude of ingredients comparable to specks of dust, it insists rather on the massive effect of an *élan vital* or on the power of a *totum simul,* albeit limited, at least provisionally, to an order immanent to duration.

Nevertheless, Blondel suggests that such an *élan vital* is not totally divorced from the analytical science it spurns, and that it stands to gain in its very spontaneity from the intellectual asceticism that analytical science represents. In fact, Blondel claims, notional thought and materiality have to be integrated into the total unity where everything has to take its place and have its efficacy. Pure intuition is not sufficient for an adequate grasp of the whole, which after all is made up of different parts. Without a clear appreciation of how notional knowledge is a necessary moment of any real knowledge of the whole, one cannot but lose one's way in the reversal of perspective that the view of the whole is supposed to imply, with the result that one falls back into the same kind of essentialist and immanentist thinking that plagued Leibniz at the end of his life, as he was struggling with the idea of a *vinculum substantiale* in relation to his metaphysics of a world made up of monads.

All in all, according to Blondel, both Leibniz and Bergson failed to take any properly moral or spiritual content into account, in defining their supposed intuition into unity. Leibniz spoke only of a "God who produces possibles and essences as in a flash of lightning, who sorts out and combines mathematical compossibles, who realizes them through a moral necessity whose true figure is an automatic predestination" (1930a, 108). For Bergson either "the *élan vital,* even if it were to be declared divine, which identifies freedom to spontaneity, or the spiritual energy, even if it were glorified as a triumph of the immaterial or as a miracle of faith, remains in the final analysis only a force of nature" (1930a, 108). It has nothing that is intrinsically spiritual about it. "What we are shown in the *Monadology* or in *l'Évolution créatrice* is mathematical, aesthetic, logical, metaphysical, empirical, anything one might wish for; but however beautiful, however stimulating, however architectonic it may appear and be, the edifice that rests on this foundation, even illuminated by the most marvelous of fireworks, does not have the light and the warmth of the true sun" (1930a, 108). It is still only the organization of a force given once and for all, the triumph of an architect or a spontaneity, the result of a *vis a tergo.* It is not what Blondel is looking for in the life of spirit: "the Vocation from on high, the attraction of the Good, the cooperation that enriches unto the infinite, the only truly intelligible finality of Love communicating itself in order to associate new beings to a life that is always more abundant and beatifying, the effusion of the Spirit who engenders a life that, without metaphor or trope of any kind, we can call new and divine" (1930a, 108). Without some understanding of a finality that is implanted in human existence from on high, one cannot appreciate the real content of the spiritual life in all its richness. Blondel is interested in looking for this finality, which is the beginning of true transcendence, not outside of human nature or experience, but as a seed for a new life of communication and freedom among human beings as well as with God.

What this implies is not a detachment from all analytical or notional science, but a reversal of purely analytical perspectives that the sciences themselves can appreciate. Blondel looks for examples of such reversals of perspective even within the positive sciences themselves, when they appear to be looking for a theory that will unify all the elements they have distinguished, whether it be in wave mechanics or in biology, where it has been said that, from the standpoint of logical understanding, life is a sort of vicious circle. Blondel cites Claude Bernard, the great experimental biologist, as having remarked that the organized being is "a creation according to a directive idea," and that such an organized being constitutes a substantial bond that is not derived from its members. Speaking more as a metaphysician, Blondel adds that this organized being is well and good like an author of its own elements. He finds similar reversals of perspective in the medicine and the psychology of his day.

One has to wonder what he would have said about research into the human genome in our day and the attempts to break it down into so many elements, as if we were not beginning from a very unified living being in reality. Blondel would have insisted on the transcendence of this unity with respect to its components and its importance in defining life itself, let alone the higher unity of the human spirit itself, where the kind of metaphysical union Leibniz had in mind comes into its own. But in 1930 Blondel would also have insisted that such a transcendence is not foreign to our ordinary way of thinking and acting. Such a perspective is where we all start from, including the scientists, and to it we must return in a final reversal that brings us back from our reflective notional knowledge to our prospective real knowledge.

"We all think and act as metaphysicians of finality," Blondel writes (1930a, 122). This has long been known in the philosophy that he was familiar with, from Aristotle down to Ravaisson, Lachelier, and Bergson, but Blondel felt it was necessary to reestablish these theses on finality that seem to defy the rudimentary chronology and logic of modern science. For him it was one thing "to enunciate them as a view, as an interpretation, as a dream of the spirit, and another to realize them *in concreto*, to understand that efficient causality itself would be unintelligible and unreal without finality itself, and then to go to the end of the 'exigencies' and applications of finality. The *vinculum* is a step in this direction, only a step, but taken on a firm ground and to be made one's own" (1930a, 123). This is what he had begun to see in his original study of the hypothesis in Leibniz and what had motivated him intellectually to take up the question again as he was beginning to refocus on the real knowledge we all start from, even in our notional knowledge, and as he was contemplating expressing this metaphysics of finality in a more systematic and technical form.

In addition to the collaboration of Valensin and Wehrlé in giving this second version of his study of the *vinculum* in Leibniz its final form, Blondel also had that of a younger Jesuit colleague of Valensin, Father Gaston Fessard, S.J., himself an ardent reader of Blondel. What Fessard did was reinforce Blondel in his criticism of Leibniz for trying to rationalize and anthropomorphize his hypothesis of a *vinculum,* which even in the mind of Leibniz himself would depend on another will of God than the will that had given us the original, or the natural, order of the monads and their pre-established harmony (1965a, 158-60). With all this interest and participation of Jesuits like Valensin and Fessard in the work, however, it was not certain that the *Archives de Philosophie* would publish its final version, or under what form. The Society of Jesus exerted some control over what appeared in the journal and it was leery of seeming to give its approval to a philosopher who had yet to publish his final work. The editors decided that the work was too long to appear as an article or a series of articles in the journal itself. They decided to publish it as a separate volume in the *Bibliothèque des Archives de Philosophie.* Even so, that decision itself had to be approved by two committees made up of professors at the two French Jesuit Schools at the time, one at Vals-près-le-Puy and one still on the Isle de Jersey. The approval of the committee at Vals, where Valensin was stationed, was more or less assured, but not so with the committee in Jersey, where Pedro Descoqs, whom Blondel had criticized twenty years earlier for his advocacy of participation in *Action Française* by Catholics, sat on the committee. Descoqs, a staunch Suarezian, was opposed not only to the thought of Blondel but also to the neo-Thomism of the Rousselot-Maréchal school as well as to the paleo-Thomism of Garrigou-Lagrange. Descoqs opposed publication of Blondel's work by the *Archives,* but he was outvoted by the rest of the committee. The work was published by Beauchesne in 1930.

X

The Question of a Catholic Philosophy

By the time Blondel was finished working on the Leibniz volume for the *Archives de Philosophie,* it was already about a year-and-a-half since Wehrlé had received the papers he had to sort through, in order to organize them into the work on *Thought* they both wanted to see published, and he did not seem to be making much headway in this monumental task. To help him along, in March 1929, Blondel wrote or dictated a *Précis* of what he had in mind for this work. In December of the same year, he dictated a set of dialogues as a complement for the *Précis,* and as something that might also serve as "a sort of introduction to the ensemble of a philosophy that disturbs, so to speak, the usual perspectives." As Paliard remarks, when he later published these dialogues after Blondel's death, this is Blondel commenting on Blondel and saying that he is less interested in constructing a system than in gathering elementary truths and showing how reason finds its good in the totality of such truths (1954, 6).

In all Blondel composed fourteen such philosophical conversations at this time, not counting two different introductions for the characters in these exchanges, one of them in dialogue form as well. In these dialogues he runs through the different problems of thought, or rather the different parts of the unique problem of thought he is interested in exploring, starting from the appropriate method of implication for this exploration and going on to the various levels of thought in the universe, from the unconscious to the conscious, from unthinking thought to thinking thought, all the way to the highest causes, immanent and transcendent, for the unification that takes place in this process. This was to introduce the subject matter of volume one of *La Pensée*. It stopped short of the discussions that were to take place about the proper nurturing and education of thought and the proper virtues required for thought in its natural way through this world, not to mention the ultimate incompleteness of thought in any created intelligence that opens a hiatus in human consciousness for religion and the supernatural, which was to be the subject matter of volume two of *La Pensée*.

When Blondel began dictating these dialogues, he had every intention of publishing them. He would prepare each session of dictation with notes he scribbled to himself, and after each session he would add remarks on separate sheets of paper that were to be incorporated into the written text. But there was no going back over an earlier session. Blondel spoke as one who was introducing the secretary herself into the subject matter. He did not want to force her to go back over things mechanically or just to patch up things. Each session would simply go forward into the subject planned for that session. It was the press of other interests, especially that of getting his principal systematic work itself on track, that forced Blondel to break off this dictation and leave the dialogues unfinished. He remembered this later on, in 1942, after the Trilogy had been published, and began thinking of finishing these dialogues as a way of answering some of the criticisms he had received due to an inability on the part of readers to shift paradigms, as he thought was necessary. He thought then of finishing these dialogues, but he did not get beyond the point of writing a new preface for them. He was diverted once again by other activities and by the preparation of the volumes on *Philosophy and the Christian Spirit*. The text that Paliard published in 1954 as the third fascicule of *Études Blondéliennes* under the title, *Dialogues sur la pensée: Conflits et éclaircissements dialogués*, shortly before his own death, is mostly the one that Blondel had dictated in the winter of 1929, with the additions Blondel made each day to the dictation inserted in the appropriate place.

What there is of these dialogues has not been given much attention, but they could serve as a good introduction to the perspective Blondel adopts in *La Pensée*, in contrast to other perspectives in philosophy that different characters or spirits in the dialogue represent for him. Blondel takes the name of Paleoneos for his own spirit, one who is young but who tries to be faithful to the human tradition of old. Other spirits invited to the dialogue include Polymath, the one conversant with all philosophical systems but committed to none, Eutrapelos, the conciliatory spirit who wants to gloss over all differences of opinion, Kinesis, the spirit in perpetual motion, always ready to take on a new form whether as evolutionist, transformist, symbolist, intuitionist, or modernist. Then there are Monotime, the opposite spirit of fixity in a system that is exclusive of any other, and Dynast, a name Blondel picked up at the École Normale to brand the sons of official dignitaries, the heirs of a name or of a university caste who were first to arrive on the scene and who would not admit newcomers on a par with them, let alone allow for any broadening of outlook.

In addition there was also Polyeucte, who was full of zeal and devotion for the interests of Paleoneos but made the latter wary of himself by reason of this confidence, and finally Logophile or Logodoule, the rationalist and immanentist who rejected out of hand any view prior or ulterior to that of his own supposedly adult and liberated thought, the one who had opposed Blondel's suggestion of a philosophy of the supernatural from the beginning.

The idea of Blondel was to bring together all the different spirits who had objected to one or another of his proposals and to confront them in a dialogue that would be fruitful for every spirit present. "Philosophy can and must tend to be a collective task; it must confront living thoughts. I shall therefore be consoled and happy, given my present inability to complete in detail, as I had dreamed, this book on *La Pensée,* if from this very imperfection there can come an encouragement for other spirits and if a few barely sketched indications leave more ample matter for new initiatives. The excessively individualist conception of a system of defined and closed notions is obviously insufficient and stifling; what is important is a spirit, firm in its orientation, but open to any increase, to all diversity. That is, the participation of many interlocutors in a sincere dialogue is the natural instrument for a cooperation that leaves to each one his legitimate preferences, while allowing all to cohabit together in trustful quest, in charitable peace and even, differences notwithstanding, in spiritual communication" (1954, 20).

This is the spirit Blondel had already begun to see emerge in philosophy at the end of the *Letter on Apologetics,* a spirit of accommodation or of flexibility in adjusting to the thinking of others that he thought more required for philosophy perhaps than for religion or theology. It was also the spirit he wanted to return to, in dialogue with other philosophers, as he was struggling to gather his own thoughts together in a Trilogy he was beginning to feel might slip away from him, because Wehrlé appeared to be making little headway in organizing the mounds of material Blondel had sent him. With the dialogues he felt he might get something done of the grand project he had in mind, while allowing more time for his friend to piece the larger, more technical work together. But even the dialogues, which he characterizes as prosaic in a letter to Brémond (1971b, 352), had to be set aside to address philosophical questions about Saint Augustine on the occasion of the fifteenth centenary of his death in 430.

The Philosophical Retrieval of Saint Augustine

Blondel saw this centenary as an opportunity for refocusing on the philosophy of Augustine as something to be valued not only for Christians but also for philosophy as such. Hence when asked to contribute to two different commemorative collections of essays on Augustine, including one in English, he was more than willing to comply, on the basis of his earlier research on the one he was to call the Father of Christian Philosophy. But he wanted to do more than write for an audience that was already receptive to the religious side of Augustine's thinking. He wanted to write as well for a more strictly philosophical audience, like the readers of the *Revue de Métaphysique et de Morale,* who were perhaps more critical of introducing any religious dimension into philosophy, and where, as he wrote to Brémond, "it is not easy to integrate catholic philosophy" (1971b, 391). Blondel wanted to make the case, not only for Augustinian philosophy among Christians, who at this time were more heavily engrossed in the philosophy of Aquinas, but also for Christian philosophy as such among non-Christians as well as Christians.

He began working on this in November 1929. Ironically, he begins by remarking that he had not been directly influenced by Augustine in the original elaboration of his philosophy, as Archambault appeared to be supposing in his letter of invitation to contribute to the forthcoming volume on Augustine in the *Cahiers de la Nouvelle Journée,* given the kinship in thought that Archambault saw between the Bishop of Hippo and the Philosopher of Aix. It will be remembered that Blondel never mentions Augustine in his *Itinerary* among those who had influenced him, even though there were Augustinians among those he does mention, like St. Bernard and Pascal.

Blondel came late to the study of Augustine, even later than he did to the study of Aquinas. Neither of these two authors was on the program at the University when he had been a student. In fact, it was Blondel who put Augustine on the program for philosophy at Aix around 1920-21, as he had done earlier for Aquinas. Many of his early contacts with Augustine were through others who thought of themselves as Augustinians, like the Jansenists or Malebranche, but whose reading of Augustine was questionable for him from the philosophical as well as from the orthodox point of view. In a way Blondel was forced back into a study of Augustine himself, as he was into the study of Aquinas, by disciples whose interpretation he could not accept as definitive of what the Master had really thought and taught. This was not to say that Blondel owed nothing to Augustine, but rather that he had come spontaneously to the same sort of ideas in his own reflection, which Blondel took to be a proof of their universal validity, wherever they came from.

In his article for the volume of *La Nouvelle Journée,* however, titled "The Ever Renewed Fecundity of Augustinian Thought," Blondel does not try to cover a wide range of Augustine's ideas. He decides to dwell only on the first point of the questionnaire Archambault submitted to his prospective contributors, which had to do with the *method* of Augustine. It has been said that the essential of Augustine's thought passed over into Aquinas, there to be made more precise, better organized, and even redressed, to forestall excessive interpretations. But what strikes Blondel more is a tendency to oppose the method of Aquinas as heterogeneous to the method of Augustine among historians of philosophy like Étienne Gilson. Blondel had already taken exception to this tendency in the interview with Lefèvre, in connection with Gilson's book on St.

Bonaventure, the contemporary of St. Thomas who had championed Augustinianism against Aristotelianism. But now he also had Gilson's book on Augustine himself to contend with, where the dichotomy between two methods is deemed absolute, so to speak, as if each method were complete and closed in upon itself apart from the other. Augustine's is said to proceed only from a spiritual experience, while Aquinas's is said to proceed from the order of the senses by abstraction to general ideas. If each system is supposed to contain the fullness of the catholic sense, as Gilson claims, Blondel asks, how can they be thought of as coming together within the integrity of Christian life and teaching with this partiality of intellectual constructions? Instead of insisting only on the differences that have separated the two systems historically, Blondel would rather seek to understand how the two principal philosophical systems come together in a single catholic speculative tradition and converge on one another, to the advantage of both Thomism and Augustinianism. Beyond the antagonism that seems to separate them, one has to come to what unites them in the differences that they emphasize.

To do this, Blondel insists that we must broaden our understanding of each method and see how they compenetrate one another in the examination of one and the same historical reality. Gilson describes the vibrancy of Augustine's thought very well, its charm and enthusiasm, its capacity to rejuvenate and to draw us forward, but he finds a complete scientific method only on the side of Thomism. But to insist on the analytical and didactic method of Aquinas in this way is to insist only on the anatomy of his thought, a skeleton of abstractions without any flesh and blood. Augustine did not overlook this sort of rational skeleton, but he viewed it more as wrapped and nourished in a living flesh. Even though Thomas dwelt longer with abstractions, while Augustine was more concrete, both were concerned with finding the living Truth as well as the meaning of Charity. Augustine's method was no less intelligent, no less intellectual, no less scientific than an abstract anatomism, which says that real life is found only at the point of a scalpel dissecting a cadaver. It is important to bring out how the Augustinian method arrives at a certain intellectual precision and justification, even as it describes very personal experiences. The story of a soul that it tells, the itinerary of its thought, is of universal value and validity. On the other hand, the method of Thomism must not be reduced to a didactic apparatus, a mere dialectic of ideas and argumentations in its organization. This sort of technical exactitude in Aquinas is nourished by concrete sources, by spiritual experiences, and the reestablishment of historical and traditional realities. To lose sight of this is to reduce Thomism to the sort of abstractive science that has become prevalent in modern thought, to the exclusion of the more concrete spiritual science one can actually find in Aquinas.

The two systems thus must be brought together for the progression of Christian thought and speculation. Blondel would include further study of St.

Bonaventure, the Teacher of interior ways, and Saint John of the Cross as well, for the same purpose. But here he satisfies himself with making two or three points indicating how St. Augustine and St. Thomas can be thought of as completing one another in finding solutions to questions that still trouble us. From Augustine we can get the idea of Truth as a light to be sought after, and of philosophy as a primitive *élan* of the spirit that bears us toward the epicenter of divine light and love. With him we can also say that the Christian inspiration is everywhere equally, because in the depths of nature and of the soul there is one and the same clarity, one and the same love that assigns both the universe and humanity a single end of supernatural union in the City of God. But we must also say that, due to his insistence on original sin and its consequences, in opposition to gnostic illuminism and to Pelagianism, and due to his own personal experiences as a sinner and as a convert, he was not always clear about what is a properly human gift in us of reason and will in their natural integrity and what is gratuitous and supernatural vocation that is not congenital or naturalizable in any created being.

To help clarify this distinction, and to avoid the errors that have come from this lack of clarity, the Thomistic distinction between what is natural and what is supernatural in man's concrete historical existence has been very useful. It has helped to keep philosophy distinct from theology for one thing, within Catholic thinking, but not by separating them from one another on the question of religion in the concrete. Thomas did not become an advocate of natural religion in philosophy in distinguishing the natural from the supernatural, and philosophy from theology. He continued to think as a philosopher that there is a natural desire to see God, even though he thought of such vision as entirely beyond the capacity of any created intelligence. Blondel is always happy to point out the recent studies that have brought out this aspect of Aquinas's teaching as a philosopher. They show how the Augustinian inspiration and the Thomistic precision of thought can come together in a doctrine that maintains both the incommensurability and the compenetration of reasonable nature and supernatural life, which Blondel did not want to lose sight of in the Catholic tradition. If the distinction, which is essential for a proper philosophy of religion, is not turned into a separation, as has been done even by many Thomists, along with many others in modern philosophy, beginning with Descartes, it becomes possible to render an account "of our undeniable obligation to adhere rationally to catholic truth and to safeguard the free and gracious gift, which, as supernatural and even as *unnaturalizable* as it is, can justly be imposed under the most rigorous sanction and invisceprated into the most profound depths of even unconscious human life without losing the purity and the transcendence of its origin" (1966a, 232-33). Blondel is back waging the battle he had waged during the modernist crisis against the twofold error of extrinsicism on one side and excessive intrinsicism on the other regarding the mystery of

Christian life. This is an example of the benefit that can come from bringing Augustinianism and Thomism together for the work of a higher spiritual synthesis in the Catholic tradition.

The second essay Blondel wrote on Augustine, for the English volume *A Monument to Augustine*, edited by Martin D'Arcy, S.J., appeared in August 1930. It was the first thing ever to appear in English by Blondel. The original text was written in French, of course, and Blondel did not get the chance to review the translation, which must have made him somewhat uncomfortable, careful as he had become about everything that appeared under his name. The original French was never published during his lifetime, except for a part of it, in the *Revue néo-scolastique de Philosophie* in Louvain, where he made corrections, which he later wanted to be taken into account if ever these essays on Augustine were to be reunited in a volume, as was in fact done after his death in the volume titled *Dialogues avec les philosophes*. In that volume it is the original French text sent to the English publisher, as found in the Archives, that is published, with Blondel's corrections, as the editor is careful to note. Typically, the essay is titled "The Latent Resources in St. Augustine's Thought." It discusses some of the more systematic aspects of this thought that are often overlooked by historians. What he proposes is to ascertain why this "Catholic philosophy" offers us something more than just another system among many, but rather "a unity of thought and life, a new and higher kind of philosophy in relation to the aspirations and the needs of many contemporary minds" (1966a, 193–94).

Blondel proceeds by answering difficulties or objections that have been raised against Augustinian philosophy by historians or by critics of the saint's thought. The first one is that historians frequently imply there is not systematic teaching in Augustine of the kind Blondel is suggesting. Blondel answers by saying that one has to know how to look for such a unified teaching philosophically, as well as historically, in an author like Augustine. The second objection comes from a tendency to separate two different approaches to philosophical and Christian thought, one that proceeds by rational demonstration and another that proceeds by vital enthusiasm. Augustine is said to be more a soul burning with charity than a mind of pure light and scientific exigency. But Blondel rejects this way of separating light and love, as if they had nothing to do with one another in Christian thinking. One cannot play St. Thomas off as the formal rational thinker, as if he never appealed to his personal concrete experience as a Christian, against St. Augustine as the writer of confessions expressing his affective orientation toward God as absolute good. Both saints shared in the same tradition that combined these two approaches, intellectual and affective, to the ultimate Reality, and Augustine is an excellent example of how one works toward the light and truth, toward a teaching that is valid for all, in disclosing an intimate reality that can be illuminating for all, in a sense that is fully catholic or universal.

A third objection is taken from a tendency to juxtapose the realm of philosophy and the realm of religion, again as if they should be kept strictly apart from one another. Gilson, as we have seen, lends himself to this objection by insisting on the heterogeneity between the two systems of Augustine and Aquinas, both of which he has so admirably described, as if they were irreducible and even incompatible with one another. For Blondel, however, this is to fix these two systems of thought in two different sets of historical expression, looming across from one another without contact and without communication. It would be a mistake to think that, in Augustine, philosophy gets lost in theology, or theology in philosophy. It would also be a mistake to think that Aquinas tried to set up a philosophy separate from theology. Those who have interpreted Thomism along this line have not only betrayed the thinking of their Master, but have also found themselves at odds with Christian teaching itself, as in the case of the Thomistic supporters of *Action Française*. Studies on the natural desire to see God in the philosophy of Aquinas have proven them wrong, both in their interpretation of Aquinas and in their understanding of the relation between philosophy and theology in the living unity of Christian thinking.

Other difficulties are brought up against the thinking of Augustine, such as his reliance on a theory of illumination that seems to dispense with the necessity of starting from sense knowledge, or his doctrine of intelligent faith and submission to the authority of God without sufficiently clear distinctions for a didactic science or a systematic philosophy. But Blondel answers these by highlighting the principle of unity in Augustine's thought, which is its fundamental orientation to the truth and to happiness in God. Here too Blondel tries to show how Augustine is a systematic philosopher in his own way, referring especially to those last conversations with Monica at Ostia, where he teaches us that "God, touched at the high point of demonstration, implied by the entire movement of sensibility and knowledge, also can and must be taken in by the whole soul, obeyed by a purified and submissive will, loved under the inspiration of grace, which, offered independently of us, cannot fructify without us" (1966a, 208). *Quaeritur non ambulando, sed amando.* What could be more opportune, Blondel comments, for showing in current debates about atheism and the problem of God the necessary role of rational proofs and the implied presence of spontaneous certitudes as well as the importance of moral rectification in resolving this supreme problem of the living God? (1966a, 208).

Blondel, however, is not satisfied with treating Augustine's thought from the viewpoint of a spectator or an observer. He wants to enter into the very center of his perspective, the profound unity without which we cannot grasp his real thought, what became for him the decisive and unforgettable experience of his conversion, a transforming evidence, a vision and a disposition of his entire soul. This was the realization that man is not a light unto himself and that nothing of what we know is luminous in itself. To look for the light, to seek truth, is not just to know things, objects, facts of consciousness, rational ideas, transcendentals, all things that we believe we start from in ascending to God, all things that are themselves in need of illumination, that are without the truth that comes from God. *Ubi inveni veritatem inveni Deum.* Augustine reverses the ordinary way of moving from creatures to God and thereby renews all the movement of inquiry, showing how it is tied to a spiritual conversion. For Blondel this was a liberating view amid the controversies about immanence and extrinsicism he had suffered through.

It has been said that Augustine's conception of the nature of man remained equivocal or confused, lending itself to the aberrations of Jansenism in a backwash of contrary predestinationisms or concupiscences, one for evil and one for the good or the supernatural. But Blondel blames these aberrations on the abstractions of Jansenism itself, not on Augustine, who never lost sight of man's freedom in the work of salvation. Blondel gives credit to Aquinas for clarifying the notion of an absolute supernatural in relation to the Augustinian fluidity in passing from the order of nature to the order of grace, which clarification should have prevented the deviations of Jansenism. But then he insists all the more on the necessity to unite, to make nature and grace cooperate, where Augustine excels in stimulating a science of the interior dynamism. In this respect the renewal of Thomism makes the renovation of Augustinianism all the more desirable, inoffensive, and beneficial, especially in philosophy. One gets the impression that Blondel was perhaps thinking of his own philosophy as part of this complementary renovation for Thomism, even though it was not directly tributary to Augustine.

The problem of the supernatural as something totally gratuitous on the part of God and yet as obligatory on the part of man, as Blondel had already argued in the *Letter on Apologetics,* can be seen as the most formidable obstacle that stands between modern philosophy and Christianity. This is the problem he had set out to solve to the satisfaction of both philosophy and theology, from the beginning in his own philosophy. In Augustine he finds a solution to this problem already implied in the idea that every intelligence aims at knowing and possessing the God of Truth from whom proceeds all light, that of the sensible order, that of the rational order, that of the aesthetic, that of the moral order, and that of the religious order, understanding at the same time that this truth cannot be encompassed by any simple metaphysical curiosity or by simply overcoming some material or intellectual obstacle through rational argument. If we remain on the purely intellectual level of essences and natures, the interior union of man and God will continue to appear impossible. The mysterious marriage of the soul and God takes place in the order of the will and love, through the gift of the Holy Spirit, the help of grace, which could never be absorbed in any nature. This is a new way for metaphysics that Augustine opens up for us, a metaphysics of *charity* as well as intellectual light.

Blondel goes on to show how this new way requires humility, more than any sort of triumphalism, before referring once again to a tradition of Catholic philosophy that stems from Augustine, which, while being more singular and concrete in its personal dimension, is at once most universal and catholic in meeting the test of any critical intelligence. He ends by reintroducing his own notion of the *transnatural* as part of the debate in answering the question of how historical man is called concretely to a life that transcends historical consciousness itself.

Blondel spent two months all by himself, in July and August 1930, as he told Brémond (1971b, 386), working on the article that was to appear later that year in the *Revue de Métaphysique et de Morale* under the title "The Fifteenth Centenary of the Death of St. Augustine: The Original Unity and the Permanent Life of His Philosophical Teaching" (1971b, 430). In it he wanted to be especially careful to bring out the rigorous philosophical aspect of Augustine's thought by explaining what he thought was the central core or the unifying principle of this philosophy, as well as what he thought has to be preserved of this philosophy for modern times against the aberrations of tendentious interpretations that have pulled it to one side or another in the past, contrary to its universal or catholic intent, which was as traditional as it was original. Blondel presents Augustine as a model for thinking personally, on the basis of one's own experience, through confession so to speak, at the same time as universally, in a way that appeals to any rational being, whence the permanence of its interest for the life of the human spirit.

What Blondel finds in Augustine, which he had regretted not finding in Leibniz, is an intense spiritual life as the basis for his philosophical realism. What he wants to insist on, in the *Revue de Métaphysique*, is the philosophical character of the thought of one who seems to have absorbed the light of reason into the irradiation of the divine Word and to have subjected philosophy to Christ, even to the point of treating certain natural virtues as splendid vices. What he wants to argue is that, in spite of all this, Augustine belongs to the line of the highest metaphysicians and psychologists of all times, that, even when he speaks as a theologian, he remains always a philosopher, and that it is the philosophical aspect of his thought that constitutes the true unity of his vast and very diverse work. In fact, Blondel wants to argue that this paradoxical extension of Augustine's thought into the religious quest of faith is indeed in answer to the secret wish of the philosophical spirit in its highest form.

Blondel begins by bringing out the peculiar turn of Augustine's thought, how it tries to maintain an interior coherence in order to tie all the parts of his highly disparate work together intelligently, and how it is constantly in contact with the realities to which he is trying to relate his thought, his will, and the whole of his being. It is a philosophy always ready for retractations, as it searches within its profound experimental and spiritual realism for new developments and for renovation without limits, while at the same time, through its intellectualism, looking for reassurances against the fallacious intuitions of one's own private sense and the superficial partialities of moral empiricism. Blondel distinguishes between two kinds of implicit thought: "one that remains *enveloped* in sentiments that may be vivid but confused, serving as matter for analysis; and one that, after having used the primitive data and the discursive knowledge, is *enveloping*, more comprehensive, more certain of itself, more full of real truth than abstract definitions or notional frameworks could be" (1966a, 148). For him Augustine was a master at pursuing the second kind of implicit thought, without ever losing sight of the first kind, at which he was also very good in his probing psychological analyses. It is the second that made the strength of his philosophical method, much more than the first.

Again, Blondel distinguishes two seemingly heterogeneous elements that are integral to Augustine's philosophical outlook: one a "systematization of ideas aiming at a coherence of organized truths, and seeking in this cohesion itself a formal proof of their scientific value," the other "a finalist intention and living response, not just to some curiosity, but to the human disquietude and to the problem of universal becoming" (1966a, 148-49). Augustine was able to combine these two elements in a synoptic view that did not close in upon any system of ideas, which were plentiful in his mind, but remained open to the fullness of reality. "He is not content with thinking and acting *sub specie partis;* he lives, he philosophizes *in realitate totius*" (1966a, 149).

This is the center of Augustine's way of thinking according to Blondel. It is difficult to place oneself at this center, but it is essential that we do so, if we are going to read him with the same kind of consistency that he used in tackling so many divergent problems as a Christian philosopher. If we can place ourselves at the center, Blondel says, we can see that "the speculative and the ascetical method are wed, in such wise that rational investigation, the singularities of psychological and moral experience, Christian data, all come together, without having the philosophy thus deployed confused with positive Religion" (1966a, 151). It is often said or thought that philosophy and theology remain confused in Augustine. It is true that we do not find in him the distinction made in the same way that it would be made later on in the Middle Ages, as Blondel will recognize later on. But the distinction between the two is clearly there to see and understand, Blondel maintains, if we can place ourselves at the center of Augustine's thought, to which Blondel is trying to call philosophical attention.

The first thing Blondel insists on at the intellectual center of Augustine's philosophy is the living unity of speculative effort and moral purification. Augustine's was a work of dialectical and critical science, but having to do with the task of beatitude and salvation. Rectification of the will and action as well as reorientation of thought and knowing were two essential parts of one and the same effort. For him there was no opposition between the way of truth and science and the way of salvation and beatitude. Indeed, there was no way of entering into the truth without charity, just as there was no way of finding true love of the good without the critical reflection of intelligence. *Intellectum valde ama*, Augustine used to say.

The second point Blondel insists on, which is closely related to the first, was the better-known theory of interior illumination that runs through all of Augustine's work. This was the truth of truths for Augustine. What it meant, according to Blondel, is "that things are not of themselves enlightening, that the spirit is not unto itself its own light, that we could not find in things or in the spirit any primitive light, any intrinsic clarity.... There is no luminosity in anything that is not the sole truth that shines in the darkness" (1966a, 155). We have a propensity to ignore the darkness in which we find ourselves and to attribute to ourselves the luminosity that makes all things visible to us intellectually, but that is to ignore the true source of light that illumines our soul as well as things, the source toward which Augustine is ever striving to return out of the darkness that he recognizes in himself, the divine Word who creates and illumines every man who comes into the world. To find truth for Augustine is ultimately to find God, as another one of his sayings has it: *ubi inveni veritatem, inveni Deum* (1966a, 156).

Blondel understands all this as part of the philosophical quest in Augustine, where the human being comes to understand his aspiration to the fullness of truth and yet finds himself incapable of reaching it adequately on his own resources alone. To become attached to things, as if they were knowable by themselves, to become fixed in our own ideas, as if they were intelligible essences by themselves, all that is a sort of philosophical sickness, a way of seeing things apart from their true foundation. What we want ultimately is a contemplative union with the true Source of light and being, but it takes a spiritual dialectic to bring us back to this, *per grados debitos*. Blondel was ever conscious of the need to proceed according to a universal order in the philosophical ascent to God, and he finds the same kind of concern in Augustine at every turn, including that of the final conversation with his mother, Monica, at Ostia.

However, the theory of exemplarism in Augustine is not the same as those that came before it or after it. Augustine has been called the Christian Plato. But Blondel sees an important difference between Augustine and Plato in relation to this first basic truth. Plato looked for the truth in a world of ideas that was illuminated by a Sun that was only intelligible. For Augustine, the divine source of truth was a union of intelligibility and charity. "For him the Ideas are not in themselves, apart from things, apart from us or even apart from God" (1966a, 156). In this sense, Augustine is much less an idealist than a realist. Yet it is not in God himself that we see things, as Malebranche and others have suggested with their theory of "Vision in God." For Augustine, to be sure, "all truths, all particular realities we know are known and knowable only with the help of the irradiation in them, and the illumination in us, of God; but we do not see them in Him, and our ideas, those that we form of beings and of ourselves, are not the thoughts of God, not even in the case of supposedly exact and necessary sciences" (1966a, 157). In all of our ideas there is a sorting out to be made between the part that is from God and the part that is from our darkness, from our human indigence and from our natural inadequacy, the admission of which, at least implicitly, must keep us on our guard against the presumption of constituting ourselves or finding in things a principle of subsistence, of sufficiency, and of intelligence that is somehow autonomous and immanent. In Augustine's doctrine of illumination there is no trace of ontologism, illuminism, or pantheism. There is only a dialectic that is at once rational and ascetic, open to every rectification and progression of explanatory and discursive thought, while recognizing the inadequacy of our own being, our own ideas, and even our own presumptions.

Blondel points out how every finite intelligence, because it receives the light of the divine Word, is naturally inclined to make itself the focus of light, to make its own reason the norm, to confer an apotheosis upon its conceptions, "to make what it sees, in the light of God, profit from this origin, as if the object basking in the rays of the sun were the Sun itself, the Sun that is not seen as if we were facing it, but that makes everything visible, and without which things, being only what they are, would be only darkness" (1966a, 158). Whence the importance of humility, not just because of one's failure to grasp the true meaning of things in human experience, but also because in the dialectic one finds oneself always in the Presence of God. For Augustine, scientific systematization and spiritual purification always go hand in hand. It is not that our ideas cannot be solid. It is rather that at their core there is an opening, an emptiness that remains to be filled by something other than themselves. Augustine is anything but an immanentist, an idealist, or a subjectivist. What he shows, according to Blondel, is that "if there are in us light and darkness, fullness and emptiness, this positive emptiness, this illuminated darkness is from us, whereas the light in this darkness, the infinite appetite that is in us cannot be from us" (1966a, 160).

Along with this unitive aspect at the center of Augustine's thought, which functions as illumination from on high, and intellectual humility from below, there is also a discursive aspect of searching, which is in solidarity with it and which is required to give our thought consistency. These are two vital functions for Augustine, both essential. Blondel tries to show how Augustine keeps them in solidarity with one another in the way he proceeds philosophically. To begin with, Augustine has his own way of abstracting the data of experience. He does not start only from sense data, but from anything that is given in human experience, which is spiritual as well as sensible. Nor does he just accumulate abstract notion upon abstract notion, as if they were levels of being or echelons in an intelligible and ontological hierarchy. What he sees rather are concepts that point to the subsistent truth in God, recognizing that the concepts are but anthropological expressions. They are nevertheless occasions or indications that we must take advantage of, to go through them and to rise to the pure light that illumines us. "In our ideas, we become attached, not to our ideas, but to what gives them light and to what makes of them a demand for truth, a vehicle toward being: purification by extraction, which in one sense can be immediate, *ictu oculi interioris*, but which requires at the same time an interior conversion, a spiritual ascetic . . . that implies a unitive disposition of the soul and a comprehensive attitude of intelligence, of which Plato said that it was proper to the philosopher, *sunoptikos tis* (Rep. 537c)" (1966a, 162).

The analytical and didactic precision of Augustine's thought has been noted before, but it should not be separated from its dynamic thrust toward the light that illumines everyone who comes into the world. Augustine was fascinated with numbers. He was a mathematician in his own way, as Plato was. He was a theoretician of order. He excelled, according to Blondel, "at divining the rational armature that holds up the universe and grounds the infinitely diverse movement of singular beings on the immutability of a universal and intelligible plan at the service of charity" (1966a, 163). For him the divine exemplarism was a translation of this requirement of order, *numero, mensura et pondere*. Only, he never confused "our notional constructions with this providential ordinance that proceeds from the whole to the parts and aims at individual beings, without passing through generalities" (1966a, 163). Far from being a march toward conceptual generalities, Augustinian abstraction frees us from them and elevates us to the universal present in all singulars. And with Leibniz in the back of his mind, Blondel adds: "It makes all events, all concrete beings enter into the infinitesimal calculus that solves without any artificial simplification the problem of the whole in function of each point" (1966a, 163). God does not first see and will abstract types; he sees, wills and loves beings, and it is to the being who is loved that Augustine wants to go in keeping with his concrete realism.

What we all have to start from is our own self-consciousness, which underlies and is included in all our knowledge, and which entails a certain concrete certitude that we cannot escape from. But for Augustine this certitude hangs from another certitude that is higher and more necessary. Descartes has often been seen as tributary to Augustine with regard to this certitude of self-consciousness, given the similarity of the *cogito, ergo sum* of the father of modern philosophy with the *si fallor, sum* of the ancient Church Father. But Blondel sees an important difference between the two. What follows from Descartes's *cogito*, as the sequel of modern philosophy has shown, is a certain idealism, a conviction that thought is in itself the true reality, the subsistent truth, the source of light, even though Descartes himself thought he had to consolidate this conviction in what was for him still only the thought or the idea of God. For Augustine, according to Blondel, it was the other way around. It was not his idea of himself that was certain, but his experience in which he was only discovering himself. The discovery, although certain, was tentative, expressed in the optative: *noverim me,* and it implied a deeper discovery that was also expressed in the optative: *noverim Te, Deus.*

Descartes began by separating himself and the world from God, only to bring God back in on the rebound, to overcome the separation between the *res cogitans* and the *res extensa*. Augustine was looking within his own reality, and the order of the universe, in order to find God present there, *intimior intimo meo*. For a long time he did not know what he was looking for, immersed as he was in human and even material conceptions. He had to run the risk of complex dialectical and ascetical ways, all of which contributed to what he was finally able to see of God, in himself and in reality, if not in God himself. But he did not do this by first absolutizing himself or his idea of himself and the world, and then looking for the ground of such an absolute. What he did was rather relativize himself and his ideas in the light of who God is as the Teacher within, in the Person of the Word who is all Truth for our thought.

Augustine was not averse to rational arguments for the existence of God, whether cosmological or psychological, as Augustinians have often contended. What he thought was that every rational argument has to be accompanied and vivified by a purification, as he had learned in his own conversion. Even the *Confessions* can be read as a demonstration, but for the demonstration to be complete or for it to have its effect it has to become a conversion that is at once spiritual and intellectual. Augustine was not one to separate the God of the philosophers from the God of Abraham, Isaac, and Jacob, but he did consider the dispositions of the will and even the habits of the flesh as part and parcel of the intellectual process of conversion, along with the insights of the spirit and the teachings of tradition.

From this followed the unique relation between knowing and believing that Augustine entertained. For him, according to Blondel, there was not just a connection of reciprocal causality of *crede ut intelligas* and *intellige ut credas*. In addition there was a higher metaphysical and religious truth. "When there is question of attaining any concrete being whatsoever, better still, if there is question of a spirit knowing itself, even though it already possesses the secret of its own consciousness, and finally infinitely more so, in the presence of the divine mystery itself, the most objectively certain, demonstrated and demonstrable knowledge calls for the complement, also essential, of a belief, of a confidence to which corresponds the possibility or the desire for a manifestation, a revelation. And thereby we touch on the philosophical aspect of the religious problem, on a first extension of the rational systematization into a domain or into assertions that appeared to exceed the limits of philosophy" (1966a, 169).

If we are to understand how Augustine relates reason to faith, or faith to reason, we must understand this higher metaphysical and religious truth that transcends the capacity of philosophy to understand, and yet that philosophy cannot ignore or simply set aside. It is interesting to note that Blondel specifies this truth philosophically, not only with reference to the supernatural as such, but also with reference to knowing any individual in the concrete or any spirit knowing in its own self-consciousness. This is no doubt how Augustine would have seen the problem in his realism, prior to the formal distinction that was made later on in the Middle Ages between the supernatural and the natural order of reason. In his way of conceiving the relation between knowing and believing, Augustine was already touching on this religious and philosophical problem that had become uppermost in Blondel's mind.

Augustine did not formally elaborate on this problem as such, as Blondel had done and was intending to do further, but his way of relating faith and reason never separated the one from the other, as was to be done later on, once the formal distinction between supernatural and natural was made. Augustine never considered either realm as a self-enclosed set of quiddities, essences, or intelligible natures. There was no neat or pat compartmentalization, or juxtaposition, between the two. There was only a profound cooperation and compenetration, a living unity between the two that was the subject for critical analysis and reflection as well as the object of teaching in a community of belief. Augustine did not confuse the two orders in his own mind, nor did he find them incompatible in his own historical experience. He saw them rather as one spiritual reality to be promoted by reason and in faith. Keeping in mind that he is speaking only about Augustinian philosophy, and not theology, however, Blondel suggests that, "without going beyond its competence and its proper function, and without blurring anything in theology, it could and perhaps even should have raised from its own standpoint the problem of the supernatural and of salvation, made it the center of its metaphysical and ethical speculation as well as of his psychological observations and experiences, and thereby found the secret of its unity, its integrality, its universality and its perennity" (1966a, 172). Blondel goes on to show how there was implied in the work of Augustine such a philosophy of the supernatural, even though it was never expressed in so many words.

This follows from Augustine's fundamental idea of Truth, and of God, with whom Truth is identified. Our ideas always fall short in some way. They never exhaust the truth to be known. They do not attain God or the beatitude we are looking for. There is for Augustine a double aspiration that we cannot deny in our intelligence and in our heart, *mens insatiata, cor irrequietum*. But there is also a double inaccessibility that is not merely accidental, but metaphysical and necessary: "for if man has his own secret, God has his as well, and we cannot hold Him unless he gives Himself and unless we accept Him. The end that we cannot but conceive and will is naturally beyond our grasp. From this there emerges, within the field of philosophy itself, the hypothesis of a supernatural that is possible and desirable, even though it is entirely gratuitous on the part of the One who commands what he wills, only in giving what he prescribes" (1966a, 172-73). Augustine never put it precisely in these terms, but it was implied in many of the things he said, as for example in the saying, *jube quod vis, da quod jubes*. Blondel quotes this phrase from memory and, in a note, apologizes for not being able to quote from many other texts that he had gathered at an earlier date when he still had his sight, acknowledging that he is trying to make explicit propositions that were unformulated but still to be found at the basis of Augustine's thought.

If in speaking of the original state of innocence, before the Fall, Augustine did not think of distinguishing within man's original integrity between the *gift* properly attributable to the rational being and the *grace* that is specifically supernatural and incapable of being naturalized in any creature whatever, "it is because the distinction is implied inasmuch as the spirit, participating in the light of the Word, can both know that God is and know the deficiency of this knowing, so that the natural desire to know God better and to possess Him beatifically is naturally impossible" (1966a, 173). The expression is close not only to Blondel's own way of expressing the problem, but also to that of Aquinas, who had made the distinction between supernatural and natural more explicitly, and whose idea of a natural desire to see God, a vision that would be quite supernatural, was being brought out in several studies at the time that Blondel repeatedly refers to, as if to justify his own philosophical stance, and Augustine's, in the eyes of neo-Scholastic theologians.

What follows from this expression that can be found in Augustine is the opening prepared in every spirit to an order of grace that is gratuitous but not just an add-on or something anti-natural, because this order serves and is *fitting* (or *conveniens*, another expression dear to Aquinas) in fulfilling the undetermined desire or filling the emptiness that is felt by any finite spirit left to its own resources. What also follows from this expression is that, for man to assimilate this grace that is more than just a metaphysical curiosity, but rather a transforming union from within, it was necessary even in an original state of innocence, for him to go through a test by being exposed to a fall, "a possibility that was the condition for his merit and his supernatural elevation. We see thereby how Augustine succeeds in inserting and, as it were, inviscerating within his speculative philosophy a religious doctrine that, while keeping its autonomy from the standpoint of theology, nevertheless has, on the rational and moral side, an absolutely radical grounding" (1966a, 174). We see here too how Blondel is trying to steer a very narrow course in the philosophy of religion between a Hegel and a Kierkegaard, neither of whom he had studied in any great depth. Unwilling to give up the idea of philosophy when it comes to the problem of religion and faith, he looks for the philosophical reason why it is necessary to go through a test or to actively dispossess oneself of oneself, as Abraham had to, in order to accept the divine life within oneself.

The main difficulty with pursuing a philosophy of the supernatural in the Catholic sense is that one has to deal with a reality to which, by definition, human reason and critical reflection have no direct access, not even in the sense that one has access to one's spiritual life. There is a lot that we can know about ourselves absolutely, but that cannot encompass how God is concretely and mysteriously present within us. There is a lot we can know absolutely about the world, but that does not include how God reveals and offers himself in history. Philosophically speaking, Blondel would maintain, one has to be systematically open to this surplus gift from God, but one can never take rational hold of it, even as one believes in it and responds to it. One has to face up to facts in which something supernatural that may affect one's destiny may appear, but one can never see directly the grace that is given or the promise that is made, any more than one can have a direct vision of God by human reason alone.

Neither the Resurrection nor original sin are matters that lend themselves easily to the historical method or to a purely rational dialectic. If, however, one wants to go further than just affirm a bare necessity of taking supernatural facts seriously, let us say, affirm the Incarnation of the Word, for example, and its meaning for the future of mankind, and then reflects on the consequences of accepting such truths for one's life on earth, one has to find a proper method for capturing within a philosophical framework, not the divine life itself, but the effect it has in human life itself when the truth is freely accepted and ratified within one's spirit. This was the sort of method Blondel was working on for the philosophical reflection on the Christian Spirit he was projecting, a reflection on how man is to relate to God within a Christian community. What he found in Augustine was an excellent example for doing just this, if we read this church father as the philosopher that Blondel claims he was and continued to be, and not just as a theologian.

In the midst of all his confessions and professions of faith, Augustine remained a philosopher of human experience in its intimate relationship with God. He was able to profit from his speculative analyses with neo-Platonism and the positive experiences that brought him to recognize the normal deficiencies and failures of a human being, in order to take into account the less normal falls, the weaknesses of the flesh, or the wonder of liberation. "He never tires repeating that, held back by the servitude of passion and a will cast in iron *(ferrea voluntate mea)*, he was helped in ways that were marvelous and hidden — *miris et occultis modis*. It is not that he claimed to grasp in his consciousness the divine reality and the supernatural aspect of grace as grace, but he takes notes, under their psychological and moral aspect, which is itself quite accessible and certain, of the most decisive, the most profoundly human facts, those that novelists can describe as blatant truths and which, for Augustine, are the very realities of his life: the realities of our human condition" (1966a, 176).

According to Blondel, Augustine could not have been satisfied with a purely rational ethic. For him it was not enough to subordinate action to general concepts. Practice had to rise to the highest value and the highest dignity it was capable of, through a convergence of all the powers of nature, reason, will, and grace. His philosophy was never separated from the religious elements that are, in fact, intermixed with everything else in our personal activity. The essential infirmity that he found in man simply as man served as an opening in his philosophy for a doctrine of sin and the ravages of sin as well as of the conditions for a liberation. Blondel shows how Augustine integrates into his philosophy the teaching of St. Paul about my doing what I do not will to do and my not doing what I will, or my radical inability to bring to completion what I set out to achieve as a human being.

Moreover, Augustine did not work all this out philosophically in isolation, as if only within himself face to face with God. In all his soliloquies and intimate confessions before God, or in his detachment from earthly contingencies, he was not leaving the society of human beings behind. His spirit was still filled with the world and with a sense of the unity between men and the universe. From a religious standpoint he was a herald of Catholicity and of the Church, of a Communion that makes of the faithful a unique body and soul, like the bread made up of many grains. Believing in the solidarity of all men in a hereditary evil and in the chains of sin, he was led to practice a philosophy of the concrete, the singular, and the spiritual. But he did not conceive this science except as implicitly disindividualizing us, so to speak, "in order to constitute the human person in a form that is universalist, 'catholic,' and divine." What Augustine was saying about himself as a philosopher, he was saying for every man. The drama playing itself out in his life was the universal drama, "so that the history of the world, the conflict of the two cities is at once a reality of fact and a reality of soul, a one on one and an all on all, in a continual mêlée that will be sorted out and fully illuminated only in eternity" (1966a, 178).

In his reflections on time and eternity, especially in Book XI of the *Confessions*, Augustine shows that "our actual sense of duration is not a physical reality or an ontological law, but a psychological perspective, a condition of our moral experience and our spiritual growth. It is a given in motion that has its measure, its meaning, its consistency only in a reality, and with a measure, that are transcendent" (1966a, 178-79). Augustine was intent on showing this by what Blondel would earlier have called a method of immanence, and what he would now call more a metaphysical and a moral method, echoing the more technical title of the journal for which he was writing, the *Revue de Métaphysique et Morale*. His point was to show that Augustine, whatever else he might have been, was indeed a philosopher according to the highest standards of modern critical philosophy.

In the end, Blondel recognizes that, in trying to bring out the thought that was at the center of Augustine's philosophy, but that Augustine did not always explicitly formulate, he may have gone beyond where Augustine actually stood, thereby stretching Augustine's teaching somewhat. There are many assertions requiring formal or rational justification in modern philosophy that Augustine did not stop to elaborate on, as Aquinas would do later on or as Blondel himself was continuing to do. But Blondel insists that the thought was *really* there in the conviction that to aim at the truth and happiness as Augustine did in a unified effort, is to do the work of a philosopher as well as of a believer. There is for man only one destiny, not two different intelligences, two separate wills, two kinds of possible salvation. Augustine's intention was to integrate all the elements of the drama that is playing itself out within each one of us into an intelligent and salutary unity. "It is through this intention of integrality, more than in the detail of his arguments or the elaboration of his particular theories, that Augustine has, in the general history of thought, an original value; and that is what also explains the inexhaustible value of his inspiration" (1966a, 179). In the eyes of the historian of ideas, according to Blondel, his essential merit is "to have implied in his effort an explanation and a realization of all that Catholicism encompasses metaphysically, historically, psychologically, ascetically, mystically, and this he did under a law of intellectual homogeneity, which, while leaving its very diverse elements their proper character, confers upon them nevertheless a formal coherence sufficient to make them thinkable in solidarity with one another" (1966a, 180).

We could take this as a formal statement of what Blondel thinks a Christian philosophy should be, pulling together the diverse elements of human experience as they relate to the transcendent end of human existence. He found in Augustine the makings of such a philosophy in a way that had not been found earlier in the Christian tradition, not even in the one who was called earlier Justin the Philosopher, so that Augustine should be called the Father of "Christian philosophy," in the technical and legitimate sense of the term, because he gave it the synthetic principle it needed for an infinite renewal and growth of the human spirit.

We can see here how Blondel thought of himself as in continuity with this ancient Christian philosophy stemming from Augustine, which antedates the great philosophical syntheses of the Middles Ages, even though he had not started his own philosophy with any direct reference to the Bishop of Hippo. He only found in him a kindred philosophical spirit, which he had to dig out from under a long series of misinterpretations and misrepresentations that often distorted what Augustine was driving at, while missing the central thrust of his thought. Blondel had the idea that one could use these distortions to highlight what was truly essential to Augustine's philosophy, even when it was left unspoken. From this central core of his thought one could then find the way of correcting for the misrepresentations that stifled the true course of Augustinian philosophy and so account for its continuing vitality, which has survived all attempts to bury it or to pull it to one side or another away from its Catholic truth.

It is not the case, however, that Blondel finds nothing to criticize in Augustine's philosophy. This would have been surprising for one who had almost never found a philosophy that he did not want to criticize under one score or another. Here he ends by bringing up several points that he thinks should be improved upon in Augustine's philosophy, recognizing that this is quite in keeping with the spirit of that philosophy. First, he mentions a certain naïve reliance on sense data at their face value, without enough critical discernment of the kind we have become accustomed to with modern science. Using an expression he had used in speaking of how Leibniz had criticized Descartes and Locke, he refers to this as a kind of "dogmatism of the senses and of the understanding" that sometimes compromises his more profound spiritual and even material realism. Augustine had to struggle to free himself from Manicheanism, but he remained somehow caught up in it, in the way he thought of the world largely as a place of darkness to push away from and not as a means of illumination and elevation.

Second, Blondel brings up a certain moral counterpart to this scientific insufficiency, that of maintaining a certain simplistic dichotomy between, on the one side, all that is obscure and evil, and on the other side, all that is clear and good. Augustine was well aware that things and human beings in their historical complexity could not be divided so easily into two separate camps, City of God or City of Man. He saw that every spiritual being has a natural inclination toward God and a freedom without which there can be no personality and no moral destiny, but he did insist also on man's inability, by reason of his natural limitation as well as his sinfulness, to attain salvation on his own. For him these two theses were not incompatible with one another. In fact, they were tributary to one another in his way of thinking. Sin made it all the more evident that man needed divine help and concurrence to attain his final end, but it did not take away man's ability to choose responsibly and to achieve some good in history. There is a natural and rational morality that can comport very well with the Christian conception of human destiny, but Augustine did not attend to that very much, except perhaps in dealing with certain particular issues such as just war theory. This is a criticism of Augustine that Aquinas probably would have concurred in, given the way that he spoke more positively of imperfect happiness and human virtue in the *Summa Theologiae*.

Third, Blondel mentions the absence of any clearly articulated social and political philosophy for this world in Augustine. What Augustine says in this regard is suggestive at times, but it is often confused with what he has to say about the City of God, not the City of Man, which he tends to treat rather negatively. He did see something of the natural foundations, the moral reason, and the spiritual services that political and social organization could offer man in his pilgrimage on earth. He also understood how the distinction of the two powers, political and ecclesiastical, could be liberating and salutary. But what he had to say concretely about the political was quite limited to the historical circumstances of the decadent Roman Empire in which he found himself. He was more interested in showing how the City of God had to liberate itself from these ties with the *Res romana* than in finding a new conception for the order and peace of civilization.

Finally, Blondel criticizes a certain lack of formal clarity on the complex questions that he raised in the philosophy of religion and in the conception of divine transcendence in relation to human destiny. To be sure, Augustine was the first to open up new avenues for human thought in this regard, but he was not able to give these new ways a sufficient technical expression. This is why, according to Blondel, the interpretation of Augustinianism through the ages has been plagued with so many aberrations about the original state of man or the current state of fall and redemption in which man finds himself. Blondel tries to sort out some of the things Augustine said about these states and about how man is thought to exist and to act in them, in the light of Augustine's own central doctrine about divine illumination and man's tendency to know God and to participate in his happiness, but he recognizes a certain oscillation and indefiniteness in the way he spoke about immanence and transcendence, or about the natural and the supernatural, ideas that came to be clarified in their solidarity as well as their distinction only later on in the tradition of Christian philosophy, thanks not only to medieval theologians but also to Blondel himself in the context of modern philosophy.

Blondel ends by bringing the debate about Christian philosophy, first inaugurated by Augustine 1500 years earlier, up to the present. He recognizes that, in talking about Augustine he has suggested things that Augustine had not said, in a philosophical language that is obviously posterior to the Saint. But that is inevitable if one is to give a living account of a thought that was formulated in the past. "The historical truth of a system — of this one no less than any other — is not totally enclosed in the terms in which it is enunciated" (1966a, 188). The spiritual drama that Augustine depicted in his philosophy is one that plays itself out in every consciousness. A true history of this truly philosophical thought cannot be written except by entering oneself "into the metaphysical epic and the spiritual tragedy that leaves out nothing and no one. If we feel this and realize something of it, Augustine keeps an indestructible vitality" (1966a, 188). Augustine continues to speak to unbelievers as well as believers, which is what makes his thought genuinely philosophical, at least in the sense that philosophy has to do with the spiritual life of a human being. "Whoever has the sense and the need for intelligible unity, for an interior life, for a moral and religious faith, for human communion, for spiritual purification and ascension, for union with God, for an explanation satisfying to the spirit and to the heart of the universal drama, will find profit and joy in commerce with Augustine" (1966a, 189).

All this is what Blondel was looking for as a philosopher. As a believer he was also looking for an understanding of how faith and reason, the order of grace and the order of nature, come together in our human historical consciousness. Many, in philosophy and in theology, have thought that the distinction between the two orders meant that the two had to be kept separate, opposed, or juxtaposed and superimposed on one another, always with the fear that one would encroach on the other, as if they excluded one another if one did not take control over the other, either as theology or philosophy. But Blondel found in Augustine a way of unifying the two orders in human experience by going back to the sources of intelligence and charity, to find principles that would explain and vivify the two orders in their historical unison, without blurring or compromising the distinction between them, but rather by bringing the distinction to its perfection in a solution to the problem of human destiny.

This too Blondel was looking for as a believer and as a Catholic philosopher. His search had begun independently of Augustine, but he rejoiced in finding an enunciation of such principles at the head of a tradition of which he felt he was a part, a tradition that was not just Augustinian but more fundamentally Christian, a tradition that constantly implies that "our concrete state is neither pure nature in an intrinsic self-sufficiency nor some naturalizable supernatural, but a *transnatural* state" (1966a, 190), the term Blondel had come to use to characterize the dramatic tension in which we find ourselves as human beings, as a result of our call to a supernatural life in God, a term he had succeeded in having accepted in Lalande's *Vocabulaire technique de la philosophie*. This was a key term for his Catholic philosophy of the concrete order of things. In studying Augustine he had succeeded in bringing its importance back to the forefront of philosophy as an intellectual discipline.

Defense Against the Backlash of Would-Be Separate Philosophy

Blondel's renewed insistence on "Christian philosophy" in its catholicity did not go unnoticed by others who held a less open conception of philosophy. In a note to his *Introduction to the Study of Saint Augustine,* Gilson had begun to suggest that the concept of Christian philosophy needed to be re-examined. Émile Bréhier, another eminent historian of philosophy, followed this with a complete rejection of the very idea of a Christian philosophy in the pages of the *Revue de Métaphysique et de Morale,* only a few months after Blondel's article on the permanence of Augustinian philosophy. Bréhier stood for a complete separation between philosophy and the Christian tradition guided by an authoritative Magisterium. He argued that there had never been anything but a separation between the two, even in the thought of Augustine and Aquinas, as well as in the thought of modern thinkers like Descartes, Malebranche,

Spinoza, and Leibniz. If there appears to be any common ground between Christian teaching on the one hand and philosophy on the other in Hegel, it is only because the Christian dogmas about the Trinity and the historical reality of the God-Man get absorbed into philosophy as symbolic representations of the infinite movement the human spirit finds within itself. What is Christian about this philosophy, according to Bréhier, gives way to nothing more than pure philosophy, untainted by any external authority such as the Church. Even in Blondel's philosophy of action, Bréhier goes on to argue, there is no properly Christian philosophy, that is, a philosophy born of Christianity itself, but rather an apologetic for his faith in Christianity. When Blondel speaks about the unrest and the impossibility of finding satisfaction within the human spirit alone, Bréhier maintains, he is not speaking about anything that has a special connection with Christianity or that could not be found in the ancient wisdom of the Stoics, the Epicureans, or the Skeptics. Hence, starting from a conception of pure philosophy supposedly exemplified in the Hellenic conception of eternal laws and principles governing the universe, Bréhier concludes that "we can no more speak of a Christian philosophy than of a Christian mathematics or a Christian physics" (1931, 133-62).

In effect, Blondel had re-opened the debate about philosophy he had provoked earlier, at the beginning of his career, with his dissertation on *Action* and the *Lettre* of 1896. He could not let Bréhier's negative stance about philosophy in relation to religion go without an answer, at least for the sake of his readers who had come to think with him that there is a Christian philosophy and that it is alive and well in the modern world. The reply appeared within a few months in the pages of the same *Revue*. It was brief but to the point of how philosophy is to be conceived. For Blondel the question was not just a matter of words, as they appear to a historian, or of how philosophy might be used in Christian apologetics. It was a question of the fundamental attitude and the normal function of pure philosophy itself, so highly prized by Bréhier, but perhaps not as fully understood as it should be. Bréhier was forcing Blondel to re-examine his own position in a radical way and not to be satisfied with mere approximations, let alone equivocations, in such a complex and delicate subject matter, but he had to expect the same readiness to examine anew from Bréhier as well, whose idea of Christian philosophy was not exactly what Blondel had in mind.

What Bréhier was demolishing was a certain concordism between Christian ideas and philosophy, a certain conflation of philosophy with ideas from outside philosophy. But this is not what Christian philosophy is about as philosophy. To demolish this kind of concordism, as Blondel himself had done in approaching his own philosophical method in the *Letter on Apologetics*, is not so much to nullify the idea of Christian philosophy, but rather to open the way for reinstating it as part of an authentic and autonomous philosophical tradition in contradistinction from both theology and atheology.

If one followed the course of Bréhier's historical recital point by point, it would be possible to show that even as he describes the different episodes in his story of "Christian philosophy," albeit with some literal exactitude, he often distorts the spirit in which it was lived. Notwithstanding the notional oppositions and ambiguities that he rightly points out, his general interpretation of Augustinianism and Thomism, not to mention other efforts as well, unduly sets aside or ignores what, under less than adequate garments, constituted the life and made possible the continuity of an intellectual tradition. In fact, one could show that the very dogmatic rationalism of this historian becomes irrational, and seems to mutilate both history and philosophical speculation itself, with regard to modern philosophy as well as ancient and medieval. But Blondel cannot pursue any of this in detail in the space allotted to him. He can only try to specify the kind of dogmatic rationalism that leads Bréhier to miss the point so systematically in his reading of what is alleged to be the history of Christian philosophy. He identifies philosophy with its supposedly narrow Hellenic conception, and he identifies this conception with a certain block of propositions that he describes as "an ensemble of doctrines that are systematically tied together and that bear on all realities" (1931a, 601). Is this supposed to be the last word in the history of Hellenism, Blondel asks, or more importantly, is it the best one can come up with in scientific and metaphysical speculation?

As an alternative to such a closed philosophy, Blondel talks about "entertaining the idea of a God transcending the world, conceiving eternity as irreducible to duration, seeing in time less a physical reality than an aspect of becoming and the condition of growth, finding the distinction between the indefinite and the infinite rational, recalling that from the beginning philosophy has been not a *sophia* but a search, a progress, an *inventum semper perfectibile* [according to the word of Aquinas already quoted in connection with Augustinianism], recalling and developing its double function as explanatory and humanizing, broadening and opening up science and intelligence to comprehending the dignity of singular facts and human persons, reconciling in thought as they are in life what abstract understanding thought incompatible, bringing in everywhere a genetic and dynamic viewpoint that makes of the physical and spiritual Universe an immense history and a drama" (1931a, 601-2). To excommunicate all this from the realm of rational discourse in the name of a cult of reason is nothing less than a reverse apologetic, a betrayal of real philosophy about the real world. It may be that Christianity has added its own share to the advent of this humanism where "the problem of universal intelligibility appears compatible and even complementary with subjectivity and the progress of the interior life," but that is no reason for banishing it from philosophy, if it has truly brought something to humanism itself, as Blondel claims it has, thereby elevating philosophical discourse to a higher plane.

Blondel then turns to what Bréhier has done with Blondel's own philosophy of action, by totally ignoring the method used, by metamorphosing its content, and by omitting the qualifications and limits of its conclusions. Here Blondel finds himself in more or less the same situation as the one he had found himself in, when he had to defend his dissertation before a jury of philosophical examiners at the Sorbonne. He has to argue that philosophy cannot be reduced to the canons of a purely objective rationalism of the understanding, such as one finds in mathematics or physics. Philosophy has always had a dual function in the Western tradition, one that is speculative and one that is practical and humanizing, so that, from Socrates on, it has aimed at self-actualization and the ideal of a sage in his relation to the universal order.

In effect, Bréhier has turned Blondel's method upside down, by treating it as an apologetic for the Christian faith. Blondel argues that, from the introduction in his dissertation on, he had proceeded only according to the requirements of a rational science, by an indirect way of negation that examines the different solutions that have been proposed to the problem of action, such as dilettantism, nihilism, scientism, and so on. Nowhere does he introduce or go into any assertion or content of the Catholic religion. The philosophy of the dissertation was not an apologetic, nor was it intended to be such. Its strictly philosophical nature had been recognized by the examiners of 1893, who voted unanimously to give it their philosophical approval, even though they were less than enthusiastic about its conclusions.

The method of Blondel's endeavor was seen to be strictly philosophical more widely later on, after Blondel explained it more carefully in the context of Christian apologetics, in the *Lettre* of 1896, even by colleagues who remained adversaries in philosophy. At no point did Blondel ever think of himself as doing Christian apologetics in the strict sense of the term, even during the years when he was so preoccupied with the question of apologetics. He never wrote the book on apologetics he kept thinking about, but if he had written it, it would have been a philosophical critique of apologetics, not an apologetic as such. What it eventually turned into many years later was a philosophy of the Christian Spirit in the Catholic sense, which was still a critical reflection on the human side of the Christian experience, and not an apologetic, since apologetics is a part of theological discipline, and not philosophy pure and simple, as Blondel understood very well. The reason why Bréhier did not find any "Christian philosophy" in *L'Action* is that he was looking for a kind of concordism that Blondel always found, not only equivocal, but also dangerous and ruinous for both philosophy and religion. Blondel was not one to indulge in such concordism or merely notional conformism. In fact, he criticized such conformism even more severely than Bréhier wherever he found it. But he never ceased advocating what he insisted should be called a Catholic philosophy.

This response of Blondel to Bréhier, however, did not end the controversy about the legitimacy of a properly Christian philosophy; far from it. Gilson, the historian of medieval philosophy, whose view of Christian philosophy as split apart between Augustinianism and Thomism had been challenged by Blondel, not only called for a re-examination of the idea of Christian philosophy, but also offered his own idea of what "Christian philosophy" was supposed to mean, in the *Bulletin de la Société française de Philosophie*, taking issue with Blondel as well as with Bréhier. Against Bréhier, Gilson argued that one could speak of a Christian philosophy in the sense that, at some time in the history of philosophy, philosophy had in fact been strongly influenced by Christianity, without ceasing to be authentically philosophical, as Gilson himself had shown in his own work as a historian of philosophy in the Middle Ages. In this, he appeared to be taking Blondel's side in the controversy with Bréhier, but his way of talking about how philosophy remained authentically philosophical under the Christian influence showed that he was more on the side of Bréhier in his conception of philosophy as a closed system, separate and exclusive of religion, let alone of Christianity.

For Blondel, the question of the relation between philosophy and Christianity is not just a question of historical fact. It is a question of philosophy itself, if one abandons the prejudice that philosophy is only a closed system of concepts, rather than an open system calling for a surpassing of itself in the relation to an infinite, as Blondel had argued in *L'Action* of 1893. This does not mean that the data of revelation as advanced by Christianity can become simple ingredients of philosophical speculation, as they do for example in Hegel, without losing their specificity as Christian and supernatural, but it does mean that philosophy can become systematically open to the reception of such a higher teaching, insofar as it has to do with human destiny as such or the true vocation of humanity in reality. This is why Blondel will insist on using the term *Catholic philosophy* instead of *Christian philosophy,* because many who think of themselves as Christians do not have this precise Catholic sense of the supernatural, which Blondel wants to insist on, paradoxically enough, as Kierkegaard might say, but precisely as a philosopher, which Kierkegaard might be less willing to say. For Blondel the possibility of a Catholic philosophy stems from a recognition that philosophy raises and studies problems that it cannot solve on its own. It consists, not so much in an expression of some religious experience, but rather in a critical analysis of the presence of the supernatural.

Consequently, philosophy should not be conceived as a complete set of doctrines that can be closed in upon itself at whatever stage of development it may have reached, as Bréhier and Gilson seem to presuppose. It should rather be conceived as having to recognize rationally that it is constitutionally incomplete, so to speak, as opening up within itself, and before itself, an abyss, "not only for its ulterior discoveries within its own proper domain, but also for additional enlightenment of which it is not itself and cannot be the real origin" (1931b, 122). This, according to Blondel, is an idea that can be philosophically defined and maintained, which, without coming from a revelation, is also spontaneously and profoundly in accord with a Christianity that affirms its supernatural origins. It is not one that is imposed by any teaching Authority of the Church. It is arrived at by critical reflection upon human experience in action, as he had tried to show in his dissertation on *Action*.

The Case for a Catholic Philosophy

Blondel, however, was not merely responding to Bréhier or Gilson in their own terms. Even before these two began calling into question the idea of a Catholic Philosophy, Blondel had been working on a book that would appear in the *Cahiers de la Nouvelle Journée*, on *The Problem of Catholic Philosophy* in general, while still waiting for the results of Wehrlé's work on the notes for *La Pensée*. Once again, Archambault, ever solicitous to advance the thought of Blondel before the public, had offered the pages of the *Cahiers* for reissuing his earlier articles on method, in which he had first expounded how such a Catholic philosophy could be instituted, but which had become difficult to find since the demise of the *Annales de Philosophie Chrétienne*, especially in the case of the *Lettre* of 1896.

But Blondel could not accept to just have those articles reprinted as they had appeared originally. There had been too much of a negative reaction to them, especially on the part of theologians, and he had second thoughts of his own on some of the things he had said about different methods in apologetics. He felt the need for a certain "retractation" of the entire matter, in the etymological sense of the term, not so much a taking back as taking a second look at some things he had written perhaps too impetuously in the heat of argument. Blondel felt chastened by the reaction of certain theologians who had misunderstood or maligned his earlier work, and he wanted to explain himself and his method a little better, at least for the benefit of those who were open to his broader conception of philosophy as one, integral and universal.

In his prefatory letter to Archambault he insists that his intention had never been to do a work in apologetics, but rather of pure philosophy. His idea was not to propose as a philosopher any doctrine that was even vaguely religious as a result of Christian influences and aspirations. It was a question for him of inquiring "whether a philosophy that is technically developed can in all its spontaneity cohabit with Catholicism, viewed under its properly supernatural aspect and according to the requirements that seem to oppose its *totaliter* to the *totaliter* of reason; further still, it is a question of knowing not only whether we can, but also whether we must accept and justify this symbiosis, whether, in a word, a Catholic Philosophy is not, absolutely and truthfully speaking, Philosophy simply, a philosophy that is one, integral and universal, if not in fact, at least in principle" (1932, 6).

This is the question, which was still so startling to those who held a more limited or immanentist view of philosophy, that Blondel wanted to put once again before philosophers in the early 1930s, as he had done forty years earlier in the 1890s. But it was the question that both Bréhier and Gilson were ignoring, whether by positing a fundamental incompatibility between philosophy, "domain of the rational," and Christianity, supposedly "quite irrational," or by suggesting certain "common elements" that can be found in both Christian revelation and philosophy through a sort of intellectual exchange. Both of these positions, whether of incompatibility or of compatibility, tend to adulterate alternatively both philosophy and Catholicism. To find a true symbiosis between the two spiritual powers in the presence of one another, one must not look for how one might have borrowed from the other, or for mere coincidences in terminology between the two. One must look rather to the heterogeneity that moves each of these two spirits and see how the two must come together in this very heterogeneity, without confusing the two incommensurable orders or reducing them to an easy but ambiguous concordism. This is the way Blondel had seen the problem earlier in 1896, and it was still the way he saw it forty years later. He was still doing battle against mere juxtaposition or separation between the two, as well as against opposition or elimination of one power through superimposition by the other.

Part One of the book on *The Problem of Catholic Philosophy* frames the question precisely as he had framed it in the second part of the *Lettre* in 1896: "in search of the point where the problem of philosophy and the problem of religion run into one another." In fact, for this part of the book, Blondel falls back mainly on the text of 1896, but with some qualifications, explanations, and omissions to forestall any further misunderstandings of the sort he had encountered earlier. He explains the circumstances that had led to this discussion of his philosophical method in the context of religious thinkers who were reading him as anything but a critical philosopher. But he does not repeat his long critique of the six apologetic methods that, in his view, were failing to meet the exigencies of philosophical thought in the question of religion. This was the part of the *Lettre* in which he had stepped on so many toes and that had brought so many recriminations against him. He only lists the six methods he had criticized briefly.

In connection with the fifth method he had criticized, that of his friend Fonsegrive, he explains the idea of different historical states for humanity, in Augustinian fashion, and presents his own understanding of what he referred to as the concrete *transnatural* state in which we find ourselves, thus clarifying the ambiguity or the confusion in a method that had simply identified the laws of Christianity with those of human life as such. With regard to Thomism, the sixth method he had singled out for criticism, which he had characterized as "the ancient doctrinal apologetics," realizing that he had come to a better understanding of the real philosophy of religion in Aquinas, he now admitted that he had changed his mind.

Blondel explains that his earlier criticism had been aimed, not so much at St. Thomas himself, whom he had not read at the time, but rather at certain Scholastic manuals, purportedly Thomistic, which he had in fact read and reviewed while he was a student at Dijon, and which he had found wanting in any sort of critical reflection on human experience. After reading more of Aquinas himself and the more recent studies on his intellectualism and the natural desire to see God, he stood corrected. The method of Thomism did not have to be relegated to the past, as he had intimated, but it had to be made more consistent with modern critical philosophy. This meant that there were still certain assertions in Thomism that cut off access to Christianity, or to the examination of what it meant for minds that had some concern for philosophical exactitude. Blondel lists several of these assertions, but this time he sets them apart between brackets and in smaller print so that they will not be taken as his own ideas, as had been done in the past despite his protestations to the contrary. What he mentions are some of the obstacles he still found among Catholics in his controversies against monophorism and its brand of obscurantist extrinsicism, against the purely affective kind of connaturality allowed by Maritain in matters supernatural, and against the positivistic kind of politics advocated by *Action Française*. These different kinds of "integrism" were not essential to Thomism, but somehow or other Blondel always seemed to find too many Thomists associated with them.

The more important part of the *Lettre,* in which Blondel had taken care to explain positively what was necessary for a proper understanding of the relation between philosophy and Christianity in their very heterogeneity, he reproduces almost word for word, with some omissions, thus showing that he remained faithful to his method as well as to his original way of conceiving the problem of religion, even as he was thinking of the Trilogy he was contemplating.

The same three points have to be made in the movement toward a properly Catholic philosophy. First, the problem of religion or of the transcendent, even in the sense of something supernatural, that is, of something formally inaccessible to philosophy itself, must be raised from within a philosophy that claims for its part total immanence as the condition for considering any idea or any problem as valid or real. This is where the radical heterogeneity of the two orders, natural and supernatural, immanent and transcendent, has to be brought out along with a way of bringing them together existentially that does justice to the exigencies of both orders, one order that is supposedly autonomous and self-sufficient, and another order that, while insisting that it is gratuitous and inaccessible from the standpoint of the other order, nevertheless claims to impose itself as obligatory in the concrete existential order of humanity.

This, for Blondel, is the only way of raising the problem of religion philosophically. One has to understand that religion entails a gift from beyond anything that can be thought or achieved by human being as such, a gift that is not merely coincidental or in juxtaposition to the "gift" of nature, but one that changes the very destiny of every human being into something supernatural, so that, while one cannot achieve this destiny on one's own, one can still damn oneself eternally by refusing the gift when it is offered. It is the Catholic religion that makes this problem so acute for philosophy, and requires a special method for resolving this essential problem of religious philosophy without watering down either the notion of rational philosophy or the notion of supernatural religion.

Blondel's second point, then, was to determine a method for dealing with this problem of supernatural religion philosophically. For Blondel this means having recourse to a *method of immanence* that will take its stance within philosophy, but in order to show that the very *notion of immanence* is not realized in our consciousness except by the effective presence of a notion of the transcendent. This passage in the original *Lettre* had given rise to many misunderstandings as to what Blondel was up to. In a footnote to this reproduction of it in 1932, he tries to clarify what it means by distinguishing three stages in the ascension of philosophy to its religious standpoint. First, one has to answer the objection of those who claim that the idea of transcendence is nothing but an empty pseudo-idea, by showing that it is real in consciousness, that it is even the most positive of all ideas, since "without it, if we were totally immersed in the immanent and the relative, we would have no consciousness of the whole, not even the slightest idea of the relative (1932, 35). This is what Blondel had shown in Part Three, Stage 2 of the 1893 dissertation.

From this come the possibility and the access to a second stage, by showing that our real idea of a transcendent implies the admission and the effective presence of that which is irreducible to anything we can produce or draw out of ourselves *(ex nobis)*, even when we recognize some effect or some clarity from it in ourselves *(in nobis)*. This is what Blondel had argued in Part Four of the dissertation. Finally, this opens up to the possibility of a third, ulterior question: "Can this absolutely inaccessible transcendent, naturally inscrutable and impossible to lay hold of in its depth, reveal and give itself supernaturally, and under what conditions?" (1932, 36). This had been the burden of Part Five of the dissertation. If Blondel had appeared too elliptical in describing his method in the *Lettre*, the way he had carried it out in the dissertation had been much clearer for readers to see. Far from being inconceivable, inadmissible, or even non-philosophical, the problem of the supernatural had been shown to be the very condition for philosophy itself, precisely as it presents itself in its own intransigent independence. It is at the apex of its own development that the problem of religion arises, as it had previously in Hegel and Kierkegaard, though without the Catholic insistence on the supernatural.

The third point of Blondel's method was to show that, in order to pass from a philosophy of the natural to a philosophy of the supernatural, one had to go by way of a *necessary* connection between the two. This, he knew, was the most controversial point for Catholicism, for it seemed to go against the idea of the gratuity of the supernatural, as it relates to the exigencies of any natural order. But Blondel had to insist on this, because it was for him a matter of philosophical science, which proceeds by finding *necessary* connections. He did not proceed, however, from a mere analysis of nature or of human nature as such, to show this *necessary* connection, as if the supernatural were an exigency of nature itself within the capacity of reason itself, but rather from the determinism of human action, which, at the highest point of human freedom, places the human being before a totally transcendent necessary Being, having to say *yes* or *no* to a will that may offer itself as a gift that may be in keeping only with the demands of nature, or in keeping with a wholly supernatural set of demands. It is in the presence of this totally transcendent necessary Being that the ultimate destiny of each individual human being is played out as a matter of choice between *yes* or *no* to the whole of what comes from the will of the necessary Being. The hypothesis of a totally supernatural gift occurs *necessarily* in the dialectic of a will seeking an object that will be the equal of itself and, once the hypothesis occurs, philosophy has the task of reflecting on how such a hypothetical gift could be realized in the human condition of existence, where choices have to be made that have eternal consequences. Philosophy has to show that, while human beings cannot demand or achieve on their own the ideal they may be aspiring to supernaturally, they still have the capacity to say *no* to any gift from God, natural or supernatural, and so turn away from their ultimate destiny as human beings.

In the book that now reproduces pages written thirty-six years earlier, Blondel expresses a certain reserve on the way the problem was initially presented for minds that were not ready for it. Too many side issues had been brought up, having to do with apologetics, and not with philosophy pure and simple. Even then, however, the distinction had been made between the two, apologetics and philosophy, in terms of the nature of the questions raised and of the bearing of conclusions to be drawn. For Blondel only philosophy can "set aside [the] prejudicial objections [of immanentist philosophy], bring to full light the exigencies and the insufficiencies of nature, and consequently bring precision *a contrario* to the notion of the supernatural" (1932, 39).

In the book of 1932, Blondel does not reproduce much of the long third part of the *Lettre,* barely two or three paragraphs, in which he had tried to envision a reciprocal renewal of perspectives for both philosophy and religion, by pushing the development of modern philosophy to the fullness of its consequences. He goes on rather to discuss how the letter was received, which did anything but follow the scenario of mutual enrichment between philosophy and religion he would have liked to see from the introduction of his method for bringing the two together, in a search for truth that took nothing away from the essential differences between the two and the different positions one could adopt with regard to religion in philosophy, his main point being that these were matters for philosophical discussion as well as religious belief.

The reaction to the *Lettre* on the side of philosophy had been more favorable than he had dared to hope for. Other philosophers came to see in him a genuine philosopher in his argument about religion as a philosophical subject, even though most did not agree with the conclusions he was coming to. Blondel reminds the reader that he was accepted, not only as a professor of philosophy in a system that prided itself in doing the purest of philosophy, but also as a peer in journals and in professional associations of philosophy. The only thing Blondel had to regret on that side of the question was that some came to take him as a pure immanentist in his rationality, which of course was the opposite of what he intended rationally, while others continued to see him as a simple apologist of supernaturalism or transcendentism. The two misconceptions should have canceled one another out, but they persisted in spite of Blondel's arguments against a rationalism that was exclusive of anything transcendent and for a humanism that was receptive of a gift that could only come from above. The misconception he regretted more was the one that attributed to him the mentality of an apologist, because that detracted from any intrinsic examination of analyses that he thought were properly rational. He did recognize, however, that his long involvement with theologians and methods in apologetics during the modernist crisis did little to clarify his proper standing as a philosopher, rather than as an apologist.

It was the reaction on the side of religion that had shocked Blondel and had taken him by surprise. Instead of taking his intentions and his faith at face value, and then going on to examine the problem, the method, and the solution he was proposing, many religious writers turned against him and accused him of betraying the cause of religion, of becoming a dupe or an accomplice of "the enemy." We have seen to what extremes of denunciation and obfuscation this led, and how he suffered from it as from a sword of Damocles hanging over his head, when he was trying to be nothing else than a faithful son of the Church. Here, in 1932, he recalls how, following the advice of certain proper authorities, he refrained from entering personally into the controversies for fourteen years, even though he did throw in a word here and there under pseudonyms or under the name of friends like Monsignor Mallet. Now, in retrospect, he still wants to point out possible deviations against which he wants to defend himself.

First he points out that the words *apologetics* or *method of immanence* appear nowhere in *l'Action*, which had been for him the principal focus of attention as he was writing the *Lettre* of 1896. Where others saw an apologetic, Blondel had seen only a method in philosophy, without any pretension of saying anything specifically Christian concerning the supernatural or the transcendent in human action. It will be remembered that where Blondel had written the name of Christ in early versions of *l'Action,* he scratched it out in later versions, to remain only with the philosophically definable term of *mediator* as part of what is *necessary* for connecting the divine and the human in action. He had never had the intention of giving a lesson, *faire la leçon,* to theologians or to the Magisterium of the Church. Moreover, he points out that his criticism of the classical methods of apologetics, which remain for him a legitimate form of Church teaching, had never been an absolute rejection. It had been rather a rejection of philosophical shortcomings in certain manuals that, in fact, could be made up for by other works like those of Aquinas himself or Dechamps. Unfortunately, as Blondel now recognizes, in speaking of "the traditional apologetic" or of the "fundamental doctrine of the ordinary teaching" in his blanket condemnation, he had gone beyond the legitimate point he was making as a philosopher, and had to accept some responsibility for at least some of the complaints brought against him.

Blondel protests that he had never intended to shift the debate from philosophy into apologetics or even theology. He only wanted to get beyond the idea of a philosophy separated from religion, or of a mere juxtaposition between the two, without any living connection, where a reciprocal relation could be examined without any infringement of the one on the other in their respective autonomy. The only problem is that he had not seen clearly what he was letting himself in for in tackling this problem. "I did not suspect then, I only began to glimpse much later the ways required for raising a problem in all its amplitude and for solving it with true precision, for which I now hope, in the Trilogy I am preparing, to bring out the data and the conditions" (1932, 49). Blondel now realizes that the full retractation, in its literal sense of treating over again, of the problem of Catholic Philosophy raised in the original work on *Action* and the *Lettre* of 1896 can only be given in the work that still lies before him. To get to that, however, one has to recognize the tremendous difference between the world as conceived in medieval philosophy and the world as conceived in post-Cartesian philosophy. For Blondel conceived of his task as starting from modern philosophy, and its presuppositions, and not from medieval or ancient philosophy, no matter how modern philosophy appears to be the enemy of religion. His position was analogous to that of the early Church Fathers, who had to start their philosophizing in the context of a pagan world, as St. Thomas had noted in praising the method of the ancient teachers, who, having lived among non-believers and pagans, had started from their erroneous and incomplete standpoint in order to draw the truth out of their error and their deficiency.

Blondel, however, did not think he could, as a philosopher, pass over from philosophy into theology or into any sort of religious teaching, especially if it entailed any sort of supernatural dimension. This is something he was adamant about, even though there were others who were inclined to fudge ideas on both sides of the problem in order to bring them together as one discipline. Blondel was more concerned with working out ideas philosophically and technically, as he liked to put it, to satisfy the strictest exigencies of the rationalists, even if this seemed too tedious for the more religious-minded. He had to show that he understood rationalism, so to speak, in order to tap its internal surge toward transcendence. On the other hand, he did not think it wise to leap into easy accommodations or premature applications of religious ideas, where in fact a more critical reprise had become necessary. No doubt, some crossover, some mutual adaptation of ideas might be beneficial for both philosophy and religion, but not if it became a *hybridation* of perspectives or a superficial and falsifying *concordism* between the two. For him, what had to be marked first was the radical heterogeneity of the philosophical and the theological, by bringing out the apparent, albeit provisional, conflict between nature and supernature and then by showing how a pacifying light and a vivifying union can emerge through this confrontation. The rational passage from philosophy to religion could not come as easily as some religious thinkers might think, but for Blondel this was in keeping with the exigencies of Catholic religion as well as of the most rational of philosophies. Contrary to all modernist tendencies, one had to understand first and foremost how the supernatural was literally unnaturalizable and inconfusible, even if it entered the historical movement of humanity.

In his article on the so-called "method of immanence" for the *Dictionnaire Apologétique,* Valensin had spoken of Blondel's philosophy as "an apologetic of the threshold." Now the fear and danger that Blondel had to guard against, as a philosopher, was that the momentum of his ascent to that threshold did not carry him over that threshold into the domain of theology. But he also thought that theology had to guard against the opposite fear and danger, namely that of exporting into philosophy supernatural truths as if, in their descent, they became part of or limited themselves to the requirements of philosophy. "What has to be underlined more than ever in response to our intentions and the conclusions of our philosophical effort is what there is that is superhuman, unattainable, even mortifying as well as paradoxically vivifying in the given exigencies of Revelation, in the inalienably Christian virtues, in the passive purifications of the transforming union, of which grace, even in its most embryonic form, is the seed" (1932, 52). This is what the *Lettre* of 1896 had tried to do in examining fragmentary methods, in order to block the way of any illusory concordism and to prevent any watering down of a religious sense that implies a premonition of the inaccessible divine mystery, accompanied nevertheless with a desire for some alliance with this reality beyond our grasp. The last thing that a philosophy of the supernatural would want to do would be to anthropomorphize the higher gift of divine Charity, because that would be to reduce it to the first gift of a nature that is reasonable and free in its human initiative, without any understanding of how God destines us to an infinitely higher gift — "a paradoxical gift of something metaphysically *incommunicable,* of something that, in order to become a reality of life and love, presupposes in effect a transformation, a *denuo nasci,* hence a sort of death to ourselves to make room in our human being for the spirit and the will of God" (1932, 53).

Philosophical Reassurance from the Side of Religion

As sure as he was of his position as a philosopher, Blondel also needed some reassurance that he was on the right track from the religious standpoint. That is why as a young man he had shown his work to a Dominican friend of his in Aix-en-Provence, Father Reginald Beaudoin, O.P., before any of it was published. While recognizing that some theologians might find some difficulty in understanding it for what it said, Beaudoin, a professor of theology who was later to become Socius to the General of the Dominicans in Rome, had made a point of approving Blondel's approach to the supernatural through philosophy and his way of characterizing the kind of transformation it required of human nature. Not all Dominicans had been opposed to Blondel's efforts as a Catholic philosopher, especially not this one, who had perhaps had something to do with keeping his fellow Dominicans from going too far in their attacks on Blondel. But as a religious thinker Blondel had also found some reassurance in the work of another religious authority, Cardinal Dechamps, Archbishop of Malines in Belgium, whose views had been decisive in the First Vatican Council's pronouncements on Faith and Reason, and approved by the ultraconservative Pope Pius IX.

What Blondel found in Dechamps that was important for him was the indication of a philosophical method that needed to be explicated and justified in more technical terms, but that could be taken up in a modern spirit, and completed. This is why he devotes almost a third of this book on the problem of Catholic philosophy to a description of this "method of Providence," as Dechamps called it. It was a way of showing how the problem of Catholic philosophy had been viewed by a theologian who was also a philosopher, albeit not as rigorous as Blondel wanted to be, as well as a way of reassuring hesitant theologians that his philosophical efforts were not as unorthodox as they might appear to be.

The first part of this book on the Problem of Catholic Philosophy was mainly a re-edition of certain parts of the *Lettre* of 1896, where he had first explained his method for such a philosophy, with some commentary appropriate for the context of the renewed controversy. The second part was a re-edition of another earlier study by his friend, Monsignor Mallet, on Dechamps's Method of Providence, which Blondel thought might clarify how his own method could relate to a more theological method of apologetics capable of using a philosophical method without absorbing it into theology. In devoting so much time to a method of apologetics Blondel may have been playing into the hands of Bréhier once again, who had accused him of being only an apologete for Christian religion and not a philosopher, something Blondel wanted to defend himself against, but Blondel does not say at any point that his method was the same as that of Dechamps. In fact, he explicitly acknowledges that Dechamps's method left much to be desired from the standpoint of philosophical explication. What was important for Blondel was to show how a properly philosophical method could be distinguished from a theological method of apologetics without setting up a wall of separation between the two.

What Dechamps had insisted on in his "demonstration of the faith," as Mallet brings out, was the necessity of appealing to two "facts," the external fact of the history and teaching of the Church and the internal fact of consciousness or conscience. For Dechamps these were "two facts to be verified, one within yourself, the other outside yourself; these facts reach out to embrace one another, and the witness for both of them is yourself" (1932, 62). For Dechamps, as Mallet notes approvingly, this method was "essentially philosophical," grounded in a rational process that is common to both the simple, for whom it is sufficient, and to the learned, for whom it is necessary. What made it especially interesting to Blondel as a philosopher was that "in the facts which are proposed or even imposed from the outside it seeks a light for reason, a nourishment for the will; hence it finds therein an intrinsic sense and not just a content with a simple *juxtaposition* of heterogeneous data; it brings out the correspondence that makes them *assimilable* and even *obligatory* for us" (1932, 62). It considers supernatural facts as facts within man as well as without, and it examines them first as "psychological and metaphysical truths." It observes the fact before inquiring into its nature. Moreover, it makes these facts enter into the determinism of our life as it is *necessarily*, in virtue of the positive determination that results from the free and gratuitous design of God. It inserts itself into the heart of a philosophy that would falsely claim self-sufficiency and freedom to get along without Revelation, by remaining faithful to itself alone, this being "the psychological thesis of the permanent, subsistent, intrinsic insufficiency of reason, even the most advanced, to resolve the religious question as it arises inevitably from the state of humanity" (1932, 62-63).

All this brought Dechamps's method in line with what Blondel had proposed as the philosophical exigencies, not only for a proper philosophy of religion, but also for a properly Catholic philosophy. It took the internal fact as a fact of consciousness and of conscience, not as a certain content to be analyzed, but rather as a real opening within us that does not allow us to remain closed up within our nature without giving the lie to the intimate experience of our soul, so that wanting to stop at a separate philosophy and at a natural religion would be to succumb to a "positive" temptation. Commenting on Dechamps's idea of a fact of consciousness taken as an opening or an insufficiency, or as a need that should be felt by all of humanity, Blondel adds that "to justify the use he makes of this observation, an immense and methodical investigation is required," of the kind Blondel has in mind in the three books he is projecting on Thought, Being, and Action (1932, 65, note). A mere statement of the fact is not enough. A more critical examination of the human condition is also required. In the projected Trilogy, Blondel was not setting aside his original intent of developing a philosophy of the supernatural. He was only expanding it to include a greater complexity in this fact of an opening at the heart of human thought and being as well as of action.

The interior fact, however, is not the only fact to be considered in an apologetic such as Dechamps has in mind. There is also the exterior fact that reason itself calls for, a religious authority that is conceived as somehow necessary. This is where the proper name of Catholic tradition comes into view for the apologist, but this authority is not always known under its true form. According to Dechamps the exterior fact of a religious authority is taken to be real and actual by the man of good faith who, in his ignorance, imagines that he belongs to a religion for all men, the religion of his fathers, a divinely instituted religion. This exterior fact should not be examined independently of the interior fact of a rational opening, but rather in the light of it. It is a fact that is of interest to us interiorly as human beings. Nor is it enough to study it historically or objectively, in order to discern the supernatural in it. It must be discovered in its present actuality as supernatural. Otherwise we would not be able to discover it in the past as such. This is why Dechamps insisted on the present actuality of the Catholic Tradition as the key to a successful apologetic for faith in the supernatural, much as Blondel himself had insisted, against Loisy and proponents of a purely "historical method" in *History and Dogma* on the living Tradition of the Church as the key to a true interpretation of the historical facts in which Christianity has its origin and its development.

In the end, of course, these two facts, the interior and the exterior, have to be brought together. This is where Dechamps speaks of a mutual penetration by a sort of *circumincession,* a term Blondel was especially fond of. One can consider the relation between these two orders of fact objectively and intellectually, but that is to view them only in the abstract. Concretely they flow into one another in our consciousness as our conscience and our reason assimilate this twofold and yet single fact. The interior fact alone cannot reveal to consciousness its true origin, nor reveal to analytical reason the supernatural end toward which it tends obscurely because it proceeds from this fact secretly. The exterior fact, for its part, in spite of the motives of credibility that render it certain, cannot by itself generate a beginning of faith. Even if they were clearly in the presence of one another, the two facts cannot combine into one by themselves, no matter how they might seem to fit one another. The flow of the two orders into one another does not take place by a mere observation of the facts, or by the consciousness of needs and satisfactions that can be found in Christian truths and practices through the force of intellect and science. The circumincession takes place vitally in action and in concrete thinking that takes place beyond the realm of clear and distinct ideas, as reasonable as it might appear to be, without being able to be reasoned out absolutely as integrally rational.

In other words, the real relation between the two orders of fact cannot be directly perceived or made scientifically intelligible. To enter into it really, more is needed, a movement of grace, but also an intelligent effort of will, whence the role of freedom and merit in Faith. A moral preparation is necessary as well as an intellectual preparation, which is not prior or extrinsic, but rather intrinsic to the practical validity of the demonstration. There is no purely natural certitude in the motive of faith and, even if there is no perception of the supernatural as supernatural, the real presence of the supernatural can make itself felt. There are psychological facts that can express it for a consciousness in search of it, and help it on the way of discovery, and that can also mysteriously confirm the consciousness that has found it. The circumincession takes place in an act of faith that is at once human and divine.

One final point to be made about this circumincession is that it is not an act of individuals taken in isolation from one another. In the mystery there is light to be found, just as in the rational there is always something mysterious that remains. The Christian tradition has always maintained this twofold openness of reason and mystery to one another. The facts it insists on are not only psychological and rational, but also social. Even the relation between civil society and religious society should not be construed as one of separation or mere juxtaposition. Just as reason is not free to get along without Revelation, if it is to be faithful to itself, or the will is not free to get along without grace, so also civil society is not free to get along without religious society. The two must somehow come together in history without diminution of autonomy on either side. For, as Dechamps says, "Christianity is not, like other religions, something set apart and outside the history of the world. No, Christianity affirms that it is itself the history of humanity" (1932, 73).

All this is said in the context of an apologetic by Dechamps, but it is easy to see why it was of interest to Blondel as a philosopher of the concrete movement of spirit in history. Dechamps spoke of his method as the method of Providence, thus emphasizing that it tried to follow the movement of how God himself enters into history. It was a method adapted to the simple as well as to the learned. It was more concrete than the method of the schools, which Dechamps maintained is not the one more ordinarily taken by divine Wisdom or by the exigencies of reason. What Dechamps was doing, according to Mallet, was introducing into the *theory* of apologetics what hitherto had been only in the *practice* of the Church, where the natural and the supernatural come together without confusion but with a practical efficacy that a purely abstract science of separate spheres cannot produce. Dechamps's method could explain how faith can always be reasonable, even before or during the critical examination of its own foundations, by taking reason as fundamentally open to Revelation or to enlightenment from God. It was this fuller scope of reason in the face of a supernatural intervention on the part of God that Blondel was interested in developing as a philosopher, prior to any apologetic intent on the part of theology or of the Church. If Blondel thought he had a mission as a Catholic in the intellectual community, it was to develop the philosophical side of this movement toward transcendence in its most critical fashion.

In a note to Mallet's text on Dechamps (1932, 79-80), Blondel adverts to the fact that Dechamps speaks of *apologetics* in a way that is not consonant with his own insistence on a philosophy of religion, which remains for him essentially a philosophy rather than an apologetic. He notes that the use of this term, apologetics, was in keeping with Dechamps's viewpoint as a theologian and as an apostle. But Blondel adds that this did not keep Dechamps from making the same kind of distinction that Blondel wanted to make. For Dechamps, there was a *grande apologétique* that dominates and opens the way to arguments for credibility and for partial apologetics. This greater apologetics, according to Blondel, constitutes, in a rational order, a coherent ensemble of intellectual, moral, and metaphysical dispositions whose normal and autonomous character does not prevent this veritable and true philosophy, the only one that is completely true, from being in harmony with human destiny, with the Catholic teachings, and with the intimate stimulations and the effective operations of grace. In other words, in speaking of his "greater apologetic," Dechamps was thinking of it in the higher sense of a Christian philosophy, or a religious demonstration that was more like what Blondel had in mind than the more partial apologetics one finds in theology.

Mallet goes on to discuss the various objections and difficulties that had been brought against Dechamps and his method, along with the "victorious responses" Dechamps had countered with. He also adds a chapter on Dechamps's counteroffensive with regard to his detractors. But the discussion has to do mostly with theological points. In his notes on this discussion Blondel points out how, in his search for an apologetic that is complete and efficacious, Dechamps tends to show constantly that apologetics presupposes a religious philosophy whose fundamental tenor is at once psychological, moral, and rational. "It is this philosophical aspect that should especially be highlighted in order to discern and justify the original meaning of this 'method of Providence' that he also names 'the greater apologetic' or the apologetic that corresponds to 'the most developed philosophy' that can be conceived" (1932, 90).

In the end, however, Blondel concurs with Mallet's judgment that, however philosophical Dechamps wanted his method to be, it left much to be desired from an analytical and technical standpoint. Dechamps was not consistent and rigorous enough in his way of proceeding in problems of human destiny, where a certain affirmation of necessity or principle was called for. He was not able to penetrate to the most secret sources of thought and action, where ideas are considered not only as the expression of a reality other than the subject and taken as the principles of deliberate decision, but also are themselves the fruit of action, as Dechamps put it, and the expression of natural aspirations, of attitudes adopted, of graces received. What was needed, according to Mallet, was a philosophy that, not content with a science of good faith and an analysis of the "interior fact," as if it were entirely elicited from nature, could also make room in this interior fact for a gift that is already supernatural, a principle of restlessness and of religious expectation (1932, 111).

There is no doubt that Mallet had been influenced by Blondel in originally coming to this assessment of Dechamps. In repeating the assessment, Blondel was reinforcing it. For him Dechamps had had an intimation (but only an intimation) of the ideal and total itinerary of philosophy, in keeping with its essential role or "in keeping spontaneously and discretely with the demands, not of Christianity taken in some indeterminate sense, but with the precise and supernatural character under which Catholicism presents it imperiously" (1932, 113-14). In this, Blondel saw a precious and double service that the Cardinal had given him in his mission: that of setting things right with theology by placing us on the road that leads us to and obliges us to set things right with philosophy. What fooled a lot of people was his use of the term *apologetic* for a method that had to be strictly philosophy. What Blondel came to realize, after Dechamps, was the necessity of proceeding as rationally as possible in the development of the Catholic philosophy that was called for in terms that could be understood and verified by any rational being.

Confronting the Refusal of Any Properly Christian Philosophy

In Part Three of *Le problème de la philosophie catholique*, after mainly repeating certain passages from the *Lettre* of 1896 in Part One and reproducing Mallet's study of Dechamps in Part Two, Blondel finally comes to the actual state of the problem, after Bréhier's denunciation of the very idea of a Christian philosophy, and to what he refers to as the prerequisite conditions for a solution to the problem. Before confronting the more radical refusal of Bréhier regarding any philosophy claiming to be Christian, however, Blondel addresses what appears to be the more moderate position of Gilson as a historian of philosophy who sought to bring out a certain historical interlocking of philosophy and Christianity, at least during the Middle Ages, in response to Bréhier. Gilson, in fact, along with other historians and philosophers, agreed that the expression *Chris-*

tian philosophy did entail a hybridation that could not be justified speculatively. In fact, he went so far as to say that it was not just the exclusive rationalists who reject this rapprochement, but also certain "recent interpreters of Saint Thomas [including himself, for whom] the expression *Christian philosophy* makes no sense and the notion to which it supposedly corresponds is impossible" (1932, 129). The assertion of Gilson may seem surprising to those familiar with the English title given Gilson's book on St. Thomas, *The Christian Philosophy of St. Thomas,* but in 1931 Gilson appears to have been much clearer and more one-sided about where he stood with regard to the question of philosophy, at least independently of his thinking as a historian of philosophy.

Blondel takes him at his word as a philosopher when Gilson maintains absolutely "the formal distinction between the philosophical order and the Christian order" as between two solid blocks with fixed and impenetrable borders. The surprising thing for Blondel was that in the domain of history as such, Gilson thought that the expression *Christian philosophy* as he had encountered it in the past could still make some sense, more than in the present, where Bréhier was arguing that it had never made sense. But Blondel wants to know what sense it would make, if one takes for granted Bréhier's closed conception of philosophy. Gilson makes the point that the expression was associated especially with the thought of Augustine, but he does not acknowledge that the thought of Augustine was properly philosophical, contrary to what Blondel had tried to show in his article on Augustine for the *Revue de Métaphysique.* In this, Blondel says, Gilson remains faithful to his cult of human concepts to the point of ignoring their shortcoming, both congenital and acquired. Borrowing a phrase from Augustine, Blondel writes, "the internal illumination that is true is the one that, inseparable from intellectual humility, frees rational speculation from an anthropomorphism that is both anti-rational and anti-Christian" (1932, 130). This was an incontestably philosophical stance that Gilson could not recognize in Augustine's thought, a stance that made it characteristically Christian as well as philosophical, and that Gilson also tended to overlook in other medieval authors whom he could not take seriously as *philosophers,* St. Thomas not included. Blondel does not try to redo the history of medieval philosophy in opposition to Gilson, but he does point to certain factors that have been brought out by others, that show more of a kinship between the "Augustinians" and the "Aristotelians" of the thirteenth century, a Christian-philosophical kinship, rather than the kind of opposition modern rationalist philosophers, including Gilson, like to bring out in speaking of the thought of medieval theologians. On one side the original unity and the animating inspiration of Augustinianism is stripped of its "Catholically philosophical spirit," and on the other, Thomism is mutilated in its historical equilibrium and in its Christian soul by making of it a "separated philosophy, an immobilized rationalism."

Gilson appears to be so far encrusted in his "formal distinction between the philosophical order and the religious order, let alone the Christian order, that, in the name of these hypostatized concepts, he is ultimately forced to exclude even the concept of natural religion and to admit as philosophical only irreligion, or if one prefers, areligion" (1932, 132). Even his attempt to preserve some historical meaning for the notion of Christian religion runs into the difficulty of the kind of concordism and compromise that Bréhier is attacking as a phony kind of philosophy, or as watered-down theology. Blondel has two objections to what Gilson is trying to do. First, how can philosophy, which by hypothesis is presented as completely rational and conceptual, owe anything of what constitutes it to something that, also by hypothesis, is given as irrational and non-conceptual? If the two are declared heterogeneous to one another in their origin, their method, and their content, must we not exclude rigorously any reflected connection between religious dogmatics and rational speculation? Second, and more fundamentally, in this show of doctrinal historicism, does not the historian come up against a dilemma that undermines what he wants to conserve and safeguard? For what is Christianity supposed to bring to philosophy, what can its irrational and aconceptual contribution be to "philosophical systems that are purely rational in their principles and their method," when we are told that the existence of these ideas cannot be explained without the existence of the Christian religion?

If we accept this way of patching philosophy and the Christian religion together, Blondel argues, we are left with either one of two positions, neither of which is acceptable to both philosophy and Catholic thinking. On the one hand, we have to suppose that the adventitious data of the Gospel are assimilated, as is being suggested, into an intellectual civilization and into the mental organism of humanity, which transubstantiates the data into its own human thoughts, thus betraying the supernatural origin that Christianity claims for itself. Everything is reduced to a natural origin, an immanent drive, a divinatory anticipation of what the human spirit can achieve on its own. These supposedly Christian ideas, circulating among consciences and philosophical systems, become humanized, naturalized, dismantled into something purely immanent. Such a "Christian philosophy," according to Blondel, dechristianizes Christianity in two ways, in its origin, and in its newly conceived finality.

On the other hand, if we try to maintain the Christian data under the form of their supernatural exigency, that is, under their authentically Catholic form, then philosophy is forced to suffer an intrusion that is absolutely unjustifiable from the standpoint of a philosophy that is supposedly self-sufficient, as both Gilson and Bréhier will have it. In this instance the Christian idea can never appear except as an intrusion into philosophy that poisons it from the inside, for, as Blondel insists, even identical assertions that could be made in the name of reason or of science or of history on the one hand, and in the name of faith or according to their supernatural value on the other, would have to be understood as spiritually different.

What Blondel concludes from this rejection of the Gilsonian compromise is, not that the two sets of ideas cannot be brought together in any way, but rather that they cannot be melded into one in the way that has been proposed. The problem of the relation between philosophy and Christianity, or between the natural and the supernatural, in human existence cannot be resolved in historical terms alone, or in terms of mere facts of consciousness, or of acquisitions for a civilization, or by way of a mere absorption of ideas. A mere sorting out of concepts will not do. It will either cause oppositions or else it will make Christianity an unbearable burden for reason. "If supernatural revelation is 'generative of reason' as we are led to hope for, then we must first be shown how reason, far from stabilizing everything into closed concepts, discovers within itself needs that nature cannot satisfy, something unfinished, ever unfinishable naturally and yet uncoercibly avid of fulfillment" (1932, 135).

Having thus restated his fundamental position about having to show a necessary connection between philosophy and the Catholic understanding of the supernatural for his fellow Catholic, Gilson, Blondel then goes on to deal with the more radical objection of Bréhier to the very idea of a Christian philosophy. There he concurs in Bréhier's rejection of the kind of "Christian philosophy" that Blondel calls *concordism*. In asserting the necessity of Catholic philosophy, Blondel is not looking for any sort of concordism between philosophy and Christian ideas, especially not the idea of the supernatural. In this respect Blondel could not but agree with Bréhier against Gilson. But what he could not agree with was Bréhier's way of denaturing the way of thinking that had brought philosophy and Christian faith together in a living symbiosis. Blondel goes to some length to show how Bréhier had missed the point of this coming together, starting from the New Testament on down to St. Justin the Philosopher, Clement of Alexandria, Tertullian, St. Augustine, and St. Thomas Aquinas. When he comes to Schelling and Hegel, whom Bréhier had indicted along with the more traditional Catholic philosophy, Blondel concedes that this German idealist departure from the tradition is not what he had in mind for an authentic Catholic philosophy. In his view these later philosophers, in using Christian ideas, had betrayed in part, but in an essential way, the Christian spirit they were invoking by rationalizing it and hence immanentizing it, without regard for the heterogeneity between the rational sense and the Christian sense of assertions that were verbally similar. From this point of view, Blondel writes, Bréhier's criticism of Schelling and Hegel is justified and beneficiary. But does this not mean that Bréhier has stopped mutilating the ideas he is playing with, whether they be those of philosophy or those of the Christian spirit? The fact that the Christian spirit has transfigured the cosmological speculation of the ancients, without suppressing it, by bringing it to a theandric humanism, does not mean that speculation has been vitiated, or that philosophy must fall back on a divinized naturalism and logicism falsely attributed to Hellenism by a mutilated modern conception of philosophy.

Blondel is now more prepared to recognize a positive orientation in Greek philosophy toward the totally transcendent and supernatural than he had admitted in his earlier criticism of the medieval synthesis between Aristotelian philosophy and Christian theology in the *Lettre* of 1896, thanks to his clearer understanding of how nature has to relate to the supernatural. But he does not develop this point here. He goes on rather to defend his philosophical method in *L'Action*, as showing the necessity of this relation of the natural to the supernatural in a way that is indirect, negative, but exhaustive, in dealing critically with all solutions to the problem of action that stopped short of the hypothesis of the supernatural. He points out that he had never called that philosophy Catholic in the sense that would have brought him over the threshold into the temple. From the speculative and rational standpoint he had taken, he had never made any assertion that he could have made only as a believer concerning the reality of the supernatural. In other words, he had never crossed over into the murky terrain of apologetics, into which Bréhier wanted to relegate him. The reason why Bréhier thought he had, is that Bréhier thinks "that philosophy begins and ends with concepts, that it shuts itself in this representational and surreal domain, that consequently its encounter with religion comes as a clash of rational dogmas with the irrational, that there is an apparent compatibility only through an illusory concordism of notions defined in an absolute truth, incompressible and full on both sides, as if we were trying to push a compact content into an already full receptacle, whence the idea of a crushing, of a repression, of an attempt on 'the rights of reason,' unless we canonize a passivity that is docile to such an intrusion" (1932, 153).

This is where Blondel found a denaturation of both philosophy and the Christian contribution. The spirit of faith is not in the business of hurling concepts against concepts materially. On the contrary, it seeks a cooperation where each of the spiritual powers has its proper and distinct part to play in a compenetration that allows each to complete itself without interference from the other in its spontaneous initiative. In opposition to Bréhier's view of the history of the philosophy of religion, Blondel cites the view of his friend Delbos, no less of an authority in the history of philosophy than Bréhier, assessing the philosophy of *Action*: "The philosophy of religion has almost always taken an artificial form, seeking constantly to live by borrowings, by *utilizations*, which explains why its own vitality has been so feeble and inconsequential. Whether it is ordinary spiritualism, or idealism, or criticism, or, as has happened strangely, positivism, or any other *existing* doctrine that supposedly supplies faith seeking understanding its rational anchors, it always appears that the soul of Religion puts on a foreign body. It was on the contrary the original thought of the book on *Action* to attempt to dominate the order of external and conventional relations through which Philosophy and Religion had been hitherto brought together in order to establish a philosophy that was religious, not by accident, but by nature, without nevertheless being so by prejudice. And this intention alone was enough to inspire much more confidence than the search for new compromises between reason and faith. . . . It comports both a method and a doctrine wrapped into one" (1932, 153-54). Moreover, Delbos added, much to Blondel's satisfaction, this philosophy is not only religious in its essence, but Catholic, in that it is free, full, and integral, embracing the full scope of the most intellectual speculation as well as of reality in the concrete. To further reinforce his philosophical credentials, Blondel cites the judgment of those who had to be convinced of the strictly philosophical character of his dissertation, much against the grain of their own preference for keeping philosophy separate from religion, especially Catholicism.

In the end, however, after opening the way for a Catholic philosophy, against the narrow rationalism of modern philosophers like Bréhier and Gilson, Blondel recognizes that the epithet or the enterprise can easily be misunderstood and give rise to unwarranted claims that would militate against a proper access to the Christian spirit. He lays out three successive stages that philosophy must cross in order to avoid these pitfalls. First, it must lay out the essential metaphysical conditions under which a question of the supernatural, such as the one proposed under Catholicism, can be raised. This is to bring philosophy to the fullness of what it has to discuss concerning man's vocation in his historical actuality. Second, if the hypothesis of the Supernatural understood as something rational is taken to be realized in fact, philosophy has to come to terms with such a concrete order in which a unique and precise solution is imposed on human destiny. Even if it does not know this order to be the fact, since it is gratuitous from the standpoint of nature and reason alone, it must examine this sort of exigency that gives itself as "catholic," that is, as universal *de jure*, but without secularizing it or immanentizing it. This is where it must get into what are called "preambles of faith" in theology. Third, starting from the real state of humanity, philosophy can and should take facts into account that, as different as they are in their origin and their nature, nevertheless shape within us a life that is one, a unique destiny, with only one precise solution. This is where philosophy would get into the study of the repercussions within natural human being of the diverse states — transnatural, supernatural, or rebellious — that bring up for consciousness and the will data or reactions that differ from those a pure state of nature would present. It is what Blondel was intending to propose in his book *Philosophy and the Christian Spirit*, which was to be for him a philosophical science of human being in the concrete, but not as purely natural or separated from God. Blondel argues that all this is in keeping with an integral conception of philosophy that does not cut itself off from human existence, in the concrete realm of choices to be made. He is also happy to be able to add that all this is in keeping with the teachings of the First Vatican Council on faith and reason, understood in the light of Dechamps's Method of Providence for human beings in history.

Overcoming the Catholic Resistance to the Idea of Catholic Philosophy

Blondel was not happy with the book on *The Problem of Catholic Philosophy* he sent to the publisher in 1932. He had had to put it together under very difficult circumstances. Unable to review for himself the arguments he had made concerning the method to be used in the philosophy of religion in the *Lettre* of 1896 or the articles Mallet had written on the views of Dechamps concerning the Method of Providence, or on the Problem of Catholic Philosophy as seen by a philosopher-theologian, he had been able only to pick and choose the texts he wanted to use, without being able to rewrite much, and with only the barest commentary to connect them to the problem now under discussion, always with the help of a secretary who had to do the sorting out for him, without entirely understanding all that she was dealing with and to whom he had to dictate whatever else would go into the book. The older texts still had the ring of the earlier debates about apologetics and did not explain just how Blondel was trying to justify the idea of Catholic philosophy precisely as philosophy. In Part Three he had tried to focus more directly on the actual status of the question, in order to explain in what sense there has been a properly Christian philosophy in the past starting with Justin and Augustine, notwithstanding Bréhier's failure to recognize it as such, and why Bréhier and others, like Gilson, had failed to recognize it as such by reason of their rationalist presuppositions about the nature of philosophy. But the argument remained less than well knit. He fell short in his attempt to state how a properly Catholic philosophy could be conceived, in what sense and with what reservations. Later on he would express his own reservations about the book to Mademoiselle Panis, the secretary who was to help him with the publication of all his later books, about its failure to present a united front.

But this was not Blondel's final chance to make his case for a Catholic philosophy. The following year he was invited to present a communication on the subject by the *Études Philosophiques*, which was then circulated among a wide diversity of authors to be commented upon in a special issue of the journal. In his answers to each one of his commentators, friend and foe alike, Blondel insisted on the doctrinal aspect of the problem, rather than just its historical context, on the concrete dialectic it required at the intersection of rational exigencies, historical data, and intimate experiences, and on the compenetration of philosophy and a religion that purports to be "catholic" in the sense of "universal" as well as supernatural, rather than settle for a mere juxtaposition of the two, or for the misconception of the relation between natural and supernatural he had been fighting against since the beginning of his philosophical career.

Resistance to Blondel's idea of Catholic philosophy, however, did not cease, even among Catholics and Thomists who had an interest in speaking about "Christian philosophy." The question was debated at a meeting of the Thomist Society, which was attended by luminaries from all over Europe and reported on by F. Van Steenberghen in the *Revue néo-scolastique de Philosophie*, in November 1933. A wide diversity of opinions was expressed, but there was a general consensus among the participants on several points. First, it was agreed that Christian teaching had exerted a real and profound influence on the historical evolution of Western philosophy, especially through the philosophy St. Thomas and Duns Scotus. On this crucial score, none of the Catholic historians agreed with Bréhier, though they did not argue against Bréhier in precisely the way Blondel did. Second, it was agreed that no philosophy in the proper sense of the term could formally be characterized as "Christian." When this view was expressed quite emphatically by Dominicans like Chenu and Sertillanges, not to mention Gilson, who had taken a similar position earlier, there was no protestation from anyone in the audience. Third, as to the relation between faith and reason, or between Christian teaching and philosophy in the mind of a Christian, it was thought that there should be neither separation nor subordination pure and simple, but a union, and something reciprocal, in keeping with a longstanding intellectual tradition in the Church, on the relation between faith and reason in theology as well as in philosophy.

But Van Steenberghen himself was not satisfied with the lack of consistency he found in this position, where, after denouncing a certain lack of rigor and impropriety in the expression "Christian philosophy," such learned people still insisted on keeping it in vogue. For him it implied having to carve out a sort of speculative middle ground for "Christian philosophy" between philosophy and theology that showed a lack of precision concerning the nature of philosophy and theology, and concerning the relation between them in the general order of the sciences. What was needed was a more consistent position on the nature of philosophy that would make room for a consideration of Christianity in philosophy, without setting aside the strict requirements of rationality itself. Van Steenberghen proceeded to defend a more rigorous kind of philosophy as a general account of reality in strictly rational terms, and the legitimacy of Christian thinkers pursuing this kind of rational investigation, prescinding from what they happened to believe about reality as Christians. In this regard, faith could have no direct bearing on their philosophy, so that their concern was not with a Christian philosophy as such but with a philosophy that was true. The only way that Christianity could influence philosophy was to foster the proper dispositions for doing philosophy critically, not by adding anything specifically Christian to the content of philosophy or raising it higher than reason, let alone making it infallible. The most that their philosophy could do was to aim at interpreting so-called religious facts as well as other facts. In this way philosophy in general could include a branch called *philosophy of religion,* in the same way that it included a philosophy of the sciences, a philosophy of history, a philosophy of civilization, and so on. Within the philosophy of religion there could then be a *philosophy of Christianity* that would study, in the light only of philosophical principles, Christianity as a historical fact and as a social reality. Such a study might generate some apologetic interest for Christianity, but it could not invoke any theological principle based on revelation and faith.

This is where Van Steenberghen thought he could locate the work of Blondel, not as a Christian philosophy, but as a philosophy of Christianity, regardless of how it appeals to religious needs in man and how it recognizes the insufficiency of philosophy in answering these needs. Every philosophy would encounter the religious fact, and in particular the Christian fact, which justifies speaking of a philosophy of Christianity. But we should not call a philosophy of Christianity "Christian philosophy" any more than we would call a philosophy of civilization "civilized philosophy" or a philosophy of history "historical philosophy." Even if one argues that all philosophy has to end up as a philosophy of insufficiency and must thereby find its completion in a philosophy of religion and of Christianity, it still should not be characterized as Christian, according to Van Steenberghen, because that would be to contaminate, in a way that is unacceptable from the standpoint of reason, one of the branches of philosophical knowledge with a *material object* that is foreign to its domain.

Over and above this philosophy of religion, or of Christianity, as well as philosophy in general, Van Steenberghen still had a place for two kinds of theology, a theology in the broad sense based on philosophical principles, of the kind Thomists could recognize among the ancient Greeks, for example, and theology in a stricter sense based on principles rooted specifically in the Christian revelation. But this further elaboration Blondel had no quarrel with. Like the Thomists, he recognized the specificity of Christian theology as transcendent and supernatural or, as Aquinas would have said, as beyond the capacity of reason to investigate. It was with the closed conception of philosophy itself, which these Thomists held, that he had a quarrel, and Van Steenberghen did not satisfy him with the seemingly conciliatory distinction between "philosophy of Christianity" and "Christian philosophy."

In his reply to Van Steenberghen, which followed in the next issue of the *Revue néo-scolastique de Philosophie* under the title *"Pour la philosophie intégrale,"* Blondel acknowledged once again the hybrid nature of the expression "Christian philosophy," which he had shunned, but only to add that we could still speak of the truth of "Catholic philosophy," if the concept of philosophy itself was properly understood. As for Van Steenberghen's idea of a philosophy of Christianity in contradistinction from the hybrid notion of "Christian philosophy," Blondel found no improvement in it as far as trying to determine the relation between philosophy and Christianity was concerned. Either it kept philosophy at arm's length from examining the interior life of Christianity, allowing only for an extrinsic rational examination of a message that was vital for human fulfillment, thus consecrating a rigid separation between the two, or else, if philosophy tried to penetrate more intrinsically into the Gospel message, it would find itself as either having to abandon its own autonomy as philosophy and subordinating itself to a regime of specifically supernatural positive religion, or else as having to reduce what is by hypothesis supernatural and incommensurable to philosophy in the Christian life, to something purely rational and abstract. That is not where Blondel thought the center of the question could be found, much less the vital point where all the difficulties come together.

To understand what is meant by properly Catholic philosophy, according to Blondel, one must start from the twofold truth: first, of an essential incommensurability between the Christian order and the philosophical order, so that reason can never exhaust, perceive, or assimilate the mystery of truth and grace hidden in history, but that radiates from the Redeemer universally; and second, of an essential role to be played by philosophy in developing dispositions that are required for an access into the supernatural order that is open to all, even though philosophy itself cannot penetrate the secret of this supernatural order. This is not a matter of competition between philosophy and Christianity over the soul of man or of some sort of rational concordism between the two, but of preparing an opening on two sides, one on the side of philosophy and one on the side of religion presenting itself as a free gift to man. This implies recognizing a certain insufficiency in philosophy, but this recognition must be turned into a philosophy of insufficiency, so that philosophy can no longer be conceived as separate, or as self-sufficient in its accounting for reality, or exclusive of any conception of the supernatural or of readiness to accept it.

Some Thomists have accepted this idea of a philosophy of insufficiency, but they have not drawn the necessary consequences from it concerning the nature of philosophy. They have taken it only as a static statement about philosophy in general, without understanding that it arises from "the total dynamism of the human being and expresses a congenital and incoercible desire in any created spirit" (1934c, 53), something that was not ignored by St. Thomas with his idea of a natural desire to see God. Some critics of the idea of Christian philosophy have tried to neutralize the idea of this total dynamism of the human spirit, or have failed to integrate it into their conception of philosophy. Instead of considering the vital problem of how the surge from which the quest and the goal of philosophy arises relates to the exigencies of our religious aspirations and of a supernatural vocation, they have taken refuge in an abstract terrain of separate disciplines and separate methods to be maintained, ignoring the living thought that animates and dramatizes philosophy as well as Christianity, and that vivifies souls, with its salutary truths and its divine exigencies. That is where the problem of Catholic philosophy lies, and not in an abstract discussion of scientific criteriology.

Moreover, it is not enough to affirm merely a simple theoretical opening to the possibility of the supernatural as a consequence of philosophy's insufficiency in relation to our certain notion of God, of our ignorance concerning our final destiny, or of our vague aspiration to beatitude. If we are to maintain the extension of philosophical reflection to the whole of reality, we cannot restrict it to the domain of concepts, essences, possibilities, or metaphysical necessities. We must also push it to an examination of the historical, psychological, moral, and religious fact as part of what it has to study, in view of leading to a more complete human action. We must not stabilize our intelligence in our concepts of God or of possible beatitude. We must rather use it to go forward in an exploration that might satisfy our quest as a positive state, as the expression of a presence, a power, a duty for our thinking, which is already moved by a real aspiration and by a vocation set in history, or even by a stimulating grace that should not be declined.

What is required then is a philosophy that is willing to go forward with the dynamism of the spirit, not one that is concerned only with fixating on concepts acquired in the past, one that is intent on reaching out to the real in its integrity. What keeps certain philosophers from going forward is the temptation only to juxtapose heterogeneous orders of reality as determined abstractly by divergent sciences, without going back to the principles that tie them all together as sciences of one and the same reality, and in the case of the natural and the supernatural, without going back to the principle that governs and that alone can prepare and even realize a union, without confusion, of philosophy, history, dogma, and the Christian life. This is the old temptation that Blondel had been trying to overcome since the beginning of his career. Here he does so by arguing that "each one of these elements can be viewed under two aspects, that of a historical *fact* in space and time and that of a supra-temporal and extra-spatial *act* that essentially constitutes Christianity" (1934c, 56). This *act* is prior to the facts that it compenetrates, and through it philosophy can have access to what remains invisible to discursive thought and to a standpoint apart from which everything remains mixed up and undecipherable, in the vital problem of our unique and undeniable destiny. The order in which we approach the various data for these problems is important for the validity of whatever solutions we can come up with.

This unifying approach to facts has not always been sufficiently recognized, but here Blondel lays out three stages through which one must proceed successively, similar to the ones he had laid out in *The Problem of Catholic Philosophy*.

First there is the stage of what he calls "the traditional effort of speculative metaphysics that surveys all conceivable hypotheses: What are the necessary conditions that make possible the existence and the destiny of spirits?" (1934c, 57-58). This is the stage where intrinsic necessities are established and certain errors are excluded. Conscious that he is addressing Thomists for the most part, Blondel mentions such necessities as the distinction between essence and existence, the truth of creation, the knowledge that God is and that he is our principle, our end, and the source of our happiness. Then he mentions the admission of the incommensurability between God and creature, and consequently the natural inaccessibility to man of union and assimilation with God. All of these are truly philosophical assertions that prepare and even impose the idea of a supernatural that is conceivable as well as desirable, and that one could hope for obscurely but without efficacy. In this way, Blondel thinks of intellectual speculation as opening up a void of some practical consequence, even though it does not have the wherewithal to fill this void, but all this only on the condition that philosophy does not become stabilized in the concepts of these essential possibilities and metaphysical necessities.

Once philosophy has advanced to this point of rationally recognizing man's inability to limit his *élan* toward the infinite, no less than to arrive at the possession of this object on his own, can philosophy then avoid raising the question of whether this idea of the supernatural, corresponding to this normal need in man, might not be, or if the truth of a revelation and a divine elevation of man can be entertained, recognized, brought into practice, without any legitimate opposition from philosophy, once such a reality is proposed or even imposed, as the Catholic teaching would have it. This is the second stage in the development of what Blondel wants to call Catholic philosophy, and he argues for it on the basis of the idea, recognized by Van Steenberghen and other Thomists, that philosophy has the whole of reality, *la réalité intégrale,* for its object. Is it not still the part of philosophy, logically speaking, to bring the historical, moral, and supernatural truth of Christianity that is living into the philosophical organism itself, especially insofar as philosophy has to be concerned with the final destiny of man? It is not under its empirical aspect that the Christian teaching must be integrated into philosophy, but rather under the ever-mysterious aspect of its supernatural formality.

This is where Blondel sees the danger lurking in speaking of Christian philosophy, rather than Catholic philosophy. "Christian philosophy" for him is too equivocal or too pretentious, as if philosophy could absorb into its rational process a reality that has to remain totally mysterious or, as Kierkegaard would say, totally paradoxical to it. If Revelation and grace are necessary for the reality of the Christian mystery to be known, however, it still remains that the Justification for it must be accessible, through the soul of the Church, to all who do not sin against the light and their interior call, "even if it presents itself anonymously under forms that are sufficient for a salutary supernatural option" (1934c, 59). Because Blondel thinks that no one is absolutely deprived of this possibility of salvation, he wants to characterize as catholic the spiritual and voluntary disposition that philosophy, in keeping with what it can do and should do, "can determine effectively in whoever remains docile to the solicitations of conscience. Thus it is legitimate to call 'Catholic philosophy' the teaching that focuses on the necessary and sufficient attitude for a human being to participate in the invisible universal Church, even if this being would remain, without fault of his own, ignorant of the Christ, of His truth and of His law" (1934c, 59).

It is not enough, then, for philosophy to arrive at some theoretical possibility or some vague obediential potency that could close itself off from any wonderment about a reality that might correspond to the undeniable aspiration of reason. A philosophy of insufficiency cannot restrict itself to some vague and sterile concept. Appealing to what he calls the reality of the invisible soul of the Church, a dogma that would be denied by any refusal to scrutinize what might open up access to the supernatural for one in invincible ignorance of Revelation, Blondel argues that philosophy has to inquire into the reasons for the hypothetical necessity of the supernatural as affirmed by the First Vatican Council. "What is necessary is subject to rational analysis and since, hypothetically speaking, the supernatural vocation is recognized as possible, there are consequences that reason can analyze in view of enriching the very notion of an eventual revelation, of a human obligation and a strict responsibility: all truths that follow one another in a strictly rational order and for which one can still develop the philosophical sequence" (1934c, 60).

This is the kind of strict philosophical argument Blondel had tried to develop in the original philosophy of the supernatural of his dissertation in 1893 and to defend in the discourse on method of the *Letter on the Exigencies of Modern Philosophy in Philosophy of Religion* in 1896, for the benefit of Catholics who were enthused about his philosophy for the wrong reasons. But now, in 1932, he wants to include a third stage of penetration for philosophy into the domain of Christian practice and the life of grace that joins together the life of God and the life of man in a theandric action. Here he refers to St. Bernard's way of speaking of this life of union as a reality, where God and man, without confusing their being and their action, join together, not as two separate parts of something to be accomplished, but as a single work where each one affects the whole — *sed opere individuo totum singuli peragunt.*

This is a representation of the Christian life here on earth he had also dwelt on in his dissertation, but here he wants to draw it out further into something we can be conscious of as philosophers. What is true of the core of the theandric operation can also be true of the consciousness we have of it. Even if we think of these actions as supernatural and, as such, inaccessible to the investigation of reason, they are still human actions, something in our consciousness under their psychological and moral aspects and, as such, accessible to a description of an original and nuanced perfection that a natural ethic would be unable to attain by itself. This is the kind of life Kierkegaard eulogizes in Abraham, and in any man of faith, as something beyond the grasp of philosophy, but Blondel thinks of it as something that can be thematized in philosophy as something real, something concrete, something that is lived humanly. "If philosophy is to encompass the integrality of what is true and lived, should we keep it from contemplating what is most beautiful in humanity?" (1934c, 61).

This presupposes a much more open view of philosophy than we find in either Kierkegaard or Hegel, even as it recognizes its inability to transgress into the divine origin of this graceful elevation. Blondel alludes to certain seeds planted in human consciences, certain seminal virtues, which may not derive from nature alone, but which can present for philosophy a rich harvest as a science of human resources. Along the same line he speaks of a certain aspect of the union with God and of mystical life that does not altogether escape philosophical analysis. If we speak of philosophy as concerned not only with possibles, essences, or concepts, but with anything real in our experience that is part of the lived history of our souls, the contemplation and the action of a Christianity that is known and lived in its highest degree can offer to philosophy a surplus of ideas, sentiments, and aspirations that can be assimilated philosophically, as long as we avoid a twofold misapprehension: that of secularizing or reducing specifically Christian virtues to something that would result from a natural progress of civilization, and that of judging chimerical or inhuman the humility, the asceticism, the follies of the cross, and all those aspirations and immolations that have their meaning only through grace and in view of the supernatural elevation of human beings.

In speaking of this third stage for Catholic philosophy, Blondel had in mind a work that he was still only projecting, one that would come after his Trilogy on Thought, Being, and Action, and that would bring to light ideas he had begun to explore as far back as when he was embroiled in his controversies about apologetics at the turn of the twentieth century, ideas that he would publish not as apologetic, but as straight philosophy under the title *Philosophy and the Christian Spirit*. Having laid out the three stages for an integral philosophy such as he has in mind, Blondel then comes back to a discussion of how such a philosophy should be named in the conclusion of his response to Van Steenberghen and other Catholic historians of philosophy. Van Steenberghen had spoken of theology in a broad sense, to include under this rubric the theology of the Philosopher along with that based on Revelation. Blondel turns this around to speak of philosophy in a broader sense, in accordance with its own formal and rational principle so that it will extend as far as the universe, as far as humanity, as far as the soul of the Church, as far as the human spirit can go toward its highest destiny, without ceasing to be human. Van Steenberghen had dismissed the expression "catholic philosophy" without any justification, but Blondel insists on it as the most comprehensive and appropriate term of all, as St. Augustine had remarked, since it applies to the integral truth under whatever aspect we consider it. There are those who would say that a "philosophy that is true" would be enough. Blondel argues that we could not make an integral use of our reason and our will without encountering and implicitly resolving the problem of our attitude with regard to the One who, even if he be unnamed, illumines, attracts, and fortifies every man who comes into this world. For Blondel, one has to allow for true "believers" even among those who appear as unbelievers in the external forum.

This does not mean that philosophy can simply take over what are thought of as Christian dogmas about man in the world, as some philosophers have tried to do. In fact, it is precisely for this reason that Blondel rejects the epithet "Christian philosophy." "Christian," according to him, refers directly to a historical reality and as such it is too restrictive. It can apply to philosophers who do not deserve it, as Kierkegaard might have said of certain Hegelians, if not of Hegel himself. On the other hand, the epithet "catholic" that Blondel is reproached for having used in two apparently equivocal senses, encompasses, on the contrary, the integral truth from whatever point of the horizon and under whatever anonymous form there may be along with the ideas and the persons who participate in a right direction, a good intention, a salutary inspiration. Even in saying that revealed assertions and philosophical teachings cannot be simply fused in some kind of material or formal concordism, we are not prevented from seeing in the word "catholic" a double meaning taken as something unique with regard to a vivifying truth, and yet as diversified with regard to the methods and the ways of access to salvation. The point is not to bring philosophy into accord with Christian teaching or Christian teaching into accord with philosophy. "On the contrary," Blondel writes, reverting to Van Steenberghen's words, "true philosophy is the one that not only remains open and plastic, but also contributes to total life in order to shed light on it as well as to accept light from it" (1934c, 63). This is how Blondel himself had come to philosophy as a Catholic in the completely rational sense of the term, without falling into the false concordism of any Christian philosophy or any false regime of separation between the two spiritual powers of philosophy and Christianity.

PART TWO

The Systematic Summation

While Blondel was thus defending the idea of Catholic Philosophy, he was still at a loss about how to go about finishing the work he most wanted to publish before his death, his Trilogy on Thought, Being, and Action. He had been working on this for years. He had copious notes accumulated, but was no longer able to read them, much less organize them into a coherent whole. The nature of his blindness was such that he still had some peripheral vision, so that he was not completely in darkness, but he could not see anything directly in front of him, so that he could not read or find things he would be looking for. With very careful attention he could write with his own hand, the only way he knew how to, but he could not read what he was writing. Thus, he was able to write directly to friends like Brémond, who were able to follow his handwriting even though it no longer had the careful delineation it once had. But other than that he was totally dependent on others to read to him, to read his own script, and to take dictation for anything he wanted to send to others or publish.

In the early months after the hemorrhage to the retina of one of his eyes on March 17, 1926, forcing him to nurse what little sight he had left even with the other eye, his children helped him while he still had some use of his quickly failing sight — Elisabeth mainly, whom Brémond dubbed "the perfect secretary," also Charles, who was married and living in Paris but came to visit often, and André, who was still living with his father working on a dissertation in Law. Elisabeth, however, was also married, with children, and living in Paris, and André, having finished his dissertation and all requirements for the degree in Law, moved out of his father's house in January 1928, in search of his own career, leaving Blondel to his own resources in a large house with his neuritis and other ailments, at the mercy of whomever he could find to take care of the house and himself, whether in Aix during the school year or in Magny-la-Ville in Burgundy during the summer, feeling very much alone and ever more frustrated in trying to work. Efforts to read and write had to stop after only a few minutes because of increasingly blurred vision. By February 1927, after consultation with doctors in Paris as well as in Aix, he had lost all hope that the deterioration of his eyes could be reversed. He could only continue to make what little use he could of them as long as that would last.

In addition to his immediate family, Blondel also began to seek the help of secretaries who came to help with his work at different times. Over the years from 1926 to 1931 there were four of these, judging from the dictations that can be found in the Blondel Archives. Two of them were graduate students with Blondel working on their Licentiate. One of them, Mlle. Isambert, worked over a period of three years, from 1926 to 1928, and the other, Mlle. Giannorsi, a Corsican, over a period of two years, in 1929 and 1930. Both went off to teach on their own once they had finished their studies. Another, the daughter of an Italian diplomat, came from Marseilles, also during 1927 and 1928, to work when the graduate students were not there. There was even a fourth, who worked on a single text during those same years, albeit a relatively long one. But in all of this Blondel found himself incapable of pursuing any continuous work such as would be required for the production of a book.

Early in his life, when he had tried dictating parts of his dissertation on *Action*, he had found himself distracted by a certain human respect for the secretary, as he wondered what was going on in the secretary's mind instead of wondering what was going on in his own. Here again the same kind of problem arose, as he explained to Wehrlé in July 1929 (1969b, 663). What he dictated to the different secretaries and what he wrote in his own hand did not seem to go together. What came out were many different pieces that were very uneven in quality, some of which corrected one another while others seemed to exclude one another. More often they complemented one another, but they still had to be reconciled with one another. "The dictations have both an advantage and an inconvenience: they have forced me to explicitate, in a continuous fashion, ideas that had to be drawn out from their internal 'ineffability'; but on the opposite side they are caught up in the impression of the moment, in a detail that is at times accessory but that they exaggerate and thereby denature. Hence the necessity of personal glosses to remedy the childish unilaterality of my oral expositions, in which, as I am constantly improvising, I give in to the hazard of the associations of ideas and to human respect for the secretary before whom I do not want to fall short, so that I push on, at whatever cost, even with the feeling of a clumsy phrase or of a development that is tedious and disproportionate."

This was hardly the stuff that good books are made of, and Blondel knew it. The dictations and the notes were materials that had to be used liberally and shaped so that the essential ideas could be drawn out as part of a whole leading to an end. Blondel appears to have used these secretaries mostly for taking dictation, but none of them stayed long enough to get into his work with him and to come to some understanding of what he was trying to do. How often he had them come to work or for how long is hard to tell, but in his letters to Brémond he complains of being alone a lot, like a saddened widower of many years, and helpless, especially during the summer months at Magny. It is a wonder that, in spite of all this, he managed to do so much during these years of working alone in large part, in spite of his handicap, from the volume on *Action Française* to the one on his *vinculum,* the *Itinéraire Philosophique* with Lefèvre, and the controversy over the idea of Catholic Philosophy, not to mention his continuing correspondence with Brémond, Wehrlé, and others.

None of this, however, was bringing him any closer to the publication of the work he held most at heart. Working with secretaries in this way, almost randomly, as it were, did not lend itself to the sustained effort that was required for the series of books he had in mind. Blondel had the sad experience of this with the book on the *Problem of Catholic Philosophy,* two thirds of which only repeated an edited version of texts written thirty years earlier in different circumstances, with notes added here and there and a final chapter relating directly to Gilson and Bréhier. On the whole it remained quite disjointed. Blondel was quite disappointed with the result. He realized that the longer, more systematic books he was contemplating could not be brought to term in this way. So too did his friend Wehrlé, who still thought of Blondel as his philosophical mentor and who wanted him to come out with his book on *Thought* above all else, berating Blondel for spending so much time on other things instead of what he thought would be his *magnum opus.*

And so it came that, in December 1929, Wehrlé offered to take up the task of pulling all of Blondel's papers together and ordering them into a consistent whole, even though he was working on a book of his own on their mutual friend, Victor Delbos. Blondel was delighted with the offer and seized upon it, thinking that perhaps the publication of his thought could finally appear at least under joint authorship. This spurred Blondel to compose yet another set of notes and instructions on how to proceed in the elaboration of a systematic order for all that he had already set down on paper. It was a heavy package that Blondel sent his friend to work on and that Wehrlé undertook to read and organize as best he could with great zeal. In a letter to Brémond, Blondel joyfully announces that Wehrlé, after ingesting some twenty or so kilos of notes and dictations, will "solemnly" begin writing the volume on *Thought* (1971b, 374).

But things did not turn out as well as Blondel had hoped for. Wehrlé did get to work on the notes and dictations for *La Pensée.* He wrote to Blondel asking for clarifications and Blondel answered him with further outlines of what he was driving at with the two kinds of Thought he was distinguishing and the dialectical relation between them. At the same time, however, Blondel was also having Wehrlé review the text on Leibniz's *vinculum substantiale,* which was being readied for publication during these first efforts to pull the volume on

Thought together. As usual, Wehrlé acceded to this request from Blondel, but not without insistent protestation that they should be devoting their time and effort to Blondel's own thought, and not to that of another, even if it was Leibniz. "I assure you," he wrote to Blondel, "that there is a great inconvenience in having always to judge with the criteria of a metaphysics that has yet to be published: for, after all, this metaphysics has never been formulated *ex professo*, for its own sake and methodically. You must, you must give us *La Pensée* and not let yourself become once again the victim of a search for perfection that, as you look for more of it, becomes more and more impossible" (1969b, 662). Wehrlé was not asking that the notes and dictations be published in the state that he had received them, but he also knew that his friend would be very demanding about how they were to appear in their final revision.

Wehrlé worked at this revision for almost two years, trying "first of all to *read* everything, to digest it all, and then to transubstantiate it through a decisive response of 'my' pneumatic to 'the' noetic . . ." (1969b, 665). This allusion to one of Blondel's key distinctions about thought shows how aware he was that he would have to put a good deal of his own thinking into the final product. It was perhaps the difficulty of this third and final phase of his work that proved insurmountable to Wehrlé, who was also in poor health as well as perhaps overly devoted to getting the thought of his friend out as perfectly as possible. His effort to bring Blondel's thought on Thought to completion went on for about two years, but in the end he had to admit that he could not do the job satisfactorily. In March 1931 he sent all the notes and dictations back to Blondel with his apologies for not being able to do what both would have liked him so much to do.

Needless to say, Blondel was very disappointed with this failure of what had appeared as his last best hope of getting a systematic exposition of his ideas published. Brémond suggested that he look for a layman instead of a cleric to help with the completion of his work, but Blondel does not seem to have taken to that. In fact, one young man by the name of Léon Delpech, who had probably come from Algiers to study with Blondel, is reported to have offered his services as full-time secretary, but Blondel turned him down, not wishing to cut short his career. Delpech did in fact go on to pursue a career in psychology and would later come back to write a few articles on Blondel at the time of the latter's death, among them one on "the psychological conceptions in *La Pensée*," as part of an homage to his departed teacher. After Wehrlé sent him back his papers in March 1931, Blondel was left to make do as he had been doing for three or four years with different part-time secretaries. While this could work for taking care of his correspondence and writing articles like the ones on the question of Catholic Philosophy, it left him in a kind of limbo as to how he could go about pursuing his more systematic work on Thought, Being, and Action.

This problem was not solved for him until a few months later when, out of the blue, or providentially, as he more likely would have said, a certain Mlle. Nathalie Panis, having heard of his plight, wrote to him from Paris to offer her services as secretary on a long-term basis. She had been a graduate student of Blondel in Aix during the First World War and, after getting her Licentiate in Philosophy, had gone on to teach at a French Lycée in Athens, Greece, for years. In 1931 she was back in Paris, relatively unattached, but still very much interested in the thought of her former teacher and perhaps even more devoted to him than his friend Wehrlé. Blondel had no problem remembering her and began to think that perhaps she could do on a long-term basis what others could not do on a short-term basis. Seeing that she was eager and that she was ready to make a long-term commitment to the task, he invited her down to the house in Aix. She came in December 1931, and, as she was fond of saying, she never left his side after that. This became for her a second career in which she would look after the intellectual affairs of the one she would call *Maître*, not in the sense of Master, but in the sense of *Magister*, Teacher. She moved into the large house on rue Roux-Alphéran with Blondel, to be at his side, just the two of them for the most part, except when family and friends came to visit, and worked with him for the rest of his life and beyond, taking care of the Blondel Archives after his death for as long as they were in that house. The arrangement was as simple as could be. There was not even any question of a salary. Blondel assured her that she would be taken care of as a member of the family in exchange for dedicating herself totally to the support of Blondel in his work, becoming his eyes and his hands, as it were, by reading to him and taking down dictation, and most importantly by being there consistently at his side day in and day out with her enthusiasm and her interest in seeing that Blondel's work be brought to completion and broadcast as widely as possible, including through translation into different languages, which she was always eager to urge on those who came to visit the Blondel Archives from abroad.

This proved to be the answer to Blondel's problem, short of restoring his sight. It enabled him to start a second career of writing from his solitude in Aix, not unlike the first one, when he first conceived his original dissertation on *Action* in the solitude of Saint-Seine. It was what he had been dreaming of being able to do for a long time in order to give a more complete expression to his philosophy in terms of Thought and Being as well as Action. Together, he and Mlle. Panis developed a daily routine of work that would take them through the five volumes of the Trilogy and way beyond. Each morning they would attend the early mass at the nearby parish church of Saint Jean de Malte and come back to the second floor study to prepare for the morning's work. While Mlle. Panis prepared the coffee and bread for their *petit déjeuner*, before the arrival of the housekeeper who took care of the other meals, Blondel would sit by himself scribbling notes and preparing in his mind what he wanted to get into for that day. Morning sessions, which lasted three or four hours, were reserved exclusively for work on the books that Blondel wanted to compose. Afternoon sessions, after *déjeuner* and a siesta, were devoted to other business, such as the ample flow of correspondence that never slowed down, keeping up with the literature on philosophy and education that always interested Blondel, and responding to proposals of others in discussions that went on in the Société de Philosophie Française in connection with Lalande's *Vocabulaire* or in *Les Études Philosophiques,* a journal edited by Gaston Berger, a former student of Blondel. Also included was a certain amount of political commentary as a regular contributor to the review *Politique,* which his son-in-law, Charles Flory, had founded in 1926. With the collaboration of Mlle. Panis, Blondel was able to get back into the swing of things almost as well as when he had been able to see for himself, in what has been called his second career as a publicist.

The first order of business in this new career was the publication of the two volumes on *Thought.* Blondel had begun drafts for these two volumes even before going blind. The notes he had for this first part of the Trilogy, not to mention the dictations to various earlier secretaries, were more amply developed than any for the later parts. They showed more of his earlier vigorous style as a writer and were more ready to go into the kind of book he wanted to put out. The procedure was for Mlle. Panis to read these notes and earlier dictations, or at least parts of them, back to Blondel, and then for him to reprocess them in his own mind in order to see how he would use them in the text he was now composing from all this raw material of his thinking. The idea was not just to find texts that he wanted to use again and simply copy down as parts of a "new" book, as had been the case in the production of *Le problème de la philosophie catholique.* It was rather to review what he had elaborated over the course of many years and to integrate it into a new synthesis that had to be worked out step by step, precisely what Wehrlé had been unable to do on his own with the same papers. After the early-morning preparation, when Mlle. Panis came in to start a session of dictation, Blondel would sit in an easy chair and dictate slowly and deliberately, with occasional interruptions when he asked to hear once again something written in his notes, what he wanted written in the final version of his thought. He did so, according to Mlle. Panis, out of his own abundance, but with a movement of his right hand as if to spur himself on.

To understand what Blondel was up to in his own mind in beginning this Trilogy, we must refer back to his interview with Lefèvre in 1927 and to notes dictated around the same time in view of a possible re-edition of his work of 1893, long since out of print. In answer to the question why he had never allowed a second edition of his original dissertation on *Action,* he answered that it was for him only a part of what he originally had in mind for his philosophy as a whole. "Without the requirement for my career that forced me to publish *Action* and use the beginning of a fragment as a school exercise, I think that this book, or rather this chapter, would not yet have appeared" (1928a, 63). At the beginning what he had had in mind was "a metaphysics common to nature, science, and religious morality," which would have included a treatment of the problem of agency in general *(l'agir)* for a finite being, but "in view of a thesis written for the Sorbonne, I had artificially narrowed down a subject that was too vast and I limited myself to the human and moral aspect of an infinitely broader problem" (1951, 11-12).

Most readers, including the jury of examiners, did not notice how Blondel had narrowed down his original subject. They took his dissertation to be the whole of his philosophy, thus branding him as "the philosopher of action," something that eventually came to irritate him. But two had noticed and called it to his attention. One was the Dominican, P. Beaudoin, to whom he had shown the proofs for the dissertation. His observation was that while titling his thesis *Action*, Blondel was confining his study not even to human action as a whole, but rather to the moral dimension in the search for a solution to the problem of our free and ineluctable destiny. Of course, Blondel had a right to specify the scope of his study as he wished, but Beaudoin was saying that the moral problem was not convertible with the problem of action as a whole, as his title seemed to imply. The other one who pointed out how Blondel had restricted his problematic was his friend Victor Delbos. He is the one who urged Blondel to add a final chapter to the thesis he had defended at the Sorbonne in order to bring out the metaphysical dimension of his philosophy. As we know, Blondel did this in a long, hastily written chapter titled "The bond of knowledge and action in being," added on to the text he had submitted to the Sorbonne, "with the purpose of keeping a *philosophy of action* from being taken as an intellectual abdication and for a flight from metaphysics," but by his own admission "the execution did not measure up to the intention" (1951, 9).

Hence, notwithstanding the success the dissertation enjoyed, Blondel was not satisfied with the impression of his philosophy that it had given. This impression had to be broadened to include not only the problem of action, but also the problem of thought and being, and this is what the Trilogy was intended to do. This was not to be a second philosophy for Blondel. He always maintained that it was his philosophy from the beginning that had received only a truncated expression. Nor was it any less rigorous in his own mind than the original dissertation on *Action*. If anything, it was more rigorous in that its implications were more completely articulated. It showed a philosopher more in control of his own thought in the face of views that remained shortsighted or one-sided for him, one more ready to expose the universal content of his thought in relation to the most singular initiative of any human experience in the world.

XI

The Question of Thought

The more complete exposition of Blondel's philosophy had to begin with a study of Thought, the more universal theme he had only touched on in his earlier studies on the "elementary principle for a logic of moral life" or on "the point of departure for philosophical research" in the spontaneous activity of prospection and reflection in human experience. Whereas the earlier philosophy of action may have left this intellectual side of the human experience too much in the background, and perhaps might have given the impression of being opposed to it, Blondel now wanted to bring it to the forefront and study it as an integral part of human activity, bringing this activity of thought to its properly spiritual dimension, as the philosophical tradition had long maintained.

For the first part of his philosophical Trilogy, on *Thought* or *La Pensée*, Blondel has two volumes clearly in mind, one on how thought is constituted in the universe and how thought constitutes itself in the spiritual experience of human beings, and the other on how thought has to be exercised responsibly in the pursuit of science, including the science of itself, in its own progressive education as a social form of culture, art, literature, and even of metaphysics and morals. Ultimately even with regard to a rationally conceived final perfection for it, thought remains problematic for any finite spirit by reason of its natural insufficiency, but it is still of essential interest, in the hypothesis that a supernatural dispensation has been offered to an intelligent creature, free to accept or to reject such a gratuitous gift from the Creator. This is to be a science, not of thoughts or ideas taken in abstraction from the activity of thinking, but of the entire activity of thinking as a whole, from its emergence as something real in the world to its highest accomplishments in the realm of spirit, including the idea of God as totally transcendent even to itself. In its first part, it will proceed phenomenologically from thought in its lowest forms, as cosmic, as organic, and as psychic, to a thought that awakens and thinks itself as a new invention in the universe, even as it thinks of objects and subjects in the universe. In its second part, it will rehearse the problems thought finds within itself in dealing with the world and with others in the normal course of its spontaneous development, ending with the most fundamental problem of them all, concerning what to do about our own natural aspirations toward divination that we are naturally incapable of fulfilling for ourselves, but that could be fulfilled by God.

In beginning this study of thought, or in trying to specify the subject for such a study, Blondel notes that, somewhat surprisingly, thought had never been properly studied as a whole in the way he thought it should be, at least not in modern philosophy, which is where he was situating himself. One would have thought that Descartes, more than anyone else, would have focused on the subject of thought as such, with his insistence on the *Cogito* as the start of philosophy, but Descartes did not dwell on thinking as such. He was looking for a metaphysical response to the question of thinking, to grasp it ontologically in its being, or as a thing, *res cogitans*. He did not articulate an intrinsic view of thinking itself. To the question, "Is there thought?" he answered yes, but when it came to the question: "What is thought?" he turned away from any intrinsic view of thought itself, at least not as "taken in its essential unity, in its simplicity, infinitely rich in internal determinations, toward an enumeration of the most heterogeneous operations. It was no longer thought according to what is substantial and unifying about it, or to what is common to all its uses and its productions [that Descartes was studying], but rather the multiplicity of thoughts in us, that is, a hybrid mixture of objective data and subjective activity" (1934a, 217), including doubting, conceiving, affirming, denying, willing, not willing, imagining, and even sensing, as Descartes himself says in his second *Meditation*. Instead of studying thought for what it is as thought, he turned to the study of ideas, intellectual objects, rational truths, and scientific laws. It was an evasion of the problem he seemed to be raising, in raising the problem of the *Cogito*.

In raising the question of thought, according to Blondel, one appears to be raising a two-sided question. On one side, thought appears to be an interior light without which there would be nothing for us. Far from receiving any radiation from objects, this light appears to illuminate them out of its own focus from a critical and reflective standpoint. As enlightening, it cannot be enlightened by the reverberation of rays that serve to make it conscious of this interior source. On the other side, that which is enlightened, even in contributing to the revelation of light, does not disclose it as it is at its center, so that we are forced to turn our gaze away from this center, as prisoners in a cave, toward a mixture of shadows and clarity that make up the shape of our world. Thus, in thinking about thought, we oscillate between objects that are thought and a subject who is thinking, without knowing which side to begin with in figuring out what is enlightening and what is enlightened. We take the notions of subject and object as primordial, obvious data of consciousness, when in fact they are latecomers on the scene, artificial, and unverifiable. For Blondel, one cannot start from this separation of subject and object in a proper study of thought as an activity.

If one does start from such a dichotomy, one ends up in a theory of knowledge that can only fall short of any proper understanding of thought as we exercise it spontaneously in our life. Modern criticism and relativism, as Blondel sees them, only introduce a third term into the dichotomy of subject/object they start from, that of a relation between the two, which is the relation of truth or verifiability, and which reduces the question of thought to a matter of knowledge that cannot be verified. In a long *Excursus* complementing his introduction to the problem of thought as the proper subject for a philosophical inquiry, Blondel goes into a long discussion of how this inquiry has been short-circuited in modern philosophy after Descartes. After bringing out the discrepancies of Descartes's theory of ideas and his failure to resolve the bipolarity of his view into a unified theory, he goes on to examine attempts to come at the problem from the side of the object in what has been called a natural metaphysics of thought, or naïve realism.

Thought, *la pensée*, it is said, is essentially what is thought, *le pensé*, not as a subjective phenomenon, but rather as a real object that informs the power of thinking with its intelligible nature. Prior to this informing, consciousness is empty, unthinking, even unthought and unthinkable, as long as it has not been colored or delimited by something from the outside. Blondel had run into opponents who held such a view, but he did not think any serious philosopher had ever held it in such simple or uncritical naïveté. Nevertheless he found something approaching this view in many philosophers who had tried to approach the problem of knowledge from the standpoint of its material conditions, without giving due consideration to the spiritual side of this activity and to the mode of its operation. "It is wrong to ignore the idea of a pre-existing and specific initiative without which a spirit could not think any more than a stone, however many the occasions or stimulations may be. Nothing is more misleading than the word of Locke claiming that God could have made it such that matter as matter could think. We must not render intelligence totally unintelligible nor should we speak of an intelligible that remains intrinsically unthinkable, which is what happens if we claim that thought proceeds from a pure passivity, in the sense of inertia that we often give to this word" (1934a, 227).

There is, underlying the experience of many objects that we can discern in the world, the secret striving of a thought that is in search of itself in depth as well as in breadth, that gives us some perspective on the origins, the nature, and the destiny of the human spirit, a latent dynamism that turns spontaneously to objects but that has its own constitutive principles that we think of as rational, or better still intellectual. Through these principles we come not only to a distinction of objects or a diversification of natures in our consciousness, but also to an ordering of this multiplicity and diversity into a world. For a proper study of thought, we must not only gather the data that are the genetic preparation for thought, which usually presupposes a long experience. We must also develop a higher, more methodical consciousness in pursuit of a science of thought as an activity that will take us into its infinite ramifications. "In short, it is not enough to ground a study of thought either on the banal appearances or the observations of common sense or some impoverished science; the question is to find the means for examining the origins of thought that tie it to its distant conditions as well as its highest developments, whose prodigious richness both the positive and the mystical sciences attest to" (1934a, 231).

Finally, if consideration of the subject alone, or the object alone, cannot properly ground a science of thought, can a consideration of the relation between them serve that purpose? This is the way that criticism and relativism have taken in modern philosophy, in making the theory of knowledge the summit of philosophy. Thought is taken to be a relation, that between "an object, a given, a matter" of knowledge on the one hand, and on the other, a subject, a synthetic activity, "a form." This relation is taken to be the fundamental datum from which critical reflection takes off, without even asking whether its *fundamentum* can be thought of as the pure relation it is supposed to be. Blondel calls this a relativist point of view because it reduces thought to a theory of knowledge, of which there have been many, each one shot through with insoluble difficulties from their own standpoint. In none of them is the problem of thought resolved. It does not even seem to be raised. Worse still it is made to appear insoluble by the way it is "masked by words and images that not only keep us from perceiving it, but also accumulate contradictions" (1934a, 234-35).

Critical idealism, for its part, tries to resolve these contradictions, but it does so only from within thought itself. It tries, not so much to make the object disappear, but rather not to posit it at all, and to remain within interiorized thought or thought reduced to itself in some kind of absolute knowing. All that is left as matter for thought, as Blondel sees it, is "some immanent elaboration, the immense edifice of the sciences, a reflection on the secular process of consciousness and civilization, and they call that spiritual liberation" (1934a, 235). For Blondel, critical idealism was attempting, at the limit, to eliminate all differential aspects of thought. Its failure to do so was proof of a necessity to consider thought more seriously in the concrete, as it is lived in the world by different people.

It is thought in itself and for itself that must become the problem for philosophical science. How does it reconcile within itself what appears to be a twofold exigency of duality and unity? Can it resign itself to a split between two blocks, where it seems to be divided from itself unto infinity, or is there a tendency deep within it toward a unity that it cannot attain but that it cannot renounce trying to attain? Indeed, within human consciousness, "in order to think itself, thought needs to distinguish itself from its object. It has long been recognized that thought is the other with regard to being and, in keeping with the scholastic formula, it comes to know itself only in also knowing others as others.... But on the other hand, thought is only in view of unity: in the mind of everyone this need in it is undeniable..." (1934a, 236-37). How does this need of duality and unity cohabit in thought? "How can we understand this double tendency in thought toward what comes before it, what produces it, what justifies it, and toward what it produces as a new synthesis that would not exist without it?" (1934a, 236-37). These are the questions that must be explored in a concrete science of thought, to make thought intelligible to itself within the solidarity of conditions from which it emerges, on the way to an end that we have yet to determine.

Blondel begins this inquiry by indicating different ways in which thought in act tends to reconcile, at least partially, what speculative reflection is tempted to make exclusive in the abstract. Prior to any distinction between subject and object, he considers how thought presents itself in act, first, in language, then, in the spontaneous logic of grammar, and third, in the implicit metaphysics that forms the atmosphere of any spirit. He refers to linguistic studies of different languages, to semantic and logical studies that have focused on thought as an operative principle, and to certain prospections, a term that had become a regular part of his vocabulary in thinking about thought since his article on "The Point of Departure for Philosophical Research," in affective life, in artistic intuitions, in a certain speculative vision that, in a concrete way, makes every human being a metaphysician and a poet at least in embryo. According to Blondel, these were all matters of fact that one had to attend to in order to bring out, according to a method that is genetic and integral, what is implied in the possibility and the fact of thinking, beginning with the simple act of thinking and following the implications of this act to whatever end they would lead us.

Implication, or disimplication of all that is implied, laying out what is necessarily implied in the initial prospective act we start from, was to be the essential characteristic of Blondel's method. The full scope of this method would both define and justify itself only as it developed step by step in the process of the investigation, for, as Blondel writes, "every true method is in truth a science or a teaching in act" (1934a, xxx). What Blondel was looking for in his science of thought was what is implied, and all that is implied, in each thought and in any thought, something concrete that would be present both universally and singularly, independently of any particular uses of thought, of their imperfections or their mistakes, something that could be taken as proper to any individual and yet as common to all who think, the effective and even efficient presence of a dynamism binding together seemingly scattered and mutually exclusive states. More than just a phenomenological description of states of consciousness, this was to be a search into the real and intelligible conditions that precede, prepare, accompany, support, and bear toward their end all the thoughts that constitute the world of nature and of spirit. It was to be an attempt to understand how they all come together as a whole not only in our representation but also in their deepest reality. The force of the method of implication is to show how all of our assertions of detail and all of our progressive observations depend on one another and are interconnected in such a way that, without this necessary connection, there could be no real data and no intelligible consciousness of them. What Blondel was interested in pursuing systematically was nothing more nor less than what was required by the totality of our experience of thought in a world that is as much a thought as a reality.

Real Cosmic Thought

In a move that took many by surprise, Blondel began his study with a consideration of what he called "real thought apart from thinking or thought thought — *la pensée réelle hors de la pensée pensante ou pensée*," prior to any discussion of thinking or thought thought as such, which is thought at the level of self-consciousness. For him thought was already a norm for the orientation of things in the physical world, as it was for scientists like Claude Bernard in biology or physicists interested in the cosmic motion. Hence, the study of thought had to begin from this profound reality in things in order to find the first signs of its élan and to follow its progressive steps toward a more conscious kind of thought. This is part of what is implied in our very activity of thinking, if not as cause of this activity, at least as a concrete condition for it. Thought does not come to us out of the blue, apart from the world in which we find ourselves. It begins from the bottom up, and Blondel wants to follow its emergence from its most humble beginnings.

In this first part of his study, on "real thought" prior to thinking thought, Blondel distinguishes three degrees of thought: cosmic thought, organic and organizing thought, and psychic thought. He describes each one of them in succession, but the one he knows will be most difficult to convince people of is the first. If we leave out every type of psychic or organic thought, how can we still speak of thought in an order whose sole characteristic is to be physical and material, or thoughtless? But Blondel finds thought even in the most purely physical aspect of the universe by the mere fact that we still speak of it as the universe in which we find ourselves. We cannot isolate ourselves from this universe, nor can we isolate the universe from ourselves. Physicists have come to realize this in recent times with their idea of an anthropic principle in physics, but Blondel realizes it in a way that is the reverse of how physicists come at it, not in the sense that he is formulating a theory of the cosmos as a whole, but in the sense that such a formulation already implies a certain degree of thought in that a plurality of otherwise thoughtless elements is unified and interconnected into a whole, for that sort of unification is a proper function of thought as we come to know it in our experience. This physical world that we think of as something solid, we also think of effectively as a thought that is at once diffuse and synergetic. It is given and thought of only under the species of multiplicity, diversity, and motion. What we find in fact, however, is a universe not only in motion at a single degree of stability, but one incessantly passing from homogeneity to a highly diversified qualitative heterogeneity, going, under the impulse of thought, toward beings that are ever more complex and yet more centered in their identity than lower forms of existence, opening the way for the ascent of life and thought.

Blondel presents this ascending motion not so much in terms of some purely mechanical push from below as in the Darwinian conception of evolution in which a mere abstraction such as "the survival of the fittest" is taken as a norm, but rather in terms of the rich diversity we find concretely implied and implicated in the unity of an order in the making, each new degree of complexity and identity adding a new qualitative dimension to a universe still in process of becoming. Diversification might appear to abstract thought or to a monistic form of speculation as a breakdown of unity and universality, but by his method of implication Blondel finds the reason for greater unification through thought itself. For what is implied in this diversity of qualities and of beings that are multiplied in the universal becoming? If they are to be understood specifically in their individual and moving singularity, "These forms of existence and of knowledge entail two symmetrical traits: on the one hand there is in them a determination that makes of them a relative unity, a kind of original quiddity, something more definite than the universe in its unlimited becoming could be ... something real that can be thought, or better still something thinkable that is realized; on the other hand [there is] this beginning of a singular unity, which is not an entity abstractly isolated for the purposes of science, but a concrete given that, by its very singular existence, is inserted into the total becoming" (1934a, 11). Abstract science, like physics, has a tendency to reduce everything to some lowest common denominator. But that is not the way we think of the world concretely. To follow Blondel in his elaboration of cosmic thought we have to insist more on what is original about the many different kinds of being, or intelligible natures, in the universe and about their very singularity.

The importance of this sort of insistence may be clear enough in the consideration of living things and human beings in their self-consciousness, whose unique and original identity is more obvious to all, but Blondel wants to make the same point about originality and identity with regard to lesser beings. They too have to be understood in their diversity and singularity, and this precisely is what he means by the thought realized in them. The universe is not a monolithic, compact sphere, as Parmenides still thought of it. Nor is it merely an interplay of merely physical forces, as some modern physicists would have us think. It is a wide diversity as well as a great multiplicity of beings in search of some unification. What we find in cosmic thought is a very original and essential fact: "an instability that undermines any pretense of taking the world, whether as a whole or in any of its fragments, as a foundation that is solid and sufficient" (1934a, 15). Blondel is well aware that he is not the first to have made this kind of observation about the world in which he finds himself as a thinking being, but he comes back to this in terms, not just of being, but also of thought, that is, cosmic thought.

What he says, however, that is perhaps original about this cosmic thought is that it is what accounts for the movement of the universe through diversification toward some unity in its deepest reality. To show how this is the case, Blondel distinguishes between two "aspect/elements" of thought, even on the cosmic level, that relate to one another in this movement, prior to any explicitly conscious thought. These two elements both repel and attract one another, imply and exclude one another, not only within thought itself at all its levels, preconscious, conscious, reflected, and even contemplative, but also in the order of existence or in the relation between what is real and what is thought. The distinction runs through the entirety of the universe viewed in its physical aspect as well as in the spiritual realm.

The first of these aspect/elements is spoken of as *noetic*, in that it corresponds to the descriptive and explanatory requirements of knowledge, while it is also seen as constitutive of things themselves in their existence. "It consists in what there is that is already unitary and universalizing in things and that is thereby rational and connective, so to speak, in the world" (1934a, 17). Such a real and rational connection, Blondel adds, "serves to solidify and make intelligible, up to a certain point, as a principle of order and necessity in the very midst of becoming and contingency, all that is possible and given for us to experience or to conceive" (1934a, 17). But this noetic element, however, is spoken of as only an epithet at this point in the consideration of cosmic thought, not as a substantive expressing an absolutized substance. It has to do with what is only a beginning, something unfinished, passing, even something perishable and incapable of reaching completion, even though it is already a realized thought and an object proportionate to a knowledge that does not have to fabricate it or impose it from the outside in accordance with some subjective necessity.

The other aspect/element, which is symmetric to the first, is also one of thought, but in an irreducibly different way. "In contrast to the first or, so to speak, in a perpetual encounter with the noetic, this [second] element expresses what is diverse, what is multiple, but that is such only because it is also the singular, the unique, the ineffable, that which has nothing comparable ... what the Greeks spoke of as a *hapax legomenon*" (1934a, 18). Because this element participates at once in the connection with all the rest as well as in the originality that interiorizes each singular in itself and in the power of reacting on all the rest, where it impresses itself and makes a mark of its own, Blondel speaks of it as *pneumatic,* a term borrowed from ancient philosophy that seems to suggest, albeit in a premature fashion, a breathing exchange that entails a reception, an interiorization and, under a new form that is at the same time innovating, a restitution of an infinity of conditions and real interactions. Through the pneumatic element in things, each thing is not only linked to all other things, but also responds to them in its own original way.

We can understand more readily how this takes place on the level of conscious thought, but Blondel wants to affirm the same kind of thought-dynamic at the level of "mere things," as Kant would say, in the cosmos as such. "It is the associate presence of these two elements that launches in a certain way, in keeping with an alternating rhythm, motion in all its forms and that, reconciling necessity and contingency, order and initiative, determinism and the inventive genius of nature and of spirit, will lead us all the way to the problem of a final union from which hangs the universal dynamism" (1934a, 19). In this perspective, matter does not appear as something apart, as a being independent from the rest of things and from a creator, even less as a creature *sui generis.* "It presents itself as the in-between, so to speak, of two aspects, or rather of two realities, in becoming, each diversely and incompletely intelligible" (1934a, 20-21).

Organic and Psychic Thought

This dynamic relation of the two elements of thought is given only in its most tenuous sense on the cosmic level, which does not yet entail any organic or psychic order. Blondel goes on to show how this dynamic of thought on the cosmic level already implies the more intrinsic dynamic that characterizes an organism, as distinct from the more extrinsic dynamism that binds things together on the cosmic level. He analyses this more intrinsic dynamism in its original and histological nature and in its essential modality, in the form of vibrating undulation. Then he goes on to show that it does not limit itself to determining merely organic systems. It also goes on to use what is organized as a base and as a point of departure for life, a life that already incarnates a thought ready to become organizing and inventive in its own right. With all that the positive sciences can determine in this transition, the movement is essentially a reality in the order of intelligibility where thought must discover its own germination and its own field of action. In it, according to Blondel, we can see thought progressively seeking its own realization, its own clarity, still in search of itself. What he insists on more than anything else is an internal finality of organisms that opens the way to life and to higher levels of thought.

Before going on to thinking itself, as consciously so and as conscious thought, however, Blondel distinguishes a third level of thought which presupposes the first two but is necessary for the advent of reason, and without which "the birth of intelligence" would be incomprehensible and unfeasible, what he calls psychic thought, which is still without a consciousness of itself as thought. At this level of emerging thought, Blondel discusses animal life and what is improperly called animal consciousness as a new kind of concentration of "impressions gathered by the senses under the form of excitations where there is no automatic reaction without going through a nerve center that organizes, modifies, and elaborates external data in view of counter thrusts that will express the unity and the specificity of the living being" (1934a, 47-48). Without this sort of mediating elaboration through the senses and the imagination, thinking thought could not emerge or become efficacious. But such sense activity must not be confused with self-conscious thought as such. It has to do, not with a beginning of thinking thought as such, but a prior condition for reflection that is nevertheless a kind of noetic reality, an integration of intelligible elements and of thought present in the world of life, an *élan vital* no doubt but not yet an *élan spirituel*.

Psychic thought is a sort of reduplication of life on a higher level through which consciousness will take hold bodily and "enter into the general dynamism of the world under the nascent form of a properly psychic energy, an imaginative representation, and a finality that becomes an effective causality and has a real influence in the complexus of this world, where there should be some communion between the apparently brutal concatenation of blind forces and the power of ideas as forces" (1934a, 51). Instincts, which lack any sort of self-conscious deliberation, are a part of this reality of transition between two worlds where thought, not yet disengaged from the immanent order of the universe, tends nevertheless to surpass it in relation to an order that is properly ideal. Even civilization can be thought of as a product of this psychic activity in its historical determinations. But when we come to the level of thinking thought or self-conscious thought, we come finally to a still more original form of thought with transcendent ramifications beyond the immanent order of the universe.

The object of Blondel's inquiry thus far has been to explore the cosmic and geological, the physical and biological, and even the psychic setting of thought that opens the way for thinking, what he refers to as *le penser*. Though he refers to all of this as a kind of thought, none of it is thinking in any self-conscious sense, or thinking thought, as he puts it when he speaks of *la pensée pensante*. Much less does it account for thinking thought as such, which constitutes an entirely new initiative in the world and requires or implies a new, transcendent principle of its own. The point of this initial exploration of what Blondel calls "real thought outside of thinking or thought thought *(pensée pensante ou pensée)*" is to show how the thinking or self-conscious thought of human beings, no matter how transcendent it may appear in its own right, is deeply implicated in the different levels of process and internal unification already taking place in the world prior to self-consciousness. Without the mediation of this kind of elaboration in the world itself, thinking thought could not come into its own, or become efficacious of its own order. All of it, however, is not a beginning of thinking thought as such. It is only a prior condition for reflective thought, a kind of noetic reality, an integration of intelligible elements and of thought present in the world of life. For thought that thinks, there has to be a return into self, something that has been implied all along in this initial exploration of real thought outside of thinking thought, inasmuch as there cannot be a consciousness of things without a consciousness of self. Now, for Blondel, this consciousness of self already implies consciousness of a transcendent, which will present a whole new kind of problem for the realm of thought. But before going into anything having to do with transcendence, he is careful to examine how self-conscious thinking thought itself emerges and makes its way into the world.

The Invention of Thinking Thought Through Language

This is an important step in Blondel's elaboration of thought in its many and diverse aspects. It brings out the essential difference between human thought, or thought on the spiritual level, and what he has already referred to as psychic thought, or thought on the merely animal level. It shows how, with thinking thought, we enter into a whole new order of diversification and unification that has not been seen even in the order of organic or of psychic thought. He refers to this as a dawn, an awakening, or the rising of the interior life of thinking, recognizing the ambiguity that surrounds this term "rising," since it refers both to the rising of the sun, drawing us from the state of rest to renewed activity through the arrival of its light, and to our own awakening in a new light of our own day. This is evidence that there is a thought that can be thought prior to thinking thought and that nourishes thinking thought, but it does not take away from the fact that there is a new initiative on the part of the conscious being giving rise to a new order of thought as it raises itself little by little to a properly rational life. This is a thought that begins to appear to itself self-consciously and interiorly as well as exteriorly, in an expansion of activity that can transform the world. It is something new in the universe, something given concretely, a new fact that illuminates itself from an act that is interior, as in a phenomenology of spirit coming into its own realm of illumination on the world.

To bring this new fact out, in the genesis of thought, Blondel begins by analyzing the very subtle differences there are between the psychic life of a child and that of primates in the purely animal kingdom. He refers to empirical studies where the behavior of children has been compared to that of other animals in ordinary life situations, including the studies of Piaget in the development of the child. What he brings out is, not how close animals come to being human, but rather how the child distances itself from non-rational animals in its approach to life and in its solutions to the problems of life. There is a time when the primate is ahead of the child thanks to the greater subtlety of its sense perceptions, its greater agility, its more specialized needs. It can satisfy its avidity more quickly than the child. But then "there comes a moment where the child takes an advantage that is definitive and decisive: the day when a flash of reflection makes it substitute for purely empirical agitations a curiosity about objects to be overcome, a way of proceeding based on a search for causes and means, in short an explanation that can already be characterized as rational and general" (1934a, 71). In other words, instead of proceeding purely by trial and error, the child begins to proceed in a way that can be termed properly only as *methodical.* Instead of proceeding *à l'aventure,* so to speak, the child begins to construct plans of action, so that it can look much farther ahead in its prospection as it reflects much farther back in its experience.

There are those who would insist that animals too have method in their life, something like human method, which can give them an air of being rationally conscious, as humans are, but Blondel speaks of this sort of insistence as a kind of anthropomorphism for which there is no justification. Blondel would insist much more on the difference even in psychic life itself or in sense activity as such between humans and other animals. Sensation in humans is much more open to the universal dimensions of reason than it is in animals. The analogy that would reduce human sensation to purely animal sensation is one that is false, and Blondel has empirical studies to show that they are contrary to fact. "There are other senses than ours, and if reason is a universal instrument, we must admit that it has at its disposal only incomplete and partial tools, whence the need to devise artificial instruments and to borrow from physical forces new means of investigation and action" (1934a, 79). This is something non-rational animals do not do or recognize any need for doing. Only human initiative and consciousness overcomes this incompleteness of its sense organs and thereby multiplies the value of what it has to work with from nature, especially if we think of the way the hand becomes the organ of thought par excellence, as Aristotle noted long ago. "Even in what seems purely animal in us there is already a preparation, a reason ready to appear and to reign, a sort of throne where thought can come to take its place" (1934a, 79).

On the other hand, however, Blondel also notes that thought in ourselves, no matter how pure it may be, cannot in its present circumstance do without its ties to its lower attachments. Hence, even as we insist on the heterogeneity and the originality of rational thinking in the world, it is still necessary to affirm and to understand the solidarity within ourselves between humble organic and psychic functions and the highest forms of rational thought. There is no other way of conceiving rational thinking as it presents itself for us. "If nature were not penetrated by a noetic element *(natura ut ratio)*, if reason were not infused in our nature prior to being purified in itself *(ratio ut natura)*, the life of our rational thought *(ratio ut ratio)* would not be possible" (1934a, 80). These are *implications* that we must take into account as matters that run deep in our experience and that will bear rich fruit in our understanding of how thought runs its course in the universe.

To bring out the original aspect of this outbreak of rational thought in the universe, Blondel speaks of an *invention*, a stunning discovery that leaves the inventor in a new state of joy and enlightenment, "the disclosing of a reality, that has not come out from behind what was hiding it, but that was already existing under obstacles that were preventing its manifestation and its useful exercise" (1934a, 84). We have no direct access through analysis and reflection to such moments of invention, where we could grasp its first blush in the quick of experience. It normally takes place very gradually, bit by bit, and we only notice it once it has taken place, in a new resourcefulness of thought. We look for signs of it in every infant and perhaps even "find" some before the invention has really taken place in a particular individual. What is crucial, however, is the invention itself that takes place within every child as it comes to human consciousness, the discovery of itself as a thinking rational self and of the interior light that makes it so.

There is, however, a way of coming closer to this moment of first human invention in an individual consciousness that Blondel explores, by examining the case of individuals who have been deprived of the normal psychic experience that contributes so much to the emergence of rational consciousness. Normally, the individual has a rich sense experience that includes much rational sedimentation through hearing and seeing to draw from in coming to its own reflective self-consciousness. But someone who is deprived of these activities from birth, or shortly thereafter, does not have such a rich experience to draw from in making rational connections and may be retarded in the emergence of its properly human consciousness. For such an individual, Blondel notes, "the act of thinking will arise from much lower, from the depths of organic life, from which will appear its original elevation" (1934a, 84-85). Reflection on the experience of such individuals can represent a certain philosophical advantage for Blondel in bringing out the subtle beauties of thought in its forms and in its movements without the swaddling clothes of sense activity in which we normally find them. And so in the second moment of exploration of the new and original fact of rational consciousness in the world, he turns to a consideration of individuals who appear to have come to their own rational consciousness much later in life than usual, thanks to the special efforts of teachers who took great care to reach into the intelligence buried in the depths of their psyche.

He cites the story of Marie Heurtin, which he had used frequently in his classes on the subject of human consciousness and which was widely known in France, and he even refers to Helen Keller, without mentioning any of the specifics in her case. What is noted about consciousness in all such cases is an apparent lack of intelligence, a darkness from which they cannot be drawn, or a dungeon from which they cannot be liberated, at least not by any normal intelligent means of communication. The problem is to find means of communication that will reach the intelligence hidden within the recesses of a psyche closed in upon itself because of handicaps that cannot be directly overcome, whether they be handicaps of sight or hearing or just a prolonged absence of human communication at crucial moments of growth, much as an animal is closed in upon itself by its shortsighted reaction and adaptation to its environment. The genius of the teachers who have found such means has been that they were able to find ways of tapping into the native intelligence of these sensibly handicapped individuals in new and original ways that got around these handicaps, in a first confrontation with the internal self of such individuals recognized as being human without any sign of acting consciously as humans on their part.

What Blondel wants to insist on in such experiences, however, is that we are assisting at the *invention*, not of something that did not exist in any degree, nor of something that would be simply unconscious, though already real, but the *invention* of a latent energy striving to come forth but still losing itself in darkness and floating about in vagueness, "without thereby ceasing to come up against the unknown barrier, to suffer indistinctly and unspeakably from it and without ceasing to continue in a movement of internal growth that makes the suffering worse, without finding any means of discovering its cause, articulating its meaning, and even getting an idea of it" (1934a, 86-87). This is how Blondel explains the state of individuals who are struggling for intelligence but who do not yet know what they are struggling for. The task of teachers is to help them to become conscious of what they are struggling for before they even know what they are struggling for.

The thing that makes all this pent-up energy of thought and intelligence most interesting, philosophically speaking, is that it revolves around language. From the standpoint of those still in their unwitting search for self-understanding or understanding of any kind, the problem is to find a means for expressing what they are looking for. "They are unable to help themselves for lack of being able to make themselves passive and witnesses to their own initiative as inventing intentional signs. In their solitude, reduced to tactile impressions, they remain incapable of inventing a language for them to begin hearing themselves" (1934a, 88). From the standpoint of those who would draw them out of their mute solitude, the secret is to begin communicating through language with those who have no sense of language to begin with. Language has long been invented among humans. But one cannot simply and directly invent it for another from the outside, so to speak, especially not for one who has been deprived of most means of recognizing language in the way that it presents itself in normal visual and auditory human intercourse.

Even creating a special language suited to those who have only tactile impressions to go by will not do the trick. For language is not a trick. It is something that has to be invented from the interior by each would-be self-conscious individual, which is especially true for the very first invention of it in anyone's life experience. It has to happen interiorly as a new initiative before one can begin to borrow and to interiorize the language already devised by others. Learning a language from others always entails reinventing it for oneself, especially in the case of doing it for the first time. Like the proverbial eye of the needle, language is a narrow gap indeed that one has to pass through in order to enter into the world of understanding, but once one has passed through this gap, it is a much broader world that opens before the one who has come to self-consciousness. Everyone goes through such a determinate gap, even those who emerge to their own consciousness more gradually and in more normal ways. We usually do not remember these subtle moments of awakening in our later, more self-conscious life, but they were nevertheless real moments of invention from the inside as well as in response to external impressions in the shape of words. For the handicapped who come late to such moments, it is easier to remember such moments because the difference they make is so dramatic in their own lives as well as in that of others; and it is easier to represent the difference a spiritual awakening makes in the life of an individual, who might otherwise have remained walled in by immediate sense impressions of touch and reaction to them. The proximate cause of this sort of awakening, Blondel points out, is in the act of symbolizing or of instituting intentional signs for ourselves, which opens up for us a whole new realm of thought that goes far beyond the physical and the organic realm we start from.

The rest of Blondel's investigation into thought will have to do with this new realm of self-conscious thought that we see now emerging for the first time. In this realm there are new problems that will have to be resolved, but before moving into this discussion Blondel pauses to make a quick inventory of what can already be seen about thinking thought in this first moment of its emergence into its own light of consciousness. No matter how humble the occasion and the origin of this rudimentary consciousness, its first awakening already entails a complexus of sentiments, movements, and aspirations that call for careful analysis of essential implications representing universal and necessary components in any particular experience. By looking at the contours of thinking in this nascent state, which is more one of thinking than of thought, we can see it as it arises spontaneously as a nature, so to speak, before it becomes an object of thought as such. We speak of this spontaneous act of invention as if it were simple in comparison to the complex material preconditions it presupposes, but in itself it is not a simple act. It is made up of many essential ingredients that come together simultaneously in concurrence with one another. For Blondel it is important to make an inventory of these ingredients in philosophy at the outset, but with the *caveat* that none of them is to be understood independently of the others. They are only different aspects that appear simultaneously in the unity of a spiritual act.

Blondel enumerates twelve of these ingredients, many of which overlap and flow into one another. First there is (1) an affective disposition, a sort of Spinozist *conatus*, which connotes a certain need for infinity. Then there is (2) a surpassing of what is merely given, *un dépassement*, which is the result of an unrest and gives rise to a kind of prospection about what one is to make of oneself. Third, there is even (3) a certain leap into the infinite that surpasses all its physical conditions. In fact, this leap is (4) acosmic; it is not something of this world as given. There is in this act (5) a certain duality, a kind of internal conflict that becomes a test or a challenge, which forces it to reflect and take hold of itself. In this act there is also (6) a determinate form that results from its own initiative, the sign that comes, not from the preconditions of thinking, but from the depths of thought itself, which is not yet expressed but is beginning to emerge in the light of day. Then there is (7) the fabrication of the representational sign that becomes an instrument for the spirit in its coping with the world. There is also (8) a supra-natural character in this creation of a sign, something almost divine, which conveys upon this experience a certain religious, if not superstitious, dimension. Beyond the opposition of subject and object, there is (9) a certain assimilation of thought with reality and of reality with thought with a purpose of universalization within the pneumatic singularity of a singular spirit. With this there is also (10) a transcendence that becomes the common principle of art, science, morality, and even religious aspiration. In its surpassing of all that is given to understand, there is also in this act (11) a capacity to dominate all of nature, to go beyond what is given and to become a giver of meaning for things. Finally, there is the intimation of (12) a radical crisis, a metaphysical unease, a hidden antagonism that will have to be pacified in relation to the principle of its power and of its light.

All this implies many more things in the life of the nascent spirit, but Blondel does not elaborate on them at this point. In this initial inventory he is satisfied with only giving a suggestion of the kind of life we are getting into as conscious, thinking beings. The next step in his elaboration of the genesis of thought, after this initial taking stock of what there is in the first awakening and invention of consciousness, is to follow how this new intellectual spontaneity deploys itself in the normal course of human experience. This will take him through three stages: first, how we come to know or even construct objects in our thinking; second, how from this we come to know ourselves as subjects, through a higher construction of reflected thought; and finally, how through a purification of our knowledge of both objects and the subject we come to understand that the knowledge of this duality implies a constant recourse to a knowledge that is no longer that of the senses or of consciousness, but one that raises us to rational principles and to affirmations that surpass all our experience, necessary and universal truths without which neither our sense knowledge nor our psychological or moral consciousness would be possible or conceivable. These are three distinct domains for analysis, but they must not be separated from one another. They must be understood in relation with one another as aspects of the movement of thought as it seeks its own self-actualization and unification.

The Problem of Knowledge

We saw how from the very beginning Blondel distinguishes the problem of thought from the problem of knowledge, the latter being only a particular problem within the broader problem of thinking as a whole. Here, however, we see how the problem of knowledge enters into the problem of thought, for it is through knowledge that thought develops spontaneously. Thinking begins as a striving to know, and such a striving requires an effort on the part of the one thinking. This is why there arises a problem of knowledge, as if there were a gap between the one striving to know and what there is to know. This gap is usually represented through a distinction between two terms, object and subject, that somehow have to be brought together in a single act of knowing. If we start from the supposition of a gap to be bridged between these two terms, there is no way of solving the problem of knowledge directly. Any attempt to bridge the gap, whether from the side of the subject or from the side of the object, will always appear as interference or falsification in the act of knowing, so that true knowing of anything substantial will appear as impossible. The only way to solve the problem of knowing is to recast it as a part of the problem of thinking as a whole, which is where the distinction between subject and object is made to begin with.

Blondel does not undertake to solve the problem of knowledge frontally, so to speak, in his science of thought. He shows rather how it is solved spontaneously and critically in the exercise of thinking itself. Thinking thought as its emerges in human beings begins by turning naturally toward objects that appear external and prior to the knowledge it has of them, and even to the knowledge it acquires of itself. Thinking does not know itself before turning to objects. It discovers itself only in this turning to objects. It is not that objects are the true principles of knowing, but rather that we would not start thinking without reference to obvious objects that seem to impose themselves on a thinking subject. For Blondel these objects appear to have an undeniable solidity, and yet they are only unstable points for thought to touch on, like shaky stepping-stones one has to tread on lightly and quickly in a brook in order to cross over to the other side. Conscious thought uses objects to reason from, in search of a more complete truth it is looking for. The question for Blondel is why we have recourse to such supports in our thinking, how we use them, and to what shore they lead us beyond themselves as objects.

To begin with, they are part of the problem in the way we come to think of the universe in its diversity and unity. In discussing this problem of a universe that is not one on the level of real thought, prior to thinking thought, movement was seen as a solution of unification in nature, in life, and in consciousness. What we have to work with is a rich elaboration and many partial victories of different kinds of individuals that have a standing in the world. As conscious thought emerges, the world appears to present it with an interconnected set of distinct and unified objects, "each one resolving somehow the fundamental problem of the one and the many, the continuous and the heterogeneous" (1934a, 128).

Under the general term of "object" we usually include a wide diversity of things in motion given in experience, ranging from the most inert to the most active, from the sensible to the perceived, the conceived, and the real. Through the latter term, *real*, we tend to fix things in some kind of stability and to absolutize them as atomized beings, as if we were purely passive in their regard. And yet we know that objectification is as much a function of the subject as it is a fact on the part of the object. We reify the world much as we tend to produce different artifacts, constructed beings as distinct from natural beings, in order to reshape and dominate it. The advance of positive science and technology shows how successful we have been in this manipulation of objects through concepts, which tends to reinforce our tendency to absolutize the way we objectify or reify the diversity of things given in experience. But we also know that what we know exteriorly in experience is not static, that it is made up of distinctly subsistent realities, different centers of outlook and action, which are not complete and independent in themselves, but are nevertheless original in their spontaneity, in a way that entails some intelligibility, some noetic aspect, as well as objectivity. These are things we had to advert to in following the traces of real thought in the cosmos, prior to the appearance of thinking thought. Here, with the advent of thinking thought, we see how the world presents itself objectively as that which thought has to attend to first in its first initiative. The world of objects is not the principle of thinking, but it is a necessary condition for thinking. We do not begin thinking except with reference to things we can objectify in our experience.

These objects are the first solution, at many different levels, for the problem of unification that thought finds amid the multiplicity of things. Thinking seizes upon them in its own synthesizing activity. But they are only partial solutions, incomplete solutions of a world still in motion toward a higher unification, where conscious thought has its own dimension to add to the equation. Thus, from the object, we are led back to the thinking subject, who needs objects to think about, but who can encompass the totality of objects in the scope of its activity. It is important to recognize that this subject is no less an object in the world than anything else, but at the same time it is essential to see that it entails an internal initiative irreducible to anything objective. "The objective order as a whole implies a subjective reality without which nothing of the object would be thought. . . . Even where we seem to be conscious of objects before being conscious of ourselves, it is already the indistinct but real presence of the subject to itself that is the effective condition for thinking thought" (1934a, 133).

Thus, in this transition from object to subject, or in the fertile marriage of the two, as he also calls it, Blondel comes to a second crucial moment in the elaboration of thought, the one that takes thought itself as its object, so to speak. From the standpoint of thought itself, which is always in quest of a more comprehensive synthesis, one that brings about greater unity in diversity as well as multiplicity in harmony, in a union without confusion, the purpose of the confrontation with objects in the first exercise of thinking can be seen as serving the awakening of thought to itself as well as to the things of the world. This is why it is an error to absolutize objects into atomized beings. Blondel is more interested in seeing them in motion as part of the movement of thought itself in the universe, and in stepping on them only lightly in order to get to the shore of thinking itself as a real constituent of our experience. Far from belittling the validity of the objective sciences, he wants to affirm their necessity as a first step in the exercise of thought about the world, and about itself as part of the world, through a sort of objectifying introspection. But he does not think that thought can stop at that. Thought must also turn upon its own act reflectively and think through what it brings to the world as well as what it has to aim at in its own right as thought. It must pass from what is external to it to what is internal, *ab exterioribus ad interiora*, according to the phrase of Augustine that Blondel cites more than once. This opens up for it a whole new realm of knowledge that must be articulated for consciousness itself in terms of its subjectivity.

It is generally thought that the subject is more the domain of philosophy than objects in the world. Blondel avers that this is true for ancient philosophy as well as modern. But in his attempt to make explicit what is implicit in the genesis of subjective life, in the strong sense of this expression, he begins by noting how different modern philosophies have not gone far enough in their turn to the thinking subject. Psychologism focuses on so-called "facts of consciousness," not to mention the supposedly primitive fact of an internal sense, but in treating these "facts" it only objectifies them as another set of things in the world to be taken into account, like things that are still exterior to the subject. It does not get to the surge of subjective life itself in its proper actuality as thinking thought. Starting from an abstract transcendental analysis, Kant gets back to the subject as a unity of apperception, but this is seen as only a function in an objectified scheme of how knowledge takes place, not as the real subject that experiences itself in its thinking. In the subjective order that we are entering with the genesis of thinking thought, "we cannot have the least sense of a real life without encountering the concrete, personal reality of the thinking subject and of its spiritual realism" (1934a, 151). "What experience offers us, is a circumincession between diversely conscious phenomena and the concrete union that initiates the original certitude of our personal singularity" (1934a, 150). What Blondel wants to look into is the spiritualist realism of the thinking subject, as he calls it at one point, not just its function in the generation of objects of experience.

Blondel even refers to a certain "pure and integral phenomenology" as insufficient for expressing what every subject knows about itself in the experience of its own act of thinking, inasmuch as such a phenomenology tries to prescind from any ontological commitment. To be sure, such a phenomenology constitutes a certain concrete return to facts or to the "things themselves," including consciousness itself, but what are such facts if we do not include in them their actuality? Blondel knew how far such a method could go in the science of subjectivity. He had pushed it to the hilt with his own phenomenology of action in the central part of his dissertation on *Action* in 1893, considering only what it is that we think necessarily in the deployment of action, apart from any ontological commitment, and putting off to the end the question of the being of action and of the transcendence beyond any immanent order of concepts. But, in the more mature expression of his thinking, he finds this kind of reserve too artificial, too restrictive, in its assessment of what there is in the genesis of the thinking subject as an original act of unification in the experience of the world. The idea of a "subjective fact" is still too ambiguous. What Blondel wants to explicitate in this part of his reflection is the *act* implicit in everyone's thinking, through which the subject constitutes itself as thinking that is implicit in everyone's thinking. Here in *La Pensée,* having explored the preparation and the condition for the emergence of thinking thought in the cosmic, the organic, and the psychic order, he goes directly to the knowledge we have of ourselves as thinking, spiritual beings, whether as child or as more learned.

The Constitutive Act of Thinking and Its Principles of Reasoning

This knowledge consists in a kind of looking within, at the subjective realities within ourselves, where there is more being still than in everything objectified knowledge has to offer or can contain. It is a sense of one's own interior life as something real spiritually. What it focuses on is not just the superficial subjectivism of the phenomena of consciousness, but the real intimacy of a soul in act in its initiative of thinking on its own. What this initiative discloses is not just what we can call instituting the facts of consciousness, but also what we have to think of as the affirming of itself as a substantial reality. This does not mean that we have to go back to some primitive fact of an interior sense, something merely given like a surge of nervous energy on one side or resistance on the opposite side, two things that would remain unconscious in isolation from one another, unless consciousness related them to one another. It is impossible that such a primitive fact should spark the light of consciousness itself. We must rather look to the initiative of the consciousness itself in its endeavor of unification, and we must do so reflectively, that is, by drawing out the self-conscious reflection that is already at work in this new initiative. This is where the cause or the reason for this new initiative must be sought, not just in the intuition of psychological facts. In other words, we must pass beyond, not just objective data, but also subjective facts, to a more interior act and a higher order of reality.

"Is it true," Blondel asks, "that the thinking subject, as tied as it may be to its antecedent conditions and to its own phenomena, reaches itself directly either in a primitive fact, independently of the particular occasions where it embodies itself, or in its own meta-empirical reality?" (1934a, 153). The answer would be easy, if we could say we experience ourselves as absolute in a sort of spiritual atomism that closes in upon itself. But that is not the way we experience our spiritual reality as we come to an act reflecting upon itself. In this budding reflection that we are trying to focus on, there is implied what Blondel calls a certain impersonal and universal dimension that draws the subject out of the privacy of its individuality, the dynamism of a living reason within our person. Along with this reflection, there is also a prospection with an underlying requirement for achievement, a tendency and a demand that is intrinsic to thought itself. "This living truth acts effectively in the thinking being to make it capable of knowing not only empirical or subjective realities, but also needs a presence that is demanding, the duty of an order that is real in itself and to be realized in ourselves" (1934a, 156f.).

All of this shows that the thinking subject has its origin and its principles in something broader than itself and that it is called to go out of itself toward something greater than itself. Its living thought implies an affirmation of something absolute, something universal, first truths, and everything that can be called the principles of reason, something that will have to be explained at some point. But at this point Blondel is more interested in showing how these principles are inserted into the thinking subject as if they were its very own. They "appear to have their subsistence only by actualizing themselves in the living thought, in the personal reality that is thinking them, affirming them and applying them as the effective norm of the intelligible — the intelligible, always tied to an intelligence" (1934a, 158).

These principles of reason are not in facts as such, but in the thinking subject. The order that they constitute can be thought of in either one of two ways, either as flowing necessarily from the nature of the subject, "so that the order would be ideal only if it is concretely real and personalized," or as relating to our thought, which thinks and vivifies these principles, spontaneously and necessarily "to a thought that is even more thinking, an ideal that is more living and more concrete, an absolute where there could be a reconciliation of terms that up to now have appeared to us as irreducible, incompatible and indestructible" (1934a, 158).

Blondel draws out the implications of each one of these hypotheses. In the first case we would have to limit thought to some sort of cyclical movement or to the immanence of an eternal return, an immanentism that would be open but that would nevertheless close in upon itself, like a movement that can only start over and over again. "In the second hypothesis, subjective thought, far from taking itself as the sufficient source and term of thinking *(le penser)*, refrains instead from attributing to the objective idea it has of an absolute truth a validity equal to the transcendence that it affirms" (1934a, 159). To be sure, subjective thought recognizes that our interior life implies the immanence within us of such an idea and even the active efficacious role it plays in our knowledge, but from there to identifying this notion and this real action to the full reality of the transcendent that is conceived and affirmed, there opens up an abyss that we would be blind to ignore, deluded to deny, and absurd to claim to be able to bridge.

Of the two hypotheses, Blondel clearly thinks that only the second does justice to the rational experience of the singular thinking subject as it relates to the universal, in contrast to Hegel, who appears to settle for the first. But before trying to make the case for what he wants to affirm, Blondel pauses to draw out the truths implied in a subject who is conscious, not only of objects within itself, but also simultaneously of itself in the knowledge it has of everything else it knows. In the connection between these two affirmations or these two sides of consciousness he finds a twofold genetic sense. On a superficial level, truths proceed from the bottom up, or, to use the Augustinian phrase, *ab exterioribus et inferioribus ad interiora*, which corresponds to appearances in the chronological development of thought. On a more profound level, however, the dependence of these intellectual phases is determined by an inverse subordination, from the top down. Again, for Blondel, it is the second of these two levels that is the more essential, so that the history of our thought could be summed up by saying that, if reason seems to result from a progress in experience, consciousness itself is produced by reason and for reason. "Already indispensable for the knowledge of distinct objects, rational activity underlies subjective life even before this very life, unable to close in upon itself and to justify and perfect itself, erects above itself, if not at its own summit, an ideal order" (1934a, 160). Such an order is neither entirely unreal nor entirely subjective, because it has a twofold efficiency, that of bringing forth the subject conscious of itself and that of inducing this subject to go out of itself and to always surpass its own consciousness and its own action.

We see why Blondel is not satisfied with starting from a simple fact of consciousness, no matter how interior or primitive we might imagine such a fact to be. What is at the origin in the genesis of rational self-conscious thought is an activity of reason itself that makes its appearance in the discourse of objectification. There is no positive grasp of this activity, as in some intuition. There is only an elaboration that recovers itself reflectively in its own act. It is launched, so to speak, by a principle that is broader than itself, or even infinite in its scope, toward an end that also surpasses it as it is given in its singularity, so that the self-conscious subject is not an end unto itself, nor does it find within itself the desired equation with itself. All of this implies the presence of something really transcendent at the origin of subjective thought and in the end toward which it is spontaneously and necessarily oriented as rational. This is why Blondel can already begin to characterize anyone who would restrict thought to some internal immanent dimension of the subject, not only as idealist in some way, whether it be individualist, personalist, humanistic, socialist, or communist, but also as idolatrous and superstitious. Any such attempt to keep the subject turned in upon itself in some immanent order is an abuse of a power that is within ourselves but that is not entirely from ourselves or for ourselves. One has ultimately to refer to a reality that is beyond ourselves as well as beyond the universe we hold in our gaze, before one can do justice to subjective thought in our experience.

In this analysis of the thinking subject as it emerges in thought as well as in its own thinking, Blondel argues not only for the first part of the Augustinian dictum, *ab exterioribus ad interiora,* but also for the second part as well, *ab interioribus ad superiora,* no matter how one might conceive this higher order for the moment. His point is to show that this higher order is not something added on to rational consciousness, once it is constituted in its own experience, but rather it is something already present and real as principle and end in the very genesis of rational self-consciousness. It is part of what is implied in our own self-consciousness as well as in our consciousness of the world. Blondel proceeds to show how this is so in the way rational thought itself develops.

Insufficiency and Aspiration to a Higher Order in Rational Thinking

What remains for Blondel to do in this deployment of what is normal in the intellectual spontaneity of consciousness is to bring out the rational ordering that takes place in relation to the higher order of things, the *superiora*. This he thinks of as the ladder of reason reaching toward the idea of God or the divine, which resolves certain problems for reason, but also presents new ones for it. He begins with the observation that we cannot hypostatize or absolutize the subject in such a way that we can be satisfied with it as we find it in experience. We are constantly going beyond it, and this in two directions: below or in depth, in that we never exhaust the least fact of consciousness, so that our reflective thought never adequately represents the spontaneous life of the subject, and above or in elevation, in that, for us to ground this ever-inadequate knowledge, we are always appealing to assertions that somehow belie and exceed our experience. "Self-consciousness would remain incomprehensible and unrealizable without this implication of an order that we have to call rational and, in a sense that has to be explained, transcendent" (1934a, 169-70).

What makes us conscious of the insufficiency of our knowledge of objects and of the subject is an immanence of reason in all the lower forms of thinking thought. Through reason we come to principles and to ideas of real existence, of true unity and personal identity, or other essential truths regarding data that do not realize them and experiences that do not contain them in their indivisible purity. Without claiming that such principles and ideas are innate to human thought as such, Blondel wants to show that they are virtually included and even effectively present in the various states of our consciousness so that they make our intellectual experience of things and of ourselves possible, even though they do not proceed from our sensations, our perceptions, or our reflections as such, whether subjective or objective. For there is nothing in the latter that meets what thought is looking for or that satisfies its essential exigencies. Because of the incompatibility or the incommensurability between the empirical and the intelligible, some have resigned themselves to agnosticism or they have concluded to a strange sort of dualism between the rational and the irrational, but Blondel tries to refocus on the truths themselves as they are present even in those we misrepresent, and then he follows step by step how living thought proceeds effectively.

He begins with the tendency everyone has to set up, alongside or above the data we experience, the vision of another order that is different from the impressions received by our sensibility, our intelligence, our will. "We live," he writes, "we think, we will only for what is not and for what we would want to be. This is the principle of the congenital unrest that is the specific trait of being human" (1934a, 171). What is involved in this universal need, if we judge it on the basis of its genesis and according to the end toward which it tends? It is not just a dream based on pathological states, or the *libido* of pleasures that are unsatisfied, or a curiosity that is insatiable, although these can be thought of as changing proximate conditions for this more fundamental desire. It is rather a desire or a love of something beyond that already implies a presence of what is still desired in a mysterious interchange with a transcendent that is already immanent somehow, and yet remains inaccessible to our grasp. It is an invisible active principle within our thought from which this fundamental inclination flows, so that, as Augustine and others have said, we would not be looking for it if we had not already found it. What comes into play here are not merely regulative principles or constructions superimposed on our consciousness or on the reality of things, but real truths that cannot be fitted into objects or the subject we experience without or within ourselves, truths that are affirmed as constituting an order of higher realities, no less than they are necessary to the empirical order. This is why we find reason arrogating to itself an original realm of its own over and above the merely empirical order. Blondel sees in this a threefold affirmation of ideas: "There is a transcendent principle; — this transcendent does not apply to real objects; — it nevertheless has an objective value that has no adequate application except in some ideal reality" (1934a, 172-73).

The question for philosophy is to figure out what this reality consists in that is irreducible and yet indispensable to everything we know experientially. Many answers have been given to this question in the abstract, but Blondel wants to approach the truth in question as it presents itself concretely in the progression of thought through objects and the subject that has brought us to this question. How are we to think of these ideas and principles of reason that have been shown to be at once immanent to every conscious thought and yet transcendent to every experience, whether exterior or interior? Are they real in an objective sense only insofar as they result from a propulsion of nature and consciousness following from the momentum of an inexhaustible becoming in the world and in spirit? Or does the consciousness we have even of the immanent data of our thought, on the contrary, depend on an effective presence, on a real transcendent? It is important to sort out the differences between these two alternatives in order to get at the truth concerning the transcendent order of reason.

In the first case, the entire logical, metaphysical, moral, social, and religious structure in our thought would be founded on a category of the ideal that could lead to nothing more than some overman *(surhomme)*, which would be only a cult of humanity projected into an indefinite future. In this case all the effort of the human being to rise to a higher order would rest on our imagination, not anything real. In the second case, on the other hand, it is the term itself, as hidden as it may still be, that furnishes all our effort, all becoming, not just with a fictitious or anthropomorphic ideal, but with a positive stimulation, the leverage of an infinite power to raise our contingent and indigent being to some participation in a creative cause. Far from settling for some sort of *Übermensch* in the human aspiration to a higher order, Blondel finds in it something that relates it directly to a cause that surpasses even the most universal immanent will to power.

The choice between the two alternatives he lays out cannot be arbitrary. If thought remains coherent with itself, if it follows the spontaneous movement that has already brought it to this threshold, from which it must now find its course deliberately as well as necessarily, it cannot avoid affirming a transcendent that is not only objectively ideal but also ontologically real. This affirmation of an absolute is contained in every consciousness, even of the relative, not just as a dialectical and formal interplay of notions, but through the indispensable and acknowledged efficacy of a pure act higher than any of our passive or active states, and yet buried in what there is of force and clarity within us and within the world. What we undergo most fundamentally, then, in our thought, is the *idea* of a real transcendent from which a certain necessity flows that is associated with a natural conviction among human beings and a religious instinct that hinges on the affirmation of a first cause, a mysterious power, a superhuman reality. This is so fundamental to our way of thinking, according to Blondel, that there is no such thing as an atheist in the strict sense of the term. If there is a problem of atheism, which parallels the problem of superstition, it is because the idea of God has not been properly understood. There is always a certain confusion that arises when the idea of God is introduced, or rather brought out from its embeddedness in the contingencies of our experience. The task of philosophy is to keep this idea as clear and distinct as possible without separating it from the very act of thinking in which this absolute transcendent reality presents itself.

Blondel recognizes that the sense of the divine, as it presents itself in ordinary experience, is ambiguous. It can lend itself to a denial of any clear idea of God as well as to all sorts of superstition or exaggerated claims even about our idea of God. First of all, it is not the easy idea that many make it out to be, the solution to all our problems about the world, the absolute equation we would like to jump to in our assessment of reality. Whatever idea of God we may have, no matter how purified, it does not disclose or contain God, as he is or even if he is. Whatever we come to know about God arises from a laborious genesis in which our thought is always torn between the noetic ideal of a reason taken up with a universal and impersonal unity, and the constant aspiration of thought toward a concrete reality in a singular and inaccessible intimacy that Blondel characterizes as pneumatic. To speak properly about God as he presents himself in our rational experience, we must always keep track of these two lines of thinking, one dialectical and rational and the other spiritual and aspirational, that, together and in tension with one another, have brought us to conceive of him in the first place. For Blondel there is no way of separating the God of Philosophers and the God of spiritual and religious Tradition. The two can only be conceived in relation to one another. As a philosopher, he will insist more on proofs for the existence of God, but only insofar as these complement, clarify, and purify the initial spiritual sense of God we all start from in the real movement of our thought toward God in the concrete, a Reality that is neither without reason nor merely ideal.

The Problem of God for Rational Thinking

Thus, for Blondel, there are two aspects to the problem of God in his transcendence, one that is rational and ideal, and the other that is spiritual and vital. Far from deducing the affirmation of God from abstract principles, he shows how these intellectual premises flow from a more profound realist conception of a divine subsistence. At the same time, however, he sees this implicit and concrete certitude of a real transcendent as always elaborated, infinitesimally at least, by the requirement of some incipient speculation. These are two distinct *élans* that converge on a being that is Infinite. And the convergence must not fall short either with only our idea, finite and always abstract and inadequate, of the real infinite realizing itself in our immanence, or with falsely identifying our idea with the transcendent absolute that comes precisely into question for us. In an immanentist idealist view, where the transcendent absolute is simply identified with the idea we have of it, there is no question of a really transcendent absolute. Rational discourse ends with the noetic identification of the absolute with our idea of it.

For Blondel, on the other hand, there is also the pneumatic aspect of thought to be brought into consideration, where the singularity of each consciousness is to be seen in confrontation not only with objects, or with others in the world, but also with the radical otherness of the Transcendent as real. This is not for him a matter of some new intuition or of some mystical religious experience. Discursive reason itself is necessary for coming to a proper idea of God as transcendent, but reason as preceded, sustained, nourished, and perfected by a more concrete living thought, which, for its part, would remain vague and dreamy and perhaps die of inanition, if it did not come by some precise contours, some alimentary sustentation in ideas that proceed from the labor of reason. For Blondel, it is the symbiosis of these two thoughts, the noetic and the pneumatic, within ourselves that brings us to a proper understanding of who or what God is in himself as well as for us. The dialectical argument is valid only if it aims at a living object. Our concrete affirmations gain precision and efficacy only through forms that are at once definite and plastic. Both are equally essential modes of thought.

In exposing the ways of discursive reason for validating and demonstrating the affirmation of God *per gradus debitos,* Blondel distinguishes nine degrees of clarification, so to speak. The first is the fundamental assertion of something beyond the real data of nature and of consciousness that we have already seen him insist on repeatedly, and that he sees as inevitable in the way we consciously experience the world. This gets him beyond both the atheism that would deny this necessary idea of a Transcendent and the dualism that would posit a reality independent of this Reality in itself. The second degree begins to deal with the problem of superstition and idolatry, both of which fall short of what is meant by the affirmation of a God who is totally transcendent, and the parallel problem of atheism, which is satisfied with false images of God or the limited freedom of human thought that goes with these images. At this level one has to argue methodically against such hasty and temerarious conclusions in order to bring out the convergence of both rational and spiritual thought toward something higher than the world and consciousness in the concrete. At the third degree Blondel recognizes that a legitimate and valid case can be made for the existence of God starting from the visible world and the physical order in what have been called cosmological proofs. He does not elaborate such a proof, but he notes that in distinguishing between the noetic and the pneumatic even in cosmic thought, he has already set up the dynamic for such a proof by showing what there is that is solid in the universe and what there is that is deficient in this passing being, requiring a cause that does not pass.

Blondel runs through the dynamic of other proofs as well. At the fourth degree he suggests a sort of teleological proof starting from the reality of organic life and conscious thought, which is also experienced as requiring a foundation that comes from deeper within each living or conscious thing and raises it to a higher level of aspiration. What "these fertile organisms and these comprehensive consciousnesses reveal through their failing ambitions and their encouraging achievements is the propulsive presence, the attractive expectancy, the necessity of the one Aristotle called the unmoved mover, the Thought of thought, the pure and eternal act" (1934a, 186). What this proof shows, that may not have been clear in the cosmological proof, is that we cannot stop at the universe or the consciousness we have of it. The invention of our consciousness and the surge of our thought give us an experimental ground that becomes more and more intelligible for affirming something transcendent that is not to be confused with the organic, the rational, or the spiritual realities, for which it appears necessarily as principle and as end.

Higher still, at the fifth degree, Blondel introduces another aspect that must be present in these arguments requiring that God be and affirming demonstratively that God is. This could be thought of as a sort of ontological proof, but Blondel speaks of it as the traditional proof through first and eternal truths. This proof loses none of its force because of the first two, starting with the fundamental assertion of something transcendent in the way we experience the world and arguing toward something higher than the world as we experience it through a convergence of the two irreducibly distinct elements/aspects of our thought, the noetic and the pneumatic, or the rational and the spiritual. In fact, for Blondel, this proof acquires a more precise and commanding force "by the fact that it shows how all rational principles, all transcendent assertions are called for, and not produced, by the entire movement of the universe and of knowledge" (1934a, 187). This proof focuses on the global aspect of our thought, which contains the passing, finite character of things in becoming, and of our thoughts, and relates it to what is beyond all limits of time and space and consciousness as an absolutely subsistent and intelligible reality. If this appears as too much of a leap all at once, Blondel reminds us that the third proof does not stand alone. It comes rationally only after the first and the second and it has been prepared by them. "In fact," he writes, "all these proofs complete one another in the notional realm and fortify one another in the more profound zone of our living thoughts" (1934a, 188). If there is an ontological argument for the existence of God, it does not proceed purely and simply from an idea we have to something in existence. As such it would get us nowhere. It works only if it takes its place "in a demonstration that is modestly progressive. There it has an irreplaceable role to play for the good of reason" (1934a, 189).

It does not work, however, unless we recognize that the idea we start from, or the idea we have of God, is not equal to God as he is in himself or to his existence. Such an equality would completely stabilize and satisfy the two aspects or the two *élans* from which thought proceeds in a perfect unity. But reason has to show that we have not reached such an equation even with the proper idea of God as necessarily existing. This is the sixth degree reason must come to in its elaboration of whatever it is that is totally and absolutely transcendent. Following Bossuet, Blondel remarks that we do not equal even the least of our thoughts, let alone that of God, and we must always look for more than what is contained in our consciousness. With regard to God, whom we do not and cannot equal in our thought, we can ask whether a thing such as we are thinking of is even possible, but we cannot answer the question directly by laying hold of his presence, or his absence, once and for all. We can only answer it indirectly, on the basis of what has already brought us to affirm the presence of such a being in our experience. Having clarified all that is implied in the idea of such a being, which includes its necessary existence, we have to say that it is possible, from which it follows that it necessarily exists. There is no simple intuition into this essence on our part. There is only a growing realization of a living idea and an effective presence within ourselves that remains ultimately mysterious in its core and in its ways.

This brings us to the seventh degree of rational clarification concerning this presence of the divine in our intellectual experience. The ontological proof gives us, at best, a beginning of what we have to think when we try to think of God. Even though we have to think of this divine identity as in itself, we can only think of it in relation to our way of conceiving and being. When we try to pass beyond the limits of our consciousness, we are afraid that we might be uttering pure nonsense, something that is totally impossible. We try to pacify all the conflict in our thought that has brought us to the affirmation of this absolute, in order to rest in this divine abyss, as if it drowned all the troubles of our thought or reconciled all its contradictions. But that is only a lazy solution to our problems, "a suicide and not a glorification of pure thought" (1934a, 193).

In this thought of God as the perfect resolution of all the problems we have with thought itself Blondel sees a resurgence of the false opposition between the God of Philosophers and the God of spiritual and religious Tradition, or a separation between the two. This is exemplified in deism, which claims to stabilize and fully exhaust the idea of God, without any reference to the initial religious sentiment from which the entire process of rationalization of experience began. The abstraction of deism is not all that the rational demonstration of God amounts to. On the contrary, it raises a more dramatic question before consciousness, a more intense and vital desire, an ulterior striving that has to be thought of rationally as normal, obligatory, and decisive for human consciousness, which brings us to the eighth degree of our rationalization regarding the affirmation of God.

The difficulty to be resolved at this eighth degree is that we seem to be merely juxtaposing our dialectical satisfactions concerning the idea of God as cause of the world and of our spirit to some quasi-mystical adherence to a hidden God as that which surpasses all human capacity to know. How can we bring together or reconcile the two tendencies we have found in our thought that correspond to these two sides of our idea of God, the one that orients us toward the category of the ideal and of principles, toward the God who seemingly is thought and understood only as not being, and the one who draws the soul toward some reality wrapped up in folds where reason loses its hold? Is this the point where we must pass beyond the limit that up to now we have said we cannot pass over, except by some arbitrary or subjective extrapolation? Blondel sees in this question a culmination of all the conflicts that have gone before in thought, and from it he thinks we can draw a new clarity and a new spiritual *élan* that we cannot turn down without some fault and some loss. How does it come about that, where we hoped we could find rest, we encounter yet a higher exigency for movement and a more serious risk to run in the actualization of our own thought? Does this mean that we know more about God than what we have admitted can be demonstrated up to now, or does it mean that we can demonstrate more about how we actually encounter God in our own self-actualization?

Blondel is careful to delineate the ways in which we do not know God, how he is not contained in our ideas or defined by them any more than in the feelings of fear and love inspired by the mystery in which humanity spontaneously locates the object of its terrors, its adorations, its cult, or its invocations. All we know about God is that he is. We surround this fundamental assertion with a method of negation, of elimination, and of purification with regard to all that he is not. God is not contingent, not finite, not relative, and so on. In a way this takes us further than any direct and positive assertion, as when we say that God is necessary, infinite, or absolute, in addition to saying that he is. Yet it does not give us any purchase on what he is in himself or the mystery of his existence.

Even if our thought subsists only by participating in the light infused in this mystery, it does not follow that we reach this mysterious Being in its center or that we are justified in setting up our mode of thinking as the norm for this Thought in itself. Yet in the face of this known unknown, we are not left without some rational way of proceeding in conjunction with the heart, which is what brings us to the ninth and final degree of rationalization that we have to come to in this clarification of what to think and what to do about God in our lives. It is not enough just to affirm God in his ineffable mystery; it is necessary also to adopt a personal attitude toward this personal God who is present at the very origin of our thought.

The Turn Toward a Need for Practical Resolution

Up to now in this study of thought Blondel has been following what he refers to as the spontaneous genesis of thought as it is implied in our experience. Starting from real thought as it is found outside of thinking thought or the thinking subject, he has traced its emergence in cosmic thought, organic thought, and psychic thought as a search for higher degrees of unification and consolidation of disparate energies into single beings, culminating in the invention of a thought that thinks itself or a properly self-conscious thought. In his exploration of this thinking thought he has shown how it spontaneously turns toward objects, both without and within itself, prior to turning upon itself reflectively as thinking subject that also thinks itself. Rational discourse about the world and about self-thinking thought has been shown to be part of this spontaneous genesis of thought, even to the point of elaborating an ascending order toward the affirmation of a Being who is totally transcendent and absolutely unified in its existence, albeit in a way that we cannot comprehend. The various proofs for the existence of such a Being — cosmological, teleological, and ontological — have been brought in to bolster this affirmation as well as to clarify its meaning and intent, especially as they complement one another in complementing the thrust of living thought itself. The proofs have been shown to be valid and rationally effective in demonstrating that there is One whom believers call God and that there has to be such a One as principle and end of all there is. But they have also been shown to be inconclusive in demonstrating *what* such a One is to whom all else is related, including ourselves as thinking subjects. The ninth degree in the rational process of recognizing how we ultimately relate to God in our experience as enlightened intellectual beings, consists precisely in facing up to the problem, as rational beings, that this final lack of clarity about *who* God is in his mystery and *what* he wills in his infinite power presents us with — namely, recognizing him as the God we have to relate to personally in religion.

The problem here for one who wants to combine rational precision with the aspirations of the heart, as Blondel does, is that the demonstrative argumentation that goes on about God cannot close in upon God in his infinite mystery. How can one place a content in or find a verification for this affirmation of a mysterious reality? What is one to make in practice of this affirmation that could still be only the expression of our own past or present sense of incapacity in the face of an obscure consciousness of some indefinite capacities in our human development? At the summit of our thought, in the rational affirmation of God, we are left with this opening between our affirmation and what it is that we affirm. We are left in a state of doubt and hesitation that we have to resolve rationally, not by a sudden and arbitrary decision, but by a methodical examination of the intelligent and free fidelity to what Blondel calls our intellectual duties, an examination that has to complement the more spontaneous movement of our thought up to this point.

This is the complement that had brought Blondel's original philosophy of action to a philosophy of the supernatural. It is the complement that now opens his reflection on thought to a whole new dimension of deliberation and choice, beyond the necessary realm of spontaneity in the emergence of thought. For him the idea of God within us, as deficient as it may be and by the very fact of its deficiency, "becomes principle of freedom, requirement of option, source of responsibility, confirmation of certitudes, condition of a destiny that does not allow human thought to close itself up into a philosophy that is stabilized, separated, self-satisfied and exclusive of any other spiritual discipline" (1934a, 196-97). The idea of God, such as it is in its necessity and in its inadequacy, brings us to a new realm of consideration in thought, one of responsibilities in view of a possible fulfillment, one of "decisive option among ways where the intervention of the most enlightened thought and the most responsible freedom have to be engaged in their integrality" (1934a, 196-97). The conclusion of our intellectual genesis that this idea of God in his mystery represents for us does not take away the risk of losing our way amid obscurities that persist in our thought, but it does make a necessary connection to a realm that becomes decisive for our destiny as thoughtful beings.

This conclusion marks the end of Blondel's first volume on Thought at the same time as it opens the way to his second volume, which will deal with the responsibilities of thought and the possibility of its reaching fulfillment. The new fact, which the idea of God introduces into our thought, far from suppressing the duality of aspects in our thought between the noetic and the pneumatic that ever sets us in motion toward some greater unity, opens up a more profound abyss that calls for greater union still with the One who is Thought thinking itself. The inevitable thought of God within us "creates a conflict between all that we are in the world and all that our thought conceives and requires with regard to Being and beatitude, so that we cannot avoid coming to an alternative that sums up, prolongs and surpasses all the oppositions and all the provisional conciliations provided by the progressive genesis of the world, life, and consciousness" (1934a, 197). It places before us the question of a necessary participation that is conscious and free, of all that we are, in all that is, through consent or refusal. This is the question that remains to be elucidated rationally for thought and in thought for Blondel. Having climbed the ladder of thought from the cosmic, the organic, and the psychic to conscious and thinking thought, from the exterior to the interior and from the interior to the higher, "it is the deployment of a ladder now tied to its higher point of contact that must now draw all our attention" (1934a, 202).

XII

The Responsibilities of Thought

The second volume of *La Pensée* presents itself as a continuation of the first. It begins with Part Four, on the duality of thought, which was first adumbrated in connection with cosmic thought, but will now be more fully articulated in terms of thinking thought and of liberating alternatives it is presented with. It goes on to three more parts, on the education of thought, on its natural inability to complete itself, and on the necessity of some spiritual integrity for it. In actuality, however, it represents an important shift in perspective on the problem of thought. In volume one, what we have is "the descriptive inventory of a spontaneity viewed from the outside so to speak" (1934b, 419), a sort of phenomenology of thought in its genesis and in its ascension through the different levels of its realization, from the cosmic and organic to the more properly self-conscious and rational, and finally to its highest possibility in a perfect coincidence between thinking thought and thought thought.

At every level, from the cosmic on, we found a tension between something noetic and something pneumatic in thought that propelled it to ever-higher forms of unification amid universal forms of diversification. But in the end we were left with a problem of how we are to exercise thought in a situation where we are unable to reduce its two aspects/elements to a simple unity. It took both aspects of our thought to properly affirm and to clarify the idea of God, the perfect unity of Thought in itself, in its own transcendent reality, but even this left us at odds within our own thought, not only in relation to the mysterious Transcendent, but also in relation to the cosmos in which we find ourselves and in relation to our own consciousness of this world and of ourselves. In volume two Blondel turns to explore this internal oddity or, as he puts it, to "explain internally how such a thought takes itself in hand, examines itself, deploys itself, seemingly wills to conquer itself, partially succeeds in doing so, but finds in its feeble successes a more vivid sense of its great indigence, of its great hope, and of the great exigencies that correspond to its incoercible desire" (1934b, 419). In a word, in going from volume one to volume two of *La Pensée*, we pass from a phenomenological to a more existential consideration of thought within ourselves, where the will and responsibility come into play in what Blondel calls an intellectual sense of duty, the sense of something to be done in the continuing disarray of our thought.

This more existential consideration of our own thought stays within the ambit of the science of thought as a whole, however. It takes us within ourselves, so to speak, but it does not take us out of the mode of rational inquiry that has led us to the necessity of this turn to our own subjectivity in the study of thought. The aim is to pursue a systematic study of this strange complexity of our thought, to look for its origin, to understand its meaning, to discern its consequences, to show its finality, and perhaps even to open the way to a point where these two parallel ways of thought might converge, following the secret resource from which this double life surges.

The Noetic and Pneumatic Duality of Thought

Blondel begins this new stage of his inquiry by revisiting the distinction he first made between the noetic and the pneumatic in relation to cosmic thought, now in the much more personal terms of human experience, where the distinction, which is seen to run through the different levels thought, can be understood much more readily and much more concretely, in a way that explains how we can adopt different spiritual attitudes as a result of what we come to understand. He takes it as the primordial fact about human thought that has to be taken into account, and that has been generally remarked upon by philosophers like Pascal *(esprit de géométrie/esprit de finesse)* and Newman (notional knowledge and real knowledge), but that has not been sufficiently reflected upon as the origin of the necessity for us to exercise our own intellectual responsibility in thought with regard, not only to the immediate objects of our experience, but also to the final destination of our thought itself in its spiritual actuation.

Blondel examines the problem of this irreducible duality in our thought from three different viewpoints, that of the origin of these two different modes of our thought, that of their essential nature in relation to one another in the actual exercise of our thought, and that of their finality in the search for some unification of the two. He shows that no solution can be found for this dichotomy from the standpoint of its genesis or origin, or from the standpoint of their interplay with one another or their alternating dynamism in the actual exercise of thought, but that perhaps a solution can be found in its final destiny, which, as its final goal, would determine the two distinct functions of this movement, in view of the end toward which thought must tend. But this is a "perhaps" that opens the way to a long search through the many partial ways in which human thought does manage to pull itself together in different accomplishments such as science, art, and even metaphysics, without sacrificing either of its two basic modes. For launching this search, Blondel is satisfied with defining as closely as possible how each one of these modes is in tension with the other, as well as complementary to it, in the concrete process of thinking.

Putting it in terms of the distinction he had made long before this, in 1906, in speaking about the Point of Departure for Philosophical Research, he speaks of abstractive thought as "the condition, the vehicle and, at times, even the logical aim of reflective consciousness. [As such it] appears as a retrospection concomitant with and consecutive to a prospection. In this sense, we can always say that the advance of the human spirit is always an analysis between two syntheses — an analytical regression aiming at a restitution or a synthetic construction, even the beginning of some unification" (1934b, 51). The ordinary function for this analytic mode of thought is to determine elementary conditions, discursive means, scientific precisions, general laws, and ideal types. While it appears to start only from appearances, from simplified and representative notations, this way of extracting from realities different aspects immanent in them takes place only by an appeal to some transcendent and essential truth, "whence the normal tendency of the spirit to look into ideas and, through thought, for the ground and the explanation of nature as well as of conscious life. Thereby it seems that abstractive and ideal knowledge overflows, at both ends, the order of contingent realities and of the concrete bits of knowledge contained in them, without the container joining with them well enough to coincide with them" (1934b, 51-52).

On the other side is the more concrete mode of thought to which this abstractive mode has to relate in the human experience. This thought is assimilative and global, even when it has the finesse of seeing realities in their singularity. "It bears within itself, as long as it remains direct and concrete, the implicit presence of the whole. The universe reverberates in every sensibility, in every particular consciousness, just as every singularized being impresses its original effectiveness into the milieu that has contributed in shaping it but that it modifies and adds to in turn" (1934b, 52). From this it follows that this concrete thought is no longer simply contained or surpassed, but that it brings something new into being, that it is a perpetual going beyond *(dépassement)*, and that it aims at something other than just some exhaustive analysis, a static representation, or a science relevant only to the immanent order. What it expresses is some indefinite aspiration, if not, perhaps, an infinite one, which remains to be seen. Beyond what it can comprehend of the past and the present, it anticipates something that will be and even that must be above the flow of duration, a flow that nevertheless remains necessary for its development. "And what is this power of moving forward," Blondel asks, "without which a retrospective consciousness would be vain and impossible, if not a spiritual élan toward the unitive and solely pacifying term toward which tend the universe in its becoming and the restlessness of a thought doubly hungry for unity and ever in disequilibrium, ever divided from itself?" (1934b, 52).

Lest we get the idea that abstractive analytical thought is totally absorbed with management of life in the physical world, however, we should note that it too is part of the élan that promotes the spiritual life in its metaphysical dimension. To be sure, it proceeds by the elaboration of signs and expresses itself in discourse, ideas, conceptual systems that appear as constructions that do not adequately represent the concrete complexity of the real order. Far from encompassing the totality of all that is given, it also falls short of all there is in the least singular being. Nevertheless these same ideal conceptions witness to a richness in thought that far surpasses any knowledge of particulars. Without them and the lift they give to our intellectual outlook, we would not even have any clear consciousness of empirical data. More importantly from the standpoint of our spiritual élan, through their indigence as notions, they also express a superabundance of thought, a *sursum*, as long as we do not absolutize them or keep them relative to the total movement of the universe and the spirit. To take them as fixed would be illusory, but to take them as promoting the higher life of spirit in conjunction with the more unitive form of thought is salutary. Human thought thus appears "not as a subsistent being in itself, not as two beings coupled together and living off their mutual relation, but as a becoming with a mixture of non-being and being, as a rising to something higher, as a postulation of unity and as the expectation of a complement, an end that would bring to completion its incipient and progressive effort" (1934b, 46).

This being said, we have to recognize still, that what we begin with is not the unity that we may be looking for, but rather two distinct modes of thought and knowing, which, though tied together, cannot be reduced to one and the same method. Hence it is that "they can be studied, used and perfected only in and through the movement toward the end that, perhaps, will unite and reconcile them" (1934b, 56). Blondel writes "perhaps" here because it is not a foregone conclusion that they can be united, when we find so much incompatibility between them in our aesthetic and spiritual experience. It is from this very dichotomy, from this double sort of vision in our thought, that he proceeds in the existential exploration of our thought. From it derives his idea of a necessity to choose in the development of our thought, where nothing ever seems to be settled once and for all.

This idea of a necessity to choose within human consciousness is one of the key moves in Blondel's existential philosophy. He had argued for such a necessity at the end of his phenomenology of action, where he spoke of it in terms of two alternative attitudes in the face of God or the necessary Being, to be god with God or to be god without God, each of which had its own consequences that could be determined rationally, fulfillment of our deepest aspiration or total frustration of the desire that frees us from the material conditions of our existence. Here he speaks of the same sort of radical alternative as both liberating and exacting for human thought. It may seem overly precipitous, from a critical standpoint, to speak of this radical alternative in terms of the divine at this point, in his science of thought, but there is no other way of understanding this alternative in its comprehensive form. One has to see it in terms of one's final end, and that is precisely where God presents himself in human thought.

Blondel is not interested in keeping this view of the radical alternative in the depth of our life a secret. By stating it openly early in the exposition of human thought in its development, he hopes to make the way clearer toward this end or this problem of human fulfillment, by giving his discourse the rational direction it needs long before getting to a critical examination of the ramifications of this ultimate problem for human thought. But he does not think that the view he is stating here, concerning the ultimate alternative, is completely absent from the ordinary way of choosing and making responsible judgments about what to do in life for thoughtful human beings. Implicit in our decisions or in the totality of our decisions in life, is always some decision about our attitude toward our final end. This is already part of the prospection in the unitive and global aspect of our concrete thinking. Deciding will be the part of a reflective scientific discourse on the activity of thought as a whole, so that it will be spelled out more critically step by step.

What Blondel does that has never been done by other philosophers who have reflected on the irreducible duality of human thought, is to show how it hangs from the very alternative that is presented in our consciousness regarding the final end of our existence, which defines our very being. The line of argument he wishes to follow is the following: "From the apparent duality and dichotomous nature of our thought follow progressive implications that first of all raise an alternative between two global orientations; — from this alternative, which arises spontaneously and goes unnoticed, all the more because it is embodied in thought as it first comes into its own, arises a judgment, that is, an affirmation that takes on an intellectual shape and a personal value only through an arbitration between yes and no, between two orientations of our thought" (1934b, 65). The essential and constitutive act of thinking is to judge, as he also says. "The verb that is the soul of affirmation is always in fact the taking of a position, an attitude of the spirit in the face of its objects as well as of itself" (1934b, 65). This spontaneous necessity for an option implies a certain freedom that reveals itself and begins to realize itself in particular choices of everyday life, but the reciprocal causality between the two fundamental modes of our thought promotes this free enterprise to ever-higher accomplishments, and so prepares us to raise the ultimate question of a destiny that transcends our thinking: "the supreme option in which will be expressed the free choice of a thought that can either restore to God His divine totality or artifactually limit itself to the finite goals among which the infinite condescends to take the rank of a competitor" (1934b, 66). This is the ultimate drama for any singular human thought that has its roots at the intersection of our intelligence and our freedom as imperfect beings who "make their own history and whose spiritual élan knows itself in this very imperfection only to tend toward its own completion" (1934b, 67).

Going back to the same kind of argument that he had developed in his reflection on the subjective principle of human action in *L'Action (1893)*, Blondel claims that the alternative that makes this deliberate option possible is also what makes the very act of thinking conscious, knowable, and perfectible, for two reasons. First, if we had only one idea or if all our ideas came only from outside a thought that is supposedly one, we would not have the kind of consciousness that can inhibit and free us from the motions that come to us from outside our thought. There would be no possibility of subjective deliberation in what we do as thoughtful beings, unless there were within our thought itself a principle of multiplicity and a necessary possibility of choosing. There has to be room for alternatives, for ulterior aspirations and for interventions that give meaning to the spiritual élan, without which we would remain merely passive things incapable of developing any personality of our own. Second, looking at it from the side of the object that serves to nourish the interest of the subject in relation to its end, we see how "the internal alternatives are embodied, so to speak, in the goals, whether near or far off, immanent or transcendent, that come into our view and into our grasp as stages to be traversed in our itinerary toward the ontological mystery and the intelligible unity to which thought does not cease to aspire" (1934b, 69). As long as we are on the way, everything remains partial, divided, inadequate. The inadequacy between any given object of choice for us and our ultimate aim remains constant and deficient, by nature. Whatever truth we arrive at, whatever good we accomplish, always leaves us calling and searching for more. The fundamental error would be to cut the search short, to settle for what is acquired, to wrap up within a cycle of eternal return what is intelligible and real only by proceeding from an infinite principle toward an end that is infinite, *une fin infinie*.

The Radical Alternative in Relation to Our Final Fulfillment

The incommensurability between the two modes of our thought thus cannot be made whole or brought into one, short of the infinite. This, however, is not a mere deficiency on our part. The fact that the modes are such is for us the origin of freedom, the necessary condition for having to choose, the principle of movement, obligation, and responsibility within ourselves. We cannot stay with either one of these thoughts without the other, because their role in tension with one another is to tie us into the infinite and because whatever consciousness we have of things within our experience is due to the hidden presence of a reality and a truth that surpasses any positive datum in our thought and in our action. The internal tension between these two modes is what makes our thought conscious of itself as a problem to be resolved through its own activity. Without their internal incompatibility everything would remain flat and stagnant. "In one sense distinct consciousness seems to go before, and condition, the incipient effort of an option imposed by a spontaneous alternative; in a more profound sense, it is the alternative tied to the infinite divergence of the contrasting terms of thought itself that makes thought conscious of itself, produces its freedom and engages the responsibility of its option" (1934b, 78).

To see what this fundamental option consists in, we have only to look at how we exercise each one of these two modes of thought. At first sight it appears that we have only to choose among diverse objects or directions that are interchangeable. But that is not the way it goes most profoundly in our spirit. Whatever use we make of our thought, whatever path we choose to follow, however legitimately, there is always a bifurcation between two conceptions in our thought, between two spiritual attitudes guiding our life. "On one side there is a presumption of self-sufficiency in our intellectual effort, which, however incomplete it may be in fact, should by right find within itself enough light to satisfy itself. On the other side there is the sense of a growth and fidelity to the call of a truth and a perfection that, in spite of the paradox joining the two terms, sees only the *infinite* as the end (*fin*) of thought" (1934b, 79). Whatever success thought may find in solving its transitory problems, "it has the possibility of its existence, no less than a docility to its inborn exigencies, only in finding and in seeking the solution to its first and final problem in the infinite" (1934b, 79).

All of this makes it incumbent upon Blondel, then, to examine the ways that open up to an option that is not arbitrary, but whose consequences can be rationally discerned in relation to how we conceive the final end of thought. The logic of thought is not determined to allow for only one way in seeking the fulfillment of thought. It allows for new initiatives and options in conjunction with the part of passivity that thought experiences, along with the impulse that propels it forward. What Blondel wants to get at is the fundamental option that underlies all particular options that thought goes through in the course of a life filled with objects, occupations, and vocations. Without taking anything away from the reality and the value of these particular options in building up a life, he wants to get to the more profound choice or election we are exercising in making any of our particular choices, the option regarding the whole of life upon which depends the failure or the possibility of a fulfillment for our thought, the choice that governs the fundamental spiritual attitude we bring to everything we undertake.

Strictly speaking, this fundamental option is not a preferential choice of one of our two modes of thought over the other. Those are not matters of choice for us. They are necessary aspects of our thought that interplay with one another in whatever we think and initiate. It would be illogical and perilous to thought itself to exclude either one from the other. One cannot be a scientist independently of one's spiritual life, for example, nor can one's interior be detached from the real world of social and practical interests. What we have to choose from at the summit of our thinking is between two horizons, so to speak, whether we will be satisfied with an immediate exploitation of what we have achieved in thought, as if we could limit ourselves to such transitory and partial successes, or whether we shall continue to search for a solution that none of our own thinking activity can bring, but that any such activity calls for, no matter what its shortcomings. This is not to depreciate the value or the validity of any intellectual activity, but rather to start from its power of achievement within itself as well as in the world, in order to raise for it a dilemma regarding something that lies beyond its power to resolve.

There are two ways of working towards one's fulfillment in thought. One is to make use of the world and of one's own being in becoming, in tending, through this very becoming, toward an order and perfection, a unity, not to be found in any realized object or in any return into self, in fidelity always to one's spiritual élan, by going beyond any stage of advancement. The other is to let oneself get caught up in a cycle of subordination, either of the world to the self or of the self to the world, as if reality could be encircled in this way and thought could find satisfaction in such an enclosure. These are the two visions that are in the balance and that thought must pronounce itself on, if it is to be consequent with the élan from which it proceeds. Blondel wants to show that ultimately thought has to opt for one or the other, transcendence or immanence, and to seek in all responsibility to enlighten itself here and now on the error or the truth of these absolutely contradictory conceptions, without absolutizing either the self or the world or the combination of both in a sort of eternal return.

In this, thought must also face the paradox of an end that is truly infinite, that is, not an end or a limit. Thought cannot but aspire to some sort of adequate unification. As a spiritual reality conscious of itself in the world, it has to contribute to its own genesis, whence the possibility of fallibility and error. In becoming conscious of itself and acquiring its spiritual value, it is necessarily aiming at a transcendent object and an infinite progress. Yet, it can nevertheless confine the infinitude of its aspiration to finite terms and to a totally immanent conception of how it is to be used, given that it is left always with an option. Its "relative autonomy is conceived and effective only by surpassing the horizon of the universe and seeing, as in a mirror, truths and ends of an order that is higher than anything limited or taking place in duration, space and becoming.

The difficulty is to understand how one of the eligible alternatives can be to choose and will infinitely what is finite or even indefinite" (1934b, 99). The truth is that the infinite is infinitely more than the finite or the indefinite, the indefinite being nothing more than an accumulation of finite upon finite without ending, what Hegel calls the bad infinite. To have an infinite aspiration to an end that is truly infinite is to aspire to something more than can ever be achieved by an endless succession of finite acts in the world, no matter how high or indefinite their aim may be. And yet, according to Blondel, that is what thought aspires to, even though it cannot conceive how such an end could be achieved, given the duality of its own constitution in its becoming. The inconsequence of thought comes in only when it chooses to remain with the finite or the indefinite it can conceive, and to find sufficiency in that rather than recognize the insufficiency of it all in relation to its own infinite spiritual aspiration.

Blondel asks himself how it is possible for us to opt in this finite way for a solution that is speculatively illogical, even though it is the only one that is within our grasp. On the one hand, he finds that we are always tempted to attribute a certain totality and sufficiency to the world of becoming that appear to satisfy our need for security, for conquest, and for unlimited inquiry. But we must be prepared to question such an extrapolation, which may be contrary to both critical reflection and our ethical consciousness. On the other hand, as if to compensate for upsetting the balance in favor of things over the spirit, we succumb too easily to a symmetrically opposed but no less tendentious temptation: we attribute to thought, even in its inadequacy or deficiency in us, a certain power of domination, "as if, in the act of confining itself and losing itself in the universal immanence, the idealist pretense could realistically rely on its indefinite becoming, its inventive power and its unending rhythm of failure and successes, to close off or to deny any ulterior horizon for this perpetual mobilism" (1934b, 100). Blondel sees in this an attempt to exorcize the idea of an infinite transcendent by taking advantage of the fluid and anthropomorphic character of deism, to drag the divine down into the turmoil of an unending genesis and a total relativity. There is a certain logic in this sort of position that Blondel wants to bring out, but it is contrary to the original élan from which our thought emerges, and to the highest exigencies to which it must respond. His ultimate aim in this science of thought is to show that this immanentist option cannot be justified.

In order to come to that more logically and more positively, however, after having shown how deviations are possible in the process of thought, he turns to an exploration of the ways that can lead us closer to our true end, which means a consideration of the normal development, or of the straight line that thought can and should follow in what Blondel calls its civilizing work. Blondel devotes the entire Fifth Part of *La Pensée*, titled "The Education of Thought," to this immanent development of thought where he wants to show how spontaneity and freedom concur in the normal progress of thought. While trying to avoid becoming fixated in any immanent achievement of thought or in its indefinite virtualities, he also wants to show thought's rootedness in reality and its effectiveness in transforming itself and the world. These are not matters of indifference to thought. Blondel thinks of them as stages in the development of thought, as it works its way toward its most fundamental option, or as it ascends to its highest confrontation with its innermost transcendent reality. For him such stages represent a rational progression of partial successes and partial failures, on the way toward the recognition of what will have to be thought of as the ultimate success and perfection of thought, or its ultimate failure.

A simple list of the themes he explores for this education of thought will indicate the richness of the spiritual life and humanism he wants to fall back on for his argument about the insufficiency of human thought in a purely immanent order. He talks about the organic development of the diverse forms that make up civilization, the alliance of intelligence and sensibility, and how affection and prospection must be integrated into any culture. He speaks of the scientific culture as quite progressive, as well as having its own limitations, of the human sciences and the formation of social thought, of the aesthetic urge in thought and the intellectual function of art and literature. He even brings in the idea of different metaphysical and ethical systems, and the function of philosophical thought, as part of any civilization, always with the intention of bringing out both the validity as well as the precariousness of all forms of civilization for thought.

Insufficiency and the Metaphysical Problem of the Infinite

Armed with this spiritual revaluation of civilizing thought and healthy humanism, however, Blondel then returns to the ultimate problem thought must resolve regarding the final unification of its two modes and how it can be resolved, even if such a resolution lies beyond the capacity of human thought to achieve by itself. Such a problem, he insists, comes up beyond the historical or the scientific order as such. It pertains to a metaphysical order having to do with the infinite. It can be formulated in terms of the antinomy within thought itself. "For thought to be in us under a conscious form, it has to somehow touch on a foundation and be limited even as it is indefinitely active and busy. It has no knowledge of either this mobile limit or this absolute infinity without some knowledge of the other. The relation between these two necessities or the living bond of this double reality remains hidden for it, like a painting behind closed shutters. Thought is thus rationally brought to this question: can we think the infinite? And if the infinite is, can it think? Moreover, if we are finite, can we think it, by falling back on it, at the same time as all foundation seems to fall away from a thought in need of encountering an end to reflect and to know itself?" (1934b, 215).

If these questions were to remain insoluble, thought itself would become unintelligible and perish as thought. What they presuppose is the idea of an absolute infinite distinct from our thought, to which our thought is necessarily related in its very immanent movement of progression. This is the metaphysical problem Blondel says we must now face up to by placing in evidence "what is universal, permanent and inevitable in the achievements as well as in the insufficiencies of any finite thought, whether in the face of a world that is indefinitely changing and reshaping itself or in the presence of the true or the transcendent object alone capable of satisfying thought, but that seems to remain intrinsically inaccessible to any finite spirit" (1934b, 223). Such is the idea of the true infinite Blondel is working with in order to shift the idea of absolute knowing away from the human spirit into the divine, without however abandoning the idea of some absolute knowing as a proper end for the self-conscious human spirit. The problem we must face up to in thought according to him is how we can attain such absolute knowing, something we aspire to spontaneously and by nature, even if we are congenitally incapable of achieving it on our own initiative.

In his approach to this ultimate problem for a thought in quest of a perfect unification, Blondel begins with a reflection on what is for him a matter of observable fact, the experience of dissatisfaction we feel even with our successes in thought, let alone our failures. Such an experience is a constant in human thought at whatever level of achievement it attains, whether it be in the realm of empirical science or human science, of mathematics or even of metaphysics. Everywhere we look we find ourselves still drifting in a becoming where our thoughts are incomplete or unfinished. The metaphysical implication to be drawn from this, according to Blondel, is that such a perpetual and ever recurring feeling of insufficiency connotes a congenital or natural insufficiency on the part of our thought, a consistent absence of adequacy between our thought and being, between thought and action within ourselves, and an imperfection that persists in our thought no matter how high it rises.

Along with this is also implied the further idea of a real thought, other than ours, that is perfect in itself where thought and action are perfectly one and where there is a complete adequacy of thought and being. Even if we cannot attain such perfect adequacy on our own, by reason of the natural insufficiency of our thinking — that is, its inability to come to a complete unification — it is something we aspire to as to an end or to a complete satisfaction for our thought. It is by reason of this aspiration that we experience the natural state of our thought in the world as one of insufficiency. In fact, as Blondel argues, it is by reason of this aspiration that our thought comes to self-consciousness and the sense of its own freedom and responsibility in striving for any perfection.

Also implied in this perennial sense of insufficiency is the thought that we cannot attain any sort of sufficiency for ourselves, such as the sufficiency of a thought perfectly one with being, without the intervention of the one we have just spoken of as a real thought other than ourselves, the Thought that is already thinking itself in perfect unity with its being and that in fact already constitutes us in our thinking. From the experience of our being unfinished, Blondel wants to move step by step toward the fundamental difficulty and toward what is a crucial truth for human thought: "in us thought is naturally and metaphysically unfinishable *(inachevable)*" (1934b, 231), that is, "unachievable" as something complete in itself. This truth is all the more crucial for our thought, if our innermost desire, that which makes us self-conscious and free, is to attain such a completion. The questions that this state of affairs raises for human thought is precisely what makes necessary the "philosophy of insufficiency" he had spoken of earlier in his controversy against Bréhier and Gilson over what he wanted to call "Catholic philosophy." What Blondel has in mind now is to develop such a philosophy of insufficiency by exploring these questions surrounding our profound sense of insufficiency, and by relativizing a metaphysics, or an ethic, or a civilization that has become overly confident in its stability and in its power to go on indefinitely, without giving any thought to a true Infinite that is real.

As part of his philosophy of insufficiency, Blondel goes into what he calls the metaphysics of death, something that he says philosophy rarely pays attention to, but that is important for understanding the destiny of any individual human thought, not just of thought in general. To all appearances death marks the ultimate proof that our thought remains inevitably incomplete. But that is only the empirical side of the fact. There is also a metaphysical side to it from the standpoint of thought, which protests against this finality of death. There has always been a special consciousness about death among rational beings, one that goes back to the earliest signs of human habitation in the world and that remains even among "the post-civilized, those who think themselves free of any superstition or religion. Respect for death shows itself even where all other respect appears to be abolished" (1934b, 245).

Blondel sees in this a sort of ontological argument for immortality or for the eternity of thought. "If we did not have some metaphysical sense to posit, on the other side of phenomena that succeed one another and disappear, a permanent reality, we could not conceive either an afterlife or, what is more paradoxical but no less certain, a death in the sense we give to this word. The idea of death is possible and real only by the implicit certitude we have of immortality" (1934b, 245). From this certitude comes the metaphysical side of the problem of death for us, which Blondel takes very seriously. It shows that death is somehow contrary to our nature and that human thought is somehow torn between two worlds, that of the here and now and that of a truth that is eternal or a thought of thought itself. It is the latter tendency, Blondel has argued, that gives the impulse toward ever-higher realizations of thought in the world. When the possibility of such higher realizations comes to an end, the question of yet a higher realization of one's thought itself in its eternal sphere remains.

One could suppose that, once liberated from its material conditions, human thought immediately comes to its own perfection by making its own place within the realm of pure thought thinking itself, but Blondel says the problem of our final perfection cannot be resolved so simply, as if by an absorption of the individual spirit into a pantheism of thought. The conviction we have that all is not ended with death is true, based on the spontaneous élan of our most intimate thought. Empirical death, so to speak, does not cut us off from this dynamic of our thought. However, it is presumptuous to assume that we automatically fall into the completion of our thought by simply and totally coinciding with truth once individual thought is disincarnate. The arguments Blondel has used to show that human thought cannot in principle bring itself to its own complete unification militate against the idea of any such natural absorption into the infinity of spirit. In fact, they still leave us with the problem of how to attain a final unification of our thought without losing our individual identity. What the meditation on death in its twofold aspect, metaphysical as well as empirical, brings out is a greater clarity about the radical incapacity of our thought to bring itself to the absolute perfection it aspires to, at the same time as it introduces us to the more profoundly ontological dimension of the problem. What remains incomplete at the end of our temporal existence does not automatically become complete in eternity. There are still problems to be resolved in the metaphysical dimension of our thought that can lead us to a better solution to the question of our final destiny. Torn between the need within ourselves to suspend our thought from a truth that is real and transcendent and the incapacity that remains within us to equal ourselves to this necessary affirmation, philosophy still has to keep both of these requirements in mind simultaneously and seek to make the conflict that results from them intelligible. "As logical and positively necessary as it is to affirm the divine absolute, it is no less rational and inevitable, in order to remain coherent, that we affirm the impossibility for us to be this absolute whose real and actual truth our thought cannot not imply" (1934b, 256). There is no other way of affirming the absolute while maintaining our relation to it in our finite thought.

The question then becomes for Blondel how the perfection of thought in ourselves is conceivable and whether that has to relate to a God who remains mysterious to us at best, if not downright impossible to conceive as an actual perfection of thought distinct from human thought in the world. He argues, first of all, that it is intrinsically impossible for a thought that has its beginning in time to find completion in itself, even if it passes over and loses itself in eternity. We are caught in a tragic conflict between exigencies that appear incompatible, and yet that may not be sacrificed one to the other. Our personal consciousness, as he has argued at great length earlier, is rooted in the entire cosmic and psychic order. If we try to think of it as simply uprooted from this invisceration in the world, either we have to think of it as annihilated through absorption into an eternal truth, of which we would have to say "that it is unthinkable for us or that it has the intelligibility of pure nothingness for our reason, or else we have to find another way of tying the life of our thought, now dying, into a substantial and immortalizing thought, one that is not a matter of succession or of automatic evolution" (1934b, 264). Blondel's argument seems to be tailored very precisely to the view of both Spinoza and Hegel concerning the end of personal life for thought. One cannot accept sheer annihilation for a thought that has constituted itself out of an infinite dynamism of its own, and yet one cannot expect to grasp the infinite itself with means and thoughts that are finite or at best indefinite, that is, open only to more finite accomplishments.

For Blondel the progression of thought toward its absolute fulfillment is never just an advancement toward an ever-higher point of view. It is always at the same time a new realization of how far removed we remain from our infinite goal. We never come to a place where we can stop once and for all. Nor can we ever be satisfied with any sort of movement, even one that encompasses the totality of ourselves and our thought in the world. We have to come to a philosophy of insufficiency regarding the very end we aspire to in our thought, a kind of reversal in our thinking concerning being. "What is true paradoxically in the historical and moral order has to be turned around for a truth of a higher order still to appear: the higher thought rises, the more conscious it is of its incommensurability with its perfect object and its total destiny" (1934b, 266). We cannot escape the necessity of being tied to duration, and yet it is impossible as well as irresponsible for us to go back, or to embrace nothingness. Nothingness can no longer be for us. We remain what we have made ourselves, even in death, but if we try to go forward on this new front of metaphysical thought for us, we find ourselves without the further resources we need to advance. It is impossible for us to stay put in this halfway house for thought, and yet we do not have within ourselves the wherewithal to go forward any more.

Thus, in the fading light of its highest metaphysical speculation, thought finds itself obliged to examine as methodically as possible the problem that surpasses all others, "that of the very possibility of a God who is one, infinite and perfect, a God who would not be a mirage appearing to the soul at the edge of the desert, but who, through the very distance that separates us from him, would appear as the only solution, ever near and intimate, ever naturally inaccessible and nonetheless irrecusable, ever fundamentally desirable and desired, but who is so often misconceived or rejected because, even if the solution is offered, it implies in the human being dispositions that do not pertain only to rational evidences or that become intelligible only by supposing, within our very thought, some meritorious response to a call heard within the generous sincerity of one's spirit" (1934b, 268-69). Blondel speaks of obligation here, rather than just necessity, because the supreme problem he refers to arises not just out of some perceived metaphysical necessity, but also out of a sense of one's own rational responsibility in facing this ultimate problem of our final destiny, namely, whether it is possible for our thought to reach completion in any way.

Rational Responsibility at the Brink of Mystery

The question as stated by Blondel is inescapable when we have come to the end of what we can do on our own in pursuit of the absolute perfection of our thought, but the answer people give in life is not always the same. According to Blondel, there is only one that is "positive and coherent in keeping with the exigencies of an exploration that is intrepid" (1934b, 269-70). Before positing such an answer, however, he goes into what he thinks is the root or the fundamental principle of any denial of the reality of the problem, in order to show all the more clearly the meaning of the answer we can give only by entering more deeply into the mystery of the divine life, a mystery we surely cannot penetrate, but one that is still illuminating enough to give the lie to any objection to the ultimate truth. Blondel has already made the point that there are no atheists. There is only an infinite number of ways to disfigure or to deny God and to become deicidal. "The most intellectual way of all consists in using all the force of our thought to take hold of the very source from which it arises, in order to turn the conditions of its human course into an unconditional law and to transform this becoming, this relative, this immanent, with its limitations and unending initiatives, into an absolute, a transcendent, a divine" (1934b, 270). This is tantamount to saying that, if we conceive God as perfect or as complete (*achevé*), we have to think of him as not being; and if he is, it is on the condition of remaining always incomplete (*inachevé*) and imperfect. What is illogical or inconsequential about this stance is that it takes a purely abstract notion of becoming, or of what Whitehead calls process, as a fixed measuring stick for the real, as if change itself were simply a given, prior to the things that change.

In opposition to this view, Blondel quotes the question of Bossuet: "Why should the imperfect be and the perfect not be? Perfection is not an obstacle to being; it is its *raison d'être*" (1934b, 271). Real thought has a direct realist sense even in metaphysics which should not give way to any sort of immanentist idealism, especially when the latter takes itself, as movement or process, to be the absolute reality. When we say that all reality is definite and hence hemmed in in its very indefiniteness, and when we add that in affirming God as real we imply in this assertion the idea of a limitation, are we not diluting the pure notion of being into an image that is still too gross for pure thought? Are we not subjecting thought itself to an understanding oriented to materiality and subservient to spatial configurations? Blondel has made a point of showing the superiority of thought and intelligence with regard to abstractive constructions that can so easily be manipulated. Now, in the face of the question of God and possible divinization of the human, he warns against letting dialectic give way to its exclusive bent, at the risk of missing the most fundamental and the highest implications of our thought.

The point Blondel wants to make is to avoid naturalizing or humanizing the divine, or subordinating it to becoming, even in the form of a sublimation into the category of the ideal, either as an impulse of the animal instinct, or as an end that recedes indefinitely into the future never to be attained. It is not enough to gaze backward into our origins or within our human reflection, as if the consciousness we have of "the lower conditions of our personal life immunized us against the temptation to twist discursive reason and our dialectical conclusions around into a universal mobilism, where personality itself appears to be no more than a brilliant floating piece of wreckage and where the notion of human being and of God, of nature and of spirit, cling together in a common succumbing" (1934b, 272-73). On the contrary, we must look forward and see if thought in itself is in fact contradictory, unacceptable for a finite spirit that is not caught up in words, or if it is not something realizable in a being for whom essence and existence, knowing and subsisting, are one and the same, without being confused or immobilized, and without remaining incomprehensible and barren. Blondel does not think that we can adequately penetrate into the mystery of such a being, but he does think that we can know enough about it to think rationally about what we aspire to infinitely, without imposing on it the contingent relations and the dependencies that condition the exercise of our thought, even though they do not constitute it in its core.

It is difficult to neutralize these impressive objections to the thought of a thought that is perfect in itself, and real in contradistinction from anything natural and human, but that is because we tend to represent the object thought and the thinking being as two things congealed in time and as antithetic in space. Blondel's thinking here is quite in line with that of Hegel when the latter rejects every representation of the absolute, or of God, as beyond *(jenseits)* anything finite. But he differs from Hegel in trying to think of the infinite as a life of perfect coincidence between thought and being, unlike any thought of ours where we always have to struggle for whatever such coincidence we can achieve. For Blondel the true infinite in thinking is "this strange reciprocity of an object and a subject coinciding and perfecting one another, both simultaneously faithful to what is generative in an infinite fecundity" (1934b, 275). He notes that many who want to argue for a personal God do not understand the force of the reasoning that leads many philosophers, especially in modern philosophy, to reject such an idea. For his own part he welcomes this kind of rational objection to the idea of a

Thought that is perfect in itself, without struggle and without any limit whatsoever, because it forces us to recognize the metaphysical aporia in which we find ourselves as spiritual beings. There is something to be gained spiritually in overcoming such objections rationally, a new realization of what life must be in the divine, where, "for Being and Thought to subsist in a perfect unity without confusion, where, instead of a subservience to the necessary law of a dualism, there must be, at the heart of the Being that thinks itself and of the Thought that constitutes itself into a substantial perfection, an initiative whereby the one who is already fundamentally Being, Spirit and Charity engenders an other itself; this Word, itself also Being, Spirit and Charity, must restore itself as in a filial immolation, as mediator and eternal pontiff, to the Father who has given himself totally to him and to whom he gives himself entirely and eternally; this twofold love that is so personally diverse and so substantially identical must itself be Spirit, Life and perfectly subsisting Charity" (1934b, 276).

Again, Blondel makes no claim to penetrate into the mystery of this divine life, but the Trinitarian relation he can articulate rationally in it enables him to get around to the fixated idea of a god relegated to some inert and dead solitude, a total stranger to the life of nature and humanity and even to itself, because it is without soul, without warmth, without love, and without intelligibility. Blondel's intellectualism requires an intrinsically ethical element. "Perfect thought cannot be realized or understood if it does not breathe in an atmosphere of divine charity" (1934b, 276). This will have consequences for the way we are to relate rationally and responsibly to such perfect thought. But for now Blondel remarks that the objections that have been raised against the idea of a perfect Thought that is in itself, to which we have to relate, can be seen as a springboard to overcome the weak, obsolete, and dangerous conceptions of thought when it is spoken of as divine and even as it comes forth in our humanity. If we are to relate properly to the divine in our infinite aspiration toward the perfection of our thought, we must recognize the infinite difference that separates us from the divine perfection of thought itself, and that we nevertheless aspire to, even as we recognize our radical inadequacy to overcome this difference from our side alone.

The next step in Blondel's argument is to examine critically how the final problem of a perfect unification of the two modes of our thought can be resolved rationally, even if it cannot be resolved successfully by reason alone. We have just seen that we cannot legitimately deny the possibility or even the necessity of perfect thought. The question is now to see how we can benefit from the light of this thought in the halting exercise of our own thought, and then to see how we cannot but desire to commune with this perfect thought, as we seek to bring thought to completion within ourselves. If this seems naturally impossible for us, as we see in the radical distinction between an eternally perfect thought and our own imperfect thought, can it still be achieved in another way?

Thus the question of a supernatural intervention of the perfect Thought in our own thought recurs at the end of this dialectic of thought, as it had at the end of the dialectic of human action. Blondel will treat of it here only in terms of thought, which is only one ingredient of human action as a whole, albeit the most intellectual and the most expansive, as he had always thought from the beginning of his philosophizing, and as he now finally had the occasion to show more convincingly.

For him the problem is to steer a very narrow course between two extremes, the presumptuous claim to overtake divine thought in our own thought, in a sort of pantheistic idealism, and the reverse attitude of total abdication or discouragement in pursuing a task we appear to be made for. This calls for a more precise weighing of the rational exigencies we find within our spirit and the all-too-real deficiencies of our thought than we have seen up to now. He distinguishes between three moments in the articulation of our spiritual life that must be emphasized anew. First, there is the necessity of recognizing a guiding principle, a presence, a support for our thought without which it could not function. From this comes a certain natural stability in our intellectual efforts that reinforces the reality of these efforts at the same time as it reveals the weakness of our indigence. What Blondel recognizes in this is the undeniable transcendence of God present in our thought where it is most immanent to itself.

With this recognition he can then speak of the second moment as one where our thought, having become conscious of itself and of the divine concurrence without which it would not know itself, finds within itself a need to tend toward a union with the one who is the principle and the end of our thought. What this means is that it desires a more intimate presence and communion with God that would require a higher assistance, something that would also have to be recognized, accepted, and even deserved, not so that our thought could use God for its own purposes and partial achievements, but rather so that it would surrender and join itself to the divine truth.

Then comes the third moment where the difficulty, if not the illusory temerity of such an aspiration, comes to the fore, the moment where we are most tempted to abandon the aspiration at the core of our thought and where we have to recognize the deficiency of our thought in bringing about what it aspires to be most intimately. Blondel has shown how we cannot back away from any of these moments. He must now show how we can go forward rationally, from where we find ourselves in this presence of God who both inspires us and summons us toward the perfection of our own thought.

With a clear idea of a real Infinite at the origin and at the end of our thought, promoting our thought every step of the way in its infinite thrust, Blondel returns once again to examine the principles that have led the exercise of thought to the realization of this problem it must face in relation to the Infinite of total perfection. Unlike Descartes, he is not satisfied with just affirming the existence of God and then just using it to solidify his scientific exploitation of the world, without any concern for how God is actually present in the concrete operations of nature and of thought. He wants to be more concrete and realistic in his metaphysics by following the progressive incarnations of thought in a properly spiritual life, that of the scientist as well as that of the philosopher. What he proceeds to do, then, is a new examination of conscience, or of consciousness, along rational lines that are left unexplored by Descartes or other idealists. "After having recalled the active and secret presence of divine thought in human thought, we have to bring more precision to the explicit and deliberate or reflected use we have to make of this truth, once it is recognized, and to the salutary exigencies of which it is the source" (1934b, 287).

Blondel is still doing battle against merely juxtaposing two intellectual lives, one that is merely formal and speculative and one that is concerned with achieving ends. At the root of our thought, we are never just dealing with speculative or practical problems we have to contend with in the immanent order of things; at the same time, we are also imitating God, by taking our own initiative and action, and we are seeking ways to become assimilated to him. If there is any truth to the active presence of God in our own thought and action, and to the sense of our natural insufficiency in the kind of perfection of thought and action that God represents for us, it is to bring out a certain "obligation on our part to conceive, to desire, to solicit, to accept another presence, a more intimate concurrence, a more personal cooperation than that of a spontaneity oriented to utilitarian or even to simply speculative and metaphysical results" (1934b, 289). It becomes illogical and false to use this source of infinite vitality only for our benefit and lower purposes. It is not enough to have reverence for the one from whom we have the strength to go for the infinite, and then to turn to the pursuit of egotistic or lesser interests. If we take the spiritual life of human beings as a whole, we have to see it rationally, that is, not just as an effort to make our own way in the world, but also and at the same time as an *illuminative* and *unitive* way toward something divine. Those who are familiar with the language of ascetical and spiritual writers will recognize that Blondel is here presenting a rational justification for this conception of life that he learned from his Christian ascetical tradition.

However, it would be a mistake to think that we can pass immediately from the human to a properly divine life, solely on the natural power of reason we already have from God as human. When he speaks of the divine immanence in nature, in consciousness, and in human action, that is not what he thinks of as the participation of a spiritual being in the divine life by grace, which gives rise to a transforming union. The latter is something more properly supernatural in Blondel's way of thinking, and therefore beyond the scope of philosophy to comprehend, although philosophers have sometimes vaguely or falsely appropriated Christian terminology in expressing their conception of the human spirit in its perfection.

Blondel wants to maintain a strict rational distinction between two ways of divine cooperation, one natural and one supernatural, and he will not rush to a consideration of what the second might possibly be before bringing to the fore again the natural insufficiency of human thought to achieve its goal of perfect unification with itself and with God that he has been insisting on all along, an insufficiency that shows itself in our inability to penetrate fully into the matter of our thoughts and actions, into the infinite mystery of our action, and even into the secrets of nature, as Bacon had to admit in his *Novum Organum*. The most crucial aspect of all of this, which it cannot penetrate into, is the invisible presence of God, which only shows how far removed our thought remains from the perfect unification it aspires to with respect not only to God but also to itself and the world. What this insufficiency shows is a certain dependency of our thought as well as of everything else on God, along with a certain need and obligation, given the exigencies of our thought, to recognize it for what it is, to ratify it and to use it as a way of preparing ourselves for a spiritual cooperation that our lowly nature exists only to prepare and to make way for.

A Paradoxical Logic for Natural and Supernatural Cooperation

It is impossible to imagine or to represent this double presence of God in our thought and in creation as a whole, but we can try to think it philosophically as a kind of immanence of something transcendent. The first, which we can think of as natural or as constitutive of our very being and thought, we may forget, misrepresent, or even deny, but we cannot do as if it were not. The second, which we would have to think of as supernatural, we can misuse, but it remains as an interior beacon or requirement that is at least tacit. If we turn away from this double presence, it may be because of illusions or obstacles within ourselves, but none of these can completely obscure the radical aspirations of our consciousness and the light of reason searching for its ultimate perfection. If philosophy cannot entirely probe the depth of this double presence, it can at least clarify the difficulties we encounter, both real and imaginary, in facing up to it to the full extent of our rational capacity. This is where metaphysical speculation has a special role to play in the understanding of our spiritual life.

Blondel reiterates his argument that, for us to go from our desires, our knowledge, and our will, not only to external reality but even reflectively to ourselves, there has to be within ourselves the transitive operation of something infinite. This is something for us to appreciate speculatively as well as to respond to actively in the attitude we adopt toward this necessary presence of the transcendent. If there is a secret presence of the divine within, beyond that which we can barely discern naturally, what would be the higher end to which it calls us? Could we rationally remain indifferent to it, since by definition it transcends the capacity of our nature, or would we have an obligation to respond to all its exigencies? That is the aporia that presents itself at the summit of thought we have reached. That is the problem of our attitude, no longer just with regard to nature and humanity, but now with regard to this God "whom reason can demonstrate as the unique and ultimate principle, mediator and end, in spite of its incommensurability with everything that is generated, finite, changing and imperfect. What is implied here is that all the spontaneity maintained by the immanent and transitive action of God leads up within us to an alternative that brings into play a freedom of option between two terms" (1934b, 295).

Blondel describes these two terms as follows. One would be to recognize this necessary concurrence of divine assistance in the physical and scientific order, where we take hold of nature, but then to use it only to accomplish what depends only on ourselves, leaving God and his action aside, to think only of our own action in our management of the world and the organization of humanity. Blondel calls this a sort of metaphysical positivism that suppresses the inquietude of the soul and that sees religion only as an arbitrary add-on to our consciousness. The second term of the alternative would be, in keeping with the original and constant élan of our thought and reason, to affirm that our certain, rationally grounded knowledge of God requires of us, at least implicitly, a constant disposition that would keep us from limiting ourselves to the enjoyment of the world and ourselves to the exclusion of God, who reveals himself in this very capacity to enjoy. "There is everywhere in fact a specifically spiritual or 'religious' obligation, to tend toward God and to 'bond' with him, instead of just using him as a bond, so to speak, to capture everything else without him. What this truth contains, what this obligatory option requires is an attitude of intellectual humility, of unwavering quest, of indestructible expectation, of invincible confidence, all rationally justified dispositions even though they surpass any deism, any natural presumptuousness" (1934b, 296). In this ultimate spiritual option we find the culmination of the total drama of our thought.

Thus we find ourselves in a sort of spiritual no man's land that is difficult to describe, but the ramifications of which must be clarified philosophically, for us to understand what is at stake in this spiritual drama. We cannot say that *thought in itself* is in us, but we have to say that we are in it. Here Blondel recalls Augustine's saying that it would be easier for us to doubt our own existence than its existence. But we cannot leave the problem in terms of vague impressions or mere dialectical constructions. We have to reflect more carefully on what comes into play at the moment of the supreme deliberation. Blondel offers three ways of putting things in perspective. We can think of using the transcendent light and force we have from God to master nature and our own destiny and then, by a sort of reversal, turn this illumination and power on God himself, treating him like one of the things we can overpower with our own thought, going thereby against the normal élan of our thought, which is more one of desire and docile expectation.

In another way of understanding our situation, we begin to fear not ever attaining the perfection we aspire to spiritually, especially when we understand that it is not within our capacity to do so. Then we begin to think less of the spiritual values implied in this aspiration and to set them aside, in order to devote all our power to the management of exterior things, to the neglect of what is commonly called our interior life. Finally, in an exaggerated esteem for the power of thought we do have over ourselves and the world, we lose sight of any philosophy of insufficiency, as if insisting on deficiency in our thought were to abdicate from it or betray it in its highest achievement, and as if admitting that our thought cannot close in on itself did not imply an essential inadequacy in it in relation to its highest object. Blondel wants to propose a philosophy of insufficiency that will steer clear of both presumptuousness and abdication in this ultimate dilemma for our thought.

He notes that it is by a series of precise and coherent implications that we have been led to the problem we must now face. What we have come to understand speculatively must now be coordinated with the responsibility we cannot but exercise in the face of alternatives where our destiny is at stake. There is a concrete but secret logic that governs our thinking life, even though our abstract science, far from being equal to this logic, can be satisfied with partial and therefore perilous views. Blondel sums up this logic with six assertions that mutually presuppose and imply one another.

First, there is the consciousness we have inevitably of our insufficiency and our incompleteness, which has been shown to be not just a matter of fact, but a metaphysical necessity. Second, for this consciousness of something that cannot be completed within ourselves, to be and to be thought, there must be the assertion of a perfection that is conceivable and desirable, but that we are naturally incapable of attaining even as we aspire to it in affirming it. Third, in the face of this mysterious paradox, we are inevitably led to a twofold observation: on the one hand we feel moved by the active presence within us of the living idea of the perfect without which we would not have a sense of our imperfection, our aspiration, our existence; on the other hand, no matter how inaccessible the divine end we are tending toward may seem, we cannot deny or repress this élan whence our thought proceeds and that bears us along invincibly toward this endless end *(fin infinie)*.

Fourth, there is in all this, therefore, a rational and irrecusable attitude to be taken: we cannot remain disinterested, overtake, or deliver ourselves from this demanding condition seemingly imposed on us. "We have neither the power to abolish our being and its undeniable aspirations, nor the right to reject the ascensional vocation imposed on us, nor the faculty of evasion that would allow us to turn away from a gratuitous gift under the pretext that it is onerous, that it would take us away from ourselves, that seems to require of us what we are unable to give" (1934b, 302). Fifth, there results from all this a conception that can be integrated, not only in a primitive soul, but also in a most highly critical and rationally developed philosophy, a conception that condenses all these ingredients that have just been analyzed, namely, the conception of a *supernatural*, that is to say of a complement alone capable of bringing to completion what cannot be humanly and metaphysically completed. Such an increase in what is offered to our choice would not be due to or required by anything in our nature, but, if it were offered or given, it could not legitimately be neglected, repelled, or deflected from its aim and its true end with impunity.

The intricacy of Blondel's concrete logic of implication here cannot be denied, even as it leads to one more assertion that may seem all the more shocking to abstract reasoning on our natural capacity to act but that follows no less rationally from all that has been asserted up to now. From the accumulated light of all these assertions that mutually complement and reinforce one another, Blondel concludes that "any doctrine systematically closed up in a purely human and rational sufficiency would sin against the essential law of its intrinsic development" (1934b, 303). The sense we have of our natural deficiency does not leave us in a darkness without contours any more than it enables us, by itself, to enter into a mystery that it only prevents us from ignoring. The insufficiency we have to recognize has to be seen as the positive privation, so to speak, of a perfection that, without being owed, since it is inaccessible to nature, is nevertheless defined precisely and justly required in the hypothesis that the gift is offered and placed at the disposition of a thought called to its own perfect fulfillment. It would be illogical to maintain that the rational being could be free to refuse this offer and remain in its own nature with impunity, when this same rational being is conscious of its metaphysical indigence and its moral insufficiency.

With this, Blondel is back to where he wanted to be philosophically with his original philosophy of the supernatural in the dissertation on *Action*, only now he has come to this point through a science of thought alone rather than a science of practice as a whole. What he has done is develop a dialectic of thought that had remained hidden in the background of the original argument, but that had been the moving force of the ascension from the lower forms to the higher, more spiritual forms of human action, which he can now speak of more explicitly. What remains for him to show is how and why we do not escape from this interlocking sequence of truths that seems to force us into submission, but that in fact assures us of our freedom in choosing the only way we can bring ourselves to completion. The drama of our existence as thoughtful beings is not yet ended. There is still a spiritual struggle to go through and to overcome for this liberation that cannot be automatic, if it is to be salutary for a spiritual being. The philosophy of insufficiency is only provisional. There is still a philosophy of superabundance to be developed. "For an imperfect spirit to participate in plenitude, there is, under necessary exigencies and moral conditions to be realized, a life of the spirit to be developed or to be taken in. To study the life of the spirit in finite thought will be the object of the seventh [and final] part of this science of thought" (1934b, 306).

Doing Justice to the Human Spirit with the Divine Cooperation

Blondel titles this last part of his science of thought "The Integrity of Thought." What he wants to convey by the title is both a certain steadfastness in thought itself, in the pursuit of its end, and a readiness to use all its resources in applying them unfailingly to complete its spiritual task. For him this means developing a broader idea of spirit that will encompass the different element/aspects of thought and accommodate the presence of the divine in human thought, without reducing the divine to the human or absorbing the singularity of the human person into some impersonal universality. What has been said regarding the essential insufficiency of human thought remains crucially true, especially with regard to attaining the divine in itself, where human thought would find its perfect unification. But there is still something to do for human thought in pursuit of its own fulfillment, even after it has come to the realization that it cannot achieve this end on its own, or without some additional or supernatural gift from God. There is still an attitude to be taken that will define a spirit further, whether it will stop short and use its natural ability only to manage the things for which it is adapted in nature and history or society, or limit its relation to God only to what can be known of him in some abstract metaphysics, or whether it will continue to try to break out of these limitations in a way that can identify more closely and intimately with God. For Blondel, only the second has any chance of doing justice to the human spirit, while the first has already been shown to be illogical and irrational in failing to take into account the full scope of human aspiration.

The term *aspiration* here should not go unnoticed. Like many other terms, such as *inspiration* and *expiration*, it is made up of the same root metaphor as the word *spirit* itself. Blondel uses this metaphor to describe the life of spirit as a kind of breathing in of the whole universe and breathing out of one's self in the universe. Given the pains Blondel has gone to prove the total transcendence of God, however, as well as our deficiency in reaching for such transcendent perfection in our temporal lives, he cannot settle for a spirit that is only immanent to the world. The life of the spirit he wants to describe is the one that reaches out beyond anything finite, even if it be the indefinite succession of finite after finite. The human spirit does not stop short at the finite. Even if it recognizes that it cannot transcend its own finitude absolutely, as it would have to, in order to achieve its own perfect unification, it still wants to and, Blondel adds, it has to make its own contribution to its ultimate perfection. Hence there can be no legitimate philosophical abdication even in the face of supernatural demands, just as there should be no presumption that we can be satisfied with what lies within our capacity to achieve. Rational initiative cannot be left out of the picture, even where there is a question of some supra-rational achievement.

These are the intricacies that Blondel wants to pull together with the idea of spirit and its life. In this life there is an interweaving of noetic thought and pneumatic thought that arrives at some perfection and unification in different cultural achievements we can rightly boast of. These achievements, however, are only partial and passing. The unification and perfection are real for thought, but they are never fully satisfying. They dissolve into new kinds of opposition and tension that give rise to an ever-progressive movement toward higher forms of unification. Even if these achievements of thought are perceived eventually as essentially deficient from the standpoint of a perfect fulfillment, they do give us some inkling of what such a perfect fulfillment might be, if we can abstract from their partiality. That is why the achievement of philosophy in affirming the existence of God, and recognizing the consequences of our attitude in responding to this presence of God, is an important part of the spiritual life Blondel is interested in. It raises our spiritual life to a metaphysical level it otherwise would not have.

However, philosophy does this, not by bringing God into the world, as some philosophers would have it. Blondel considers every attempt to bring the infinite into the finite, whether it be some crude totem or our finite idea of the infinite, a form of superstition or idolatry. We have seen how severely he criticized this attitude of spirit at the end of his phenomenology of action. If there is a truly religious attitude in our spirit, it cannot be based on anything we have achieved or conceived, no matter how transcendentally. It has to be based on the realization of a presence of God at the origin of our thought and at every moment of its unfolding. We do not place him there. We find him there, and philosophy has a crucial role in bringing this realization out in our spiritual life, as a higher dimension that we can never reach by ourselves. This is over and above the essential deficiency of our thought in relation to that higher dimension. At the same time it also has a crucial role to play in showing the way this higher dimension can be joined to the lower dimension through cooperation with the divine in the spiritual life. Blondel's conception of the spiritual life is thus one that pulls together the divine and the human in a cooperation that stimulates the activity of thought with the two element/aspects that have been distinguished from the beginning of this study of thought in search of ever-higher degrees of unification and perfection.

With a clear consciousness of the radical transcendence of the divine even as present in the human spirit, Blondel warns against any premature mysticism which, "for lack of ascetical purification and critical science, would lapse all too easily into quietism and illuminism.... In fact, spirit remains a mystery in us. It is what cannot be brought to completion by us and what entails or what calls for completion by God: *initium aliquod creaturae quod Deus ipse perficiet* [a certain beginning of a creature that God himself would perfect]" (1934b, 319). To be sure, this created spirit can repulse God and pretend to be self-sufficient, but it does not thereby annihilate itself. It remains profoundly attached to the being it has received and to the truth it has perceived, which makes it worse than nothing. "Spirit is thus this power of balancing, as if on a sharp peak, whence, through quite partial and contingent options, it must put into play a deliberate judgment that has a bearing on the whole, so that it comes down finally entirely on one side or entirely on the other. This dignity of a judge that follows on the alternative, whose origin and urgency we have previously demonstrated, corresponds within us to the evocative presence of the Spirit to make us equal and ready to decide our destiny. Thus sustained, stimulated, enlightened, we become, without losing sight of the first Cause, the artisans of our spiritual being; for there is no spirit who is not, under the conditions just stated, cause of what it becomes, *causa sui*" (1934b, 320).

If we keep in mind this divine cooperation that sets in motion all beings and all our aspirations, we are led then rationally to raising an alternative before God and to reflect on the rational consequences that it implies necessarily. Yes or no, is God the cooperator hidden in all our endeavors? Is his solicitude for the world and for ourselves in particular limited to providing the imperfect joys of a temporal life or even of some vague immortality in Elysian Fields? Or is it for us to cooperate in the divine ends? Once we have tasted life for ourselves, do we not have more and better to do, "even to justify, elevate and eternalize this love of ourselves, by living for God, *sunergoi Theou* [co-workers of God], and would we not cease to love and help ourselves, if we did not prefer a voluntary and loving conformity to perfect truth, to universal charity, [rather than] to our own perishable and limited desires?" (1934b, 323). Thus, coming back to his basic metaphor, Blondel speaks of living by the spirit as breathing, in an exchange that benefits the cooperator by the very generosity it shows to the original generosity expressed in the very gift of being and by the highest aspiration of thought. But he warns against thinking of this cooperation as a simple alliance of friendship among equals based on a natural order of direct exchanges with God. If we were to settle for a simple equality between the human and the divine in this cooperation, which would be bringing God down to the proportions of our reason, we would be selling ourselves short, along with all that God may be intending for us, as seen in the aspiration to absolute perfection he endows us with.

Blondel notes a certain pessimism in the ancient spirit of Aristotle and the Greeks, when faced with the lack of all proportion between the human and the divine, a spirit of infinite resignation, as Kierkegaard would have called it. To entertain any thought of friendship, which presupposes some kind of equality, between God and man, was bound to appear extravagant and beyond the bounds of reason. The best that reason could do was study nature and, after Socrates, work toward the organization of the city. *Ne quid nimis,* nothing in excess, was the injunction: nothing too profound, nothing too far-fetched, nothing too elevated for human enterprise and generosity. But here we find ourselves before another injunction, the injunction to go higher, to reach further and to seek union with God, in whom is our perfection. The fault would not be in aspiring too high, but rather in failing to respond to an interior calling, a rising force, a supreme invitation. Blondel has tried to show that this would be the ultimate sin against the spirit, a failure in the light of nature and of reason itself, which, at this point in the ascent of thought, calls for letting go of our spontaneous natural selves and our own limited achievements, to take one final step toward our final fulfillment. The role of spirit is to tie together within ourselves all the incomplete aspects of our thought as they culminate in the final alternative that presents itself for each one of us. It has to do with a binding that is "rational and vital, noetic and pneumatic, logical and spiritual, enveloping and surpassing the entire scope of nature and conscience, and reaching all the more forcefully toward the unitive solution — apparently quite close by, but perhaps at a distance that is manifestly infinite — the universal integration of earth and heaven that thought, from its humblest origins has not ceased looking for, not without achieving marvelous results" (1934b, 326).

What all this consideration of thought and its achievements as well as its essential deficiency brings us to, then, is to recognize the need, the nature, and the obligation of a life that is truly spiritual and that touches on religion. Philosophy does not end in pure speculation or theories. There is religious thought as well, and the philosophy of spirit at the end of the philosophy of thought finds itself, not undermined, but challenged from within to explore the conditions for entering a life that remains mysterious for it, but that it cannot but sense it may be called to in its search for perfect unification. Metaphysics, at its summit, can and does open within itself a necessary abyss that it cannot clearly delineate, but whose sides and contours nevertheless prefigure the virtualities for what could be an eventual solution. What we have seen of the cooperation between the human and the divine at the core of our spiritual life will suggest the ways in which we access this life, in which we come face to face with God.

After carefully considering how we can deviate and fall short in the pursuit of the spiritual life to which we are called by the very dynamism of our thought, Blondel now turns to what he sees as the normal development whose implications he is trying to describe and whose rectitude he wants to discern philosophically. What he wants to come to is the generous simplicity that can be found in any straightforward exercise of thought as well as in the highest spiritual speculation. He distinguishes between three births to be considered in our spiritual life, or three thresholds to be crossed. The first is the threshold when our thought first appears to itself or is born to itself. In this moment there is also the consciousness that we are not alone in our self-consciousness, that our spirit is not entirely ours alone, but in communication with another spirit. This is the birth we have just been considering in describing the wakeup call within our thought to a higher life of spirit, if not to the highest life of unification possible.

The second birth is the one where our thought, finding itself unable to be sufficient unto itself or to find perfect unity with its principle, its object, its light, and its end, must go out of itself and its isolation, as well as its fallibility, in order to suspend itself from "the Thought of Thought," "the source necessarily affirmed of all internal illumination as well as of all aspiration toward the perfection of being, of knowledge and of beatitude" (1934b, 346). This is the threshold where thought must die to itself because of its incapacity to realize the union without which the life of the spirit, though indefectible, would remain as it were dead. It is the passage that Blondel now proceeds to analyze in a chapter titled "Access to the Spiritual Life." A third chapter will then follow to go into a third birth for our thought in the Spirit that it is impossible for philosophy to delineate with any sort of detail, but that remains something to be examined critically according to the rational method Blondel has long been following.

Dying to itself, for finite thought, means trying to enter more deeply into the mystery of being and of divine thought to which it has been brought, at the limit of its capacity to achieve, or of its essential insufficiency. It means looking for a second birth. The first impulse of the spirit has resulted in our conceiving the idea and the desire of a new life other than that of a perishable world or an earthly science. Now a new impulse comes to the fore that must be analyzed in the light of all the implications that have been brought forth in the final moments of this dialectic of thought, all of which are profoundly rational, but some of which seem incompatible with one another. Blondel sums these up once again in order to define the conditions for this second mode of access to a superabundance of the spiritual life.

First, there is the incommensurability between Thought conceived and affirmed as metaphysically necessary and perfect, and the mode of any thought in becoming and always incomplete. Perfection is not a sum of successive states; nor can thought be reduced to mere agglomeration of data upon data. If we think of perfection as absolute, we cannot think of it as merely strung out in a series of contingent and relative facts. Hence the metaphysical incompatibility between the absolute thought of God and our own mode of thought as we experience it in the world.

The second point, however, is that there is no spirit capable of affirming the absolute and the perfect (since otherwise it would not be spirit) that does not tend, by a congenital aspiration, to inquire more deeply into this perfection of being and thought, no matter how inaccessible in itself it may appear to reason. Along with this there is also a natural desire to participate in the joy that would go with knowing and tasting such perfection. Is it possible to reconcile the affirmation of this natural necessity to see God with the affirmation of a necessary incommensurability between the absolute perfection of God and our capacity to see? Are we bound to say only that our natural desire to see God is incurably frustrated, or is there some other more positive attitude that can be taken with regard to this inclination within our spirit?

There is something to be said for the Hellenic wisdom, of staying within the bounds of reason, or for the modesty of the scientist before the infinite distance that seems to stretch beyond what he speaks of as his findings. But such dispositions are not entirely in keeping with the infinite thrust of reason or the interior duty of thought to seek where the ultimate truth lies. They risk cutting us short of where we can go rationally with the power to think we already have from God. "We do not have the right to hold ourselves to this prostration which is not the only and the ultimate role for a cooperator summoned, from below and from on high, to a true participation in the movement of nature and in the total design of the first Cause" (1934b, 337). This is the third point Blondel says has to be made. Having recognized that we cannot go forward by ourselves, we must now add that, since we are never alone in our endeavor, we must still go forward, even though we do not see clearly how far we are being sustained, led, or aided in what would be for philosophy a third birth in the spiritual life.

Going Forward with Dispositions of Readiness to Accept a Positive Offer of Supernatural Grace from Religion

Far then from selling philosophy short in its natural initiatives and its spiritual spontaneity, Blondel is trying to keep it from closing itself up in its own systematic achievement. He sees a new field of life and abundance opening up before it for exploration according to its own rational method of inquiry. Once we have recognized the possibility and the desirable advantage of a more intimate cooperation with the One who is already the principle of its natural light, it remains to be asked whether, "if such a higher union is in fact offered, thought can and must take it into account somehow, even without having an express knowledge of it, as long as it remains faithful to solicitations that remain quite anonymous. For the science of thought, or true metaphysics, which has a bearing on all possibles at the same time as it makes itself docile to the whole of what is real in nature and in consciousness, goes beyond pure hypotheses, when it is a question of the integral conditions of thinking and the final destiny of the spirit" (1934b, 338). If there is truly a natural, congenital desire to know and to possess God in his beatitude, albeit an inefficacious one, the hypothesis that God might be offering a special dispensation for achieving such a goal cannot be thought of as purely arbitrary and gratuitous from our point of view. If it were to answer to our inmost desire, it would have to be taken seriously and a place would have to be made for it in our rational accounting for ourselves and for the world in which we live.

Blondel does not believe that philosophy can prove such an offer has been made. He thinks of it as so far surpassing the power of reason that we can already exercise, that it remains hidden in the wide-open mystery of how God *de facto* cooperates with us and how we cooperate with God in spirit. But he does think philosophy must go out of its way to inquire as to whether God has in fact offered a solution to this most profound human predicament. In this respect Blondel is still trying to answer the question asked of him at the École Normale, as to why anyone should be interested in some obscure individual in an obscure part of the Roman Empire centuries ago, or in any individual for that matter, when one is trying to orient one's life by universal rational principles. Here at the end of his philosophy of thought he lines up his answer to such a question in three steps. First, it has been shown that the problem of a complete fulfillment is real for us and that its terms must be enunciated very precisely, so that we understand how difficult the solution is, if not simply impossible. Second, the mystery is not seen as entirely opaque, so that thought does not have to remain paralyzed in its activity as it faces this problem. It can learn something in contemplating this mystery. Third, proceeding from all the effort of thought that has led to posing this problem for our thought, and using the momentum acquired in the process, we can start tending toward a solution without pretending that we already have it within our grasp, as a philosophy of absolute knowing might. This means striving not to be unworthy of such a solution by closing our mind to its very possibility, let alone its necessity. It means also looking into the dispositions of spirit that might be required for us to receive and accept such fulfillment from on high, and then beginning to ask what signs there might be that such a gift has been offered to our free choice, and what might be the requirements on our part for entering into such a communion with God. As open as these questions might be for a proper philosophy of spirit, they are still within the scope of what Blondel calls the integrity of thought and the care we must have for its total coherence in terms of all that it might require of itself.

What the questions suggest is that this philosophy of spirit, at its pinnacle, must look anew to history, to the movement of the spirit in individuals and communities, in order to discern whether a solution has in fact been proffered to the problem of its ultimate fulfillment and, if so, where and how. Blondel ends his argument with a caution, however, ever solicitous not to transgress into the domain of religion, where the answer to the ultimate problem of philosophy may be given but remain mysterious for it. Even when philosophy thinks it has found what might be the answer to its ultimate problem it cannot take hold of that truth as if it were its own. Beyond the metaphysical necessities that it can grasp there is a life that is more than human and that flows into human life within the confines of our personality, as it draws us back to itself. What this life is in itself and even as it communicates itself supernaturally remains hidden from philosophy. For philosophy it can only be a hypothesis, not a thesis, albeit a necessary hypothesis for the perfection of human thought that is compatible with the most rigorous of reasons.

With the thought of this radically new life for human thought comes the thought of the third birth in the spiritual life Blondel has already spoken of, the birth to a strictly supernatural life that can only come from a God who is totally other in his own spiritual life. This has to be represented as an immense flow of theandric life in the society of spirits freely convened for a more intimate participation, the possibility of which philosophy can conceive but without having the means of defining it or acquiring it effectively on its own. This is the threshold philosophy cannot cross in the strict sense of the term. It is guarded by the divinity itself as understood metaphysically, or as totally transcendent to anything we can conceive. But it is a threshold that comes at the summit of thought that allows for a certain leeway for speaking of it indirectly. It does not leave us deaf, blind, and dumb at the door of an inner sanctum that is now properly a religious life, for, by hypothesis, we now have to think of a new teaching addressed to our human intelligence as something assimilating and vivifying. Even if it is directly from God in a way that transcends the way he is already the principle of our being and the natural light of our intelligence, there are still some things philosophy can say about it, to keep it pure in its transcendence and elevation and to determine the human conditions for its proper assimilation into our spirit, or better still for our own due and deliberate assimilation into it.

One of these things is to prepare and ratify the necessary dispositions of spirit, even for acknowledging the very offer of such a gift, if it is made, as something that is in line with a complete rectitude, sincerity, and readiness to learn what might be to our ultimate advantage, even if that is beyond our power to achieve. This is the thing that Blondel has already taken great pains to put in place philosophically in this dialectical elaboration of thought. Whatever the case may be about the actuality of such an offer, the total good faith that such dispositions would imply, even in the absence of any positive faith or explicit knowledge, could not be without salutary effect on an individual spirit. Another thing for philosophy to show would be the necessity or the obligation to search in the historical order of positive facts to see if there might not be a sign given in response to the solicitations of our thought for a higher light to achieve complete perfection. Because Blondel does not think we can attain any sort of absolute knowing purely from within, without the help of some higher assistance from without or from deeper within ourselves, he understands the necessity of some positive religion in history that would meet our deepest rational exigencies and answer the questions left open for us at the end of philosophy. The endeavor of his philosophy of insufficiency has been to keep reason from falling asleep about its ultimate concern, not to let it sin against the little natural light we already have and for which we are constantly responsible, and not to let it repel the stimulations that may be secretly at work in our good faith. For, what we have to start from in our spiritual endeavor is always a twofold activity: our own rational initiative and God's advances of light and power to our credit.

Another thing philosophy can do for religion, or about religion, is keep the religious sense from becoming atrophied and from falling back into superstition. This is especially important for a religious spirit that has to show itself in positive external facts and that requires some external practice. The temptation is to see these external facts and practices as the essence of religion, whereas the essence of religion is in the way God calls us to himself as something quite transcendent and infinite, and how we respond to this call. To be sure, the call takes place historically in positive facts, and the response takes place in chosen particular practices, but the true meaning of the religious spirit cannot be limited to those facts and practices. Focusing on bare facts and practices is something we learn to recognize as another form of superstition from a proper metaphysics of God in his transcendent being, as another way of trying to have the infinite under our control in something finite. Nor can we limit the religious sense to any of our metaphysical concepts of the divine, or of thought thinking thought, or to our conception of absolute knowing. That would be to take away from God his initiative, by which he moves our spirit to be itself. It would be to replace God's initiative with the human initiative alone in the theandric equation of cooperation. The attempt to supersede religion by reason is only a higher form of superstition, another way of trying to fit the infinite into something finite, or at best indefinite. Reason itself must be critical of this superstition as well. That is, it must remain open to the full extent of the infinite and thus become religious itself in relation to the true Infinite, by recognizing its essential deficiency with respect to the real Infinite it can only aspire to. It must recognize the necessity of a mediation from the Infinite to meet the exigency of its own aspiration. Religion has to be understood as this sort of mediation from God, which may result in some kind of absolute knowing, but cannot be presumed as coming from a finite spirit alone, not even from what has been called a World Spirit. If there is some religious knowledge in the world, it too cannot be called absolute, even if it presupposes a mediation from God, because, as long as it is in this world, it too is finite and subject to the temptation of superstition. We cannot make an idol of God, as Blondel says elsewhere, or of his Word. We can only seek to be faithful to this Word rationally and responsibly in all that it offers and requires.

Purgative, Illuminative, and Unitive Stages in Thought's Progression

Beyond all this, philosophy can also inquire into what would be the ramifications of a de facto supernatural intervention, or of a positive call to a supernatural life in the natural life of the human spirit. This, for Blondel, would not presuppose any knowledge of any positive religious content that might have resounded externally at some point in time and space, or made itself known internally to a human soul, for the message may be given, indeed must be given, in the internal forum as well as in the external. It would only presuppose an understanding that states of consciousness, moral obligations, and spiritual attitudes can and do relate to the kind of faithfulness we can exercise, even when God is not named, in response to the common motions of reason, freedom, and grace we have from him, either by translating them into action in some positive way or betraying them by withholding our cooperation. Blondel eschews any apologetic intent here for affirming the fact of a supernatural intervention on the part of God in world history. All he wants to do is "define and obtain as much as possible all the dispositions that are integrated in an implicit faith and that tie a human soul into the invisible soul of the living Truth" (1934b, 354). This is to be done not by gazing directly into a brilliance that would only blind us, but rather by trying to glimpse it indirectly through the rays that emanate from it in order to enlighten and rally the society of spirits in the world.

To describe how this enlightenment and this rallying of spirits take place, Blondel borrows the language of spiritual or ascetical writers who have had much to say about how God works in the souls of people and who have distinguished three ways in which this work takes place: a purgative way, an illuminative way, and a unitive way. In his systematic reflection on how human thought progresses by nature, Blondel proceeds to show how each one of these ways proves to be necessary for the spirit to strive effectively toward its goal of divinization. With respect to the purgative way, he shows that it is normal for any finite spirit to go through some sort of purification, for it to enter into the way of divinization. It is normal for our thought to spontaneously rely on itself in achieving its goals. But when in the normal course of reflection we come to realize that we are not our own light or that we are not in complete possession of ourselves, that in fact we are operating with some help on loan from another, for which we have to render some account, then we come to realize that we have to let go of our spontaneous but still perhaps too-proud tendency to want to go it alone, with only our native or natural capacity.

This is perhaps the most fundamental reason for the necessity of some purification to enter into the way of our lofty ambition, the pride we take in our own initiative as thinkers that would turn us away from looking at any higher goal we might also have as thinkers. But it is not the only reason. There is also the fact that we have committed positive faults in choices we have made precipitously, or under the sway of partiality or passion, or following the ever-present temptation to make ourselves the center, the sole arbiters of the truth, glorifying in our free thought without any sense of intellectual responsibility. The first reason for the need of purification, namely that of a certain self-confidence in the power of our thought, is not necessarily bad, unless it turns into a pride that is exclusive of any further assistance. Blondel is far from wanting to destroy the spontaneous confidence we have in our thought. He is more interested in building on it by adding confidence on a higher principle still. But the second reason for the necessity of purification is one that calls for correction, for letting go of tendencies that have drawn us off course, for a purging of inclinations that we have allowed to build up within ourselves as a kind of resistance to any transcendence.

As for the illuminative way, that is where the purification of the senses and of the understanding is confirmed and perfected as a new orientation for the spirit. This too is a necessary facet of our spiritual life in explicit cooperation with God. "Even when we have recognized that the source of our illumination is within us without being from us — to the point that in this light we have to acknowledge that it is we who are exterior to ourselves and that our thoughts become idols the moment we start thinking of them as both ours and sufficient at the same time — we find it difficult to really take this truth into account and to avoid either exaggerating or depreciating these certitudes that force us out of ourselves, instead of taking satisfaction only in our own light" (1934b, 359). This coexistence of two thoughts within our spirit has been demonstrated in many ways throughout this study of thought. It is something that we cannot but recognize as necessary for the very existence of consciousness, let alone its progression through the world and through itself toward some unifying goal it cannot but intend. But now the question is how we come to consent freely and meritoriously in this spiritual union of wills. What we know of natural causes, of rational science, or of moral activity, is no longer enough to raise us to this new level of consent. What we need now is the more intimate light of divine Truth itself, which it would be presumptuous and incomprehensible for us to think we have, without the gift from God and acceptance on our part. It is not for philosophy to try to enter into what such graceful giving and acceptance might actually entail in a properly religious spirit, but it is for philosophy to show that it would provide a necessary illumination for raising our spiritual life to a new level of efficaciousness.

Beyond the illuminative, spiritual writers also speak of a unitive or contemplative way for the spirit elevated by God, not without the free response from the creature. This third way is associated more with the end of the religious cooperation between God and the human being than with the progression toward that end, for union with God in an absolute perfection of thought is what we aim at, rather than what we start from or already have along the way toward that end. Nevertheless, in a properly conceived religious activity that is essentially theandric, we can also speak of the end of union as actually present in the labor toward the end, not just as a beacon shedding light on the nature of the spiritual struggle, but as a real communion here and now between the human spirit and God leading the way by bonding between the two natures, one finite and the other infinite. Here even the number two becomes mysterious for philosophy. Blondel prefers to speak of heterogeneity between the two "natures," thereby keeping the aspect of mystery always on the side of the divine or the supernatural. But here he has to speak of the union between the two in the religious spiritual life and show its necessity at the very core of that life.

Going back to the hypothesis about the possibility of a free and graceful intervention by God in the spiritual life of human beings, and the necessity of such an intervention, if any human being is to attain the kind of perfection in thought we aspire to by nature, but cannot procure for ourselves by reason of the essential deficiency in our thought, Blondel then brings up a second hypothesis for the philosopher to consider, one in which there is no consciousness that any supernatural gift has been offered: "If this grace of union that would constitute the fulfillment and the salvation of our thought were really offered, how would it be possible and obligatory for us to take advantage of it, even unwittingly?" (1934b, 362). What this implies for thinking beings who are aware of no special revelation, either internal or external, and who therefore have only what their consciousness and the probity of their reason tell them to go on, is that they must ask themselves what steps must be taken by their thought — if not speculatively, at least actively in a life of reason — in order to maintain the unified integrity of both science and generosity in thought. Knowing that as a philosopher he cannot in principle penetrate, through speculation, into the content or the truth of any supernatural intervention in the spiritual life of human beings by God, Blondel turns more to the practical side of the question, that of how contact or union of the two spirits is to be established or viewed from the side of the human being. This would not be a matter of trying to figure out what God might be saying or doing in human history, but rather of figuring out what we would have to do, or rather what disposition we would have to make of ourselves, if such a grace were offered.

Thus, the unitive way in the spiritual life has to be thought of as something other than a metaphysics or a simple monistic ethic of the kind Spinoza envisioned with his intellectual love of God, which is no more than an absorption of the intellectual soul or the individual thought into God. It has to be a union of two self-conscious wills in loving response to one another. Analytical and discursive thought, as normative and as indispensable as it is, cannot remain alone or aloft in abstraction from life. It "lives by and for a thought that is quite concrete, quite universal, and that by reason of its extension goes far beyond the limits of our nearsightedness. That is why at the depths of our thought there is always implied a state, which, by reason of its virtualities known only indistinctly and by reason of the access it opens up to any divine touches and initiatives, deserves the name 'mystical'" (1934b, 364). But such a state is more than philosophy can attain in its systematic articulation.

We saw earlier, in this dialectic of thought, how Blondel rejected any suggestion of something mystical about the philosophical discipline of metaphysics. We saw even earlier, in his article on Philosophy and the Mystical Life, how he was careful not to let philosophy intrude into the content or the truth of what such a life might entail for the mystic, choosing rather to limit himself to what he thought were the conditions for the possibility of such a life for a human being. We even saw how he refused the name "mystic" for himself as a philosopher from the very beginning, in the defense of his dissertation on *Action*. This was because he wanted to speak only as a philosopher, and not as a believer, much less as a mystic, though he did see the continuity there could be between the normal experience of faith in the spiritual life of a Christian and the exceptional experience of the mystic. He will have more to say of this continuity later on, in *Philosophy and the Christian Spirit*, when he comes to speak of the grace initiated through Baptism, which can rise, not just to ordinary states of faith-full consciousness, but also to the highest mystical experience. Here, at the end of *La Pensée*, he is satisfied with speaking of the mystical as an expression for the union that must take place, on the level of loving intelligence and enlightened loving, which philosophy can envision rationally between a finite spirit and the infinite Spirit of God. Such mystical life has to be taken for granted rationally in the very concept of a spiritual life in supernatural communication with God. There is some mystical knowledge in such a life, but not without a loving response on the part of the finite spirit to the advances of the Infinite.

All this is to be taken, not as an argument or an apology for Christianity, or for any other form of religion that would add certain more explicit determinations to the basic mystical knowledge Blondel wants to speak of here as related to some specific historical origin, but rather as a way of alluding systematically to the existence of a religious organism that is still thought of as hypothetical and hidden from the clear discernment of philosophical thought. Blondel is not trying to pass through the visible body of any church. He is only trying to bring out what there is in any properly spiritual religious life that any upright and generous soul would have to respond to, in response to a light it sees interiorly. This is the light and the life that can rebound to eternity, in a thought that is fully enlightened on the gifts it has received unbeknownst to itself and on the meaning of its mysterious aspirations toward an object beyond its capacity to understand. To be able to point meaningfully and rationally to all of this mysterious life within one's spiritual experience, one has to marshal together all the implications that follow one another in the dynamic of our thought. To see it as something we are responsible for, we have to be ready to accept whatever gifts it might entail generously, no matter what the sacrifice to ourselves and to our nature.

One last thing to be noted about this religious aspect of the spiritual life of thought as Blondel conceives it, is its inherently social dimension. The union between the human and the divine in this life is not just a one-on-one relation. To be sure, it is that for every individual spirit that enters into such a relation. That is why it points to some kind of immortality for any individual human being. The union begins in a reverential fear on the part of the human spirit, and it dilates the soul into a sort of compassionate piety that is merciful and universally comprehensive. We have seen Blondel speak of the pneumatic element/aspect of our thought always as both concrete and universal at the same time. Most recently we saw him invoke this pneumatic element of our spiritual life as the one in which the supernatural would insert itself in mystical experience. The universality in question is one that takes the concrete living spirit out of its individuality into the broader perspective of diversity in nature and more specifically in civilization, which is built up by the spiritual enterprise of people. The virtue of intelligence consists, not just in discerning and distinguishing, comparing and constructing, but also in embracing, in comprehending and uniting. As it looks on high to a totally transcendent Good, it discovers a way of encompassing the good of all things in the universe, especially the good of other human beings and other civilizations. It discovers its social function as well as its critical function, and it becomes more modest in deference to others. It discovers its community with others as a source of light even more than its own reflective consciousness. That is where the spirit comes to life in its purest and most primitive form, in living traditions that give witness to the light that illumines every human being who comes into the world. When that light is deemed supernatural it can be called mystical. When it is natural, it is called rational or philosophical, but it still has to relate to its origin and to its end as totally Transcendent in its universality. That is what makes authentic religious thought, in union with God, truly the most universal form of thought, ready to appreciate the full value of the widest diversity of human spirits and civilizations, something philosophical thought can only aspire to, by not closing in upon itself in its always partial outlook.

Circumincession of Thought, Being, and Action

In the end of this long study of thought, or better still, of thinking in its diverse functions and in its aspiration toward a perfect unification, which has turned out to be a phenomenology, not of one absolute spirit, but of two spirits, one finite and one infinite, in essential communication with one another as conceived in their heterogeneity, Blondel offers a summation of the way we have come from the humble beginnings of cosmic thought to the height of a thought that thinks itself in relation to a Thought that it cannot fully comprehend but that is the principle and the end of its own thinking. With the understanding of the Thought that thinks itself absolutely as the principle, not only of any finite thought, but also of all that is in becoming, Blondel can now explain better how he could begin his study with a thought that does not think itself in any conscious way, but that nevertheless manifests the dynamic nature of thought. With the understanding of the essential deficiency of any finite thought in becoming, complemented by the thought of a superabundant spirit that can overcome this deficiency through a supernatural communion that the finite spirit can and must respond to, we can say that the study of thought has come to a conclusion. This is as far as we can go in a philosophical reflection on the human exercise of thought. It is not, however, as far as thought has to go. There are still *aporiai* concerning being and action that have surfaced in the course of this study, and that have still to be resolved at the end.

Clearly Blondel is thinking ahead to the two other parts of his Trilogy that will complement this science of thought, but he wants to show how they are called for by thought as having to do with something other than thought. Given all that Blondel has included in this study of thought, from the cosmos to the perfect identity of thought and being in absolute Thought, and given that he has considered thought itself as being in its own right and as an action, one could wonder what more there is to consider, other than thought. But Blondel is not willing to let it go at that. This would be giving in too much to idealism. He wants to maintain that being is something other than thought, at least for a finite thought, even though he has shown that there is no being without thought, no brute reality totally deprived of intelligibility, which would be tantamount to nothing.

To do this, he goes back to an internal criticism of the notion of intelligibility, which expresses for him a facet of being as it relates to intelligence. As intelligible, being is taken as the principle of intelligence. On the other hand, intelligence cannot be understood except in relation to the intelligible. Clearly the two cannot be understood except in relation to one another, but the two must not be confused, in what he calls "a reality where being and thinking entail a true distinction in a real unity" (1934b, 385). The unity may be perfect in God, to the point of a simple identity, but not for a finite thought that has to find intelligibility in something more than itself. This does not mean, however, that there is intelligibility somewhere without intelligence. Can we really conceive of a thought as objective and merely thinkable without some thought? In dealing with such questions we must keep in mind the dual function of thinking, the noetic, where idealism or any sort of abstract science tends to confine itself, and the pneumatic, where the realist principle comes into play in the life of our intelligence, including the reality of the necessary Being, even though we do not always discern the presence of this Being for all that it is and can mean for our thought and action.

To account for this unity in a distinction of thought, being, and action, Blondel uses the term *circumincession*. Earlier, the Scholastics had spoken rather abstractly of a convertibility between being, truth, and the good. Blondel specifies that, in act, they are one, though not the same. They are distinct, at least in finite beings, but they cannot be conceived except as flowing into one another. This circumincession can be viewed from the standpoint of being and of action, and Blondel plans on getting to that later on, but here he wants to view it from the standpoint of thought and intelligibility. If we go back to the distinction between a perfect thought and an imperfect thought still in becoming that we had to make in our reflection on the functions of thinking, we find ourselves before a fundamental antinomy. On the one hand, if we manage to conceive the possibility, and posit the necessity of perfect thought as full and exclusive intelligibility, then it seems impossible to understand how and why a deficient thought is constituted with its mixture of darkness and light, something that appears more incomprehensible than pure darkness would be. On the other hand, what appears to be given in fact is this disconcerting mixture of light and darkness, so that it would seem that we have to turn these antagonistic terms around and declare, as some metaphysicians have done, that the incontestable existence of our imperfect thought, with its strict laws of rationality, forces us to cast the ever-receding conception of a pure thought into the realm of a dream about some vague ideal, beyond our grasp because it would be unreal. Blondel casts this antinomy as a struggle unto death between two ways of conceiving the divine, the immanentist way that, in the name of a living, moving thought, relegates the idea of God as its term to a category of constructive reason, and the more traditional way of a philosophical and religious faith in a living God.

This antinomy cannot be resolved if we remain within thought reduced to what pertains to it alone, or to a role of merely mirroring or repeating passively what there might be beside it. In either case thought cannot go out of itself. Closed within itself, it could not find anything like its own reality, or that it would have to integrate into itself. Pure thought would be immobilized in a sterility that would isolate it in some abstract identity. Thought in becoming would be drawn into an indefinite process far from any possession of self or any possibility of unity. For the two thoughts to subsist and for thought to be thinkable at the same time as fertile, there has to be something other than just a matching of intelligible and intelligence. There has to be reference to *being* as other than just thought, and to *action* as generous response to thought. Blondel has shown this by talking about cosmic thought before talking about thought that is thinking itself in consciousness, and by showing how thought in us cannot remain withdrawn into itself, without adopting an attitude of responsibility toward what it comes to know. He has shown this necessity of thought relating to being and action also with his triune conception of God as Spirit, who first presents himself as perfect Thought thinking itself. Such a thought is not just a thought remaining hidden in itself. It is an eternally flowing spring of being, a reciprocity of power, truth, and love in the unity of a living substance. Spinoza had it wrong when he spoke of thought as only a mode of absolute substance among many. The absolute substance is Thought as Spirit that gives itself in love when it creates other thinking beings and enlightens them to think and to respond in return. The incompatibility between perfect thought and an imperfect thought that seems to exist in a purely conceptual order can be resolved thus by an intellectual metaphysics of charity that does not just oscillate between pantheism or nihilism, where consciousness is incomprehensible in its genesis and collapses in some sort of endless reiteration. Nor is it rational to abandon the personal consciousness of a finite spirit when it enters into union with the infinite Spirit, which is the finite spirit's highest aspiration.

Two things must be kept clearly in mind in this circumincession of thought, being, and action. The first is that being and acting cannot be reduced to thought. Part of the deficiency that we must recognize in our thought is, not just that we cannot attain on our own the fullness and perfection of thought we aspire to, but also that there is more to being and action than our thought of them or what we can conceive of them. We are always still striving to make our thought equal to them. Being is the principle, the focus, and the end of our thinking and of our acting. There is always more in our acting than we can conceive. There is a constant going back and forth among the three, an *in-between* that remains to be explored by thought, the in-between in which we have seen the ultimate aporia between imperfection and perfection, finite and infinite, insert itself. The second thing, however, is that by pulling being and action back into thought, or by reintegrating them, as Blondel prefers to say, into the dynamism of our thought, we are opening up within them the same kind of fundamental aporia we had to face between infinite thought and finite thought. Just as we had to face the difficulty of maintaining the personal identity of a finite spirit when it is in communion with the truly infinite Spirit, outside of whom there is no other or for whom the only "other" is no spirit, so also we shall have to face the difficulty of explaining how there can be a plurality of beings, when there is one Being who is the fullness of all being, or how there can be secondary causes or secondary agents when there is one Cause who is the universal cause of all there is, and of all action in the universe. These are not the questions one ordinarily starts from in the philosophy of being or in the philosophy of action, at least not phenomenologically, but they are questions one can proceed to from the metaphysical perspective Blondel has arrived at with his philosophy of thought or, better still, of spirit. They are questions Blondel proceeds to explore in the other two parts of his Trilogy.

XIII

Ontology of Consolidation in Being In, Through, and Of Itself

Blondel's work on Being in the Trilogy is much less complicated than his work on Thought. A lot of what he had to say in metaphysics and about the reality of spirit, including God as the absolute spirit our spirit aspires to, he said in the work on Thought, which had become the primary focus of his attention in his later years, after his earlier focus on Action. It is not that he had never focused on Thought in his earlier philosophy, but he had not said much about it as a component of his dissertation on action, leaving many with the impression that he was anti-intellectual and anti-metaphysical, when in fact his intention had been to open up intellectual discussion to new dimensions in his science of practice and to push metaphysics to new limits in the discussion of the Transcendent. His friend Delbos had known this already in 1893 and had urged him to add a final chapter to his dissertation before releasing it for publication, to make this metaphysical outlook more explicit, but, as we saw, the added chapter at the end of *l'Action (1893)* was not successful in clarifying the issue to Blondel's satisfaction. This was part of the reason why he resisted appeals to have the book published again for years after it was out of print, as he explained in his *Itinéraire* in 1929. He had a lot more to say about Thought before his philosophy of transcendence in human action could be understood in its proper context.

When, in 1934, he had finally published his critical examination of Thought in all its ramifications, however, he did not think he had finished presenting his entire philosophy or all that philosophy had to go into. Blondel was not one to think that everything could be reduced to the dimension of thought or logic, especially not to human thought or logic, which could only yield some sort of immanentist idealism, unable to give its due to *being* and to *action* even within the human experience. We saw how at the end of his study of Thought, in its genesis and in the exercise of its responsibilities, he insisted on returning to these open questions of being and action for thought, at the level that it has reached in its relation to the supernatural. In a way, this is where Blondel began his philosophizing, and this where he intends to pursue the question of being and the question of action in a systematic fashion, in a sort of face to face with God.

We should note that this is not where most philosophers begin their philosophy of being or of action, except probably Augustine, Anselm, Spinoza, or Hegel in their more systematic modes. But Blondel is not beginning as if from scratch. He is beginning as one who has already explored the realm of thought as a whole, including the idea of a Thought thinking itself to which human thought aspires in its twofold dynamism as noetic and pneumatic. He is proceeding here in the same way as he proceeded in the dissertation on action, where the question of the necessary being of action was introduced only after the entire phenomenon of action had been explored and found wanting in its ascension toward a fulfillment that it could not achieve on its own. He is proceeding also as he said one had to proceed in his earlier article on the Point of Departure for Philosophical Research, that is, after having come to a cohesive understanding of the whole of experience, as at the end of a phenomenology.

With what, then, does Blondel begin his exploration of the problem of being at this point in the Trilogy? What he finds in this problem is a combination of both evidence and enigma that cannot be taken apart from one another. In fact, the problem arises for us because we find ourselves alternating between what we take to be a certain evidence about being and a mystery about it that seems impenetrable to us. These two aspects of being are not merely alternative. They are wrapped up in one another in our spontaneous consciousness and, together, they simultaneously provoke us to reflection. They cannot be reduced to one another, and thereby comes what we can call a metaphysical inquietude. Blondel takes this to be a primordial fact for our consciousness, a first paradox, a first problem that we cannot escape from, for to choose one side or the other of the two, evidence or enigma, is to find oneself in a crisscrossing between an equivocal sort of realism and an unstable idealism. How, then, are we to proceed in this exploration of a problem we cannot evade?

Each one of these two aspects of our attitude or our consciousness toward being must be taken seriously. Each one of us starts off with an attachment to our own being, in a confrontation with other beings that cannot be denied. Pure nihilism is unthinkable. Even to try to imagine it is still to exist and to be. We are in being, indubitably so, and are part of it. We do not have to cross over some spatial abyss to get to it. We cannot separate ourselves from being or being from ourselves, as we sometimes do in a prematurely critical attitude that parcels being off to one side or another and leaves us empty or unknowing on some other imagined side. This is contrary to the first evidence of being we start from in our experience.

On the other hand, this being that is so evident and so certain to us is at the same time an enigma to us. It is not so much a given, but rather a problem for us in the immense field of becoming, where everything *is* only by letting go of itself in search of itself, in tending toward what is not yet, in a perpetual exodus aiming at an end that is hidden and that seems to fade away into the infinite. This problem lies at the core of all reality. "It is the spring for all the dynamism we bear within ourselves and that seems to extend and transfigure the élan of the universe" (1935, 10). It has to do not only with the contingent existences in movement we are so well aware of. It also brings before us the mystery even of the one Aristotle called the unmoved mover, the thought of thought already spoken of in the study of Thought, the pure act, the mystery of "that Being in itself where essence and existence are incomprehensibly conceived as one, and who, incommensurable with every other being, lends his name — incommunicable nevertheless — to the imperfect realities that our human language, not knowing how to do otherwise, analogically adorns with the title of beings" (1935, 10).

We see here the full scope of what Blondel has in mind with his title *Being and Beings*, as he sets up his ontology in the same way as he had originally set up his science of action and his science of thought to deal with problems in the concrete. "How can beings be called such if not in the measure that they tend to make themselves equal to all their virtualities and with their total end?" (1935, 10). If Blondel begins with the certainty of beings that are in evidence before us, including our own selves, it is not to absolutize them in their isolation from one another. It is rather to see them in their complexity and in their solidarity, so as not to isolate them in our thought as subjects and objects in utilitarian fashion, where we attribute to them an independent sufficiency or a sort of ontological autonomy. Blondel is ever on his guard against this sort of metaphysical precipitation. He is more inclined to take what is given initially as a beginning, "as a provision of strength, a viaticum destined to facilitate the genesis of beings toward the end where they will be able to rejoin their principle and accomplish their destiny according to the function they have to fulfill at their rank in the universal order" (1935, 11). The worst thing we could do for philosophy, that which vitiates philosophy from the start according to Blondel, is to imagine either that reflection takes us out of being, so that we then have to force our way back into it, or that we can dispel, as if it were a naive illusion, our spontaneous certitude about being. This would be to take ourselves out of the reality that penetrates us to the core and that we bear within our hidden-most selves.

Put in more personal terms, as in the dilemma of Hamlet, "to be or not to be," this becomes a question of what it means for us to be. "If we are really beings, in what sense, at what price, under what conditions is this possible? What is our power, what is our dependence, what can our obligations and responsibilities be with regard to other beings, ourselves, and to the unavoidable idea of a Being in itself?" (1935, 13). Ontology for Blondel is not a matter of abstract possibilities, or of excessive realism or idealism with regard to one modality of being or another. It is more a matter of exploring the entire chain of being, whose two ends we have to hold on to from the start, the real beings we take for granted and the idea of a Being in itself that is the compass for our becoming. It is a matter of seeing how things are in the concrete and asking how they are to be thought of as consolidating themselves in their becoming and their interaction. The subtitle for this probe into the evidence and enigma of *Being and Beings* is *Essay in Concrete and Integral Ontology*.

In his preamble Blondel warns against looking for being where it cannot be found, that is, in abstract ideas that supposedly manifest an inner structure of beings, as in some noumenal thing in itself. If we look for it where it is not and where it cannot be, or in a manner that is inappropriate for finding it, he warns, we either affirm it massively from the start as an immediate and definitive given, or else we surround it with an impenetrable smokescreen at a distance without limits, or else we hold these two extremes together without shedding light "on the in-between that separates intuition and mystery" (1935, 15). For Blondel it is the in-between, "the interval that must be explored, because that is where we have to live and to discover at the same time as realize the sense of our life and come to our own standing in being" (1935, 15). What we have to look into is not just essences detached from existence. Nor can we be satisfied with a speculative theory of essences and existences. What we need is a philosophy, not only of intelligible nature or generic existences, but also of beings "laboring in a sort of parturition, beings that are not restricted within their ideal definition, but rather, through their mutual subjection and their real dependence, are looking to enrich themselves, perfect themselves and find their singular and common destiny as it can be assigned to each and to all by a providential design able to respect for its part free options where they are possible and obligatory in the plan of intelligences" (1935, 16).

Clearly, this has to be an ontology that includes human initiatives as well as the effectiveness of nature. The problem for Blondel is to conceive of it as something that starts from concrete experience but tries to go deeper than what appears to us immediately. Without denying that appearances are already real, he thinks of ontology as an inquiry into something more real than just the subjective or objective fact of appearance, "an existence that is more real yet, as if the entire phenomenon were on one side and the subsistent were on the other" (1935, 18). This is not to be taken in the way that critical philosophy distinguishes between a noumenal object and the phenomenal, as if the thought of a noumenal object could be taken independently of the phenomenal, whether as subject or object. Blondel views such a dichotomy as all too abstract and as engendering an artificial abyss between appearance and things as they are in themselves, which only creates false problems against all knowing, even of appearances, and leaves us always with insoluble antinomies. Far from getting caught up in such global oppositions that only keep us from entering into any true knowledge of being, Blondel proposes to study, degree by degree, those realities that present themselves in experience invincibly withstanding all negation, but that, through their becoming, fall short of the idea and the exigency of being, which are at once evoked and frustrated by these very realities (1935, 19). The task for him is not to set up road blocks to knowledge of being of any sort, but rather to follow the real progression in the parturition of beings, through any initiative, no matter how insufficient, or any effort, no matter how faltering, by which they tend to their end.

If ontology is not to collapse into an abstract gnoseology, or an overly fixated ontologism, not to mention an incurable agnosticism, it must take advantage of a proper study of thought, which includes a theory of the knowledge of being, rather than agnosticism, and proceed to its own task of exploration into what thought has to relate to, thereby opening up for thought itself a new outlook that will fortify its spiritual dynamism. The way to do this is not to fix on things as given in experience, as if they were absolute in themselves, without reference to other things or to what might be a truly absolute Being. Nor is it to reject any exigency we associate with the idea of being out of hand as irrational or as self-defeating. It is rather to take the things of experience as a first evidence of being, the evidence Blondel claims we all start from in our quest for being, and to proceed from there, critically, with the question of what it means for them to be: in what way are they subsistent and in what way are they dependent, how are they in solidarity with one another, for what end do they exist, and can they be thought of as really being without reference to some Being in itself? Even if we think of them as only participating in Being, can we think of them as purely passive? Or do we have to think of them as active, that is, as actively seeking their own perfection as being?

Such questions might be thought of as arising only with regard to human beings, who strive for their own perfection in being consciously. But Blondel thinks they can and should be raised for anything we take to be a being in our experience, including those that give no evidence of consciousness. For him, so-called realism and so-called idealism have to come together in ontology. The method of ontology cannot be reduced either to any empirical method in the study of nature or of the spirit, or to a critique of such methods as falling naively under the realism of the senses, the imagination, or discursive understanding. Nor can it fall back on some kind of intuitionism such as that proposed by idealism after Kant, or by Bergsonism in Blondel's day. What ontology has to do is follow "the exigencies of being, of its genesis, and of its perfecting of itself" (1935, 28). This is what he calls a "normative method," one that he cannot fully describe at the beginning, but that will determine itself little by little as it is put in practice. This method relates back to his "method of implication" which, he says, "as long as it is applied to being, brings infinite suppleness to the enterprise of knowledge and philosophy" (1935, 29). Harnessed to the study of being, the method of *implication*, without losing any of its extension or suppleness, becomes a method of *application* for affirming and excluding, to be deployed even in the extreme consequences of the drama of beings capable of enriching or ruining their very being.

In this, Blondel is alluding to the ultimate question, or the ultimate drama he always returns to at the end of each part of his Trilogy on Thought, Being and Action. Here it is cast in terms of being: to be or not to be? It will not be enough to have recourse to the order of phenomena and to stop at a science or a philosophy of generalized relativity. Ontology, which cannot be satisfied with abstraction or speculative transcendental principles, "requires an experimentation and a norm of another type than the one positive researches in the physical, biological, psychological, or social order can be satisfied with" (1935, 30). For Blondel, this experimentation at the core of ontology comes with the exercise of free choice in the face of Being itself, as we seek to enrich and perfect our own being, where a means may be offered that we can accept or refuse. The method of *implication* brings us to the point where we must face the necessity of choosing *for* or *against* the proffered gift of the most high Being. The method of *application* takes us to the consequences of either option in their absolute difference of being and non-being, of total perfection or total frustration of our being. Blondel casts this ultimate drama for our being beyond physical death, as Heidegger would have it, to a choice we have to make in the face of an offer made to us that would secure the perfection of our being for good absolutely.

It is not death that will resolve the problem of Hamlet every man raises for himself in the most secret depth of his being, Blondel suggests, bringing Parmenides into the picture as well as Shakespeare. No metaphysical concern about our being would warrant this brusque and total intervention of suicide against what the energies of life and conscience call for. On the contrary, these energies of life and spirit open up another way for us that may be less direct and hasty, but that is all the more enlightening and decisive for us, in terms of the being we aspire to in our present uncertainty. Instead of sudden death, this way opens for us a way of mortification, a way of growth by asceticism "which, by silencing the clamors of the world and the passions, reveals the truth hidden under the appearances. And thanks to this method, which sets aside the prestige of what Parmenides was already naming 'non-being, becoming, the reign of illusion and of falsehood,' we are able to see what subsists that is permanent, substantial, ontological running through all the phenomenology of time and space" (1935, 30).

This, of course, is not where Blondel purports to be at the threshold of this concrete ontology. There is still the entire phenomenon of all beings to be run through before we can come to this ultimate threshold for us, in our seeking the perfection of our being. But what Blondel says in alluding to Parmenides gives us an idea of what he has in mind when he speaks of his ontological method as normative, or as defining consequences of a choice that can be totally satisfying or totally frustrating, to the exclusion of any middle or third possibility. Early in his career, in his attempts to work out a general logic based on the study of action he had begun to map out a position where the principle of non-contradiction, the absolute opposition of being and non-being, would be seen as strictly applicable only in relation to the act of saying *yes* or *no* to God, the author of all finite being, where the principle has its ultimate application. But he had not pushed through to this position as a matter of logic, perhaps due to a realization that this would leave him still too much in the abstract. The insight, however, stayed with him and came back to him as a matter of concrete ontology rather than abstract logic. It became the guiding light for the development of his ontology seeking to clarify the middle ground between our first certitude of being and the hiddenmost secret of Being in itself. Thus even ontology became for him a key to the solution of the problem of life and our highest destiny, not just for human beings but also for anything that is thought of as a being. "The theory itself here is an experience of life and of ascetics that requires of us, at the same time as intellectual rigor, a constant effort of uprightness, of exigency, and, so to speak, of spiritual actualization. We know being better only by applying ourselves, by managing to be more" (1935, 31). Hence the method of application as well as the method of implication.

Ontology, then, for Blondel, is an inquiry that takes us beyond any merely phenomenological description of beings in the world. More than a static theory of knowledge, it tries to penetrate intellectually the mysterious X that is always left open at the end of our critical reflection on what we know or what is in our mind. Unlike idealism, it takes being as something more than what is secretly produced by a thought in need of an obstacle, a *choc*, or an *Anstoss*, to bring itself to its own act of consciousness. Instead of bringing ontology back to what we can know about being through thought, Blondel thinks we must proceed inversely, "seek what we do not know about being, in order to arrive at a final discernment of what there is in being that we allow into our thought, to shed light on thought as it sheds light on itself, and that, by a reciprocal causality, will show us how the interior life of being, inaccessible to an inspection that is purely speculative and exterior, as it were, to its intimate life, can develop and manifest itself not just through the phenomena, but through a spiritual growth that might possibly be shown to constitute a truly metaphysical experience" (1935, 382).

Included in this final discernment will be explicit reference to the Being that we are already thinking of as absolute in itself, to which all particular beings relate as well even more deeply than with one another. This is something a purely descriptive phenomenology of beings cannot get at, especially one with the pretense of being an adequate science of being by substituting its own integration of all phenomena to the deeper reality of beings, in a way that is systematically closed to the claims of an authentic ontology. Blondel thinks of metaphysics as surpassing any descriptive phenomenology. It is something he has already brought up in his study of thought. However, he does not think of metaphysics as the equivalent of ontology as "properly specified by the singular and universal character of beings, and of Being itself, required of its study" (1935, 383). Metaphysics serves as a transition from the empirical and immanent order to the order of absolute truths. However, "in turn ontology uses these metaphysical certitudes to discern the hierarchy of beings, to justify their relative consistency relative to absolute Being on which they depend, without its ceasing to be independent of them" (1935, 383). In a way, in his science of *Being and beings*, Blondel was taking ontology, not just beyond the abstract ontologies of modern philosophy, where absolute Being in itself was left out of consideration, ontologies that were replaced by immanentist phenomenologies after the onslaught of critical philosophy, but also one step further than the more ancient focus of ontology, or science of being as being that only led up to absolute Being, but did not inquire into how we can come back from the discovery of such a Being and show how it is normative for the beings in the order of becoming. This shows how Blondel's ontology represents a new departure in the service of being, which he thought had to be made clear from the outset.

Blondel presents his ontology in three parts. The first presents itself as a liminal discussion in search of Being, not just of particular beings as they present themselves in our experience, but of Being as we think of it as somehow absolute, necessary, and perfect, as in itself, but that we nevertheless think of in conjunction with the ones we initially identify as being, no matter how relatively, contingently, or imperfectly. This is the part where discoveries are made, ranging from material beings, to living organisms, to persons, and finally to the universe in its physical and ideal integralness, but where also reason finds itself wanting for more in what it takes to be real here and now in the whole of experience. Part Two takes up the central question plumbing the depth of the idea of being that we associate with the total order of beings we experience in the universe, whether we truly conceive such an absolute Being, whether we can affirm such a Being, and in what sense we can affirm anything about *what* this Being is. This is the part where Blondel discusses what can be said of Being in itself and how the beings we do know can be thought of as actually created by It, without taking anything from its absoluteness. This is where ontology normally ends, in a sort of negative theology. But Blondel adds a third part by returning to a consideration of the beings in our experience previously found wanting, but now considered as finding their consistency in the absolute Being. This is where he explains his idea of real norms and how such norms play a constitutive role in the ontological logic of beings, including an elaboration of the normative function found at all four levels of being previously distinguished — the material, the organic, the personal, and the universal — in a consolidation of all beings in the process of their mutual confirmation and realization.

It is impossible for us to go into the details of this complex elaboration of a normative ontology that relates the human being to the absolute Being as creator and final end for all beings in conjunction with one another. But it is important to have some idea of the whole and its parts to understand where he is coming from and where he is going with this method he has so carefully mapped out from the beginning. The most we can do here is highlight some of the more significant indicators along the way.

The Search for True Being from Matter to Organic Life

Blondel begins his preliminary exploration into beings by asking what is meant by being: what is it to be — *qu'est ce qu'être?* The question is not as simple as it sounds. We come to it with two different senses of "being" as Blondel has already noted, one of immediate evidence about ourselves and things that we cannot deny, and one of dynamic openness toward something mysterious, "in the coexistence of true beings in relation to an absolute Being in its necessary unity, uniqueness and plenitude" (1935, 46). The history of metaphysics is fraught with many different ways of parsing this simple word, *be,* in relation to general ideas of substance, essence, existence, and the many different ways of being that are not themselves beings. Blondel, however, is not interested in pursuing such specious dissections of being. He is more interested in figuring out how essentially heterogeneous beings such as we find in our experience can be related "to the unity of a principle and an end able to confer on the word being a meaning that is neither univocal nor simply equivocal" (1935, 60), but quite analogous according to the wide diversity of beings encountered in experience.

For him, there is one ontological antinomy to be resolved, not between a vaunted phenomenal and a dubious or problematic noumenal, but rather between our spontaneous and confused sense of being as of something present, solid, and subsistent, and a sense of something mysterious, if not absent, that makes of the profound reality we cannot doubt, not an object of well-defined knowledge, but of endless inquiry. On the one hand, we seem to find being within ourselves and without, in realities that impose themselves in our experience and our action, as if it were by abstraction from these data that we come to our generalized notion of being. On the other hand, we cannot but confer upon being attributes other than those suggested by the realities we experience within ourselves and without. These are notions of unity, permanence, absoluteness, autonomy, productive causality, supreme finality, substantiality, and perfection, all of which Blondel thinks of as "evidences" that are really and necessarily implied within beings we experience, including ourselves as being, even before we recognize them in or attribute them to the being we take to be "Being in and for itself." These are the notions and principles that polarize us and set us in motion or spark the development of our knowledge. They are transcendent to the immanent order of our universe, but they are not known by abstraction or extrapolation from the beings we encounter in experience. They are known quite concretely and rationally as we draw on them to name and to make sense of the beings present to us in reality. The dilemma of ontology is to see whether there is any compatibility in the two ways we have of speaking of beings and of Being. "Is there a metaphysical incompatibility between absolute Being and true beings that, without being by themselves, would nevertheless be capable of real consistency, a definitive and indelible perennity, a destiny of their own that would depend on an option by which they would cooperate in their very destiny?" (1935, 68). The dilemma arises most acutely for human beings, but it also brings in any lower being worthy of the name and capable of its own actions.

In fact, Blondel begins his exploration of this ontological antinomy between beings as given and Being as absolute with beings that have to be taken into account in our experience, starting from matter as the first thing that presents itself as being, however remote that may appear from the absolute. As attentive as he is to the interconnections of the rational implications he insists on in our Transcendental conception of being, he never fails to start from reality as given, real data that also have their interconnections in the global fact, and that must also be recognized in their consistency. There is a history of being to be investigated, an ascension and a drama to be sketched. His aim is to reintegrate everything we call phenomena "into the history of being, into the science of Being and into the realization of the total ontological plan" (1935, 73). Everything has to be explained, "matter, living organisms, spiritual persons, even the ideal and metaphysical world in the twofold light of positive data and the most inflexible rational exigencies" (1935, 74).

To follow him in his ascension from the being that is most immediately given in our experience to the highest Being we are able to conceive rationally, we must see how he applies the transcendental notions we necessarily associate with being, such as unity, permanence, absoluteness, or perfection, to the different kinds of being we experience in the world or to the world itself as a whole. These notions are for him part of what is evident in our very conception of being, by implication, if not in immediate reference to any particular thing.

The first question to ask, then, in this ontology is whether matter is a being: *La matière est-elle un être?* This is not to ask whether matter is real. Blondel has no doubt, as Descartes did, about conceiving matter as real. His problem is to see whether matter can qualify as a being in the full metaphysical sense of the term that is implied in our rational conception of being. Is it a substance, for example, in the full force of that term? Blondel alludes to Leibniz's refutation of the Cartesian theory of an "extended substance," and to the way such an idea has been discredited by the progression of modern science toward the infinitely small and the infinitely large in the material universe. As a metaphysician, however, Blondel argues that there is a contradiction between what he calls the "factitious idea of a substantial materiality and the necessary idea we have of being" (1935, 78-79).

The argument hinges on the convertibility of being and the one. Every being has to be thought of as one and there is no way we can conceive or comprehend *one* as a physical mass or as a moving synthesis, much less as a numerical abstraction. "Everything we can discover in materiality affirmed as most real is absolutely repugnant to the possibility of seeing in it an authentic being" (1935, 79). There is no substantiality in it apart from the other beings. To conceive it as real is to conceive it as a force at work in the entire physical and spiritual order. It is at once a principle of individuation and a medium of communication among higher beings, as it serves to keep them separate from Being in itself so that they can participate in him without confusion or absorption. It is also a stimulus that is partially docile and usefully resistant for a spiritual life that arises in it in view of higher ends. "It resists indefinitely and at the same time it encourages, it provokes, it even helps the struggle of thought, the effort of the will, the achievement of a personal life" (1935, 81).

With all of this, nevertheless, matter cannot be said to be a being that is one, or that merits the name of being. The most that can be said for it is that it is a principle of limitation and inherent imperfection for spirits that are created. It represents more an exigency for perfection than any sort of self-contained flat extension. For that reason, Blondel concludes that we shall have to "accompany and keep finding matter even in the highest forms of being" (1935, 83), beings that we have yet to encounter, as we continue the history of matter's genesis and the study of its complete function. For Blondel this means moving on to examine the order of living things, to see if there are any that subsist in a way we could recognize as true beings and "in what measure they can contribute to transforming matter itself and make way by their passing existence for the advent of a spiritual order, where it will be even more true to apply the important name of being which is so easily misused" (1935, 83).

With this first consideration of matter as real, but not yet worthy of the name *being,* Blondel sees himself as having overcome a whole set of views that are for him inadequate in the consideration of being as a whole. These include both *dualism,* which posits a second cause of being in opposition to the creator as first cause, and *monism,* which fails to account for how particular finite beings can subsist in contradistinction from absolute Being in itself. At the same time he claims to overcome *idealism* as well, as a superficial form of spiritualism that only juxtaposes two kinds of substance, one material and one spiritual, each of which could be understood as subsisting in isolation from the other or as absorbing one another, whether as materialism or spiritualism, as in the opposition between Marxism and Hegelianism. For Blondel, matter cannot be understood except as it relates to spirit and finite spirit cannot be understood except as constrained by matter.

The next step in his ontological inquiry into being, however, is not to move directly to spirit. It is rather to move to an intermediary between matter and spirit, or a preliminary form of unification between the two, which we think of as the living organism as such. Ontologically speaking, the question is whether organisms that live and die can be counted as beings in the proper sense of the term. What characterizes such organisms is already a certain characteristic and specific *unity* that we do not find in merely material things. "Strictly speaking, the living thing, as rudimentary as it may be, is intimately one and singularly specific: as a metaphysical center of perception and expansion, it engages and organizes, in a way that is inaccessible from outside, all the observable manifestations of a directive idea incarnating itself" (1935, 85).

What is especially important for Blondel in this metaphysical characterization of the organism is that it exhibits a certain degree of unity, specific spontaneity, and perennity not found in merely material things but that is nevertheless a mark of true being. Even if individual living things come alive only to die eventually, they are not without an identity of their own, as fugitive as that may be, for as long as they live, and they do pass on that identity to other individuals who perpetuate their species. Here one has to think of the entire order of ontogenesis and phylogenesis in which this history of living things on earth takes place. One cannot think of all this only as an immense course toward evanescence. One has to see it also as tied to something higher that can assure the consistent reality of life, which it cannot find from below from a purely temporal and spatial point of view. In other words, according to Blondel, "the ontological reality of life and its essential function has a higher basis" (1935, 88) than anything found in non-living matter. It is this higher basis of life that warrants our speaking of organisms as more properly being or beings.

The question remains, however, as to whether they are beings in any absolute sense. We have seen that there is being only where there are unity, spontaneity, and perennity. But can we speak of merely living things as achieving unity, spontaneity, and perennity in any complete sense, whether individually or collectively, or is this only a passing kind of spontaneity, a relative sort of autonomy that leaves these organisms in a state of being halfway, that is, of being further along ontologically than just matter, but not yet what would qualify as being in a full sense of identity and perennity? What is lacking in simple living organisms, for them to constitute true beings, is a lack of unity, due to an essential failure on their part to act on their own and to exercise true autonomy, which is why they are wanting in the sort of perennity, whether individual or collective, "without which a truly substantial existence could not be called literally a being" (1935, 91-92). Hence living organisms that come and go, even though they exhibit a certain unity, spontaneity, and perennity for as long as they are, cannot be termed beings in any full rational sense. As long as thought has not found "the sense of what passes, the reason for what lives and what dies, it does not yet dare to speak, from its necessary point of view, of an authentic being" (1935, 93). It has to find a more profound meaning, a more intimate unity, a more permanent reality in living things, before it can be in a position to recognize in them the true traits of being and integrate them into the ontological certainties implied in our first conception of being. For Blondel this means finding our way into a higher kind of life, the realm of personal consciousness and of reflected life, which brings us to the third question in this ontological ascent: Are persons beings?

The Search for True Being in Interpersonal Life

Blondel's answer to this question, not surprisingly, is *yes*, even more so than for organisms that have some reflected life. Persons are commonly thought of as beings on two counts, one, their tangible existence, and the other, the order of thought and will in which they operate. As such, they deserve the name of being more than anything else we know in the world. To emphasize this point ontologically, Blondel refers to the three criteria he has already used in assessing matter and organisms under the rubric of being: unity, spontaneity, and perennity or subsistence.

With regard to unity, we find in the person not just an external unity, but more importantly and more emphatically an internal unity, an invisible and indivisible center that analysis cannot break down into parts, in spite of the virtual expansion of thought and action. As proof of this, Blondel points to the fact that the person draws in the entire universe to know it and responds to it in using it and mastering it. With regard to spontaneity, there is not just an élan vital, but something more spiritual with an initiative of its own, drawing from its own higher enlightenment and raising itself to a more discretionary and effective power to act on its own. With regard to perennity or subsistence, the truly spiritual being of the person is one that defies the passing away of lesser living things, not by being trapped in some imagined "eternal return," but by surviving in its spiritual identity as one who has to decide about its ultimate destiny. Personality, according to Blondel, "is a reality far more consistent than material and organic realities, although our present existence does not seem able to get along without them" (1935, 98). But the question that remains for him in this ascensional ontology is to see whether it is being itself, a being able to consolidate itself as a self-sufficient substance in its own unity, its autonomy and its persistence, as defined and definitive in its own right. Conversely, if it is not Being in itself, how can it be thought of as truly a being within absolute Being itself? How can it remain separate from this infinite Being that encompasses all beings?

To discuss this strange relation of identity and difference between Being and beings at the level of personality and spirit, Blondel goes back to the three ontological criteria he has laid out for assessing the ontological status of different kinds of being. For each one of these criteria, he shows how the personal consciousness we know is affected by matter, no matter how personally or spiritually it is unified, spontaneous, and subsistent. Personal consciousness, as we know it, is never perfectly unified in its reflection and prospection, no matter how hard we try to pull ourselves and our world together. We always find ourselves scattered, our attention pulled one way and another by different thoughts and desires, unable to concentrate ourselves fully or totally.

Another thing about the person is that we cannot be alone. We cannot center only on ourselves and make the universe turn on our egoism. Blondel makes this point by saying that personality must become a consciousness of the impersonal. It grows above all by giving itself and by devotion to all. There is in this a moral antinomy in mutual recognition that touches on the core of the ontological problem. "The person cannot be alone: it cannot be itself except by a sort of exodus and generosity: and just as the individual, in spite of the etymological sense of the word, exists only in function of what limits it and separates it from others, so also the person seems to subsist only by going beyond itself and by taking as its motto: *vae soli!*" (1935, 101). One is not a person except in the presence of another person.

On the score of spontaneity the same kind of reservation must be made as on that of unity. In the initiative that engenders the person in a truly spiritual manner, the spontaneity is not entirely original and the élan is not entirely its own. It is not a force that is truly creative of its own being. Its origins proceed from below, and from what is higher than consciousness itself. Our free choice is never without initial impulses from outside and attractions from on high and, in the choices that we do make, there is always a part we have not chosen. If we think it necessary to say that, for someone or something to be truly, it must contribute to its own life and accomplish its own destiny, for which it becomes responsible, we have not yet found how such being is realized in the course of human events where persons are in search of themselves more than in possession of themselves. Though we *are* in a very true sense of the term, we are still only in the beginning of our being.

At this point the third aspect of the ontological problem for the person comes into view, its perennity or its subsistence. How truly a being is the person, and in what sense ultimately? In answering this question Blondel has to steer a course between two shoals that could bring the proper idea of a personal being to an end. One is the supposition that a person is only an unstable concentration of forces, subject to deception and self-deception, and destined to dissolution like any other organism. The other is the tendency to sublimate the intellectual and ethical element of personal life in such a way that in the end only an impersonal trace of thought remains, detached from all contingency and all individuation and deprived of whatever personal being there might have been.

In his critical approach to this question, Blondel acknowledges that living persons, while being real as persons, still have to develop themselves to become beings in the full sense of the term. Hence he has to examine under what conditions and with what reservations we can say that persons achieve the plenitude of being proper to them as persons. This will show for him how persons take up within themselves the lower forms of existence and assure for themselves a stability that will result from their common participation in the Being that is their principle and their end. But to do this is to challenge the all-too-facile attitude of confidence with which the solidity and the immortality of persons are sometimes celebrated. It is to show how, phenomenologically, we do not ever succeed in overcoming the dispersion, not just of things as they affect us in time, but of our own consciousness in its struggles with these things. We are never completely clear about who we are or what we are.

This, however, may still be too sentimental a way of looking at the way we come to our own personality. Blondel wants to look at it in a way that is more rigorously metaphysical. How can the synthesis of a personal history, as a synthesis, become a unity that we can call truly a being? Can we take any moment of a person's life, that of the child, or that of the adolescent, that of the adult, or that of old age, or even the moment of death, and say that is where the true personality is to be found? Or do we have to collapse all these images of a self into a sort of blur where nothing of a true personality can come through? Can a true personality be formed without going through a process, but on the other hand, can a process yield a true personality on its own? Can any phenomenology of the spirit make a unity of the multiple that is not just another abstract sum of many parts posited as somehow absolute? One could think of Hegel's *Phenomenology of Spirit* here, but Blondel has Spinoza more in mind, who was in the back of Hegel's mind as he was working his way toward Absolute Knowing. It was Spinoza, who from all the struggles of thought with the passions, had first concluded to an intellectual love of the single, impersonal, eternal Substance, where nothing was to remain of any individual personality. In his own phenomenology of the personal spirit, Blondel wants to resist such a leap into the absolute, where individuals can only be absorbed and lose all being of their own. The being of the person cannot be thought of independently of the individualizing process by which it comes to be, even when one thinks about how this being has to relate to the absolute Being alone worthy of such attribution in its complete and absolute sense.

The Search for Being in the Universal Becoming

There is more to be said about how the person necessarily relates to the unique and absolutely necessary Being in its individual as well as spiritual identity, but Blondel does not immediately go into that in his critical ontology confronting the beings we encounter in our experience. Even if it is true that persons are the ones that approximate our conception of being most as one, spontaneous and subsistent, there is yet the totality of all beings as unified in our consciousness to be critically evaluated. Can we say that the universe itself in its physical or ideal integrity is truly a being, so that we could say we find verified in it all the criteria of unity, identity, and perennity? Or will we have to say that it too, along with the persons who conceive it, falls short? This is the last question Blondel has to entertain in this ascending critical ontology before he can turn to the final question of how we conceive a yet higher Being that is truly or absolutely One, in a way that nothing else can be. This question of the universe as a single being has always haunted humanity, like a sort of recurrent millenarism, in the guise of a great Being realizing itself whether in the form of a superhuman people or state, in the form of a cult of becoming as a total immanence, or in the form of an anticipated fulfillment through some divine incarnation.

Blondel argues against each one of these three kinds of universalist pretensions to the fulfillment of Being, especially the third, which is most seductive, because it attributes "to the immanent life of the world and humanity the power to realize within itself and to perfect by itself the idea and the presence of the divine" (1935, 111).

Against the first, which he calls ontological sociologism, insofar as it claims that only social being is real, he argues for an irreducible personalism, where individuals have to be taken as seriously in their being as the whole. This is not to say that there is no solidarity among human beings or that such solidarity is not essential to persons. It is to say that "even in the highest forms of the spiritual, solidarity is more than an ideal interpretation of relations among persons: it tends to form a body with the free spirits where we can, even before the perfect bond of charity, already observe the beginning of a communion where the word [of St. Paul] can already be applied: *unum corpus, multi sumus in eodem spiritu* (one body, we are many in the same spirit)" (1935, 113).

To found society on the impulses of blood and race, or on the fear of violence that comes from unbridled desires and passions, according to Blondel, is to dehumanize persons by putting intelligence and will at the service of brute forces within them, even when those forces are hypostatized in the form of an overman who lords over all as a herd. For Blondel, spiritual solidarity among persons cannot be accounted for except on a spiritual level of mutual recognition, which is a reality of vital moral, spiritual, and even religious proportions even more than it is material. "There is nothing truly social without something psychic, psychological, rational and transcendent" (1935, 116). In fact, if we take this last trait at its face value as transcendent, we have to say, not only that there is more to persons than what can be included in any social ideology, but also that persons cannot find their ultimate perfection as beings in any purely immanent association.

When we move to a higher level of abstraction, that of becoming itself as a totality, we find ourselves still at a loss for representing a being that would fulfill the ontological criteria for any true being. Here Blondel brings out the double ambiguity in any attempt to affirm becoming, conceived as a whole, as if it were purely immanent to itself and able to be self-sufficient in its indefinite expansion. On the one hand we seem to have in mind things moved or in motion, without reference to any moving cause that might lead to metaphysical questions transcending becoming itself. On the other hand, as concrete as our attention might seem in focusing on things in motion, we fall back on a simple abstraction, a general idea of the concrete that is fraught with difficulties, when we try to analyze what it is supposed to refer to. We have the illusion of a *totum simul,* when in fact becoming is never at any point simultaneous and coextensive.

We know this as an illusion through what Blondel calls the secret logic of being that inspires our discourse. A more critical attention to this logic warns us that any attempt to ascribe ultimate ontological reality to becoming alone, and to universal immanence, is bound to fail. Our view of what passes in our thought as well as in the world is irremediably incomplete, since it has to renew itself with every passing moment, and it is so *ad infinitum.* This does not mean that we have to think of becoming as unreal, but rather, that we would not even be conscious of becoming or of any desire to seek its development and its full realization without a fundamental certainty of Being itself as principle and end.

This leaves Blondel with the third universalist pretension to ontological fulfillment to contend with, which is to bring the divine into the universe itself as the "being of beings," *l'être des êtres,* while denying all transcendence. The problem with this sort of view according to him is that it eliminates the notion of incommensurability between beings and the principle of their élan and their sublimation. In connection with our synthetic or objective view of becoming, he has shown that we inevitably affirm something infinite, something absolute and atemporal, something that preoccupies us spiritually even in the way we conceive of ourselves and the universe. Many are willing to speak of this as something divine or God, but only "to establish a natural continuity between contingent realities and absolute and necessary Being" (1935, 425), thus allowing for a natural religion of progress or even a sort of theogony for humanity in history.

This view of the divine and divinization is very seductive, according to Blondel, but it too is fraught with ambiguities. In opposition to it, he brings up his earlier critical clarifications concerning the ontological status of things that could not be thought as self-sufficient and stable in their being, namely, matter, organisms, and persons. The pretense to think of the world itself, the One and All, as it is also called in this context, as something divine and self-sufficient, is only an extrapolation that cannot be justified ontologically. There is nothing in becoming, or in the expansion of the cosmos as such, that allows us to cut our affirmations short in any stable or definite state. "To unify the universe as an integral sum and attribute to it the solid subsistence of a true being, is not only a fiction denied in mathematics where there is no infinite number, and in the experimental sciences that do not reach the origins and the ends of the moving realities they study, but, worse still, it is to mistake one plane for another and to pass unduly from one order to a quite different order" (1935, 128). Even if we can speak of a divine plan in the world from a natural and historical standpoint, it is another thing to think of that plan as coming from God, who remains incommensurable to anything in the world and in relation to whom the world and persons remain radically insufficient. No amount of supernaturalizing, superhumanizing, or superchristianizing of beings, from their own standpoint, will overcome this insufficiency. If there is to be any such divinization, it will have to be from the standpoint of a totally other Being, the absolute Being who realizes in Itself all the criteria of perfect Unity, perfect Spontaneity, and perfect Subsistence, all of which distinguishes It from any of the contingent beings we have spoken of thus far, including their totality.

The Central Probe into Being In, Through, and Of Itself

Blondel has been referring to a Being, in, through, and of itself, from the very beginning in his elaboration of our primordial conception of being as both certain and mysterious. Now he must turn his ontological critique on the idea we have of such a Being as absolutely one and perfect. This will entail stepping out of the realm of becoming in order to begin scrutinizing "the order of necessity and transcendence, by confronting the most ontological problem of all, that of a God in all the purity of Being affirmed as one and unique" (1935, 131). Needless to say, this has to be the key to his ontology, which he has been leading up to step by step, and which must now be put to the test of critical examination in what he calls a central probing — *sondage central*. His argument up to now, in the preceding analysis, has been to show how reflection on the insufficiencies of either material being, the being of persons or even the being of the universe as a whole, forces us to acknowledge Being in itself as a necessary conception for any Thought and as an underlying presence for any reality. Such an acknowledgment is already enough to cast some doubt on any peremptory negation of such a Being or any indifference in entertaining the thought of such a Being. But for Blondel it means also a rational requirement to examine and enter into what such a Being might consist in. "From the beginning of our inquiry," he writes, "we had to observe that being is at once manifest and obscure to us: this above all is where the evidence remains mysterious and where the mystery makes itself evident" (1935, 141). Blondel now has to probe this relation between evidence and mystery in our conception of being, as it puts us in a new relation of responsibility to the absolute Being.

Blondel sums up this central probe of his ontology in three questions. First, do we truly conceive an absolute Being, or is our seeming conception of Being in itself and by itself just another illusory projection? Second, supposing that we do truly conceive such a being, can we legitimately affirm that such an absolute Being is real, and not just an ideal or a necessary category of our reason, a subjective construction of our spirit? Third, if Being in itself is affirmed as subsistent no less than as conceivable or possible, are there not difficulties in admitting an ontological argument on our part, even if it has its own necessary force in itself? Moreover, does not an admission of an absolute Being in itself raise many metaphysical and moral dilemmas for us as human beings, and do not these dilemmas bring us to the necessity of recognizing in this Being the God of charity?

The third of these questions is the one he discusses at greatest length, but in order to get to it, he must discuss the first two, showing that we do necessarily conceive of an absolute Being, and arguing from that conception or that possibility from our standpoint, in Leibnizian fashion, that such a Being must be affirmed as Being in itself one, unique, and subsistent par excellence. In answer to the first question, whether we truly conceive an absolute Being, Blondel tries to overcome the many obstacles that have been stacked up in the history of philosophy against the very coherence of the idea of being, on empirical grounds or on grounds of incompatibility between components that have to be included in the idea. Underlying our conception of things in the world as beings, including ourselves as well as others, there is an overarching conception of being that encompasses them all. "It is not from phenomena and empirical realities, nor even from our personal experience, that we go to the idea and the conviction of Being: whatever the chronological or psychological aspects of our mental genesis, it is within our profound sense, within our implicit and primitive idea of being, that we find the necessary resources to know that we are and to recognize in other beings what reality they have in becoming" (1935, 155). According to Blondel, this profound sense or this primitive idea of being, from which we come to know that we *are* and that others *are* as well, is a necessity of fact that overrides any theory obfuscating our consciousness and that makes itself known sooner or later infallibly in the internal forum of our sincerity. To bolster this claim, Blondel repeats an argument he has made at the various stages of his ontological ascent. "We would not have any idea of any sort, any conscious image, any known experience, if, from the beginning, some notion of being, as undisclosed as we want to suppose it, did not condition all sensible perception, all empirical and scientific elaboration" (1935, 156).

Hence, according to Blondel, we do not go from beings and becoming to some abstract entity or to an *ens generalissimum,* as discursive understanding would have it, when it reacts as it were to data or to some initial genesis. Rather we start from beings in the concrete with the concrete conception in our consciousness of a being that owes nothing to these beings, but on which we sense these beings depend both as being and as perceived. This suggests for Blondel an *ens concretus et absolutus,* in the masculine, that has nothing in common with what is mistakenly spoken of in the neuter as *ens generalissimum.* The fact is *not* that we have a secret intuition into being whose content we have only to develop by reflection or even that our primitive and confused idea of being is enough to ground an ontological proof or an auto-affirmative conception of being. This implicit and real idea of Being that is congenital to every spirit remains hidden in our experience, though it is not empty or deprived of all sense. It is enough to shed light on the steps we have to take in order to rise or to penetrate to a clear apprehension of its mysterious notion, or to order the questions it raises for us in the ascent to a clear conception of it.

Blondel's logic of being here is not to immediately affirm the reality of our fundamental idea of an absolute Being. It is rather to show that we cannot eliminate this conception from our consciousness, since it is the condition for the possibility of our consciousness of ourselves and others as beings. What he wants to show from this impossibility of annihilating our conception of being is only a subjective necessity concerning which we have to raise the question of the objective sense of such an idea, its intellectual value, and its bearing as at least an ideal force. For, as he writes, "it is on this power of affirmation, this intrinsic dynamism, this efficiency of the concept of being that we have to bring a motivated judgment to bear" (1935, 157).

Hence, Blondel's second question has to be raised in this central probing of his ontology. Can we affirm absolute Being and in what sense do we do so necessarily? Is this only a regulative idea for our thought in our search for what there is, or is it something real in itself to which we must relate in a unique way? Is it only an obstacle of sorts that our spirit projects outside itself in the effort to realize itself as idea, or is it truly something transcendent even to the highest reaches of our activity, something "irreducible and transcendent to the immanent and inexhaustible fecundity of our spiritual becoming" (1935, 160)?

Blondel notes that we do not come to this question except at the end of an ascending order of questioning concerning different degrees of being that we find in experience, that is, *a posteriori,* and not *a priori,* on the basis of only an idea of an absolute Being. The idea arises in our consciousness through an internal determinism and a certain force of nature, to become in turn the spring of a dynamism that generates science, art, morality, and even a certain mystical life. But it cannot be accounted for in terms of a pure immanence in an order of becoming, which would encompass its transcendent reality, not to mention its independence and absoluteness. There have been many attempts in the history of philosophy to circumscribe the dynamism of spirit, and of the idea of the absolute, into a pure immanence of nature and history, but few of them have done justice to the proper light of the principle we come to with the idea of a Being in itself, perfectly one in itself and the cause of being for all other beings. "The study of the genesis of any consciousness implies the active presence and the affirmation — at least implicit but real — of a supra-temporal and properly transcendent reality" (1935, 162). It is not for any philosophy to use these ideas of spirit and the absolute against the principle from which they are derived. We cannot reverse the proper order of derivation here, as if it were we, in thinking about God, who confer being on him, and freely concede him existence, by an affirmation that we could just as easily withhold.

That would be the worst of illusions, "because, in a radical sense, our idea of God had its origin, not in any light that would be proper to ourselves, but in the illuminative action of God within us" (1935, 162-63). If our thought participates more fully in Being, it is by docility to this light that takes hold in us through God's prevenient action, and "by affirming the reality of the One of whom we had only the idea" (1935, 163). There is more in this affirmation than just our idea of the absolute Being. There is a certain *conversion* of our consciousness and a certain acceptance that is nourishing for our thought. Far from being just an abstract speculation or a theoretical assertion of Being, this is the culmination of a concrete science of being that implies a recognition on our part of the substantial truth of this existence of Being, on whom we depend and who is independent of us and of all contingent realities.

The upshot of this affirmation of absolute Being in itself, which is at once recognition of something totally Other in being than what has led us to this affirmation, is that we cannot but want to scrutinize it better as something more than an impersonal law of nature and history, as something personal with perfections that are more satisfying for the spirit and the heart, and as something absolutely incommensurable with anything we know of ourselves, of others, and of the world as a whole. For Blondel this means that the science of being as being cannot stop at a bare assertion of a totally transcendent Being, or of a Thought Thinking itself, as Aristotle leaves this science at the end. To be sure, it must know where to stop in recognizing the incommensurability of an absolutely First Mover. But it also must know enough not to stop. Agnosticism in the face of the mystery of Being is not enough of an answer. Even if we recognize the necessity of a negative method in speaking of the perfect Being, who is *not like* any of the imperfect beings we know in experience, whether that be matter, organisms, persons, or the universe as a whole, we must also recognize that such a method is grounded "on positive exigencies, on an aspiration toward plenitude alone capable of arousing our sense of insufficiency in our knowledge and in our proper reality" (1935, 167). From these exigencies and these aspirations comes a twofold duty *(devoir)* or a twofold sense of what we have to do; first, to go from the world to God; and then, in order to examine what it is important for us to know in our attitude toward him, through the very mystery of his creative design, it is crucial for our science of being not to lose interest in the transcendent Being, once we have come to know of his Being as principle of our being, either by keeping him separate from his creation, as Descartes did, or by submerging him in our immanence, as Hegel did. What we find in affirming the absolute transcendence of Being in itself as principle of our being, is not that we have to undergo some subjection, but rather that we are sustained and raised bit by bit to the light and to liberation. There are difficulties in working out this mysterious sort of relationship with God in our world, but it is the part of ontology to clarify in what these difficulties consist, and in answering some of the questions that remain once we have affirmed a totally Transcendent Being in itself, the first among which has to be concerning *what* this Being is in itself that we affirm.

In fact, this question concerning *what* Being is in itself is the opening to the third set of questions Blondel has in mind for this central probe of his ontology. He begins by taking stock of how we arrived at the point where we are. "We know that, since Being is, it still cannot consist in a subjective fiction, nor merely in an ideally regulative principle, nor in the obscure force of an indefinite becoming, nor in the sum of the physical and spiritual universe, nor in the confusion of the 'One and All.' These diverse forms, whether of monism, pluralism, or immanentism, are not only arbitrary hypotheses or errors lacking in intellectual coherence; they are positively unintelligible and unreal . . ." (1935, 172). From the beginning we have been asking what it is to be according to some exigency that now forces us to ground thought, life, and universal existence on a Being in itself, "whose unity, radically distinct from the multiplicity or the totality of subsistent or conceivable things, imposes itself as a truth so impossible to escape from, that we seem to reject it only by implying it more profoundly still" (1935, 172).

In affirming such a Being in itself, however, we also know that we cannot pierce the mystery of what such a Being is in itself. Apart from affirming it as the absolute Being in itself, we are somehow reduced to a respectful silence in its regard. It is *not* that we think of it as something *beyond* other beings we think we can know. If anything, it is more *within* the beings we know than beyond them, as the principle or the source of all being outside of Itself. But our interest in this Being is not ended. Our inquiry into it is not closed. "We cannot, we must not abandon it. If there is mystery, all is not darkness in it; otherwise we would not even know that it is a mystery and why" (1935, 172). Even if we have to proceed very prudently in a negative way, there is still a way of inquiring further into it by examining the difficulties we have in conceiving such a Being, as if they were ramparts, surrounding its citadel. In this way, Blondel says, we might gain a bit more territory for ontology, and some access, not just to obtain at least some partial views on the secrets of the impenetrable sanctuary, but also so that "the expression of a Being in itself will not remain a term so vague and cold that it has no meaning and no bearing on our life" (1935, 173). For Blondel, the God of philosophy is none other than the God of religion, even in Its transcendence, and philosophy has to explore this relation to a Being in itself that cannot, by definition, be absorbed into philosophy or, as Aquinas put it, that lies beyond the power of reason to investigate.

Aporiai Concerning What Being in Itself Is

Blondel knows he cannot gain further light on Being in itself by direct assault, so to speak. But he thinks he can tease further light from that Source of all light by examining a series of *aporiai* that engender one another around this mystery and following the salutary rigor that ties them together as they introduce us more deeply into the secret of the ultimate enigma. He runs through nine of these *aporiai*. The first of these is whether it is intelligible, legitimate, and useful to say of Being that it is *in itself*. This is a crucial one for understanding how God is in truth transcendent to our very affirmation of his transcendence. Once we are led to the logical necessity of affirming Being in itself, the same rational exigency forces us to recognize a certain interiority, sufficiency, and independence, in other words, a transcendence of such a Being that, far from denying any dependence on the part of beings in becoming with regard to this Being, expresses its supreme power and its incommensurability with regard to all contingent realities and possibilities. It is a matter of rational necessity for us to affirm such a Being, but can we posit it in the absolute, so to speak, independently of our relative point of view or our anthropocentric language? Is Being in itself anything more than the way it is viewed and posited in our own thought?

The answer to this question cannot be conclusive without reference to the responses to the other *aporiai* about this Being, as *of* itself and *through* itself, but Blondel begins to answer here by indicating how the certitudes we have been operating with in affirming this Being in itself are not merely subjective and ideal, but are really participating in the ontological truth they express, however inadequately and analogically. We would not be conscious in the way we are, or have the intellectual life we do, without a light that proceeds from the Being in itself, a light "that comes not from ourselves and that hence supplies and shines within us a ray from the source that is Being itself" (1935, 175). What this presupposes, however, is that this light must first enlighten itself and that Being in itself can and must, *of itself*, be an absolute truth in possession of itself, which remains to be shown in the following aporiai, having to do with how we affirm Being as *of* itself and *through* itself. It is through these two prepositional phrases, so commonly used in our ordinary speech, that Blondel proposes to zero in on the Being we affirm, not only as *in* itself, but also as absolute and independent of all relativity, whether to our thought or to the world.

To speak of Being as, not only in itself, but also as of itself, is to speak of it as without any antecedent or any physical or metaphysical ground, that is, as a primordial and original wisdom, power and goodness. "It is of itself, not as a consequence or an effect, but as a cause ever adequate to its principle and its end ... the living and eternal fecundity of freedom and necessity" (1935, 177). To be sure, we know this as a consequence of our own thought process, but no matter how elevated this process may be, it is not what makes Being in itself be in any way whatsoever. There is no making of the eternally necessary and free Being, not even by itself. Nor is there any fabrication of a conclusion regarding this absolute Being through some contingent connection, logical deduction, or speculative construction. What there is is an implication, a term that has been much used by Blondel in his exploration of Thought as well as Being, but that he now uses in an absolute sense, surpassing all mental constructions, including those we have used to get where we are. To speak of Being *in* itself as also *of* itself is, by implication, to speak of it in its very mystery without any claim to have penetrated that mystery.

However, that is not to say this Being in and of itself has nothing to do with us or that we should have nothing to do with it, not even try to see more of its mystery. Blondel brings in another phrase we can use with reference to this Being, in addition to the two he has been probing, the one of Being *through itself* (*par soi*). This one will open the way for him to speak more positively of a certain exchange within the absolute Being. Unlike the beings he has spoken of previously, none of which exists through itself alone or perpetuates itself really through its own power, the Being that is *through* itself or *by* itself exists totally and absolutely on its own initiative, so to speak. It is difficult, if not impossible, for us to think of such a Being without thinking of it as creating itself or causing itself, as if it were lifting itself out of nothingness, but we must free ourselves or our thought from such images in order to come to a justification of the more traditional idea of a Being *through* itself in its eternal perfection. The flat idea of eternity alone here will not do. We have to have the idea also of a surge, *un jaillissement*, that we can relate to a total possession of itself in a knowledge of its intimate truth and perfection. "There is no priority conceivable or desirable within the Absolute between its infinitely pregnant power and its intrinsic light through which it illuminates and literally gives itself to itself. There is no limitation that conditions this intimate and integral generation, independently of any duration, any fatality, any extrinsic necessity. There is only an unchanging truth, extrinsically founded in the excellence and the beauty of a perfection without beginning, without darkness and without decline, that necessarily unites freedom and love" (1935, 180).

To speak more concretely of this Being whose mystery escapes our grasp, Blondel puts it in the context of the perfection that we aim at in our thought and action, but that we cannot actualize for ourselves. The Being perfect in itself is, as it were, the aim of our knowledge and our aspiration that is ever open before us and desired. "In this Being are found in effect eternally attained the perfect end that escapes us, the distinction and the adequate union of the intelligible and intelligence, of being and knowing, of truth and life that equal one another and hold one another in an unceasing and total embrace" (1935, 181). All this is said, not of any human spirit, no matter how perfected, nor of any world spirit, in which one would still have to distinguish priorities in a process of coming to be perfect, but of a Being in absolute possession of its immutable spiritual perfection and its infinitely abundant simplicity.

To speak of the absolute Being in itself in these terms, however, as intelligible and as intelligent, as the living truth in its substantial unity of knowledge and the absolute, gives rise to the next aporia Blondel has to face. Is that not falling back into some sort of anthropomorphism or, worse still, is it not bringing the Transcendent back into some sort of immanence, the difficulty philosophy is ultimately brought to in speaking of any sort of divine transcendence? Can we affirm Being as a unity of intelligibility and intelligence or as a living truth of the kind we can conceive?

To answer this question Blondel goes back to the law of doubling we find in our knowing: we have some truth; we are not the truth. This comes from our way of knowing, where we always represent for ourselves what we take to be present as object. The representation may be more or less inadequate, at the same time as original and innovative, in spite of its fidelity to the object, which, for its part, does not pass over into our knowledge of it. Our knowledge of the object is something other, more and less, than the distinct reality represented in it. But how much of this is to be applied to Being in itself when we speak of its intelligence of its own intelligibility as absolute living truth? When we think of our goal as a real perfection subsisting in principle in the absolute Being, we cannot think of it as just another object we can represent to ourselves. The goal we have in mind is something naturally inaccessible to this manner of representing. The intelligible for this absolute Intelligence is not some partial object in juxtaposition and somehow opaque to it before being pierced by the light of reason or thought. It is rather itself precisely as intelligence in a perfect coincidence of knower and known. If there is any duality or exchange in the knowing of this Being, it does not prevent a perfect adequation. It only concentrates a perfect unity that cannot be found in any finite intelligence, which always represents any object, including itself, as other than itself. What we have in the knowing of the Absolute is a "unity without confusion and without passivity: a fully pregnant generation of a Word that is absolutely expressive and restorative to its Principle of the plenitude it has received of it while keeping this gift in the integrality of its infinite richness" (1935, 183).

With this thought of absolute Being as thought thinking itself, *noēsis noēseōs*, where being and truth are taken as one, however, do we not run into another problem, not only of losing sight of any distinction in it, but also of failing to recognize the superabundant richness of its perfection? Do we not run the risk of seeing it lost in the monotony of a contemplation lost in some immutable and sterile embrace? Are we not reduced to immobilizing it in a fixity that seems incompatible with its life and beatitude, in contrast to the imperfect beings we find in our experience, always in search of greater perfection, greater adequacy to what will satisfy their desire? This is the fifth aporia Blondel has to confront, which he frames as the question: "Can and must Being be affirmed as being solitary?" (1935, 184).

Here Blondel is very conscious that he is treading on very delicate ground as a philosopher, not to say sacred ground. But he pushes on to make as much rational sense of the Being we affirm as *in* itself, *of* itself, and *through* itself in its mystery, even if we admit that we cannot enter into the very core of this mystery. Even if we admit a certain duality of intelligence and intelligibility in the supreme Being, and immediately add that this intelligence that is generated adds nothing to the profound reality we are affirming, are we saying enough of the richness and perfection of this reality? Can we leave this mystery simply to itself as a sort of rational blank for us, or can we say more of what makes it the perfect Being that it is? We have already seen how this Being can be thought of as generating its own Word, which is nothing but itself as Engendered, in a sort of eternal mutual contemplation, with nothing hidden from either side in a perfect union of the two, but could we not conceive this as a sort of narcissistic solitude lost in an unending gaze into a reflection of oneself? Blondel wants to deny this, and to do so he pushes the analogy from the human being one step further, this time on the side of what is called the heart, the soul, or goodness in the human order, or what is called charity in a higher order.

The point is not to introduce a third party, so to speak, to stir up a self-enclosed intellection of intelligible and intelligence. Nor is it to tack on to the eternal substance an accidental fulguration that would spread goodness about as though radiating from a burning center. It is rather to recognize a reality and a truth that proceeds from the reality and the truth we have already affirmed, without any separation from that reality and truth, a reality that we have to accept as a complement that is not tacked on but is rather intrinsic and essential to the very Being we are affirming.

Blondel argues that it is not enough to think of the intelligible and intelligence as face to face with one another in Being itself. Even if we fix on truth alone as the absolute and total expression of Being in itself, that is still only an abstraction that cannot withstand a more fundamental analysis, as if the absolute Being were merely gazing into a mirror image of itself. "Could we say that this image, passively received and sent back to the original, reproduces it entirely or equals it absolutely? No, since what is passively expressive remains irremediably unfaithful to the act it represents in a copy that can offer the whole of an exact figuration, save what is the initiative and the fecundity of Being itself" (1935, 185-86). We cannot isolate the terms and the conditions of intellectual life, even for the absolute Being, as if they were self-sufficient in this sort of abstraction. Such a solitude would stifle the two terms or would not allow them to exist, for they would have to appear as either coinciding purely and simply, or as opposed to one another in an exclusive manner. From this, Blondel adds, comes "the point of departure of so many doctrines that end up in the incompatibility of the real and the rational or in pure agnosticism or in a groundless idealism" (1935, 186). The imperfection of human knowing may appear to lend some plausibility to one or another of these alternatives. But concerning absolute Being and absolute Knowing we cannot continue to oscillate between the two escape hatches that drain our mental life of any adequate content or leave it with a purely abstract intelligibility. We must reflect more attentively on the kind of duality we affirmed earlier between being and knowing in a Being that is without any need of anything other than itself. How are we to conceive the unity of the two in such a happy duality without going into anything that is extrinsic to either one or to their unity?

Blondel here averts to ancient doctrines that spoke of an internal procession or an eternal genesis of Being as one and triune, including the Christian teaching on God as a Trinity of persons. But his aim is not to invoke these teachings as a solution to the problem he is now facing philosophically. They are only ways of speaking about the mystery he is probing, no matter what authority they might otherwise have of themselves. His aim is to pursue whatever further knowability there might be in this Being we have to affirm, for "independently of religious teachings, our reason is not dispensed from, nor is it entirely incapable of gathering some rays of light among the hidden recesses of the mystery itself" (1935, 187). His probing thus far has led us to the thought of Being in itself, in its absolute unity, as conscious of itself in a world distinct from it and yet as totally one with it, and to the impossibility of representing this unity as a somber egoism or as a dualism without meaning. What further resources does our language provide in the analogy of human beings to the mystery of Being in itself that can bring more of its light to shine in our reason?

Blondel's reasoning to a third ingredient in the thought of the absolute Being can be summed up as follows. From the depths of its substance, Being gives itself totally to another Itself, contemporaneous with it in every way and the integral beneficiary of its power and fecundity. This other Itself, however, is what it is only by giving itself in return in a permanent and integral oblation of truth and love. This sacrificial act proper to the other Itself is that by which it expresses the plenitude of Being, from whom it receives all it is. Now, the third ingredient in the thought of this absolute Being has to be thought as this mutual exchange of truth and love, a common re-spiration, a primitive love that is uncreated, a reciprocal fecundity of the first two. Such a reciprocal love between the substantial Being and its substantial expression as Word cannot be thought of as adventitious to their relation within the identity of the One and the Other, nor as something accidental to them, nor as in any way passive on either side, or without any initiative and without substantial and essential efficacy of its own in the common life of all three. Far from compromising the intelligence, the unity, or the perfection of Being, this triple and unique life of spirit constitutes it essentially and substantially as one in whom all is being, all is life, all is light, and all is charity. Having said all this and having brought in the affective side of the human analogy to God, Blondel can now say that the One he has been speaking of metaphysically as Being *in, of,* and *through* itself can also be spoken of in religious terms as God. The God he has been speaking of philosophically is indeed the God of religion, not the god who can be absorbed into philosophy, but the God who has to be affirmed as hidden within the deep recesses of his own mystery, whatever light reason may be able to gather from this Being.

This marks the high point of Blondel's central probing into the inevitably mysterious Being affirmed as *in, of,* and *through* itself. Recognizing the resonances of his elaboration on how to make more sense of such an affirmation with the Christian mystery of God, understood as charity as well as Being in itself even in the contemplation of itself as *noēsis noēseōs*, he pauses to insist on the philosophical nature of his argument. "The metaphysics that can and must justify the mysterious aseity of the necessary Being is not without all reasonable argument to show that God is good, of course, in a way that is ineffable for us, but that nevertheless allows us to glimpse, if we dare use human words here, into the intimate liberality, the sublime devotion, the exchange of love that makes up the happy eternity of the one an Aristotle already knew enough to call *pure act* and thought of thought, without arriving at the full idea of charity, lacking which the frame still leaves empty the place open to the vivifying Spirit" (1935, 193). The point is not to show that we can penetrate into the inner sanctum of the divine Life itself, but rather to take in as much light from it as we can through reason, so that we can not only overcome the reluctance of certain rational thinkers to admit the possibility of such a triune Being but also find in it more convenience and relief for our reason than "the all too simple assertions of a dry and clear deism" (1935, 192) would offer. "As impenetrable as may appear, and as may in fact be, the Trinitary Unity, the synthesis of Essence and *Existence* would be all the more so, if the identity of these two terms were not founded on a reciprocal gift, on a perfect circumincession of love, on an absolute and perfect unity in a generation and procession where Power, Wisdom and Charity are coeternal and equally substantial" (1935, 194). Blondel pulls out all the stops of his philosophical language to make his point that the God he is talking about is indeed the God of religion. To stop short of that would be to cut reason short in its task of opening up the religious ways of faith.

The resolution of this fifth aporia, however, leaves us with a sixth one: Can the divine Being be thought of as personal and, if so, can it be only one person? Can we be satisfied with speaking simply of a divine personality? Blondel views this sort of appellation as inadequate and denaturing on three scores. First, a person for us is inconceivable as a unique singularity. By definition, according to Blondel, a person asserts itself, develops, and acquires its value, only in a confrontation, a collaboration, and a devotion to another, that is, in a relation with other existences. Such a relation of dependence is incompatible with the affirmations implied in the idea of Being in itself. Second, supposing that we raise the reality of the person above all the contingencies of moral and psychological interactions with other persons, do we not lose what dignity and generosity are inherent in a person only to find ourselves in some sort of solipsism or metaphysical egoism, which Blondel has already shown to be unintelligible and intrinsically contradictory? Third, in speaking of Being in itself as a single person, we would be implying that the knowledge it has of itself presupposes, as in our own consciousness, an obscure point of departure and a development due, if not to the trying experience of other beings, at least to the necessity for the purportedly absolute person to produce other beings to realize itself, see itself distinctly, and know itself fully, much as German idealism has been inclined to do, but contrary to and incompatibly with what we have already had to say about the absolute Being as *in*, *of*, and *through* itself.

Some of this difficulty could be obviated by saying that the perfect Being, complete in itself, is not one person, but at least something eminently personal. Blondel is reminded here of a reading of Plato by his teacher, Boutroux, who had spoken of three Ideas in themselves, the One, the True, and the Good, as of three realities subsisting separately but as constituting together a kind of consciousness of personal self, life, and goodness. This tells us something of how he had come by the idea of threefoldness in God philosophically, as well as through his Christian faith. But Boutroux's way of speaking of the threefold aspect of the personal in God does not meet with Blondel's philosophical exigencies concerning a perfect Being that is complete in itself. It still seems to suggest a kind of composition, or some ideal necessity, or a kind of *fieri* in the divine *esse*. What Blondel has argued for earlier is a Being that is absolutely perfect and complete in itself, without becoming of any sort and without necessity from anything other than itself. If we are to think of a threefoldness in such a Being in personal terms, we have to think of it as "three Persons perfect in the eternal unity of an absolute Transcendence" (1935, 197). Hence the difficulty of speaking of Being simply as personal if, in doing so, we represent the person as an absolute self, an individual closed in on itself and despotically lording over all that is not itself. This is a view that must be rejected with regard to both God and human beings. If we are going to speak of the eternal Being as personal, we are going to have to find better ways of speaking of its Goodness, its Holiness, its substantial Generosity. "If in his isolated attitude God were only one person, this word could have for God only an egocentric meaning, without any altruism whatsoever" (1935, 198). What Blondel sees in this is a crumbling of the entire spiritual edifice he thinks of as grounded in the Being posited as absolutely necessary and as indissolubly linked to this Being in its Transcendence.

The thought then of a spiritual edifice, including other beings along with absolute Being in itself as threefold, brings up another kind of aporia for a reason that Spinoza would have been very conscious of. If we say that Being is perfect and complete in itself without movement or coming to be of any kind, how can we continue to speak of ourselves as being or as beings in the face of this absolute mystery of Being? If being connotes a certain clarity of reflective insight, a certain independence of selfhood, are we not brought up short of being by the enigma of our own obscurity, our dependence, our incommensurability, even our divine appetite, face to face with the inaccessible Being? In other words, is our affirmation of Being compatible with other beings than this Being, and, if so, does it follow that God has to be thought of as creator, as well as totally self-contained in God's triune perfection?

The problem is very real for a philosopher who, like Blondel, starts from a concrete experience, in search of what brings our idea of being into play and what seems to correspond to it in realities positively given, such as matter, organisms, and persons, only to be led to the affirmation of a higher being that is most certain and most substantial, the only Being that is absolutely consistent *in, of,* and *through* itself as *Ens concretissimum, absolutum et unice perfectum* (1935, 199-200). From this conclusion in the search for a being that is Absolute, are we to turn around and deny all being, all truth, all goodness of whatever else we might still be thinking, as if whatever else there might be were absolutely contrary to what there is in all Truth and all Goodness? Do we have to choose, as many metaphysicians have thought they had to do, between absolutizing the Absolute in opposition to the relative and absolutizing the relative in opposition to the Absolute?

Aporiai Concerning Created Being as Such

We have seen how Blondel proceeds from the very beginning of his ontology by refusing to absolutize any being as given in experience. This is what enables him to rise to the true Absolute in his dialectic. In reaching the Absolute in this way, however, and in affirming the interior generation of Being as absolutely exhaustive, without precondition and without any need for completion, he realizes that he cannot fall back into the kind of oppositional thinking that would have kept him from the true ontological relativity of the beings he was starting from. He has to find another way of conceiving how the plenitude and beatitude of the divine Being can reasonably insert into itself, so to speak, and not opposite to itself, beings, or even phenomena and becoming, that cannot be thought of as anything but contingent and relative to absolute necessity. Hence the philosophical idea of creation.

This idea, for Blondel, ties not only into omnipotence in God, where absolute Being is understood as willing itself necessarily, and willing other beings as well, no less for itself or, as it is sometimes said, for its eternal glory. It also ties into the goodness and generosity of God producing other beings, for them to participate in diverse degrees in the perfections of the one true Being. God is not just a calculating architect for the universe. God is at the same time a loving communicator, a giver of being itself to others who are made actual in this giving, and who are beings for themselves, able to imitate God not only as being, but also by imitating God and uniting themselves to their Creator in "celebrating the creative goodness and participating in some measure in the generation of the Creator" (1935, 202). This can already be said, in a remote way, of beings on the physical and organic levels of existence in the universe. One can even hypothesize that God could have added to the immensity and the prodigious diversity of beings we find on these levels, not knowing why he willed it precisely as he did in his wisdom, power, and goodness. But one can also suppose that such a spectacle of nature, whose magnificence already strikes us as so sublime, "would not have been as worthy of his power and liberality without calling spiritual beings to the life of intelligence and freedom, making of the universe the scene for a drama where the regularity of a cosmogony opens up the way and the risks for a participation of spirits in God's work in the world" (1935, 203). This is a way for us to say that nothing is created except *for* God, just as everything is made *by* God. "But this metaphysical necessity implies also that the true accidental glory of God supposes among creatures the homage of their free and loving submission, and on the side of the Creator, the aim of communicating something of its own felicity" (1935, 203).

Just how this ontological drama is supposed to play itself out in the universe is something Blondel intends to work out later. He speaks of it here only to show that it has to be included in the metaphysical concept of creation, along with the sheer power and wisdom of the creator, which is not without an infinite goodness to be communicated. In the following aporia, now the eighth, he examines how *creation*, which cannot be observed as a matter of fact, is still by right compatible with the absolute of Being, a problem that has to be resolved in any claim referring to the Absolute as origin of being.

The objection is that, if we accept the necessary affirmation of self-sufficiency, a plenitude and a perfect saturation of Being in itself, there is no room for other true beings. The idea of an open space or a lacuna to be filled, an emptiness, a matrix, a receptacle, or whatever else one might imagine, perhaps even a nothingness, appears to the more critical thinker as little more than a myth fraught with contradictions, not the least of which is its incompatibility with the supreme intelligibility attributed to the Absolute. Even the idea, advanced by Blondel, of a spiritual reality and a generosity giving of itself is sometimes viewed as a depravation and an infantile image of the perfect Being, seen by reason, in its highest form, as the only reason for being, and the basis for its supreme value, to the exclusion of any other value or any other being.

Blondel's response to these objections is to get beyond these images and to go back to the reasoning that has led him to include the element of goodness and generosity within the process of eternal generation in the Absolute itself. "If, in itself, Being is perfect and reciprocal gift, are we to interdict, is it repugnant for its all-powerful charity to communicate freely some of the light from this source, not of course to add anything to its own beatifying warmth, but in order to make other happy ones, to associate to itself living images of its own substance, to communicate what is communicable of its life, its incommensurability, its transcendent felicity?" (1935, 207). If there is no intelligibility in Being except through its trinitary internal generation, why can we not admit at the same time that, if there are beings, and for there to be beings within *(au dedans)* the Absolute, creative intentions on the part of the Creator are the only way of explaining such beings?

We cannot think of this idea of divine creation without images, but Blondel proceeds by turning the image of the objection around. For him creation is not to be pictured as taking place outside the Absolute. There is no way we can understand creation with that image. For Blondel creation takes place within the Absolute, though by a distinct process from the one by which It generates itself eternally in its perfect Sufficiency. We cannot think of the Absolute as Parmenides did of being, as if it were a compact and opaque sphere outside of which there could only be illusion and nothing. To express how creation takes place as within the Absolute, Blondel borrows the Pauline phrase, *semetipsum exinanivit*, he emptied himself: "Being has withdrawn from a part of its own plenitude, as it were; it has opened a void in order to put in it, not nothing, but what would be able to restore it to itself, what would, by rendering, so to speak, God back to God himself, through a free gift and a meritorious renunciation, allow this lesser conditional being to add in some way to the divine glory, [a being] which becomes its own through the acceptance it makes of the gift and through the transformative abnegation that results from its voluntary fidelity to this divine destiny" (1935, 208). It would be difficult to express the entire idea of creation Blondel has in mind in a less complicated way. But it is also possible to see how much reasoning has gone into it.

Blondel has concentrated a good part of his philosophy of Thought and his philosophy of Action in this definition of creation by the *Ens concretissimus*, in view of having "others of itself," *d'autres lui-même*, now in the plural. He goes on to reflect further on this relation of creatures to Creator, in view of bringing creation as a gift of being to perfection, but only to bring up one final aporia or objection that has been raised against Being in itself from the side of beings. Does not the existence of the beings we have before us constitute a setting aside of Being in itself? The objection is not so much one of saying that the existence of the free beings that we are has to nullify the existence of a supreme being over us, as it was to be stated later on in an atheistic humanism and existentialism. It is rather the more classical objection of the existence of evil in the world, both moral and physical. How can we say that there is an omnipotent and benevolent God at the origin of being, if there are so much imperfection and downright evil in actual existence? But it is this objection also with an added twist, concerning the possibility of success or failure to reach the end for which at least human beings are created, with the consequent fulfillment of the call to beatitude on one side or the curse of eternal frustration on the other. How can the risk of such dire consequences for beings who are free to constitute themselves as they will, be justified in the face of a God who chooses to communicate not only his being but also his beatitude to those he creates?

In a way Blondel had spent a good part of his philosophical effort in answering this objection, beginning with his dissertation on *Action* and the *Letter on Apologetics*. Here he intends to spend a longer time still, answering it in the remaining part of his ontology on becoming and on how beings are solidified through their own initiative, under a normative of being. But before going into that he wants to give a shorter answer to the speculative embarrassment the objection presents from a rational standpoint, even if it be only to open the way to the normative part of his ontology.

The speculative answer to the aporia that Blondel feels he must give, before going into the more practical side of his ontology, in response to the objection, begins with a reflection on what is affirmed in a rational affirmation of creation and on precisely what is taken to have been created. From the standpoint of Being in itself, it might seem that *its* truth would exclude the likelihood or even the reasonable possibility of true being, whether apart from it or within it. In overcoming this difficulty about the very thought of creation, Blondel had introduced the idea of goodness to complete our metaphysical understanding of Being in itself as creator. This was an issue of greater intelligibility, if not of the only intelligibility, regarding absolute Being, as well as an issue of greater moral value for the creature. From this, however, we find ourselves in even greater difficulty when we contemplate the poverty of the beings created, yes, and even their abjection and sinfulness. Does this not take away from the speculative thesis of a creative omnipotence through love? At first we had to figure out how there could be any other beings than the Absolute. Now we have to figure out how these other beings have turned out so badly, without taking back anything of what we have said about the creative wisdom and goodness.

If we were to adopt an attitude of pure pessimism, we would have no way of escaping the difficulty. We would be locked in a circle of pure dissatisfaction, by reason of a radical immanentism avid only for passing joys. Blondel has already shown the inconsequence or the psychological and rational impossibility of such immanentism. Here he proposes to go one step further and maintain that "if the whole of nature is groaning, it is so that no being may become acclimatized to it, hold itself to the present or even to the future, come to a halt in the ascending movement opening the way toward a change of state, even more than toward eternal returns going around in circles" (1935, 212).

Blondel is alluding once again to his ever-present idea of a vocation to a supernatural state of being created, a state of completion and goodness that would surpass any natural power of achievement by any created being. But how could this solve the difficulty of continued suffering in the world and the presence of sin, if the will of God is in fact always for a greater happiness, at least for human beings, if not for lesser beings in nature? Indeed, if we have the further idea that such a state of union with God and of beatitude cannot be attained by beings, if they remain entirely passive and subject to a heteronomy, but that they must choose it for themselves, with the understanding that a refusal of the gift that would free them from their narrow egoism would entail falling short of their destiny and the worst possible loss for them, does this not aggravate the difficulty even more into a complete contradiction in being? *Yes,* says Blondel, for the being that refuses the gift that would fulfill its destiny. But more importantly, *no,* for the one who accepts the gift, for then the call to happiness and goodness that comes with creation is fulfilled. The fact that such fulfillment does not come automatically or naturally cannot rationally be held against the call, given the freedom and responsibility of the one called. Nor can the failure of responding to the call positively, however it may be heard, be held against the generosity of the call. A gift so generous cannot be offered except to one who can will it for itself, as well as refuse it, one who has to will it in order to receive it. If there are those who love themselves wrongly by refusing the gift, and who end up hating themselves and the divine life to which they are called, is that a reason for divine charity, in order to avert all voluntary aberration, to renounce any "design of raising intelligent and free creatures, with the entire cortege of the universe they bear with them, toward a communion and felicity of which no one is deprived without its own express fault" (1935, 213)? If there is sin and evil in the world it is not because God wills it. It is because there are creatures in the world who have to freely accept the gift offered by the Creator, but who can also use the gift only to refuse it.

The argument is cast first in terms of moral good and evil or, more precisely, in terms of attaining one's true destiny, or failing to do so. But it can also be cast in more general terms of any creature relating to the Creator in its own striving. Once the problem of the existence of imperfect beings coming from an omnipotent and benevolent perfect Being has come to the consciousness of philosophical reason, it cannot be set aside or repressed. Nor can it be justified or maintained as a problem, unless we include in it the idea of a possible assimilation to God, an idea Blondel loves to quote, *omnia intendunt assimilari Deo*, which he attributes to the metaphysical tradition here, and more particularly in other places to Thomas Aquinas. "In spite of the objections and the scandals that imperfections, sufferings, depravations, and eventual sanctions provoke, it seems necessary and possible that creation is worth something that is not entirely unworthy of its author. We should even say that the more the work can be degraded, the more it proves the vigor of the initial gift and the immensity of the destiny offered to the creature" (1935, 213). We could also say that, the more vigorous the initial gift, which is a gift to act as well as a gift of being, the more keen is our sense of evil or of failure, when we do not measure up to it in action.

Blondel has every intention of pursuing this theme of a relation to a supernatural end in the creature in his later works on *Action* and the *Christian Spirit*. Here he is careful to make a disclaimer he has long been accustomed to making, concerning any knowledge of what the supernatural gift might entail or even if any such gift has been given in reality. As a philosopher here he has only spoken of the idea of the supernatural and how a creature would have to relate to that, if the additional gift were offered. He has spoken of assimilation to God as only a tendency in nature, or in the created being. He has used the idea of the supernatural only to show how it is possible and even necessary for the Creator to allow for evil in a world he wills only out of goodness and charity, as the flip side of the good he intends but not without the decisive approval or refusal of the creature. This is not an argument for a dialectical necessity of good and evil in being. Nor is it an attempt to reduce all evil to good as in some neo-Platonic schemes of a necessary return to the One and the Good. For Blondel there is not even any necessary emanation from the One. There is only creation out of sheer goodness and liberality, with a consequent call to use the initial gift to aim at some still higher gift of being. The only necessity that Blondel has invoked is the necessity of responsibility on the part of the created being to the call to seek its own ultimate goodness and perfection in the only One who can make it possible. What this entails for the creature is a willingness to deny itself in its own egoistic interests, to suffer the loss of itself, in order to enter into a more perfect kind of selfhood in communion with the threefold divine life.

Nothing apodictic can be said about how this perfection of created being is to be realized or what precisely it will consist in, no more than we can say *what* the perfect Being is in itself. But it is possible to say something of the rationality in the "mysteriously metaphysical necessities" (1935, 214) of the relation we find from created being to the Uncreated. "The divine art in creation is one of clarity in obscurity and the shadows are themselves a beauty and a truth" (1935, 215) to be explored. The more practical and longer answer to the question as to how there can be beings other than the absolutely perfect Being is to examine how created beings, as imperfect as they may be in themselves, have to relate back to the Perfect Being. This is something they must do of themselves in striving for their own perfection, which is not given to them immediately from the beginning of creation, but communicated to them liberally as they exercise their own responsibility, for they can refuse as well as accept this final gift of perfection in being, which would be a participation in the divine life of Perfection itself. What Blondel wants to show is that, even if this gratuitous achievement is liberally offered by God, it is no longer legitimate for a creature to prescind from it in the exercise of its responsibility and, if it is true that it is a necessity for the creature's perfection, it is no less true that in rejecting it "our being suffers a disaster" (1935, 216).

To show this will be the burden of the third part of this ontology, which Blondel conceives as a *normative* of created beings, a logic inscribed in the very being of things, especially as they find their consistency in connection with the beings capable of freely setting their own course toward their own perfection in being. This final part of the ontology will consist in trying to understand how the becoming of so many beings, on the way to being more fully, forms a *complexus* where, on the one hand, the foundations given de facto necessarily sustain one another and, on the other, "existences are constituted susceptible of acquiring a relative autonomy and of cooperating in a decisive manner in their own destiny" (1935, 216). Blondel has in mind the metaphor of a structure reaching for the heights of perfection where the human spirit soars above its material ties to the universe, but without being able by itself to place the capstone of perfection, which would solidify the whole structure. The capstone for this human spirit in the world can only come from the divine Perfection of Being in itself, no less than creation itself as ontological foundation. Unlike the originating creation, however, it cannot come without the cooperative intervention of the creature already constituted in its own natural being. Hence the awesome ontological responsibility of the creature with intelligence and will in the world, which is not without its necessary norms. It can accept this rightful presence of God in the world, and thereby restore it to the place God has emptied out of his infinite being to make room for finite being, or else it can refuse this presence offered as new fulfillment and stay with the frustration of its most profound ontological aspiration.

The Idea of an Ontological Normative for Created Beings

Blondel's ontology thus does not end with a consideration of absolute Being in, of, and through itself. He has shown that we have to affirm such a Being as totally transcendent and self-sufficient, without any need for other beings, and he has drawn all the intelligibility he could reasonably extract from the necessary affirmation of this mysterious Being. He has also shown how it is possible for this infinitely perfect Being to make room within itself for other beings, to create beings other than itself that can be thought of as being in a lesser sense as finite, but nevertheless as truly being in their own right, so to speak, and as truly capable of their own initiative in bringing their own being to perfection. Supposing, then, that there has been such a creation, since it is from created being, now properly known to be created, that this entire ontological consideration has had its beginning, Blondel proceeds to examine what there is in created being as such to consolidate it as being and as acting in its own right toward its own perfection.

Earlier the consideration of things given in experience had been of them as fleeting and as unable to stand in themselves or by themselves or meet the criteria we associate with Being as absolute. Beginning with matter, we had been forced to go on to organisms, and then to persons, and finally to the All of being, in search of a Being that would meet the criteria we associate with our fundamental conception of Being. This is what brought us to the affirmation of a Being that met these criteria and that Blondel presented not only as intelligent and free, but also as a loving giver of gifts, the first of which is the very being of the recipients themselves, leaving aside for the moment whatever additional gifts might be offered by this giver of life. Now, however, after our central probe into this absolutely perfect Being in, by, and through itself, we must return to these passing beings of our experience, examine how they are solidified as beings through creation, not as fixed in any sort of absolute existence, but rather as called to work out their own perfection in relation to the absolutely perfect Being.

This is a question that arises for ontology inasmuch there are beings in this secondary and derivative sense, including imperfect spirits who have to work out their own perfection. It devolves upon reason to ask why there are such beings, all the more so because of the evil and imperfection found in a world that flows from an omnipotent and benevolent Creator. Is there an explanation to exonerate perfection from all these deficiencies and failures we see around us and within our spirit? Is there any way of reconciling our imperfection with the perfection of Being in itself? Through this question Blondel is led back not just to the question of how there can be beings other than only the Absolute, but also to the question of a design for creation as expressed in nature and history. This is a question for ontology, according to him, because it has to do with certifying existences that seem as nothing "next to the Absolute," or as only running away from Being in itself.

Now it is payback time for these beings and ourselves in this ontology, to enrich our knowledge of them and of ourselves and perhaps to build up our own being into something more solid by way of a more conscious participation in the solidarity and the elevation of this universe, in which we have a singular role to play through thought and our own resolve in bringing it all back to the Being who, being the principle, must also be its end. In this third part of his ontology, then, Blondel returns to the world of becoming to examine what will make for its solidification in being, at least for individuals capable of thought and responsibility. At the end of part one, it might have seemed as if there were not true beings apart from the Absolute. Now after the central probe into Being in itself in part two, we can see how there are indeed beings other than the one absolute Being, not outside of it, to be sure, but still not just attributes of it, as Spinoza would have it, real beings with their own standing and orientation toward some perfection by assimilation to the perfect Being in itself. These beings are not to be thought of as merely juxtaposed, in isolation from one another and diversely perishable. Together they constitute a universe of nature and spirit in which a drama is being played out according to what Blondel will insist on calling norms inscribed in the very being of things and persons. It is the task of this third part of ontology to lay out this normative as it unfolds like a substantial law internal to beings and persons, directing their development and their relations to other beings as well as to the totally transcendent Being.

For Blondel this means asking, not only about the *existence* of particular beings which seems to keep them outside of one another, as the term *ex-sistere* seems to suggest, but also the *consistency,* which suggests to him a twofold idea: "that of an internal or, better still, an intrinsic coherence to be considered and that also of a solidarity among the diverse existences that we are tempted to abstract and oppose to one another" (1935, 229). The question is to see whether there is enough in the *consistency* of things in the universe of becoming to constitute a recipient for the substantiality we look for in beings worthy of that name. This will mean keeping track not only of how all things come together in world history, but also how each being truly worthy of the name finds its own particular consistency, by taking initiative for itself in the way the whole relates to the Transcendent, for we must not lose sight of this ultimate dimension as required for the final consolidation of created beings.

Two extremes are to be avoided in this consideration of *consistency* in created beings: (1) to insist too much on the true reality, the dignity, and the grandeur of the destiny of creatures as such, or (2) to worry about compromising the divine sovereignty, of which it is said that it effects everything in all things. We cannot understand the full consistency of created things without reference to the Creator not just as their principle but also as their final end. But neither can we understand the consistency of these very beings without the order within them, which comes over them in their contingency and multiplicity and in which these beings find their support, their development, their form, and their value, a rule, so to speak, or more precisely, a norm that is at once intimate and transcendent, and that both stimulates and judges them. At this point, the ontology of the concrete has to become an ontogeny, in search, point by point and step by step, of "the efficacious presence of the norm that is, within us, the call of the being that has to be, that will be and that is already on its way" (1935, 234). How does this normative influence make itself felt as a matter of fitting and adjustment in a universe that has to be returned to the Creator as to its final end?

In a sense, with this idea of a normative in ontology, Blondel is returning to a theme of necessity in being he had begun to develop earlier with the philosophy of action, as he notes in an Excursus. At that time, more than thirty-five years earlier, when he was just beginning his philosophical itinerary, he had spoken of a general logic that would encompass both formal logic and applied logic, the logic of both speculative science and moral action, and integrate them into a single logic of how we relate to things in the concrete synthetically as well as analytically as free agents. His insistence had been on how we can arrive at such a logic through reflection on the activity of a subject, who has to be analytical and speculative as well as synthetic and ethical. Now, however, he wants to bring out the more realistic side of this reflection, its more ontological bearing, so to speak, by insisting on norms rather than on rules of logic.

The reversal of perspective is almost imperceptible from the standpoint of logic, but it is important for understanding Blondel's ontology of the concrete. It was already implied in the earlier approach through logic, but here Blondel makes it quite explicit. Rules, like the ruler with which they are associated, are imposed from the outside of what they are applied to. Logically they flow from the thinking subject and tend to remain subjective in their content, even in their engagement with objects, thus giving rise to what Blondel thinks of as idealism. Norms, on the other hand, suggest something more realistic to him, something found in the things themselves, which is what he wants to get at in his ontology. For him, they are real and have a "constitutive role in the ontological armature of beings" (1935, 237). "It is not in subjective inventions, but in the profound reality of beings and in the truth of their interrelations that we must look for the secret of an order that has always, in effect, to be repaired and renewed, but is never one to be improvised from the bottom to the top" (1935, 239). This order is where the consistency of created beings lies, what there is in them that is at once most intimate and most universal in the relations of interdependence and finality that make up the total ordering. It is not a static juxtaposition of things that can be grasped in abstraction from one another. It is a design in process of realization with its own effective principles that can be discerned as internal regulations of beings, as they are and as they strive toward their own perfection.

The norm here has to do with a certain qualitative precision to be obtained, something that allows for only one perfect way to go. It necessarily includes an element of value in the reality to be produced. It is not arbitrary, artificial, approximative, imprecise, or something merely agreed upon. It is something to be discerned as accurately as possible, but still as "a supple, delicate, precise, stimulating and demanding adaptation of the singular resources of each individual to what is its true possibility, its having to be *(son devoir être)*, its value, at each moment of its becoming, all the way to the final point of its destiny" (1935, 241). It is in such norms that individuals find consistency in their being, not in a way that precludes free choice, but in a way that promotes and requires an ever-higher sense of choice in the face of Being in itself, "a power of consolidation or of ruination for beings that were able either to cooperate with or resist these promptings within themselves" (1935, 242). Even in his ontology, when Blondel is thinking of the normative ordering of created beings, both within and among themselves, he always has in mind the singular role spiritual beings have to play in this ordering both with regard to themselves and with regard to the whole.

In the opening part of his ontology, he had gone through the diverse stages of being in a critical way, from matter to organisms to persons, in search of what would satisfy our intimate sense of Being in the complete and absolute sense of the term. At each stage, short of Being in itself, he had argued that none of the things we distinguish in the universe of our experience satisfy our fundamental notion of Being, or qualify as beings in the full sense of the term, as we find them in the realm of becoming, even though he had used the varying degrees of oneness and completion among the material, the organic, and the personal as a way of ascending toward the Being that is perfectly one and absolutely complete in itself. In the final part of his ontology, Blondel now returns to these same appearances of being in becoming, now understood as created in their own being, to reaffirm what there is of being in them, not in a static way, but in the very dynamic of their becoming. What is most real about them, which is the concern of ontology, is the norm that governs their becoming and orients them toward the fullness of their own being, both as individuals and as a universe.

It is possible to think of a wide diversity of particular laws or norms that govern the different kinds of being we find in experience. These can be thought of as governing the becoming of these particular sorts of being in becoming. But to inquire into these norms, which can go on indefinitely in many directions, is not the task of ontology. Blondel does not question the reality of such particular laws. He thinks of them as the concern of more particular sciences, not of ontology. His aim is to bring out the norm of all these norms as it pertains to the fundamental exigencies of contingent beings as a whole "without which no creature would be properly speaking a true being" (1935, 254). The issue for him is "to establish how a created being, whatever it may be, can become a being deserving of the name" (1935, 254), which can be done only through a certain norm governing all created being simultaneously and correlatively.

This is what he calls a normative, a logic that is effective of being and that differs from any logic of abstract thought. He refers to the logic of Aristotle, which is based on the radical opposition between affirmation and negation, or contradiction, *apophasis* and *antiphasis*, and tends to treat of opposites as exclusive of one another, or of any middle. The more *effective* logic of the norm Blondel has in mind is one that pertains to the kind of binding that establishes the solidarity of each being with itself, with other beings, and with the final end toward which all are tending. Something of this logic was already contained in another fundamental distinction of Aristotle, that between possession and privation, *hexis* and *sterēsis*, which pertains to the dynamic of being in terms of perfection and imperfection. What characterizes this logic is less a matter of opposition and more a matter of vital assimilation, a real exchange, an enrichment or an impoverization, in short, possession or privation of perfection in being.

The first logic, that of affirmation and negation, proceeds by way of elimination for what does not fit into its rational scheme. It divides according to affirmative inclusion or negative exclusion, as if between pure being and pure nothing. Not so, however, for the real normative Blondel has in mind. What is repelled in it is not *ipso facto* suppressed. Blondel cites moral experience as an illustration of this kind of logic, where temptation serves to focus and enrich one's moral energy, or else, if there is failure, the evil is made worse in proportion to the consciousness and the value of the good that is betrayed, and to the will letting go of its own purpose. We find this kind of logic at play in the physical world, where forces that are overcome are not exterminated, as well as in the spiritual order, where different alternatives do not annihilate one another or keep one another from having a double-edged role. It is a dialectic of being, the truth of which is fundamental and universal for the total organization of being. Not to take it into account "would render anemic and even compromise the concrete truth of any ontology. It would be to expose oneself to losing sight of the interaction and the destiny of beings" (1935, 258).

Normative Ontological Exigencies in Matter, Life, and Personality

Blondel finds the first trace of this real normative truth in matter itself. After taking a critical stance with regard to various ways of representing matter, whether as support for all other beings, or as a potency containing the diversity of ulterior determinations, or as a primordial being independent of all others, at the beginning of this ontology, he now returns to the question of its reality as part of the order of being. His aim is not to undermine our sense of matter as real in any idealist fashion. It is rather to overcome any tendency to absolutize matter as a being in itself, whether in the form of dualism, monism, materialism, or what he calls false realism, as well as what he had spoken of earlier as illusory idealism. Matter as such is not a being in itself apart from anything else we might consider as real, such as form. Neither can it be thought of as apart from any other conception of reality. But even if we place it at the limit of the indeterminate, and assimilate it almost to nothing, it is not nothing and it has within itself some virtuality, some real capacity, which enables us to affirm it as something, an x, that is somehow known, even when we say that we do not know it directly, as we know material things, which are already more than just matter as only virtual or potential.

This something or this contour for our thought is not just some dark, impenetrable hole. It is a darkness or an obstacle that is everywhere permeable to light, not just for the progress of the positive sciences, which are not at issue here, but for the metaphysical and the moral probing of an ontology interested in seeing how actual beings are elaborated and how even our personal being has to develop under its material conditions. This is what Blondel sees as the normative role played by matter in the total and highest plan of creation. It is ontogenic, indispensable and indestructible, and therefore real, though not a being in itself. Even if it is not by itself a sufficient cause for the ascent of the universe toward the higher forms of life and spirit, it is a necessary condition for this ascent. Matter is like a springboard that has to be used for this ascent. "It is not that the lower conditions are the cause of the ascent, but the *élan* that comes from above needs to descend to the bottom in order to rebound from the obstacle, from what we have called the springboard, at once resistant and nevertheless ever elastic, that any metaphysical imperfection opposes to the most unifying design of uncreated perfection" (1935, 263).

Thus, even if matter cannot be termed properly a being, it has a necessary role and function to play in the constitution of beings more deserving of the name. As such it is real and irreducible to our idea of it, even though, as normative function, it has a twofold aspect, one of opposition and one of stimulation, one as instrument of perfection and one as instrument of degradation, one as occasion for merit and one as occasion for sanction. This function remains indispensable for the evolution and even for the final state of spiritual beings, a function that, "in contributing to their realization, their obligation, their consolidation and their sanction, must therefore be considered as co-substantial to the beings that could not have risen without it" (1935, 264). Matter thus does not appear as a being alongside other beings, something existing separately by itself, but as a reality tied to all other realities, "as the universal expression of their contingency, their imperfection, their dependence, their aspiration, their mutual obstacle, their reciprocal stimulation, their total complexus, and their possibility of union or antagonism" (1935, 264-65). The reason why Blondel will not admit that matter is not a being absolutely in itself, no matter how real it is in its normative function, is that nothing of what can be said of matter can be said of absolute Being in itself. The same will not be true of life, the next stage of normative function in the created universe Blondel proceeds to examine.

His probing into life, however, will not be as it is found in the subsistence of the absolute Being in itself, but rather as it is found among observable realities, those that "constitute organisms endowed with a relative unity, a power of assimilative expansion and a fecundity that prolongs and multiplies their existence" (1935, 265). These are already beings of a sort, but still perishable, unable to close in on themselves in any sort of immortality. Blondel will consider them in the same way as he considered matter, as opening the way for the advent of higher forms of existence that do not pass away or die without recourse, that is, as forms that are organic but not yet spiritual. Here Blondel speaks of the *élan vital* that Bergson had made so much of, which constitutes living things in a perennity of their own, whether in their individual ontogeny or their more historical phylogeny, both accessible to the biological and social sciences in their successive phases and in the phenomenological symbiosis of their perishable life. But what Blondel wants to bring out in the ontological role of life is its normative function in the preparation of true beings, in whose constitution it contributes and to which it owes, keeping and developing its own proper virtualities and its permanent reason for being. From an existential point of view, Blondel views this initiative of bodily life as a substrate for the person capable of thought and self-consciousness, which, in order to develop its proper powers, needs this support, this setting in motion, this instrument, at once attuned to the new exigencies of spiritual beings, which for their part remain in accord with the organic exigencies that serve as partial norms for the life of spirit itself.

In response to a conception of spirits as detached from all material and biological conditions and separate from any organism or animal life, Blondel falls back on three basic points he keeps on making concerning any created being. First, if it is the case that there is no created nature that is without imperfection or without some inequality between its essence and its existence, there is no absolutely pure spirit other than the first Cause. There is no creature that is without any shade of materiality, without any obstacle to overcome or without a test of its own to undergo. Second, it is wrong to imagine the purest of spirits as apart from one another, apart from any solidarity with the humblest of tasks, apart from any vital connection or any duty of perfecting themselves through some work of charity and humility. Blondel will elaborate on this point further in terms of mutual recognition and mutual service among spiritual beings, when he comes to deal with personality on the third level of his ascent through the normative functions. His third point here is one that results from the first two: "All spiritual life, as created, dependent and obliged to some option, finds in the spontaneous and controlled organization of the biological order as well, as in the physical laws, a principle of regulation, a stimulating and supportive dynamism, but also a force of contradiction from which free wills can try to liberate themselves, without however remaining caught in their reprise and their sanction" (1935, 268).

Thus Blondel will argue that organic life is essentially good in the sense that, without constituting by itself beings that are fully realized, it nevertheless enters into the substantial order of a universe designed to produce true beings in the bosom of absolute Being. He introduces here the idea of an *élan spirituel*, which he is more interested in getting to in this normative ontology, in contrast to the *élan vital* he has been speaking about, but only to show how the two flow together to promote the fullness of a life that is spiritual at the same time as organic. Spontaneous life, to begin with, is already an effort of organization and unification, of interiorization and expansion and proliferation, which marks an advancement over the conditions that prepare it. It also shows a certain egocentrism that is vital, healthy, and normal. It is on this platform of realization, so to speak, that consciousness appears with a new effort of its own, one that is spiritual and oriented toward an infinite goal. This new life does not minimize or repress the first vital élan, but raises it to a new order, disciplines it so that it will become more fecund as well as more worthy of a rational and providential being. Even when it appears to be refraining or mortifying the vital élan, the spiritual élan is only elevating it, perfecting it, to make it reach the abundance of a universal and indelible life through participation in the permanent solidity of beings capable of infinite perfection, or else of definitive defection.

Blondel then passes on to the third degree of this ascent toward what can count truly as being in this normative ontology of the created universe, what he refers to as the person, which also has its own normative exigencies. Here he takes issue with the common modern representation of the person as an absolute being by itself, or as an end in itself. Personal life is something other than merely organic life, but it is not something sufficient unto itself. It is subject to norms that come from below and from above. But it is also subject to norms on the personal level itself that transcend the purely individual sense of personality. It would be an ontological mistake to represent any individual person as a complete being in itself, especially if we wish to take this being as the basis for a system of rights to the exclusion of anything or anyone else.

Here Blondel is taking aim, not only at the Hobbesian conception of personality, but also at the sociological materialism of a Durkheim, which remains derivative from the Hobbesian view by grounding collective consciousness on the rational division of labor, instead of the spiritual ascent of social life that brings human beings together. What constitutes personality is a spiritual élan, a moral dynamism over and above the merely vital dynamism. Blondel first speaks of this spiritual élan as open to the infinite. Personal life, he writes, "as rooted as it is in the cosmos, is therefore acosmic through an emergence that makes it into a need of infinity, a virtuality that has been defined by saying *capax entis, capax Dei*" (1935, 277). In a sense, the élan vital already brings repercussions in from the whole of reality into each living thing and stamps its own singular originality into the history of the world through a proliferation of consequences and interminable existences, but in the spiritual élan there is more than just the entire world of things. There is a world of spirit rising above the visible universe organized by reason imitating and using the creative force, working toward a community of spirits where the many recognize one another as in one another "in a multiple unity resulting from a multiplicity perfectly united with its highest principle" (1935, 278).

Such an ideal of spiritual communion may seem too far-fetched in an ontology of the normative functions of the spiritual being we experience. But it does say something of the scope our spiritual élan opens us to. Blondel will have a lot more to say about it later on. Here, however, he wants to say more about how we experience the exigencies of this spiritual life methodically and ascetically, as we grow to adulthood. He shows how the spiritual élan entails a reversal of the vital élan in this process. As we have seen, the vital élan builds up to a certain egoism in the living being. This is something we like to see in a child. It represents a healthy and necessary movement toward a robust self-consciousness. But it is not something we like to see in an adult, when it becomes selfishness that recognizes only its own desires and its individual rights. What we look for in the adult is a readiness to turn one's own sensibility around and to act in the service of others by decentering oneself and embracing less "personal" causes, a service of others and even the higher interests of truth, equity, and the common good.

Blondel speaks of this as an ontogenic virtue in the spiritual order. "Once our particular egoism has easily taught us that we are, we have to learn that others are as well, that we have to 'realize' them by placing ourselves actively in their place, that if they are through us and for us in many respects, we are also for them and through them, and that even our personal life opens up, enriches and realizes itself only at the cost of this exodus from a false egoism, and through this sort of paradoxical mortification that alone is vivifying for any true and strong personality" (1935, 279). This sort of realist and normative doctrine of true personality has sometimes been vilified as false virtue, a slave morality or an aberration for subjects who are supposed to be masters of their own destiny. But Blondel sees in such vilification a reduction of the person to only the basest elements of the vital élan, a vehemence of blood and race, a personal or collective pride, violence, and a passion for domination and pleasure. These are not ways of surpassing the world and oneself. They only mask the true goal of personality from itself and keep it from transcending the narrow confines of its egoism.

The person is not just a self-enclosed monad. Nor is it limited to seeking only its own individual advantage. It does not come to be in the fullness of its being except through some reciprocal gift that follows from mutual recognition with other persons, through a union of spirits, not by eradicating differences down to some lowest common denominator or by neutralizing ambitions, but by some comprehension, cooperation, and elevation that are mutual among members of a community. Blondel has in mind here the classical conception of the virtues, which are properly spiritual and relate to the vital appetites of our organism as means for growth under the material conditions of life. Such are the virtues of temperance and courage, for example, and the concern for justice as a true progress of humanity. These may not mark the highest perfection possible for truly spiritual beings, since they are realized in the immanent order of history, but they are exigencies or normative functions of personality that open the way toward higher achievements still in the order of spiritual perfection. The life of the person in the "city of man" is only a beginning of a transition toward a higher order that emerges above, and encompasses all the lower orders we have seen succeeding one another in this ontological scale of beings, without taking anything away from any of these intermediate degrees.

Here Blondel evokes the geometrical figure, not of the self-contained circle, but of the cycloid he liked to use to illustrate the kind of upward movement he is describing in this normative of becoming toward a perfection of being. Personal life is not just something superadded to a structure that is already stable and complete in itself. "Is it not rather a cycloidal progression? Does it not go down into what is lowest in order to rise higher, to raise and bring along with itself the entire mass in which it plants itself and nourishes itself in order to transubstantiate this mass as it were?" (1935, 283). This is not just a matter of positing one on top of the other different elements, given apart from one another. It is a matter "of an organic function subordinated to the unity of an end that magnetizes, so to speak, and animates all the components" (1935, 283). It is a norm inscribed into the movement of creation as a whole that comes to fruition in spiritual beings as such.

Ontological Consolidation of Finite Spirits, and of the World, in the Perfection of the Infinite Spirit

The question that remains for Blondel is whether we have gone far enough with this ontological normative. Can we speak of these spiritual creatures, through their beginning of communion, as a reality that is completely stable and consistent in itself, summing up the whole world in a common cohesion? Or do we have to think of the whole of creation as still aspiring to some participation in absolute Being in itself? Unlike Hegel, Blondel does not think that any created spirit, or any world spirit for that matter, can pass over simply into absolute Knowing or absolute Being. But he does think that there is some aspiration, in the spiritual being, summing up the universe within itself, to become a being in the fullest sense of the term, the sense that is found only in the Creator itself. This is what he has in mind when he speaks of beings that will be "truly worthy of the name." The problem for him is not to maintain the total transcendence of the Creator or of Being in, of, and through itself. He has already established that at some length clearly in his own mind. The problem is to see how the creature can be consolidated as a being in a way that shares in the necessary Being of the Creator. This is a problem that arises from the very mystery of creation for Blondel, for there the problem was "to produce beings that would not be a vain image, a semblance unworthy of him, but that would be *d'autres lui-même* [others of itself], capable of justifying the sense of creation as a whole, and of realizing a destiny enabling spirits to become the arbiters of their own existence" (1935, 284). It is this problem that he proposes to discuss in the fourth and final degree of his ontological normative.

The condition of personal beings in the universe, even understood as a community of spirits in the historical process at the end of a normative ontology of created being, remains unstable. These beings still aspire to a higher union among themselves and a greater consolidation of their being in the absolute Being of the Creator, but they can also settle for the lower conditions of their existence. They must rise above themselves, or fall back into what is lower than themselves. But there are problems with conceiving how this rising is to take place, and what precisely it is supposed to accomplish. To begin with, the spirits we are talking about are finite spirits, with only finite powers of unification and concentration, whereas what they aspire to is a totally transcendent end and an infinite Perfection of their own being. The unification they aspire to cannot take place without a new initiative on the part of the infinite Being itself, over and above the initiative already taken in the design of creation itself. But then, supposing that some such new initiative takes place, how are we to understand that the finite spirit, along with other beings in the universe, is not simply absorbed back into the Infinite from which it was drawn? How are we to understand that the final perfection of such finite beings has to be a consolidation of their own being, and not just a disappearance into the abyss of the Infinite, an affirmation of their very being instead of a final negation?

These are questions philosophy must explore, even if it cannot offer any final solution to them by itself, because the human spirit's own sense of responsibility for its own being has to come into play in any solution to this problem of a final perfection in being. Created as a free and rational spirit, the person cannot be raised or rise to any higher perfection in its being without its willful consent. It has to enter willfully into the solution of its own problem because, as Blondel will show, that is a condition for the consolidation of its own being, precisely as finite or as other than the Infinite. It is what makes for all the drama in the final reconciliation of beings and Being, as well as for the possibility of there being two very different issues for this drama, one that is fulfilling and consolidating for the finite spirit and the other that is absolutely frustrating for a being that does not cease to be.

Blondel begins by speaking of an initial ontological solidification of beings, a certain substantial realization of things in the universe as a whole, stemming from the divine initiative in creating. This includes the cooperation of personal beings who not only bring their own orientation to the realization of the design, but also gather all things into an order of their own making as a community. "Faithful to the norms that sustain them from within, that order them among themselves and subordinate them to the principle of truth and goodness whence they proceed and to which they tend, such beings, each according to what is from itself and all according to what composes them into a total harmony, organize themselves, edify one another, confirm one another and deploy themselves as if in the infinite solidity of the God who has called them to the dignity of being themselves beings in the divine Being, who has become in a way their cement, their armature, their form, their indefectibility" (1935, 289-90). This is the perspective one gets from thinking of the world of human spirit or of history as created by the absolute perfect Being in itself.

Such a perspective, however, entails a consciousness of certain paradoxes in the relation between finite spirits and the Infinite Spirit that must be elucidated. On the one hand, there is an irreducible metaphysical incommensurability between Being in itself and beings in becoming that assures absolutely a distinction not to be glossed over, between the necessary and the contingent, between the perfect and the finite. On the other hand, there is a freedom, on the side of the origin of all good, to raise to itself these inchoate beings, or to bring them to a perfection that they would be incapable of by themselves, without lowering itself into them and without sublimating them or making their proper nature vanish along with their originality and their power to enjoy a beatitude of their own. These are not opposing aspects of the relation between finite spirits and the Infinite Spirit, but mutually reinforcing necessities in any spirit, and in the fundamental option that opens up for any finite spirit in the presence of the Infinite.

It is reasonable to think of the world and of the nature of finite spirits as having a certain consistency of their own even as we think of them as still yearning for a fulfillment of their own. Such a consistency is conceivable without the implication of any internal necessity or any justified claim for an additional intervention from the infinite Spirit, without which a complete perfection could not come to be. It is still rational to think of a finite spirit as really incomplete, and as in motion toward its own perfection. Blondel suggests the mathematical image of an asymptotic line in nature that can go on indefinitely, without ever attaining the true infinite and yet without ceasing to be a curve with properties of its own that make it an intelligible object still. What he wants to focus on, in the finite spirit as this sort of object tending toward the Infinite, is its own power of choosing for or against what would bring it to its own perfection, and the consequences that follow necessarily from either accepting to be elevated, in fidelity to its own true aspiration, or refusing what would be an additional gift, and finding itself totally frustrated in its very being.

Blondel maintains that there is a positive ontological value to the practice of virtues according to the norms of science and duty, even when this entails sacrificing passing inclinations to one side or another, without any mercenary intentions or any ulterior ambition surpassing the order of truth and rectitude we come to as finite spirits. "For there is really more being in the option in keeping with the norm, even if it is not crowned with a final triumph, than in letting go evasively toward the incoherent concupiscences of passionate attractions" (1935, 293). Even for people of conscience, who do not know how to attach their own sense of obligation to metaphysically established causes or to transcendent ends, or who do not will to do so, there is still a realist value for moral choosing in the light of principles that they perceive as in a dark night, and there is a loss of value for those who refuse the norm and choose contrary to it.

But Blondel wants to say more than this about the spiritual élan that moves us. There would be no conscience or consciousness, no occasion for deliberation and choice, not even any notion of an immanent order or of transitory realities, if there were not a sense of the infinite to illuminate and to penetrate interiorly any spirit capable of reflection and choice, a sense that already bears it toward the unique and supreme object of its aspiration. "There is thus an infinite virtuality in every spiritual élan, but what makes for the tragic grandeur of the destiny in which all these spirits must cooperate is that, to respect free choice, to open the way to merit and to have the rational creature contribute to the Creator's design, the infinite takes on the aspect of a finite end among other possible objects of election, while passion ordinarily paints its covetous desires with the prestige of an incomparable beauty, a joy and a fictive infinitude" (1935, 294). It is from such a mixture of the infinite with the finite that deliberate human action has its origins, as he had explained in the original dissertation on *Action*. Here he wants to make the point that the same kind of disciplined and even sacrificial action constitutes a veritable ontological experimentation. It builds up imperishable being in what is perishable. It incarnates the universal and the infinite in existences that are singularized and yet indestructible. It communicates eternal meaning to what is otherwise only temporal.

From this we see the immense responsibility of one who would will the finite infinitely, and thereby realize within oneself and within the universal community only disorder. Such a being already bears within itself what condemns it to perdition. As far as its election is concerned, it destroys within itself the reason for its existence, the end toward which it was tending normatively in its initial and ineradicable sincerity, even though this finite spirit does not thereby destroy its very being or annihilate itself. It only sets itself up to be in contradiction with itself, to be deprived of the perfection it yearns for most fundamentally, no matter what that perfection might turn out to be as willed by the Creator. This is the normative rigor Blondel has found in the logic of beings that is so much more complex than a dialectic of concepts. "Beings do not eliminate themselves as if they were mistakes, even when they are mistaken or tend to destroy themselves in order not to fulfill the conditions of their own genesis" (1935, 295-96). They continue to subsist, even to the point where it would have been better for them not to be, or where, irretrievably indebted in the way they have exercised their power to be or make themselves be, they see themselves as deprived of what they should have had or been, of what they do not have and are no longer. To justify this view Blondel has had only to tie his concrete ontology into the dynamism of a finite spiritual life powered by an infinite desire.

But that is only one side of what can happen in the life of a finite spirit, the negative side or the side of depravation. There is also a positive side to be considered, or the side of possession, which remains wide open or infinite for reason to enter into. Blondel turns toward this side in his normative logic of finite beings by raising the question of such a wide dissymmetry between two outcomes that are so logically tied together for the finite spiritual being. On the one hand, we can know absolutely, so to speak, the negative consequence of willing only the finite with our infinite power of willing. On the other hand, we do not know positively all that would be entailed in our willing the infinite infinitely, by sacrificing our finitude, because we do not have any direct access to the will of the Infinite or to what he makes accessible to us for our ultimate perfection in being. We can only hypothesize about that, but for Blondel we have to hypothesize rationally about it, in keeping with the norm that commands all the genesis of beings we have seen, and that does not abandon us at this decisive moment concerning a final solution to the question of what we are to be.

The paradox in which we find ourselves at this supreme moment of our existence, as Blondel has argued most of his philosophical life, here in his ontology as well as in his philosophy of action and his philosophy of thought, is that, as spiritual beings we tend toward a union with a supreme object that is infinite and toward a perfect unity in our own being, on the one hand, and that, on the other hand, we find ourselves radically incapable of fulfilling this aspiration by ourselves, an incapacity that does not suppress the aspiration but that leaves us in suspense as to what is to be the final determination of our being. It is the misuse of this aspiration, which is a precondition for the very infinity of our consciousness in the exercise of free choice, that explains the gravity of the failures of a spiritual being that lets itself go, as it engages a superior force with all those of a lower nature. But it is the good use of this same aspiration that can open the way toward an acceptance of a more positive solution to our quandary about what we are to be ultimately. And that is what Blondel wants to concentrate on here in this final moment of his concrete normative ontology, knowing that he has to thread a very fine line between pushing his philosophy to the limit of its rational aspirations, where it encounters religion, and overstepping this limit by replacing religion with his concept of infinity, or trespassing into a realm of theology where he says he cannot go as a philosopher, the line that distinguishes the supernatural from the natural as it unites them in the concrete.

Blondel has come to this line only philosophically, although as a believer he is well aware of many things on the other side of that line, things that he intends to explore philosophically later on in his work of *Philosophy and the Christian Spirit*. Here, in his normative ontology of beings and of Being, however, he wants to remain strictly on the side of philosophy, in a rational account of the dilemma in which the finite spirit finds itself, in the face of an Infinite it aspires to but cannot attain on its own. It might be tempting to settle for some abstract attainability, or a willingness to remain unsatisfied as the noble end of an aspiration that gives rise to the insatiable drive found in science, art, and human civilization, as if we could transpose the spiritual élan that urges us toward the Infinite to a never-ending horizontal series of conquests over nature. But Blondel will not settle for that. He wants to remain focused on the vertical transcendent Being we aspire to as spiritual beings as the true End, even if it remains unattainable. Even if we take this to be only a disposition of good faith and good will on our part, he sees in it already what we can call "a virtual participation, a spiritual attitude that makes up in a certain fashion for the metaphysical unattainability, thus allowing, for rational beings, a connection that can be said to be really, albeit imperfectly, ontological to God" (1935, 299).

Two errors are to be avoided here, which Blondel was not as careful to point out in his earlier formulations of this argument. The first would be to make the existence of finite beings contingent on an elevation to something higher than their proper nature, as if the world could not have been left in a state of pure nature. The other would be to think that what is metaphysically unattainable could not be made attainable by a free and gratuitous invention or re-creation on the part of a charity that is almighty. The question here is no longer one of necessary and undeniable truths. The question is one of a communication through grace that leaves open the abyss between the created and the uncreated, but creates a bridge over these unfathomable depths. It is not Blondel's intention here in his ontology to explore what might be entailed in such a solution to the problem of unattainability, if it is offered in fact and discernible by reason. It is enough for this ontology to follow the movement in the dialectic of being and to examine what results from this dialectic, so as to enunciate the problems to which the ontological normative has led, without going into the questions of fact or of faith that are of an other order.

The problem is to determine what should be our spiritual attitude with regard to this final alternative to which we are led in this dialectic of finite beings.

What is it rational and reasonable to consider at this point of ultimate bifurcation in our being? "How are we to understand that a natural desire of reason should remain inefficacious and unsatisfied, especially when this élan of our intelligence toward a universal and infinite object turns into an obligation to aim at the absolute Perfection, thereby subordinating and, if need be, sacrificing everything else, and when, failing to submit to this truth and this desire, spirits, which cannot be annihilated, 'lose' their being?" (1935, 300). Given the place of spiritual beings in the entire order of the created universe, and the role they have to play in this universe, the being of the universe is at stake in this question, since it is through the finite spiritual beings that all other beings are effectively tied back to their Creator as to their Perfection. Is it possible that this entire order of contingent beings could acquire a higher order of solidity in their being, a higher degree of being and perfection that would make them less unworthy of the Cause? And if so, under what conditions could it be acquired on the part of the creature or the finite spirit?

At this point Blondel is interested in clarifying the notion of a supernatural gift that would come as a complement to our nature, which is the gift we already have from the Creator, and as a way of bringing our being to the Perfection we aspire to in our spiritual élan. Reason cannot penetrate into what such a gift would be, on the grounds that, *ex hypothesi,* such a supernatural gift would surpass anything we have by nature, which reason can penetrate, in striving for the perfection of our being. But it is a supposition philosophy can make some sense of, as it relates to our nature and to the destiny that the ontological normative of beings places before us. To make this clear Blondel speaks in terms of two hypotheses that seem to present themselves at this moment we have come to, in the acquired momentum and concentrated force of beings reaching for their perfection, one that would remain in the realm of the natural, and the other that would suppose something supernatural, but as fulfilling something divine we aspire to naturally without having the power of achieving it in our nature alone.

If we are unable to let go of a more elevated sense of our destiny, a religious need, a cult of God, an homage our finitude has to pay to infinite Perfection, and if we are unable to satisfy this higher elevated sense on our own, can we still make rational sense of it on the supposition that no further gift is offered that would enable us to satisfy it? Would it still be worth the price of creation to have spirits that remain radically unsatisfied in the very orientation of their being? Yes, Blondel says, if we think of the noble élan that makes us feel this lack of satisfaction, that which sustains and renews the generous search of spirits who do not find but who draw ever closer to the divine mystery. "The beauty of such an attitude in spirits animated with a humble disinterestedness in the pursuit of truth could already constitute the true bond, the ideal attraction, which, according to the Peripatetic doctrine, lifts and suspends the entire universe to the unmoved and impassible Mover. We see in this how inadequate it is to say the natural desire spirits have for their divine end is inoperative and sterile" (1935, 303). Even the movement of civilization and the achievement of any good in history depend on this desire for the divine, as does the sense of obligation and of a cult that is due to something greater than ourselves, an Infinite. Far from minimizing the realism of nature, the principles of reason, or the normal order of created finite beings, in his concern about a supernatural end Blondel wants to go to the deepest desire of the given nature of finite spirits as to what is most real about them. If that natural desire were to remain unfulfilled for finite spirits, it would still be a way for them to fulfill themselves to tend endlessly toward the One who invites them to recognize his incommunicable secret. In fact, Blondel insists, the attitude of the finite spirit he is describing is one that reason would have to acknowledge as necessary for itself, even if it were not destined to a higher end, an attitude that it has to maintain under any circumstance, and that must therefore keep it in a disposition of dependence and humility even in its highest achievement on the world-historical stage.

The second hypothesis, however, is the one Blondel is more interested in, and the one that presents more speculative problems in itself for philosophy as well as in comparison with the first hypothesis. This is in effect the hypothesis of a supernatural gift that will enable natural reason or the finite spirit to actualize the final perfection of its being in union with infinite perfection of Being in itself. This entails a gift of grace, over and above the gift of reason itself, that would unite reason itself to its Creator, in a way that does not destroy reason, but that rather enables it to actually achieve the perfection it can only aspire to on its own. Such a conception would not contradict reason in any way, nor any religious aspiration, nor the spiritual attitude we have just defined as normal and natural. It would correspond to the twofold exigency of not collapsing finite beings into Being and of extending to finite beings the benefit of a solidity that can only come from Being in itself.

To be sure, nothing in such an order of liberality and grace, which would complete without contradicting the order of nature and of reason alone, could be postulated, much less required, estimated, or defined by a purely philosophical reason in the absence of any divine teaching or any historical data, but just thinking of such a hypothesis as legitimate or even as rationally normal is enough to shed new light on the sense of beings as they approach the steep incline that goes up to the inaccessible Being. Even if we insist on the incapacity of finite spirits to scale the heights of this incline, we can glimpse "how the incipient beings, which, without this support from the cliff, would remain fluid and forever incomplete, can be consolidated and arrive at what is the place for spirits, their *ubi*, and, according to the Augustinian expression, their form and their consistency.

This is the consistency we are looking for as finite spirits that Blondel spoke of as the problem that remains to be resolved at this highest level of spiritual life, a divine consistency, access to which would result in an ontological solidity to the whole of creation. Solidity is the term he uses in contrast to the fluidity of beings and spirits as they are found in the universe, a solidity where the contingent and the singular do not cease to be themselves, but where they enter into communion with the plan for the whole and bear within themselves the total value of the universe. Note that this solidity is expressed with reference to the universe and not with reference to the mystery of God himself, which remains inexhaustible for any created being, spiritual as well as material. Reason alone cannot fathom how such a consolidation would take place or come about for created beings, but the hypothesis does not contradict reason in any way. Better still, the hypothesis, or this conception of the spirit in a new form and consistency, alone brings a luminous coherence to the whole as it assures a cohesion of all beings among themselves and with their principle and their end.

As good and as fulfilling as this conception of the spirit might appear to reason, however, it does not mean that we are entitled to pounce upon it and to stick by it as if it were ours to choose in affording us a solution that is complete and satisfying to our natural, ontological aspiration. There is more to reaching this solution than merely knowing about it as a possibility. In fact, philosophy alone has no way of entering into this domain directly, which is more one of religious faith than of pure reason. Blondel makes no claim to have arrived at this conception of the spirit purely by a dialectic of ideas. All that he claims is that there is in this conception a rational necessity, "a rational continuity in the concatenation of data that, more or less obscurely, solicits our consciousness and serves as a norm, even an implicit norm, for the spiritual being" (1935, 308). One does not have to suppose that philosophy can replace or supersede religion or faith in following this sequence of ideas. In fact, in showing that the hypothesis in question has to do with something supernatural, Blondel has shown that philosophy cannot do this. Philosophy can only show the necessity of such a hypothetical gift for the spiritual creature, if it is freely and gratuitously offered by the Creator, and show this necessity in the context of having to make a choice, to accept or to reject whatever gift is offered, whether supernatural or merely natural, that is, in keeping with the capacity of reason alone. This is what forces the logic of an integral realism, such as the one Blondel has in mind in the study of being, to extend to what he calls the "supreme conditions of possession or privation that beings can receive from their end" (1935, 309). A complete ontology cannot stop short of a consideration of these alternative conditions that open up before any finite spirit.

XIV

Action as Cooperation with the First Cause

Blondel thought of the three different parts of his Trilogy as representing three distinct problems for philosophy as a whole: the problem of thought, the problem of being, and the problem of action. When we think of all that has gone into his discussion of the problem of thought seeking the perfect equality with itself, and then of the problem of beings seeking equality with the perfect Being in, of, and through itself, it is difficult to imagine what more there could be to discuss as a general problem for philosophy that has not been included under the problems of thought and of being. What more is there to the problem of action that has not already come into the problem of thought or the problem of being? And how is it that this problem deserves equal attention in this systematic elaboration of an integral philosophy, in addition to the problem of thought and the problem of being, as it had been the case in most of modern philosophy? For even where there has been a reference to action in philosophy, it has usually been to consider the multiple aspects of particular facts we apply to the term *action*, rather than to *acting itself (l'agir lui-même)* or, to use the pleonasm Blondel himself indulges in, *the act of acting ("l'acte d'agir")*, as distinct from productions or diverse modes of action. Whatever else other studies may focus on when they speak of action, Blondel wants to go to the heart of the matter, the *acting* itself in any action, in a way that is most precise and most universal at one and the same time, precisely as he has already done for the problem of Thought and the problem of Being. Action, for him, "has to do with a reality that is coextensive to all that is and to all that thinks" (1936, 10). The philosopher cannot ignore it and cannot fail to explore it in all its ramifications, from the lowest to the highest dimensions of the universe, reaching all the way to what we have to think of as a primary pure acting, from which all secondary acting originates.

This is a difficult idea for anyone to take in all at once, but it is what Blondel has in mind as he begins on the third leg of his Trilogy. It is the idea he tries to lay out schematically as he enters into this philosophy of action as a whole. He recognizes that we often speak of action as simply transitive, as a sort of movement that cannot cease without ceasing to be what it is, but he also wants to speak of a certain immanence of action to itself, as in the intimacy of a life that grows and determines itself in its own specific way, something not incompatible with the pure essence of an absolute Acting. He wants to speak of action, not just as an idea that the philosopher has, but as something, in the speculative order as well as in the practical, that "precedes, prepares, nourishes, verifies, enriches and completes thought" (1936, 11). Action, as Blondel understands it, is not just the counterpart of thought. It gives rise to thought and is itself enhanced by thought in a sort of alternating cycloidal upward movement. We cannot leave thought out of action, but neither can we reduce action to thought. Nor can we leave action out of thought, but always think of each one as surpassing the other in their mutual promotion of one another, as they rise to an ever-higher sense of perfection and coincidence with one another. "For action seems on one side to be tied to the evidence of a successive operation that cannot be fixed in a concept without self-contradiction, and on the other side it is affirmed as a transcendent perfection which, above all passivity and all change, appears to be the incommunicable privilege of the absolute Being, the only one we can call pure Act" (1936, 11). From this comes the problem that occupies the entire first volume of this second philosophy of action: to understand how there can be secondary causes active on their own account, or how these contingent agents, coming from the pure Acting, become capable of returning and participating in the pure Acting itself.

Blondel had not raised the philosophical problem of action in these terms up to this point, prior to his systematic works on Thought and Being. In introducing the problem of Action this way, he had, first, to set action off as a distinct universal theme for philosophy to explore, in contradistinction from Thought and Being; and second, to raise the level of discourse in this philosophy of action to that of a metaphysical and ethical science similar to those of the philosophy of Thought and the philosophy of Being. We shall see, in fact, how the order of discourse in the first volume of this expanded philosophy of action closely parallels the order of discourse in the philosophy of beings as they relate to Being, when he comes to discuss the problem of secondary causes in relation to the pure Acting of the first Cause.

But in starting with a metaphysics of action, Blondel was not setting aside his first approach to the philosophy of action, through human acting as we know it in experience. He recalls at the beginning of *Action I* how he first came to the problem of action in philosophy as irreducible to the problem of thought or the problem of knowledge, including the date and time, November 5, 1882, when he first started gathering notes on the theme of action in Aristotle, that is, action as "unifying, supra-discursive and pregnant with infinitude as well as precision and perfection" (1936, 324), something real belonging to "the category of substance, expressing and even realizing and constituting the truth of being that entails a simultaneity of contraries and a unitive convergence, whereas the other categories, by reason of their abstractive and relative character, exclude this conciliating dynamism" (1936, 325). Blondel explains that he never used action in the divisive sense of categories, where Aristotle had originally situated it, but always in a composite sense that is comprehensive and substantialist with reference to the universe as a whole. He had originally thought of action in this way in the context of Leibnizian philosophy, where the idea of a *vinculum substantiale* for the universe of monads had emerged. Here, however, he cites Aquinas to reinforce this comprehensive sense of action as pertaining to the perfection of everything in creation.

For this metaphysical study of action, Blondel proposes what he calls a method of *efference* or of expansiveness reaching out to the totality of things, one that considers acting as a real enrichment, a productive unification through which being completes itself. This is said in contrast to the method of *implication* that he used in his philosophy of thought and of knowledge. It is also said from the standpoint of the agent who must go out of himself and encounter the other, an *afferent*, in his own self-actualization or his own striving for perfection. Action condenses within itself everything that is imposed on the spiritual agent, the arbiter of his own destiny, by the logic of thought, by the normative of being, and by the obligations or the sanctions of a life that comes around only once. It is for the philosophy of action to unpack all this organic growth and all the internal exigencies of action, not just according to its essential structures, open to the discernment of phenomenology, but also, and more importantly, according to the full extent of the unitive initiative of an act with metaphysical ramifications — from the lowest kind of agency in nature, shot through with passivity, to the highest kind of pure acting we can conceive. Even as philosophers, we find ourselves inevitably, as actors, with a necessity and an obligation to cooperate in a drama that surpasses us, but in which we cannot be dispensed from participating. For Blondel, action remains the hinge on which his philosophy turns in the push toward completeness and integrity.

It is with this kind of question that his original philosophy of action had begun: Yes or no, does human life make sense and does the human being have a destiny? I act and I am told that my acts have an eternal bearing on my being, but I do not know what precisely action is or how it places me before the question of my destiny. As a philosopher I must examine critically what action is and how it places me before this responsibility with regard to the completion of my being. The same question remains for Blondel at the end of the Trilogy, after the philosophy of Thought and the philosophy of Being. He intends to return to it in what will be the second volume of this later philosophy of action. But before returning to this more experiential method of exploration of action in its fullest sense, according to its internal principle of willing, he must raise the more speculative question of action in order to arrive at a more formal specification and a more intelligible definition of *acting* in its pure form as well, in contrast to what will turn out to be its secondary form in our experience. Blondel now wants to do a theory of action as a whole as well as a reflection on our own spiritual endeavor to actualize ourselves, in order to open up the full scope of the latter in its metaphysical dimensions, through a proper conception of pure acting.

Action I in the Trilogy will study what essentially constitutes acting in God, and then the action of creatures elevated to the dignity of being causes themselves through cooperating in the achievement of their own destiny. *Action II* will "show how this destiny can and must be accomplished, starting from the humble origins of a good will still unknowing or uncertain about its ways and its final end, and able, by using the universal order as a means to raise itself up to its transcendent goal, to open itself to, or close itself off from, the action that liberates it and gives it the power of actualizing its spiritual acting" (1936, 31-32). The point in this later philosophy of Action will be to study, first, not particular actions, but "the metaphysical possibility, the ontological reality, the dignity of acting," in view of raising these fundamental problems of action under two symmetrical aspects. Blondel will thus express in the Trilogy the metaphysical intent that underlay his study of human action from the beginning, but that he had systematically held in reserve earlier in his first scientific articulation of the phenomenon of action, leaving until the end of his dialectic the question of its necessary being. In this later version of his philosophy of human action, as we shall see, no such methodological reservation will be made in reflecting on how we come to an action of our own, allowing for a fuller conception of action as real from the beginning and letting the rigor of the dialectic work itself out in more realistic, rather than just phenomenological, terms.

In the first part of this metaphysics of action, therefore, the point will be to work out what Blondel calls an *essential* definition of action, a way of specifying it that will confer a real intelligibility to our certitude about a first Cause and about secondary causes. The second part, in *Action II*, will try to go beyond this relatively speculative consideration in order to bring out more of the richness and the lessons that our human action brings, in the concrete, to our knowledge of, and to the sense of obligation, of merit, and of value we have as spiritual beings, as we receive the higher lights and resources of Thought and Being already elaborated upon. The first task, therefore, is to show how the philosophical problem of acting arises from the way we think about acting and action.

The Initial Conception of Essential Acting and Action

Blondel begins his metaphysical study of action in the same way as he did his study of being, by a reflection on the way we speak of acting in action. If we go back to the etymological roots of the word *acting* or *agir*, in Sanskrit, from which the Greek term *agein* and the Latin term *agere* derive, we find an idea of pushing forward and even of leading, an image of moving and propulsion. In French, Blondel adds, the sense of acting, *le sens d'agir*, has turned back and concentrated on itself. Instead of looking only to the deployment or to what results from acting, it looks also to the prior and interior cause from which imperceptibly these various movements and external shifts in direction flow. As a whole, then, our sense of acting expresses "the notion of an internal initiative, both immanent and transitive, the source of which remains invisible and can be suggested only by its effects related back to an intrinsically inaccessible cause" (1936, 37). Hence the necessity of a method of *efference*, to bring us back to the *act* from which action flows.

This is the primordial concept from which the problem of acting arises. It can be taken as a verb and as a substantive. As a verb, *acting* is closely associated with being, and seems to express an *essential* function of any being, which is to act, so that we have to say that whatever does not act *is not*. Nevertheless, there is a distinction to be maintained between the two terms, being and acting, especially in the way we experience the two. Acting seems to suggest intermittent states of being, while being seems to be more comprehensive as a source of diverse and successive initiatives. Yet the relation between the two appears to be *essential*, something for philosophical reflection to contend with.

As a substantive, however, *acting* does not seem to have the same versatility as the substantive *being*, which was shown to play a triple role in the philosophy of Being — that of a verb, that of a proper name for Being in itself, and that of a common name for the plurality of beings. Acting does not lend itself to naming in this way. But it does lend itself to express a proper relation within being, between what a thing is and what a thing does. If acting is taken as an essential function of being, it can be thought of as an excellent way of specifying what is most essential and most vital about being, both with regard to the pure act of the Being in itself and with regard to the inherent initiative of beings endowed with a secondary causality of their own. Taken as a substantive, in contradistinction from the names *act* and *action*, *acting* distils from these words what is most dynamic and what is richest in initiative, in a way that can be expressed both as a proper name for pure Being in itself and as a common name for the plurality of beings in the universe. This is what enables Blondel to state the problem of this first part of his study of Action as "the problem of the secondary causes and the pure acting."

Blondel admits, however, that using *acting* as a substantive rather than just as a verb may be forcing our language too much. To correct against what could be an excess in this abstraction, he maintains the more direct way of speaking about *action* and *act*, which, he says, is engendered by this substantive way of speaking about *acting*. Viewed in this more concrete way, "*action* implies an elaboration, something that is done not from nothing, but from what expresses itself as the truth or the aspiration of a being realizing itself and realizing its proper work, whether it be from the start, or through its own essential initiative, or through multiple operations amid resistances and contentions" (1936, 40). The idea is loaded with ramifications in experience. Blondel wants to insist on three of them in a special way: (1) the indication of a primordial initiating élan as a vital and productive intention, (2) a continuous and progressive series of means used toward an end, where a discursive and complex operation becomes necessary for an action to realize itself, and (3) the result obtained, the work acquired, or the achievement realized in the agent.

In this more complex sense, the term *action* takes us to more than the abstract term Blondel has already begun to think of as *pure act* or *pure acting*, but it does not take anything away from the idea of *pure acting*. It only brings in different aspects to the idea of *acting* that we must discern in the way it realizes itself in our experience, the different kinds of action that a philosophy of action must study in its pursuit of a clearer idea of acting in its purity as well as in its complexity. For it is in the distinction between *acting* and *action* that philosophy finds itself engaged, where we find ourselves torn between a primitive conviction of a pregnant initiative, on the one hand, and on the other a sense of elaboration that is not so immediate, so automatic, or so completely efferent. On the one hand we have in mind an original efficiency that supposes an absolute beginning and an autonomy, such that it is not modified by the recipient in which the action is realized. But on the other hand we have the experience that we do not act without modifying ourselves or without being modified and fashioned by the reactions, the opposition, or the collaboration of forces against which or with which our own initiative deploys itself.

From this follows the further complexity of action that we cannot prescind from in a philosophy of action. For we do not think that there is acting in the proper sense of the term where there is only blind impulse fatally transmitted. There is acting only where the agent, even under the influence of some prior motion, gives evidence of an efficiency that is singularized by the originality of its own being, and its own initiative. For Blondel this kind of initiative is inconceivable among secondary causes, except where there is consciousness and knowledge of where they draw their determination from, and of where their mysterious finality is tending. Yet we do speak of action outside of ourselves and even within ourselves, where this essential condition of consciousness is not realized, not to mention those who think of action as anything but self-conscious. The extension of the idea of action to something outside of consciousness has to be justified and criticized from the standpoint of our first conception of action as something that flows from consciousness and knowledge of how we are influenced, and of what we are aiming at in acting, whether within ourselves or beyond ourselves. What sort of knowledge does real action presuppose concerning these influences from our past and from the ends we are aiming at in our future? Could the spiritual agent exercise its ideal action without the concurrence of subalternate energies and lower stimulations in its consciousness? But at the same time could we think of a spiritual agent acting without implying a real effectiveness and a certain sense of responsibility as a proper cause?

These are the problems that present themselves for Blondel at the beginning of this philosophy of action. They arise from a latent antagonism between "a secret ideal we bear within us of an acting that is pure, free and perfect, and the weaknesses, the promiscuities that subject our liberating élan to passivities that are natural or acquired" (1936, 45). Can we go forward in the study of this tension between an ideal liberation and a real dependency on forces external to consciousness, or do we have to remain in nothing but a constant oscillation between two antagonistic extremes? Clearly, Blondel's aim is to make intelligible this very dynamism of action in the light of what he has already referred to as *pure acting*, where there is no passivity whatsoever and no antagonism to overcome. Recognizing that he cannot start from a simple definition of action, he will proceed by critically examining the concrete ways in which action is commonly spoken of, in order to move toward a more precise and more philosophically technical understanding of both *action* and *acting* in its purest sense. In this he will be following an order similar to the one he followed in his elaboration of the philosophy of Thought and the philosophy of Being, starting from the lower instances where we seem to find a semblance of action, and rising through intermediate instances all the way to the highest and purest form of *acting*, which is that of the pure *Act*.

In Search of an Authentic Action

Action and *acting* are terms used in a wide diversity of senses and attributed to a wide diversity of beings. Like the term *being* itself, they range across the spectrum of the universe in a way that unifies all things at the same time as it recognizes their diversification. The philosophical problem of action, then, as Blondel understands it, is to work toward some conceptual specification of what we mean by action in its most proper sense, and what we mean by it in its *purest* sense, where there is no passivity to be understood. Hence his fundamental question: Where can we find an authentic action? Can we find such an action in physical beings or what we call physical agents, or is this attribution of agency to physical beings merely a metaphor? To answer this question concerning authentic action will result, not only in a process of elimination for what things qualify as truly active, and in what sense they do, but also in an enrichment of our idea of action that we do not have from the beginning of our reflection. Blondel is careful to proceed step by step in this process of enrichment, starting from the lowest kind of agency we seem to find among beings where there is no sign of life, let alone of consciousness. The strategy here is the same as the one he followed in the philosophy of Being and in the philosophy of Thought, where we found a wide-ranging application of basic terms neither purely univocal nor purely equivocal, to the order of things in the universe.

In beginning this search for an authentic action with what are called physical agents, Blondel has in mind both the organic and the inorganic, everything in the order of the universe that falls short of human beings, that is, beings with self-consciousness and a clear sense of exercising an initiative of their own, which is taken by many as a minimum for having an authentic action. Blondel comes at this question wondering whether there is not a certain anthropocentrism in attributing action to merely physical agents lacking in consciousness, or whether we do so only as a sort of metaphor rather than in any scientific sense. Whatever spontaneity we may find in nature, it does not measure up to the kind of initiative we think is proper to human action.

Modern science tends to speak of movement and efficient causality in mechanical terms, with the implication that things in themselves are purely passive transmitters of force or energy, without any addition of their own in the ongoing process. For Blondel, this view calls for a twofold correction, if we are going to think of things as physical agents — one, having to do with how we conceive passivity, and the other, with how we conceive activity. With regard to passivity, we must not think of something as purely passive or static, lacking in any natural movability of its own. When we think of something coming under the influence of another thing already in act, we must think of the recipient as being set in motion according to virtualities of its own. These virtualities are not sufficient to set themselves in motion by themselves, without the influence of another already in act, but they are potentialities in things ordering them to one act or another, a sort of pre-ordination or affinity to certain acts, "without which the causal excitation would be without effect" (1936, 59). Borrowing an expression from Aquinas, Blondel speaks of this potency, even in merely physical things, not only as dynamic, which is another word for potential in the classical sense we are recalling here, but also as obediential, as an ordering in the passive toward a response.

This ordering or this pre-ordination in the potency of physical things, however, or in the responding to physical influences, does not of itself constitute an action in the proper sense of the term. It is still only a potency awaiting the act of the causal agent to set it in motion. But this act of the agent itself must not be understood in purely mechanical terms, as defined in positive sciences. To understand how physical things can be thought of as acting, we must rise to a more metaphysical conception of act as a principle of action. For Blondel this already suggests something about a pure act that would be a universal first cause in all particular agency, such as that of physical things on one another. For the moment, however, he is interested in pursuing the idea of act in physical things only as the jumping-off point for pursuing how there can be secondary causes, even on the physical level of things, without derogation from any primary cause in any and all particular causation. Indeed, to preclude all proper action or causation on the level of physical agency would be to preclude all further investigation into higher forms of action and causation, let alone the highest and the first.

In fact, if we were to think of the physical universe as purely mechanical, and of things as purely inert in the face of a totally extrinsic stimulation, then the use of the term *action* with regard to the elements and the movements of nature would be a misleading metaphor. We would have no way of distinguishing different kinds of things in the dynamic reality of contingent things, and we would be ultimately reduced to a sort of pantheistic monism. If all things are purely passive, if there were no activity of secondary causes in the physical universe, there would be no way of arriving at true principles of explanation and of reality in the process of universal becoming.

For Blondel, this is not the way we view order in the physical universe. We view it more as a progressive integration that goes from automatism in lower, non-living things, to the different degrees of spontaneity in life, and ultimately in consciousness. This implies a certain finality in nature that brings out both "the idea of a progressive genesis and the initial necessity of a supreme end that inserts into the apparent evolution, from the beginning and at every stage, the transcendence of its pure and sovereign acting" (1936, 61-62). But to grasp this finality in nature, one cannot stay with only the two extremes in the way we speak of action, pure acting and sheer deployment of physical forces. One must also take into consideration the many intermediaries we find in the course of our experience.

In doing so, moreover, we must attend not only to the organization that takes place in the dynamism of the physical universe, to what Blondel calls "a noetic order that is as extensive and unitary as possible," but also "to the internal originality that is no less unitive and comprehensive on the part of a singular being that is finite and active, one that is knowingly active" (1936, 63). What emerges from reflection on this sort of causal and singularized initiative among natural agents, amid the give and take they are caught in, is a sense that they are reacting "on one another not just according to the sensible and scientific representation we have of them, but also according to a deeper influence, that of a reciprocal and metaphysical causality" (1936, 63), as if from a higher motion that transcends the entire series of actions and interactions. In other words, to arrive at a proper conception of action in physical things, we must not try to fit them only into purely spatial and temporal images, or into a pure phenomenology. We must view them in an ontological order according to a metaphysical perspective that includes the presence of a creative truth and love.

The conclusion Blondel comes to, then, in this first stage of his inquiry into action, focusing on physical agents, is to say that "on the one hand, there are real and progressive activities in the world of nature, in the physical elements and in living organisms, but that, on the other hand, even as they develop indefinitely their growing complexity and their more than apparent initiative, these secondary causes are nonetheless passive in their origin, relative to an absolute in their coordination, subordinate to a transcendent end that commands and surpasses them" (1936, 65). This, of course, does not mark the end of the inquiry into action, in search of one that is authentic. It is only an opening into another kind of action, one that is more spiritual and conscious of its resources, its means, and its ends. Will this more conscious and spiritual kind of action satisfy the notion of action we have implicitly from the beginning, and the one we try to realize explicitly in all its richness and vigor?

The action that comes to the fore in the opening at the summit of the order of what Blondel speaks of as physical agents is, of course, that of human agents — conscious, not only of the resources they draw on in nature, but also of willing and realizing more or less laboriously goals they envision as desirable. Such action is a new synthesis of all the powers in our nature, where we make these powers our very own as we integrate them into a higher level of personal being. We humanize them, and the world from which they come, as we humanize ourselves. Not only do we assume them into our selves, we also elevate them into the service of ideal ends that we conceive and pursue, at the same time as our action incarnates these ideals in our very reality and in that of the universe, by a sort of re-creation.

This is the idea of action we have as fully conscious human beings, the idea we have in mind as we try to discern what action there is on the level of merely physical agents lacking in consciousness, the idea of a genuinely spiritual action that transcends all the different sorts of physical action and interaction, as it labors to integrate them into its higher unification. We can think of it as a progressive liberation from the passivity of its origins in nature and from the burdens that weigh it down from all sides. But we also have to think of it as entering into a new kind of order determined by ideals, with sanctions of their own. It is not a pure evasion into some indefinite future.

In its purest form, this is action that is fully conscious, characterized by tradition as *actus humanus,* a properly human act. But before going into his exploration of this properly human action, Blondel pauses to examine a realm of action in human beings that is less properly human, but still that of a human being as a thing of nature, what tradition referred to as *actus hominis*. This is a distinction Blondel had recognized and insisted on in approaching his original dissertation on action, to clarify in what sense he was studying action, that is, as *actus humanus* and not merely as *actus hominis* (see 1893a, 121 [116]). But here, in this more speculative study of action, he pauses to speak briefly of action as specifically human even on the level of nature, namely, as an impulse ordered to the highest initiative of spirit in the human being, unlike any other impulse in lower physical agents.

Already in speaking of action and secondary causality on the level of merely natural agents, Blondel had insisted on a certain originality coming from physical agents, even as they reacted to other physical agents, as irreducible to a mere transmission of mechanical impulses, the originality of a certain dynamism, or spontaneity in things, irreducible to a mere determinism. Here, as he comes to human action, Blondel has to insist on an even greater originality and an even higher dynamism introduced by the rational soul, so to speak, into the organism, opening the way to the fully rational *actus humanus*, the fully rational human acts, "to an efficiency that is truly causal and to an acting that is finalist, free and responsible" (1936, 70). This specifically human impulse from human nature as such, is, for Blondel, a link that must not be neglected in the series of conditions indispensable for the advent of a true freedom, in the midst of an enchainment that seems to tie the entire contingent and immanent order of this world to a determinism. If the human body were just another body like other natural agents in the world, a bit more complex perhaps, but still simply caught up in the immanent order or the flow of the visible universe, we would have to think of the human being, body and spirit, as subject to the universal relativity, over which science would supposedly give some relative control. But that is not all there is to human natural impulses, if we think of the organization of the body and the senses as instruments of the spirit, indeed as necessary instruments, wherein are already incarnated requirements, aptitudes, and higher aspirations than in activities and exigencies that are purely animal. "If we were immersed in the moving ocean of phenomena and relations that make the universal flux, the consciousness of an initiative on our part could never emerge. Even science itself cannot begin, except thanks to an aspiration that transcends infinitely the entire domain of relativity in which it maneuvers" (1936, 72).

What this means for Blondel in the search for an authentic action, is that we must now turn to an entirely new order if we are to understand the scope of human action, an order for which the actions of the body are only a preparation, an order of transcendent truths and transcendent ends. When we look into human action, we must see not only a succession or a system of phenomena. We must recognize also a metaphysical reality that is more than just a matter of fact. What we take to be facts are for the most part abstract interpretations of data, a regrouping into partial tendencies, amid a vast array of interferences and interdependencies. "Acting, on the contrary, whatever the ingredients and the conditions of actions, proceeds from an internal unity, from a cause that sets in motion an initiative perduring through its irradiations, and from a finality responding to the *primum movens* animating the entire deployment of the persistent operation" (1936, 74). Blondel has taken some time going through various degrees in his approach to this full conception of human action, but it is now to this degree of action that he turns his attention, to see if it fulfills our implicit conception of a pure acting.

The Human Sphere of Action

Human action, or *actus humanus*, is the degree of action that had been Blondel's main preoccupation in his original dissertation of 1893, but his approach to this sort of action here is not the same as it had been in that earlier study. At that time the question had been whether we can make sense of human action as a whole, or as an engagement with others in the world, with some finality toward an accomplishment of our destiny. He intends to return to this question later on, here in the Trilogy, in the second volume on *Action*, which will deal with *Human Action and the Conditions of Its Fulfillment*. Here, in the first volume on *Action*, he is examining human action as a degree, on a scale that goes from a minimum of initiative intermingled with a lot of passivity to a maximum initiative without any passivity whatsoever. On this scale, human action presents itself as a much higher degree of initiative than the lower forms of action already considered, but still with a measure of passivity, as he is about to show.

He distinguishes three different types of human action, corresponding to the way the Greeks had distinguished between *poiein*, *prattein*, and *theorein*: *making*, *doing*, or *actualizing* humanity in ourselves, and *contemplating* or, as he puts it, "assimilating and . . . acting the most pure act possible for a second cause" (1936, 79). The first is the elementary type of human action that consists in making, fabricating, or working over some matter, the sort of activity that comes from *homo faber*. This includes a wide range of activities, in which we fashion and refashion our world, from working with putty, to sculpting a statue and even "incarnating pure poetry in the precious matter of evocative words and condensed sounds" (1936, 80).

Conscious of the peculiarly human dimension of such initiative taken in the world, Blondel calls it an "idealist fabrication," an animation, a transfiguration, a sublimation of matter, by reworking it into something that will serve human ends. From this characterization of this elementary type of human action, he draws a twofold conclusion, one, concerning dependence, and the other, concerning the beginning of a desired independence. The human being does not fabricate or produce anything without leaning heavily on the forces of matter, and even of words that name and rename the world. It is labor for it, to produce things anew in an upward movement of the human spirit. At the same time, however, this labor, this dependence that conditions all fabrication, would not be conscious, does not come into being or provoke useful efforts without "the idea, the hope, the implicit encouragement of a partial and progressive liberation" (1936, 81). What Blondel had brought out earlier in the sense impulse of the human being was a certain openness to the higher activity of reason. Now he brings out the other side of this openness, the cunning of reason in finding connivances and contriving affinities in matter to suit its purposes. If there were not this hope and this cunning, if all were resistance and brute force, there would be no practical initiative, no delighting in taking action, in short, no consciousness, no science, no aesthetic or moral activity whatsoever.

To this twofold conclusion concerning genuinely productive activity, Blondel adds another important remark. "The ideas that orient us higher are not entirely from ourselves: they bring into us the force of a presence that is truly transcendent" (1936, 82-83). We do not see this immediately in our productive activity. But little by little reflection has to tie back into its true source an initiative that, at first, appears to come only from the obscure depths of our being, but that in fact comes from heights initially hidden. It is the task of a reflective philosophy of action, here, to make the connection between the lower impulses of our spontaneous activity and the higher force of a transcendent presence, and the liberating exigencies action must satisfy in order to become fully itself through the mediation of a middle zone in action that has already been named "doing" or *prattein* by the Greeks, but that Blondel speaks of as *actualizing* humanity in ourselves.

This actualizing of humanity, or humanizing as such, is the second type of human action, which must be distinguished from the first. We can speak of it as humanizing action inasmuch as it remains in ourselves and transforms us as human and as spiritual beings, even as we try to shape and reshape the world around us. There is a certain opposition between the action that strives to reshape the world and the action that strives to reshape the human being according to the exigencies of its own perfection, but there is also an intimate connection between the two, again, a twofold relation that must be explored anew in the context of this study of action according to its varying degrees of purity and impurity. Blondel had already explored this twofold relation in terms of determinism and free choice at great length in a key passage of his dissertation, where he went from the threshold of consciousness to the voluntary operation, by an elaboration on the moment of deliberation that precedes any free initiative on the part of the human being (1893a, 109 [103] ff.). Here he returns to that original insight into how properly human action is conceived as something other than just a passive reaction to physical and animal forces agitating within one's nature. These forces limit what we can and cannot do, but the plurality of them within our consciousness at any one time can also be liberating as they become an occasion for deliberation to intervene, to hold them at bay momentarily, and then to choose which one of them to follow. In other words, the power of reflection appears as a new force amid this plurality of forces vying for attention in our consciousness, where "using the very passivities that seem at first to oppress it, the human agent draws from them the means and the merit of its liberation" (1936, 86).

From this analysis of how human action is conceived in consciousness, Blondel draws four interrelated conclusions. First, there have to be impulses in our nature that evoke needs, desires, and aversions, to set our consciousness in motion. Second, such needs cannot be spontaneously and fully satisfied, so that a further effort is provoked in the agent who remains disappointed and anxious amid the plethora of impulses. Third, the cause and the end of such aspirations inevitably bring into play an intellectual activity that will take over these natural impulses and spontaneous inclinations, with which it is in some accord. Fourth, there has to be a goal or an end proper to the intelligence itself, more or less obscurely defined, but always really distinct from all particular transitive operations, to explain the reflective, deliberate, and voluntary action of the human being. For Blondel, the impulses or motives for action they give rise to are not merely views or theoretical hypotheses about human action. They are integral parts of what is really given in human experience. "If we suppress any phase of this progression, everything falls back into unconsciousness and passivity" (1936, 88).

Of these four implications in the fact of deliberative consciousness in human action, the one that interests Blondel most here is the fourth, the one that points to a metaphysical reality from which human activity seems to draw the idea and the force of its own real agency. The other implications refer back to the human being's capacity for production by appropriation of the forces of nature and by disciplining our faculties, in view of ends that transcend the physical universe and express our spiritual nature. The fourth implication opens the way to a higher vocation on our part in this effort to master nature and ourselves, a consideration of a higher mode of acting to which our more worldly mode is now to be subordinated. What we call our subordinate actions, as we exercise them in history, cannot be confined to the limited objects that occupy them in our day-to-day historical activities. If they were, they would remain deficient and illusory, merely subject to our passions, as Spinoza would claim. The subordinate actions "do not liberate, they are not an *acting* except in the perspective that refers and orders them, at least intentionally, to the supreme end that provisionally we can call an *act* purified of the original passivities and of the ties of passion holding back, skewing, or reversing the forward look and the orientation of man in search of his destiny" (1936, 89). It is to this higher mode of *acting* that Blondel now wants to turn, which traditionally has been called *theorein*, and Blondel now refers to as *contemplative action*.

The question for Blondel here is whether *contemplative action* represents a pure act that would exclude all passivity. This will appear strange to anyone who sees only an opposition between action and contemplation, as if contemplation could not be the highest kind of action of which we are capable, let alone an *acting* of any kind. Maine de Biran, an earlier writer in the French tradition of spiritual philosophy, viewed by many in French philosophy as their Kant, had described the final state of the human personality, coming after the more discursive states of deliberative efforts at building up humanity in ourselves, as a passive quietude, symmetrically analogous and antithetical to the initial passivity of sense immediacy. In opposition to this view of a double passivity, one initial and one final, Blondel finds a twofold failure to see what activity there is at either end of the spectrum. Passivity is never quiet in the order of sensation, not even in its first immediation or in its most rudimentary form. There is always implied some tendency, some motoricity, without which no mediating effort could be conscious or efficacious. Much less is it quiet or inert, in what is called its final state, which would reduce the agent to unconscious inexistence. What Blondel prefers is to characterize this final state as a triumph, harmonizing and unifying all our energies in a sovereign act of perfection and beatitude in possession of what Aristotle called its abiding work, *oikeion ergon*. It is difficult for us to think of this abiding work as a final state for all our striving as human agents, but Blondel marks it as an act of contemplation in which all things come together for us, an act that surpasses any empiricism or didacticism, one that is the culmination of all our discursive actions and our personal lives. We can think of such a supreme act of contemplation as acquired through discursive thought and experimentation, but masters of the spiritual life also speak of it as infused. The problem for the philosopher is to sort out what sort of passivity might still remain in this summit of activity for a human being, and what further idea of an absolutely pure act there might be for us to entertain as something to be assimilated to in the supreme act of our own contemplating.

It is at this highest level of contemplative action that Blondel encounters the most serious objections to any idea of an absolutely pure act, and the most far-reaching attempts to preempt the necessity of affirming any such act as *real*, and as *active*, in a way that no secondary cause or agent, such as we have been considering thus far, including ourselves, could replicate or equal. What he presupposes is that contemplation or speculation in its purest form is still an action, and that it is for the intellectual being the highest form of action attainable, one in which a spiritual being might realize its ultimate perfection and salvation. The question thus becomes for Blondel whether the human being can realize for itself, and by itself, the essential and pure idea of action through some personal contemplation, as one might think happens in a Hegelian science of logic, for example, given the more humble origins of human thought as it comes to us in our experience as makers and as doers in the world.

Blondel wants to envisage this problem at the highest point of human activity, where man seems to triumph over everything, as the stoic sage claims to do, even over God or the *logos*, as he enters into his own kingdom as contemplated. But Blondel does not approach this culmination of human activity without recalling the original dependence and the more pedestrian material to be assimilated, whence this activity has to arise by a transformation of all that is given in our common life by nature, by our sensibility, by the understanding, and even by asceticism itself. Blondel alludes to three ways or three stages traditionally distinguished by masters in the spiritual life: the purgative, the illuminative, and the unitive. He points out that one does not go from one stage to the next without some laborious analytical discourse, followed by a more synthetic grasp of what there is in the concrete and in reality. And when one finally comes to the unitive way, it is never with an adequate grasp of what he calls the ontological and causal unity of our being, or of other beings. "The mystery of acting is not penetrated; and it is by an imperfectly justified extension that contemplation is referred to as a higher form of acting" (1936, 96). In other words, there always remains some degree of passivity even in this highest form of activity for us as spiritual agents, even as we affirm or demonstrate the necessity of a pure *Act*, to which we have no direct access.

Moreover, there always remains some necessity to struggle against this duality of passivity and activity in our nature, another sign of how imperfectly we dominate in our most triumphal activity. Each one, even in the highest moment of contemplative action, always continues to depend not only on his own nature, but also on the social interaction that pulls the being and the action of all together into one. Even in his cell, the pure contemplative is never completely himself and "possesses his soul only by making of it a universal suppliant surrounded by an impenetrable shadow" (1936, 96). We have to recognize that no human contemplation can quite equal the ultimate secret of action and of our destiny.

At this point Blondel is ready to conclude that human action cannot purify and complete itself except to the extent that, while confessing that it is not and cannot be pure acting in itself, it tends toward a principle and an end higher than itself. But as he stands on the brink of such a conclusion, he finds that there have been other forms of contemplation that have stopped short of any such conclusion, using contemplation instead either to enter into the impersonal order of an abstract noeticism, where all action is denied except for that of an absolute substance in which only modes can be distinguished, not *really active beings*, or to settle for an evanescence of all personal being, at the limit, where speculation makes a pretense of coinciding with absolute science and perfect *Acting* in a sort of indeterminate nirvana. Blondel mentions no names as proponents of such doctrines, though it is clear to whom he is alluding. He only identifies them in terms of variations on the theme of monism, where all differences in being and action seem to vanish or, more precisely, are transferred either to the totality of a unique Substance, from which proceeds all force and all modes, or to some indefinite recurrence of universal relativity that appears to make an integrality of becoming, or finally to some vague mysticism, where renouncing all particular activity and all determinations of consciousness turns out to be a melding of both motion and rest in an attitude that would deny all desire and all suffering.

These are three forms of monism Blondel usually has in mind when he makes the case for an absolute transcendence of what we have to think of as pure *Being* or, in the present case, as pure *Acting*. He brings them up now, in this reflection on the action of secondary causes, as it relates to the action of what we have to think of as the primary Cause, no less than as a pure Acting, not just to refute these forms of monism, so that he can pass on to a contemplation of the mystery he says we have to affirm at the summit of our contemplative action, but more properly to show the necessity of having to rise higher, if we are going to be fully rational. He goes into each one of these forms of monism, or immanentism, at some length in order to show how each one is inconsistent with the very rational principle from which it proceeds, as from an action of its own. The lack of consistency shows a lack of rationality on the part of any immanent rationalism or any contemplative action that would claim to capture within itself all that is entailed in the idea of pure *Acting*. Logically, Blondel argues, we are driven back always to some dependence on other factors in our own initiative, to some passivity in our own action, and to the necessity of affirming some first *Act* as the source of our own acting, even in the highest moment of contemplation or speculation. This is the only conclusion that is consistent with the principles we start from in taking any rational initiative, whether as makers, as doers, or as contemplators of truth.

The argument against monism here, which denies real action on the part of secondary causes, and against immanentism, which remains satisfied with an indefinite running on of spirit in becoming or an evanescence of personal action into some sort of nirvana, is similar to the argument used earlier in the Trilogy in the approaches to pure Thinking and to pure Being. Faithful to the scientific method he has followed from the beginning, he examines, criticizes, and eliminates false solutions to the question he is asking, in order to open the way to the one solution he thinks is possible and necessary. If anything, the argument in relation to pure *Acting* is more complete and more decisive than it is in relation to pure Thinking, "because the exigencies of action are such that, if they were not met, nothing, absolutely nothing would subsist, whether as intelligible or as effective" (1936, 117). For Blondel, we come here to the certitude of certitudes: "and, for philosophical reason, the problem of pure acting is the capstone of everything" (1936, 117).

This is not to say, however, that everything falls into a fixed place as we come to this problem. There still remains much obscurity that surrounds it for us. Blondel will speak of it as a mystery, but not in order to settle into a false mysticism he likens to an ideal or a metaphysical suicide, a spiritual attitude that is totally evasive. He thinks of it rather as a new kind of clarity and intelligibility, something profoundly realistic that we must explore as far as we can, even if we cannot approach all by ourselves this new light that is dawning in our consciousness. If at the end of his defense of his dissertation he had resisted being characterized as a mystic, here he is more willing to say that there can be a true mysticism, and that philosophy is not entirely excluded from exploring this realm of truth, even if it is not able to take hold of it completely. He had published a long article on "the problem of mystical life" to that effect in 1925, some ten years earlier, before he lost his sight.

Aporiai on the Triune Mystery of Pure Acting

Thus Blondel launches into the central part of this reflective study of action, titled the "Mystery of Pure Acting: Approaches to the Inaccessible," much as he had launched into what he had called his central sounding on pure Being as one and absolute, transcending all beings and drawing all to Itself. It is for him at this point in the Trilogy as if the central affirmation of the earlier volumes, that of a perfect *Thought* and that of an absolute *Being*, were to remain unintelligible if we cannot conceive a pure *Acting*. "For does not acting imply the image of a transitive operation? And how are we to discover a repose immanent to the very transcendence of an act that would be only act?" (1936, 126). The obscurity of this mystery casts its shadow over the destiny of all other beings, particularly the spiritual agents. "For if action were conceivable only as a perpetual transition and without having the *infinite* itself appear as an end (*une fin*), there would be no way of conceiving of a fulfillment combining consistency, conscience, and an inexhaustibly active vitality" (1936, 124). Blondel sees the whole of his philosophy of Thought and of Being as riding on his philosophy of Acting, and he sees in this philosophy its greatest difficulty of coming to a proper conception of pure Acting even as a mystery inaccessible to pure philosophy.

His strategy then is to face up to all the objections and difficulties that can be brought against the idea and the affirmation of a pure Acting, in the form of *aporiai* once again, as he had done before in the run-up to the idea and the affirmation of an absolute Being, complete and perfect in itself. He formulates ten aporiai that could be construed as obstructions in the passage to the idea and the affirmation of a pure Acting, ranging from the problem of applying the very words *action* and *acting* to God, to whether a true Acting is compatible with the affirmation and the certain reality of absolute and omnipotent Acting. The endeavor is to go from a consideration that begins with how we use language derived from our own conception of action, as we experience it in ourselves and in the world, to a penetration of what is meant and signified by the affirmation of a pure Acting that is real but has to remain mysterious to us. Put in terms of causality, the difficulty comes from trying to understand how action, which in our experience supposes some relation between a productive cause and an effect produced, does not preclude an *acting* in which there is no such duality, no such dependence of an effect on a cause, which would sully the sublime and unique purity one has to preserve with regard to Acting in and through itself.

The dialectic at this point becomes very dense and closely knit. The resolution or the dissolution of one aporia into the next follows all the way up to a final affirmation of a pure Acting, transcending all lower forms of acting, whether physical or spiritual. It begins with a dilemma we find in our own spirit between, on the one hand, our way of conceiving action as a transitive operation that goes out from an agent into the world while at the same time modifying the agent and bringing the latter to some further perfection and, on the other hand, the necessity we find ourselves in, to free acting, especially in its self-conscious self-actualization, from any centrifugal or centripetal movement, and to lock it up, so to speak, within itself. At this level of reflection into our own mode of action, it is our own acting that posits itself as contradicting the very possibility of an act that would have nothing transitive about it. This is what leads many to say that there is no action in God, especially not in the sense that we can speak of a plurality of actions.

But this way of setting up an opposition between action and acting is doubly false for Blondel. It overlooks something he thinks is necessary for the very consciousness of having an action of one's own. "The idea of an imperfect and transitive action does not come to the fore except thanks to an antecedent real idea of an authentic initiative and of an efficient energy" (1936, 132), the very thing that Blondel has taken great pains to make manifest at least in his philosophy of self-conscious agents, if not in merely physical agents as well. It is out of such an antecedent real idea of acting that we come to the consciousness of any real action on our part, even when it is transformative of something outside ourselves. Second, this way of opposing action and acting leaves us with only a pseudo-idea of acting, as if it were a fictitious extrapolation, contrary to what acting really is in our action. Far from being only an extrapolation into some remote territory, the conception of a true acting comes "first in our living thought and it is from experience that we learn the limits of our power and the repressions that come to bear on our *élan* and our insatiable desires" (1936, 132).

The first antinomy between action and acting is therefore false. But overcoming this antinomy brings us to another contradiction within the very idea of "pure acting" as we apply it to something divine. Instead of entering into the mystery of divine acting itself as well as we can, in thought, we fall back into thinking of it only as productive of something *ad extra*, under the name of *first cause*, not as immanent to itself, as if it were impossible to come to it conceptually *in itself* and finding some light in it as such. Blondel notes that *acting, agir*, is not an active verb in the strongest sense of the term. "It is a neuter that does not need to produce or to make something, or to spend itself copiously: to do that is only to agitate oneself, quite the opposite of the interior and rich life acting in its unity, higher than any spatial expression and temporal succession" (1936, 134). We have to think of pure acting as something other than first spending oneself out in a world. But how can we do that positively and intelligently without abandoning all the content we have in the notion of action and acting, from experience? Affirming pure acting as a metaphysical principle for all things, but of which we have no intuition, will not entirely resolve the dilemma for us. For we will find ourselves having to say, on the one hand, that action is not in the agent, but in what receives it, as the Schoolmen used to say *(actio non est in agente, sed in passo)*, or on the other hand, that there is no reality or intelligibility in a *pure cause* if there is no recipient to undergo and realize in itself the acting of the cause deploying itself.

What results from this is not just one, but two *aporiai*, one on the side of saying that action is not in the agent, but in the recipient of it, and the other on the side of saying that there can be no thought of a pure cause unless there is a recipient to undergo its causality. Blondel tackles the latter first, as easier to deal with and as leading to the other, which is more profoundly discomforting, and also more far reaching in its solution. In our experience of action in the world, we find multiple causes acting and interacting, with a mixture of passivity and activity — some things, including our own initiatives, stimulating others and being in turn stimulated by others. There is a constant reciprocity in this cooperation of causes that we have to think of as secondary in relation to what we would think of as the primary cause operating in the whole. From this immanent and contingent order, however, we cannot extrapolate to what comes into question as the primary or the first Cause, as if it were just another particular cause in the universal concatenation. In other words, the idea of an absolutely first Cause is that of one whose acting cannot be conditioned by any of its effects. In fact, these effects of the first Cause, thought of in the plural, would not be anything like the effects we produce ourselves, or that envelop one another around us and within us. It would be a paralogism to argue from the fact of mutual subordination and relative interdependence among agents in our experience against the purity of a first Act in the first Cause.

What we are coming to with the idea of a first Cause is the idea of a *pure acting*, in which the initiative cannot be subordinated to results or to mutual influences due to the imperfect characteristic of secondary causes. The pure acting we are coming to conceive cannot be made subject to the accidental conditions of mixed and transitive actions, as if the latter could determine the intelligible law of a properly perfect Acting that is absolute. We cannot legitimately transfer into the absolute at this juncture what is characteristic of the action and the interaction of secondary causes in our experience. There are a continuity and a certain infinity in the flow of interaction among secondary causes, but it is not the infinity of an *acting* without any passivity whatsoever. What we have to understand is that, even when we think of the actions of the absolutely first cause *as effecting* the immanent order of secondary transitive causes, we cannot think of it as giving up its purity as pure Acting in the absolute. In this regard, even the name of first Cause may be too relative, suggesting we can only think of the pure Act as dependent on its having effects, when in truth it can be pure Acting only as absolute in itself. There is no necessity for such Acting to exteriorize itself in a transitive fashion, or to produce something other than itself, in order to be or to become itself, much less to produce itself as something other than what it is in its absolute identity.

In this regard, Blondel cautions that we should use the name first Cause only with great reservation in speaking of pure Acting. As first and pure Acting it is not subject to any law or order among any secondary causes it might produce, nor does it even produce itself in any proper sense of the term, as we might say a human being produces itself in the expression of its free initiative. Pure Acting is incommensurable to any such necessity that would imply some passivity in what we can only think of as pure Acting. Passivity can be associated only with secondary or transitive causes that produce themselves as they interact with other causes in an immanent order of creativity.

On the other hand, there is the other aporia that flows from the dichotomy we found at the end of the first, namely from the side of saying that action is not in the agent. How are we to rationally conceive an Acting that is supposedly pure, absolute, and transcendent with regard to any becoming and to any solidarity with other agents, without reintroducing into it some human dimensions and some immanence such as those we associate with human relativity and the universal dynamic of nature and spirit? How can we escape from the antinomies in which we go back and forth between the relative and the absolute, the finite and the infinite, the imperfect and the perfect, without verging into the unintelligible and the irrational? Does acting just for the sake of acting, without even the trace of a necessity to actualize oneself, make any rational sense for us? And if so, what sense can we make of it, from the limited and relative perspective in which we find ourselves?

Not satisfied with any answer that would leave us totally in the dark concerning a transcendence that would remain unthinkable and without name, Blondel wishes to push on with this question clearly in mind. Can we think of an absolute transcendence without secretly introducing into it something contradictory to it, some idea of indwelling, some taking hold, some doubling upon oneself, or some immanent determination, or are we left always going back and forth between immanence and transcendence? After having come to the proper idea of pure Acting, it would be a mistake for reason not to push forward into this idea. However, in doing so, can reason avoid reintroducing into it a nature that pure Acting would be submitting to, or a sort of imposed immanence that would close it in upon itself?

This is the fifth aporia Blondel wants to work his way out of. The problem is not just one of playing with words, or of artificially opposing mere abstractions, such as "total transcendence" and "total immanence" to oneself. The problem occurs in any attempt to rationally affirm a totally transcendent being, as it did when Aristotle affirmed the "unmoved mover." He called it "pure Acting" and "Thought thinking Itself" or, more precisely, "Thought of Thought," *noēsis noēseōs,* as if "the divine cycle of transcendence were closed in on itself and this immanence of the transcendent were contained in an absolute and total return of Thought into Thought, quite apart from all things in motion" (1936, 141). This is a conception reason cannot settle for, according to Blondel. Apart from the ambiguity of the very expression "unmoved Mover," there is the difficulty of thinking of a Thought that, after going out of itself, is supposed to return purely and simply to itself, in a sort of absolute knowing or thinking. The line of thinking here may be more Hegelian than just Aristotelian, but, as a way of introducing the intelligible into the divine, it brings us back to the unacceptable aporia of mixing immanence in with transcendence. Similarly the expression "pure Acting," which would seem to bring some correction against introducing this impurity into the Transcendent, falls short and remains ambiguous still, because it brings with it, not merely the ideal intention from which a concrete action flows, but also the entire retinue of operations in which the intention is realized. It could be thought of as referring "to a physical force or an ideal or logical determinism, a *natura naturans* or a *natura naturata,* [so that] its pure act would remain actuation rather than an acting properly speaking. The God we would get thus would have and undergo its nature rather than be itself its being, its life, its acting" (1936, 143). Blondel's solution to this Spinozist aporia is not to abandon the language of pure Act or pure Acting, but to clear up, in a manner that is more rational than anything we have seen so far, this ambiguity, which is still incomprehensible and irrational.

The next two aporiai mark two steps in clearing up this ambiguity surrounding the language of pure Acting, by recalling two of its aspects that should not be overlooked. The first is *thought,* which is always implied in the consciousness and the reality of acting. We do not act or take any initiative without some thought of an end or some goal to be actualized. Acting is always somehow using an ideal force or some consciousness of something to be achieved. There is an integral connection between knowing, willing, and doing, not only in our day-to-day experience as human beings, but also in the highest form of contemplation and the most ideally unified action. At the limit, we have to think of a compenetration of both pure acting and pure thinking. But if we think that, do we not find ourselves in yet two more aporiai? Such an identification, on the one hand, annihilates both pure acting and pure thinking, with acting passing over entirely into knowing and knowing open only to acting, each one disappearing into the other simultaneously, leaving us with no possibility of affirming any sort of personal consciousness or active resourcefulness for a supposedly pure acting and pure thinking. If, on the other hand, we have recourse to what the world of becoming offers us, or to our own actions and thoughts, fraught with all sorts of impurity and passivity, in order to escape from this annihilation of pure acting and pure thinking, are we not falling back on something that is even more obscure in a sort of *petitio principii*, by supposing that our actions and our thoughts are derived from a pure acting that could not subsist except "by manifesting itself through the flow into some shadowy light of a source that remains ever obscure, hypothetical or perhaps unthinkable" (1936, 145)?

For Blondel these questions stretch, to the utmost, the difficulty of understanding how we can affirm a pure Acting that is truly transcendent and intelligible as well as independent of all contingent realities, when we start from a reflection on our own acting and thinking. We use these contingent realities within ourselves, as well as without, as occasions or as grounds for tracing all activity and all consciousness necessarily back to the free and sovereign initiative of some pure Acting, but we have to recognize that they shed no light into the reality of what we are affirming. We remain on the obscure side of a light whose source is even more obscure to us.

There is, however, the other aspect of pure Acting that can be brought out, along with Pure thinking, that Blondel now refers to in the seventh aporia as *uncreated Love*. Blondel has been very patient in getting to this mysterious aspect of the spiritual life or, more exactly at this point, of the pure Spirit itself, but only so that he could enter further into it as a philosopher. To do so he borrows a comparison from Trinitarian theology. He recalls how this analogy has already been worked out in his probing of Being in and through itself, in terms of an immanent life and an eternal generation within its absolute Perfection. The difficulty, as it now stands in this ascending dialectic toward pure Acting, is that we cannot think of such pure Acting without thinking of it as pure Thinking, which leaves us in a sort of speculative no-man's land, caught in a light that would be either emanating from a source that is no more than an unconscious force, or a necessity without reason or soul, or else that would be only reduplicating a light that is intrinsically indeterminate and becomes intelligible only through its reflection, as if from something other than itself. The only way out of this speculative going back and forth where being and thought, intelligibility and intelligence, seem to be irreconcilable in the Absolute, is through another light that filters down from pure Acting as well as pure Thinking, not one that is hypnotic for contemplation, but one of newness of spirit breaking forth, "an action of love and compenetration, thanks to which being and thought are no longer two things that are neither identical, nor extrinsic, nor stagnant, but *really living* by being at once, though differently and in an equally personal fashion in their substantial unity, Omnipotence, omniscient Wisdom, uncreated Charity" (1936, 148).

The names, of course, correspond to the three persons of the Blessed Trinity in Christian theology, the third referring to the Holy Spirit, who is spoken of as proceeding from the Father and the Son. Blondel focuses on this idea of procession as attributable to pure Acting, to bring out its aspect of uncreated Love. From the eternal engendering of the Son from the Father, without succession or change of any kind or without any difference of nature, proceeds the Spirit, not as a going out, but as a reciprocity of the two, by which they are penetrated and unified in a perfect and loving distinction. To complete this concept in its integrality Blondel adds the term he always likes to use in this context, that of a *circumincession*, the way in which the highest action of spirit completes "the intimate 'process' of a pure acting that surpasses infinitely all anthropomorphic objections and all idols that theosophies try to project in the esotericism of initiations that lead to pure indeterminacy" (1936, 148). In fact, it is in the intimate triune Life of Pure Acting that the most perfect kind of *circumincession* is to be found, which is only imperfectly replicated in the lesser spirits we know.

Blondel thus uses the doctrine of procession within the life of the pure Spirit to mark the aspect of pure Loving in pure Acting. This gives him a more complete conception of what there is necessarily in pure Acting. But even that is not an adequate conception of what is essentially a pure coincidence with pure Acting in pure Thinking and pure Loving, as one might think in a supposedly absolute knowing, where all difficulties are resolved and all oppositions are supposedly reconciled. For even in this more complete conception, a further difficulty arises, another aporia presents itself for philosophy to entertain. If acting can be distinguished from thinking, even as we recognize that it uses the resources of thinking, can we say that it proceeds on its own without thinking or that it surpasses thinking altogether? The difficulty appears in purely formal terms at the level of pure acting, but it comes from a way of conceiving action in our own experience, as if it could be divorced from intelligence. For Blondel, this is a misconception of action that he will try to resolve in what follows of this philosophy of action, which will include the action of secondary causes as well as that of the first Cause, but he thinks it must first be set aside with regard to the very first principle of all acting. To insist on the originality of action is not to set it outside of thought, as if thought were only a contour of action, a way of channeling it one way or another, leaving out much of its force and energy and vitality. On the contrary, thought opens new ways for initiative in action, as it learns from what is effected through these initiatives. "This discursive history of human actions with their reciprocal causality cannot be what it is, unless the first and constant initiative dominates from the start and encompasses the entire series [of means] through more or less confused prospection of the end to be attained" (1936, 149).

The truth of this is all the more certain and necessary when we consider the absolute Acting whose internal *circumincession* has already been suggested as a triple acting within a perfect unity. The diverse operation of this pure and unique Acting entails no division, no isolation, no becoming, no dependence whether internal or external. This is the kind of Acting we implicitly refer to in our own acting, "a transcendent notion of initiative, without which would disappear and become impossible all consciousness, not only of our own power, but also of our being, of other agents, of all knowledge and all perception" (1936, 150). Blondel always distinguishes these different aspects of action and consciousness, including the relation of the immanent to the transcendent, or of the finite to the infinite, only to tie them all the more closely together into one, in his rational discourse. His study of action does not take him outside the realm of Thought or the realm of Being and beings. It serves rather as a complement to these studies to bind them together as a way of explaining and realizing all these aspects of an integral philosophy, by manifesting its coherence and its dynamism.

The insistence on the complement of action for this integral philosophy, however, brings up one more difficulty that could undermine this entire philosophy, if it were unduly considered as a subordination of thought to an impulse that is initially blind and that, after crossing the luminous zone of consciousness, only plunges all acting into the obscurity of a terminal monism, like a firework that flashes for a moment out of the darkness only to fall back into the darkest of nights. This is one more aporia that Blondel must work his way through to keep his philosophy properly oriented on a truly infinite pure Act. "Could it be that the notion and the reality of an absolute acting came from an occult influence of the universe whose empire would be deemed absolutely unconditioned, under the pretext that it synthesizes all the integrated conditions in the totality of reality?" (1936, 154).

The question, and the presupposition it conveys, could be understood as coming from many quarters in philosophy, whether from a conception of total determinism in the universe, with consciousness appearing only as a momentary epiphenomenon, or from a conception of determinism within consciousness itself, both psychological and social, where human beings are seen as acting completely under the influence of infra- or extra-personal impulses, no matter how conscious and free they appear to be in choosing their own ways. On the whole, it suggests a mystical view of action as coming from below a threshold of clear consciousness and as exceeding any of the calculations that deliberative reason can fathom. But Blondel will have none of this belittling of the moment of consciousness and of rational prospection in human action as a whole. Whatever can be said for a primitive force that moves the universe, or for individual impulses that surge within the field of consciousness prior to any sort of deliberation or choice, there remains the argument made earlier in this ascending dialectic of action for the originality of consciousness itself as a force for an ever-new initiative and as a power to grasp the ideal ordering of the universe, in which consciousness is called to play a role of its own. It is from this original and originating dimension of rational consciousness that even the arguments for some universal infra- and supra-conscious determinism draw their strength. Without insisting on the transcendent aspect that this dimension takes on at this point of the dialectic, Blondel simply calls back or vindicates the permanent truth it entails, even in the deviation that would consign it to some blind force, no matter how progressive it might be judged to be. Even the idea of progress implies a logic of spiritual ascent that cannot be confined to a purely naturalistic conception of action.

Blondel speaks of doctrines that advance this darkness or this nihilism of the beyond in action as unstable, inconsequential, and deceiving. They have "the fundamental incoherence of theses one would like to construct in the place of a transcending order, under the guise of an immanentism that abuses the very term 'pure Act' in order to canonize negations and violations" (1936, 153). They set aside the role of conscious thought in order to latch on to that of a purely vital or gregarious élan, an *élan vital* or an *élan social*, while keeping "the idea of an orientation and a value, to the point of constituting a sort of axiology and theory of progress with respect to human tropisms valued with reference to an ideal and finalist term" (1936, 154). There is no proper logic in this nihilistic attitude, according to Blondel. The only thing that is logical is to keep in mind for consciousness a principle of judgment and of ideal finality, even if we cannot fully represent what such a principle might be. In short, our personal acting does not simply annihilate itself, nor is it sufficient unto itself in its dependence on a pure Acting. Nor can it be confused with pure Acting, even though it finds in it its principle and its end.

At this point we come to Blondel's tenth and final aporia, the supreme difficulty that arises, not from below but from above and from the unique sovereignty of a pure Acting. Even if it is not a lower nature weighing on us, it is not the divine who alone is the agent in all things. If it were the sole agent, how could it allow us or confer upon us a genuine activity? "How is a true activity on our part compatible with the affirmation and the certain reality of the absolute and omnipotent Acting?" (1936, 155). This aporia is similar to the one Blondel had come up against in his probing into the absoluteness of the Being that is perfect in and through itself. "Can Being, must Being be affirmed as compatible with other beings and as creator?" (1935, 199). This is the aporia that Spinoza and Hegel try to finesse in their talk about the absolute, by fudging about the ontological status of individual persons or finite spirits in an Ethic or a Logic supposedly of the absolute, but that falls short of a proper conception of the Absolute, whether as pure Being in and through itself or as pure Acting in a totally self-contained life, without motion and without dependence of any kind, not even that of having to go out of itself in order to return into itself as absolute. Blondel is trying to be as clear as possible about both the infinite Being outside of which there is nothing and the finite being that has a standing of its own, not outside of the infinite, but within it somehow, and yet with an identity and an activity of its own. This is the very precise notion of *creation* he wants to talk about, not only in terms of *being*, as he has done already, but now in terms of *acting*, where the problem is to conceive how there can be a secondary cause acting in the universe, even though there is already such an omnipotent universal primary cause at the origin of all activity. It is the central aporia of this entire study of action that must now open the way to a more existential study of human action in particular. For if Blondel cannot resolve this dilemma about a true creation of finite spirits or a true acting on the part of human beings, there would be no way of rationally justifying the study of any other action than that of pure Acting.

The task of resolving this dilemma, however, is not just a matter of a few pages so that one can then go further into something else. Blondel has taken a long time to get to this precise aporia. He now intends to dwell on it at some length. "To tell the truth, it will take all the rest of this work to elucidate the very terms of this problem that sums up and rises above all the others for us" (1936, 155). What he proposes to do, therefore, without presuming to "shed a complete light on the very depth of a mystery where the infinite comes into play," is first to gather together all the convergent aspects of action that can shed some light on our affirmation of pure Acting, "something absolutely real and transcendent to all manifestations of secondary activity that are for us the contingent occasion for our necessary certitudes," and then in a second moment, "according to what this higher inquiry will have shown us, to try to give an account of the possible functioning and of the real efficiency of second causes under the divine action" (1936, 156). Much as he had done in the volume on *Being and Beings*, Blondel begins by honing what can be said dialectically about a mystery of pure *Acting* that remains unviolated by our probing, and then he proceeds to show how second causes have access to the first Cause, and how their actions get specified as their own, at least in the case of spiritual agents.

The Immanent Life of the Totally Transcendent Pure Acting

Blondel's approach to any question concerning the totally Transcendent is always one of cautious conceptual daring, desirous to push philosophy to the fullness of its task in examining such questions. We have seen how far this can go in connection with the questions of pure Thinking Thought thinking itself, and of absolute Being in and through itself. But we should also keep in mind that it was a mark of his thinking from the beginning, in the original philosophy of the supernatural of his dissertation on action and in the discourse on method of 1896.

Here, in this approach to pure Acting as totally transcendent, Blondel thinks he has come as far as philosophy can go into the mystery that remains impenetrable at its core for philosophy. Still, action is for him a handle he did not have with *thinking* or with *being,* for dealing with the totally Transcendent as something that is not inert or static. It is a concept that is about to lead him more deeply into the mystery of a transcendent life, and yet it is one that recognizes shortcomings within itself for conceiving clearly and distinctly all that is implied in a pure Acting that is utterly free of any passivity antecedently or subsequently to its acting, or which is totally immanent in its very transcendence.

At this point Blondel is well aware that he must sharpen his method even more carefully than it has been up to now. To get to this point of scrutiny into the very act of pure Acting, he has run through a number of aporiai as a preliminary effort to bring the focus of attention on what he refers to as "the real problem of Acting" (1936, 124). This was for him like going through a number of problems we have to resolve just to conceive the real problem of pure Acting, like running through an interplay of lights and shadows that surround the mystery he was leading up to. As he prepares to enter into the mystery itself, he is aware that he cannot leave it simply as a black hole, without any light of its own for the philosophic spirit trying to come to terms with it. We must not "remain in the black night of a complete indetermination in the face of [this] inviolable secret" (1936, 162). There is more light to be drawn from it regarding *acting* than we have already seen in getting this far into the problem. Even if we cannot say that we will ever dissolve the mysterious aspect of this totally transcendent pure Acting altogether, we cannot abdicate our task as philosophers to inquire as far as we can into this light that seemingly blinds us. There is a certain discretion of certitude and humility to be maintained that Blondel will not deny. But it is also indispensable "to overcome any agnostic discouragement or any collapse into a mute and formless indetermination" (1936, 164).

Going forward, however, will require tightening up the philosophic method, so that it can advance as deeply as it can rationally into the conception of pure Acting, while recognizing that it cannot close in on its inviolable mystery even as revealed in the Christian teaching on the triune God. Ever cautious about transgressing into a domain reserved for and by a supernatural theology, he falls back on the use of "two traditional methods: a way of elimination or negation and a way of affirmation and analogy" (1936, 162). But true to the reproaches he had made repeatedly in the past concerning the way these methods have been used by those who keep them separate from one another, he adds that it is not enough to juxtapose, much less to oppose these methods. They can and must be used jointly to counterbalance one another, so as to prevent falling from the tightrope of reason, either by presumption on a false light or by abdication and giving in to confusion in the dark of night. Blondel has the image of the tightrope walker with his long balancing pole to keep him centered, and to keep him from leaning too far to one side or to the other in his walk over the abyss. Taken by itself, neither side of the pole, neither method, can yield a sufficient expression for the Acting we are trying to enter into. Each one needs correction from the other. But together in the proper balance with one another they can keep us surefooted in a direction that keeps us in line with the truth and the light that beckons from the Infinite. If Blondel is willing to fall back on those traditional methods, it is not in the way that they have typically been used on either side of the rational tightrope. What he will do is work through a series of couplings of an affirmation and a negation, where the affirmation has to be purified of all undue limitations and the negation compensates for what is lacking in the affirmation, as it stimulates reason toward a higher conception of what may be involved in pure Acting as such.

Starting, then, from the formula of *pure Act* that we have from the Aristotelian tradition, to speak of the divine infinitude, Blondel proceeds to examine what is to be included with that formula and what has to be eliminated from it, since the one it designates is not an idol or a mummy, or some anthropomorphic idea or a mere intellectual category. The term *act* presents both an advantage and a disadvantage for speaking of the one Blondel has already designated as a Thought of Thought, *noēsis noēseōs*, and as Being in and through itself. "On the one hand, it has the merit of suggesting something spiritual, immediate and superior to our discursive efforts and to the resistances that often retard, embarrass and complicate our action" (1936, 168). In this sense it seems to fit what we have to think of as the intimate decision of a pure Spirit for whom there is no resistance and no delay in realizing all that it wills in an instant. "On the other hand, however, the word has the disadvantage of being derived from the past passive participle of *agere*, *actus* or *actum*, thereby suggesting the idea of a result that is reached rather than a living initiative" (1936, 169). In other words, when applied to the initial acting, the term *act*, as something that has been actuated or that is now in act and no longer in potency, seems to take away from the purity of Acting we wish to affirm, by introducing a certain passivity into it.

At best the term *act* remains equivocal when applied to what we affirm as divine Acting, and at worst it could convey the wrong idea of what such acting is. A similar shortcoming had been pointed out earlier by Aquinas with another term that is frequently applied to God in the Aristotelian tradition, *perfect* or *perfectum*, which is also derived from a past passive participle, this time from the verb *perficere* or simply *facere* without the prefix, rather than from the verb *agere*. *Facere* is the verb for *making* in Latin, or *poiein* in Greek, and in the passive, *fieri*, it is the verb for *becoming* or for *being made, factum*. As past passive participle in the infinitive, it is *factum esse* or, with the prefix, *perfectum esse*, meaning something that has come to the completion of its coming to be or has reached its perfection. Now when we attribute perfection to God, or speak of him as most perfect or absolutely perfect, we do not speak of him as having come by his perfection in any way, out of any sort of imperfection, as the etymological origin of the term would suggest. Strictly speaking, as Aquinas put it in his *Summa Contra Gentiles*, I, c.28, "what has not been made *(non factum est)* cannot be said to have been perfected *(perfectum esse)*."

Blondel is trying to make a similar point about the Latin verb for doing, *agere*, or *prattein* in Greek, when it is used as a past passive participle. Put in the infinitive as *actum esse*, it suggests that something has come to its actuality from some potency or other. And this cannot be said of God, or of pure Acting in the strictest sense.

What this means for Blondel is that we must look more deeply into acting as an active intransitive verb or, essentially, as a "perfect immanence at the heart of absolute transcendence" (1936, 170). At least that is what we should be thinking as something positive when we speak of *pure Acting*. To reinforce this idea Blondel cites the medieval adage, which said (1) that acting, even when it produces an effect, is not passive of what it effects, and (2) that the modification is in the patient, not in the agent. More qualifications will have to be introduced into the use of this formula, but Blondel sees in it a rigorous translation of "the simple and perfect idea of the absolute Acting, in which no passivity is imposed by any rebound on the pure Agent" (1936, 170).

With this purified idea of pure Acting, however, we must not be deceived into thinking that we have grasped pure Acting absolutely, as some modern philosophers such as Hegel would seem to suggest. To the extent that this idea of pure acting begins to make sense for us, on the basis of our human experiences, and on the basis of our own directed but derived causality, it remains fraught with a residue of perhaps presumptuous obscurity. No matter how much we try to deny it, our notion of acting seems to imply for us certain dependencies that we cannot overcome, and that we must keep the first Cause free of any such dependency in our thinking, lest we fall into what Blondel calls "fallacious obsessions" (1936, 170). Acting for us suggests a goal to be attained, and a productive operation, coming from and for the sake of something that is not yet. The initial agent is thus made to seem as if it "somehow goes out of itself, even if it be to better enter into itself, undoubtedly for some gain (but a gain that supposes an original need), and with some shock on the rebound that makes it appear as passive, happily passive perhaps, but to some degree dependent on the operation from which it profits" (1936, 171). For some in modern philosophy, this might seem a sufficient way of characterizing the absolute or divine Acting, but true to his determination to pursue superstition under any form, no matter how philosophically sophisticated, Blondel will not settle for this sort of temporizing about the Absolute or the divine Acting.

One could conclude from this renewed affirmation of the total transcendence of the divine Acting in its eternal immanence, that we are reduced to a metaphysical silence concerning this absolute Acting. Religion and faith in the supernatural have often been invoked to reduce philosophy to such silence, lest it trouble the faith of true believers. But there has always remained a tradition of speaking about attributes and names for this God, to express some of the light we still have about him and to give further access into his intelligibility. These are names and attributes that cannot be understood independently of one another as they apply to God. Through bringing them together from the standpoint of acting, Blondel wants to show how they "imply one another in a primitive unity where, according to our way of thinking and speaking, they vivify one another, however different they may seem to our discursive understanding" (1936, 172). Even if we run the risk of unduly separating by our analytical efforts what is utterly one and simple in the Absolute, it is important and legitimate, from a rational standpoint, that we try to work through this diversity of divine names and attributes, if only to prevent adulterations of the metaphysical spirit and of the authentic religious sense itself, or to avoid verging into religious agnosticism, not to say skepticism and atheism. Even if any name we use, including that of pure Acting, will always fall short and remain unclear as it pertains to the Absolute, "it would be even more impertinent and misleading not to name it in any way, and to turn our rational endeavor away from any consideration of the approaches or the aspects of this mystery par excellence" (1936, 172).

Blondel's argument here is addressed to those who not only recognize the total transcendence of the divine, but also want to maintain a total separation between what can be said of God in philosophy and what can be said of him in religion, or in a theology based on revelation, starting from an assertion that the "God of philosophy" is not the "God of the Gospel." Far from denying the heterogeneity he has always maintained, ever since his first discourse on method in 1896, between philosophy and theology, he continues to see this difference of method as assuring the autonomy of both philosophy and theology in the study of objects that appear common to both, in this case, God and the Trinitarian view of the divine he is about to move into. He also sees it as requiring that philosophy itself enter into such a Trinitarian view of the immanent life of the Transcendent, even though such a view has always been held in the Christian tradition to be a strict mystery, known only by some supernatural revelation. Blondel, of course, has no doubt about the impenetrability of this mystery in its essence, but that does not mean that philosophy should show no interest in it or remain disinterested in it, in a sort of agnostic extrinsicism. He has already argued that we cannot reduce this immanent life of the divine to any sort of human dimensions. But he has also maintained a certain necessity for human reason to get a more vivid or more spiritual view of the living God, lest we remain agnostic even as people of faith, or fall into even worse errors such as atheism or indifference to God.

There are not two infinites, "one that satisfies the philosopher, the other that, for those privileged by grace, would raise souls above a world left to its sciences, its industries, its human aspirations" (1936, 399). This would amount to another kind of juxtaposition between the natural and the supernatural that Blondel has always eschewed. "The infinite of the God of reason is not a boundary at which we stop after touching it as one touches a mountain, according to the expression of Descartes: it is already a life, a stimulation, a goodness, an exigency that no rational being can escape from" (1936, 400). The idea of two infinites, or of two gods, so to speak, one for the learned according to the world and one for believers according to some arbitrary grace, makes no sense and is unintelligible before reason as well as before the most authentic Catholic tradition. Hence, to speak of God as one and simple in his substance and to speak of him as triune is to speak of one and the same God, and it is as much the task of philosophy to make as much sense of this as it can, as it is for a theological faith seeking some understanding of what is revealed as pure mystery.

Besides, it is not as if Christian theology had been the only one to come up with the idea of a trinity in the divine. There have been other places in the philosophical tradition where a triune view of the divine has been advanced, so that Blondel is not alone as a philosopher in pursuing this line of thought in his reflection on the divine names and attributes. His purpose, however, is not to review all the ways in which philosophers as well as theologians have spoken of the attributes and names of God. It is rather "to concentrate his effort on the typical problems where the most essential difficulties converge relative to radical heterogeneity and to the similitudes that it is equally important not to ignore" (1936, 173-74). These are the difficulties that hinge on the disparity we have already been speaking of between pure Acting and the mixed activity of secondary causes. They are the difficulties a philosopher must resolve, if we are to think of God as pure Acting, without thinking of him as static or as passive of his own action in any way.

Blondel sums up where he takes his stand in two points. First, we have to affirm "that it is legitimate and indispensable to build as it were rational bridges and not to hold ourselves from the start to a more or less skeptical or mystical agnosticism," when it comes to the divine (1936, 173). At the same time, however, we must maintain an attitude that is rightly critical of any assimilation between the human and the divine that would be premature and unwarranted. The divine *acting* cannot be compared "either to anything accomplished once and for all, whether by a necessity of nature or by a power resting in this perfection of a result supremely willed and obtained, or to the indefinite remaking of a productive activity that would remain itself only by breaking up any apparent and provisional determination" (1936, 173). If there is nothing transitive, nothing fixed in the divine *acting*, nothing dependent on some future acquisition or perfection, how then are we to conceive it as ever living and ever fecund?

The simplest way tradition has found for speaking of this purely immanent acting in the divine has been through an idea of *engendering*, but one that has been purified of any semblance of passivity in a *generation* that would imply an effect separate from its cause or a cause relative to what it engenders. Blondel brings up the difficulty there is for us to conceive of such an engendering in the absence of any interdependence of reciprocal causality among complex conditions and unceasing reactions, as happens in the engendering of a human being. The problem for us is to conceive, within absolute transcendence, "an acting that in fact would be the only acting perfectly specified as such, an acting that would be neither moving nor moved, not subordinated to any reciprocal law of passivity, one that proliferates without being modified in return by this real production and without the proliferated itself ceasing to be itself also pure acting, notwithstanding the expression that seems to require a passive participle to signify the origin whence it issues" (1936, 174).

Blondel had already had recourse to the idea of *generation* to express and to justify in part a conception of this kind of interrelation within Being in and through itself. Here he considers it again in terms of pure Acting, appealing to the intimate mystery of a life that goes on in a sort of darkness, where continuity is reconciled with the distinction of beings united by blood. The human term of *generation* suggests something of a reproductive action that is most intimate and most productive in a real sense, as it prolongs itself in other agents who are both united and separate. To be sure, this is only a metaphor. It does not adequately represent the true transmission of life from the engendering to the engendered in the pure Acting of the one and the other, without any precedence or contingency on the part of the engendering or any dependence or passivity on the part of the engendered, as is always the case in any secondary or finite engendering of life, but it does express in a discursive way a total and incomparable transmission of life: *genita, non facta, vita*, where the engendering and the engendered are coeternally one and equal in their very distinction.

Such a generation in pure acting is a living and perfect immanence of thought to itself, but not in a way that would hold this generation in a simple but static reciprocity of intelligibility and intelligence. Already in speaking of absolute Thought and of Being in and through itself, Blondel had argued against any static conception of Thought-thinking-itself in any sort of mirroring from thought to thinking and from thinking to thought, or from intelligibility to intelligence and from intelligence to intelligibility. But it is here, in terms of pure Acting, that he finds his strongest argument for the purest life of

Spirit, where subject and object are no longer opposed and beings are no longer limits for one another, but are altogether a subsistent plenitude, both as thinking and as thought.

Blondel tries to enter further "into this intellectual action at the heart of the pure, intelligent and intelligible acting" (1936, 177). In the human order the father has to recognize his son amid the obscurity of his origins, as the son recognizes his hidden filiation, so that there comes a double acknowledgment expressed in the Latin verb *agnoscere*. "In the intellectual order," Blondel writes, "a similar *recognition*, an *agnition* confesses and seals, so to speak, the double relation of generation that assures the authentic unity of race and spirit" (1936, 177). From this natural truth, Blondel rises to what would be the perfect type of such relating in the pure, divine generation where all is light, unity, recognition. Indeed, in this light the term *recognition* reaches a fullness of sense in a twofold way: "for to *recognize* is, in one sense, to see, to admit, to ratify the knowledge of the received truth authenticated by the reflected and somehow verified adherence of the two terms, [or] of the two agents to the accord; but it is also, in another sense that could be deemed moral, to *express gratitude* for what is received and for what is returned, where the perfectly consummate unity implies an exchange and, as it were, an infinitely rich circulation from the one to the other of those for whom all is common" (1936, 177-78).

In this carefully crafted articulation of the twofold sense of *recognition*, in the pure Acting of one who engenders and of one who is engendered, Blondel is trying to show in a measured way not only how pure Acting can be conceived only by integrating intelligence and intelligibility, that is, the Thought of Thought, into pure Acting, but also how a moral element, not to say a charitable function, has to be introduced into this conception of pure Acting. Some who have conceded the more intellectual element of the conception have objected to the introduction of this moral element, usually associated with action, but Blondel insists that it must be brought in as part of the conception of pure Acting, which has to include more than what pure Thinking would entail by itself, even when it is the pure Thinking of pure Thought. It is this moral element in the conception of pure Acting, which already integrates within itself perfect Thought, that leads to the necessity of including in the conception of the transcendent immanence of pure Acting what Blondel now calls the Spirit of *Charity*.

Thus, through the twofold sense of recognition, between the engendering and the engendered in pure Acting, between uncreated Thought that is eternally generative and the Word that, in expressing the Being whence it is generated, is also expressing itself as perfectly as the One whence it is, Blondel penetrates more deeply into the conception of the divine as triune. Mutual *recognition* between the Two is not just an act of intellectual ratification of a truth received and authenticated, so to speak, on both sides of this pure Acting.

It is also an act of *gratitude* on both sides for what is received and for what is given in return, in a consummate unity that has to be thought of as a third, which is a bond of love between the first and the second in their perfect equality, and equally a pure Acting with them. This third is named Spirit of Charity, but the conception of it is necessary for making sense of the distinction and the living unity of the first Two, which are conceived as pure Thought of Thought in pure Acting constituting Being in and through itself.

To show this necessity of conceiving a third, Blondel argues from the inconceivability of thinking only of the Thought of Thought, either as an identity, where the one generated would be only a reiteration of the first, a verbal tautology, or as a pair of thoughts, where the second would be a conscious replica of the first, so that the first would be somehow different from the word that expresses it, supposedly in an adequate fashion. Thought of in this way, the concept of pure Acting would consist only of a going back and forth between affirming the primacy of *intelligible* being and affirming the primacy of the *intelligence* that knows it and expresses it to itself, which is not anything truly conceivable, even in the mystery we are trying to penetrate. It is rather, in effect, "an annihilation that would suffuse the two confronted terms into an indetermination, or into a hypothesis, removing from Being any possibility of knowing itself, existing for itself, or subsisting in itself" (1936, 179). The only way of escaping this incoherence in conceiving a pure Acting that is absolute is by affirming in it a life that is not absorbed in any sort of egoism, which ultimately is deadly, but that is fully personal and willing that others be in a way that makes others be. And this is what Blondel calls "the perfect function of charity, thanks to which what is, is never solitary, what knows, is only for what is known, and what loves, only for the mutual love" (1936, 180).

Blondel is fully conscious that he is skirting around what others in Christian theology have called a mystery known only by divine or supernatural revelation, surpassing any power of reason to investigate. He recognizes that his own faith in this revelation has prompted much of his own investigation into this mystery of pure Acting. His claim, however, is that he has come to this conception of the Trinitarian mystery of Being and Acting only by a rational process that can be followed by anyone following the light of reason, whether a believer or not. He is speaking to universal reason in its infinite dimension, and not just to a believer in the Infinite whose belief might be bereft of any conception of the infinite as absolute, or as having a life of its own in its very transcendence. It would be a serious mistake for him to fall back into a false extrinsicism on the part of faith, or a false intrinsicism on the part of reason, at the height of this reflection on the God who has to be thought of as absolute Being in and through itself in its pure Thinking and pure Acting.

On the part of faith, the mistake would be to shut our eyes to the very mystery that is revealed. Even if we cannot penetrate into the divine action itself, as it reveals itself, without some express positive revelation that philosophy cannot fully comprehend, it remains that the revelation is addressed to spiritual beings who have to receive it meaningfully, not to say rationally. "Besides the double grace of its external manifestation and its veiled assistance within us interiorly, the words that formulate it, the ideas it suggests, the practical commitments it requires of us have to have some meaning for us, correspond somehow with the working of our spirit, and come to some accord with the secret harmony of our soul" (1936, 406). Working from the side of the soul and the human spirit, philosophy reaches out, not only to touch the Spirit in the mystery of its transcendence, but also to open itself up to the infinite Spirit of Love as well as of Thought in its absolute Being in and through itself.

On the part of reason, however, it does this only by reaching out beyond itself into the true infinite of pure Thinking and pure Acting, where pure Being is at once giving of itself to another, whether that be within the immanent life of the Transcendent itself, or to yet other beings and finite spirits that are also the products of the eternal Charity. For Blondel, to remain within the parameters of finite spirit, no matter how dialectically that is done, whether in a rationalist pantheism, in deism, or in agnosticism, not to mention atheism, is to fall short of where reason has to lead us. The same would have to be said of a purely natural theology that cuts reason short of any attempt to penetrate the mystery of a truly transcendent Being with an immanence of its own, though not undergone as a nature with a sort of fatality. Following his own dialectic of pure Thinking and pure Acting in absolute Being in and through itself, Blondel speaks of this immanence as freely necessary and necessarily free, as a perfect initiative that entails a perfect conformity achieved uniquely through an uncreated love, a reciprocal giving, and, in a way that rejoins much of the expression found in the reflection of Christian theology on the revealed mystery of divine Trinity, as an intimate and substantial *circumincession,* wherein is "realized and explained the action such that the Spirit of Charity (consubstantial itself with and proceeding at once from the two whose personal distinction is perfect in their unity) consummates and vivifies the eternal generation and procession" (1936, 180).

With the inclusion of this Spirit of Charity as a third personal relation in the divine immanence, we come to a certain completion in the conception of pure Acting as totally transcendent. Blondel is then able to reflect on this conception of the divine as a whole, as it relates to the God who remains mysterious and hidden to our probing mind. We cannot say that we have fully entered into this truth of the divine as triune, or even as one, in its pure Acting. But we can say that it has a life of its own, that it is not a static identity in its own unmoved immanent activity. We can also say that it cannot be identified simply as the first Mover of other things or as the first cause of secondary causes, according to how we first come to know of it. Strictly speaking, absolute Acting cannot be named first cause or even cause of itself in any sense that would imply an effect other than itself, or its being somehow passive of itself. All we can say of it is that there is generation and procession in it without efficiency or fabrication of any sort, even of itself. "There is pure acting only where the act itself is totally immanent and adequate to itself, but where nevertheless the surge remains eternally and totally live and productive" (1936, 183). At the same time, however, even when we think of it as also the first Cause of secondary causes, we cannot think of it as reducible to this role or this function. Perfectly self-contained, so to speak, in its very pure Acting, it is in no way dependent on anything outside of itself or any necessity to go out of itself, to actualize itself, as some idealist philosophies would have it. Probing the Trinitarian aspect of the divine mystery in pure Acting, even while affirming its incomprehensible reality, has made this clearer for Blondel than a reflection on the thought of an uncaused Cause or an unmoved Mover alone could have.

Nevertheless, when we do turn to the thought of pure Acting as first Cause or as Creator of things other than itself, this same reflection on what we can conceive of the inner life of a triune God in its mysterious transcendence can keep us from misunderstanding what is implied in this action of God *ad extra*, or rather what is not implied in any such action on the part of the totally transcendent Agent. There are those who have attributed to the divine a need or a necessity to produce creatures in the exercise of its activity, or even to become conscious of itself through this world emanating from its unconscious. On the other hand, theocentricism itself is also seen as requiring that the divine action draw all things back to itself exclusively, as if to a Transcendent egoism. But Blondel points out how a proper conception of absolute and pure acting in itself can show both of these representations of the divine action *ad extra*, to be not only a dilution of the perfect self-containment of divine action in itself, but also a short-changing of the actuality of creatures themselves and their action.

There is an ambiguity, if not a certain lack of logic, or at least a serious inconvenience in maintaining that the divine, in its amplitude, as perfectly independent of anything else, can only act *for itself,* so that as the unique principle it is necessarily the unique end of everything. The idea that God acts only for himself applies strictly only to the pure act and its Transcendent immanence. When it comes to thinking of God's creative and providential work, however, we have to think of the divine acting in a different way. When we think of *creation* we cannot speak of God acting only in and for himself, as even Blondel himself does elsewhere in his reflection on Being and beings. When we think in the Absolute terms of *acting*, however, even with regard to a gratuitous creation *ad extra*, we have to understand that God is not acting for himself, as if he needed something new to bring himself to completion. Such transient purposefulness, which is implied in our representation of one acting for itself, has to be excluded from God, even in thinking of the eternal generation and procession of the three personal relations, let alone of any action or creation *ad ex-*

tra. But the cloud of this representation, or misrepresentation, which is inevitable in our way of thinking, becomes doubly confusing and misleading when we come to think of the divine action *ad extra*. Whereas the terms *pure act* and *absolute acting* could still apply in the case of the divine generation and processing, they no longer apply to what is only a production of things, visible and invisible. To say that God creates only for himself, as if to produce a good that would only return to him egotistically, would surely be wrong, both from the standpoint of the divine spirit and from the standpoint of any creature, which is incommensurable for satisfying any necessity in the creator. Even supposing that there could be some necessity in the creator, no creature could be the equal of that necessity.

Acting *in itself*, without undergoing any passivity whatsoever, implies "an eternal and ever immediate adequation of omnipotence, omniscience and omnigoodness" (1936, 191). Acting *for itself*, on the other hand, on the level of pure Acting, implies the "unity of a threefold giving where there is room only for devotedness and, if we dare say, for the tenderness of the most abundant and the most intelligent charity" (1936, 192). What the study of *acting* has brought for Blondel is a way of going beyond a representation of the divine in the study of thought and being that still remains relatively static. In thinking about the pure and transcendent Acting, the unique principle and end of all the secondary causes, including ourselves, he is using all the resources we have to sort out, within the realization of our own action, as the conscious point of departure for seeking, and for affirming, a much more synthetic and demanding conception of all that is involved in absolutely pure Acting.

Creation and the Acting of Secondary Causes

This study of acting, however, does not end with this affirmation of the pure absolute Acting in its mysterious transcendence, for the acting of the secondary causes remains to be considered in this new light that comes from the conception of the pure Acting as giver and gift, or as Creator of secondary causes or agents with an action of their own. These actions of secondary causes, including our own initiatives as self-conscious agents, are for us the point from which we start in our search for and in our affirmation of a first, pure, and transcendent Act. Now the question is to see how, in spite of its perfect self-sufficiency, this absolute Acting is, nevertheless, First cause of secondary causes capable themselves of acting on their own initiative. The problem for Blondel is to understand how, after having placed *acting* in its purest sense so completely on the side of absolute Being in itself, with the implication that anything else depending on its sovereign and universal causality has to be seen as necessarily passive, there can still issue forth a real causality in the created universe, not just in a sort of mutual influence and interaction that mimes the creative initiative, but also on the level of spiritual agents in relation to God with a free will that empowers them to exercise, not just an immanent causality in the world, but also a certain resistance even to omnipotence itself. For Blondel, there is within us a power that transcends the entire universe, and that we can now characterize as "powerful even against God," implied in the very consciousness we have of our own initiatives. How is this to be reconciled with any sort of necessary passivity on the part of created agents, with regard to the pure Acting of the absolutely universal Cause of all secondary causes?

The crux of the difficulty lies in the consciousness we have of being true agents on our own, without which we would not even be conscious of ourselves. The temptation is to turn this experience of our own self-conscious action against the very idea of an absolutely unique first Cause and a perfectly pure and independent Acting, as for example, in atheistic existentialism, where it is said "if I exist, God cannot exist." Or, to put it the other way around, as Blondel now puts it from the side of the first universal Cause, if God is omnipotent, how can we say that he somehow delegates something of his creative omnipotence? If we insist only on the necessary self-sufficiency and supreme transcendence of pure Acting, which is unto itself its own ground and its own end, it becomes difficult, if not downright impossible, to understand how there can be other agents or secondary causes, let alone agents or causes that can go against this first Cause of all causation. How can we help but think that God would not be willing to go against his own willing, as purely self-contained absolute acting?

If we remain exclusively in the order of power and intelligibility, an order of metaphysical truths that are necessary for anyone considering the relation of creatures to the Creator, the difficulty can only result in an insoluble dualism where both sides are absolutized in their opposition to one another. For Blondel, however, there is another aspect of pure Acting to be considered, the aspect of goodness and charity that he has been careful to elaborate on and that can now be brought in to give a better rational solution to this paradox of a created will capable of resisting the uncreated Will. The full name of God is not just one of intelligence and intelligibility, but one of wisdom and generosity. "It is therefore through pure and gratuitous liberality, without necessity, that creative action was exercised in order to organize a universal order where everything conspires toward a supreme end, about which St. Thomas could say: the entire movement of nature and thought tends to multiply spirits for eternal life" (1936, 196). We could say that this is only a matter of contingency and convenience ordained by God, not out of any metaphysical necessity for his own perfection that we can conceive, but rather out of sheer loving generosity that takes nothing away from the purity of the transcendent Acting, and in no way compromises the order of necessity in its willing of itself, though not of creation.

What has to be clarified in this understanding of the creative action, according to Blondel, is how a space is opened up, so to speak, for the total passivity of creatures in their very originality as agents and how, while remaining incommensurable to the first Cause, these secondary causes can accept, use, and acquire a power they can, on their initiative, not only use but also abuse. The problem, as Blondel approaches it from the side of pure Acting, or the first Cause, is to understand how, from his own free goodness, God can create, through his power and wisdom, true *secondary causes* in the precise sense of this appellation — *secondary*, in the sense that they depend constantly on the one from whom and in whom they have their being, their life, their movement, their will, and their action, and that they are nevertheless true *causes*, in that they are to decide their destiny by accepting or rejecting what Blondel now calls the divine loan *(prêt divin)* of power in their freedom to act against God as well as in step with God. For, as Blondel points out, if the secondary cause can act against God, it is a sign that, even if it *acts* with God and for God, "everything is not submission in their elected lifework" (1936, 198). Blondel thinks of this as a paradox that can be made intelligible and justified by a consideration of how power and wisdom serve charity in the work of creation.

On the side of metaphysical necessity, we have to say that pure Acting cannot alienate itself. God cannot annihilate himself, redouble himself, or abdicate what he is. But this does not mean that there is no possibility of created agents. What is also absolutely necessary is a total incommensurability between the Creator and any creature we could suppose, even a creature that would be active in its own right. In fact, Blondel argues, this incommensurability is the very thing that assures contingent beings of what belongs to them, according to the nature they have received. What God gives, out of his gratuitous charity, is real and without reservation. His is a goodness that bestows being, enriches beings, and entrusts them with what they need to achieve their proper good for themselves. In endowing the creature with riches of its own, God gives up nothing of himself.

Yet, have we said enough to get to the heart of the matter on the side of the creature? If we were to think of creation only as a sort of play or spectacle that God produces for himself, as a sort of cosmic machine where everything develops automatically, without any consciousness or knowledge or spirit or freedom, would there be any true secondary causes with an activity of their own, and could we make sense of creation as a work of wisdom and goodness? "What brings sense and value to the universe is the presence in it of spiritual and active beings; for it is by such beings and for such beings that a drama arises, that of secondary causes with a responsibility of their own in the face of an absolutely first cause of their very action as well as of their being" (1936, 199). This is for Blondel a decisive point to be taken into account when thinking of creation.

He speaks of a long process of gestation in the universe preparing for the advent of consciousness and reason, of spiritual beings gifted with a divine loan, so to speak, which comes as an aspiration that is at first confused and implicit, but which reflective thought and action gradually bring to greater precision in a way that cannot be ignored. This is the emergence of a consciousness that is somehow infinite, as it takes root in the world, an emergence that Blondel has followed in its ascension through both thought and action. As spirit, it is divinely endowed, and on this endowment is grounded all that it is and all that it has to do with things, with itself, and with God. It is in this virtually infinite advance of spirit that "the very principle of all power and all consciousness of acting in secondary causes resides" (1936, 200).

This is an argument we have seen Blondel use time and time again, concerning what is implied in the very consciousness of our being agents on our own. Here we see how it relates to the very notion of having spirits as secondary causes in the universe. The world is not just a wondrous structure where the omnipotent alone is at work. There is more to it, in that God comes down himself into his work where there are workers working both for themselves and for him, without always knowing precisely whence they are or whither they are going. God offers himself to spirits in a hidden way through the physical grandeur of the universe and in the obscurities of our unconsciousness, but only to be discovered by those he stimulates from within and from without through a pedagogy of nature and of the soul. What Blondel sees in this is a design aiming at having us "earn the initial loan so that this acquisition will allow the transformation of the loan into a gift" (1936, 200). What is on loan is the divine power and light, which empties itself of its infinity to make room for spiritual creatures to develop and to become active on their own account. What is gift is the actual conscious exercise of this power to act in freedom and in response to a loan that is recognized as such.

Two things have to be kept in mind in this mysterious strategy of the divine loan to spirits that are free to set their own course: (1) how God offers his power and light to make it ours, without its ceasing to be his, so that he wills and makes free acts of which he remains the master and the instigator; and (2) how he does this without taking away the free choice and the just responsibility of the human agent. One condition is that God does not lend himself all at once, with all his imposing necessity and his immediate acting. This would not only be a metaphysical impossibility with regard to a spirit that is finite, but it would also be contrary to the design of goodness itself, which aims at calling forth truly active beings that relate to the infinite from which they come and to which they are called to return. For secondary causes that are nevertheless active, action must be rooted "in obscure states of consciousness that develop in the shadows of an ascension toward an intellectual and moral order that makes room for reflection, the appeals of conscience, and for reasonable and voluntary choice" (1936, 201).

Human beings are not just extras in the very personal drama that is playing itself out in creation. They are at center stage in their relation to the first Cause, in accordance with the way Blondel has been thinking about this ever since his first approach to the philosophy of human action. It may seem strange that the divine action should stay hidden in this way, and limit itself, so to speak, by suspending its brilliance and its power and appearing only in partial truths and occasional or particular goods that do not compel our judgment or our resolve. But, Blondel asks, "is that not the way, the only true way for a finite and imperfect spirit to bring something of its own, to take in the light and the goodness rather than reject it, to use what we are calling the divine loan, to restore it by making it bear fruit, and to receive it as a gift, but now a gift in which has been incorporated the good will of the spiritual agent who, so to speak, has brought something to God by making it so that, what could have been refused, profaned or lost coming from him, should be handed over to the master of the field along with the fruit of human labor and of the earth divinely seeded?" (1936, 202). It is not hard to see how Blondel is back to thinking of his philosophy of action as a philosophy of the talents spoken of in the Gospel.

There remains, however, one more difficulty to be dissipated in this account of a paradox that brings together an absolute and transcendent Acting and a mutual participation of responsible creatures where the Creator cannot be disinterested, inasmuch as he gives them something of his power and glory to be safeguarded. How is this to be understood now, not from the perspective of the divine, but from the human standpoint? Is it not strange that so much is at stake in our action without our knowing clearly from the start, the origin, the bearing, the eventual sanctions or the complete destiny of our action? Can there still be a design of goodness hidden under such perhaps fatal exigencies? If they came from a blind necessity, we would simply have to accept them. But can we resign ourselves to them when we claim that they are the free inventions of a perfect Charity, even when this Charity would appear to become victim and passive of a design that would put it in contradiction with itself?

The difficulty Blondel is referring to is one he had led up to in his original philosophy of action, where he had tried to account for the necessity, not only of saying *yes* to God in fulfillment of one's action, but also of a sanction of eternal frustration for saying *no*. This is the difficulty he intends to return to in the second volume on *Action* in the Trilogy, starting once again from human action as it is exercised in the concrete, and running through the entire course of its deployment to the limits of the universe. Thinking in anticipation of what that articulation will bring to the solution of this metaphysical problem of secondary causes related to a first universal Cause of all action, Blondel refers to what will appear as a law that is proper and internal to the secondary causes, even if the conscious and exacting truth of that law is not always clearly in the creature's mind. What human agents have to do in acting humanly is discern the conditions required for them not to go against the light they already have in their conscience. If they fail to act according to that light, this does not indicate in any way a failure in the creative design itself, nor does it take anything away from its proper transcendence. Nor does it entail any diminution of the divine goodness, for there is always mercy as well as justice. What it helps us to understand "is the mystery of suffering, both culpable and innocent, in the spiritual agents that make up the fearsome drama of humanity" (1936, 204).

This will be understood more clearly after the articulation of how this drama plays itself out in human action, but before going on to that Blondel thinks he has to give a more positive account of the action of creatures themselves in their relation to the pure creative Acting, which has now become the model, so to speak, for fulfilling our own role as causes in the universe. We would not be causes if we were merely pawns in the immanent order of things, without any sense of transcendence and without any call to realities beyond space and time, indeed, without the beginning of a participation in a divine offer that cannot be dismissed out of hand. In the first part of this study of secondary causes as they relate to pure Acting, Blondel had considered the various kinds of agency in the world, from the physical, to the organic, to the properly human, in search of our fullest idea of *action*, or of what could be thought of as *acting* in the purest sense. He found each level wanting from the standpoint of a realized pure acting, which remains always as a mystery of pure Acting without passivity whatsoever, transcending all other types of activity in the universe, each of which is always tainted by some passivity. Now, having explored the mystery of pure Acting in itself, he comes around full circle to these various degrees of created activity, as they come to be and as they are actually exercised, to determine what specific traits they have in the accession of secondary causes to the first Cause. The question is to examine how this mixture of activity and passivity is composed, to see whether it is fixated in the way it is immediately given, or else whether it can "either deprave itself by falling under the yoke of passion, or tend toward a purification capable of assimilating it more or less completely to pure Acting as to its end, just as it has it for its principle" (1936, 213).

In his approach to the specification of the different kinds of activity among the secondary causes, Blondel is thinking primarily of the actions and interactions, or the mixture of activity and passivity in the world as a whole, and of the special role spiritual agents have to play in this cosmic historical order. In fact, he has in mind that, only on the level of spiritual agency, do we have secondary causality in the full sense of the term, which can be assimilated to the first universal Cause as to its principle and its end. He does recognize, however, a certain dynamism in the physical order as such that can be viewed as a beginning of activity, a force, something intrinsic to material things that is a metaphysical principle of initiative giving rise to more manifest forms of more organized and concentrated acting. We cannot think of the universe except in function of action and reactions, in things and among things, that specify themselves and organize themselves through a continuous reciprocal causality among different elements or agents responding to external stimuli from other elements or agents, with each one constituting itself through the interconnections of the whole into a center of some particular initiative reacting to others in its own way. This is not to be thought of in purely mechanistic terms for Blondel, or as a mere reiteration of always the same. On the contrary, the physical order is already a history, an incessant initiative of irreversible movement going forward from the cosmic order to the apparition, not only of organisms, but even of spirits.

Two truths are involved in this conception of physical action and interaction among elements of the universe. First, there is activity properly speaking in the physical order and amid cosmic connections, only to the extent that there are different kinds of being, different centers of reaction already specified, whose traits can be defined by the positive sciences, but which also constitute metaphysically determined natures. Second, Blondel adds, "there can be action even in the elemental and unconscious sense only because, in this very obscurity, there is already a virtuality tending toward an ideal order, toward a living and acting thought" (1936, 223). We find in the human composite a compenetration, a synergy, a reciprocal subordination of corporeal energies and ideal powers that embody and spiritualize themselves in an unceasing struggle.

Vital spontaneity and the initiatives of organic agents bring a higher degree of activity into the world. In comparison, merely physical agents would appear to be capable of little more than reaction to external excitations, while living things appear much more as centers of concentration and diffusion with an even greater diversity of activity. The universe is not just a clock, made up of inert gears, moved as if by an unwinding of solely efficient springs. If it is not living, it at least has a history in which living things have consolidated themselves in innumerable variants. Echoing Leibniz, Blondel writes that "what characterizes life is not the ensemble of phenomena that compose its external history; it is a metaphysical unity thanks to which life expresses the universality of what there is by responding to it through a synthetic and original unity" (1936, 226). What Blondel sees in this is already a loan *(un prêt)* from the one who is Life and Light, though one that is still submerged. It is a light ready to "illuminate a thought that will gather into a budding consciousness, into a power capable of summing up and dominating the forces of lower nature because it proceeds and benefits from the transcendent principle that has prepared for it both the universal dynamism and the certitude of the divine acting itself" (1936, 226). What Blondel sees, therefore, is a genesis of secondary causes that starts from near passivity and rises to ever greater plastic spontaneity, thereby composing the means for intelligent beings to take over in becoming conscious of their power of free choice and their obligations, as they envisage a destiny that brings them squarely before a supreme option: for or against God.

Life thus represents a step higher than merely physical agency in this ascent of secondary agency toward a fully conscious kind of action, but it is not yet the kind of *acting* Blondel has in mind when he speaks of it in its fullest sense. Physical things and living things in the universe can be spoken of as secondary causes in their own right, agents that must be recognized and respected for what they are and what they do, but not as much as fully conscious spiritual and rational beings. These are the agents Blondel has primarily in mind when he speaks of secondary causes in the truest sense of the term, and these are agents whose activity he is most interested in specifying, as they concur in their destiny in the context of a universal design, in solidarity with other causes and in subordination to an end that requires active engagements on the part of all with the conscious power to act.

If Blondel thinks primarily of spiritual agents as secondary causes, it is because for him there is an ideal element implied in acting itself, which is most evident in the self-conscious deliberate agent acting in view of an end. But this is not to deny that there is properly some agency, with a finality of its own, in lesser agents that contributes to the goodness and the beauty of the universe as well as to the drama that is playing itself out in this universal order for spiritual creatures as secondary causes moving toward a participation in the pure Acting of God. Blondel rejects the kind of dualism that simply opposes the blind forces of nature and the spiritual forces that would appear to take them over as purely mechanical and technical tools to be conquered and used for whatever purpose the rational agent may decide. There is something to be said for that attitude of control over the forces of nature, but it is too exclusive and it fails to respect the significance of the action of these forces as part of the total plan for the progression of the work of creation, which is not limited to what man may devise for himself in the immanent order. Nor does this materialist, utilitarian, and industrial conception of the world set us properly on a prudent course for our due liberation as spiritual agents. How we think of the world, and how we live in society, must be integrated into the way we think of ourselves as striving for a higher end than ourselves.

Indeed, in this context, Blondel repeats his argument that we would not have any consciousness of the power over nature that liberates us from the passive and passionate impulses that surge into consciousness, unless we had some consciousness, as obscure as it may seem, "of some point of reference that is absolutely higher than all finite objects, than all subalternate enticements around which our conscious and antagonistic desires oscillate. This presence, in the conscious and free agent, of an idea of the infinite, of the universal, of the good transcending all the particular determinations that can solicit it, is the condition *sine qua non* of any consciousness of being a cause, of any acting proper to an agent no matter how imperfect, of any really efficacious initiative" (1936, 234-35). This argument, which was at the dialectical core of Blondel's original philosophy of action, will return to set the second version of this philosophy in motion in the second volume on *Action* in the Trilogy.

Blondel uses this argument with reference to the infinite in consciousness whenever he wants to show that there is more at stake in human action than just carving out for the spiritual agent a place of its own in the world. It is not enough merely to use the idea of the infinite as a lever to raise the world or to fabricate our own little heaven, as one more thing in the finite order of things of our own doing. Such a poor ambition would not only be absurd or chimerical, but even "contradictory, culpable, hostile to itself and condemned at its own tribunal. For the congenital élan that constitutes the reasonable and free agent cannot, with impunity and sincerely, shut itself in, satisfy itself, finish with itself in the immanent order of finite and perishable goods, as long as consciousness and will exist only in function of a transcendent finality" (1936, 238). This is the way Blondel thinks God, or pure Acting, communicates his goodness to us, by creating us as free and active, and by calling us to submissiveness and charity, so that we can actively be assimilated to God's life, God's goodness, and God's beatitude.

In the end, then, Blondel concludes that the spiritual agent as secondary cause must be thought of as active in a twofold order, the immanent order of our universal reality and the transcendent order of assimilation to the pure Acting of divinity. Created spirits, who find themselves engaged with cosmic forces as well as with one another, and passively dependent on the initiatives of other things as well as on one another, must rise historically to a free initiative of their own in responsibility, as they exercise a role of providence similar to that of the Creator, in accord with his plan for the universal common good of a community of spirits. Such an action has to be one of conforming and decentering of oneself, one of compassion and cooperation with forces that affect the entire course of creation. It requires detachment from self in a way that attaches us to all and to everything, by developing in countless ways an action of solicitude, of readiness to succor, and of efficacious devotion. "From this point of view and concerning the immanent order of creation as a whole, we can conceive and launch an action on the whole that could be called a form of pure acting accessible to the spiritual agent within the entire universe of secondary causes" (1936, 249).

At the same time, however, and already implied in this order of immanent activity among created spirits, is also a higher kind of aspiration to a transcendent order more directly related to the pure Acting of the Creator. For us to conceive and to realize such an active communion of beings as we have just been entertaining, must we not implicate the first Cause and its creative intervention, at once hidden and manifest in the universal synergy and in the converging aspiration of the secondary causes? "To reach, to unify and to act on beings and to suffer them as we should, we have to pass through God, so to speak" (1936, 250). From this another question arises: "Is it possible, and is it not obligatory to tend to participate in some way, through and above the created solidarities, in the pure and transcendent acting of God, without thereby losing sight of the incommensurability of the infinite and the finite that is metaphysically necessary and insurmountable?" (1936, 250). The question arises for Blondel in human acting even while recognizing the total transcendence of the divine pure Acting. Reason has to recognize this question, even if it has no way of answering it on its own, whether it be regarding the mode of access for such a participation or how it could succeed in such an endeavor.

At the end of this discourse on the relation of the created acting of finite spirits to the pure and infinite Acting of the Creator, Blondel finds another reason for raising the question of the Trinitarian unification of intelligence and charity within the divine Substance. The reason why we cannot remain indifferent to God in our action is that God has not been indifferent to us. It is by a loan from God that we have become secondary causes capable of conquering the world as well as the passivities and passions within ourselves. It is incumbent upon us to inquire how far this loan is meant to take us: all the way back to God himself or not? To remain closed in within ourselves with it, or even within the immanent order of the universe, would be a failure, not only in exercising our free initiative as far forward as we should, but also in making full use of the divine loan on which our freedom is based, especially if we are created to seek our fulfillment in the divine life.

In this sense, the final specification of action for spiritual agents such as we are remains shrouded in the mystery of the divine pure Acting. It takes place within the universe, but always with some deference to creative providence for all things and especially for the created spirits themselves. At the same time, it takes place within ourselves on a higher plain, in that, as a specifically spiritual activity, it tends toward an assimilation to its paradigm, the divine Acting. This can be spoken of as a natural desire of finite spirit, or as a rational appetite. Given the incommensurability between the infinite paradigm and the finite aspiration, it would require an attitude of receptivity and openness on the part of the finite spirit with regard to all that is offered from the paradigm, including the loan already made in the very desire that liberates us from our passivity in the world. The very fact of having become rational and free is already a fulfillment of our spiritual desire for assimilation to the divine.

In addition to this, the thought of a higher fulfillment still occurs, the hypothesis of something more, a supernatural elevation for human action, especially in the context of Christian revelation and divine Incarnation. Blondel recognizes that philosophy cannot properly conceive what such a higher supernatural life would consist in for human being, nor how it would transform human action into something even more divine than it already is, but he insists that such a hypothesis could be entertained rationally, as a higher form of the assimilation we are already capable of with regard to pure Acting. Reason could also ask whether such assimilation to the divine might not be the only thing that could fully specify the action of a finite spirit, and what would be the requirement, on the part of the finite spirit, for it to reach this higher, supernatural specification. If there is to be a transformation that does not simply suppress the original and natural created agent, the latter must, in a supreme act of renunciation, let go of the being it has in its possession as a free agent, and disappropriate itself, in order to exchange this gift of nature and of the entire world for an infinitely higher gift, that of divinity itself. In this way the creature is both raised to the divine and preserved in its own personality, "maintained at the core of a divine appropriation that lets the creature subsist and thus confirms that initial gift without regret, but enlarged infinitely and completed as both active and actuated. Such is the logic required by this conception [of a supernatural gift] presented here [in philosophy] simply as a hypothesis" (1936, 262).

What remains to be seen is how this spiritual kind of action is exercised more concretely by secondary causes in a world that crowds in on them from all sides, and how this exercise itself opens them up to the infinite action of the Creator, as it offers itself to the creature. This is the task Blondel goes back to now, after these more metaphysical elaborations of how secondary causes relate to the ever-first universal Cause.

XV

The Original Philosophy of Action Revisited

In the second volume on *Action* of the Trilogy, Blondel returns to the original method of his earlier philosophy of action as conceived prior to any engagement with a systematic metaphysical view and as dealing directly with human action in its immediacy, that is, as exercised by human beings in good faith and in good conscience. In the first volume on *Action* of the Trilogy, having to do more with a metaphysics of secondary causes in their dependence on the primary Cause, and the general conditions for such a derivative causality, he had already made the point about a necessity to examine this entire question on secondary causality from the standpoint of humans, who ordinarily exercise such causality without a distinct knowledge of the origin, the bearing, the eventual sanctions, or the destination of their action, but still with a necessity to take all this into account, even though they do not entirely understand it from the start or in setting out to make their mark in history. If everything in the action of spiritual creatures followed from a blind necessity, there would be no problem of action as such. There would be only unthinking submission to some natural determination. But if there are exigencies that come with action as conceived by human beings, exigencies that weigh in on the consciousness of free agents and that can turn the gift of freedom against itself, if it cuts itself short of accepting the gift in all its fullness, then it becomes necessary to examine how the drama of human action plays itself out concretely in the life we choose to lead.

That is where Blondel's original philosophy of action and of the supernatural had begun, unsupported by any metaphysics of secondary causes relating to the primary Cause, although such a metaphysics was already implicit in the way he approached that original philosophy of action in the concrete, as he tried to show in the final chapter, added to the dissertation for its eventual publication five months after the defense. It will be remembered that Blondel himself was not satisfied with his attempt to add this more explicitly metaphysical dimension to his thought at the time. But as he returned to this philosophy of human action in the concrete at the end of his Trilogy on Thought, Being, and Action, he could assume that the metaphysical context of this thought had now been sufficiently brought out. He could also be more confident that his scientific method could be applied all the more surely and concretely to the reality of action, and not just to the phenomenon or to the idea we have of action. Though the method was to remain essentially the same in its critical tenor, the restriction to a purely phenomenal consideration of ideas as they present themselves in action would no longer shape the argument, as it had in 1893, where the Part on the Necessary Being of Action had been set off from the Part on the Phenomenon of Action.

The point of returning to this more concrete consideration at the end of the Trilogy, according to Blondel, is that there is still something to be learned from action for philosophy. Raising the philosophical question of human action will eventually show, or had already shown in the dissertation, that there is something to be learned for philosophy from human action, especially concerning the full spiritual scope of its bearing. Blondel had begun his philosophical journey at the point where he thought action could bring new light to philosophy. Action had been for him the locus for probing more deeply into the concrete of human experience, as he explained in the *Itinerary* of 1928, and for raising the human spirit to new heights, heights he had now explored at some considerable length in the volumes on Thought, on Being in and of itself, and on pure Acting as first cause of all secondary acting. But having explored these heights, there was still something more to be explored in concrete human action as integral to a philosophy that wants to encompass the whole universe as the stage for unfolding the drama in which human action plays itself out. This was the part left for the second volume on *Action* to explore, according to a method that could now take the more technically elaborated philosophy of the Trilogy for granted.

Sameness and Difference of Method

In our earlier presentation of the original philosophy of human action, we spoke of it mainly as a philosophy of the supernatural, taking our cue from the fifth Part of the book, where Blondel had pushed his phenomenological analysis into what presented itself as a hypothesis, one necessary but impossible to achieve in human terms alone, the hypothesis of the supernatural, to show certain exigencies that would follow for human action, if such an offer of a higher gift of divinization were actually made, for human action to accept or to reject. We have seen how the same sort of hypothesis is brought up for consideration in the more metaphysical context not only of the relation between human beings as secondary causes and God as the primary Cause, both efficient and final, of all action in the universe, but also of the relation between the gifted finite being and the pure infinite Being in and of itself, or between a thought that remains inadequate in striving for its own perfection and the total adequacy of pure Thought thinking itself. Here, in the second volume on *Action* of the Trilogy, we shall see the same hypothesis arise again as a rational hypothesis concerning a supreme and exotic sphere of divinization for human action, as a rational possibility to be examined critically with the conditions it would imply for how human action could attain fulfillment of its destiny, or fail to do so. But we shall not see any prolonged discussion of the shape such a supernatural gift would have to take as revelation and as call to a higher level of responsibility in human action, such as was found in *Action* of 1893. Blondel had another plan for that part of his discussion which would fit in with his idea of Catholic philosophy. That was to appear in a further work on *Philosophy and the Christian Spirit*, which was projected as a three-volume work to follow the first Trilogy. It is only in the latter that he would return to a more complete elaboration of his philosophy of the supernatural with explicit reference to how such an idea has been revealed in history.

To begin this return to human action in the concrete, Blondel points out that his prior volume on *Action* has shown that "moral speculation does not absolutely coincide with the exercise of human activity" (1937a, 8). This opens the way for a direct exploration of action that is unfettered by metaphysical speculation and does not presuppose any systematic conception of what human action must be or, as Blondel puts it, a philosophy that is outside of any technical framework. For one thing, this direct study of action has to stand as a relatively autonomous inquiry, for anyone who might not be initiated to other technical disciplines of philosophy. At the same time, however, this exploration has to be included as an integral part of philosophy as a whole. What it will show is that, as philosophy brings itself to a certain completion in its rationally autonomous order, it cannot close in on itself in any self-sufficient autonomy. "On the contrary, it will open up new views and issues concerning the depths where action receives its stimulations and brings up its own enrichment and the heights toward which speculative certainties and spiritual aspirations make us tend" (1937a, 11).

We see here how Blondel understood his original philosophy of action as it related to the classical tradition of philosophical speculation. It was a matter of "incorporating a popular philosophy of action into the technical system of philosophy" (1937a, 409), as something called for by that very living tradition of philosophy itself. It had to do with raising some fundamental questions in a new way by studying action through action itself, not just the idea of action, thereby leading to a more intimate confrontation of theory and practice. From this confrontation was to come a new precision concerning "the original role of action with regard to thought itself, the reasons why the theory of practice and the practice of theory remain disjointed and alternatively inadequate, and the decisive consequences that result from this strange and yet salutary disproportion" (1937a, 409-10). From this systematic inadequacy of thought in relation to action and of action in relation to thought, Blondel had positive conclusions to draw concerning the human being's opening to the divine, as we have seen already from the side of human thought. It remains to be seen how he draws similar conclusions from the side of human action.

From the standpoint of this direct consideration of action in the concrete, the preceding volumes of the Trilogy on Thought, Being, and Action can be seen as a certain speculative preparation for what is now to be a "practicing philosophy," or a philosophy of practice, which will itself be scientific, through a process of elimination of all false solutions to the problem of action, in order to lead us to conclusions that are certain and necessary. But for the reader who has not been initiated to these higher philosophical elucidations, it is important to emphasize that no such initiation is necessary to enter into this direct philosophy of action, because this philosophy examines the itinerary any spiritual agent has to follow, whether in all simplicity, or armed with sophisticated thought patterns, as long as one is looking for a right intention amid all the byways that human existence presents with its crisscrossing of circulating ideas and passions. In fact, a certain innocence of any philosophical system that tends to bias the mind in one way or the other can be an advantage here. It liberates us from any set way of thinking and leaves us free to examine critically any frame of mind that may present itself. What Blondel wants more than anything else in this investigation is a certain sincerity in pursuing the question of what one wills ultimately in willing anything in particular here and now.

How, then, does Blondel begin this new version of his original philosophy of action? In much the same way as he had begun the first version some forty-four years earlier. Many modifications to the original text were to be made in most of the argument from beginning to end, including the suppression of certain parts and the addition of new explanations and transitions from one stage to the next. All this was to reflect a certain change from a strictly phenomenological method in relation to experience to a more straightforward, openly realist attitude in relation to the life of the spirit in the world. But to introduce it he simply reproduces the introduction as he had written it for the earlier work, as he notes himself (1937a, 442), although he does touch it up here and there to make more explicit the spiritual aspect of the life he was inquiring into, as distinct from its two-sided phenomenal aspect as both objective and subjective.

Repeating the same introduction, which shows the necessity of raising the scientific question of action and justifies the method for dealing with it philosophically, indicates a certain continuity of inspiration between the two works, or what Blondel calls a fidelity to his original intention in redoing the work he had launched his career with in philosophy. The touch-ups suggest a new light in which the dialectic is to be recast, that of self-consciousness as spirit in its own reality. It is not that the light of this self-conscious spirit had been totally absent from the first version of the direct philosophy of action. It had only been left too much in the background in order to show that the critical science of action presupposed nothing as given or affirmed at its inception, not even that there was a problem of action. Much of the dissatisfaction Blondel felt regarding *Action* of 1893 in the years after it was published stemmed from a realization on his part that he had conceded too much to his opponents by going in their door of negation or of phenomenalism without sufficiently highlighting the reality of spirit he wanted to get at, beyond all factious oppositions that mark the immanent order of consciousness. This is the systematic reason why he had resisted suggestions to have his first work re-edited once the first printing was exhausted shortly after its publication in 1893, and why he began to think of a two-volume work on *Action* as early as 1901 (1957b, 312). His outlook on the problem of human action had greatly expanded, as he indicated in the *Itinerary* of 1928, where emphasis was placed on the *élan spirituel* rather than just the Bergsonian *élan vital*. In the modified introduction for *L'Action II*, Blondel was merely reinserting into the texture of the argument the ontological dimension of a spiritual life that he had long had in mind, even though earlier he had strategically decided to meet phenomenalism on its own grounds before trying to raise it to the higher ground of a spiritual realism.

The difference between the first version of Blondel's philosophy of action in 1893 and its second version in *L'Action II* of the Trilogy raises a more general question of the distinction between what some have called the first or the early Blondel and the second or the later Blondel. Many philosophers are thought of as having gone through two or more phases, often with dramatic and systematic differences between the two or more phases. There is no evidence in all of Blondel's work that he ever had to go through such a radical switch in his thinking. Whether or not he was completely in possession of his intention from the beginning or in the early years of his career, when he was struggling with questions of apologetics and the exigencies of modern philosophy in matters of religion, it was one and the same intention that drove him throughout his life both as a philosopher and as a religious thinker, as is clear from what we have seen of his philosophical career thus far, and as we shall see more clearly when we come to his work on *Philosophy and the Christian Spirit*. The same unity of intentions can be seen even as we compare the early and the later version of his philosophy of human action in the concrete.

To be sure, there are differences between the two versions. Those having to do mainly with style are due to the different circumstances under which each was written. The first was written by a young man of thirty or so, filled with enthusiasm for his subject and able to piece together a closely knit argument for a jury that he knew would be hostile to his conclusions. It was breaking new ground for philosophy, and Boutroux, who was patron and first reader for the dissertation, was there to insist on greater coherence and cogency for an argument that took in so many aspects of life and practice. It was also quite eloquent and personal in many of its parts, as well as rigorous in its structure. This is what makes it still a very engaging philosophical work to read as both rational and existential at the same time. The later version, on the other hand, appears comparatively flat and subdued at first sight in comparison to the first, which remains the favorite of many readers of Blondel, and has been translated into many other languages, including Japanese. *Action II* is more difficult to read because of the way it was pieced together with the help of a secretary who had to both read and write for him because of his blindness. It was composed from an old text into which he was making significant cuts while adding a new perspective to an argument that did not entirely match the earlier text in style and crispness.

A close analysis of *Action II* reveals not only a difference of outline in the book, but also two or three different layers of writing in what found its way into the final text. Large segments of the 1893 book are simply omitted, like the chapter on subjectivity (1893a, 87-102) or the section on muscular effort (1893a, 153-60), because Blondel thought them unduly confusing for a spirit clearly conscious of itself in the act of doing science or of exercising its will. Other parts were taken up into the new text, sometimes without modification, but more often with some additions and subtractions and even some substitutions of key words, all of them designed to transpose a constrained earlier text into a more open spiritual outlook. Not all of these transpositions achieved the clarity Blondel would have desired or could perhaps have achieved, had he been able to read himself and make corrections with his own hand. Blondel himself remarks to his friend Wehrlé, in 1937, on how this recasting, or this "*refonte of L'Action* was much more necessary, laborious, and slow, than he had foreseen" (1946, 705).

Moreover, the differences between the two versions of *Action* are not just a matter of style. They are also a matter of substantive content. Blondel tried to put much more of the spirit in its concrete form or as real into this second version of his direct philosophy of action. This not only complicated his argument, as we shall see, but it also made it more rigorous from a critical and scientific point of view. Though Blondel thought of *Action II* at the end of the Trilogy as still accessible to those without any technical background in philosophy, as he thought his first effort in *Action* (1893) had been, it became a more difficult book to follow in all its ramifications, now seen as ontological in its bearing from the beginning as well as phenomenological. Some commentators, like Henri Bouillard, have seen this more explicit admission of the spiritual and the ontological into the tenor of the argument as a shift in method from "a phenomenology of existence to a classical type of metaphysics. A development, no doubt" *(Recherches de Science Religieuse*, 36 [1949]: 367). But this is clearly contrary to what Blondel says about his method and the principle of judgment in both versions of his philosophy of action.

To begin with, his method was never purely a "phenomenology of human existence." Even in the early version of the dialectic, the phenomenology was designed to raise the question of the necessary being of action. Putting that question off to a later part of the dialectic, after a full elaboration of the phenomenon of action, did not mean that it was excluded, in principle, from the phenomenological elaboration of human action. On the contrary, in the final chapter of the published version of *Action (1893)*, added after the defense of the dissertation, Blondel had sought precisely to correct for the mistaken impression that metaphysics had been left out of his phenomenology. On the other hand, however, the metaphysics he wanted to allow for was not the kind Bouillard had in mind when he speaks of a classical type, with "being" as principle of judgment. This would have been for Blondel an abstract metaphysics of the understanding. In fact, in the later version of *Action*, he was no less critical of such metaphysics, which verges on superstition when it turns into a religious practice, than he had been in the earlier version. Blondel was thinking of a metaphysics of the concrete in human action from the beginning. The principle of judgment he fell back on for the development of his dialectic in *Action II* was exactly the same as the one he had come to in *Action* of 1893, what Bouillard refers to as the spiritual dynamism that animates human action in its development. What would it take to make human action the equal of itself or, in more technical terms, what would it take to make the willed will equal to the willing will?

In fact, in both versions of the dialectic, Blondel comes to this principle through precisely the same reflection on the internal conception of action in human consciousness, where a metaphysics of the will comes to the fore at the same time as a metaphysics of reason. The only difference between the two versions of the argument is that in the first he had taken only the phenomenological aspect of the principle explicitly into consideration, while leaving its metaphysical or ontological aspect to be brought up later on, when he would face up to *the necessary being of action*, however that would be conceived in the end. In the second version of *L'Action*, he abandons this strategic contrivance and lets the metaphysical side of the human spirit speak for itself from the beginning, so to speak, without abandoning the methodological principle that nothing is to be admitted into the science of action except what comes from action itself. The reason for insisting only on the phenomenological in the first place had been to show how one can "reintegrate into one and the same determinism all the forms of life" (1896a, 64), prior to bringing up the question of the necessary being of action, but even that was to "describe *sub specie necessitatis* a real connection of states" (1898, 98). It was to get to the real, beyond the ideal, that he had decided to study action in the first place. This had to include, beyond our consciousness of the world, the real world itself and the spiritual activity we insert into it.

Clearly, then, Blondel was thinking of the real life of the spirit in the world as something transcendent that philosophical thought had not yet begun to grasp adequately at the time. "Even if it were ideally parallel or identical to the real of the act done *(l'acte opéré)* and of the being thought *(l'être pensé)*, philosophy must always bear in mind that in us concrete thoughts and lived life are transcendent with reference to our immanent knowledge even of the transcendent and even of the supernatural" (1896a, 67). What he was striving for in his systematic elaboration of the phenomenon of action was a way of speaking about the transcendent in human thought and action on the basis of a principle that has ramifications in a reality both immanent and totally transcendent at the same time. Only thus could he speak legitimately and rationally, not only of the immanent and the natural, but also of the transcendent and the supernatural.

Blondel had a keen sense of an eternal responsibility in his action. That is why action became for him the philosophical problem par excellence, one that could encompass all other problems, including that of being. At the end of his introduction to the first *Action*, in order to give an indication of where he was going with his science of action taken as "common knot of science, morality and metaphysics," he points out that it is not only life that is in question, but "the very reality of being" (1893a, xxii). For, ultimately, if I cannot choose to be free one way or another, I simply cannot *be* free. "If I am not what I will to be, what I will, not on my lips, not in desire or as a project, but with all my heart and all my strength, in my acts, I am not. At the core of my being, there is a willing and a love of being, or else there is nothing" (1893a, xxiii). In the introduction to the second *Action*, Blondel reiterates this way of posing the ultimate question, but perhaps with a greater consciousness of its metaphysical ramifications for a spiritual being. For at this point he adds a new sentence for *Action II*, to make explicit what had remained implicit in the earlier version. "In a nature that is reasonable and free, being, which finds in it its essential form, if it were entirely involuntary and constrained, would cease to be, which is contradictory to the congenital and indestructible reality of any spirit" (1937a, 34).

If there was an anti-metaphysical strain in what became the third and longest part of *Action* (1893a), on the *Phenomenon of Action*, it was only in opposition to a certain kind of abstract metaphysics, said to be of the understanding, one that reduced being to the idea we have of it. In turning to action Blondel was trying to get beyond this sort of metaphysics back to something real, action as concretely exercised, from which there was something to be learned metaphysically as well as phenomenologically. His method of studying action had to begin phenomenologically, as it did in the second *Action* no less than in the first, but it could not limit itself a priori to this immanent order of experience. Blondel's aim was to show the necessity of passing on to a transcendent order that manifested itself in human action as such, and to reason about what was implied in such an order for human action. Sooner or later what began as only a phenomenology of action according to a method of immanence was bound to turn into a metaphysical consideration, not as a regression to some abstract metaphysics of the understanding discredited by critical philosophy, but rather as an intellectual step forward into something that transcended not only the categories of our understanding but also the totality of all the things we are involved with in our immanent historical action. In the second *Action*, this turn came sooner in the dialectic, in comparison to the first *Action*, but it did not replace the phenomenological or existential approach Blondel had taken earlier. In fact, that approach remains a mark of this philosophy as a direct philosophy of action in its second version. The second version only took the existential phenomenology one step higher, to arrive at what Blondel calls a "more rationally coherent organization of this new study" (1937a, 412). For Blondel there is no opposition between phenomenology and metaphysics. There is rather a reciprocal necessity of passing from the one to the other and for maintaining ties between the two, for anyone who would study human action concretely in its integrity.

We see, then, why Blondel could repeat the same introduction for the second *Action* as he had used for the first. In it, after raising the question of action in human life as a whole, he makes the same distinction made earlier between *practical science*, the science concerning human life as a whole that one acquires through the moral experience of following the light of one's conscience, dim as that may seem at the beginning, and the *science of practice*, the science we acquire more immediately in the present by the critical question concerning everything that is presupposed or anticipated prospectively in the practical science of a conscience that strives to be true to itself. In both versions he shows the necessity of doing such a science of practice, not just for those who are critical of all-too-naïve consciences, but even for those who are prepared to follow their conscience sincerely, at whatever sacrifice. The first question to be raised in the science of action is the most radical that can be raised concerning the problem of action, which is whether there is even a problem of action. Answers are to be sought only in action, without appealing to anything from outside of action. And if some judgment is to be arrived at, it must be rooted in action, which contains its own principle of judgment. This was to hold for Blondel in this second version of his science of action no less than in the first version.

Restructuring the Argument

What Blondel had in mind all along in both versions of *Action* was to study the movement of the human spirit in its aspiration toward equality with itself, an equality it could not attain by itself without the intervention of a totally transcendent Being and pure Acting eternally equal to itself. For this, as a philosopher, he had to start from where human action begins in human consciousness and follow the expansion of this action from the interior of consciousness to the external world through physical effort, to the world of others through co-action, and to the entire immanent order of universal morality. The way he chose to do this in *Action II*, after having abandoned the contrivance of a strict immanentist phenomenology as a set of stepping-stones to the question of a real transcendence, led him to what he thought would be a more rationally coherent science, with a way of laying out the entire subject matter systematically that differed from the way he had proceeded in the first place. This meant he had to restructure his argument so that it would be more in keeping with his way of thinking both phenomenologically and metaphysically at the same time, as can be shown by a comparison of the two outlines or tables of contents we have for this dialectic.

Action (1893) was divided into five parts of very unequal length, two short ones at the beginning, one on dilettantism and one on pessimism, and another relatively short part at the end, on a hypothetically conceived fulfillment of the human spirit in religious action. Most of the book, and certainly the most important part of the argument, was contained in Parts Three and Four, the first on the *Phenomenon of Action* and the second on the *Necessary Being of Action*. In fact, Part Three was more than four times as long as Part Four, comprising almost half of the entire book in its systematic exploration of the *phenomenon of action*, beginning from the lowliest consideration of action as an object of empirical science, and rising, through a turn to subjectivity, to its highest and most universal pretension as ethical and as religious, or as superstition, as Blondel characterized the first semblance of religion in his critique of the fifth and final stage of the spirit's appearing.

In fact, in the process of elaborating this *phenomenon of action*, precisely at stage two, which is on the conception of action in self-consciousness and on the free exercise of the will, Blondel worked his way into the dynamic principle of spirit that became the engine, not only for moving from one stage to the next in the phenomenon of action or the appearing of spirit — from individual consciousness to social consciousness and from social consciousness to universal humanitarian consciousness — but also for moving on beyond the very phenomenon of action and its immanent order to a transcendent order, where the *necessary being of action* comes into view, the being that all human action must ultimately acknowledge within itself and without. The transition from Part Three to Part Four thus takes place on the basis of a dialectical principle that had been presented initially as a stage in the natural phenomenon of action, the second one of five. And it was left for Part Four to show how the dialectic of human action comes to a climax regarding man's destiny in the face of an inevitable transcendence. The general thrust of the argument was to go from the immanent to the transcendent, but it was presented almost as if there had to be a break between the two before one could begin talking about transcendence as placing us before the *one thing necessary*, God, with the alternative of saying *yes* or *no* to his necessary presence in our action.

In *Action II*, Blondel thought it would be more rational to reorganize this argument and to simplify it in outline, if not in the execution of its various parts. The major division between Part Three, the *Phenomenon of Action*, and Part Four, on the *Necessary Being of Action*, was let go, as was much of the elaboration on the conflict necessitated by this division, in which the will finds in itself a desire to equal itself and a radical inability to do so on its own. Instead, for the second version of this dialectic of action in the concrete, Blondel chose to follow a method of *deployment* into concentric waves that took human action from its emergence as an initiative of individual self-consciousness, through different spheres of expansion in personal and interpersonal action, in social life as family and as homeland, in a universal ethical life, all the way to the human being's effort to absorb the transcendent into its own acting, with a risk of deviation into superstition, but still leaving room in the end for a moment or a wave of properly religious dispositions as part of action in the world. What characterizes this new method of expansion into concentric waves is a movement of transcendence from the very beginning, a process of unpacking that is still phenomenological for each new moment, but that also allows for seeing how each new wave is a moment of consolidation in human action at a higher level than in the previous wave. The metaphor of the concentric waves serves to illustrate this twofold method, first, of looking forward in transcendence to a higher level of action and, second, of looking back at each level to integrate what has gone before into the higher level. The dialectic thus rises from one level of transcendence to the next in the immanent order, now viewed as real and no longer as merely phenomenal or ideal, until it reaches a critical point on the level of ethical action, where the object becomes one of realizing a metaphysical ideal in history. At this point the question of a real transcendence of the entire immanent order comes into view along with the human being's effort to integrate such a totally transcendent being into his ever-immanent, historical action. The entire movement is presented as a continuous line of argument, laying out the different waves of action the human will must go through in search of an object that will be the equal of itself, including a religious wave at the end, where more questions are raised than philosophy can answer, but that a philosophy of action must still take into consideration, if it is to go to the end of its universal concern.

All of this movement is spelled out in carefully modulated details, in a series of nine concentric waves that now make up the major part of this exposition of human action in the concrete, using phenomenology to bring the philosophy of action to its highest metaphysical considerations. This part of the book takes up about half of the text, not counting the 150 pages of supplementary explanations and historical confirmations Blondel adds to the text in this volume, as he does in all the other volumes of the Trilogy. It ends with a brief consideration of a hypothetical supernatural gift that would enable the will to come to completion in its quest for equality with itself or with its infinite power of willing, but that Blondel now conceives as a tenth and exotic wave, because it exceeds anything that the natural will could do for itself. Hypothetical though it has to be from the standpoint of philosophy, Blondel still sees a certain necessity in this supernatural gift, in that it would satisfy a natural aspiration of the human spirit. But he does not elaborate on this necessity as much as he had done in the dissertation of 1893, leaving that sort of elaboration for a later work more explicitly on the Christian Spirit. In *Action II* he is satisfied with showing how the offer of such a gift would answer all the highest exigencies of reason, and more.

Prior to this long elaboration of the phenomenon of human action in concentric waves, however, Blondel made important adjustments in the way he led up to it. In 1893 he had devoted two brief parts justifying his science of action, one criticizing dilettantism, which denied there was any problem of action, and one criticizing pessimism, which claimed nothingness as the answer to the problem, prior to coming to the *phenomenon of action* as the problem to be explored. This, however, had not brought him to the standpoint he needed to launch the kind of subjective science he was seeking to elaborate. Included in the *phenomenon of action,* as he had originally thought about it, was another science that could stand as an obstacle to a proper science of the subject as the initiator of its own proper activity. This was the purely objective science of positivism even as applied to human behavior.

In the first version of his own science of action, Blondel had chosen to deal with this remaining obstacle as part of the first stage of his elaboration on the *phenomenon of action* as a whole. Against the sheer positivism of objective science, which tended to reduce consciousness to nothing more than its material conditions, he had argued for the necessity of a science of the subject as the initiator of its own action, including the action of doing science itself. More than that, using the language of objective science, he had spoken of elements of consciousness in a way that was deliberately ambivalent, in order to reverse the way of considering subjective consciousness, from a perspective that was purely objective and external to one that was properly subjective and internal, the perspective he thought necessary for a proper science of action. What he was attempting was a tour de force that could work only within a phenomenology of science, as the action of a scientist who remains in a state of confusion concerning the internal and spiritual aspects of his own activity, even as a scientist, let alone as a human being with purposes of his own.

In the later version of his dialectic of human action in the concrete, Blondel not only revised his approach to the phenomenon of action as a whole, distinct from the necessary being of action, but he also dropped this attempt to make a direct transition from a purely objective standpoint in science to one that was subjective as well, in exploring the *positive something* about action that comes as an admission with the refutation of pessimism or the nihilistic attitude toward action. There is no trace of this chapter on "the elements of consciousness" from 1893 in the later version of *Action*. What is kept from the argument against positivism is simply that positive science alone cannot give an adequate answer to the question of action, because positive science itself is an action that begs the question. And the case for this is made in 1937, not as a stage in the elaboration of the phenomenon of action, but as a separate preliminary chapter along with those on dilettantism and pessimism, prior to a central chapter on the internal ingredients of action that had previously appeared only as a second stage in the *phenomenon of action.*

In 1937, Blondel considered the argument against positivism as a necessary step in clearing the ground for a proper science of human action, a *pars purificans,* in the same way as he had originally considered the arguments against dilettantism and pessimism. The purpose of the chapter on positive objective science was simply to open the way for a proper consideration of the subject in its spiritual and even its metaphysical reality, as the initiator of action in historical actuality. "It has always been possible to note that, amid the churning and under the universal shove and pull of things, acting and having the consciousness of acting implies an initiative capable of holding up this crushing passivity. There has to be both a victorious transcendence of the total immanence and a finality that is irreducible to all the apparent determinism of nature and science. It is clear, therefore, that action as such belongs to an order that is original and ulterior to or higher than scientific data and conclusions" (1937a, 120). This is the order and the dynamism of a consciousness that is thoughtful and active, which a proper study of action must get to, the order of an *élan spirituel* that is internal and irreducible to its subalternate conditions, the order that manifests its own "original nature through the development of its own proper virtualities. Already the activity that brings forth and indefinitely prolongs the effort of the positive sciences derives from and depends on, even in the immanent order, transcendent needs of human action" (1937a, 121).

The philosophical question of action thus becomes for Blondel one of exploring this human order, no longer as an object seen from outside and serving as a basis for the prestigious symbolism of the positive sciences, but as a reality that is grasped only from the inside. Blondel is thinking of action as something centered in self-consciousness and as deploying itself out from this center into the ever-broadening spheres of the individual person, society, and the entire order of the universe. His purpose or his method is no longer just to offer a phenomenological description of our mental activity. It is rather to get back to the primitive élan of human acting and to examine how "it determines itself little by little according to the ends toward which it is drawn or it draws itself, and the entire question is to learn how the initial act of the willing will will find its equilibrium according to how it will be in equation or in discordance with the final term toward which it tends spontaneously" (1937a, 127-28). The entire science of action will now consist in refocusing on this center of self-consciousness in act and then in following how it transcends itself as well as the world in which it finds itself, in the concrete exercise of the willed will, without admitting any sphere of influence unless it proves itself necessary for achieving an equation of the willed will with the willing will.

In the first version of *Action*, the turn to the subject had come only at the second stage in the development of the *phenomenon of action*, the first stage having been devoted to how we try to restrict science to purely objective or positive considerations of action. In his critique of the positive sciences, Blondel had tried to show the necessity of a subjective science of action even from the standpoint of objective science, or of the scientist doing positive science. He had even included a chapter where he attempted to turn objective science itself around into subjective science, by playing on the notion of *elements* in consciousness that could be identified objectively but that could not be properly understood except subjectively, from the standpoint of an agent. In the later version he dropped this chapter altogether as no longer necessary to make a transition from positivism to a reflective science of the subject, and as perhaps still too ambiguous or misleading about the nature of subjective science itself. By the time of *Action II* positivism had become only a third obstacle, along with dilettantism and pessimism, to be overcome along the way to the really positive science of the subject he wanted to come to, that center of consciousness from which action surges in ever-broadening waves of encompassment, and what he had come to refer to as "the permanent opening that assures access to one's most intimate life for transcendent stimulations and the possibility for man to accept not only the influences of his state of nature or the external teachings that history and the use of reason may enable him to utilize, but also certain solicitations and enablements at the greatest depth of action as into the secret of a covenantal arc" (1937a, 130). These are the broad lines of the universal development Blondel wanted to come to in this dialectic of action. What he had to do next in this dialectic was find the principle in the historical subject upon which such a spiritual development could be based.

Worldly Ingredients and Internal Parturition of Action

Thus, by restructuring the preliminaries to his argument, Blondel brought into new prominence what had been the essential part of his argument from the beginning but had been buried, so to speak, in a long exposition of the phenomenon of action, with little or no reference to the fullness of spiritual transcendence already at work in human action. In *Action II* this essential reflection on the ingredients of action and on the internal dynamism of consciousness is included as a principal part at the head of the argument in the book, before the deployment of action in its concentric waves, and as what will rationally account for that deployment. What were previously spoken of only as "elements of consciousness" will now be seen as ingredients to be integrated in human action, in a description of "the phases of what one could call the embryogenesis of human acts. For all the forces of life, of thought, of willing come secretly into play to compose — in fostering it — this initiative where Descartes saw something marvelous whereby the Creator seemed to delegate to man something of his own forever" (1937a, 131).

Two sorts of things come into play in this internal dynamism Blondel now turns to analyze, natural forces that affect our sensibility and an initiative of our own that sets a new course for action in the world. The initiative stems from ideas that Descartes thought of as innate and separate from all preconditions in the world and in sensibility, but that Blondel thought of as emerging phenomenally in consciousness due to essential ties they have with things and other subjects in the world. Even if we act freely and in an original way in the world, thanks to the ideas we form in our consciousness, it is never independently of these many ingredients from the world that have penetrated into our unconsciousness. Even with his renewed insistence on the original and originating act at the core of properly human initiative in the world, Blondel continues to see this act as emerging from pre-conditions that the science of action must take into account as part of how action comes to emerge.

He goes back then to his earlier assertion: *Il est de science que la conscience est* (1937a, 133; 1893a, 103). It is a matter of science that there is consciousness and conscience. In French, *conscience* has both meanings and Blondel has both in mind as he begins this inquiry, the prospective view of consciousness as well as the reflective. It is not enough to study *consciousness* and/or *conscience* in function of the external phenomena to which it is tied as to necessary conditions. It must be studied as an *act* irreducible to any fact, an *act* that is "certain, precise, positive, scientific as much and more than any physical data, any mathematical truth" (1937a, 134). This assertion is taken to follow from the critique of a purely positivist or objectivist approach to facts or to action, one that presupposes but cannot encompass the act of *consciousness* and of *conscience* from which it flows. "Consciousness takes its nourishment from the immense milieu that has repercussions in it and that it organizes within itself, but it contains this milieu only by surpassing it. Also, once consciousness appears under the form of appetite or of an instinctive need, there is a victorious spontaneity" (1937a, 134). The fact of this spontaneity is undeniable for any self-conscious being. The problem is to study it as a new force, a new act, no less methodically in all its ramifications than in its preconditions, starting from the principle that will disclose itself through reflection on this act, which is one of both intelligence and will at once, amid the stirrings of one's sensibility. The life of practice has a dialectic of its own, and it is the task of a philosophy of action to follow this logic, or this order of practical reasoning, as it presents itself in the necessary sequence of our states of consciousness. The difficulty in doing this will come from the combination of characteristics that action presents for any human subject, its singularity at the same time as its universality, and its internal unity even as it relates to the external. Hence, there is the necessity of following a specifically designed method to get, not only to the bottom of this *act*, but also to the fullness of the *end* toward which it tends.

When Blondel speaks of the *conception* of action he is usually referring to the way we conceive action rationally, or to action as first conceived in its very originality by the human agent. Without some conception there is no properly human action. There is only the reaction of an automaton, connoting more passivity than activity. This conception of action, however, does not spring forth in consciousness as from a clear blue sky. It goes through a period of gestation amid other acts that precede and prepare this birth of action in the concept. Blondel is concerned with analyzing how this birth takes place concretely in human consciousness, because in it is already at stake the question of human freedom itself and of "the highest option on which hangs our destiny" (1937a, 137). He knows that there are all sorts of subconscious forces influencing his consciousness, but he does not try to probe into what these might be as a psychologist would, in doing what has been called an archaeology of the subject. For that would be to move back into an objectivist point of view on the subject. What he does is examine how these forces emerge in consciousness as impulses for action that one must contend with in determining one's own course as a human being. A desire or an image has appeared in consciousness. There is no need or no way of knowing whence or how an instinctual urge has come into focus, or how the brightness of an idea has revealed itself. All one needs for a science of action is to examine how these impulses fare with all their determinism once they cross the threshold of consciousness.

Blondel distinguishes within consciousness what he calls *mobiles* and *motives* for action. Motives are ideas that draw to action. Mobiles are forces or impulses that incline us to act. The two are dynamically related in consciousness in the sense that motives are ideal representations of what the mobiles at work in our psychic makeup would have us do. There is no motive that is real for us unless it corresponds to something indigenous in our nature. "Our desires are and express what we are and what we make of them; the idea goes through the sentiment or else it remains a dormant seed. . . . The motive is in fact only the repercussion and the synthesis of a thousand unheard murmurings that is the reason for its natural efficacity" (1937a, 139-40).

At the same time, however, no mobile is truly a mobile for human action unless it is taken up by thought as an idea or a motive. Merely instinctive impulses, or the power of images, are not enough for an act to be human. There has to be some quickening of ideation from a motion higher than the impulses of animal life or the attractions of desire. For the diffuse energies of our nature to become efficacious principles of action in our consciousness, they "have to be gathered up in a mental synthesis and represented under the single form of an end to be realized; they are confirmed and vivified by the effort expressing them, as attention is fortified by the tensing of organs" (1937a, 141). The dynamogenic influence of mobiles takes place only if it is expressed in a definite representation and a determinate movement, "so that the final cause becomes moving cause and ideas and signs are the indispensable condition of the dispositions they manifest" (1937a, 141).

Indeed, Blondel uncovers a still-higher motion in human consciousness than the motive and the mobile, which remain intertwined with one another as indispensable conditions for one another. This is the motion on the side of the motive, or the idea itself in consciousness. "The motive itself is no longer a motive unless it becomes in turn a mobile" (1937a, 142). Once the hidden causes of our emotions have provided themselves with an aim for their tendency, they are no longer one with the total flow of life. They constitute a distinct end for themselves. They are no longer merely a summation of the subalternate determinism that nudges them into the light of consciousness. They take on a dynamism of their own as they bring a new perspective, the promise of an unknown to be achieved. We do not always know all the reasons why we do what we do, nor are the reasons we give ourselves always the only ones or the truest ones. They are usually approximative, alongside other reasons that we sense vaguely summed up in our natural inclinations, in hereditary habits, desires we have grown into, or in our entire organism and even the universe. "More profoundly still," Blondel adds in 1937, to emphasize the spiritual character of this new dynamism, "and more broadly, this congenital motion of our rational nature oriented by an infinite aspiration is nourished by the still confused presence of truths and realities transcendent to the entire empirical order" (1937a, 142). The motive that at first was charged only with the energy of emotional forces can now dominate all these antecedent energies and exploit them in view of ulterior ends that surpass the passive experience, and even what may be anticipated from it. Somehow or other, at the *decisive* moment of our action, something unforeseen carries the day by a sort of reversal of perspective, where thought takes over the motion in view of higher ends that it only begins to conceive. "Issued from force, the interior light is an origin of force; the image that results from movement is cause of movements, and thought, ceaselessly fecundated by nature, fecundates in turn, as an organism that digests and vivifies all that it takes in" (1937a, 143).

At this decisive moment in the internal embryogenesis of action, then, when the motive conceived becomes itself a mobile oriented to further ends than the one its antecedent mobile had determined, an important turn takes place in the science of action. Action can no longer be seen as determined only by its antecedents in the past, or in nature. It is now self-determined, and this in view of ends that cannot be reduced to anything external to self-consciousness. If we are still acting in the world and on the world, it is only by surpassing it in order to transform it. Marx would understand this kind of humanistic practice quite well, but Blondel sees a much more spiritual dimension in it when he insists there can be no true humanism without some clear consciousness of an end that is at once interior and transcendent to the agent. Man does not live only for what is not yet, for the future, for progress. Underlying all this striving in time, this broadening of one's consciousness to new horizons for conquest, there is an aspiration to a higher order that raises the human élan to a level that surpasses time and space. In fact, Blondel adds, using the argument by implication we have seen him use frequently, "we would not even have any consciousness of the future or of progress if we did not have implicitly a need for liberation and infinitude" (1937a, 143). This is the point in the philosophy of action where the argument seems to be most telling for raising reflection to a higher, inner level of activity, where new models of initiative are invented and ideas are produced in view of new realizations.

Indeed, further reflection upon this phenomenon of multiple ideas for action in consciousness will bring greater clarity about how freedom and infinity are associated in the transcendence of human action with its antecedent conditions. Blondel avers that "a motive is not a motive if it is alone. If it is alone it is animal desire, an instinctive image. If it appears alone in consciousness, it is an impulse of spontaneity or of mechanical habit, a delirium for one who is sick or alienated, a suggestion for a sleepwalker, an automatism for a daydreamer; it is a fixation, not an idea" (1937a, 144). For an idea to be really an idea in human consciousness it has to be accompanied with other ideas that we contrast and oppose to one another. A clear consciousness of ideas, even as motives for action, comes to the fore only by a process of discrimination and of relativization among different and antagonistic tendencies in our psyche. If there is a mechanism of negation at work in our consciousness, it is because it sets in motion a pairing of rival affirmations of which one succeeds in excluding the other, but without eliminating it altogether. "In short, to conceive an act sharply is to imagine at the same time at least the vague possibility of different acts, which play the role of highlighter and serve to make more precise by elimination and by approximation the initial conception" (1937a, 145).

What this plurality of solidary and opposed states of consciousness in the discriminative process serves to bring out for Blondel is the presence and the immanent action of a power able to encompass them all in a higher kind of unity, namely, that of *reason,* which is not only a speculative function, but also and more radically a power of promotion, elevation, and liberation. In the interplay of forces and tendencies within itself, consciousness discovers, also within itself, a higher force of *reflection* able to hold all these antecedent forces in check, at least momentarily, in order to deliberate about choosing to go with the one or the other. As the diverse ideas for action emerge from their obscure origins through confrontation with other ideas in the clear light of reason, reason encompasses all of them in a system. It contains them all as it sees each one as one among many in contention with one another. It drains each one of its spontaneous energy and uses them all to hold them all at bay for at least a moment of deliberation, before giving itself to one or the other of them for its own actualization.

Through this analysis of the mechanism of free choice in human action, Blondel can explain how we can have a consciousness of determinism in our action. We think of the necessity of an act following from fascination with a mental representation only by imagining that the system of the successful motives has eliminated any adverse tendency and has become a total part, so to speak. That is, as we consider this dominant motive as the only real and effective one, in abstraction from all the rest, we maintain in opposition to it the idea that it could be only a part in a whole; so that we maintain the thought of determinism only by finding within ourselves something to surpass it with, namely, deliberative reason.

The same analysis can also explain how we can have the illusion of acting freely when, in fact, we are under the influence of a single idea or suggestion. Once an action suggests itself along with the retinue of motives that reinforce it, the suggestion can have the effect of chasing from the field of consciousness all contrasting or alternative tendencies in a kind of subjective anesthesia. These different, antagonistic tendencies are not thereby suppressed. They are simply ignored, leaving the subject, or the patient, who is executing the suggestion with the impression that, in the absence of any other motive, there is only one goal to be pursued, and in pursuing it one is totally free. In the case of determinism, the illusion was in thinking that one partial tendency in one's behavior can totally dominate all other tendencies. In the case of illusory freedom, all sense of antagonistic tendencies is lost and with that also any sense of a need for discrimination and struggle in the actualization of one's freedom.

Action is thus seen as a movement of discernment and liberation within human consciousness. As we deliberate we liberate ourselves, momentarily at least, from the spontaneous impulse of any tendency within us. At the level of reflected consciousness, there is a twofold synthesis: first, the synthesis that each motive represents of a tendency or a set of tendencies, and second, the representation of these representations that holds them in suspense to be assessed in the light of a higher tendency or a higher goal more proper to it as *reason.*

Viewed from the past or from the antecedents of any moment in human consciousness, everything seems to be determined by different tendencies in our nature or our history. But through the determinism of these different tendencies in their very diversity, a new movement, a new moment of consciousness emerges, that is not accounted for by this antecedent determinism of tendencies, but that in fact accounts for the emergence of what are only obscure tendencies, or forces, or mobiles, as motives and ideals for consciousness. Viewed from the bottom up, everything in this ascending movement seems necessary. But this is only a buildup to a point or a moment where a new movement takes over. Blondel has tried to show how this higher movement was already at work in the lower tendencies leading up to it, through his analysis of the dynamic of mobiles and motives in human consciousness. What he wants to do now is show what comes from this higher movement in terms of its own ends, or of what it wants fundamentally to achieve or actualize for itself. This he does by elaborating on how reason functions both as decisive and as liberating, in transcending what is given to it by the spontaneity of nature.

What we have, then, in the reflective conception of an act accompanied by contrasting projects and prospections, is a new, more complex kind of activity that transcends the primitive automatism of tendencies. A new power has emerged that has given rise to consciousness itself with this plurality and diversity of ideas and motives for action, a power that was at first hidden in the obscurity of these tendencies but that now comes to the fore as having to choose among these tendencies in the light of ends of its own. This power, now seen in the light of day, has been an active presence in the parturition of motives for action in human consciousness and must now be recognized for what it is, as a spiritual *élan* that transcends the diverse motions it stirs up and that must now serve as the *norm* and the moving force, not only for what precedes its emergence as consciousness, but also for all the deployment of action that is to follow. The antecedent mobiles and motives are already constitutive of human action in one sense, but in the broader more spiritual sense they are only preparatory for action. Blondel recognizes how the human spirit is quite engaged in a physical organism, from which the possibility of many operations and successive horizons can arise, but in all of this he wants to point out that a properly rational activity will have ends of its own to pursue and a necessity to become equal to itself in a "term capable of making the willed and elicited will equal to the willing will that sustains, commands and sanctions all our thinking and all our acting" (1937a, 151). This is what distinguishes his understanding of the *élan spirituel* from the Bergsonian *élan vital,* even as something secretly at work in the immanent order of motives and mobiles, and this is what he must now bring the science of action to consider as it begins to transcend the immanent order in which it appears.

To do this Blondel does not try to step out of the immanent order in which human consciousness is engrossed. He tries to see rather how reason is tied into this immanence, as it connects the transcendent and the absolute to the contingent. His concern is with "the real link that ties together affirmations that would have neither life nor possibility without one another" (1937a, 153). Reason cannot remain up in the air, even in seeking its own ends. It has to choose how it will approach this end concretely; and what it has to choose from are particular mobiles and motives that now represent for it different objects to be willed. In choosing, however, it cannot be purely indifferent to any motive, since it is itself a mobile oriented to an end of its own, something transcendent and absolute to which all that it chooses somehow has to be related. Reason somehow touches on the two extremes of an order that action has to ascend and that science has to consolidate, for a consciousness that is still tentative in its search for the practical truth about itself.

To illustrate how the dynamism of reason reaches out to these two extremes in its conjunction with the dynamism of nature, Blondel takes a closer examination of how it comes into play in the contention of motives and mobiles within consciousness. These motives and mobiles are the repercussion in our consciousness of the entire world and the expression of our own nature. The consciousness that perceives them from its singular point of view is at the same time perceiving the universe and its total solidarity. For such a knowledge of the universe a new relation has to be established by that very knowledge; "the better we understand the vastness of the universe and of this immense duration in which we roam, the more we rise above it. To know is to possess and to rule" (1937a, 153). To become conscious of them is to begin to take control over the subalternate forces of the physical and biological world. Even as reason appears to dispense itself in our experience of multiple motives and mobiles that pour into our consciousness, it never loses the character of universality and transcendence that makes possible its immanent activity and that raises the particularity of our contingent acts to a higher order than that of simple becoming.

We cannot understand parts, Blondel argues, without the idea of the whole. Nor do we come to know the whole except by distinguishing ourselves from the *universe,* as we perceive the *universal.* Everything we have seen in the dynamic organization of motives and mobiles in our consciousness points in this direction. There was no consciousness of a motive without the presence of other motives. The consciousness of multiple reasons for acting did not come without at least some confused view of their mutual conflict and of the system that they form in a single consciousness. Finally, our "consciousness of these contrasts within an organic unity does not take place without the thought of what is inaccessible to relation and limitation, without the presence, known and possessed, of an absolute, or without the regulative idea of the infinite" (1937a, 154). We cannot doubt the presence of these "rational notions" in our consciousness, nor of the role they necessarily play in the way we come to manage our personal behavior and take initiative of our own in the world. We have to see rather how they converge with motives and mobiles in the human consciousness of action, not just to open up our perspective on life, but also to explain the sense of freedom we have in acting as we do. Blondel puts it as succinctly as he can when he writes: "the consciousness of action implies the notion of infinite; and this notion of infinite explains the consciousness of free action" (1937a, 155).

For Blondel this is not just the conclusion of a philosophical reflection on the embryogenesis of action in consciousness. It is something in the consciousness of anyone who has a sense of inserting or adding something of his own in the immense mechanism of the world of which we are conscious. There is no *act*, no state of consciousness that does not somehow transcend its conditions, and thought has everything to do with this transcendence. Reflection is not just a damper on the spontaneity of action. It is the force of these forces taken together. Leveraged by the idea of the *infinite*, it can raise the entire universe, as ideas have always done in the formation of civilizations.

The decisive reason for a genuinely human act does not reside only in one or another of the partial tendencies that stirred in our consciousness to make it possible. It lies rather in this power of reflection that can dominate the various forces that make themselves felt, whether as physical energies, appetites, tendencies, motives, or some sort of pressure both of nature and spirit. If an action is truly and expressly willed, the total reason for it has to be found in a principle that is irreducible to any of these impulses that have found their way into clear consciousness as particular motives for action. It can only be found in a principle that transcends them all. The sense that we take initiative of our own in action implies a character of infinitude and transcendence in that very principle. What reflection does is dispose for itself the resources of spontaneity. Thanks to its own resourcefulness and invention it takes over the expansion of its natural energy and turns it into a new effort of its own, toward a goal it formulates for itself. The reciprocity of mobiles and motives, or of means and ends, that had manifested itself in consciousness, as if from a still-extrinsic source in the dynamism of nature, is now illuminated by reason itself with its own internal dynamism and finality, the dynamism that the science of action must now explore step by step, by showing that it rises necessarily amid the interplay of motives and mobiles to a consciousness of a free power.

Blondel has thus brought to the fore the essential role of action itself in the constitution of reason and in the idea of freedom. In the original version of 1893 he had done this strictly in terms of ideas or phenomena that appeared in consciousness as a consciousness, not only of being in action, but also of being a new source of one's own action. At that time he had been concerned primarily with bringing out the necessity in this phenomenal concatenation of ideas in an active self-consciousness, without regard for any consideration of whether these were only ideas or whether there was any reality in them, in keeping with the restricted phenomenological outlook he had designed for this part of the dialectic, keeping the question of the necessary being of action in parenthesis for a later consideration in the dialectic. In 1937, he follows largely the same method of analysis almost word for word, except for the passages in which he had earlier explained how he was prescinding from the question of reality with regard to the interplay of ideas he was discussing. In fact, instead of the phenomenologically restrictive passages he omits, he introduces new passages to show the substantial value of the idea he deems necessary in the parturition of action, namely that of the *infinite*. As important as it is to call upon the infinite and the transcendent implied in the consciousness of one's own originality in acting, he writes, "it is no less capital not to confuse this infinite with an indeterminate, this transcendent with an immanence that is indefinitely variable and perfectible" (1937a, 157). This would amount to nothing more than a bad or a false infinite, one that would offer no leverage for consciousness to rise above the world pressing in on it from all sides. The *true infinite* as contained in reason entails a precise *norm* for reason to follow. Reason is not just a regulative power. It has within it a "substantial truth. Transcendence is not a category of the ideal. Even if we can speak of its vital immanence in the intelligence and will of spiritual agents, its presence in them is well and good the presence and the stimulation of a subsistent absolute that remains incommensurate with any contingent reality" (1937a, 157). One no longer has to wait until the end of the dialectic to find out that the presence of the infinite and the absolute in the consciousness of the free agent is real and consequential in the very production of something truly original in action. It is the very presence of this infinite that makes the agent spiritual as well as incarnate in the world.

We do not, however, come to the full knowledge of all the ramifications of this spiritual dynamism of reason in an instant or in a way that can be clearly defined by the understanding in conjunction with only a particular act. Even in 1937 Blondel continues to maintain that the life of the rational spirit discloses itself phenomenologically in the exercise of reflection upon particular, antagonistic motives for action. After bringing out the character of universality and fecundity that reason displays in relation to the various complementary possibilities for action that occur in our deliberative consciousness, in its subjection to influences from nature, so that a properly reflected act is never merely a reflex act, he goes on to show that "under the conditions that our way of thinking and looking forward necessitates, what we call our reason is never from the start in full and distinct possession of all its light and all its sovereignty" (1937a, 158). Human reason is always in a struggle where it must serve as an impartial judge or arbiter among conflicted motives, even as it has to become partial to one or the other of them in rendering its judgment. Even if it rises above the fray in a moment of deliberation, it still has to choose one or the other of these as the one that will be victorious over the others in the action that is to follow. In doing so, reason conveys upon a motive, hitherto caught up in an immanent determinism of mobiles and motives, the force of its own efficacious transcendence. It confers upon what was only a relative good among other relative goods a universal value it did not have of itself. In doing so, reason also implicates that universal good, or the view it has of its own final end, in that particular value, so that the ultimate and absolute good of action becomes immersed in a particular good that hides it from view and that may become a false substitute for the true end of human action.

From this arises a new problem, not just for the science of action, but also for the agent in the process of making a decision among the various impulses that move it. After showing that freedom arises necessarily from the interplay of diverse motives and mobiles through the power of reflection, we must now ask ourselves how freedom maintains itself or develops, as it lends itself to forces and tendencies that are still exterior to it and that draw it out of itself. After showing how the light of reason serves to illuminate motives in relation to one another, making them reasons for action, we must now wonder how this light keeps on shining in all its fullness even as it becomes partial in one or the other of its particular applications. Blondel has made the case for the necessary idea of infinite and transcendence in the genesis of self-conscious action. How does this necessary idea play itself out in the particularization of human action and how can we remain faithful to it in all its universality and openness, as we go from one particular choice to another in the concrete exercise of our will? How can science keep track of the universal intent of reason in action as it expands beyond the particularity of any willed object in the effort "always to rectify our aims and our efforts, to make our reason reasonable, to liberate our liberty" (1937a, 159-60).

What we start from in our conscious action is a certain primordial *act* in the élan of our spirit. This act, infinitely rich as it may be in virtualities and exigencies, cannot remain indeterminate. One intention or another comes to the fore in some vague or rudimentary fashion. One reason or another begins to determine a second act that is the embryo of a thought, or of what Blondel calls a willed will, *une volonté voulue*. The infinite in the primordial élan partializes itself in a particular motive before and in view of recovering itself and of making itself equal to itself, as an aspiration that is always tentative in the search to know itself better and to satisfy itself less imperfectly. This is how Blondel comes to think of that primordial act as the willing will, *la volonté voulante*, and of reason as starting from a congenital knowledge of essential truths and principles embedded in this fundamental and transcendent motion that launches all the appetitive, the cognitive, and the liberating powers of the spiritual being. Once we have penetrated to this inner core of our rational appetite, we can understand how it is a stimulation for advancement and the deployment of an intellectual and voluntary activity that will actualize little by little an agent oriented to a destiny in which it can knowingly cooperate. We may not know clearly from the beginning in what that destiny will consist concretely, as we reflect still only on how action is generated internally in consciousness, but we can know that human action as a whole is oriented to something infinite and transcendent to all or to any of the particular motives and mobiles that punctuate our search in time and space. Instead of looking only at this or that particular action in a fragmentary way, or according to the trifling value of a finite good, the science of action has to look more to the dramatic unity of a human life that, far from tarrying in what comes and goes and is limited to this or that, goes "from the infinite that launches it, penetrates it, attracts it, and is waiting for it" (1937a, 161).

The purpose of this entire reflection has been to bring to the fore of consciousness this primordial and profound principle of all human action, which we can now refer to as the *willing will*, and to show the necessity of following this principle wherever it may lead us, as we move out of the epicenter of our consciousness into a world of motives and mobiles still conflicted with one another. Initially starting from the efficient causes of what penetrates into our consciousness, Blondel has turned this immanent necessity around into a transcendent finality that we must pursue step by step in our exercise of decision-making. Action brings a new energy into the world. It is always somehow beyond what it starts from. And it is from this sense of a beyond that we must now proceed "as from the true and solid origin of the movement that turns man toward known and willed ends" (1937a, 163). It is not enough to look back to where we come from. True men of action always look forward, and rightly so, for they do not merely give in to the necessities from the past. They take over the determinism of unconscious life and give it a direction of their own, finding in the future the decisive reason for their resolve. They do not take the universe to be a closed cycle. As long as man is in it, the spirit is in it as something infinite, capable of dominating natural forces, even if it does not know all that there is in them and even if its freedom is very shaky and tenuous at first. "Voluntary action appears as a creation within creation; it is an infinite gathered in a point, rising above universal oppression and raising the world" (1937a, 164). The task of the philosophy of action is to examine how action does this concretely, by insinuating itself into the very tendencies that have made it possible, both within the individual agent and without, even to the ends of the earth.

What the analysis of the internal parturition of action has revealed, then, is a necessity for the self-conscious subject to go out of itself. Necessarily brought to consciousness, freedom has to exercise itself necessarily. "Once this liberating reason has flashed through reflection, the die is cast; its light has shone forever" (1937a, 166). Rational responsibility has been brought into play along with responsiveness. This ulterior necessity of a responsibility is an integral part of the actual determination in any concrete action, a norm to be followed. It is for the science of action to examine all that it entails and for reason itself to consent to it in all sincerity in the very use it makes of its freedom. Once reflection has awakened in us the sense of our own freedom and remanded us to our own counsel, we cannot go back to irresponsibility. To will not to use this power is still to use it. Freedom is not a purely arbitrary power that can lend or withhold itself, or the mediation of reason. It arises from the dynamism of spontaneous action and it issues in the dynamism of reflected or deliberate action. It brings with itself the mark of the movement from which it issues and a logic internal to willed action as such. The will cannot withdraw from this necessity, since to will not to will is always still to will. Even in willing a particular motive deliberately, it is never just that motive that we will in these particular circumstances at this particular time. It is the will itself that we engage in submitting to a particular motive or in using it for the purpose of liberating ourselves from other determinisms. The actually willed act always surpasses what is known, analyzed, or determinate in any particular deliberation. It reaches out to all that we are seeking in acting, something that transcends any configuration actually conjured up of the world at any given moment.

Free will thus arises in us necessarily and takes over its origins, including the will itself as willed. It appears to be hemmed in by determinism in everything that precedes it, accompanies it, and follows it, but in consenting to will and to act, to exercise itself, it takes on the necessity that results from its willing. It has only itself to blame, so to speak, for the consequences that follow directly from what it wills or excludes. What makes a science of free action possible is precisely this seriation of conditions and goals that the will sets for itself in the very act of willing, no matter what it may be willing in particular at any particular moment. Thought does not remain lost in the infinite variety of decisions and possible acts one can perform. In the concatenation of its indefinite particularizations, it also grasps a universal thread common to the singular destinies of all willful agents. The power of willing defines itself by its very *act* of willing, not by what it happens to will at any particular moment. It is in this *act* of willing, where the end it is aiming at and the means it has to use are disclosed, that a reflective science of action can find its proper determination as a necessary logic of freedom.

The task of the philosophy of action from this point on, then, after having unpacked how action originates in an individual self-consciousness, is to develop the content of what the will wills necessarily in willing any particular thing freely. Blondel thinks of this as developing "the content of the will that follows the very movement it imposes on itself in its primordial *élan*" (1937a, 169). If there is a rule to be observed, an operation to perform, moral and social relations to be instituted, it is by this expansion of outlook that they will be discovered, "thanks to a method that is incomparable. For it is the *a priori* initiative of this free activity that, in deploying itself, must reconstitute the necessity it is subject to *a posteriori*, so to speak, so that the heteronomy of its law will correspond to its interior autonomy" (1937a, 169).

We see here how Blondel proposes to get beyond the formalism of Kant with regard to moral law, seen from the standpoint of pure practical reason. Practical reason is never purely *a priori*. "When we truly do what we will in all sincerity, we are obeying an obligation that, far from depending on our decree, is for us an imperative end" (1937a, 169). The problem for us is to discover all that that end requires in what Blondel calls a practical experimentation. What we do in acting voluntarily is appropriate the very transcendent motion from which our action proceeds. We provoke responses from without to better define ourselves. The will "draws from the apparent subjections and the provisional heteronomy under which it develops a means of acquiring the only true autonomy that conforms it with its fundamental destiny" (1937a, 170). What we have to learn is how to become truly autonomous, and all the teachings that bear down on us from without or from on high are already wrapped up in the willing and acting we experience historically. The task of a philosophy bearing directly on action in the concrete is to unravel all these teachings step by step as provoked by the internal stimulations of the rational appetite or the willing will.

And so, having elaborated on the ingredients and the internal parturition of action within consciousness, and having established scientifically the necessity of going out from consciousness to learn from experience all that is willed in willing freely and responsibly, Blondel launches into his examination of the proliferation of the will in act in what he calls its metaphysical history. This will be more than a description of facts considered from without and according to experimental relations. It will be an attempt to penetrate the inner being of the power of willing through its actual exercise so as to preserve and develop the freedom with which it is endowed, going all the way to "where action meets its final end, its equation with itself and, as much as possible, with the original Principle from which proceeds its élan and its destiny" (1937a, 172). More than just a phenomenon and an accident posterior to being, as if it added nothing to the determination of being itself, human action is constitutive of something essential and substantive in being that must be studied, not just by reflection on its internal constitution, but also and more importantly in the lived experience of persons and humanity, in order to learn from the experience, or *a posteriori*, so to speak, all that is contained in its ideal, or *a priori*, internal principle.

Deployment of the Internal Act into the Ethical Sphere of History

Blondel proceeds first to examine the emergence of action as intentional effort and as external sign in the use of one's body as instrument. Then he looks to the action of the human agent on itself in going from being just an individual to making oneself a person, before coming to the more important and more crucial expansion of self-conscious action into interpersonal life. Once on the level of interpersonal life, he examines how concrete action coalesces into conjugal and familial life, then into a more universal form as patriotic life that allows for a plurality of different unifications of spirit and of civilization, until it finally opens up to humanity as a whole and to the universe itself as the stage for the human drama in history, the point where he begins to consider action as moral and as the realization of an ethical ideal.

These are the stages in the elaboration of human action as willed in the immanent order of the universe. Blondel examines each one of them successively, going from the most constricted concentric wave in the physiology of the self-conscious individual to the most expansive wave in humanity as a whole and in the universe. Each new wave of this consideration of willed action in the concrete brings new insight into what is contained in the mysterious power of willing that the expansion starts from, the willing will. Each is admitted scientifically only upon seeing the necessity of it, or the necessity of going beyond the previous wave. At the same time, however, each wave is presented as a necessary consolidation of willing in its own right, so to speak, or as a way in which the will has to form itself, if it is to remain faithful to its initial thrust as a spiritual élan. Far from leaping immediately into the abyss of an infinite that makes itself felt and known in the first stirrings of the will, Blondel dwells on the many ways in which this stirring makes itself known step by step in an ever-expanding perspective on others and on the universe.

Morality, in this version of *Action,* thus appears as an ulterior sphere in this dialectic of a will in search of a willed object that will be the equal of itself, a sphere of total transcendence with respect to humanity and the universe. It is another concentric wave that the will must pass into, so to speak, given the insufficiency of humanity or of the universe for fulfilling the infinite aspiration of willing. At the same time, however, it is a further level of decentering for the individual self-consciousness unmatched by anything considered so far in the spheres leading up to it. In effect, the dialectic until now has been a decentering of conscious willing into ever-broadening spheres of willed objects, but always within an immanent order, no matter how universally conceived, where everything is seen as relative to something else. Now, with morality as Blondel sees it, the decentering takes a new turn, so to speak, in relating to something absolute or irreducible to anything in the immanent order, including that order itself. Until now we have been going from one finite sphere to another that was less finite, or relatively infinite. With morality we seem to come to a sphere of action that relates to the absolutely infinite, which Blondel thinks of as totally transcendent, and not immanent in any way, not even as an interchange among finite opposites. Speaking of conjugal action as something spiritual as well as physical going on between two self-consciousnesses, Blondel writes that "we cannot capture the infinite élan of willing between two" (1937a, 265). More generally, he would say that, no matter how far we extend finite opposition of any kind, true infinity will always be something else, a third or an other than any two, or more, already in relation with one another.

The question for him then as he comes to the limit of the immanent universal order is to understand how we come to think of ourselves as transcending this very order in our action. "In what sense can human acting, for it to be truly what it is and for it to be conscious of its initiative, surpass all the given on which it leans, the entire immanent order into which it inserts itself, all conceivable achievements even of the most evolved humanity in the spontaneous movement of collective civilization?" (1937a, 293). The question is most carefully worded in order to bring out how we seem to be leaping out of the universe at this point in the dialectic, by bringing out the universe's insufficiency to satisfy all that the will wills, and by using the will as a new leverage that would raise us and everything else in the universe above itself. Such pretentiousness on the part of human acting might seem illusory or chimerical at first sight, but reflection will show that it is a constant law of the human condition. "We do not act and we are not conscious of acting and willing to act except for what is not yet, to change things and to change ourselves, to introduce something new into a reality that does not match our aspirations or our passions, to incarnate an ideal without which we would have no grasp of positive data" (1937a, 293). What is at issue here is the emergence that raises us above the universe, so that we may know it, tend to take it over as we are enabled to discern the higher exigencies or the expectations we have as willful human beings, as empires in our own right within the empire of the universe.

Blondel's reflection here goes back to the point where self-conscious action takes hold in the world of experience. Earlier, before setting out on the odyssey in search of how the power of the willing extends beyond the confines of our first, immediate consciousness as individual beings in action, he had shown how this very consciousness, with the sense of freedom it entails in initiating its own action, over and above the action that comes to it from the universe, emerges from the interplay of a plurality of mobiles and dynamisms within its own unity as a consciousness that encompasses all of them from its universal perspective and holds them in check, at least momentarily, in order to bring its own stamp to the action that is to issue from its own will. Consciousness is what transforms mobiles into motives, or into ideas for action, because it has ideas of its own that it is pursuing in its action, including the idea of the infinite. Now, in the dialectical expansion of all that has to be included in what the will wills according to the exigencies of our willing, he returns to that same point of insertion of a universal consciousness into the universal immanent order in order to highlight what the flow of the ideas themselves brings to action.

We should note, however, an important change in the way he introduces morality at this point of the dialectic in the concrete deployment of action. In the 1893 version of *Action*, Blondel had begun to speak of morality and obligation in conjunction with his initial reflection on the parturition of action within consciousness, as part of his argument against the formalism of Kant, in order to show that the willed act could not remain closed in on itself. As willing, the will has to go out of itself in search of an object or a content that will be the equal of itself, in the body, in another, in society, in humanity, or in the universe as a whole, however far the search may take it. There is a sense of obligation tied to the idea of an end we are necessarily seeking in our action, but that is not the concrete moral sense as it emerges in the exercise of our will, once we have come to the limits of the immanent order we can affect, which is where Blondel first introduces the order of morality in the later version of *Action*, after having omitted any talk of morality in showing the necessity of the willing will to go out of itself in search of an object equal to itself.

Instead of using the concrete sense of morality in human action as a way of setting his dialectic in motion, Blondel is now using it only as a step along the way, as the step in which the universal in its transcendence begins to appear in the deployment of action. This is not contrary to his original strategy in the science of action, for it was not the concrete moral sense of *practical science* Blondel was invoking against Kant's formalism. It was only the necessity of the will to will more than itself in a freedom that was still to be actualized by choosing one thing in particular over another. The full force of practical science in the moral sense is brought into play only later in the dialectic of *Action II*, at the end of the expansion of action within the limits of the universe, in order to make the transition from the immanent order of the finite to the transcendent order of the infinite. Using the practical science of morality in this way was only a moment in the science of practice as it came to the recognition of an absolute transcendence in the end it was searching to illuminate. It did not have to be used at the moment of parturition of action, as Blondel realized in the second version of his dialectic, but only at the moment when the science of action seems poised to pass over concretely into the totally transcendent or the absolutely infinite. Then he does not hesitate to invoke our spontaneous moral sense of duty as somehow practically open to something that cannot be encompassed by finite choice of one thing or another, even as it translates itself into such a finite choice.

This is the moment when Blondel begins to pass inconspicuously from one meaning of the French term *conscience* to the other, as noted earlier, from its meaning as *consciousness* to its meaning as *conscience*. What conscience adds to consciousness in the constitution of a human act is a more metaphysical dimension to the action that goes with the sense of duty, or with *devoir*, from which it flows. *Devoir* too, like duty or oughtness in English, has a double meaning in French: one, the sense of something we *ought* to do here and now, and the other, the sense of what *ought* to happen in the future as a consequence of what we do here and now. Ideal human action is brought into concrete, particular choices through consciousness as conscience.

This ideal or moral action, moreover, is not detached from the ingredients of the universe that have impressed themselves on the consciousness of the deliberative agent. The free agent acting out of his sense of duty always finds himself having to act amid circumstances of an immanent and natural order. In thinking of the moral order as a new wave unfurling before us, beyond the world given to us as a matter of fact, beyond the shores of this world, so to speak, Blondel thinks of it at first as an "ideal flow that seems to be more real than the real, since without it we would neither be conscious of the real here and now nor have any hold on it. As it overflows in this way, this new wave takes, so to speak, shapes that are more varied and less regular than the concentric circles already described and explained [in this expanding dialectic of the will seeking an object equal to itself]" (1937a, 294). The purpose now is to follow how this moral influx permeates the world of action according to various contours, beginning from the rising aspects of a natural or *a posteriori* morality, still emerging from the natural order of things in history, toward the ever-more transcendent order of a moral or *a priori* morality with its own metaphysical resonance.

"In acting, man does not limit his élan and his scope to the family, the city, or humanity. He casts his intention further still. He inserts himself, as the stoics rightly said, into the entire universe" (1937a, 294). Voluntary action has to do with the entire system from which it draws its nourishment and in which it claims to take hold as spirit. In it converge both a certain egoism of individual will seeking its own satisfaction and another infinitely complex more general movement of life that seems to envelop the individual. This comes as part of one and the same movement flowing spontaneously from the willing will in the deployment of willed action. As man remains faithful to his willing will, he rises toward an ever-more disinterested attitude, even as he continues to strive in the direction of his destiny and to concur in his own best interest.

At the phenomenal level, which we are now preparing to surpass dialectically, acting appears as a way of leaping into the universe. It means letting go of one's egoism and entrusting oneself to the forces of the universe, gambling on them and speculating on what they will do, almost like a grasshopper leaping with abandonment, without seeing where it will land. Utilitarian calculations can go only so far. In order to really take action in the world we must go beyond them and seek what we really will to be amid an infinite complexity, where we have to forget ourselves or abandon ourselves to something beyond our control. It is not possible for action to be a pure calculation. There is in it a broader scope than all the combinations it can entertain at any given time, a scope that

Blondel is willing to characterize as *ethical* at this point in the dialectic, after having shown how in acting we inevitably let go to external operation, to co-action with another, with the family, with a nation, and even with the universal assembly of the human generations. What justifies the introduction of the term *ethical* at this point is that the will is now being considered as seeking its "equilibrium in the total system of the world. Action is a function of the whole" (1937a, 296).

What this means for Blondel, however, is that we are no longer concerned merely with inserting our action into the succession of phenomena or into the moving complexus of becoming. The question now becomes one of inserting ourselves "into the reality of a substantial order through which is fixed forever the being and the act that, once it is subsistent and accomplished, can never again not have been" (1937a, 296). This is something Blondel would not have said at this point of the dialectic in the 1893 version, where he was still arguing only from a phenomenological standpoint, resisting any idea of an ontological commitment on the part of the will prior to coming to the end of what had to be included in what he then referred to as the phenomenon of action, that is, prior to considering the necessary being of action as something more than this phenomenon. Here, in 1937, he acknowledges this ontological commitment of the will as it first presents itself by superseding the more utilitarian sense of morality, still immersed in what he calls the natural order of the phenomenal universe. "There is a moral sense," he writes, "only where one has a presentiment and one sees, under the passing and utilitarian forms of action, a bearing that surpasses the immediate result and the simple consequences immanent to historical becoming, be it that of the entire universe" (1937a, 296). The human act is not just another fact among others. It expresses in its cosmic context "an intention, a supra-cosmic realization, an ideal that tends to incarnate something that was not, something that, without the human effort, would never have been in the universe" (1937a, 296). That is what constitutes and determines the ethical character of the human act in its essence.

We should note, however, that this ethical character of human acts at the level of the willing will of a fundamentally rational spiritual being does not flow from the natural forces in the midst of which our experience is deployed and through which we learn the meaning of our ideal initiatives in the world. Morality in a properly conceived human action is not detached from the world in which we have to act, as if in a purely formal sense of duty, like a kite that supposedly would hover on high without even a string to hold it in place. Blondel sees it more as immersing itself in the phenomenal order of history and emerging first in that natural order for the human being, not to be submerged in that immanent order, but to emerge in a transcendent order where a human agent still has to choose how he will relate to his destiny. It is as if "the entire movement of the universe were disposed in view of enabling the advent of spirits capable of orienting their destiny and making the world the theater of morality and the vestibule of the temple of the spiritual life" (1937a, 297). Human action is the organ that pulls these two realms together, the physical world and the ideal world, as complementing one another.

Starting from this complementarity of the natural and the moral in human action, Blondel finds merit in utilitarianism, when it shows that, where formalism sees only an ideal duty, there is already an inevitable matter of fact. To bring this natural morality to its true meaning, however, we must look upon it in its twofold aspect, one *a posteriori* and one *a priori*. The first brings in the experimentation that we cannot do without and that we cannot avoid in action. In conscience we have to learn from the milieu in which our action has to deploy itself. We can only form ourselves through the wear and tear of interaction with others and the world as a graduated whole. Customs, *mores* in Latin, and rules come to the fore through secular traditions and establish themselves in ways that allow morality to emerge. At the same time, however, what was initially only a *fact*, under an interior pressure as well as the exterior one, becomes the consciousness of a duty *(d'un devoir)*, a matter of *conscience*. The external constraint opens the way for an internal disinterestedness. The *a posteriori* necessity comes to be seen as resulting from an *a priori* movement of the will. The fact of the moral ideal thus distinguishes itself from any practical empiricism, thanks to an internal aspiration "without which a passively felt pressure could not evoke any glimmer of ethical consciousness" (1937a, 299).

There is thus a certain continuity between a natural order that emerges in utilitarian fashion and the moral order that supervenes in human action. Morality is not contrary to what works according to nature. But it does introduce a certain disinterestedness into the calculus of consequences. Each individual must act in view of an end, but it is impossible to figure out ahead of time every outcome of whatever it is we do in taking action. A purely utilitarian arithmetic falls short of whatever the egoist has in mind in seeking his good. Our action is never ours alone. We have to cast our acts amid the acts of many others, where we find indifference and disorder as much as advantage and coalescence in a seeming chaos of universal life. Little by little, however, through obscure compensations and the confused reactions of impulses thrown in together, different currents and patterns emerge in human consciousness. Different conceptions of human life emerge in keeping with an interior *norm* of sincere willing, a sense of what is right for human action and a sense of failure that has to be compensated for, one way or another.

From the experience of life there emerge maxims, empirical precepts, popular "moralities" that somehow sum up the wisdom of centuries and of peoples, folkways, or customary practices conducive to the welfare of societies that we call *mores*. What makes these customs moral, however, is that they have to be understood from the standpoint of the whole, the universal, and not just that of the individual or of a particular society. At this point Blondel takes issue with sociologism, which excludes, not only the psychological and personal from its consideration, but also the cosmic and the metaphysical aspect in its analysis of the problem of human life as a whole. It looks only to how the social models the individual and the political. It does not look to the truly practical science Blondel sees as developing from a real experimentation with life reaching out into the universal immensity of things, not to say into the infinite, and listening for echoes or feedback from this vast expanse. As he comes to the moral dimension of this practical science, it is its universal aspect Blondel wants to insist on, which is arrived at more by "a concrete experience *sub specie universi*" than by a merely critical analysis of data (1937a, 302). What he has in mind is more the classical notion of a moral *synderesis*, rather than a purely formal categorical imperative of pure reason. With the insistence on the universal aspect of a properly moral consciousness, however, he wants to bring out "a transcendence of the ideal over the real, a recognition of human superiority over the forces of nature and over the goals the world can offer our will" (1937a, 302). Beyond any natural, utilitarian, or sociological morality, and even to make such subalternate forms possible, there is "a truly moral morality, that is, one that prescribes and realizes a moral ideal to be incarnated by action into a world that does not contain it spontaneously" (1937a, 302). This is the most original factor human *acting* brings to the universe, "the production in man and by man of a reality that transcends all conditions and all that is given as a point of leverage, but not as an adequate end for our thinking, our willing, our acting, or our entire being" (1937a, 303).

Blondel calls this the realism of the ethical ideal in human action, something metaphysical as well as physical or temporal in the historical order flowing from the very power of willing, the principle of any properly human action. What gives us a sense of duty concerning any personal action we may take, any willed will on our part, is the connection it has with the élan of our willing seeking a term that will be the equal of its primordial impulse, the *act*, once again, that has elicited all the successive waves of willing from the individual, to the social, to the universal, in the search of an object to equal its infinite power of willing. It is here that Blondel justifies, in the dialectic of 1937, the idea of *obligation* as binding on a will that has to go out of itself to realize its own freedom. To speak of obligation as a moral ideal transcending all matters of fact is not to speak of it as unreal, as only a subjective projection, a myth of one kind or another. It is to speak of it as more real than the real we take to be only a matter of fact. Deontology for Blondel is not opposed to ontology. It is a passage to a higher metaphysical realm than is evident in mere matters of fact. It is more real than what we take to be the real in these matters of fact. The argument he gives for this is one he has used consistently in the past. This consciousness of a higher ethical order flowing from the will is "the *conditio sine qua non* of the very consciousness we have of the entire empirical order, of our science and of our *conscience*, of our reflected activity and of the sense we have of our free willing" (1937a, 304). It is part of the light that brings reflective reason to distinguish itself from any and all particular motives and mobiles in action.

What remains to be done at this juncture in the expansion of the scope of action, then, is to purify and to enter more deeply into the sense of transcendence, at once ideal and real, that has shown itself at the limit of our universal perspective in acting freely. Blondel now sees the role of the metaphysician in a science of action as one of looking more deeply beyond the superficial matters of fact to "the truths and the duties from which our action must take its inspiration in rising to a life that will unify all our actions, past, present and future under the law of an intention entirely oriented toward the one transcendent end" (1937a, 305-6).

Far from eschewing the thought of metaphysics, as he had done in his earlier elaboration of the phenomenon of action, Blondel goes on to describe the dynamism of the will in metaphysical terms as relating to the true end of acting in its transcendence. Metaphysics here serves as a passage from the finite order of our understanding, as it focuses on the world of means we have to use to achieve our end, to the more metaphysical order of the end itself. Metaphysics is no longer for him an understanding that closes in on the world where action takes place. It is a systematic opening to the transcendent, "a passage that enables the movement of life by moving itself" (1937a, 307). It affirms the transcendent and shows it to be a higher rung to aim at necessarily, though it is not itself the transcendent end we have in mind. It only presents us with a new critical situation, as we have to face up to a goal that exceeds our limited or partial capacity to act at any moment in the immanent historical order of our action.

Blondel characterizes morally moral action as relating to an end that is transcendent and immutable, as joining becoming with the absolute. As moral, it is truly a disinterested action that can go on without the support of any exterior pressure. It goes forward with a rectitude that has no need to turn to one side or another "as it follows the normal élan that bears it toward the light of a circumspect prospection, in the simplicity of the good intention" (1937a, 315). The willing will does not find itself in any of the particular goals it sets for itself. It always finds itself higher than any of its willed objects, always more ample than any or all of them. It proclaims itself free in choosing to pursue any particular interest, but it cannot give itself only to itself. That would be like giving in to its own emptiness. "It can take hold of itself only by assigning for its initial indetermination an end that can be neither inadequate to it, nor its own proper inanity, nor its own indefiniteness, but that obliges it to place the term of its aspiration above all contingent and finite reality, beyond its own indetermination" (1937, 316). That is why action, "having become conscious of itself and of its excellence, and in keeping with the élan it has received and that it ratifies by making it its own, has to tend toward what it is not yet, toward what has not yet been realized anywhere in the universe, toward what is an ought *(un devoir)* for it and a good in itself" (1937a, 316).

The Perversion of Transcendence in Superstition

Going forward, however, into what is now seen as a metaphysical realm of accomplishment for human action, presents one final challenge for a will in quest of an object that will be the equal of its infinite power to will. If there is still an absolutely transcendent end to be attained in the élan of our spiritual life, how is it to be brought into what we do immanently as part of what we will necessarily? Up to now in the deployment of action into successive waves or spheres of influence, each time the will came to a higher stage of development, a more universal scope of intention to be realized, the will was able to consolidate itself anew around an object found in the immanent order it had to will necessarily. So it was at the stage of the person and then of interpersonal life. So it was also at the level of familial life and at the level of social life in a homeland, all the way up to the cult of humanity as a whole. At each level of deployment, the will found something to satisfy itself with, but also a necessity to move to a broader, more universal sphere. Each time also, the will was able to acquiesce in the higher sphere as something it could will naturally or immanently, as we have just seen it can do by realizing an ethical ideal and a natural morality in the historical order. What Blondel comes to now, in this expansion of spheres for the will to go into, presents a difficulty unseen at any of the earlier stages of deployment. If we have come to the limit of the universe itself, the entire immanent order of human action, how can we even think of going further into a transcendence that now appears clearly limitless or infinite? And yet, how can we not think of going further, if we have not yet found the object that will be the equal of our infinite power of willing? That is the unique question that remains to be dealt with at the end of this dialectical deployment of action in the concrete.

Up to this point in the dialectic, morality has given us some inkling of the ideal transcendence we bring to our action in the world, but it has not resolved the radical problem of transcendence we encounter on the plane of a metaphysical reality we have yet to conceive in its very transcendence. How are we to relate to such a reality in our action and how can we find in it a way of making our willed will equal to our willing will?

Blondel distinguishes two more waves of expansion in his conception of action expanding toward something ever-more infinite, in search of an object that would equal the power of willing, one way inconsistent with the logic of action that has brought us to this radical problem of transcendence, and the other, more consistent with that logic, but which still only leaves us open to a resolution that cannot come from ourselves. The first he describes as an attempt to resolve the problem of the infinite object we are seeking in only immanent terms, in what he calls superstitious action. The second he describes as properly religious action in the face of an "object" that we cannot properly take hold of, but that can take hold of us as it wills, namely, the one, true God. As he had done in *Action* of 1893, it is through the critique of superstition that he leads us to a proper understanding of the religious attitude in human action, with the possibility of some cooperation with God in this action.

Blondel speaks of *superstition* in the context of a human effort to bring the transcendent into the immanence of human endeavor. Superstition is a misfiring of this effort in resolving the problem of transcendence that arises after there has been nothing to confront the initial movement of the will as infinite. This movement has superseded all the spheres of resistance, as it were, encountered in the expansion of its intention toward an object that would be the equal of its power. At each new wave it has found a partial satisfaction of its fundamental élan, but always only to rebound again toward a more ample object, even to the very limit of a moral universe. "Coming from the infinite power hidden in the depths of the subject's life, action appears able to reach some leverage and conclusion only in an infinite reality. Where can it find such a total use of itself, such a perfect equation with itself that would establish a reciprocity between the necessary expansion and the return of a freedom ever in progress?" (1937a, 319). After running through the gamut of the forms of personal, social, and moral life, there is still at the heart of human action a mysterious amplitude that cannot be filled by the magnitudes of science and of conscience, affections, ideas, duties, or whatever else our casting about has brought into our consideration. As broadly as we have now cast the lines of our inquiry into what has to be the necessary object for an infinite power to will, we can no longer simply call back the search and retract the end, as if to close the circle of action upon ourselves or upon some object in our world. Morality has given us some inkling of the ideal transcendence we bring to our action in the world, but it has not resolved the radical problem of transcendence we encounter on the plain of a metaphysical reality we have yet to conceive in its very transcendence. How are we to relate to such a reality in our action, and how can we find in it a way of making our willed will equal to our willing will?

We have gone through all the various stages of development, and all the partial satisfactions that the will can find in the immanent order of the universe, without having found anything that will completely satisfy the will in its search for an object that will equal its power to will. In expanding and in realizing itself outside of itself, the will cannot find in what it has done objectively up to now all that is hidden in the sanctuary of its interior life. The infinitude we feel within ourselves, and the need to be all that we will to be, still seems beyond our grasp. How can we think of reaching into it without going beyond ourselves and the entire universe? And yet what would it mean to reach it, if not to pull it once again within our grasp as we would any object?

This is the strange and paradoxical problem of a religious dimension that presents itself in human action even at the highest level of morally moral consciousness. At the summit of its actualization, there remains in human action a mysterious depth that no form of personal, social, or moral life can fill. Even after we have brought into it all the riches of science, of consciousness and of conscience, of ideas, affections, and duties, there remains an abyss to be filled. Hence a necessity to push further on beyond any finite satisfaction we could find in the order of historical phenomena. At the limit even of the moral universe, there arises inevitably an ulterior need. Even if this need were to obtain only an illusory satisfaction, Blondel writes, it is still a real need that the science of action must take into account. The infinitude that we sense obscurely within us as we exercise our freedom amid so much determinism, and that we wish for in order to be all that we will to be, looms before us paradoxically in a beyond that we somehow wish to master, as we master everything else in our universe.

What happens under this strange metaphysical condition, even in the most ordinary circumstances of life, is a double movement always running in opposite directions. First, the secret we cannot grasp within ourselves or produce on our own, we make into an *object of cult*, with the hope of better attaining it by keeping it at an infinite distance. But then, in no less surprising fashion, this object, which we have placed infinitely above us, we try to dominate or take hold of, as if we had divinized it only to demand of it a response that will satisfy our still-avid hearts. In this way, Blondel writes, we come "to realize outside of ourselves what escapes us within ourselves, with the secret intent of capturing this infinite somehow in the finite of a real object, and with the intimate hope that this is the true means of conquering and holding this infinite finality in a perfect action" (1937a, 320), that of a *ritual*, in which the infinite is taken as something finite, possessed, and even employed for human purposes. What makes the ritual or cultic action perfect at this point of the dialectic is that it joins together in a single religious embrace, as it were, the infinite that remains hidden and beyond our reach and the finite of any object of choice at our disposal, thus apparently bringing action to the completion it has been seeking in all of its deployment in the universe.

The religious or cultic sphere of action Blondel is talking about is one that arises spontaneously in human consciousness, going all the way back to the most primitive societies and coming all the way up to the most modern. It is a pervasive part of any human culture that goes to the end of its spiritual exigencies. Blondel's aim in the science of action has been to demonstrate how this religious dimension of action arises necessarily through the dynamism of a will moved by an infinite power, in search of an object that will be the equal of that infinite power. The object of a cult for him is something projected outside the religious subject in which the will can find a reflection of its own interior movement, so that it can know itself better and learn how to make itself the equal of itself. But the question that arises at this point in the science of action, as it did in all the previously disclosed spheres, is whether this endeavor of the human spirit to take hold of the infinite, or the divine, can be taken as a legitimate extension of our reach in human action, or whether it should be judged to be temerarious or illusory, not to say downright impious. Everything will depend on how these cultic forms of human action have been conceived in the past as well as the present. Some may have been mere superstitions or aberrations in the orientation of the will, while some could be viewed as authentically religious. It is through a critique of *superstition,* in its modern as well as its ancient forms, that Blondel comes to what is for him a proper conception of human action in its religious form.

Prior to any critique of *superstition,* however, he explores whence religious initiative as such originates in the human subject, even at the risk of deviating into superstition, for that is where the natural basis lies for proceeding further in this dialectic of action, into a sphere that appears totally transcendent. This basis lies in the surplus of the human act that always exceeds sensible facts and social life. It is a remainder of force and of will, as it were, one that has yet to find its proper object, but to which we spontaneously and naturally assign an object that is finite and insufficient like any other, one that is unworthy of the homage it is given, but that precisely because of this unworthiness satisfies our twofold need of fabricating and mastering a god for ourselves. We see this happen in fetishism, for example, one of the more primitive forms of superstitious action known to anthropology, but we can find traces of the same kind of cultic attitude in our more advanced societies, where an object found in the series of things given to us in the world is assigned a special place outside the series, something at once "visible and mysterious, incomprehensible and accessible, menacing and protective that sums up the divine; as if the finite could become the very reality of the infinite" (1937a, 323-24).

It is remarkable that this kind of superstitious action can take anything for the object of its worship or cult, something human in form or even something quite inhuman. But always there is some ambiguity that surrounds these objects, and the cult that surrounds them, some equivocation concerning a transcendent power that lies beyond our grasp and yet allows us some ways of taming it for our purposes. People make idols of these objects, which at first are taken to be only imitations or receptacles of invisible forces or of diffuse powers, but then become total and exclusive representations of the mysterious power itself. Ultimately, Blondel explains, man wants to invade the secret of things. He wants to disarm and subjugate the hidden power that weaves itself into his acts. "And when he is persuaded that in effect he has succeeded on his own initiative in this prodigious enterprise; when he begins to boast of having placed his hand on the hidden powers hidden in nature that surpass it; when he has raised his conceptions and his heart to the level of the idol he proposes to himself for adoration, that is when undoubtedly his action seems consummated to him and he feels reassured. There is no act, as disreputable as it may be, where the divine has not been placed, no act that has not evoked an idolatry" (1937a, 324-25). This can be said even of the more reputable acts so highly touted in modern social and scientific life.

What Blondel sees in the object of the superstitious cult is ultimately, under a borrowed form, the expression of the unfathomable depth of an interior life that no particular act can equal, a desire for an infinite response to an infinite tendency. What man adores is the impenetrable secret of his conscience and, as he becomes more and more reflective, he is brought to conceive this object under the form of humanity, albeit of a humanity that cannot be realized within oneself and that represents an ever-moving ideal in advance of its real development. This is how Blondel explains the solitary evolution of the idol, of the cult, and even of the mediator, in what has been called religious consciousness. Once the idol ceases being some inanimate, dark, mysterious thing, once anthropomorphism is added to fetishism, the ritual act ceases to be the only superstitious act. Superstition overtakes all human acts and confers upon them an aura of prayer and sacrifice. For, once the idol is thought of as having a consciousness analogous to one's own, and once this consciousness of the idol is thought of as penetrating into what escapes us in our own consciousness, we begin to think that we must appeal to it in suppliant mediation for its supreme concurrence, in order to consecrate all our undertakings, none of which can be achieved without this almighty power. At this point cult ceases to revolve around only one object or another. It comes to permeate all of our actions, as if to complete and sanction them. A certain spirit insinuates itself into every literal practice, that of a god who demands that human actions be what they should be in accordance with a total harmony.

There is much that is legitimate and necessary in this superstitious act of the human being, but also much that needs to be clarified and purged, if it is to become true to the need for associating a truly infinite and transcendent object to our own finite capacity. Once the sacred object is conceived in the image of spirit itself, "it would seem that its transcendence can become immanent to each one of our particular actions, to consecrate that action and impress upon it the seal of the finite infinite that human consciousness demands" (1937a, 326). This is the way many a philosophy of religion would have human action go, but Blondel is not prepared to let things stand as simply as that. Having brought us to this kind of synthesis between finite and infinite for conceiving the fulfillment of human action, he finds in it the idea for taking us one step further, for not closing the circle of action in on itself, as if in a totally immanent system. The fullness of human life cannot be wrapped up or encapsulated into a perfect concentration of itself within itself, even as it encompasses the entire universe, where everything becomes end and means for everything else.

What Blondel claims we have to look for instead is a *positive* cult that cannot be conceived as coming purely from the human spirit immanent in the world, but that has to be conceived as coming from on high, from the divine and from nowhere or no one else, no matter how compatible it may be with the human spirit and its exigencies. Such a *positive* cult would be the reverse of any superstitious cult added on to action by human ingenuity, to give it an aura it does not have of itself. It would be a divinization received in human action rather than one fabricated by man.

Blondel notes how much we are attached to the ceremony that surrounds all the important events of both family and public life. Even those who consider themselves free of all superstition still feel a need for some ritual as a counterpart to ceremonies of a true cult, as if there were a need for enhancing, through some liturgical performance, actions that otherwise are all too bare by themselves. It seems that we cannot be satisfied with just doing simply what we have to do. This need for elevating our acts to a higher degree of transcendence is grounded in the very dynamism of our will in search of an object that will equal the power of willing. This is what leaves us in suspense between two opposing tendencies in our consciousness with regard to the transcendent. One sets the transcendent far above or deeper within ourselves than anything we can know, take hold of, or do for ourselves. The other tends to take over whatever transcendence there may be in ritual practices and to make the divine immanent to the human itself. While the first of these tendencies may correspond to a normal élan and a legitimate need in ourselves, the second "results from a lack of coherence, if it does not express a hope, a possibility that, once purified of superstitious illusions, will constitute the religious sentiment" (1937a, 329).

This hope and this possibility conceived in conjunction with the tendency to set the transcendent far above ourselves is what will distinguish an authentic religious sense from any semblance of superstition, the belief that only God in his transcendence can initiate an action that will effectively bring human action to fulfillment, that is, render it an object that will be the equal of its infinite power to will. As long as man thinks he can draw from himself alone such a transcendent object and keep it strictly within himself or the immanent order he can more or less dispose of, he is in contradiction with himself, and abusing the sincere and primitive élan of his will that has brought him to surpass himself and to conceive this higher order of total transcendence.

Having gone through all the various waves or spheres of action, from the personal to the social and from the social to the universal, we come to a threshold as if between two worlds, that of our own making amid the immanent realities of the physical order, and that of something totally transcendent from which something can be drawn that would surpass all contingent existence and all particular ends marking the varying degrees of partial fulfillment in our acts. In a sense, immanence and transcendence have worked in concert with one another in this rise from particular to ever-more universal ends to be achieved by our action, as if a natural religiosity were urging us on at each new level of transcendence. But now we have come to the point where this natural religiosity must be purified of all superstitious contamination, by rectifying our intention anew and in a more radical way toward a transcendent that is not where we are, even in the use either of our appetite for it or of the function accorded to the divine in our acts. This is not just a matter of affirming the idea of the reality of a transcendence, from which all our acts hang as from what would be their highest fulfillment. It is also a matter of knowing how we might make use of this transcendence, whether to take advantage of it for our own human ends, or to serve it and thereby find through this disinterestedness a supreme fidelity to what is most generous in our nature and most in conformity with our profound willing.

There is only one way in which this fidelity to the primitive élan of our will can be thought through toward its logical end of real transcendence, but there are many ways of cutting it short to only a partial transcendence in one sphere of human activity or another, while acting out of reverence for an object that escapes our grasp. Before going on to the conception of the only properly religious way to act as the ninth and final wave of expansion for the will in action, Blondel pauses to contemplate various ways in which human action can still fall short of its proper end by taking itself as the end or as the fulfillment it is seeking. In this reversal of perspective, religion, instead of appearing as the end, is still taken as a means. It is judged in the light of human means and of human ambitions. Religion becomes purely ostentatious ceremony. "Instead of orienting man toward an external or a higher object, one tries to call him back toward his conscience and toward his thought. And the consequence of this inversion is, in a certain fashion, to reduce to two the three terms of superstitious action: sentiment, object, and rite. It is to suppress any transcendent object of cult, to place man in the presence of the content he bears in his own conscience" (1937a, 33). For Blondel this comes down to looking for the object of adoration within the adorer, as if that were the true cult in spirit and in truth, the only way of ridding human life of the demeaning mark of superstition. Left to itself, then, and reduced to its simplest expression, action would thus appear to be self-sufficient in the fullness of its autonomy.

Blondel recognizes this attitude as a summit in human action, but not as one that is legitimate. He sees in it one more form of superstition, in the guise either of a modern savant dedicated to the search for total truth, striving to become the high priest of a future already present, or that of a metaphysician advancing his own brand of natural religion, or that of the beautiful soul of conscience finding satisfaction in its own austere practice of duty, or that of the pharisee infatuated with his own confiscation of the true God. These are for him still different types of superstition that abound in the modern form of consciousness that show disdain for ancient traditions and for what he calls positive Religion. It is not surprising for him to find a new kind of polymorphous mysticity that affects every sort of recurrent millenarianism such as progress, evolution, permanent revolution, anarchism, exclusive totalitarianism, or whatever other ideology may come along in the course of history. For him, the worst kind of superstition of all would be to believe that we can escape, through a liberation from all superstitions, from having to admit any transcendence whatever, or from all religious obligation. "Acting for the sake of acting, acting to satisfy an instinct for the unforeseen, for leaping into the unknown, for perpetual risking, out of devotion for anything or anybody, that is the religion of those who maintain a need for generosity, a desire to give of themselves and to insert into their life something other than too direct a return into their egoism" (1937a, 337). Acting in this way, however, for the sake of acting, with a semblance of generosity, remains evasive with regard to true transcendence. Blondel detects in it a strain of superstition as well as of irreligiosity, a spirit that is still closed in upon itself. The generosity he is advocating for in the human spirit is an antidote for what he calls the superstition of irreligiosity. Action that takes itself as its own end is an illusion snuffing out the infinitude within itself, now seen as an élan of authentic religious expectation in the presence of a transcendence that no one can entirely disavow because it is already secretly at work in each one, in the very exercise of freedom.

The conclusion that Blondel draws from this ruthless critique of superstition in its highest humanistic form is the same as the one he had drawn from his earlier critique of superstition as part of the phenomenon of action in 1893: a double impossibility and a double necessity. It is impossible not to recognize, not to feel the inadequacy of the entire immanent order wherein our action deploys itself in response to the capacity or the exigencies of our willing will. From this follows the necessity of looking higher still for the highest and the true end we aim at in our human action. At the same time, however, it is also impossible to remain consistent with our willing will and find within ourselves or our willed wills the satisfaction we aspire to necessarily and have to pursue freely. From this twofold bind in which we find ourselves inevitably, and yet willfully, of having to go forward and of being incapable of doing so, there results a twofold acknowledgment from which we cannot escape: "indeclinable, impracticable, those are the two traits that, in the face of transcendence impose themselves in fact and at once for our action to follow in its course, according to the primitive motion of its essential nature and the necessity of the profound willing that ratifies it" (1937a, 338).

Out of this paradoxical situation for the human will, at the end of its deployment in the phenomenon of action, or in the immanent order of the universe, comes the question of yet another concentric wave that could bring some resolution to this double bind in which the will finds itself, from the side of Transcendence itself now, rather than from the side of immanence. This is the question of a ninth wave of deployment for action, which takes us out of superstition and brings us into a sphere of authentic religion, where initiative on the part of the divine is to be taken into consideration as coming from the Transcendent as such.

Ascent to True Transcendence in Authentic Religion

In the articulation of the phenomenon of action of 1893 there had been nothing that would correspond to this ninth wave. The deployment of the phenomenon had ended simply with the exposition of superstitious action and Blondel's criticism of it. It had been followed by another part of the dialectic on the *necessary being of action,* in which the will found itself contradicted and having to face the source of its being as other than itself, whence came its inevitable transcendence. Religion had been brought in as part of the hypothesis of a supernatural gift that would enable the will to bring its action to full equality with itself. Here, in 1937, Blondel thinks of religion proper prior to any hypothesis about the supernatural as something in the natural order of human action, even though it has already been represented as a positive phenomenon in history. What he does is take this phenomenon of religion as a sign of the necessary transcendent aspiration of the human spirit ever working toward its own transcendent end in all that it does in the world.

The religious sense of the human spirit comes on the scene in human action after the moral sense and the superstition that can go with it have run their course. Even after the broadest limits these forms of the spirit can reach, there remains a dimension of willing, or of something to be willed, that has not been reached and that cannot be included in what we actually will. There is something in our willing that has not been satisfied, but that calls for satisfaction. *Aliquid super est.* Transcendence remains as the crucial problem for our action. Giving in to the temptation of superstition has not solved the problem, because it reduces what we think of as infinite in its transcendence to something finite or to an indefinite succession of finite acts stretching before us in an unattainable bad infinite. If we cannot stop at superstition and if we must go further, what are we to do? Each time in the earlier concentric waves of expansion, Blondel had found something to take him beyond in a broader sphere, whether it was from the physical to the personal, or from the personal to the social, and so on, all the way to the sphere of a metaphysical ideal for man to realize in the world. Here, after the critique of superstition, he must find the way of facing up to the problem of transcendence in a positive way, even if it cannot be solved by man alone without falling once again into superstition. The only place where a solution might be found was in a final wave of deployment for human action defined in properly religious terms, that is, a generous willingness to turn the will around in a total reversal of perspective for a will still in search of a satisfaction that it cannot find in the immanent order, so that it now has to accept from the transcendent what it cannot will of itself. The problem of transcendence for human action cannot be solved by superstitious clinging to anything in the immanent order, not even by acting or willing itself. Indeed, it cannot be solved by anything man can do for himself in the world. It can only be solved from the side of the transcendent, and man's part in the solution can only be one of rising to a proper disposition, what Blondel now calls a religious disposition, which is anything but a superstition, but which has to be seen as a necessary disposition of receptivity toward a transcendent that is otherwise inaccessible to us.

Blondel approaches this final problem for human action as one of a singular conflict between the charm of the present world and the mysterious attraction of a higher world toward which we somehow feel obligated to orient our life. Philosophical reflection on Thought and Being has done a lot to heighten our metaphysical and religious sense of the Transcendent, but one does not have to wait upon such systematic or technical reflection to come into a proper sense of the Transcendent as something we must relate to. Action itself has its own lessons in this higher regard as well as in the earlier, immanent waves of its expansion. Earlier, in 1893, Blondel had shown how the dialectic of action unifies the various proofs for the existence of God — the cosmological, the teleological, and the ontological — into one single affirmation of a totally transcendent God. But that was before he had written the volumes on Thought, Being, and the Action of a first Cause. Here he merely alludes to this intellectual effort of the Trilogy to elaborate technically what now has to be seen as the ground and the scope of an action that starts from a secondary cause but must somehow rejoin its first cause. This is a dynamic found in the ordinary action of ordinary human beings, who may have only a rudimentary and obscure knowledge of anything properly metaphysical or religious, perhaps little more than a certain expectation of something they may not be able to name or conceptualize clearly, but that is nevertheless very real for them and must somehow come to some expression in their own action. The more speculative side of the approach to transcendence is not a matter of indifference or of superfluity for Blondel in this ultimate moment of his philosophy of action, but at this point in this philosophy of the concrete he is concerned more with bringing out the very concrete and living meaning that transcendence must have for us and in us, if we are to conform to what it implies for us in our very power to know and to act. Recognizing that this living mystery so far exceeds any idea we may have of it through speculative reflection, Blondel looks for further enlightenment about it in action itself, which, "by its complexity and its realism, becomes the irreplaceable and inexhaustible vehicle we cannot do without to support and enrich our being on the way to its term — *in via*" (1937a, 342).

Blondel has taken great pains to show all that man wills and does to conquer the universe in order to satisfy himself and gain his own spiritual ascendancy. It is not from the weakness or the fragility of the human spirit that he argues for the necessity of moving into a realm of transcendence, beyond the universe and everything the spirit can accomplish for itself in it. It is rather from the insufficiency we still experience at the highest point of our accomplishment. *Misère de grand seigneur,* he calls it. No matter how much we have done in the world, in all sincerity we still find reasons for willing more. That is how the question of transcendence arises for us concretely in action in its simplest form. Is there any way of gaining a complete satisfaction for ourselves, one that would equal the power of willing within us, a higher satisfaction still than the self-satisfaction we can gain by ourselves? That is how also the question of a truly religious dimension in action arises in a science of action that wants to encompass all that the will wills necessarily. Even if we do not have any clear proof for the existence of God, in his transcendence or in any well-reasoned way of conceiving such as existence, there are within us dispositions that relate us to such a transcendent Being by reason of their openness to the universal and the infinite that cannot be contained within the universe.

Blondel's argument here remains quite straightforward, in keeping with the logic of this entire scientific deployment of ever-broadening spheres in human action, on the basis of a principle he has uncovered at the core of its origin in human consciousness, its fundamental spiritual élan, or the willing will, with its infinite power of transcendence. He does not go into the more metaphysical elaborations on Thought, Being, and Action given in the earlier parts of the Trilogy. Nor does he go into how this élan toward transcendence relates back to proofs for the existence of God, as he had done in 1893. All he appeals to is the spontaneous and implicit faith in God that expresses itself as a relation to something transcendent in our action and as a need for something more in our search for complete satisfaction.

Whether or not we admit the validity of dialectical proofs as justification or clarification or enrichment for this spontaneous idea of a transcendent Being, or of a God whose name is incommunicable, there is still a need in an integral philosophy of action for examining how the idea, as obscure and rudimentary as it may be, has repercussions of its own in our action. "Resting on the entire élan of human life, the certain affirmation of a transcendent being adds to, fortifies, perfects the élan itself. To remain faithful to the initial motion, by virtue of the acquired momentum and of the progressively developed spiritual forces, the living idea of the transcendent God is itself efficacious; and we cannot run away from this proper efficacy without betraying, at least in part, a sort of obscure loyalty" (1937a, 345). Moreover, to the extent that our actions flow from this spiritual élan, within us, they bring into play the stimulating and cooperative presence of the transcendent Being, thereby adding a grave responsibility to our acts, as well as a metaphysical consistency surpassing what might otherwise be deemed only a passing phenomenon. The attitude we must take under the most varied circumstances of our life regarding our final end does not depend only on discursive views or ethical theories that we can share with others. In our most deliberate actions, in those that are most decisive and thereby most complex, Blondel tells us, there is always a singular part that escapes the grasp of any general speculative science and that belongs properly to the calling of each singular agent, and to a *norm* that is most personal at any given moment of life. That is why an action that is faithful to its end bears within it a truth that illuminates us on ourselves and contains more, in the present, than we can fully comprehend on our own destiny, on the concurrence we have to bring to it, and on the helps we could expect in securing it. Even if we cannot define how far an authentic religious disposition towards transcendence might take us in our concrete action, there is much more to look forward to in that opening, as Blondel sees it, even before we begin thinking of it as supernatural.

Blondel is well aware of the different developments that can occur in this spiritual and religious attitude among different peoples and at different times. We have seen how superstition in all its forms is, for him, only a perversion of the authentic religious sense that undergirds the human spirit. He does not want to do the history of this religious sense as it runs through the different forms of human consciousness, from the primitive to the modern, as he has done in part for its perversion into superstition. He is more interested in showing how the religious sense in the human spirit always entails a reference to something transcendent, something he looks for in all authentic religious practices, whether ancient or modern, wherever there has been some sense of cooperation with a really transcendent God, in what one does in the world and in what one has to make of oneself. This is what a methodical and integral study of human action in the concrete has to bring to philosophy, a new way of looking further into the interior and the ulterior sphere that has always inspired conscientious spirits, even if this includes some positive religion that exceeds the capacity of human reason to achieve or to comprehend. All the argument of this dialectic up to now has been to show that we cannot stop short of an authentic belief in a transcendent who is already present at the conscious origin of our action, and who can still reveal himself further in the way he cooperates with us. Our willed will cannot legitimately or rationally keep us from where our willing will would take us. We have still to learn how we must ratify this profound willing we all start from in our action, as from an originating necessity we have not chosen, but that we must exercise freely and responsibly.

In the context of this relation to some transcendence, we find ourselves deeply conflicted between the charms of the world we find ourselves in and the mysterious attraction of a higher world that calls us from within, between the motives and mobiles that push and pull us in so many different directions and the single end that alone can satisfy our desire for equality with ourselves. In this final sphere of expansion for our action, this conflict comes to a climax in a drama Blondel has already alluded to at the end of the first volume on *Action* in the Trilogy, having to do with how the action of secondary causes relates to the pure Acting of the first Cause. Here, as he had done in 1893, he presents the climax in the simplest and ultimate terms, without going into any kind of rational calculus to show how in choosing for a lesser good we are in fact choosing against what would be the infinite good we actually desire in our willing will. Nor does he go over the philosophy of death and mortification he had used to convince a more academic philosophy of the necessity to give up our present self-made life, if we are to accept a new kind of life from on high, consistent with what we aspire to in our willing will. What we have seen here in going through the expanding waves of action and in the spiritual advancement of civilizations is not only an augmentation of power and enjoyment, a certain magnanimity of spirit among people, but also a growing sense of dissatisfaction and deception, even with the best of what has been achieved by human action. Blondel alludes to ever-recurring perturbations in the historical order of human action as signs both of a strength in our spirit, and of a lack of strength in our will, once the idea of a transcendent end, from which we draw our power to deliberate and choose, enters into composition with our acts. What we find at the end of our consideration of human action is that it "rises above space and time, and that, going beyond our isolated personality, it brings into play, along with other human persons, the transcendent cooperator whose loan of power it uses abusively and whose intention it denatures" (1937a, 351).

From this Blondel draws the positive truth of affirming for human willing an impossibility of keeping only to its own action, and a necessity of placing the center of its moving equilibrium and its abiding aim, no longer in a false egocentrism, but in a transcendence where the true love of self will coincide with a theocentric truth and love. If we come up against a final incapacity in our will to will all that we will to be, it is because we are called to a higher amplification, a higher kind of growth where human willing is finally called to ratify itself, something it can do only by acceding, through a kind of submission, to a creative design of love and to the happiest of freedoms.

At this culminating point of Transcendence, then, one does not lose one's freedom, but rather one rises to a new way of exercising it, not just in relation to the plurality of motives and mobiles toward particular goods that agitate themselves in our consciousness, but now in terms of a more fundamental option that presents itself regarding our very being, or the being of our willing will. We are at a point where the influx of the divine, in giving us the infinite power of a willing will, and a reflux of the self-same divine calling us paradoxically to an infinite end, seem to meet and present us with what Blondel calls an *alternative,* the alternative of one's life. On the one hand, we seem crushed between an initial will that is imposed on all of us and a final will we have only to submit to. On the other hand, if we are to escape a forced consent that would be more demeaning than an absolute constraint, we have to recognize that we can be strong even against God, and that our submission can become a double victory, that of the sovereign master and that of ourselves, through a free and complete ratification of the willing and of the destiny assigned to us. None of the particular goods we will by and for ourselves satisfies our willing will in its virtual infinity. None can satisfy our freedom in its ambition for what Blondel calls a generous autonomy.

In fact, the fundamental generosity of willing is the theme we must go back to in order to work our way out of the dilemma in which we find ourselves at the peak or in the depth of our willing, a generosity that extends beyond the universe, not to say transcendence itself as something we could capture or would undergo only passively. For Blondel, as well as for Aristotle and Kant, the grandeur of man is to find happiness only in something one is worthy of. What we all have to face up to is a certain dependence in our initial willing, "since it is undergone at its core, imposed with its modalities, imperiously oriented toward an end from which (supreme oppression) it cannot subtract itself, even though it may fail to attain it and suffer from it incurably" (1937a, 354).

These are the severest terms in which Blondel presents this problem of problems, this alternative that presents itself at the peak of human action. The question for the willing will is whether it can still will itself as a willed will that is rationally ratified and sincerely generous, knowing that its initial investment of responsibility is involuntary on its part. We have not chosen to be free. Why should we be held eternally responsible for our choices? This is the ultimate crisis of consciousness for spiritual beings obliged to contribute to their own destiny. "They are called without prior warning and without any original admission on their part, to will no longer the object, no longer the fact, but the first act and the very being of the will" (1937a, 355). Faced with this seeming imposition of our very will upon us by a transcendent will, we have only two ways to go: use this will to ratify our own willing and its necessary consequences, or else use it to say no to the giver of this will and to whatever else he may wish to give in addition. Blondel knows that the second alternative is possible. It is even a sign that the first alternative is real and ontogenic in a very positive sense, that is, in keeping with a will that is free and generous to the point of giving itself up for the other. What he wants to show is that the ratification of our own willing, even as originally imposed on us, is not only free and rational but also quite in keeping with the exigencies of our own willing itself. These are exigencies that will serve to clarify the sort of spiritual and religious dispositions we must now make our own, in order to remain faithful to the élan of the will whose expansion we have followed to the limits of immanence.

What creates the problem for us is this insertion of a transcendence in our spirit that at first we thought to be our own, but that in the end seems to be in us only to claim us for itself. How can we accept such an intrusion when our first instinct is to desire a god who will serve us? "To have God within us without belonging to Him: or else belonging to him to the point of going out of oneself, prior to and in order to come into full possession of oneself in full enjoyment of truth and mutual charity" (1937a, 355). That is the dilemma that arises at the heart of human acts and consciences. To represent the problem merely as an opposition between divine willing and human willing is not to see it in the proper light. God is not one we can conquer by our action. He is pure Act and Subject in himself, to whom the human subject must configure his own willing by a rational and free adherence to a divinely providential order, where subjects capable of their own providence have their own role to play in managing their ascent toward a transcendence of their own. We must not therefore erect another god besides this One to do battle with in our will. We have only to recognize God as the one we aspire to be like in our action. *Assimilation* to God was a theme Blondel found in Plato and one that he made much of in his own philosophy, as we shall see in the last work he published at the time of his death.

Here, however, as an answer to the problem of how we are to accept the presence of God in our acts, assimilation alone appears too idealistic and unrealistic. It is easy to say, let us go to God and try better to resemble him, but it does not take a metaphysician to recognize that, literally speaking, this is rationally impossible, morally presumptuous, and religiously unacceptable. Philosophy has to preserve a more precise sense of the mystery that surrounds the divine, even in our lives. So too must a healthy conception of what destiny means for us. Even if we admit a power and an obligation to pursue indefatigably the knowledge and the service of the God of reason and of aspiration, it would be vain to suppose that the search will ever come to an end or to hope that it could ever be exhausted or useless. "The rational and free being that we are can never be dispensed from a philosophical and religious inquietude, it can never be authorized to be content with a metaphysics acquired once and for all (as Descartes thought of it), never allowed legitimately to confine himself to positive science and to the organization of the order immanent to human societies or the entire universe" (1937a, 359). If there is a natural religion, something Blondel was more willing to concede in 1937 than he had been in 1893, it is not one that can stop at a static deism with self-proclaimed rites, for that would be one that would close itself off from the true infinite. No matter how inadequate man may be in his search for God, his action cannot be dispensed from this mission of exploration, submission, and adoration toward the divine power and majesty. From this comes the trait of generosity that Blondel associates with any authentic religious sentiment, in which there is acceptance of one's reason and will as a gift that cannot be rationally denied or voluntarily refused. Blondel speaks of this trait as one of infinite aspiration, one that finds itself in contention with an insatiable élan of egoism within us, but that little by little builds itself up into a spiritual disinterestedness of personal liberation able to enjoy a rightly deserved fulfillment.

Three more difficulties remain to be resolved in this point of contact where the finite spirit finds itself at a point of influx and reflux in relation to an infinite that surpasses it, even as it empowers it to be and to act on its own account, difficulties to be assuaged rationally in a critical philosophy of religion. The first of these comes up as we think of the strange and obscure responsibility our action seems to fall into, especially when it deviates from the right path and finds itself incapable of undoing what it has done, unable to recover itself in its integrity, stuck in a debt it cannot pay back or annul. We can understand passing hardships or humiliations, when action is rising toward the glory of some eternal felicity. But how can we understand that action can ultimately fail and find itself confirmed in this failure, especially when the failure seems to be due to some trivial act, a passing desire, an incidental intention, or a confused effort at best? Blondel's analysis of action has shown that our choices always relate back to motives and mobiles that come and go in our consciousness, never anything that is strictly equal to our willing will. However, in the experience of the will itself there is something that surpasses all these passing motives we contend with, and that builds within us an abiding substantial being. We do not think of each one of our acts in our conscience as affecting our very being all in the same way. Some are seen as having a negligible effect. But others, those that bring into play a more serious responsibility for ourselves and for others, have to be seen as affecting our very attitude toward the good we are aiming at in forming our character.

What Blondel says we have to think about in all this is our action *as a whole,* in which all these individual acts expended over time coalesce into a dominant willing that perseveres and builds itself up into a final whole that endures in being. If there is generosity toward the infinite in this overarching willing, then the subject is ready for eternal fulfillment. If there is only closing in on oneself or on anything in the immanent order, then the subject finds himself stuck in the immanent order, or rather condemns himself to an immanent order that can never bring him the fulfillment he aspires to in his still infinite willing. He has placed himself in contradiction with his own fundamental willing and being, without the possibility of redeeming himself. This is a hard saying to come to, at the end of a philosophical exploration of action, but Blondel sees it as flowing from the logic of action, no less than from the more positive religious sentiment of generosity toward the infinite.

The second and penultimate difficulty to be resolved in this philosophy of action, after all this, is the inadequacy we are ultimately left with between what we can grasp of action in our scientific reflection and what is effectively realized in action that simultaneously falls short and is more comprehensive than anything our human science encompasses. This is the kind of disequilibrium he has pointed out in each one of the earlier volumes of the Trilogy, with regard to Thought, Being, and Action. He comes back to it here as something written into human nature. As rational, the disequilibrium moves us toward a spiritual life that surpasses time and space, so that we cannot simply close ourselves up in humanism or immanentism of any sort. For in that there is no fulfillment for us. We cannot escape the immortality of our congenital élan. The action we accomplish in the world cannot be self-contained. The law of growth, of humility, or of abnegation and sacrifice that action exemplifies, is the condition for accessing a higher life, a truly spiritual freedom, and even a transcendence we can only think of as beyond all limits.

What makes this possible, however, is that we are never alone in our action. There are always a stimulus and a secret cooperation from the other who communicates his infinite power, a force we have on loan that "confers upon our personal efforts a vigor we can use and a bearing for which we become responsible as an advance we have to make fruitful" (1937a, 364). The acts in which we place ourselves already surpass and escape the parameters of our clear consciousness. When we add to this fact the idea of an impulse or an attraction from a higher source than anything we can draw from in our own thought or our willing, it is no wonder there is always some mystery hidden in our action, something we can never adequately grasp, even though the willing will, in its profound *sincerity,* another term that Blondel likes to invoke at this point of his argument, along with generosity, can never disavow or fail to ratify the complex reality that, amid all these shadows, we can still make intelligible and recognize as good.

The third and final point of the enigma Blondel wants to shed some light on, in this sense of a cooperation between man and God, is the fact that the end toward which we have to tend is not only obscure and mysterious for our thought, but also inaccessible to our action, even of the most generous sort. This is a point Blondel had made most emphatically in his original philosophy of the supernatural, precisely with the idea of the supernatural in mind as something *hypothetically necessary* for the ultimate perfection of human action. Here, where he has not yet introduced any such hypothesis into the study of the expansion of action, and is still working only within the realm of what he would call its natural expansion, Blondel responds to the problem of this irreducible obscurity and the inaccessibility of any final fulfillment for our most generous efforts, by acknowledging that what we do know of the world and of the Creator, and what we can achieve with the power that has been given to us to dominate and master the world, can already be thought of as a fairly high destiny for us, even if it does not entail being able to capture God in himself.

It would be wrong to say that, in a natural order, human life would not be worth living, or that the sense of an incommunicable and despotic transcendence would make this life something mutilated or miserable. Nor would the incommensurability between transcendence and the transitive acts of contingent beings leave us without any conception of participation in the divine at any degree whatever, "so that the only religion exempt of superstition would be agnosticism or pure indetermination" (1937a, 365). Religion is not opposed to humanism or to naturalism. What it does is take us beyond naturalism and humanism into a realm of higher need, of hope, of confidence, and of expectation for a possible alliance with the divine or a new intervention in favor of man. This is not contrary to anything in human nature, let alone spirit. It is a sense that flows from the deepest aspirations of the human spirit and of the willing will. The only thing that would be contrary to nature, Blondel observes shrewdly, "would be the pretense of a natural religion reduced to some dry deism without any positive element or without any specifically religious act. By what it contains of transcendence in it, of tacit recourse to the cooperation of the first cause, action, for whoever becomes conscious of all that it implies and all that it tends to, always has an intrinsically religious character" (1937a, 365). This is said as a direct counterpoint and correction for the natural tendency we also have of making an idol or a superstition of almost anything we find in the world of man. In this ninth wave, on authentic religious dispositions in human action, Blondel has turned the tables on what had started as only superstition in the eighth wave, leaving us with the possibility of considering a more positive kind of religion as an exotic wave for action to expand into.

Having gone as far as we can go in the normal and natural expansion of human action, however, Blondel now notes that in the end we are not really decentering ourselves in broadening and transferring little by little our intention as spiritual agents outside of ourselves. We are only centering or recentering ourselves into a common and universal perspective that is transcendent and divine as it radiates from without, so to speak, through the universe. To illustrate this, Blondel repeats what has been his conception of action from the beginning, only to show that it is our way of cooperating in the divine plan. "The entire order of things is nothing but the order of means we must will and use to realize our own person in communion with the design for the whole and the will of the Creator" (1937a, 366). To turn all this back only on oneself or on anything immanent in the universe, be it a world spirit, would be to vitiate it at the very core of action. So too would be any type of self-sufficiency. The ideal that we aspire to in our action is so far above anything we can ever achieve on our own that we are always left with a profound sense of inquietude. If human endeavor is indefinitely progressive in the world, it is because it is oriented toward a divine transcendence.

We have a need to draw closer and closer to God. But this is something we can never finish doing, because the closer we draw to such a destiny, the more we become conscious of "how unreasonable it would be for a finite thought or a contingent being to pretend to comprehend the infinite and possess the absolute" (1937a, 367). Such a humble admission is the expression par excellence of the necessary religious dispositions we must rise to in our action.

The Supernatural as Exotic but Supreme Sphere for Human Action

Blondel ends his systematic deployment of human action into concentric waves with this one on the religious dispositions the created spirit must rise to in tending toward an end that will equal the principle from which it flows. He has spoken of a necessary place for positive religion in what action has to include in its expansion, beyond a purely immanent order, but only in general terms that could be deemed part of the natural exigencies that mark human action as a whole, the exigency to turn the will around at the summit of its expansion, so that it will accept itself and its own action in the world as a gift from God in all generosity and in readiness to sacrifice itself and the world to the mysterious transcendence from which it comes and toward which it tends. Anything short of that, any attempt to find complete satisfaction in the immanent order or in self-sufficiency of any sort, would be a form of superstition, not a truly religious attitude for a finite spirit. In the final estimation of our life as spiritual beings, we must always recognize that we want more than what we can lay our hands on, even if that be our power to will and to act. We must recognize that we are incapable of willing more, unless we will it through the *one thing necessary*, the transcendent Being who wills us and our action in the first place. Such is the ultimate religious situation in which man finds himself.

We could say that the philosophy of action in the concrete ends here, but Blondel does not end it there. He finds in this ending a reason to rebound to the rational possibility of a higher wave of expansion that he now speaks of as exotic and supreme, but that he has long spoken of as the philosophical hypothesis of a supernatural gift, to complement the natural gift that brings us to this final religious disposition as finite spirits. Such a wave would be exotic in the sense that it would not follow necessarily from what we can accomplish with the natural gift that constitutes us in our being and acting. It would be gratuitous from the standpoint of that gift and of the Giver. However, it would be in keeping with a rational necessity we still experience at the end of our action in its religious dimension, when we realize the insufficiency in which we still find ourselves with regard to willing an object that would be the equal of our power to will. It is already a lot to be able to will ourselves and the world we create historically, but it is not enough to provide the full complement of what would satisfy or equal the infinite power of willing within. If we wish to think of such a full complement for our action, we have to think of it as *supernatural*, transcending our own capacity to accomplish. Yet in thinking of it as a complement to our power to act, as something that would satisfy or equal our infinite power of willing, we have to see in it a certain rational *necessity* in relation to the principle that has motivated the science of action from beginning to end.

The orchestration of this question, or of this hypothesis of a supernatural gift to complement the gift of nature itself at the end of this second version of Blondel's dialectic of action, is more subdued than it had been in the first version, but it is governed by no less of a rational necessity to pursue the question of human action to the end of what would be its perfection, even if that should prove to be beyond its capacity to accomplish by itself. Philosophy cannot shirk its responsibility to examine this hypothesis and the rational conditions it would imply for human action, because of the way such a hypothesis would seem to fulfill the aspiration of the will at the end of its trajectory in the universe.

The logic of concentric waves continues to play here, bringing with it an added necessity for considering the hypothesis of such an exocentric wave, as something to be critically evaluated along with the waves already considered in the normal expansion of action. Though Blondel does not insist as much on this necessity here as he had in the original dissertation, and in defending the idea of an integral Catholic philosophy, he still wants to present it as a truly rational possibility, something that cannot be a matter of indifference for a will in search of an object that will be the equal of its power to will. The method he follows in bringing up this final question of divinization for the human spirit at the end of *Action II* remains as scientific and rational as he had made it out to be in the *Lettre* of 1896.

Blondel realizes, however, perhaps better than he had earlier, that he is now venturing into what he has already spoken of as the mysterious aspect of action, into ways of access to a Transcendent we know of, but more as an unknown, and as incommensurable to anything we know even of spirit. The idea of doing so in philosophy comes with the thought of finding a more complete fulfillment than we can achieve through the powers of reason and will we already have, a closer union of human action with the divine transcendence whence it proceeds and to which it aspires, whatever obscurity such a supernatural realization may still entail for us. We have already traced the progressive expansion of waves that come from the personal center of human agents under the influence of a will infused in the depth of our rational nature. But the movement we would have to suppose now, with this hypothesis of a supernatural gift, would make sense and serve the higher purpose we are envisioning only if it were to proceed directly from an antecedent divine initiative, and not just from the gift we already have that constitutes our rational nature and our own proper will. In other words, along with the infinite power of transcendence we have already seen at work in human action leading up to authentic religious dispositions in human action, we would now have an infusion of a different kind leading to an actual cooperation between the human and the divine in a properly theandric action. What makes such a hypothetical gift interesting for philosophy, as paradoxical and mysterious as it may sound, is that it would enable us to reach the fulfillment we aspire to in seeking to make our willed will equal to our willing will, in an action that would be truly perfect or absolute in its transcendence.

To be sure, there is something more than paradoxical about the hypothesis to be examined, but Blondel is intent on showing its rational aspect as something in keeping with the fundamental aspiration of the human will. It would not just be an arbitrary fiction that philosophy could legitimately ignore as a pure figment of our imagination or a mere pretension of our reason. "Even if we have to conceive the supplement now in question as gratuitous, it does not thereby appear either as without a point of insertion that is possible and prepared for, or as a matter of indifference for us in the manner of a tacked-on or elective juxtaposition" (1937a, 375). Mere juxtaposition between the hypothesis in question and what is natural to man is a conception Blondel had fought all of his philosophical life, as something to avoid and exclude in a true philosophy of religion. What is implied in this hypothesis as conceived by Blondel is not only a matter of metaphysical possibility for man, alongside another perhaps more natural possibility. It is rather an offer that would respond more fully to what has been seen as a radical insufficiency in human capacity, something more fitting or convenient *(convenant)* to its need. In the final analysis what we find in the exercise of reason is a certain "disproportion between the indefinite in our religious aspiration and the infinite of the object toward which it tends by a desire, undoubtedly obscure and inefficacious, but by that very fact nostalgic and unsatisfied" (1937a, 375). The principle of this indelible desire for an ulterior shore adds to our very rational notion of the transcendent "the very human idea and the very religious sentiment of a supernatural" (1937a, 375).

This is not just an idea Blondel comes to at the end of his science of human action. It is one he finds expressed in the broad religious experience of mankind. Philosophy of religion should not get stuck in the "prelogism" and the frequent absurdities of primitive cults. Nor should it be afraid to approach the higher, more profound spiritual life of a communion with the universal and the absolute, under the light and the influence of a supernatural that transcends, not just space and time, but also the discursive mode of our thoughts and worldly actions. Philosophy has nothing to fear from a higher illumination coming from action in the concrete. It only has more to learn about how far its rational task must go into the mystery that presents itself through such human and divine action.

The hypothesis of a higher gift gratuitously offered to a rational nature does not jar in any way with a pre-established order that cannot require more than what is already given. All it presupposes is a new gift that may come as a surprise for an order that tends to close in upon itself, or upon finite objects in the immanent order, in superstitious fashion, but a gift that nevertheless shows some convenience or appropriateness for a spirit that aspires to the infinite and the absolute, but can never simply identify with it by reason of the latter's irreducible transcendence. Blondel is intent on preserving both the immanence and the transcendence of divinization in human action at one and the same time.

Thus the hypothesis of a supernatural can be said to enter into the realm of metaphysically intelligible necessities for the human spirit. It can also be seen as compatible with the contingent ways in which human willing actualizes itself in the world. But there is no way it could be perceived directly in experience or grasped effectively by our reason and our will. Even if it were offered *de facto*, this hypothetical gift, as good as it may be conceived to be for us, would still remain inaccessible to the natural control of our spirit, apart from some divine revelation. It would be imperceptible to our natural ways of knowing. We could not discern its supernatural and gratuitous character as such any more than we can comprehend its transcendence over the natural gift we start from in this philosophy of a finite spirit. We cannot command or demand it, let alone define what it would be, even with our metaphysical idea of its hypothetical necessity. Without further illumination from within as well as without, our consciousness, moral as well as psychological, is naturally incapable of discerning by its own natural light what it would be, or even if it is, precisely because, as supernatural, the new gift proceeds from an absolutely gratuitous initiative from God. To be sure, such an initiative would insinuate itself into the most intimate depth of our life, to transform it from the inside, but precisely for that reason it would be mixed in with the human ways of knowing and acting, where it would have its effect as grace. It would be impossible for us to discern what in our conscious life is from the gift of nature and what proceeds from the gratuitous gift, let alone discern the new presence and efficaciousness of the gratuitously infused support for our reason and will. It would be impossible for us to unravel this new support from the natural support we already have by nature and from the normal course of our acts.

This is not to say that we could not know of such a gift, if it were offered. The supposition of Blondel is that we would have to know about it, because it would create a new level of responsibility in our action, which, as we have seen, is already of eternal consequence. It is only to say that we could not sort out the supernatural in its purity from the rest of our experience by the light of our own consciousness alone, which remains confused about so many other things in our actions, even after the kind of existential analysis we have gone through in this science of action. Blondel wants to maintain the incommensurability and the inconfusibility of the directly divine wave that would represent a supernatural gift in relation to all the natural waves at work in the world and in the human being. He does not, however, want to keep the supernatural separate from the natural or from our action, as we come to know it in the concrete. Nor does he want to think of it as juxtaposed or as superimposed on the natural, as a layer or as a surface that would not penetrate it. He wants to think about it precisely as something that would enter into the world and into our spiritual élan to create new exigencies in action for our willing.

Even if we can think about it only as a hypothesis in philosophy, he wants also to draw on the authentically religious experience of man, his justified inquietude in the world, as it is on the whole and in so many disturbing details for a would-be self-sufficiency, in order to formulate what would have to be our spiritual attitude as human beings, if we were to suppose that such a hypothesis of a supernatural is realized in fact. He recognizes that his very formulation of such a hypothesis has been influenced by the historical experience of a Christian civilization, but that does not deter him from thinking about it as a philosophical problem to be analyzed critically, not to pronounce himself as a philosopher on whether such a gift has been realized historically or not, but rather as a matter of integrity in the pursuit of philosophy's own task of shedding spiritual light on the human experience, or on human action as a whole.

The hypothesis is rationally conceivable and, as gratuitous or gracious as it might be on the part of the divine, it would answer to a real aspiration on the part of the human being. All the prior dynamism of human acting, whether in its striving for transcendence or in its insufficiency and its failures, arouses within us a vibrant interest in what could be a solution to the problem that surrounds the secret of our destiny. Even if we cannot determine philosophically whether the gift has been proffered, much less claim it as owed to our nature, Blondel thinks we can determine certain conditions that would be entailed in the communication of such a gift, on the basis of the very reasons that have justified our entertaining the thought of such a supernatural gift as hypothetically necessary for a will seeking equality with itself. In the final part of this discussion of a hypothetical, exotic way of expansion for human action, he elaborates briefly on several of these conditions, which must be understood prior to any elaboration on the experience of the Christian Spirit itself that may follow.

The first condition is to remain rigorously true to the character of gratuity of the gift hypothetically in question, though conceived as a supreme wave of expansion for human action. Though it can be thought of as perfecting for human action, in accord with action's own spontaneous aspiration, it cannot be thought of as flowing from the spontaneous initiative of the human will itself or of any other created nature. The hypothesis stipulates precisely that it can come only from a new and totally gratuitous initiative on the part of the Creator toward a creature that has no right to expect such an initiative, and has no way of giving itself this subvention, since no action of a creature could contain, produce, or acquire it on its own initiative. For all his insistence on transcendence in human action, Blondel is prepared to resist any attempt to immanentize what he still thinks of as absolutely supernatural, even when he thinks of it as a gift designed to penetrate the very core of human action, where the infinite power of willing still has to embody itself in particular choices.

The second condition is that, as the wave of this new gift penetrates deeply within the created spirit, without coming in any way from it, from its nature, or from any of its efforts, it is not absorbed merely in the manner of a material and intellectual nourishment that we are conscious of ingesting, digesting, or using up. The new gift is not unrelated to the prior gift of creation. It presupposes the prior gift of thinking and willing itself. It is offered to free agents who have a role in accepting it or rejecting it. Yet, as this mysterious new force works its way into us and through us, it does not become confused with anything in the prior gift of our reasonable nature or in the habitual divine concursus that sustains the acts of a finite spirit. Even as it penetrates to the most mysterious depths of our consciousness, in order to unite itself secretly to human actions for all they are capable of, it does not lose any of its divine originality and transcendence.

From this a third condition becomes clear. What the supernatural brings to human action cannot be naturalized. If it appears that God is descending into the depths of man, while man is tending toward the summit of God, it is not as though they were simply converging confusedly toward something indefinite in the future, no matter how dialectically conceived as a true infinite or a unity of opposites. As gifts of one and the same God, the natural and supernatural are not opposites in any way. If we speak of two gifts, it is only in relation to us or to different ways God has of giving himself to us. Even in giving himself, God remains himself. He is himself in man in two different ways. "At first He lends Himself so that He may be sought, but He can also give Himself more, so that the seeking may find Him more completely than it could ever attain by its natural resources" (1937a, 382). We know that human action always has a religious dimension. It supposes the divine from its conception on, and invokes it in the end. It can become receptive of two gifts that, without confusion, can come together in a symbiosis that is utterly theandric without thereby compromising the incommensurability and the absolute distinction between creature and Creator. This is something Blondel will have much more to say about in the coming volumes on the Christian Spirit.

A fourth condition flows from the foregoing three conditions. Even if we were to suppose that a wave of divine grace has been granted, it would not come under the empire of our ordinary means of knowing and of taking initiative. It is not given through the original gift of nature, where its divine originality as supernatural would be absorbed or lost. But even as it descends into the depth of our subconscious life in order to rise with it to the highest operations of the spirit, it remains hidden, within or above what our consciousness and our discursive operations can discern, analyze, or lay hold of by themselves. We can have no direct view into the kind of supernatural life we are hypothesizing. This is for him by definition, as it were. Nor can we arrive at it by any inference from human thought or action. It can be known expressly only through some positive revelation, thanks to signs that authenticate it and an integration of many reasons for believing. Far from regretting the intrusion of positivity in religion, Blondel sees it as a necessity for a religion that purports to be truly supernatural as well as historical.

There is, moreover, what Blondel calls a compensating condition that he infers from this rational elaboration of the different aspects of the hypothesis in question. Given the mystery in which this wave of supervenient grace would be enshrouded, and given that, according to the hypothesis, it would be "calling or recalling the human being in the depth of his intimacy to an elevation incommensurable with our natural knowledge and with results unachievable by man, the condition for a salutary use of such a grace — if it were granted — does not depend essentially on the science or the consciousness we could have of it" (1937a, 383). What this means is that ignorance, which is not the same as ignoring something of which we are not totally ignorant, "is not an insurmountable obstacle to a fidelity that would suffice for adhering to a truth, hidden in apparently natural intentions and acts, as adherence in fact to a supernatural elaboration" (1937a, 383). There is an awesome responsibility implied in the idea of a new solicitation coming from a supreme wave of grace to be taken into account by human action. It might seem unfair or even scandalous that such a responsibility should have to be exercised without a clear and distinct consciousness of the specific originality of God's gratuitous intervention as absolutely transcending our natural powers of reasoning and willing. Yet, what other way would there be of assuring and reassuring all the susceptibilities of reason itself, of justice, of human dignity, and of divine charity itself, in what would be a new alliance of human and divine initiatives in one and the same action? The mysterious and shadowy realm in which this responsibility of man would have to play itself out would be what allows initiative on both sides, as it were, that of the creature and that of the Creator. It would bring human responsibility to a new level, one that touches on the supernatural as well as the natural.

From this ignorance, however, or from our natural incapacity to discern by ourselves whether or not we are in fact destined to a higher end, Blondel points out, we cannot argue against what we already know is a possibility, by right of its being something that could be realized eventually in our favor. Blondel takes the knowledge of this possibility as a very positive conclusion concerning what we are to do in the state of spiritual hesitation we find ourselves in on the religious level of action. The very hypothesis of a possible supernatural elevation has arisen from the dynamic of our spiritual élan seeking an object it is incapable of attaining by itself. Now the hypothesis itself reinforces the dispositions of thought and action that have led us to this thought of a supernatural gift enabling us to attain perfect satisfaction in the first place. "From all these connections there comes an obligation of sincere inquiry, of eventual docility, of submissive and loving cooperation that, even if the order of grace were not to be for us, would constitute a generous and true attitude able to perfect what we had to say about a religious disposition that is most normal and most essential" (1937a, 384-85).

The last thing Blondel would have us think is that all this talk about a hypothetical supernatural wave of expansion for human action has to do only with some fanciful pie-in-the-sky or some vague desires running wild beyond the pale of legitimate philosophical inquiry. Much less does he think he is in the business of "rationalizing unduly certain teachings that can come only from another source and another order" (1937a, 386), as one might suppose concerning a theology, or an apologetic that is out of touch with human action in its concrete expansion, or a philosophy of religion that is uncritical and merely dictated extrinsically by a religious magisterium. On the contrary, in raising the question of a hypothetical supernatural gift that would fulfill the human aspiration in a way that human nature cannot by itself, Blondel is still proceeding strictly as a philosopher out of a necessity he has found essential in human willing and acting, the necessity to bring the willed will into equation with the willing will. This has been the essential point of his philosophy of action and of the supernatural from the very beginning, the point he had insisted on against all other methods of apologetics in his discourse on method of 1896. Here at the end of this second, more metaphysical version of his philosophy of action in its concrete expansion, he returns to make the same point over again, but now in the more classical context of what had come to be spoken of as a natural but inefficacious desire to attain God. However else one might speak of such a desire in theology or in religious discourse, Blondel claims to have come to the idea "in the language of the most rational thought and of the most reasonable will," from an ontological standpoint, while "meditating on truths that are necessary and rigorously exact" (1937a, 386). Without such careful reasoning from the fundamental principle that governs and commands the action of a free self-conscious subject, even the alleged natural desire to see God would remain effectively vague, irrational, or even unreasonable. One has to show how willing itself in the human being "raises the hypothesis of a sublime and gratuitous effusion of divine charity" (1937a, 386), an effusion that would restore the free spiritual being to itself in the end, in a way that cannot be realized by any finite spirit left to its own resources.

We see here why Blondel wanted to take the idea of an integral Catholic philosophy much further than any of his fellow Catholic, mostly Thomist, philosophers. At the end of this second version of his philosophy of the supernatural, as he is contemplating taking philosophy one step further in the more explicit consideration of the Christian Spirit as it has made itself manifest in history and in the human experience of the world, he remains no less rigorous in maintaining the strict heterogeneity of what this super-added gratuitous gift would be in its content relative to the natural gift he has done so much to explore, as far as it would take him, in the question of transcendence in human action. All that he has affirmed is a hypothetical necessity of an exotic wave that would bring completion to an otherwise insufficient action, a necessity philosophically recognized to be such in its own right in relation to a will that is incapable of willing an object that is equal to its power of willing, without appealing to any theological *datum* or to any *fact* of revelation, and without transgressing into the domain of any supernatural religion. Even after speaking of a supernatural gift as hypothetically necessary for fulfilling aspirations of the created spirit, philosophy is still not in any position to take the place of a theology based on faith in a revelation, with a content such as that of the Christian religion. With the idea of a hypothetical necessity of a supernatural dimension for human action, however, he has also affirmed the relational necessity of considering the union and the interpenetration of the natural and supernatural in human experience, once the offer of a supernatural gift has been entertained.

What follows from this is a certain obligation for philosophy to continue searching in the direction of such a satisfying gift, which already can be viewed as a certain perfecting of the will in its fundamental religious disposition, though not with any expectation of attaining a truth that remains beyond its grasp, whether as a matter of fact or even of factual possibility. For philosophy to try to define what the supernatural gift would entail, in terms of what we know and will naturally in our action, would be to betray what it says is transcendent and supernatural about it. Philosophy can only bring us to the necessity of a further, perhaps more properly theological kind of inquiry. It cannot, however, as rigorous philosophy, cross over into such an inquiry, due to the total heterogeneity it acknowledges between the two kinds of inquiry. Philosophy has nothing to fear from this other kind of religious inquiry, which cannot replace the philosophical inquiry that it presupposes. Neither does religious inquiry have anything to fear from philosophy, even as the latter entertains the hypothesis of a supernatural gift in its relation to the natural gift of thinking and willing. Indeed, Blondel thinks of the necessary rational connections he has made between the two as not only legitimate, but also as profitable for both disciplines, "which cannot ignore one another with impunity" (1937a, 387). In the work he still has in mind to pursue on *Philosophy and the Christian Spirit*, he will take philosophy one step closer to the mystery of the divine ordination for the world, in order to arrive at a new depth of interpretation for the human experience, as it relates to its highest aspiration for divinization, without confusing or hybridizing the two orders he has taken such pains to distinguish as well as to unite, in a philosophy that wants to be integral with regard to all that can be found in historical human action.

XVI

The Expanded Philosophy of the Supernatural

Blondel must have felt a tremendous sense of relief when he came to the end of the fifth and final volume of his Trilogy on Thought, Being, and Action. This was a work he had begun planning almost from the days when he felt compelled to add one final chapter on "the bond of knowledge and action in being" to his original dissertation on Action in 1893. The dissatisfaction he felt about that chapter opened up for him the necessity of rethinking, not only his dialectic of *Action* in the concrete, but also the conception of both *Thought* and *Being* that underlay the entire enterprise of his philosophizing from the beginning, but had remained unspoken in this first expression as a philosophy of action only. Thinking and Being had been an integral part of his thinking from the beginning, as Blondel explained in the account of his *Itinerary* later on, so much so that he thought of the original dissertation as only a part of his philosophical project produced in the context of satisfying an academic requirement. Looking back at the end of his life, he spoke of his two Trilogies as an unfolding, an explication, of the thesis on *Action* into all its ramifications of Thought and Being as well as the explicitly Christian concepts of the supernatural.

The recasting of the original dialectic of *Action* in the concrete in more spontaneously metaphysical terms, which we find in the final volume of the first Trilogy, shows not so much an evolution in Blondel's thinking as a revolution back to its origins in a philosophy of Thinking and of Being, brought on, not so much by an external critique from those who accused him of idealism, as by an internal critique of the philosopher himself, as he looked back on that first expression of his thought. His friend and philosophical soulmate, Victor Delbos, after the successful defense of his dissertation before a jury that remained largely hostile to its conclusions even though they recognized the critical value of its method, made him aware of the metaphysical dimension of his thought left unspoken in a method that purported to be purely phenomenological. After the defense, and in writing his discourse on method, the *Letter on Apologetics*, in which he was defending himself against those who showed no proper critical sense in their approach to the question of religious philosophy, he was becoming critical of the critical method itself, thus raising it to a higher level of systematic consideration, to include Thought and Being as explicit presuppositions in his consideration of Action, both in the concrete, and as it relates to Pure Acting in its transcendence.

Blondel worked on this systematic expansion of his perspective on and off throughout most of his teaching career, producing notes and papers that were eventually to be gathered up into more coherent wholes. This he did even while he was still preoccupied with the controversies over apologetics during the modernist crisis, but he did more of it once he was freed from that drag on his intellectual energy. He wrote more and more about Thought and Being and even taught some courses on these subjects, always in anticipation of volumes that were to follow and that had taken a definite shape in his mind at the time of his interviews with Frédéric Lefèvre in which he was laying out the future course of his *Itinerary*.

When disaster struck, however, in the form of blindness, all this planning went into a holding pattern, with all sorts of materials strewn about, so to speak, and no way of gathering them together on his own, as one usually does in coming to the final draft of a book. We have seen something of the first futile attempts to work with secretaries, who did not know enough about Blondel's thought and who did not stay long enough to find out more about it. We have also seen how another soulmate of Blondel, Abbé Wehrlé, tried to do with the copious notes on Thought what Blondel could not do by himself or with transient secretaries. All this highlights the handicap Blondel was under in composing these final volumes of a Trilogy he had been working up to, to the point that he probably gave up hope of ever publishing all this work he had so carefully planned over many years. It also highlights the importance of Mlle. Nathalie Panis and her collaboration in the actual production of these final works of Blondel. Having been a student of Blondel and knowing him and his work as she did, she not only was able to help him pick his way through piles of notes and manuscripts, but also was interested and devoted enough to stay with him for as long as the task would require.

The outcome of all this patient and persistent effort day after day, however, was not all that it could have been, had the author been able to review his own work with his own eyes. His original science of action as expounded in the dissertation of 1893 had gone through a sevenfold revision before it was submitted for review by the jury of examiners, in an effort to bring every part into a closely knit argument rigorous enough to convince the severest philosophical critics of the day. Looking back on it, Blondel thought of it as a well-constructed cathedral. His comment at the time of the publication of a loose collection of *Pages Religieuses,* taken mainly from *L'Action* (1893), selected and tied together by Yves de Montcheuil in 1942, as recalled by Mlle. Panis, was more an expression of disappointment than of satisfaction: "They have demolished my cathedral," he is reported to have said. Blondel was more concerned about the philosophical rigor of his work than about pious uses it could be made to serve, though such uses were not contrary to his intention. The metaphor of the cathedral would be even more apt for the Trilogy in the way Blondel conceived it, not as an appendage to his philosophy of action in the concrete, but rather as a broader, more systematic nave for the cathedral in support of rising higher aloft into the mystery of the divine. Blondel's problem was not in conceiving the broad lines of this more metaphysical and spiritual move of Thought, Being, and Action, but rather in laying it out in all its details in a way that would bring out how all of them hung together in no less rigorous fashion than his first Philosophy of Action.

The difference between the later and the early Blondel was not one of method or of system, but more one of emphasis and style. In his early work he had insisted on the critical and phenomenological aspect of this thought in confrontation with either a philosophy that was satisfied with dealing with ideas about action, instead of action itself, as it presents itself in human experience, or one that jumped too easily into metaphysical claims independently of action and its real content, when it came to transcendence. In his first work, he had appeared as anti-intellectual, when in fact he was trying to be more intellectual or thoughtful than those whose ideas he thought too short. He had also appeared anti-metaphysical when in fact he was trying to make more serious metaphysical claims in his approach to the transcendent, not apart from human action but in human action. These are impressions he wanted to correct even as he was adding the final chapter to his dissertation before publication after defending it. They were also impressions he sought to avoid by not allowing his early work to be re-edited as it had originally appeared without making all the adjustments that would recast it in its true light, once the fuller dimensions of Thinking and Being he was presupposing were better laid out.

The result of this recasting in the final volume of the Trilogy was a much more coherent book in its general outline, albeit one more difficult to read in the details, because of the patchwork effect in its composition. Many parts of the new version were simply lifted out of the first version of *L'Action,* sometimes *verbatim,* sometimes with systematic, minor adjustments in terminology, calling attention to *spontaneity* in action instead of *determinism,* for example. Other parts were written specifically for this new version to replace the more restrictive critical parts of the earlier version, in an effort to keep the new version more critically open to each new wave of deployment in action, as the deployment coursed from the spiritual interior of the subject through the body to others and to humanity as a whole toward a rendezvous with a transcendence that it cannot entirely encompass on its own. What gets confusing at times is, how these two layers of redaction, dating from two very different times with a forty-year interval between them, are meshed together in a new weave that is often poorly smoothed over. The new unity of spirit that runs through the book does not always permeate through to the parts taken from the earlier version. In fact, some of these parts, simply lifted from the earlier work, can be understood better if they are placed back in their earlier context, almost as if it were necessary to read both versions in comparison with one another to get Blondel's full intent in *Action,* the final version of his philosophy.

Another thing to be noted is that, whereas the first version of *L'Action* culminated in a briefly elaborated philosophy of the supernatural, the second version stops short of that. The first Trilogy in each one of its three parts brings us to the question of the supernatural, but does not at any point cross over into it. This is not because Blondel had lost interest in the question. On the contrary, his interest in the question had only grown and expanded after his first brief sortie into it in his early writings. Blondel was reserving a larger place for it in his conception of his philosophical task later in life. More than just a philosophical Trilogy on Thought, Being, and Action, Blondel had in mind a Tetralogy, an ensemble of four works where the new version of the philosophy of human action and the conditions for its fulfillment mediated or served as a transition for the passage from the natural domain of philosophy to the supernatural as necessary complement for a complete fulfillment of human spiritual aspirations.

The fourth component, to be titled *Philosophy and the Christian Spirit,* had yet to be written, but for it Blondel was projecting three volumes: one on how rational initiatives mesh with what we are told of the divine plan to elevate the whole of humanity to a higher calling and destiny, a second on the needs and the risks humanity must face in the pursuit of such a destiny even with the resources God puts at its disposition to sustain the faith and hope of a Christian life in pursuit of eternal life amid the trials of this world, and finally a third on the actual problems in making peace and creating justice in the world, through an exercise of divine charity, out of a tradition that has always to renew itself.

In a sense, then, the Trilogy on Thought, Being, and Action, solid as it was in its own right, was only a warm-up for the fourth part of this Tetralogy, a more amplified version of the supernatural brought up at the end of the dissertation as a necessary hypothesis for science to consider, with explicit reference to the Christian Mysteries. Instead of considering only "the phenomenology of action" and "the necessary being of action," in order to raise the question of the supernatural for the completion of action in a supernatural transcendence, the Trilogy on Thought, Being, and Action provided a more metaphysical and spiritual outlook, and one more rationally consistent and autonomous, in keeping not only with the modern conception of philosophy, but also with the necessary connection he still wanted to argue for in relation to the Christian Spirit, or to the supernatural, as understood in the light of the Christian Mysteries. As always, Blondel was concerned with articulating an autonomous philosophy that any rational inquirer could recognize as valid and logical, but one nevertheless that would also recognize the necessity of going into what presents itself as mysterious at the core of human action in the ultimate confrontation with the divine. Before actually launching into this final extension of philosophy into the Christian Spirit, however, he had to clarify one more time what he took the supernatural to be as a specification of what we take the transcendent to be in our own experience.

Incommensurability of the Supernatural in Transcendence

The publication of the first four volumes of the Trilogy between 1934 and 1936 brought Blondel back to the forefront of philosophic discourse, much as his original dissertation had done in the 1890s. The new, more "technical" elaboration of his philosophy, as he was calling it at the time, revived a certain interest among his peers in his approach to the transcendent, even though not all of them were willing to go along with him into what they thought was beyond the scope of philosophy. This is perhaps why, at the Ninth International Congress of Philosophy held in Paris, July 31–August 6, 1937, in honor of the third centenary of Descartes's *Discourse on Method*, the question of transcendence was included in the program, and why Blondel was invited to discuss it at a plenary session of the Congress. The expectation was that he would speak of the theme that was dearest to his heart.

Unable to read his communication himself, he chose Mlle. Panis to read it for him, because he thought she was most familiar with his thought, with good reason after the years of their working together on the Trilogy, and because he felt she would enunciate most clearly to an audience that would be all ears. The text of the communication would eventually find its way into the final volume of the Trilogy, *L'Action II*, as Excursus 35, near the end (1937b, 513-24). Starting from where he stood at the time in the elaboration of his thought, he chose to speak of both the transcendent and the supernatural, but in a way that would bring out the heterogeneity between the transcendent and the immanent, prior to going on to write of their necessary interconnection in the human experience of the two.

Blondel begins by warning against taking transcendence as only a relative term. Though its original and obvious sense is metaphysical and relative, its more radical and difficult sense to maintain is to signify something metaphysical and absolute, a sense that has to be justified rationally but that is also rich in its ramifications. The image we have of transcendence is of something higher, surpassing and rising as compared to immanence, which also has many senses, whether of something interior to a particular subject, as flowing from it, or as coming into it in its development. Immanence can also signify the "integral order of all that is the object of scientifically determinable and verifiable experience" (1937b, 514). There follows from this a subalternate use of the term *transcendent* as applicable to varying degrees of relative essence and existence in the universe going from lower to ever-higher forms. But the sense Blondel wants to propose is the more rational sense of an other order above and beyond the region "where experience, science, and action are deployed, [one] that is commonly represented as higher than anything over which we have any positive control" (1937b, 514).

Such an order is not to be conceived as superimposed or as juxtaposed to the immanent order, which would be to reduce it to a spatial image or a verbal entity of formal logic. For Blondel "there is a transcendent presence and action within man, or in the world we call immanent" (1937b, 515) that does not come as if from another external world. This presence is rather an internal stimulus and a call from on high that entails no local collision, no conflict, and no confusion. It is something that takes us beyond all anthropological categories as insufficient in their very sufficiency. "Transcendence and immanence, considered not as materializing images or abstract concepts, but as concrete truths, do not exclude one another. They are metaphysically conceivable in a real cohabitation" (1937b, 515).

The problem for Blondel is to find in immanence itself, and in the consciousness we have of it, the certitude of a transcendent presence and action. It seems at first that our action and our consciousness deploy themselves in a field of determinism and immanence that extends indefinitely before it, without reference to any other principle than that of a generalized relativity. As we try to discern the phenomena of experience and sort out the laws that govern it, however, we find ourselves referring to a new light, "a higher term of reference absolutely necessary for whatever particular choice of a unity made [or taken for granted], [a term of reference] without which no consciousness, no science could distinctly arise" (1937b, 516). These notions of immanence, relativity, and standards make no sense except by referring, at least implicitly, to a transcendent — a transcendent, it should be carefully noted, that is not in the series and is not relative to the relative. "It is the relative that is intelligible and real only by adverting to this necessary and incommensurable affirmation of the absolute" (1937b, 516).

Transcendence, then, is a necessary, constant, and universal affirmation implied in the thoughtful exercise of any knowledge. Blondel thinks of this transcendence as infused, though inaccessible, not only in our sciences of the relatively immanent, but also in the most primitive forms of the moral and religious sense. The highest task of philosophy, then, must be to purify this sense of transcendence in human action and science, and to react against the adulterations and the diversely opposed abuses it is subjected to. Philosophy must also labor methodically to free this sense of an absolute transcendence from all dialectical illusions or sentimental deviations, in order to assure its precise truth against all tendencies to immanentize the Transcendent, using all concrete data and all the resources of reason, to distinguish "the transcendent within us from the Transcendent in itself, to determine how from immanence itself a necessary affirmation emerges of the absolute, to which we are relative but which remains incommensurable with us" (1937b, 519).

The affirmation of transcendence thus rests on the entire order of the immanent, even as it surpasses it and gives it its initial and its final consistency. But to understand better how the transcendent is posited in itself or in its absolute independence, which, for us and in the name we give it, is still caught up in the relation that ties us to it, a stronger term is needed, one more paradoxical than just transcendent. In fact, such a term is necessary to designate what exceeds all the natural powers of the physical, animal, and human world in order to bring "this paradox of a really concrete truth that remains incommensurable to all that is relative to us and accessible to our grasp" (1937b, 520). That, of course, is the term *supernatural*, which philosophical and religious speculation has made its own in a technical and rational sense, in trying to specify the reality that remains higher than any of our human modes of thinking, being, and acting, but in a way that takes nothing away from the autonomy of philosophy as an enterprise of reason. The thought of the supernatural represents a second step in the consideration of the transcendent, one that might be aided by some positive revelation from on high or from the divine transcendence itself, but it is a step that can be taken by reason itself. "Just as we do not have the idea of immanence without positing the affirmation of transcendence, so also we do not safeguard our pure idea of a veritable transcendence without affirming in it a supernatural essentially inaccessible to the grasp of our thought and the conquering of our action" (1937b, 520). Blondel has every intention of holding on to this technical sense of the supernatural as incommensurable to anything in human thought, even in the exploration of the religious phenomenon taken as a hypothesis, in which the relations between our contingent being and the Sovereign Perfection itself might be taken to new heights inconceivable by reason alone, though not in opposition to its most profound aspirations. For him, the paradoxical hypothesis of a supernatural confirms our affirmation of an absolute transcendence by marking even more strongly the incommensurability that nothing can take away from it.

To be sure, philosophy is not in any position to determine any positive content for a hypothetical supernature, conceivable as gratuitous gift from divine charity itself. It is not even in a position to pronounce itself on the fact or on the modalities such a gift might take in us. Yet, even with these reservations, there remains, for philosophy, a twofold principle of order, one natural and one supernatural, in an open pursuit of growth and development, in what we need most to assure freedom and cooperation, or the security of peace along with a generous service of equity toward all, as we progress toward a common goal. The idea of the supernatural as absolutely transcendent does not weigh on nature as a yoke; it does not limit human endeavor; it does not oppress thought or will. "On the contrary, it keeps open immense perspectives; it excludes both fixism, which sclerotizes, and mobilism, which upsets and destroys; it elicits initiatives and emulation by condemning the abuses of authoritarianism against spiritual values; it is incompatible with the reign of force, the enslavement of peoples and the violation of consciences" (1937b, 522).

Blondel has the whole range of philosophical values in mind when he speaks of the idea of an absolutely transcendent supernatural enhancing our natural aspirations, rather than suppressing them. He does not accept any conception of religion that would cut any of these values short. Religions that do usually turn out to be only "immanent transcendences, incomplete ideologies that bring about wars over idols, with violences, incomprehensions, hatreds born of falsely religious struggles" (1937b, 522). That is why, in speaking to philosophers about the transcendence they may have been willing to admit, "in order to protect the integrity and the efficacity of a real transcendence," he urged adding to the idea "the less equivocal, more exacting, more concrete conception of the *supernatural,* so that by insisting on the exact rational bearing of this idea and of the sense that it evokes, philosophy might work for order and peace, for cooperation and progress, and for the good of humanity" (1937b, 524), as he was planning to show in the final volume of his work. This at least is what he was hoping to do with his projected philosophical inquiries on the Christian Spirit.

The Interweaving of Philosophical Enigma and Christian Mystery

This affirmation of something distinctly supernatural about transcendence had important methodological implications for the explicit philosophy of Christian religion Blondel was about to embark on. What he wanted to do was bring Christian teaching about spiritual life in the world into the pale of philosophical and systematic consideration, somewhat as Hegel had done in his *Phenomenology of Spirit,* but without reducing it to a purely immanent shape of consciousness. The idea of something distinctly supernatural affirmed by reason itself concerning divine transcendence precluded the possibility of absorbing God or the divine Transcendence into any circle human reason could encompass, whether in logic, nature, or spirit. All such rational circularity pertains to what Blondel generally calls the natural order accessible to philosophical reason, including the affirmation, not only of transcendence, but of something supernatural about that transcendence to which reason has no access, such as that which it has with regard to anything in the immanent order of nature and spirit. To say, then, that the Christian spirit has something supernatural about it is to say that it exceeds all capacity of philosophical reason to comprehend, so that, if philosophy is to take this spirit into consideration, it will require a distinct method from the more natural method required in the rest of philosophy, one that will respect the mysterious or the supernatural aspect of its specific subject while probing into this mystery as far as it can.

However, what will distinguish this inquiry from a theology elaborating on articles of faith in an explicitly religious context, is that it will follow a strictly rational process in line with the philosophy of action that has preceded it. What this philosophy has shown, in the search for clarification concerning the human being's ultimate destiny, is that we remain in an enigma about how that destiny is to be fulfilled. The same kind of enigma has been shown to exist at the end of the philosophy of thought and the philosophy of being. In the face of this enigma, as in any other enigma, it is the role of philosophy to seek further for solutions to the questions it raises about our final destiny. Recognizing its insufficiency, even at the summit of its achievement, its dependence, even at the height of its freedom, it should be willing to inquire further into what could be answers to questions it cannot answer by itself, but that religion and its mysteries might have to offer, especially when there still remains a choice to be made on how we are to relate to a final end we perceive as transcendent. That is how the question of a supernatural religion occurs at the end of philosophy. That is also how it occurs as a question that must be dealt with in philosophy, for the integrity of philosophy is at stake in this ulterior question into something that exceeds reason's capacity to comprehend. In his title for this last part of his philosophy, Blondel chose to speak of philosophy as a whole, *la philosophie,* to emphasize this integrity of a philosophy that recognizes its insufficiency, only to pursue its inquiry further into the Christian Spirit, which has an integrity of its own, to which that of philosophy cannot be left unrelated.

The outcome of the philosophical Trilogy has been to show that philosophy cannot and should not close in on itself, that it remains ever-more perfectible in its own line of endeavor, even if it is by something that surpasses its own capacity to investigate, something truly mysterious. As such, it "legitimately and necessarily raises questions about the meaning of life and the highest end of our destiny, for which it sets parameters, even though it remains ever incapable of answering them fully by itself" (1944, 214). In this sense, philosophy remains insufficient to answer its own questions. Yet, this sense of its own insufficiency, "while proving the force of the human élan, born for the infinite, opens it naturally to a desire, an expectation, an activity of a religious character that will never allow it to legitimately close itself up either in an exclusive sufficiency or in a skeptical immanence" (1944, 214). The human spirit cannot be indifferent toward the transcendent or the divine of which it is conscious at bottom, in the very exercise of its self-consciousness. There are two voices it has to listen to in its Christian historical context, that of its own aspirations and insufficiencies and that of more satisfying offers and promises from on high that are neither opposed to our human aspirations, nor superimposed on them, but rather are complementary to them. Philosophy has to probe further than itself into the meaning of what has to remain for it unfathomable mysteries.

To distinguish a strictly supernatural sphere of expansion for the transcendent in human action, as Blondel does, is not to separate it from the rest of the spheres deemed natural or immanent for the human spirit in the world. On the contrary, we have seen how Blondel always rejected such a view of separation or even of juxtaposition for the supernatural, let alone a superimposition on an order already thought to be complete or closed in upon itself. In the debate about a properly Catholic philosophy, we saw how he objected even to the idea of "Christian philosophy," as too hybrid and confused about how philosophy and Christianity have to relate to one another as natural to supernatural, *not* to locate the supernatural or the Catholic religion as it presents itself in experience *beyond* the pale, but rather to show how it can shed some light from within a philosophical reflection on the human spirit. This had been his purpose from the beginning in undertaking a philosophy of action in the concrete, for that is where, as a religious philosopher, he saw the light shining in a religious practice that was authentically divine, transcendent, and supernatural as well as human, natural, and historical. In the dissertation of 1893, and in the discourse on method of 1896, he had barely sketched his philosophy of the supernatural, arguing anonymously, that is, without naming Christ in any way, for the necessity of a revelation, the necessity of a mediator, and the necessity of a religious practice, under the necessary hypothesis of a supernatural gift that would fulfill the human spirit in a way that the rational will could not manage by itself. Here in this final systematic work of his he was prepared to go in much greater detail into the Christian mysteries according to what he knew of them and according to how they relate to the enigmas about human life in the universe that remain at the end of a philosophy that has run its course to the limits of its capacity and has recognized its insufficiency in relation to the transcendence it has to affirm as necessary.

Blondel's idea of the true infinite was not one reducible to a dialectic of opposition between two finites. It implied a total transcendence of the divine, even as it is affirmed immanently by reason, so that while there is a necessary relation of reason and of immanence to the Transcendent, there is no such necessary relation that reason can affirm from the Transcendent or the Infinite to the immanent or to anything finite. The idea did imply, however, a way of conceiving how the infinite could be found in the finite both at the origin and at the end of its spiritual élan, and in the intervening spheres of its expansion from that of the singular self to ever-more universal spheres, such as the interpersonal, the social, the familial as well as the political, all the way to a moral sphere that includes humanity as a whole. The method used for the systematic elaboration of these spheres was anything but circular or cyclical, but more one characterized by Blondel as *cycloidal*, where reason advances by considering a higher viewpoint, which it then takes to be necessary for its own integrity.

This is a method we have previously encountered in Blondel's way of philosophizing. It will now mark this final venture into the infinite and the transcendent as it has been mapped out in the mystery, or the mysteries, of the Christian Spirit. At each point in the investigation the mystery will be related to an enigma that remains for philosophy at the end of its course through the immanent order of nature and history. We have seen how, already in the Trilogy, Blondel touches on the central Christian mystery of the Trinitarian Life in connection with pure Thinking, with Being in and through itself, and with pure Acting. But that was proceeding only from the bottom up, from what we can say rationally about the Creator from the standpoint of the creature who thinks, is, and acts. Here in the final work of the Tetralogy he will proceed more from the top down, that is, from what we are told about the mystery to how it resonates with the experience of the rational being concerned about its own destiny. This time, in the cycloidal method, the mystery as contained in the Christian Spirit will take precedence in shedding light for the enigma that remains in the philosophical spirit as it relates to the divine.

What Blondel was working toward, then, was a truly rational symbiosis between an autonomous philosophy willing to go as far as it can in the exploration of questions that arise for it in the realm of transcendence, now taken in its incommensurate sense, and a religion whose mysteries are "authentically irreducible to the conquests of reason while being rationally admissible and inviscerated into the destiny of humanity, as it is concretely according to the order of history and divine providence" (1944, 5). This meant going beyond any Enlightenment idea of philosophy as separate from religion, whether as abstract deism or as rational agnosticism, professing ignorance concerning the religious or the Christian idea of God. For Blondel, deism and agnosticism were only opposite views of one another within one and the same idea of philosophy as "either establishing a self-enclosed, separate philosophy, or excluding the religious idea of God from philosophical and social teaching, or using Christianity [only] as a spiritual reservoir to be drained progressively" (1944, 5), in the progress of a civilization enlightened only about itself.

He had long argued against any such idea of an intrinsically self-sufficient philosophy, even in its autonomy, and against any attempt to use Christianity as a prop for advancing any worldly cause, as Charles Maurras, an avowed atheist, had done in the movement of *Action Française,* or perhaps even as Hegel had done to give his philosophy a better boost toward absolute knowing. Blondel was steadfast in his affirmation of the supernatural dimension of the Christian religion and of its irreducibility to anything purely rational or logical such as the Idea. Mystery remained for him an essential feature of anything affirmed in the Christian religion, and this was precisely what philosophy had to engage with, as it came to the realization of its own insufficiency and its own enigmatic character in relation to everything having to do with transcendence. Supernatural transcendence is what made symbiosis with the Christian mysteries possible and necessary for philosophy in the end, presupposing that these mysteries could lend themselves to some understanding as they were realized in human history and experience, even though they remained ultimately beyond the grasp of reason itself. Such understanding of the Christian mysteries, especially as they relate to man's desire for perfection in his action, was not excluded by anything in the Christian teaching, which was in a sense begging for understanding as a calling for man toward a higher destiny.

What would come of this symbiosis would not be a "Christian philosophy," for that would connote hybridization and confusion of radically distinct and heterogeneous disciplines, something that would offend against the very idea of the supernatural in the Christian teaching, and against a properly Christian theology as distinct from any philosophical theology. Nor would it be a "philosophical Christianity," for that would offend against the idea of an autonomous philosophy and dilute it into a mere instrument for a theology that cannot be fully understood. The two ideas of philosophical enigma and of Christian mystery have to remain distinct at all times in the symbiosis, so that bringing them together will enhance the rational connection between the two as well as enrich each side in its own integrality. From the autonomy of philosophy Blondel had come to the necessity of exploring the Christian mysteries as they relate to man's free choice with regard to his destiny, not in opposition to religious authority, but in symbiosis with it, for the functioning of that authority in religion was itself part of the mystery, just as the functioning of reason is part of philosophy itself.

Blondel projected three stages for this philosophical exploration into the mysteries of Christianity as they relate historically to the human endeavor. In a first volume he would bring to the fore an alternation between the rational initiatives of human beings and certain contributions from the divine plan for one and the same human being, in order to show the higher kind of destiny to which humanity is called obligatorily. This would be to show the ever-increasing generosity, suppleness, and richness of the divine plan not only for human beings, but also for creation as a whole.

In a second volume, he would show the risks for humanity as it enters historically into such a plan, the needs it will require and the resources God places at humanity's disposal to meet these needs, to sustain the faith and permanent vitality of Christianity as it struggles to sustain itself until the end of time. In this he would deal with the more pragmatic stuff of leading a Christian life in this world under the guidance of the Holy Spirit, in the Church and its mystery, through the sacraments and everything that promotes the Christian symbiosis uniting transcendence and immanence on earth.

In a third volume, he would come back to what he calls "our present perspectives" (1944, xv), the kinds of problems Christians have to face in their own time, as every generation does in the long religious tradition, in order always to bring out something new from what has been handed down, solutions that will renew the face of the earth. Blondel died before he could actually write this third volume, but notes he had prepared for it show that he would have written mainly of the social constitution of human beings in civilization, beginning with the man-woman relationship and going on with marriage and the family, then to the broader moral and political life, and ending with universal humanitarianism as part of the Christian way of relating to God, an integral philosophy shaped by a total Christianity, a truly Catholic philosophy.

Triune Life as Inscrutable Essence of the One, True God

In volume one of *Philosophie et Esprit Chrétien*, Blondel begins his philosophic engagement with the Christian Spirit as articulated in the mysteries of the Catholic religion at the highest point in what reason has to say about the divine and with what has been termed the mystery of mysteries in the Christian religion, that of the Trinity in Godhead itself. This is the mystery in which, Blondel notes, William James found no pragmatic significance for philosophy, and which idealism tried to water down, if not simply set aside, in its endeavor to fit the divine into the immanent historical order of spirit, as Hegel attempts to do, for example, using the idea of the Trinity only to distinguish different moments in the self-actualization of absolute spirit in the world. Blondel thinks of these two ways of thinking about the mystery of the Trinity as either trivializing, in the case of pragmatism, or ignoring, in the case of idealism, this mystery in Godhead itself, or as excluding from philosophy "the swelling spring of all fertile truth and of all progress in the spiritual order, the order that proceeds entirely from this illuminative mystery" (1944, 28). The mystery that most people are inclined to bypass or to prescind from in modern philosophy, not to mention what was called natural theology, is the one Blondel wants to start from for shedding light on how the Spirit really comes alive in the world, not just as philosophy in the abstract, but also as religion in the concrete. Bringing such an impenetrable mystery before human reason in a light that can take the human spirit beyond what it can achieve by its own power of investigation is for him the justification for contemplating this Mystery we know of only by Revelation.

He begins with what he has maintained from the beginning about the human spirit and its spiritual élan as oriented to a supreme end, "to which all intelligence and all appreciation of values are referred, as to an absolute standard, a sovereign God — without which nothing would be conceivable, nothing would be thought and nothing would take hold in our consciousness" (1944, 1). Without such a term of reference for human intelligence, there would be no science, no moral life, no metaphysical speculation. All spiritual activity we take to be fully human presupposes "the higher idea of a relation to what serves to measure all things and to bring all things to a universal mediator, whether it be the Unity of the whole or absolute Perfection" (1944, 2). Associated with this notion of an absolute, transcendent and divine, as it were inviscerated in every form of philosophizing and of spiritual life, is also the even more positive notion of an infinite found in the principle of all science, especially that of a self-conscious subjectivity, such as the principle he had elaborated in his original science of human action. The principal problem for philosophy, concerning the Infinite recognized concretely in human action, according to Blondel, has always been to determine the various aspects of this implicit idea of the divine that make it conceivable and affirmable, but that have given rise to various contents in different philosophies, each of which was bound to be deficient and inadequate with respect to the idea or the reality being referred to.

This did not mean that reason cannot demonstrate that God *is*, in the fullest sense of the term, or that God is certain and "concretely real" (1944, 4). Blondel recognizes at this point in his philosophy a better capacity for a rational metaphysics to prove the existence of God than he had earlier on, but he still affirms the other side of this certitude about God, which is to say that he remains beyond our grasp "in the secret that cannot be violated by any finite intelligence" (1944, 4). The truth about God is not only that he is, but also, and at one and the same time, that what he is in his essence or existence escapes us as something totally incommensurable to anything in our experience or in our discursive ways of knowing. Any conception of God we might have is bound to be anthropomorphic. Such a conception would not only denature and compromise the idea or the concrete reality we are referring to. It would also belittle the spontaneous faith of humanity in a truly transcendent Being.

From the standpoint of reason, according to Blondel, there are no atheists or people who do not somehow aspire to be God. There is always reason enough to foster all sorts of idolatry, including what he calls modern autolatry. But the common claims of our basic human consciousness and the exigencies of reason have a way of going against one another, "as if metaphysics were killing the 'God of good folks' and as if the soul of people remained rightly hostile and closed to the ontological abstractions and the frigid ideal of deism" (1944, 6). The conflict is not as simple as one might think. With the rise of reason and its exigencies, at times critical and at times also constructive and generous, the intestinal conflict within our human ideal can become quite complicated and, in the process, generate problems of its own that were not in evidence when reason was only denouncing superstition among the less critical. The current crisis concerning the problem of God, as Blondel saw it in modern philosophy, had come to the point where the God to which rationalism or idealism was trying to convert us was opposed "to the God of tradition and was declared to be the one that is not as the God of philosophers" (1944, 6). But Blondel was not prepared to admit any such separation in our idea of God as it presents itself in the concrete of human action.

Blondel refers to Leibniz's attempts to prove the existence of God from the possibility of God, relying still on some necessary connection between the ideas of perfection and of existence, as in ontological proofs. But the solution he finds in this *Theodicy* is still only anthropomorphic at best. It has nothing to do with the concrete reality of God unifying absolutely, in his simplicity, all the attributes that rational discourse is led inevitably to recognize in him. Blondel alludes also to other rational attempts to "realize" our idea of God as substance in its own infinite perfection, as in Spinozism or Hegelianism, but he finds in all of them a failure to speak adequately of the God who is affirmed in his own transcendence by both reason and religion. All of these endeavors end up in some form of immanentism, activism, or actualism that brings everything back to little more than our own conscious experience of spirit in the world. If reason must affirm a supernaturally transcendent being, as it must necessarily at the end of its course through the world of experience, it must also recognize that it finds itself before an enigma, both within itself and without. This is an exigency of reason that is not only legitimate but also salutary for its own sake. It is a duty for it to recognize its own embarrassment before a perfection in being it cannot fathom.

Blondel thus rises to a consideration of the central mystery of Christianity through a metaphysics of what he calls deism in general, but he does not stop at the abstract results about the divine essence, which such a metaphysics can yield. He recognizes that the God of critical philosophy represents a certain purification of grosser beliefs found in certain forms of religious consciousness, but he questions whether the critical representation of God is itself adequate to the object of its affirmation. Surely, it does not equal the living God of Christianity who reveals himself in history. Nor does it equal the God who is real and totally transcendent, incommensurable with anything in our experience, including the whole of experience itself. It is rather a God reduced to "a category of the ideal, pure becoming, a god that makes itself little by little in history through something like a superhumanity ever in perpetual evolution ... a god that is not, one where the highest philosophic conversion comes down to a cult of progress in scientific relativism, a stranger to anything that is not continuous invention in technical methods and discoveries, an anomy exclusive of any fixed law in whatever order there is" (1944, 8-9). This was hardly purification and sublimation enough for the more profound religious consciousness Blondel had in mind. In fact, he had argued, it still amounted to no more than a kind of superstition that reason itself could not sanction. Even if reason has no way of speaking consistently of this Being, who surpasses any idea we can have of him, it still has open before it more positive ways of speaking of this reality, ways that reason can accept as coming from the living God himself through Revelation.

Blondel finds difficulty even with conceiving God in a dry monotheistic fashion, as if God were solitary and walled up within himself. Such a God could not be thought of as wise and just, or as infinitely lovable and good, especially if we think of him as a consciousness absorbed only in an immutable contemplation of himself, a mere *nous noēseōs*. If we wish to think of him as lovable and good, we have to think of him as relating to others, as we do for ourselves in our own personal consciousness. In Leibniz, the solution to this rational impasse of a solitary God is to admit that God has to shape a world for himself, in order to become conscious of himself and to have other beings to love. From this follows the well-known idea of God having to create only "the best possible world." But such a resolution of the impasse, according to Blondel, is not only contrary to reason as it contemplates God, who is absolute Perfection in himself; it is also an evasion of the real problem of God, who still has to be thought of as personal, wise, just, and infinitely lovable *in himself.* This is the inescapable enigma before which reason finds itself in affirming an Existence whose Essence remains incommensurably beyond reason's grasp.

Blondel uses the term *enigma* here to make a special point about how reason has to relate to religious mystery. He takes the cue from St. Paul, who warns us that in this world we do not see fundamental realities face to face, but, for lack of intuition, they appear to us *tanquam in speculo et aenigmate* — as if in a reflection and in a perplexity. Blondel will use the term *enigmatic* for many other realities in the Christian dispensation, but here it is used for the way we come at the reality of God rationally and in the concrete. That reality, even as rationally affirmed, has to remain enigmatic and perplexing to us, given the way we arrive at it discursively, but not as putting a full stop to discourse. It is rather an invitation to seek further for a resolution of the perplexity. The mystery, on the other hand, will be seen as bringing a resolution to the perplexity, what Blondel refers to as the *word* of the enigma, even though it is a word that reason alone cannot fully encompass.

The term *enigma* is less technical than the other term, *aporia*, which he had used more freely and abundantly in the Trilogy on Thought, Being, and Action, with reference to the Transcendent, and how we and the world relate to it. *Aporia* is suggestive of many risks we must run, many obstacles we must overcome, much human stumbling and much providential rectification in the course of our human journey toward our destiny. Blondel does not want to use it here in the relation of reason to mystery because the term also suggests something of an impasse, at which we cannot stop and from which we must find a way out. It may be apt for speaking of a philosophical itinerary, where difficulties occur and recur dialectically from one another, opening new ways of penetrating more deeply into the truth and into salutary outcomes for the life of spirit. But when it comes to opening the way into the mysteries that surround the Transcendent, both in itself and in its supernatural immanence in history as a whole, Blondel prefers to stay with a less technical term, one less loaded with philosophical pretensions of encompassing all that there is in concrete reality. The enigma Blondel has in mind is not just a particular riddle for which there is a one-word answer. It is a whole series of interconnected enigmas that open up into a new unexplored territory in the life of the spirit as it ascends toward the Transcendent.

The method here could still be characterized as phenomenological, as it was in the original philosophy of the supernatural of 1893, prior to the explication of its metaphysical presuppositions in the Trilogy on Thought, Being, and Action, but not as one that leaves us in the immanent, where the enigma appears. With the metaphysics now brought explicitly to the fore, so that the enigma appears at the highest level of rational discourse relating to a Transcendent affirmed as incommensurable to anything reason can encompass, Blondel thinks of his method more as *cycloidal*, rather than as phenomenological or as circular in the way Hegel comes to see his philosophy at the end of his *Encyclopedia*. This is due to Blondel's affirmation of the divine as totally Transcendent and incommensurable to anything that can be brought into a dialectical unity of opposites, even if it be thought of as infinite. The affirmation of a totally transcendent incommensurate Being, however, does not preclude any further exploration into a mystery that might bring some relief to reason's perplexity over the unresolved enigma. In fact, if anything should present itself that could bring some resolution to the enigma, even if reason cannot entirely encompass it, then it becomes incumbent upon reason to look into it. Hence the cycloidal aspect of the method.

One has to have advanced a certain distance in the life of the rational spirit in order to come to any true enigma concerning the Transcendent. But one also has to understand that the enigma, for which reason has no adequate answer, does not necessarily mark the end of the line for reason. For Blondel the Christian mysteries, precisely as mysteries, offer new light in the obscurity of the enigmas that reason is left with at the summit of its ascent, so that reason can roll on further, so to speak, in keeping with the figure of the cycloid, seeking further satisfaction for aspirations that remain unsatisfied from the standpoint of reason alone. Rational reflection on the mystery will not do away with the enigma, once again precisely because the appropriate mystery for each enigma remains a mystery for human reason, something it cannot properly demonstrate, as it can demonstrate that there is a God with certain attributes who is ever-radically enigmatic for reason — indeed, a God who is bound to remain mysterious in all that he is essentially and in all that he does supernaturally. Such reflection, however, precisely as it relates to rational enigmas, can lead philosophy ever deeper into the truth and the Being it is trying to equal. Reflection on the enigma opens the way to the relevance of a Christian mystery that brings a better appreciation of the importance of the enigma for advancement in a properly spiritual life, which in turn leads to a new point of reflection on the Christian mystery itself. In the reflection on the philosophical enigma of God, and on the mystery of the Trinity, we have the highest kind of example possible for the use of this cycloidal method.

The enigma we are left with in philosophy concerning the God affirmed in religious consciousness has to be made clear. How can we think of God as solitary in his total transcendence and yet as perfectly Good in himself, loving and lovable, in a monotheistic isolation? When reason attempts to reintegrate the infinite into the finite, by denying it as a concrete reality apart from all finite opposition, or as a subsistence in itself, or as "a perfection absolutely realized in a somber and isolated transcendence" (1944, 16), it is running contrary to its most fundamental affirmations as reason, which include that God remains unknown even as we affirm that he is. There is no reciprocal analogy between the absolute and the relative. No dialectical interplay between finite and infinite can bridge the gap between a totally transcendent Being we affirm as concretely real and what we know of ourselves and of the world. The fundamental affirmation of God in his Infinitude and the systematic but futile attempts to deny this total transcendence, or to reduce it to something immanent, display a sense of mystery and a religious attitude that, in one form or another, Blondel reiterates, oscillates between a reverential cult and an idolatrous superstition. Reason cannot rest in such oscillation.

The oscillation can also be found between rational assertions and Christian teaching, where one-sided or verbal rapprochements between the two also prove deceiving, for both philosophy and the Christian sense of mystery. Blondel goes to some length to show that philosophy should suffer some embarrassment in speaking about a God who is pure spirit and perfect unity, for whom there is no analogy even in our own spiritual experience, let alone in the lesser beings we know of in the world. After all the classical proofs for God, we are bound to find some incoherence in the concept of a perfection that combines *omnipotence, wisdom, and infinite love all in one*. Blondel sees in this *aporia* a kind of oscillation in rational monotheism itself between agnosticism and pantheism. Echoing Leibniz, he asks, "How can personality and goodness be found in a complete solitude and a total egotism without there being consciousness of the impersonal or without there being a necessity to produce other beings than Being itself so that the transcendent God would be subject to an imperfection and to a going out from itself?" (1944, 19). How many forms of theologizing in modern philosophy and theosophy do we not see coming from this oscillation within the enigma of a God who is known to exist but whose essence remains unknown to us, and unknowable, according to our natural, God-given rational power to investigate?

Blondel, however, does not stop at the statement of the enigma in the religious context in which he finds himself. Besides showing how irrational it is to try to bring God down to the dimensions of anything in the universe in idolatrous fashion, even if it be an actualization in process of perfecting itself or a spirit realizing itself in history, he also tries to show how in the mystery of the Trinity as spoken of in the Christian religion we have a better way of satisfying the exigencies of reason within the philosophical enigma of God. This is not to say that he tries to reduce the mystery to the enigma, for this too would be to sell the mystery short, another kind of superstition. Blondel continues to insist on a complete incommensurability or heterogeneity between what is affirmed about God in the Christian teaching, or in the mystery of the Trinity, and what is affirmed about God in a properly understood philosophy, or in the enigma of God. Indeed, he argues that it is unthinkable for us even to demonstrate the Trinity, let alone explain adequately its inner workings. It is very much a mystery for us, the mystery of mysteries, and it remains ever such for any finite spirit, even one with theological or supernatural faith. Yet, revelation of this Mystery brings new light into the rational enigma, from which reason can profit in its affirmation of God and in its appreciation for what God is in his inscrutable essence. This is what Blondel endeavors to show positively for a reason that is still in search of a Truth it can never fully equal or encompass.

There is something supernatural about that Truth and about the way we aspire to it. Blondel warns his reader: "God's providential plan [for humanity] is founded on the model and at the instigation of the Trinitarian life itself" (1944, 21). This is where Blondel thinks William James falls short in his failure to appreciate the pragmatic significance of the mystery of the Trinity. Understanding our supernatural vocation in history is not independent of our knowledge of the Trinity. Blondel speaks of a precaution we must take even in assessing what we can know and prove of God rationally, as if it were without some concurrence or what he calls an "afferent help" from God. That would be an error or a fault, "as if we could attain, by our own efforts alone, an exact notion or possession of the Being whose transcendence we must admit" (1944, 23). Strictly speaking, though the expression is justified by our need for analogy in speaking about God, we have no knowledge of a divine nature. God is not known as one born *(natum)* or as undergoing a nature, as if by some fate. With the idea of the divine transcendence clearly in mind, Blondel refers to the theme that had surprised everyone at the end of the dissertation of 1893. "From the standpoint of reason, so-called *natural* religion is irrational and thereby artificial: if God is, he is supernature and without common measure with what is born" (1944, 23).

Whatever we can say rationally about God will always be partially anthropomorphic and, by reason of its abstract character, it will never equal the concrete plentitude of this Being in itself. It is this insufficiency of reason, known by reason itself, that keeps reason open to other assertions about God that are heterogeneous to those reason can make, coming from a further revelation from God, or from religious experience, but assertions that can be seen as complementary to those of reason, albeit without any apodictic connection between them. Reason has no way of rising to such assertions on its own, but it has an interest in following up on such assertions because it recognizes the inadequacies of its own assertions. This is how Blondel sees the realm of mystery entering into the realm of philosophical enigma. And this is how he brings consideration of the Trinity in God into the philosophical consideration of the one, true God.

This is not just a question for him of remedying what appears unintelligible and even absurd to human thought in the affirmation of a God who is at once triune and one. It is as much a meditation on the mystery itself, in order to enter into a sphere that is still luminous for us, but wherein a divine irradiation is now diffused, so that our discursive mode of thinking can catch a glimpse of the intimate life of the Divinity itself as a spiritual union of three Persons, a life we are ultimately called to enter into. In the Trilogy on *Thought, Being,* and *Action,* Blondel had already speculated on this triune life in connection with *Pure Thinking*, with *Being In and For Itself,* and with *Pure Acting,* not without the recognition of some influence from the Christian teaching concerning the divine mystery. Now, in weaving the mystery into the enigma, he wants to suggest something more concrete, in more religious terms, on how the Father and the Son *are substantially* in their own light in an identity that does not preclude reciprocity "by reason of the double love that is itself so personal and so unifying that the distinction of Persons is supreme condition for this interior richness, ever infinitely active and fruitful" (1944, 25).

It is not as if the Father existed first in some sort of substantial autocracy. The Son would not be the Word and the adequate knowledge of the principle of Pure Acting if he were not himself Principle and Acting. And the personal distinction between the two, the Father and the Son, would remain unintelligible and unreal if each did not give itself back entirely to the other through a Love that unites them, thereby personalizing them in a triple way within a unity of substance. All of this, Blondel adds, is without opposition of the sort we find in human language between principle, means, and end, or between efficient causality and finality. Christian theology has developed a language of relation and procession to express how the Son comes from the Father eternally and how the

Spirit comes from both — *ab utroque.* But Blondel prefers the language of *circumincession,* to suggest how the Word expresses the Father completely, and how, in giving himself back to the Father, he gives the Father back to himself in a Love that is adequate to both Father and Word, and that has nothing egotistical about it, because it is made up of an integral double donation. The Love, which is also personal and substantial, perfects and accomplishes "Being in Itself" in its infinite fecundity and in its absolute plenitude. None of this implies a mere circularity or a mere emanation in the neo-Platonic sense, but rather a *circumincession,* which Blondel takes to be proper and reserved to the Christian mystery of Trinity. That is why we have from St. John a definition of God that is realist, simplified, and exhaustive, "the only one that is not deficient: *Deus caritas est*" (1944, 26).

Blondel sees in this and in the triune God "the only and the absolute response that relieves, vivifies and exalts religious anguish onto a contemplation and a generosity as nourishing to an intelligence avid for clarity as it is to a spiritual as well as a mystical aspiration" (1944, 27). For him, the mystery of the Trinity, by reason of what the Trinity is in itself, represents the nourishment, the exemplar, and the highest goal of what has been his concern from the beginning, our destiny as it must be worked out amid the obstacles of history. In it is found the only true spiritual climate, what Hegel would call the element, for the parturition of a properly eternal life in human beings stemming from that of the triune God himself. William James could not have been further from the truth when he said that the Trinity was of no pragmatic value for religious life and of no speculative value for philosophy.

The Mystery of a Supernatural End for the Created Spirit

Blondel's interweaving of Christian mystery and philosophic enigma does not end with a better, more lucid appreciation of the incommensurable Trinitarian life. It only begins there. It goes from there to what we know about God as Creator and the mystery of his purpose in creating a universe of finite beings destined to return to himself and to partake of his divine circumincession. Blondel's cycloidal method is designed to follow this mysterious purpose in what has been called the divine economy in the world and in what Blondel thinks of as the "substantial truths, ontological data, ideal and effectively subsistent realities, all generative of spiritual life" (1944, 13). These too are matters for philosophy to be interested in, given its own orientation toward what remains hidden in Being and in beings that concerns our destiny and that of the world. History, for Blondel, is "always simultaneously metaphysical and religious, where mysteries bring to rationally raised enigmas, [new] obligations, solutions and resources leading man to his [divine] end" (1944, 31). There is a logic or a necessity implied in this relation of historical enigma to God's mysterious purpose, and Blondel's purpose is to bring that divine purpose out at the various points in which the drama of human relations to the triune God is playing itself out.

He begins with creation as the initiating point and with the mysterious sense of a divine purpose he finds associated with it. What he finds philosophically enigmatic is the existence of contingent beings in the face of an all-wise, all-powerful necessary Being, whose creation cannot be but unequal to the Creator. How is it that there is anything besides this Being In and Through Itself, who is absolute and fully self-sufficient? How is it that this plurality of beings that come to be in succession, and that are clearly a falling away from the perfection of the absolute Being, does not seem to be unifiable, whether by reason of the sheer distinction of individual persons, or by reason of impassioned conflicts between them, or by the very heterogeneity of multiple forms whose combination as a universe appears only to trail off asymptotically in what can be called a false infinite or an indefinite? The idea of creation, that is, the idea of an ontological dependence of the entire order of universal history and nature on the Being of beings, brings to philosophy a number of questions of its own that go begging for answers in philosophy. Hence the philosophic enigma that the idea of creation represents in the face of a Christian mystery associated with it in the mind of the philosopher.

It is the very idea of creation that is problematic for philosophy. Blondel does not think creation itself is the mystery. It is an idea we can arrive at through the notion of causality pushed to the extreme of a necessary and certifiable first Cause that is supreme and unique. But there is an aura of mystery that surrounds the idea concerning "the very sense, the ultimate and the higher finality of the creative work" (1944, 42). Even the idea itself is difficult to come by. We find it difficult to think, let alone imagine, an absolute beginning of everything from nothing, by divine *fiat* only: *dixit et facta sunt*. In the pessimism or the nihilism concerning anything but the supreme Being that goes back all the way to Parmenides, Blondel suggests, we do not know how to find a place even for God, let alone for anything else. "The most radical nihilism would destroy itself, and the cure for all illusion would suppress every conceivable problem and existence" (1944, 39). On the other hand, in the all-too-facile but perhaps specious optimism that sees the good as diffusive of itself, there is always the supposition of something other for a demiurge to work on, what Blondel calls a dualism or a pluralism that obscures "the sharp and firm notion of a true *creation*" (1944, 40), presupposing nothing but the creative act itself.

Blondel remarks that such a sharp and firm notion has not been found elsewhere than in the Judeo-Christian tradition. "Though such an idea does not seem absolutely inaccessible to human speculation, this capital truth has never been elaborated in all its purity without the help of Revelation" (1944, 40-

41). Left to its own resources, human thought seems to be excessively tied to the sense data from which it takes flight, so that we are unable to free ourselves from images, so that we fail in representing for ourselves the living and acting truth of a supra-sensible order. "Unable to imagine for ourselves anything that does without materially pre-existing conditions, we subordinate all innovation to an empirical datum as to a substrate that conditions it" (1944, 42). On the one hand, we cannot represent for ourselves an absolute beginning, an absolute origin of time and space, let alone the finite or the infinite character of time and space. On the other hand, in addition to the ancient repugnance to thinking of a God who is transcendent and omnipotent, there is also the more modern and opposite Leibnizian repugnance to thinking that the divine power could create an imperfect world, which would give the appearance of failure on the part of God, instead of a manifestation of an all-wise and all-powerful goodness.

Blondel calls special attention to this Leibnizian difficulty concerning the radical idea of creation, which will not allow for anything less than "the best world possible," but which, he says, stems from our moral consciousness. He takes it as an objection that can be used to prepare for a better reception of the most essential secret of the evangelical message, "for only the supernatural order in its eternity can answer successfully this sublime objection that proceeds apparently from a high religious susceptibility and from a preoccupation to save God from any plausible reproach" (1944, 43-44). For Blondel, it is important to get past, not just the dualist conception that imposes on our way of thinking some pre-existing matter or some prior possibilities that God would have to choose from in creating, but also the sort of Leibnizian calculus concerning a best possible world that would, incorrectly, subordinate the divine inventiveness to the discursive ways of our conceiving, deciding, and executing. Such a subordination of the divine willing and love to mathematicism and to supposedly pre-existing forces is a denaturing of the Trinitarian life already indicated in the Creator, and of the union in it of *absolute power, perfect wisdom,* and *immense charity.* "Not to find the means of unifying supra-temporally these infinite perfections, is to falsify, to ruin the essential of divine transcendence" (1944, 45).

The problem, then, for a rationally alert philosophy with a clear idea of creation as the act *ad extra* out of the plentitude of a Trinitarian perfection, without any prior necessary conditions or even intrinsic possibilities, but simply *ex nihilo,* is to discern how or why, in the presence of the reality of a world absolutely distinct from the living God in his independence, "we can recognize in this divine absolute a reason that would render creation worthy of its Author and capable of receiving in its contingency a prize that justifies calling it to existence" (1944, 45). The suggestion has been made that God, in creating, wanted to display his power, wisdom, and goodness, as if to prove these to himself, thereby adding an external glory to his essential internal glory. For Blondel, however, this still smacks too much of a divine egoism that knowledge of the Trinity has already led reason to set aside. Instead he harkens back to another mystery, that of God's intention in creating. If God has created, it is surely for an end worthy of himself, of his freedom and of his supreme charity, whatever the required inventions of his power and wisdom may be. The question for philosophy would be to wonder how such a worthy program for the divine charity might be fulfilled, and what obstacles it would have to overcome in order to attain such an end. "That is the effort we must exert in order to enter, thanks to Revelation, into the secret of the divine plan whose enigma critical reason requires us to face up to and whose revealing mystery it requires us to take into consideration" (1944, 46).

In keeping with his cycloidal method, Blondel recalls the difficulties and the exigencies that philosophy encounters in dealing with problems of human existence that it cannot resolve to its own satisfaction, along with some of the failed attempts to resolve these problems. Among the latter he cites a certain resignation to a *status quo* or a giving in to the idea of eternal returns, "repeated beginnings without end, in order to reconcile the finitude of things with the infinite or the indefinite of human aspirations" (1944, 47). Such an attitude has no place in our historical consciousness and is morally untenable. The human being is not designed to oscillate between progression and regression forever. Historically and philosophically, he "is a perpetual surpassing, and if he does not rise above what he is, he falls below what his nature seemed to offer or even to require of him" (1944, 48).

What we must wonder about is not just God's reasons in the work of creation, but also man's reasons concerning his own exigencies with regard to his own nature and his highest destiny. Would it be enough to create spirits that would attain the Creator only from the outside, or admire him only from a distance? One could say that that would already be an enviable fate, namely, to belong to the royal retinue at least, if not to be admitted to the reserved quarters or the inviolable intimacy of the deity itself. But for Blondel that would not meet the exigencies of any living spirit such as we know in the world. Falling back on the assertions of his original philosophy of the supernatural, he recalls that "every spirit, every will that exists only to tend toward the infinite, because they do tend toward it, can know fulfillment only by tasting and possessing beatitude" (1944, 49), which, for Blondel, can only be found in God himself. To admit that we can and must aspire to this beatitude without ever attaining it, is "to confuse an indefinite with the infinite" (1944, 49). It is to foster a nostalgia that is all the more excruciating for bringing us so close to the treasured abode, but that leaves us outside, still panting for ever more.

There is no reason for limiting the magnanimity of God in this way. Blondel's thought turns rather to the possibility that the divine *Omnipotence* could overcome the obstacle of a finite spirit actually entering the infinite, so that one could "justify creation in a more complete fashion for both Creator and creature by an adoption that, by making the asymptotic line, so to speak, passes to its limit, unites created nature to uncreated supernature" (1944, 50). The thought of the Infinite at the end of the finite spirit's aspirations, given in the exercise of that spirit's own activity, suggests something beyond all nature and all possibility conceived by man or natural reason, a real supernatural in itself. And the thought of such a supernatural allows for finding a better reason for justifying creation, which is the gift of nature, by allowing for a supernatural gift that can raise the creature into the very life of the Creator. The mystery of the Trinity is thus expanded, so to speak, into the life of the created spirit, as the created spirit itself is brought into the life of the Trinity.

All of this is said without compromising the total transcendence of God, for it means elevating the creature into the Trinitarian life without any loss to the creature's identity. But it is said only in the light of a Revelation that gives the word for the enigma of human existence in the world. Such a word could not have been foreseen by man alone, and is so disconcerting to his habits of mind, that Blondel feels a need to verify whether such an unimaginable and almost unreasonable destiny, to the exclusion of every other, is really part of the divine revelation. He finds his reassurance not only in the entire biblical tradition running from the Scriptures to the Fathers of the Church and the later teachers and theologians, but also in the definitions of the First Vatican Council, which had a significant impact on the elaboration of his own thought during the modernist crisis. He sums up the teaching of that Council's constitution *de Fide* as follows: "There is not for man, as he is in fact and as God has willed him, any different issue, any facultative option, any effective salvation apart from this singular and binding destiny, supernatural life, without which there is eternal death; hence there is no legitimate possibility for the human person apart from faithfulness to an elevating vocation; no, it is not a matter of an offer that commits us to nothing: we have only one destiny, unique and 'indeclinable,' and this destiny is essentially supernatural at the same time as reasonable; for, to rebel against it and to refuse it, would transform our reasonable and immortal nature into a failure, a death, eternally conscious of its culpability and its just sanction" (1944, 51). This is the idea of our supernatural destiny Blondel will come back to repeatedly in this philosophical exploration of the Christian Mysteries.

This is no doubt a difficult teaching for reason to absorb, but Blondel sees it as necessarily tied to the very idea of a supernatural offer made to the rational and free spiritual agent as such, an offer now to be understood, thanks to the Revelation, as integral to the Trinitarian design of creation as a whole. Before trying to explain how such an offer can be understood as truly equitable and charitable, and as anything but an abusive constraint or an unbearable responsibility, he tries to enter more deeply, as a philosopher, into the mystery itself of an infinite supernatural destiny for a finite spirit, by revisiting the philosophical resistances he finds to such an idea, stemming from the dualism of principles in the conception of creation spoken of earlier, and from a certain conception of natural beatitude that would limit man to what he is capable of achieving on his own, a beatitude that has appeared to some as reason enough for creating finite spirits, though not one that would satisfy an infinite desire such as Blondel has unearthed in the dynamism of human action.

Aquinas had spoken of the happiness man can achieve by himself as imperfect, in contrast to the perfect happiness of a supernatural vision of and adherence to the Trinitarian life. But Blondel contests the very idea of a natural happiness for man, just as he contests the idea of a natural religion, based on no more than human musings about the divine, without some revelation from God in his transcendence, that is, for a nature whose very élan is a quest for the infinite, an aspiration at once congenital and inefficacious by itself, for a knowledge that saturates and a fruition that leaves nothing to be desired.

There is a long philosophical tradition that has recognized this sort of infinite aspiration in the finite spirit as such, a tradition Blondel added to considerably with his earlier dissertation on *Action*. What we are told in the Revelation is, not that this aspiration has been fulfilled as if from outside, nor even that it requires fulfillment by reason of its nature, but rather that to this "*original motion* of reason, which would attain only a nostalgic sort of powerlessness, is added a *higher motion,* a directly divine grace that would confer, to what would otherwise remain a disappointing powerlessness, the power to become a participant and an adoptive child of God" (1944, 54). What is there in this, Blondel asks, that is not coherent, convenient, benevolent, and entirely justified from the standpoint of man as well as of God? Would it not be unreasonable and unworthy of human dignity to expect to taste happiness, perfect happiness, as Aquinas called it, without having made itself worthy of it?

The supernatural gift in question should not be conceived as just an extension of the natural gift already granted to the finite spirit from creation. It should be conceived rather as an elevation, a higher motion granted to the finite spirit itself, raising it to a higher degree of responsibility in the exercising of its freedom and in choosing to accept or to reject the proffered gift. As a second gift added to the first gift of creation, it calls for an exercise of the first gift, which is free to accept or to reject the added gift, but has to face the consequences of its choice as regards attaining happiness or failing to attain it altogether. This is the idea, not just of a relative transcendence, or one that is merely ascensional, but of an "infused elevation" or a "divine assumption" that cannot be taken lightly by any rational spirit caught up enigmatically but rationally in the question of its final destiny. Without taking anything away from the freedom of the divine Goodness in communicating itself supernaturally as well as naturally, we can say that God's creative design is indeed justified by this vocation "to a new order that confers to created spirits and, through them, to the immense universe, a value, a participation, a divine adoption that no creature, however high we may conceive it, could contain of its own nature, nor attain by its own strength alone" (1944, 55).

The sense of mystery here is heightened by the thought that God does not have a nature, as every creature does, and hence cannot be assimilated to anything other than himself. For him to confer upon a created spirit a power of assimilation and even of proper filiation into the familial life of the Trinity, the Uncreated in every way, is itself a mystery of mysteries, that of the supernaturalization of creatures: "the mystery of adoption that alone conveys an adequate sense of all that is being prepared in time and will be consummated in eternity" (1944, 58). It is to this mystery, Blondel concludes, that reason, which is enigmatic even to itself, must be raised by a light and a grace that is itself mysterious, and therefore an added light for reason to follow and to seek.

The Mystery of Supernaturalization for the Enigmatic Rational Creature

The problem here is most acute for a philosophy that affirms the transcendence of God, not only as supernatural in its own triune life, but also as incommunicable in its own mysterious light. God is not a nature to be assimilated to created nature. And yet to speak of supernaturalization is to speak of God as somehow making himself present in the creature as God, as Uncreated, and as Supernatural in the strictest sense of the term. Blondel never loses sight of this central affirmation about the incommunicability of the divine even when he comes to speak of divinization or adoption into the triune life through a supernaturalizing gift. Supernaturalization remains supernatural even when it is brought before the rational creature. The difficulty he finds for philosophy at this point, or the natural resistance reason finds before entering into the mystery, stems from this precise meaning Christian teaching attaches to the term *supernatural* as something beyond the pale of philosophy even when it is offered to the rational creature as something for it to take in. Not only is the offer gratuitous from the standpoint of the expectations of reason or nature, but even when it is offered, it is offered only and precisely as a mystery, secretly, as it were, because it surpasses our capacity to understand what it is that is being offered, let alone to will it or to act upon it. As such, it does not come directly under our consciousness or any of our initiatives. What is reason to do before such a jealously guarded secret? How is it to understand that it must respond freely to such an offer, and that on its response, for or against the gratuitous offer, will depend the whole of its destiny, either as fulfilled in a way that it cannot grasp at the moment, or as eternally frustrated from a satisfaction it could have had but knowingly rejected? How can there be such immense responsibility on the part of a finite spirit in spite of such insurmountable ignorance concerning what is being offered?

To answer these questions, Blondel brings back into play his entire philosophy of human action, as it culminates in an enigmatic confrontation with God. The mystery that presents itself as supernatural at that supreme moment, by definition, surpasses all human experience and remains inaccessible to human or philosophical discernment. Yet, in the Christian dispensation it takes some historical form recognizable and intelligible to the rational spirit in a way that is precise, operative, and sanctioned, albeit through a veil that cannot be torn asunder. As supernatural offer, it cannot be thought of as assimilable to human nature or reason, even in its infinite movement. To treat it as anything less than heterogeneous and totally transcendent would be to fall back into superstition, to make an idol of God and his supernatural offer, at this moment of a supreme call for a higher integration into the divine that runs mysteriously throughout the historical drama of mankind's engagement with God.

Blondel begins his discussion of this moment in the mystery of supernaturalization by reasserting his philosophical clarification of the very idea of *supernatural,* as something higher than any nature associated with finite spirit, incommensurate with any determinate nature, something that even the term *transcendent* cannot convey. The strict idea of supernatural, as incommunicable, excludes all thought of transition or ascension from a lower to a higher stage, all thought of a phenomenological breakthrough from below on the basis of anything growing or developing in nature or history. It might seem that only God in his triune life could be spoken of as supernatural in this strict sense. But the challenge of Christian revelation is to claim that it is the very incommunicability of the divine itself in its perfect and eternal aseity that is being offered for some communication between the divine supernature and the human nature in the supernatural vocation, or elevation, of a creature called to accept a gift it cannot refuse without falling below its own nature and without falling short of its own aspirations and its own sense of obligation. Can philosophy even think of such a vocation as rational, let alone possible? Could it be that Blondel's effort to explain or justify the plan of creation itself would leave us with an insurmountable scandal for philosophy, or a sacrilegious reversal of the incommunicable into something communicated? Before he can go on to explore the historical realizations of this supernatural order that has come so acutely into question, he must show how such an order is conceivable or possible for man even as it is divinely infused. For that is how he conceives of his critical method in his approach to the history of the Christian mysteries. "Before enunciating the facts, it is good to understand precisely how they are intelligible and realizable" (1944, 66).

The problem for philosophy is to understand how there can cohabit in one and the same human being a twofold gift from the Creator, one of which is strictly incommensurable with the other: first, a reasonable nature viable in itself, and second a supernatural reality, which, by its intrusion, would seem to set aside or crush the first. How can two such gifts without any common measure between them be understood as compatible in an order that is real and so highly charged for a being with only finite powers of understanding and action? Blondel explains the problem in terms of two gifts that come into play in the exercise of any human living. On the one hand, there is the gift that is constitutive of human nature itself, with "reason, freedom, the life of the spirit, the joy of possessing truth, beauty, wisdom, the power of mastering oneself, of dominating the forces of the universe" (1944, 67), all things that go into man's own capacity to transcend the given universe in realizing his own perfection. On the other hand, there is another gift, one of a totally other value, offered at first as a sort of loan that, it seems, we cannot make use of and take full possession of except by renouncing our natural sufficiency, the one so highly prized by man purely as man. This second offer, which presupposes the actualization of the first by man himself, comes in the form of a barter, where we are asked to sell all that we have and all that we are in order to buy the "pearl of great price" spoken of in the Gospel. It places us in the frightening dilemma of having to renounce all that we are and all that we have achieved, in order to enter into a yet-higher spiritual life that by ourselves we could not have ambitioned for ourselves.

If we stay with the language of appearances and of discursive thinking in speaking of the divine plan for man as revealed in the Christian teaching, we have to say that man receives two gifts, radically distinct and intrinsically heterogeneous from one another, but not in a way that keeps them separated from one another. The second presupposes the first and the first serves, so to speak, as the currency for an exchange, so that the second may compenetrate the first with all its supernatural value. In other words, through the second gift, presupposing a willingness to enter into the deal, so to speak, the human is assumed into the divine, in a manner that is at the same time, by reason of the same willingness on the part of the recipient of the gift to accept the loan, a meritorious ascension into a higher life. This is the complex idea Blondel understands as following rationally from a series of truths that have been previously established, ranging from an established capacity in any spiritual creature to affirm God as incommunicably transcendent, without any requirement of any further communication from God other than that of first gift of creation according to a natural order, and without relativizing God in any way even to the spiritual creature he so generously endows with being and power, all the way to recognizing that God does not give himself except to one who has opened up a place for him in his spirit, to the point that no one sees God without dying to self, which is to say that, for man to access the supernatural loan, he must restore to God the gifts of nature itself, even though he could use these gifts only to exalt himself, and thereby fail in attaining his one and only destiny, which is supernatural and which he cannot decline with impunity since it is in keeping with the spiritual reality of his most profound aspirations.

This is the series of truths to keep track of that Blondel has taken great pains to elaborate, not only in his original dissertation, but also in the Trilogy on Thought, Being, and Action, now summed up concretely in this final version of his philosophy of the supernatural, with its insistence on the incommensurability, not only between the human and the divine, but also between the two gifts offered to the rational creature, that of human nature and that of divine elevation. Blondel is careful to justify before reason in yet another way the grave imperative that comes with a gift that is not only supernatural and gratuitous from the standpoint of reason and moral obligation, especially since it entails such grave consequences for the creature failing to answer a call that can hardly be perceived by conscience by reason of its very incommensurability. For Blondel this was a matter of faith as well as reason. He speaks of the movement of nature as preparing the way for the advent and for an open aspiration of finite spirits. He speaks of self-conscious spirits as avid for domination and happiness. But for a spirit that knows and wills the infinite, a merely conquering expansion can hardly be satisfying. Indeed, Blondel argues, "it can only make one hungry for more by preparing souls in their depth to receive an entirely other motion, an absolutely new gift that cannot be confused with the first gift of nature, no matter how richly endowed or generously spiritual" (1944, 70). What is thus dispensed into what is most intimate to these spiritual creatures is not some other nature like the one they already have, but something purely and directly from God, a grace, "as if God were depositing Himself as a seed in this emptiness ... [God] divinizes [man] so that He will be at the center and so that we can pass from ourselves to ourselves only through Him and by living for Him" (1944, 70). God gives himself to us so that we may give him back to himself. He becomes our captive, so to speak, to the point that we can refuse to have him live in us and have him fructify as the new seed he plants in us, in what amounts to a kind of deicide, killing God, who has placed himself at our mercy within us. In giving himself supernaturally to us, God gives us a new power over him with a new responsibility concerning what we do with that gift. If man has a supernatural vocation, as Christian revelation maintains, this is what is entailed rationally for the philosopher as well as the believer.

Having spoken rather objectively of a single human destiny, which Christian revelation tells us is of a supernatural order, Blondel then turns to consider the problem from the standpoint of the subject, which also calls for some further clarification and justification of the Christian claim. What constitutes man in his nature, and as the compendium of the world in which he finds himself, is a union of matter and spirit. Man is twofold, we are told. But now the supernatural has been brought into the picture as a third. Are we to say that man is now threefold in the Christian economy? Not necessarily, for that will depend on how God gives himself in that new dispensation. In the first dispensation of creation as such, we come to know ourselves as matter and spirit, and God as essentially incommensurate and incommunicable to anything we know of our nature or of the universe. We are called to exercise our responsibility as self-conscious agents within these parameters. What is shocking about the Christian revelation, however, is that we are also told that we are called to exercise our responsibility in a higher order still, one that presumably strikes us in two ways, exteriorly through the senses and interiorly in heart and soul, but that we are unable to perceive as present or as operative within ourselves through our natural powers alone. Blondel is very sensitive to the difficulty this represents for any rational creature called to exercise its responsibility in an order where it does not know clearly what is at stake, especially when the stakes are of eternal and infinite consequence. How can anyone be held responsible for an act in which he cannot know all the ramifications?

Blondel explains why a properly supernatural motion that engages our destiny in a new order cannot but remain something of which we are not directly conscious, as we are of other facts in our experiences or, as he puts it, in the actual of our existence. The reason is that, even in giving himself directly as supernatural or as incommensurable, God remains hidden in his very presence and in the operations of his grace. He inserts himself not only into the affections of our soul but also into the solicitations and the accomplishment of our moral duties, thus raising them to a higher order of responsibility regarding the divine within us, while disappearing at the same time, in his infinite incommensurability. If we are to distinguish between the two motions we are speaking of in the Christian dispensation, it can only be by a careful discernment of spirits within ourselves, and a careful reading of the signs of the time without, in history. We can be responsible for our opposition or for our fidelity to this grace that keeps its secret, even though, when we rebel, we may not have the same sense that we are failing in a fundamental motion that is decisive for our entire destiny, and not just in some subalternate duty.

According to the order of our supernatural vocation there is bound to be a veil of mystery surrounding our deliberate attitude as it affects the orientation of our life as a whole. Along with the natural aspect of our moral duties there is also a certain touch of grace, which, when it intervenes, entails a responsibility all the more serious by bringing into play "a force that should have been sufficient, by adding itself to that of the natural law, for a favorable solution to the problem brought before our option" (1944, 75). It is not so much a question of our destiny being played out in some impenetrable darkness for us. It is rather a question of not sinning against the light coming from a double source, the normal one of moral consciousness and the supernatural one bringing new assistance in the face of decisions that engage our immortal future. If the Scriptures speak of a certain exchange or negotiation in this relation of the human to the divine that is at once natural and supernatural, it is not to say that nature must sell itself short in order to access the supernatural. Blondel has a much higher spiritual reading of this apparent deal between the human and the divine, reaching more deeply into the revealed mystery in order to bring out the higher meaning our own reason aspires to in relating to it.

The supernatural destiny to which we aspire by the grace of God so far surpasses our capacity to achieve, that we could never merit it in any natural sense of the term. On the other hand, considering human dignity itself and its own sense of responsibility, a happiness that we would not have merited in any way would not be satisfying or ennobling, as many philosophers have recognized. If our supernatural vocation does not make itself heard in the fullness of our conscience and in the clear light of our consciousness, it is not only because it remains hidden from us in its incommensurability with anything we can take hold of on our own. It is also to show respect for our freedom and leave our will master of its own choice in our present historical state, unlike what we could suppose would be the case in a final state when the full disclosure of the divine glory would captivate us infallibly. The half-light in which we become conscious of our supernatural vocation, which we are free to acquiesce in or to refuse, is an invitation for us to be generous and disinterested in our acts, in provisional sacrifices that "confer on our spiritual life a value that is incommensurable with any seeking after lucre and even with the semblance of a wager" (1944, 76). What we have to contribute in this new symbiosis of the human with the divine is a certain energy of our own by making a place for God within ourselves, by emptying ourselves so that God may come in, in a supreme act of sacrifice that will allow God to come flooding in.

What this requires is not just an exchange of energy between a stem or a trunk and a graft inserted into it, as suggested in the metaphor, not of the vine and the branches, but rather of inserting a new shoot in a wild product of nature. That sort of exchange is still only a biological phenomenon. The new symbiosis requires rather a new kind of secret mediation between the aspirations of our human intelligence and will and the divine breath or the supernatural seed that is infused into our very nature, taken as at once physical and spiritual. Blondel will enter further into this function of mediation that now comes to the fore, in order to account for an action that is truly theandric. He will enter into the mystery of the Mediator to which this enigma relates, in the next part of his exploration of how the conjoining of the human and the divine, or of the natural and the supernatural, is possible or actual in historical fact. Before turning to that, however, he pauses to show how refusal of the supernatural call, gratuitous though it may be in itself from the viewpoint of our nature or our autonomous spirit, or rebellion against it, has to be thought of as unreasonable and contradictory to our best interest. The call is indeed a gift, an inchoation of divine adoption within us in keeping with our most profound aspirations, over and above anything we could hope for on our own. To refuse it, to betray it or to rebel against it, is not only a sort of deicide against the God who gives himself, a stubborn ingratitude against him. It is also a self-condemnation to eternal frustration coming from ourselves as from a self-sufficiency that would substitute itself for what only God can bring, and thereby abolish God from our lives. This is no small rebellion, but one that affects the course of one's life, with eternal consequences the offender can only blame himself for.

Using an argument he had first developed at the end of his dissertation on willed action, Blondel writes that the rebel against the supernatural calling in question, wills to be God without God. He has to face up to what he has willed: his own deification and autolatry, "for one does not refuse to be God, not any more than God can annihilate Himself; and if it is given to man to aspire to divine adoption, man cannot get around this vocation except by trying to raise himself to it by himself, without his failure ever suppressing the consciousness of his aspiration, of his error and of his senseless presumption" (1944, 78). All this is now said clearly with reference to a supernatural vocation that remains mysterious to us in the historical state of our existence. But it also clarifies something about the logic of the rebel in refusing the gift. He cannot but recognize and love passionately what happiness would be. If his mistake leads him to be deprived of it, he cannot thereby commit metaphysical suicide, "for it is essentially illogical and perverse to imagine that, placed in the presence of immortal and perfect happiness, he could so belittle it as to annihilate himself" (1944, 78). It is not God, therefore, who is to be incriminated for the rebel's fall from grace, not to say into eternal punishment. God has exhibited nothing but the greatest generosity to one who still has his own generosity to exercise, by accepting the gift. It is only the rebel, who says: I will not serve — *non serviam* — who must then face up to the consequences of his choice according to the conditions and exigencies of a gratuitous, yet obligatory supernatural vocation. All this follows from a concrete and integral philosophy intent on exploring all the exigencies that come up in connection with the problem of God, the meaning of creation, and the ends of human destiny, for a nature and a spirit shot through with an aspiration for the infinite.

The Mystery of the Incarnate Divine Mediator and the Enigma of a Constant Mediating Function

Given this understanding of the radical incommensurability of the supernatural, even as it offers itself on loan to a created nature that remains at odds with itself, if it turns the offer down, the next question to be explored in this expanded philosophy of the supernatural is that of how it is communicated to a creature to comprehend the infinite actuality of what is being offered. The philosophy of action has already demonstrated that, at the summit of the ascent, at the moment of finding the object that is the equal of its power to will, the finite spirit finds God, the Infinite itself, as the necessary Being to mediate between itself as willing and itself as willed, so that it cannot will itself without willing the God who creates it. That is mediation at the highest metaphysical level for a spiritual creature seeking to equal the source of its true being. But in speaking of the supernatural as a gift or as a calling for this same created spirit, we have to speak of mediation in a new way, as coming down from the divine into the human and enabling the creature to do something it cannot do by itself, even if it be choosing against the gift. We have to think of this mediation as taking place in history, where the drama of human existence is being played out. The calling is taking place in history, as obscure or mysterious as it may be to our consciousness, and consciousness of it is bound to fluctuate between many highs and lows among those so called to what we now have to think of as a *theandric* action. Man's cooperation with this supernatural gift is not assured, for he is free to reject it as well as to accept it. The success of the plan of supernaturalization is not assured for everyone, because that is conditioned by man's willingness to accept rather than resist a mediation that now takes a historical form, that of the Mediator who remained unnamed in the original philosophy of the supernatural. Christian revelation identifies Jesus as this Mediator, and Blondel will now take him as *the Mystery* in relation to the enigma of salvation history. He will argue that the supernatural order in history presupposes a constant mediation that is certain in our experience of the universe, and that the mystery of Christ as universal Mediator is the only reality that can explain or justify this constant function of mediation for human being.

Blondel thinks of mediation as pervasive of everything we do as human beings, from the way we perceive things, to the way we integrate our perceptions into sciences, purportedly about ontological reality, to the way we come to think of the world of things as one, and even to the way we have to take action in relation to the universe understood as the series of means at our disposal in working toward our final end or our own final integration as spiritual beings. His own philosophy of Thought, Being, and Action has been nothing other than the kind of mediation we find in these three realms, not only as they can be distinguished from one another, but also as there is mediation among them. Mediation runs through the heart of philosophy in its highest metaphysical and spiritual dimension, as it does through our simplest perceptions of sense data, our sciences, and our conscientious deliberations in view of taking action. Blondel has even argued for a necessity of God as mediator if we are ever to come to a perfect adequation with ourselves. But with all of this he still thinks of mediation as an intractable problem for philosophy, as the supreme enigma at the heart of philosophy itself, the enigma in which philosophy has to recognize its own incapacity to deliver the access it needs, not just to the Absolute or to the supernatural reality, but even to the created reality of which it is itself a part.

By mediation Blondel understands a function of unifying things or aspects of reality that are and remain heterogeneous. For example, in our perception of a thing there are always varieties of sense data that are taken as proper to this thing in their combination. To illustrate this function, Blondel turns, not to the Hegelian logic of opposition between finites, but to the Aristotelian logic of gathering all the other categories around that of a substance, even as he recognizes that the function of mediation itself can be traced back "to the Pythagorean discovery of a presence of the infinite in the finite" (1944, 85). Mediation is a function that runs through all the sciences of nature and of the spirit, but that remains an enigma for philosophy to this day, even as it is brought more and more to the forefront of attention. The genius of Aristotle was to show how we classify things according to different categories that are irreducibly distinct from one another but that are also combined with one another as cohabiting in different ways, in spite of their heterogeneity, in one and the same substance and across the different kinds of substances. By singling out the category of substance as the most fundamental and as the only one that could serve as the subject of inherence for all the other categories, such as relation, quality, quantity, and so on, Aristotle showed how all the different aspects of thought and being could be attributed diversely to substantial being. Blondel speaks of this substantial being or this subject of inherence for other categories as ontological reality and calls attention to the habit of mind, which is anything but natural, that so easily and so fruitfully reunites or recombines such diverse categories in relation to the different things we come to know in the world.

Blondel notes how Aristotle takes language to be a replica of reality as an astute way of gathering the diverse aspects of reality as properties of things, through the grammatical strategy of the substantive noun or name that serves as subject of predication. From this can come different dialectical and scientific developments in search of new and more precise predicates to be attributed to what we take to be things or substances, one in themselves. The thing we take to be one in itself is one only in our thinking through a synthesis of what Leibniz spoke of as unconscious minute perceptions, or through a convergence of what Blondel calls heterogeneous influxes, in short, "through a hidden mediation we can call providential established by and for an order inserted into the ensemble of data that contribute in posing for us the problem of our integral destiny" (1944, 270). From sense data such as color and sound to scientific conclusions gathered from multiple and heterogeneous conditions, to the discernment of all the forces that affect our consciousness in our experience and thereby add to our knowledge as well as our reality, all of this presupposes a mediation, or what Blondel calls a unitive finality associated to our own finality as spiritual beings.

Blondel's intention is not to belittle the validity or the importance of this mediating function in our activity of thought. He refers to it rather to show how it remains problematic for philosophy and for critical thinking because it always presupposes some irreducible heterogeneity in things. Analytical judgments may be only articulations of one and the same content expressed in the subject. But synthetic judgments express in the predicate something other than what is contained in the subject, and thereby bring something more into play, something to be explored further in an order of truth that remains ever-incrementally open. Even in a priori deductive sciences, Blondel adds, "truth is never closed and our thought always has movement to go beyond the world of ideal realities" (1944, 271), that is, to get back to the concrete reality of being as well as action. Even in the demonstrative syllogism, the act of reasoning par excellence, there is the artifice of a mediation that brings in a third term, the middle, to mediate between the terms of the conclusion.

With all this, however, mediation remains an enigma for philosophy, one that is at the very core of the philosophical enterprise, and one that it cannot round off in some sort of absolute knowing. Heterogeneity among things, not to mention the individuality of persons in the historical order, remains irreducible. Indeed, the heterogeneity between finite and infinite, which it is beyond the capacity of any finite spirit to supersede, is even more irreducible than any other in logic or in ontology. The highest function of reason is to recognize that it cannot manage any mediation of its own in this ultimate heterogeneity, no matter how necessary it might consider such mediation to be.

To illustrate how the problem of mediation can be resolved at least in part, Blondel appeals to both Aristotle and Kant. Contrary to the sophist maxim about "man the measure of all things," which gave free rein to any individual caprice and to the variations of a sensibility left to its own devices, Aristotle advanced the idea of the earnest man, *anēr spoudaios*, the man who acts in accordance with his reasonable nature, his social formation, or with virtue conceived as an excellence in a properly human activity, even with a certain ascendance toward contemplation, all of which raises man above the realm of mere generation and corruption, and raises him, at least in certain moments, to something of a divine life. In this, according to Blondel, Aristotle was associating his human language to something analogous to the divine *Logos*, thanks to a mediation that, through what seemed a simple artifice of grammar, "associated our intelligence to the divine vision of intelligences and of providential relations among all the elements of nature and the destiny of spirits" (1944, 88-89). Without knowing it, Blondel adds, the Philosopher was beginning to open the way toward an idea, not just of a secret and inexplicable mediation, but also of a higher, universal and perfect mediator, not just of the worldly-man who is somehow divinized, but of the God-man, the incarnate Word. Not unlike Aquinas, Blondel saw Aristotle as somehow opening up to what would be the Christian Faith.

But he also saw Kant as shedding new light and broadening this Aristotelian intuition, though in a very different way. After taking mathematical science as the type of all exact sciences and as yielding synthetic a priori judgments independently of any experiential domain, Kant, with his cult of duty and detachment from anything not purely formal, reduced the world to little more than a "theater for morality." Blondel agrees with this in part, but not without affirming the reality of the material universe as something more than an occasion or a stage for human agents, or a nourishment for their knowledge and action. The world can serve both as obstacle and as vehicle for the development of spirits, as an occasion for acquiring virtue and overcoming temptations for a freedom on its way to God. But the finite spirit can also fall by the wayside, by preferring the present over the eternal, or its own independence over its liberating submission to God. Blondel had already argued at some length to work his way out of Kantian formalism with regard to duty and moral obligation in his dissertation on action (1893a, 128ff.), but not to do away with the idea of autonomy. It was rather to find strength for it by passing through the heteronomy of the external world of sensibility, through mutual recognition with other selves in social interaction, in order to rise even higher to a final encounter with God face to face.

Kant had a moral vision of the world in the presence of an eternal lawgiver for pure reason, but this vision went begging for the kind of mediation we learn about in Christian revelation, where, in the prologue of John's Gospel, we are told of the Word, the *Logos*, who was from the beginning, in the bosom of the Father and in the ardor of the Holy Spirit, the one by whom all things were made, the one who was the life and the light for all those who come into the world, and who became man to renew the face of the earth or, to put it in more technical terms, to communicate some historical form of supernatural life, so that all men of good will could have the power of being made children of God. Blondel sees in this the announcement of a new initiative, a new ferment for those who would let themselves be penetrated by its action, an action at once absolutely transcendent at the same time as immanent and stimulating for a new life at the very core of our being, a supernaturalization of our nature, which up to now we still find so difficult to conceive and yet so desirable for our indigent finitude. This is the prologue to a new way of life that was to spell itself out in the sacraments and the mysteries of a Church that would spread across the face of the earth, an expression of this wondrous presence of the Emmanuel, the God with us, in the life and unity of a Mystical Body that would bring all things together as one, from the humblest material being to the highest, most divine.

Blondel had in mind to describe different spiritual aspects of this mystery, or of the mysteries of the Church, in the next volume of this work on *Philosophy and the Christian Spirit*, but here in the first volume he is still intent on showing the intelligibility of this new kind of mediation that has come upon the world stage, without reducing the transcendent or the truly divine to the immanent, or to the merely human or rational, as other philosophers of Christian religion have tried to do. In relation to the Kantian idea of freedom and the moral vision of the world, he recognizes that God must somehow be passive of creatures or suffer some influence from them, especially from creatures that are themselves spirits with free choice. This follows from his conferring upon them what Aquinas called the dignity of being causes themselves, but not in any way that would make God subject to change as any contingent being is bound to be. As pure Act in his absolute Transcendence, God cannot become passive or entangled in the contingency of creatures, even as he communicates himself in willing them to be and in loving those he so wills. The only way in which he can be thought of as passive is if he becomes a creature without ceasing to be God, which is precisely the mystery of what John calls the Incarnation of the Word in Christ Jesus.

This mystery has to be understood very precisely without taking anything away from transcendent divinity and the immanent humanity of the one in whom both are found at once. How this is so in one human individual is even more mysterious to us than how God is in himself. But the mystery as revealed is a solution to the problem of mediation in a philosophy where the finite has to be related to the infinite. It is not enough to say that the universe exists in its consistency through the mediating act of creation. It is also important to bring out that God confers upon things, and especially upon spirits, "the dignity of being causes on their own account," according to the expression of Saint Thomas Aquinas. This allows for a certain convenience for Blondel, in saying not only that God wills them and loves them, "but that he is passive in their regard in some way" (1944, 90). Strictly speaking, God as pure Act, in his absolute transcendence, cannot become passive or enmeshed in the workings of contingent beings. Yet it is possible to show how some passivity can be associated with the Godhead, if we think of the God-made-man, *factus homo*, thereby taking a place in the universe in order to become passive as well as active.

Blondel finds an admirable expression of certain intelligible aspects of this mystery in St. Bernard's treatise *De libero arbitrio et gratia:* "God, made man, knowing all things himself in their identity in a twofold way, one way through divinity, another way through flesh, sees all things, wills them, rules them, and somehow suffers from them *(patitur)*, as agent, witness, mediator, judge and, if necessary, healer and savior of all" (cited in Latin 1944, 90). The expression is perfect, Blondel comments, in that it gives everything its due on both aspects of the mystery while asserting the universal historical significance of the Mediator on whom all mediation between the human and the divine must rest, without confusion and without absorption or hybridization of the one by the other. To all who would accept or believe freely in this Mediator would be given the capacity not only to be made children of God, but also to enter meritoriously into an action that was already *theandric* in this world and so to become part of the mediation. Bernard had another succinct way of expressing the expansion of this mediation through the exercise of human freedom from the same treatise on *Free Will and Grace* cited earlier in the dissertation of 1893: "Grace stirs free will, as it seeds what it has in mind; heals it, as it changes its affection; strengthens it, as it leads it to take action; sustains it, so that it will not feel faint. However, it operates with free will in such wise that at first it only prompts it; for the rest, it accompanies it. It goes before it only so that from then on [the will] co-operates with it, in such a way that what has begun only from grace, is brought to perfection by both operating mixedly, not singly, simultaneously, not successively at each moment of advancement. It is not grace that does one part and free will that does another, but both perform the whole in each individual work. Free will does the whole, and grace does the whole, but so that as the whole is in free will, so also is it from grace" (cited in 1893a, 403-4). Thus, Blondel can say, while *theandric* action is entirely based on the divine will, human will remains coextensive to it. "It is a gift, but one we acquire as if it were gained" (1893a, 403).

Mediation understood in this way does not require that we reduce the transcendent to the immanent, or the divine to the human. On the contrary, it requires that the human is assumed into the divine, to use the traditional term Blondel borrows from the tradition going back to the Church Fathers — *assumptus homo*. Such assumption is quite in keeping with the ascensional movement of a finite spirit seeking its perfection in the infinite, though it is not something any finite spirit can pass into or achieve through its own initiative alone, without the incitement of a supernatural grace inserted into its deepest spontaneous élan. The grace, though gratuitous from on high, does not remain extrinsic to the natural movement of the human spirit. It is infused into its very élan, to use another consecrated expression, so that reason can have some inkling of it. It vivifies from the inside out, where the rational spirit can recognize the historical signs of its conferral. It is for a philosophy of the supernatural to gather the rays of light that the revelation of this Christian mystery projects in our thought, even though the source of this light remains hidden from it. Far be it from Blondel that we ever attain absolute knowing, let alone absolute identity with the divine, in this life. Even as a Christian, Blondel still can only reason from the world he finds himself engaged in.

The thought of the Mediator who unites within himself both extremes to be reconciled, the human and the divine, the natural and the supernatural, the created spirit and the uncreated, marks the culmination of philosophy's engagement with the mysteries of the Christian dispensation. This engagement began with the mystery of the Trinity, where a more concrete conception of God emerged as an eternal life shared by three Persons, Father, Son and Word of the Father in an eternal generation, and Holy Spirit as the Love that binds them together and is equal to them eternally, so that we can say with the Evangelist: *God is Love.* In keeping with the divine power, the resourcefulness of its Wisdom, and the solicitude of Charity, it was brought out in connection with the question of a motive for creation, that the happiness of spirits, called to know God and desire a union worthy of him and of themselves, would have to entail a relation of knowledge and love that might be adumbrated but not bridged by any created spirit alone. From this impossibility of bridging the abyss between God and the created spirits aspiring to know him, serve him, and love him, from the idea of a possible participation, of a mediation overcoming the incommensurability between the Creator and creature, came the suggestion of an obscure desire, apparently quite chimerical from the standpoint of the creature, of a supernatural vocation, a mediating grace able to bring what is contingent and relative together with the Absolute. What we are told by Revelation is that this has been done, that the call has been offered, that the assumption has begun, made possible by the divine gift of a grace of union that would otherwise be inconceivable for a finite spirit. At the intellectual core and at the heart of this entire scheme of creation and of elevation or of return to the divine itself in its triune life, is the Mediator, who not only makes it possible but actualizes it in himself before actualizing it in others as well. The Word has come down and become flesh, so that all who would believe in him and serve him lovingly could be made children of God and co-heirs with him of divinity itself.

In this perspective, the entire natural order, on the one hand, is seen as constituted to serve and to promote, at diverse degrees, occasions for posing the problem of finite spirits and for resolving that problem. This interconnection of things in the immense diversity of the universe already implies the mediating active presence of a "universal witness, an infallible arbiter, a judge sanctioning the development of all free agents more or less faithful to their providential destination" (1944, 93). Such is the force of the language taken from Revelation. The eternal Word, in incarnating himself, inserts himself into the movement of the universe, a witness to the creative work in which he has cooperated to the point that it would not be without him. While it is all well and good that things are and have a consistency of their own in which and in whom their Author has a loving interest, it becomes necessary that they tie themselves back into him through an intimate bond, and thereby penetrate to the majesty and the truth of God. The primordial role of the Mediator is to provide for this by forming the bond in himself and by opening the way that rises from the lowest degree of the created order to the mystery of divine love as Creator and Vivifier. Theologians may debate over the motive of the Incarnation, *cur Deus homo,* whether it was for the redemption of sins or whether it would have taken place even if man had not sinned. But Blondel finds the reason for it in the very intention, not just to create, but to elevate created spirits, independently of the twists and turns these creatures might introduce into the deployment of the divine plan and its providential ends.

On the other hand, as reason itself urges us and, more especially, as the firm teaching of Revelation indicates, we are led to profess the truth of a destiny that is undeclinably supernatural. Logically and irrefutably, we are to consider the incarnation of the divine Word as the source *sine qua non* of elevating and beatifying grace. To reach God as our only true and fulfilling end, we need a mediator to bring us not only to the brink of the universe, but also over the abyss that reason alone cannot fathom, because of the incommensurability between the uncreated and any conceivable created nature. Only the incarnate Word, not reason or any concept, can join the natural order and what is above nature, not only as the *truth* and the *light*, but as himself the *life* we must live by. With St. Paul, Blondel avers that we see all this only "in part, as if in a mirror and in an enigma," but there is in it also a certain intellectual satisfaction to be found, a moral security and a spiritual well-being. Without the thought of the mysterious Mediator having come into the world, "no other conception of the world and of the spirit could satisfy in the least" (1944, 94). Nor could any attempt to reduce this mystery to something purely rational or conceivable by man.

Historical Realization of the Supernatural Ordinance in the Face of Man's Sinful Rebellion

It should be noted, however, that the combined logic of reason and revelation has given us only the essential idea of a plan of supernaturalization for the whole of creation, a plan offered principally to the rational creature and requiring a Mediator who would unite within himself both the nature to be supernaturalized and the mysterious supernatural that would satisfy the plan as well as the most profound aspiration supernaturally offered on loan, for the spiritual creature to use and profit from, or to abuse and suffer from, in its confrontation with the divine, a supernatural now within itself as well as without. Nothing has been said yet about the actual realization of this plan in creation, or about the historical form it must take, since it is addressed to the rational creature, which has its own initiative to take in history, and which is created free to accept or reject the gift divinely offered in taking these initiatives as a spiritual being in the world of nature.

What this means for the realization of the divine plan is that it will be subject to some variation, so to speak, depending on how the rational creature responds to the offer. It also means that we have no way of knowing in advance how this realization will take place, or of deducing logically what modalities it will take, merely from the concept we have of this supernatural calling at this point, or of the Mediator who will be required in any eventuality. In some respects, God has made himself passive of the rational creature in the way that his plan is to be realized, not just in the end, but in the process it will take to get there.

We have learned of this supernatural calling and of the Mediator it will require, not just from looking at the mediating function of the rational creature in the world of nature, but also from historical circumstances that contain a revelation of the living God, such as the call of Abraham and the story of Jesus' life as told by St. John, beginning with its prologue on the Word-made-man. Blondel has used both of these sources to arrive at his idea of an essential plan for supernaturalization and its necessary inclusion of the incarnate Word as mediator for effecting the plan, whatever historical modality it would take as a result of man's response or his failure in responding to the offer. Having distilled this spiritual meaning of our supernatural calling and of the revealed mystery of the universal Mediator, Blondel then turns to consider the history in which it has been realized or is still to be realized, for that is part of the mystery of the Christian spirit itself as it responds to what remains enigmatic in the history of humanity itself.

What we have spoken of as an eternal plan in God must now be spoken of in its temporal deployment. The eternal role attributed to Christ as mediator must now be seen as playing itself out in the real world of human action in a kind of genesis of the supernatural order amid the historical realities of a spiritual parturition, but not without keeping the spiritual dimension of history always clearly in mind. For Blondel history now was this twofold sense: "that of transcendent realities which play into an earthly life of humanity laboring to engender new life, and that of a positive order of factual realizations forming an ensemble of vicissitudes and dramas in the immense epic deployed by the supernatural design permeating all human accidents" (1944, 103). The Mediator is not just eternal Word. The Word became man, born of a woman. He played his role as Mediator as a man in history, calling upon others to follow him in fulfilling his mission historically or "until the end of time." What now has to come into view is this supernatural ordering of universal history as the Mediator immerses itself into the real history of human beings and into the experiences of our collective and individual lives.

The cycloidal method here takes on a new level of complexification due to the Incarnation now seen as indispensable for a solution to the problem of mediation that runs through all the different aspects of the relation between the supernatural and the natural. How is the realization of the supernatural order in the spiritual history of mankind to be understood, which is the only way it can be made known to those called to it? But, on the other hand, how can it be made known if this order, in its incommensurability, remains beyond the grasp of our actual consciousness? Blondel is not about to become an immanentist in his appreciation of the Christian mystery of Incarnation, but he has to examine critically as philosopher of religion how this order or how this new economy makes itself known historically, so that human beings can respond to it in this life as they exercise their option for or against it.

Blondel scrupulously maintains that there is no purely historical science that can establish the authenticity of something that surpasses the entire order of phenomena, or of anything we know in the order of physics, biology, psychology, and metaphysics. Most scientists would agree that there can be no demonstration properly speaking of anything supernatural, which is by definition beyond the realm of science. But for Blondel and for the Christian revelation, the matter cannot be left at that, as long as the offer is made of a supernatural gift that would fulfill the aspirations of a finite spirit in a way that nature cannot. Such an offer would have to come in the form of a confrontation between the self-conscious being and the Creator. God would have to find some way of making it known in our historical circumstances, if the human being were to have anything to say about accepting or reflecting it. The central moment of this disclosure in the Christian revelation is, of course, the Incarnation of the Word itself, but then there is also the divine pedagogy in history itself leading up to that moment and following rigorously from it in the Church and its sacraments. Far from being purely theoretical or abstract, the doctrine about the supernatural is also about historical facts in which the mystery is hidden as it reveals itself over the course of history. This is the problem Blondel now sets out to elucidate, in the way God makes the supernatural offer known historically, without taking away from the incommensurability of the gift itself.

The problem had vexed many Catholics during the modernist crisis in the early years of Blondel's philosophical career, whether on the side of the extrinsicists, who were getting nowhere with their objective proofs for the truth of revelation, or on the opposite side of the historicists, who interpreted everything said in the Scriptures, especially the Gospels, in purely humanistic terms as grasped by critical-historical research. We have seen how Blondel had intervened in the debate between these two irreconcilable points of view by pointing out the one-sidedness on each side and showing the need for a different kind of method that would do justice to the problem as it presents itself historically to human subjects invited to cooperate in a theandric work. At the time he had proposed *tradition* as the only way of doing justice to the problem, a living tradition in a Church that traces its identity all the way back to the Mediator, who had himself walked the earth with his own consciousness of who he was and what he was about in the world, a *tradition* guided by the Holy Spirit more than by any merely human authority, as part of the divine pedagogy. Here he takes this idea of *tradition* to include the entire biblical story of mankind and of a chosen people in anticipation of a Mediator who had yet to come, so that the philosophy of the supernatural would now include not only doctrinal truths concerning God and man's special calling, but also "doctrinal facts," such as the Incarnation and the Resurrection, in addition to Original Sin and the special calling of Abraham and his progeny, where the transcendent truths about man's calling were already adumbrated.

The mystery of mankind's supernatural calling to divinization begins to make itself known, for Blondel, and for the Christian spirit he is exploring, from the very first moment of history as narrated in the book of Genesis, in the story of Adam and Eve, the original human couple, and of an original sin that marked the subsequent course of history in both human and divine terms. The narrative is not written in the form of a modern historical account, recreated from eyewitness accounts, documents, or monuments that supposedly bring us back to facts seen in themselves, so to speak. The account is more in the form of a parable that Blondel takes to be about a matter of historical fact in which much more is going on spiritually than could appear to the naked eye, or even to the critical examination of the philosopher or the historical criticist. Indeed, the story is told from the standpoint of one who is believed to have had an inside track on the spiritual drama that was playing itself out in this first moment of history, and who has to be thought of as having a much better understanding of all that was at stake than even the protagonists themselves in the event, though the latter were not without some appreciation in their own consciousness of what their choice meant in relation to their own destiny and that of mankind as a whole.

Blondel's reading of the Christian belief concerning this first moment of history has it that the original human couple was not created in a state of pure nature, though they did exist in a state of innocence where they could enjoy the many benefits of nature and exercise choice in their use of these benefits. In addition to the gift of creation, or of their very nature, which enabled them to act responsibly as rational beings, there was also from the very beginning a higher gift, a higher calling to something that has to be thought of as supernatural in relation to the Creator. For Blondel this higher gift was not strictly another creation, but rather an elevation of the given nature, presupposing the creation of a responsible agent with a dignity of its own, in accordance with the way he had come to understand the mystery of the human being's supernatural vocation as intended by God from the moment of creation on. In fact, the idea of a twofold gift from the beginning, one of nature and one of elevation to a higher order, was important for understanding this story of an original test and its outcome, not just for the original couple, but for humankind as a whole. Without the idea of a higher calling for the free creature, to say *yes* or *no* to, there would be no way of understanding how there could be a test for a creature that had everything going for it in a state of innocence, or how a negative response to the test could have such dire consequences as we are told of in this story of a fall from grace.

Blondel sees in the story of Adam and Eve a first historical instantiation of the drama provoked by a grace given to mankind from the beginning, obscurely to be sure, but nevertheless clearly enough to meet the original couple's level of responsibility. The story does not presuppose, in these individuals, originally interpolated by God in their state of innocence, the high level of historical consciousness the modern critical thinker or the more articulate theologian might suspect. Nor is the gift itself addressed only to such highly reflective individuals. Still, in his own philosophical reflection on the story, Blondel finds enough to explain why there had to be an initial grace given, presupposing a supernatural end of creation worthy of the Creator and of the spiritual creature itself, why this grace had to be only the loan of a divine power, so to speak, so that the spiritual creature could exercise its own free choice in response to it, and why saying *no* to it changed or is still changing the course of history for all human beings, not to mention the eternal outcome for those who persist in saying *no* to the end. The story of Adam and Eve is not just the story of a couple eating of a forbidden fruit in a garden of natural bliss. It is the story of a disobedience to God, of saying *no* to God by a creature endowed with a power to become one with God, by letting him in freely in a fundamental option, rather than excluding him. Eating the fruit of a forbidden tree was the exercise of such an option portrayed in a parable of immediate confrontation with God.

Blondel, like many other commentators, highlights some of the psychological refinements in the story that make the temptation, or the test, so penetrating to the core of the human spirit and so devastating for this spirit in its first negative outcome, without however ruining the natural capacity to reason and to will freely. Blondel takes note of these more spiritual aspects of the temptation and of the sin in keeping with both the Catholic teaching and his own experience as a philosopher of human action. He also shows how the evil spirit, who had already exercised his own choice of *non serviam*, is brought into the picture in the form of a serpent to shine the spotlight on the element of pride and self-satisfaction in man's ceasing to will to obey God — "you will be like God, knowing good and evil" — even though it is not said in the story what kind of immortality this would entail for the one who refuses the gift of a higher life with God.

Blondel also calls attention to an aspect of the soteriological problem that has not been noted much, when we think of how that problem might have been resolved, if the original couple or humankind in general had not failed the original test at that initial moment or at any later moment in what would have been an otherwise sinless history. Revelation tells us nothing of what might have been the passing from Eden in this world to the life of beatific vision in God himself, had man remained faithful to the original calling. It was not predetermined that man should choose as he did. It was necessary that there be a choice on the part of man, so that he might enjoy the supernatural life in God as something willed by himself with the élan of grace already given with the supernatural calling. "For the dignity of a free being, made in the image and resemblance of God and, consequently, participating in some way in this aseity, calls him to become in some way the arbiter of his own destiny, either by accepting or by refusing the indispensable conditions for an elevation that obliges him to surpass himself if he is willing to confirm within his obediential potency the supreme gift of grace" (1944, 122-23).

There could have been another outcome to the test or the temptation, but we are not told what that would have entailed for the passing from this life to a life of perfect happiness in the triune life of God, though the plan of perfect beatification for spiritual creatures that motivated creation of such spirits from the beginning remained in effect even after man's initial refusal. What we learn about the plan, at least as far as it concerns human beings, is that it is quite plastic in its ability to take human choice into account in the pursuit of a destiny that man can refuse. What might have happened historically, had man never chosen to refuse the plan, is not something we have to know in the way we still have to relate to the plan as we know it in our real history. What we have to know are the real and necessary historical consequences of a sin freely committed against grace, against reason, and against the élan of our will and our sensibility, with repercussions even against God in his twofold plan of creation and sanctification. What we have to enter into now is the new historical phase, the postlapsarian phase of the immediate consequences due to the fall from grace, which is one of the new promises opening the way "toward a long convalescence from an ill that, without the immediate charity of the Mediator [already spoken of], would have remained deadly, that of a pedagogy, amid many misunderstandings and relapses, preparing the advent of the restorative Messiah" (1944, 125-26).

How is it and why is it, Blondel asks, that sin, or the offense of the creature against God's gift of himself, does not turn out to be a definitive failure of what has been determined to be the providential plan giving creation its truly transcendent sense, to wit, the call to supernatural life for spiritual creatures? It would seem that the revolt of original man, with all his natural, preternatural, and supernatural gifts, should have been decisive enough to put an end to the plan. But that is not what we are told of God's abiding love for mankind in the biblical story after the fall. "God's gifts are without repentance": he does not take them back even when they are refused or set aside by ingrate or sinful people, who turn to other gods for their protection and satisfaction, or make other gods for themselves as so many have done and continue to do. Blondel has maintained that the offense or the fault is naturally irreparable, since it would have to make up for some infinite damage in what has been done irrevocably, even though man's natural powers to choose and to repent freely have not been undermined to the core. If, however, we broaden this philosophical reflection to include the ties of the entire universe that pull the hierarchy of beings together, from the lowest material things to the highest spiritual creatures, we can find a better reason for the kind of plasticity God reveals in a plan that goes to the heart of our very moral being as integral to the entire order of creation. Composed of matter and spirit, the human being serves as the universal bond in the hierarchy of beings, surpassing it by its own act with a higher perspective of its own, thereby summing it up as a sort of mediator, as if toward the supreme Mediator, through whom all of creation returns to God, whose munificence is the origin of all there is in creation. The historical exercise of man's free will still has within it the power to orient itself, and the things it touches, toward their true end, even if it has not exercised that power adequately yet. It has not yet cut itself off from that end definitively, as it might do in the final moment of its earthly existence.

From this, Blondel concludes, "man, called to serve as incarnator and realizer for the assumption of all nature, could not by original sin ruin the supreme finality of the creative intention" (1944, 128). Before coming to how the divine plan of supernaturalization is in fact being realized in history, Blondel has already shown the necessity of the supreme Mediator, through the Incarnation of the Word, in relation to the supreme finality of creation itself, prior to any consideration of sin on the part of the one who was to serve as Mediator in the entire order of spirit and matter. What we have to think of as a consequence of sin is not an abandonment of God's plan, or even a change in the plan, strictly speaking, but an enhancement of the plan to include a rebellious creature in need of mercy as well of justice to reenter into the plan. Grace was not withdrawn, but offered in a new way, in the form of a promise that accompanied the condemnation and the banishment from the original state of innocence and relative happiness. Man was not left entirely to his own resources in suffering the consequences of this. He was given some hope in what remained an aspiration for him toward some higher beatitude mysteriously conceived as another Eden or as a promised land.

Blondel notes that we do not know precisely what the role of the Mediator would have been in the final divinization of man, had there been no sin. What we do know from Revelation is that, as a result of sin, that role would now include that of Redeemer as well. Mankind would still have to wait and see what difference that would make in how this role would play itself out in the historical event of the Mediator/Redeemer's coming. All that we can say, according to Blondel, is that the necessity of the redemptive aspect in the role of the Mediator was contained in germ in the ordering of the creative plan spoken of from the beginning, which had to allow for the possibility that the free creature would reject the initial offer of supernaturalization rather than accept it forthwith. The rational creature was not predetermined to sin, but sin it did, as happened historically, and if the offer of supernaturalization were to remain in effect, as the promise that accompanied the banishment from the earthly Eden continued to indicate, then the necessary mediation for supernaturalization would take the form of Redemption. There are theologians who have been known to argue that the Incarnation was only for the sake of reparation from sin, as if Mediation were only a matter of Redemption. But Blondel has a more universal view of Mediation as it relates to supernaturalization as such, independently of whether or not the rational creature were to stand in need of redemption for it to finally be able to accept the proffered divinization. Redemption is only an aspect of that more universal Christological view, necessitated by man's fall from grace due to an offense against God.

The historical period that followed the fall of the original couple was thus a time in which the consequences of sin and rebellion against God became manifest. But for the Christian Spirit looking back on it, it was also a time of gradual and progressive preparation for the human race looking forward to a Savior who was to come under very paradoxical circumstances. It was a time stretching forward from the fall toward the proclamation of the Good News. Reflecting back on that time through the lens of the Christian Spirit, Blondel examines it critically, not as a historian or as an exegete, but as one concerned about where humanity stood in its relation to God and to its supernatural calling. What he finds as a philosopher is a very enigmatic character of this historical existence of a humanity in need of redemption and being prepared to enter into a mysterious solution for itself to a problem it does not fully understand. The enigma is still one of a relation to something absolute and infinite. In religious terms, it is still one of people dimly wanting to be faithful to the one, true, totally transcendent God, but falling constantly into superstitious practices of all sorts, as the Bible tells us even of the Chosen People. The view of a higher life that human beings aspire to remains confused and is often mixed in with magic, rituals, and cults that prevail among nations, in a kind of hybridization found already in the moments leading up to the temptation and the sin of the original human couple. All this history of rebellious resistance to the call of true divinization is a result and a continuation of original sin, and in it all humankind is still torn between trying to capture whatever vaguely divinized powers they think they perceive, and submitting to them, thereby rendering them favorable "by circumventing, so to speak, through a science and through obligatory practices, the inevitable influence that, without the cult, would be contrary and punitive" (1944, 134-35). For it is still the original temptation that finds its way into what we have come to think of as the most frustrated and frustrating religious practices, even those with a spark of the true spirit behind them.

The shapes of idolatry and human prostitution became innumerable. In the story of Noah we are told of a new alliance between man and the God of nature, followed surprisingly "by a first realization of the merciful announcement, this miracle of the call of Abraham" (1944, 136). The reason for naming this call, along with Abraham's response to it, a miracle is that it represents a new departure in the course of history, leading up to the definitive advent of the One who was to be the light of mankind in the return to God. For Blondel, as for Kierkegaard, not to mention St. Paul and the Four Gospels, and contrary to Hegel's religious put-down of this Patriarch of the Jewish spirit, Abraham was a pivotal figure in this return, as the Father of faith in a God who was truly transcendent, and whose promises as well as commands truly superseded those of nature or of any earthly society. The call of Abraham marked a new beginning in the supernatural rise toward what would come to be an authentic Christian spirit. To be sure, there would still be many setbacks and many delays, even partial obstacles and moral failures, among the children of Abraham following in his footsteps, but through it all God was preparing his people to accept what Abraham could believe in only obscurely, a *providence* that was already a mystery working its way through history. Blondel speaks of Abraham as a hero, not in some grand human scheme, but as a hero of faith in this mystery that contained a solution to the enigma of man's religious aspirations.

In the retelling of this story of a fall from grace and of a promise to restore the gift of a supernatural calling through the Redeemer-Mediator, Blondel focuses on philosophical enigmas of universal import for mankind for which he finds some illumination in the different aspects of the Christian mysteries playing themselves out in this history. The idea of a fallen humanity is one such enigma, and in response to it Blondel introduces what he calls the mystery of a *transnatural* state for humanity in history. This is an idea he had introduced into André Lalande's *Vocabulaire Technique et Critique de la Philosophie* as early as 1921, to characterize the state of humanity after the fall as provisional, as unstable and transitional, where the supernatural life to which man is called is no longer or has not yet been restored, but where this vocation still has its repercussions as a point of insertion and an aptitude for the restoration of the gift lost in the fall. This state is no longer the supernatural that has been lost. Nor is it the supernatural that is yet to be restored or offered anew. It is simply the tension or the élan toward a proper divinization that remains in man, who somehow experiences himself as fallen, or deprived of something he aspires to. The story of the first couple in the book of *Genesis*, which was first recorded long after Abraham and his people came to their faith in a transcendent and provident God, speaks to this enigma of human experience. Man was not created in an original state of pure nature. He was called from the start to rise, even to something supernatural for him, but on the condition that he would freely accept the gift by submitting to a command from the One offering such a supernatural gift. In refusing the gift, however, the original couple and their offspring did not fall back into a state of pure nature. The offer of supernaturalization was not absolutely rescinded. It was rather postponed, due to the original refusal of man, for a later time, to be offered again, while in the meantime humanity suffered the historical consequences of its refusal in all sorts of aberrations and confusion. Given the promise of redemption that had accompanied the banishment from Eden, the providential plan of supernaturalization continued to have its repercussions in the human spirit even during this time of deprivation of supernatural grace, as a desire for something that it could not achieve on its own.

What Blondel had in mind in speaking of a *transnatural* state for mankind in history is this resulting condition that runs through "the diverse phases of humanity, a humanity marked and stigmatized in all epochs by original sin, but diversely and progressively prepared by the promise made to the first couple, a promise frequently reiterated in the aftermath" (1944, 136). This is a condition that remains true for all, even after Redemption has been consummated, for all still have to go through their own test, so that "the grace of the Savior may be applicable in diverse ways to those who, until the earthly end of humanity, are born or will be born with this stigma of the hereditary sin and will find themselves in a state to be crossed and to be transcended" (1944, 137). In this mystery of original sin and its consequences Blondel finds an answer for the enigma of man's lack of equilibrium on a road we might otherwise think of as without fault. But the answer remains a mystery, because it is naturally impossible for man "to discover by himself the reality and the causes of such a state that no psychological or moral analysis can discern in fact or define according to its origins or consequences" (1944, 137).

The mysterious *transnatural* state Blondel speaks of is not just one for the chosen people of the Old Testament who were alerted to it in their consciousness by the story of the Fall and its consequences, accompanied by a promise of future restoration of the gift that had been lost. It is one for the whole human race as well, as it is descended from the original couple and as it keeps on repeating the offense against a God who still would raise everyone to a higher life. For Blondel the authentic religious aspiration in question has never been absent from the human race, even as something oriented to a supernatural vocation. What happened as a result of the original sin was a loss of clarity as to what this attitude entailed in relation to the one, true God. People lost their bearings and turned to all sorts of other things in superstition and idolatry, in attempts to take control of God and of the world, as the original couple had originally tried to do in the Garden of Eden.

Revelation tells us that God, in keeping with his promise of a Redeemer for everyone, had to intervene all over again in mysterious ways to bring people to a better consciousness of the need for redemption and of what they had to do concerning a gift that was still being offered, though it was hardly perceived in all its grandeur and exigencies. Blondel thinks of the Old Testament as a long history of such divine interventions with a people, to prepare them to accept the gift when it would present itself again in human history, through the Incarnation of the Word.

Blondel did not, however, think that explicit historical confrontation with the Redeemer who was to come, or who has come and consummated his work of salvation for the nations, was the only way possible for bringing all human beings to the sense of a choice to be made in response to an offer they could refuse, but that they had to accept humbly to gain its supernatural benefit. There could be other ways in which God, in his universal salvific will, can bring people to a sense of their supernatural vocation and the choice they have to make about it, as he did for example with the original couple and as he can still do for all those who have never historically encountered the Biblical Revelation or the mystery of the Redeemer. We are not told about such ways in Scripture or how they would work their way into the secrecy of souls. We are told only of the way in which God worked his way into the soul of a Chosen People from whom a Messiah was to come, where both the way, the historical facts themselves, and the telling thereof by patriarchs, lawgivers, and prophets is suffused in a mysterious *transnatural* movement of spirit that should not go unnoticed by philosophy.

Blondel reads this history of the chosen people as a philosopher reflecting on the enigma of human existence in need of rehabilitation and a long convalescence, with many transitions toward "a light and a religion that would be fully spiritual . . . in order to bring out the rational sequence and disclose the intelligible structure that the philosophical spirit has to find in the cooperation that human wisdom itself can furnish in considering providential intervention in the course of human history" (1944, 139). It is not for human wisdom, or philosophy, to substitute itself for this providential enlightenment from on high, concerning an end that surpasses history itself, though many an immanentist philosophy would have it so. Nevertheless, it remains for philosophy to explore the intricate ways in which the call of a totally transcendent God wends its way back into a rational consciousness that has refused it a first time and is to be given a second chance historically, once again to accept or to reject, this time perhaps for the last time.

This conditional rehabilitation of humanity in view of a supernatural end is itself an enigma that the Biblical story speaks to as preparing a people for the mysterious advent of a Messiah, who would exceed all human expectations. Blondel reconstructs the spiritual history of the Old Testament to show how this preparation was done through different prominent figures. In the story of Abel, a just man killed by his brother Cain, he sees a prefiguring of Christ. Noah too is seen as a figure of the Savior rising above the deluge of sinfulness. In these two figures, and in the line of Patriarchs, Blondel acknowledges a sign that not all was universally perverted or damned as a sequel to original sin. In some rudimentary form, even amid superstitious practices most likely, there emerged a certain purposefulness, "a certain fidelity to duty, a *sursum* that could serve as a vehicle for a true regeneration" (1944, 140). Little by little primitive savagery and confusion of tongues were replaced by a culture with certain material, social, and even spiritual resources, so that a new kind of message could be understood by a people with a purified tradition leading back to the one, true God.

With Abraham came a new era, the era of *faith*, inaugurated by the heroic faith of one called out of his own land to wander, to believe in the promise of a son in his old age, and, paradox of paradoxes, to believe that he would have this son, and the progeny that would come through him, even though he was commanded to sacrifice this son. In this faith of Abraham in God's providence, and that of those who would follow in his footsteps, Blondel finds a new openness and readiness for the mysterious Redeemer to come, not just for the "chosen people," but for the whole of mankind as a spiritual humanity. With Moses came a more determinate shape for this people who had wandered into the "fleshpots of Egypt" and fallen into slavery there. Moses, with all of the strange circumstances that were to assure his survival as a male Jewish child under threat of extinction by Egyptian authorities, became not only the liberator of his people, but also a leader as they wandered in the desert for forty years, an educator, a lawgiver, and the organizer of a religious cult centered on the one, true God who revealed himself on Mt. Sinai. Out of this mysterious meeting of a people with its God came divine ordinances once again, a pure moral law, Blondel says, "graven on stone tablets as the expression of the eternal and universal Decalogue for a humanity faithful to God and to the steadfastness of conscience proclaiming and thus clarifying natural religion and morality in opposition to the 'golden calf' and rampant idolatries everywhere" (1944, 143). Again, for Blondel, Moses is more than just a lawmaker. He is precursor and revealer of a cult in spirit and truth that was to come.

Of special importance in the continuing history of this people, once it was established in a land of its own, however tenuously that may have been, was the emergence of *prophets*, especially the great ones like Isaiah, Jeremiah, and Ezekiel, who were forever calling back this errant people to the purity of their own religious spirit, toward their God, and keeping alive the hope of a Messiah who would take on the burdens of his people due to their sins, thereby redeeming them and restoring them to a new covenant, one written in their hearts of flesh, and not on stones. Blondel calls attention to the rich spiritual texture, as a model with a universal intent for all nations in this teaching of the prophets that was far from being appreciated for all its spiritual significance by the people to whom it was addressed and by the authorities at their head. He does the same with the poetry of the *Psalms*, which the Christian tradition has always read figuratively as well as literally, representing man as conscious of his dire need and complete dependence before God, for relief and salvation. So too, the suffering servant announced by Isaiah who would take this need upon himself as a way of atoning for sin, that is, of making humanity once again at one with

God. These are all facts in a long historical consciousness having this about them that is particular and even unique: "The facts include at once the annals of a diminutive people and the immense prelude of human destinies in all their height and depth, not just for the goings on unfolding in the passing centuries, but for the total, spiritual and supra-temporal history of humanity" (1944, 148). Understanding the spiritual dimension in all these facts, and in the narration of these facts, and in the accounting for them by the prophets, presupposes a much more complex reality than the banal methods profane history can lay hold of. Far from reading the Jewish spirit as only closed in upon itself and its utter dependence on a God who remains distant and aloof, Blondel reads it more as a spirit struggling to overcome its limitations, its infidelity to a God it most profoundly aspires to, its continuing sinfulness in the face of a covenant that it cannot fulfill without the Mediator, now seen more than ever as necessary, not only for rational beings to have an authentic sense of their supernatural vocation, but also to make up for the original prevarication that has set them apart from God.

Even the advent of the promised Messiah himself into history is an enigma to be wondered at, after this long period of spiritual preparation following the fall from grace. Foretold by the prophets of old, this advent was to be of universal significance for all men of good will, the incarnation of the universal Mediator for the supernaturalization of mankind and of the world. And yet, with all this universal religious significance, it took place in the most ordinary circumstances of a single individual being born and taking his place in the world, with very few people, other than some already imbued with religious fervor, taking note. Blondel has in mind the mystery of the Man-God among men hidden in these enigmatic events recounted in the Synoptic Gospels — though not in John's Gospel, which spoke rather of the Word becoming man, insisting more on the mysterious aspect of the event, or that of the incarnate Mediator for all of creation, spoken of earlier in the previous part of Blondel's elaboration on the Christian spirit. Here he wants to insist more on the human side of this Mediator and how he comes to play his role in history as man, even as the eternal Word. He alludes to the wondrous circumstances that surround the narrative of his birth and of a certain youthful episode in the Temple of Jerusalem at age twelve, but he remarks that these were not enough to set him apart from others in the eyes of most people, or of the religious authorities of his time, except for his mother, "who kept all these things in her heart." What he contemplates is a man who for the better part of his life did as most other men do, took care of ordinary business, worked as a carpenter with his putative father, and became very much a "Son of man." This is what he did for the first thirty years of his life in what Blondel calls the "realism of action," learning and growing in wisdom and in age, and preparing for a more public mission that was to come. This was the Word incarnating himself in actual, historical fact, though most of the world did not see it as such, and still has great difficulty recognizing this Jesus of Nazareth for what he truly is as "Son of God."

Other wondrous events marked the transition of this Jesus from his hidden life to a more public life, such as the temptation in the desert, the acknowledgment of John the Baptist at the Jordan, and the descent of the Holy Spirit, with the acknowledgment from his Father in heaven. But Blondel contemplates more the teaching inaugurated by Jesus in his brief public life, as the Gospels do for the most part. He insists especially on what was *new* in this Good News that would initiate a supernatural life for those who would become faithful to the grace at hand and join in the universal Church, of which it is written that it is the "Spouse" and even the "Mystical Body" of Christ. For Blondel, this *new* in this Good News "was something other than a metaphysical ideology or a speculative vision, something other than a myth or a parable or even a historical fact with a tomorrow of universal youth" (1944, 157). It was a reality no human being could have invented or even thought of, the advancement on a promise, the certitude of a substantial truth already initiated in its realization and destined for a perfect and eternal fulfillment. This was a teaching to illuminate the spirit in its depths and in its heights, a way to follow even in the obscurity of the senses and in the dark night of the spirit.

The fullness of the message was not understood immediately by the hearers of this new Word, not even by those who became personally faithful to this teacher, so capable of understanding and stirring their soul. They did not yet have "the ears to hear and the eyes to see" into this new life that was to come. Picking up from St. John again, Blondel points out that more light was to come later, after the death and resurrection of Jesus, when the eyes would be opened more fully to the mystery, with another sending of the Holy Spirit, who would lead them deeper into the truth of the New Teaching, so that they could announce it to all the world. Indeed, those first hearers of the Word did not understand the depth of the renunciation and emptying of oneself the Mediator still had to go through before the proclaimed new life would be inaugurated in history itself, the mystery of a passion and death that the Redeemer saw himself headed for from the beginning of his preaching, the mystery Blondel himself was most interested in elaborating on, given the special difficulties it presented for right reason and conscience.

The Enigma of Reparation for Sins Culminating in the Mystery of Redemption

Blondel's approach to the Christian mystery of redemption is one of profound spiritual realism concerning a historical event in which a man who is said to be Son of God undergoes a most ignominious suffering and death in order to redeem mankind from its sinfulness. Blondel's is not the idea of a speculative Good Friday that every man has to go through to supersede the limits of a finite understanding on the way to becoming absolute spirit in an infinite movement. It is more the idea of a historical fact witnessed and narrated by many, in which a lot more was going on spiritually and mysteriously than meets the eye, or is understood by merely rational spectators of the event, but a fact of universal import for the whole of mankind. What Blondel wants to do as a philosopher is make as much sense of this event as he can, in the light of the spirit in which it is told. There have been many misunderstandings as well as misgivings concerning this story and its import for mankind, no less than concerning the kind of mediation it represents. There is, nevertheless, a lot that reason and conscience can do even from a natural standpoint to overcome these resistances to what is essentially the restoration of an offer or a loan to be used once again, or abused, in the achievement of a supernatural vocation, or in the frustration of such a call. The supernatural character of our destiny and of our actual historical state adds a new dimension to the extreme difficulty of remedying the faults of mankind and their eternal repercussions, but there is already a kind of rigorous determinism at work in the event of Christ's passion and death, both physically and spiritually, that has to be understood properly.

Blondel begins by examining the very idea of *sin* as it is proposed in the Christian perspective, whether as original sin or as personal sin. What *sin* entails is not just a matter of imperfection or of dereliction in an order of passing and reparable contingencies. Much more is at stake in acts that deliberately and freely orient our destiny than just temporal interests and contingent goods. For in deciding anything seriously in our lives we are also adopting an attitude toward God, using the double motion of a right reason and of a divine impulse. In *sin* we are abusing something ontological, departing from an eternal order, going against the divine motion itself. For Blondel, as he tried to show from the beginning, in his philosophy of action, this is part of the logic of a conscience that is free to say *yes* or *no* to the stirrings of the Spirit.

Making reparations for this fall from a due order does not mean undoing the wrong that has been done. It means more a spiritual *conversion,* a reversal of attitude toward the divine, drawing from what has been done new virtues, compensating merits, reasons for loving and surpassing more. Always, Blondel notes, along with the idea of a fall, there has been in philosophy and in the religious instinct a trace or a foreshadowing of a restitution and some unforeseen amelioration. He alludes to Plato and Spinoza and their sense of a need for restoration and liberation from the pull of phenomena in our experience. In Aristotle's idea of contemplation, as touching on an eternal order, and in Kant's theory of an atemporal freedom exerting itself once and for all, prior to all temporal occasions, and determining the total orientation of each individual destiny, he finds further indications recalling what our real destiny is to be in relation to our original vocation, amid personal chains and the wages of sin, from which we cannot free ourselves. These philosophical indications, however, remain deceiving and imperfect, enigmatic at best, unable to express distinctly the goal to be achieved, or to escape completely from the sense of being imprisoned or from the temptations of chimerical illusions. In all of this, humanity shows signs of being "stirred by an obsession about no longer being what it should be and stirred as well by a desperate effort to attain or to return to its liberation" (1944, 163).

But this is so only for the human order of things as a consequence of sin. In the divine order made known in the Christian spirit, there is a twofold higher responsibility to be considered. Violations of justice go against not only our duties to ourselves and to all other beings in the world, but against the very Author of nature and of the laws that govern the universal order of things. On a higher spiritual level, there is also the proffered supernatural vocation that we cannot escape from without sinning against ourselves as well as against God. What this higher responsibility adds to the evil that we commit in abusing our free will is a dimension "that cannot be expiated, repaired, or pardoned by a simple admission of guilt, a remorse, a change in attitude, or an ever-insufficient compensation for a past deed, a past henceforth sealed in what can no longer not have been" (1944, 164). There is no easy way to escape from the justice due for an evil recognized as *irreparable in its eternal gravity*. Blondel intends to show, in the light of the mystery of Redemption, that, as onerous as the reparation was bound to be, "infinite charity and omnipotence did not shrink back from remedying the evil, but did not triumph without paying a divine price for this victory" (1944, 164). This will be understood as following from two necessary truths already adumbrated: the impossibility of humanly repairing or absolving the past, and the indelible need to satisfy the exigencies of a justice surpassing any excuse or any partial transaction. Blondel is once again defining an impasse for a humanity that cannot undo its past or make its way out of the bind it has placed itself in, not even to find a ray of hope.

He is conscious of the ambiguities and the uncertainties of the ancient prophetic announcements concerning the Messiah or the Lamb of God, who was to be the savior of his fellow human beings, and of the need to understand the literal sense of the language in which this coming of the Son of God was foretold, along with "the inconceivable rigor of the reparation he was to accomplish" (1944, 164), in that it was necessary that the Son of God should die, so that humanity could be revived to the eternal order of grace, and so that the original intention of a supernatural destiny could once again be brought to perfection. The stakes in this drama of the Son were higher than anything we can imagine or understand on our own. Blondel is careful to lay out the language in which they were expressed as precisely as possible.

Expiation suggests the idea of impiety, a sacrilegious offense, a debt to be paid in justice to erase a crime against God for refusing the advances of a supreme divine love. More than just some vague convalescence, this situation of humanity entailed a salutary fear before the ineluctable demands of absolute justice that could not be met by any imperfect compensation. *Reparation* adds to the idea of expiation by indicating that compensation is not just a matter of replacing or partially remaking an old structure that has deteriorated, but more positively, a matter of renovating it radically so that it can satisfy new needs and serve higher interests resulting from the very defects of past experiences. In other words, fallen and wounded humanity had to be repaired and raised to a situation higher than its original primitive state, or the state of pure fallenness and pure expectation, though not without some sense of repentance and moral suffering of its conscience.

Satisfaction is another term in soteriological language that must be understood carefully, especially in its original sense of a "vicarious satisfaction." What it recalls is that, for purposes of expiation and reparation, the ones who alone are truly culpable are powerless unless they find another "who can answer, a voluntary victim, a merit equal to the offense and to the offended ... the incarnate Mediator who is alone up to obtaining the salvation of those for whom he offers himself in holocaust and who are at once his tormentors and his saved; for he takes their place and undergoes the punishment whose ignominy and total cruelty they could not have borne usefully" (1944, 169). This is much more than a matter of *quid pro quo* in a simple exchange of one scapegoat for another. It is a matter of getting something done that a fallen humanity could not have done by itself. Similarly, the term *redemption*, which is the one most commonly used to express the historical mystery we are trying to penetrate, needs careful articulation. Indeed the history of this dogma shows that it was not completely understood from the beginning of its promulgation, especially as it relates to what was lost in the supernatural order and had to be gotten back as if by ransom.

At first the metaphor of buying back was seen as a kind of deal to liberate from captivity the human beings held in bondage by evil spirits, the enemies of God and of his anointed one, as if the entire Passion were in payment of a ransom through the suffering due on the culpable slaves demanded by the usurper of this world before he would let go of his prey. The allegory was later thought to be too simplistic and in need of being transposed into a more spiritual understanding of the redemptive drama as suggested by the idea of "vicarious satisfaction," as previously explained in terms of the more spiritual aspects of the New Alliance in the making. The Redemption was not merely a settling of accounts for a reimbursable debt; it was "the instauration, at once renovating and enriching, of a new divine intervention that went far beyond what was offered or acquired, as if to manifest the inexhaustible character of the divine mercies and generosities" (1944, 171). If the perfidious angel remained part of the drama as the one who has ensnared and duped the human race into the throes of hell itself, it was to show that these captives had to be liberated. "That is why," Blondel adds, "the Christ took the form of a slave, waged war through his hidden humility, by the Gospel of gentleness against his enemy who seemed assured of a definitive domination over the world of all sinners" (1944, 171-72).

There was no deal, with any particular spirit in the event, good or bad, as if the Redeemer were paying back debts accrued by a captive humanity. The incarnate Word was submitting to a corporal death, to a letting go of all the vicious causes of the fall and of the loss of eternal life that still afflicted man, and passing on to an exemplary practice of human and divine virtues formulated in the Sermon on the Mount. For Blondel, the mystery of the Passion of Jesus Christ has to be read, not as an isolated fact at the end of his life on earth, but in the light of the entire Gospel and its call to a supernatural life of virtue, both human and divine. It was a culmination, and not just an end in a whimper, as some have made it out to be, and as some of the disciples thought it to be for a time. That is why the Passion and Death of Christ was also called a *consummation,* which for Blondel expresses better than any other term the plenitude of the testament and the supreme holocaust of the dying Christ, the *consummation* of a new Alliance that would have no end. For, in this idea of *consummation,* he found the integrative principle for unifying the various sensible metaphors encompassed in this mystery into its spiritual meaning and its supernatural efficiency.

What Blondel has to integrate in his philosophical appreciation of the mystery of Redemption through the Passion of Jesus Christ are two sets of propositions, two truths, that are simultaneously formulated and clearly insisted upon concerning this historical event, but that seem exclusive of one another. The first has to do with divine justice, in that Christ is condemned to a most cruel and ignominious death on the Cross, out of submission to a divine law, in order to repair a sacrilegious offense to God. This is the requirement that draws from Jesus a sweat of blood and a supplication that he be spared this chalice, which seems to go unheard — the requirement that makes him the Man of Sorrows or the Son of Man representing a weak and sinful humanity to be immolated according to an inexorable logic of both the natural and the supernatural order. The other truth, to be reconciled with this one, is the one of divine mercy, namely, that this same agonizing Christ was not only obeying his Father, but at the same offering himself in the fullness of his own will to love and to sacrifice himself for the good of mankind. It is to undergo this cruel expiatory suffering that he came into the world, the hour of darkness he longed for, in order to make known his compassionate mercy and bring new light and salvation to his fellow human beings.

This is the paradox that lies at the heart of the drama of the passion and death of Jesus Christ and that must be seen as unfolding in this tragic historical event of both human and divine proportions. The two antithetic aspects of the mystery must be closely intertwined to make sense of the seeming harshness of the divine exigencies on the one hand, and to appreciate the salutary effect of a Christ who is sacrificed at the same time as glorified, on the other. Taken together they shed light on one another in the mystery of Redemption, but taken in isolation from one another they yield only contradictions that reason or conscience cannot accept. To bring out the only synthesis that would satisfy the exigencies of reason and human conscience before this immense divine paradox, Blondel analyses different hypotheses on ways of representing what is supposed to have happened in this momentous event that do not take both sides of it at once into account.

For example, what if we think of this passion and death as nothing more than a severe punishment exacted of his own son by a god seeking compensation for the offense and the disobedience of its creatures against his law and its majesty? Would that not be like measuring the fault to be remedied and the punishment to be required only according to the grandeur of the one offended, without taking into consideration the weakness or the lack of consciousness of a child who does not know clearly all that is at stake in its disobedience? Blondel recognizes a certain righteous indignation on the part of moralists and of common sense at the representation of such a punishment for an act that was only semi-conscious, but he does not see this indignation as completely justified, because it seems to trivialize the seriousness of the moral life and to be inconsistent with the sense of a human dignity that is supposed to rise above the foibles of passion and is called to a higher life. Whatever excuses we may make for our betrayals to this higher calling, and whatever we may do as a consequence, we cannot set aside our infinite spiritual aspirations or escape our divine calling.

We could also suppose that Christ, the Mediator, in making reparation for the offense against God, was only obeying this exigency of justice passively, merely undergoing death as the necessary expression of "the deicide included in the rebellion of man against his supernatural vocation and against the offer of a divine adoption, too heavy to bear for his pride" (1944, 176). Then we could only shudder at the harshness of this execution of a sentence so inexorably just from the Father toward the Son, without recognizing the divine pity for man in the Son's self-inflicted distress, which is what motivated both the condescendence of the incarnate Word and the order of suffering from his heavenly Father to begin with. To leave out this element of pity for man, this concern for remedying his sinful condition, in the mystery of Redemption, is to turn it into nothing more than a barbaric satisfaction for a Moloch only seeking revenge, from which nothing good could come for mankind. In fact, if this element of mercy is left out of the Mystery, the expiation required by the Almighty would only have made matters worse, adding to the culpability of mankind the worst crime of all in a way that even the sovereign Judge would have found unacceptable. The idea of a purely vindictive God without mercy is no more acceptable to what is best in human conscientiousness than that of a paternalistic God who would let himself be ridiculed or mocked when he makes an offer of adoption into a higher life. What we look for in good conscience, according to Blondel, is, obscurely perhaps but still indubitably, "an exact justice that would still be a consequence of [God's] mercy, that would be an occasion of making more manifest a paternal love" (1944, 177).

Such is the mystery revealed in the Gospel when we are told that God so loved the world and "so exalted humanity that he gave it his only Son, as if he preferred the salvation of men to the tenderness he felt for this beloved Son" (1944, 177). If the Father does so, it is because the Son has no less compassion for the guilty and consents as well to undergo the suffering required by the realism of a strict equity, not just with acquiescent resignation but with an impatient generosity capable of touching even the most hardened hearts through this redemptive Passion. In the harshness of the sacrifice exacted by justice and in the spiritual immolation of the Son's personal will that draws blood from him in the garden, even before the cruel assault of the executioners, Blondel suggests, one could think of one more reason for the Father to love a Son so willing to express his generosity toward creatures he wished to be able to adopt anew, and one more reason for the Son to love a Father so willing to pardon at whatever price by reopening access to the heavenly joys for those excluded from it, "without the possibility of recovering them except through the sacrifice *consummated* on Calvary" (1944, 178).

In his concern to bring out the internal and transcendent realities that are witnessed to in the facts and in the words of the dying Christ, Blondel delves deeper into the mystery where the paradox of the very Son of God abandoned by his Father appears most acutely as the ultimate suffering of the God-man. We are told in Christian dogma that Christ was never without the beatitude of the Trinitarian life, of which he remained a part in his divinity. Yet, at a decisive moment on the cross he had the feeling of having been abandoned by his Father: "My God, my God, why have you abandoned me?" This sense of abandonment and dereliction was for Blondel one of the terms that marked the mystery of our Redemption most profoundly. What reality was hidden in this internal suffering, more radical than every other, the only one that was absolute and total and that we have yet to comprehend? Was it not the suffering of *damnation* itself that the Mediator had to experience by becoming personally conscious of the extreme states into which sinful creatures fall as a result of rejecting God, or of trying to be God without God, so that nothing of man would remain outside of him and unexperienced by him? Having made himself sin in the place of all sinners, "Did the implacable logic of the divine realism require that Jesus should experience profoundly and really this nameless horror that is the hatred of God and the desire to destroy his kingdom?" (1944, 181). Or is that the wrong way of conceiving in what this ultimate suffering of Christ consisted?

According to Blondel's way of understanding this ultimate dimension of the Redeemer's suffering, there was no question of God hating the sinner, nor even of the sinner hating God, once the sinner becomes conscious of his own irrationality in the light of eternal justice and his inexcusable ingratitude to the One who should have meant everything good to him. It is against himself that the culpable one turns with the feeling of a worm that eats away at him from the inside, a fire that consumes him, without his having to blame anything on the one who is, from the beginning, pure love. What Jesus felt in that moment of being abandoned was not being a sinner himself, but the weight of all the sins of the world with all its monstrous ugliness to be offered up before God. This is what grieved him so that he felt overwhelmed and cut off from his Father. This was the ultimate torture, the most humiliating suffering he had to offer God as the loving Savior of a wretched humanity. For, as Blondel concludes, "that is where was *consummated* most completely the quite spiritual holocaust that the divine horror of sin required" (1944, 181).

Blondel thus insists on the sacrificial aspect of the mystery of Redemption as the moment in which it was *consummated*. To take the measure of it, he takes himself back to the deliberation of the Trinitarian council spoken of in the book of *Genesis* leading up to the creation of humanity, as he has done from the beginning in contemplating this entire mystery of supernaturalization. By reason of the divine prescience of what would happen with man's refusal of the first call to the divine life, it followed that the Christ would accept his role as crucified and would consent, not just out of obedience, but more importantly out of love, to undergo the worst bodily and spiritual suffering that his humanity could experience. This was in keeping with an image suggested in the Scriptures of "the lamb immolated from the origin of the world." This meant for Blondel that the sufferings of Calvary had to be taken as "a reality to be called permanent and eternal, even as the title to glory as well as the justification of the reign of Christ conquering his royalty through this sacrificial love in order to procure an ineffable glory to the Father . . . and meriting by his heroic Passion his body of which he is the head in all its members" (1944, 182). All this was consummated on Good Friday, though what was to come from it for the world, for humankind in history, and for those who would believe in his accomplishment for themselves, still remained to be seen in the mysteries that were to follow, beginning with the mystery of the Resurrection.

To highlight the spiritual character of this complex mystery of Redemption, Blondel contrasts it with an opposite view, one that sees in it only a divine vengeance and an accumulation of crimes by executioners unaware of what they were doing. When Christ prayed for his executioners he was not praying just for those inflicting physical torture on him, but for all sinners who, in doing evil and remaining hardened in their impenitence, add to his corporal suffering the deeper suffering of the soul, that of a love unrequited and obstinately rejected. The realism Blondel points to in the Passion and Death of Jesus Christ is a sign for him of how God takes us seriously in our dignity as human beings and in our sinfulness as these relate to the end he has in mind for us. What he calls us to is not just some mediocre good that we might tentatively enjoy by ourselves, but an elevation into the intimacy of the divine life itself. The necessary condition for meeting such a call on our part, however, entails a test that our reason and our freedom cannot but see as legitimate, indispensable, and beneficial. Given our need for infinitude, we cannot be satisfied with any banal human happiness. We have to be dilated to the point of suffering our own Good Friday, of crying not to be abandoned, in order to become open to the amplitude of the divine gifts and joy. In becoming man, the Son of God was not just emptying himself of his divinity to become a mere man according to our natural capacities. Rather he was coming to raise us to the measure of his own divine life by adding to our ambitions as spiritual beings an infinite extension. Having become man, he too had to go through his own Good Friday, which was to become the model for all those who would come after him and follow him in this fearsome broadening of our natural capacities and in a passive purification that would give way to a transforming union with God himself.

For a true redemption of mankind it was not enough to have a sacrifice adequate to the offense against God in sin, since it was by sinful man himself that the Passion would be inflicted on the One taking upon himself all the faults to be repaired, including the one of deicide. For the ultimate crime contained and culminating in this suffering of the Just One par excellence to be wiped clean of humanity, it was necessary that what was being endured and consummated through rigorous obedience also be accepted freely and pardoned by the one suffering himself. In other words, all this flow of blood and evil had to be absorbed in what Blondel calls a meritorious charity, for only thus does the Victim of the sacrifice become the Savior of humanity. Such is "the astounding and magnificent generous logic" (1944, 184) of the mystery of Redemption. In it two extremes, one of rigor and another of tenderness, come together, without commanding one another as if by dialectical necessity, but still complementing one another as a consonance of both severe exigency and condescending gentleness. Taking these two extremes together in the mystery of Redemption, we can understand how this passion and death, now the inexhaustible source of purification and of all grace, is the accomplishment of the Mediator's redemptive work of supernatural revivification in accordance with Christ's final words on the cross: *consummatum est,* before commending his spirit into the hands of his Father. What comes after that is history, but a new kind of history in which the struggles and the suffering of humanity can become meritorious of a supernatural life, something that philosophy itself cannot fully fathom.

The New Mystery of History as an Immediate Consequence of the Redemption

In conclusion of his consideration of the Christian Spirit coming into the world, *Blondel turns to what he sees as the immediate historical consequences of the consummation* of this mystery in the Passion and Death of the Mediator. What results from this Redemption is a new stage in world history, for mankind, that reason alone could not have anticipated. What Blondel now sees opening up before the human race as a result of this labor of love consummated on Calvary is a new historical state where consciences are stirred by needs, by temptations, and by graces stemming from this historically momentous justification, obtained for all, and offered to all, although not all have had or will have had an equal consciousness of it. All that Blondel can say concerning this new state of challenge for humanity is that no more will be demanded of anyone than he has received or than he has been able to do with the grace actually given, however secretly it may be given. What remains to be analyzed by the philosopher is the condition of this redeemed humanity as a whole, where, according to the logic of the divine plan, this state following on the Redemption differs from all three states already encountered in the light of Revelation, that of original innocence already endowed with a supernatural gift, that of fallenness after the rebellion, and that of the promise renewed through the calling of Abraham and developed through the history of a people that had to struggle, not always successfully, to understand "the coming of the true universalism of a 'catholic' religion effectively realizing all the promises of salvation and supernaturalization" (1944, 186).

Focused as he was on the supernatural gift at stake in the providential ordering of history, Blondel does not lose sight of the world-historical role the children of Abraham had been chosen to play in this drama, notwithstanding what he calls the "narrow-mindedness and the false ambition of a universal domination" (1944, 186) shown at times by this chosen people. What comes into view in the end, however, is a whole new way of characterizing the spiritual situation of a redeemed humanity, one still connected with the divine plan of supernaturally divinizing a humanity, once lost, but now redeemed through the sacrifice of Christ the Mediator consummated on the Cross. Before going on to analyze the conditions of a humanity now to be considered redeemed as a whole, in the second volume of this philosophical reflection on the Christian Spirit, Blondel pauses to consider the immediate consequences of the new spiritual situation that now results for humanity from the divine plan, said to have been *consummated* on the Cross. In this new phase of the human drama, everyone is still marked with the stigma of original sin, even prior to any personal sin, but everyone is also called in one way or another to benefit from the merits of Christ, whether it be by the grace of *sacramental baptism*, or by that of what

Blondel calls a *baptism of desire*, for one who leads an upright life upon reaching the age of reason, or even a *baptism of blood*, in the performance of a heroic act for the good of others, or by other graces that God secretly dispenses in hearts amid the infinite variety of historical circumstances in which human beings find themselves.

Without the Revelation we would not know with any certitude or precision of the real state in which we find ourselves as a result of original sin. But neither would we know clearly the extreme issues that are at stake in the alternative that still presents itself to any rational being in this life, whether to surrender ourselves to God through the trials of this mortal life or to place ourselves ahead of God and turn in on ourselves through carnal enjoyment and proud satisfaction over a civilization of material achievements. It is still in time and through choices of a free conscience that we come to what will be either an eternal happiness or an irreversible privation. It is in the context of this new historical state that Blondel comes to what is for him a more precise and definitive meaning of what he has already begun to speak of as the *transnatural* state of humanity. What he has in mind about this state is something quite compatible with the rectitude of a moral consciousness and a good will capable of responding to the secret and indiscernible touches of a grace that infiltrates all the activities of the human being.

Blondel now characterizes this *transnatural* state as morally and religiously more delicate and more difficult to maintain in proper equilibrium than ever. On the one hand there is given a profusion of prevenient and supportive graces flowing from the Passion, but on the other hand, for anyone to benefit from them, he or she must accept the divine advance and commit to the duties that result from this acceptance. The Savior has placed at the disposition of everyone an ocean in which to purify and feed oneself. But each one still has to consent to taking certain steps to become faithful and participate in this life of grace, and this not by some power drawn from ourselves alone, but rather by a docile receptivity to what is given by Christ, without presumption and without self-sufficiency. Nothing can be truly salutary for the human being without this attitude, at least implicit in the manner of our action, the attitude that raises us to a spiritual truth, for, in this order, we are always only cooperators with the divine.

Moreover, through this attitude, when there are sufferings or faults to be expiated, or hopes to sustain and hopes to develop within ourselves or in those around us, it is in union with Christ, who suffered because of us and for us, hoped for us and even within us, that our role, after his Passion, is amplified and, as it were, divinized, so that for ourselves and for others we have to become co-redeemers, and thereby fulfill, according to the word of St. Paul, those things that are lacking in the passion of Christ. The reference to others as well as to oneself in fulfilling this co-redemptive role humans are called to is an allusion to the communion of saints, to be elaborated on more fully later on. But here Blondel mentions it only as a characteristic of the new life that is understood to be flowing immediately from the *consummatum est*, as a sort of mutual intercession for the exchange and the growth of merits and expiations among souls.

From this central mystery of Redemption through Christ will follow, not just a spiritual community of mutual co-redeemers with Christ, but also a whole ensemble of institutions and providential supports, sacraments, whose coherence and inexhaustible richness the second volume on the Christian Spirit will delve into. Blondel recognizes that there is something surprising in ending this first volume on the mystery of Redemption, without going into the mysteries of the Resurrection, the Ascension, Pentecost, and the Church, all of which seem to complete what he calls "the series of truths indispensable for the solidity of Christian foundations" (1944, 193). While these are essential to the mystery of the Christian life as such, however, they present a different character from those that end at the mystery of Redemption, which Blondel still understands as the final moment in the *realization* of a plan of supernaturalization conceived at creation itself. All the mysteries that come to a term in the Redemption represent "an absolute necessity for establishing the Christian order and for reopening the flow of grace indispensable for the supernatural order" (1944, 194).

The mysteries that come after follow from these as proof, application, and diffusion of this surge of life and of preparation for eternal life. "While the first are intrinsically constitutive while hiding rather than revealing the internal depth of the supernatural vocation, the second make manifest by their dazzling splendor what might otherwise have remained more or less hidden, without thereby suppressing the supernaturalization" (1944, 194). From the standpoint of God, so to speak, what is most at issue is concentrated in the passion — a Passion that in its depth lasts as an agony until the end of time. From the standpoint of the human being, the drama rises to a higher level of tension and becomes more and more tragic by reason of the state resulting for us from the Passion, which brings us deeper and deeper into the combat and the extreme conflict of the spiritual struggle.

To be sure, Blondel argues, the series of the glorious mysteries that are interconnected and serve as proof in the propagation of the supernatural are *morally* necessary for the establishment of Christianity in the world. But, *ontologically*, so to speak, "the efficacy and the sufficient proof of a way to salvation reopened for fallen humanity are a reality achieved on the cross and by the last word and the final sigh of the Christ" (1944, 196). Blondel cites the words of Jesus to the "good thief" as an indication of this radical ontology of the deed *consummated* on the cross: "Today you shall be with me in paradise." To one who has reflected on the entire mystery of redemptive supernaturalization, this could only mean an immediate application of the merit realized in the Passion itself to one suffering with Christ and transformed into a just man by the spectacle, and by a certain comprehension of the mystery of innocence and of love emanating from one so divine in his suffering. For Blondel the death on the cross is a "total reality," whereas the mysteries of Resurrection and Ascension, for all their value as theophany, are not the exhaustive truth or the full expression of divinity, either in its incarnation or in the future vision reserved for the elect. As necessary as such signs may be, these facts are still only signs or demonstrative evidences of the exact and total reality they express. The same could be said of the mystery of Pentecost, which represents the birth of the Church, itself another mystery. The manifestation of the Holy Spirit and of the superhuman effectiveness of such an outpouring is tied to a reality that remains invisible, more than to the paradoxical fact of miraculous tongues as if of fire and a no-less-miraculous speaking and being heard in various tongues, the reality of which is a secret grace of conversion to a new spirit.

Thus the first volume on *Philosophy and the Christian Spirit*, as announced from the beginning, has considered the part of God in planning and realizing the supernaturalization of man, including the perpetuity of grace amid the vicissitudes of human waywardness. Blondel speaks of a plastic tenacity in the realization of this plan culminating in the redemptive sacrifice of Christ. What remains to be done in volume two is an exploration of man's cooperation in the *theandric* action that maintains the presence of the Christian life in the world and of all the resources man has at his disposal, at once divine as well as human, for the maintenance and the propagation of this life. In conclusion of this first volume, Blondel begins to anticipate on the difficulty human beings find in responding to solicitations and to resources offered by the divine initiative to the creature, for one does not enter into such a supernatural life, or become pregnant of the Creator within oneself, without labor and without dying to self and to the pride of egoism.

The difficulty comes from the creature most desirous of infinity having to accept the infinite as it is. Without such acceptance there is no access to an order that is not only supernatural but also superhuman. It is not Christianity that shrinks from transcending merely historical man, but those who resist or are hostile to it, those who would transcend without letting the divine, or the supernatural incommensurate to our humanity, insinuate itself into themselves. As a philosopher Blondel is well aware of the many objections that motivate incomprehension and failure to appreciate the gift of elevation for human beings that the Christian Spirit represents, especially of those who belittle the humble methods and practices required by Christianity for inserting into our present life the resources for a higher life. His aim is to explain and to justify these methods and practices as conducive to a higher life, because, though they are of divine origin, they require the free cooperation of human beings to have their efficacity in persons and in societies.

This is the other side of his speculative task, concerning now, not just how man's call to the supernatural life of the triune God is to be conceived in relation to creation as a whole, but also how such a life is realized as a religion in the world through an effective consent on the part of believers to authentically religious practices dictated by the Founder of the Christian Church. It is through communion in an effective practice of precepts and sacraments that the unity of doctrine is maintained historically in what Blondel calls *tradition*. It is also through such fidelity and devotion to the laws of Christ that Christ lives on in the soul of the faithful and in the community of a truly sacred union. Hence there is a necessity for Blondel to prolong his investigations into the practical order itself where the mystery of the supernatural takes many different shapes. It follows from the paradox that the institution of Christian religion, as divinely ideal and as supernatural as it may be, is at the same time something positive in history, both incarnating and fulfilling the promises of eternal life.

In the original dissertation on *Action*, Blondel had only sketched a necessity of religious practice generally, or anonymously, so to speak. Here, however, he proposes to go into the organic detail of this life on earth which is at once moral, social, and Christian, where "philosophy keeps its need for elucidation in all things and its duty to cooperate, always keeping in mind the speculative conclusions brought together and harmonized in this first volume" (1944, 202). This will entail going into three things: another sequence of mysteries that have served to illuminate and to reinforce the intelligent assent to the essential and constitutive mysteries already spoken of in relation to God's work of supernaturalization; then, the ensemble of supports established by Christ and proposed by the Church in order to maintain a living faith in practice and to perpetuate the real presence of Christ in a life of grace overcoming all resistances, difficulties, even faults due to weakness or infidelity; finally, the recurrent objections to this life due to misunderstanding, hostility, or betrayals that distort the true face of Christianity. What he will show is that many of the objections to the Christian Spirit proceed from a false way of raising the Christian problem in the effort of bringing philosophy and Christianity in closer collaboration with one another for their mutual improvement. What Blondel is aiming at is for philosophy to learn from the Christian experience and for Christian thought and life itself to adjust better to the "living suggestions of the Spirit of truth and charity through the very striving of a civilization ever more faithful to the twofold interior norm of Christianity, learned reason and permanent inspiration" (1944, 208). This is the same irenic goal of mutual enrichment between Christianity and philosophy he had set for himself in the third part of his discourse on method of 1896, except that now it was to be more explicitly in terms of the Christian mysteries.

XVII

Symbiosis of the Human and the Divine in History

It would be difficult to exaggerate the universal sweep of Blondel's thought as he thinks of the relation between philosophy and the Christian Spirit. What he has in mind always is philosophy as a whole and the Christian Spirit as a whole, both operative in the world as a whole, and in the historical drama of humankind struggling to achieve an end worthy of its profound spiritual aspirations.

In volume one of *Philosophy and the Christian Spirit,* starting from the initiatives and enigmas of philosophy that find in the Christian mysteries some light and some encouragement, he had swept all the way back to the beginning, and even to the Trinitarian life of the Godhead, through what he calls a logical reasoning, *un enchainement logique* (1946, vi), leading him from philosophical enigma to enigma in the spiritual life of man to engage the various mysteries of the Christian Spirit, from the creation of the world, through the fall of man, all the way to the consummation of the divine plan of Mediation and Redemption in the Passion and Death of the God-Man. This was for him the logical way of connecting facts and ideas in what we know of the history of humanity in its spiritual ascent. It was a kind of demonstration of how the Christian spirit is to be understood as coming into the world in order to revivify the human spirit toward new heights.

Starting from this demonstration, he proposes to follow all that it leads to as a *norm* for evaluating all our duties and all our responsibilities in a human action now seen in a new light. The question is now to study the *symbiosis* where the natural and the supernatural calling of man come together in a theandric action, where a more complex and a more vital principle comes into play for man in history than was suspected by any ancient conception, when man was still viewed as subject to occult powers in the universe. Through modern science, man has mastered over many of these powers. He has liberated himself from what was fated for him in them by progressively overcoming the determinism they entailed for him. But he has not freed himself from another problem, ignored by the ancients, that an integral philosophy of action still places before us, as we master nature in relation to a destiny that remains imperious for us.

Blondel alludes to a number of philosophical attitudes prevalent at the time of his writing shortly after World War II as having misunderstood this problem, or twisted it around and mutilated it: a decapitated positivism, an atheist humanism, a wish for cosmic suicide, a philosophy of anguish or of the absurd, an existentialism, and an activism, all of which were the sequel of "the most audacious speculative ardor" (1946, vii). None of them, however, had come to any kind of norm or principle for solving a problem he had raised for modern man many years earlier, in his dissertation on Action, and that he thought he could now work on in joining philosophy and the Christian Spirit. Detached from their origins and their final end, Christian ideas may appear wild, preposterous, or even criminal. It is not for philosophy to take over these ideas, and then to drop them after using them, much less to suppress them in order to raise man above nature by claiming to surpass it. Nor is it for philosophy to misconstrue, as we liberate ourselves from certain material servitudes, either the source or the ocean from which we draw and toward which we are aiming "the true course of a life, destined for that total liberation that Spinoza called a union with the infinite and the eternal" (1946, vii-viii).

Even while seeming to be turning away from religion, Spinoza was still raising what was for Blondel the religious problem par excellence, the best answer to which Blondel found in the Christian religion, if one was willing to push reason to its most learned, its most speculative, and its most active extreme in "an ever-progressive synthesis toward what Christian language calls the consummation of time and of eternal life" (1944, viii). This is the way Blondel conceives his undertaking as a philosopher in this second volume on the Christian Spirit. He will draw not only from the advances of human civilization in its progression toward ever-greater sufficiency and freedom, but also from the light and the viaticum that has been introduced into the historical subconscious of this civilized humanity by the Christian religious tradition, as an accompaniment in the journey toward our final end. Even if philosophical reflection has no direct access to these supernatural gifts proffered to an ailing and struggling humanity, we cannot say that there can be no knowledge of them. Moreover, if in the end of it all, "human freedom cannot renounce its right to choose, its duty to act, its requirement to contribute to its victory, our reason and our will will have to extend their critical examination and their own concurrence into these indications and resources that our integral spiritual tradition offers" (1946, ix). Christianity, as it presents itself in history, cannot but become manifest to what concerns the human spirit at its core.

The exposition Blondel wants to give of this human activity is not an apology in favor of the Christian Spirit. Nor is it a theology. It is no more than a succinct résumé, as faithful as possible, of an authentic teaching that anyone has to be aware of and even understand in some sense, before it can be contradicted or honestly appreciated for what it has to say, what bearing it has on human life, or what justification it has to offer for itself. Blondel's aim is not to make a complete exposé of the Christian teaching about life in the world. All he wants to do is say enough to deflect false critiques of this spirit and to persuade certain minds to reverse their cavalier attitude toward what Christianity has brought to civilization, so that this spirit can continue to influence public life and the moral education of peoples. Having set forth as much as he could of God's initiative in the providential plan for creation in volume one, his aim now is to elaborate on how the divine motions and human efforts join together in an active symbiosis when these efforts are docile and truly faithful to the conjoined callings of reason and grace. *Symbiosis* is the watchword for this further elaboration on actual Christian life in the world, where man has his role to play in working toward his destiny and in the achievement of his supernatural vocation. At issue are not proofs for matters of faith, but a discernment "of the data and certitude that good faith can humanly gather as it confronts conclusions already endowed with historical and rational guaranties" (1946, xi).

The endeavor will be divided into three parts. The first will consider the glorious mysteries that mark the departure of the vanquishing Mediator Redeemer from this world after the consummation of his mission on earth, those of the Resurrection, the Ascension, and Pentecost. These mysteries are to be taken as proven and probative, but more precisely as *probant* or conclusive, without any sort of vicious circle, by bringing together material facts and a spiritual intelligence adhering to a truth interiorly justified. The second part will hearken to the impressive and discrete voice of Tradition, in the strongest religious sense of this word, as it designates the progressive perennity of an ever-fruitful truth and vitality under the guidance of the Holy Spirit and with the oversight of a Magisterium. Then, in part three, will come an unfurling of the aids and supports offered in the Christian revelation for the wayfarer wishing to know where he is going and what means he can use to get there. This will include not only the organism of the seven sacraments, beginning with baptism and culminating in the Eucharist, but also the preaching of the Beatitudes as a program for uniting immanence and transcendence in this life, prior to a final consideration of the Last Things as they are usually spoken of in the Christian Tradition, such as the "communion of the saints, " the "remission of sins," death and personal immortality, the resurrection of the body and, in a more philosophical vein, the twofold aporiai of time and space on the one hand, and of duration and extension on the other, and last but not least the idea of final sanctions in "eternal life," which has been a matter of preoccupation for him since the beginning of his career as a philosopher.

The Supernatural Life as Made Manifest in the Glorious Mysteries

It is surprising that Blondel chose to speak about the glorious mysteries in a volume separate from the one in which he ended with the mystery of the God-Man's passion and death as the consummation of his redemptive labor and suffering. Christian tradition had always hearkened to these soteriological mysteries in tandem with one another, going back not only to the Fathers of the Church but even to the very first tellings of the evangelical stories, which focused originally on the Passion, Death, and Resurrection of the Lord, as the essential message of salvation for the human race. Recent theological writing, dating back to the time when Blondel was making his own philosophical presentation of these mysteries, has insisted on the redemptive value of the Resurrection, a value that Blondel seemed to reserve for the Passion and Death that the Redeemer had steadfastly looked forward to in his life, somewhat in keeping with earlier theological insistence on satisfaction for sin, punishment, and reparation. But Blondel has a reason for making this break in his depiction of soteriological action that did not in any way contradict the earlier tradition of keeping all these mysteries as part of one and the same action. What he looked for in these Glorious Mysteries was a way of satisfying the need for a higher revelation of the supernatural mystery for disciples who still had not gotten the full force of the instauration of a new life inaugurated by the redemptive sacrifice of the God-Man.

Blondel refers to the dismal state in which the followers of Jesus found themselves after the events of Good Friday. They had believed in him and followed him, even in the triumphant entry into Jerusalem on the previous Sunday. They were the ones who were to carry on the work of the Savior in the world, become witnesses of it, *martyres,* and yet they thought all had been lost. They had hoped, but now were at a loss about what to do with this hope. They had believed in what the prophets had said about the one who was to come, even that he was to suffer and die for his people, but they still could not grasp the spiritual force of what had been wrought. The idea of an immediate resurrection, as something discrete in time, had not entered into their minds, let alone made itself explicit in their conviction. All this had to be brought home to them anew in a convincing way, and that is precisely what had to be done by the Resurrection, the Ascension, and Pentecost as the parting events of the divine Word's passing on earth. That is why they deserve special attention as mysteries in themselves, even apart from their soteriological connection with the Passion and Death of the Savior.

Blondel is as much a realist about the *Resurrection* as he was about the suffering and death of Jesus. The same Jesus who died and was buried rose from the dead. This was a sensible fact of which the first followers of Jesus became very much aware, much to their astonishment in their incredulity. More importantly, however, this second fact of the risen Christ opened their eyes and their minds to a dimension of spirit that they might have suspected before in their Teacher, but that they had not appreciated fully for all that it entailed. It is in this sense that Blondel speaks of these three Glorious Mysteries of Resurrection, Ascension, and Pentecost as "a teaching, a proof, a fecundity" (1946, 3). Regardless of how one might try to conceive the mechanics, the chemistry, or the psychology of this event of resurrection, which Blondel showed no interest in doing, enigmatic as it was bound to be, what was important about it is the *new life* that it not only displayed, for the disciples to see, but also infused into these disciples, which would enable them to give witness of it, and even to remit sins for which satisfaction had been given. It is this spiritual sense and its supernatural reality that is made manifest in the Glorious Mysteries that come after the passion and death of Jesus, more than in any other mystery of his earlier life and preaching. In them the supernatural aspect of the gift being placed in the balance for the human spirit is to be seen better than ever before and is to become the principle of spiritual revivification of the community still gathered around Jesus, the community to whom Jesus had promised to send his Spirit, so that they could enter more deeply into all that he had taught them, the community that did in effect receive that Spirit at Pentecost, ten days after the Ascension, before setting out to give witness and to conquer the world for the Lord who had died and was risen for its glorification.

As conclusive as the truths made manifest in these mysteries may be, it is not unexpected that there are still some shadows surrounding them, for ourselves as well as for those who first experienced them, as we see in the story of the doubting Thomas. This is what leaves us in an attitude of faith in their regard, rather than simple vision, as all the saved would have in the end, or as Thomas thought he already had in touching the fleshly wounds of Jesus. But the spiritual faith of identifying with Jesus in these mysteries as "my Lord and my God," in the words of Thomas, who was the first to put this faith in these words concerning Jesus, is not something separate from reason, for the certitudes of reason itself "help us to accommodate higher truths more rewarding for our aspirations toward an immortality and even a participation in eternal life" (1946, 5). Contemplation of the glorious mysteries opens before us the way of our pilgrimage toward a final fruition of our beatitude, ready to travel all the byways that this may entail and to make use of all the resources placed at our disposal for the attainment of an end now seen more clearly than ever as supernatural in the contemplation of these mysteries.

Blondel notes how the dawn of Resurrection came as something quite unexpected by the followers who still had much to learn from it. He notes also that Christ, in taking up his corporal life once again, now transfigured and liberated from all material subjections, did not present himself before the crowds or the public authorities, as if in order to vindicate himself and his divine mission.

The point was not to exploit a physical feat; nor was it to launch a political coup to get some servile adherence due to fear or human aspirations. It was rather to appeal "to a spirit of faith and love in order to grant access to the spiritual city of true messianism in spirit and in truth" (1946, 8). To be sure, this was to be done in a sensible experience that could be controlled and verified, but not by any sort of vulgar experimentation or touch, though such experimentation was in fact given to the doubting Thomas. What was necessary for the disciples was that, through the circumstances of this apparition of the risen Christ, there came about a transposition from the empirical and carnal order to the truths of the spiritual, and even the supernatural order. There was more than just a brute fact here, and to perceive that a certain moral and religious disposition was required to arrive at another kind of certitude than that which comes from merely physical verification. To appreciate something of the new, suprasensible state Christ had attained in his Resurrection there had to be something disconcerting about him, and all the more indicative of his supernature, which, in itself, remains really transcendent to all our present experiences. "The immediate data of the senses, the very certitudes of thought and of the heart are not enough to efficaciously take in the testimonies of remembrance, of reason, nor even the suggestions of grace; to all this a decisive synthesis must be added, without which the supernatural meaning of the provocative mystery does not lead to the act of faith" (1946, 9). This act does not fall short of reason or true conviction in the face of some puzzlement in experience. It transcends reason in a higher synthesis of certitude concerning a reality we cannot fully comprehend. Blondel wants to show how this takes place in relation to the mystery of the Resurrection, as we learn about it from the Gospel narrative.

While showing himself physically in the various episodes, Jesus also says: do not touch me, not as if to guard against a certain fragility in himself, but rather to prevent his disciples from trying to cling to him physically. Even as he shows himself, he also shows himself as coming and going without constraint from any physical barriers, *januis clausis,* as if to show that he is no longer bound by any terrestrial obstacles. What he wants to show from his former body more than anything else are the profound traces of his wounds from the nails that pierced his hands and feet and the spear that pierced his heart, as a reminder of what he went through before becoming the risen One, and what others will also have to go through in order to rise with him to a new life. Earlier he had promised his disciples that he would be with them until the end of time. Here in the Resurrection he was showing that this presence would take place in a real way without being visible or tangible, even under sensible and historical species, all this being part of his supernatural triumph over death and sin.

Easter thus marked the consummated advent of the Good News and the return to life for all men represented and assumed by Christ in this triumph over death and sin, a life not just of natural immortality, but "a recovery of the supernatural state, of sanctifying grace, of the divine life in our nature elevated anew and called once again to divine friendship and adoption" (1946, 12-13). As a realist about all this, Blondel argues against anyone who would be satisfied with a symbolic and mystical interpretation, not just of the teaching of Easter, but also of the facts in which this teaching took place, as if the Resurrection meant only an invisible diffusion of a vanquishing spirit into a regenerated world and into the bodies and souls of believers whose faith in this vanquisher awakens a naturally invincible force. There have been several philosophical versions of such an interpretation, but Blondel considers them as essentially reductionist with regard to the supernatural he takes to be real, as well as to the facts in which this reality has been made manifest. To accept this reductionist reading of the facts would be "to compromise, even to evacuate all the divine realism of the Mediator and the Savior, truly incarnate, suffering, glorified in his own flesh and arrived at what can be called his normal state, *in carne propria*" (1946, 13). The purely symbolic or natural view of resurrection, no matter how spiritual it may be, would betray the supernatural transcendence of the life Christ has come to restore for mankind, which is not what the person of faith would want.

Blondel argues against this sort of immanentism concerning the mystery of the Redemption, by showing how the interpretation of such facts depends on the convergence of certain testimonies analogous to any that establish the historicity of events and, on the other hand, "the arrangements, the requirements of a reason coherent with the whole ensemble of the truths constitutive of the entire Christian organism" (1946, 13-14). On the one hand, we do have the authenticated testimony of witnesses who were indeed slow to believe what they were seeing, one to the point of demanding to see and touch for himself. On the other hand, there is the need to approach this fact warily and spiritually, because its meaning cannot be understood except in function of the soulful questioning of the witnesses themselves. More than just the brute fact restricted to itself, what counts is the spiritual value it had for the witnesses, the substantial truth or the divine presence for which it is the vehicle and the content. The profession of faith Thomas expressed after touching the wounds of the risen Christ did not come from the touching as such, but from one searching for something he thought too good to be true. Touching only gave him, and many who would come to believe as he did later on, a reassurance he needed as a human being.

Blondel speaks of a reciprocal causality here between sense realities that are at once *proofs* of a fundamentally rational credibility, and *proven*, or tested, in turn by the religious efficacy of the mystery clad in flesh that leaves its role essential for the internal striving of the faithful soul to the stirrings of charity and grace. There are two movements here and the efficacy of a mutual certitude. What confirms the need for both is that, in the many apparitions of the risen Christ, some who had seen and known him before his death, and who even ate with him after the resurrection, did not believe in him, a sign, according to Blondel, that they did not have in their soul the desire for the Good News and for the coming of the spiritual kingdom of God. Even the story of the empty tomb enters into the argument of faith, for if the tomb had kept the body placed in it and death had kept its prey, the role of the incarnate Word as mediator would have been belied, along with the call of all the members of Christ to rise again in body and soul. Without the Resurrection of the individual Christ, witnessed factually as well as spiritually, none of this supernatural ordinance would have been believable, let alone conceivable as a hoped-for ultimate good for the human being.

The mystery of the Resurrection, more than just a spectacular fact like any other, is a promotion of a spiritual intelligence, a passage from true appearances to an intussusception into a life that is to go on in this world as a preparation for entering into the Trinitarian life in the next life. "The message of Easter thus continues, completes and illumines the *consummatum est* of Good Friday. It reveals the supreme goal, which, in time, entails stages and progressive realizations, but which, from the supra-temporal and unifying standpoint, encompasses the entire economy of the work of salvation" (1946, 22). It is not only a historical fact of very peculiar spiritual dimensions; it is a truth signifying, by translating it into a miraculous appearance, a supernaturally incarnate substance, expressing thereby in an anthropomorphic form, to make it accessible to our terrestrial way of knowing, our existence whose real totality, partially and even according to what is essential about it, escapes our actual experiential and discursive mode of knowing. If this reality is made manifest in a way that is attenuated and fleeting as it were, it is only to give a foundation for the faith in this new life and to provide an initiation into that life with a taste for the higher life humans are called to live even now in history.

What the twofold certitude concerning the prodigious fact of Resurrection entails, however, that of a historical fact full of promises and that of an eternal life already begun in the world, but that will find its fulfillment only after we pass out of this world, is for Blondel a matter of ontological significance both for the risen Christ and for the one who rises to faith in this Lord of the universe who shows himself. Christ's humanity did rise from the tomb to prove that he was more than human and that he was free of all sin. But to initiate us to his own true, supernatural life, he had also to convert us from our natural way of looking at things so as to take us from the mere terrestrial order to the reality that makes us eternal already by his presence in us and his life hidden in the bosom of the Father. Everything that we know and can say about the historical reality of the Resurrection is but a transition to a certitude that sight and touch know nothing of, a certitude "converted into a faith more comprehensive of the spiritual order and even of the transcendent life that can and must unite us to the transfigured and glorified Christ" (1946, 24). Blondel remarks that this may come as a surprise to believers, but he wants to insist on it to point out how faith in the mystery of the Resurrection already engenders within us eternal life and the promises it contains of a future beatific vision. What the Resurrection does for us is raise us from the terrestrial order and from our human certitudes to an order that is actually invisible, but the one that is absolutely and definitively true, something that philosophy could never do by itself.

Recalling the sinful state of man after the fall, and the death that had come as a consequence of sin, Blondel speaks of Christ's overcoming of death as "a metaphysical miracle shrouded in what at first seems to be only in a chronological succession" (1946, 26). Given what Blondel had said earlier, not only about the rational and metaphysical gravity of sin, but also about its supernatural gravity as deicide, it followed that the fault was irremediable. "The most absolute logical realism seemed to imply that, man being inexterminable, the deadly fault, at once homicidal and deicidal, that he could commit was and remained impossible to erase or to make disappear as if it had never been" (1946, 26-27). Yet in the logic of the Resurrection, under a light that was more than metaphysical, was revealed the almost inconceivable invention of divine charity bringing "the indestructible eternal Word to immolate himself in a human flesh so as to destroy the very reality of sin in the flesh" (1946, 27).

We see here one more dimension of the logical organization and the effective realization of God's grand design of a supernatural elevation for man, spoken of from the beginning in conjunction with creation, but now seen as redemptive after the fall, and as a return into grace through an ever-more intimate insertion of created beings into the intimacy of the Trinitarian life. We see also the continuity that binds together the successive aspects of this mystery and that ties them all to the essential aspirations of man, *tel qu'il est fait,* as he exists in fact, and to the unforeseeable supports of Revelation, as inexhaustible as its mysterious depths remain. All this converges in the mystery of the Resurrection, which is why, as extraordinary as it is, it can become as disconcerting as it is enlightening. In the next glorious mystery, the bodily Ascension of Jesus into heaven, Blondel will indicate how obscurity itself, not obscurantism, remains part and parcel of this revelation of a truth inaccessible to our sight about a life of glory whose vision and participation cannot be encompassed in the earthly test we still have to go through as rational beings.

What should be clear, however, is that the Resurrection, with its twofold character as tangible fact for certain witnesses and as unfathomable in a transcendent life that surpasses our common notions of living matter, could suffice to ground an entirely new historical development at once visible and invisible, terrestrial and celestial, a spiritual city to be constructed little by little through innumerable generations upon generations. What distinguishes the mystery of the *Ascension* from that of Resurrection is that, after forty days of intermittent apparitions, the Christ now manifests himself in all his splendor and all his power on a mountain where many of the disciples who have been with him in his journey are now gathered for this momentous event. What they are to witness is the final celestial triumph of the One who, on his own initiative, rises corporeally to the Father, at whose right hand He is to sit, according to the expression of the Scripture.

What Blondel calls special attention to is the cloud that envelops the risen One as he disappears from their sight, as a fact once again for them, and as a sign that he will no longer be with them physically, as he had been in his public life and even in the forty days of risen life he has given them a glimpse of. He will be with them henceforth in a new way, but not in a way that would allow them to cling to him in human fashion. "Do not cling to me," he had said to those who rejoiced in his resurrection, "for I am not yet ascended to my Father." Loyalty to the risen Christ could never be a mere clinging to a thing or a human being in the past. It had to be a following after one who had gone ahead to prepare a place for us in the bosom of the Father. How the disciples were to follow after, more concretely, would be made known in the mystery of Pentecost, but to come to that mystery in the proper light, there had to be the mystery of the Ascension in which the followers were to discover that they had to go their own way in this life, take up their own task and their own cross, under the guidance of the Spirit who was to come and teach them anew all that Jesus had taught them.

Blondel sees the mystery of the Ascension as part of the integral realism that characterizes the Christian teaching concerning supernaturalization, which joins the foundations of the physical universe with the higher construction of the spiritual order in a movement of spirits that goes from the principle that launches them to their final destination, starting from creation, and rising to the heights to which divine wisdom and charity beckon them. Even without having the same kind of ontological efficacy as the Incarnation and the Redemption for this divine purpose, the Ascension discloses an essential aspect of a truth still pregnant with immense promises, the full extent of which the disciples were only beginning to discover in their spiritual journey. What they learn as witnesses to the mystery of the Ascension is that, henceforth, in order for them to follow their Lord, and in order for him to remain with them in the world, they would have to look up more to the things of the spirit.

Blondel points to two sides of this mystery. First, there is its sensible aspect that causes astonishment in all those who were witnesses to it, a historical fact before a large crowd of spectators in full possession of their senses. This, like the fleeting apparitions of the forty days of risen life on earth, served to strengthen the faith of the disciples in a way that had not been possible before the Resurrection. It is this aspect of the Glorious Mysteries that had led Blondel to keep the Glorious Mysteries separate from that of the Redemption through suffering and death, of which they were a consequence. It was the miracles of Resurrection and Ascension that made all the difference in the world in the disciples' understanding of the events that preceded them, where they had seen nothing but defeat and loss. The apostles, and the Church that was to come after them, needed the Resurrection and Ascension to renew their faith in the divine power of the Redeemer, for these were facts that clearly surpassed any human power to realize.

The other side of the mystery, however, is the one Blondel thinks more important for philosophy to bring out. For "faith can and must find another reason, an enlightening lesson, a motive more intrinsic and more fecund, a reasonable mobile for the Christian belief. The Ascension of Christ contains enlightening stimulations to justify convictions resting even more on invisible grace than on a spectacular and ostentatious feat" (1946, 33). In this new convergence of the literal fact and of the spirit bringing new nourishment and progress through this mystery, Blondel finds another way of uniting faith and reason. The "heaven" to which Jesus ascends, where he now sits at the right hand of the Father, is not a determinate place in the material world, "not an elite residence of a compartment of the cosmos." It is a transfigured and real state of life that, for man, as a composite and natural whole, will be a state "that the supernatural order must reconstitute and perfect for eternal life" (1946, 33-34). The metaphorical way of speaking through the physical aspects of the phenomenon must not obscure the higher meaning contained in the mystery of the Ascension, which Blondel says we must take in its most realist as well as spiritual sense. It has to do with the supernatural life wherein God enables us to aspire, to tend toward, and to attain through faithfulness, not just to the reason and principle of our will that he had argued for in 1893, but to the elevating grace that beckons us toward God and raises us effectively all the way up to God. The mystery of the Ascension is another episode in the long line of teaching concerning our supernatural vocation going all the way back to creation and now converging on these glorious mysteries of the risen Redeemer.

One lesson of this mystery is that of a certain detachment from earthly tasks that might tie us too closely to things of this world. The Ascension is the image of an orientation that will affect the entire future march of the itinerant Church and the generation of the faithful toward the One who is now invisible to the senses but all the more present in this community. "Jesus leaves in order to remain all the more with us, for his sensible absence stimulates and increases the exercise of faith, hope and charity" (1946, 35). What he wants is to unite us to his Father and to the beatific life of the Trinity, and he does this inchoatively in this life by making us brothers, adoptive children of God. He appears to leave but only to draw us closer to his divinity, not only by effecting in us a transposition from the flesh to spiritual being, but also by a certain "divine symbiosis reconfiguring human nature and its ways of thinking and acting with the perfect type that we have to more than imitate and reproduce — albeit always imperfectly — because we have to adhere to, participate in, and realize within ourselves, beyond all sentiment, Christ himself: *mihi vivere, Christus est*" (1946, 35-36).

The mystery of the Ascension came at a time in the history of the divine missions when the task and the responsibility of propagating the divine message was to be handed over from Christ himself in his human nature to his disciples and to his future Church, now to be taken as the mystical body of Christ, resulting from the faithful being born spiritually into a new life in Christ. Blondel's meditation on this mystery brings him back to his fundamental idea of a *theandric* action that humans now become capable of in the world, in union with the Christ who has departed sensibly but remains ever present in his Mystical Body. In a way that is adapted to both simple folk and to philosophers, the mystery opens a vista that is infinitely rich in metaphysical truths concerning our nature and our destiny, and rich as well in the most sublime of religious teachings, with practical as well as mystical ramifications, at least for one who knows how to reflect on it rationally in the kind of spiritual faith that it builds up and justifies.

The mystery of the Ascension opened up broad supernatural vistas for others who were to follow in the mission inaugurated by Christ. It did not, however, inaugurate the Church itself that was to take up that mission. That was to happen ten days later in another mystery, that of *Pentecost*, the third of the Glorious Mysteries, in which the role of the mission of the Holy Spirit, third person of the Holy Trinity, was made known in the community of those who were to continue the work of calling all men and making them disciples.

Though the disciples must have felt new hope and enthusiasm in witnessing their Lord's final triumph over death and over the limits of his human nature that tied him to an earthly life, they did not yet understand all that this would mean for them and for the task of evangelizing they were to undertake in embracing the risen life of Jesus. They were still like the bedraggled and befuddled group they had been when they scattered at the hour when their master had been taken and put to death. Jesus had promised that he would send them his Spirit after his final departure from this world and his return to the Father, but that Spirit had not come yet. They were simply to regroup in the upper chamber, where they had celebrated the first Eucharist with the Lord on the night before he was to die, and wait in prayerful expectation for the One who was to lead them into a fuller understanding of all that Jesus had taught them, including the injunction to go and teach all nations, the thing that Jesus himself had not done but that he had left for his followers to do. And so they waited for ten days, until the Jewish feast of Pentecost, when the Spirit came over them "from heaven like the rush of a mighty wind, filling the house where they were sitting. And there appeared to them tongues as of fire, distributed and resting on each one of them. And they were filled with the Holy Spirit and began to speak in tongues, as the Spirit gave them utterance" (Acts 2:2-4).

In his realism of the Christian Spirit, Blondel takes this as an account of something that really happened to this group of men, which transformed them into something they had never been before. He takes what they did immediately after, in going out to speak to "devout men from every nation under heaven," who had been attracted by the sound and bewildered by it, as a further indication that this was truly a historical event of some magnitude to further assure that it was not just the hallucination of a small group of men closed up in a room. This was the factual aspect of the mystery that Christianity has always insisted upon, just as it has always insisted upon a resurrection of the body and a physical ascension of Christ in his humanity. This historical aspect of the facts did add certitude, further proof, so to speak, to faith in this Lord as divine and all-powerful. But Blondel is more interested in bringing out the spiritual aspect of these facts and relating them to the divine plan of divinization for man. For the Spirit is sent in order to unite the disciples all the more really to the divinity of the incarnate Word in what has now become for the disciples the night of sensible absence. It is not the charms of a visible presence of Christ, or of his most captivating dedication that suffices to make our affections, our will, or our human actions rise to participation in the Trinitarian life, free of all egoism in its pure spirituality. It is rather for the Holy Spirit to consummate the effusion and the donation of the Man-God requiring a prior and total renunciation of self, "only to restore the personal appropriation of every human being to keep of his individual particularism only the means and the merit of making himself everything for everyone" (1946, 44).

Where the sacred authors write only of the most complete realizations of these mysterious insinuations of the Spirit into the souls of the apostles, Blondel reflects on how they are woven, in a manner that is dialectically expressive and charitably inventive, into a design of harmonious plenitude that, on the one hand, responds to the needs of aspirations that humanity cannot satisfy in answer to questions philosophy cannot answer, and on the other hand, in the solutions given, even though they offer some purchase for intelligent and systematic reflection, remains an unfathomable mystery for reason alone, surpassing all reasons that reason can attain and anything that the human heart could have dared to conceive or to realize.

If we look back on this design, which Blondel has related to the Trinitarian life from the beginning of creation itself, and on the action proper to each of the divine Persons in this work of power, wisdom, and love, we can see better the profound meaning of the descent of the Holy Spirit at this moment of history in the Cenacle, something that human thought and action can assimilate to, but not fully penetrate. It is not just the Father or this eternal Word, who are spoken of as Creator of heaven and earth, of things visible and invisible. It is also the Holy Spirit, who is the very union of Father and Son, without whose sending creation would not seem to have been or to have taken place, and who consummates the deed of gratuitous love that creation is, let alone the consummation of this work of power and wisdom in a communion of charity with the divine beatitude. That is why he is called the Creator Spirit. And if he had a role in the creation and mediation of finite spirits, all the more did he have a role in their vocation and elevation, and in the supernatural reparation this required. "Since it is a question of depositing, nourishing and making flourish in man the divine seed of supernatural adoption, it is indispensable that the spirit of union and charity contribute in forming, in perfecting the real bond, *vinculum substantiale,* that answers to the supreme wish of the dying Christ: *sint unum*" (1946, 47-48). It is in the logic of the entire divine plan that the Holy Spirit makes himself present and known in this moment that has come to be known as the birth of the Church as the body of Christ with its initial excellence and its original perfection. Without the effusion of the Holy Spirit, the nascent Church would have been lacking, not only in any effectiveness to proceed in its task, but also in one of its essential components for the symbiotic life it was to represent and promote among mankind.

Blondel reflects on the different spiritual stages these early proclaimers of the New Alliance had to go through under the divine pedagogy. What had to happen was not a suppression of the sensible and natural order in their consciousness, but a transposition to a transcendent truth that requires a conversion that can go from simple abnegation to the supreme sacrifice of martyrdom. The Old Law is not denied. The law of fear remains the beginning of wisdom. But it is said that to enter into the law of love, everything must be made new — hearts, voices, and works. The Holy Spirit is a spirit of newness for every age that is to come spiritually and socially. The new that is to come is not merely one to be superimposed on the old order. The supernatural of which we are speaking is not just an addition, as if nature and reason could simply step forward into grace and salvation. "To acquire the precious pearl and have access to divine adoption, the creature must strip itself of any false sufficiency, free itself of its egotistic limits, use its natural gifts as currency for exchange or a toll to cross the abyss over which divine mercy spreads a bridge and a way to draw it on and lead the creature to the supreme union" (1946, 50). This is the sort of transformation that the Holy Spirit secretly effects in souls, usually quite gradually, but also at times quite surprisingly, as at moments like that of the Pentecost.

What we witness there is a sudden transformation of Peter and the other Apostles, who were moved to rush out into the street to begin preaching the Good News of salvation through Christ in the face of both Jewish and Roman authorities, whom they had feared until then and who did not want to hear more of this commotion about the Nazarene. To be sure, their life with Jesus earlier and their witnessing of the Resurrection and the Ascension had prepared them for this, but it was the new rush from the Spirit that put them over the top, much to their own astonishment as well as that of the crowd that met them. This was a miracle of human achievement mobilized by an interior presence of the Spirit they had not known. The miraculous preaching that followed was a wonder, not just by reason of the polyglot phenomenon that everyone present attested to, each from his own language, knowing that Peter was speaking only in his own language, but even more so by the fact that the message was heard by such a diversity of spirits from all over the world, and that all had found within themselves the ears to hear about this new life in Christ. It is in this hearing of the message that the mystery of grace resides, Blondel points out, "to realize all at once the unanimity of the nascent Church, a truly unforeseeable and in a way incomprehensible success to strengthen the paradoxical confidence of the Apostles in their future preaching and to guarantee the indefectibility of the Church" (1946, 51). The mystery of the Church itself, of which Blondel will say more later on, began in this extraordinary moment of the Spirit moving both preachers and hearers of the Word entering into a community of faith, hope, and charity around their risen Lord. Blondel takes this polyglot Church that so quickly coalesces around the Apostles on the first Christian Pentecost as a symbol of the universal extension of a unique language that was eventually to speak to all human beings, regardless of culture, race, or ethnic identity.

The Supernatural Life as Continued in the Church

While the glorious mysteries of the Resurrection, the Ascension, and Pentecost mark a certain completion and culmination in the realization of the divine plan of Redemption and Salvation for mankind, they do not tell us about how this good news was to be spread abroad for all men to know about and to consider in their own aspirations for completion and beatitude. The revelation so far had reached only a few who had come to believe in the divine power of the risen Christ, but a few whose mission or commission was now to spread the good Word to all mankind from generation to generation until the end of time. In the first volume of this work on the Christian Spirit, Blondel had probed into the intentions of the divine plan leading up to the sacrifice of the Word incarnate on the cross in overcoming man's culpable resistances to the plan as well as the faults they opened up in man that could not be cured naturally. The Resurrection and the Ascension had demonstrated how these faults and their consequences were indeed overcome, with Christ leading the way into the bosom of the Father and the fullness of Trinitarian life in God, in keeping with an intention of supernaturalization already traced back to the very first moment of creation.

In that same first volume he had also worked out a way of distinguishing different historical states for mankind according to the way it was relating to its supernatural vocation, dating back to before original sin. After the Fall, there came a *transnatural* state of fallenness and of supernatural death, a time of waiting for the divine intervention that would restore the possibility of supernatural life for men in history through the mediation of the incarnate Word. But now, after the Resurrection and Ascension, we find ourselves in a new historical state, a state Blondel speaks of as one of "redemption and convalescence," in a life that is already supernatural in its orientation, though it has not attained its fulfillment as eternal life in the Trinitarian God himself. It is against this broad universal and historical panorama that Blondel introduces, not just the Church as a human institution, but the mystery of the Church as the visible continuation of the invisible presence of the risen Christ for all ages. This is not an easy idea to catch, as if in some sort of phenomenological or sociological analysis. It is an idea that was formed in the faith of a community called together by a risen Lord and solidified in its historical presence to the world by the coming of a Holy Spirit who is himself God as the Spirit of Jesus. But it is an Institution designed to meet the needs and promote the supernatural life of a mankind that is still only convalescent in that life.

All this historical and theological background is important for understanding how the Church is indeed a mystery in the world. Blondel notes how the name itself came into use early on, to identify it as a radically new phenomenon in the world and as unique in its kind, by reason both of its origin and its purpose of divinization for mankind. From this mystery will follow the enactment of many other mysteries or sacraments in the world in the work of perpetuating the mission and the spirit of Christ, and adapting it to all generations and to all crises of humanity, according to a logic that is coherent with our spiritual needs as well as with the systematic and practical structures of Christian institutions.

The Church Blondel is thinking of, however, is not one defined primarily by its hierarchy. The term as it was originally understood designated first, in the internal forum, the assembly of the faithful gathered together, and then, by extension, the place built for the cult to be celebrated in common under the leadership of the apostles. Then, in a broader, more historical, and spiritual sense still, "Church" came to mean a universal unity of the faithful, "united together among themselves, both visibly and invisibly, under a supreme authority that governs them and maintains a rule of faith and of morals, establishing thereby a living and operative communion among successive generations, under the governance of the invisible Head, who is the Christ, and of his representative, his Vicar, invested with the power and the mission of seeing to the permanent unity of the visible body and the invisible soul of this Christian universalism" (1946, 56). This is the understanding of "Church" Blondel wishes to elucidate on as a mystery, while paying special attention to the distinction between the visible and the invisible. For the unanimity in question is not one that can be reduced to external appearances measurable by statistics, or external deportment. It refers more to the faithful struggling in this world, to the suffering souls still expiating their sins in purgatory, and to the crowd of the elect who have come into their glory. Like Augustine's *City of God,* Blondel's *Church* is one defined by the faith of those who are moved by God and who are returning to God. In it are to be included, not just those who have come to believe in Jesus Christ, the risen Lord, but also "those souls of good faith and good will who, while ignoring positive revelation and remaining docile to the secret motions of grace — which are not lacking absolutely for any man in possession of his conscience and will — belong invisibly to the Church" (1946, 56). Even if we do not know how God, or the Spirit, works secretly in the souls of those who have had no contact with the visible Church on earth, or who have been repelled by the human failures of that Church, Blondel is mindful of the universal salvific will of God for all human beings and of the only way the rational creature can have access to the divine fulfillment willed by God, which is by deliberate choice in saying yes to God. The drama that Blondel thinks is playing itself out between man and God in the Church is one that has to play itself out for all mankind, whether in direct relationship with the visible Church or not. Blondel does not see any of this as happening outside the Church, defined in the broad spiritual terms of faith, hope, and love, or even apart from it. He sees it rather as coming under the invisible side of the Church where God has other ways of working his grace into the souls of good faith and good will, other than those institutionalized in the visible Church, otherwise known as the Mystical Body of Christ with a visible body and an invisible soul.

Speaking of this Body, Blondel wants to show how and why it remains mysterious in its essence, even as it answers to the normal aspiration of human beings who, in developing their inalienable personality, need nevertheless a spiritual community in which to flourish. He notes the twofold tendency in human nature he has long analyzed in his philosophy of action, one egocentric and in need of concentration and indefinite expansion, and the other, no less real, an élan of decentering and of expansion unto the infinite. Each one of these tendencies, left to itself, runs a danger of excess, either of egoism on one side or of generosity without rational limits on the other. But left to themselves in relation to one another they cannot come to a perfect equilibrium or to a unity in which they perfect one another mutually, whether in individuals or in society as a whole. When Jesus prays that his followers may be one, the resolution of this antinomy he has in mind for the religious community of those who are to carry on his work is not one that can be accomplished by simple contract, by majority decision, or by some traditional convention of merely human origin. Nor can it be constituted by a simple mutual recognition that is arbitrary from the standpoint of the sovereign will of the individuals in confrontation with one another. For Blondel it takes a higher principle to account for the Christian sociability, or what is also called the communion of the saints, one that is transcendent in the strict sense of the term and one that has not been conceived in any school of sociology or social philosophy.

As natural as it may be for the human animal to be social, nature and feeling are not enough to found a truly human society. Even Aristotle, who recognized that man was instinctively social, saw in addition "the necessity of reason to intervene to attain an intelligence of common interests and the formation of virtues that consolidate and perfect the social order into a higher principle, ideal in character and even already transcendent" (1946, 64). It is not the spontaneous grouping of the horde or the clan that gives rise to the subjective life of persons becoming conscious of what Blondel calls "their human and generous character" with regard to one another. This does not come from confrontation for Blondel, but "from higher aspirations that are the seeds of a truly social life, the condition for personal dignity and the guaranty of moral integrity" (1946, 61-62). From this comes a sense of authority and discipline consented to in a society that rests on a principle of reciprocal subordination and discipline between the members and the authority, normally in a relation of final mutuality.

The social life of a community is never just a juxtaposition of spiritual beings, independent of one another and each participating as it sees fit in injunctions emanating from some conception of the common good. It presupposes an ideal character of a transcendent nature that historical societies or communities strive to attain, but cannot equal by reason of the infinitate at work in their aspirations stemming from the mediation of the incarnate Word, who suffered, died, and rose from the dead. The Christian Spirit of faith and hope raises the natural sociability of man through virtue to a higher degree on the basis of a higher calling and a divine commandment, "the law of charity that sums up and perfects the moral law, the prophets, the regime of fear, and all the attempts at a civilization that, by itself, would always fall short, halfway, or fall back under the regime of a brutality and hatred born of egoisms made worse by science without God" (1946, 60). For Blondel, the supernatural law of charity that binds the Christian community together is not one that is detached from the world, transcendent though it may be. He has reserved an entire volume of this work on the *Christian Spirit* in which he will explore what this Spirit has to say in the face of problems that continue to arise for a modern technological society that may be seeking peace but that still finds itself caught up in the worst kind of war and violence.

Here, still in the second volume, while he is exploring the mysterious aspect of the Church as an institution in the world, he turns to consider how power and authority are constituted in this Christian community. Unlike civil power, which can still fall short of its proper end or even pervert its legitimate function, Church power, which is of divine origin, rests on an assurance that it will not deviate from its purpose in maintaining dogmas, precepts, discipline, and all other means that pertain to the attainment of its end, which is the salvation of souls called to the higher Trinitarian life. This is so even for those who are called to a special function of teaching in the Church and presiding over its activities and practices. They are functioning in a supernatural order that transcends the human need for collective order and, though their human frailty and faults, not to say their positive shortcomings, may stand in the way of others perceiving the divine function they exercise, and perhaps even betray that function at times, the community has the assurance from its Founder that they will perpetuate the Spirit that moves the entire community in matters of faith and morals. Such was the promise of Christ, who said that he would not leave his followers as orphans in a hostile world, and such has also been, Blondel adds, the experience of the community historically, to the point that the survival of the Church in its supernatural integrity is often referred to as the most significant of all Christian miracles. There is this perpetual infallibility in the Church, and in the exercise of its teaching authority, that follows from a principle that rises above the fluctuations of times and of spirits. The problem Christians have, including those in authority, is keeping track of it as they keep reorganizing themselves to meet the new challenges of their vocation in the world.

Blondel speaks of the Church as having to organize itself and providing a spiritual sort of equipment to engage in a drama that is essentially theandric. The Church itself is Christ's instrument for creating solidarity with all men of all ages, notwithstanding human infirmity. Like Christ, it assumes a sinful humanity through solidarity with its debt and its sufferings in order to complete what, according to the words of St. Paul, "is missing in the Passion of Christ." Conscious of their own sinfulness, Christians have to become all the more understanding of others and draw from their personal experience a keener sense of forgiveness, of mercy, and of revivifying penance, something they could not do without the example and the teaching of the Mediator who has gone before. In this sense, the militant Church is not just a means of solidarity, a stimulant of mercy and of apostolate as well as zeal. It is as much a testing ground, a place of struggle, a sign of contradiction, a touchstone, a preparation as suffering Church for the triumphant Church and the entire society of the glorified and the blessed. "The Church in this way partakes in every stage of the life, death, and glory of its Chief: it follows the ways He has taken himself, not just to fully humanize and spiritualize, but to supernaturalize a redeemed humanity" (1946, 65). That is how it becomes part of God's providential plan to elevate human beings through the concerted resources of nature and grace God places at its disposal for pursuing its continuation of Christ's mission on earth, namely, the spiritual equipment Blondel has already alluded to.

His intention is not to do a history of how the Church has advanced its supernatural purpose through the ages, but rather to make manifest what is reasonable, and even rational and philosophical, in the way that the Church has operated in the world, showing a wisdom that can be justified by a moral and intellectual value, even where a supernatural bearing reveals itself, starting from "the logic of the glorious mysteries, their demonstrative value and their specifically religious intent in the education of primitive or of progressing Christianity" (1946, 68-69). The history of the Church is a sacred history starting from the risen Christ manifestly glorified. It is the Incarnation prolonged and effectively permanent in those who call themselves vicars and servants of this risen Lord, whether as authorities for this Christian community or simply as faithful in that community, faith being the fundamental condition for belonging to that community. Blondel makes a special case for some permanent infallibility in this community rooted in the divine will itself, for the sake of those called to exercise a role of teaching and guidance in it, going back to the special role assigned to the apostles and their successors by Christ himself, but this is mainly to reinforce a "principle of confident docility" among all the faithful, a willingness to learn from the institutions and the control of sacred science on the part of all, including those who exercise this power within the Church.

It is with this supernatural character of the Christian's vocation in mind, and the faith that places it above mere morality or religious sentiment, not to mention other social or individual initiatives, that Blondel speaks of the exercise of authority in the Church and the permanent presence of Christ's action in how that authority exercises its function. Fidelity to that supernatural character requires that believers avoid two extreme attitudes in listening to the voice of authority, first, the pretension of grasping the Word of God completely on one's own within one's conscience or consciousness alone, or second, the pretension of organizing merely conventional or bureaucratic collective directives and legislations. "With such attitudes," Blondel writes, "we run the serious risk of regarding Christ only as an elder brother, as a rouser now gone to sleep" (1946, 72), not the risen Mediator still exercising his function through an authoritative voice in the Church.

Moreover, if anyone claims only to go back to the origins, one ends up temporalizing what is of an eternal significance, without understanding that it is for mobile duration, through the changes that it entails, "to spell out little by little the total message, a message that shows its meaning only by a continually new development in order to remain in conformity with the permanent and universal Mediator, whose inexhaustible newness the Spirit perpetuates by the developing of it" (1946, 72). The total message of the Good News for man cannot be fixed in any single stage of its expression, not even in what has been called the "deposit of faith," which, we are told, was closed in the Church with the apostolic age. Always, in the history of the Church, Christians and those in authority are called to ever-new riches for the spiritual life of mankind from a deposit that contains an infinity of plastic plans for a humanity still on the way to its final divinization. Such is the progressive role Blondel recognizes for authority in the Church as part of a living tradition going back to the authority of Christ himself and reaching forward to a proper supernaturalization of believers in the Word. It is, or should be, supernatural in its own right.

Tradition and Magisterium

The Church Blondel is talking about is one with a universal spiritual role to play in history. As conceived in the mystery of Pentecost itself, it is a continuation of Christ's exercise of mediation for a proper divinization of man reaching out to all peoples and all civilizations through all ages. In considering this universal historical import of the Church, Blondel singles out two functions in it that are essential to its supernatural, and hence still mysterious, character, but that are often seen as problematic, if not downright absurd, by a critical philosophical reason bent on showing how everything has to be rational, functions that have been the butt of much derision and rejection by modern Enlightenment philosophy. These are the functions, *Tradition* and the *Magisterium,* the authority functioning in the Tradition to assure its development in accordance and in continuity with its principles and its origins as expressed in the deposit of faith left to the Apostles and the first community of the faithful gathered about them, and as leading up to the supernaturalization of all those who were to choose to accept this vocation. Blondel thinks of these functions exercised by human beings in history, not only in relation to the mysterious and supernatural character of the Church as embodiment of the Christian Spirit, but also as themselves working in mysterious ways to bring about a clearer understanding of the Christian teaching regarding man in his historical situation, and a more effective religious practice to keep this new Spirit alive in the world as an imitation in time of its promised fulfillment in eternal life. What he wants to show as a philosopher is that these functions, as exercised in the Church, are necessary and rational, in keeping with the suppositions of faith concerning Christ as the head of this Mystical Body and concerning the mission, or the commission, given to the Church to go in this life and teach all nations and make disciples of all men. For the Church itself is something to be *believed* in as an extension of the incarnate Word's mediation in time.

Concerning *Tradition,* Blondel points out that, in the Christian language, the term has a much stronger and more real meaning than it has in the more conventional language that applies to a wide diversity of cultures and communities that come and go in the fluctuations of history. He depicts it as a flow in the world of Spirit, coming from God and taking up all of nature with it to unite it with the providential plan. It is a Sacred History in the proper sense of the term, which Blondel extends back to the call of Abraham and the choice of a people to prepare the way for the Messiah to come. It goes back even to the story of creation and of the fall that preceded this call of Abraham that gets its full complement only with the coming, the suffering, and the resurrection of the one Mediator for all and with the sending of his Holy Spirit. Blondel takes all this mediation as very real in human history, and he understands Christian Tradition as an extension of it in spiritual time that is no less real in the community of faith that propels itself across the ages and all the civilizations that mark the passing of time. It is not directly discernible to the sense or to the human intellect, but it discreetly reveals itself in the effects it has on the Christian experience of the world and in the light it reflects back on itself in this experience. It is Christ handing himself over to us — *ipse tradidit semetipsum* — and ever interceding in our behalf as the community comes to a better understanding of the plenitude of what has been handed over.

The operative term for the Christian spirit here is that it is himself that Christ hands over to be handed on to the generations of those who would come to believe in him, himself the man who is at the same time God, the incarnate Word, the second person of the divine Trinity made man. This is not something that can be fully grasped in a moment by human intelligence, or even over a long period of time by those who have accepted the revelation and are laboring for its propagation, not only within themselves and their community of believers, but also in the entire human race. Christ himself, in a most solemn moment of his leave-taking with his apostles before going to his passion and death, told them that they could not then bear all that he had to say to them, but that when the Spirit of truth whom he had promised them comes, "he will guide you into all the truth" (John 16:12-13), as if to say that there was much more for them to learn and come to understand better in all that they had heard and seen of him, and that they would yet hear and see in the mystery of his Resurrection and Ascension before his return to his Father. This was an eternal truth encompassing the whole of creation and a supernatural vocation for rational creatures squeezed into a moment of consciousness that could not express all the richness and the infinite spiritual newness it was introducing into the world. It was a deposit whose understanding would have to grow and develop, assisted by the Holy Spirit.

"We cannot exhaust God," Blondel writes; "and Tradition is, we repeat, God handing himself over to humanity, in a possession ever assured and whose satiety remains forever the freshness of a spring and Good News. In the whole of its scope in the earthly life of the Church and of each of the faithful, Tradition appears therefore as a disbursement of eternity, in anticipation of coming into possession of the entire treasure, whose total evaluation will give the simultaneous certitude of an immensity definitively possessed, but always inexhaustible" (1946, 81-82).

This is not a tradition as normally understood, a wisdom accumulated over the ages in societies growing old, something semi-historical usually expressed in stories or fables that fix an ephemeral mobility into successive tableaux. Tradition in its essence, as it is to be taken in the Church, is not reducible to anything that can be expressed in words. What it transmits is precisely what cannot adequately be named and mummified in sensible or intellectual aspects. It is "a living transmission no longer merely in words, but in acts, in signs, through contacts among living persons, gestures that exclude doubts and second thoughts because they surpass the plasticity of deliberations and of mental hesitations" (1946, 80). For Blondel, Tradition takes the form of a self-conscious action in and by the community of the faithful energizing itself spiritually and propagating itself from generation to generation, stemming from a wealth of knowledge and power that is inexhaustible. Its function in the history of a Church, called ever, not just to renovate, but also to *innovate, vetera novis augere,* to augment the old with the new, is to serve as a compensatory balance that allows the Church to go forward, so to speak, on the tightrope of the future, high above the pitfalls that would sidetrack it from attaining its true end, so that nothing is innovated that is not in keeping with what was handed over from the beginning, *nihil innovetur nisi quod traditum est.* More than just being conservative of the past, or of past encapsulations of the infinite truth and power it vehicles, Christian Tradition is a continuous movement subject to modifications and even radical renovations that do not foreclose on anything positive, but leave us open to whatever the Spirit holds in store for us still. It is what vivifies the Church and each one of its members, enabling all of them to exercise the charisma by which they communicate and multiply the supernatural seeds Christ has sown through his own actions and through his Passion.

In this perspective the canon of Sacred Scripture as established by the Church can be seen as an integral part of Tradition, the part that expresses its message of Good News as originally revealed through the inspiration of sacred writers. Included in the Canon are texts that speak of the Tradition as flowing from Christ handing himself and his Spirit over to the community of his disciples, so that the Tradition can draw strength and light from the Scriptures as well. But that is all within the logic of a community and a movement that grounds itself and finds its confident security in events remembered by the Tradition and narrated in the Scriptures, which include the mysteries of the Resurrection and the Ascension as well as the coming of the Holy Spirit at Pentecost. These events themselves are not pastiches that one relegates to a past all bandaged up and left behind. The narration of them is the beginning of a new supernatural stage in the spiritual life of humanity that is to spread to all corners of the earth. Fidelity to the Tradition that narrates these events and spells out their significance for the human spirit is what makes the Church the mystery that it is and has to be as a beacon for a fallen humanity that is still struggling for redemption, but now with the grace of Christ and all sorts of new aids to come to its support.

If Tradition is a continuous flow of the supernatural experience of faith and practice, there is also in it an exercise of authority by a *Magisterium* to assure fidelity to the original endowment in its movement of unceasing innovation. Blondel recognizes this function of authority in the Church as essential to its mysterious perpetuation in history, as an extension of Christ's own authority through time in matters of teaching and of disciplinary power. To those who object to the presence of such human imposition on a life that is supposedly so sublime, spiritual, and free, or who misconceive its functioning as part of the essential unity in the supernatural perspective of the Christian spirit, Blondel explains that the order of grace where it is operative does not come from below, through a progressive evolution of our natural faculties or through a collective growth of obscurely religious aspirations. That would represent only a naturalist or idealist conception of a gift that may indeed correspond to the primitive motion of a reasonable nature and a religious need, as Blondel had tried to show in his philosophy of human action. In the Christian perspective, the gift remains totally supernatural in its origin and its communication. The grace and the vocation in question cannot be naturalized in any creature, even if it passes through the most intimate sources of the human spirit or the lowest foundation of the human composite, for as properly Christian, it "proceeds integrally from above, *desursum*, even if it appears to rise from the unconscious or from most humble forms of personal life" (1946, 90). That is why, in the diffusion of the Christian order in and through the body of the entire Church, it is imperative that the head command, dispense, control, and judge any authentically faithful action and restore it to its principle as to its end. So it is for the conception of Christ, the supreme authority, as head of his mystical body. So it is also for those to whom he delegates the exercise of this authority in the spreading of this Body through history.

What constitutes the Church of God is not the society of Christians bringing about an explication of the content in its beliefs and in its religious experiences through the ages. Nor can it be said simply that the progressive evolution of its religious aspiration only expresses more clearly and more completely the primitive and fundamental truth of a destiny congenital to ourselves as human beings. That would imply that the supernatural order of the Christian Spirit is no more than "the full blossoming of human nature in the process of realizing itself all the way to its perfection, as if in a sort of exchange between two wills, that of God, our heavenly Father, that of man, adoptive son, to whom God gives himself so that man may give himself to God" (1946, 91). The exchange that takes in the supernatural order of Christian religion is not one between equals facing one another, as in mutual recognition between particular human beings. It is an exchange of receiving for finite spirits so that they can give back and thereby merit entering into the infinite totally transcendent life of the Trinity. Mere historical evolution of human consciousness cannot account for that. The development of Christian consciousness always has to go back to its source in the gift at the origin, the deposit of faith which it has from Apostolic times, and assure fidelity to that gift even as it innovates and renews itself in its religious teaching and practice. The development stems directly from the divine authority of Christ, who is Mediator, and remains subservient to the vicars of that authority appointed by Christ to ensure fidelity throughout the ages.

This is not to say that the Christian consciousness is enslaved either to Christ, or to his vicars on earth, or to some particular encapsulations of its spirit in the past. Christ himself is not slave to any letter or to personal ambition for himself. He is the *servant* of those he has come to command and to liberate from error and evil. This teaching concerning *service* is the secret of all authority worthy of the name in an authentically Christian Church, a necessary safeguard against all presumptions of what Blondel refers to as *sens propre,* which is a way of reducing any universal teaching to one's private understanding of it, and against all deviations due to a lack of discipline in morals as well as ideas.

When Christ tells his disciples "the truth will make you free," he takes the truth to be a discipline for thinking and living rightly in the world. And when in addition he promises the assistance of the Holy Spirit, whose role will be to suggest by interior motion what is to be recalled from the deposit of faith handed over to the Church that will be appropriate to succeeding generations, he is giving some assurance that what will be brought forth from the Good News will not be just any sort of rash novelty, but a wealth that was already implicit in the original teaching, so that those who are encouraged to go forward with discernment, discretion, and patience may proceed into the future according to the markers from the past. This assistance is promised in a special way to the apostles and to those who would succeed them in the exercise of authority, not so that it would prevent any innovation in the history of the Church, but rather so that it would encourage all necessary innovation called for by a deposit that remains mysterious to this day.

Indeed, one could rightly expect the Magisterium, as guardian of that deposit, to be as ready for innovation as anyone else in the Church, lay, clerical, or religious, given this special assistance it is assured of to stay within the firm but supple bounds and counsels set by Christ and elaborated further by the Holy Spirit in the historical experience of the Church as community of believers with a mission to all ages and civilizations. The Magisterium becomes a dictatorship only when it loses sight of this universal mission and becomes entrenched only in a particular ideology or culture subject to its administration or control, contrary to its character as *catholic,* a trait that Blondel now insists upon, following St. Augustine, to bring out not only the universal purpose of the Church in history, but also its consistency as one religious community exercising its functions in a wide diversity of civilizations.

Blondel recognizes the Papacy as playing a central role in this mysterious Magisterium of the Church, mainly because the Pope is seen as the successor of Peter, who was assigned a similar role by Christ in the original college of the apostles. But he sees that role mainly as one of unification for all the faithful from all parts of the world, each with its own cultural particularities, in keeping with the prayer of Jesus that they all be one — *ut unum sint*. The fact that the Pope is Bishop of Rome is not an essential part of the mystery that authenticates his function as Vicar of Christ on earth. Nor is the curial bureaucracy that has grown around the Papacy over the centuries. All this is a matter of particular historical and cultural circumstance that accompanies the embodiment of Christ in a community with a visible head. The Pope is Bishop of Rome because that is where Peter and Paul ended up as apostles and where the successors of Peter in the Church have stayed for the most part. Blondel is not concerned with doing a history of the Church as such. He is concerned more with understanding the essential character of the Church as supernatural embodiment of a Spirit. What he wants to bring out is the strategic importance of having a central authority of the church, not only to promote the charitable union of all Christians, but also to address opportunely the wide diversity of problems, doctrinal as well as practical, that are bound to arise in the innovation it is fostering for so many peoples across the ages. Even if the Roman curia are not always up to performing this task in as creative a way as they should, Blondel believes in a Pope and a college of bishops, *local ordinaries* around the globe, who are supernaturally assisted to do it, so that the Church will not just stay put and miss out on its mission to evangelize the world, or deviate from its universal discipline for bringing a transcendent means of salvation for all human beings in a symbiosis of reason and Christian faith, but bring forth New Things of faith that will command the attention of people of good faith ready to hear about what they must do to attain salvation and about what aids or supports there might be to enable them to do what they must to enter into the kingdom of God.

Symbiosis of the Natural and the Supernatural in Its Sacramental Ordering

Blondel, however, does not stop his critical considerations at the universal functions of Tradition and Magisterium. In keeping with his cycloidal method he comes around again to examine the detailed application of this mysterious life of the Church to the lives of singular human beings in an action that he thinks of as *theandric*. The universal framework of the Church is not just a blank that we are left to fill in according to whatever devices might occur to our good will or intention. It also includes a certain discipline to which the rational creature must submit, a certain "spiritual hygiene" it must follow, along with what Blondel has begun to call an *equipment* given to us by Christ to be exercised in the spiritual combat. These are what have been called the literal and sacramental practices to be engaged in to let the supernatural life and the kingdom of Christ into our souls, to preserve it there, and to fortify it. These are the Christian practices that had originally suggested to him the idea of beginning his philosophy as a philosophy of action, for it was there, in action, that he found the normal receptacle for incoming grace adapted to "the union of our rational and moral nature with effective presence or the Trinitarian inhabitation in our personal life" (1946, 102). Hence the importance of a philosophy of action to complete a philosophy of knowing and willing. "For it is through action that the symbiosis of nature and grace, of the human order with the divine life, can be realized and come to fruition in man" (1946, 102).

The domain of grace and of the entire supernatural order, even when it is conceded to exist for human beings, is usually thought to be off limits or untouchable for a philosophy of ideas, such as that of Descartes, which does not find anything more in action than what is in the idea of action. Blondel's endeavor in his philosophy of action had been to show that there is more to be learned from action in the concrete than a purely rational speculation can explicate, something that may be acknowledged by critical reason in a sort of *agnition*, as something it would have an interest in, but that could not be encompassed by any natural or abstract means of *cognition*. What Blondel was thinking concretely was, first, a necessity to open thinking up to something in experience that could not be encapsulated or conceived in any philosophical system, and second, the necessity for reason to take such a thing seriously into consideration, if it showed any signs of satisfying some fundamental human aspiration. This was, of course, his way of raising in philosophy and for philosophy the question of a supernatural as hypothetically necessary, that is, as something to be considered seriously in anyone's philosophy and in the conduct of one's life. It was also a way of bringing philosophy to show interest in the literal practice of a religion such as that of the Christian Spirit, even with its claim of transcending anything philosophy could conceive, again if it showed any signs of offering a solution to the problem of human destiny, as Blondel thought it did. But until now he had not tried to show how the literal practice of sacramental life in the Church, which is an integral part of the living Tradition in the Christian Spirit, is itself rationally integrated in God's providential plan for the supernaturalization of mankind, something that philosophy would require in the consideration of the hypothetically necessary gift.

What he sets out to do here is not a theology or a history of the sacraments in the Church. The philosophical spirit is not in a position to penetrate these mysteries, as if from within the living consciousness of the catholic Tradition itself. It can only look upon them as having some meaning to the philosophical spirit, which finds something to mull over "only where there is a unity in some complexity that corresponds to its need to integrate multiple data into an order that is at least partially explanatory" (1946, 126). The practice of a sacramental life according to the seven sacraments in the Church presents itself as part of the way the supernatural we have been reflecting upon is being communicated historically in an action that is at once divine and human, or theandric. Even while showing respect for the essential mystery of the life that is coursing through this action, philosophy still has to take hold of the ordering these sacraments represent in human experience, "from baptism to what can be called the sacrament of sacraments, the Eucharist, and to tie them back to the One who makes men Christian" (1946, 126).

Blondel begins this critical inquiry by recalling the idea of the historical stage in which the sacramental life becomes part of the supernatural ordering of man toward his divine destiny. As we understand from revelation, the first state of man was one of innocence, when man was already called to a higher life, but had not yet exercised his freedom to refuse. The second state, which Blondel calls *transnatural*, resulted from man's refusal of this higher calling, which left him in serious disequilibrium in the exercise of his natural faculties and "in a state of supernatural death that no human effort was enough to bring back to life" (1946, 109). We are also told that the incarnate Word offered himself in sacrifice to satisfy both justice and mercy as Mediator, to restore some equilibrium to man's natural capacities and, more importantly, to restore access to the supernatural life by rising from the dead and ascending to his Father as man. The state Christians now find themselves in, after these momentous events narrated in the Good News, is a state of being redeemed, of no longer being blocked by an insuperable obstacle from returning to God and from having recourse to a grace newly offered. It is not a state of innocence, nor a *transnatural* state of irremediable sin and condemnation.

However, it is not a state of automatic justification applicable to all, without any cooperation from man, without any willingness, implicit or explicit, to accept the renewed offer under conditions to be worked out, without some individual assistance, and "without a regime of convalescence and tonification," all things that human beings would need in order to enter into a collaboration that would be different from anything in the preceding states, and that would entail new responsibilities, new labors, new moral testing as well as new advantages in our capacity to go forward in a life we could not undertake by ourselves, let alone succeed in attaining its fulfillment. This is a new state for actual humanity according to the Christian Spirit about which philosophy cannot remain indifferent or disinterested since, as mysterious as it may still seem, it has to do with things that may count for the personal salvation of human beings.

What is new in the historical situation for mankind after Christ is clearly a religious factor for philosophy, but for the Christian spirit it is not a religious factor like any other that one might associate with what has been called "natural religion" or with various religious initiatives associated with diverse cults that often verge into superstition and idolatry. Blondel has not forgotten his radical criticism of superstition in the name, not just of reason, but of the Christian Spirit itself. Even when psychology and sociology recognize an authentic religious instinct operative in many historical societies of the past and the present, these tendencies and inclinations are never seen as rising to the level of the Christian Spirit. Blondel warns against analogies that would reduce Christian practices that have developed historically in the journey toward Christian fulfillment to the practices of other religions with a less clear conception of the total transcendence of God, and no conception at all of a supernatural calling. Such analogies bring into Christianity itself a tendency toward superstition and idolatry, even regarding the means or the instruments used in the Christian practice, if not the practice itself as well. They imply the same kind of attitude found in many so-called natural religions of taking control over the mysterious powers of the divine in human experience and turning them into a presumptuous magic. This is entirely contrary to the Christian ordering of things in human action, though it is something Christians themselves are often tempted to in their natural anxiety to get things done with, or to be in complete control. The exercise of any Christian action in the world, even if it be the celebration of the Eucharist, must free itself from any semblance of superstition. God, as present in any sensible species, cannot be turned into an idol any more than he can be naturalized in these species.

Blondel's critique of any purely natural attitude in religious practice, however, is not meant to deride or to devalue anything in the authentic practices of the Christian Tradition. He criticizes this naturalistic attitude in religion as immanentist, as failing to recognize both the divine origin of the practice and its totally supernatural character, even as it takes shape in history. It is not enough to see in the acts and in the literal practice prescribed in Christianity only a utilization of natural procedures or of psychological and moral laws of education and spiritual ascetics. Even if we recognize in them a discipline susceptible to mold our natural faculties into some spiritual character, it would be a mistake to overlook "the more than human reality and the transforming efficacity of the divine pedagogy using all the stages of our being or of the resources inserted by Providence into the entire organization of the human composite, in view of its ongoing transformation and its future transfiguration" (1946, 118). The resources Blondel has in mind are not only those of a spiritual resilience in our nature, but also those of a prevenient grace to open our soul up to the possibilities of our supernatural vocation.

Blondel's view of how all these resources, human as well as divine, converge in the development of Christian consciousness through faith and religious practice as theandric action is quite complex. First of all, the Christian supernatural is not just an afterthought arbitrarily tacked on to a nature complete in itself, without relation to anything divine, or even human, beyond itself. It presupposes a nature already constituted in itself with spiritual faculties grounded in lower principles, but at the same time apt to receive gratuitous gifts from on high "that have to penetrate and to do over, so to speak, *reprendre en sous oeuvre,* all this complex edifice" (1946, 120). To bring about this higher elevation, it seems that the entire series from its lowest foundations to the peaks of the Spirit, must be imbued with the vivifying breath of the entire ensemble.

At the same time, however, it must be understood that this entire surge of new life in the human spirit has to come from God himself, or Christ the incarnate Word, to begin with in the natural order, where divine concurrence is necessary for all thought as well as for all action, but even more so and especially when there is question of acceding to a supernatural life, for which a gratuitous impulse remains the indispensable source. This is what Blondel takes Jesus to mean when he says: "Without me, you can do nothing." On the other hand, it must also be understood that God does not save us or elevate us to a higher life without our own consent, at least tacitly, and our willingness to suffer the purification this requires. There is in this passivity with regard to the divine willing "an activity that, in identifying itself with the divine willing and acting, realizes the most perfect act human willing can accomplish" (1946, 112-13). Implied in this summit of activity is a sense of insufficiency on the part of human nature to bring itself to perfection and a conviction that God supplies what is lacking to our capacity when we do as he commands us to do in remembrance of what Christ did. Without Christ, Christians can do nothing in the sacramental life of the Church, but with him they can do many things that go far beyond any external appearances in entering into communion with Christ and one another. The supernatural efficacy of their action stems from Christ's divine will that his followers do things as he has commanded out of love for them. Such is the power of the lived Christian liturgy, its literal practice and its sacramental action.

In his study of human action, Blondel had made a lot of the solidarity between thought and practice, and of the reciprocal causality between what is known and what is to be done in the normal deployment of personal and social action. The same sort of solidarity and reciprocal causality is to be found in the historical ordering of the Christian community between the exercise of faith and the elaboration of its sacramental practice. In fact, Blondel wants to show "how and why the Christian order requires even more this interdependence as a sort of circumincession between dogma to be believed and a divine fidelity to be practiced" (1946, 113). For, both faith and piety have their origin in a divine motion whose initiative and progress men cannot take up within themselves without accepting the divine solicitudes, according to the form in which they present themselves for their own generous acquiescence. Christians are not at liberty to act in any which way in the world. Nor are they able to create within themselves dispositions or practices that will be adequate to the will of the One who has loved them first and prescribed to them how to return love for love. They have to think and act according to a twofold reasonable truth and exigency: for the cult to be appropriate to God, for the means of access to him not to be temerarious or vain, it is necessary for man to take into account what the divine power and charity have wisely established and mercifully furnished to enable him to run the immense course that will raise him from his wounded nature and elevate him to an eternal life of beatitude. This is not something that can be done by magic or any other idolatrous practices devised by human resources alone. It can only be done by means positively indicated by God for purposes of a true divinization and supernaturalization of man. Positivity is not something to be eschewed in the Christian Spirit, according to Blondel. It is something to be contemplated in fear and trembling, as it was in the story of Abraham, in the story of Moses and the law, and most of all in the story and the teaching of Jesus of Nazareth, risen from the dead, body and soul.

Blondel takes issue with Renan's idea that action materializes and besmirches the purity and the freedom of a thought and "a contemplation that allows at once for all contraries and even for contradictions whose implacable logic seems to kill fecundity" (1946, 115). Blondel sees this as a specious idealism that is shortsighted and deceivingly generous. He calls it a dilettantism lacking in spiritual vigor and generosity of heart, bereft of any élan of faith and devotion. The salutary truth of the Christian is quite the opposite of this. There is in faithful and faith-filled action, "in the divinely prescribed letter, infinitely more reality than can be furnished by or contained in the most free-floating intelligence or the most humanly cultivated spirit. It is discursive science, the most dialectically systematic ideas, that always fall short in some way and eliminate, unknowingly, the essential of the total truth, of concrete life, of infinite wisdom" (1946, 115). That is why, when it comes to positive prescriptions, which in the Christian language express the whole of what is called sacramental practices, "this authentic letter is more spiritual, more full of reality, more vivifying and sublimating than the human spirit, all philosophical syntheses and all inventions of art, science or poetry could conceivably be" (1946, 115). When Blondel, in the introduction and the conclusion of his original philosophy of the supernatural in 1893, was affirming the priority of practical science over the science of practice, it was already this Christian view of practical science in the concrete he had in mind, a science conscious of the mystery in the theandric symbiosis it is living and of the unanimity of spirits to which it aspires in an integral Catholicism.

If the Christian community rested only on a speculative credo, he argues, and if it were up to each individual believer or each generation to interpret and to assimilate an ideal nourishment, so as to transform the biblical formulary into a humanly established church on the more or less minute or late-coming elaboration of a profession, there would follow a profound dispersion of souls, even if it were masked by some common appellation lacking in any organic cohesive power. There is no way that words, ideas or verbal professions of a faith personal to individual people can equal the realism of sacramental life Blondel wants to highlight in the Christian Spirit. This is the life that infuses into all, to the depths that no divergence of thoughts or sentiments can touch, the vivifying graces, the nourishment constitutive of the spiritual body permeated by the hidden life of the Christ, who is ever present and living in all. Thanks to the mystery of the Incarnation, and thanks to Christ's command to "do this in memory of me," positivity and realism in Christian action and Christian tradition are elevated into the reality of a Spirit that transcends all material conditions. That is what philosophy must understand when it looks down from its perch upon the lowly instruments that God has chosen to advance his work of supernaturalization in history. The institution of the ensemble of the sacraments to be administered by the Church, and the authority vested in it to keep this *equipment* intact, is a consequence of the Christological mysteries, as an application of these mysteries in view of and in preparation for the sublime ends to which the Church and souls are called and destined.

There is more here than an anthropomorphic fiction working itself out in time. What there is is God placing himself, so to speak, in each agent to cooperate and to enhance the part each one brings to what is accomplished, in a condescendence that expresses his goodness lending itself in its entirety at each moment of time. Time, in this light, is seen as "the symbol of the supratemporal option on which depends the free destiny of each free spirit" in what Blondel calls "this mysterious passage from time to eternity," where time and space are not seen as realities imposing a norm on eternity and divine immensity, but rather "as abstract figurations that must, as St. Augustine shows most profoundly, be interpreted in function of their spiritual significance and their moral and religious finality" (1946, 123). If the final option that decides the spiritual creature's destiny for eternity is a passage from the temporal to the eternal, it is because that decision sums up for that spirit the entire order of time and space, or the series of means it has traversed in coming to its decision, including the use it has made of sacraments in the Christian dispensation.

Thus, to explain and to justify the real efficacy of sacramental action in the militant Church on earth, Blondel appeals to the entire supernatural order and to the role the sacraments were instituted to play in that order by Christ. "Literal practice is not fully justified and does not show its true sense and its salutary efficaciousness except in function of its supernatural origin and orientation" (1946, 125). It is part of what Christ wills for his Mystical Body extending itself in history, and it works, so to speak, or has its real effects in the spiritual life of Christians, because Christ wills it to be used or put into practice as real support for that life and for fulfilling its mission. That is what sets the sacraments of the Church apart from any sort of magic or incantation devised by man, as if to lay hold of hidden forces to benefit the interests or the passions of a still-too-carnal humanity. They are an integral part of the Tradition going all the way back to its Founder and Head and leading forward to the future life of the Church on earth and in its eternal fulfillment.

What Blondel has in mind more concretely in speaking of this literal practice of Christians in the Church are the seven sacraments that Christian Tradition has always conceived, at least in the Catholic Church, as an organized, and even as an organic way of distributing grace where needed. What he sees in these sacramental practices is the way that Christian authorities have come to adapt the means of supernaturalization inspired and established by Christ himself and passed on to the Church to actual religious exigencies in diverse historical circumstances. They represent a certain culture peculiar to the Church as a religious institution in the world oriented to its supernatural end, but one with an ordinance of its own, covering a range of aspects in the life that makes human beings Christian, beginning with Baptism as initiation into that life and culminating in the Eucharist, which Blondel thinks of as the sacrament of sacraments. It is part of his interest as a philosopher to inquire into something of this ordinance as a historical phenomenon affecting human consciousness in its spiritual aspirations.

Blondel considers each of the sacraments as they transform the earthly life of Christians interiorly both individually and socially. *Baptism* is seen as doing two things, repairing the sinfulness into which every descendant of Adam and Eve is born, and giving birth to the life of divine grace that comes from Christ, the second Adam. This presupposes the human being is not, from the first instant of his or her life, in a normal state concerning his fundamental spiritual orientation. There is something missing in him, even a certain indebtedness from a troubled heredity with a penchant for error and evil. We are heirs, not just to some original sin, but also to a certain rebelliousness toward our higher destiny. Baptism is the initial solution to this enigma in which all human beings find themselves as they enter into the world.

Baptism is at once a cleansing ablution, a restitution of the grace that goes with our supernatural vocation, a reconciliation with our heavenly Father, and a rebirth of the spirit of adoption that has to grow into ever-closer union with the risen Christ. It is not a restoration to an original state of prelapsarian innocence or to any preternatural gifts concomitant to a supernatural vocation given at the beginning, prior to original sin. Human nature remains troubled as a result of sin, but with the grace of baptism, it now becomes curable through participation in the ascetics and the sacrifice of Christ. What baptism brings is a certain gratuitous motion from which something supernatural can begin and develop in the baptized, something the free human being will be held accountable for in his good will according to the measure of the "talents" and the lights given to each.

Blondel thus speaks of baptism as the beginning of a long passage from what he calls the transnatural state, which is still one of death, to grace, to one of conversion and successive ascents, starting from the "narrow gate" of a prevenient grace, without which there can be no supernatural life for man, and rising, through overcoming indifference and resistance, to the new birth of sanctifying grace. Blondel sees this grace as having its own influence on the spontaneity of Christians, their sentiments and their actions, shaping them into a Christian temperament, Christian habits, and a Christian comportment. All this is taken as a matter of Christians responding to prevenient grace and using it to elevate themselves to a higher life on earth in anticipation of their final elevation into the divine life. Blondel even alludes to those who make more than ordinary, or heroic, use of these graces and gifts of the Holy Spirit, and rise to mystical union through passive purification and infused contemplation, as examples of what the grace of baptism can lead to. Without understanding what such mystical states consist in, reason can still see how the attainment of such states is in line with how far the development of the Christian Spirit can go with the grace that comes from baptism planted in the soul of the baptized, like a seed that has only to grow to reach the transforming union of the heavenly life. That seed, as Blondel writes, "already contains all the spiritual proliferation for which the highest fruit will be the beatific union" (1946, 131). This is what he calls the theandric instantiation that is already a beginning of eternal life. He speaks of it with reference to the simple ritual act by which a child or an adult is initiated into the Christian community, but in a way that allows for a broader conception of baptism, such as the "baptism of desire" or the baptism of heroic sacrifice to one's duty, where prevenient grace is offered as to anonymous Christians in other mysterious ways known only to God, to those who do all that is within their power for the good.

What this normative conception of baptism within the Christian community shows, however, is that the supernatural life it inaugurates does not attain its sublime end or its further development in an instant or without a struggle against the resistances or the forces of evil that remain in our lives. To sustain us and to give us new strength in our ascent, which always presupposes a divine prevenience and assumption, it becomes clear that "other sacramental aids are required by our weakness as they are also prepared, confirmed, and imparted through other divine institutions" (1946, 132). There is more Christian equipment, as Blondel puts it, for Christians to avail themselves of to meet their spiritual needs and to assure the perennity of the Church. These are the sacraments of Confirmation, Penance, and Extreme Unction, to provide for key moments in the life of individuals, and of Marriage and Orders, to provide for social needs of the Church, not to mention the Eucharist, which sums them all up in itself.

Confirmation is a second sacrament of initiation designed for Christians as they approach the age of responsibility in undertaking their own tasks in the community and in facing a world that still shows hostility to the progression of the Christian community. What is presupposed here is the need for an added strength, for confirmation, to meet the challenges for and against the Christian community in carrying out its mission on earth. Through the mystery of Confirmation, the Holy Spirit, who is in on the plan of salvation from creation on, is understood as perfecting the graces already initiated and as enriching the soul further with gifts said to create anew the face of the earth. For Blondel, "confirmation" means "a bolstering added originally and completely to the invisceration of the supernatural order into the spiritual organism" (1946, 133). For a better philosophical appreciation of these gifts of the Holy Spirit, and how they perfect the human spirit from the top down, Blondel suggests studying their progression from the bottom up as they come to exercise themselves, fortify one another, and tie into one another ever more and more.

Even with Confirmation, however, there is no guaranty that there will be no fall from grace. Sin remains a reality in the lives of Christians, and provision must be made for repairing all-too-frequent faults. Otherwise, the fallen would have to be understood as being definitively excluded from the Church. Hence, there is a necessity for the sacrament of *Penance* as an integral part of the ongoing life of the Church. Blondel speaks of it as a benefit that is both human and divine, "a marvelous double extension of God's charity for men and of the duties of justice and love for men among themselves. Is it not by this reciprocal absolution that Christians can imitate the Savior, satisfy their debt toward him, prove their mutual generosity and their recognition of Christ who, dying for them, asked them to forgive one another?" (1946, 136). Blondel speaks of Confession in the church as a discipline of fraternal correction or as a compassionate remedy for sinners, who come to examine themselves in their own internal forum, accuse themselves, and submit to salutary counsels and necessary reparations, so as to obtain pardon from God and even from other men, in order to be reconciled once again with Christ, who "died for their acquittal, to the extent that those who have failed recognize their weakness, their faults, and their debts" (1946, 137). As embarrassing as the practice of sacramental confession might seem to individuals unable to recognize their own sin, there is no question that such voluntary confession is in keeping with the highest form of spiritual awakening not only to God but also to others in a communion of saints.

This presupposes in the Christian dispensation, that the one before whom one confesses is more than just a counselor, a judge, or a human supervisor of conduct in our regard and that of others in society, more even than an appointee of religious law. Sacramental confession presupposes that the one who hears confessions is a representative of God himself in whom the penitent sees "Christ himself who, while prescribing to all that we not judge one another, is himself the arbiter in this Tribunal of mercy" (1946, 138). For his part, Christ does not have to judge as if by external appearances, since he resides at the heart of every conscience, whence he draws any sentence as from ourselves, "inasmuch as He is within us the light, the living norm, the universal Mediator, the only true and total retributor" (1946, 138).

What the sacrament of Penance takes care of is the particular sins of individuals who have fallen from grace, not the original sin committed before any injury to nature in relation to the first elevation of grace that was already supranatural. What the original rebellion required was a Redemption consummated by the sacrifice on the Cross for the sake of all humanity. This is not so for the individual infidelities of those who have received the grace of Baptism, even infidelities grave enough to place the guilty soul in a state of spiritual death. For the latter there is an absolution that can be repeated, unlike the absolution of Baptism, in conjunction with a sincere repentance and a sacramental application of the merits of Christ to the contrite sinner with a firm resolve to sin no more. In fact, the availability of Penance in the Church, as a sort of second baptism that can be repeated when needed, is a sign of some divine realism with regard to the human condition and a willingness to accommodate to human contingencies in the plan to elevate all human souls who remain receptive toward the supernatural offer. In fact, Blondel takes it as a sign of even greater plasticity, in cases where there is no confessor to go to for absolution or where there is not even any knowledge of such confessors so empowered, at which time an act of perfect contrition out of a pure love of God is enough to repair the lost life of grace. This is similar for him to what he called the baptism of blood, that is, confronting death and undergoing it to fulfill an important duty of obedience and sacrifice. This, too, can purify one of sin. Blondel suggests that even fidelity to the exigencies of a just war can serve as a vehicle God uses to save souls who, without this heroism, could not have found or regained the way of salvation.

The sacrament of *Extreme Unction* serves to help those undergoing illness or approaching death to stay the course in these especially trying moments of any human life. There are two sides to this sacrament, also known as the Sacrament of the Sick: one of bringing relief to the sick through a serene consolation, with an influx of strength to help prolong the benefit of life here and now, and one of a purifying grace and a docile attitude in facing life or death in one's extreme circumstances. Blondel speaks of this grace as one of a new Baptism at the hour when we may be approaching life beyond the tomb, or what the Christian language has called our true date of birth — *dies natalis*. This is the sacrament in which the Christian Spirit shows its profound compassion for the human body, which can be a body of sin, but which can also be purified through ascetic discipline and the active presence of grace from Christ himself to serve a higher state of untrammeled purity. People hesitate to speak of this sacrament of the sick to those who are in need of it, but Blondel is struck by the extreme regard the Church shows in prescribing it to help dissipate the apprehension of those at risk, entertain the hope of some convalescence, and reassure the suffering of a complete purification of body and soul for the passage to eternity, through the prayers that accompany the anointing of a human being in extreme distress. He regrets that this most compassionate expression of the Christian Spirit for the good of our physical life is not invoked more often during the times of our serious physical need.

Concerning the sacraments of *Marriage* and *Orders,* he points out that they are meant to maintain and develop the communal life of the Church, the first to increase the people of God, the second, "to recruit the magisterium and to assure a sacerdotal ministry to re-enact the permanent sacrifice of Christ through Mass" (1946, 147). With regard to *Marriage,* he points out that the sacramental grace has to do, not so much with sheer multiplication of progeny through fertile unions of man and woman, but rather with promoting union among the conjoined and their offspring, in accordance with the prayer of Christ that all may be one in a theandric life. The sacrament in this case symbolizes the intimate union of the incarnate Word and Redeemer with the entire Church of the saved. With regard to *Orders,* he refers to a need for a continuous transmission and a proliferation of the supernatural deposit to be perpetuated according to its original purity, its authentic authority, and a ministry of the sacraments proceeding from a divine investiture. This implies that the calling, or the vocation, to such a ministry is not purely an impulse of piety or an aspiration of the human soul. It has to be a calling from God, something for the faithful to discern under the guidance of a hierarchy charged with the transmission of sacred powers by Christ, the high Priest, in view of keeping alive the sacred flame of the Spirit and perpetuating the Good News for the spiritual enlightenment of souls. The ordained priesthood in the Church to which he had aspired for a time as a young man, and among whom he had found so many close friends and counselors, for following his own vocation as a philosopher in the world, is the prolongation of Christ's own Priesthood as mediator and savior for all. Through it is to be "realized the total plan of adoptive assumption and of supernaturally transformative union" (1946, 163). It is the "social sacrament par excellence" in which all the others concur as conditions for its existence in the Christian community and as preparation for its final attainment in the performance of the Eucharist.

Blondel ends his consideration of the sacramental ordinance in the Church, Mystical Body of Christ acting in the world, with the *Eucharist.* Whereas this sacrament is more commonly spoken of as the third sacrament of initiation into the life of the Church, after Baptism and Confirmation, Blondel, who attended daily Mass faithfully at his parish church, Saint Jean de Malte, near his home in Aix, highlights it more as the sacrament of sacraments prolonging the effective presence of the incarnate Word and his redemptive sacrifice through time and in all places on earth. What Blondel saw in the Eucharist, more than anywhere else, was a condensation of the "whole of Christian thought and life, the whole of the destiny offered to humanity, the whole preparation for eternal life into this Guest of the Tabernacle and this Sacrifice of the Mass, which is not just a figurative, but a realist summation giving us the One who intercedes at all times for us, or better still, gives himself to us to unite us to his mystical Body, to serve as viaticum and enabler for the eternal life, inaugurated in this world already in Baptism but nourished by the Bread of life, *Panem de coelo*" (1946, 163).

Blondel's conception of the "real presence" of Christ in the Eucharist was anything but an empty formula. To explain the central place of the Eucharist in the divine plan, Blondel goes back to the ontological significance of the Incarnation as ordered by divine Wisdom and Charity for the elevation of the universe into a participation, an assimilation, an adherence to God. More than just a juxtaposition or a gluing together, this adherence is better understood as an organic compenetration in keeping with the true meaning of life as principle of spiritual unity transcending the sensible appearances of material extension. Citing Pascal, and not Hegel, Blondel refers to the true universal, not as an abstract generality, but as "a concrete reality, invisibly and totally present in each of the singular beings participating in it: *totum in singulis*" (1946, 165). This allows him to think of Christ, universal principle of a new life, as wholly in each and wholly in all. The Savior's vitally spiritual and properly supernaturalizing function thus is to make himself intimately and totally present, living and acting in each one of the cells, so to speak, that makes up his mystical Body, so that each one brings its own hidden identity to perfection in him through him. When Christ makes himself present in the Eucharist, as consecrated Host, he is exercising this function in as concrete and realistic a way as we can think, but not just to remain confined in some material singularity. Through this concentration in the singularity of bread and wine, he is bringing a way that is positively practical in solving spiritual problems for the faithful struggling to accomplish their mission in the world and to fulfill the plenitude of their vocation here and now in anticipation of the fulfillment that will be eternal.

What the Eucharist brings to the life inaugurated in baptism for Christians is a presence of Christ that is singularly concrete, quite real, as Blondel repeatedly insists, but as nourishment for a life that is supernaturally spiritual, not just physical or animal. In fact, as nourishment in the supernatural life, Christ gives rise to a certain transubstantiation into his person, body and soul. "Through his transubstantiation," Blondel explains, "Christ has recourse to a reverse transubstantiation, so to speak, in order to insert us into his life by giving his life to the extent that we give him ours" (1946, 168). However, it is still not an exchange between equals. It is a transfiguration of the human into the divine, a divinization. Blondel pictures it more as a kind of endosmosis, where a less dense fluid passes over into a more dense fluid. Assimilation of the heavenly nourishment in the Eucharistic communion is more of an assimilation of our life to that of Christ than an absorption of Christ into our life. This is the reverse of assimilation in earthly nourishment. God gives himself to assimilate us to himself. Adherence to the action of grace in our souls brings new energy in our spiritual life, liberates us from our narrow egoism to participate meritoriously in what Blondel calls "the requirements of Christian heroism" (1946, 169). This is how a true symbiosis of the divine and the human comes to take place in history without reducing the divine dimensions of history and without negating the singularity of individual spirits in body and soul.

The place where this human and divine symbiosis is realized most effectively for the Christian community in its historical peregrination is in the celebration of the holy sacrifice of the Mass, which is at the central core and the highest summit of its religious cult, its literal practice of the sacramental order. Blondel's fascination and absorption with this mystery was not just that of a devout Catholic who as a young man entertained the thought of being ordained to celebrate, and who attended daily mass throughout most of his life, including the years when he was writing this work on the Christian Spirit and its sacramental ordinances, but that of a philosopher who saw in it a beacon of light for the enlightenment of a humanity in search of a destiny that would be worthy of its highest aspirations. He recalls how Christ first spoke the words of consecration, "this is my body, this is my blood; take, eat and drink," in the context of what the Incarnation, the Redemption was for, the sanctification and divine adoption of people in all ages, and how Christ then empowered the apostles to do the same in memory of him, whence the spiritual realism of this Eucharist reaching down into the depths of our humanity. "Nothing is more logical, more salutary, more justly commanded than this participation in this supra-temporal, so to speak, synthesis of the Mass, uniting us, as contemporaries, at all dates of duration to our Mediator, our Savior, our deifier" (1946, 174).

In the continuous re-enactment of this mystery, we are assimilated to God in a way that philosophy cannot comprehend, but that becomes problematic for it when rational speculation is conjugated with the revelation of these mysteries as they affect humanity in what Blondel calls a "symbiosis of human docility and of divine grace" (1946, 172). Ever mindful of the incommensurability and of the essential autonomy on both sides of the distinction between the philosophical order, summing up into a single order the whole of nature and the human being at its head, and the Christian order, raising this humanized order into the higher order of adoptive filiation through incorporation into Christ, Blondel continues to insist on a necessary connection between the two, from which he derives his logic of the symbiosis between the two. From the side of philosophy this necessary connection begins to appear at the summit of human achievement, when reason, aided and abetted by grace, recognizes its insufficiency, its incapacity, in the face of a divine order, to satisfy the infinite power that moves it or, to put it in terms of the philosophy of action, to find an object of the willed will that will equal the power of the willing will. Satisfaction at this highest level of human achievement can only come from a divine order duly recognized as totally transcendent. Yet, from the side of the Christian order, it must be said that this supernatural order cannot establish itself without the good will of human beings and without an effective action that, with all its universal ramifications, is the toll of access and the receptacle for the superhuman supplements, without which the plan of the supreme and all-powerful charity could not realize itself.

This is how Blondel justifies his philosophical incursion into the mysteries of the Christian Spirit as a matter of rational necessity. The philosophical enigmas that remain at the end of a proper philosophy of action are not matters of indifference to human prudence and true wisdom. They follow from a properly humble philosophical attitude, and from properly religious expectations at work in the human way of experiencing the world. The sense of our insufficiency, Blondel writes, "comes from a conviction, a hope for an assimilation to a more perfect order of justice, truth and goodness" (1946, 174). The idea of human destiny, what we hope for as human beings, cannot be framed in static concepts or in any closed system of world history, at least not in a conception that is both truly philosophical and Christian at the same time. Looking back over the history of philosophies from antiquity to modern times, Blondel sees a progressive synthesis having emerged dialectically from partial systems correcting one another's insufficiencies and complementing one another. All that is true in the progressive synthesis of these partial systems has a place "in the synthesis made possible by the integral doctrines of Christian assimilation" (1946, 175). In fact, with his friends, Pierre Duhen, historian of science, and Victor Delbos, historian of philosophy, Blondel was of the opinion that modern operative science and the true conception of philosophy as unitive came only with the advent of Christianity. Before that, man was seen as only a piece in the mechanism of nature "that he could master only by his resignation and by his knowledge, without modifying its occult powers. Philosophy itself was undergoing the destiny and the mystery of the infinite without participating in the *fatum* against which the gods could do nothing" (1946, 175). Modern civilization and philosophy, under the influence of the Christian idea of the infinite, has changed all this, but only by exaggerating human transcendence and its growing domination over the forces of nature, and losing sight of the true transcendence of the triune God and the supernatural order designed for man in the world through the mediation of the incarnate Word and the sending of his Spirit. Blondel's instinct as a philosopher is to recall to mind this entire Christian order, which is at the origin of our modern civilization and philosophy, and to restore it in its own true light, so that it will better serve once again "the human and divine truths from which depends the only true civilizing progress for our present and future life" (1946, 175). That is why his consideration of the

Christian spirit had to come down to such practical matters as the sacramental order and, above all, the celebration of the Eucharist as the epitome of this order of real divine presence in human action.

The Paradoxical Ethic of the Beatitudes

Beyond this consideration of the sacramental order culminating in the Eucharist as integral to Christ's providential plan for disseminating his life and his Spirit to generations around the world, Blondel goes on to explore how immanence and transcendence come together in an ethical practice that draws spiritual creatures into communion with one another as well as with the triune God. He finds this more practical side of the Christian teaching expressed in what has been called the first programmatic statement of Jesus for the coming of the kingdom of God, at the beginning of his public teaching, the Sermon on the Mount. He takes this statement as a challenge addressed to human beings to rise to new, paradoxical heights and as requiring superhuman courage in working through the trials of history toward a fulfillment, a beatitude, that surpasses the capacity of any created spirit. It represents for Blondel a philosophy expressed in the form of eight sublime paradoxes concerning true beatitude, and how to strive for it, that is consistent and heroic, in keeping with the sublime ideal it is aiming at.

Blondel contrasts this Christian ethic with one that comes only from an egocentric perspective on the basis of a utilitarian principle, or what he calls "the calculus of a collective protection focused on the disproportion there is always between those who despoil and those who are despoiled with an eye to minimizing one's own individual risks" (1946, 180). The latter is an ethic of maintaining one's might, regardless of social consequences for others. Writing in 1946, Blondel sees this calculating ethic as having infected personalism and polymorphic existentialism, which denature the dignity of man by considering him as an absolute in isolation and in abstraction from any other, and by forcing everyone into a defensive posture, ever ready to become aggressive against other individuals and collectivities that have the same ambition of independence, expansion, not to say exclusive domination at the expense of others. This is not an ethic out of which ancient traditional communities were formed, much less that of the Good News propounded by Christ. It is the ethic of a war of everyone against everyone that remains in force even after agreements or contracts have been signed not to pursue the war beyond certain limits set by contract or treaty. The Christian ethic is an ethic of peace from its very inception, a promise of peace on earth to all men of good will, not just in the interior life of individual consciences, but more universally in relations of mutual recognition and regard toward all human beings.

Blondel has always maintained as a matter of essential truth, both speculative and vital, that "for the person to become fully herself, she must be dedication, consciousness of other persons, justice and charity and, one could say, an image — from afar no doubt, but already in an embryonic or an incipient way — of that Trinitarian life which is the perfection of one being, the unique Being, in a reciprocal love" (1946, 182). It is in their assimilation to this supreme reality, which is their Cause as well as their End, that beings gifted with knowledge, freedom, and fecundity have to unite in their multiplicity in a way that surpasses all utilitarian calculus reducible to the animal interests of man rather than his authentically spiritual interests. Having brought man back to his first Cause and to an order of supernatural ends as the ultimate reason for his existence, Blondel takes the presence of the Mediator and the universal Savior as well as the Creator in human beings as the principle for the devotion and love among them, without which the person and society close themselves off from their destiny and fall back into disorder, dissatisfaction, and fratricidal combats, in a sort of indefinable vacuum due to being cut off from their divine vocation. Consciousness of this divine vocation, made known within conscience itself and through explicit or implicit faith in Revelation, brings knowledge and action together so that they may compose the masterpiece of a transformative union that "puts Christ in man and in humanity and humanity in each one of his members and in all, called as they are to form a unified organism" (1946, 184). What the Beatitudes express are the ways Christians must take, the ethical dispositions they must develop, to enter into such a high level of communion and peace, at once among men and with God himself. They cannot be anything but paradoxical even in the rational order that Blondel finds among them.

Blondel elaborates on each one of the eight Beatitudes as spiritual dispositions conducive to greater mutual recognition and assistance out of love of God and neighbor, insisting always on a certain heroism to be shown in the pursuit of a truly communitarian life. He speaks of the spirit of *poverty*, not only as a heroic detachment from the goods of utilitarian life in this world, but also as heroically fecund in attaining the "pearl of great price" in a show of humility and charity. He speaks of *meekness* as a kind of liberation from the hardness of heart that braces us up in opposition to others, not one that is timid or fearful of standing up to blows and risks of suffering or death, but one that does not flinch when truth and duty call and that does not retreat in defending just causes or giving witness to the truth, a meekness that is heroically decided to uphold necessary affirmations even in the face of martyrdom. He explains how those who *mourn* are blessed in the hope that sustains and allows them to feel the desolation that comes from loss and deprivation, so that they will be consoled in a way that Stoic ataraxy cannot appreciate, in a future life of communion with others that begins right now. Those who *hunger and thirst for justice*, for others as well as for themselves, also will be satisfied, for they become part of the total concert of humanity and of all creation that divine Providence is composing for the elevation of mankind, where justice has to do "with equitable relations among the diverse creatures cooperating in our existence, in our social functions, in our universal duties with regard to God as well as our neighbor" (1946, 195).

But then, in the fifth place, so too are the *merciful* happy, for they will obtain mercy, the condition for entering into communion, not only with God, but also with any other human being. Blondel notes that mercy, *miséricorde,* is a term that has no equivalent in antiquity and seems to have disappeared from much of modern philosophy. The word sounds hollow to all those fearful of being taken advantage of by others. But the Christians have the heroic benignity of the Savior to go by, in their exercise of supernatural charity, who, by examples and by command, as expressed later in the Sermon on the Mount, enjoins them to love their enemies and to will and do good for them. Again, it takes heroic restraint of legitimate aversions to show genuine mercy to one's enemies, but it can move the offenders toward more just sentiments and it does bring some relief to the suffering of the Crucified one. As for the *clean of heart,* of whom it is said that they will see God, Blondel thinks of them as liberated from troubled passions in their exercise of charity toward God and other loved ones. This is pertinent for all Christians of every state in the Church, married as well as unmarried, but Blondel sees it also as "an encouragement or even a call to those who, chosen by God, have a vocation to disengage themselves more from earthly bonds, worldly riches and human attachments" (1946, 199). Cleanliness of heart is another indication of the heroic heights to which Christians are called in this life, in preparation for a more penetrating and more beatifying vision in eternity.

Writing at the end of World War II, Blondel attaches special importance to the seventh Beatitude: Blessed are the *peacemakers,* for they shall be called children of God. What is meant by *peace* here is not just an interior disposition that comes from realizing that one is a child of God; it is also an attitude of friendliness and civility within a Christian community that can become fragmented because of deficiencies in teaching and practice, and within the broader civic community among social classes as well as among families and fellow citizens. The model that comes to mind is that of the early Christians, of whom it was said: "see how they love one another." That was the mark by which Jesus wanted them to be known as his disciples, the actualization of divine charity in the world. But the model was not designed for just a small community. It was meant for all men, to bring them into a single fold. The model may not have worked yet to bring the true peace of a Christian charity in all parts of the universal Church, let alone civil society, national and international, for all sorts of reasons, but Blondel sees this law of love prescribed by the Gospel, as its characteristic principle, as the one to be applied in the resolution of all conflicts. That is the one he appealed to in a work titled *Lutte pour la civilisation et philosophie* de la paix in 1939, as the storm clouds were gathering and one he was intending to return to later in discussing the actual problems Christianity has to face up to in volume three of this work on *Philosophy and the Christian Spirit*. The fundamental challenge that remains for all Christians in the world is: How do we exercise heroic charity in the struggle for a truly peaceful civilization?

The eighth and final Beatitude speaks to this question in a paradox that sums up all the other paradoxes in this discourse, and in a way that highlights the heroism of the Christian ethic of love more than any other. "Blessed are those who suffer persecution on account of justice; the kingdom of God is theirs." Blondel notes that this one is spoken of in the present, unlike the others, which refer to the future. He takes it to be "the affirmation of a fidelity already enjoyed amid the persecutions, the contempts, the insults, the martyrs of this world" (1946, 204). Implicitly, it is referring to every manner of suffering Christ had to endure in his passion and death, and to the spirit in which it was endured, which was peaceful and merciful, and anything but cowardly or slavish. Blondel reads it as offering encouragement for all those still caught up in the spiritual struggle against those who pride themselves as incarnating human wisdom and heroic virtue when they "denigrate, ridicule, condemn Christian life as a slave morality, a life of sadness and servitude" (1946, 205). In presenting each of the beatitudes as heroic in its requirement, Blondel has been counteracting this dismal view of the Christian ethic that understands nothing of the profound hope and joy that motivates it. In their struggle and in their suffering Christians are actualizing the kingdom of God on earth, as Christ was doing in his passion and death. Needless to say, all this presupposes faith in a totally transcendent triune God who has sent his only begotten Son and the Holy Spirit to establish this kingdom among all men.

In a final comment on this synthetic summation of the ways of accessing to our final beatitude, Blondel takes exception to the pacifist view of Tolstoy that would advocate "non-resistance to evil," as if to accept any intrusion of violence and crime against the rights and the duties of civilized life. Such was not the teaching of Jesus, who did not belittle the necessity of just laws and of legitimate authorities to secure the human person and an equitably established order. What this Master of the interior life, "this educator for the supernatural life and for the future city," was addressing was this inner disposition of souls where his Spirit cannot reside unless one's "most profound will dominates all egoism, all anger, all avidity for reprisals and for earthly advantages" (1946, 206). What is promised in return for this resignation and this abandonment of all vengeance as integral to the Christian spirit is a peace that surpasses all feelings of bitterness, all egoistic intransigence, leaving our interests in justice in the hands of God alone, for "he has reserved the matter of sanctioning to himself while associating us to his work of clemency in our own regard as well as that of those who offend against us" (1946, 206).

The Christian Outlook on the Last Things in Human Life

The Sermon on the Mount goes on to say more about how the New Law of Christian beatitude is to relate to the Old Law, by perfecting it and by making it even more demanding in a higher spirit of charity, but Blondel does not go into that more legal aspect of Christian prescription for life in this world. Nor does he go into the parables Jesus later used to indicate how the Kingdom insinuates itself mysteriously into the world of human spirit like a good seed amid bad seed or a pearl of great price, hidden but ready for the taking. Instead, in keeping with his constant preoccupation with the thought of our final end, he turns to consider what are called the "last things" in the Christian creed, having to do with the transition from a life of meritorious action in this world to a life of eternal reward or punishment in the next. Of special importance to philosophy is the spiritual bond that ties the past, the future, and the eternal together in these "last things," and the conception of how time ends and how eternity begins for man in a face to face with the Absolute or with the triune life of God himself in his total transcendence. Questions of the communion of the saints and the remission of sins arise in this eschatology, along with questions of death and afterlife, of personal immortality and the resurrection of the body, but those that are of greatest philosophical interest are those having to do with thinking of the historical universe as a whole, the aporiai of time and space, and what Blondel calls "final sanctions" in eternal life for having done good or evil in temporal life.

Eschatology has to do with things coming to an end, not as into nothingness or mere cessation of being, but rather as coming to something that surpasses time and space, to a "one thing necessary," a supreme reality to which the human spirit is oriented from its beginning. We have no clear vision of this end we are destined for, just as we have no clear vision of our origin, but the Christian spirit has clear indications of how we can come to terms with facing such an end. What the question comes down to ultimately is how we have to think of the universe as one in its extension and as somehow finite in its seemingly indefinite expansion. This is so, not only in the physical order of conception, but also in the religious order relating to the Creator, at least as this is understood in the Christian Spirit. It seems that, just as the world of creatures had a beginning in duration, it will also have an end, though we are not given any precise indications of how this limitation in time is to be conceived. One thing, however, is certain for Blondel: neither counting nor duration, neither space nor time, entail any true or real infinity. At the most they can only be thought as indefinite in relation to a *finality* of an other order, that of a spirit at once human and divine. The problem of the true and the false infinite in the universe can only be resolved by what Blondel calls "the normal and providential transfer of the cosmological problem to the level of the spiritual and even the properly supernatural order" (1946, 229).

Blondel derives his understanding of the cosmological problem, not from the Newtonian absolutization of space and time, but from the more recent developments of astrophysics in the first half of the twentieth century as formalized in relativity theory. From the evidence that points back from the seemingly indefinite expansion of the physical universe to an enigmatic point of origin in the distant but numerable past, he draws a further inference concerning what would be a no less enigmatic point in the future where this immense movement would come to an end as counterpart to its origin. Physicists are far from having come to any agreement as to how such an end would come about, but Blondel points out that the problematic of modern cosmologies concerning the beginning and the end of the universe is not unlike the problematic of ancient cosmologies, when it came to final resolutions. Cosmologies always leave us in spiritual suspense. Even with the supposition of a Creation in time, there is no reason for putting a limit on the inexhaustible proliferation of diverse forms in a universe emanating from divine generosity.

To work toward a better resolution of this aporia of indefinite progression in time and space, Blondel introduces another aporia between duration and extension, much as Bergson had done in dealing with the more concrete problematic of life as such in the universe, as this problematic of duration and extension now relates for him to the relation between immortality and eternity, that is, to a life with a beginning in time but without end, as distinct from a life without beginning and without end on the side of eternity, as it were. Philosophers have come up with diverse ways of pulling these interlocking aporiai together, often exclusive of one another, but Blondel wonders whether distinguishing between concrete duration and abstract time could not bring a final resolution to a problem that has become all too generalized as a progressive relativism in higher mathematics. If we distinguish concrete duration as a psychological factor in reality from abstract time as measured in and through space, philosophy can formulate a much more open conception, not only of life, but also of intellectual spontaneity and freedom in the conquest of new orders, spiritual and scientific, including some more metaphysical and mystical or religious, and perhaps even of *eternity* itself as living Absolute. Through his renewed insistence on concrete duration, Bergson opened the way to such broader perspectives on reality, but it was Louis Lavelle, friend and colleague of Blondel, who had pushed his philosophical analyses and syntheses to the point of realizing a certain virtual participation in the eternity of being and truth on a conceptual level. Beyond this, Blondel had to insist on the realism of such conceptions in relation to the universe, in order to assess the more positive resolutions offered by Christianity to the remaining problem of opposition between duration and extension subject to the completely heterogeneous forms of time and space.

Through generalized relativity theory Einstein had come to some point of reference, chosen to serve, so to speak, as a relative or conventional absolute, the speed of light. Blondel argues, however, that discursive thought cannot come to any such sample of an absolute in the order of our spatial and temporal experiences without some reference to "the true Absolute, the Absolute in itself, thanks to eternity which is itself only by being entirely in itself" (1946, 236). For a better way of representing what is not merely an indefinitely prolonged duration, Blondel goes to Aristotle's idea of the *now* without duration, either past or future. This enables him to think of spirit as an ongoing life drawing from the past and reaching into the future, where the problem becomes one of joining this life of movement and deployment to that of the Absolute or Eternity.

If we think of the eternal only as unmoving and immutable, we could reduce the problem of our "final end" to little more than a word game, an end "that is not an end, but an infinite beginning of what will have no end" (1946, 237). But such a purely notional and discursive way of thinking would not be true to the inexhaustible plenitude that has already been shown to be implied in the philosophy of *Action*. Not only is Trinitarian life itself a genesis without beginning or end, but the possession of beatitude as well implies "an inexhaustible affluence of a richness that is ever total" (1946, 237). The notion of such an infinite and eternal affluence is not entirely foreign to us. It is secretly *in act* in our experience of all forms, all encounters, all oppositions, all analyses and all syntheses that coalesce, positively or negatively, in our sensible, our intellectual, our moral, and even our religious life. This presence *in act* cannot be systematically synthesized intellectually in any sort of pantheism, but it does remain vitally inviscerated in all of our being, present and future, requiring of us a spiritual transformation, a dilation unto death, so to speak, "through the intrusion of the infinite into our natural limits, in order to regenerate us to the measure of God and eternal life" (1946, 238). This new life rises and raises us above all duration and all extension, regardless of how real and burdensome the toll we have to pay on "the bridge of which Christ is the eternal Bridge-Builder or *Pontiff*" (1946, 238). Far from minimizing the empirically amalgamated notions brought out by critical reflections on our experience, Blondel draws on them to prolong their apparent parallelism and to suggest how and why they converge, come together, and enrich one another in the infinite of eternity through the opening of our supernatural destiny unto an eternal beatitude that has been shown to be the highest and most justifying aim of creation.

All this presupposes that we take the two abstract notions of time and space, concretized in the terms of duration and extension where human action takes place, as intelligible data expressing a divine ordering that is good, flowing from the Good as an immense generosity whose aim is not only to create an image of its own power and wisdom, but also to realize itself effectively through love and gifts in the creatures themselves. Only by taking such a high perspective of creation as transcending all notions still too caught up in the speculations of philosophy and science, can we escape from any relativized conception of the Absolute, and from any exclusively immanentist approach to the problem of transcendence. "It is therefore normal, necessary and even inevitable to elevate a debate that is insoluble if we do not tie it into the problem of eternity and our participation in eternal life" (1946, 240).

Within this complex of abstract aporiai between time and space concretized for human beings into aporiai of duration and extension, where action is exercised in relation to the eternal Absolute, however, there remains another aporia within the Christian notion of the "last things" that is even more difficult for philosophy to resolve than the first two. For when we do raise the level of discourse to that of a spiritual fulfillment and beatitude through regeneration into adoptive filiation with God, we are told in Revelation that not all attain that beatitude equally, and even that some do not attain it at all, though they do not lose their necessary connection with the eternal. All are called to a supernatural life with the Eternal, but not all attain it. Whether one attains it, and by how much, depends on how each one responds to the call, whether through positive acceptance or negative rejection, and in the case of positive acceptance, with how much generosity and self-sacrifice. Whence comes the idea of eternal sanctions for acts taken in time and space that we cannot but find mysterious, if not at odds with the just exigencies of reason itself. For, if reason is willing to accede to some eternal reward for a temporal good act, it is not so ready to accept an eternal punishment for an evil act that is equally temporal and passing.

This is a philosophical problem for Blondel, not only because he takes eternal life itself to be totally transcendent and supernatural, beyond the pale of any natural or immanent life for a finite spirit, but also because he takes each individual human being to be called to eternal life and to have to respond to the call one way or another. God does not save or bring anyone to perfect fulfillment in himself, without each one actively choosing to be saved, explicitly or implicitly, and meeting the conditions of self-abandonment necessary for salvation. The counterpart of this is that one can also choose not to be saved and refuse to meet the conditions for salvation, as the first couple did in the garden of Eden and as many others appear to have done since then. Blondel is careful to point out that it is not for us to judge absolutely concerning other individuals in this regard, or even concerning our individual selves in this life. The choice each one exercises concerning our final destiny is one that is usually exercised over a series of acts strung out in each one's duration and spread out over a broad extension of reality, including other selves in a common civilization. But the suggestion that some will suffer eternal punishment rather than an eternal reward implies that there are sinners, and that they have done what should not have been, according to the supernatural order ordained by God. In the case of a grave or a mortal sin, the past would be irreversible, so that the sinner as such cannot enter into eternal life, unless he were redeemed by Christ, who underwent the punishment for all sin, and unless the sinner accepted the Redemption voluntarily with all the conditions for entering once again into the way of salvation.

There are not two orders of creation, one natural and one supernatural. There is only one order of nature that has been elevated through man to a supernatural destiny. It is up to man to achieve this destiny, with the help of grace, in the light of Revelation that places our natural immortality in relation to "eternal life" itself. It could have been that there be no sin, but we do not know what history would have been in that case. What we do know from Revelation is that sin has been from the beginning and remains a refusal of the supernatural destiny offered to us, for us to take or to set aside. If sin is left unrepented, it leaves the individual outside looking into a beatitude the individual could have had, and that he or she desired congenitally, if not naturally. Whence the idea of a punishment willed more by the sinner himself rather than by God. Blondel maintains that, even in this life, we live in a perspective of atemporal truth under the aspiration of the infinite. This makes us imperishable in being. We subsist already under a mark of eternity — *sub specie aeternitatis*. What is more, we have seen how God's providential plan destines us, not to be absorbed into some impersonal divine totality, "but engages us in a supernatural order offered to a free and normal option, respecting and affirming our personality" (1946, 361). What results from this option is either an introduction into life eternal, or an irremediable failure "conscious of its incurable misreasoning [*déraison*] and of the inextinguishable suffering that follows from it; for the supra-temporality of the perdition is an effect of the eternalizing purpose of the docility to the election" (1946, 361). For those who willingly refuse to enter into the fullness of being to which they are called, there is, not annihilation, but an awakening, so to speak, to the dire conditions of deprivation and self-contradiction in which they have willfully placed themselves irrevocably.

For those who will have willfully benefited from the universal mediation of the Man-God, the Sun of spirits and intimate confidant of each of the beatified, on the other hand, there will be not only the supernatural union with God that all aspire to, but also a communion of saints where each one rejoices for all the others in a single possession of the Spirit who proceeds from the Father and the Son. "Such is the expression," Blondel concludes, "of a hope quite different from that of the pantheism that reduces us, in this world even more than in the next, to a fugitive instantaneity that depersonalizes us in affirming the Great All. Such a disappropriation — which in certain regards can be admired or pitied — could not be anything in effect but a resignation mixed with proud serenity and vanishing hope. How different is the multitude of souls formed in the practice of the eight Beatitudes who, without egoistic second thoughts, without limits in their commitment to the works of mercy, beyond all calculation, consecrate themselves in a life of full generosity" (1946, 248).

Far from abandoning itself to any sort of infinite resignation such as the one Kierkegaard found in Hegelian philosophy, the Christian Spirit goes forward to meet God on his own grounds, ready to accept more than what it could have bargained for. Blondel's insistence for this Spirit is not just on its totally transcendent and supernatural character as it affects human destiny, but also on an equally high regard for every fully conscious individual in his or her freedom to say *yes* or *no* in all responsibility to the gift of elevation into the eternal life of the triune God. Thus, what started off as a simple reflection on what he called the philosophy of the Gospel in his *Carnets Intimes,* by a young man preparing to enter into the fray of philosophy, with his philosophy of action bearing within it a philosophy of the supernatural, grew to a full, systematic expression, able to distinguish itself from any and every sort of immanentist or dualistic sort of philosophy, religious or not, even as applied to the question of eternal sanctions for individual acts committed in space and time, but with a will that has eternal consequences. Blondel understood very well how the one with Christian Faith could "get it all back," after sacrificing everything for the pearl of great price, supernatural life as such. But he also understood how one could lose it all, eternally, because each individual has God-given power to say *no* to the gift proffered gratuitously by God, but in line with the highest aspirations of the human spirit.

XVIII

Christian Spirit and Historical Civilization

Blondel was eighty-five years old when volume two of *Philosophie et Esprit Chrétien* was published. He had been laboring, unable to read or write for himself, with Mademoiselle Nathalie Panis for some fourteen or fifteen years to bring to the light of day his long-planned Tetralogy, or his two trilogies, the one on Thought, Being, and Action, and the other on the Christian Spirit in its various historical phases. Not only were his sight and hearing impaired, but so too was his general health. Like that of many others in his time, it had long been frail, his longevity notwithstanding. Yet he was still determined to bring his project of a third volume on the Christian Spirit to completion, as a philosophy of history open to the insertion of a supernatural end of communion and peace. Even before volume two appeared in print, he had begun to write a general plan for the work and to elaborate on what were to be his essential themes.

In a transitional conclusion to volume two of *Philosophie et Esprit Chrétien*, Blondel asks: After we have come to the highest extremity of all knowledge and of all destiny conceivable, can we go further, beyond eternity and beyond infinitude itself? Where another philosopher, with a less strict sense of the supernatural than the one Blondel associates with the idea of the transcendent and the Absolute, the eternal or the infinite, might answer yes, with an ever-transcendent movement of spirit in the world, Blondel answers with a peremptory *no*. There is no going beyond what we can only accept on faith, or what we can only conceive as a final destiny in which we pass over into eternity, or into the Absolute itself, though he will speak of eternal life itself as a certain progression for us into higher perfection. Going beyond in a third volume on the Christian Spirit for Blondel meant coming back "to the itinerary of the time in which we are living, facing up to the risks we have to run, and looking for salutary solutions to be brought forth in action" (1946, 249). In other words, going beyond in this reflection on the Christian Spirit immanent in history meant coming back to action in the concrete, to the state of the world in which that human action takes place concretely and historically, with its recurrent problems of war and violence, as evidenced in the paroxysm it had reached at the end of World War II. At that time, there were those who spoke of the need for a new order to surpass the Christian order that had become part of the historical order of civilization, but Blondel saw things differently. Even with his idea of the totally transcendent good of communion with the divine, toward which the human spirit was moved by grace as well as by nature, he still thought that the Christian Spirit could offer solutions for the immanent good of history and civilization on earth, in keeping with what Augustine had called a tranquility of order, for the benefit of all in their pursuit of a vocation of love and mutual regard, not only with the triune God, but also with one another in a communion reaching out to all humanity.

For Blondel the life of Christians in the world could not be separated from that of humanity as a whole. That is why this Christian life on earth had become a matter of interest for him as a philosopher, no less than he had tried to make the question of our eternal destiny a matter of human interest. The two orders of questioning were intimately bound up with one another for him as both philosopher and Christian. In volume one of the *Christian Spirit*, where he follows the history of how God's plan for a higher supernatural vocation is made manifest from creation on, through the fall of the human race and on to the redemptive sacrifice of Christ, he is careful at every turn to show how the revelation plays into questions or enigmas that remain for human understanding regarding where we stand as spiritual beings in history. Similarly, in volume two of the *Christian Spirit*, in pointing out the spiritual force of the Resurrection and of the Ascension for launching the properly Christian community in the world, followed by the effusion of the Holy Spirit and the prolongation of Christ's life in the world through the Church, the sacraments, and tradition as a discipline for life in the world, he indicates how all these are supports and resources placed at our disposal for sustaining faith and vitality as well as the permanence for a community still very much in action, in a world that does not recognize it for all that it is or for all that it is aiming at, but that should be of interest to an integral philosophy of the human spirit. Now, in volume three of the *Christian Spirit*, as he turns to a consideration of his own conflicted historical actuality, a matter of concern for both Christianity and philosophy, it is for the same integral philosophy, at once Christian and universally rational, *catholic* in every sense of the word, to look for solutions to the impasses of war and violence that have accumulated in his time. The need for innovation in the philosophical spirit in dealing with these problems of historical actuality strikes him as coming from the traditional Christian spirit itself, going back to the New Testament.

What his systematic work has brought forth up to now in the Trilogy on

Thought, Being, and Action, and in the first two volumes on the Christian Spirit, focusing on the divine initiatives in history for the divinization of mankind and on the symbiosis of both natural and supernatural initiatives in the ongoing Christian life on earth, is a certain ordering, an internal logic, and an immanent norm in creation itself as a motion toward transcendence. What has been shown is a certain interdependence of things and of human events going back to the origins of the cosmos and of historical experience, and reaching forward to a final end that is no less mysterious than its origin in the divine will itself. All the world and mankind have been shown to be in a universal movement, defined at once from the top down and from the bottom up, depending on whether we view it from its final spiritual end or from its cosmic origins in matter.

In this vast itinerary, however, human beings have not always been in accord with one another or with any overall plan of human betterment through historical civilization. Taken in isolation and often absolutized in opposition to one another, human beings also create impediments to the sort of universal peace envisioned in the Christian spirit, or even in the ancient philosophical spirit of human community. Blondel thought of his time as having come to an extreme crisis in this regard, a crisis that his Christian philosophy had to contend with, in order to come up with more positive solutions for what he chose to call *civilization* as the universal good of mankind in history. The reason why a third volume on *Philosophy and the Christian Spirit* was called for was to fulfill a responsibility that an integral philosophy of action had to exercise in the concrete historical situation in which he found himself. His philosophy of history was to be one of the rise of civilization to a proper social and universal dimension of spirit, in opposition to the more materialistic and antagonistic forms of social philosophy that had come to prevail in modern thought.

Insufficiency of the Modern State

We have only fragments of what this final volume on the modern crisis in world history would have been, most of them dictated to Mlle. Panis during the last four or five years of Blondel's life, but these are enough to give us some idea of what he had in mind for what he called this integral philosophy of action in relation to the Christian Spirit at work in the world. In a general overview of his plan, dictated over a period of several weeks during December 1945 and January 1946, he speaks of "the divorce and the reconciling convergences between integral philosophy and Christianity as a whole, and of conditions for a peace to be grounded in natural rights and on essential duties for all nations that have attained the level of pacified and liberating life" (1948, 23). What he had in mind was the concrete actuality of civilization as he knew it in Europe at the end of World War II, attempting to step back from the precipice of a war that had shaken the very foundations of civilized life. The problematic as he conceived it was one of finding ways to go forward with civilization on the basis of both natural and supernatural principles simultaneously at work in world history. His plan was to work out a "sequence of advances to be realized through the conjunction of the philosophical order and of the insertion, into the natural and scientific order, of the obligation entailed by the anonymous but real penetration of the supernatural vocation and the responsibilities it introduces even into the apparent ignorance of these responsibilities" (1948, 23).

Every word in this programmatic statement is carefully measured. It speaks of an insertion and of a penetration of the supernatural into the natural order, but only as addressed to free and responsible agents. It speaks of this addressing as anonymous, in order to include all human beings in this calling to a supernatural spiritual life, even those who have never heard the name of Christ, or who think of themselves as anti-Christ. For, as Blondel had always maintained, if there is an offer of supernatural fulfillment made to man, as Christians believe explicitly, it has to engage every man's responsibility through some necessary moral as well as historical connection as an obligation. The problem he had to contend with was not just that of ever-recurrent war and violence in human history, but also that of a social philosophy that could pit man against man in a constant struggle for domination.

This was the problem of modern social philosophy as Blondel saw it, a philosophy he would have to bring back in line, not only with the Christian spirit of charity and mutual regard, but also with the more ancient forms of human sociability and respect for consciences in communal life. For he saw the modern synthesis, not exactly as an atheistic humanism, but rather as an autolatrous humanitarianism, or a theogony seeking the realization on earth of the deceptive promise that we should become gods in our own right, able to achieve our own happiness on earth. What he saw in the total secularization of the State, the schools, individual and family life, of science, and of the new social order, was a secretly coherent complexus of ideas that had all the earmarks of a "theology" in reverse, constructed by an emerging science bent on a new idolatry that he had long branded as a form of superstitious autolatry.

For all their utilitarian ambitions for domination in the world, he would show that these ideas did not and could not bring true peace to human society without a more spiritual education, without the development of civic and spiritual virtues, as a way toward Christian virtues, for there is a necessary "connection between an integrally moral and human civilization and the vocation of the Good News, alone capable of bringing peace with liberty and fraternity among nations and persons" (1948, 25). The modern sloganeering about "liberty, equality, and fraternity," detached from its roots in the ancient social ethic of the cardinal virtues and in the calling of the Good News to the virtues of faith, hope, and charity, had resulted too much in everyone seeking only the gratification of self-interests, in competition with others, and a will to power proclaimed by prophets of modernity like Nietzsche and others. Against these prophets of modern "liberty, equality, and fraternity," Blondel would try to restore the true meaning of these terms in the context of a profoundly spiritual social ethic, including that of the Beatitudes, which express for him the Christian ideal of justice and charity, in opposition to the modern spirit, where the dignity of human persons is sacrificed to a utilitarian will to dominate and control over all the facets of human sociability.

In opposition to the secularization and the consequent absolutization of the modern State, as he saw it functioning in his own country as well as others in Europe in modern times, he would advance a more spiritual idea of political association with an authentic religious dimension and openness to the transcendent. His preferred term for such an idea, going all the way back to the dissertation of 1893, was *patrie*, which designated for him both a people and a country, or a people in its own country, conscious of the traditions and the customs out of which it had grown as a nation. Such an idea of political sociability could be traced back all the way to ancient societies, and had always included a religious function as essential for any sort of civilized life. In fact, many of the secularized nation-states in Europe could be said to have lost touch with such traditions and customs, including those instilled by the Christian Spirit, however anonymous or religiously neutral they had become in their alleged break with the ancient order.

Blondel's aim was to show that this same religious function, whether explicitly Christian or anonymous, was still essentially operative in the life of any city, nation, or even of what he referred to as a "normalized international life," not just in matters of economic and political order, but in what pertained to any sort of moral and spiritual concord, which was and remains of highest human interest. Life within various nations could be said to be *normalized* up to a point in the way the State relates to families and individuals, with respect for personal consciences, but the same kind of normalization had to be transposed to the relations among the supposedly sovereign states as they moved toward an international civilization, so that war, or the struggle for domination, would cease being the determining factor in international relations, and a true universal peace could be achieved on the basis of mutual respect and cooperation among all peoples. For Blondel it was the *catholic* dimension in the religious function that required this internalization of the ethical sense toward all peoples, rather than nationalism of any sort, or of the supposed manifest destiny of any State lording over states. While each people has to be conscious of its own *patriotic* originality and its own right to independence, it also has to recognize a higher law of spiritual value in all peoples and of fidelity to its own singularity as found in other peoples, much as persons must respect personality in others as well as in themselves.

This *catholic* dimension of the spirit was one of justice and charity towards all human beings, those of other nations as well as those of one's own. Instead of restricting the intent of human sociability to only one nation or another, he saw it as extending to all nations and as bringing greater hope for perpetual peace, not only within souls, but also "among peoples with their twofold patriotic and humanitarian sense" (1948, 31). The ideal of a durable peace among nations, which was very much in the air at the end of the Second World War, had something of the mythical about it for him, "a dream one could call religious," something that only a supernatural spirit could bring about, by overturning the egoisms and the passions that troubled social relations among nations as well as among individuals and families. Moving forward toward such an ideal civilization of peace for all men and women of all nations and tribes would require another way of conceiving human sociability than the one that had taken hold in modernity, beginning with Hobbes and a social contract theory requiring an absolute ruler.

The Spiritual Basis of Human Sociability

Blondel remarks on the brutal nature of this Hobbesian theory. It begins by absolutizing individuals in relation to one another, all in a state of war with one another, so that it becomes necessary to impose on them an absolute ruler to maintain a semblance of peace, while the turbulence of war and competition for domination continues to seethe beneath the surface, always ready to erupt at any moment. Even for Rousseau, who had a more benign idea of the state of nature, there was a similar paradox in the social contract, in that the general will had to force everyone to be free, leaving those in opposition with only one alternative: either liberty or death, as happened at the time of the Convention during the French Revolution, when the guillotine was used to solve the problem of practical differences. Blondel points out as well that, for all of his insistence on the rational being as an autonomous end in itself, Kant did not shrink from appealing to an absolute master in political affairs, the good tyrant who was King of Prussia, while in France, the neo-Kantian Renouvier would follow the same logic, in advocating absolutism for the republican government according to the rule of the majority, leaving all minorities without recourse.

All this amounted to setting up the State as an end in itself, for Blondel, and as a master over consciences dominating the entire spiritual life of persons, denying in effect that they were indeed ends in themselves or that they could have a destiny that surpasses all earthly interests. All the State does in fact is preside over a submerged war of everyone against everyone, not only among individuals within one and the same nation, but also among nations, in a free for all, or in a struggle for domination of one nation over another. Hence the recurrent problem of war that had reached its climax in the Second World War, and that seemed to call for a merging of nations under a higher authority still, perhaps a United Nations, where, Blondel wryly remarks, "even in reunions for peace, we find, under forms of violent politeness, brutal regimes bent on world domination." Blondel had pondered at length this ever-increasing problem of war and violence for modern society — magnified by the development of science and technology and the production of ever-more destructive instruments of war — in a short book titled *Lutte pour la civilisation et philosophie de la paix* first published in 1939 and revised for a second edition after the war. In this book he had already begun to show how the Christian Spirit could be brought to bear in the solution to this problem, which Kant had been unable to resolve with his idea of a cosmopolitan perpetual peace, and which Hegel had only exacerbated with his idea of progression in world history as a struggle for domination by one national spirit over others. But in that book, Blondel had not shown how the problem arises from the way the origins of human sociability were still being conceived in modern sociological thinking, like that of Emile Durkheim, a prominent contemporary of Blondel.

For Durkheim, there was a purely natural way of accounting for the emergence of human sociability from a purely animal ancestry, rising little by little through the development of organs and then of cooperation among individual animals, "as the point of departure for a true sociability organized under the direction of chiefs, and for the benefit of a natural, intelligent and hierarchical finality" (1948, 188). For Blondel, however, this was not enough. To account for the originality of properly human sociability, one had to put more emphasis on the spiritual ingredient of human experience, on its psychological aspects of intelligence and will, as he had already maintained in 1893, without naming Durkheim, in his dialectic of the phenomenon of social action (1893a, 234 [245]ff.), but without invoking the Christian Spirit as such. At the end of his life he now intended to show, in this more explicit reflection on the Christian Spirit as such, by speaking of the human spirit as divinely infused, "deliberately fashioned in the image of the Trinity and destined to be assimilated to it — an assimilation surely not by way of a confused mixture, but by way of a supernatural condescendence" (1948, 188), for the constitution of human sociability in the world.

Mere gregariousness in an animal herd adjusting to an interplay of physical and biological forces in order to survive or, as he had also put it earlier in the dissertation of 1893, "a merely regulated exchange of self-interests ... limited to economic phenomena" (1893a, 250 [263]), would not be enough to account for human sociability in all its ramifications. For Blondel, it took much more to set the process of human civilization in motion, a kind of "reciprocal respect" with regard "to an end higher than each individual taken in isolation" (1893a, 238 [249]). As an original form, the social life of human beings in civilization is more than a remodeling of older forms, a physical kneading, so to speak, to make them less incompatible with one another.

Even technical innovations were inventions that nature could not produce by itself, let alone language by which humans communicated with one another, and came to respect one another as selves. Human sociability is something spiritual, born of much more than felt needs in the appropriation of physical and biological forces. It is a matter of intelligence and will that eventually becomes a matter of justice and charity in mutual regard for one another.

It is from this appeal to intelligence and will in the constitution of human civilization that Blondel argued for the necessity of considering the Christian dimension in spirit, with its supernatural intent, going all the way back to the creation itself of contingent spiritual beings. Two things were implied in this supernatural ordering of created spirits, with an initiative of their own in the world, not just the elevation of these creatures to a participation in the inner life of the Trinity itself, something they could not have envisioned, let alone achieved, by themselves, without the aid of grace, but also a call to join with other spirits in working for peace and communion in this world for all the human race, a peace that could not come from the mere interplay of biological and economic forces corralled by some external State authority. The Christian view of sociability came rather from internal dispositions of human beings with a spiritual regard for one another that could not be imposed by an external authority, a view with the divine Trinity "as its model, principle, and final end" (1948, 188). It is not the State that makes the human being initially and ultimately sociable. Nor is human society conceived only as a reaction to mechanical or biological evolution amid discordant and dislocating forces. Organically speaking, "it is an instrumentation at the service of a spiritual life and a religious union tying the whole history of creation to its divine origin and its highest end, through which its destiny is supernaturalized" (1948, 188).

Threefold Level of Human Sociability

What Blondel had in mind for the third volume on the *Christian Spirit* was to show what had to be done to insert this spirit of both justice and charity into a historical process that was constantly hampered by selfish interests of individuals and of nations, all constantly in violent opposition to one another. He had in mind three levels of sociability, which he had already distinguished in the dialectical elaboration of the phenomenon of action of 1893, the familial, the patriotic, and the international or humanitarian as a whole. Each of these he saw as spiritual and religious in its own right from creation on, not as granted by the State, and each with exigencies of its own for a moral conscience and a religious consciousness called to act in the world, in view of a common good that would encompass the whole human race, and in view of an ultimate end that supersedes time and space.

Blondel cautioned, not only against absolutizing individuals in isolation and in violent opposition to one another, but also against absolutizing any sort of organization in like fashion, whether civic, economic, or national. As essentially sociable, man is "destined for a unifying spirituality." He should not subject himself to limited societies that would enslave him to subordinate or narrowly partisan interests, no matter how useful these might be for a time as he had long before argued against those who were willing to join *L'Action Française*. Political, economic, and scientific organizations are correlative means, not ends in themselves, much less obligations to which we could sacrifice the ultimate ends of a destiny that supersedes time and space. The same has to be said of the State. As necessary and legitimate as its authority might be, it cannot be a dominant goal of human life, as it has been represented in many modern philosophies. Nor do persons have their rights from the State. They have their most fundamental rights in themselves, from their very creation as human beings. When the powers that be clearly defy the common will and the essential rights of a nation, it is not only legitimate, but it may also be obligatory to resist and to overthrow such abusive power. Ancient pagan philosophy had already recognized this duty of resistance to abusive power for the unanimity of a nation, but even in a context where we might say that all power is from God, this duty of resistance might become more obligatory and urgent, to maintain a spiritual life or a religious institution imperiled by an authority that abuses its prestige and its physical force. Ignoring the duty to resist in this case would be, not just "a national betrayal, but an apostasy of conscience, a denial of the highest truths to be served and safeguarded with the greatest vigilance."

Blondel had no intention of belittling the importance of establishing political associations, or nations, for the spiritual kind of association he calls civilization and for establishing a universal peace on earth. For him, the *patriotic* level of sociability remained essential and integral for the historical progress of humanity as a whole. What he wanted to insist on was that such political association did not come about without a sense of equity for others as well as for oneself, for other nations as well as one's own, a sense always ready for sincere and utilitarian compromising with others, with a sincere "good will" inspired by a generosity toward others. Even within a nation, without the meritorious intervention of a common effort toward comprehension, and a willing of the good for one another, there can be no properly national order in the face of growing tensions due to scientific developments and competition among materialistically oriented enterprises. Blondel saw the formation of national spirits as a realization of the Good News on earth, by overcoming the powers of destruction and enslavement, through what he called a spirit of dedication and Christian concord, superseding all forms of class or partisan as well as individual egoism, and all foregoing pretensions of domination, including that of majorities over minorities. Far from thinking that it was the State that conferred rights and duties upon persons and the different social elements that make up a national unification, Blondel saw these rights and duties as flowing from the very spiritual nature and willful constitution of human beings, as exercised in action. If there were an *absolute*, to which the human spirit had to refer ultimately, it could not be the State or any particular national unity. It could only be the divine, properly speaking.

In fact, Blondel intended to argue that other forms of spiritual unification were no less natural and rightly willed, on the way to our final unification in the Trinitarian life, than the prized national unification of the modern State, operating under the false or ambiguous pretenses of an absolute "liberty, equality, fraternity," which often masks one form of group egoism over another, whether it be that of a majority over a minority, or that of one State over another. Against the absolutization of the State, he would argue for the inalienable right of the family to exist, and to develop socially according to its own spiritual constitution, not just as a first step in the socialization of human beings that would later give way to some national constitution, but as a permanent form of socialization for the perfection of human beings, with its own exigencies and rights that the State could not supersede.

For Blondel, the family was not just a natural first stage on the way to the more spiritual socialization of the nation-state. It was already the embodiment of a spirit in which human beings learned to have regard for one another, and for the higher things in life, including religion and concern for one's ultimate destiny, where some form of unification with the absolute and with all human beings was at stake, in accordance with the wish of Christ, "that all may be one." These are things Blondel himself had learned in his family, before seeing them in the context of any national unification, even though he did see that the nation had its own degree of spiritual unification, over and above the economic and civic interests that tied it together in a certain geographic territory.

What Blondel valued socially and spiritually as a human being, he learned from the family, in conjunction with the Christian Spirit that was such an essential part of his education. Even though outside the family he encountered an official State that was largely antagonistic to the Christian Spirit he had profoundly internalized as a human being, he did not turn against the State as something purely secular and destructive of spiritual values, as many staunch Catholics were doing in France in his day, even in his own family. He continued to value his own nation as the "organic instrumentation at the service of a spiritual life" he experienced as a Frenchman, but he condemned its officialdom for betraying the religious tradition that had added so much to its civilizing influence over the centuries. What he saw in the antagonism of French officialdom to religion, and more specifically to the Catholic Spirit, was an attempt to dominate over souls in violation of the freedom of conscience, relating to the divine, that had long been essential to the Christian Spirit, even more than the vaunted modern or "enlightened" secular spirit, now cramped into nothing more than what he saw as a totalitarian immanentism. In his reflection on the Christian Spirit as a philosopher, Blondel was calling the modern European State back to its Christian roots, through a full exercise of true religious freedom for its citizens and its families.

In doing so, he was calling upon the State to recognize its limitations, not just in dictating to the spirit of a people as actualized in individual persons and families, but also with regard to other peoples with a civilization of their own. The Spirit he was starting from was one with much more universal ramifications than could be contained in one State, or in any particular combination of states such as Europe. It was a Spirit that flowed from the universal salvific will of the Creator, through Christ, the universal Mediator and Redeemer, to all peoples and all human beings. The fact that it was supernatural and divine made it all the more universal or *catholic,* so that it could not be contained in any particular nation or civilization. In fact, French national though he was, Blondel had the idea that a plurality of diverse civilizations would better represent this universal World Spirit in history than any single State at any given time, given the incommensurability that always remains between a supernatural grace that is totally transcendent and any human appropriation of that grace expressed in history. He remarks at one point, quite significantly, that "separate philosophy," or any secularized philosophy that loses sight of its religious roots, or any reference to a totally transcendent God, tends to conceive of civilized human spirit only in terms of one nation or another, and to put down other nations or civilizations as less than human or as less worthy of respect.

The Greeks did this with regard to the *barbaroi,* and enlightened modern European thinking has done the same with regard to other peoples deemed less civilized and therefore apt for being colonized. Hegel, whom Blondel does not mention, can be seen as having done this even in his philosophical appropriation of the Christian Spirit to his own immanent conception of the Germanic "northern European Protestant spirit," something that the French Catholic Blondel is sure to have noted precisely as a philosopher. In opposition to this idea of superiority for the Germanic Protestant spirit, Blondel did not argue for a superiority of the French or Latin spirit. That would have been to immanentize the supernatural Christian Spirit in the same way as Hegel was doing, contrary to his own belief that the Christian Spirit cannot be immanentized or naturalized, even as it inserts itself into the historical economy and calls for a free acceptance by human beings, in view of a life that is eternal. Instead he used the transcendent universality of a truly *catholic* spirit to broaden the conception of human dignity and civilization beyond the limits of any nation or set of nations he knew, including those that could be said to have absorbed something of the Christian Spirit, whether Protestant or Catholic.

What was at issue for Blondel was a more fundamental principle of sociability for mankind in history, which came from going back, reflectively, to creation and to a first cause, with a universal intent of supernatural salvation for mankind, working its way through history amid the actions and interactions of peoples in a process of universal civilization and spiritual pacification. The model or the exemplar for this process is the first cause itself in its Trinitarian life, as it is also the end to which human life aspires at the head of all material creation.

Blondel's conception of a supernatural life stemming from the Trinitarian life itself and calling us back to itself had everything to do with his conceiving of a universal civilization and peace among diverse peoples as an ideal to be realized on earth through human initiative. Such a conception of creation did not take anything away from the necessary role human action was to play in the pursuit of an end that had to be historical as well as eternal. On the contrary, it required the action of all in consort with one another, according to principles of justice and charity, an action to build up to diverse civilizations, depending on how diverse peoples would constitute their social life, all of them progressively coming together in peace and harmony as one universal civilization made up of many civilizations, each with its distinct right and form of existence in history, to be respected and to be honored as human and spiritual.

Normative Immanence of Spiritual Transcendence

It is with this ideal of a universal civilization in mind for mankind that Blondel approaches the problems of violence and war in modern society, as they had come to a head for Europeans in the Second World War, and consequently for the rest of the world, by reason of the widespread colonial dependence on Western Europe. Against the spirit of violence and competition for domination that had become the norm of modern secular society, not only among factions and classes within nations, but also among nations, he would argue for a fundamental sociability in the human spirit at every level — the family, the nation, and among nations — on religious grounds as well as on anthropological and political grounds. He would denounce not only the onslaught of Nazism or of atheistic communism looming on the international horizon, but also every form of self-centered nationalism, including that of France and its allies. While affirming *patriotism* as standing up for the country of one's origin and for its own form of civilization, he would also insist on respect for the social spirit of other nations. For him, true patriotism was more than mere nationalism. It was a spiritual consciousness open to a wide diversity of civilizations as they present themselves in history, each with a right to assert themselves in their civilized originality, and to maintain and to defend themselves against aggression from other civilizations.

The most difficult part of his task, however, would be to show how this universal sociability of all human beings in history follows from a Christian Spirit that, while remaining mysterious in its ways, challenges human beings to rise to new heights in the advancement of civilizations, and in the promotion of universal peace among them, not by attempting to dominate or to exploit them, but rather by entering into mutual cooperation with them, on a basis of justice and charity. This would require him to show how the Christian Spirit does in fact insinuate itself into the historical consciousness of human beings, or into the constant movement of civilization in the world, through the thought of a final end that surpasses our capacity to achieve, whether as individuals or as human civilizations, but that draws us all to one common life in the life of the Trinity. "There is for us, human beings, at every moment of our history," he writes in 1948, "a kind of judgment, a transformism with indefinite possibility and variety, subject to an internal norm whose secret and absolutely sanctioned inspiration we have to take hold of and follow" (1948, 244). It was to bring out the presence of such a norm in our historical consciousness of daily life that he had traced the deployment of human action step by step, from the individual to the familial, to the patriotic, and finally to humanity as a whole, in his elaboration of the phenomenon of action, arguing all the while that we would not be conscious of ourselves in all this, without some sense of a higher end we are striving for, an end normative for action, a sense of some future good to be attained that sheds light on our experience and turns us toward a future that opens up infinitely before us. The conception of that end may be restricted to what is possible for a created nature to attain with regard to the infinite Transcendent, but if the idea of a supernatural possibility is introduced even by supernatural revelation, it is the idea of the end itself that is affected as a real norm for historical consciousness, in keeping with philosophical reason itself, as it assesses the exigencies and the responsibilities of taking action in the world.

A self-enclosed nationalism may claim to exclude every idea of a supernatural order, under the pretext that the only field open to philosophy is immanence, but for Blondel, it is still within the scope of reason to examine not only how a supernatural end may present itself for humanity, but also how it can become a norm for judgment in orienting human action in world history. This is how the Christian Spirit comes to penetrate human consciousness and consciences with its own exigencies and responsibilities. Even if Christianity presents itself in the light of an eternal and supernatural end, it is not expedient for an integral, historical philosophy to show no interest in it, especially if it offers solutions to the problems that plague humankind in history, not thought of by philosophy.

Blondel alludes to Spinoza and his sense of the eternal dimension in human existence: *sentimus nos aeternos esse.* For Blondel, in the framework of a philosophy that recognizes the total Transcendence of God and of God's supernatural offer to man, without taking anything away from the historical substantiality of the human creature, this means understanding how we must pass from time to eternity in our consideration of the final end for all that we are to be, even as we approach the detail of our daily life in our decisions.

Blondel's philosophy of spirit had been existential from the beginning, but one that was systematically open to the divine in its Transcendence, rather than being merely anti-rationalist and atheistic. It was through a prolongation of this rational existentialism that he wanted to extend the reach of philosophy, into a realm that could not be rationally discerned by human consciousness alone, but whose historical penetration into that consciousness could not be a matter of indifference to an integral philosophy, one willing to entertain all the exigencies and responsibilities of life in the world. Just as the deployment of the infinite power of the will in its exercise of free choice amid immanent motives and mobiles had led up to the necessity of a final option before God, *for* or *against,* so also could he now, in a philosophy of the Christian Spirit, explain and justify before reason how the supernatural motion of that spirit can insert itself, however secretly and mysteriously, into the ongoing natural and socio-historical motions of human experience and civilization, to raise and elevate human life in the present life as well. However that divine motion or grace may remain mysterious in itself, it offers itself as a mobile or motion in our consciousness, to be accepted or rejected by choice, personally and freely, just as other motions of natural or social origin do, or better still, within those natural and social motions themselves, as a return to Blondel's original "method of immanence" would show.

What distinguishes the divine supernatural motion of grace from any other natural or social motion is that, if freely and personally accepted, it empowers us to act in unison with the divine itself, in a theandric action that brings together the first Cause itself and our own reason and will, as second but true cause, where the Transcendent is not only higher than the human, but also interior to it, by a sort of incarnation such as we find in the sacramental life of the Church. Blondel here cites the phrase of Augustine: *tu forma mea Deus — interior intimo meo, superior summo meo.*

The external historical way in which this supernatural ordering for mankind made itself known and insinuated itself into the consciousness of human beings was through a revelation that had its own history, starting with the calling of a Chosen People out of bondage to sin, as well as out of bondage to another people, and going back even to the very beginning of history, with the failed test of original sin, a revelation that was pointing forward to the Incarnation of the divine in history in the man called Christ, as Mediator and as Redeemer for all mankind, who came to announce the Good News and institute a historical Church with a sacramental order, as a way to prolong the mission of announcing the Good News to all men and providing the socio-historical means for sustaining a supernatural life of grace and good will toward all men, as well as toward God, already begun in history. Looking back on the history of the Chosen People and of the Church that succeeded it in the New Alliance, Blondel thought that any rational observer should be able to see that this Spirit did have a civilizing effect on many nations as well as many people, even if the full scope of what was involved in a "Christian Civilization" is not entirely recognized, where all will be one not only with another but also with Father, Son, and Holy Spirit in the eternal life of the Trinity.

Blondel had already gone to great efforts, in volume two of *Philosophy and the Christian Spirit*, to show how the mysterious call to the supernatural insinuates itself historically in a rational consciousness through a Church that gives witness to Christ and his salvific role in history, and thereby challenges the rational being to a higher level of responsibility in accepting or rejecting the freely proffered gift. All of this was in keeping with the way the supernatural has made itself present to the consciousness of rational human beings going back to Christ himself, if not to Abraham as well, the Father of Faith. It spoke of explicit encounters between individual human spirits and Christ himself, or his Spirit and his disciples, in which new levels of consciousness and responsibility did come into play.

This philosophy of the Christian Spirit did not, however, suppose that, in the encounter with Christ, rational thought had a direct access to the supernatural as such. There is no man who can know with certainty of the presence of this superhuman reality within himself, even when the secret offer of it entails and justifies a higher responsibility that is tacitly infinite. The option we face when it comes to our supernatural destiny remains anonymous for us, precisely insofar as it bears on something that is more than human. Blondel, however, maintains that this is as it should be for a rational philosophy, and for human beings with a true sense of justice. Even without knowing the fullness of the reality they are contending with, supernatural as well as natural, all are normally conscious of their moral responsibility, with the concomitant possibility of salvation, or damnation, for themselves.

The Gospel itself allows for this anonymity of the supernatural in human history, Blondel notes, when, in answer to those who ask when it was that they served Christ, bound his wounds, fed him when he was hungry, or visited him when he was in prison, in the final analysis or judgment on their action, they are told that whenever they did any of these things to the least of their brethren they did it unto Christ, and were indeed the blessed of the Father. One does not have to know all of the ramifications of one's choice to choose for the better part, even when that entails a supernatural good. Nor does one have to have understood all that one would be missing in choosing the lesser part, or in refusing a higher calling by remaining earthbound and egotistical, to be held accountable when one learns one's error in the final judgment. In every choice that we make in a historical order that is at once supernatural and natural, there is always more at stake than what we can name or clearly define for ourselves, even for those who have not heard the Good News of Christ.

It is difficult to conceive how those who have not heard this Good News, or who apparently have no consciousness of their supernatural vocation, can respond to it in any way, positively or negatively. Those who have responded to it explicitly "by name" are thought of as belonging to the Church of Christ or to his Mystical Body, and as on the way to salvation. Blondel had a very determinate idea of this Church operating in history and giving witness to Christ as a means of salvation, a Catholic Church that included many members of many civilizations sharing in the common Christian Spirit. He was also well aware of many people in history, past, present, and future, who have never heard or who would never hear of this Church of Christ, or who would never come to a true grasp of its message because of miscommunication, through no fault of their own. The existence of such people presented a problem for his anonymous philosophy of the supernatural, because in their ignorance of the historical Christ and his Church as universal Mediator for the elevation and divinization of mankind, it seemed that they were being denied access to what was supposed to be a supernatural vocation for all human beings of all ages. In his view, God would not save any rational being for this supernatural end without that being's own willingness or acceptance to be saved, nor would he damn such a being without its own willingness to be damned. Yet, if the historical Christ were the only mediator necessary to make such a fundamental option possible, to say *Yes* to the supernatural as well as to say *No* to it, how could this question of a possibly true divinization arise for a rational being, let alone call for a possible resolution on the part of the creature?

Blondel's entire philosophy of the supernatural had been developed in the context of a Christian Spirit at work in the world, a spirit stemming from a certain Jesus of Nazareth, understood as Redeemer for mankind and representing a higher challenge to the free rational being, to remain true to his rationality, by accepting the challenge as a gift from God, and by following a way of life in keeping with this acceptance, a way of true justice and peace, a way that had been prescribed by Jesus himself as what would mark his followers in what Blondel was naming the Christian Spirit. In an essential respect, Blondel's philosophy of action had been developed to show the necessity of coming to a confrontation with this obscure individual who had lived and been crucified in an obscure part of the Roman Empire, for any rational being in search of a destiny that would equal his power of willing, and to show the necessity of a historical religious practice in any Church that would gather within itself those who accepted the challenge, that is, those who were willing to enter into the new historical way of life instituted by Christ, for what was to become the Catholic and Apostolic Christian Community.

Church: Visible and Invisible

With this idea of a necessary confrontation with Christ, as a historical figure or as a Mystical Body propagating itself in world history, however, there was also the problem of accounting for the possibility of a supernatural salvation for all those who, through no fault of their own, would never have any apparent contact with Christ or his Church in their historical consciousness. How could such people be held responsible in the supernatural order mediated and established for all created spirits? The ordinary way, or what Blondel as a philosopher of the Christian Spirit would have called the *normal* way, of bringing people to their responsibility regarding their supernatural end, was through revelation or what we would call some spiritual contact with the historical Christ or his Church, with its own sacramental order instituted by Christ. This meant that the visible Church on earth, Mystical Body of Christ, had the mission of making known the Good News of salvation through Christ to all peoples and providing specific means for a supernatural salvation. It is in relation to this Church that Blondel had come to his understanding of how we have to exercise responsibility with regard to our supernatural end. But then he had to ask himself, how could the exercise of such responsibility even become possible for anyone who had never heard of Christ or his Church?

In answering this question, he notes that when God or Christ communicates himself in the visible and normal ways of the Church, that communication, which is always a challenge to the soul, remains mysterious, even where there is explicit faith that one is confronting the divine. This entails an element of anonymity even in recognizing Jesus as Lord and Mediator for all human beings. In this mysterious anonymity there is also something that allows for a certain catholicity in the way God can enter into communication with all rational beings and raise them to a new level of responsibility concerning their eternal destiny, even through the merits of Christ, who eternally remains the universal Mediator for everyone in history.

To make this intelligible, Blondel distinguished between an invisible Church and the one he took to be the visible Church of Christ on earth. Both are part of one and the same Mystical Body of Christ, the universal Mediator for all human beings, but the invisible can include many who have not had any visible or tangible contact with the visible Church, or with Christ himself, but who have been touched by God in some other spiritual way, so that they could exercise their own responsibility regarding the Supernatural, even without naming it as such, as those who were seen to have served Christ in the Gospel in sacrificing themselves for others without knowing he was present. As a philosopher Blondel of course had no way of describing such mysterious and anonymous ways in which rational beings could be brought to a confrontation with their supernatural vocation. That was something that, by definition of such supernatural intervention from the Creator and Savior, remained beyond the grasp of philosophy. The idea of such an intervention, nevertheless, implied an opportunity for the created spirit to acquiesce in it freely or else to turn away from it, in an attitude of self-sufficiency, even outside the normal channels of such confrontation advanced in the teaching of Revelation proposed by the Church. In fact, as a philosopher, he had no way of describing such a supernatural confrontation in the intimacy of any personal spirit, even where there were all the external signs of an explicit confrontation in the historical context of a duly announced Good News, for that too is bound to remain secret and mysterious for any human being to perceive or judge with any certainty, even in one's own case, let alone the case of another. In this regard, Blondel took the Gospel injunction as absolute: *Thou shalt not judge.*

What he did instead was develop a philosophy of action in which he opened up a clearing in human consciousness, for the light of our destiny to come in, along with whatever resources it would require, so that "no man attaining a level of reasonable choice would be deprived of the possibility of acceding to the order of grace and salvation" (1948, 250). Notwithstanding the paradox of affirming such a philosophical ignorance of the supernatural as such, even when it is offered *de facto*, while requiring some responsibility in accepting or rejecting it, he saw in this integral philosophy of action the possibility of affirming categorically "that the consented adherence to anonymous and even totally unsuspected grace is the very condition for a teaching and a realization of the supernatural order and of the entire economy of Christianity" (1948, 250).

Blondel had thought as an existentialist philosopher from the beginning, but as one interested in discovering the integral series of truths and actions where the natural order and the supernatural order meet, either to clash or to unite. Against a University that was refusing to admit *action* as a worthy subject of philosophical research, he had asserted the right and the highest duty of reason to study and to exercise human action. Secure in his own position as a philosopher at the end of his life, Blondel could now say that any so-called separate or atheistic philosophy is not only dead, but also one that "kills in its pure and impossible autonomy." Just as metaphysics is possible, legitimate, and even necessary, only on the condition that it ties into a religious perspective, so also "and more opportunely still," Blondel maintained at the end that "there is no fully legitimate and resourceful philosophy except in one that reaches the study of the supernatural, the highest aim and reason of nature, of thought, of activity and of felicity for creatures."

This followed for him from the priority and the indispensable initiative of the first Cause in everything that any creature is and does, something that is often lost sight of in an exclusively humanistic philosophy of existence. It is thought, in our sufficiency, that we are in full possession of our strength, and that divine intervention in human affairs is only that of an observer from a distance, or, at most, that of a judge. With regard to the birth of a human being, we imagine that this singular procreation is the labor only of parents, and that what counts for the child is "the physical or artistic heritage of the temporal being born thus like a statue proceeding from the genius of the artist." What is forgotten is the creative presence and action of the first Cause in the very coming to be of this or that spiritual being. Existence, and the determinations of each one, never depend only on a simple complexus of genes, humors, and talents. Nor is it ever purely a fortuitous innovation, no matter how else a good physical and spiritual heredity may count. "There is," Blondel writes, "in all that exists, a newness due to the primordial act of the Creator, without whom there is no new life or even existence sustained and prolonged, subject to judgment and ultimately responsible in man for the part he has chosen, docile or rebellious, in his relative autonomy" (1948, 251).

It is important for a truly existential philosophy to take this into account. It is not enough to simply declare that existence is independent of any generic essence, or of one only partially transmitted, as if there were no objective validity to thought, or no intelligible and constitutive reality in existence itself. The very idea of a Creator as first cause operative in any particular human being precludes such absurdism. More than just a humanism, true existentialism has to be a response to the supernatural within, either positively unto eternal life, which is not immobile, but a perpetual enrichment, or negatively, in a willed refusal of the one thing necessary for fulfillment of our most fundamental human aspiration, which is to be divinized, in seeing God — Father, Son, and Holy Spirit — face to face.

Christian Existentialism

In response to the atheistic existentialism of his time, Blondel's intention for the third and final volume of his philosophical work on the Christian Spirit was to show the possibility, and even the necessity, of *inviscerating* the Christian mystery into consciences, into history, into civilization, so that people would see reciprocal causality and finality between knowledge and Christian life. From the standpoint of philosophy, he would argue that agnosticism is not the end of the line for a critical spirit that still has to contend with the problem of its destiny in its historical existence. This is a problem modern thought cannot legitimately ignore, much less resolve in a purely negative fashion. Even if we recognize that we have some absolute truth in human existence that we cannot comprehend, we still have a positive perspective on that unknown that we cannot logically declare to be unknowable. Such abstract speculation cannot be the last word in human existence, when there is more to be learned from action and from facts, including those Christian revelation speaks of as significant for resolving the question of one's destiny and as having an eternal, absolute, and universal value, indispensable for the salvation of all. From the standpoint of the revelation itself, he had to show how the truth of the Christian Spirit made itself known in a series of temporal, relative, and contingent events clearly enough to engage human responsibility, but still without lifting the veil of incommensurability that kept the mystery hidden from our historical and critical way of knowing. All this had to be shown according to the strict rational method he had set for himself early in his career, in the discourse on method of 1896, but now in a much more complicated way that encompassed the historical facts as such, in which the natural and supernatural do come together existentially and historically.

His examination of these Christian facts and mysteries had to be no less critical and philosophical than that of any idealist, willing to bring everything in action and reality back to what were taken to be principles of strict science. At the same time, however, he would have to show how these same principles do relate existentially to the supernatural aspects of reality that were revealing themselves in the common experience of people in history. Blondel did not think that the philosophical order could confine itself to a lower order, leaving above itself another order to which only faith could raise us, as if philosophy could remain alone, separate, self-enclosed, without raising the question of the strictly supernatural in religion. Philosophy, like everything else in human action, springs from an élan that cannot be contained within any finite object. It is "an effort always encouraged by certain advances and conquests, to be sure, but always unfinished and leading, for what is essential, to raising questions whose complete answer escapes it" (1948, 61-62). Part of its duty is to remain attentive, prudent, and open to such questions, without credulity and without prejudice. Only thus can it fulfill its function fully and integrally, of forming human consciousness and conscience, in relation to the final destiny of human beings. Far from being just a vague, preliminary attitude in the search for truth and fulfillment, this was for Blondel a disposition requiring to be brought to ever-greater precision, with scrupulous exactness, through a steady and integral study of all the elements human action calls into play, where a solidarity of progressive spiritual states strives to get organized and to complete itself without ever succeeding in closing itself up entirely within itself.

Only thus also can philosophy open up a perspective for entertaining the possibility of a fulfillment that reason cannot attain by itself, but that a supernatural offer could enable. Having come to the limit, where the offer of a supernatural gift to the rational creature could be understood as fulfilling its most intimate concrete aspiration, philosophy can then examine how such a gift can be assimilated existentially into the natural organism and the interior life of the finite spirit, without losing its transcendent and incommensurable value as divine mystery. Philosophy can then speak of a true convenience, a *convenance* of this gift, as meeting the needs made manifest by the prior critical inquiry into human action, and as laying out from the side of the human being "the modes of insertion and utilization that correspond to all the exigencies of our spiritual life and of human civilization," in opposition to any form of self-sufficient naturalism and immanentism (1948, 63).

To emphasize this philosophical side of his endeavor, Blondel spoke of it as one of understanding, in the sense of *intelligere,* a scrutinizing of all that "reason and experience can perceive of continuity, universality, and unity in existence and in the destination of the universe, which seems to subject us to it, at the same time as we have the feeling and the pretension of dominating it" (1948, 263). This is the condition of human consciousness and existence as he had described it originally in the subjective science of action, at the beginning of his career as a philosopher. His intention from the start had been to carry on an impartial search for coherence in his life as a rational being and for a serene comprehension of the whole to which he was relating. For him, understanding meant trying to see as far as one can into *what* is, no more, no less, "with all the essential unity, the intimate connection and the final consequences that integral truth entails" (1948, 263). From the beginning, his intention was one of systematic exploration of all there is to be taken into account in leading a human life as well as one can, including objections one might encounter at times that could shed new light and new riches of intelligibility, justice, and goodness on the life he was leading as a Christian philosopher.

The order disclosed in his systematic understanding, however, was not immobile or static, nor was it reducible in its apparent dynamism or becoming to a principle that is "confusedly immanent to the seriality of things or ideally transcendent to all its possible developments" (1948, 264). At the end of its exploration of all there is to be seen and understood of a universe that encompasses man and is encompassed by man, Blondel's philosophy becomes systematically open, in religious expectation, to the totally transcendent reality, to which all things, including rational beings, must be related as "to a thought, a power, an acting *(agir)* that, perfect in themselves, cannot be conceived unless being, intelligibility, intelligence, and love are intimately one, without confusion among them, and without the creation of the contingent universe being anything other than a free and gratuitous manifestation of the divine and supernatural charity" (1948, 264), not just in the sense of allowing for such a reality in the abstract, but also in the sense of requiring a response to it, in any new initiative it might put on the table of responsibility for the created spirit. All of his systematic philosophy on Thought, Being, and Action had led him to the consideration of something that cannot be systematized, by reason of its incommensurability with anything accessible to human reason, but that at the same time must be taken into systematic consideration by human intelligence, by reason of the paradoxical end to which the created spirit aspires.

With regard to the Christian mystery itself, understanding came to mean explaining the possibility of an elevation, through unnaturalizable grace, of the rational nature of creatures endowed with free will and personality, with the complication of responsibilities that this entails for rational creatures having to choose between accepting the offer, and so entering into eternal life, or refusing it, and consequently suffering eternal death. Understanding in this case came to mean recognizing as well the eventuality of a fall, with the consequences of a refusal, not just of proffered graces, but also of the conditions that accepting the marvel of supernatural elevation can lead to. "In all of this," Blondel writes, "one also has to glimpse how this unforeseeable liberality cannot be justly refused, given that the supernatural gift, anonymous or revealed, brings into the spiritual being a motion destined to fulfill an incipient desire and a first gift that, in its essential goodness, is inalienable and cannot be disavowed on the part of the creature, just as it is without reproach on the part of God" (1948, 264). Even if it takes a positive revelation for us to know of this supernatural vocation, there is a continuous linkage that enables human reason to find the satisfaction of a conformity in all this "with the profound need for logic, for moral aptness, and for religious plenitude that constitutes our spiritual being" (1948, 264).

It is through this systematic opening of a philosophy that wills to be integral, without closing in on itself or on the immanent order of history, that the Christian Spirit enters to raise human life itself in history to a supernatural and supra-rational level. Blondel had worked at developing this systematic opening all his life, in keeping with the exigencies of both reason and the Christian faith. In a brief note dictated in the summer of 1946, highly reminiscent of the 1896 *Letter on Apologetics*, he speaks of returning to the true sense of what had been spoken of as the "method of immanence," which, he says, was a matter "not so much of transcending oneself as it is of discovering and hosting transcendence within ourselves" (1948, 169). What has to be understood here is the necessity of extending philosophy to the full integrity of its domain by deploying it anew in the structures of Catholicism, the ensemble, as he calls it, "whose coherence and complementarity my entire effort has tended to develop from the thesis on Action to the Trilogies that are an explication of it" (1948, 170). If we are to understand and justify the divine plan and the possibility of our acceding to a supernatural path, whose undeclinable offer we cannot reasonably refuse, as sublimely desirable and as adapted as it is to all our just aspiration, we must become aware of "this complex organization as the secret of the universe and the masterpiece of perfect charity. Christ died to restore this plan that admits of no legitimate protestation, no conceivable escape" (1948, 17).

Blondel thus thought of his two Trilogies as an integral elucidation of an essentially philosophical character, where nothing is brought in except under the aspect that is open to reason, for reason to find some satisfaction in. In his way of thinking, there was not a word in them of exhortation or of apologetics to take it out of the realm of philosophy. His aim from beginning to end had been simply to make the truth known, "not in a fragmentary fashion, but in the integrality of what it holds and what it leads to, so that the truth itself is the criterion for itself, because there is no longer, outside of it, any real cause for doubt, for the possibility of resistance, or for any pretext for negation that could take hold" (1948, 265). Outside the truth there is nothing that is of interest to reason. Blondel does not claim to have arrived at this totality of truth in any sort of absolute knowing in his philosophy. On the contrary, he has argued that philosophy is insufficient to answer all the questions it raises about the totality of what there is in universal history and in the agents who move it forward, divine as well as human. By placing this ideal limit before reason, however, he has tried systematically to open up for any rational being and to assure for all of them "the duty of humble sincerity in the effort of the beneficial task of intellectual and charitable cooperation among all spirits, who have to mutually confront, correct, and complete their own itinerant wisdom and their own outlook, which always falls short" (1948, 265). One cannot be *truly* intelligent according to Blondel, without this openness of spirit and soul, where there has to be both "plasticity and firmness," along with "dedication to truth and infinite solicitude for each spirit in search of its spiritual nourishment" (1948, 265).

What the original philosophy of action, as philosophy of the supernatural, had brought out, independently of faith and consequently also of Christian practice itself, was the necessity and the cohesion of the Christian message as it relates to the whole of creation, and to the human spirit in particular, as this spirit looks for its way through the universe. In the end, however, it came to the conclusion that intelligence alone cannot be complete, and that intelligibility itself remains deficient, even unintelligible, as long as we look on the mystery of the Christian Spirit from the outside in a purely speculative attitude, as if we had to do only with a well-constructed story or some abstract possibility. What is true in the order of nature, of morality, of metaphysics, with respect to circumincession of theory and practice, is true also in the religious and the supernatural. The Christian Spirit requires a compenetration, a symbiosis of the human and the divine, of the natural and supernatural, in the historical order, from which follow a certitude and a possession, no doubt still obscure, but still legitimate and fulfilling of the whole truth of human existence, at once intelligible and good. To emphasize this intimate accord between light and life, Blondel recalls how Christ himself says that he is the Truth, the Way, and the

Life, and how at the core of Deity itself, Being is not without the Word, just as neither the one nor the other is without the Charity that fuses them, without confusing them, in a perfect unity.

What the Trilogy of the Christian Spirit added that was not in Blondel's original anonymous philosophy of the supernatural was a certain verification, a certain confirmation from the tradition of faithful religious experience, or the life of faith and charity in the Church, that could be traced back to Christ himself and his messianic proclamation of the Good News, "not just in the clear-obscure of each personal conscience, but also in the secular effort of a historically lived tradition disclosing little by little from its inexhaustible treasure ever new and ancient resources — *nova et vetera*" (1948, 266). This living tradition, rooted in a positive Revelation and stemming from Christ himself, the universal Mediator, is itself in the form of a universal civilization, capable of inserting itself, even anonymously, into any particular civilization open to the Spirit who moves in all sorts of mysterious ways, not just those embodied in the visible Church of Christ.

Blondel had thus labored mightily to make philosophy conscious of all the exigencies implied at once in the fundamental and final élan of the human spirit in the idea of a divine charity that creates it, and in the justification of that creative act by the supernatural vocation of the human being to the divine life itself. His philosophy of the supernatural was a radical theocentrism called for by reason itself, but one that maximized anthropomorphism beyond anything that it could wish for itself. It is in the Christian mysteries that Blondel finds the key to all the enigmas that surround our destiny, including the justification for a paradoxical exigency that seems to mortify us in our natural life. God does not leave us to ourselves in the world. Nor does he offer us satisfactions only proportionate to our human nature. It is himself that he wills to give to us, "and it is to make this donation possible, exceeding all that we could gain or receive lower than this supreme gift, that everything has been brought into concert in the universal drama of life and of humanity" (1948, 269). That is why we are left with a fundamental option in relation to this offer, to accept or to reject, each with its own eternal consequences, about which we have no choice. Blondel has shown not only that choosing anything less than the maximum that divination represents is not only inferior and insufficient, but also illogical and culpable as an effort to keep ourselves within our finite boundaries, self-satisfied with a good that cannot satisfy us.

The exercise of this fundamental option in the face of our eternal responsibility, however, normally does not take place in a single act of an individual or of a civilization. In the normal course of events, it is exercised through a series of particular choices about one thing or another, wherein we develop a fundamental attitude that is generous toward God or any other spirit, or one that remains closed up within oneself clinging to whatever each one has made of itself.

The integral task of philosophy is to teach human consciousness and consciences how to become aware of all that is implied in our making particular choices, including the fundamental option relating to our ultimate destination as spirits, and to help overcome, not just the egoism of human persons, but also the exaggerated prestige of science, the human ambition to dominate nature, and even the ambition to master oneself fully. It is to promote a hierarchy of spiritual values in civilization, where all are subordinated to the final end assigned for our fundamental spiritual élan, not just by discerning something of the content entailed in that final end, but more importantly by encouraging fidelity to the inner motion that moves us forward and upward bit by bit in the small change of our daily lives.

It is this upward tick of decision-making in human action that Blondel intended to promote in his third volume on the Christian Spirit, by turning to practical implications for the human spirit in the solution of problems affecting social life in modern civilization, on the threefold level of family, country, and international relations. As supernatural as Blondel thought the Christian Spirit to be, and as paradoxical as it appeared in its most radical exigencies of self-sacrifice to obtain its pearl of great price, he still saw it as the best way of conceiving how all things converge for critical reflection on sensible and historical data, on the positive sciences, on metaphysical speculation, on moral consciousness, on religious history, and even on Christian experience itself, toward a unified humanity. This was something not just for unbelievers to think of, but also for many who "believe they know the true message [of Christianity] and have not fallen away from Christian practice" (1948, 270). If there is a divine providence at work in history, it has to have some bearing on how human beings organize their life in civilization, and how they work toward universal peace on earth.

The Philosophical Exigencies of Christianity

During all this time, when Blondel was working on his notes and outlines for the third volume of *Philosophie et Esprit Chrétien,* and participating for the third time in the *Semaines Sociales de France* which were, in 1947, on the way of conceiving a truly universal social order, the thought of the Christian Spirit as supernaturalization for the entire human race remained uppermost in his mind. Realizing perhaps that he would not be able to bring this final project to completion, due to his failing health, he began to think of publishing two shorter essays that were among the papers he was working with, written some twenty years earlier, as he was beginning work on his final Trilogies in which he was arguing for the necessity of a Catholic philosophy. Less technical and more succinct than the three-volume work on the Christian Spirit that was then to follow, these essays could serve as an introduction to that Trilogy as well as an expression of what had been the guiding principle of his Catholic philosophy from the beginning. As he had always done earlier when hesitating about publishing something, especially during the modernist crisis, Blondel sought the counsel of two close confidants, Jean Trouillard and Henry Duméry, who knew his work well and could estimate how these two essays would be received by the reading public. Recognizing that the essays did express the central idea of Blondel's philosophy of the Christian Spirit, and that they could stand on their own as written, both friends argued and urged him to seek publication immediately.

There did remain, however, some hesitation concerning how to title them and join them together in one book. The two had originally been conceived as a single essay on the legitimacy and the necessity of treating the Christian Spirit in philosophy. They had been split up into two essays when one chapter, on "the doctrine of the supernatural considered under its triple aspect as metaphysical, ascetic, and mystical," took on a life of its own, as it were, and required further amplification, in connection with a theme Blondel had found in the *Summa contra Gentiles* of St. Thomas Aquinas, to the effect that "all things tend to be assimilated to God — *omnia intendunt assimilari Deo*" (1950a, 221).

Blondel had seen in this phrase a way of summing up the movement of all nature and, more especially, of spiritual beings, toward the divine. As assimilation, it could be taken as referring only to a resemblance or an imitation on the part of an essential nature that reflects the divine perfection, more or less according to a similitude that remains detached from the divine life it can only mimic from afar. This was perhaps the way many philosophically inclined Thomists were interpreting the phrase. But Blondel saw a deeper way of taking this idea of "assimilation to God," one more akin to St. Augustine and St. Bonaventure, who spoke more of interior illumination and of a spiritual assimilation to the divine life itself in a vital union of filiation and participation in the triune paradigm of Father, Son, and Holy Spirit. The latter view was a way of conceiving the final end of creation as something more than just an order of multiple copies analogous to a divine object. It was a way of conceiving that end as an "authentic and vivifying incorporation of beings into the divine Subject attaching them to Himself as the shoots to the stem of the vine" (1950a, 222).

For Blondel, these two views of assimilation to the divine were not exclusive of one another, though he was leery of those who would reduce it to one of only intellectual resemblance, by analogy. What he was trying to elucidate in his philosophy was the more vital kind of assimilation elevating the finite being into the infinite being itself, as necessary from the standpoint of the finite being itself and of its exigencies for fulfillment. This is called the amplified development. "On Assimilation" was seen as a culmination and as a transposition of the theory of analogy between creature and Creator, requiring now a truly vital participation, a new labor of love, a new birth, and a new assimilative theogony requiring renunciation of the self on the part of the creature.

This second essay, however, was only an aside for the main theme of the book as a whole, for which Blondel and his confidants still had to formulate an appropriate title. The different ones that came to mind, as indicated in Blondel's notes, tell us something of how Blondel conceived the content of this book. One was *"Extension d'une philosophie ouverte,"* which said nothing of the content, but merely stated that from which this extension was to start, the idea of an open philosophy. Another suggested title was *"Les exigences rationnelles d'une philosophie chrétienne, conditions et exigences d'une philosophie intégrale,"* terms that Blondel was fond of using, to show how his idea of Christian philosophy came under a philosophy prepared to pursue all questions that occur in a human spiritual life, including those of religion and of the supernatural. The third title suggested was the simplest of all: *"Le sens chrétien,"* the Christian sense. This one referred to the content of the book, but it left too much unsaid, especially regarding "the philosophical exigencies of the religious problem" as conceived by Blondel, both at the beginning of his career as a philosopher in the *Lettre* of 1896 on "the exigencies of contemporary thought in matters of apologetics and on the method of philosophy in the study of the religious problem," and now at the end of his career in this more concrete exploration of the Christian sense in the world, in life, and in history.

What was settled upon was the simple title, *Le sens chrétien,* for the first and principal essay of the book, with *De l'assimilation* for the second essay, and *Exigences philosophiques du Christianisme* as the title for the book as a whole. The latter was a compromise of sorts, but it did cover the line of thinking that ran through both essays by expressing the necessary connection Blondel had always seen between philosophy and the Christian Spirit.

The book proved to be one of Blondel's best in his later life, for many readers, as a concise presentation of his philosophical approach to the study of the Christian Spirit as historically relevant and philosophically legitimate, in connection with the question of the rational being's destiny with respect to a supernatural order that could not be refused with impunity. What this philosophical method shows systematically is how Christianity presents itself historically in matters of fact, how it ties all things together intellectually in a permanent unity that runs through the course of nature and spirit, and how it has to be taken up internally, by intussusception, so as to vivify anew the human spirit into one that is properly divine and supernatural, beginning in the present life, but only to be fulfilled in eternal life.

In it, Blondel discusses various ways of conceiving the principle of essential unity for this Spirit in relation to the threefold idea of God we have, the God of power, the God of truth, and the God of charity, with the caveat always that the God we are relating to, and the divine life we are speaking of, remains unfathomable to us, totally heterogeneous to anything in our created nature. All of this development is shown to depend on a philosophy of human and rational insufficiency, which alone allows for some access to this domain, where the Christian Spirit itself lives in its indissoluble unity.

In a chapter on "catholic unity," Blondel shows how the three parts of the Trilogy on Thought, Action, and Being (and beings) converge on this unique center of perspective, when the Christian Spirit, derivative from the light of the Word made man, who comes from the Father and returns to him in a Love that is eternal, is woven into the reflection on *thought* and *action* that prepares us for confronting *being* in its most mysterious dimension. What this philosophical achievement prepares is not just an opening to the Christian Teaching, but also a readiness to recognize in it an unexpected response to our rational expectation and a marvelous convenience, or *convenance,* for satisfying our most fundamental spiritual élan, all of which takes nothing away from the possibility of a natural order that could subsist, without the supernatural, in some viable but imperfect equilibrium of nature. It is in the context of this radical disequilibrium in our thought and action that the inventions of divine charity and the supernatural are brought in, as if by the intrusion of a higher destiny offered and imposed on man, requiring a radical mortification of our natural and human being to make way for the coming of the supernatural and divine Being within our created spirit. "The measure of the supernatural in man, and of his future beatitude, is the very degree of his courage in the test that substitutes for his self-will the exigencies, apparently cruel, but in reality tenderly paternal, of the One who can place himself only in the standpoint of truth eternal and perfect joy" (1950a, 138).

To make all this more intelligible, the essay on the Christian Sense brings it back to the work of creation itself, as the first volume on *Philosophy and the Christian Spirit* does, and to the initiative of supernaturalization added to creation, so to speak, from the very beginning, surpassing the entire created order as such. With the idea of two incommensurables, the Creator and the created, ever present in his mind, Blondel explores the conditions for realizing the divine plan by overcoming the difficulty of uniting the two. This requires an invention of divine charity to bridge the abyss, through the Word made flesh and the hypostatic union and, on the side of the creature, the testing that the transforming union imposes. The idea of the supernatural at issue is not just some vague transcendence surpassing some nature or other, nor is it something merely preternatural. It is not something created, stuck onto the human being or added to it from the outside. Nor is it God in himself. It is a new relation between God and man, spoken of as a marriage of the soul with God, or an adoption, an assimilation, an incorporation, a consortium, a transformation, all terms that assure both the union and the distinction of two incommensurables, through the bond of charity. What is at issue is not just the highest explanation our intelligence can attain in holding its divine object. It is more a matter of accepting a friendship that, freely offered, requires that it be freely taken in by man. In the essay on *assimilation*, Blondel explores how this new relation of man to God is lived, where we learn that the participation in question is not just an ideal one, but a vital one requiring an onerous test on the part of the creature, to bring about a new birth into a higher life, or even conversely to give God new birth within oneself.

Such an order of grace has to be understood as completing nature and forming with it, within ourselves, a life and a personality that is truly one in the practical order as well as in the intellectual order. From this comes the idea of a civilization inspired by this new unity in a transcendent symbiosis, where the natural inclination for domination is left behind, in favor of a more realistic unification among diverse human societies based on the law of *forgiveness* that runs through the Christian Spirit. This Spirit is anything but the kind of perpetual oscillating between opposites that characterizes the pantheistic absolute. Rich as this pantheistic spirit may seem for souls enamored of the spiritual life, it turns out to be the "privation of infinite Transcendence for the sake of an immanence that is ever movable and indigent in its indefinite extensions" (1950a, 185). Pantheism, as it is found in Spinoza and Hegel, is but a caricature of the truly Catholic unity.

Blondel distinguishes two kinds of unity, that of monism and that to which Christianity leads. In the first, starting from an identity of nature that joins contraries together, there is a mixing of all the diversity in things and of all differentiation of beings, into a single impersonal being or a substance that contains all becoming, all the relative, all imperfections, but that excludes thereby the perfect, the absolute, pure thought and existence in and for itself. In the Christian perspective, on the other hand, "true unity consists in the presence in all and in everything of a single real mediation of a concrete universal that, without mixing in with the imperfections of creatures or with their finite mode of existing, is nevertheless everywhere itself in its entirety, the *God of power,* who makes all things subsist, the *God of light,* who illuminates every intelligence in making it participate in the clarity of the Word and the life of the Spirit, the *God of charity,* who enables all faithful souls for the union in which He gives himself entirely to all those who consent to receive him" (1950a, 185). Sanctity thus comes to be seen as a philosophical problem in the light of a spirit that is deemed *catholic,* not just with regard to all men, but also with regard to the ontological order of creation as well, because the truly catholic spirit is one with God, the Creator and the Redeemer of all human beings and of all things.

All this is but the skeleton of the richly endowed spiritual life Blondel lays out as both Christian and supernatural. Writing these essays in the late 1920s had served as a warm-up for the more elaborate task of the Trilogies that were yet to come. At the end of his life, when he saw that he would not be able to complete his project as he would have wished, he seized upon these essays as a way of making one last statement concerning what his Catholic philosophy was all about, as philosophy and as a critical message of good news for the world. Blondel spoke and wrote, not just for philosophers, but for all men of generous good will, for good and loving human beings of all times, anonymous Christians as well as those belonging to the visible Church. He was a man of his time, but also a philosopher for all times, and for all who were willing to push the limits of reason beyond the limit.

The way these essays on the *Philosophical Exigencies of Christianity* came to be published at the very end of his life is an indication of how Blondel was able to transcend his own time in his writing. With the reassurance he had sought from Trouillard and Duméry concerning the timeliness of these manuscripts, he had hastened to submit them for consideration at the Presses Universitaires de Frances (PUF), who were then quick to accept them for publication. The contract that would set the presses in motion was sent by mail and arrived in Aix-en-Provence on Friday, June 3, 1949. Conscious that he was nearing the end of his life and realizing that this was important business to take care of without delay, Blondel immediately signed the contract and instructed Mlle. Panis to send it back to Paris by return mail the same day. He died quietly and peaceably the next day, knowing that an essential part of the final volume he had projected on the Christian Spirit would be published.

News of his death, however, reached Paris and the editors at PUF on Sunday, while the signed contract was still en route to them, which gave them to think that perhaps the opportunity for publishing this last manuscript from the Philosopher of Aix was lost. They, of course, found out otherwise when the signed contract arrived a day or two later, giving them clearance to proceed with the publication. Blondel had cheated death, old age, and blindness one more time to fulfill his mission as philosopher of the Christian Spirit to the world.

Index of References to Blondel's Works

I refer to the writings of Blondel according to the year of their publication, including those that were published after his death, which even for the works published in his lifetime is not always the year in which they were written. I list here only the works actually referred to in my philosophical narrative. Also listed according to the year of their origin are unpublished materials from the Blondel Archives at Louvain-la-Neuve.

For a more complete and exhaustive bibliography of Blondel's works and of works about him, see René Virgoulay & Claude Troisfontaines, *Maurice Blondel: Bibliographie Analytique et Critique*. Louvain: Institut Supérieur de Philosophie/Peeters.

   I. *Oeuvres de Maurice Blondel (1880-1973)*. 1975. Centre d'Archives Maurice Blondel, 2.
   II. *Études sur Maurice Blondel (1893-1975)*. 1976. Centre d'Archives Maurice Blondel, 3.

This bibliography was supplemented for later years by Albert Raffelt, Peter Reifenberg, and Gotthard Fuchs, in *Das Tun, der Glaube, die Vernunft: Studien zur Philosophie Maurice Blondels "L'Action" 1893-1993*. Würzburg: Echter, 1995, pp. 216-38.

1893a   *L'Action: Essai d'une critique de la vie et d'une science de la pratique*. Paris: Alcan.
   – reprinted as *L'Action (1893)* in *Les Premiers Écrits de Maurice Blondel*. Paris: Presses Universitaires de France (PUF), 1950 & 1973.
   – reproduced in *Oeuvres Complètes*, Tome I: *1893, Les Deux Thèses*. Paris: PUF, 1995, pp. 15-530.
   – translated by Oliva Blanchette, *Action (1893): Essay on a Critique of Life*

and a Science of Practice. Notre Dame: University of Notre Dame Press, 1984.
I cite according to the translation and include the pagination of the original French edition in brackets.

1893b   *De Vinculo substantiali et de substantia composita apud Leibnitium.* Paris: Alcan.
– re-edited and translated by Claude Troisfontaines, *Le lien substantial et la substance composée (1893).* Centre d'Archives Maurice Blondel, 1. Louvain/Paris: Nauwelaerts, 1972.
– reproduced (with the French translation) in *Oeuvres Complètes,* Tome I: *1893, Les Deux Thèses.* Paris: PUF, 1995, pp. 538-687.
I cite according to the Troisfontaines edition and translation.

1894a   Une des sources de la pensée moderne: L'évolution du Spinozisme. In *Annales de Philosophie chrétienne* 128 (1894): 260-75 & 324-41. [Pseudonym: Bernard Aimant].
– reproduced in *Dialogues avec les philosophes: Descartes, Spinoza, Malebranche, Pascal, Saint Augustin.* Preface by H. Gouhier. Paris: Aubier, 1966, pp. 11-40.
I cite according to *Dialogues.*

1894b   Lettre au Directeur de la Revue de Métaphysique et de Morale. In *Revue de Métaphysique et de Morale* 2 (1894): 5-8.
– reproduced in *Études Blondéliennes* I, Paris: PUF, 1951, pp. 100-104.
I cite according to *Études Blondéliennes* I.

1895   Lettre sur l'apologétique philosophique. In *Annales de Philosophie chrétienne* 131 (1895): 188-89.
– reproduced in *Les premiers écrits de Maurice Blondel.* Paris: PUF, 1956, pp. 3-4.
I cite according to *Les premiers écrits.*

1896a   Lettre sur les exigences de la pensée contemporaine en matière d'apologétique et sur la méthode de la philosophie dans l'étude du problème religieux. In *Annales de Philosophie chrétienne* 131 (1896): 337-47, 467-82, 599-616; 132 (1896): 225-67, 337-50.
– reproduced in *Les premiers écrits de Maurice Blondel.* Paris: PUF, 1956, pp. 5-96.
– translated by Alexander Dru and Illtyd Trethowan, in Maurice Blondel, *The "Letter on Apologetics" and "History and Dogma."* London: Harwill Press & New York: Holt, Rinehart & Winston, 1964. 2nd ed. Grand Rapids: Eerdmans, 1994, pp. 125-208.
I cite according to *Les premiers écrits.*

1896b   Le christianisme de Descartes. In *Revue de Métaphysique et Morale* 4 (1896): 551-67.
– reproduced in *Dialogues avec les philosophes* (1966), pp. 41-59.
I cite according to *Dialogues.*

1898   L'illusion idéaliste. In *Revue de Métaphysique et Morale* 6 (1898): 726-45.
- reproduced in *Les premiers écrits de M. Blondel* (1956), pp. 97-122.
- translated by Fiachra Long, "The Idealist Illusion," in Maurice Blondel, *The Idealist Illusion and Other Essays*. Dordrecht: Kluwer, 1997, pp. 75-94.

I cite according to *Les premiers écrits*.

1900   La psychologie dramatique de la Passion à Oberammergau. In *La Quinzaine* 35 (1900): 1-18.
- reproduced in *"Art et Littérature," Science et Religion*, n. 574. Paris: Bloud et Cie., 1910.
- reproduced in *Oeuvres Complètes*, Tome II: *1888-1913, La Philosophie de l'Action et la Crise moderniste*. Paris: PUF, 1997, pp. 291-307.

1903   Principe élémentaire d'une logique de la vie morale. In *Bibliothèque du Congrès de Philosophie* II (1903), pp. 51-85. Paris: Colin.
- reproduced in *Les premiers écrits de Maurice Blondel* (1956), pp. 123-47.
- reproduced in *Oeuvres Complètes*, Tome II: *La Philosophie de l'Action et la Crise moderniste* (1997), pp. 367-86.
- translated by Fiachra Long, "The Elementary Principle of a Logic of the Moral Life," in *The Idealist Illusion and Other Essays*. Dordrecht: Kluwer, 1997, pp. 95-113.

I cite according to *Les premiers écrits*.

1904   Histoire et Dogme. Les lacunes philosophiques de l'exégèse moderne. In *La Quinzaine* 56 (1904): 145-67, 349-73, 435-58.
- reproduced in *Les premiers écrits de Maurice Blondel* (1956), pp. 149-228.
- reproduced in *Oeuvres Complètes*, Tome II: *La Philosophie de l'Action et la Crise moderniste* (1997), pp. 387-453.

I cite according to *Les premiers écrits*.

1905a   Notre Programme. In *Annales de Philosophie chrétienne* 151 (1905): 5-31. [In collaboration with Laberthonnière].

1905b   L'oeuvre du Cardinal Dechamps et la méthode de l'apologétique. In *Annales de Philosophie chrétienne* 151 (1905): 68-91. [Pseudonym: François Mallet].

1906a   Les controverses sur la méthode apologétique du Cardinal Dechamps. In *Annales de Philosophie chrétienne* 151 (1906): 449-72, 625-46. [Pseudonym: François Mallet].

1906b   Le point de départ de la recherche philosophique. In *Annales de Philosophie chrétienne* 151 (1906): 337-60; 152 (1906): 225-50.
- reproduced in *Oeuvres Complètes*, Tome II: *La Philosophie de l'Action et la Crise moderniste* (1997), pp. 529-70.
- translated by Fiachra Long, "The Starting Point of Philosophical Research," in *The Idealist Illusion and Other Essays*. Dordrecht: Kluwer, 1997, pp. 114-48.

I cite according to the original article in APC.

1907a   L'oeuvre du Cardinal Dechamps et les progrès récents de l'apologetique. In

Annales de Philosophie chrétienne 153 (1907): 561-91. [Pseudonym: François Mallet].

1907b Qu'est-ce que la foi? In *Science et Religion*, n. 450. Paris: Bloud et Cie.

1907c Une soutenance de thèse. In *Annales de Philosophie chrétienne* 154 (1907): 113-43. [Pseudonym: J. Wehrlé].
— reproduced in *Études Blondéliennes* I (1951), pp. 79-98.
— reproduced in *Oeuvres Complètes*, Tome I: *1893, Les Deux Thèses* (1995), pp. 696-745.
I cite according to *Études Blondéliennes*.

1909 La semaine sociale de Bordeaux et le monophorisme: Controverses sur les Méthodes et les Doctrines. In *Annales de Philosophie chrétienne* 159 (1909): 5-22, 162-84, 245-78; (1910): 372-92, 449-72, 561-92; 160 (1911): 127-62. [Pseudonym: Testis].
— reproduced in a separate volume: *Catholicisme social et Monophorisme*. Paris: Bloud et Cie., 1910.
I cite according to *Catholicisme social*.

1910 La psychologie dramatique du mystère de la Passion à Oberammergau. In "Art et Littérature," *Science et Religion*, 574. Paris: Bloud et Cie.
— reproduced in *Oeuvres Complètes*, Tome II: *La Philosophie de l'Action et la Crise moderniste* (1997), pp. 697-707.

1913a Note de la Rédaction. In *Annales de Philosophie chrétienne* 166 (1913).

1913b Lettre aux lecteurs et abonnés des Annales de Philosophie chrétienne. In *Annales de Philosophie chrétienne* (1913). [In collaboration with Laberthonnière].

1916a L'anti-cartésianisme de Malebranche. In *Revue de Métaphysique et de Morale* 23 (1916): 1-26.
— reproduced in *Dialogues avec les philosophes* (1966), pp. 61-89.
I cite according to *Dialogues*.

1916b Un problème de psychologie sociale: La correction du retard chronique de l'heure civile. In *Séances et Travaux de l'Académie des sciences morales et politiques* 76 (1916): 45-60.

1917 Victor Delbos (1862-1916). In *Annuaire des anciens élèves de l'École normale supérieure Paris* (1917), pp. 47-69.
— reproduced in *Dialogues avec les philosophes* (1966), pp. 239-69.

1921a Un rapt. In *La nouvelle Journée* 16 (1921): 234-37.

1921b Le procès de l'intelligence. In *La nouvelle Journée* 19 (1921): 409-19, 30-39, 115-33.
— reproduced in *Le procès de l'intelligence*. Paris: Bloud et Gay, 1922, pp. 217-306.
I cite according to the volume of 1922.

1921c   Un interprète de Spinoza: Victor Delbos 1862-1916. In *Chronicon Spinozanum* I (1921), pp. 290-300.
– reproduced in *Dialogues avec les philosophes* (1966), pp. 271-80.

1922   Lettre à l'Ami du Clergé (dated May 14). In *Ami du Clergé* (June 1922).

1923   Le jansénisme et l'anti-jansénisme de Pascal. In *Revue de Métaphysique et de Morale* 30 (1923): 131-63.
– reproduced in *Dialogues avec les philosophes* (1966), pp. 91-128.

1924   *Malebranche:* "Papillon" présentant l'ouvrage de V. Delbos, *Étude de la philosophie de Malebranche,* publié par J. Wehrlé (1924). Paris: Bloud et Gay.

1925   Le problème de la mystique. In *Qu'est-ce que la mystique? Quelques aspects historiques et philosophiques du problème.* In *Cahiers de la nouvelle Journée* 3 (1925): 1-63.

1926a   Lettre concernant le rapport de M Brunschvicg, Les conditions d'existence de l'enseignement supérieur de la philosophie. In *Bulletin de la Société française de Philosophie* 26 (13 February 1926): 4-7.

1926b   Note liminaire au *Bulletin de la Société d'Etudes Philosophiques du Sud-Est.* Reproduced in *Études Philosophiques* 1 (1926): 1-2.

1926c   Remarques touchant la communication de M. Paliard, Le Conflit de l'idéalisme et de la psychologie. In *Études Philosophiques* 1 (1926): 5-7.

1926d   *Vocabulaire technique et philosophique de la philosophie.* André Lalande, 2 volumes paged continuously. Paris: Alcan.

1927   Les conclusions d'une expérience personelle. In *Un grand débat catholique et français. Témoinages sur l'Action Française.* In *Cahiers de la nouvelle Journée* 10 (1927): 177-215.

1928a   *L'Itinéraire philosophique de M. Blondel.* Coll. "La Nef," no. 5. Paris: Spes.
– new edition, Paris: Aubier, 1966.
I cite according to the 1966 edition.

1928b   *Patrie et Humanité: Cours professé à la Semaine sociale de Paris,* Juillet 1928. Lyon: Chronique Sociale de France.

1930a   *Une énigme historique: Le "Vinculum Substantiale" d'après Leibniz et l'ébauche d'un réalisme supérieur.* Paris: Beauchesne.

1930b   Le quinzième centenaire de la mort de Saint Augustin (28 août 430). L'unité originale et la vie permanente de sa doctrine philosophique.
– reproduced in *Dialogues avec les philosophes* (1966), pp. 143-91.
I cite according to *Dialogues.*

1930c   La fécondité toujours renouvelée de la pensée augustinienne. In *Saint Augustin* (Blondel et al.). Paris: Bloud et Gay.
– reproduced in *Dialogues avec les philosophes* (1966), pp. 223-35.
I cite according to *Dialogues.*

1930d   Les ressources latentes de la pensée augustinienne. In *Revue néo-scolastique de Philosophie* 32 (1930): 261-75.
– reproduced in *Dialogues avec les philosophes* (1966), pp. 193-222.
– translated by Fr. Leonard, "The Latent Resources of Saint Augustine's Thought," in *A Monument to Saint Augustine: Essays on His Age, Life and Thought*. London: Sheed & Ward, 1930, pp. 319-53; and in *Saint Augustine*. New York: Meridian, 1957, pp. 317-53.
I cite according to *Dialogues*.

1931a   Y a-t-il une philosophie chrétienne? In *Revue de Métaphysique et de Morale* 38, no. 4 (1931): 599-606.

1931b   Lettre concernant le rapport de M. Gilson, "La notion de philosophie chrétienne." In *Bulletin de la Société française de Philosophie* 31 (1931): 86-92.

1932   Le problème de la philosophie catholique. In *Cahiers de la nouvelle Journée* 20 (1932): 5-177.

1934a   *La Pensée*, Tome I: *La genèse de la pensée et les paliers de son ascension spontanée*. Paris: Alcan, 1934.
– new edition Paris: PUF, 1948.
I cite according to the 1934 edition.

1934b   *La Pensée*, Tome II: *La responsabilité de la pensée et la possibilité de son achèvement*. Paris: Alcan, 1934.
– new edition Paris: PUF, 1954.
I cite according to the 1934 edition.

1934c   Pour la philosophie intégrale. In *Revue néo-scolastique de Philosophie* 37 (1934): 49-64.

1935   *L'Être et les êtres. Essai d'ontologie concrète et intégrale*. Paris: Alcan, 1935.
– new edition Paris: PUF, 1963.

1936   *L'Action*, Tome I, *Le problème des causes secondes et le pur agir*. Paris: Alcan, 1936.
– new edition Paris: PUF, 1949.

1937a   *L'Action*, Tome II, *L'Action humaine et les conditions de son aboutissement*. Paris: Alcan, 1937.
– new edition Paris: PUF, 1963.

1937b   Aspects actuels du problème de la transcendance. In *Travaux du IXe Congrès International de Philosophie* (Congrès Descartes). Paris: Hermann et Cie.
– reproduced in *L'Action* II (1937a) as Excursus no. 35, pp. 513-24.

1939   *Lutte pour la civilisation et philosophie de la paix*. Paris: Flammarion.
– new edition with revisions, Paris: Flammarion, 1947.

1942   *Pages Religieuses. Extraits reliés par un communitaire et précédés d'une introduction du R.P. de Montcheuil, S.J.* Paris: Aubier, 1942, 1945.

1944   *La Philosophie et l'Esprit chrétien*. Tome I: *Autonomie essentielle et connexion indéclinable*. Paris: PUF, 1944.
— new edition Paris: PUF, 1950.

1946   *La Philosophie et l'Esprit chrétien*. Tome II: *Conditions de la symbiose seule normale et salutaire*. Paris: PUF, 1946.

1948   Archival materials in preparation for Volume III of *Philosophie et Esprit Chrétien*. I cite according to volumes 18 and 19 of the Méry typescript of these materials available at the Blondel Archives at Louvain-la-Neuve University, Belgium.

[Posthumous Publications]

1950a   *Exigences philosophiques du christianisme*. Paris: PUF.

1950b   *Mémorial* (or: *Généalogie*) *de la famille Blondel*. Dijon: Massebeuf.

1951   *Études Blondéliennes* I. Paris: PUF.

1952   *Études Blondéliennes* II. Paris: PUF.

1954   *Études Blondéliennes* III. Paris: PUF.

1956   Lettre sur les exigences de la pensée contemporaine en matière d'apologétique (1896) — Histoire et Dogme. In *Les premiers écrits de Maurice Blondel*. Paris: PUF.

1957a   *Maurice Blondel — Auguste Valensin: Correspondance (1899-1912)*. Tome I of II. Paris: Aubier.

1957b   *Maurice Blondel — Auguste Valensin: Correspondance*. Tome II. Paris: Aubier.

1958   William James and Maurice Blondel. Frederick J.D. Scott, S.J., in *New Scholasticism* 32: 32-44.

1960a   *Au coeur de la crise moderniste. Le dossier inédit d'une controverse. Lettres de Maurice Blondel, Henri Brémond, Fr. Von Hügel, Alfred Loisy, Fernand Mourret, J. Wehrlé*. Edited by R. Marlé, S.J. Paris: Aubier.

1960b   Ébauche de logique générale. Essai de canonique générale. In *Revue de Métaphysique et de Morale* 1 (1960): 7-18.

1961a   *Lettres philosophiques de Maurice Blondel. Lettres à É. Boutroux, V. Delbos, L. Brunschvicg, J. Wehrlé, Henri Brémond Éd. Le Roy, etc. . . .* Paris: Aubier, 1961.

1961b   *Maurice Blondel — Lucien Laberthonnière: Correspondance philosophique*. Edited by C. Tresmontant. Paris: Seuil.

1961c   *Carnets intimes*. Tome I (1883-1894). Paris: Cerf.

1961d   Le dernier chapitre de *"L'Action (1893)."* Édition critique, H. Bouillard. In *Archives de Philosophie* 24 (1961): 29-113.

1965a	*Maurice Blondel — Auguste Valensin: Correspondance*. Tome III (1912-1947). Annotated by H. de Lubac. Paris: Aubier, 1965.
1965b	*Genèse de l'Action*. Raymond Saint-Jean, S.J. Paris-Bruges: Desclée.
1966a	*Dialogues avec les philosophes: Descartes, Spinoza, Malebranche, Pascal, Saint Augustin*. Preface by H. Gouhier. Paris: Aubier.
1966b	*Carnets intimes*. Tome II (1894-1949). Paris: Cerf.
1969a	*Blondel — Wehrlé: Correspondance*. Vol. I. Commentary and notes by H. de Lubac. Paris: Aubier-Montaigne.
1969b	*Blondel — Wehrlé: Correspondance*. Vol. II. Commentary and notes by H. de Lubac. Paris: Aubier-Montaigne.
1970	*Henri Brémond — Maurice Blondel: Correspondance. I: Les commencements d'une amitié (1897-1904)*. Edited A. Blanchet. In *Études Brémondiennes* II. Paris: Aubier.
1971a	*Henri Brémond — Maurice Blondel. Correspondance. II: Le grand dessein d'Henri Brémond, 1905-1920*. Edited by A. Blanchet. In *Études Brémondiennes* II. Paris: Aubier.
1971b	*Henri Brémond — Maurice Blondel. Correspondance. III: Combats pour la prière et pour la poésie 1921-1933*. Edited by A. Blanchet. In *Études Brémondiennes* II. Paris: Aubier.
1972	*Le lien substantiel et la substance composée d'après Leibniz: Texte Latin (1893)*. Introduction and translation by Claude Troisfontaines. *Centre d'Archives Maurice Blondel*, 1. Louvain-Paris: Nauwelaerts.
1995	*Oeuvres Complètes*. Tome I: *1893, Les Deux Thèses*. Paris: PUF.
1997	*Oeuvres Complètes*. Tome II: *1888-1913, La Philosophie de l'Action et la Crise moderniste*. Paris: PUF.
1999	*"Mémoire" à Monsieur Bieil: Discernement d'une vocation*. Présentation de Michel Sales, S.J., Texte établi par Emmanuel Tourpe. Paris: CERP.

Name Index

Abraham, 705, 708, 719
Aimant, Bernard (pseudonym for Blondel), 110
à Kempis, Thomas, 48
Anselm, St., 494
Aristotle, 4, 43, 131, 146f., 163, 176, 210, 213, 215f., 222, 244, 253, 268f., 270, 293, 331, 355, 361, 401, 431, 447, 478, 513, 520, 533, 549, 561, 568, 575, 643, 691f., 711, 741, 770
Aquinas, St. Thomas, 130, 132, 179, 231, 243f., 248, 267ff., 275, 289, 295, 313, 338, 360, 362ff., 365, 373, 376, 379, 398, 400, 381, 386, 390, 406, 409f., 527, 549, 554, 575, 585, 682, 692, 694, 799
Archambault, Paul, 290, 292, 299ff., 323, 360, 384
Augustine, St., 9, 245, 255, 268, 276, 295, 359ff., 379, 398, 400, 403, 411, 438, 441f., 444, 473, 494, 740, 748, 775, 787, 799

Bacon, Francis, 215, 472
Beaudoin, Reginald, 175, 179, 392, 419
Berger, Gaston, 319, 418
Bergson, Henri, 3, 213f., 219ff., 222f., 286, 291, 325f., **353ff.**, 497, 535, 769
Bernard, St., 9, 48, 119, 130, 158, 338, 360, 409f., 694f.
Bernard, Claude, 355, 425
Berkeley, 267
Bertrand, Alexis, 33

Bieil, Abbé, 99, 101, 327
Blondel, Georges, 234, 279
Boehme, Jakob, 53
Boissard, Adéodat, 118, 223f., 234f., 238, 278
Boissard, Henri, 224
Bonaventure, St., 338, 361f., 799
Bossuet, 448, 467
Bouillard, Henri, 600f.
Bourdel, Charles, 37
Bourget, 179
Boutroux, Émile, 3, 6, 7f., 38f., 40, 43f., 59, 61, 90f., 96f., 120, 211f., 214, 266, 306, 521, 600
Bréhier, Émile, 379ff., 385, 397, 403, 415, 464
Brémond, Henri, 171f., 175, 214, 224, 259, 279, 281, 290, 299f., 307, 320, 323f., 413, 415
Breton, Marcel (pseudonym for Blondel), 329
Brochard, Victor, 16, 96f.
Brunetière, Ferdinand, 179
Brunschvicg, Léon, 21f., 106f., 132, 161, 213ff., 318f., 350

Cajetan, 289
Cézanne, Paul, 164, 327
Chateaubriand, 179
Chenu, M.-D., 404
Claudel, Paul, 329

Clement of Alexandria, 400
Combe, Charles, 223f.
Croce, Benedetto, 334

d'Alès, A., 288f.
de Biran, Maine, 33, 267, 328, 561
de Broglie, Guy, 301
de Lubac, Henri, 171, 232, 266
de Montcheuil, Yves, 659
de Tonquédec, Joseph, 258, 289
Dechamps, Cardinal, 228, 231, 244, 246, 390, 392ff., 396
Delbos, Victor, 3, 108f., 110ff., 131, 135, 137, 147f., 173, 290ff., 297, 307, 401, 415, 419, 493, 657, 763
Delpech, Léon, 416
Denis, Abbé Charles, 122, 225
des Bosses, 33f., 61, 95f., 346ff.
Descartes, 10f., 14, 162ff., 218, 267, 270ff., 305f., 328, 349f., 362, 370f., 377, 379, 421f., 471, 502, 514, 578, 609, 644, 661, 750
Descoqs, Pedro, 256, 356
Duhem, Pierre, 3, 120, 301, 763
Duméry, Henry, 288, 799, 803
Durkheim, Émile, 3, 536, 780

Eckhart, 53
Einstein, Albert, 769
Eucken, Rudolf, 181

Favre, Paul, 4, 119f., 181
Fessard, Gaston, 171, 356
Fichte, 113, 350
Flory, Charles, 284, 418
Fonsegrive, Georges, 122, 128, 179, 192, 227, 385
Fontaine, J., 243
Forest, Aimé, 288
Franck, Adolphe, 4
Frémont, 179
Freud, Sigmund, 328
Froude, Margaret, 181

Gallois, Étienne (pseudonym for Blondel), 323
Garrigou-Lagrange, Réginald, 257, 284
Gaudeau, Abbé, 243
Gayraud, Abbé, 179, 184, 191

Gentile, Giovanni, 332f.
Gide, André 277
Gilson, Étienne, 267, 338, 360, 364, 383f., 385, 397ff., 403f., 415, 464
Goethe, 112
Gonin, Marius, 234
Grassi, Ernesto, 333

Haruack, Rudolph, 182, 185, 187, 190
Hegel, 5, 14, 86, 93, 110, 113f., 116f., 135f., 147f., 154, 160, 210f., 215f., 222, 295, 298, **337f.**, 341, 345, 380, 383, 387, 400, 410f., 373, 441, 461, 466, 468, 494, 507, 514, 538, 561, 568, 572, 576, 664, 667, 669, 671, 673, 677, 705, 761, 773, 780, 784, 802
Heidegger, 333
Herder, 112
Herr, Lucien, 5
Heurtin, Marie, 433
Hobbes, Thomas, 536, 779
Hume, David, 178, 350
Huvelin, Abbé, 165
Huysmans, J. K., 179

Ignatius of Loyola, 48

Jacobi, Friedrich, 112
James, William, 216, 267, 286, 325, 669, 675, 677
Janet, Paul, 13f.
John of the Cross, St., 306, 317, 362
John, St. (Evangelist), 677, 693, 698, 710, 745
Joly, Henri, 33f., 318
Jousse, Marcel, 325, 328
Justin Martyr, St., 400, 403

Kant, 7f., 15, 43, 70, 86, 90, 96, 112f., 116, 148, 174, 176, 178, 181, 212, 219, 349f., 428, 439, 497, 561, 624, 643, 692f., 694, 711, 779f.
Keller, Helen, 433
Kierkegaard, 66, 86, 318, 339f., 373, 383, 387, 408, 410f., 705, 773

Laberthonnière, Lucien, 179, 225ff., 229, 235, 258ff., 262, 290, 322, 324
Lachelier, Jean, 42, 355
Lacordaire, 179

NAME INDEX

Lalande, André, 179, 214ff., 258, 291, 379, 418
Lasson, Georg, 117
Lavelle, Louis, 769
Le Roi, Édouard, 214, 227, 229, 353
Lefèbvre, Frédéric, 164f., 322, 324ff., 360, 658
Leibniz, 33ff., 43, 61, 89, 95f., 112, 306, **346ff.**, 354, 357, 366, 376, 377, 380, 415f., 502f., 511, 549, 590, 671f., 674, 679, 691
Lemius, Joseph, 230
Lena, Maurice, 29, 167, 171
Leo XIII, Pope, 233, 235, 243f.
León, Xavier, 106, 108, 210f.
Lessing, 112
Locke, 178, 350, 377, 422
Lorin, Henri, 234, 254
Loisy, Alfred, 179, 181, **182ff.**, 196, 208, 230, 280, 322, 394
Lévy-Brühl, Claude, 291

Mallebranche, 245, 267, 272ff., 305, 360, 368, 379
Mallet, François, 191, 224f., 318, 389, 392f., 396
Maréchal, Joseph, 301, 356
Marion, Henri, 14f.
Maritain, Jacques, 292f., 299ff., 311ff., 318, 323, 331f., 386
Maurras, Charles, 51, 236, 250ff., 322f.
Milhaud, Claude, 214
Mill, John Stuart, 267
Montaigne, 331
Mourret, Fernand, 191ff., 196, 225f., 227, 229, 232, 259, 264, 280, 287
Mulla, Ali, 282ff., 307

Newman, John Cardinal, 295, 454
Nietzsche, 275, 337, 444

Ollé-Laprune, Léon, 3, 5, 7, 38, 41, 44, 51, 53, 126f., 143, 172f., 179, 223, 302

Paliard, Jacques, 277, 289f., 307, 319
Panis, Nathalie, 417, 658f., 661, 774, 776, 803
Parmenides, 498f., 524, 678
Pascal, Blaise, 38, 47, 49, 162, 267, 295, 302ff., 323, 331, 350, 360, 454, 761

Paul, St., 48, 130, 165, 524, 672, 697, 705, 720, 742
Payot, Jules, 256, 263f.
Pératé, André, 36, 41, 119
Piaget, Jean, 431
Pius IX, Pope, 392
Pius X, Pope, 230, 235, 323f.
Pius XI, Pope, 284, 323
Plato, 176, 222, 368, 370, 374, 521, 711

Rahner, Karl, 232
Rauh, Frédéric, 40, 110f.
Ravaisson, 355
Renouvier, 779
Rimaud, Jean, 287
Rollin, 214
Rousseau, J.-J., 779
Rousselot, Pierre, 179, 243, 269f., 301, 356

Sailly, Bernard (pseudonym for Blondel), 227f.
Saint-Jean, Raymond, 50
Scheler, Max, 181
Schelling, 53, 93, 112f., 148, 400
Scheuer, Pierre, 301
Schiller, 112
Schopenhauer, 13, 60, 267
Schwalm, M.-B., 174, 179, 181, 191, 213, 227, 257, 288
Scotus, Duns, 404
Séailles, Gabriel, 18
Semaria, Giovanni, 181
Sertillanges, 405
Shakespeare, 498
Spalding, Bishop, 181
Spinoza, 39, 89f., 93, 110ff., 116, 131, 137, 147f., 160, 176, 183, 218, 222, 271, 293, 306, 337, 341, 380, 435, 466, 487, 492, 494, 507, 522, 530, 560, 568, 572, 671, 711, 725, 787, 802
Suárez, Francisco, 289, 356

Taine, Hippolyte, 149
Teilhard de Chardin, Pierre, 171
Tertullian, 400
Testis (pseudonym for Blondel), 234ff.
Theresa of Avila, St., 306
Trouillard, Jean, 288, 799, 803
Tyrrell, 181, 230

Valensin, Albert, 289
Valensin, Auguste, 38, 171, 234, 258, 287f., 333, 342, 346, 349, 356, 391
Valéry, Paul, 331f.
van Steenberghen, F., 404, 408, 410f.
von Hügel, Friedrich, 179, 181f., 190f., 230, 280

Weber, Louis, 214
Wehrlé, Jean, 7, 53, 98, 103, 172f., 182ff., 191, 196, 225f., 228f., 231, 235, 262, 264, 280, 288f., 291, 307, 344, 346, 356, 357f., 384, 414ff., 600, 658
Wolff, Christian, 350

Analytical Index

absolute, 75, 774
action, 2, 12, 65ff., 83f., 108f., 276, 326, 418f. (Action), 491, 493f., 547ff., 551, **556ff., 609ff.,** 658, 660, 684, 774f., 792ff., 796, 801; philosophy of, **65ff.,** 327, 750, 774f.; phenomenon of, 58, 66, 234; subject of, 66, 80, 85, 87f., 96, 223, 244, 309
acting itself, 547, **550ff.,** 560, **564ff.**
adoption, 682f., 689, 693, 716, 730, 737, 762, 771, 811
aestheticism, 10, 332
aesthetics, 343
afference, 233, 242f., 246f., 255f., 309, 549, 675
agnition, 580, 750
agnosticism, 513, 519, 574, 577f., 582, 647, 667, 674, 792
alternative, 60, 74f., 223, 456f., 473, 478, **643,** 605, **645f.,** 720, 771, 773, 797
analogy, 501, 515, 519, 569, 574, 674f., 799
apologetics, 2, **124ff.,** 177, 257, 279, 381f., 384, 388ff., 392f., 396, 401, 485, 655, 658, 735f., 796
aporiai, **515ff., 522ff., 564ff.,** 672, 674, 726, 768ff.
Ascension, 721f., 727f., **732f.,** 775
assimilation (to God), 333f., 340, 353, 393, 403, 471, 483, **529ff.,** 644, 683, 761f., 763, 765, 780, **799ff., 801f.**
assumption, 685, 695

atheism, 364, 380, 445f., 467, 577f., 582, 585, 725, 777, 791f.

baptism, 719f., 726, **756ff.,** 761; of blood, 720, 757, 759; of desire, 140, 720, 757
beatitude, 734, 764, 767, 770, 772, 801
beatitudes, 726, **764ff.,** 767, 770, 772, 778
being, **89ff.,** 92, 216f., 257, 290, 327, 329ff., 334f., 348, 419 (Being), 491, 493f., 658, 801
Being In Itself, 497ff., 500, 506, 508, **510ff.,** 569, 572f.

Catholic, 775, 778f., 784, 795, 798f., 802f.
Catholic philosophy, 360, 379, **383f.,** 578, 597, 655, **668f.,** 719
Catholic religion, 748, 754
charity, 338ff., 344ff., 361, 363, 391, 492, 520f., 663, 677, 696, 712, 718, 777f., 781, 785f., 794, 796, 801; uncreated, 569f., 580ff., 588, 734, 761, 766
Christian community, **740ff.,** 746, 748, 754, 757, 762
Christian philosophy, 45, 57, 64, 88f., 94, **104f.,** 107, 123, 128f., 141, **146ff.,** 161, 180, 245, 249, 251, 257, 262, 273f., 279, 321, 376, **378ff.**
Christian spirit, 179f., 191ff., 209, 251, 253, 301, 325, 342, 358, 374, 382, 402, 527, 597, 606, 652f., 655, **660, 665ff., 723,** 719, 724, **774ff.,** 787ff., 796, 799, 801

Analytical Index

Church, 721f., 723, **735ff.**, **739ff.**, **744ff.**, 775, **790ff.**, 797; invisible, **408f.**, 410
circumincession, 394f., **489ff.**, 520f., **570f.**, 582, 677, 796
civilization, 429, 766f., 776, 778, 782, 785, 792, 802
communion of saints, 720, 726, 734, 741, 745, 758, 768, 772, 774
concordism, 380f., 391, 400f., 405f., 411
confirmation, **757f.**
conscience, 15f., 156, 337f., 479, 603, 609, 624, 627, 629, 631, 644, 664, 686, 708, 710, 720, 740, 743, 765, 777, 781f., 784, 792f., 798
consciousness, 66ff., 310, 536, 565, 568f., **571f.**, 587, 591, 599, 604, 607f., 609, 624, 640, 743, 746, 752, 794, 798
consistency, 530f., 545f.
consummation, 714, **717ff.**, 719, **721**, 724f., 729, 731, 736
contemplation, 757
contrition, 759
conversion, 364, 368, 370f., 513, 711, 722, 757
cooperation, 472ff., 476ff., **547ff.**, **641f.**, 647, 650, 655, 720
creation, **522ff.**, 523, **573f.**, **583ff.**, 619, **677ff.**, 681, 724, 732, 768f., 770, 775, 781f., 801
cult, 632ff., 635, 754, 762
cycloid, 538, 548; cycloidal method, **667f.**, **673f.**, 677, 680, 698, 749

death, 61, **464f.**, 480, 498, 642, 711, 728f., 732, 768ff., 770
decision, 66ff., 611f.
deicide, 686, 689, 715f., 718, 732
deism, 449, 461, 473, 520, 582, 644, 647, 667, 670f.
deliberation, 559, 591, **613ff.**
demonstration, 692
destiny, 65, 334f., 457, **464ff.**
determinism, 10, 12f., 16f., **67ff.**, 72f., 84f., 92, 96, 112, 137, 139, 198, 205, 557, 559, 568, 571f., 601, 607, **610ff.**, 619, 632, 659, 662, 711, 725
dilettantism, 10, 66, 382, 604, 606, 754
divine loan, 586f., 590, 593f.
divinization, 686, 700, 719f.

dogma, 107, 109, 159f.
dualism, 446, 503, 514, 523, 585, 678f., 682
duration, 769f., 771
duty, 624f.

efference, 233, 246
élan spirituel, 328, 362, 429, 456, 460, 505, **535ff.**, 599, 607, 614, 667, 670, 801
élan vital, 353ff., 429, 505, **535ff.**, 572, 599, 614
elevation, 722
engendering, 519f., **579ff.**, 583
enigma, 346ff., 352, 494ff., **664ff.**, 672, 681, 704, 709, 724, 763, 775, 797
eternity, 768ff.
ethical consciousness, 626f.
ethics, 764ff.
eucharist, 726, 735, 756f., 757, **760ff.**
evolution, 426
exigency, 595f., 599, 606, 623, 632, 637, 643f., 670f., 675, 680f., 715, 781, 783, 786f., 794, **800**
existence, 454, 456, 475
existentialism, 764, 787, **791f.**
expiation, 712
extension, 769f., 771
extreme unction, 757, **759f.**
extrinsicism, **194ff.**, 246, 301, 362, 365, 386, 581, 699

faith, 38, 46, 78, 80f., 84f., 87, 123, 126, 131, 148, 174, 228, 234, 251, 262, 270f., 315, 337ff., 341, 371f., 373, 379, 395, 402 (preambles of), **640f.**, 656, 670, 675, 686, 705, 708, 723, **729f.**, 734, 741, 743f., 752, 765, 774, 790, 793, 796, 777
family, 344
fideism, 219, 236
freedom, 12f., 16f., 53, **67ff.**, 96, 112, 139, 338, 498, 559, 590f., **610ff.**, 631, 637, 642f., 769, 773

generosity, 643, 645, 648, 688f., 771f.
gift, 651, 794; of divinization, 596, 606, 651, 656; of existence, 679; of freedom, 595, 642f., 645, 656; of grace, 702; of nature, 681f., 648, 653, 685f., 700, **790f.**
gifted finite being, 597, 606; twofold gift, 695

God, 46, 56, 73ff., 76, 337, 340, **445ff.**, 466, 499, 508f., 515, **520**, 550, 562, 577, 587, 605, 631, 658, **639f.**, **647f.**, 667, **670ff.**, 675, 686; proofs, 62, 257, 447
Gospel, 338, 710, 729, 748
grace, 338f.

Hellenism, 401, 481
heroism, 720, 757, 759, **765ff.**
historicism, 182ff., 186f., 194, **196ff., 338**, 362, 699
history, 168, **192ff.**, 195, **197f.**
hope, 734, 741, 765, 777
humanity, **344ff.**
humanization, 559ff.

idealism, 13, 113, 169, 174, 214, 217, 222, 297, 332f., 347, 368f., 370, 423, 497, 499, 503, 519, 531, 534, 671, 754
identity, **504ff.**, 510
idolatry, 670, 674, 684, 706, 777
illumination, 364f., 368ff.
immanence, 22, 60, 71, **76ff.**, 93, 107, **114ff.**, **133ff.**, 245, 258, 334, 341, 356, 365, **386f.**, 399, **567f.**, 576, 581f., **662f.**, 726, 764
immanence/transcendence, 334, 341, 356
immanentism, 441, 491, 514, 526
Incarnation, 692, **694ff.**, 707, 709, 724, 730ff., 745, 755, 764, 801
incommensurability, **661ff.**, 670f., 683ff., 762, **683ff.**, 784, 793, 795, 801
infinite, 10, 17, 19, 52f., 54, 59, **69ff.**, 73, 86, 162f., 269, 381, 383, 428, 435, 442, **446ff.**, 449, 455, **458ff.**, 462f., 470, 484, 492, 495, 509, 516f., 536, 540ff., 548f., 564, 571, 573, 587, **592**, **612ff.**, 623, **630ff.**, 666f., 670, 680, 722, 725, **763**, **768**, 774
inspiration, 723
insufficiency, 420, **442ff.**, **462ff.**, 472, 474f., 484, 510, 514, 597, 623, **640**, 648f., 662, 665f., 676, 753, 763, 801
intellectualism, 177, 179, 215, 220, 222, 227, 234, 292, 369, 493, 659
international order, 778, 781, 798
intersubjectivity, 508, 521, 535ff., 605, **622**, 740f., 746
intussusception, 293f., 309, 800
invention, **432ff.**, 450

Jansenism, 302ff.
justice, 714f., 765f., 767, 777, 779, 781, 785f., 788, 794

language, 342f.
last things, 768ff.
liberation, 559f., 591, 613, 618, 645
logic, 64, 152, 167, **210ff.**, 222f., 293f., 275, 420, 472ff., 499, 509, 528, 531, 549, 610, 620, 640, 711, 724, 743, 795; by connaturality, 295f., **313ff.**, 317, 332, 386; knowing, 217, 436; prospective/reflective, 217f., 219f.; real/notional, 294ff., **296ff.**, 312f., (existence) 328ff., 335, 340, 354f., 454

Magisterium, 726, **744ff.**, **747ff.**
marriage, 757, **760**
matter, 501ff., 534
mediation, 83ff., **690ff.**, 724, 743
mediator, 83, 392, 689; Christ as Universal Mediator, **690ff.**, 696, 702, 704, 709, 745, 751, 762, 765, 784, **790f.**
mercy, 714f., 765f., 772
metaphysics, 50, 70, 90ff., 111, 160, 167, 186, 262, 273, 275, 327, 349f., 350ff., 365, 419, 422, 424, 472, 481, 492, 455, **482ff.**, 486, 493, 499f., 548, 550, 595ff., 601, 621, 629, 659, 791
method, 1, 8ff., 13f., 52, 55, 98, 114, **122ff.**, **167ff.**, 174, 182ff., 194, **217ff.**, 223, 235f., 275, 307f., 318, 328, 360f., 382, 596, 658f., 666, 673; of application, 498f.; of deployment, 605, 609, 614, **620f.**, 630, 649, 659; of *efference*, 549, **551f.**; of immanence, 23, 93, 107, 115f., 132, 231, 258, **288ff.**, 375, 386f., **389ff.**, 603, 614ff., 787, 795; of implication, 72, 216, 357, 367, 424, 426, 475, 497, 516, 549, 612; ontological normative, **497**, **499ff.**, 525, **528ff.**, 546; of ontology, 497, 513
mobile, 66f., 80f., 608ff.
modern state, 776ff., 778, 781, 783
modernism, 7, 156, 191, 234, 699
monism, 446, 503, 514, 523, 555, **562f.**, 571, **802**
monophorism, 232, **242ff.**, 301, 386
monotheism, 672, 674
morality, **624ff.**, 632

Analytical Index   819

mortification, 49, 61f., 82f., 339, 392, 410, 498, 537, 801
motive, 66f., 75, 458, **610ff.**, 645, 734, 787
mourning, 765
mystery, 258, 395, 458, 495, 496, 563ff., 573f., 577, 660f., **664ff.**, **672**, 709, 719, **726ff.**, 739, 795f., 797
mysticism, 258, 299, **305ff.**, **336**, 488, 512f.

nation, 344ff., 778, 784f., 798
necessary hypothesis of the supernatural, **76ff.**, 125, **136ff.**, **139ff.**, 141, 483, 542, 597, 606, 646, **648ff.**, 750
neo-scholasticism, 146ff., 155, 160, 363, 373, 385, 404
nihilism, 58f., 60, 66, 250, 382, 492, 572, 678

Oberammergau, 58, 279
obligation, 624, 628, 684
omnipotence, 674, 680
ontogenesis, 504, 535
ontology, 90ff., **330ff.**, **493ff.**, **496f.**, **500**, 505, 513, 600, 628; normative, **497**, **499ff.**, 525, **528ff.**, 533ff., 546, 549
order, 23, 128, 131f., 134f., 158f., 195, 245, 248, 300, 306, 313, 350, 370, 776, 794; natural, 8, 12, 15, 64, 71f., 74f., 76, 81, 83, 85, 126f., 180, 202, 207, 236, 241, 243, 300, 314, 338, 379; supernatural, 8, 22, 64, 72, 80, 85, 126f., 139, 180, 236, 241, 300, 338, 379; twofold, 365, 385, 386f., 394ff., 398, 406, 664f., 757, **760**
organic life, 501ff., 535
original sin, **701ff.**, 706, 719, 724, 739, 756, 759, 795

panchristicism, 232, 247, 317f., 339, 349, 409
pantheism, 492, 674, 770, 772, 802
paradox, 472ff., 714f., 764ff., 791, 795, 797
peace, 764f., **766ff.**, 774, 776, **778ff.**, 782, 785f., 798
penance, **757ff.**
Pentecost, 721f., 727f., 733, **735ff.**, 744
perennity, **504ff.**, 510, 535
person, **505ff.**, 508, 536
personalism, 764
pessimism, 478, 526, 604, 606f.
phenomenology, 439f., 549f., 600f., 604, 659f.

phenomenon of action, **66ff.**, 550, 601f., 604, 608
philosophy, 1, 16, 49, 79, 90, 98, 123, 140f., 144ff., 207f., 244, **774ff.**, 792ff., 799f.
phylogenesis, 504, 535
positive science, 3, 17, 66, 124, 271f., 355, 437f., 606ff.
positivism, 66, 332, 606ff., 725
positivity, **85ff.**, 654
practical science, 15, 55f., 65ff., 207, 211, **217ff.**, 221, 296, 603, 624, 628, 754
pragmatism, 214f., 332
predestination, 365
primary cause, **547ff.**, **565ff.**, 573, 582f., 595, 597, 639, 642, 647
privation, 213
prospection, 333, 349, 353, 420, 424, 431, 435, 440, 455, 457, 506, 571f.
psychologism, 438
pure acting, 548ff., 552f., **561ff.**, **564ff.**, **573ff.**, 658, 753

rationalism, 381f., 384, 398, 402, 671
realism, 13, 35, 169, 174, 241, 243, 332f., 368, 422, 439, 497, 531, 534, 546, 599f., 617, 628, 640, 716ff., 730, 732ff., 736, 755, 759, 761f., 769
reason, 67, 123, 131, 134, 174, 337f., 341, 354, 371f., 379, 402, 432, 613, 711, 723, 731, 734, 775, 791, 794
recognition, 580f.
redemption, 704, 707, **710ff.**, 713, **721f.**, 724, 727, 762, 772, 775
reflection, 349, 420, 431, 440, 506, 613, **616f.**
religion, 1ff., 19, 22, 59, 62, 65, 78f., 80, 103, 107, 144ff., 167, 183ff., 228, 251, 271, 335, 358, 369, 387, 399, 445, 450f., 464, 473, 479, 577, 644, **632ff.**, **638ff.**, **646ff.**, 665, 708, 725, 751ff.
religious practice, 50, 60, 84, 86f., 104, 109, 303f., 744, **750ff.**, 755, 762
reparation, 713
responsibility, 454, 458f., 463, **467ff.**, 474, 486, 491f., **586ff.**, 592, 641, 645, 651, 597, 602, 619f., 643, 645, 654, 682, 686f., 712, 724, 751, 777, 786f., **790ff.**, 794
resurrection, 721, **727ff.**, 731f., 768, 775
revelation, 1, 19, 80, 109, 135, 137, 155, 180, 188, 197, 393, 675, 678, 690, 693f., 696ff.,

703, 720, 727, 732, 738, 740, 751, 765, 771, 787, 790, 793
ritual, 632, 635

sacrament, 726, **739ff.**, **749ff.**, 755f., 775
sacrifice, 339f., 603, 685, 688, 737, 771
satisfaction, 713
science, 382, 455
science of practice, 55f., 65ff., 117, 139f., 207, 211, 217ff., 296, 375, 493, 598, 603, 624, 754; objective/subjective, 60, 96, 130, 174, 177, 223, 308f.
secondary cause, 595, 597, 639, 642
secondary causes, 547f., 566f., **584ff.**, 595, 597, 639, 642
sin, 711, 717, 728f., 732
sincere will, 59, 77, 140, 156, 300, 467, 483, 541, 592, 598, 603, 620, 635, 640, 643, 646, 796
social concern, 31, 37, **210ff.**, 774ff.
sociologism, 628
space, 768ff.
spirit of poverty, 765
spontaneity, **504ff.**, 510, 555, 557, 590, 609, 640, 659, 670, 769
subjectivity, 381, 439, 454, 600, 604, 606f., 645, 670, 794
subsistence, **504ff.**, 510
suffering, 589, 593, 716f., 718, **767**
sufficiency, 70ff., 76, 79, 135, **146ff.**, 149, 158, 162, 183, 248, 304, 315f., 369, 383, 393, 399, 405, 406, 409
supernatural, 1, 3, 7f., 15f., 19, 46, 49, 53, 59, 64f., **76ff.**, 82, 92, 100, 103f., 109, 123, 125f., **133ff.**, 137f., 148, 174, 180, **182ff.**, 197, 200, 237f., 241, 248, 255, 310, 318, 336, 340f., 358, 362, 365, 372f., 387, 402, **475**, **483f.**, 470f., **472ff.**, 543ff., 526, 578, 593, 595, 602, 638, 646, **649ff.**, 653, 655, **661ff.**, 675f., **677ff.**, **681ff.**, 719, 721, 726, 728f., 730, 750, 768, 788f., 793f., 796, 801
superstition, 15, 60, 68ff., 78, 86, 109, 442, 445ff., 464, 477, 484, 576f., 605, **630ff.**, 648, 671f., 674, 684, 704, 706, **752**
symbiosis, 87f., 89, 668, 688, 724, **726**, 737, **749ff.**, 762, 796, 802

tala, 98
tetralogy, 660

theandric action, 76ff., 340, 650, 653, 688, 690, 695, 722, 724, 735, 742, 749f., 752, 754, 760, 787
theology, 1, 18f., 23, 79, 93, 107, 123, 126, 128f., 138, 140f., **150ff.**, 178, 182, 186, 208, 244f., 337, 380, 390, 401, 569, 577, 578, 656, 665, 675, 726f., 750, 777
Thomism, 7f., 124ff., 169, 173f., 181, 243, 267, 301, 311, 318, 356
thought, 213, 216, 227, 327, 334, 357, 415f., 418, **420ff.**, 493, 497, 598, 658, 801; noetic/pneumatic thought, **427f.**, **445f.**, 451, 453, 477, 490, **454ff.**, 494; thinking thought, 213, 216, **264f.**, 275, 303, 332f., 429ff., 453; thought thought, 213, 216, 332f., 429ff., 453
time, 768ff.
tradition, 86, 189, **201ff.**, 394, 681, 699, 723, 725f., **744ff.**, 775, 797
transcendence, 73, 76, 78, 148, 183, 258, 334, 341, 356, 443f., 446, 557f., 559, **567f.**, 574, 589, 602, 604f., **616ff.**, 629, 632, 639, **661ff.**, 726, 764, 768, 771
transcendent, 493, 502, 509, **510ff.**, 515, 539ff.
transcendental notions, 502
transnatural state, 232, 245, 337, 366, 379, 385, 402, **705f.**, 707, 720, 739, 751, 757
transubstantiation, 87, 761
Trilogy, 63, 90, 94, 216, 223, 262, 275, 285, 325, 327, 334f., 349, 358, 386, 390, 394, 416f., 418f., 657f., 660, 672, 775f., 798
Triune God, **518ff.**, **564ff.**, 569f., 574, **577ff.**, 593, **669ff.**, **675f.**, 723, 724, 731f., **735f.**, 747, 763, 764f., 768, 770, 773, 797, 799, 800f., 802
truth, 45, 49, 292, 361f., 501ff., 504ff.

universal, 615
universe, 508ff., 615, 608f.

vinculum substantiale, 33ff., 39, 89, **95ff.**, **347ff.**, 355f., 415, 548f., 696, 737

willing, 10, 292, 549; willing will, 15, **58f.**, 68, **72f.**, 76, 82, 88, 139, 292, 608, **614ff.**, **618ff.**, 622, 629f., 640, 762; willed will, 15, **58f.**, 68, **72f.**, 76, 82, 85, 139, 292, 608, 614ff., 618ff., 622, 630, 763

www.ingramcontent.com/pod-product-compliance
Lightning Source LLC
Chambersburg PA
CBHW032125010526
44111CB00033B/79